THE ROUTLEDGE HANDBOOK
OF MAGAZINE RESEARCH

Scholarly engagement with the magazine form has, in the last two decades, produced a substantial amount of valuable research. Authored by leading academic authorities in the study of magazines, the chapters in *The Routledge Handbook of Magazine Research* not only create an architecture to organize and archive the developing field of magazine research, but also suggest new avenues of future investigation. Each of 33 chapters surveys the last 20 years of scholarship in its subject area, identifying the major research themes, theoretical developments and interpretive breakthroughs. Exploration of the digital challenges and opportunities which currently face the magazine world are woven throughout, offering readers a deeper understanding of the magazine form, as well as of the sociocultural realities it both mirrors and influences.

The book includes six sections:

-**Methodologies and structures** presents theories and models for magazine research in an evolving, global context.

-**Magazine publishing: the people and the work** introduces the roles and practices of those involved in the editorial and business sides of magazine publishing.

-**Magazines as textual communication** surveys the field of contemporary magazines across a range of theoretical perspectives, subjects, genre and format questions.

-**Magazines as visual communication** explores cover design, photography, illustrations and interactivity.

-**Pedagogical and curricular perspectives** offers insights on undergraduate and graduate teaching topics in magazine research.

-**The future of the magazine form** speculates on the changing nature of magazine research via its environmental effects, audience, and transforming platforms.

David Abrahamson is a professor of Journalism and the Charles Deering Professor of Teaching Excellence at the Northwestern University's Medill School, where he teaches courses exploring the changing nature of long-form journalism. He is the author of *Magazine-Made America: The Cultural Transformation of the Postwar Periodical* and editor of *The American Magazine: Research Perspectives and Prospects*.

Marcia R. Prior-Miller is an associate professor emeritus of Journalism and Mass Communication at the Greenlee School of Journalism and Communication at Iowa State University, where she led the magazine program. She is the compiler of the *Bibliography of Published Research on Magazine and Journal Periodicals*, now in its 9th edition, and serves on the editorial board of *Journalism & Mass Communication Quarterly*.

THE ROUTLEDGE HANDBOOK OF MAGAZINE RESEARCH

The Future of the Magazine Form

*Edited by David Abrahamson and
Marcia R. Prior-Miller*

Foreword by Bill Emmott

NEW YORK AND LONDON

First published in paperback 2018
First published 2015
by Routledge
711 Third Avenue, New York, NY 10017

and by Routledge
2 Park Square, Milton Park, Abingdon, Oxon OX14 4RN

Routledge is an imprint of the Taylor & Francis Group, an informa business

© 2015, 2018 Taylor & Francis

Library of Congress Cataloging-in-Publication Data
The Routledge handbook of magazine research : the future of the magazine form / edited by
    David Abrahamson, Marcia Prior-Miller.
        pages cm
    ISBN 978-1-138-85416-1 (hardback) — ISBN 978-1-315-72228-3 (ebook)   1. Periodicals—
History—20th century.   2. Periodicals—History—21st century.   I. Abrahamson, David, editor.
II. Prior-Miller, Marcia, editor.
    PN4832.R68 2015
    050—dc23   2014045151

ISBN: 978-1-138-85416-1 (hbk)
ISBN: 978-1-138-29744-9 (pbk)
ISBN: 978-1-315-72228-3 (ebk)

Typeset in Goudy
by Apex CoVantage, LLC

Praise for *The Routledge Handbook of Magazine Research*

"If you are looking for an idea or an angle for research, begin here, and you will discover what topics have and have not been researched in the magazine literature. You will discover the major authors in the field. This 650-page volume will become an indispensable "bible" and starting point for any kind of magazine research."

—David E. Sumner, *Journal of Magazine and New Media Research*

"Magazines have contributed much to the development of literary journalism. Therefore, it should come as no surprise that magazine professors would champion the genre in a handbook of magazine research. With that in mind, it is only fitting that Abrahamson and Prior-Miller's thorough and meticulously researched volume should find its way onto the bookshelves of professors, practitioners, and students at the undergraduate and graduate interested in the field of magazine journalism."

—Amber Roessner, *Literary Journalism Studies*

"This handbook will prove to be an invaluable resource for anyone involved in periodical studies."

—Maaike Koffeman, *Journal of European Periodical Studies*

"This comprehensive, 33-chapter compendium of essays is bursting with theoretical insights and analysis, all underpinned by a clear understanding of the practicalities of magazine-making. Synthesizing research in a diverse range of areas including design, literary journalism, editorial practices, religious magazines, globalization, and curricular perspectives, Abrahamson and Prior-Miller's volume is likely to be regarded as the seminal text on the subject for many years to come."

—Richard Lance Keeble, University of Lincoln, UK

"Focusing on the vibrant and continually evolving magazine form, this anthology brings together 38 top scholars and educators to document the major themes and theoretical perspectives occurring in magazine research in the last 20 years. Their comprehensive approach provides a new benchmark in the study of magazines."

—Sammye Johnson, Trinity University, USA

For Francis T. Taliaferro (1922–2011)
and, of course, Barbara
and
For Joe, Amanda and Jacob

CONTENTS

CONTENTS

CONTENTS

FIGURES AND TABLES

FIGURES

TABLES

FOREWORD

Bill Emmott

It might seem eccentric to some readers that the foreword to this volume about the future of the magazine form has been written by someone who spent a quarter-century working for a publication that looks like a magazine but insists on calling itself a newspaper. But bear with it: There could be method in this apparent madness.

Magazines come in many different shapes, sizes and styles, but no one who looks at the *Economist* will have any doubt that it is one. Yet my distinguished predecessor, Geoffrey Crowther, who was the longest-serving editor of the twentieth century (1938–1956), made a particular effort to ensure that it described itself as a newspaper, an effort that all his successors have found awkward or undesirable to change. This is in part because to be different—and, especially, quirky—is an advantage in a competitive media world, a trait shared with the publication's other idiosyncrasy, that of anonymity for its writers. But there were other reasons for it, at least in Crowther's day, that are more related to the issues being discussed in this book.

Crowther's stubborn eccentricity was substantially a competitive reaction to the success of two relative youngsters in the field of weekly news and current affairs journalism, *Time* (launched in 1923) and *Newsweek* (1933), both of which called themselves *newsmagazines*. So he determined that the *Economist* (1843) must be called a newspaper. His reason for that insistence was not, however, based on a desire to pretend that his publication was competing with the dailies as a purveyor of up-to-date information about what was happening in the world. It was based, most probably, on a desire to associate his publication with the characteristics or values that he believed in that period were most closely linked to newspapers, at least in Britain, at the time: seriousness, reliability and analysis. A newsmagazine, by contrast, was something more flippant and decorative, he felt, something read for leisure and consumed without a sense of urgency.

Times, very plainly, have changed, and newspapers have changed with them, especially in response first to competition from television and then from the digital world. They now are often the flippant and decorative ones. Trapped between the 24-hour news cycle and the difficulty of providing sound and efficient analysis or original content on a timely basis, many have opted instead, because of the pressures on editorial budgets, for entertainment over deeper forms of journalism.

Magazines—including, yes, the *Economist*—have fared better in the digital age because their revenue model has tended to be less prone to disintermediation by the Internet than has that of newspapers. Many magazines depended less than did newspapers on classified advertising of jobs, property and cars. Thanks to often being less local or regional in their circulations, they also depended less on retailers' advertising. Most of all, though—and this no doubt is a view shaded with more than a little self-interest and professional pride—the magazine form retains the potential to offer something scarce and valuable to both readers and advertisers in an era in which attention spans seem to have shortened and simple information has become a commodity.

That something has long brought to my mind a sound bite once heard from a chief executive of the German luxury car firm, BMW. "Yes," he said, "I am always hearing that the world market is flooded with cars. But there is a world shortage of BMWs."

Creating scarcity by giving your product and your brand a premium value and characteristics is one of the great business challenges of our time, in all sorts of sectors. The media are no exception. Indeed, thanks to plunging barriers to entry, the ubiquity of free content and the collapse of old business models, this challenge is at least as great in the media as anywhere else. But in meeting that challenge the magazine form has, in the view of this former magazine editor, a number of substantial advantages.

The first advantage is especially clear in my old field of news, current affairs and business journalism. Information is cheap and ever-more abundant. *Understanding* of that information is scarce—and is what readers, who are time-poor or simply with short attention spans, most need and are willing to pay for. The journalist's classic role as a reliable intermediary, as a trusted gatherer, processer and interpreter of information, is alive and well and living in the magazine form. This can still be done in daily or 24-hour newspapers, but time is short and the analysis is always in danger of either being crowded out or indistinguishable from the rawer information.

The second and third potential advantages are pluses for advertisers and thus for the business model. What advertisers crave, in all sorts of fields, is a combination of attention and precision. By attention is meant the likelihood that readers' eyes will dwell on the advertisement for a sufficiently long time for it to have a chance of having an impact. By precision is meant the likelihood that the readers paying that attention are actually people the advertiser wants to reach.

Neither is easy to achieve in the digital era. Barriers to entry in the magazine form have fallen too, and the battle to be noticed is fierce. But both characteristics are typically easier for the magazine form to achieve than for others. Analysis, interpretation and depth all draw on and demand more time and reflection from the reader. Those features can also benefit from multimedia formats. A reflective read, on whatever topic, is a more attentive one. And magazines in all their varied fields typically lend themselves to more specialized audiences, in niches large or small, national or international, which potentially offer the precision targeting that advertisers have always wanted.

Nowadays, a Geoffrey Crowther would not be preoccupied with the need to differentiate his publication from the newsmagazines, which have typically fared a lot worse than his former title, in their being less analytical, less demanding of attention and less precise in their demographics. But what name he would choose in order to ensure that the *Economist* was not confused with Google News or Buzzfeed is not obvious. Which might be why his successors have stuck doggedly to the word *newspaper*, while they carry on, well beyond the foreseeable future, producing their *magazine* in print, on-line and mobile formats.

PREFACE TO
THE PAPERBACK EDITION

Exciting times, these. Staying abreast of the growing body of scholarly work that spans the myriad aspects of the multi-disciplinary sphere of magazine and journal periodical inquiry is a wonderful challenge. It is surpassed only by the revolutionary changes that continue to occur in the industry's subsectors, whose creative and knowledgeable professionals work tirelessly to meet the challenges to producing these print and digital publications that keep the world informed about every imaginable topic, issue, . . . the list is long, in ways that amaze.

This edition includes updates to some data in the book's last chapter to reflect industry changes, economic and otherwise, as those continue to evolve and grow in response to contemporary technological and global influences coming from every direction. Also for this printing are included a few other changes and corrections to source listings from the first.

And we thank you, our colleagues, present and future, in the academy and industry, researchers, students—future industry professionals and scholars—who have found this resource a valuable addition to your toolkits. Our great thanks also to our publisher and their incredibly supportive staff as we take this next step.

D.A. and M.P-M
April 2017

PREFACE

Prefaces can serve a variety of functions. We would like this one to speak in somewhat personal terms about how we came up with the idea for and embarked on the creation of this volume.

The narrative opens on a sultry afternoon in St. Louis as one of this book's editors—a bit tired and a bit early to a session at the annual conference of the Association for Education in Journalism and Mass Communication (AEJMC)—wanders into a cavernous meeting room containing an imposing rostrum, perhaps 50 chairs, 10 tables and only one other person, sitting quietly and alone in the center of the first row. Professional colleagues of more than two decades standing, the two greet each other warmly. They sit next to each other. And then one asks, "Given all the research that's been done in the magazine field since your scholarly anthology was published in the mid-1990s, don't you think that it is about time for a follow-up?" To which, in the slimmest instant, the other replies: "Only if we can be co-editors." And the response, again in a heartbeat, is: "Okay, done." Such was the impulse—instantaneous, collegial, rigorous and pure—that gave birth to this volume.

Whether more accurately attributed to Sir Isaac Newton or Bernard of Chartres, the quiet but profound aphorism, "If I have seen further, it is by standing on the shoulders of giants,"[1] may through the centuries be best understood by scholars and researchers. Each generation gives large portions of their lives to searching, pondering and sharing past and present knowledge so that the next generation may see further still. So, too, this book stands on the shoulders of those who have both gone before us and—in the face of their own unique challenges of culture, time and circumstances—dared to dream and share.

In the opening paragraphs of the introduction to *The American Magazine: Research Perspectives and Prospects*, editor David Abrahamson described the volume as having been "born, in roughly equal measure, of both synergy and serendipity"[2] when the idea for that first scholarly anthology emerged in the fall of 1992 at the mid-year meeting of the Magazine Division of the AEJMC.

> Some forty scholars of the magazine form assembled . . . [and] after considerable reflection . . . concluded that the existing body of scholarly knowledge about magazines seemed to lack a larger coherence. . . . An informal but fervent consensus was reached that, should the sum of magazine research ever be assembled into a rational corpus of knowledge, it would then be possible to identify important theoretical and/or methodological issues and perhaps even to suggest promising new directions for further research. Further than that, it was agreed that such an effort, in addition to its potential to advance magazine scholarship, might also prove a valuable teaching tool.[3]

Almost exactly two decades later, serendipity and synergy again converged when the editors of this volume had the aforementioned conversation at the 2011 annual meeting of the AEJMC in St. Louis. They were convinced the veritable explosion of research on the magazine form since the first volume's 1995 publication begged a second.

There are other parallels. The first volume's named editor, 19 authors, 10 editorial board members and publisher's editors were supported in their work by a legion of unnamed peer reviewers, industry professionals and academic colleagues, research assistants, students and others, as well as the hundreds of scholars whose work was cited in the chapters. So, too, here. Known only to the individual researchers and scholars whose work appears herein are the substantial contributions of a legion of people whose names and specific tasks supported their work. It is impossible to name them all. However, as editors we want to give public credit to several individuals and groups of people who deserve mention: for long hours, meticulous work and deep dedication. Without their contributions, completing this project would have been impossible.

Our first thanks go to the authors of the chapters, who shared both our vision and, from their respective areas of research, their expertise. As a result the frontiers of scholarly knowledge on the magazine form can continue to be pushed forward. A second round of thanks goes to a team whose names do not appear in this book. Words are inadequate to describe the contributions made by Iowa State University honors research assistants, Sarah Korneisel, music performance major, and her successor Courtlyn Rentschler, double major in communication studies and psychology. Their keen eyes and attention to detail made them invaluable members of the book's editorial team. Thanks must also be given to the thirty-four ISU graduate and undergraduate research assistants and Honors Program Mentees who since the late 1980s helped with the labor intensive processes of identifying, collecting and mapping the emerging research on the magazine form that has expanded exponentially over the past two decades.[4]

Finally, we want to thank our two faculty colleagues, Prof. Susan Mango Curtis, instructor of design at Northwestern University's Medill School, and Sherry Berghefer, graphic designer and design lecturer in the Greenlee School of Journalism and Communication at Iowa State University, who with their students accepted our challenge to design a possible cover for the book, all without promise of its being used. The visual skills of the current and next generation of media professionals give ample evidence that the media are in good hands.

—David Abrahamson and Marcia R. Prior-Miller
September 2014

Notes

1 In the original, "If I have seen further it is by standing on ye sholders of Giants"; Letter from Isaac Newton to Robert Hooke, 5 February 1676, as transcribed in *The Correspondence of Isaac Newton*, vol. 1, H.W. Turnbull, ed. (Cambridge, UK: Cambridge University Press, 1959), 416; Robert K. Merton, *On the Shoulders of Giants: A Shandean Postscript* (New York: Free Press, 1965), 8–9, 37, 40–41.

2 David Abrahamson, "Brilliant Fragments: The Scholarly Engagement with the American Magazine," in David Abrahamson, ed., *The American Magazine: Research Perspectives and Prospects* (Ames: Iowa State University Press, 1995), xvii.

3 Abrahamson, "Brilliant Fragments," xvii–xviii.

4 Marcia R. Prior-Miller and Associates, "Bibliography of Published Research on Magazine and Journal Periodicals," 9th ed., research database (Ames: Iowa State University, last modified, 31 August 2014), MSWord file, 2–3 <mpm@iastate.edu>.

Bibliography

Abrahamson, David. "Brilliant Fragments: The Scholarly Engagement with the American Magazine." In Abrahamson, David, ed. *The American Magazine: Research Perspectives and Prospects*. Ames: Iowa State University Press, 1995, xvii–xxi.

Merton, Robert K. *On the Shoulders of Giants: A Shandean Postscript*. New York: Free Press, 1965.

Newton, Isaac. Letter to Robert Hooke, 5 February 1676, as transcribed in *The Correspondence of Isaac Newton*, Vol. 1. H.W. Turnbull, ed. Cambridge, UK: Cambridge University Press, 1959, 416.

Prior-Miller, Marcia R. and Associates. "Bibliography of Published Research on Magazine and Journal Periodicals." 9th ed. Research database. Ames: Iowa State University, last modified, 31 August 2014, MSWord file <mpm@iastate.edu>.

Introduction

SCHOLARLY ENGAGEMENT WITH THE MAGAZINE FORM

Expansion and Coalescence

David Abrahamson

Many media scholars agree that magazines—even more than newspapers, which are geographically limited, or the broadcast media, which are largely derivative, amplifying rather than creating social and cultural trends—serve both as a mirror of and a catalyst for the tenor and tone of the sociocultural realities of their times. A few historical examples can illustrate the point. In the 1950s, the glossy photographs of *Life* and *Look* defined a new era of postwar abundance in the United States. The political activism of the 1960s and early 1970s, reflected in publications such as *Ramparts*, later gave way to the Me Decade of the 1980s, with city and regional magazines such as *New York* taking the lead in extolling passions for consumer goods and the politics of the personal.

In the 1990s and the first decade of the current century, an era defined by the globalization of commerce and communication, magazines entered a period of evolution, distinguished by niche marketing and a fertile interaction between print media, the World Wide Web and proliferating digital media forms. Exactly where these developments will lead in the future is not entirely clear, but it is certain that magazines are likely to benefit from their unique ability to provide specific information of perceived value to a definable group of reader-viewers who are both attractive to marketers and for whom the content of magazines they value is an informational good worth paying for.

Equally notable, the last 20 years have seen enormous change in the industry, with much of the innovation in these new media areas led by magazine firms. In the main, the reason for this has been the fortuitous convergence between the strengths (and needs) of the magazine industry and the emerging directions in which the Web seems to be evolving. These include at least four significant trends, the first of which is specialization. In many ways, the development of the on-line realm has followed the historical model of magazine development: mass vehicles that, over time, evolve to define and serve specific niches. In the beginning of the on-line world, many of the newly created sites were fairly general in their orientation. Today, however, despite the success of portals such as Google and Facebook, the dominant on-line trend seems to privilege substantial content specialization. As in the conventional magazine world, beyond the gateway afforded by the portal, there will be more different sites serving more different audiences—and, driven by diverging audience interests, the content of the sites themselves is in turn becoming more differentiated.

A corollary of specialization will be that fewer magazine Web sites will identically mirror the hard-copy print version of the publication. No longer will the Web site be a mere archive of the print product. Many magazine publishers will come to believe that other principles of conception and presentation apply on-line. However, no industry-wide agreement has as yet emerged on the operative principles to be applied when taking information originating in print form and putting it on-line. Some publishers, for example, believe that the average reader's on-line attention span is limited to one screen's worth of information; others think that as many as five screens are acceptable. Some believe that on-screen flashing banner advertising makes no difference; others find it an abomination. With all the different on-line presentation solutions currently in use, it is evident that there is as yet very little unanimity on trade practices.

It is likely that the historic adaptability of the magazine form will serve exceedingly well in the future. The basic strategic model of *narrow-casting*—serving the specific information needs of specific audiences for whom advertisers will pay a premium—will certainly continue to prevail. In large part due to their skill in applying this niche-driven economic model, successful magazine publishers will remain active in World Wide Web development, providing on-line information derived from, yet not identical to, that contained in their printed versions. Despite the importance of the Web, it is clear that both as a self-contained, highly targeted information vehicle and as a core brand from which other products will be extended, the magazine in its contemporary printed form will continue to demonstrate its efficacy as a source of information and pleasure for its readers, its utility as a marketing vehicle for its advertisers and its viability as a business enterprise for its publishers well into the twenty-first century.

As a concomitant result of all of the above, the last two decades have seen a flowering of scholarly research focused on the magazine form. Much of it, however, has been published in inordinately diffuse circumstances, making it relatively inaccessible and difficult to retrieve. What is lacking is a coherent scholarly anthology that will provide not only the much-needed coalescence of the recent research by scholars around the world, but also a coherent information structure that will facilitate further research into diverse aspects of the magazine form as manifest around the world.

To accomplish this, this volume comprises six parts and includes a total of 33 chapters. Each chapter surveys the relevant scholarship of roughly the last 20 years in its subject area, identifying the major research themes, theoretical developments and interpretive breakthroughs.

The Central Argument

The intellectual underpinning, as well as the over-arching rationale, of this volume can be explicitly stated: Scholarly engagement with the magazine form has, in the years since 1990, produced a substantial amount of valuable research. However, the best of this scholarly effort needs to be assembled into an interpretive anthology that will both document the recently created new knowledge and encourage further research. Through the use of discursive articles authored by the leading academic authorities in the study of the magazine, the hope is that this volume has created not only an architecture to organize and archive the new knowledge but also explicitly suggests possible new avenues of future investigation. The ambition of this book is undergirded by a tangible argument: that there is a genuine need for such a volume that might further broaden and deepen our understanding of the magazine form, as well as the sociocultural realities it both mirrors and influences.

Moreover, it must be acknowledged that there is no dearth of books related to the current state of affairs in journalism, but these vary in their attention to the magazine form, from little to none. It is further worth noting, moreover, that a great deal of highly germane research has been accomplished since the publication of an earlier scholarly anthology.[1] So the underlying premise of this volume is to organize and interpret the last two decades of scholarship related to the magazine realm.

Structure of the Volume

One of the interesting challenges faced in assembling this volume was establishing its organizational structure. At the very start of the project, it was, as a friendly colleague observed, a little like dancing with a partner of unknown dimension. It quickly became apparent, however, that with the expansion of research on the American periodical since 1990, a certain structural coherence was lacking. To quote from the earlier anthology:

> There are perhaps a number of reasons that the scholarly engagement with the magazine form has long suffered from a degree of fragmentation. In the absence of any overarching intellectual structure, many researchers have often pursued their studies in relative isolation. As a result, they have often produced what might be characterized as "brilliant fragments"—worthy research of clear merit, but, it might be argued, occasionally unconnected to any larger framework.[2]

Determining and applying that framework is one of the central tasks of this project. The structure of the volume is divided into six thematically organized sections—labeled, in the language of publishing, *part titles*. They are: Part I, "Magazine Research: Methodologies and Structures"; Part II, "Magazine Publishing: The People and the Work"; Part III, "Studies in Content: Magazines as Textual Communication"; Part IV, "Studies in Presentation: Magazines as Visual Communication"; Part V, "Pedagogical and Curricular Perspectives"; and Part VI, "The Future of the Magazine Form."

Part I. Magazine Research: Methodologies and Structures

Part I investigates the approaches and parameters of magazine research, as well as studies of the various genres of magazine publishing. It includes Chapter 1, "Theory and Methods of Analysis: Models for Understanding Magazines" (Carolyn Kitch, Temple University); Chapter 2, "Magazine Typology: Using Operational Classification Theory" (Marcia R. Prior-Miller, Iowa State University); Chapter 3, "Methodological Studies: Interdisciplinarity Is the Key" (Kathleen L. Endres, University of Akron); Chapter 4, "Magazines as Historical Study Subjects: Reflecting the Sociocultural Reality" (Cynthia Lee Patterson, University of Southern Florida); Chapter 5, "Source and Citation Analysis: An Epistemology of Magazine Research" (Dominic L. Lasorsa, University of Texas-Austin); Chapter 6, "Business-to-Business Media: The Informational Needs of Professional Life" (Abe Peck, Northwestern University); Chapter 7, "Organizational Magazines: Addressing Captive or Cautious Audiences" (Michael Heller, Brunel University, and Michael Rowlinson, Queen Mary University, London); and Chapter 8, "International Magazine Publishing: The Transformative Power of Globalization" (Leara D. Rhodes, University of Georgia).

Part II. Magazine Publishing: The People and the Work

The second section explores the research into the contributions of prominent individuals and the factors which define the roles and performance of magazine professionals. It includes Chapter 9, "Autobiography and Biography: Lives Well Lived in the Magazine World" (Elizabeth Meyers Hendrickson, Ohio University); Chapter 10, "Editorial Roles and Practices: Exploring the Creative Enterprise" (Susan Greenberg, Roehampton University, London); Chapter 11, "The Business of Magazines: Advertising, Circulation and Content Issues" (Sela Sar and Lulu Rodriguez, University of Illinois); and Chapter 12, "Magazine Management: Publishing as a Business" (Hanna-Kaisa Ellonen, Lappeenranta University of Technology, Finland, and Anette Johansson, Jönköping International Business School, Sweden).

Part III. Studies in Content: Magazines as Textual Communication

Part III was the most challenging section to define, for it attempts to summarize the studies framed with a focus on the subject matter, the textual content, of magazines. It includes Chapter 13, "Gender, Race and Ethnicity: Magazines and the Question of Self-Identity" (Cheryl Renée Gooch, Lincoln University of Pennsylvania); Chapter 14, "Covering Public Affairs: The Arena of the Newsmagazines" (Isabel Soares, Universidade de Lisboa, Portugal); Chapter 15, "Business Journalism in Magazines: Wrestling with Economic Issues" (Dane S. Claussen, Shanghai International Studies University, China); Chapter 16, "Societal Considerations: Uses and Gratifications of Magazines" (Vincent F. Filak, University of Wisconsin Oshkosh); Chapter 17, "Creating Consumer Lifestyles: Esteem and Enjoyment, Influence and Appetite" (Yanick Rice Lamb, Howard University); Chapter 18, "Magazines and Popular Culture: Exceptional People, an Exceptional Medium" (Elizabeth Crisp Crawford, North Dakota State University); Chapter 19, "Religious Magazines: Keeping the Faith" (Ken Waters, Pepperdine University); Chapter 20, "Covering Science and Technology: Opportunities for Greater Scope and New Methods" (Lulu Rodriguez, University of Illinois, and Michael F. Dahlstrom, Iowa State University); Chapter 21, "Magazines and the Visual Arts: The Ideal Showcase" (Sheila M. Webb, Western Washington University); and Chapter 22, "Literary Journalism: Journalism Aspiring to Be Literature" (Miles Maguire, University of Wisconsin Oshkosh).

Part IV. Studies in Presentation: Magazines as Visual Communication

Part IV addresses the research into aspects of visual presentation used by the magazine form. It includes Chapter 23, "The Magazine Cover: The Craft of Identity and Impact" (Ted Spiker, University of Florida); Chapter 24, "Magazine Design: Defining the Visual Architecture" (Carol Holstead, University of Kansas); Chapter 25, "Photography and Illustration: Power and Promise of the Image" (Berkley Hudson, University of Missouri-Columbia, and Elizabeth A. Lance, Northwestern University in Qatar); and Chapter 26, "Infographics and Interactivity: A Nexus of Magazine Art and Science" (Carol B. Schwalbe, University of Arizona).

Part V. Pedagogical and Curricular Perspectives

Part V is centered on studies dealing with the teaching of magazine journalism. It includes Chapter 27, "Magazine Journalism Education: The Challenge of Assessing Outcomes" (Elliot King, Loyola University of Maryland); Chapter 28, "Teaching Magazine Writing: The Long- and Short-Form of It" (Kim Martin Long, Delaware Valley College); Chapter 29, "Teaching Magazine Editing: Part Art, Part Science, All Craft" (Bill Reynolds, Ryerson University, Canada); and Chapter 30, "Teaching Magazine Research: Explicating Theory and Methods" (Carolyn Ringer Lepre, Marist College).

Part VI. The Future of the Magazine Form

The final section concerns the future, both the possible opportunities and the apparent obstacles. It includes Chapter 31, "Magazines and Sustainability: Environmental and Sociocultural Impacts" (Helen Kopnina, The Hague University of Applied Science, the Netherlands); Chapter 32, "The Changing Magazine Audience: Enriching the Reader Relationship" (Rachel Davis Mersey, Northwestern University); and Chapter 33, "Digital Transformation, Print Continuity: Magazine as Art Form Rather Than Platform" (David Abrahamson, Northwestern University).

In closing, it might be worth noting that the animating principle behind this scholarly anthology is that magazines are uniquely suited as a worthy scholarly study subject. The measure of the volume's success will be if it succeeds in definitively identifying, organizing, evaluating and summarizing the working state of the academy's engagement with the magazine form. But only you, dear reader, will be the proper judge of that.

Notes

1   See David Abrahamson, ed., *The American Magazine: Research Perspectives and Prospects* (Ames: Iowa State University Press, 1995).
2   Abrahamson, *The American Magazine*, xviii.

Bibliography

Abrahamson, David, ed. *The American Magazine: Research Perspectives and Prospects*. Ames: Iowa State University Press, 1995.

Part I

MAGAZINE RESEARCH
Methodologies and Structures

1
THEORY AND METHODS OF ANALYSIS
Models for Understanding Magazines
Carolyn Kitch

Over the past quarter-century, magazine scholars have been influenced by many of the theoretical ideas that have informed the larger field of communication inquiry, as well as other disciplines in the social sciences and humanities. The resulting work has offered new understandings of magazines and magazine audiences as economic, social and cultural forces. This chapter surveys those developments, considering how they add to the literature and yet also underscore some central tensions in beliefs about the role of media in society.

In simplest terms, theory can be understood as our central assumptions about how the world around us works. Such assumptions are inherently historical, influenced by time and place. Researchers' uses of theory, therefore, shed light on not only the institutional and social climate of the subject at hand—the topic of study—but also the scholarly climate of the discipline in which the topic is studied. In other words, trends in theory tell us about our own academic enterprise as well as about the media world. This essay reviews applications of theory, and their consequent implications for methodology, in recent magazine scholarship. Because another chapter of this book discusses methods in more detail, this essay focuses primarily on philosophical views about the role of magazines in society (i.e., theory) and on how those perspectives affect scholars' views of what is worth studying and how it should be studied (i.e., topic and method).

Magazine scholars long have brought theoretical concepts to their research, whether or not explicitly; even those who have disavowed "theory" nevertheless have had to design their studies based on certain assumptions about what magazines are and do (or should be and do) and how they do or do not affect society. Even so, for many years magazine research was dominated by descriptive studies of magazine institutions and documentary studies of magazine content. More than a decade ago, scholars such as David Abrahamson urged researchers to go "beyond the mirror metaphor,"[1] in which magazines are seen merely as a reflector of an independent social reality, accepting that they play an important role in constructing that reality. This shift has occurred. In fact, in recent years, the construction view has become the default assumption—in a vast amount of scholarship about all kinds of media, including magazines—by scholars drawing on largely European theories from sociology, anthropology and literature that have taken hold across academic disciplines. Although many of these ideas, some of which are more than a century old, were initially articulated without specific regard to media, they have become popular in media studies, including magazine scholarship.

Most researchers today agree that magazines are prescriptive as well as descriptive: They convey messages about not only how society is, but also how it should be, constructing ideals to which readers should aspire. The "should" in this premise prompts some scholars to view magazines negatively, as commercial vehicles of control in service of economic profit and the political status quo, while it prompts other scholars to view magazines positively, as cultural vehicles of aspiration drawing together imagined communities of like-minded people.

This chapter considers how such differing beliefs have affected the shape of magazine scholarship by briefly discussing the broader theories at hand and then noting how they have been used in recent research. Those studies are offered merely as examples and are not necessarily the definitive works in each area, although some of them have been quite influential. Similarly, this chapter offers a discussion of some noticeable trends but is not an exhaustive survey of all theoretical approaches employed within what is, across many disciplines, now quite a large body of research that in some way involves magazines.

In the following sections, recent scholarship is sorted into three different models for understanding magazines: as a form of control, as a form of community and as a form of culture. The first two models are (or seem to be) parallel to the philosophical split described above, while the third model combines elements of both. The chapter concludes with some thoughts on the implications of theory for the possible future of magazine scholarship, especially in light of current challenges facing the journalism industries.

Magazines as Control

Critical theorists have tended to embrace an essentially Marxist belief that magazines (among other kinds of media) are influential players in systems of power, serving the economic imperative of profit as well as the political regime in which that economy exists. Political-economy theory draws on the philosophy of not only Karl Marx but also Louis Althusser, in whose model media are one of many societal institutions that dispense official ideology and that limit citizens' identities and power by addressing them in certain ways ("hailing" or interpellation).[2] To explain why such top-down power systems survive, many media scholars turn to political theorist Antonio Gramsci's notion of hegemony, a process in which powerful institutions convince the public that the status quo is in their best interests[3]; others use philosopher Michel Foucault's concept of discourse, the circulation and reinforcement of certain ideas at the expense of others.[4]

In all of these views, magazines are instruments of power, and the typical research question investigates how they work to maintain it. Usually part of that question has to do with representation or rhetoric, how ideals are verbally and visually constructed and emphasized in order to promote certain kinds of behavior that maintain the existing economic and political system. This kind of research is further interested in how those messages address and assemble readers as groups of consumers, as markets rather than people, thus commodifying the readers as well as the topics of the magazines.

The two most common kinds of magazine research—historical studies and studies of body image among female magazine readers—frequently take this theoretical route. Quite a number of historical studies have explained magazines as key players in the emergence of modern commercial culture at the turn of the twentieth century. That era was the focus of several influential books that were published within just a two-year period during the mid-1990s and were written by scholars of sociology and literature as well as history: Richard Ohmann's *Selling Culture: Magazines, Markets, and Class at the Turn of the Century*; Helen Damon-Moore's *Magazines for the Millions: Gender and Commerce in the* Ladies' Home Journal *and the* Saturday Evening Post, *1880–1910*; Jennifer Scanlon's *Inarticulate Longings: The* Ladies' Home Journal, *Gender, and the Promises of Consumer Culture*; and Ellen Gruber Garvey's *The Adman in the Parlor: Magazines and the Gendering of Consumer Culture, 1880s to 1910s.*[5]

As their titles suggest, all of these works connect the emergence of mass-audience consumer markets to magazines' strategic constructions of class and gender. Scanlon writes that during this era magazines promoted a "'consensus' view" by publishing "stories, editorial pieces, and advertisements [that], although seemingly fragmentary and perhaps unrelated, actually worked together to provide [a] larger, dominant picture."[6] Damon-Moore contends that they "creat[ed] . . . a gendered commercial discourse and a commercial gender discourse" through a "hegemonic" process in which both audiences and producers were participants and yet were "unequal players."[7] Their work provided a theoretical foundation for other research on the same time period, an era when mass-circulated magazine artwork created "a visual vocabulary of womanhood that now seems natural."[8]

The role of mass media in defining and naturalizing female beauty ideals was a primary focus of the earliest generation of feminist research during the 1970s, when popular-culture scholar Judith Williamson published *Decoding Advertisements*[9] and sociologist Gaye Tuchman declared "the symbolic annihilation of women by the mass media,"[10] and it remains probably the most common topic of research on current magazines. Another influential early work was Angela McRobbie's ideological analysis of the content of the British teen magazine *Jackie*, which inspired many other works about magazines for adolescent girls.[11]

This kind of scholarship, which has emerged alongside a similar body of criticism in the popular press, often focuses on magazine content, embraces a strong-power model of media messages and uses several methodological tools that are linked with particular theoretical perspectives. Some researchers perform semiotic analysis in order to study the patterns through which images "signify," as initially described by semiotician Roland Barthes.[12] Others, drawing on the work of sociologist Erving Goffman and political theorist Robert Entman,[13] employ framing analysis, the study of how media emphasize certain aspects of events or phenomena in order to create a sense-making *frame* for their meaning. Still other researchers use focus groups, surveys, observation or interviews with audience members to measure their reactions to media content. The shared assumption is that magazines' messages limit readers' knowledge or negatively influence their self-image and behavior. This is an especially common theme in *media literacy* research, which focuses on media effects among children and young teens.

Given the extent to which magazines are part of a broader and aggressive commercial culture, these concerns are warranted, yet they have become problematized by newer ideas about the nature of audiences and identity. During the 1980s researchers began to suggest that while ideological messages are encoded into media texts by producers, they also must be decoded by audiences, whose readings can be "negotiated" or even "oppositional." Those terms were used by Stuart Hall[14] and other British cultural theorists involved in the Birmingham Centre for Cultural Studies, which turned a critical spotlight on working-class subcultures—the audience itself. Angela McRobbie's early work was an attempt to consider the role of gender within the Centre's focus on class, and in subsequent essays she noted the importance of studying readers as well as text, acknowledging that magazines are not merely "a massive ideological block in which readers [are] implicitly imprisoned."[15]

Frequently citing Janice Radway's influential 1984 book *Reading the Romance*, which used reader-response theory to argue that female readers can make their own, productive meanings from what are assumed to be ideologically restrictive texts, more recent magazine scholarship has made similar claims.[16] Joke Hermes, who interviewed 80 Dutch readers of women's magazines, concludes not only that they "are neither cultural dupes nor silly housewives" but that magazine stories give some of them a sense of "connected knowing and emotional learning."[17] In her study of teen-magazine readers, Dawn Currie argues that "the process through which dominant meanings are able to provide satisfactory accounts [of readers' social reality] is never seamless or uncontested," and that girls "draw upon experiential knowledge of the social world during meaning-making."[18] Several other studies have indeed found that readers' upbringing and social norms may make them more capable of negotiated readings. In a longitudinal study of white and black girls reading teen magazines, for instance, Lisa Duke learned that "[w]hile

Black girls . . . sought out mainstream teen magazines for what they saw as relatively generic content on topics like social issues and entertainment, these girls were largely uninterested in teen magazines' beauty images because they conflict with African-American standards of attractiveness."[19] While not necessarily refuting the strong-power model of media effects, such findings complicate it by positing that "the peer group is of crucial significance," writes Meenakshi Gigi Durham.[20]

Magazines as Community

A magazine's readership may itself be a peer group, even if its members are not physically together. As David Abrahamson and others have noted, because of their thematic segmentation, one "exceptional" aspect of magazines (as compared to other kinds of media) is the homogeneity of their audiences: They are ready-made social groups, collections of people united by shared interests and worldviews.[21] Thus they are fruitful groups to study as "interpretive communities," a term coined by literary scholar Stanley Fish. His original definition of this concept was more about the reader's own interpretation of a text (based on assumptions about how other people would interpret it),[22] yet researchers of mass media were quick to embrace the term to refer to groups of media audience members and sometimes media producers as well. Media researchers also have enthusiastically taken up political scientist Benedict Anderson's notion of the "imagined community," a feeling of connection to strangers based on their presumption of shared identity.[23] Finally, drawing on the ideas of literary theorist M.M. Bakhtin, some scholars analyze the magazine text as a form of conversation among readers, producers and subjects, a dialogue that is "multivocal" (multiple voices) and "polysemic" (multiple meanings).[24]

Such views constitute a departure from the model discussed previously, in which texts inflict normative ideology on readers (even if some readers may be able to *resist* it). Instead, the power to make meaning and construct identity lies with the audience, or at least they share that power with the media producers. In this second model, magazines are forums for productive and organic expressions of social and cultural identity.

Sheila Webb found this model even in the politically conservative content of Reiman magazines (or Reiman Publications), whose "reader-written" shelter and women's magazines solicit readers' anecdotes, advice, recipes and memories; the result, in Webb's view, is a "social space readers share."[25] In their study of alternative magazines, Bill Reader and Kevin Moist contend that such connection among readers is not imagined but real. Borrowing from the language of on-line media scholarship, they see audiences as "virtual communities . . . made up of like-minded individuals who transcend limitations of space and time to commune via media."[26] Like Webb, they analyze this reader phenomenon through the lens of magazine content, in their case letters to the editor, which "can provide insight into the shared values of the virtual communities and how readers . . . play a constitutive role in developing those values."[27]

Alternative magazines are, of course, one sector of the medium that is by definition a critique of the mainstream ideologies with which magazines are usually associated. In identifying and challenging those mainstream ideas, alternative magazines perform "oppositional decoding as an act of resistance," to use Linda Steiner's phrase from her study of the content of *Ms.* magazine. Writing 25 years ago, Steiner concluded: "We need not so pessimistically concede unitary effects of mass media on mass audiences. Indeed . . . looking at alternative publications may suggest how to teach oppositional and critical thinking."[28]

As Katherine Sender has noted, "oppositional" can be a fluid concept over time as alternative cultures are accepted and absorbed into the mainstream (an assimilation process that is part of hegemony). She saw that outcome in her study of 25 years of the *Advocate* magazine, concluding that it had succeeded in fostering a sense of "cultural belonging" among its readers but also in constructing "a unified [and exclusive] gay discourse" that enabled its publisher to "sell a homogenized gay readership to advertisers."[29] Yet her theoretical model, based on sociologist Pierre Bourdieu's concepts of *habitus* and *taste cultures*, is a useful framework for understanding the "cultural capital"[30] acquired by the active audiences of other kinds of alternative media.

Reader and Moist understand such publications as processes as well as products, writing, "In alternative media, social and creative aspects are emphasized as much as content related to the subculture in question; such publications encourage, even rely upon, engagement, participation, and interactivity with their audiences."[31] This is, in Tony Harcup's terms, a form of "active citizenship," a practice of participatory democracy in which editors' and readers' goals are aligned and their contributions are entwined. Harcup writes that "alternative media participants do not concern themselves only with the production of alternative content; they also embody alternative ways of producing such content. By doing so, they disrupt established 'power relationships' on multiple levels."[32]

Chris Atton describes music fanzines, for instance, as a "community of interest" in which readers "contribute reviews, interviews, discographies, histories, analyses . . . [and] artwork" and "display . . . expert knowledge [that] can challenge professional notions of expert authority."[33] Echoing Harcup, Atton contends that "[p]articipatory, amateur media production contests the concentration of institutional and professional media power and challenges the media monopoly on producing symbolic forms."[34] Based on values including "connection" and "authenticity," zines, writes Stephen Duncombe, "privilege the ethic of DIY, do-it-yourself: [M]ake your own culture" as opposed to "consuming that which is made for you."[35] While these scholars write about on-line as well as paper fanzines, Alison Piepmeier focuses on the role of physical form in the social experience of readers. Contending that their literal circulation is as important as their content, she writes,

> Zines instigate intimate, affectionate connections between their creators and readers . . . embodied communities that are made possible by the materiality of the zine medium. . . . In a world where more and more of us spend all day at our computers, zines reconnect us to our bodies and to other human beings.[36]

Magazines as Culture

Piepmeier's further point is that magazines are cultural artifacts, and that is the third perspective this chapter will assess. This view problematizes the dichotomy between the *top-down* vs. *bottom-up* models discussed previously, containing elements of both. Magazines are studied as culture in at least three overlapping ways: as a cultural form in their own right; as an expression of the ideals of the surrounding culture; and as a statement about cultural identity.

First, magazines are physical repositories of text and art whose form itself is the focus of researchers interested in narrative and iconology. Scholars search magazine content for recurring stories and symbols, drawing on ideas about representation and structure from theorists such as folklorist Vladimir Propp, semiotician Roland Barthes and literary and art historian W.J.T. Mitchell.[37] Such research understands magazines as systems of symbols arranged according to "culturally specific storytelling codes," in the words of S. Elizabeth Bird and Robert Dardenne.[38]

This structural analytical lens has been applied to magazine images as well as text. When Wendy Kozol studied the construction of the ideal (yet also "representative") American family in *Life* magazine photographs published after the Second World War, she "examine[d] composition, lighting, framing, and subject matter of the photographs in conjunction with written texts," concluding, "Analysis of the layout of photo-essays reveals the narrative drive of *Life*'s format for reporting the news and the ideological power of that narrative."[39] Narrative analysis also has been employed to study the role of magazines in the construction of social memory through, for instance, the "core plots" of decade-in-review issues or the visual iconography of masculinity that emerged across all types of magazines after September 11th.[40]

These works additionally qualify as examples of the second (and related) way scholars view magazines, which is that they are *windows* on cultural conditions in any given time and place. In another book about *Life*—a collection of essays on its treatment of topics ranging from war and peace to religion and race—Erika Doss argues that the magazine both "structur[ed] visual experience" and functioned as a "visual theater of postwar national identity."[41] Here theater is a metaphor for the audience as well as the magazine. Their inseparability is similarly suggested by the model of magazines as a set of "culturally specific"[42] stories.

"If culture is the stories we tell about ourselves, then magazines are prime examples of cultural resource," writes Tim Holmes. "They are full of stories which we tell about ourselves, which we make up about ourselves, which we accept as being about ourselves. . . ."[43] His phrasing deftly implies that magazines both reflect and construct reality and that they reveal the wishes of the readers as well as the goals of the editors. Magazines construct an ideal world and disseminate that vision, yet they reference a real world, a culture that is external to magazines and inspires their creation.

This has been the argument of several ambitious cultural histories in which magazines are understood as powerful influences and yet also as expressions of audiences' wishes, imaginations and sensibilities at historical moments of great social change. As have many other researchers, Matthew Schneirov studied the emergence of mass-circulation magazines at the turn of the twentieth century. In his view, however, the new, popular magazines did not merely create consumer markets; they articulated social "visions of the future" that were in circulation throughout the broader culture. "These magazines were not superstructural reflections of economic changes that somehow operated 'behind their backs,'" he explains, but instead were "part and parcel" of the cultural ideas that constituted a "new social order."[44] Another example of this more complex view is Richard Popp's study of the emergence of travel magazines and tourism advertising during the mid-twentieth century against the backdrop of not only a strong economy and increasing leisure time (i.e., a new economic market), but also the "middlebrow ethos" and "wanderlust" of postwar Americans. Thus this new sector of publishing was not "simply a mirage conjured up by advertisers, publishers, and ideologues," but the result of "a cultural moment in which vacations and mobility captivated the public imagination. . . . Genuine excitement thus converged with marketing strategy."[45]

Both Schneirov and Popp study magazine content as evidence of, to use Raymond Williams's well-traveled term, the "structure of feeling" of a historical time and place.[46] This also is a primary goal of scholars of literary journalism. Like structural analysts, they are interested in the literal form of such journalism, its aesthetic elements that align it with literature as a form of cultural production. Yet they also attend to the cultural insights that such writing contains, its mission of conveying not only facts but also "feelings, emotions, and expectations—the consciousness behind events and actions that can provide reflexive cultural insights into other times and places," writes Norman Sims.[47]

Finally, magazines have been analyzed as the constructors of shared (even if invalid) definitions of the cultural identity of particular social or national groups. These studies, while focusing on ideas about culture rather than commerce and in some cases drawing on theory from cultural anthropology, have much in common with the ideological critiques that embrace a strong-power model of media. One especially influential investigation, published two decades ago, was Catherine Lutz and Jane Collins's *Reading National Geographic*. This was a pioneering work on magazines methodologically as well as theoretically, in that its authors researched production and reception as well as content, and they analyzed the relationship between text and visual images. Ultimately they concluded that the magazine's role is a mentally colonizing one, as its editors and photographers "objectify" and then "appropriate" non-Western cultures in service of "the imaginative spaces that non-Western peoples occupy and the tropes and stories that organize their existence in Western minds."[48]

Recent scholarship has offered a more optimistic picture, taking into consideration how globalization, the concurrent rise of nationalism and a preoccupation with "authentic" ethnicity have combined to create "glocal" cultural forms. Because they are audience-specific and yet global, magazines have become an excellent lens through which scholars may view "processes of cultural hybridization that allow active audiences locally to resist globally dominant cultural forms," writes Fabienne Darling-Wolf.[49] Many magazines have national editions across the world that carry both western and local content or that locally re-edit foreign content for local audiences[50]; what's more, some recent cultural trends (expressed in magazines as well as other media) have traveled from east to west, rather than the more common opposite direction of "cultural imperialism."[51] The hybridity of both content and audiences invites future studies of magazines as cultural processes as well as cultural products.

Future Research

This essay began with the premise that theory is historically grounded, shaped by prevailing beliefs about what matters more or less at any given time. So, too, is the question of what topics are worthy of study, including not only specific magazines or themes but also the magazine medium itself. Today we may be at a crossroads in terms of how we answer that question. Why and how do magazines matter?

One recent answer is that magazines are "exceptional," that they are special and different from other kinds of media. This may remain an important distinction for some kinds of research questions (such as, for instance, studies of magazines' value as material culture, as physical objects to be shared and saved). Yet perhaps the magazine medium is not so exceptional after all—especially when considered in light of developments in the broader world of journalism.

So much recent research has identified key concerns regarding the future of journalism: the need for smaller, thematically defined audiences who demonstrate a high level of reader engagement and are willing to pay for specialized content; the realization that those audiences want coverage of longer-term issues that apply to their daily lives rather than breaking news they can get elsewhere; the need to integrate images and words within new kinds of narratives; the proposition that journalism should be less didactic and more of an interactive conversation; etc. Yet these are not new concepts. Their precedents lie in magazines: in the editorial and business models set in place at the end of the nineteenth century; in the specialization that swept the industry in the middle of the twentieth century; and in the long and evolving relationship between written narratives and visual aesthetics that magazines pioneered.

Certainly the professional perspective of magazine experts should be valuable to the rest of the journalism world now more than ever. So should academic scholarship on the magazine medium. In the meantime, the current "crisis" in journalism reminds us that the industry remains important to study. Major works tracing the magazine medium over time—such as John Tebbel and Mary Ellen Zuckerman's *The Magazine in America* and David Sumner's *The Magazine Century*[52]—are not merely descriptive profiles but shed light on an evolution of media models that should be of broad interest to observers of the shifting sands of the journalism profession. Moreover, institutional histories do not have to be atheoretical.

Recent years have seen some fine works that blend cultural and business history. Kelley Massoni's book about the early years of *Seventeen* magazine in the 1940s uses oral histories with the original editorial and promotion executives to provide corporate context for the emergence of teen culture.[53] Douglas Ward's study of the innovative research operations of the Curtis Publishing Company in the 1910s sheds light on the origins of the business strategies and conceptualizations of audiences that shaped modern magazine publishing.[54] Richard Popp's study of magazines' role in the creation of travel marketing similarly uses business archives to provide evidence for a cultural argument.[55] Anna Gough-Yates analyzes trade-press characterizations of the editorial and marketing strategies of women's magazines, especially with regard to their ideas about how to sell to a professional "new woman."[56]

Two noteworthy recent works also offer new approaches to researching the production of women's magazines, the industry's biggest and most-criticized sector. Elizabeth Hendrickson's study of *Jezebel*, an on-line magazine for young women, considers how an alternative (feminist) editorial point of view is expressed on a new media platform; in her observation of its editors' work, she also discovers that the long-held principles of journalism sociology do not work well to explain the values and economy of "convergence culture." Calling for "a theoretical shift," she concludes, "As old models for understanding media cease to support the complex structures of new organizations, we must look to other frameworks. . . . "[57] In her 2013 book *Remake, Remodel: Women's Magazines in the Digital Age*, Brooke Duffy draws on trade-press coverage and interviews with some 30 magazine professionals to paint a portrait of "an industry straddling two seemingly different media eras,"[58] a time when technological evolution has meant "the evolution from magazine as *object* to magazine as *brand*."[59] This transformation, she argues, has affected not only the magazine product, but also the professional identity of magazine editors and the nature of the industry itself, including "longstanding production roles and routines, assumptions about the audience, and deeply embedded relationships with advertisers."[60]

This is the kind of research that can propel journalism theory forward while positioning the magazine medium at the center of that discussion. And it emerges in a media world in which, in many ways, theory seems quite real. Social media have made everyone aware of the idea of the imagined community, as well as the potential for the reach and power of amateur, bottom-up communication. At the same time, journalism companies' dissolution or diminishment have revitalized public interest in ownership issues and concerns about influence and commodification, the focus of political-economy theory and ideological top-down models.

The current climate invites us—indeed, it requires us—to remember that theory is useful. Theory answers the how and why questions, not only the what, who, and when questions. How do magazines function, as forms of control, community and culture, as well as forms of commerce? How do they preserve or challenge the status quo? How and why do readers use and need them? Why do they matter in relation to the broader culture? These are the questions of theory, and of the fertile landscape of future scholarship.

Notes

1 David Abrahamson, "Beyond the Mirror Metaphor: Magazine Exceptionalism and Sociocultural Change," *Journal of Magazine & New Media Research* 4.1 (Spring 2002): n.p.

2 Louis Althusser, *Lenin and Philosophy, and Other Essays*, trans. Ben Brewster (New York: Monthly Review Press, 2001; originally published in 1968).

3 Antonio Gramsci, *Selections from the Prison Notebooks of Antonio Gramsci*, trans. and ed. Quintin Hoare and Geoffrey Nowell Smith (New York: International Publishers, 1971).

4 Michel Foucault, *Power/Knowledge: Selected Interviews and Other Writings, 1972–1977*, ed. Colin Gordon; trans. Colin Gordon, Leo Marshall, John Mepham and Kate Soper (New York: Pantheon, 1980).

5 Richard Ohmann, *Selling Culture: Magazines, Markets, and Class at the Turn of the Century* (London and New York: Verso, 1996); Helen Damon-Moore, *Magazines for the Millions: Gender and Commerce in the* Ladies' Home Journal *and the* Saturday Evening Post, *1880–1910* (Albany: State University of New York Press, 1994); Jennifer Scanlon, *Inarticulate Longings: The* Ladies' Home Journal, *Gender, and the Promises of Consumer Culture* (London and New York: Routledge, 1995); and Ellen Gruber Garvey, *The Adman in the Parlor: Magazines and the Gendering of Consumer Culture, 1880s to 1910s* (New York: Oxford University Press, 1996).

6 Scanlon, *Inarticulate Longings*, 7.

7 Damon-Moore, *Magazines for the Millions*, 3.

8 Carolyn Kitch, *The Girl on the Magazine Cover: The Origins of Visual Stereotypes in American Mass Media* (Chapel Hill and London: University of North Carolina Press, 2001), 3.

9 Judith Williamson, *Decoding Advertisements: Ideology and Meaning in Advertising* (London: Calder and Boyars, 1978). Also in this era Erving Goffman published the influential book *Gender Advertisements* (Cambridge, MA: Harvard University Press, 1979).

10 Gaye Tuchman, "Introduction: The Symbolic Annihilation of Women by the Mass Media," in Gaye Tuchman, Arlene Kaplan Daniels, and James Benét, eds., *Hearth and Home: Images of Women in the Mass Media* (New York: Oxford University Press, 1978), 3.

11 Angela McRobbie, Jackie: *An Ideology of Adolescent Femininity* (Birmingham, UK: The Centre for Contemporary Cultural Studies, University of Birmingham, 1978). Other important works published during the 1980s and early 1990s include: Marjorie Ferguson, *Forever Feminine: Women's Magazines and the Cult of Femininity*. London: Heinemann, 1982); Ros Ballaster, Margaret Beetham, Elizabeth Frazer, and Sandra Hebron, *Women's Worlds: Ideology, Femininity and the Woman's Magazine* (Houndsmills, Hampshire, UK: Palgrave Macmillan, 1991); and Ellen McCracken, *Decoding Women's Magazines: From Mademoiselle to Ms.* (Houndsmills, Hampshire, UK: Palgrave Macmillan, 1992).

12 Roland Barthes, *Image–Music–Text*, essays selected and trans. Stephen Heath (New York: Hill and Wang, 1977).

13 Erving Goffman, *Frame Analysis: An Essay on the Organization of Experience* (Cambridge, MA: Harvard University Press, 1974); Robert M. Entman, "Framing: Toward Clarification of a Fractured Paradigm," *Journal of Communication* 43.4 (Autumn 1993): 51–58.

14 Stuart Hall, "Encoding/Decoding," in Stuart Hall, Dorothy Hobson, Andrew Lowe and Paul Willis, eds., *Culture, Media, Language* (Birmingham, UK: Centre for Contemporary Cultural Studies, University of Birmingham, 1980), 128–138.

15 Angela McRobbie, *Feminism and Youth Culture: From "Jackie" to "Just Seventeen"* (Boston: Unwin Hyman, 1991), 141.

16 Janice A. Radway, *Reading the Romance: Women, Patriarchy, and Popular Literature* (Chapel Hill: University of North Carolina Press, 1984).

17 Joke Hermes, *Reading Women's Magazines: An Analysis of Everyday Media Use* (Cambridge, UK: Polity Press, 1995), 150, 152.

18 Dawn H. Currie, *Girl Talk: Adolescent Magazines and Their Readers* (Toronto: University of Toronto Press, 1999), 13.

19 Lisa Duke, "Black in a Blonde World: Race and Girls' Interpretations of the Feminine Ideal in Teen Magazines," *Journalism & Mass Communication Quarterly* 77.2 (Summer 2000): 367–392. In other studies, J. Robyn Goodman and the team of Donnalyn Pompper and Jesica Koenig found that Latino women also may resist (although to a much lesser extent) magazines' definitions of ideal body image. See J. Robyn Goodman, "Flabless Is Fabulous: How Latina and Anglo Women Read and Incorporate the Excessively Thin Body Ideal into Everyday Experience," *Journalism & Mass Communication Quarterly* 79.3 (Autumn 2002): 712–727; and Donnalyn Pompper and Jesica Koenig, "Cross-Cultural-Generational Perceptions of Ideal Body Image: Hispanic Women and Magazine Standards," *Journalism & Mass Communication Quarterly* 81.1 (Spring 2004): 89–107.

20 Meenakshi Gigi Durham, "Girls, Media, and the Negotiation of Sexuality: A Study of Race, Class, and Gender in Adolescent Peer Groups," *Journalism & Mass Communication Quarterly* 76.2 (Summer 1999): 193.

21 David Abrahamson, "Magazine Exceptionalism: The Concept, the Criteria, the Challenge," *Journalism Studies* 8.4 (July 2007): 667–670. This point also is made in other scholarship including Sammye Johnson and Patricia Prijatel, *The Magazine from Cover to Cover*, 3rd ed. (New York and Oxford: Oxford University Press, 2013), 5–6.

22 Stanley E. Fish, "Interpreting the *Variorum*," *Critical Inquiry* 2.3 (Spring 1976): 483.

23 Benedict Anderson, *Imagined Communities: Reflections on the Origin and Spread of Nationalism* (London: Verso, 1983).

24 M.M. Bakhtin, *The Dialogic Imagination: Four Essays by M.M. Bakhtin*, ed. Michael Holquist and trans. Caryl Emerson and Michael Holquist (Austin: University of Texas Press, 1981).

25 Sheila M. Webb, "The Narrative of Core Traditional Values in Reiman Magazines," *Journalism & Mass Communication Quarterly* 83.4 (Winter 2006): 865.

26 Bill Reader and Kevin Moist, "Letters as Indicators of Community Values: Two Case Studies of Alternative Magazines," *Journalism & Mass Communication Quarterly* 85.4 (Winter 2008): 823.

27 Reader and Moist, "Letters as Indicators of Community Values," 824.

28 Linda Steiner, "Oppositional Decoding as an Act of Resistance," *Critical Studies in Mass Communication* 5.1 (March 1988): 14.

29 Katherine Sender, "Gay Readers, Consumers, and a Dominant Gay Habitus: 25 Years of the *Advocate* Magazine," *Journal of Communication* 51.1 (March 2001): 74, 95.

30 Pierre Bourdieu, *Distinction: A Social Critique of the Judgement of Taste*, trans. Richard Nice (Cambridge, MA: Harvard University Press, 1984).

31 Reader and Moist, "Letters as Indicators of Community Values," 825.

32 Tony Harcup, "Alternative Journalism as Active Citizenship," *Journalism* 12.1 (January 2011): 17, 26–27.

33 Chris Atton, "'Living in the Past'?: Value Discourses in Progressive Rock Fanzines," *Popular Music* 20.1 (January 2001): 40; Chris Atton, "Alternative and Citizen Journalism," in Karin Wahl-Jorgensen and Thomas Hanitzsch, eds., *The Handbook of Journalism Studies* (New York and Milton Park, UK: Routledge, 2009), 271.

34 Atton, "Alternative and Citizen Journalism," 268.

35 Stephen Duncombe, *Notes from Underground: Zines and the Politics of Alternative Culture* (London and New York: Verso, 1997), 3, 2.

36 Alison Piepmeier, "Why Zines Matter: Materiality and the Creation of Embodied Community," *American Periodicals* 18.2 (2008): 214.

37 V. Propp, *Morphology of the Folktale*, 2nd ed., trans. Laurence Scott; ed. Louis R. Wagner (Austin: University of Texas Press, 1968; originally published in 1928); Barthes, *Image–Music–Text*; W.J.T. Mitchell, *Iconology: Image, Text, Ideology* (Chicago and London: University of Chicago Press, 1986).

38 S. Elizabeth Bird and Robert W. Dardenne, "Myth, Chronicle and Story: Exploring the Narrative Qualities of News," in Dan Berkowitz, ed., *Social Meanings of News: A Text-Reader* (Thousand Oaks, CA: Sage, 1997), 338–339.

39 Wendy Kozol, *Life's America: Family and Nation in Postwar Photojournalism* (Philadelphia: Temple University Press, 1994), ix.

40 Carolyn Kitch, *Pages from the Past: History and Memory in American Magazines* (Chapel Hill: University of North Carolina Press, 2005).

41 Erika Doss, "Introduction: Looking at *Life*: Rethinking America's Favorite Magazine, 1936–1972," in Erika Doss, ed., *Looking at Life Magazine* (Washington, DC: Smithsonian Institution Press, 2001), 11, 13.

42 Bird and Dardenne, "Myth, Chronicle and Story," 338–339.

43 Tim Holmes, "Mapping the Magazine: An Introduction," *Journalism Studies* 8.4 (August 2007): 515.

44 Matthew Schneirov, *The Dream of a New Social Order: Popular Magazines in America, 1893–1914* (New York: Columbia University Press, 1994), 255–256.

45 Richard K. Popp, *The Holiday Makers: Magazines, Advertising, and Mass Tourism in Postwar America* (Baton Rouge: Louisiana State University Press, 2012), 2–6, 143.

46 Raymond Williams, "Film and the Dramatic Tradition," in John Higgins, ed., *The Raymond Williams Reader* (Oxford, UK: Blackwell Publishers, Ltd., 2001), 33.

47 Norman Sims, "The Problem and the Promise of Literary Journalism Studies," *Literary Journalism Studies* 1.1 (Spring 2009): 15.

48 Catherine A. Lutz and Jane L. Collins, *Reading National Geographic* (Chicago and London: University of Chicago Press, 1993), 2.

49 Fabienne Darling-Wolf, "The Men and Women of *non-no*: Gender, Race, and Hybridity in Two Japanese Magazines," *Critical Studies in Media Communication* 23.3 (August 2006): 181.

50 Fabienne Darling-Wolf and Andrew L. Mendelson, "Seeing Themselves through the Lens of the Other: An Analysis of the Cross-Cultural Production and Negotiation of *National Geographic*'s 'The Samurai Way' Story," *Journalism & Communication Monographs* 10.3 (Autumn 2008): 285–322.

51 Fabienne Darling-Wolf, *Imagining the Global: Transnational Media and Popular Culture Beyond East and West* (Ann Arbor: University of Michigan Press, forthcoming), n.p.

52 John Tebbel and Mary Ellen Zuckerman, *The Magazine in America, 1741–1990* (New York and Oxford, UK: Oxford University Press, 1991); David E. Sumner, *The Magazine Century: American Magazines since 1900*, Mediating American History Series (New York: Peter Lang, 2010).

53 Kelley Massoni, *Fashioning Teenagers: A Cultural History of Seventeen Magazine* (Walnut Creek, CA: Left Coast Press, 2010).

54 Douglas B. Ward, *A New Brand of Business: Charles Coolidge Parlin, Curtis Publishing Company, and the Origins of Market Research* (Philadelphia: Temple University Press, 2010).

55 Popp, *The Holiday Makers*.

56 Anna Gough-Yates, *Understanding Women's Magazines: Publishing, Markets and Readerships* (London and New York: Routledge, 2003), 24.

57 Elizabeth Meyers Hendrickson, "Refresh: Examining the Production of Celebrity News in an Online Environment" (Ph.D. diss., University of Missouri-Columbia, 2008), n.p.

58 Brooke Erin Duffy, *Remake, Remodel: Women's Magazines in the Digital Age* (Urbana, Chicago and Springfield: University of Illinois Press, 2013), 5.

59 Duffy, *Remake, Remodel*, 136.

60 Duffy, *Remake, Remodel*, 5.

Bibliography

Abrahamson, David. "Beyond the Mirror Metaphor: Magazine Exceptionalism and Sociocultural Change." *Journal of Magazine & New Media Research* 4.1 (Spring 2002): n.p.

Abrahamson, David. "Magazine Exceptionalism: The Concept, the Criteria, the Challenge." *Journalism Studies* 8.4 (July 2007): 667–670.

Althusser, Louis. *Lenin and Philosophy, and Other Essays.* Translated by Ben Brewster. New York: Monthly Review Press, 2001. Originally published in 1968.

Anderson, Benedict. *Imagined Communities: Reflections on the Origin and Spread of Nationalism.* London: Verso, 1983.

Atton, Chris. "Alternative and Citizen Journalism." In Wahl-Jorgensen, Karin and Hanitzsch, Thomas, eds. *The Handbook of Journalism Studies.* International Communication Association Handbook Series. New York and Milton Park, UK: Routledge, 2009, 265–278.

Atton, Chris. "'Living in the Past'?: Value Discourses in Progressive Rock Fanzines." *Popular Music* 20.1 (January 2001): 29–46.

Bakhtin, M.M. *The Dialogic Imagination: Four Essays by M.M. Bakhtin.* Edited by Michael Holquist. Translated by Caryl Emerson and Michael Holquist. Austin: University of Texas Press, 1981.

Ballaster, Ros; Beetham, Margaret; Frazer, Elizabeth; and Hebron, Sandra. *Women's Worlds: Ideology, Femininity and the Woman's Magazine.* Houndmills, Hampshire, UK: Palgrave Macmillan, 1991.

Barthes, Roland. *Image–Music–Text.* Essays Selected and Translated by Stephen Heath. New York: Hill and Wang, 1977.

Bird, S. Elizabeth and Dardenne, Robert W. "Myth, Chronicle and Story: Exploring the Narrative Qualities of News." In Berkowitz, Dan, ed., *Social Meanings of News: A Text-Reader.* Thousand Oaks, CA: Sage, 1997, 333–350.

Bourdieu, Pierre. *Distinction: A Social Critique of the Judgement of Taste.* Translated by Richard Nice. Cambridge, MA: Harvard University Press, 1984.

Currie, Dawn H. *Girl Talk: Adolescent Magazines and Their Readers.* Toronto: University of Toronto Press, 1999.

Damon-Moore, Helen. *Magazines for the Millions: Gender and Commerce in the* Ladies' Home Journal *and the* Saturday Evening Post, *1880–1910.* Albany: State University of New York Press, 1994.

Darling-Wolf, Fabienne. *Imagining the Global: Transnational Media and Popular Culture Beyond East and West.* Ann Arbor: University of Michigan Press, forthcoming.

Darling-Wolf, Fabienne. "The Men and Women of *non-no*: Gender, Race, and Hybridity in Two Japanese Magazines." *Critical Studies in Media Communication* 23.3 (August 2006): 181–199.

Darling-Wolf, Fabienne and Mendelson, Andrew L. "Seeing Themselves through the Lens of the Other: An Analysis of the Cross-Cultural Production and Negotiation of *National Geographic*'s 'The Samurai Way' Story." *Journalism & Communication Monographs* 10.3 (Autumn 2008): 285–322.

Doss, Erika. "Introduction: Looking at *Life*: Rethinking America's Favorite Magazine, 1936–1972." In Doss, Erika, ed., *Looking at Life Magazine.* Washington, DC: Smithsonian Institution Press, 2001, 1–21.

Duffy, Brooke Erin. *Remake, Remodel: Women's Magazines in the Digital Age.* Urbana, Chicago and Springfield: University of Illinois Press, 2013.

Duke, Lisa. "Black in a Blonde World: Race and Girls' Interpretations of the Feminine Ideal in Teen Magazines." *Journalism & Mass Communication Quarterly* 77.2 (Summer 2000): 367–392.

Duncombe, Stephen. *Notes from Underground: Zines and the Politics of Alternative Culture.* London and New York: Verso, 1997.

Durham, Meenakshi Gigi. "Girls, Media, and the Negotiation of Sexuality: A Study of Race, Class, and Gender in Adolescent Peer Groups." *Journalism & Mass Communication Quarterly* 76.2 (Summer 1999): 193–216.

Entman, Robert M. "Framing: Toward Clarification of a Fractured Paradigm." *Journal of Communication* 43.4 (Autumn 1993): 51–58.

Ferguson, Marjorie. *Forever Feminine: Women's Magazines and the Cult of Femininity.* London: Heinemann, 1982.

Fish, Stanley E. "Interpreting the *Variorum*." *Critical Inquiry* 2.3 (Spring 1976): 465–485.

Foucault, Michel. *Power/Knowledge: Selected Interviews and Other Writings, 1972–1977.* Edited by Colin Gordon. Translated by Colin Gordon, Leo Marshall, John Mepham and Kate Soper. New York: Pantheon, 1980.

Garvey, Ellen Gruber. *The Adman in the Parlor: Magazines and the Gendering of Consumer Culture, 1880s to 1910s*. New York: Oxford University Press, 1996.

Goffman, Erving. *Frame Analysis: An Essay on the Organization of Experience*. Cambridge, MA: Harvard University Press, 1974.

Goffman, Erving. *Gender Advertisements*. Cambridge, MA: Harvard University Press, 1979.

Goodman, J. Robyn. "Flabless Is Fabulous: How Latina and Anglo Women Read and Incorporate the Excessively Thin Body Ideal into Everyday Experience." *Journalism & Mass Communication Quarterly* 79.3 (Autumn 2002): 712–727.

Gough-Yates, Anna. *Understanding Women's Magazines: Publishing, Markets and Readerships*. London and New York: Routledge, 2003.

Gramsci, Antonio. *Selections from the Prison Notebooks of Antonio Gramsci*. Translated and Edited by Quintin Hoare and Geoffrey Nowell Smith. New York: International Publishers, 1971.

Hall, Stuart. "Encoding/Decoding." In Hall, Stuart; Hobson, Dorothy; Lowe, Andrew; and Willis, Paul, eds. *Culture, Media, Language*. Birmingham, UK: Centre for Contemporary Cultural Studies, University of Birmingham, 1980, 128–138.

Harcup, Tony. "Alternative Journalism as Active Citizenship." *Journalism* 12.1 (January 2011): 15–31.

Hendrickson, Elizabeth Meyers. "Refresh: Examining the Production of Celebrity News in an Online Environment." Ph.D. diss., University of Missouri-Columbia, 2008.

Hermes, Joke. *Reading Women's Magazines: An Analysis of Everyday Media Use*. Cambridge, UK: Polity Press, 1995.

Holmes, Tim. "Mapping the Magazine: An Introduction." *Journalism Studies* 8.4 (August 2007): 510–521.

Johnson, Sammye and Prijatel, Patricia. *The Magazine from Cover to Cover*. 3rd ed. New York and Oxford: Oxford University Press, 2013.

Kitch, Carolyn. *The Girl on the Magazine Cover: The Origins of Visual Stereotypes in American Mass Media*. Chapel Hill and London: University of North Carolina Press, 2001.

Kitch, Carolyn. *Pages from the Past: History and Memory in American Magazines*. Chapel Hill: University of North Carolina Press, 2005.

Kozol, Wendy. *Life's America: Family and Nation in Postwar Photojournalism*. Philadelphia: Temple University Press, 1994.

Lutz, Catherine A. and Collins, Jane L. *Reading* National Geographic. Chicago and London: University of Chicago Press, 1993.

Massoni, Kelley. *Fashioning Teenagers: A Cultural History of* Seventeen Magazine. Walnut Creek, CA: Left Coast Press, 2010.

McCracken, Ellen. *Decoding Women's Magazines: From* Mademoiselle *to* Ms. Houndmills, Hampshire, UK: Palgrave Macmillan, 1992.

McRobbie, Angela. *Feminism and Youth Culture: From* "Jackie" *to* "Just Seventeen." Boston: Unwin Hyman, 1991.

McRobbie, Angela. Jackie: *An Ideology of Adolescent Femininity*. Birmingham, UK: The Centre for Contemporary Cultural Studies, University of Birmingham, 1978.

Mitchell, W.J.T. *Iconology: Image, Text, Ideology*. Chicago and London: University of Chicago Press, 1986.

Ohmann, Richard. *Selling Culture: Magazines, Markets, and Class at the Turn of the Century*. London and New York: Verso, 1996.

Piepmeier, Alison. "Why Zines Matter: Materiality and the Creation of Embodied Community." *American Periodicals* 18.2 (2008): 213–238.

Pompper, Donnalyn and Koenig, Jesica. "Cross-Cultural-Generational Perceptions of Ideal Body Image: Hispanic Women and Magazine Standards." *Journalism & Mass Communication Quarterly* 81.1 (Spring 2004): 89–107.

Popp, Richard K. *The Holiday Makers: Magazines, Advertising, and Mass Tourism in Postwar America*. Baton Rouge: Louisiana State University Press, 2012.

Propp, V. *Morphology of the Folktale*, 2nd ed. Translated by Laurence Scott. Edited by Louis R. Wagner. Austin: University of Texas Press, 1968. Originally published in 1928.

Radway, Janice A. *Reading the Romance: Women, Patriarchy, and Popular Literature*. Chapel Hill: University of North Carolina Press, 1984.

Reader, Bill and Moist, Kevin. "Letters as Indicators of Community Values: Two Case Studies of Alternative Magazines." *Journalism & Mass Communication Quarterly* 85.4 (Winter 2008): 823–840.

Scanlon, Jennifer. *Inarticulate Longings*: The Ladies' Home Journal, *Gender, and the Promises of Consumer Culture*. London and New York: Routledge, 1995.

Schneirov, Matthew. *The Dream of a New Social Order: Popular Magazines in America, 1893–1914*. New York: Columbia University Press, 1994.

Sender, Katherine. "Gay Readers, Consumers, and a Dominant Gay Habitus: 25 Years of the *Advocate* Magazine." *Journal of Communication* 51.1 (March 2001): 73–99.

Sims, Norman. "The Problem and the Promise of Literary Journalism Studies." *Literary Journalism Studies* 1.1 (Spring 2009): 7–16.

Steiner, Linda. "Oppositional Decoding as an Act of Resistance." *Critical Studies in Mass Communication* 5.1 (March 1988): 1–15.

Sumner, David E. *The Magazine Century: American Magazines since 1900*. Mediating American History Series. New York: Peter Lang, 2010.

Tebbel, John and Zuckerman, Mary Ellen. *The Magazine in America, 1741–1990*. New York and Oxford, UK: Oxford University Press, 1991.

Tuchman, Gaye. "Introduction: The Symbolic Annihilation of Women by the Mass Media." In Tuchman, Gaye; Daniels, Arlene Kaplan; and Benét, James, eds. *Hearth and Home: Images of Women in the Mass Media*. New York: Oxford University Press, 1978, 3–38.

Ward, Douglas B. *A New Brand of Business: Charles Coolidge Parlin, Curtis Publishing Company, and the Origins of Market Research*. Philadelphia: Temple University Press, 2010.

Webb, Sheila M. "The Narrative of Core Traditional Values in Reiman Magazines." *Journalism & Mass Communication Quarterly* 83.4 (Winter 2006): 865–882.

Williams, Raymond. "Film and the Dramatic Tradition." In Higgins, John, ed. *The Raymond Williams Reader*. Oxford, UK: Blackwell Publishers, Ltd., 2001, 25–41.

Williamson, Judith. *Decoding Advertisements: Ideology and Meaning in Advertising*. London: Calder and Boyars, 1978.

2

MAGAZINE TYPOLOGY

Using Operational Classification Theory

Marcia R. Prior-Miller

The magazine and journal periodical is a form of mediated communication that serves a wide variety of functions in society. It contributes to dialogue and debate on critical social and political issues, increases public knowledge that allows for participation in civic and community activities, disseminates and helps define shifts in lifestyles and preferences and offers opportunities for recreation and leisure.[1] With the advent of the twenty-first century, communication media in all their forms are undergoing major changes. Many result from the adoption of digital age technologies, such as the Internet, tablets and proliferating social media, among others.[2] These changes alone may prove to be as revolutionary as the printing press and movable type, invented first in China almost a thousand years ago, followed by Germany's Gutenberg press in the mid-1400s.[3]

Moreover, trends in both print and electronic news and information delivery have shifted, becoming less verbal, more visual and entertainment-driven.[4] Post-2000 research suggests U.S. residents read less, watch and listen more than they did a generation ago. There is reason to believe the trend is global.[5] In the more than five decades since Jürgen Habermas ascribed to mass media the loss of a public sphere open to everyone,[6] the media and their influence have become so pervasive that sociologists, cultural and media scholars increasingly describe contemporary society as a media culture. In Nick Stevenson's words, "The emergence of global forms of mass communication . . . has reworked the experiential content of everyday life."[7]

In this mediated environment, the non-newspaper periodicals commonly known as magazines and journals remain a major social force that affects far more than the general public. The medium is diverse, providing a means of communicating critical information in the workplace, within and across the boundaries of informal and formal communities and organizations of interest, including scientific and scholarly. While some predict new communication technologies foreshadow the demise of the magazine form, others argue the medium will simply adopt and adapt as it has in the past.[8]

In the face of these changes, there is increasing interest in better understanding the sociocultural and organizational factors that influence and shape the medium, its content, effects and role in society. Scholarly inquiry has only begun to examine the multiple facets of the magazine, even as growing evidence suggests systematic research on and related to the medium has begun to achieve critical mass on multiple dimensions and find its place in the larger academic enterprise.[9] New research increasingly draws on prior studies. As scholars around the world engage with the periodical and all media forms from increasingly diverse critical cultural, interpretive and social scientific perspectives, inquiry is being enriched by careful articulation of theoretical and empirical questions, as well as advances in methodological approaches.[10] The parallel infusion of multiple intellectual streams of thought gives increasing evidence of maturation in the scholarly work on the medium, from studies of its history and ongoing social system within the field to questions related to communication problems and structure as they occur in the medium and the institutions that produce its content.[11]

Yet barriers to formal inquiry on the magazine form remain. Some have deep roots in a scholarly community that traditionally defined journalism research as excluding magazines.[12] In the roughly two decades surrounding the turn of the twenty-first century, scholars repeatedly noted weaknesses in the literature that was both widely dispersed[13] and too limited in quantity to provide a foundation on which to build new studies.[14] As recently as 2010, British sociologist and mass communication theorist Denis McQuail compared a continuing lag in research on magazines with formal inquiry on communication as it occurs through other media forms.[15] The "diffuseness and uncertain impact" of the periodical magazine, he wrote, "have led to a general neglect by communication research," even though the medium is "the single most significant . . . [of the] forms of publication" that followed the development of the printing press, other than books and newspapers.[16]

In attributing the neglect of communication research on magazines in part to their diffuseness, McQuail points to a core, defining characteristic of the medium: its diversity. This in turn begs an answer to the ongoing question of definition and kinds. This chapter reviews the literature on classifying magazine and journal periodicals and points to new theorizing on the question, research needs and opportunities.

The approach of this study is to examine three broad bodies of literature that bear on questions of classifying magazine and journal periodicals. The first is the specific literature related to *defining* and *categorizing* the broad range of serials that are non-newspaper periodicals, more commonly referred to as magazines and journals.[17] The second is the *taxonomic* literature—that is, the literature that focuses on systematic classification for identifying and developing taxonomies, typologies and, from the humanities, genres. And third is the *social communication* and *interdisciplinary* literature that includes scholarly inquiry related to categorizing all forms of magazine and journal periodicals. The search for the literature was strategic to answering the questions posed in the sections that follow, not a census or systematic sample of the literature in each areas' literature.

Defining Magazine and Journal Periodicals

The universe of non-newspaper periodicals is large. Conservative contemporary counts suggest anywhere from 9,000 to between 250,000 and 300,000 worldwide; the total may be higher.[18] The wide variance in these numbers results in part from there being no source capable of providing a comprehensive count of the total population of periodicals. That lack in turn is partially a function of how the extant directories, listings and databases define the medium for inclusion or exclusion.[19] Thus the question of how to define the scope of the medium and what is or is not a magazine or other non-newspaper periodical is core to studying the magazine, as attested by multiple scholars over time.[20]

Of the multiple factors that contribute to the difficulty of defining the magazine, the most pressing are issues related to the fact that defining the magazine periodical in the context of scholarly discussion requires using everyday language. "Clarifying ideas in the humanities and social sciences is an especially difficult undertaking," Patrick Dunleavy wrote, because "unlike the physical sciences . . . [these fields] do not have a separate sphere of 'scientific' discourse in which meanings are single-valued and unambiguous."[21] Dunleavy's further account of the resulting challenges to the humanities and social sciences[22] captures several aspects of the problem as it relates to systematic scholarly study of the magazine form. In addition to its multiple contemporary denotations by use and strict definition, the word *magazine* carries additional connotations that arise from its etymological French (*magasin*), Arabic (*makhāzin*) and Old Occitan origins.[23] From these, the original meaning of a *storehouse* or *warehouse* is frequently conferred on the contemporary reading material—that is, a mediated form of communication serving a conceptual storehouse of diverse ideas, information and means of presentation, both verbal and visual.

The word *magazine* also carries an additional range of meanings specific to users' personal, educational and professional experiences and backgrounds, as well as norms that differ within and across both academic and industry sectors. The body of professional and scholarly literature gives substantial evidence of the variances in the common-sense definitions[24] magazine professionals and scholars bring to the study of the medium. Even the most carefully articulated definitions differ, sometimes contradicting each other, particularly when used in contexts designed to describe and categorize the medium's various forms.

Form and Content Considerations

A second challenge to studying magazines is the form. No systematic studies appear to have been done of definitions over time, but source definitions reviewed for this study demonstrate the difficulty of framing a succinct, unique and ahistorical description of its essence. Defining the magazine periodical also poses challenges unique to time, culture and technology. As the population of magazines has grown ever larger, so too has its diversity increased, constantly changing and evolving. A wide variety of periodicity, material and content characteristics have been associated as definitive of the medium. Lyon N. Richardson, for example, found it necessary to specify that his history of the first nearly five decades of American magazine publishing (1741 through 1789) would not include *books*, a publication that at the time was sometimes designated a magazine.

> In general, the term *magazine*, as its name implies, was used to designate a general miscellany or repository of instruction and amusement. It was also used commonly in the eighteenth century as a title for books which were collections of information on various subjects, such as *The Young Man's Magazine: Containing the Substance of Moral Philosophy and Divinity, Selected from the Works of the Most Eminent for Wisdom, Learning, and Virtue, among the Ancients and Moderns* (Philadelphia, 1786) and *The Young Misses Magazine, Containing Dialogues between a Governess and Several Young Ladies her Scholars* (Philadelphia, 1787).[25]

Frank Luther Mott's working definition of *magazine*, " . . . a bound pamphlet issued more or less regularly and containing a variety of reading matter,"[26] similarly reflects the historical context his first volume encompasses.

Other scholars have identified content, rather than any specific format or other physical or material dimensions, as the essence of the medium. Indeed, in spite of the fact that Mott's operational definition pointed to the bound pamphlet form of early periodicals, he identified content as critical when he wrote, "Originally the term referred to contents only and had no connotation of form."[27] J. William Click and Russell N. Baird similarly differentiated between content and form when in 1994 they noted that to the then-common television magazines were being added more magazines retrieved through computer systems. They wrote, "Today, magazine refers more to an approach or a process rather than to a format (bound periodical)."[28] More than a decade later, Tim Holmes wrote, "If 'magazine' signifies no uniform reality . . . to demand homogeneity would be . . . to deny the very nature of the subject matter."[29]

Working Definitions

A starting point for an operational definition of *magazine* for the purposes of this chapter is the lay, dictionary definition, "a periodical containing miscellaneous pieces (as articles, stories, poems) and often illustrated; *also*: such a periodical published on-line."[30] To build on this base, two additional definitional needs exist. The first is to expand the working definition to include more than the periodicals published for members of the general public—that is, in advertising terms, consumers. Commonly and globally referred to as *consumer magazines*,[31] at one end of the continuum is a tendency to use the term *magazine* in ways that restrict its meaning to include only these periodicals. When that is true, the term still carries, almost 100 years later, what Mott recognized as "a strong connotation of entertainment,"[32] translating in contemporary society to *products* to be purchased, enjoyed and cast aside when the next issue appears.[33] Marketed to the general populace, this form of the medium is suggested in the description McQuail gave when he pointed to the lack of communication research on magazines: "The periodical magazine still belongs largely to the domestic and personal sphere and supports a wide range of interests, activities, and markets."[34]

Magazine scholars have long defined the medium more broadly, observing that of the thousands of non-newspaper periodicals published in every country around the world, more are designed in both content and purpose to meet critical information needs than to entertain. "Magazines disseminate more specialized information and commentary on a regular basis to diverse audiences," wrote Click and Baird, "than any other medium of mass communication."[35] Mott, too, differentiated between the entertainment connotation and the "professional and technical periodical for psychiatrists [that] would call itself" a *journal* or *review*.[36] He included both in the scope of his definition of *magazine*.

At the other extreme is the question of which of the broad range of publications defined as *serials* are to be included in the definition of *periodicals*, of which magazines are one form.[37] Again, the literature differs, even contradicts. Contemporary lay and scholarly definitions of the terms *periodical* and *magazine* variously exclude and include newspapers and scholarly journals. Margaret Beetham, in her exploration of periodicals as a publishing genre, includes newspapers,[38] as did the founders of the interdisciplinary, American Studies journal *American Periodicals* in defining its scope.[39] Mott excluded newspapers, because they were "not usually called periodicals," but acknowledged his doing so had "never been universally accepted, perhaps because it [was] not indicated by the etymology."[40] He included scholarly journals as "a more serious or technical publication; [that is] one speaks of the learned and professional 'journals.'"[41] Contemporary ambivalence about where scholarly journals fit is illustrated in the present volume, which does not include a chapter on scholarly journals in any of its humanities or sciences disciplinary forms. However, its importance and role is evidenced in every chapter.

Mott's strategies were echoed almost a half century later in Fritz Machlup, Kenneth Leeson and their associates' 1970s definitional research at New York University.[42] They identified nine "serials" categories, of which "Newspapers, daily weekly or biweekly" and "Periodicals (magazines and journals, published more than once per year)" are two separate classes, by definition. The periodicals category is further subdivided into two subclasses, *magazines* and *journals*.[43] Current international Anglo American Cataloging Rules, including revisions to account for digital media and databases, are used on at least five continents and echo Machlup, Leeson and Associates' definitions.[44]

Mott may have played a major role in the label *magazine* replacing the more inclusive term *periodical* early on, particularly in scholarly work on the magazine form. Of historical note is his self-described choice not to use *periodical* in naming his histories, even though he acknowledged the word "would perhaps be the most concise word to use in the title of" his work. Instead, he chose *magazine* "as the more popular and meaningful term."[45]

Magazine as Non-Newspaper Periodical

As used in this chapter, the terms *magazines*, *journals* and *periodicals* will draw on the medium's etymological roots, historical and contemporary constructions, as well as international serials cataloging guidelines, to position magazines and journals as subclasses of related periodicals, defined to exclude newspapers. *Magazine* and *journal periodicals* are further defined within the broad scope of formal, structured social behavior—a medium of communication that includes traditional formats, such as hard-copy paper, and digital forms distributed in the twenty-first century on the Internet and electronic devices. The terms *magazine* and *journal* are used interchangeably in noun and adjectival forms with the term *periodical*. Other terms commonly found in research, academic and professional literature will also be used for maximum clarity as to the scope of the medium. These include *non-newspaper periodicals*, *business magazines* and *business publications*, *organization* and *trade publications*, *monthlies*, *quarterlies* and *reviews*, among others.[46] Because magazines and journal periodicals come in a wide variety of formats, any one of which may carry the connotation of being a magazine, the contemporary term *magazine form*, which is less burdened by a history of common-sense and industry definitions and connotations, will also be used to refer to the medium.[47]

Taxonomy, Typology and Genre Literatures

The body of literature on developing taxonomies and typologies is extensive, spanning the centuries and centering in the fields of the physical, biological, behavioral and social sciences.[48] It can also be found in sectors of the humanities, where it takes two forms: the development of typologies[49] and, from critical theory and genre studies, *genres*.[50] Defined in general as an overarching inquiry, that is, the "theoretical study of classification, including its bases, principles, procedures, and rules,"[51] the term *taxonomy* also refers to taxonomic research as practiced primarily in the physical and biological, or life, sciences. There, research draws on classification philosophies and methods that result in *taxonomies*.

Pertinent to study of the magazine and journal periodical are two diverse streams of classificatory work: taxonomic work that produces *typologies*, or theoretically based systems used primarily in the social and behavioral sciences,[52] and *genre studies*, as widely used in multiple disciplines of the humanities—particularly for identifying and naming styles and forms, especially of content, that is, literary, artistic, musical and linguistic materials.[53] Not typically found in the traditional typological and taxonomic literature of the social sciences, the term *genre* shares with typological work the common goals of organizing and categorizing. However, with overlapping definitions, social and cultural meanings and applications, the processes of identifying, conceptualizing and naming genres and typologies also differ in a number of ways. Genre categories often either overlap or are embedded within each other with impunity. *Typologies*, by contrast, identify and cluster phenomena with shared characteristics and dimensions within groups, so as to clearly differentiate between groups, based on carefully articulated theoretical foundations.

It can be argued that the complementarity of the two strategies lies in different dimensions of the magazine form. Social scientific typological inquiry and development appropriately focus on identifying patterns, characteristics and dimensions of social communication behavior as it shapes and occurs through and in relation to various media forms, structures, verbal and visual content. Genre development focuses primarily on *treatment*: identifying and analyzing the literary, artistic, musical and linguistic styles and forms, particularly of media content, including, but not limited to, verbal and visual; the list is long.[54] Thus, as with differences and similarities between taxonomic and typological work, the classificatory processes of typology and genre development draw on principles that are simultaneously different and similar, discipline-specific and common to the broad spectrum of classification inquiry.

A critical starting point for developing the social scientific typology is the first assumption of science: that the world is ordered and patterned.[55] Paul Davidson Reynolds posits that the several tasks of building a body of scholarly and scientific knowledge involve describing the objects of study and, following closely as the first order of business, *classification*—that is, providing "a method of organizing and categorizing 'things, a *typology*.'"[56] On these definitional foundations, he says, science can move on to predicting future events, explaining past events and providing a "sense of understanding about what causes events."[57] Sociologist Kenneth D. Bailey expands on these concepts when he writes, "Classification . . . is the foundation not only for conceptualization, language, and speech, but also for mathematics, statistics, and data analysis in general."[58]

Yet developing a theoretically grounded typology useful for systematic inquiry into the wide range of unanswered questions about communication as it occurs through the periodical medium is largely virgin territory. This is true even though published scholarly research on the magazine form dates to the first three decades of the twentieth century and includes specific references to different kinds of magazine and journal periodicals.[59]

Importance of Typologies and Genres

Among the reasons for the failure to develop a systematic typology of the universe of periodicals may be that, although providing and clarifying definitions are processes almost as old as the scientific enterprise,[60] views on the role and importance of taxonomic work have changed over time. So great is the change that in 2011, Chunglin Kwa of the University of Amsterdam's Department of Political Science and Sociology observed that "of all the styles of science, the taxonomic is the least respected."[61] Yet Kwa argues that it is "shortsighted" to view the taxonomic style as "somehow inferior to other scientific styles."[62] Starting with the periodic table's ordering of chemical elements long before its core theoretical base was discerned, he identified the work of scientists whose taxonomic work in the physical, biological and social sciences advanced their respective fields, laying foundations for contemporary research. In each case, Kwa pointed to the classification work that did "what all taxonomies do—namely, bring order to a chaos of facts."[63] Daniel Chandler similarly points to genre studies as bringing order to large quantities of diverse texts in the world of literature.[64]

Scholars' disagreement on the value and role of classification in social inquiry[65] coincides roughly with the last quarter of the twentieth century's debate over whether the study of human social behavior is a science or a humanity. If a humanity, the argument is that social behaviors, including human communication, are best analyzed from qualitative, critical and interpretive perspectives, rather than social scientific, which historically drew heavily on quantitative measures of theory.[66] In the first decades of the twenty-first century, an increasing number of social communication scholars have begun to see the perspectives as complementary, not in opposition to each other.[67] The body of published inquiry on magazine and journal periodicals reflects this shift, as does the broader literature of mediated communication, with both theory and research, qualitative and quantitative methods enriching and expanding the extent to which old and new perspectives intersect to inform study in this sector of the field.[68]

Social scientists and some other scholars consider the taxonomic work of building typologies a foundational, definitional task.[69] Clear definitions are, in turn, essential for every aspect of scholarly inquiry, whether identifying a problem and choosing a research topic, developing or testing theory, designing data collection or discussing results and suggesting new directions for future research.[70] By extension, clarifying definitions and bringing order to the chaos surrounding magazine and journal periodical classification are important to inquiry on the medium. Scholars build on these core definitions whether the medium is their primary focus or part of broader multimedia or interdisciplinary research.

Typology and Genre as Medium Theory

The development of a theoretically based typology of the non-newspaper periodical can be argued as contributing to the theory of the medium, which, by extension, is part of the larger body of medium theory in the study of mediated communication.[71] McQuail describes *medium theory* as having shed the strong technological determinism attached to work that originally grew out of the Toronto School. In its more mature forms, the theory focuses on identifying the range of medium biases,[72] explorations that McQuail positions within the "media-materialist" quadrant of mediated social communication theory and research.[73] The biases that uniquely define each media form are what McQuail defines as "distinctive characteristics, in respect of technology, form, manner of use, means of encoding or social definition."[74] Scholarly work designed to define and classify the biases of the periodical form is limited, but has been given new impetus in the past two decades through the work of critical and social scientific scholarship.[75] To this end, identifying a theoretically based typology of the magazine form lends to laying a foundation upon which can be built the broadest range of media-centric, sociocultural, humanities and social scientific approaches to inquiry on the medium. These in turn will lead to greater understanding of the multiple facets of the magazine form.

Scholars agree that taxonomic work is not easy, but point to a paradox: Organizing and categorizing the objects of study is, Reynolds wrote, "the easiest [of the purposes of science] to achieve, because any set of concepts can be used to organize and classify." The problem is that not all ways of identifying and classifying are "useful."[76] Explanation and prediction cannot occur when no agreement can be reached on naming and categorizing. The answer to the question of what is useful takes different forms, with insights coming from the differing paradigms of critical scholars and social scientists.

Operational Theories of Classification

That there exists no overarching, theoretically grounded typology of magazine and journal periodicals is obscured by the fact that media industry professionals and scholars alike regularly break the universe of non-newspaper periodicals into multiple categories, referring to the resulting clusters of titles as "types" of magazines.[77] A few scholars use the terms *type* and *types*, but acknowledge the frameworks they describe do not meet one or more typological criteria.[78] Some differentiate among categories without calling them *types*,[79] but more common is using the terms *type* and *types* as synonyms for *kind*, *kinds*, *sort* and *sorts* without qualification.[80]

The current practices are a double-edged sword. On the one hand, they signal agreement that there are, among the thousands of periodicals published worldwide, sufficient differences to prevent their all fitting into a single, homogeneous group. On the other hand, referring to a named title or clusters of titles as a *type* or *types* implies the existence of a systematic, theory-driven base for categorizing the universe of non-newspaper periodicals that is both generally accepted and meets accepted standards for scientifically based classification, when analyses of the current strategies do not support that assumption.[81] An alternative is working within the genre framework, with its less rigorous requirements for clarity between groups. However, doing so might only further complicate the existing mix of terminology. For the social scientist, the rigor of the typological framework would allow for pulling cross-sectional samples, useful for the building and testing of theory that explains and predicts communication behavior as it occurs through the medium.

Searching for Theory

The literature on defining and building theory—like that of taxonomy, typology and genre development—is broad and grounded in almost every academic discipline. Discussions and definitions of what constitutes theory are similarly broad-ranging, from higher level conceptual questions of ontology and epistemology[82] to practical, sometimes strongly normative, guide-lines. Out of this somewhat complex, even confusing literature, Denis McQuail has provided a summary definition for emergent mass communication scholarship.

> There are different kinds of theory, . . . but most basically a theory is a general prop-osition, itself based on observation and logical argument, that states the relationship between observed phenomena and seeks either to explain or to predict the relations, in so far as this is possible. The main purpose of theory is to make sense of an observed reality and guide the collection and evaluation of evidence.[83]

From this foundational definition McQuail identifies five kinds of mass communication the-ory,[84] of which one is *operational theory*. Named *working theory* in his first editions,[85] operational theory is, by McQuail's definition,

> the kind of knowledge about the media [that] refers to the practical ideas assem-bled and applied by media practitioners in the conduct of their own media work. Similar bodies of accumulated practical wisdom are to be found in most organiza-tional and professional settings. In the case of the media, operational theory serves to guide solutions to fundamental tasks, including how to select news, please audi-ences, design effective advertising, keep within the limits of what society permits, and relate effectively to sources and society. At some points it may overlap with normative theory. . . . [86]

To McQuail's description of practical knowledge can be added the several widely used and accepted approaches to categorizing periodicals that magazine publishers, editors, writers and advertisers use to find solutions they need to complete the fundamental tasks of producing issue after issue of titles in the diverse sectors of the industry. Almost a half century ago Benjamin M. Compaine argued that resolving problems in defining the different kinds of magazines "is of more than academic curiosity."[87] He named multiple, specific tasks for which knowing and identifying classes of periodicals can be critical.

> [M]any advertisers could be served by understanding how different types of publica-tions are more or less indigenous to their products. . . . Second, editors must know what should be the orientation of their copy. . . . Third, consumers want to know what to expect from a magazine, more these days than ever as rising subscription rates force the reader to more carefully weigh his media choices. Fourth, the publishing logistics of magazines vary by type.[88]

There remain, however, unanswered questions about the strategies as they have been and can be used to meet scholars' needs.

McQuail's summary definitions of theory for mass communication scholarship and opera-tional theory provide critical links for moving through the quagmire that marks the current state of magazine classification. Outlining and linking the current strategies, their roots, core characteristics and relationships to the broad body of literature is a critical first step in articu-lating the traditional approaches as *operational theories of periodical classification*, useful to maga-zine mediated communication theory and research with applications for practice.

Three Operational Theories

A number of commonly used, basic strategies for categorizing magazine and journal peri-odicals have been identified and described. Based on an analysis of researchers' direct and implied definitions of "magazine type" in 223 studies published over the 14 years from 1977 through 1991, the approaches have been labeled the (1) *general-specialized dichotomy*, (2) *editorial interest area approach*,[89] (3) *information function approach*, and the (4) *multiple characteristics approach*.[90] Further review of the larger body of scholarly and industry literature gives evidence that the first three of the four are commonly used, first-level categorization strategies in industry practice. Moreover, the *multiple characteristics approach* is shown to be extensions of each of the first three, not a separate approach. Stated differently, the first three approaches to classifying periodicals—the general-specialized dichotomy, the editorial interest area approach and the information function approach—are described in the larger body of scholarly and professional literature as first-level classification systems that have one or more additional levels, or sub-classes. Thus, each of the three can be identified as a multiple characteristics approach. Moreover, careful examination shows the descriptions of sub-classes to incorporate, in every case, one or more dimensions of the first-level classification strategies, taken to the next sub-level or levels.

The ways these strategies fail to meet typological tests are described in the earlier research.[91] Thus, the goal here is to link the three classification strategies to the larger body of scholarly and professional literature in order to (1) provide brief, summary definitions of the strategies' characteristics, dimensions and suggested relationships, as well as indicators of sub-class strategies as found in that literature; (2) give summary descriptions of the strategies' roots in industry, again as reflected in the literature, that provide support for their being defined as operational theories of periodical classification; and (3) provide sources for the strategies of choice, both for further study and grounding in the literature in future research.

General-specialized classification. The simplest strategies for classifying non-newspaper periodicals divide the universe of magazines into two first-level groups, with the most common strategy, as found in the pre-1995 research literature ($n = 67$; 30.1% of 223 studies),[92] calling one group *general magazines*; the other, *specialized*. This dichotomous, general-specialized approach to classifying magazines is also found in the broad range of scholarly and professional literature. There the implied and direct descriptions for the terms focus on magazine content or audience, or both, as was true in the research literature, and uses are consistent with core definitions in everyday language,[93] though definitions are not stated in the literature. Recent scholarship suggests researchers are giving increased attention to describing the basis for designating periodicals as general or specialized, whether based on characteristics of content, audience—or a combination of both.[94] Global industry use of the approach and its variations is also suggested in two recent studies, Kineta Hung H., Flora Fang Gu and David K. Tse's study of Chinese advertising media-decision making and Anniken Westad's exploration of the magazine publishing industry, resources and scholarly research in Norway.[95]

Although found nowhere stated as such in the literature, it may nonetheless be appropriate to credit Frank Luther Mott with having in his 1930 summary description and definition codified the outlines of the general-specialized framework of everyday industry parlance, before, during and after his time. Mott wrote, "The general magazine's audience must perforce be a popular one, and . . . the specialized periodicals['] . . . appeal is limited to particular classes . . ."[96] Embedded in his description is the key to the relationship: the "appeal" of content to readers for whom the magazines are designed, using a meaning consistent with the common definition of *appeal*, as having "the power of arousing a sympathetic response" or attracting a response from an audience.[97]

The roots of the general-specialized terminology appear to go deep into the earliest years of periodical magazine publishing, in both the United States and Europe. Algernon Tassin in 1916 described the nearly 45 magazines that were started in the colonies between 1741 and the end of the eighteenth century, as including some " . . . addressed to a more general audience" and others focused on specific subjects.[98] Benjamin Franklin's 1741 magazine, historically one of the first two magazines published in the British-American colonies, was titled *The General Magazine*.[99] Richardson described early magazines as having a broad range of content for narrowly defined, small audiences.[100] Dorothy Schmidt described "the idea of such periodicals" as having arisen "almost concurrently in France, England, Germany, and other European countries," where periodicals had reached similarly small audiences another hundred years earlier: in Germany since 1663 and, in France and Italy, also since the mid-1660s.[101]

From historians' early descriptions of general and specialized magazines that trace to the founding years, through to the turn of the twenty-first century, the dichotomous division of magazines has remained a core framework for describing the medium as divisible into two groups. Definitions of the terms general and specialized have, however, shifted over time. A brief summary of the evolution of the framework shows them to variously, and in different time periods, refer to the population from which audiences were drawn, e.g., members of the general public, as did Tassin; to the geographic location of audiences, as did Theodore Peterson and others in their descriptions of magazines' ability to reach the increasingly regional and national audiences that spread over a growing nation when local newspapers could not; to size of audience, as in the mass audiences of millions that publishers were targeting when advertisers shifted their moneys to television's even larger audiences at the mid-twentieth century. As audience sizes increased, use of the terms broadened to include content that was designed to reach as many people as possible.[102] Habermas ascribes to advertising similar changes to the media throughout Europe,[103] and Sigfrid Steinberg argues that major changes in periodical content occurring in Scotland and England precipitated similar changes in U.S. periodicals.[104] These forces combined in the near century between the 1870s and the 1960s to define the editorial content and publishing economics of what came to be known as the general or mass-circulation magazine, also at times called the general consumer magazine.[105]

Magazines' survival of lost advertising to television in the mid-twentieth century resulted from publishers' refocusing, providing specialized editorial content for carefully defined audiences, whether by subject content interests or audience demography. In the process, the era of specialized magazines came to the fore. The 1960s and 1970s trend to identifying magazines by their more specialized content and specialized audiences was accompanied and followed by changes in publishing's economic model, with readers picking up a greater proportion of the costs that advertisers had been carrying.[106] Both trends continue unabated to the present, intensifying even as magazines expand print formats to include digital.[107] While some magazine and media industry professionals expect the new wave, digital technologies to trigger the death of the magazine,[108] others anticipate magazines will again survive, with specialization the key to adapting to what David Abrahamson describes as a new century's technological and social-cultural realities.[109]

The literature cited to this point refers to the two broad categories of general and specialized magazines as a first-level classifying strategy. Five sources were identified that expand the two first-level categories into second- and third-level sub-categories, with an apparent goal of describing the real world of magazine publishing. The most recent of the five, Ray Eldon Hiebert and Sheila Jean Gibbons, bring the framework into the twenty-first century, describing a first, *general interest* category that has no sub-groups. They also call these consumer magazines for general audiences.[110] Their second, *special-interest* category has two sub-categories, the first of which they call "dominant categories" or "magazines distinguished by content." They describe six groups "aimed at a fairly broad range of readers, almost broad enough to be considered general interest, but the contents of the magazines themselves are specialized."[111] The groups are identified by a combination of editorial topics and genre labels. The second group they call "dominant types," and define those as "magazines distinguished by demographics" of audiences.[112] They again identify six groups, using both labels that are clearly demographic and not. Their descriptions of these clusters include multiple, third-level clusters that they identify by commonly used editorial interest, or subject classifications. Their approach can be read as suggesting general and specialized are subcategories of the consumer magazine category as a whole, without reference to magazines of other kinds.

The remaining four frameworks were published prior to 2000, beginning with Mott's first volume in 1930[113]; Roland Wolseley, in 1965; James L.C. Ford, 1969; and a second by Wolseley, in 1977.[114] These sources call the two first-level groups, general and specialized, also occasionally adding consumer as a qualifier to or synonym for the general category. Each source sub-divides and names sub-classes in different ways. Sub-category labels are a mix of terms that include reusing the general and specialized labels, grouping by content—that is, subjects and audience characteristics, or editorial interest areas—and information functions. Mott's classifications, carefully detailed and inductively derived, are almost universally subject and topically based. Wolseley draws on both topical and genre terms, particularly in his more detailed 1965 analysis; Ford's system is almost fully topical. Interpretations of what constitutes general or specialized magazines and their sub-categories, and the specific magazine titles that fit into respective classes and sub-classes, differ, even contradict at times.[115]

Simplicity is a key strength of the general-specialized approach to first-level magazine classification. The enduring use of the strategy for categorizing the magazine form points to its ability to describe quickly and succinctly the relationship between two core dimensions: the appeal of content to audience. This may explain in part the ease with which the terms are used in the context of magazine publishing as operational theories for classifying magazines. A key weakness is applying the approach for classification. What one person views as a general magazine or cluster of titles, another may view as specialized, or the inverse. This is evidenced by variances across the schematics described by Hiebert and Gibbons, Mott, Wolseley and Ford.

Finally, in the literature, as in this brief summary, there is evidence that the terms general and specialized are also used to describe the population of magazine and journal periodicals as a whole, as well as trends in information presentation over time, as comparatively more general or specialized. In these contexts, magazine content, audiences, or both, are defined as being more or less general or specialized by comparison with preceding and subsequent time periods. Thus, patterns of relative specialization, or lack thereof, emerge and shift, as multiple factors, including but not restricted to technology, economic, social and cultural shifts, come into play.

Editorial interest area classification. The second classification strategy clusters periodicals at the first-level by the similarities in their shared, over-arching subject, topic or unifying theme for editorial content. Identified as the *editorial interest area approach*, this strategy was the second most used in the 1977 to 1991 research literature (n = 61; 27.4% of 223 studies).[116] As an operational classification theory, it not only names the unifying topic for content, it is frequently used to identify titles that are direct competitors for readers. Based on editorial content, the strategy is strongly related to advertising content,[117] which in turn creates a strong relation to the economics of publishing, including subscriptions, newsstand sales and advertising revenues.[118] Category labels designate specific subject or topic areas and thereby focus on content with greater specificity than in the general-specialized dichotomy. At face value, the approach is intuitive and transparent. No analyses appear to have been done of labels that are used in directories and reference books, but a cursory examination of labels used in multiple directories shows category names pointing to content by single-valued subjects (e.g., sports); indicate other dimensions, such as a range of content designed for specific audiences (e.g., women's interests); and describe content treatment characteristics (e.g., literature, or literary magazines, or newsmagazines).[119]

Magazine and mass communication textbooks commonly refer to these topical clusters without reference to the universe. Scholarly research similarly names a title or cluster of titles as part of study designs in isolation, while also typically identifying the editorial interest area as integral to the study. Examples include analyzing women's magazines' framing of empowerment versus victimization for abused women[120]; the relationship between reading women's sports magazines and adolescent female self-objectification and mental health[121]; or textual analysis of a literary magazine.[122] The global use of the strategy is illustrated in the work of Copenhagen Business School's Brian Moeran, who explored how ongoing relationships are negotiated between fashion magazine staff, readers, advertisers and the fashion world.[123]

Subject classification appears to derive from both the library sciences and media industries, for which directories and reference books are key providers of subject classification as a first-level categorizing strategy, albeit not universally,[124] providing a full range of categories under which titles are classified. One of the more comprehensive is the international *Ulrich's Periodicals Directory*, which has used subject-based classification as a first-level strategy since its inception in 1932.[125] From the first directory's 6,000 titles in roughly 450 subject categories have grown current annual editions that list more than 225,000 serials in upwards of 900 categories and sub-categories.[126] The U.S.–Canadian *Bacon's Magazine Directory* has approximately 350 classification and sub-classification groups for its 18,000 periodical listings.[127] The magazine industry also uses subject-based classification in multiple settings that include circulation data bases at auditing companies such as the Alliance for Audited Media (formerly the Audit Bureau of Circulations) and BPA Worldwide (formerly Business Publications Audit of Circulations)[128] and for magazine audience research, conducted by companies such as Mediamark and Simmons.[129]

Editorial interest classification can also be traced to early writing about magazine publishing. Tassin, for example, named music, military, German religious, and children's magazines that were published before 1800, and Richardson compared and contrasted periodicals that covered religion, education, literary issues, science and politics.[130] Internationally, classifying early magazines by subject also points to the essential dimensions of subject, audience and content treatment, specifying relationships that identified what periodicals were about, for whom and how content was treated. Steinberg described magazines that "sprang up almost simultaneously throughout Europe," beginning in 1663 through the end of the seventeenth century, for men and women and that focused on literary criticism or consisted largely of book reviews.[131]

Directories that use first-level, subject-based classification and sub-subject categories typically include individual profiles for each title that falls into the respective classes. Profile descriptions vary in length and content, but in general give insights into the editorial content, purpose and audience. Profiles also include cues to the title's place in the directories' sub-classification frameworks. *Bacon's*, for example, identifies each title by one or a combination of two or more of seven publication descriptors that reflect information function, geographic coverage and audience demographic.[132] *Ulrich's* also lists each title alphabetically within subject classifications. Shorter profiles give a description of content and categorize each title using a somewhat more complex, two-level, sub-classes identification system: The first is called "serial type"; the second, "subject type." Of the 11 serial type categories, three designate non-newspaper periodical groupings: magazine periodical, journal and bulletin, where *bulletin* is defined as "a periodical published by an organization or society."[133] Subject type categories include seven specific to magazine and journal periodicals, for which the definitions encompass topic, target audiences, publisher source and distribution methods.[134]

The directory designation of first-level editorial interest area and sub-categorizing *kind* of publication suggests a relationship between the level(s). Editorial interest areas span sub-category kinds. Thus full identification of a periodical suggests naming editorial interest area and periodical class, as indicated in the respective directories. Editorial interest area labels are typically succinct. As a categorizing system, the operational classification theory's several strengths are simplicity and ability to point to the unifying topic or subject area as an essential, concrete dimension of content. It is arguably the most consistently tested approach to categorizing magazines: Whether in standard reference directories or industry specific processes, such as circulation auditing, titles are matched to subject area, year after year. A key weakness is a lack of parsimony, a problem that increases over time, as evidenced by comparing *Ulrich's* 1932 and 2014 counts.[135]

Information-function classification. The third operational theory for classifying magazines creates categories by the over-arching purpose, use or function the periodicals are designed to serve. Used in magazine, advertising and other industry sectors, the umbrella term *information-function* classification was applied to the range of labels that fell into this approach as it emerged from the analysis of research literature. In the 1995 report, the strategy was used in the research literature only half as often, in 33 of 223 studies, or just under 15% of the cases (n=33; 14.8%),[136] as either the general-specialized or editorial interest area approaches. By contrast, the review of the larger body of industry and scholarly literature on which this chapter is based shows it to be the approach of choice for describing the universe of magazine and journal periodicals: A total 27 sources published immediately before and since 1990 use the approach.

Historically and in the current literature, authors use terms that designate a number of different content characteristics and dimensions—both editorial and advertising, whether advertising is content, a source of revenue, or both—and audience. The terms are also used to suggest marketing and economic functions, with suggested relationships between the characteristics and dimensions variously described as between editorial, advertising and identified target audiences, as well as between source publishers, editorial or advertising content and audiences.

Tracing the use of the information-function approach over time suggests that Theodore Peterson in his *Magazines in the Twentieth Century* may have brought the industry outlines of the information-function framework to the scholarly literature on magazines. Peterson wrote,

> I have limited my subject to commercial magazines edited for the lay public. Therefore, this book does not cover several categories of magazines: . . . trade and technical publications and scientific and professional journals. Nor does it treat in any detail the farm magazines, which are essentially trade journals for the farmer. . . . Also excluded are house organs, which are supported by big and little businesses to tell their stories to employees or to the public at large; fraternal and organizational magazines, which draw all or part of their support from the organizations publishing them; religious periodicals, which for the most part have church affiliations; and the so-called "little magazines" of literature and criticism, which generally are not published with commercial intent.[137]

Like Mott before him, Peterson was a journalist. His book was based on his doctoral dissertation in one of the early U.S. doctoral programs in mass communication[138] and occasionally uses language that hints at the social scientific, structural-functional perspectives on communication that were taking root in the late 1940s and early 1950s. However, he described his research as drawing heavily on industry sources,[139] and the dominant language derives from the magazine industry. Peterson used the general-specialized terms to introduce and describe the early years of magazine publishing that led to "the birth of the modern magazine" in the United States,[140] but the chapters that follow analyzed social and economic forces on the contemporary industry.

J. William Click and Russell N. Baird may have solidified the approach. In the 1974, first of the six editions of their widely adopted magazine editing and production textbook, they described the universe of magazines in broad, general-specialized terms, then identified groups that parallel Peterson's.

> Although several magazines built tremendous circulations to reach "mass" audiences, others long ago defined their specific audiences and have been serving them for decades. These are special interest magazines, the majority of which are business publications. There are also thousands of magazines issued by companies for . . . groups related to their communications and public relations programs.[141]

Click and Baird broke the first-level, specialized magazines into five sub-classes. Their descriptive use of the general-specialized terms took second place to a greater emphasis on the "types of magazines" presented in information-function terms: consumer magazines, business publications, association magazines and public relations magazines, followed by a third level of selected editorial interest area groups.[142]

From the early 1990s to the present, use of the information-function approach has increased in professional and scholarly literature for magazines, journalism and mass communication textbooks and other media-based sources, as well as media-based and general encyclopedias. Wide variances in the frameworks are found in this literature and indicate research needs.

That more than 25 contemporary sources used information-function approaches suggests there is substantial agreement that the approach has greater descriptive power and usefulness in outlining the universe of magazine periodicals than do the general-specialized and editorial interest area approaches. Conversely, the sources describe roughly as many frameworks: None are exactly the same—in number of categories, labels for categories or identification and naming of sub-categories.

All sources agree there are multiple classes of periodicals. Sources also agree on two categories for which the magazines aligned, but the labels varied: First, a category, variously labeled, *consumer, general, general interest* or *specialized consumer* magazines. Second, a category that carries some variation of labeling that includes the terms *trade, technical, business, specialized business, business to business* or *professional* publications.

Here the agreement in the strategies largely ends and the challenges become apparent. The number of categories in source frameworks range from a low of two (2)[143] to a high of fifteen (1).[144] Within a few frameworks, one or more sources identified a specific number of categories, then added an "Other" category, which included one or more additional clusters, judged not to fit the original groups. Three two-group sources added an "other" category (3).[145]

Organization publications were the third category in three-category schematics, where clusters were variously labeled *company, organizational, sponsored, public relations, association* and *in-house* and *industrial*, for six sources (6).[146] The organization category is also included in four-category frameworks (2)[147]; six-category (4)[148]; seven-category (2)[149]; the fifteen-category (1)[150] schematics; and for the Other category for two-category framework (2),[151] for a total of 18 that designated organization magazines and publications as a separate category. Other sources either collapsed organization publication into the business-trade-industrial category or did not mention them.

Scholarly journals were identified as constituting a separate category and labeled using one or a combination of the terms *scholarly journals, little magazines, academic journals, literary reviews* and *literary magazines*, as the third category in three-category schematics for three sources (3)[152] and a five-category (1)[153] schematic; and in four-category (1)[154] and five-category (1)[155] frameworks. The remaining sources place scholarly journals in the business-trade-industrial category (1),[156] organization category(3),[157] or do not mention them.

Farm and agriculture publications are a separate category in a three-category system (1)[158]; four-category (2)[159]; six-category (2)[160]; and fifteen-category (1),[161] for a total of 6.

Across the remaining sources, some 17 clusters of magazines were mentioned only one or two times as discrete categories, and included magazines distributed in newspapers (2)[162]; digital and on-line magazines (3)[163]; as well as newsletters (2)[164] and comic books (2),[165] among others.

Strategies for sub-categorization vary across source frameworks, from none to clearly identified subjects, numbers of subject classes or audience categories. Again, there was some, but not total agreement on either the sub-categories or the criteria for categorization. Benjamin Compaine's strategy of designating the consumer magazines as having general and specialized dimensions appeared in several frameworks,[166] and the advertising industry's sub-division of business or trade publications into horizontal and vertical categories appeared in one.[167]

Citation and source use remained uneven. Authors who used information-function approaches in contemporary texts and professional books cite primary or secondary sources more often than did researchers in the 1995 study. Three gave no sources, three used industry-based, advertising rate and data sources. The most frequently used, single source was Click and Baird's textbook.

Discussion

Three broad bodies of literature provide insights to the on-going questions and issues related to identifying, defining and classifying magazines and journals periodicals. This chapter has focused on several dimensions of definition and problems related to defining what a magazine is by drawing on its common-sense meanings in daily experience, concurrent but different sets of meanings from within the distinct spheres of the magazine publishing industry, and the overlapping worlds of the library sciences and inter-disciplinary and discipline-specific scholarly work. Specific attention was paid to a lexicon of terms that have particularly nettlesome dimensions and diverse meanings, creating confusion about the nature of periodicals, journals, newspapers and their relationships to each other.

The review of the taxonomic literature focused the language and work of systematic classification for identifying and developing taxonomies and typologies, while calling for consideration of the complementary work of the social science and humanities traditions' respective knowledge and uses of typologies and genre studies as those apply to different dimensions of the magazine form.

A body of literature that shares classification problems similar to those that surround the magazine form can be found in the management and complex social organizations literature. Drawing on this body of research, scholars D. Harold Doty and William H. Glick argue that classification systems can meet the most basic, typological decision tests for fit—that is, that a system may be comprehensive, or exhaustive, and provide clarity for determining which item fits into which group, that is, mutual exclusivity, and still be nothing more than a non-theoretical classification strategy. Theory, Doty and Glick argue, differentiates the simplest levels of classification from higher level conceptual constructions.[168] The goal in their field as well as in magazine classification is to move beyond what Doty and Glick would call "sloppy categorical classification system[s]" because they are not based in theory,[169] to make sense of the highly diverse, fascinating magazine medium, using classification that is solidly grounded in theory.

To that end, the chapter has sought to build a bridge between the on-going need to make sense of the three traditional approaches to classifying magazine and journal periodicals by positioning them as operational classification theories that derive from the everyday work of media professionals. From the further review of the literature published since 1990, this chapter has sought to identify characteristics, dimensions and the relationships between the two that mark these operational classification theories, to ground the operational theories in the scholarly and professional literature, and to identify from analyses of descriptions of the approaches in that literature that suggest needs for research to move the theory of the medium forward.

Conclusion

A theoretically based framework that clearly articulates the core characteristics and relationships among the multiple dimensions of non-newspaper periodicals would serve both scholar and practitioner, equipping them with new tools to enable them to explore multiple facets of communication as it occurs through periodicals in all their diverse forms and philosophies. The maturation of communication theory and research is intensifying the need for a cogent approach to classifying magazine and journal periodicals. The growing body of theoretical perspectives and methods from social-scientific, cultural and critical perspectives is tapping into increasingly important dimensions of mediated communication. Identifying such a framework could provide a solid foundation for research on the magazine medium, overcoming past tendencies toward fragmentation and barriers to communication research on the magazine medium.

Operational classification theory provides a needed tool to build the conceptual bridge between traditional approaches to classifying magazine and journal periodicals and the higher level, social scientific foundations for a theory-based typology of the medium. Benjamin M. Compaine has described multiple tasks for which the daily work in industry draws on these operational classification theories. From these he argued that resolving problems in defining the different kinds of magazines "is of more than academic curiosity."[170]

To Compaine's list of applied industry uses, given earlier in this chapter, might be added the very practical needs of young professionals, who, upon entering the field, would know available industry options far exceed the well-known titles they see on the newsstand. Given educators' greater sensitivity to preparing students to observe, report, write and edit for the spectrum of the medium, young professionals could take into entry-level and later positions both a better understanding of where they might best contribute their talents and a stronger working knowledge of how communication can be better effected through different magazine forms. So, too, scholars embarking on the research path would know the horizons are broader than those defined by the so-called general or consumer magazine, whether historical or contemporary.[171]

Notes

1 Robert D. Putnam, "Technology and Mass Media," *Bowling Alone: The Collapse and Revival of American Community* (New York: Simon & Schuster, 2000), 216–246.

2 Pew Research Center, "Overview," State of the News Media 2013: An Annual Report on American Journalism (Washington, DC: Pew Research Center, 2013) <http://stateofthemedia.org/2013/overview-5/>, accessed 3 December 2013; Jane Sasseen, Katerina-Eva Matsa, and Amy Mitchell, "News Magazines: Embracing Their Digital Future," The State of the News Media 2013: An Annual Report on American Journalism (Washington, DC: Pew Research Center, 2013) <http://stateofthemedia.org/2013/news-magazines-embracing-their-digital-future/>, accessed 3 December 2013.

3 Zhou He, "Diffusion of Movable Type in China and Europe: Why Were There Two Fates?" *Gazette* 53.3 (1994): 153–173.

4 Jim Lehrer, "The New Age of Journalism," NewsHour with Jim Lehrer, 19 January 2000 <http://www.pbs.org/newshour/bb/media/jan-june00/new_journalism_1-19.html>, accessed 20 February 2006; Neil Postman, *Amusing Ourselves to Death: Public Discourse in the Age of Show Business* (New York: Penguin Books, 1985, 2005), 112.

5 Michael E. Holmes, Robert A. Papper, Mark N. Popovich, and Michael Bloxham, *Middletown Media Studies: Observing Consumers and Their Interaction with Media, Concurrent Media Exposure* (Muncie, IN: Ball State University Center for Media Design, Fall 2006). See also, Michael E. Holmes, Robert A. Papper, Mark N. Popovich, and Michael Bloxham, *Middletown Media Studies II: Concurrent Media Exposure* (Muncie, IN: Ball State University Center for Media Design, 2006); Robert A. Papper, Michael E. Holmes, and Mark N. Popovich, "Middletown Media Studies: Media Multitasking . . . and How Much People Really Use the Media," *International Digital Media and Arts Association Journal* 1.1 (Spring 2004): 4–56; Jim Spaeth, Michael E. Holmes, Bill Moult, and Michael Bloxham, *Mind the Measurement Gap: Measured and Unmeasured Media Occasions* (Muncie, IN: Ball State University Center for Media Design, June 2006).

6 Jürgen Habermas, *The Structural Transformation of the Public Sphere,* trans. Thomas Burger and Frederick Lawrence (Cambridge, MA: MIT Press, 1989).

7 Nick Stevenson, *Understanding Media Cultures,* 2nd ed. (London: Sage, 2002), 1.

8 David Renard, "The Last Magazine (in Print)," in David Renard, ed., *The Last Magazine* (New York: Universe Publishing, 2006), 14–15; Anika Anand, "Is Print Really Dying, or Just Getting Nichier?" *Upstart Business Journal*, 8 March 2013 <http://upstart.bizjournals.com/companies/media/2013/03/08/time-inc-no-sign-magazines-are-dead.html?page=all>, accessed 3 December 2013; Mark Hooper, "Who Says Print Is Dead?" *Guardian*, 3 June 2012 <www.theguardian.com/media/2012/jun/03/who-says-print-is-dead>, accessed 2 May 2014; see also, Theodore Peterson, *Magazines in the Twentieth Century* (Urbana: University of Illinois Press, 1964), 44–45.

9 Scott Fosdick, "The State of Magazine Research in 2008," *Journal of Magazine & New Media Research* 10.1 (Fall 2008): 1–4; see also, Marcia R. Prior-Miller, "Core Knowledge: Scholarly Research on Magazines" (panel presentation, Magazine Division, at the Annual Meeting, Association for Education in Journalism and Mass Communication, August 2008).

10 Edward J. Fink and Walter Gantz, "A Content Analysis of Three Mass Communication Research Traditions: Social Science, Interpretive Studies, and Critical Analysis," *Journalism & Mass Communication Quarterly* 73.1 (Spring 1996): 114–134; W. James Potter, Roger Cooper, and Michel Dupagne, "The Three Paradigms of Mass Media Research in Mainstream Communication Journals," *Communication Theory* 3.4 (November 1993): 317–335; see also, Marcia R. Prior-Miller and Associates, "Bibliography of Published Research on Magazine and Journal Periodicals," 9th ed. (research database, Ames: Iowa State University, last modified, 31 August 2014), MSWord file <mpm@iastate.edu #x003E;

11 Prior-Miller and Associates, "Bibliography of Published Research," 9th ed., 2–3.

12 Wilbur Schramm, "Twenty Years of Journalism Research," *Public Opinion Quarterly* [20th Anniversary Issue] 21.1 (Spring 1957): 91.

13 Marcia R. Prior-Miller and Kellie L. Esch, found from their analysis of an 11-year census of *Communication Abstracts* listings that the comparatively scarce research on and related to magazines was marked

by information scatter; see "A Census and Analysis of Journals Publishing Research about Magazines, 1977–1987" (paper presented at the Annual Meeting, Association for Education in Journalism and Mass Communication, August 1990).

14 Peter Gerlach, "Research about Magazines Appearing in *Journalism Quarterly*," *Journalism Quarterly* 64.1 (Spring 1987): 178–182; see also, David Abrahamson, "Brilliant Fragments: The Scholarly Engagement with the American Magazine," in David Abrahamson, ed., *The American Magazine: Research Perspectives and Prospects* (Ames: Iowa State University Press, 1995), xvii–xxi; Margaret Beetham, "Towards a Theory of the Periodical as a Publishing Genre," in Laurel Brake, Aled Jones, and Lionel Madden, eds., *Investigating Victorian Journalism* (Houndmills, UK: MacMillan Press, 1990), 19–32; Kathleen L. Endres, "Research Review: The Specialized Business Press," in David Abrahamson, ed., *The American Magazine: Research Perspectives and Prospects* (Ames: Iowa State University Press, 1995), 72–83; Tim Holmes, "Mapping the Magazine: An Introduction," in Tim Holmes, ed., *Mapping the Magazine: Comparative Studies in Magazine Journalism* (London and New York: Routledge, 2008), xv; originally published as Tim Holmes, "Mapping the Magazine: An Introduction," *Journalism Studies* 8.4 (August 2007): 510–521; Sammye Johnson, "Why Should They Care? The Relationship of Academic Scholarship to the Magazine Industry," *Journalism Studies* 8.4 (August 2007): 522–528; Carolyn Kitch, "Making Scholarly Use of Magazines: What Counts Most? What Gets Left Out?" (panel presentation, Magazine Division, at the Annual Meeting, Association for Education in Journalism and Mass Communication, August 2008); Judith Yaross Lee, "From the Field: The Future of *American Periodicals* and American Periodicals Research," *American Periodicals* 15.2 (2005): 196–201; Dorothy Schmidt, "Magazines," in M. Thomas Inge, ed., *Handbook of American Popular Culture* (Westport, CT: Greenwood Press, 1981), 137–162.

15 Denis McQuail, *McQuail's Mass Communication Theory*, 6th ed. (London: Sage, 2010), 31.

16 McQuail, *McQuail's Mass Communication Theory*, 31.

17 For an exploration of terms and definitions used to designate the medium, including *serial, periodical, magazine* and *journal*, see Marcia R. Prior-Miller, "An Organization Communication-Goals Theory of Magazine Types: Toward an Integrated Conceptual Framework of Magazine and Journal Periodicals as a Medium of Communication," Manuscript in preparation.

18 No precise, worldwide count of magazine and journal periodicals is available. The estimated range, with a low of 9,000 and a high of between 250,000 and more than 300,000, is based on numbers drawn from current national and international periodical directories. No directory is fully comprehensive; some are partially redundant and simultaneously do not include magazines and journals that are not listed in any directory. Directories consulted were, in alphabetical order, *Bacon's Magazine Directory 2011*, 59th ed. (Chicago: Cision, 2010); *Gale Directory of Publications and Broadcast Media* (Detroit: Gale Cengage Learning, 2014); Standard Rate and Data Service directories (*SRDS Business Media Advertising Source*, Part 1, which includes listings found in *SRDS Business Media Advertising Source*, Part 2, including Healthcare Publications; and *SRDS Consumer Media Advertising Source*, 2013, which includes a Farm Publications section; all include international publication listings); and *Ulrich's Periodicals Directory 2014* (Vols. 1–4, 52nd ed. New Providence, NJ: ProQuest, 2013). The estimate also draws on Sammye Johnson and Patricia Prijatel's counts in *The Magazine from Cover to Cover*, 3rd ed. (New York and London: Oxford University Press, 2013), 16, drawn from the *Standard Periodical Directory, National Directory of Magazines*, the Custom Content Council (formerly, Custom Publishing Council) for custom magazines, and other magazine publishing associations, including the MPA–the Association of Magazine Media, the American Society of Association Executives (ASAE) and the ABM–The Association of Business Information and Media Companies (U.S.). Johnson and Prijatel included *Ulrich's Periodical's Directory*, but also did not draw from the *Burrelle's/Luce Directory*; from Association Media and Publishing <http://associationmediaandpublishing.org>, accessed 20 March 2014 (formerly, Society of National Association Publications, SNAP); the Society for Scholarly Publishing <www.sspnet.org>, accessed 20 March 2014; or directories and other industry resources outside the United States. The latter includes the International Federation of the Periodical Press, FIPP <www.fipp.com>, accessed 20 March 2014. See also, Holmes, "Mapping the Magazine," ix.

19 Careful attention must be paid to directory and industry source self-descriptions of which periodicals are included and excluded from available counts. Johnson and Prijatel provide a careful outline of periodical counts that are *not* included in most sources: See *Magazine from Cover to Cover*, 16.

20 See, for example, J. William Click and Russell N. Baird, *Magazine Editing and Production*, 1st to 6th eds. (Dubuque, IA: Wm C. Brown / WCB Brown & Benchmark, 1974–1994), 1994: 4–5; Sammye Johnson and Patricia Prijatel, "The Magazine as a Storehouse: The Scope of the Medium," *The Magazine from Cover to Cover*, 3rd ed. (New York: Oxford University Press, 2013), 2–21; Frank Luther Mott, "Introduction," *A History of American Magazines 1741–1850*, vol. 1 (New York: D. Appleton, 1930), 1:1–9; Peterson, *Magazines in the Twentieth Century*, 1964, ix; Lyon N. Richardson, *A History of Early American Magazines: 1741–1789* (New York: Thomas Nelson and Sons, 1931), x; Schmidt, "Magazines," 137–138; Algernon Tassin, *The*

Magazine in America (New York: Dodd, Mead and Company, 1916), 1–27; Roland E. Wolseley, "Magazine Types," *Understanding Magazines* (Ames: Iowa State University Press, 1965), 3–12; 255–355.

21 Patrick Dunleavy, *Studying for a Degree in the Humanities and Social Sciences* (Basingstoke, UK: Macmillan Education Ltd., 1986), 66.

22 Dunleavy, *Studying for a Degree*, 66–74.

23 Scholars and dictionaries traditionally and variously identify the English word *magazine* as originating from French, Arabic or both, in each case designating a *warehouse* or *storehouse*. Contemporary lexicographic and linguistic scholarship suggests the conjoined, sometimes apparent contradiction may also result from the term's having come through Old Occitan, the "Romance language spoken in southern France," in the 1100 to 1500 period, followed by Middle French in the fourteenth to sixteenth centuries, both of which were heavily influenced by earlier North African invasions that brought Arabic to southern Europe; cf. *Merriam-Webster's Collegiate Dictionary*, 11th ed. (Springfield, MA: Merriam-Webster, 2004), s.vv. "magazine," "Middle French," "Occitan," "Old Occitan." See also, William D. Paden, *An Introduction to Old Occitan* (New York: Modern Language Association of America, 1998), 3–9; The "Langue d'Oc" and the "Langue d'Oil" <http://www.medieval-spell.com/Langue-d-Oc.html>, accessed 2 April 2014.

24 Defined as "a body of shared and relatively standardized explanations and interpretations" that represent "personal experience and the accumulated experience of one's culture"; see George. A. Theodorson and Achilles G. Theodorson, *A Modern Dictionary of Sociology* (New York: Barnes & Noble / Harper & Row, 1969), s.v. "common sense."

25 Richardson, *History of Early American Magazines*, x. Capitalization per original text.

26 Frank Luther Mott, *A History of American Magazines*, vol. 1, *A History of American Magazines, 1741–1850* (New York: D. Appleton, 1930), 7.

27 Mott, *History of American Magazines*, 1:7.

28 Click and Baird, *Magazine Editing and Production*, 1994: 5.

29 Holmes, "Mapping the Magazine," 2008: xv.

30 *Merriam-Webster's Collegiate Dictionary*, 11th ed., s.v. "magazine." Emphasis in the original.

31 Evidence of the overtime adoption of the *consumer magazine* terminology in international publishing is given in, for example, Anthony Davis, "The Magazine World," *Magazine Journalism Today* (Oxford, UK: Heinemann Professional Publishing, 1988), 3–14, 10; Sonja Narunsky-Laden, "Consumer Magazines in South Africa and Israel: Toward a Socio-Semiotic Approach to Magazine Research," *Journalism Studies* 8.4 (2007): 595–612; and *Stern* Magazine, *Consumer Magazines in Europe* (Hamburg: Gruner + Jahr AG & Co., 1981).

32 Mott, *History of American Magazines*, 1:7.

33 See, for example, Beetham, "Towards a Theory of the Periodical as a Publishing Genre," 19.

34 McQuail, *McQuail's Mass Communication Theory*, 31.

35 Click and Baird, *Magazine Editing and Production*, 1994: ix.

36 Mott, *History of American Magazines*, 1:7.

37 Mott, *History of American Magazines*, 1:5–6.

38 Beetham, after defining *periodicals* to include "newspapers, journals, reviews and magazines," focused on "the periodical," the use of which in this context might or might not be read to include the newspaper form; see "Towards a Theory of the Periodical as a Publishing Genre," 19.

39 James T.F. Tanner, "From the Editor," *American Periodicals: A Journal of History, Criticism, and Bibliography* 1.1 (Fall 1991): iii.

40 Mott, *History of American Magazines*, 1:6.

41 Mott, *History of American Magazines*, 1:9.

42 Fritz Machlup, Kenneth Leeson, and Associates, "Terminological Notes," *Information through the Printed Word: The Dissemination of Scholarly, Scientific, and Intellectual Knowledge* (New York: Praeger, 1978), vol. 1, *Book Publishing*, 15–22; Fritz Machlup, Kenneth Leeson, and Associates, "Scope, Structure, and Market of the Journal-Publishing Industry," *Information through the Printed Word: The Dissemination of Scholarly, Scientific, and Intellectual Knowledge* (New York: Praeger, 1978), vol. 2, *Journals*, ii–iv, 3–37; Richard D. Johnson described their work as "seminal" in "Machlup and the Information Age," *Scholarly Publishing* 18.4 (July 1987): 271.

43 Machlup, Leeson, and Associates, "Scope, Structure, and Market of the Journal-Publishing Industry," 3–11; *Ulrich's Periodicals Directory* uses an 11-category definition of serials, separating newspapers from non-newspaper periodicals; Shawn Chen, e-mail to author, Senior associate editor (*Ulrich's* Serials, New Providence, NJ: Serials Solutions, 14 July 2011).

44 Anglo-American Cataloguing Rules, AACR2.org, 2006 <http://www.aacr2.org/>, accessed 16 April 2014. The AACR is a cooperative effort of the American Library Association, the Canadian Library Association and the Chartered Institute of Library and Information Professionals that includes more than 13 countries

on five continents. See also, "What Is a Serial?" *CONSER Cataloging Manual*, Library of Congress, <http://www.itsmarc.com/crs/mergedprojects/conser/conser/module_2_1__ccm.htm>, accessed 18 April 2014; Cathy Sagendorf and David Moore, "Module 33: Newspapers," *CONSER Cataloging Manual*, Library of Congress, 2006 <http://www.loc.gov/acq/conser/pdf/CCM-Module-33.pdf>, accessed 18 April 2014; Jean Hirons, "Revising AACR2 to Accommodate Seriality: Report to the Joint Steering Committee on the Revision of AACR," *CONSER*, Library of Congress, April 1999 <http://www.rda-jsc.org/docs/ser-rep.pdf>, accessed 2 May 2014; see also, Renette Davis, "RDA Serials Cataloging: Changes from AACR2 to RDA," Library of Congress, PowerPoint, 22 September 2010.

45 Mott, *History of American Magazines*, 1:9. By the end of his life, Mott expressed regret over that decision. See Frank Luther Mott, "Unfinished Story; or, the Man in the Carrel," *Time Enough: Essays in Autobiography* (Chapel Hill: University of North Carolina Press, 1962), 172.

46 See, for example, David Abrahamson, ed., *The American Magazine: Research Perspectives and Prospects* (Ames: Iowa State University Press, 1995); Click and Baird, *Magazine Editing and Production*, 1st to 6th eds.; Johnson and Prijatel, *Magazine from Cover to Cover*; James B. Kobak, "Just What Is a Magazine?" *How to Start a Magazine and Publish It Profitably* (New York: M. Evans & Company, 2002), 17–18; Leonard Mogel, "What Is a Magazine?" *The Magazine*, 4th ed. (Pittsburgh: GATF Press, 1998), 10–12; Mott, *History of American Magazines*, 1:1–9; Theodore Peterson, "Magazine," in Erik Barnouw, George Gerbner, Wylbur Schramm, Tobia L. Worth, and Larry Gross, eds., *International Encyclopedia of Communications*, vol. 2 (New York: Oxford University Press, 1989), 463–468; Schmidt, "Magazines," 137–162; Wolseley, "Magazine Types," 3–12; 255–355; and Roland E. Wolseley, "The Role of Magazines in the U.S.A," *Gazette* 23.1 (1977): 20–26.

47 David Abrahamson, "Magazine Exceptionalism: The Concept, the Criteria, the Challenge," *Journalism Studies* 8.4 (2007): 667–670; Holmes, "Mapping the Magazine," 2008: x–xi.

48 Kenneth D. Bailey, *Typologies and Taxonomies: An Introduction to Classification Techniques* (Thousand Oaks, CA: Sage Publications, 1994); Edward A. Tiryakian, "Typologies," in David L. Sills, ed., *International Encyclopedia of the Social Sciences*, vol. 16 (New York: MacMillan, 1968), 177–186.

49 See, for example, Sacvan Bercovitch, ed., *Typology and Early American Literature* (Amherst: University of Massachusetts Press, 1972); Peter Martens, "Revisiting the Allegory/Typology Distinction: The Case of Origen," *Journal of Early Christian Studies* 16 (2008): 283–317; Earl Miner, ed., *Literary Uses of Typology from the Late Middle Ages to the Present* (Princeton, NJ: Princeton University Press, 1977).

50 See Daniel Chandler, "An Introduction to Genre Theory," Aberystwyth University, 1997 <http://www.aber.ac.uk/media/Documents/intgenre/chandler_genre_theory.pdf>, accessed 12 April 2014.

51 Bailey, *Typologies and Taxonomies*, 6, quoting George Gaylord Simpson, "Systematics, Taxonomy, Classification, Nomenclature," *Principles of Animal Taxonomy* (New York: Columbia University Press, 1961), 11; see also, *Merriam-Webster's Collegiate Dictionary*, 11th ed., s.v. "taxonomy."

52 Bailey, *Typologies and Taxonomies*, 3–10; Aleksey Bashtavenko, *Principles of Typology* (Bloomington, IN: AuthorHouse, 2008), 3–32; Tiryakian, "Typologies," 177–186; see also, *Merriam-Webster's Collegiate Dictionary*, 11th ed., s.v. "typology"; Theodorson and Theodorson, *Modern Dictionary of Sociology*, s.vv. "type, social, 2," "typology."

53 *Merriam-Webster's Collegiate Dictionary*, 11th ed., s.v. "genre"; see also, M.M. Bakhtin, "The Epic and the Novel: Towards a Methodology for the Study in the Novel," in *The Dialogic Imagination: Four Essays by M.M. Bakhtin*, ed Michael Holquist, trans. Caryl Emerson and Michael Holquist (Austin: University of Texas Press, 1981), 3–40; Amy J. Devitt, "A Theory of Genre," *Writing Genres* (Carbondale: Southern Illinois University Press, 2004), 1–32.

54 See Dallas Liddle's prologue to *The Dynamics of Genre: Journalism and the Practice of Literature in Mid-Victorian Britain* (Charlottesville: University of Virginia Press, 2009), 1–11; see also, Beetham, "Towards a Theory of the Periodical as a Publishing Genre," 19–32; Chandler, "An Introduction to Genre Theory."

55 Tiryakian, "Typologies," 177.

56 Paul Davidson Reynolds, *A Primer in Theory Construction* (Indianapolis: Bobbs-Merrill, 1971), 3–4. Emphasis in the original.

57 Reynolds, *Primer in Theory Construction*, 4.

58 Bailey, *Typologies and Taxonomies*, 1.

59 Among the earliest known reports of research on magazines published as scholarly journal articles are two from 1934 and 1937: Winona Morgan and Alice M. Leahy, "The Cultural Content of General Interest Magazines," *Journal of Educational Psychology* 25 (October 1934): 530–536; and Paul F. Lazarsfeld and Rowena Wyant, "Magazines in 90 Cities—Who Reads What?" *Public Opinion Quarterly* 1.4 (October 1937): 29–41. Also published in 1930 and 1931 were the first volume of Frank Luther Mott's encyclopedic, five-volume *A History of American Magazines*; and Richardson's *History of Early American Magazines*, respectively. Tassin's 1916 history, *Magazine in America*, preceded both by more than a decade.

60 Marguerite Deslauriers, *Aristotle on Definition* (Leiden, The Netherlands: Brill, 2007); see also, Robert Bierstedt, "Nominal and Real Definitions in Sociological Theory," in Llewellyn Gross, ed., *Symposium on Sociological Theory* (Evanston, IL: Row, Peterson, 1959), 121–144.

61 Chunglin Kwa, "The Taxonomic Style," *Styles of Knowing: A New History of Science from Ancient Times to the Present*, trans. David McKay (Pittsburgh, PA: University of Pittsburgh Press, 2011), 165.

62 Kwa, "The Taxonomic Style," 166.

63 Kwa, "The Taxonomic Style," 166.

64 Chandler, "An Introduction to Genre Theory," 1.

65 For discussions of sociologists' diverse views, see, for example, Bailey, *Typologies and Taxonomies*, 10–16; Tiryakian, "Typologies," 177–186; and D. Harold Doty and William H. Glick, "Typologies as a Unique Form of Theory Building: Toward Improved Understanding and Modeling," *Academy of Management Review* 19.2 (1994): 230–233.

66 For a succinct summary of the anti-science argument and additional readings, see Jacob Barrie Gordon, "Can Sociologists Study Society in the Same Way That Scientists Study the Natural World?" Jake Gordon, 2002 <http://jakeg.co.uk/essays/science>, accessed 14 February 2014; see also, Pierre Bourdieu, "The Specificity of the Scientific Field and the Social Conditions of the Progress of Reason," *Social Science Information* 14.6 (1975): 19–47.

67 See, for example, Annie Lang, "Discipline in Crisis? The Shifting Paradigm of Mass Communication Research," *Communication Theory* 23.1 (February 2013): 10–24.

68 Fink and Gantz, "A Content Analysis of Three Mass Communication Research Traditions," 114–134; Potter, Cooper, and Dupagne, "The Three Paradigms of Mass Media Research," 317–335; see also, Prior-Miller and Associates, "Bibliography of Published Research," 9th ed.

69 Bailey, *Typologies and Taxonomies*, 1–16; Doty and Glick, "Typologies as a Unique Form of Theory Building"; Reynolds, *Primer in Theory Construction*, 4–5; see also, Dennis T. Lowry, "Population Validity of Communication Research: Sampling the Samples," *Journalism Quarterly* 56.1 (Spring 1979): 62–68, 76.

70 Earl Babbie, *The Practice of Social Research*, 11th ed. (Belmont, CA: Thomson Wadsworth, 2007), 22–23, 132–133.

71 McQuail, *McQuail's Mass Communication Theory*, 126–127, 143–144; see also, 102–103, 544.

72 McQuail, *McQuail's Mass Communication Theory*, 126–127.

73 McQuail, *McQuail's Mass Communication Theory*, 10–13.

74 McQuail, *McQuail's Mass Communication Theory*, 126.

75 See, for example, Abrahamson, "Magazine Exceptionalism," 667–670; Beetham, "Towards a Theory of the Periodical as a Publishing Genre"; and Ann Ardis, "Towards a Theory of Periodical Studies," Roundtable opening statement at the Annual Convention, Modern Language Association, January 2013.

76 Reynolds, *Primer in Theory Construction*, 4–5, emphasis added. See also, Bailey, *Typologies and Taxonomies*, 1–16; Tiryakian, "Typologies," 177–178.

77 See, for example, Johnson and Prijatel, "The Magazine as a Storehouse," 11–16; Kobak, "Just What Is a Magazine?" 17–18; Shannon E. Martin, "Using Expert Sources in Breaking Science Stories: A Comparison of Magazine Types," *Journalism Quarterly* 68.1/2 (Spring/Summer 1991): 179–187; Mott, "Introduction," *History of American Magazines*, 1:1–2; see also, Benjamin M. Compaine, *Consumer Magazines at the Crossroads: A Study of General and Special Interest Magazines* (White Plains, NY: Knowledge Industry Publications, 1974); Benjamin M. Compaine, "The Magazine Industry: Developing the Special Interest Audience," *Journal of Communication* 30.2 (June 1980): 98–103.

78 See, for example, Click and Baird, *Magazine Editing and Production*, 1994:6; Wolseley, "Magazine Types," 9.

79 See, for example, Mogel, "What Is a Magazine?" 10–12; Charles P. Daly, Patrick Henry, and Ellen Ryder, "Overview of Magazine Publishing," *The Magazine Publishing Industry* (Boston: Allyn and Bacon, 1997), 1–20.

80 Of the 30 sources whose classification frameworks were examined for this study, more than half (17) used "type" and "types" to refer to the classification strategies.

81 See Marcia R. Prior-Miller, "Research Review: Issues in Magazine Typology," in David Abrahamson, ed., *The American Magazine: Research Perspectives and Prospects* (Ames: Iowa State University Press, 1995), 13–18.

82 Jonathan Grix, "Introducing Students to the Generic Terminology of Social Research," *Politics* 22.3 (2002): 175–186.

83 McQuail, *McQuail's Mass Communication Theory*, 5.

84 McQuail's commonly used descriptor, *mass communication theory*, is not an exact fit for the dimensions of communication that occur through the magazine in all its forms. Neither is *mediated interpersonal communication*, as defined, for example, by Stephen Littlejohn in *Theories of Human Communication*, 4th ed. (Belmont, CA: Wadsworth Publishing, 1992), 17, 262–292. Rather, communication that occurs through

the magazine form draws on multiple theoretical streams. See also Charles R. Wright, *Mass Communication: A Sociological Perspective*, 2nd, 3rd eds. (New York: Random House, 1975, 1986), 2:6–12, 3:3–27.

85 Denis McQuail, *Mass Communication Theory: An Introduction*, 1st, 2nd eds. (Beverly Hills, CA, and London: Sage, 1984, 1987), 1: 17–18, 2: 4–5.

86 McQuail, *McQuail's Mass Communication Theory*, 14.

87 Compaine, *Consumer Magazines at the Crossroads*, 28.

88 Compaine, *Consumer Magazines at the Crossroads*, 28.

89 Researchers use a variety of descriptors for the topical categorization of periodicals, as do periodical directories. Prior-Miller, "Issues in Magazine Typology," 1995: 10, called the categories "editorial interest areas" to differentiate between editorial and advertising topical categorization.

90 The four patterns are described in greater detail in Prior-Miller, "Issues in Magazine Typology," 1995: 7, 8–13. See also Marcia R. Prior-Miller, "Research Review: Issues in Magazine Typology," *Electronic Journal of Communication/La Revue de Electronique de Communication* 4.2/4 (December 1994), <eric.ed.gov /?id=EJ494512>, accessed 30 May 2014.

91 See summary descriptions in Prior-Miller, "Issues in Magazine Typology," 1994: Unpaginated, 1995: 13–19.

92 Prior-Miller, data from research, not reported in "Issues in Magazine Typology," 1995: 8–13.

93 *Merriam-Webster's Collegiate Dictionary*, 11th ed., defines *general* as "involving, applicable to, or affecting the whole; . . . every member of a class, kind, or group . . . not confined by specialization or careful limitation," s.v. "general"; and *specialized* is what general is not: "characterized by or exhibiting . . . specialization; . . . highly differentiated, esp. in a particular direction or for a particular end," or, "designed . . . for one particular purpose," s.v. "specialized."

94 See, for example, Kineta H. Hung, Flora Fang Gu, and David K. Tse, "Improving Media Decisions in China: A Targetability and Cost-Benefit Analysis," *Journal of Advertising* 34.1 (Spring 2005): 49–63; Martin, "Using Expert Sources in Breaking Science Stories," 179–187; Christopher W. Podeschi, "The Culture of Nature and the Rise of Modern Environmentalism: The View through General Audience Magazines, 1945–1980," *Sociological Spectrum* 27.3 (March 2007): 299–331.

95 Hung, Gu, and Tse, "Improving Media Decisions in China"; Anniken Westad, "The Norwegian Magazine Industry: An Overview and Bibliographic Review" (Paper presented to the Contemporary Magazine Publishing Research Roundtable, Iowa State University, December 2010).

96 Mott, "Introduction," *History of American Magazines*, 1:2.

97 *Merriam-Webster's Collegiate Dictionary*, 11th ed., s.v. "appeal"; see also, Compaine, *Consumer Magazines at the Crossroads*, 58. Compaine's articulation of the general-specialized strategy is a second-level categorization, specific to the consumer magazine category.

98 Tassin, *Magazine in America*, 1.

99 The full title stated on the cover of the first issue, dated January 1741, was *The General Magazine, and Historical Chronicle, for all the British Plantations in America*. See Johnson and Prijatel, *The Magazine from Cover to Cover*, 68–69.

100 Richardson, *History of Early American Magazines*, 1.

101 Schmidt, "Magazines," 137; see also, Tassin, *Magazine in America*, 1–6; Colin Clair, *A History of European Printing* (London and New York: Academic Press, 1976), 296; Peterson, "Magazine," 463–468; Sigfrid H. Steinberg, *Five Hundred Years of Printing*, new ed., rev. John Trevitt (London: British Library & Oak Knoll Press, 1955/1996), 124–125.

102 Peterson, *Magazines in the Twentieth Century*, 1964: 20–59; see also, W. Ronald Lane, Karen Whitehill King, and Tom Reichert, "Using Magazines," *Kleppner's Advertising Procedure*, 18th ed. (Upper Saddle River, NJ: Prentice Hall / Pearson, 2011), 321–322; Johnson and Prijatel, *Magazine from Cover to Cover*, 59–87; William. H. Taft, *American Magazines for the 1980s* (New York: Hastings House, 1982), 15–24; Wolseley, *Understanding Magazines*, 25–98.

103 Jürgen Habermas, *The Structural Transformation of the Public Sphere*, trans. Thomas Burger and Frederick Lawrence (Cambridge, MA: MIT Press, 1989), 181–235.

104 Steinberg, *Five Hundred Years of Printing*, 162.

105 Lane, King, and Reichert, "Using Magazines," 321–322; see also, Johnson and Prijatel, *Magazine from Cover to Cover*, 59–87; Peterson, *Magazines in the Twentieth Century*, 1964: 20–59; Taft, *American Magazines for the 1980s*, 15–24; Wolseley, *Understanding Magazines*, 25–98.

106 Lane, King, and Reichert, "Using Magazines," 321–322; see also, Johnson and Prijatel, *Magazine from Cover to Cover*, 59–87; Taft, *American Magazines for the 1980s*, 15–24; Wolseley, *Understanding Magazines*, 25–98.

107 Newer audience-based approaches are indicated in, for example, Theodore F. D'Amico, "Magazines' Secret Weapon: Media Selection on the Basis of Behavior As Opposed to Demography," *Journal of Advertising Research* 39.6 (November/December 1999): 53–60.

108 Renard, "The Last Magazine (in Print)," 14–15.

109 David Abrahamson, "The Future of Magazines, 2010–2020," *Journal of Magazine & New Media Research* 10.2 (Spring 2009): 1–3.

110 Ray Eldon Hiebert and Sheila Jean Gibbons, "Books, Magazines and Newsletters," *Exploring Mass Media for a Changing World* (Mahwah, NJ: Lawrence Erlbaum, 2000), 177.

111 Hiebert and Gibbons, "Books, Magazines and Newsletters," 178.

112 Hiebert and Gibbons, "Books, Magazines and Newsletters," 179–180.

113 Frank Luther Mott, A *History of American Magazines*, vol. 1, *A History of American Magazines, 1741–1850*; vol. 2, *A History of American Magazines, 1850–1865*; vol. 3, *A History of American Magazines, 1865–1885*; vol. 4, *A History of American Magazines, 1885–1905*; vol. 5, *A History of American Magazines, 1905–1930* (New York: D. Appleton, 1930; Cambridge, MA: The Belknap Press, 1938, 1938, 1957; Cambridge, MA: Harvard University Press, 1968).

114 Wolseley, "Magazine Types," 3–12, 255–355; James L.C. Ford, *Magazines for Millions: The Story of Specialized Publications* (Carbondale: South Illinois University Press, 1969), 1–12; Wolseley, "The Role of Magazines in the U.S.A," 20–26.

115 Detailed diagrams of the sources' frameworks are available from the author. Any errors in translating their verbal descriptions into first, second and third level sub-categories are this author's.

116 Prior-Miller, data from research, not reported in "Issues in Magazine Typology," 1995: 8–13.

117 These title clusters are used as a second-level classification strategy in the Standard Rate and Data Service *Consumer Media* and *Business Media Advertising Source* directories, where they are called "Editorial Classifications"; see *SRDS Media Business Advertising Source*, Parts 1 and 2 and *SRDS Consumer Media Advertising Source*.

118 See, for example, Emma Bazilian, "Home Improvement: With Luxury on the Upswing, Shelter Magazines are Raising the Roof," *AdWeek*, 22 May 2012 <http://www.adweek.com/news/press/home-improvement-140629>, accessed 4 May 2014.

119 See, for example, *Bacon's Magazine Directory*, *Burrelle's/Luce Directory* (Livingston, NJ: Information Services), *National Directory of Magazines* (New York: Oxbridge Communications, 2014), *Standard Periodical Directory* (New York: Oxbridge Communications, 2014) and *Ulrich's Periodicals Directory*.

120 Nancy Berns, "Women's Magazines: The Victim Empowerment Frame," *Framing the Victim: Domestic Violence, Media, and Social Problems* (Hawthorne, NY: Aldine de Gruyter, 2004), 55–81.

121 Kristen Harrison and Barbara L. Fredrickson, "Women's Sports Media, Self-Objectification, and Mental Health in Black and White Adolescent Females," *Journal of Communication* 53.2 (2003): 216–232.

122 Orayb Aref Najjar, "'The Editorial Family of al-Kateb Bows in Respect': The Construction of Martyrdom Text Genre in One Palestinian Political and Literary Magazine," *Discourse & Society* 7.4 (1996): 499–530.

123 See, for example, Brian Moeran, "More than Just a Fashion Magazine," *Current Sociology* 54.5 (September 2006): 725–744.

124 An exception is the *Gale Directory of Publications and Broadcast Media*, for which the international volume, 5, and U.S. volumes, 1–4, are organized geographically: alphabetically by country (city within country) and by state (city within state), respectively.

125 Carolyn F. Ulrich, the directory's first editor and chief of the periodicals division of the New York Public Library, described the directory as meeting "the need for an up-to-date classified list of foreign and domestic periodicals"; *Periodicals Directory: A Classified Guide to a Selected List of Current Periodicals Foreign and Domestic* (New York: R.R. Bowker, 1932), ix.

126 *Ulrich's Periodicals Directory 2014*, 1: vii.

127 *Ulrich's Periodicals Directory 2014* is available in hard copy and electronic database formats and calls the categories *subject classifications*. *Bacon's Magazine Directory*, a directory for public relations professionals now available only as a digital database, calls categories *market classifications*.

128 Stuart Elliott, "Renaming the Circulation Overseer," *New York Times*, 14 November 2012 <http://www.nytimes.com/2012/11/15/business/media/renaming-the-audit-bureau-of-circulations.html?_r=0>, accessed 2 May 2014; "About BPA," BPA Worldwide <http://www.bpaww.com/Bpaww_com/Pages/About BPA.aspx>, accessed 18 April 2014.

129 Daniel Mallett, "The Relationship of Screen-In Rates and Readership Levels in MRI and SMRB (Mediamark Research Inc., Simmons Market Research Bureau)," *Journal of Advertising Research* [Special Issue: The Growing Importance of Media Research] 33.1 (1993): 18–22; Joe Mandese, "Simmons Adopts Rival's Audience Methodology: Magazine Research Change Will Cost Less," *Advertising Age*, 19 September 1994, 1.

130 Tassin, *Magazine in America*, 1; Richardson, *History of Early American Magazines*, 74–162.

131 Steinberg, *Five Hundred Years of Printing*, 124–126.

132 *Bacon's Magazine Directory*, 7, lists categories as Consumer Interest Publications; Trade (Business/Trade/Professional Publications); Newsletter Format; Local, State or Regional Editorial Emphasis; Canadian Publications; African-American Publications; Hispanic Audiences Publications.

133 [Emphasis added] *Ulrich's* 8 additional *serial types* categories define non-periodical serials: *Newsletter, Newspaper, Catalog, Directory, Monographic Series*. Three additional categories added in 2011 are unofficial: *Handbook/Manual, Report* and *Other Format*. Chen, e-mail to author (14 July 2011).

134 *Ulrich's* periodical subject categories are (1) Academic/Scholarly (defined as, "content is geared toward academic fields"); (2) Refereed Serial (keyed and defined as, "known to be referred or juried, as identified by publisher"); (3) Consumer ("content aimed at consumer interests and information"); (4) Corporate ("content specifically for a corporation or institution and people associated with the corporation"); (5) Government ("content government produced for government related use"); (6) Internal ("exclusively used by members or employees of organization"); (7) Trade ("content geared towards specific trades"); and (8) Newspaper Publication ("is distributed with newspapers"). Chen, e-mail to author (14 July 2011).

135 Ford, *Magazines for Millions*, 5, reported having grouped the 215 classifications in Standard Rate and Data Service's *Consumer, Farm* and *Business* directories into nine specialized clusters for his 1969 analysis. He did not provide details of collapsed groups; no similar reports were found elsewhere in the literature.

136 Prior-Miller, data from research, not reported in "Issues in Magazine Typology," 11, 15–17.

137 Peterson, *Magazines in the Twentieth Century*, 1956: viii, 1964: ix.

138 Peterson, *Magazines in the Twentieth Century*, 1956: vii–ix.

139 Peterson listed the trade periodicals *Advertising Age, Tide* and *Editor & Publisher*; news magazines *Newsweek* and *Time*; Ayer's directories; *Standard Rate and Data Service* and Standard and Poor's *Standard Corporation Descriptions* and *Standard Corporation Records*; as well as the magazines about which he wrote. See *Magazines in the Twentieth Century*, 397.

140 Peterson, *Magazines in the Twentieth Century*, 1956, 1964: 1–17.

141 Click and Baird, *Magazine Editing and Production*, 1974: 4.

142 Click and Baird, *Magazine Editing and Production*, 1:4–6, 14–29, 30–46; see editions 2 to 6 (1974, 1979–1994) for variations on the strategy introduced in the first edition that included a one-shot magazines category.

143 Jean Folkerts and Stephen Lacy, "Magazines," *The Media in Your Life*, 2nd ed. (Boston: Allyn & Bacon, 2001), 114–143; Holmes, "Mapping the Magazine," 2008: ix.

144 Melvin L. DeFleur and Everette E. Dennis, "Magazines: Voices for Many Interests," *Understanding Mass Communication*, 6th ed. (Boston: Houghton Mifflin, 1998), 97–126.

145 To his two categories, Davis identified as a third, *other* group, "'alternative,' underground and cult magazines," in "The Magazine World," 10–12; Samir Husni's third, *other* group named religious magazines, as organization publications, in *Launch Your Own Magazine. A Guide for Succeeding in Today's Marketplace* (Nashville: Hamblett House, 1998), 4–5; Michael Bugeja's third, *other* group included two or three clusters, identified as "association," "sponsored or custom" and Internet magazines," in "Magazine," *World Book Encyclopedia* (Chicago: World Book, 2008), 42–43.

146 Shirley Biagi, "Magazines: Targeting the Audience," *Media/Impact: An Introduction to Mass Media*, 9th ed. (Boston: Wadsworth Cengage Learning, 2010), 72–91; Ronald T. Farrar, "Magazines," *Mass Communication: An Introduction to the Field*, 2nd ed. (Madison, WI: Brown & Benchmark, 1996), G.1–18; Thomas M. Pasqua, Jr., James K. Buckalew, Robert E. Rayfield, and James W., Tankard, Jr., "Magazines," *Mass Media in the Information Age* (Englewood Cliffs, NJ: Prentice Hall, 1990), 66–83; David E. Sumner and Shirrel Rhoades, *Magazines: A Complete Guide to the Industry*, New York: Peter Lang, 2006, 5–6; John Vivian, "Magazines," *The Media of Mass Communication*, 8th ed. (Boston: Pearson, 2007), 80–99; William James Willis and Diane B. Willis, "Magazines and the Search for Specialization," *New Directions in Media Management* (Boston: Allyn & Bacon, 1993), 65–89.

147 Jay Black and Jennings Bryant, "Magazines," *Introduction to Media Communication*, 4th ed. (Dubuque, IA: Brown & Benchmark, 1995), 121–150; Peterson, "Magazine," 463–468.

148 Joseph R. Dominick, "Magazines," *The Dynamics of Mass Communication: Media in Transition*, 11th ed. (New York: McGraw-Hill, 2011), 108–129; Warren K. Agee, Phillip. H. Ault, and Edwin Emery, "Magazines," *Introduction to Media Communications*, 12th ed. (New York: Longman, 1997), 153–177; Click and Baird, *Magazine Editing and Production*, 1994:7–9, 24–26; Daly, Henry, and Ryder, "Overview of Magazine Publishing," 7–8.

149 Stanley J. Baran, "Magazines," *Introduction to Mass Communication: Media Literacy and Culture*, 3rd ed. (Boston: McGraw-Hill, 2004), 132–157; Johnson and Prijatel, "The Magazine as a Storehouse," 11–16.

150 DeFleur and Dennis, "Magazines: Voices for Many Interests," 97–126.

151 Husni, *Launch Your Own Magazine*, 4–5; Bugeja, "Magazine," 42–43.

152 Albert N. Greco, "The Economics of Books and Magazines," in Alison Alexander, James Owers, Rod Carveth, C. Ann Hollifield, and Albert N. Greco, eds., *Media Economics: Theory and Practice*, 3rd ed. (Mahway, NJ: Lawrence Erlbaum Associates, 2003), 127–147; John C. Merrill, John D. Lee, and Edward Jay Friedlander, "Books and Magazines," *Modern Mass Media* (New York: Harper & Row, 1990), 140–168; Mogel, "What Is a Magazine?" 10–12.

153 Joseph Turow, "The Magazine Industry," *Media Today: An Introduction to Mass Communication*, 3rd ed. (New York: Routledge, Taylor & Francis, 2009), 342–374.

154 Peterson, "Magazine," 463–468.

155 Dominick, "Magazines," 108–129.

156 James D. Harless, "The American Magazine: A Range of Reading," *Mass Communication: An Introductory Survey*, 2nd ed. (Dubuque: Wm. C. Brown, 1990), 148–180.

157 Click and Baird, *Magazine Editing and Production*, 1994:7–9, 24–26; Johnson and Prijatel, "The Magazine as a Storehouse," 11–16; Vivian, "Magazines," 80–99.

158 Stan Le Roy Wilson, "Magazines: The Specialized Medium," *Mass Media/Mass Culture: An Introduction*, 2nd ed. (New York: McGraw-Hill, 1992), 121–145.

159 Black and Bryant, "Magazines," 121–150; Kobak, "Just What Is a Magazine?" 17–18.

160 Agee, Ault, and Emery, "Magazines," 153–177; Click and Baird, *Magazine Editing and Production*, 1994: 7–9, 24–26.

161 DeFleur and Dennis, "Magazines: Voices for Many Interests," 97–126.

162 Agee, Ault, and Emery, "Magazines," 153–177; Johnson and Prijatel, "The Magazine as a Storehouse," 11–16.

163 Baran, "Magazines," 132–157; Johnson and Prijatel, "The Magazine as a Storehouse," 11–16; Bugeja, "Magazine," 42–43.

164 Dominick, "Magazines," 108–129; Turow, "The Magazine Industry," 342–374.

165 Daly, Henry, and Ryder, "Overview of Magazine Publishing," 7–8; Turow, "The Magazine Industry," 342–374.

166 Compaine, *Consumer Magazines at the Crossroads*, v; Compaine, "The Magazine Industry," 100–101. See Agee, Ault, and Emery, "Magazines," 153–177; Greco, "The Economics of Books and Magazines," 127–147; Johnson and Prijatel, "The Magazine as a Storehouse," 11–16; Mogel, "What Is a Magazine?" 10–12; Willis and Willis, "Magazines and the Search for Specialization," 65–89.

167 Agee, Ault, and Emery, "Magazines," 153–177.

168 Doty and Glick, "Typologies as a Unique Form of Theory Building," 231–233.

169 Doty and Glick, "Typologies as a Unique Form of Theory Building," 231–233.

170 Compaine, *Consumer Magazines at the Crossroads*, 28.

171 Portions of this chapter are drawn from the author's manuscript in preparation. See Prior-Miller, "An Organization Communication-Goals Theory of Magazine Types."

Bibliography

"About BPA." BPA Worldwide <http://www.bpaww.com/Bpaww_com/Pages/AboutBPA.aspx>, accessed 18 April 2014.

Abrahamson, David, ed. *The American Magazine: Research Perspectives and Prospects*. Ames: Iowa State University Press, 1995.

Abrahamson, David. "Brilliant Fragments: The Scholarly Engagement with the American Magazine." In Abrahamson, David, ed. *The American Magazine: Research Perspectives and Prospects*. Ames: Iowa State University Press, 1995, xvii–xxi.

Abrahamson, David. "The Future of Magazines, 2010–2020." *Journal of Magazine & New Media Research* 10.2 (Spring 2009): 1–3.

Abrahamson, David. "Magazine Exceptionalism: The Concept, the Criteria, the Challenge." *Journalism Studies* 8.4 (2007): 667–670.

Agee, Warren K.; Ault, Phillip. H.; and Emery, Edwin. "Magazines." *Introduction to Media Communications*. 12th ed. New York: Longman, 1997, 153–177.

Anand, Anika. "Is Print Really Dying, or Just Getting Nichier?" *Upstart Business Journal*, 8 March 2013 <http://upstart.bizjournals.com/companies/media/2013/03/08/time-inc-no-sign-magazines-are-dead.html?page=all>, accessed 3 December 2013.

Anglo-American Cataloguing Rules. AACR2.org, 2006 <http://www.aacr2.org/>, accessed 16 April 2014.

Ardis, Ann. "Towards a Theory of Periodical Studies." Roundtable opening statement at the Annual Convention, Modern Language Association, January 2013.

Babbie, Earl. *The Practice of Social Research*. 11th ed. Belmont, CA: Thomson Wadsworth, 2007.

Bacon's Magazine Directory 2011. 59th ed. Chicago: Cision, 2010.

Bailey, Kenneth D. *Typologies and Taxonomies: An Introduction to Classification Techniques*. Thousand Oaks: Sage Publications, 1994.

Bakhtin, M.M. "The Epic and the Novel: Towards a Methodology for the Study in the Novel." In *The Dialogic Imagination: Four Essays by M.M. Bakhtin*. Edited by Michael Holquist. Translated by Caryl Emerson and Michael Holquist. Austin: University of Texas Press, 1981, 3–40.

Baran, Stanley J. "Magazines." *Introduction to Mass Communication: Media Literacy and Culture*. 3rd ed. Boston: McGraw-Hill, 2004, 132–157.

Bashtavenko, Aleksey. *Principles of Typology*. Bloomington, IN: AuthorHouse, 2008.

Bazilian, Emma. "Home Improvement: With Luxury on the Upswing, Shelter Magazines are Raising the Roof." *AdWeek*, 22 May 2012 <http://www.adweek.com/news/press/home-improvement-140629>, accessed 4 May 2014.

Beetham, Margaret. "Towards a Theory of the Periodical as a Publishing Genre." In Brake, Laurel; Jones, Aled; and Madden, Lionel, eds. *Investigating Victorian Journalism*. Houndmills, UK: MacMillan Press, 1990, 19–32.

Bercovitch, Sacvan, ed. *Typology and Early American Literature*. Amherst: University of Massachusetts Press, 1972.

Berns, Nancy. "Women's Magazines: The Victim Empowerment Frame." *Framing the Victim: Domestic Violence, Media, and Social Problems*. Hawthorne, NY: Aldine de Gruyter, 2004, 55–81.

Biagi, Shirley. "Magazines: Targeting the Audience." *Media/Impact: An Introduction to Mass Media*. 9th ed. Boston: Wadsworth Cengage Learning, 2010, 72–91.

Bierstedt, Robert. "Nominal and Real Definitions in Sociological Theory." In Gross, Llewellyn, ed. *Symposium on Sociological Theory*. Evanston, IL: Row, Peterson, 1959, 121–144.

Black, Jay and Bryant, Jennings. "Magazines." *Introduction to Media Communication*. 4th ed. Dubuque, IA: Brown & Benchmark, 1995, 121–150.

Bourdieu, Pierre. "The Specificity of the Scientific Field and the Social Conditions of the Progress of Reason." *Social Science Information* 14.6 (1975): 19–47.

Bugeja, Michael. "Magazine." *World Book Encyclopedia*. Chicago: World Book, 2008, 42–45.

Burrelle's/Luce Media Directory. Livingston, NJ: Information Services, 2003.

Chandler, Daniel. "An Introduction to Genre Theory." Aberystwyth University, 1997 <http://www.aber.ac.uk/media/Documents/intgenre/chandler_genre_theory.pdf>, accessed 12 April 2014.

Chen, Shawn, -E-mails to author. Senior associate editor, *Ulrich's* Serials, New Providence, NJ: Serials Solutions, 6 March 2006, 14 July 2011.

Clair, Colin. *A History of European Printing*. London and New York: Academic Press, 1976.

Click, J. William and Baird, Russell N. *Magazine Editing and Production*. 1st to 6th eds. Dubuque, IA, Madison, WI: Wm C. Brown / WCB Brown & Benchmark, 1974–1994.

Compaine, Benjamin M. *Consumer Magazines at the Crossroads: A Study of General and Special Interest Magazines*. White Plains, NY: Knowledge Industry Publications, 1974.

Compaine, Benjamin M. "How Special Interest and General Interest Magazines Differ." *The Business of Consumer Magazines*. White Plains, NY: Knowledge Industry Publications, 1982, 89–104.

Compaine, Benjamin M. "The Magazine Industry: Developing the Special Interest Audience." *Journal of Communication* 30.2 (June 1980): 98–103.

Daly, Charles P.; Henry, Patrick; and Ryder, Ellen. "Overview of Magazine Publishing." *The Magazine Publishing Industry*. Boston: Allyn and Bacon, 1997, 1–20.

D'Amico, Theodore F. "Magazines' Secret Weapon: Media Selection on the Basis of Behavior As Opposed to Demography." *Journal of Advertising Research* 39.6 (November/December 1999): 53–60.

Davis, Anthony. "The Magazine World." *Magazine Journalism Today*. Oxford, UK: Heinemann Professional Publishing, 1988, 3–14.

Davis, Renette. "RDA Serials Cataloging: Changes from AACR2 to RDA." Library of Congress, PowerPoint. 22 September 2010. <http://www.loc.gov/catdir/cpso/RDAtest/RDAtest/rdatest.html>, accessed 16 April 2014.

DeFleur, Melvin L. and Dennis, Everette E. "Magazines: Voices for Many Interests." *Understanding Mass Communication*. 6th ed. Boston: Houghton Mifflin, 1998, 97–126.

Deslauriers, Marguerite. *Aristotle on Definition*. Leiden, The Netherlands: Brill, 2007.

Devitt, Amy J. "A Theory of Genre." *Writing Genres*. Carbondale: Southern Illinois University Press, 2004, 1–32.

Dominick, Joseph R. "Magazines." *The Dynamics of Mass Communication: Media in Transition*. 11th ed. New York: McGraw-Hill, 2011, 108–129.

Doty, D. Harold and Glick, William H. "Typologies as a Unique Form of Theory Building: Toward Improved Understanding and Modeling." *Academy of Management Review* 19.2 (1994): 230–251.

Dunleavy, Patrick. *Studying for a Degree in the Humanities and Social Sciences*. Basingstoke, UK: Macmillan Education Ltd., 1986.

Elliott, Stuart. "Renaming the Circulation Overseer." *New York Times*, 14 November 2012 <http://www.nytimes.com/2012/11/15/business/media/renaming-the-audit-bureau-of-circulations.html?_r=0>, accessed 2 May 2014.

Endres, Kathleen L. "Research Review: The Specialized Business Press." In Abrahamson, David, ed. *The American Magazine: Research Perspectives and Prospects*. Ames: Iowa State University Press, 1995, 72–83.

Farrar, Ronald T. "Magazines." *Mass Communication: An Introduction to the Field*. 2nd ed. Madison, WI: Brown & Benchmark, 1996, G.1–18.

Fink, Edward J. and Gantz, Walter. "A Content Analysis of Three Mass Communication Research Traditions: Social Science, Interpretive Studies, and Critical Analysis." *Journalism & Mass Communication Quarterly* 73.1 (Spring 1996): 114–134.

Folkerts, Jean and Lacy, Stephen. "Magazines." *The Media in Your Life*. 2nd ed. Boston: Allyn & Bacon, 2001, 114–143.

Ford, James L.C. *Magazines for Millions: The Story of Specialized Publications*. Carbondale: South Illinois University Press, 1969.

Fosdick, Scott. "The State of Magazine Research in 2008." *Journal of Magazine & New Media Research* 10.1 (Fall 2008): 1–4.

Gale Directory of Publications and Broadcast Media. Detroit: Gale Cengage Learning, 2014.

Gerlach, Peter. "Research about Magazines Appearing in *Journalism Quarterly*." *Journalism Quarterly* 64.1 (Spring 1987): 178–182.

Gordon, Jacob Barrie. "Can Sociologists Study Society in the Same Way that Scientists Study the Natural World?" Jake Gordon, 2002 <http://jakeg.co.uk/essays/science>, accessed 14 February 2014.

Greco, Albert N. "The Economics of Books and Magazines." In Alexander, Alison; Owers, James; Carveth, Rod; Hollifield, C. Ann and Greco, Albert N., eds. *Media Economics: Theory and Practice*. 3rd ed. Mahway, NJ: Lawrence Erlbaum Associates, 2003, 127–147.

Grix, Jonathan. "Introducing Students to the Generic Terminology of Social Research." *Politics* 22.3 (2002): 175–186.

Habermas, Jürgen. *The Structural Transformation of the Public Sphere*. Translated by Thomas Burger and Frederick Lawrence. Cambridge, MA: MIT Press, 1989.

Harless, James D. "The American Magazine: A Range of Reading." *Mass Communication: An Introductory Survey*. 2nd ed. Dubuque, IA: Wm. C. Brown, 1990, 148–180.

Harrison, Kristen and Fredrickson, Barbara L. "Women's Sports Media, Self-Objectification, and Mental Health in Black and White Adolescent Females." *Journal of Communication* 53.2 (2003): 216–232.

He, Zhou. "Diffusion of Movable Type in China and Europe: Why Were There Two Fates?" *Gazette* 53.3 (1994): 153–173.

Hiebert, Ray Eldon and Gibbons, Sheila Jean. "Books, Magazines and Newsletters." *Exploring Mass Media for a Changing World*. Mahwah, NJ: Lawrence Erlbaum, 2000, 166–186.

Hirons, Jean. "Revising AACR2 to Accommodate Seriality: Report to the Joint Steering Committee on the Revision of AACR." *CONSER*, Library of Congress, April 1999 <http://www.rda-jsc.org/docs/ser-rep.pdf>, accessed 2 May 2014.

Holmes, Michael E.; Papper, Robert A.; Popovich, Mark N.; and Bloxham, Michael. *Middletown Media Studies: Observing Consumers and Their Interaction with Media, Concurrent Media Exposure*. Muncie, IN: Ball State University Center for Media Design, Fall 2006.

Holmes, Michael E.; Papper, Robert A.; Popovich, Mark N.; and Bloxham, Michael. *Middletown Media Studies II: Concurrent Media Exposure*. Muncie, IN: Ball State University Center for Media Design, 2006.

Holmes, Tim. "Mapping the Magazine: An Introduction." *Journalism Studies* 8.4 (August 2007): 510–521.

Holmes, Tim. "Mapping the Magazine: An Introduction." In Holmes, Tim, ed. *Mapping the Magazine: Comparative Studies in Magazine Journalism*. London and New York: Routledge, 2008, viii–xix.

Hooper, Mark. "Who Says Print Is Dead?" *Guardian*, 3 June 2012 <http://www.theguardian.com/media/2012/jun/03/who-says-print-is-dead>, accessed 2 May 2014.

Hung, Kineta H.; Gu, Flora Fang; and Tse, David K. "Improving Media Decisions in China: A Targetability and Cost-Benefit Analysis." *Journal of Advertising* 34.1 (Spring 2005): 49–63.

Husni, Samir. *Launch Your Own Magazine. A Guide for Succeeding in Today's Marketplace*. Nashville: Hamblett House, 1998.

Johnson, Richard D. "Machlup and the Information Age." *Scholarly Publishing* 18.4 (July 1987): 271–276.

Johnson, Sammye. "Why Should They Care? The Relationship of Academic Scholarship to the Magazine Industry." *Journalism Studies* 8.4 (August 2007): 522–528.

Johnson, Sammye and Prijatel, Patricia. "The Magazine as a Storehouse: The Scope of the Medium." *The Magazine from Cover to Cover*. 3rd ed. New York and London: Oxford University Press, 2013, 2–21.

Johnson, Sammye and Prijatel, Patricia. *The Magazine from Cover to Cover*. 3rd ed. New York and London: Oxford University Press, 2013.

Kitch, Carolyn. "Making Scholarly Use of Magazines: What Counts Most? What Gets Left Out?" Invited panel presentation to the Magazine Division, Annual Meeting, Association for Education in Journalism and Mass Communication, August 2008.

Kobak, James B. "Just What Is a Magazine?" *How to Start a Magazine and Publish It Profitably*. New York: M. Evans & Company, 2002, 17–18.

Kwa, Chunglin. "The Taxonomic Style." *Styles of Knowing: A New History of Science from Ancient Times to the Present*. Translated by David McKay. Pittsburgh, PA: University of Pittsburgh Press, 2011, 165–195.

Lane, W. Ronald; King, Karen Whitehill; and Reichert, Tom. "Using Magazines." *Kleppner's Advertising Procedure*. 18th ed. Upper Saddle River, NJ: Prentice Hall/Pearson, 2011, 319–355.

Lang, Annie. "Discipline in Crisis? The Shifting Paradigm of Mass Communication Research." *Communication Theory* 23.1 (February 2013): 10–24.

Lazarsfeld, Paul F. and Wyant, Rowena. "Magazines in 90 Cities—Who Reads What?" *Public Opinion Quarterly* 1.4 (October 1937): 29–41.

Lee, Judith Yaross. "From the Field: The Future of *American Periodicals* and American Periodicals Research." *American Periodicals* 15.2 (2005): 196–201.

Lehrer, Jim. "The New Age of Journalism." NewsHour with Jim Lehrer, 19 January 2000 <http://www.pbs.org/newshour/bb/media/jan-june00/new_journalism_1-19.html>, accessed 20 February 2006.

Liddle, Dallas. *The Dynamics of Genre: Journalism and the Practice of Literature in Mid-Victorian Britain*. Charlottesville: University of Virginia Press, 2009.

Littlejohn, Stephen W. *Theories of Human Communication*. 4th ed. Belmont, CA: Wadsworth, 1992.

Lowry, Dennis T. "Population Validity of Communication Research: Sampling the Samples." *Journalism Quarterly* 56.1 (Spring 1979): 62–68, 76.

Machlup, Fritz; Leeson, Kenneth; and Associates. "Scope, Structure, and Market of the Journal-Publishing Industry." *Information through the Printed Word: The Dissemination of Scholarly, Scientific, and Intellectual Knowledge*. Vol. 2, *Journals*. New York: Praeger, 1978, 3–37.

Machlup, Fritz; Leeson, Kenneth; and Associates. "Terminological Notes." *Information through the Printed Word: The Dissemination of Scholarly, Scientific, and Intellectual Knowledge*. Vol. 1, *Book Publishing*. New York: Praeger, 1978, 15–22.

Mallett, Daniel. "The Relationship of Screen-In Rates and Readership Levels in MRI and SMRB (Mediamark Research Inc., Simmons Market Research Bureau)." *Journal of Advertising Research* [Special Issue: The Growing Importance of Media Research] 33.1 (1993): 18–22.

Mandese, Joe. "Simmons Adopts Rival's Audience Methodology: Magazine Research Change Will Cost Less." *Advertising Age*, 19 September 1994, 1.

Martens, Peter. "Revisiting the Allegory/Typology Distinction: The Case of Origen." *Journal of Early Christian Studies* 16 (2008): 283–317.

Martin, Shannon E. "Using Expert Sources in Breaking Science Stories: A Comparison of Magazine Types." *Journalism Quarterly* 68.1/2 (Spring/Summer 1991): 179–187.

McQuail, Denis. *Mass Communication Theory: An Introduction*. 1st, 2nd eds. Beverly Hills, CA, and London: Sage, 1984, 1987.

McQuail, Denis. *McQuail's Mass Communication Theory*. 6th ed. London: Sage, 2010.

Merriam-Webster's Collegiate Dictionary. 11th ed. Springfield, MA: Merriam-Webster, 2004.

Merrill, John C.; Lee, John D.; and Friedlander, Edward Jay. "Books and Magazines." *Modern Mass Media*. New York: Harper & Row, 1990, 140–168.

Miner, Earl, ed. *Literary Uses of Typology from the Late Middle Ages to the Present*. Princeton, NJ: Princeton University Press, 1977.

Moeran, Brian. "More than Just a Fashion Magazine." *Current Sociology* 54.5 (September 2006): 725–744.

Mogel, Leonard. "What Is a Magazine?" *The Magazine*. 4th ed. Pittsburgh: GATF Press, 1998, 10–12.

Morgan, Winona and Leahy, Alice M. "The Cultural Content of General Interest Magazines." *Journal of Educational Psychology* 25 (October 1934): 530–536.

Mott, Frank Luther. *A History of American Magazines*. Vol. 1, *A History of American Magazines, 1741–1850*; Vol. 2, *A History of American Magazines, 1850–1865*; Vol. 3, *A History of American Magazines,*

1865–1885; Vol. 4, *A History of American Magazines, 1885–1905*; Vol. 5, *A History of American Magazines, 1905–1930*. New York: D. Appleton, 1930; Cambridge, MA: The Belknap Press, 1938, 1938, 1957; Cambridge, MA: Harvard University Press, 1968.

Mott, Frank Luther. "Introduction." *A History of American Magazines 1741–1850*. Vol. 1. New York: D. Appleton, 1930, 1–9.

Mott, Frank Luther. "Unfinished Story; or, the Man in the Carrel." *Time Enough: Essays in Autobiography*. Chapel Hill: University of North Carolina Press, 1962, 169–180.

Najjar, Orayb Aref. "'The Editorial Family of al-Kateb Bows in Respect': The Construction of Martyrdom Text Genre in One Palestinian Political and Literary Magazine." *Discourse & Society* 7.4 (1996): 499–530.

Narunsky-Laden, Sonja. "Consumer Magazines in South Africa and Israel: Toward a Socio-Semiotic Approach to Magazine Research." *Journalism Studies* 8.4 (2007): 595–612.

National Directory of Magazines. New York: Oxbridge Communications, 2014.

Paden, William D. *An Introduction to Old Occitan*. New York: Modern Language Association of America, 1998, 3–9.

Papper, Robert A.; Holmes, Michael E.; and Popovich, Mark N. "Middletown Media Studies: Media Multitasking . . . and How Much People Really Use the Media." *International Digital Media and Arts Association Journal* 1.1 (Spring 2004): 4–56.

Pasqua, Thomas M., Jr.; Buckalew, James K.; Rayfield, Robert E.; and Tankard, James W., Jr. "Magazines." *Mass Media in the Information Age*. Englewood Cliffs, NJ: Prentice Hall, 1990, 66–83.

Peterson, Theodore. "Magazine." In Barnouw, Erik; Gerbner, George; Schramm, Wylbur; Worth, Tobia L.; and Gross, Larry, eds. *International Encyclopedia of Communications*. Vol. 2. New York: Oxford University Press, 1989, 463–468.

Peterson, Theodore. *Magazines in the Twentieth Century*. 1st, 2nd eds. Urbana: University of Illinois Press, 1956, 1964.

Pew Research Center. "Overview." The State of the News Media 2013: An Annual Report on American Journalism. Washington, DC: Pew Research Center, 2013 <http://stateofthemedia.org/2013/overview-5/>, accessed 3 December 2013.

Podeschi, Christopher W. "The Culture of Nature and the Rise of Modern Environmentalism: The View through General Audience Magazines, 1945–1980." *Sociological Spectrum* 27.3 (March 2007): 299–331.

Postman, Neil. *Amusing Ourselves to Death: Public Discourse in the Age of Show Business*. New York: Penguin Books, 1985, 2005.

Potter, W. James; Cooper, Roger; and Dupagne, Michel. "The Three Paradigms of Mass Media Research in Mainstream Communication Journals." *Communication Theory* 3.4 (November 1993): 317–335.

Prior-Miller, Marcia R. "Core Knowledge: Scholarly Research on Magazines." Invited panel presentation, Magazine Division, at the Annual Meeting, Association for Education in Journalism and Mass Communication, August 2008.

Prior-Miller, Marcia R. "An Organization Communication-Goals Theory of Magazine Types: Toward an Integrated Conceptual Framework of Magazine and Journal Periodicals as a Medium of Communication." Manuscript in preparation.

Prior-Miller, Marcia R. "Research Review: Issues in Magazine Typology." In Abrahamson, David, ed. *The American Magazine: Research Perspectives and Prospects*. Ames: Iowa State University Press, 1995, 3–23.

Prior-Miller, Marcia R. "Research Review: Issues in Magazine Typology." *Electronic Journal of Communication/La Revue de Electronique de Communication* 4.2/4 (December 1994)<eric.ed.gov/?id=EJ494512>, accessed 30 May 2014.

Prior-Miller, Marcia R. and Associates. "Bibliography of Published Research on Magazine and Journal Periodicals." 9th ed. Research database. Ames: Iowa State University, last modified, 31 August 2014, MSWord file <mpm@iastate.edu #x003E;.

Prior-Miller, Marcia R. and Esch, Kellie L. "A Census and Analysis of Journals Publishing Research about Magazines, 1977–1987." Paper presented at the Annual Meeting, Association for Education in Journalism and Mass Communication, August 1990.

Putnam, Robert D. "Technology and Mass Media," *Bowling Alone: The Collapse and Revival of American Community*. New York: Simon & Schuster, 2000, 216–246.

Renard, David. "The Last Magazine (in Print)." In Renard, David, ed. *The Last Magazine*. New York: Universe Publishing, 2006, 14–15.

Reynolds, Paul Davidson. *A Primer in Theory Construction*. Indianapolis: Bobbs-Merrill, 1971.

Richardson, Lyon N. *A History of Early American Magazines, 1741–1789*. New York: Thomas Nelson and Sons, 1931.

Sagendorf, Cathy and Moore, David. "Module 33: Newspapers." *CONSER Cataloging Manual*. Library of Congress, 2006 <http://www.loc.gov/acq/conser/pdf/CCM-Module-33.pdf>, accessed 18 April 2014.

Sasseen, Jane; Matsa, Katerina-Eva; and Mitchell, Amy. "News Magazines: Embracing Their Digital Future." The State of the News Media 2013: An Annual Report on American Journalism. Washington, DC: Pew Research Center, 2013 <http://stateofthemedia.org/2013/news-magazines-embracing-their-digital-future/>, accessed 3 December 2013.

Schmidt, Dorothy. "Magazines." In Inge, M. Thomas, ed. *Handbook of American Popular Culture*. Westport, CT: Greenwood Press, 1981, 137–162.

Schramm, Wilbur. "Twenty Years of Journalism Research." *Public Opinion Quarterly* [20th Anniversary Issue] 21.1 (Spring 1957): 91–107.

Simpson, George Gaylord. "Systematics, Taxonomy, Classification, Nomenclature." *Principles of Animal Taxonomy*. New York: Columbia University Press, 1961, 11.

Spaeth, Jim; Holmes, Michael E.; Moult, Bill; and Bloxham, Michael. *Mind the Measurement Gap: Measured and Unmeasured Media Occasions*. Muncie, IN: Ball State University Center for Media Design, June 2006.

SRDS Business Media Advertising Source, Parts 1, 2. Vol. 95. Des Plaines, IL: Kantar/SRDS/Standard Rate & Data Service, 2013.

SRDS Consumer Media Advertising Source. Vol. 95. Des Plaines, IL: Kantar/SRDS/Standard Rate & Data Service, 2013.

Standard Periodical Directory. New York: Oxbridge Communications, 2014.

Steinberg, Sigfrid H. *Five Hundred Years of Printing*. New ed. Revised by John Trevitt. London: British Library & Oak Knoll Press, 1955/1996.

Stern Magazine. *Consumer Magazines in Europe*. Hamburg: Gruner + Jahr AG & Co., 1981.

Stevenson, Nick. *Understanding Media Cultures*. 2nd ed. London: Sage, 2002.

Sumner, David E. and Rhoades, Shirrel. *Magazines: A Complete Guide to the Industry*. New York: Peter Lang, 2006.

Taft, William H. *American Magazines for the 1980s*. New York: Hastings House, 1982.

Tanner, James T.F. "From the Editor." *American Periodicals: A Journal of History, Criticism, and Bibliography* 1.1 (Fall 1991): iii.

Tassin, Algernon. *The Magazine in America*. New York: Dodd, Mead and Company, 1916.

Theodorson, George A. and Theodorson, Achilles G. *A Modern Dictionary of Sociology*. New York: Barnes & Noble Books, Division of Harper & Row, 1969.

Tiryakian, Edward A. "Typologies." In Sills, David L., ed. *International Encyclopedia of the Social Sciences*. Vol. 16. New York: MacMillan, 1968, 177–186.

Turow, Joseph. "The Magazine Industry." *Media Today: An Introduction to Mass Communication*. 3rd ed. New York: Routledge, Taylor & Francis, 2009, 342–374.

Ulrich, Carolyn F. *Periodicals Directory: A Classified Guide to a Selected List of Current Periodicals Foreign and Domestic*. New York: R.R. Bowker, 1932.

Ulrich's Periodicals Directory 2014. Vols. 1–4. 52nd ed. New Providence, NJ: ProQuest, 2013.

Vivian, John. "Magazines." *The Media of Mass Communication*. 8th ed. Boston: Pearson, 2007, 80–99.

Westad, Anniken. "The Norwegian Magazine Industry: An Overview and Bibliographic Review." Paper presented to the Contemporary Magazine Publishing Research Roundtable, Iowa State University, December 2010.

"What Is a Serial?" *CONSER Cataloging Manual*, Library of Congress <http://www.itsmarc.com/crs/mergedprojects/conser/conser/module_2_1__ccm.htm>, accessed 18 April 2014.

Willis, William James and Willis, Diane B. "Magazines and the Search for Specialization." *New Directions in Media Management*. Boston: Allyn & Bacon, 1993, 65–89.

Wilson, Stan Le Roy. "Magazines: The Specialized Medium." *Mass Media/Mass Culture: An Introduction*. 2nd ed. New York: McGraw-Hill, 1992, 121–145.

Wolseley, Roland E. "Magazine Types." *Understanding Magazines*. Ames: Iowa State University Press, 1965, 255–355.

Wolseley, Roland E. "The Role of Magazines in the U.S.A." *Gazette* 23.1 (1977): 20–26.

Wolseley, Roland E. *Understanding Magazines*. Ames: Iowa State University Press, 1965.

Wright, Charles R. *Mass Communication: A Sociological Perspective*. 2nd, 3rd eds. New York: Random House, 1975, 1986.

3

METHODOLOGICAL STUDIES

Interdisciplinarity Is the Key

Kathleen L. Endres

Communication scholars have challenged the field's researchers to transcend disciplinary and geographical boundaries in their work. James R. Beniger in 1993 complained of the "provincial nature" of communication research, characterizing it as an "intellectual ghetto, one that rarely cites outside itself and is even more rarely cited by other disciplines."[1] More than a decade later, Robert W. McChesney urged communication researchers to "strike out in a popular and interdisciplinary manner."[2] *Journal of Communication* editor Michael Pfau saw the continued provincialism of communication researchers: "Too often we write for others within specific narrow niches of our own discipline, and as a result, our output is not read by most communication scholars, let alone by scholars in allied fields."[3] Susan Herbst agreed. Communication scholarship and researchers could benefit from a little "disciplinary busting" in this post-disciplinary era.[4]

In the spirit of these calls for increased interdisciplinary communication research and in this period of enormous technological, business and editorial change in the media, the time seems right to examine the methodologies in published studies on magazines and the magazine industry from an interdisciplinary perspective. Accordingly, this chapter examines scholars' focus and methodological choices in peer-reviewed research on magazines, the magazine industry or both, published in refereed, scholarly journals of both the communication field and other disciplines. This research synthesis is designed to provide a fuller, clearer idea of magazine research across disciplinary lines than has been attempted before.

Literature Review

In 1987 Peter Gerlach provided concrete, empirical evidence of what many magazine researchers had long suspected: Research about magazines appeared infrequently in *Journalism Quarterly*. Between 1964 and 1983, only 6% of the journal's 1,917 articles dealt with magazines. Gerlach also found that more than 50% of the published research articles used content analysis as the methodology.[5] Things improved somewhat in the subsequent decade. Mark N. Popovich found magazine research represented 8% of the articles that appeared in *Journalism Quarterly* from 1983 to 1993. Looking only at quantitative studies, Popovich found that most researchers—approximately 76%—used content analysis as their method for collecting data.[6]

Scholars have also expressed concern about the lack of cross-disciplinary research in the communication field in general. In the 1993 special issue of the *Journal of Communication*, James R. Beniger noted that communication and information were not just the purview of one discipline. He observed a "convergence of the concepts and literature of information and communication across the range of academic disciplines—from the humanities and social sciences to the cognitive behavioral, and life sciences, computer science, and mathematics."[7] Other authors in that issue's focus on the future of the field also saw the shortcomings associated with the late twentieth century isolationism of the communication discipline. Pamela Shoemaker urged readers to "build linkages between communication and other intellectual disciplines."[8]

After 1993, the communication field grew, but comparatively few scholars seemed to have taken up Shoemaker's challenge of strengthening communication's natural interdisciplinary alliances. In 2008, Michael Pfau revisited the question in another special issue of the *Journal of Communication*. He observed that communication continues to fragment, and much communication research is only of interest to those studying and working within a narrow niche.[9] Susan Herbst, another of the scholars who in 1993 urged researchers to reach beyond their narrow communication confines,[10] reiterated the message but warned of possible dangers: "for all the talk about, and real value of interdisciplinarity and postdisciplinarity, the path is unclear. Professional risks abound for the postdisciplinary scholar." Yet Herbst also saw promise along that unclear path and encouraged her readers to contribute their work to journals outside the communication field.[11]

The conversation about the interdisciplinary possibilities has also directly touched magazine research. The very diversity of the magazine industry invites an interdisciplinary examination of the medium, concluded Tim Holmes.

> Scholars come at them [magazines] from a wide range of perspectives: history, feminism, fan culture, visual culture, practitioner culture, political economy—the protean nature of the form lends itself to meaningful analysis from all of these and more. If that is the strength, the weakness has been poor communication between individual scholars taking different perspectives in separate disciplines, largely because of the lack of a forum for the exchange of ideas about *magazines*.[12]

These calls for cross-disciplinary, trans-disciplinary and interdisciplinary research seem consistent with the history of the academic field of communication. As many researchers have pointed out,[13] communication research has its roots in multiple disciplines. Many of the so-called "founding fathers" of communication research, including Kurt Lewin, Carl Hovland, Harold Lasswell and Paul Lazarsfeld, resided in such academic homes as psychology, political science and sociology when they wrote the studies that helped ground communication research theoretically and methodologically. Notwithstanding these important influences from other disciplines, communication worked to become its own distinct academic field. In the 1950s, when the first PhDs in communication were graduated and started their research,[14] the field's leading scholars pushed for the legitimacy, uniqueness and importance of communication as a distinct academic discipline. In the process, they won isolation.[15]

But did researchers in diverse disciplines, who followed in the paths forged by the founders of communication research, give up their investigations into the field? Or have they—as Holmes and Beniger later observed—continued to study communication in general and magazines in particular from their own disciplinary perspectives? If so, what approaches have they taken and what methods have they used in their studies? This synthesis of research attempts to answer those questions.

Method

Beniger observed that communication and information research is being published in scholarly journals that serve a range of disciplines, from humanities to social sciences, life sciences and mathematics.[16] Therefore, this author sought to identify searchable databases that covered a wide range of academic fields, in order to develop a sample for this study. The following data-bases were identified and searched: (1) *Academic Search Complete* is a multidisciplinary database that provides indexes and abstracts of more than 13,600 journals, many of them peer-reviewed, in a range of disciplines from humanities to social sciences, life sciences and mathematics, the very disciplines Beniger noted in his 1993 article. (2) *America: History and Life* focuses on the history and culture of the United States and Canada, with indexes and abstracts from more than 1,700 peer-reviewed journals. (3) *Art Full Text* provides indexes and abstracts of art-related articles in periodicals, yearbooks and museum bulletins from across the United States and the world. (4) *Business Source Complete* provides indexes and abstracts of more than 1,300 peer-reviewed, business-related journals. (5) *Communication and Mass Media Complete* combines the content of *CommSearch* and *Mass Media Articles Index* to provide access to more than 620 communication-focused academic journals, magazines, trade publications, conference proceedings and monographs. (6) *Education Research Complete* offers indexes and abstracts for more than 2,400 education-related journals, monographs and conference papers. (7) *Humanities Full Text* provides indexes for more than 1,000 journals in the humanities disciplines. (8) *LGBT Life* provides access to more than 300 LGBT journals, magazines, regional newspapers, monographs and books. (9) *PsychINFO* is the database of the American Psychological Association. It provides indexes and abstracts for journals, books and dissertations in psychology. (10) *Women's Studies International* provides indexes and abstracts of almost 800 peer-reviewed journals, dissertations, proceedings, bulletins, newspapers and other materials in the field.

The database search was limited to journals published from 2000 to 2012, and was further limited to include only peer-reviewed journals published in the English language. The 10 data-bases allowed for a range of search methods—keywords by title, abstract, full text or subject. Based on the results of preliminary tests of each search method,[17] the author opted to use the keyword *magazine* in a search limited to article titles. Using this procedure meant some scholarly articles on magazines were not included in the final search because the keyword *magazine* did not appear in the title. For example, Lynn E. Couturier's "Considering the *Sportswoman*, 1924 to 1936: A Content Analysis"[18] was not included. Courtier's article would also not have appeared in a search for the keyword *magazine* in the subject listing. It would have appeared, however, in a search for *magazine* in the abstract.

The search of the databases, using the keyword *magazine* in the article title, was conducted on 4 November 2012. On that date, 3,744 results were returned from the 10 databases; removal of duplicates left 3,546 results. The author drew a 10% sample from the 3,546 unique entries. Using a randomly selected numerical starting point, the author drew every tenth title, for a total 355 entries. The 355 sampled entries and the database from which they were drawn are as follows: *Academic Search Complete* (114); *America: History and Life* (24); *Art Full Text* (9); *Business Source Complete* (39); *Communication and Mass Media Complete* (41); *Humanities Full Text* (27); *Education Research Complete* (39); *LGBT* (6); *PsychINFO* (32); and *Women's Studies International* (24). The author then either downloaded full-text versions of the sampled articles from (a) the databases (the most common method), (b) the electronic university library consortium (Illiad) or (c) the print journal itself. Missing from these sources were 12 full-text versions of the 355 sampled articles. For the 12, the author used the article abstracts to code the needed variable to gain information.

The unit of analysis was the research article or abstract. The author coded each of the following variables: *publication year*; *kind of article* (i.e., original research article, book/publication/ Web site review, editorial, essay, news, other); *discipline of journal*; *data collection method* used in the article; *focus of the article* by subject, magazine type and publication region; and *first author's discipline and geographical region*. Only the first author's discipline and geographical region was coded after a pre-test indicated only a limited number of multiple author articles.

In instances where there were two or more authors, only information about the lead author was coded, on the assumption that, across the sample, lead authors' disciplines would vary sufficiently to provide insight into the cross-disciplinary nature of the research and to prevent multiple-authored articles carrying heavier weight in data analysis. In many instances, scholars were from the same discipline. Thus, Marika Tiggemann, Janet Polivy and Duane Hargreaves collaborated on "The Processing of Thin Ideals of Fashion Magazines: A Source of Social Comparison or Fantasy?"[19] All three scholars were in the field of psychology. There were exceptions. Communication researcher Kim Walsh-Childers worked with medical and life science scholars Heather M. Edwards from the National Cancer Institute at Frederick and Stephen Grobmyer of the Department of Surgery at the University of Florida to produce the 2012 article, "*Essence, Ebony* and *O*: Breast Cancer Coverage in Black Magazines."[20] Only communication was coded, as it was the discipline of the lead author.

Overall Findings

The search of 10 databases identified a total of 3,546 discrete articles. Although the size of the population required drawing a sample for analysis for the study rather than using the total population, the population is an important finding. The total of 3,546 discrete articles gives evidence that magazines and their content are a popular subject for scholarly inquiry across many disciplines. Further analysis of the article sample follows.

Kind of articles. The sample of 355 published articles was dominated by articles that are peer-reviewed scholarly inquiry (221, or 62.3% of 355; see Table 3.1). It also included reviews of books, Web sites, and other publications, as well as news notes, editorials and a variety of essays and other kinds of related articles on magazines and the magazine industry.

Findings on Sampled Original Research Articles on Magazines

The remaining analysis is based on the resulting smaller sample of 221 articles, the total sample of published original research articles published in peer-reviewed journals.

Annual productivity. Based on the total sample of 355 articles, the data indicate that published work on magazines ranged from a low of 12 articles in 2000 to a high of 41 in 2007, of which 27 were scholarly articles. Publishing did not languish during the time period studied (see Table 3.2). Rather, over the 13-year period the number of publications increased at a fairly constant rate, more than doubling from 12 articles in 2000, to 31 in 2012. The highest annual percentage of scholarly articles came in 2009, with 20 of the year's 24 articles, for a high of 83.3%. After 2003, annual publications never dropped below 20 articles per year, but averaged 30.5 articles for each of the most recent 10 years.

Author discipline. Communication scholars (e.g., communication, media studies, journalism and public relations) produced the largest amount of this published material, although a substantial number came from scholars in the humanities (primarily history and English) and social sciences (primarily psychology and sociology). Scholars from business, education and the physical and life sciences (including engineering) also published material on magazines in scholarly publications (see Table 3.3).

Table 3.1. Sampled published material on magazines by kind of article

Article Type	N	Total % of N
Original research articles	221	62.3
Book/publication/Web site reviews	83	23.4
News, editorials, essays, other	51	14.4
Total	355	100%

Table 3.2. Sampled published materials on magazines by year, 2000–2012

Year	Total Articles Sampled	Total Scholarly Articles	Scholarly % of Annual	Scholarly % of n = 221
2000	12	7	58.3	3.2
2001	19	12	63.2	5.4
2002	19	15	78.95	6.8
2003	24	16	66.7	7.2
2004	31	15	48.4	6.8
2005	32	19	59.4	8.6
2006	29	22	75.9	10.0
2007	41	27	65.9	12.2
2008	25	17	68	7.7
2009	24	20	83.3	9.0
2010	31	20	64.5	9.0
2011	37	14	37.8	6.3
2012	31[1]	19	61.3	8.6
Totals	355	221	62.3	100%

[1] The figure for 2012 may be artificially low because the study sample was drawn on 4 November 2012, when not all the journals carrying the 2012 publication date may have been issued and entered into the 10 databases used.

Table 3.3. Sampled published materials on magazines by author disciplines

Author Discipline	N	Sample %
Communication	150	42.3
Humanities	61	17.2
Social sciences	41	11.5
Business	21	5.9
Education	30	8.5
Physical and life sciences	28	7.9
Unidentified[1]	24	6.8
Total	355	100%

[1] Includes published material carrying either no byline or bylines without disciplinary identification. In the latter, a few journals carried the scholars' university affiliation, but a check of the respective university Web sites found no listing for the authors in faculty, staff and student directories or broader searches of university listings. Thus, the authors' disciplines could not be determined.

Author region. The largest number of these scholars taught and held positions at universities or colleges in the United States (258 or 72.7%), while the next largest (46 or 13%) were affiliated with some institution of higher education in Great Britain or Europe. The remainder were affiliated with colleges or universities in Asia, Australasia (Australia and New Zealand), South America or Canada.

Kinds of magazines. The largest amount of material published in these scholarly journals dealt with consumer magazines (periodicals issued for the general reading public,[21] e.g., *The New Yorker* and *Esquire*) (313 or 88.2%). The second largest category dealt with association or

Table 3.4. Sampled scholarly material on magazines by location of focus publication

Publication Location	N	Sample %
United States	246	69.3
Europe and Great Britain	48	13.5
Asia	15	4.2
North America, excluding U.S.	13	3.7
Australasia	10	2.8
Africa	3	.8
Comparison of two or more regions	16	4.5
Unidentified[1]	4	1.1
Total	355	100%

[1] In four instances of news items or reviews, the geographical location of the magazine that was the focus of the article was not identified.

organizational journals (periodicals issued by an association or organization and distributed to the membership as a benefit of affiliation with the group,[22] e.g., *Academe*, the magazine of the American Association of University Professors; *National Parks Magazine* for the National Parks Conservation Association) (23 or 5.9%). A small number of scholarly material also dealt with specialized business publications (magazines that cover a specific business or industry, synonymous with business-to-business publications,[23] e.g., *Veterinary Economics* and *Motor Age*) (7 or 2.0%) and scholarly journals (periodicals which offer research on a specific topic, written by scholars or experts in the field, usually peer reviewed,[24] e.g., *Journal of Magazine & New Media Research* and *Journalism & Mass Communication Quarterly*) (6 or 1.7%).

Geographical region of focus magazine. Most of the magazines studied were published in the United States (see Table 3.4).

Findings on Sampled Original Research Articles on Magazines

The sampled articles were not all original research articles. As is the case in scholarly publications in the communication field, these periodicals offered a range of editorial matter relating to magazines. The largest amount of material, however, was original research articles (see Table 3.1).

Subsequent findings deal specifically with the sampled original research articles. As noted previously, 221 of the 355 sampled materials were original research articles. This segment of the findings deals specifically with the original research articles and the methodology used in those articles.

Author discipline. Communication scholars produced the largest number of research articles on magazines published in scholarly periodicals (see Table 3.5). Although communication scholars clearly dominated this field of research, academics from many disciplines studied magazines and the magazine industry and published their findings. Researchers from social studies, humanities, business, education, and physical and life sciences were all exploring topics relating to magazines from their distinct disciplinary perspectives.

Journal discipline. Research articles on magazines appeared in many different scholarly journals, which served a range of disciplines (see Table 3.6). Peer-reviewed journals of the communication field carried the largest number of original research articles on magazines. However, communication scholarly journals did not carry a majority—or even a third—of the sampled original research on magazines. Almost 70% of the original research articles were published

Table 3.5. Sampled research articles on magazines by discipline of author

Author Discipline	n	Sample %
Communication	108	48.9
Humanities and art	26	11.8
Women's studies	1	5
Social studies	35	15.8
Business	20	9.0
Education	10	4.5
Physical and life sciences	18	8.1
Unidentified[1]	3	1.4
Total	221	100%

[1] Author identified solely by institution; an investigation of the institution's faculty/staff/student directory failed to provide the discipline for coding purposes.

Table 3.6. Sampled research articles on magazines by journal discipline

Journal Discipline	n	Sample %
Communication	67	30.3
Humanities and art	34	15.4
Women's studies	46	20.8
Social studies	22	10.0
Business	27	12.2
Education	9	4.1
Physical and life sciences	16	7.2
Totals	221	100%

in journals that spanned 6 diverse disciplines (154 or 69.7%). Especially important were the scholarly publications of the women's studies field. More than 20% of the research articles on magazines appeared in women's studies periodicals. However, as the findings relating to the author's disciplines indicate (see Table 3.5), women's studies scholars were not producing the research on magazines published in that field's journals.

Focus magazine type. These scholarly articles almost always dealt with consumer magazines; that is, of the 221 scholarly articles sampled, 205 (92.8%) of the total research articles dealt with consumer magazines.

Focus magazine region. The largest number of the scholarly articles dealt with magazines that were published in the United States (133 or 60.2%). The second largest number were published in Europe or Great Britain (34 or 15.4%). This virtually mirrors the geographical location of the authors writing the scholarly articles on magazines. The largest number of these researchers were from the United States (144 or 65.2%). The second largest number of researchers were from Europe or Great Britain (36 or 16.3%).

Study focus. The largest number of the scholarly articles—almost 80%—focused on the *content* of the magazine itself (see Table 3.7). The largest category of these content-focused articles examined the editorial content of the magazine itself. These articles examined everything from health advice[25] to history.[26] The research articles that focused on advertising content ranged from nudity[27] to firearms.[28]

Table 3.7. Sampled research articles on magazines by focus of research

Research Focus	n	Sample %
Content	176	79.6
(editorial, e.g., features, depts., advice)	(108)	(48.9)
(advertising)	(43)	(19.5)
(images/photos/illustrations)	(21)	(9.5)
(other)	(4)	(1.8)
Readership/readership effects	26	11.8
Staffing/workplace culture	3	1.4
Management	4	1.8
Circ./dist./prod.	4	1.8
Other	3	1.4
Not available[1]	5	2.3
Total	221	100%

[1] Full texts of five sampled articles were not available.

Table 3.8. Sampled research articles on magazines by method

Method	n	Sample %
Content analysis (qualitative and quantitative)	124	56.1
Experimental (quantitative)	16	7.2
Cultural discourse (qualitative)	12	5.4
Rhetorical analysis (qualitative)	11	5.0
Textual analysis (qualitative and quantitative)	10	4.5
Survey (quantitative)	9	4.1
Narrative/thematic/semiotic analysis (qualitative)	6	2.7
Focus groups/interviews (qualitative)	8	3.6
Other qualitative[1]	14	6.3
Other quantitative[2]	5	2.3
Missing[3]	6	2.7
Total	221	100%

[1] Includes participant observation, field studies, law, biographical.
[2] Includes longitudinal, adnorm, linguistic, other.
[3] Method analysis required a full text of the article. Six were missing in full text.

This overwhelming emphasis on the content of the magazines explains the methodological decisions these authors made. More than 50% of the authors used content analysis as their method (see Table 3.8).

Discussion

Research that focuses on magazines is not the sole purview of communication researchers or communication scholarly journals. The findings of this study suggest that many communication researchers who study magazines are following the calls of Shoemaker[29] and Herbst[30] to venture beyond disciplinary boundaries to publish their work. The diversity within the magazine industry, magazine content and readership seem to invite publication outside the narrow confines of the communication discipline. Thus, the article ("Magazine Exposure, Tanned Women Stereotypes and Tanning Attitudes") of communication scholars Hyunyi Cho, Seungyoon Lee and Kari Wilson was published in *Body Image*, the international interdisciplinary journal serving the psychological, social, medical, and health sciences disciplines.[31] Communication scholar Mohan J. Dutta-Bergman's completed research, "The Readership of Health Magazines: The Role of Health Orientation," was published in *Health Marketing Quarterly*.[32]

This study also points to the importance of women's studies scholarly journals as a forum for research on women's magazines, the magazine industry and women readers. In a sense, women's studies scholarly publications serve as a kind of interdisciplinary mixing bowl for research, large enough to contain articles from many different perspectives: psychology, sociology, communication, English and criminal justice. All share a singular focus—women—but from a wide range of perspectives. In this study, these journals offered a breadth of research on magazines. Sociologist Elizabeth Monk-Turner and her colleagues provided a look at how sex is used in magazine advertising for scholars who read the *Journal of Gender Studies*[33]; psychologist Sue Jackson offered a unique perspective on teen letters to magazine advice pages in *Feminism & Psychology*[34]; criminal justice scholars Monica K. Miller and Alicia Summers's research on gender differences in video game magazine characters and roles[35] and communication researcher Katharina Lindner's exploration of images of women in magazine advertising were published in *Sex Roles*.[36] Women's studies journals also provided a range of international perspectives. Japanese literature scholar Ikuko Suiura wrote about lesbian discourses in mainstream magazines of post-war Japan for the *Journal of Lesbian Studies*[37] and Australian communication scholar Megan Le Masurier examined one of her country's women's magazines from an historical perspective in *Australian Feminist Studies*.[38]

Magazines also serve as an important lens through which researchers examine pressing health, environment and social issues, drawing on their disciplines' theoretical perspectives to examine the *content* of the magazines themselves. Accordingly, content analysis—be it qualitative or quantitative—was the method of choice. While exploring health issues, for example, physicians, sociologists, psychologists and communication researchers focused on the *content* of magazines and used content analysis to chart the health messages published in magazines.[39]

Some researchers were asking new questions about magazines, magazine publishing and readership effects. These questions could not be answered with content analysis. Since 2007, more researchers, especially those in psychology, business and the physical and life sciences, have used surveys and experimental design to examine non–content-related research questions. Typical of this new direction are psychology researchers Marika Slater Tiggemann, Amy Bury, Belinda Hawkins and Bonny Firth, who used experiments to study how women's body dissatisfaction was affected by the warning labels in fashion magazine advertisements[40]; communication scholars Silvia Knobloch-Westerwich and Gregory J. Hoplamazian used an experiment for their study, "Gendering the Self: Selective Magazine Reading and Reinforcement of Gender Conformity"[41]; and European business professors Alexander G. Kerl and Andreas Walter offered a unique perspective on readership effects by linking personal finance magazines' stock buy recommendations to buyer behavior after the magazines' publication.[42]

Finally, researchers, regardless of discipline, focused almost exclusively on consumer magazines.[43] While consumer magazines reach a large portion of the reading public nationally and internationally[44] and are certainly important, focusing solely on these kinds of periodicals fails to show the diversity within the magazine industry itself. The lack of research on specialized business publications is especially troubling. Many important research questions can be asked—and answered—by looking at these and at association or organizational magazines.

Conclusions

This study leads to a number of different conclusions. First, magazines represent a dynamic subject for research, which cuts across disciplinary lines. Second, although researchers from many different disciplines study magazines, they most frequently focus on the *content* of periodicals. As a consequence, these researchers—regardless of discipline—use content analysis as their method. As long as researchers focus primarily on the *content* of magazines, content analysis will remain a dominant method. However, this study also reveals a range of methods being used in magazine research. These range from rhetorical and textual analyses in studies of magazine content to experiments that study a range of issues relating to readership.

Third, the published research in the magazine field does not reflect the diversity within the magazine industry itself. This study shows how little research is done on specialized business publications and association or organizational periodicals and points to new kinds of magazines to examine. Fourth, this study suggests that there may be some shifts in magazine research coming, as more scholars, especially those from business, psychology and physical and life sciences, ask new research questions, especially as they relate to readership effects and non–content-related issues.

Finally, this study demonstrates the importance of an interdisciplinary approach in any study dealing with magazines. Researchers need to reach beyond disciplinary lines. Those who wear the blinders of discipline—any discipline—fail to see the rich bounty of magazine research that lies just outside their field of vision. The current state of magazine research is rich, vibrant—and multi-disciplinary.

Notes

1 James R. Beniger, "Communication—Embrace the Subject, Not the Field," *Journal of Communication* 43.3 (Summer 1993): 19.

2 Robert W. McChesney, *Communication Revolution: Critical Junctures and the Future of the Media* (New York: The New Press, 2007), 17.

3 Michael Pfau, "Epistemological and Disciplinary Intersections," *Journal of Communication* 58.4 (December 2008): 597.

4 Susan Herbst, "Disciplines, Intersections, and the Future of Communication Research," *Journal of Communication* 58.4 (December 2008): 612.

5 Peter Gerlach, "Research about Magazines Appearing in *Journalism Quarterly*," *Journalism Quarterly* 64.1 (Spring 1987): 178–182.

6 Mark N. Popovich, "Research Review: Quantitative Magazine Studies, 1983–1993," in David Abrahamson, ed., *The American Magazine: Research Perspectives and Prospects* (Ames: Iowa State University Press, 1995), 24–36.

7 Beniger, "Communication—Embrace the Subject, Not the Field," 18.

8 Pamela J. Shoemaker, "Communication in Crisis: Theory, Curricula and Power," *Journal of Communication* 43.4 (Autumn 1993): 149.

9 Pfau, "Epistomological and Disciplinary Intersections," 600.

10 Susan Herbst, "History, Philosophy, and Public Opinion Research," *Journal of Communication* 43.4 (Autumn 1993): 143.

11 Herbst, "Disciplines, Intersections, and the Future of Communication Research," 612.

12 Tim Holmes, "Mapping the Magazine: An Introduction," *Journalism Studies* 8.4 (August 2007): 510–521.

13 See, for example, Everett M. Rogers, *A History of Communication Study: A Biographical Approach* (New York: The Free Press, 1994); Jefferson Pooley, "The New History of Mass Communication Research," in David W. Park and Jefferson Pooley, eds., *The History of Media and Communication Research: Contested Memories* (New York: Peter Lang, 2008), 43–69; Daniel J. Czitrom, *Media and the American Mind: From Morse to McLuhan* (Chapel Hill: University of North Carolina Press, 1982).

14 Shoemaker, "Communication in Crisis: Theory, Curricula, and Power," 147–148.

15 Herbst, "Disciplines, Intersections, and the Future of Communication Research," 604.

16 Beniger, " Communication—Embrace the Subject, Not the Field," 18.

17 Searching the keyword "magazine" in full text gave more than 900,000 results, many of which had nothing to do with the publishing industry. Using the keyword "magazine" in abstracts offered 20,371 results. Upon

further investigation, however, a portion of those results was not directly relevant to the publishing industry; the search included articles that dealt with armaments and specialized tools in machining and engineering.

18 Lynn E. Couturier, " Considering the *Sportswoman*, 1924 to 1936: A Content Analysis," *Sport History Review* 41.2 (November 2010): 111–131.

19 Marika Tiggemann, Janet Polivy, and Duane Hargreaves, "The Processing of Thin Ideals in Fashion Magazines: A Source of Social Comparison or Fantasy?" *Journal of Social and Clinical Psychology* 28.1 (2009): 73–93.

20 Kim Walsh-Childers, Heather M. Edwards, and Stephen Grobmyer, "*Essence, Ebony* and O: Breast Cancer Coverage in Black Magazines," *Howard Journal of Communications* 23.2 (April/June 2012): 136–156.

21 Ralph E. Hanson, Study Guide for "Chapter 5. Magazines: The Power of Words and Images," *Mass Communication: Living in a Media World*, 3rd ed. (Washington, DC: CQ Press, 2011) <http://college.cqpress.com/sites/masscomm/Home/chapter5.aspx>, accessed 4 February 2013.

22 Sandi L. Humphrey, "Making Your Association Magazine Matter," Canadian Society of Association Executives, CSAE/SCDA <http://www.csae.com/Resources/ArticlesTools/View/Articleid/19/Making-Your-Association-Magazine-Matter>, accessed 25 February 2014.

23 Hanson, Study Guide for "Chapter 5. Magazines,"; Thad McIlroy, "The Future of Magazines," *The Future of Publishing*, 10 July 2013 <http://thefutureofpublishing.com/industries/the-future-of-magazines>, accessed 4 February 2013.

24 "Scholarly Journal," PennState Library <http://www.sgps.psu.edu/foweb/lib/scholarly-journal/index.html>, accessed 4 February 2013.

25 Susan McKay and Frances Bonner, "Educating Readers: Breast Cancer in Australian Women's Magazines," *International Journal of Qualitative Studies in Education* 17.4 (July/August 2004): 517–535.

26 Brian Thornton, "The Murder of Emmett Till: Myth, Memory, and National Magazine Response," *Journalism History* 36.2 (Summer 2010): 96–104.

27 Ying Huang and Dennis Lowry T., "An Analysis of Nudity in Chinese Magazine Advertising: Examining Gender, Racial and Brand Differences," *Sex Roles* 66.7/8 (April 2012): 440–452.

28 Elizabeth A. Saylor, Katherine A. Vittes, and Susan B. Sorenson, "Firearm Advertising: Product Depiction in Consumer Gun Magazines," *Evaluation Review* 28.5 (October 2004): 420–433.

29 Shoemaker, "Communication in Crisis: Theory, Curricula and Power," 146–153.

30 Herbst, "Disciplines, Intersections, and the Future of Communication Research," 603–614.

31 Hyunyi Cho, Seungyoon Lee, and Kari Wilson, "Magazine Exposure, Tanned Women Stereotypes, and Tanning Attitudes," *Body Image* 7.4 (September 2010): 364–367.

32 Mohan J. Dutta-Bergman, "The Readership of Health Magazines: The Role of Health Orientation," *Health Marketing Quarterly* 22.2 (2004): 27–49.

33 Elizabeth Monk-Turner, Kristy Wren, Leanne McGill, Chris Matthiae, Stephan Brown, and Derrick Brooks, "Who Is Gazing at Whom?: A Look at How Sex Is Used in Magazine Advertisements," *Journal of Gender Studies* 17.3 (September 2008): 201–209.

34 Sue Jackson, " 'I'm 15 and Desperate for Sex': 'Doing' and 'Undoing' Desire in Letters to a Teenage Magazine," *Feminism & Psychology* 15.3 (August 2005): 295–313.

35 Monica K. Miller and Alicia Summers, "Gender Differences in Video Game Characters' Roles, Appearances, and Attire as Portrayed in Video Game Magazines," *Sex Roles* 57.9/10 (November 2007): 733–742.

36 Katharina Lindner, "Images of Women in General Interest and Fashion Magazine Advertisements from 1955 to 2002," *Sex Roles* 51.7/8 (October 2004): 409–421.

37 Ikuko Sugiura, "Lesbian Discourses in Mainstream Magazines of Post-War Japan: Is *Onabe* Distinct from *Rezubian*?" *Journal of Lesbian Studies* 10.3/4 (2006): 127–144.

38 Megan Le Masurier, "My Other, My Self: *Cleo* Magazine and Feminism in 1970s Australia," *Australian Feminist Studies* 22.53 (July 2007): 191–211.

39 See, for example, Juanne N. Clarke and Jeannine Binns, "The Portrayal of Heart Disease in Mass Print Magazines, 1991–2001," *Health Communication* 19.1 (2006): 39–48; Kyle J. Tobler, Philip K. Wilson, and Peter G. Napolitano, "Frequency of Breast Cancer, Lung Cancer, and Tobacco Use Articles in Women's Magazines from 1987 to 2003," *Journal of Cancer Education* 24.1 (March 2009): 36–39; Juanne N. Clarke, "The Portrayal of Depression in the Three Most Popular English-Language Black-American Magazines in the U.S.A: *Ebony, Essence,* and *Jet*," *Ethnicity & Health* 15.5 (October 2010): 459–473.

40 Marika Tiggemann, Amy Slater, Belinda Bury, Kimberley Hawkins, and Bonny Firth, "Disclaimer Labels on Fashion Magazine Advertisements: Effects on Social Comparison and Body Dissatisfaction," *Body Image* 10.1 (January 2013): 45–53 <http://www.sciencedirect.com/science/article/pii/S1740144512000952>, accessed 10 December 2012.

41 Silvia Knobloch-Westerwick and Gregory J. Hoplamazian, "Gendering the Self: Selective Magazine Reading and Reinforcement of Gender Conformity," *Communication Research* 39.3 (June 2012): 358–384.

Table 3.9. Comparison of total consumer and trade magazines in 2008 in five countries

Country	Consumer Magazines (n)	Trade Magazines (n)	Total (N)
United States	3,187	9,607	12,794
United Kingdom	2,794	5,151	7,945
Germany	2,000	4,400	6,400
Japan	2,449	1,791	4,240
France	1,250	1,661	2,911
Totals	11,680	22,610	34,290

42 Alexander G. Kerl and Andreas Walter, "Market Responses to Buy Recommendations Issued by Personal Finance Magazines: Effects of Information, Price-Pressure and Company Characteristics," *Review of Finance* 11 (March 2007): 117–141.

43 More than 90% of the research articles studied dealt with consumer magazines. See, for example, Barbara Barnett, "Health as Women's Work: A Pilot Study on How Women's Magazines Frame Medical News and Femininity," *Women & Language* 29.2 (Fall 2006): 1–12; Pamela Hill Nettleton, "Domestic Violence in Men's and Women's Magazines: Women are Guilty of Choosing the Wrong Men, Men Are Not Guilty of Hitting Women," *Women's Studies in Communication* 34.2 (September 2011): 139–160; Crystal Y. Lumpkins, Glen T. Cameron, and Cynthia M. Frisby, "Spreading the Gospel of Good Health: Assessing Mass Women's Magazines as Communication Vehicles to Combat Health Disparities among African Americans," *Journal of Media & Religion* 11.2 (April/June 2012): 78–90; Silvia Knobloch-Westerwick and Brendon Coates, "Minority Models in Advertisements in Magazines Popular with Minorities," *Journalism & Mass Communication Quarterly* 83.3 (Autumn 2006): 596–614.

44 Figures on the number of magazines and their circulation depends upon who is doing the count. One figure puts the number of U.S. consumer magazines at 14,858 (7,385 in print and 7,473 on-line) in 2008 and a circulation of 368.4 million. "United States—Consumer Magazines," G2MI, Global Media Market Intelligence <www.g2mi.com/country_sector_info.php?sectorName=%20Consumer%20magazines&countryName=United%20States&id=155>, accessed 8 February 2013. Additionally, "Magazine Industry Sectors," Magforum <www.magforum.com/sectors.htm>, accessed 8 February 2013, noted that in most countries the number of business-to-business publications exceeds consumer magazines. This Web site provides the following country-by-country magazine information (Table 3.9):

Bibliography

Barnett, Barbara. "Health as Women's Work: A Pilot Study on How Women's Magazines Frame Medical News and Femininity." *Women & Language* 29.2 (Fall 2006): 1–12.

Beniger, James R. "Communication–Embrace the Subject, Not the Field." *Journal of Communication* 43.3 (Summer 1993): 18–25.

Cho, Hyunyi; Lee, Seungyoon; and Wilson, Kari. "Magazine Exposure, Tanned Women Stereotypes, and Tanning Attitudes." *Body Image* 7.4 (September 2010): 364–367.

Clarke, Juanne N. "The Portrayal of Depression in the Three Most Popular English-Language Black-American Magazines in the U.S.A.: *Ebony, Essence,* and *Jet.*" *Ethnicity & Health* 15.5 (October 2010): 459–473.

Clarke, Juanne N. and Binns, Jeannine. "The Portrayal of Heart Disease in Mass Print Magazines, 1991–2001." *Health Communication* 19.1 (2006): 39–48.

Couturier, Lynn E. "Considering the *Sportswoman,* 1924 to 1936: A Content Analysis." *Sport History Review* 41.2 (November 2010): 111–131.

Czitrom, Daniel J. *Media and the American Mind: From Morse to McLuhan.* Chapel Hill: University of North Carolina Press, 1982.

Dutta-Bergman, Mohan J. "The Readership of Health Magazines: The Role of Health Orientation." *Health Marketing Quarterly* 22.2 (2004): 27–49.

Gerlach, Peter. "Research about Magazines Appearing in *Journalism Quarterly.*" *Journalism Quarterly* 64.1 (Spring 1987): 178–182.

Hanson, Ralph E. Study Guide for "Chapter 5. Magazines: The Power of Words and Images," *Mass Communication: Living in a Media World*. 3rd ed. Washington, DC: CQ Press, 2011 <http://college.cqpress.com/sites/masscomm/Home/chapter5.aspx>, accessed 4 February 2013.

Herbst, Susan. "Disciplines, Intersections, and the Future of Communication Research." *Journal of Communication* 58.4 (December 2008): 603–614.

Herbst, Susan. "History, Philosophy, and Public Opinion Research." *Journal of Communication* 43.4 (Autumn 1993): 140–145.

Holmes, Tim. "Mapping the Magazine: An Introduction." *Journalism Studies* 8.4 (August 2007): 510–521.

Huang, Ying and Lowry, Dennis T. "An Analysis of Nudity in Chinese Magazine Advertising: Examining Gender, Racial and Brand Differences." *Sex Roles* 66.7/8 (April 2012): 440–452.

Humphrey, Sandi L. "Making Your Association Magazine Matter." Canadian Society of Association Executives CSAE/SCDA <http://www.csae.com/Resources/ArticlesTools/View/Articleid/19/Making-Your-Association-Magazine-Matter>, accessed 25 February 2014.

Jackson, Sue. "'I'm 15 and Desperate for Sex': 'Doing' and 'Undoing' Desire in Letters to a Teenage Magazine." *Feminism & Psychology* 15.3 (August 2005): 295–313.

Kerl, Alexander G. and Walter, Andreas. "Market Responses to Buy Recommendations Issued by Personal Finance Magazines: Effects of Information, Price-Pressure, and Company Characteristics." *Review of Finance* 11.1 (March 2007): 117–141.

Knobloch-Westerwick, Silvia and Coates, Brendon. "Minority Models in Advertisements in Magazines Popular with Minorities." *Journalism & Mass Communication Quarterly* 83.3 (Autumn 2006): 596–614.

Knobloch-Westerwick, Silvia and Hoplamazian, Gregory J. "Gendering the Self: Selective Magazine Reading and Reinforcement of Gender Conformity." *Communication Research* 39.3 (June 2012): 358–384.

Le Masurier, Megan. "My Other, My Self: *Cleo* Magazine and Feminism in 1970s Australia." *Australian Feminist Studies* 22.53 (July 2007): 191–211.

Lindner, Katharina. "Images of Women in General Interest and Fashion Magazine Advertisements from 1955 to 2002." *Sex Roles* 51.7/8 (October 2004): 409–421.

Lumpkins, Crystal Y.; Cameron, Glen T.; and Frisby, Cynthia M. "Spreading the Gospel of Good Health: Assessing Mass Women's Magazines as Communication Vehicles to Combat Health Disparities among African Americans." *Journal of Media & Religion* 11.2 (April/June 2012): 78–90.

"Magazine Industry Sectors." Magforum <www.magforum.com/sectors.htm>, accessed 8 February 2013.

McChesney, Robert W. *Communication Revolution: Critical Junctures and the Future of the Media*. New York: The New Press, 2007.

McIlroy, Thad. "The Future of Magazines." *The Future of Publishing*. 10 July 2013. <http://thefutureofpublishing.com/industries/the-future-of-magazines>, accessed 4 February 2013.

McKay, Susan and Bonner, Frances. "Educating Readers: Breast Cancer in Australian Women's Magazines." *International Journal of Qualitative Studies in Education* 17.4 (July/August 2004): 517–535.

Miller, Monica K. and Summers, Alicia. "Gender Differences in Video Game Characters' Roles, Appearances and Attire as Portrayed in Video Game Magazines." *Sex Roles* 57.9/10 (November 2007): 733–742.

Monk-Turner, Elizabeth; Wren, Kristy; McGill, Leanne; Matthiae, Chris; Brown, Stephan; and Brooks, Derrick. "Who Is Gazing at Whom?: A Look at How Sex Is Used in Magazine Advertisements." *Journal of Gender Studies* 17.3 (September 2008): 201–209.

Nettleton, Pamela Hill. "Domestic Violence in Men's and Women's Magazines: Women Are Guilty of Choosing the Wrong Men, Men Are Not Guilty of Hitting Women." *Women's Studies in Communication* 34.2 (September 2011): 139–160.

Pfau, Michael. "Epistemological and Disciplinary Intersections." *Journal of Communication* 58.4 (December 2008): 597–602.

Pooley, Jefferson. "The New History of Mass Communication Research." In Park, David W. and Pooley, Jefferson, eds. *The History of Media and Communication Research: Contested Memories*. New York: Peter Lang, 2008, 43–69.

Popovich, Mark N. "Research Review: Quantitative Magazine Studies, 1983–1993." In Abrahamson, David, ed. *The American Magazine: Research Perspectives and Prospects*. Ames: Iowa State University Press, 1995, 24–36.

Rogers, Everett M. *A History of Communication Study: A Biographical Approach*. New York: The Free Press, 1994.

Saylor, Elizabeth A.; Vittes, Katherine A.; and Sorenson, Susan B. "Firearm Advertising: Production Depiction in Consumer Gun Magazines." *Evaluation Review* 28.5 (October 2004): 420–433.

"Scholarly Journal." PennState Library <http://www.sgps.psu.edu/foweb/lib/scholarly-journal/index.html>, accessed 4 February 2013.

Shoemaker, Pamela J. "Communication in Crisis: Theory, Curricula and Power." *Journal of Communication* 43.4 (Autumn 1993): 146–153.

Sugiura, Ikuko. "Lesbian Discourses in Mainstream Magazines of Post-War Japan: Is *Onabe* Distinct from *Rezubian?*" *Journal of Lesbian Studies* 10.3/4 (2006): 127–144.

Thornton, Brian. "The Murder of Emmett Till: Myth, Memory, and National Magazine Response." *Journalism History* 36.2 (Summer 2010): 96–104.

Tiggemann, Marika; Polivy, Janet; and Hargreaves, Duane. "The Processing of Thin Ideals in Fashion Magazines: A Source of Social Comparison or Fantasy?" *Journal of Social and Clinical Psychology* 28.1 (2009): 73–93.

Tiggemann, Marika; Slater, Amy; Bury, Belinda; Hawkins, Kimberley; and Firth, Bonny. "Disclaimer Labels on Fashion Magazine Advertisements: Effects on Social Comparison and Body Dissatisfaction." *Body Image* 10.1 (January 2013): 45–53 <http://www.sciencedirect.com/science/article/pii/S1740144512000952>, accessed 10 December 2012.

Tobler, Kyle J.; Wilson, Philip K.; and Napolitano, Peter G. "Frequency of Breast Cancer, Lung Cancer, and Tobacco Use Articles in Women's Magazines from 1987 to 2003." *Journal of Cancer Education* 24.1 (March 2009): 36–39.

"United States—Consumer Magazines." *G2MI*, Global Media Market Intelligence <www.g2mi.com/country_sector_info.php?sectorName=%20Consumer%20magazines&countryName=United%20States&id=155>, accessed 8 February 2013.

Walsh-Childers, Kim; Edwards, Heather M.; and Grobmyer, Stephen. "*Essence, Ebony* and O: Breast Cancer Coverage in Black Magazines." *Howard Journal of Communications* 23.2 (April/June 2012): 136–156.

4

MAGAZINES AS HISTORICAL STUDY SUBJECTS

Reflecting the Sociocultural Reality

Cynthia Lee Patterson

Scholars have witnessed a virtual explosion in research treating magazines as historical study subjects in the past two decades. Moreover, the best of the historical magazine research of the past 20 years combines methodologies made possible by newly available, large database searches combined with careful combing of locally available brick and mortar-based archives. This well-executed research pays particular attention to the magazine as a material artifact arising out of particular historical and cultural contexts of production, distribution and consumption.

Although some historical research of the 1990 to 2012 period continues to be marked by weaknesses that include concerns James Startt and William David Sloan, in their 1989 textbook *Historical Methods in Mass Communication*, described as studies "based . . . too much on secondary sources . . .,"[1] scholars in all fields whose interests include the magazine form now have a wealth of available resources to which their predecessors often had no access. In the early twenty-first century, any scholar working with a computer at a medium to large research university can quickly access digital copies of magazines once only available in a select number of libraries and archives scattered throughout the country. A recent, ambitious partnership between the American Antiquarian Society and EBSCO resulted in the AAS "Historical Periodicals Collection," a digitization of more than 7,600 periodicals, dating from 1691 through 1877, most of which have never been available, either on microfilm or in digital format.[2] Scholars can also now access complete or near-complete digital runs of what some historians have considered the major American magazines published from the early 1900s on, and, in some cases, biographical and autobiographical material as well.

Fortunately, for magazine historians, a simultaneous blossoming of available funding for archival research has paralleled the digitization boom. Libraries and archives that could not afford expensive digitization projects became ever more eager to lure scholars to their collections—arguably to maintain their relevance in the new age of digitization. Today a scholar seeking financial assistance for an archival project may face stiff competition, but funding streams outside the walls of his or her own college or university prove increasingly available.

This chapter explores the contributions of the broad scope of research published in recent years and suggests future directions in a number of areas: (1) additions to the cumulative historiography of American and international magazines; (2) ethnological enrichment and expansion; (3) chronological expansion beyond the nineteenth and twentieth centuries;

(4) reconsiderations of the magazine as a genre; (5) the magazine's engagement with other cultural forms; and (6) moving beyond magazine feature and columns to other structural elements such as departments and the material qualities of the published and circulated magazine.

Literature Review and Method

Scholars relatively new to the study of magazines should be aware that magazines can be studied from a variety of disciplinary and interdisciplinary perspectives and that terminology not only varies from field to field, but has evolved over the past 20 years. Scholars working broadly in communication studies, or, more typically, in journalism and communication or media-based programs, refer to the material object in question as *magazines* and treat such as one form of mass media. Scholars working in English, history and art history, and in interdisciplinary fields such as American studies or cultural studies, typically use the term *periodical* to refer to any publication published in serial format, including magazines. Moreover, in recent years, the term *print culture* has emerged to refer to the myriad materials circulating in print form, to include newspapers, magazines, broadsides, circulars, advertising, signs and more.

To understand these differing approaches more fully, scholars may wish to read Judith Yaross Lee's succinct overview "From the Field: The Future of *American Periodicals* and American Periodicals Research."[3] As Lee points out, "journalism history [has] typically focused" on editors and the editorial processing, leading to a "great man" slant in the resulting scholarship.[4] Literary scholars, on the other hand, have tended toward an *apprenticeship* model, studying the periodical publications of canonical writers as one step in the maturation process toward production of the more-venerated genre of the novel. Historians, meanwhile, have generally *mined* periodicals for evidence supporting a larger project not focused primarily on the magazine as material object. Newer, interdisciplinary approaches in each field examine relationships between authors, editors, publishers, artists, illustrators and others associated with the production and circulation of magazines, in addition to examining issues of magazine readership.[5] For a more thorough understanding of the theoretical and methodological strategies underlying these approaches, see additional chapters in this volume treating theory and methodology.

In the interest of space, this research review covers primarily book-length publications: Scholars interested in journal articles would do well to query their institutions' e-journal holdings for the primary journals in the field. In the related disciplines of journalism and mediated communication, these include *Journalism History*, *American Journalism*, and *Journalism & Mass Communication Quarterly*. Well-respected interdisciplinary journals typically favored by scholars in English, history, art history and American studies include *Victorian Periodicals Review* and *American Periodicals*. While the former focuses primarily on British publications, it also features scholarship on transnational print culture. *American Periodicals*, in publication since 1991, is considered the leading interdisciplinary journal treating American magazines from an historical perspective. However, newer now-digital and *born-digital* peer-reviewed journals emerging during the past 20 years should not be overlooked. These include the *Journal of Modern Periodicals Studies*, *Commonplace*, *Scholarly Editing* and the *Journal of Magazine & New Media Research*.

Although book-length work constitutes the primary material covered in this research review, journal articles were consulted in instances where research in the field in question is either relatively new (magazines published in other countries, other languages or both) or the sources and audiences are rather more ephemeral (zines or e-zines). The bibliography of books and articles consulted for this chapter was culled from lists of published work and book reviews featured in the leading journals of the field, as noted previously. Readers will also want to consult Marcia Prior-Miller's "Bibliography of Published Research on Magazine and Journal Periodicals" for additional resources.[6] In some instances, books likely to fall under the subject matter of other chapters in this scholarly anthology were omitted from consideration.

Historiography of Magazines

A certain body of historical research continues the trajectory of earlier work in the field, building on the legacy of the scholarship left by U.S. scholar Frank Luther Mott's ambitious five-volume *A History of American Magazines*.[7] In this category would be placed some of the notable new reference books, bibliographies and general histories, as well as themed edited collections, individual magazine studies, and comparative studies that tease out differences between similar and competing magazines. For example, the Greenwood Press series *Historical Guides to the World's Periodicals and Newspapers* added a large number of new titles over the past 20 years, providing reference information to launch a new generation of magazine scholars.[8] In their 1990 *American Mass-Market Magazines*, Alan and Barbara Nourie provide entries for 106 magazines from the late nineteenth and early twentieth century—each with a circulation exceeding 100,000—and occupying "a sort of middle ground between the general magazines and the specialist magazines. . . ."[9] Emulating Mott, Nourie and Nourie provide entries on each magazine that approach in length and detail Mott's treatment of magazines in his pioneering works.

Sam G. Riley and Gary W. Selnow's 1991 volume, *Regional Interest Magazines of the United States*, provides full profiles for nearly 90 city, regional and city-specialty and regional-specialty magazines targeting a general consumer audience. Riley and Selnow located and indexed more than 900 such magazines, with more than half still in existence at the date of publication. The Riley and Selnow volume also includes Appendix A: Chronological Listing of Magazines Profiled, by Year Founded; and Appendix B, Geographical Location of Magazines Profiled, by State.[10] In his 1992 collection *American Literary Magazines: The Twentieth Century*, Edward E. Chielens extends Mott's work beyond the eighteenth and nineteenth centuries by providing in-depth discussion of 76 magazines from the twentieth century. Each entry runs five to 10 pages, and the volume includes three appendices: A., Minor Literary Magazines; B., A Chronology of Social and Literary Events and American Literary Magazines, 1900–1991; and C., The Archives: An Analysis of Little Magazine Collections in the United States and Canada.[11]

Scholars interested in business magazine histories will also want to consult additional volumes in the Greenwood Press series, beginning with William Fisher's edited collection *Business Journals of the United States*.[12] Fisher located 7,800-plus business titles and narrowed the list down to the 100-plus featured in this volume, winnowing out in-house magazines and newsletters. Sam Riley's *Corporate Magazines of the United States* then takes up where Fisher's volume leaves off—providing profiles for 324 magazines intended primarily for in-house consumption. Fifty-one titles receive detailed profiles, and Appendix C contains a list of 272 additional titles.[13]

Finally, Kathleen L. Endres's *Trade, Industrial, and Professional Periodicals of the United States* provides profiles for just under 100 specialized business and trade publications.[14] Scholars interested in research involving business magazines of any ilk would do well to begin with these three volumes. The Greenwood Press collection also includes volumes dedicated to the religious, political and military press. Those interested in the religious press should consult *Popular Religious Magazines of the United States*, published in 1995 and edited by Mark P. Fackler and Charles H. Lippy,[15] which extends Lippy's earlier 1986 work on scholarly religious journals.[16] In this later volume, Fackler and Lippy focus on religious magazines targeting a popular audience. In culling their list from 10,000 titles to the 100 included in this volume, Fackler and Lippy included some magazines no longer in print, with a goal to represent the range of religious expression in America. An Appendix categorizes the magazines included in the collection by religious affiliation.

Those interested in the political press will want to consult two volumes, both published in 1999 and edited by Ronald Lora and William Henry Longton, *The Conservative Press in Eighteenth- and Nineteenth-Century America* and *The Conservative Press in Twentieth Century America*.[17] Lora and Longton survey 38 journals from the earlier period, breaking them down into five categories: political journals (Federalist, Whig or the Civil War era's Northern Democratic); literary-cultural journals; southern reviews; nineteenth-century orthodox Protestant reviews; and Catholic and Episcopal journals. Each of the 38 profiles includes a publication history for the periodicals, as well as a list of sources for further reference. The volume covering the twentieth-century conservative press profiles 65 journals, divided into 10 categories. Two categories cover fundamentalist and evangelical, and Catholic and Episcopal, respectively; several cover roughly "right-wing" and neo-conservative journals, with one category devoted to Libertarian periodicals.

Scholars interested in the military press will want to consult Michael E. Unsworth's 1990 volume, *Military Periodicals*, which provides extended profiles of more than 150 military publications; shorter profiles of nearly 100 more, with an additional four profiles devoted to multiple edition publications. Unsworth offers a brief history of the U.S. military periodical, from its post-Revolutionary War beginnings (1796) to the date of publication.[18]

In addition to the Greenwood Press series, a spate of newer general histories appeared after 1990. In the Foreword to their 1991 volume, *The Magazine in America, 1741–1990*, John Tebbel and Mary Ellen Zuckerman note that their work builds on Mott (who covered the era 1741–1905) by targeting primarily magazines published after 1918.[19] Tebbel and Zuckerman also take advantage of the range of scholarship on magazines appearing after Mott's work, and their bibliography should be a starting point for younger scholars seeking access to magazine research published between roughly 1950 and 1990. David Abrahamson's 1996 study of U.S. postwar magazines argues that increasing affluence linked to a search for personal fulfillment contributed to the rise of special-interest magazines (such as *Boating, Car and Driver, Popular Electronics* and the like) and the decline of general interest magazines (including *Life, Look* and the *Saturday Evening Post*).[20] David E. Sumner's 2010 *The Magazine Century: American Magazines since 1900* targets popular consumer magazines. Beginning with a list of 9,000 magazines, Sumner focuses on what he sees as innovative business models or editorial approaches or market niches, organizing his study decade by decade. As does Abrahamson in his volume, Sumner provides a list of suggested readings that newer scholars will want to consult.[21]

Important edited collections also appeared between 1990 and 2012. Kenneth M. Price and Susan Belasco Smith's pioneering 1995 collection, *Periodical Literature in Nineteenth-Century America*, situated periodical studies within the emerging field known as *history of the book*, a field drawing on insights from literature, linguistics, history, sociology, anthropology and political science.[22] Featuring a veritable *who's who* list of scholars whose work continues to impact the field (Carolyn L. Karcher, Patricia Okker, Robert J. Scholnick, Kathleen Diffley and Paula Bennett, among others), Price and Belasco Smith's volume treats periodicals, in their words, not as sources to be "mined for background detail," but rather seen as "central components of culture."[23] David Abrahamson's 1995 *The American Magazine: Research Perspectives and Prospects* collects chapters from scholars in journalism, mass communication, media history and related disciplines.[24] Emerging from the 1992 fall mid-year meeting of the Magazine Division of the Association for Education in Journalism and Mass Communication (AEJMC), Abrahamson's volume includes both research reviews and scholarly articles organized into five categories: (1) general perspectives (typology issues; quantitative studies; political content); (2) professional issues in magazine publishing; (3) pedagogical and curricular issues; (4) geographical dimension, local and global; and (5) literary and historical contexts.[25]

Book-length studies of individual magazines proliferated, some scholarly, others relying primarily on observation and anecdote. An A-to-Z author list of scholarly studies would begin with Michael Augspurger's 2004 study of *Fortune* magazine, *An Economy of Abundant Beauty*: Fortune *Magazine and Depression America*, which traces the magazine's content from a Depression-era interest in art, literature and culture, to a post-WWII narrowing focus on financial issues.[26] Amy E. Farrell's *Yours in Sisterhood*: Ms. *Magazine and the Promise of Popular Feminism*, uses the Ms. archives at Smith College to chronicle the magazine from its origins in 1971 to 1989.[27] First, Catherine A. Lutz and Jane L. Collins, *Reading* National Geographic,[28] later Tamar Y. Rothenberg, *Presenting America's World: Strategies of Innocence in* National Geographic Magazine, *1888–1945*, provide historical background on that popular magazine. While Lutz and Collins focus largely on content analysis of issues from the earlier period of the magazine's publication, Rothenberg's study includes archival materials accessed at the National Geographic Society headquarters and focuses on thick description of representative issues spanning the entire period of her study.[29]

Heidi L. Nichols's *The Fashioning of Middle-Class America*: Sartain's Union Magazine of Literature and Art and Antebellum Culture examines the popular magazine during its three-year ownership (1849–1852) by John Sartain, Philadelphia's leading mezzotint engraver. Nichols argues that "*Sartain's* writers consistently describe and prescribe the attitudes and actions that should characterize this growing middle class."[30] Ellery Sedgwick's 1994 study, *The* Atlantic Monthly, *1857–1909: Yankee Humanism at High Tide and Ebb*, approaches that magazine's rise and fall via chapters devoted to the magazine's editors, from James Russell Lowell to James T. Fields, to William Dean Howells and beyond. Sedgwick traces the magazine's importance within the literary marketplace via the list of important writers, all of whom were male, contributing to it through the years.[31] Ending this selective A-to-Z list is Jonathan Daniel Wells's "Introduction" to the 2007 re-issue of Benjamin Blake Minor's *The* Southern Literary Messenger, *1834–1864*. Wells situates *The Southern Literary Messenger* within the larger history of antebellum southern magazines, arguing that it was the "most important literary periodical" in the South.[32]

During the 20-plus-year span from 1990 to 2012, a number of important comparative studies also appeared, some building on rich, but previously neglected archival materials. George H. Douglas's 1991 *The Smart Magazines: 50 Years of Literary Revelry and High Jinks at* Vanity Fair, *the* New Yorker, Life, Esquire *and the* Smart Set examines magazines targeting social elites and featuring the work of *the best* American authors. Douglas argues that the years 1900–1940 proved a high-water mark for these magazines.[33] Matthew Schneirov's 1994 *The Dream of a New Social Order: Popular Magazines in America, 1893–1914*, targets the antebellum "family house magazines": *Harper's Monthly, Century, Scribner's* and *Atlantic Monthly*. Schneirov argues that "popular magazines saw themselves as engaged in the 'whirlpool of real life,' expressing the 'moving spirit of the times.'"[34]

Cynthia Lee Patterson's 2010 *Art for the Middle Classes: America's Illustrated Magazines of the 1840s* argues for the importance of the illustrations (woodcuts, steel engravings, lithographs, mezzotints) to the popularity of Philadelphia's nineteenth-century pictorial magazines (*Godey's, Graham's, Peterson's, Sartain's Union* and *Miss Leslie's*). Working exclusively from print runs of these magazines—some found only in limited east-coast archives—and from extensive manuscript collections of the correspondences of artists, authors and editors, Patterson's study is the first to carefully analyze these magazines in relationship to each other and to the larger literary and artistic marketplace.[35] Mark J. Noonan's 2010 study, *Reading the* Century Illustrated Monthly Magazine: *American Literature and Culture, 1870–1893*, challenges the previous work of media historians that tends to lump into one group magazines like the *Century, Harper's* and *Atlantic*. Noonan claims the *Century* differed in several important ways—namely in corporate structure, a focus on artwork, and publication of serialized novels, especially from regionalist authors. Noonan also labels the *Century* as the "forerunner of the modern magazine," challenging scholarship that identifies *McClure's, Munsey's* and *Cosmopolitan* as serving in that role.[36]

Ethnological Enrichment and Expansion

Magazine research in the past often treated magazines created by and for a white, male, middle-aged, middle-class American audience. Thanks at least in part to the efforts of the Greenwood Press series *Historical Guides to the World's Periodicals and Newspapers*, noted previously, contemporary magazine scholars have begun to expand these boundaries by gender, age, race, ethnicity, language, region and nation-state.

Women's Magazines

The explosion of women's history as a disciplinary field paralleled and contributed to a similar expansion in periodical studies focused on women's magazines. Useful as a bibliographic reference is Mary Ellen Zuckerman's 1993 *Sources on the History of Women's Magazines, 1792–1960: An Annotated Bibliography*. Zuckerman provides a brief history of women's magazines from the eighteenth century through the mid-twentieth century, then identifies primary and secondary sources for the "popular" women's magazines, which she defines as those "with the largest circulations and the broadest interests."[37] Zuckerman gives special attention to 10 of the largest-circulating magazines, including *Harper's Bazaar, Vogue, Woman's Day* and several others. Expanding on this work is Zuckerman's 1998 *A History of Popular Women's Magazines in the United States, 1792–1995*, which devotes nearly half of its pages to the highest-circulating women's magazines, which Zuckerman identifies as "the big six": *Delineator, McCall's, Ladies' Home Journal, Woman's Home Companion, Good Housekeeping* and *Pictorial Review*.[38]

Two additional volumes in the Greenwood Press series provide much-needed background sketches on other women's magazines: the 1995 *Women's Periodicals in the United States: Consumer Magazines*; and the 1996 *Women's Periodicals in the United States: Social and Political Issues*, both edited by Kathleen L. Endres and Therese L. Lueck.[39] The 1995 volume on consumer magazines covers 75 publications still in print when the volume appeared, narrowed down by the editors from an original list of 500, based on the following criteria: "the magazine's editorial excellence, historical significance, and position within its niche."[40] Endres and Lueck's 1996 volume covers 76 publications over a wider historical range (nineteenth and twentieth centuries) and geographical expanse. In selecting these publications, the editors tried to capture what they identify as "a wide range of social, economic, and political issues—from abolitionism to temperance, from moral reform to birth control, from suffragism to antisuffragism, from pacifism to feminism."[41]

Several important edited collections on women's magazines also appeared during this time period, expanding the range of magazines receiving serious scholarly treatment. Martha M. Solomon's collection, *A Voice of Their Own: The Woman Suffrage Press, 1840–1910*, features chapters on the *Lily*, the *Una*, the *Revolution* and the *Woman's Journal*.[42] Aleta Feinsod Cane and Susan Alves's 2001 study, *"The Only Efficient Instrument": American Women Writers and the Periodical, 1837–1916*, focuses on the work of women writers such as Margaret Fuller, Harriet Beecher Stowe, Charlotte Perkins Gilman, Emma Goldman, Zitkala-Sa and others. Cane and Alves argue that these women used periodicals in three major ways: "for social and political advocacy, for the critique of gender roles . . . and for refashioning the periodical as a more inclusive genre."[43] Sharon M. Harris's 2004 edited collection, *Blue Pencils and Hidden Hands: Women Editing Periodicals, 1830–1910*, with a Foreword by Ellen Gruber Garvey, offers 12 chapters focusing on the work of women as editors rather than women as writers and includes editors of African-American as well as Native American magazines.[44]

Several important, single-authored works also forwarded scholarship in the burgeoning field of women's periodical studies. Sherilyn Cox Bennion's 1990 *Equal to the Occasion: Women Editors of the Nineteenth-Century West* examines women who were editors of newspapers and magazines during the period 1854 to 1900.[45] Patricia Okker's groundbreaking *Our Sister Editors: Sarah J. Hale and the Tradition of Nineteenth-Century American Women Editors*, important for its work on Hale, also provides an Appendix identifying hundreds of nineteenth-century women editors and their periodicals.[46] Jennifer Phegley's 2004 study, *Educating the Proper Woman Reader: Victorian Family Literary Magazines and the Cultural Health of the Nation*, examines the "family literary magazines" on both sides of the Atlantic, targeting *Harper's New Monthly Magazine* in the United States and *Cornhill, Belgravia* and *Victoria Magazine* in Britain. Disputing the work of earlier scholars critical of women's reading practices, Phegley argues that the "family literary magazine empowered women to make their own decisions about what and how to read" and that "this genre of magazine led the way for women to participate in professional critical discourses as both consumers and producers of literary culture."[47]

Several studies mine the same popular magazine, the *Ladies' Home Journal*, providing historical context to greater and lesser degrees. Ellen Gruber Garvey's *The Adman in the Parlor: Magazines and the Gendering of Consumer Culture, 1880s to 1910s* examines trade cards, advertising and fiction in a range of women's magazines in that era.[48] Jennifer Scanlon's *Inarticulate Longings: The* Ladies' Home Journal, *Gender, and the Promises of Consumer Culture* picks up chronologically where Gruber Garvey leaves off, focusing on the period 1910–1930.[49] Helen Damon-Moore provides a comparative study in her 1994 book *Magazines for the Millions: Gender and Commerce in the* Ladies' Home Journal *and the* Saturday Evening Post, *1880–1910.*[50] Finally, Carolyn Kitch's *The Girl on the Magazine Cover: The Origins of Visual Stereotypes in American Mass Media* draws on Kitch's own 10-plus years' experience in the magazine business, as well as archival research, to produce what Kitch herself calls "the sort of interdisciplinary communications history/American culture/ gender studies work that this book is."[51] Kitch argues that "media stereotypes of women first emerged not in mass media from the 1970s to the 1990s, but in mass media of the first three decades of the century."[52]

Children's Magazines

Scholars have also expanded the boundaries of periodical studies to include those written for, and sometimes including work by, children. For example, using what she calls a cultural studies approach, Lorinda B. Cohoon's 2006 study, *Serialized Citizenships: Periodicals, Books, and American Boys, 1840–1911,* examines such boys' periodicals as the *Youth's Companion,* the *Young American's Magazine of Self-Improvement, Our Young Folks* and *St. Nicholas.* Cohoon argues, "During the nineteenth century, periodicals, far more than novels, were influential in shaping attitudes about citizenship in a young nation."[53]

Edited collections focusing on children's periodicals include James Marten's 1999 *Lessons of War: The Civil War in Children's Magazines,*[54] and the 2004 collection, *St. Nicholas and Mary Mapes Dodge: The Legacy of a Children's Magazine Editor, 1873–1905,* edited by Susan P. Gannon, Suzanne Rahn and Ruth Anne Thompson.[55] Marten focuses on titles such as the *Little Pilgrim, Our Young Folks, Forrester's Playmate,* the *Student and Schoolmate* and others, and features lengthy examples culled from these periodicals that specifically addressed the Civil War. The *St. Nicholas* collection features 18 chapters and is divided into three parts: The Making of *St. Nicholas,* 1873–1905; "Jacks and Jills": *St. Nicholas* and Its Audience; and *St. Nicholas* and Its Worlds: Cultural Messages. In the words of the editors, the volume "is designed to bring together pioneer work on *St. Nicholas,* essential resources for its study, and new essays setting the magazine and the Dodge legacy in fresh contexts."[56] Additionally, the journal *American Periodicals* dedicated a special 2012 issue to children's magazines, with research treating such periodicals as the *Slave's Friend, Heathen Children's Friend* and *Talks and Thoughts of the Hampton Indian Students.*[57]

Some of the most exciting new magazine research to emerge in the last 20 years targets African-American periodicals. Abby Arthur Johnson and Ronald Maberry Johnson's *Propaganda and Aesthetics: The Literary Politics of African-American Magazines in the Twentieth Century* adopts a chronological approach in six chapters: the *Colored American Magazine, Voice of the Negro* and *Horizon* (1900–1910); *Crisis, Opportunity* and the *Messenger* (1910–1928); little magazines and the Black Renaissance (1916–1930); house organs, annual reviews and little magazines (1930–1940); *Negro Quarterly, Negro Story, Phylon* and *Harlem Quarterly* (1940–1960); and revolutionary little magazines (1960–1976). In the Epilogue, Johnson and Johnson argue, "In comparison to journals issued by the culturally dominant groups in the United States, Afro-American magazines as a whole have been more committed to social and political expression."[58]

Noliwe M. Rooks's *Ladies' Pages: African American Women's Magazines and the Culture That Made Them* examines eight magazines published between 1891 and 1950, by and for African American women. She traces two broad themes: the influence of migration and regional differences on the magazines and the efforts of magazines to subvert the hypersexualized representations of African American women emanating from the white press.[59]

Eric Gardner's ground-breaking, 2009 *Unexpected Places: Relocating Nineteenth-Century African American Literature* shifts the focus chronologically, spatially and geographically.[60] A body of earlier scholarship focused on novels by African Americans, published largely in the eastern seaboard cities of Boston, Philadelphia and New York.[61] Mining largely overlooked archival sources, Gardner recovers other sites of nineteenth-century African American literary production: newspapers and magazines, stretching from Indiana to St. Louis to San Francisco.

Ethnic and Immigrant Magazines

Research into ethnic and immigrant periodicals in the United States also received a boost in this period, beginning with the Greenwood Press's 1990 annotated bibliography of 290 contemporary ethnic periodicals compiled by Sandra Jones Ireland: *Ethnic Periodicals in Contemporary America*.[62] A couple of edited collections and a special issue of *American Periodicals* also contributed to this scholarship. The 1992 collection *The German-American Radical Press: The Shaping of a Left Political Culture, 1850–1940*, edited by Elliott Shore, Ken Fones-Wolf and James P. Danky, offers a dozen chapters targeting periodicals ranging from New York to Philadelphia, and Chicago to St. Louis.[63] Danky collaborated with Wayne A. Wiegand to edit the 1998 collection, *Print Culture in a Diverse America*. This later study includes chapters on the Italian immigrant press, African American periodicals and the Chinese press.[64] The special issue of *American Periodicals* devoted to immigrant periodicals, Volume 19, Issue 1,[65] includes additional selections on German and Chinese newspapers as well as the Irish-American periodical press. Finally, extending studies of ethnic and minority periodicals to non-English-language immigrant magazines as well (Chinese, French, German, Italian, Norwegian, Spanish Polish) is Patricia Okker's 2012 edited collection, *Transnationalism and American Serial Fiction*.[66]

In recent years, several book-length studies of interest covering religious and ethnic magazines also appeared. Peter Richardson's 2009 study of *Ramparts*, the Catholic magazine-turned-political publication, is notable. Richardson argues that *Ramparts* was "the premier leftist publication of its era," running from 1962 to 1975.[67] Benjamin Balint's 2010 study, *Running Commentary: The Contentious Magazine That Transformed the Jewish Left into the Neoconservative Right*, traces the trajectory of the magazine from its founding in 1945 by the American Jewish Committee to the present.[68] Balint argues that the magazine began from the Jewish community's "outsider" status but lost its audience along the way as it increasingly tailored the content to a readership predominantly "inside" the political corridors of power.[69]

Expanding both chronological and national boundaries, Nicolás Kanellos's 100-plus page introduction to the 2000 Arts Publico volume, *Hispanic Periodicals in the United States, Origins to 1960*, examines serials published in the Americas, as conceived in broader geographical terms, and pushes the chronological boundaries of American print production back to the sixteenth century.[70] Likewise, the shift from a national to transnational focus in periodical studies can be seen in an explosion of journal articles treating magazines published outside the Americas, some with connections to the geographical region, some not; some published in the English language, and some not.

International Magazine Research

A selection of primarily journal-length studies of magazines have been published about magazines originating in more than a dozen countries around the world. A selection arranged roughly in alphabetical order by country, below, demonstrates the breadth of this research. On the women's magazines of Great Britain, see the 1991 *Women's Worlds: Ideology, Femininity and the Woman's Magazine*.[71] Specifically on Ireland, see Dathalinn M. O'Dea, "Modernist

Nationalism in *Dana: An Irish Magazine of Independent Thought*."[72] Jaleen Grove's 2001 article, "A Castle of One's Own: Interactivity in *Chatelaine Magazine*, 1928–35," traces the relationship between editors and readers in that Canadian magazine.[73] Anne Jamison examines a popular Czech magazine in her 2007 study, "*Kmen*: A Faraway Magazine about Which We Know Nothing."[74]

Janet Steele's 2003 study, "Representations of 'the Nation' in *Tempo Magazine*," targets the way Indonesia's popular periodical covers its country of origin.[75] Japanese magazines are the focus of Leith Morton's 1997 study, "The Concept of Romantic Love in the *Taiyō* Magazine 1895–1905,"[76] as well as Gennifer S. Weisenfeld's 2000 article, "'Touring Japan-as-Museum': *Nippon* and Other Japanese Imperialist Travelogues."[77] Kenya's *Joe* magazine takes center stage in Bodil Folke Frederiksen's 1991 study, "*Joe*, the Sweetest Reading in Africa,"[78] while Tyler Fleming and Toyin Falola's 2005 article, "Africa's Media Empire: *Drum*'s Expansion to Nigeria," traces another popular magazine from that continent.[79]

Mexico's *Plural* magazine is the focus of John King's 2007 book *The Role of Mexico's* Plural *in Latin American Literary and Political Culture*.[80] Natasha Tolstikova analyzes a popular Russian magazine in her 2004 article, "*Rabotnitsa*: The Paradoxical Success of a Soviet Women's Magazine."[81] South African magazines receive their due in Sarah Nuttall's 2004 article, "Stylizing the Self: the Y Generation in Rosebank, Johannesburg," among others.[82] This list, by no means exhaustive, is meant to suggest the breadth and depth of scholarly research on magazines at the international level.

Into the Twenty-First Century

Magazine scholarship prior to 1990 tended to focus on either nineteenth- or twentieth-century magazines. Magazines of the nineteenth century piqued scholarly interest in the wake of American scholar Frank Luther Mott's pioneering research, and by virtue of the availability of the *American Periodical Series*, first released on microfilm, later in on-line database format.[83] Meanwhile, easy extant availability attracted scholars to magazines from the twentieth century. Recent studies have pushed back the boundaries of printing on the American continent to the sixteenth century, largely by focusing on the Americas in its broader geographical context (for example, Kanellos, mentioned previously). In particular, the past 20 years have witnessed important journal and book-length studies on early national and eighteenth-century American magazines, ranging from edited collections to single-authored, single magazine studies.

Edited collections that expand the breadth and depth of work on eighteenth-century magazines include Mark L. Kamrath and Sharon M. Harris's *Periodical Literature in Eighteenth-Century America*.[84] This collection begins with an introduction providing historical context and an overview of periodicals research and organizes the dozen or so chapters into three roughly chronological sections: Transatlantic Currents; Revolutionary Era Discourses; and The Early Republic and the 1790s. The editors assert that while methods range from historical analysis to discourse analysis, to employing theories of race, class and gender, all selections aim at the kind of "thick description" that marks the best of periodical studies.[85]

Single-authored studies challenging previous research in the field include Amy Aronson's 2002 study, *Taking Liberties: Early American Women's Magazines and Their Readers*.[86] Correcting earlier figures tallied by Tebbel and Zuckerman that America birthed only 45 women's magazines by 1830, Aronson catalogued more than 110 early American women's magazines, noting that these were only the ones she could find extant in libraries and archives.[87] Aronson argues that the "formal qualities and discursive practices" of women's magazines "enable multiple uses of the genre" across "a range of women and gender politics," contributing to the genre's enormous profitability over time.[88] Key to the success of American women's magazines, Aronson argues, is the "democratic" participation the genre extended to its readership, especially in an era before women gained political rights.[89]

The late eighteenth- and early nineteenth-century editor Charles Brockden Brown is the focus of a single-authored, book-length study by Michael Cody specifically targeting his late eighteenth-century editorship.[90] Scott Slawinski's 2005 book, *Validating Bachelorhood: Audience, Patriarchy, and Charles Brockden Brown's Editorship of the* Monthly Magazine and American Review devotes his second chapter to placing the *Monthly Magazine* with the historical context of eighteenth-century magazine publication.[91] Jared Gardner's 2012 work, *The Rise and Fall of Early American Magazine Culture*, challenges earlier scholarship that portrayed colonial and early American magazines as failures. Using Brockden Brown's editorship of both the *Literary Magazine* and the *American Register*, Gardner disputes the rationale of the profit motive as the driving force behind these early experiments in nation-building and argues, rather, for their importance as sites of early experimentation and innovation.[92]

The Magazine as Genre

While one set of scholars pushed the chronological boundaries of American magazine scholarship back into the eighteenth century and earlier, another set sought to understand new classes of magazines. Previous historical research tended to focus on what some historians refer to as the "general interest magazine" and commercially viable, mass-market magazines, or magazines that are both. Newer research questions the very definition of *magazine*—focusing not only on zines and e-zines, but also on little magazines, pulps, the flash press, magazines published by hand and magazines circulated in socially marginalized communities.

Zines and E-zines

In her groundbreaking 2009 work, argued to be the first book-length study of the genre, Allison Piepmeier provides a methodological model for scholars interested in research on zines. Employing oral history interviews, as well as close readings of zine texts, *Girl Zines: Making Media, Doing Feminism* traces the birth of the genre to the early 1990s punk subculture. Piepmeier argues that these productions not only inform scholars about late twentieth-century girlhood, but also serve as sites for examining the evolution of feminist thought.[93]

By virtue of the rather ephemeral nature of zines and their circumscribed audiences, much of the published research on these periodicals takes the form of journal articles. For example, gay zines are the focus of Tom Boellstorff's 2004 study on Indonesia, "Zines and Zones of Desire: Mass-Mediated Love, National Romance, and Sexual Citizenship in *Gay* Indonesia,"[94] as well as Daniel C. Brouwer's "Counterpublicity and Corporeality in HIV/AIDS Zines."[95] Margaret J. Finders focuses on zines targeting adolescents in "Queens and Teen Zines: Early Adolescent Females Reading Their Way toward Adulthood."[96] With the explosion of e-zines in the twenty-first century, this promises to be a fruitful subject for future scholarly investigation.

Little Magazines

While article-length scholarship on zines and e-zines has flourished, little magazines and their place within the history of literary modernism have received the bulk of book-length attention. One of the first during the 20 years under review here was Mark S. Morrisson's 2001 study, *The Public Face of Modernism: Little Magazines, Audiences, and Reception, 1905–1920*.[97] In their "Introduction" to the edited 2007 edited collection *Little Magazines and Modernism: New Approaches*, Suzanne W. Churchill and Adam McKible define "little magazines" as "non-commercial enterprises founded by individuals or small groups intent upon publishing the experimental works or radical opinions of untried, unpopular or under-represented writers."[98] Churchill and McKible further argue that little magazines share two features: "a vexed relationship to a larger, mainstream public, and an equally vexed relationship to money."[99] This collection provides 11 articles arranged into three sections: Negotiations; Editorial Practices; and Identities. Extending the conversation to include the women editors of modernist little magazines is Jayne E. Marek's 1995 *Women Editing Modernism: "Little" Magazines and Literary History*. Marek's premise is that "women had far more to do with the support and evolution of modernism than has been generally acknowledged," and she offers six chapters to support her argument.[100] Further extending the discussion to include not just the overtly *literary* aspects of modernist magazines is Robert Scholes and Clifford Wulfman's 2010 *Modernism in the Magazines: An Introduction*, which argues for the importance of examining the advertisements, editorial matter and other extra-literary content for a fuller appreciation of the contributions of the genre to "modernism."[101]

Pulp Magazines

Pulp magazines also proved popular with scholars. Researchers wishing to track down these magazines should begin with the guidebooks to library holdings, such as *The Adventure House Guide to the Pulps*, edited by Doug Ellis, John Locke and John Gunnison,[102] and Jess Nevins's *Pulp Magazine Holdings Directory: Library Collections in North America and Europe*,[103] both targeting collectors as well as academics. Mining rich archival materials and targeting a scholarly audience is Erin A. Smith's *Hard-Boiled: Working-Class Readers and Pulp Magazines*,[104] which draws on theories and methods from history of the book, working-class studies and feminist cultural studies. Also targeting primarily a scholarly audience are twin book-length works by David M. Earle: *All Man!: Hemingway, 1950s Men's Magazines, and the Masculine Persona* and *Re-Covering Modernism: Pulps, Paperbacks, and the Prejudice of Form*, both published in 2009.[105] Both volumes seek to challenge earlier scholarship both on pulps and on literary modernism by tracing the work of canonical authors for the pulps.

Other Forms

Literary forms not uniformly classified as *magazines* by some scholars comprise a final category of scholarship highlighted in this section of the research review. Urban weekly periodicals targeting men formed the focus of the 2008 release *The Flash Press: Sporting Male Weeklies in 1840s New York*, edited by Patricia Cline Cohen, Timothy Gilfoyle and Helen Lefkowitz Horowitz.[106] Lee Jolliffe and Virginia Whitehouse's illuminating 1997 article, "The Magazine as Mentor: A Turn-of-the-Century Handwritten Magazine by St. Louis Artists," published in *American Periodicals*,[107] expands the definition of magazine beyond the typeset and mass-produced to include publications honoring older, scribal practices.

Shifting the focus to include not only magazines produced under unusual circumstances but targeting audiences largely unrecognized by previous scholars are Tessa Swithinbank's *Coming Up from the Streets: The Story of the* Big Issue[108] and "'The World We Shall Win for Labor': Early Twentieth-Century Hobo Self-Publication," by Lynne M. Adrian (in the 1998 Danky and Wiegand edited collection)[109]—the former targeting a periodical published by and for the homeless; the latter, a publication by and for men riding the rails.

Engagement with Other Cultural Forms

At issue here is research that places magazines in conversation with other cultural products. Some scholars have treated magazines as isolated products of mass consumer culture that largely *reflected* their cultural context. Newer work acknowledges that magazines not only reflect, but also shape the wider culture and in relationship with other cultural products and contexts. Much of this work has been influenced more broadly by newer interdisciplinary fields such as cultural studies, history of the book and the history of print. Book-length work in this vein includes Ellen Gruber Garvey's *The Adman in the Parlor*[110] and Isabelle Lehuu's *The Carnival on the Page*.[111] Gruber Garvey's *The Adman in the Parlor* examines, in addition to magazine advertising, additional sites of advertising shaping the woman reader as consumer, including trade cards, scrapbooks, advertising contests and novels. Lehuu's *Carnival on the Page* sets *Godey's Lady's Book* in conversation with the *New York Herald* (a penny daily), *Brother Jonathan* and *New World* (mammoth weekly newspapers), as well as giftbooks and literary annuals. Taking on the classic work of cultural historian, Lawrence Levine,[112] Lehuu argues that the bifurcation of American culture occurred not as Levine suggests—at the end of the nineteenth century—but much earlier and certainly before the Civil War. Lehuu argues that even more important was the development of "a separate sphere of print culture for women," the outline of which she traces in this book.[113]

Beyond Editorial Content

Early studies tended to focus primarily on fiction, news reporting, editorial content and advertising. Research in the past 20 years has examined other genres of writing in magazines, including poetry and drama, as well as wrappers and covers, front and back matter, and other magazine features previously ignored. Though not explicitly a study of magazines, Paula Bernat Bennett's 2003 *Poets in the Public Sphere: The Emancipatory Project of American Women's Poetry, 1800–1900*, as well as much of her later article-length work, focuses attention on magazines as the site for the transmission of much of nineteenth-century American poetry written by and for women.[114] Susan Harris Smith's 2007 book, *Plays in American Periodicals, 1890–1918*, turns attention to magazines as publication sites for plays. Harris Smith chronicles the history of more than 125 plays appearing in 14 general interest periodicals—from recognized magazines, such as the *Atlantic Monthly*, to lesser-known titles, such as *Arena* and *Forum*.[115] While noting that not all these plays treated specifically American themes nor were all written by American playwrights, Smith argues that nonetheless, all "did the cultural work of American periodicals."[116] In addition to this work, scholars should consult the "From the Archives" feature of the journal *American Periodicals*, which frequently attends to magazine matter not generally discussed by scholars examining the literary content of periodicals.

Looking Ahead

As scholars look to a future of publishing work on magazines or e-zines as historical study subjects, they need to avail themselves of all the newer, digital tools at their disposal, while not abandoning the commitment to the rigors of archival research. Both for-profit and open-source digital platforms continue to expand the availability of primary source materials for the magazine scholar. Financial support for research time and travel, though increasingly circumscribed by economic factors plaguing many higher education institutions—that is, reduced state revenues for public universities, depleted endowments for private—nevertheless still remains obtainable. And although scholars have watched while academic presses and journals shutter their doors, a new generation of publishing opportunities beckons. Scholars should consider placing their work not only in the established journals in the field—*Journalism History, American Journalism, Journalism & Mass Communication Quarterly, Victorian Periodicals Review, American Periodicals*—but also in the newer now-digital and *born-digital* peer-reviewed journals emerging during the past 20 years. Among those are the *Journal of Modern Periodicals Studies, Commonplace, Scholarly Editing* and the *Journal of Magazine & New Media Research*. As this chapter's bibliography indicates, scholars working on magazines as historical study subjects have placed their work in a wide variety of scholarly venues, and the future of this research looks promising.

Notes

1 James Startt and Wm. David Sloan, *Historical Methods in Mass Communication* (Hillsdale, NJ: Lawrence Erlbaum Associates, Inc., 1989), 114.

2 AAS, Historical Periodicals Collection." American Antiquarian Society <http://www.ebscohost.com/archives/featured-archives/american-antiquarian-society>, accessed 12 February 2014.

3 Judith Yaross Lee, "From the Field: The Future of *American Periodicals* and American Periodicals Research, *American Periodicals* 15.2 (2005): 196–201.

4 Lee, "From the Field," 197.

5 Lee, "From the Field," 198.

6 Marcia R. Prior-Miller and Associates, "Bibliography of Published Research on Magazine and Journal Periodicals," 8th ed., research database (Ames: Iowa State University), last modified, 31 August 2012, MSWord file <mpm@iastate.edu>.

7 Mott, Frank Luther. *A History of American Magazines.* Vol. 1, *A History of American Magazines, 1741–1850;* Vol. 2, *A History of American Magazines, 1850–1865;* Vol. 3, *A History of American Magazines, 1865–1885;* Vol. 4, *A History of American Magazines, 1885–1905;* Vol. 5, *A History of American Magazines, 1905–1930* (New York: D. Appleton, 1930; Cambridge, MA: The Belknap Press, 1938, 1938, 1957; Cambridge, MA: Harvard University Press, 1968).

8 ABC-CLIO Greenwood, "Historical Guides to the World's Periodicals and Newspapers," ABC-CLIO <http://www.abc-clio.com>, accessed 5 February 2015.

9 Alan Nourie and Barbara Nourie, eds., *American Mass-Market Magazines* (Westport, CT: Greenwood Press, 1990), vii.

10 Sam G. Riley and Gary W. Selnow, eds., *Regional Interest Magazines of the United States* (Westport, CT: Greenwood Press, 1991).

11 Edward E. Chielens, ed., *American Literary Magazines: The Twentieth Century* (Westport, CT: Greenwood Press, 1992).

12 William Fisher, ed., *Business Journals of the United States* (Westport, CT: Greenwood Press, 1991).

13 Sam G. Riley, ed., *Corporate Magazines of the United States* (Westport, CT: Greenwood Press, 1992).

14 Kathleen L. Endres, ed., *Trade, Industrial, and Professional Periodicals of the United States* (Westport, CT and London: Greenwood Press, 1994).

15 P. Mark Fackler and Charles H. Lippy, eds., *Popular Religious Magazines of the United States* (Westport, CT: Greenwood Press, 1995).

16 Charles H. Lippy, ed., *Religious Periodicals of the United States: Academic and Scholarly Journals* (Westport, CT: Greenwood Press, 1986).

17 Ronald Lora and William Henry Longton, eds., *The Conservative Press in Eighteenth- and Nineteenth-Century America* (Westport, CT: Greenwood Press, 1999); Ronald Lora and William Henry Longton, eds., *The Conservative Press in Twentieth-Century America* (Westport, CT: Greenwood Press, 1999).

18 Michael Unsworth, ed., *Military Periodicals: United States and Selected International Journals and Newspapers* (Westport, CT: Greenwood Press, 1990).

19 John Tebbel and Mary Ellen Zuckerman, *The Magazine in America, 1741–1990* (New York and Oxford, UK: Oxford University Press, 1991), v.

20 David Abrahamson, *Magazine-Made America: The Cultural Transformation of the Postwar Periodical* (Cresskill, NJ: Hampton Press, Inc., 1996), 3.

21 David E. Sumner, *The Magazine Century: American Magazines since 1900*, Mediating American History Series (New York: Peter Lang Publishing, 2010).

22 Kenneth M. Price and Susan Belasco Smith, eds. *Periodical Literature in Nineteenth-Century America* (Charlottesville: University Press of Virginia, 1995), 7–8.

23 Price and Belasco Smith, *Periodical Literature in Nineteenth-Century America*, 14.

24 David Abrahamson, ed., *The American Magazine: Research Perspectives and Prospects* (Ames: Iowa State University Press, 1995).

25 David Abrahamson, "Brilliant Fragments: The Scholarly Engagement with the American Magazine," in David Abrahamson, ed., *The American Magazine: Research Perspectives and Prospects* (Ames: Iowa State University Press, 1995), xvii–xxi.

26 Michael Augspurger, *An Economy of Abundant Beauty: Fortune Magazine and Depression America* (Ithaca, NY: Cornell University Press, 2004).

27 Amy Erdman Farrell, *Yours in Sisterhood: Ms. Magazine and the Promise of Popular Feminism* (Chapel Hill: University of North Carolina Press, 1998), ix, 1.

28 Catherine A. Lutz and Jane L. Collins, *Reading National Geographic* (Chicago and London: University of Chicago Press, 1993).

29 Tamar Y. Rothenberg, *Presenting America's World: Strategies of Innocence in* National Geographic Magazine, *1888–1945* (Aldershot, UK and Burlington, VT: Ashgate, 2007), 21.

30 Heidi L. Nichols, *The Fashioning of Middle-Class America*: Sartain's Union Magazine of Literature and Art and Antebellum Culture (New York: Peter Lang, 2004), 7.

31 Ellery Sedgwick, *The* Atlantic Monthly, *1857–1909: Yankee Humanism at High Tide and Ebb* (Amherst: University of Massachusetts Press, 1994), vii.

32 Jonathan Daniel Wells, "Introduction," in Benjamin Blake Minor, ed., *The* Southern Literary Messenger, *1834–1864* (Columbia: University of South Carolina Press, 2007), xi.

33 George H. Douglas, *The Smart Magazines: 50 Years of Literary Revelry and High Jinks at* Vanity Fair, *the* New Yorker, Life, Esquire, *and the* Smart Set (Hamden, CT: Archon Books, 1991), 1–2.

34 Matthew Schneirov, *The Dream of a New Social Order: Popular Magazines in America, 1893–1914* (New York: Columbia University Press, 1994), 2.

35 Cynthia Lee Patterson, *Art for the Middle Classes: America's Illustrated Magazines of the 1840s* (Jackson: University Press of Mississippi, 2010), 12.

36 Mark J. Noonan, *Reading the* Century Illustrated Monthly Magazine: *American Literature and Culture, 1870–1893* (Kent, OH: Kent State University Press, 2010), xi.

37 Mary Ellen Zuckerman, *Sources on the History of Women's Magazines, 1792–1960: An Annotated Bibliography* (New York: Greenwood Press, 1991), xviii.

38 Mary Ellen Zuckerman, *A History of Popular Women's Magazines in the United States, 1792–1995* (Westport, CT: Greenwood Press, 1998), 3.

39 Kathleen L. Endres and Therese L. Lueck, eds., *Women's Periodicals in the United States: Consumer Magazines* (Westport, CT: Greenwood Press, 1995); Kathleen L. Endres and Therese L. Lueck, eds. *Women's Periodicals in the United States: Social and Political Issues* (Westport, CT: Greenwood Press, 1996).

40 Endres and Lueck, *Women's Periodicals in the United States: Consumer Magazines*, viii.

41 Endres and Lueck, *Women's Periodicals in the United States: Social and Political Issues*, vii.

42 Martha M. Solomon, ed. *A Voice of Their Own: The Woman Suffrage Press, 1840–1910* (Tuscaloosa: University of Alabama Press, 1991).

43 Aleta Feinsod Cane and Susan Alves, eds., *"The Only Efficient Instrument": American Women Writers and the Periodical, 1837–1916* (Iowa City: University of Iowa Press, 2001), 1.

44 Sharon M. Harris, ed., with a Foreword by Ellen Gruber Garvey, *Blue Pencils and Hidden Hands: Women Editing Periodicals, 1830–1910* (Boston: Northeastern University Press, 2004).

45 Sherilyn Cox Bennion, *Equal to the Occasion: Women Editors of the Nineteenth-Century West* (Reno: University of Nevada Press, 1990).

46 Patricia Okker, *Our Sister Editors: Sarah J. Hale and the Tradition of Nineteenth-Century American Women Editors* (Athens: University of Georgia Press, 1995).

47 Jennifer Phegley, *Educating the Proper Woman Reader: Victorian Family Literary Magazines and the Cultural Health of the Nation* (Columbus: Ohio State University Press, 2004), 2.

48 Ellen Gruber Garvey, *The Adman in the Parlor: Magazines and the Gendering of Consumer Culture, 1880s to 1910s* (New York: Oxford University Press, 1996).

49 Jennifer Scanlon, *Inarticulate Longings: The* Ladies' Home Journal, *Gender, and the Promises of Consumer Culture* (London and New York: Routledge, 1995).

50 Helen Damon-Moore, *Magazines for the Millions: Gender and Commerce in the* Ladies' Home Journal *and the* Saturday Evening Post, *1880–1910* (Albany: State University of New York Press, 1994).

51 Carolyn Kitch, *The Girl on the Magazine Cover: The Origins of Visual Stereotypes in American Mass Media* (Chapel Hill and London: The University of North Carolina Press, 2001), xi.

52 Kitch, *The Girl on the Magazine Cover*, 3.

53 Lorinda B. Cohoon, *Serialized Citizenships: Periodicals, Books, and American Boys, 1840–1911* (Lanham, MD: Scarecrow Press, 2006), xv.

54 James Marten, ed., *Lessons of War: The Civil War in Children's Magazines* (Wilmington, DE: SR Books, 1999).

55 Susan R. Gannon, Suzanne Rahn, and Ruth Anne Thompson, eds. St. Nicholas *and Mary Mapes Dodge: The Legacy of a Children's Magazine Editor, 1873–1905* (Jefferson, NC: McFarland, 2004).

56 Gannon, Rahn, and Thompson, St. Nicholas, 2.

57 [Special Issue, Children's Periodicals], *American Periodicals* 22.2 (2012).

58 Abby Arthur Johnson and Ronald Maberry Johnson, *Propaganda and Aesthetics: The Literary Politics of African-American Magazines in the Twentieth Century* (Amherst: University of Massachusetts Press, 1991), 201.

59 Noliwe M. Rooks, *Ladies' Pages: African American Women's Magazines and the Culture That Made Them* (New Brunswick, NJ: Rutgers University Press, 2004).

60 Eric Gardner, *Unexpected Places: Relocating Nineteenth-Century African American Literature* (Jackson: University Press of Mississippi, 2009).

61 For a summary of this earlier work, see Gardner, *Unexpected Places*, 6–8.

62 Sandra L. Jones Ireland, *Ethnic Periodicals in Contemporary America: Annotated Guide* (Westport, CT: Greenwood Press, 1990).

63 Elliott Shore, Ken Fones-Wolf and James P. Danky, eds., *The German-American Radical Press: The Shaping of a Left Political Culture, 1850–1940* (Urbana: University of Illinois Press, 1992).

64 James P. Danky and Wayne A. Wiegand, eds., *Print Culture in a Diverse America* (Urbana: University of Illinois Press, 1998).

65 [Special Issue, Immigrant Periodicals], *American Periodicals* 19.1 (2009).

66 Patricia Okker, ed. *Transnationalism and American Serial Fiction* (New York: Routledge, 2012).

67 Peter Richardson, *A Bomb in Every Issue: How the Short, Unruly Life of* Ramparts *Magazine Changed America* (New York: New Press, 2009), 1.

68 Benjamin Balint, *Running* Commentary: *The Contentious Magazine That Transformed the Jewish Left into the Neoconservative Right* (New York: PublicAffairs, 2010), x.

69 Balint, *Running* Commentary, 202.

70 Nicolás Kanellos, "A Brief History of Hispanic Periodicals in the United States," in Nicolás Kanellos with Helvetia Martell. *Hispanic Periodicals in the United States, Origins to 1960: A Brief History and Comprehensive Bibliography* (Houston: Arte Público Press, 2000), 3–8.

71 Ros Ballaster, Margaret Beetham, Elizabeth Frazer and Sandra Hebron, *Women's Worlds: Ideology, Femininity and the Woman's Magazine* (Houndmills, Hampshire, UK: Palgrave Macmillan, 1991).

72 Dathalinn M. O'Dea, "Modernist Nationalism in *Dana: An Irish Magazine of Independent Thought* (1904)," *Éire-Ireland* 45.3/4 (Fall/Winter 2010): 95–123.

73 Jaleen Grove, "A Castle of One's Own: Interactivity in *Chatelaine* Magazine, 1829–35," *Journal of Canadian Studies/Revue d'études canadiennes* 45.3 (Fall 2011): 167–194.

74 Anne Jamison, "*Kmen*: A Faraway Magazine about Which We Know Nothing," *Comparative Literature Studies* 44.1/2 (January 2007): 51–66.

75 Janet Steele, "Representations of 'the Nation' in *Tempo* Magazine," *Indonesia* 76 (2003): 127–145.

76 Leith Morton, "The Concept of Romantic Love in the *Taiyō* Magazine 1895–1905," *Japan Review* 8 (1997): 79–103.

77 Gennifer S. Weisenfeld, "'Touring Japan-as-Museum': *Nippon* and Other Japanese Imperialist Travelogues," *Positions: East Asia Cultures Critique* 8.3 (2000): 747–793.

78 Bodil Folke Frederiksen, "*Joe*, the Sweetest Reading in Africa: Documentation and Discussion of a Popular Magazine in Kenya," *African Languages and Cultures* 4.2 (1991): 135–155.

79 Tyler Fleming and Toyin Falola, "Africa's Media Empire: *Drum's* Expansion to Nigeria," *History in Africa* 32.1 (2005): 133–164.

80 John King, *The Role of Mexico's* Plural *in Latin American Literary and Political Culture: From Tlatelolco to the "Philanthropic Ogre"* [in English], *Studies of the Americas*, 1st ed. (New York: Palgrave Macmillan, 2007).

81 Natasha Tolstikova, "*Rabotnitsa*: The Paradoxical Success of a Soviet Women's Magazine," *Journalism History* 30.3 (Fall 2004): 131–140.

82 Sarah Nuttall, "Stylizing the Self: The Y Generation in Rosebank, Johannesburg," *Public Culture* 16.3 (Fall 2004): 430–452.

83 Microfilm: *American Periodical Series, 1850–1900* (Ann Arbor, MI: University Microfilms, 1971–75); On-line database: *American Periodical Series, 1740–1940* (Ann Arbor, MI: ProQuest, 2000).

84 Mark L. Kamrath and Sharon M. Harris, eds., *Periodical Literature in Eighteenth-Century America* (Knoxville: University of Tennessee Press, 2005).

85 Kamrath and Harris, *Periodical Literature in Eighteenth-Century America*, xxiii–xxiv.

86 Amy Beth Aronson, *Taking Liberties: Early American Women's Magazines and Their Readers* (Westport, CT: Praeger, 2002).

87 Cited in Aronson, *Taking Liberties*, 8.

88 Aronson, *Taking Liberties*, 9.

89 Aronson, *Taking Liberties*, 12.

90 Michael Cody, *Charles Brockden Brown and the Literary Magazine: Cultural Journalism in the Early American Republic* (Jefferson, NC: McFarland & Co., 2004).

91 Scott Slawinski, *Validating Bachelorhood: Audience, Patriarchy, and Charles Brockden Brown's Editorship of the* Monthly Magazine and American Review (New York: Routledge, 2005).

92 Jared Gardner, *The Rise and Fall of Early American Magazine Culture* (Urbana: University of Illinois Press, 2012), 172–173.

93 Alison Piepmeier, *Girl Zines: Making Media, Doing Feminism* (New York: New York University Press, 2009), 4; see also, Alison Piepmeier, "Why Zines Matter: Materiality and the Creation of Embodied Community, *American Periodicals* 18.2 (2008): 213–238.

94 Tom Boellstorff, "Zines and Zones of Desire: Mass-Mediated Love, National Romance, and Sexual Citizenship in Gay Indonesia," *Journal of Asian Studies* 63.2 (May 2004): 367–402.

95 Daniel C. Brouwer, "Counterpublicity and Corporeality in HIV/AIDS Zines," *Critical Studies in Media Communication* 22.5 (2005): 351–371.

96 Margaret J. Finders, "Queens and Teen Zines: Early Adolescent Females Reading Their Way toward Adulthood," *Anthropology & Education Quarterly* 27.1 (March 1996): 71–89.

97 Mark S. Morrisson, *The Public Face of Modernism: Little Magazines, Audiences, and Reception, 1905–1920* (Madison: University of Wisconsin Press, 2001).

98 Suzanne W. Churchill and Adam McKible, "Introduction," in Suzanne W. Churchill and Adam McKible, eds., *Little Magazines and Modernism: New Approaches* (Burlington, VT: Ashgate, 2007), 6.

99 Churchill and McKible, "Introduction," 7.

100 Jayne E. Marek, *Women Editing Modernism: "Little" Magazines and Literary History* (Lexington: University Press of Kentucky, 1995), 2.

101 Robert Scholes and Clifford Wulfman, *Modernism in the Magazines: An Introduction* (New Haven: Yale University Press, 2010).

102 Doug Ellis, John Locke, and John Gunnison, eds., *The Adventure House Guide to the Pulps* (Silver Spring, MD: Adventure House, 2000).

103 Jess Nevins, *Pulp Magazine Holdings Directory: Library Collections in North America and Europe* (Jefferson, NC: McFarland, 2007).

104 Erin A. Smith, *Hard-Boiled: Working-Class Readers and Pulp Magazines* (Philadelphia: Temple University Press, 2000).

105 David M. Earle, *All Man!: Hemingway, 1950s Men's Magazines, and the Masculine Persona* (Kent, OH: Kent State University Press, 2009); David M. Earle, *Re-Covering Modernism: Pulps, Paperbacks, and the Prejudice of Form* (Burlington, VT: Ashgate Publishing Company, 2009).

106 Patricia Cline Cohen, Timothy J. Gilfoyle, and Helen Lefkowitz Horowitz, *The Flash Press: Sporting Male Weeklies in 1840s New York* (New York and Chicago: University of Chicago Press, 2008).

107 Lee Jolliffe and Virginia Whitehouse, "The Magazine as Mentor: A Turn-of-the-Century Handwritten Magazine by St. Louis Women Artists," *American Periodicals* 7 (1997): 48–72.

108 Tessa Swithinbank, *Coming Up from the Streets: The Story of the Big Issue* (London: Earthscan, 2001).

109 Lynne M. Adrian, "'The World We Shall Win for Labor': Early Twentieth-Century Hobo Self-Publication," in James P. Danky and Wayne A. Wiegand, eds., *Print Culture in a Diverse America* (Urbana: University of Illinois Press, 1998), 101–128.

110 Garvey, *The Adman in the Parlor*.

111 Isabelle Lehuu, *Carnival on the Page: Popular Print Media in Antebellum America* (Chapel Hill: University of North Carolina Press, 2000).

112 Lawrence W. Levine, *Highbrow/Lowbrow: The Emergence of Cultural Hierarchy in America* (Cambridge: Harvard University Press, 1988).

113 Lehuu, *Carnival on the Page*, 11.

114 Paula Bernat Bennett, *Poets in the Public Sphere: The Emancipatory Project of American Women's Poetry, 1800–1900* (Princeton: Princeton University Press, 2003).

115 Susan Harris Smith, *Plays in American Periodicals, 1890–1918* (New York: Palgrave Macmillan, 2007), xi.

116 Smith, *Plays in American Periodicals*, xii.

Bibliography

AAS. "Historical Periodicals Collection." American Antiquarian Society <http://www.ebscohost.com/archives/featured-archives/american-antiquarian-society>, accessed 12 February 2014.

ABC-CLIO Greenwood. "Historical Guides to the World's Periodicals and Newspapers." ABC-CLIO <http://www.abc-clio.com>, accessed 5 February 2015.

Abrahamson, David, ed. *The American Magazine: Research Perspectives and Prospects*. Ames: Iowa State University Press, 1995.

Abrahamson, David. "Brilliant Fragments: The Scholarly Engagement with the American Magazine." In Abrahamson, David, ed. *The American Magazine: Research Perspectives and Prospects*. Ames: Iowa State University Press, 1995, xvii–xxi.

Abrahamson, David. *Magazine-Made America: The Cultural Transformation of the Postwar Periodical*. Cresskill, NJ: Hampton Press, 1996.

Adrian, Lynne M. "'The World We Shall Win for Labor': Early Twentieth-Century Hobo Self-Publication." In Danky, James P. and Wiegand, Wayne A., eds. *Print Culture in a Diverse America*. Urbana: University of Illinois Press, 1998, 101–128.

Aronson, Amy Beth. *Taking Liberties: Early American Women's Magazines and Their Readers*. Westport, CT: Praeger, 2002.

Augspurger, Michael. *An Economy of Abundant Beauty*: Fortune *Magazine and Depression America*. Ithaca, NY: Cornell University Press, 2004.

Balint, Benjamin. *Running* Commentary: *The Contentious Magazine That Transformed the Jewish Left into the Neoconservative Right*. New York: PublicAffairs, 2010.

Ballaster, Ros; Beetham, Margaret; Frazer, Elizabeth; and Hebron, Sandra. *Women's Worlds: Ideology, Femininity and the Woman's Magazine*. Houndmills, Hampshire, UK: Palgrave Macmillan, 1991.

Bennett, Paula Bernat. *Poets in the Public Sphere: The Emancipatory Project of American Women's Poetry, 1800–1900*. Princeton: Princeton University Press, 2003.

Bennion, Sherilyn Cox. *Equal to the Occasion: Women Editors of the Nineteenth-Century West*. Reno: University of Nevada Press, 1990.

Boellstorff, Tom. "Zines and Zones of Desire: Mass-Mediated Love, National Romance, and Sexual Citizenship in Gay Indonesia." *Journal of Asian Studies* 63.2 (May 2004): 367–402.

Brouwer, Daniel C. "Counterpublicity and Corporeality in HIV/AIDS Zines." *Critical Studies in Media Communication* 22.5 (December 2005): 351–371.

Cane, Aleta Feinsod and Alves, Susan, eds. *"The Only Efficient Instrument": American Women Writers and the Periodical, 1837–1916*. Iowa City: University of Iowa Press, 2001.

Chielens, Edward E., ed. *American Literary Magazines: The Twentieth Century*. Westport, CT: Greenwood Press, 1992.

Churchill, Suzanne W. and McKible, Adam. "Introduction." In Churchill, Suzanne W. and McKible, Adam. eds. *Little Magazines and Modernism: New Approaches*. Burlington, VT: Ashgate, 2007, 3–18.

Cody, Michael. *Charles Brockden Brown and the Literary Magazine: Cultural Journalism in the Early American Republic*. Jefferson, NC: McFarland & Co., 2004.

Cohen, Patricia Cline; Gilfoyle, Timothy J.; and Horowitz, Helen Lefkowitz. *The Flash Press: Sporting Male Weeklies in 1840s New York*. New York and Chicago: University of Chicago Press, 2008.

Cohoon, Lorinda B. *Serialized Citizenships: Periodicals, Books, and American Boys, 1840–1911*. Lanham, MD: Scarecrow Press, 2006.

Damon-Moore, Helen. *Magazines for the Millions: Gender and Commerce in the* Ladies' Home Journal *and the* Saturday Evening Post, *1880–1910*. Albany: State University of New York Press, 1994.

Danky, James P. and Wiegand, Wayne A., eds. *Print Culture in a Diverse America*. Urbana: University of Illinois Press, 1998.

Douglas, George H. *The Smart Magazines: 50 Years of Literary Revelry and High Jinks at* Vanity Fair, *the* New Yorker, Life, Esquire, *and the* Smart Set. Hamden, CT: Archon Books, 1991.

Earle, David M. *All Man!: Hemingway, 1950s Men's Magazines, and the Masculine Persona*. Kent, OH: Kent State University Press, 2009.

Earle, David M. *Re-Covering Modernism: Pulps, Paperbacks, and the Prejudice of Form*. Burlington, VT: Ashgate Publishing Company, 2009.

Ellis, Doug; Locke, John; and Gunnison, John, eds. *The Adventure House Guide to the Pulps*. Silver Spring, MD: Adventure House, 2000.

Endres, Kathleen L., ed. *Trade, Industrial, and Professional Periodicals of the United States*. Westport, CT and London: Greenwood Press, 1994.

Endres, Kathleen L. and Lueck, Therese L., eds. *Women's Periodicals in the United States: Consumer Magazines*. Westport, CT: Greenwood Press, 1995.

Endres, Kathleen L. and Lueck, Therese L., eds. *Women's Periodicals in the United States: Social and Political Issues*. Westport, CT: Greenwood Press, 1996.

Fackler, P. Mark and Lippy, Charles H., eds. *Popular Religious Magazines of the United States*. Westport, CT: Greenwood Press, 1995.

Farrell, Amy Erdman. *Yours in Sisterhood*: Ms. *Magazine and the Promise of Popular Feminism*. Chapel Hill: University of North Carolina Press, 1998.

Finders, Margaret J. "Queens and Teen Zines: Early Adolescent Females Reading Their Way toward Adulthood." *Anthropology & Education Quarterly* 27.1 (March 1996): 71–89.

Fisher, William, ed. *Business Journals of the United States*. Westport, CT: Greenwood Press, 1991.

Fleming, Tyler and Falola, Toyin. "Africa's Media Empire: Drum's Expansion to Nigeria." *History in Africa* 32.1 (2005): 133–164.

Frederiksen, Bodil Folke. "Joe, the Sweetest Reading in Africa: Documentation and Discussion of a Popular Magazine in Kenya." *African Languages and Cultures* 4.2 (1991): 135–155.

Gannon, Susan R.; Rahn, Suzanne; and Thompson, Ruth Anne, eds. St. Nicholas *and Mary Mapes Dodge: The Legacy of a Children's Magazine Editor, 1873–1905*. Jefferson, NC: McFarland, 2004.

Gardner, Eric. *Unexpected Places: Relocating Nineteenth-Century African American Literature*. Jackson: University Press of Mississippi, 2009.

Gardner, Jared. *The Rise and Fall of Early American Magazine Culture*. Urbana: University of Illinois Press, 2012.

Garvey, Ellen Gruber. *The Adman in the Parlor: Magazines and the Gendering of Consumer Culture, 1880s to 1910s*. New York: Oxford University Press, 1996.

Grove, Jaleen. "A Castle of One's Own: Interactivity in *Chatelaine* Magazine, 1928–35." *Journal of Canadian Studies/Revue d'études canadiennes* 45.3 (Fall 2011): 167–194.

Harris, Sharon M., ed. With a Foreword by Gruber Garvey, Ellen. *Blue Pencils and Hidden Hands: Women Editing Periodicals, 1830–1910*. Boston: Northeastern University Press, 2004.

Ireland, Sandra L. Jones. *Ethnic Periodicals in Contemporary America: Annotated Guide*. Westport, CT: Greenwood Press, 1990.

Jamison, Anne. "Kmen: A Faraway Magazine about Which We Know Nothing." *Comparative Literature Studies* 44.1/2 (January 2007): 51–66.

Johnson, Abby Arthur and Johnson, Ronald Maberry. *Propaganda and Aesthetics: The Literary Politics of African-American Magazines in the Twentieth Century*. Amherst: University of Massachusetts Press, 1991.

Jolliffe, Lee and Whitehouse, Virginia. "The Magazine as Mentor: A Turn-of-the-Century Handwritten Magazine by St. Louis Women Artists." *American Periodicals* 7 (1997): 48–72.

Kamrath, Mark L. and Harris, Sharon M., eds. *Periodical Literature in Eighteenth-Century America*. Knoxville: University of Tennessee Press, 2005.

Kanellos, Nicolás. "A Brief History of Hispanic Periodicals in the United States." In Kanellos, Nicolás, with Martell, Helvetia. *Hispanic Periodicals in the United States, Origins to 1960: A Brief History and Comprehensive Bibliography*. Houston: Arte Público Press, 2000.

King, John. *The Role of Mexico's* Plural *in Latin American Literary and Political Culture: From Tlatelolco to the "Philanthropic Ogre"* [in English]. *Studies of the Americas*. 1st ed. New York: Palgrave Macmillan, 2007.

Kitch, Carolyn. *The Girl on the Magazine Cover: The Origins of Visual Stereotypes in American Mass Media*. Chapel Hill and London: University of North Carolina Press, 2001.

Lee, Judith Yaross. "From the Field: The Future of *American Periodicals* and American Periodicals Research." *American Periodicals* 15.2 (2005): 196–201.

Lehuu, Isabelle. *Carnival on the Page: Popular Print Media in Antebellum America*. Chapel Hill: University of North Carolina Press, 2000.

Levine, Lawrence W. *Highbrow/Lowbrow: The Emergence of Cultural Hierarchy in America*. Cambridge: Harvard University Press, 1988.

Lippy, Charles H., ed. *Religious Periodicals of the United States: Academic and Scholarly Journals*. Westport, CT: Greenwood Press, 1986.

Lora, Ronald and Longton, William Henry, eds. *The Conservative Press in Eighteenth- and Nineteenth-Century America*. Westport, CT: Greenwood Press, 1999.

Lora, Ronald and Longton, William Henry, eds. *The Conservative Press in Twentieth-Century America*. Westport, CT: Greenwood Press, 1999.

Lutz, Catherine A. and Collins, Jane L. *Reading* National Geographic. Chicago and London: University of Chicago Press, 1993.

Marek, Jayne E. *Women Editing Modernism: "Little" Magazines and Literary History*. Lexington: University Press of Kentucky, 1995.

Marten, James, ed. *Lessons of War: The Civil War in Children's Magazines*. Wilmington, DE: SR Books, 1999.

Microfilm: *American Periodical Series, 1850–1900*. Ann Arbor, MI: University Microfilms, 1971–75.

Morrisson, Mark S. *The Public Face of Modernism: Little Magazines, Audiences, and Reception, 1905–1920*. Madison: University of Wisconsin Press, 2001.

Morton, Leith. "The Concept of Romantic Love in the *Taiyō* Magazine 1895–1905." *Japan Review* 8 (1997): 79–103.

Mott, Frank Luther. *A History of American Magazines*. Vol. 1, *A History of American Magazines, 1741–1850*; Vol. 2, *A History of American Magazines, 1850–1865*; Vol. 3, *A History of American Magazines, 1865–1885*; Vol. 4, *A History of American Magazines, 1885–1905*; Vol. 5, *A History of American Magazines, 1905–1930*. New York: D. Appleton, 1930; Cambridge, MA: The Belknap Press, 1938, 1938, 1957; Cambridge, MA: Harvard University Press, 1968.

Nevins, Jess. *Pulp Magazine Holdings Directory: Library Collections in North America and Europe*. Jefferson, NC: McFarland, 2007.

Nichols, Heidi L. *The Fashioning of Middle-Class America*: Sartain's Union Magazine of Literature and Art and Antebellum Culture. New York: Peter Lang, 2004.

Noonan, Mark J. *Reading the* Century Illustrated Monthly Magazine: *American Literature and Culture, 1870–1893*. Kent, OH: Kent State University Press, 2010.

Nourie, Alan and Nourie, Barbara, eds. *American Mass-Market Magazines*. Westport, CT: Greenwood Press, 1990.

Nuttall, Sarah. "Stylizing the Self: The Y Generation in Rosebank, Johannesburg." *Public Culture* 16.3 (Fall 2004): 430–452.

O'Dea, Dathalinn M. "Modernist Nationalism in *Dana: An Irish Magazine of Independent Thought* (1904)." *Éire-Ireland* 45.3/4 (Fall/Winter 2010): 95–123.

Okker, Patricia. *Our Sister Editors: Sarah J. Hale and the Tradition of Nineteenth-Century American Women Editors*. Athens: University of Georgia Press, 1995.

Okker, Patricia, ed. *Transnationalism and American Serial Fiction*. New York: Routledge, 2012.

On-line database: *American Periodical Series, 1740–1940*. Ann Arbor, MI: ProQuest, 2000.

Patterson, Cynthia Lee. *Art for the Middle Classes: America's Illustrated Magazines of the 1840s*. Jackson: University Press of Mississippi, 2010.

Phegley, Jennifer. *Educating the Proper Woman Reader: Victorian Family Literary Magazines and the Cultural Health of the Nation*. Columbus: Ohio State University Press, 2004.

Piepmeier, Alison. *Girl Zines: Making Media, Doing Feminism*. New York: New York University Press, 2009.

Piepmeier, Alison. "Why Zines Matter: Materiality and the Creation of Embodied Community." *American Periodicals* 18.2 (2008): 213–238.

Price, Kenneth M. and Smith, Susan Belasco, eds. *Periodical Literature in Nineteenth-Century America*. Charlottesville: University Press of Virginia, 1995.

Prior-Miller, Marcia R. and Associates. "Bibliography of Published Research on Magazine and Journal Periodicals." 8th ed. Research database. Ames: Iowa State University, last modified, 31 August 2012, MSWord file <mpm@iastate.edu>.

Richardson, Peter. *A Bomb in Every Issue: How the Short, Unruly Life of* Ramparts *Magazine Changed America*. New York: New Press, 2009.

Riley, Sam G., ed. *Corporate Magazines of the United States*. Westport, CT: Greenwood Press, 1992.

Riley, Sam G. and Selnow, Gary W., eds. *Regional Interest Magazines of the United States*. Westport, CT: Greenwood Press, 1991.

Rooks, Noliwe M. *Ladies' Pages: African American Women's Magazines and the Culture That Made Them*. New Brunswick, NJ: Rutgers University Press, 2004.

Rothenberg, Tamar Y. *Presenting America's World: Strategies of Innocence in* National Geographic *Magazine, 1888–1945*. Aldershot, UK and Burlington, VT: Ashgate, 2007.

Scanlon, Jennifer. *Inarticulate Longings: The* Ladies' Home Journal, *Gender, and the Promises of Consumer Culture*. London and New York: Routledge, 1995.

Schneirov, Matthew. *The Dream of a New Social Order: Popular Magazines in America, 1893–1914*. New York: Columbia University Press, 1994.

Scholes, Robert and Wulfman, Clifford. *Modernism in the Magazines: An Introduction*. New Haven: Yale University Press, 2010.

Sedgwick, Ellery. *The* Atlantic Monthly, *1857–1909: Yankee Humanism at High Tide and Ebb*. Amherst: University of Massachusetts Press, 1994.

Shore, Elliott; Fones-Wolf, Ken; and Danky, James P., eds. *The German-American Radical Press: The Shaping of a Left Political Culture, 1850–1940*. Urbana: University of Illinois Press, 1992.

Slawinski, Scott. *Validating Bachelorhood: Audience, Patriarchy, and Charles Brockden Brown's Editorship of the* Monthly Magazine and American Review. New York: Routledge, 2005.

Smith, Erin A. *Hard-Boiled: Working-Class Readers and Pulp Magazines*. Philadelphia: Temple University Press, 2000.

Smith, Susan Harris. *Plays in American Periodicals, 1890–1918*. New York: Palgrave Macmillan, 2007.

Solomon, Martha M., ed. *A Voice of Their Own: The Woman Suffrage Press, 1840–1910*. Tuscaloosa: University of Alabama Press, 1991.

[Special Issue, Children's Periodicals]. *American Periodicals* 22.2 (2012).

[Special Issue, Immigrant Periodicals]. *American Periodicals* 19.1 (2009).

Startt, James D. and Sloan, Wm. David. *Historical Methods in Mass Communication*. Hillsdale, NJ: Lawrence Erlbaum Associates, Inc., 1989.

Steele, Janet. "Representations of 'the Nation' in *Tempo* Magazine." *Indonesia* 76 (October 2003): 127–145.

Sumner, David E. *The Magazine Century: American Magazines since 1900*. Mediating American History Series. New York: Peter Lang Publishing, 2010.

Swithinbank, Tessa. *Coming up from the Streets: The Story of the* Big Issue. London: Earthscan, 2001.

Tebbel, John and Zuckerman, Mary Ellen. *The Magazine in America, 1741–1990*. New York and Oxford, UK: Oxford University Press, 1991.

Tolstikova, Natasha. "*Rabotnitsa*: The Paradoxical Success of a Soviet Women's Magazine." *Journalism History* 30.3 (Fall 2004): 131–140.

Unsworth, Michael E. *Military Periodicals: United States and Selected International Journals and Newspapers*. Westport, CT: Greenwood Press, 1990.

Weisenfeld, Gennifer S. "'Touring Japan-as-Museum': *Nippon* and Other Japanese Imperialist Travelogues." *Positions: East Asia Cultures Critique* 8.3 (2000): 747–793.

Wells, Jonathan Daniel. "Introduction." In Minor, Benjamin Blake, ed. *The* Southern Literary Messenger, *1834–1864*. Columbia: University of South Carolina Press, 2007.

Zuckerman, Mary Ellen. *A History of Popular Women's Magazines in the United States, 1792–1995*. Westport, CT: Greenwood Press, 1998.

Zuckerman, Mary Ellen. *Sources on the History of Women's Magazines, 1792–1960: An Annotated Bibliography*. New York: Greenwood Press, 1991.

Supplemental Resources

Abrams, Nathan. *Commentary* Magazine 1945–59: "A Journal of Significant Thought and Opinion." London: Vallentine Mitchell, 2007.

Beetham, Margaret. *A Magazine of Her Own?: Domesticity and Desire in the Woman's Magazine, 1800–1914*. London, New York: Routledge, 1996.

Beetham, Margaret and Boardman, Kay, eds. *Victorian Women's Magazines: An Anthology*. Manchester, UK: Manchester University Press, 2001.

Burnham, Linda Frye and Durland, Steven. *The Citizen Artist: 20 Years of Art in the Public Arena: An Anthology from* High Performance Magazine 1978–1998. Gardiner, NY: Critical Press, 1998.

Chang, Jui-Shan. "Refashioning Womanhood in 1990s Taiwan: An Analysis of the Taiwanese Edition of *Cosmopolitan* Magazine." *Modern China* 30.3 (July 2004): 361–397.

Chapman, Michael, ed. *The* Drum *Decade: Stories from the 1950s*, 2nd ed. Pietermaritzburg, South Africa: University of KwaZulu-Natal Press, 2001.

Chiang, Yung-chen. "Womanhood, Motherhood and Biology: The Early Phases of the *Ladies' Journal*, 1915–25." *Gender & History* 18.3 (November 2006): 519–545.

Chielens, Edward E., ed. *American Literary Magazines: The Eighteenth and Nineteenth Centuries*. New York: Greenwood Press, 1986.

Chin, Carol C. "Translating the New Woman: Chinese Feminists View the West, 1905–15." *Gender & History* 18.3 (November 2006): 490–518.

Christensen, Nina. "Lust for Reading and Thirst for Knowledge: Fictive Letters in a Danish Children's Magazine of 1770." *The Lion and the Unicorn* 33.2 (April 2009): 189–201.

Churchill, Suzanne W., and McKible, Adam, eds. *Little Magazines and Modernism: New Approaches*. Burlington, VT: Ashgate, 2007.

Collins, Dana. "'No Experts—Guaranteed!': Do-It-Yourself Sex Radicalism and the Production of the Lesbian Sex Zine *Brat Attack*." *Signs: Journal of Women in Culture & Society* 25.1 (Autumn 1999): 65–89.

Collins, Max Allan and Hagenauer, George. *Men's Adventure Magazines in Postwar America: The Rich Oberg Collection*. Cologne and Los Angeles: Taschen, 2004.

Gao, Yunxiang. "Nationalist and Feminist Discourses on *Jianmei* (Robust Beauty) during China's 'National Crisis' in the 1930s." *Gender & History* 18.3 (November 2006): 546–573.

Gunn, Virginia. "McCall's Role in the Early Twentieth-Century Quilt Revival." *Uncoverings* 31 (December 2010): 11–64.

Kemp, Earl and Ortiz, Luis, eds. *Cult Magazines A to Z: A Compendium of Culturally Obsessive and Curiously Expressive Publications*. New York: Nonstop Press, 2009.

Kitch, Carolyn. *Pages from the Past: History and Memory in American Magazines*. Chapel Hill: University of North Carolina Press, 2005.

Landers, James. *The Improbable First Century of* Cosmopolitan *Magazine*. Columbia: University of Missouri Press, 2010.

Matheu, Robert and Bowe, Brian J. Creem: *America's Only Rock 'N' Roll Magazine*. New York: Collins Living, 2007.

Riley, Sam G. *American Magazine Journalists, 1900–1960*. Second Series. *Dictionary of Literary Biography*. Vol. 91. Detroit: Gale Research, 1994.

Server, Lee. *Danger Is My Business: An Illustrated History of the Fabulous Pulp Magazines, 1896–1953*. San Francisco: Chronicle Books, 1993.

Suggs, Henry Lewis, ed. *The Black Press in the Middle West, 1865–1985*. Westport, CT: Greenwood Press, 1996.

5
SOURCE AND CITATION ANALYSIS

An Epistemology of Magazine Research

Dominic L. Lasorsa

Much scholarly research on magazines and other periodicals has focused on their content, with special attention to how different social groups are portrayed and how certain broad topics, such as politics and the environment, are treated. One important aspect of the content of magazines, however, has been largely ignored: the source of this content. Given that journalism is centrally about communication—that is, reporting what other people tell journalists and staff writers—and given growing concern about the general public's lack of ability to differentiate between fact and opinion (especially on-line), this lack of attention to information sourcing is surprising.

This chapter reviews the scholarly literature on the study of magazine and journal sources and will develop four principal themes: (1) *Attribution patterns*: identifying and comparing diverse practices that exist today for crediting information sources in magazines and journal periodicals; (2) *Sourcing practices*: identifying procedures beyond attribution that relate to sourcing, including selection and use of sources, writer-source prior relationships, pre-publication reviews and other writer-source agreements and issues; (3) *Model studies*: identifying and evaluating studies that are particularly strong in their analysis of magazine sourcing issues to help advance scholarship; and (4) *Promising future research*: identifying areas of research that will improve research on information sources in magazines.

Literature Review and Method

When in 1957 the eminent pioneer of communication scholarship Wilbur Schramm searched for the most important research and theory on mass communication, he found few works on magazines that he considered noteworthy.[1] The first important article he identified on magazine research was Bernard Berelson and Patricia Salter's "Majority and Minority Americans,"[2] a remarkable study of prejudice. Schramm called the 1946 publication a "well-known article,"[3] but it is likely few communication scholars today are aware of its existence. Its abstract reads,

> This is a study of prejudice—of unintentional but consistent discrimination against minority groups of hyphenate Americans in one of the last fields one might think to look for it: popular magazine fiction. The fact that it is unconscious prejudice does not mitigate its corrosive effects on the tolerance of readers: It steals in without warning when they are relaxed and unsuspecting.[4]

The only other magazine study Schramm deemed worthy of mention was Leo Bogart's analysis of the circulation of magazines since the advent of television, published in 1956.[5] Times have changed. Those interested in finding the most illuminating literature on magazine research and theory today can turn to David Abrahamson's anthology on the American magazine, which offers a variety of research perspectives and an array of additional bibliographical references on a host of relevant topics.[6] Textbooks also abound, including Sammye Johnson and Patricia Prijatel's 2013 treatment, which offers both a historical and contemporary overview of the industry.[7]

Regarding the specific topic of this chapter, research and theory on magazine sourcing, an attempt was made to identify the best literature published since 1990. An exhaustive search mined a variety of general and scholarly search engines and database indices, including Academic Search Complete, Academic OneFile, LexisNexis Academic and Google Scholar. For journal articles, filters tapped only articles published since 1990 in peer-reviewed journals, using a variety of keywords to identify the materials most directly related to the topic, including *magazine*, *journal* and *source*. Each returned entry was examined to determine its relevancy to the task at hand. To determine whether an entry was worth consideration, article titles, authors, publications and keywords listed on the entry were noted. Even in cases where a particular item appeared to hold little promise of relevance, it was given a cursory review and references were examined in an attempt to identify other possible candidates for inclusion. Although rigorous objective measures were not used to identify the items ultimately included here, an effort was made to consider the citation histories of these materials as a measure of their importance. So, for example, journal articles that have a history of being cited most frequently were more likely to be included than others. Number of citations, of course, has its limitations as a measure of influence. Articles with a longer publication history have had a greater opportunity than newer ones to be cited. Also, some journals have greater reach than others, so readers may be more likely to be able to identify, locate, read and cite some journal articles compared to others. Also, a piece might be cited not because others consider it particularly good but particularly bad (although no evidence of this was found in the relevant literature here). Despite these limitations, how often a book, book chapter or journal article is cited can give at least some indication of the attention paid to it. In addition, a judgment of value, based on personal experience and expertise as a journalist and journalism educator, was used to help select the literature recommended here. While this is a rather subjective, less-than-scientific method of selection, it is similar to how researchers often go about deciding what literature to include in their work. From a careful reading of the resulting body of literature eventually emerged the themes, conclusions and questions considered in this chapter.

Attribution Patterns: Normative Theory

This section focuses upon theory and research that deal with practices periodicals use to credit information sources. Given the wide-ranging differences in topics, publication frequency and goals, magazines and other periodicals have engaged in diverse practices for crediting information sources. However, changes in media technologies, which have led to the introduction of new media delivery services at the end of the twentieth century and into the twenty-first, have increased that diversity even more. In recent years, on-line publishers, bloggers, information aggregators and others have raised important questions about how to assign proper recognition to the originators of information. Is it acceptable to say that a food recipe comes *courtesy of* a celebrity chef when it is reproduced without the chef's consent? What does it mean to say that material in an article was *inspired by* another source? Is it appropriate for an author to copy an entire passage verbatim from a source without indicating that the words are not one's own, even though the author links to the original article from which the passage was copied? Writers recently have gotten into trouble for practices such as these, but, at the same time, others have come to their defense, often claiming that the old-school rules of journalism simply do not apply on-line. Off-line publications, in order to compete with more fleet-footed on-line rivals, may then feel pressure to relax their attribution standards as well. The result has been a rethinking in all quarters of the media world regarding the basic rules of attribution.

This section explores the literature that has contributed to an understanding of the rules of attribution. Much of this literature tends to be descriptive as opposed to theoretical; that is, it reveals much about how information has been credited in various types of periodicals and how crediting practices have changed over time, but it does not tend systematically to explain or predict well either the antecedents or the effects of these practices or the practices themselves. In addition, and related to this, the literature that is guided by theory tends to be somewhat *normative*, that is, it stems from ideas about how practices should be without much basis on theoretical approaches that might lead to specific explanations or predictions. This is not to dismiss the value of descriptive research and analyses. Indeed, good theory requires well-grounded observations of a descriptive nature. Scholars cannot hope to explain or predict it until they first know what it is. Nevertheless, the movement toward research based (a) more on theory and less on description and (b) more on social science theory and less on normative theory is a positive sign for those hoping to understand better the process and effects of magazine sourcing. Thus, the movement toward research based in theory is a positive sign.

Bill Mitchell has noted that most publishers, editors, professional journalists and journalism educators will tell you that above all else the credibility of a means of communication is the single most important property it possesses. Credibility depends centrally upon letting one's audience know from what specific sources the information comes. Long ago, audiences of nonfiction journals came to expect them to hide their sources from the public only in the rarest of cases and then only with an explanation that justifies the concealment. When a magazine uses an anonymous source it essentially is telling its audience, "Trust me." A periodical can get away with such an excuse for only so long before audience members begin to place their trust elsewhere.[8]

At the same time, however, the new media landscape has generated increased tension between journalism's two primary thrusts, accuracy and speed. Audiences have always wanted the news right, but they also want it right now. Journalists therefore have long grappled with the tension between the need to verify their facts and to do so in a timely manner. Bill Kovach and Tom Rosenstiel found that journalists sometimes have allowed their desire to get the news first to interfere with their need to get it right.[9]

Compounding this problem has been the movement in journalism toward more user-generated content. While many news organizations have been cutting their staffs to save money in a time of economic constraint, there has been a significant increase in the use of content from ordinary people, as opposed to professional journalists. While the origin of the term is unclear, these growing numbers of contributors of user-generated content are referred to as "citizen journalists."[10] Thus, as the number of professional media gatekeepers does not show commensurate growth with the increasing amount of information being disseminated, the number of non-professional media producers is increasing. Kovach and Rosenstiel argue there is good reason to believe that such trends may be leading to more concern for getting the news first as opposed to getting it right. Indeed, some audience members appear to have adopted the notion, contrary to the norms of journalism, that speed should trump accuracy, that on-line news has a self-correcting mechanism whereby any inaccurate information will be identified quickly and corrected soon enough. Now, not only media consumers but even some media producers appear to have adopted this sentiment, which may be contributing to the emergence of looser rules of attribution among some publications, both on-line and off-line. Nonetheless, there is a clear link between the identification of credible sources and the quality of the information those sources provide. Simply put, the accuracy of information depends primarily on the use of trustworthy, knowledgeable sources, and the surest way to build the audience's confidence in the accuracy of the information is to attribute it rigorously and fully to reliable sources.[11]

Sourcing Practices: Operation:

Besides issues of attribution, questions have recently been ra
generally, including selection and use of appropriate source:
pre-publication review of material and other writer-source
what recent research has concluded about magazine sour
raised about these practices in the new media landscape, frc
fore unrealized thematic areas of research.

Just as the new digital media environment has put pres:
information quickly with possibly tenuous (less rigorous) at
of that information, the new media environment has put pr
other practices that may help get information out quickly
nalistic norms designed to protect a periodical's credibility.
one way or another with reporter-source negotiations. Many
are not experts, officials or others accustomed to being inter
being interviewed may not realize that a journalist will regard
publication. These less media-savvy sources may expect ins:
wisdom in what information they use and what they do not, o
burned when a journalist includes information they never ant
but not necessarily, lead to their becoming more media savvy.
however, may desire to have greater control over the informa
sources often accomplish this goal by negotiating the rules of

Kinds of Information Sources Pr

Sometimes sources provide information that they insist is *no*
the journalist agrees to describe the source's expertise and tru
identifying the source, such as "a senior White House official c
leum accountant." Sometimes sources provide information th
In such a case, the journalist agrees to mask the source more, p
about either the source's expertise or trustworthiness, such as
tion" or "a market observer." This should not be confused with
which a reporter states a belief he or she holds but is unwilling
the belief instead as one popular among a relevant set of sourc
forms as "market observers agree" or "experts have concluded."
this as *needless attribution syndrome*[15] and suggested that it parti
ists; instead they should simply own up to such beliefs.

Sometimes sources offer *deep background*[16] information, whic
must be attributed to no one. This *trial balloon* practice is u:
public reaction to an idea without jeopardizing a link to what
ular idea. Sometimes sources speak *off the record*,[17] which me
published. Why then does the source inform the reporter? Wh
information to be made public, the source believes that the inf
understand a situation better, which might lead to what the so
at least more balanced coverage.

Post-Interview Practices: Late Twentieth-Cen

Besides negotiating whether and how information can be used
times engage in post-interview practices that also influence t
ble here is the practice of *quote approval* whereby the journa
review information attributed to them. Some uniquely powerful

demand
of this p
to Georg
ing.[19] In
as "stand
At the s
controve
to allow
reporter
the mag;
pressures
said it w:

There
informat
informat
mation,
case, a g
way to a
it for acc

Domini
regardin
further
tions ha
the imp
Newspa
mechan

A pe
is the c;
and rec
premier
gives it
with ti
esteem
publica
colleag
has bee
respons
apologi
puts th
there i
they su
writer
tal Co
stories,
Lehrer
its rela
Cortex
to foll
that o

review an entire article prior to publication and to obtain modifications. The origin
ctice is unclear. Some attribute it to Bill Clinton's second presidential term, others
W. Bush's second term,[18] but until recently the practice showed no signs of diminish-
ne summer of 2012, *New York Times* reporter Jeremy Peters described quote approval
rd practice for the Obama campaign" and "commonplace throughout Washington."[20]
ne time, Poynter's *MediaWire* reported that the practice was becoming increasingly
sial and that while a number of publications (e.g., the *Huffington Post*) continued
he practice, other publications (e.g., the *National Journal*) were banning it. After
Mark Leibovich of the *New York Times Magazine* publicly announced that he wanted
ine to strengthen its quote approval policy so its reporters could more strongly resist
to grant it, other reporters supported that sentiment. In the fall of 2012, the *Times*
. "resetting the bar" and banned quote approval.[21]

a difference, however, between a writer giving sources the right to review and modify
on attributed to them before publication and a writer requesting that sources review
on for accuracy. Especially when dealing with complex technical or scientific infor-
riters sometimes find they are not quite sure whether their report is correct. In such a
od reporter will find a way to verify the accuracy of the information. The most direct
complish this task may well be simply to ask the source of the information to check
racy.

Clear Violations of the Norms

L. Lasorsa and Jia Dai found that besides providing clear guidance to their reporters
quote approval and other interview and post-interview practices, publications can
elp their reporters by providing the support necessary to do their jobs well. Publica-
e always put considerable trust in their reporters to do the right thing. However, given
rtance of credibility, they have always done more than simply trust their reporters.
er and magazine media have discovered to their dismay that they need additional
ms in place to keep their reporting (and reporters) honest.[22]

ct example of how things can go terribly wrong in this new age of digital journalism
e of Jonah Lehrer, the *New Yorker* staff writer who was fired for fabrication, plagiarism
ling his own material in different stories.[23] The *New Yorker* may well be the nation's
news organization when it comes to verifying the accuracy of the information it
eaders. As a weekly publication, it has an advantage in this realm over publications
ter publication cycles. The *New Yorker's* fact-checking department is held in high
a journalism circles for its thoroughness and attention to detail. Yet, the venerable
on fell prey to what it would regard as a rogue reporter willing to deceive his editors,
s and readers. Whenever a well-known magazine determines that one of its reporters
fabricating, plagiarizing or engaging in some other form of audience deception, the
from the magazine is often predictable: We have found a bad apple in our midst. We
. We will take measures to ensure it doesn't happen again.[24] Such a response strategy
blame on the individual and, for the most part, spares the publication itself. However,
eason to believe that publications are at least partially responsible for the scandals
r in today's media world. In the case of Lehrer, for example, before he became a staff
- the *New Yorker* he was one of the leading reporters at Wired.com where his Fron-
x blogs attracted a large audience. When questions arose about Lehrer's *New Yorker*
Wired.com asked New York University journalism professor Charles Seife to review
Wired.com work. Seife said he found numerous journalistic misdeeds.[25] In severing
onship with Lehrer, Wired.com editor-in-chief Evan Hansen said, "Although Frontal
osts were not edited or fact checked, we expect those whose work appears on our site
· basic good journalistic practices."[26] Hansen's sentiment here may differ little from
· least some other editors of magazines, whether on-line or off-line. Some magazines

and other media expect their writers to maintain high journalistic standards, but they don't give their writers commensurate support in order to help them perform at that level.[27] This is not to excuse Lehrer or anyone else who fabricates or plagiarizes. However, it is at least worth entertaining the idea that Lehrer might have resisted the temptation to deceive if he had had at his disposal greater organizational resources that would have helped him with checking facts and other editorial tasks and responsibilities. Yet, practically no research appears to have been conducted on this important question.

Model Studies

While all published research should contribute to the corpus of knowledge, some studies are distinctly stronger than others. In this section, a review of the literature includes an assessment of studies to identify those particularly strong in their analysis of magazine sourcing issues. Here are pointed out recent studies that are especially noteworthy regarding such research questions as how to place magazines and other periodicals into theoretically meaningful categories, how to sample from these categories, how to raise innovative and theoretically important research questions, how to test interesting ideas and how to articulate critical issues for future research. Such studies can serve as models to advance understanding of magazine sourcing issues.

Compared to research on other major media such as newspapers and television, research on magazines has in the past been less abundant, and research about magazine editing practices, including sourcing practices, has been particularly scarce.[28] If we truly want to understand the magazine, we need to make observations about content, effects and production. Most of what we know about magazine sourcing comes from content analyses. In the area of effects studies, a number of theories (e.g., *feminist theory*) might guide us to identify key factors that lead to the use of particular magazine sources and to recognize where these sources come from and why. Likewise, a number of theories (e.g., *classic democratic theory*) might guide us to identify the key societal changes due to the use of particular magazine sources. *Production studies* dealing with magazine editorial practices have been especially scant. While biographies and autobiographies of individual magazine editors and journalists sometimes have shed light on magazine editorial practices, much of that information is anecdotal and, therefore, difficult to generalize. Such works can lead to intriguing research questions and hypotheses, but in themselves they do little to advance understanding of magazine editorial practices generally. In addition to biographies, research on magazine editorial policies has most often consisted of content surveys and interviews with editors. Such research can be enlightening, but it can only go so far to help us understand the source-reporter relationship and how it affects story content.

One reason why more research attention has been given to the study of sourcing in other media, compared to periodicals, may be that their audiences are assumed to be more widely exposed. Yet, were consumers to track carefully the extent to which they are exposed to information from periodicals, they might be surprised. Even if audiences were to pay little attention to much of the periodical information they receive, the sheer volume of that reception is remarkable and some magazine content clearly does make an impression on audiences. Given the amount and variety of magazine information people regularly consume, additional research should be conducted about sourcing in periodicals and their influence on their magazine audiences.

A model study of the role of sources in magazines in a democratic society (i.e., classic *democratic theory*) is Tawnya Adkins Covert and Philo C. Wasburn's analysis of the use of sources in partisan magazines.[29] Since Leon V. Sigal's pioneering study in 1973, many studies of sourcing in the mass media have found that they rely heavily on official sources.[30] However, nearly all of these studies have been based on the analysis of nonpartisan publications, which function differently under democratic theory than do partisan publications. Covert and Wasburn examined magazines over a quarter-century on four enduring topics: crime, the environment, gender and poverty, specifically scrutinizing what sources had to say about costs, causes and solutions in stories about each of these issues. Covert and Washburn found that the partisan magazines "used official sources much less extensively than mainstream publications." They added, "The pattern of information sources used by explicitly partisan magazines appears to be significantly different from that described in studies of their more mainstream counterparts. In particular, official sources are not 'primary defines' of social issues."[31]

This study is emblematic for a number of reasons. Unlike many content analyses, it did not merely count the number of stories (or paragraphs, statements, etc.) on a topic, or the number of sources. Instead, it examined specific characteristics of the coverage, in this case, mentions of costs, causes and solutions. It also did not make the common assumption that the number of sources of certain types (e.g., conservative versus liberal sources) necessarily indicates balance or bias in coverage. Instead, it looked beyond the number of ideological sources to examine just what they said and how they were treated. Covert and Washburn found, for example, that an article in a premiere conservative journal contained numerous liberal sources but that these sources were roundly attacked and treated dismissively. Interestingly, this study also did not sample content but instead was based on a census. All stories that fit the selection criteria over the study's time frame were analyzed. This removed the possibility of poor or unlucky sampling as an explanation for any of the findings.

Another study of magazine sources that shares many of these same important characteristics is Dominic L. Lasorsa and Stephen D. Reese's comparison of coverage of an economic crisis across four different kinds of media.[32] This study also examined coverage of what different sources said about the causes and effects of the topic studied: in this case, the 1987 stock market crash. The study also involved a census of the stories rather than a sample. The study found that fewer magazine stories were published on the crash than either national newspaper stories, local newspaper stories or television stories. Given these media's shorter production cycles, compared to magazines, it is not surprising that there were fewer magazine stories about the crisis. However, the magazine stories that were published contained significantly more sources per story. Also, the magazine stories included more independent sources and fewer anonymous sources, compared to the stories in other mass media. The magazines' ability to produce stories with better sources in terms both of quantity and quality may also be related to their longer production cycle, which generally allows them to dig deeper, longer.

Another study that could serve as a model for research about magazine sourcing is Shannon Martin's examination of the use of sources in breaking science stories across a variety of different types of magazines.[33] Interestingly, Martin, too, conducted a census rather than relying on a sample. Of course, there is nothing wrong with basing a study on a sample of content rather than a census; indeed, most studies use samples in order to cut down on the amount of work. As long as the sample is carefully taken, scholars can have a known confidence in the likelihood that the sample reflects what would be found in the entire corpus of material. Nonetheless, as the previously described studies well demonstrate, studies that delve into the specifics of the use of sources, rather than merely skimming the surface with an analysis, say, of how often a topic is mentioned, are likely to lead to better understanding if all the material is given a chance to inform the analysis. Martin's detailed analysis of the connections between which specific sources said which specific things in which specific magazines defied conventional wisdom, finding that science magazines did not use expert sources more than other kinds of magazines, and the readers of general newsmagazines could expect to be informed of major breaking science stories about as well as readers of specialized science magazines.

Finally, a study by Brian Thornton exemplifies an aspect of magazine sourcing given remarkably little attention in academic research: readers as sources.[34] The authors of letters to the editor represent sources of information in magazines that have received scant attention. Given that the new media ecosystem has encouraged the publication of user-generated content, this is a particularly relevant area of research. This analysis is also important to journalism and communication researchers because of the particular content that was studied: journalistic norms and practices observed in letters to the editor published in an array of 20 magazines.

Thornton compared letters about journalistic ethics in popular American magazines in the years 1902–1912 and 1982–1992. He found that letters about journalistic standards near the start of the twentieth century represented "a continuing debate among magazine readers over journalistic standards" but that toward the end of the century "the published debate among readers . . . shrunk dramatically and nearly disappeared."[35]

Cognizant of the problems of trying to explain this intriguing difference, Thornton identified possible explanations (e.g., perhaps today's magazine gatekeepers are more inclined to censor negative comments about them) and suggested why most of these explanations are not very convincing. Instead, Thornton showed how over time there has been a palpable "distancing of readers from journalists."[36] Letters from the earlier period, for example, were sometimes quite harsh in their criticisms, but the letters almost always also suggested that readers had a generally positive view about the role of magazines in society, a view that had all but disappeared by the end of the century, when readers, if they did comment on journalistic ethics, expressed considerable skepticism and cynicism about the general value of magazines to society. It seems as if readers have given up hope that magazines might help improve society, Thornton concluded, saying, "There is a supreme indifference evident . . . in the incredibly shrinking debate over journalistic standards in modern letters to the editor" in today's magazines.[37]

Promising Future Research

This leaves promising directions for future research. First and foremost, the existing body of research on magazines indicates we sorely need studies that give more than superficial attention to information sources. To anyone hoping to increase the quality of magazine scholarship, a good place to start is Sammye Johnson's essay on ways to conduct research that will offer clear, practical guidance to make magazines more valuable to readers and their communities.[38] In trying to establish what research questions to ask, why not consider asking questions the answers to which would help the magazine industry, audiences, subsidizers, sources and other stakeholders benefit meaningfully from the knowledge gained?

Further inspiration for anyone considering the study of magazine journalism comes from Abrahamson's notion of "magazine exceptionalism," which postulates that the magazine form is distinctly different from other media and therefore should be treated as such. In particular, Abrahamson maintained that while magazines and other mass media are products of and reflect the social reality of the times, magazines serve a larger and more pro-active function than do other media; that is, periodicals can also be a catalyst for change, significantly shaping the social reality of the culture of the times.[39]

In order to advance the study of magazine sourcing, in particular, magazine scholars should work on theoretically interesting ways to categorize sources. Consider, for example, the extent to which a source is partisan or not. Covert and Wasburn showed why scholars cannot assume that research findings based on nonpartisan magazines apply to partisan magazines, which have a distinctly different function from other magazines.[40] The same logic applies to partisan sources versus nonpartisan sources, which also have distinctly different functions. Given these different functions, how might different kinds of sources behave? That is just one intriguing area for future research on magazine sources.

Some studies look at the content of magazines in terms of their topics, without connecting it to the sources of that content. Such analyses can only go so far. What is needed are more studies like those highlighted in this chapter, which explore the deep connections between what topics are covered in what kinds of magazines, what positions are taken on these topics and who expresses those positions. This framework can be used to help better understand the role of magazines in society, whether they merely reflect or significantly influence culture, what magazines are like today and how they have changed over time.

Another area of magazine scholarship is the study of trends. Some of the best analyses of magazine journalism do an excellent job of exploring trends in magazine coverage of specific topics. Among these are Jennifer A. Schlenker, Sandra L. Caron and William A. Halteman's study of coverage of the feminist movement,[41] an update of Kate Peirce's equally insightful study,[42] and Christopher W. Podeschi's study of magazine coverage of the environmental movement over the second half of the twentieth century.[43] Even so, trend studies rarely have focused deeply on the sources used in magazine coverage, making this a particularly fertile territory for research.

From the examination of the existing body of research logically arise strategies for improving the study of information sources in magazines. One of the most exciting developments in this area of research may be the intrusion of non-professionals into the professional conversation. What does it mean to be a magazine writer, editor or publisher today, compared to a decade ago? Until recently, those without recognized journalistic credentials represented a group of mostly unheard of voices with little power to intrude upon the conversation. Now, through their own mass communication exploits and efforts, these non-professionals may be helping redefine not only what it means to be a magazine journalist but also the rules that apply to magazine journalists. Will magazine gatekeepers perhaps be more willing to open the gates wider to different kinds of sources? Might changes come in the kinds of sources used in magazines and other periodicals, or how sources or the rules of attribution are used?

Another intriguing question worth study is the extent to which magazine sources resemble magazine readers. Why would this matter? Might a magazine's success relate perhaps to how well its sources resemble its readers? This research would combine content analysis and readership studies. Likewise, to what extent do magazine sources resemble magazine editorial staffs? Such research would combine content analysis and production studies. As mentioned earlier, magazine production studies are a particularly promising area of research simply because so few such studies have been conducted to date. How does content come to be, specifically in terms of how sources are selected? An underused yet productive theoretical perspective for the study of magazine sources is Pamela J. Shoemaker and Stephen D. Reese's hierarchical factoring of the *influences on media content*, which easily could be adapted to the study of the layers of influence on media sources.[44]

Clearly, these are exciting times for those engaged in magazine scholarship, and, as has been seen here, opportunities to advance understanding of the use and effects of sources in magazines are abundant.

Notes

1 Wilbur Schramm, "Twenty Years of Journalism Research," [20th Anniversary Issue] *Public Opinion Quarterly* 21.1 (Spring 1957): 91–107.

2 Bernard Berelson and Patricia J. Salter, "Majority and Minority Americans: An Analysis of Magazine Fiction," *Public Opinion Quarterly* 10.2 (Summer 1946): 168–190.

3 Schramm, "Twenty Years of Journalism Research," 92.

4 Berelson and Salter, "Majority and Minority Americans," 168.

5 Leo Bogart, "Magazines Since the Rise of Television," *Journalism Quarterly* 33.2 (Spring 1956): 153–166.

6 David Abrahamson, ed., *The American Magazine: Research Perspectives and Prospects* (Ames: Iowa State University Press, 1995).

7 Sammye Johnson and Patricia Prijatel, *The Magazine from Cover to Cover*, 3rd ed. (New York and London: Oxford University Press, 2013).

8 Bill Mitchell, "Recasting the Anonymous Source as 'Exceptional Event,'" *MediaWire*, Poynter.org, 18 June 2004 <http://www.poynter.org/content/content_view.asp?id=67304>, accessed 30 November 2012.

9 Bill Kovach and Tom Rosenstiel, *Warp Speed: America in the Age of Mixed Media Culture* (New York: Century Foundation Press, 1999).

10 Dan Gillmor, "Where Did 'Citizen Journalist' Come From?" *Center for Citizen Media* (blog), 14 July 2008 <http://citmedia.org/blog/2008/07/14/where-did-citizen-journalist-come-from/>, accessed 7 March 2013.

11 Bill Kovach and Tom Rosenstiel, *The Elements of Journalism: What Newspeople Should Know and the Public Should Expect* (New York: Three Rivers Press, 2007).

12 Dominic L. Lasorsa, "Sources, Credibility of." *Encyclopedia of International Media and Communications*. vol. 4. Donald H. Johnston, ed. (San Diego, CA: Academic Press, 2003).

13 Lasorsa, "Sources."

14 David Abrahamson, "The Problem with Sources, a Source of the Problem," *Journal of Magazine & New Media Research* 9.1 (Fall 2006): 1–6.

15 Abrahamson, "The Problem with Sources," 4.

16 Lasorsa, "Sources."

17 Lasorsa, "Sources."

18 Andrew Beaujon, "The *New York Times* Bans Quote Approval," *MediaWire*, Poynter.org, 20 September 2012 <http://www.poynter.org/latest-news/mediawire/189170/the-new-york-times-bans-quote-approval.html>, accessed 1 October 2012.

19 Lasorsa, "Sources."

20 Beaujon, "*New York Times* Bans Quote Approval."

21 Beaujon, "*New York Times* Bans Quote Approval."

22 Dominic L. Lasorsa and Jia Dai, "Newsroom's Normal Accident? An Exploratory Study of 10 Cases of Journalistic Deception," *Journalism Practice* 1.2 (June 2007): 159–174.

23 Charles Seife, "Jonah Lehrer's Journalistic Misdeeds at Wired.com," *Slate.com*, 31 August 2012 <http://www.slate.com/articles/health_and_science/science/2012/08/jonah_lehrer_plagiarism_in_wired_com_an_investigation_into_plagiarism_quotes_and_factual_inaccuracies_.html>, accessed 11 November 2013.

24 Lasorsa and Dai, "Newsroom's Normal Accident?"

25 Seife, "Jonah Lehrer's Journalistic Misdeeds at Wired.com."

26 Evan Hansen, "Violations of Editorial Standards Found in *Wired* Writer's Blog," *Frontal Cortex* (blog), Wired.com, 31 August 2012 <http://www.wired.com/wiredscience/2012/08/violations-of-editorial-standards-found-in-wired-writers-blog/>, accessed 7 March 2013.

27 David Berreby, "We Want Good Journalistic Practices. We Just Don't Want to Pay for Them," BigThink.com, 5 September 2012 < http://bigthink.com/Mind-Matters/we-want-good-journalistic-practices-we-just-dont-want-to-pay-for-them>, accessed 7 March 2013.

28 Peter Gerlach, "Research about Magazines Appearing in *Journalism Quarterly*," *Journalism Quarterly* 64.1 (Spring 1987): 178–182; Marcia R. Prior-Miller and Kellie L. Esch, "A Census and Analysis of Journals Publishing Research about Magazines, 1977–1987" (paper presented at the Annual Meeting, Association for Education in Journalism and Mass Communication, August 1990).

29 Tawnya Adkins Covert and Philo C. Wasburn, "Information Sources and the Coverage of Social Issues in Partisan Publications: A Content Analysis of 25 Years of the *Progressive* and the *National Review*," *Mass Communication and Society* 10.1 (December 2007): 67–94.

30 Leon V. Sigal, *Reporters and Officials: The Organization and Politics of News Making* (Lexington, MA: D.C. Heath, 1973).

31 Covert and Wasburn, "Information Sources and the Coverage of Social Issues," 85.

32 Dominic L. Lasorsa and Stephen D. Reese, "News Source Use in the Crash of 1987: A Study of Four National Media," *Journalism Quarterly* 67.1 (Spring 1990): 60–71.

33 Shannon E. Martin, "Using Expert Sources in Breaking Science Stories: A Comparison of Magazine Types," *Journalism Quarterly* 68. 1/2 (Spring/Summer 1991): 179–187.

34 Brian Thornton, "The Disappearing Media Ethics Debate in Letters to the Editor," *Journal of Mass Media Ethics* 13.1 (November 1998): 40–55.

35 Thornton, "The Disappearing Media Ethics Debate," 51.

36 Thornton, "The Disappearing Media Ethics Debate," 50.

37 Thornton, "The Disappearing Media Ethics Debate," 49.

38 Sammye Johnson, "Why Should They Care? The Relationship of Academic Scholarship to the Magazine Industry," *Journalism Studies* 8.4 (August 2007): 522–528.

39 David Abrahamson, "Magazine Exceptionalism: The Concept, the Criteria, the Challenge," *Journalism Studies* 8.4 (July 2007): 667.

40 Covert and Wasburn, "Information Sources and the Coverage of Social Issues."

41 Jennifer A. Schlenker, Sandra L. Caron, and William A. Halteman, "A Feminist Analysis of *Seventeen* Magazine: Content Analysis from 1945 to 1995," *Sex Roles* 38.1/2 (January 1998): 135–149.

42 Kate Peirce, "A Feminist Theoretical Perspective on the Socialization of Teenage Girls through *Seventeen* Magazine," *Sex Roles* 23.9/10 (November 1990): 491–500.

43 Christopher W. Podeschi, "The Culture of Nature and the Rise of Modern Environmentalism: The View through General Audience Magazines, 1945–1980," *Sociological Spectrum* 27.3 (March 2007): 299–331.

44 Pamela J. Shoemaker and Stephen D. Reese, *Mediating the Message: Theories of Influence on Mass Media Content* (New York: Longman, 1996).

Bibliography

Abrahamson, David, ed. *The American Magazine: Research Perspectives and Prospects*. Ames: Iowa State University Press, 1995.

Abrahamson, David. "Magazine Exceptionalism: The Concept, the Criteria, the Challenge." *Journalism Studies* 8.4 (July 2007): 667–670.

Abrahamson, David. "The Problem with Sources, a Source of the Problem." *Journal of Magazine & New Media Research* 9.1 (Fall 2006): 1–6.

Beaujon, Andrew. "The *New York Times* Bans Quote Approval." *MediaWire*. Poynter.org, 20 September 2012 <http://www.poynter.org/latest-news/mediawire/189170/the-new-york-times-bans-quote-approval.html>, accessed 1 October 2012.

Berelson, Bernard and Salter, Patricia J. "Majority and Minority Americans: An Analysis of Magazine Fiction." *Public Opinion Quarterly* 10.2 (Summer 1946): 168–190.

Berreby, David. "We Want Good Journalistic Practices. We Just Don't Want to Pay for Them." BigThink.com, 5 September 2012 <http://bigthink.com/Mind-Matters/we-want-good-journalistic-practices-we-just-dont-want-to-pay-for-them>, accessed 7 March 2013.

Bogart, Leo. "Magazines Since the Rise of Television." *Journalism Quarterly* 33.2 (Spring 1956): 153–166.

Covert, Tawnya Adkins and Wasburn, Philo C. "Information Sources and the Coverage of Social Issues in Partisan Publications: A Content Analysis of 25 Years of the *Progressive* and the *National Review*." *Mass Communication and Society* 10.1 (December 2007): 67–94.

Gerlach, Peter. "Research about Magazines Appearing in *Journalism Quarterly*." *Journalism Quarterly* 64.1 (Spring 1987): 178–182.

Gillmor, Dan. "Where Did 'Citizen Journalist' Come From?" *Center for Citizen Media* (blog), 14 July 2008 <http://citmedia.org/blog/2008/07/14/where-did-citizen-journalist-come-from/>, accessed 7 March 2013.

Hansen, Evan. "Violations of Editorial Standards Found in *Wired* Writer's Blog." *Frontal Cortex* (blog). Wired.com, 31 August 2012 <http://www.wired.com/wiredscience/2012/08/violations-of-editorial-standards-found-in-wired-writers-blog/>, accessed 7 March 2013.

Johnson, Sammye. "Why Should They Care? The Relationship of Academic Scholarship to the Magazine Industry." *Journalism Studies* 8.4 (August 2007): 522–528.

Johnson, Sammye and Prijatel, Patricia. *The Magazine from Cover to Cover*. 3rd ed. New York and London: Oxford University Press, 2013.

Kovach, Bill and Rosenstiel, Tom. *The Elements of Journalism: What Newspeople Should Know and the Public Should Expect*. New York: Three Rivers Press, 2007.

Kovach, Bill and Rosenstiel, Tom. *Warp Speed: America in the Age of Mixed Media Culture*. New York: Century Foundation Press, 1999.

Lasorsa, Dominic L. "Sources, Credibility of." *Encyclopedia of International Media and Communications*. Vol. 4. Johnston, Donald H., ed. San Diego, CA: Academic Press, 2003.

Lasorsa, Dominic L. and Dai, Jia. "Newsroom's Normal Accident? An Exploratory Study of 10 Cases of Journalistic Deception." *Journalism Practice* 1.2 (June 2007): 159–174.

Lasorsa, Dominic L. and Reese, Stephen D. "News Source Use in the Crash of 1987: A Study of Four National Media." *Journalism Quarterly* 67.1 (Spring 1990): 60–71.

Martin, Shannon E. "Using Expert Sources in Breaking Science Stories: A Comparison of Magazine Types." *Journalism Quarterly* 68.1/2 (Spring/Summer 1991): 179–187.

Mitchell, Bill. "Recasting the Anonymous Source as 'Exceptional Event.'" *MediaWire*. Poynter.org, 18 June 2004 <http://www.poynter.org/content/content_view.asp?id=67304>, accessed 30 November 2012.

Peirce, Kate. "A Feminist Theoretical Perspective on the Socialization of Teenage Girls through *Seventeen* Magazine." *Sex Roles* 23.9/10 (November 1990): 491–500.

Podeschi, Christopher W. "The Culture of Nature and the Rise of Modern Environmentalism: The View through General Audience Magazines, 1945–1980." *Sociological Spectrum* 27.3 (March 2007): 299–331.

Prior-Miller, Marcia R. and Esch, Kellie L. "A Census and Analysis of Journals Publishing Research about Magazines, 1977–1987." Paper presented at the Annual Meeting, Association for Education in Journalism and Mass Communication, August 1990.

Schlenker, Jennifer A.; Caron, Sandra L.; and Halteman, William A. "A Feminist Analysis of *Seventeen* Magazine: Content Analysis from 1945 to 1995." *Sex Roles* 38.1/2 (January 1998): 135–149.

Schramm, Wilbur. "Twenty Years of Journalism Research." [20th Anniversary Issue] *Public Opinion Quarterly* 21.1 (Spring 1957): 91–107.

Seife, Charles. "Jonah Lehrer's Journalistic Misdeeds at Wired.com." *Slate.com*, 31 August 2012 <http://www.slate.com/articles/health_and_science/science/2012/08/jonah_lehrer_plagiarism_in_wired_com_an_investigation_into_plagiarism_quotes_and_factual_inaccuracies_.html>, accessed 11 November 2013.

Shoemaker, Pamela J. and Reese, Stephen D. *Mediating the Message: Theories of Influence on Mass Media Content.* New York: Longman, 1996.

Sigal, Leon V. *Reporters and Officials: The Organization and Politics of News Making.* Lexington, MA: D.C. Heath, 1973.

Thornton, Brian. "The Disappearing Media Ethics Debate in Letters to the Editor." *Journal of Mass Media Ethics* 13.1 (November 1998): 40–55.

6

BUSINESS-TO-BUSINESS MEDIA

The Informational Needs of Professional Life

Abe Peck

Business-to-business media, today more simply known as B2B, have long mirrored national economic development. Their modern history can be dated back to newsletters published by trading organizations such as the House of Fugger, starting in 1568,[1] and possibly even earlier, to trading reports in a German publication in Poland, *New Zeitung auss Linten (Recent News from Lithuania)*.[2] Since then, they have closely tracked emerging industries and professions. Pre-dating the establishment of the United States, *The South Carolina Price-Current* debuted in 1774,[3] and its successors have maintained an intimacy with the industries and professions they target. The *American Railroad Journal* appeared in 1832,[4] just two years after the first U.S. railway began service. *Aviation Week* [now *Aviation Week & Space Technology*], debuted in 1916,[5] 13 years after the Wright Brothers flew. *Computerworld* launched in 1967,[6] matching the deployment of mainframe computers; in 1980, a variant did the same thing in China[7]; *CIO* (chief information officer) *Africa* began to support tech-executive needs on that developing continent in 2004.[8]

These and thousands of other titles are more specific in their approach than such broadly circulated business titles as *Fortune* or *Bloomberg Business Week*. Rather, they narrowcast to bring key decision-makers and purchasers together through highly targeted content, when, where and how they want it. In 2014, ABM—The Association of Business Information & Media Companies—had 200 member companies and "an audience of more than 100 million professionals," whom those members reach via "nearly 4,000 print and on-line titles and over 1,000 trade shows. . . ."[9] That same year, Matt Kinsman, ABM's vice president, reported that MediaFinder.com put the total number of B2B titles at 6,044.[10]

At the same time, the recession of 2007 to 2010 had created a perfect economic storm, harming both the general consumer economy and more specifically major niches served by B2B: Housing construction was a prime example. Technological forces also disrupted B2B. An array of digital media—Webinars, on-line video, mobile, social media and user-generated content—came to enrich B2B's audience-focused mix, but at the expense of its business model. Higher-paying print ads gave way to less-lucrative digital counterparts—or no ads. Editors needed to expand their skill sets and do more with less. Sales efforts moved from *selling pages* to constructing *integrated packages* of bundled media. As B2B's cross-platform economic approach reassembled itself after the recession, many investors that had bought B2B companies at the top of the market sought to exit, with smaller publishers snapping up titles at bargain prices.

Even amid these rapid changes, B2B media remain important to readers, users and advertisers.[11] From describing how disasters such as Katrina affect their niches—the hurricane led to "the largest peacetime deployment of veterinarians in U.S. history," said Dan Verdon, editor of *DVM*, a newsmagazine for veterinarians[12]—to uncovering that many defibrillators in public places do not work,[13] its magazines and newspapers provide useful and thought-leadership information. B2B media's laser focus provides a major laboratory for audience understanding, and the frequency of stories breaking in B2B media before moving into general-media circulation alone would be a fruitful subject for comparative and agenda-setting studies. B2B titles also provide windows into issues of focus, multiple media platforms, staffing and ownership and, ironically, challenges from ever-more-precise competitors such as blogs, social media and the like.

This chapter analyzes how scholars have approached—or eschewed—an opportunity to explore a rich area that has many key facets left to examine.

A Word about Nomenclature

Terms for describing this kind of journalism have evolved over the years. One way to capture the shift is to look at how the leading association—the previously referenced ABM—has referred to itself over time. The Federation of Trade Press Associations was founded in 1906, when the word *press* covered both magazine and newspaper formats. Ten years later, the organization gave itself a perceived upgrade by renaming itself Associated Business Publications. In 1965, it became American Business Press, which it remained except for a brief stint as Association of Business Publications. In both cases, it used ABP as an acronym.[14] On a parallel path, editorial professionalization of the *trade press* and the continued need to differentiate the category from general business magazines led to the use of *specialized business publications* or the *specialized business press*.[15]

In 2000, as the first iteration of the Web began to transform companies whose ownership also included trade shows, databases and other ancillary activities, the organization became American Business Media. But as 2011 became 2012, ABM became the preferred usage. The change, ABM's Kinsman said, was made "to get away from the idea that ABM just represents ad-driven magazines (and create separation for the investment community, which considered 'media' a dirty word after the crash)."[16]

"Ironically," Kinsman continued, "'media' was included in the tagline about that same time," as it was changed from "the association of business information companies" to "the Association of Business Information & Media Companies."[17] Further evolution occurred in 2013, when ABM announced a merger with SIIA, the Software and Information Industry Association, while retaining its own acronym, at least for now. In any event, the sector is commonly known as "B2B," "b-2-b" or similar versions, such as B-to-B, of the acronym.

Literature Review and Method

In the introduction to her 1994 compilation *Trade, Industrial, and Professional Periodicals of the United States*, editor Kathleen L. Endres noted that "the specialized business press . . . [has], literally, played a role in shaping our trades, our industries, our businesses, our professions—our economic way of life."[18] Yet, Endres went on to say, the sector's "rich heritage" . . . is "albeit little known."[19]

Endres is not the only scholar to have flagged the relative neglect of and potential for research focusing on content-driven B2B media. David Sumner, for example, in his compilation of "Magazine-Related Articles" published over a period of 20 years in *Journalism and Mass Communication Quarterly*, found just 1 of 37 articles that concerned itself with a B2B topic: namely, Gerry Walter's 1996 "The Ideology of Success in Major American Farm Magazines,

1934–1991."[20] Similarly, Sumner's bibliography for *The Magazine Century: American Magazines since 1900* contained no dedicated titles covering B2B among its 80 or so citations.[21] A review of AEJMC Conference Paper Abstracts from 1997–2012 revealed just three of 215 papers dealt with B2B themes.[22] For the purposes of this chapter, unpublished papers are not included in the review.

Although no studies of the question were found in the literature, a number of factors may be contributing to this gap: (1) what Endres noted as "the lack of sources,"[23] and Dan Schiller identified as university and public libraries that do not include B2B periodicals in their collections[24]; (2) the specificity of B2B content, whose lingua franca for its professional decision-makers[25] may seem jargon-laden or arcane to academics outside the fields—and even more so to students who have not yet entered the workplace; and (3) B2B being omitted from magazine curricula that are shrinking to make room for ever-more digital instruction not tied to traditional media categories.

Terms such as *business to business, trade publications* and *B2B* were used to search scholars' bibliographies of research on the magazine form, including Google Scholar, the Communications Abstracts database and journal-retrieval services. The search provided a range of material on business-to-business media. The identified sources cover B2B as a journalistic and publishing sector and as a referent for studies of the larger society, in the United States and elsewhere. Although not exhaustive, the identified literature collectively certifies its importance even as it exposes coverage strengths and executional weaknesses.

Structurally, this chapter first notes books—practical rather than theoretical—on journalistic B2B media (as opposed to media generated by non-media companies, such as corporate or advertising agency Web sites). It then references a roster of academic publications. Unsurprisingly, a number of pieces involved media covering media (even if less specialized titles such as the *Columbia Journalism Review* are excluded). Perhaps more surprisingly, a fair amount of research has concentrated on agricultural journalism.

Research literature in 10 areas is then reviewed, with suggestions for ongoing study. In alphabetical order, these concentrations are as follows: (1) audience understanding and engagement; (2) content overview and analysis, including performance comparability with other media; (3) digital transformation; (4) ethics and professional values; (5) global media issues; (6) historical research (where a plurality of articles can be found); (7) management structure and strategies; (8) media economics; (9) staffing, including diversity issues; and (10) B2B and the general culture.

A concluding section restates areas for potentially fruitful research. A B2B Resource Guide appends industry sources of sufficient rigor that academics can draw on in this fertile, yet still under-researched, area.

Books about B2B

Book-length works of the past half-century have included David Forsyth's 1964 historical overview *The Business Press in America: 1750–1865*,[26] Don Gussow's 1984 *The New Business Journalism: An Insider's Look at the Workings of America's Business Press*[27] and Edgar Grunwald's *The Business Press Editor*.[28] Endres noted that several of these figures were business press employees, not academicians: Forsyth, an in-house researcher and consultant; Grunwald as a B2B editor.[29] Frank Luther Mott's encyclopedic five-volume *A History of American Magazines* seated specialized business publications within the larger magazine tradition,[30] but over the period covered by the previous titles, consumer and specialized business titles moved to opposite sides of the magazine aisle.

The pace of publishing books on business-to-business issues picked up in the 1990s. William Fisher's *Business Journals of the United States* appeared in 1991, with mini-profiles of more than 100 publications. These included specialized publications, magazines that covered business for members of the general population and scholarly journals that focused on business research.[31] In 1992, Sal Marino, a CEO of the large specialized business company Penton Publishing (now Penton Media), drew on his significant industry experience for his *Business Magazine Publishing*, which concentrated on the management side of the publishing enterprise.[32]

In 1994, Kathleen Endres recruited a national professorial team that profiled close to 100 key titles to "provide a cross section of the specialized business press."[33] The studies contained valuable insights into the workings of what were then known as specialized business publications, as well as comments on their impact on society. Endres simultaneously recapitulated the available academic research in this area, publishing "Research Review: The Specialized Business Press," first in *The Electronic Journal of Communication/La Revue Electronic de Communication* and again as a chapter in David Abrahamson's *The American Magazine: Research Perspectives and Prospects*.[34] The chapter's bibliography remains useful today, including as a backdrop to this chapter.

Patrick Clinton also took a tactical approach when he produced 1997's *Guide to Writing for the Business Press*[35] in conjunction with what was then called the American Business Press. Clinton, who was teaching in the Magazine Publishing Project at Northwestern's Medill School of Journalism, offered nuanced discussion of story genres. He subsequently became an award-winning editor at *Pharmaceutical Executive*, a B2B title known for its thought leadership and interviews with C-suite executives.

Another compilation of industry knowledge, *Best Practices of the Business Press*, appeared in 2005 under the imprimatur of the B2B organization American Society of Business Publication Editors. Edited by Robert Freedman, the book featured case-study chapters by nearly a score of figures with industry experience across publishing functions.[36] Topics ran from technical editing to trade shows. Just one chapter covered Web publications—a tsunami then just over the horizon.[37]

This mini-bookshelf suggests two observations. First, titles clustered around the phrase *business press*, a philosophic upgrade from the previous *trade press* that nevertheless blurred with general-business titles, such as *Forbes* or *Fortune*. Second, words such as *press* and *publication* would become outmoded as cross-platform media supplanted print-only periodicals. As with ABM's contraction, the American Society of Business Publication Editors dropped *publication* in favor of *press* and then settled on ASBPE in the hope that the acronym would prove both more durable and less complicated.

Finally, nearly all these titles approached B2B, not from a social scientific or cultural theoretical point of view, but rather from practitioner perspective: what mass communication scholar and theorist Denis McQuail would call working or *operational theory*, which, he notes, at times overlaps with *normative theory* "in matters of journalistic ethics and codes of practice."[38]

Audience Understanding and Engagement

The redefinition of the audience-producer relationship—more knowledge about audiences, more ways to reach them, more audiences active in content dialog, varied behavior when using search, tablets, mobile and other formats—requires full understanding of how, when and in what sequence audiences receive information. Surveys of users and creators in key categories (thought-leader, product-oriented, etc.) could be of value.

One effort to gain audience understanding involved the magazine-reader experience studies conducted by the Media Management Center (MMC) at Northwestern University <http://www.mediamanagementcenter.org/research/magazineexperience.asp>. Maximizing content *touch points* around a lexicon of quantifiable experiences increases media engagement, according to in-depth analysis of reader reactions to magazines (and also newspapers, broadcast and on-line media). The magazine study concentrated on consumer titles, but the Utilitarian experience[39] has been applied to B2B in executive seminars and consulting. Fifteen professors at the

Medill School of Journalism, Media, Integrated Marketing Communications discuss multiple experiences in the book, *Medill on Media Engagement*, that describes this effort.[40]

Behavioral targeting is a key goal for B2B companies now seeking to gain deeper insights into audience mindsets and use those findings with readers and marketers alike.[41] This interest area can be studied as it begins to heat up. Researchers can play a role in assessing aspects of it, such as B2B's own policing of privacy rights and intersections with consumer and government initiatives around privacy.[42]

Content Analysis and Performance Comparability

An organizational framework is important for understanding B2B, which differs from its consumer-magazine counterpart. In research published in 1995, Marcia Prior-Miller examined scholars' classification of magazines in more than 200 research reports published between 1977 and 1991. Prior-Miller found that scholars who used labels that described these titles by the function the editorial content was designed to serve provided the greatest clarity and explanatory power—thus the *trade* or *professions* the magazines covered.[43] Twenty years later, based on teaching a matrix that retained Prior-Miller's *industry* and *professional* terms, *thought leadership* and *product-centric coverage*, with *search-specific* and *social/community* emerged in this author's experience as important on-line characteristics for this sector. Contemporary examinations could explore the evolution between these category sets and explore where coverage might be going.

As with other journalistic sectors, content quality can vary widely within B2B media. How editors sort this out and what obstacles they face in doing so are important areas for surveys and other studies. At their worst, stories simply restate vendor releases or favor advertisers without even labeling the source. At its best, B2B journalism serves and leads readers or users, sets agendas, defends and challenges the bedrock precepts of a given niche, provides product information efficiently and anticipates the need for valid and valuable thought leadership. For years after the 9/11 attacks, *Engineering News Record* brought expertise to the destruction and reconstruction of the World Trade Center.[44] *IEEE Spectrum* captured the dysfunction of the Iraqi power grid.[45] "Red Gold Rush: The Copper Theft Epidemic," an enterprise story and on-line slideshow produced by *CSO* (*Chief Security Officer*), traced homeless people stealing copper wire in Detroit back to China's insatiable need for raw materials.[46]

A pair of scholarly journal articles provided the frame for "Narrative and Values: The Rhetoric of the Physician Assisted Suicide Debate." In her 2000 article, Deborah Dysart argued that seminal stories—the controversial "It's Over, Debbie," from the *Journal of the American Medical Association*, and "Death and Dignity: A Case of Individualized Decision Making," from the *New England Journal of Medicine*—demonstrated rhetoric's importance as a corollary to the scientific enterprise of medicine.[47]

With advertising traditionally comprising as much as 60 percent of print B2B magazines, their appearance and effectiveness is crucial. Professor and advertising practitioner Robert Chamblee and researcher Dennis Sandler analyzed ads from three titles across four dependent variables in "Business-to-Business Advertising: Which Layout Style Works Best?"[48] That was in 1992: The expanding areas of design—editorial and ad content; print, Web, mobile—remain ripe for study.

Magazine Writing, a 2014 book authored by Christopher Benson and Charles Whitaker, outlines the B2B realm in a chapter titled "B2B: The Ultimate in Service Journalism."[49] It covers what makes a good B2B article and offers career advice for entering the field. *Service journalism* is a term more often affiliated with consumer-magazine journalism, but the aptness of its use here suggests that comparisons with more familiar categories may spark research.

B2B's niche precision offers ample opportunity for comparing titles within or along the audience's value chain. One might follow content approaches from, say, an oil extraction magazine through refining, distribution, service station fueling and recycling titles. Or one might explore different treatments by head-to-head competitors: Say the rise of (now-digital) step-by-step coverage for hair stylists in both *Modern Salon* and *American Salon*.

The positives and negatives of B2B's niche intimacy have occasionally been explored in academic journals. For 2006's "How Do Trade Media Influence Green Building Practice?" Pernilla Gluch and Ann-Charlotte Stenberg conducted a quantitative content analysis and a qualitative text analysis of 1,324 articles in Swedish "construction trade magazines."[50] Gluch and Stenberg told a cautionary tale:

> The majority of trade magazine articles transmit information that lacks objectivity and critical reflection, thus reinforcing the idea that environmental challenges could be solved by technical solutions and/or controlling measures. Moreover, the protection of the natural environment is rarely referred to as a motive for pro-environmental behavior. Consequently, since practitioners are not encouraged to problematize environmental aspects, they may end up accepting the simplified version presented to them by the trade press.[51]

However, Philip Napoli found greater success in B2B's ability to provide information at a higher level than produced by the general press. For his 1997 publication, "The Media Trade Press as Technology Forecaster: A Case Study of the VCR's Impact on Broadcasting," Napoli examined how well the broadcasting and advertising trade press performed in their roles as technology forecaster, using the introduction of the VCR and its potential impact on broadcasting as a case study. The verdict? "The advertising trade press proved much more active and much more accurate in forecasting the future of the VCR."[52]

Perhaps splitting the difference, C. Ann Hollifield "compared coverage of an industry-related policy proposal, the National Information Infrastructure, by the communication-industry trade press, non-communication-industry trade press and newspapers."[53] Her 1997 analysis

> . . . Found that trade media appear to function as an insider channel of communication in the early stages of industry related policy processes, but that they are less likely than non-industry-related media to cover the social implications of industry policy proposals.[54]

Finally, trade shows, conferences and other events now generate as much revenue in B2B as does traditional journalism; they also increasingly spark content ideas and social media threads. Research on trade shows as communication tools, including collaboration with the associations that provide leadership in the field, such as SISO, the Society of Independent Show Organizers,[55] could be fruitful.

Digital Transformation

As in so many areas, the rise of digital media continues to affect communication at warp speed. Yet the extent to which the change is disruptive or empowering in B2B communication has yet to be explored. How major B2B magazines have capitalized on, been disaggregated by and otherwise responded to the Internet, social media and other new digital technologies offers ample evidence to parse. Digital transformation has also birthed new forms of B2B communication: blogs, chat, video, interactive tools, e-commerce. The potential of search functions to either link B2B buyers and sellers or sap the business model of legacy media deserves academic scrutiny.

Some work already has been done. In his 2003 research, "e-Newspaper: Consumer Demands on Attributes and Features," Markus Zinnbauer examined yet another emerging technology. Zinnbauer postulated that consumers would readily adapt to "e-paper" should it be deployed.[56] David Lucking-Reiley and Daniel F. Spulber have looked at e-commerce in the business-to-business setting.[57] Again, the rapid growth in this area argues for scholarly exploration and definition.

Ethics and Professional Values

With close ties to products and services, and with advertising, search and events providing the bulk of revenue, B2B titles can feel pressure on editorial independence. The expansion of digital advertising and its lower dollar payments are spurring a search for paid content—and the growth of what has been called *content marketing*. The practice raises questions about whether new avenues of closeness to the market will hamper press independence or provide audience insight and new revenue for deeper reporting?

There is a scholarly base for this exploration: "Sixty-two percent of farm journalists reported receiving pressure from advertisers, while about half said that advertising had actually been withdrawn on occasion."[58] This finding from Robert G. Hays and Ann E. Reisner's 1991 study, "Farm Journalists and Advertiser Influence: Pressures on Ethical Standards," can be explored in other niches, across media and over time.

Some companies, however, have turned editorial integrity into a competitive advantage. Paul Sullivan's 1974 exploration of the principles behind taking the high road—"G.D. Crain and the Founding of 'Advertising Age',", in *Journalism History*—noted Crain's "insistence of editorial quality and integrity"[59] from the 1930 launch onward:

> Unlike other trade publications, which were basically public relations outlets for the businesses they served, *Advertising Age* was based on hard news, investigative reporting and informative columns. Crain was a consumer activist before Ralph Nader was born, and he turned away thousands of dollars of advertising rather than let outside interests influence the editorial content of his magazine.[60]

Back then, as Sullivan notes, "'trade journal' was used as a slur."[61]

Fortunately, Crain's reputation endures at Crain Communications, *Ad Age*'s parent company: Each year ABM gives a leading B2B figure the Crain Award, a lifetime-achievement recognition for embodying editorial standards. Sullivan's journal article shows the value of examining publishing culture over time as an underpinning of quality. Scholars can also dismiss any initial aversion to mercantile editorial and examine how B2B titles negotiate coverage of products from companies that may be advertisers or whose staffs are readers. Testing is expensive, but some publications have columnists try the products; others compare specifications or they publish or post reader comments to convey value.

ASBPE's ethics committee updates its editorial standards, posts advisories[62] and offers a dialog for explorations of independence and integrity. Inversely, B2B titles can be used to study other media's professionalism. In 1987, Susan Caudill, Ed Caudill and Michael W. Singletary analyzed 60 years of ads in *Editor & Publisher*, the magazine that covered the business of newspapers. "Journalists Wanted: Trade-Journal Ads as Indicators of Professional Values" showed that hirers were "more concerned with journalism skills than with professional values."[63] How has this changed as media have become more technological?

Global Media Issues

This chapter draws on material from Australia, China, Germany, Israel, The Netherlands, Sweden, the United Kingdom and the United States, demonstrating that targeted industry-professional coverage is desired worldwide. Many B2B titles have international editions, with *Computerworld* likely leading with a claimed 16 million readers in 47 countries.[64] Global B2B brands can offer opportunities to compare technological dispersion, through adoption and diffusion studies. Scholars of rising business sectors in places such as the Middle East and Africa might use emerging B2B media to benchmark development.

In 2003, Jixiang Wang published the chapter "Scientific, Technical, Medical and Professional Publishing" in *The Publishing Industry in China*, edited by Robert E. Baensch. Wang's historical review noted Chinese innovations from publishing on paper to medical encyclopedias and the country's revived interest in these areas, then outlined the landscape for *STM* publishing via a voluminous table listing all known category publishers as of 2001 and the size of their efforts. The rise in technical and professional activity in China makes it worthwhile for a B2B researcher to update and further analyze the data provided in this benchmark table.[65]

The work of J. Ronald Milavsky in the *International Journal of Advertising* shows how researchers can elucidate or close some of the gaps cited at the start of this chapter. Seeking to "describe the studies becoming available to the international marketer for guidance," Milavsky scrutinized more than 800 scholarly journals and trade publications and located 130 articles that offered an international perspective on mass media or advertising. In his 1993 publication, "Recent Journal and Trade Publication Treatments of Globalization in Mass Media Marketing and Social Change,"[66] Milavsky reported that a multi-dimensional analysis had shown those publications to be news-oriented, general, often unsubstantiated, Eurocentric and not based on primary data. "Empirical studies of the success or failure in the use of media or advertising in global marketing, necessary to provide guidance to international marketers, were virtually absent from the body of scholarly research published in the two years studied."[67] Replicating Milavsky's study could determine whether both practitioners and researchers have addressed these gaps over the past 20 years.

Investigators have examined B2B media to understand cross-cultural communications. In one such study, Ulf Jonas Bjork used trade journals from his homeland for both a 1995 study, "'The Backbone of Our Business': American Films in Sweden, 1910–50"[68] and a 2001 follow-up, "'Have Gun, Will Travel': Swedish Television and American Westerns, 1959–1969."[69] Lighter subjects also have proved instructive. Lynette S. McCullough and Ronald K. Taylor explored "Humor in American, British, and German Ads."[70] Analyzing the content of more than 600 ads from trade magazines in those three countries, they found that almost a quarter of the ads contained humor, with the kinds of humor varying more by industry than by country.

On the organizational side, FIPP, the International Federation of the Periodical Press <http://www.fipp.com>, includes B2B publishers among its members and references national B2B organizations. FIPP produces *Magazine World* magazine and the annual *FIPP Magazine Trends*, *FIPP World Media Factbook* and *FIPP Magazines World Report*. While primarily consumer-magazine oriented, the annual FIPP World Magazine Conference includes sessions of interest to B2B practitioners that often capture local societal and publishing conditions different from those in Europe and North America.

FIPP also holds an annual Research Forum, which is described at fipp.com:

> The key objectives of the Forum are to discuss a number of topics identified by FIPP's Research Committee as the most pressing current magazine media research issues; to enable participants to debate, compare notes and learn from each other's recent experience, to the benefit of everyone's work; and for FIPP to circulate the key points, to help improve magazine research around the world.[71]

Papers are discussed at the annual event, which in 2014 was to be held 16–17 June in Hamburg. FIPP's Research Awards also are given to qualitative or quantitative papers that "deal with any aspects(s) of the power of magazine media" and "have been first published during the previous calendar year."[72] Few entries in the competition have covered B2B topics, and there is no insistence on peer-reviewed material, but it could be worthwhile to check with FIPP going forward, or to attend the event for insights into research by "some of the world's leading magazine research professionals, who meet to discuss the latest issues and developments in the industry worldwide."[73]

Historical Appraisals

Of the 10 categories for research delineated in this chapter, history has most frequently been in the academic researcher's wheelhouse. Various explorations crosscut historical analysis with factors closely associated with B2B, then and now. An early historical study, "The Genesis of the Business Press in the United States," appeared in *The Journal of Marketing* in 1954.[74] In it, Roland B. Smith established the need for specialized professional and industrial publications (as well as scientific journals) to chart "the complexity and magnitude of American economic and cultural development"[75] up to 1850. John Bidwell, in his 1977 research, "*The Engraver and Printer*, a Boston Trade Journal of the Eighteen Nineties," provided a case study of an early business-to-business publication.[76]

Media-about-media research has included how *trade magazines* home in on highly specific audiences. In "Doing the Biz: Book-Trade and News-Trade Periodicals in the 1890s," Laurel Brake charted how new titles captured changes in the book-business audience "to supplement more generic and established"[77] periodicals.

Farm publications have lent themselves to several scholarly approaches: (a) *The genre itself*: Donald B. Marti, in his 1980 research, "Agricultural Journalism and the Diffusion of Knowledge: The First Half-Century in America," charted how this sector came to rely on expertise from sources, editors and a changing concept of the audience.[78] Stuart W. Shulman studied a later period in his 1999 "The Progressive Era Farm Press: A Primer on a Neglected Source of Journalism History"[79]; (b) *Impact and regionalism*: In their 1978 "Regional Patterns of Farm Magazine Publication," Stanley D. Brunn and Karl B. Raitz studied the "vital ingredient in agricultural decision making"[80] represented by U.S. farm publications, especially as technology, marketing and capital literally transformed the landscape. They also noted how these magazines dispersed geographically to serve farmers nationwide; and (c) *Personalities*: Joseph A. Coté profiled the man behind *Progressive Farmer*, a large-circulation title especially important in Southern farming, in 1979's "Clarence Hamilton Poe: The Farmer's Voice, 1899–1964."[81]

A contrarian finding came from Sharienne Sweeney and C. Ann Hollifield. In "Influence of Agricultural Trade Publications on the News Agendas of National Newspapers and News Magazines," they "found more evidence that agricultural trade publications' news agendas were influenced by the reporting in the national newspapers than the reverse."[82] The specialized titles' "greater topical expertise,"[83] they said, yielded to the mass magazines' organizational resources and readership of investors. This yin-yang deserves greater examination.

B2B also has reflected social and political attitudes. Jeff Rutenbeck found that "newspaper trade journals provide promising locales for studying . . . the transition from partisanship to independence" of American newspapers, and discussed this in 1994's "The Triumph of News over Ideas in American Journalism: The Trade Journal Debate, 1872–1915."[84] Pama A. Mitchell showed in 1994 how periodicals covering media "cracked badly under the pressure of McCarthyism" and "fell in line with the prevailing hysteria."[85]

Of course, one cannot research what is not there. A 1989 survey of three academic libraries by Dan Schiller showed "a dramatic decrease in the proportion of telecommunications titles during a time when these publications were increasing in number and price, suggesting that the research library-centered information system was being bypassed."[86] Retrospective issues of B2B titles can fill some gaps because they often chart the twin evolution of niche and title. *Restaurants & Institutions*, a once-dominant title serving the broad foodservice industry, was, in the words of publisher David Wexler, nothing less than "a mirror of the change from food at home to food away from home."[87] An anniversary issue tied the changing nature of restaurants to such social factors as the development of the interstate highway system. Jean

Russel Moss's 1987 Iowa dissertation, "Walking the Tightrope: The Story of Nursing as Told by Nineteenth-Century Nursing Journals," was a scholarly treatment of the same linkage.[88]

Studying industry awards might also enrich historical, content and longitudinal appraisals. ABM's Jesse Neal Awards[89] are the *Oscars* of B2B. The Neal Awards celebrated their sixtieth year in 2014 and thus are a record of the evolution of B2B media and the issues these publications cover. The AZBEE Awards—sponsored by ASBPE—offer a similar pool of titles for consideration.[90] *Folio* (known for its industry-monitoring magazine) and MIN (with a flagship newsletter) judge both B2B and consumer categories and host conferences.

Structures and Strategies

Basic publishing structure differs on the B2B side. Eighty percent or more of B2B titles use *controlled circulation*: They provide their magazines free of charge to purchasing decision-makers or thought leaders, with much preference given to *qualifying* reader interest and offering advertisers an audience that *specifies* and purchases their products. Consequently, the erstwhile lay reader of *Waste Management* would be considered *waste circulation* and would not be issued a subscription. Such specificity also leads to only a comparatively few *straddle* titles being found on newsstands: for example, *Advertising Age*, city business magazines and *Variety* (which in 2013 morphed from a daily newspaper into a weekly magazine). Some on-line B2B titles even block general audiences so professionals can speak freely without *end users* looking over their virtual shoulders (e.g., veterinarians and pet owners).

In 1988, Endres studied "Ownership and Employment In Specialized Business Press."[91] A generation later, The Netherlands was the venue for a 2005 review of several B2B sectors by Richard van der Wurff. In "Business Magazine Market Performance: Magazines for the Agricultural, Business Services, and Transportation Sectors in the Netherlands," van der Wurff said that "business magazines provide need to know information to decision makers and professionals," and then investigated how competition, revenue ratios between advertising and subscriptions and publisher type determined "price, product variety, and diversity of business magazines."[92]

Organizational study can take a more *meta* approach. "The Roots of Uncertainty in Organization Theory: A Historical Constructivist Analysis"—Yehouda Shenhav and Ely Weitz's 2000 research—used primary data from the *American Machinist* and *Engineering* magazines to show how the idea of *uncertainty* spread from the technical side to organization management and how social context from 1879 to 1932 also affected discourse.[93]

Today, a range of operational concerns can be explored: (a) the optimal timing for information distribution to various multiplatform audiences; (b) whether moving from *editors* to *channel managers* privileges technocracy over journalism; (c) the erosion of editorial independence per both pressure from advertisers and agencies' increasing ability to generate their own custom media; and (d) the new rules and regulations of social media and of digital formats such as mobile and what is now known as *big data*. Also, are Web site metrics being used as a god or a guide for content planning? When do channel managers *go against the data* to use their own market intelligence and try new coverage areas that may not yet be quantifiable? Do publishers obstruct such exploration for short-term profit or encourage innovation? What is privacy today?

Media Economics

The B2B revenue mix is undergoing significant shifts, which offer opportunities for scholarly exploration. In 2012, total revenue for U.S. business-to-business media and information companies was put at $25.68 billion, according to ABM's Business Information Network (BIN) figures published in February 2014. Revenue in the third quarter of 2013 was put at $6.57 billion, a 4.9 percent increase compared with the third quarter of 2012. "The growth was driven by digital brands, primarily on-line advertising revenue, which surged 21 percent compared with the third quarter of 2012, and increased 4.2 percent compared with the second quarter of 2013," the report said. "Events and data and business information also saw solid growth for the quarter. Data revenue rose 7.2 percent . . . Event revenue rose 4.4 percent, while revenue from print advertising fell 4.7 percent."[94] Following cross-media revenue shifts and their effects on how content is produced and distributed will be of continuing interest for researchers into media strategy.

As noted earlier, ownership patterns have led to corporate consolidation. In his 2005 study, "Economic Concentration in Agricultural Magazine Publishing: 1993–2002,"[95] Mark W. Stuhlfaut studied potential restraints on an agricultural niche that had many magazines but was showing moderate ownership concentration. After the 2007 recession, though, small companies snapped up titles at sharply discounted prices as giant publishers exited traditional B2B media. In 2013 yet another round of mergers and acquisitions began. These cycles bear assessment.

Other relevant questions around B2B media economics include the following: How have format and ownership trends affected the ability to serve and lead audiences? How does equity firms' desire to maximize profit affect B2B journalism—positively through funding of potentially lucrative brand extensions and effective staff reallocation or negatively through cuts to the bone? And how can small but aggressive companies find capital for expansion?

Staffing Issues and Diversity

Across post-recession media, shrinking staffs are dealing with growing multimedia tasks. A 2009 collaboration between ASBPE's Robin Sherman and Northwestern University's Media Management Center's Abe Peck and Bob LeBailly surveyed 273 B2B editors about their digital skills and their company's training and strategies. The results were daunting: "B2B editors have been left largely to their own devices to gain the skills necessary to do their jobs across platforms."[96]

B2B also provides a window on traditional research disciplines such as gender studies. In 1987, Dennis W. Jeffers presented "A Descriptive Study of Perceived Impact of Gender on Employment Status, Type of Work, Industry Relationships, Working Environment and Job Satisfaction in Livestock Industry Magazines."[97] Jeffers examined 59 mastheads of Australian livestock titles and questioned 69 men and women to ascertain employment patterns, job satisfaction and promotion opportunities. Respondents liked the work, but underestimated the situation, namely that "Discrepancies between promotion, salary, and pay raise trends for men and women were serious . . . "[98]

After his 2012 retirement as a professor at the Scripps School at Ohio University, Joseph Bernt recalled his 1995–1996 report on a B2B shortfall:

> I did do a conference paper on race/gender images in a sample of about 300 B2B titles in the mid-1990s that showed outrageous under-representation of the usual suspects in the face of all the "workforce 2000" talk at the time. Basically the conclusion was that B2B should look to include content and images of more young, more black, more Asian, more Hispanic and lots more women as a means of keeping their titles from falling into waste-baskets rather than being passed around the office or read religiously. Essentially I was interested in diversity as competitive advantage—more diversity should put your title ahead of the competition in terms of perceived value.[99]

While women are now better represented, they are only starting to push through a top-management glass ceiling. And the presence of people of color remains woeful. Benchmark, content and organization studies all could be valuable.

B2B and General Culture

Content analysis of B2B titles has been useful in analyzing elements of popular culture. Anthony Hill, for his book *Pages from the Harlem Renaissance*, used "J. A. Jackson's Page" in *Billboard* as a fulcrum to explore the intersection of black performance and national and cultural concerns of the 1920s.[100] Decades later, a very different culture also intersected with the pages of B2B. As citizen's-band radios spread along America's highways, W. Dale Dannefer and Nicholas Poushinsky based their 1979 analysis, "The C.B. Phenomenon, A Sociological Appraisal,"[101] on not only a cross-country trip and monitoring chat but also the examination of seven previous years of *Overdrive*, a leading magazine for truckers. This content helped connect C.B. proliferation to protests over high diesel-fuel prices. C.B.s were used to organize deliberate traffic jams; letters, articles and editorials outlined the dispute and rallied the convoys.

Prior-Miller notes that the "Unit 8O Editorial Treatment of Non-Magazine Media and Communication Technologies" in her bibliography[102] includes "quite a few studies for which B2B titles are *core data* sources."[103] The Bjork study on Swedish television and American Westerns, cited previously, is among these.

> These studies suggest to me an untapped treasure for studies that could be done on B2B media. . . . For example, how do B2B publications in apparel and fashion portray women, compared with what studies have found about their portrayal in consumer magazines. . . . Are male and female models super thin? How are sports and athletes treated? Ethnic group representation? The list is long. If the same, how are they setting the agenda for the other?[104]

How women are portrayed in B2B is in fact a substantive issue.

Analyzing an historic depiction of women in *Broadcasting Magazine*, James C. Foust and Katherine A. Bradshaw found in their 1997 research, "Something for the Boys: Framing Images of Women in *Broadcasting* Magazine in the 1950s," "that positive portrayals of women as professionals were heavily outweighed in the magazine by stereotypical portrayals with far more scantily clad models appearing than female station managers."[105]

Sexism re-appeared Down Under in 1989's "Gender-Role Stereotypes in Australian Farm Advertising."[106] J.H. Bell and U.S. Pandey parsed ads in *The Land*, a leading farm magazine, and learned the role of women in family farms was underestimated. More recently, in 2004, Endres chronicled how an opinion-leader title related (or failed to relate) to changing times. In "Help-Wanted Female: *Editor & Publisher* Frames a Civil Rights Issue," Endres used the magazine's coverage of Title VII of the Civil Rights Act from 1964 to 1973 to show how the "sex amendment and its women supporters were trivialized and delegitimized in the frames crafted by *Editor & Publisher*."[107] Too much sexism—but grist for the willing researcher.

Conclusion

This chapter has essayed to explore areas where research has and can be fruitful. It has touched on intimate audience relationships, the changing scope of the B2B sector as it plunges into a multimedia world, the pros and cons of its content and content types, ethical concerns surrounding market proximity, global reach and national and cross-cultural B2B, B2B as a tool for historical and popular culture examinations, staffing, management and economics, and B2B's relationship to popular culture.

Within a perceived lack of research, it has found studies worldwide on B2B and its media effects. At the same time, B2B's dynamism suggests that far more can be done. B2B is paralleling momentous technological shifts. Clean energy has led to magazines such as *GreenSource* and *EcoHome*—and an opportunity to see how more traditional B2B magazines advance or retard energy shifts in their pages and on their Web sites. How do staffs that are still woefully undiverse prove relevance in a multi-cultural world? Perhaps studies are gestating. Perhaps this chapter can assist in tomorrow's efforts.

Notes

1 University of North Carolina at Chapel Hill School of Journalism and Mass Communication. "1500s–1800s: History of Business Journalism." <http://www.bizjournalismhistory.org/main_frame.htm>, accessed 29 May 2014.

2 Jim Bernhard, *Porcupine, Picayune, and Post: How Newspapers Get Their Names* (Columbia: University of Missouri Press, 2007), 38.

3 David P. Forsyth, *The Business Press in America, 1750–1865* (Philadelphia: Chilton Books, 1964), 20, as quoted in Kathleen L. Endres, "Research Review: The Specialized Business Press," in David Abrahamson, ed., *The American Magazine: Research Perspectives and Prospects* (Ames: Iowa State University Press, 1995), 72–83. The chapter is based on Kathleen L. Endres, "Research Review: The Specialized Business Press," *Electronic Journal of Communication / La Revue Electronic de Communication* 4.2/4 (1994) <http://www.cios.org/EJCPUBLIC/004/2/004211.html>, accessed 12 May 2013.

4 Forsyth, *The Business Press in America*, 178.

5 *SRDS Business Media Advertising Source*, part 1, vol. 95 (Des Plaines, IL: Kantar /SRDS/Standard Rate and Data Service, 2013), s.v. "Aviation Week & Space Technology."

6 *SRDS Business Media Advertising Source*, s.v. "Computerworld."

7 "*China Computerworld* Online," IDG—International Data Group <http://careers.idg.com/www/IDG-Products.nsf/ByKey/People's-Republic-of-China_WebSite_China-Computerworld-Online>, accessed 29 May 2014.

8 *Ulrich's Periodicals Directory 2014*, vol. 1, 52nd ed. (New Providence, NJ: ProQuest, 2013), s.v. "CIO Africa."

9 "About ABM." ABM—The Association of Business Information & Media Companies <http://www.abmassociation.com/abm/About.asp>, accessed 14 January 2014.

10 Matt Kinsman, e-mail to author, 22 April 2013.

11 Michael Moran Alterio, "Print Advertising Down in August, but Select Verticals Show Life," ABM—The Association of Business Information & Media Companies, 5 December 2012 <http://www.abmassociation.com/News/2936/Print-ad-sales-continue-downward-trend>, accessed 25 January 2013.

12 Dan Verdon, editor of *DVM Newsmagazine* (speech given at the Medill School of Journalism, Northwestern University, Evanston, IL, 5 February 2009).

13 Mark Harris, "A Shocking Truth," *IEEE Spectrum*, March 2012, 30–34, 57–58 <http://www.americanbusinessmedia.com/abm/C1A_Shocking_Truth.asp>, accessed 14 January 2014.

14 Debbie Humphreys, e-mail to author, 17 May 2013.

15 Endres, "Research Review," 1995: 72.

16 Kinsman, e-mail to author, 27 February 2014.

17 Kinsman, e-mail to author, 27 February 2014.

18 Kathleen L. Endres, *Trade, Industrial, and Professional Periodicals of the United States* (Westport, CT and London: Greenwood Press, 1994), vii.

19 Endres, *Trade, Industrial, and Professional Periodicals*, vii–viii.

20 Gerry Walter, "The Ideology of Success in Major American Farm Magazines, 1934–1991," *Journalism & Mass Communication Quarterly* 73.3 (Autumn 1996): 594–608, cited in David E. Sumner, "Magazine-Related Articles in *Journalism Mass Communications Quarterly* 1990–2010," <http://davidabrahamson.com/WWW/MAG2/Sumner_JMCQ_Magazine_Bibliography.pdf>, accessed 30 May 2014.

21 David E. Sumner, *The Magazine Century: American Magazines since 1900*, Mediating American History Series (New York: Peter Lang, 2010).

22 Abstracts are listed by year and with live links at "Conference Paper Abstracts," AEJMC—Association for Education in Journalism and Mass Communication <http://www.aejmc.org/home/scholarship/abstracts-archive/>, accessed 14 January 2014.

23 Endres, *Trade, Industrial, and Professional Periodicals*, vii–viii.

24 Dan Schiller, "Informational Bypass: Research Library Access to U.S. Telecommunications Periodicals," *Journal of Communication* 39.3 (September 1989) <http://onlinelibrary.wiley.com/doi/10.1111/j.1460-2466.1989.tb01044.x/abstract>, abstract accessed 20 May 2013.

25 Sal Marino noted the level of this specificity by referring to the specialized business press as "graduate school" for its readers in his McAllister Top Management Fellowship winner speech given at the Medill School of Journalism (Northwestern University, Evanston, IL, 1985).

26 Forsyth, *Business Press in America*.

27 Don Gussow, *The New Business Journalism: An Insider's Look at the Workings of America's Business Press* (San Diego: Harcourt Brace Jovanovich, 1984).

28 Edgar A. Grunwald, *The Business Press Editor* (New York: New York University Press, 1988).

29 Endres, "Research Review," 1995: 76–77.

30 Frank Luther Mott, *A History of American Magazines*, vol. 1, *A History of American Magazines, 1741–1850*; vol. 2, *A History of American Magazines, 1850–1865*; vol. 3, *A History of American Magazines, 1865–1885*; vol. 4, *A History of American Magazines, 1885–1905*; vol. 5, *A History of American Magazines, 1905–1930* (New York: D. Appleton, 1930; Cambridge, MA: The Belknap Press, 1938, 1938, 1957; Cambridge, MA: Harvard University Press, 1968).

31 William Fisher, ed., *Business Journals of the United States* (Westport, CT: Greenwood Press, 1991).

32 Sal Marino, *Business Magazine Publishing: Creative Ideas on Management, Editorial, Selling Space, Promotion . . . and Boosting Profits* (Lincolnwood, IL: NTC Business Books, 1992).

33 Endres, *Trade, Industrial, and Professional Periodicals*, vii.

34 Endres, "Research Review" (1994); Endres, "Research Review" (1995).

35 Patrick Clinton, *Guide to Writing for the Business Press* (Lincolnwood, IL: NTC Business Books, 1997).

36 Robert Freedman, ed., *Best Practices of the Business Press* (Dubuque, IA: Kendall/Hunt Publishing Company, 2004).

37 Todd Raphael, "Web Publications," in Robert Freedman, ed., *Best Practices of the Business Press* (Dubuque, IA: Kendall/Hunt Publishing, 2004), 121–130.

38 Denis McQuail, *McQuail's Mass Communication Theory*, 6th ed. (London and Thousand Oaks, CA: Sage, 2010), 13–14.

39 Abe Peck, "The Utilitarian Experience," in Abe Peck and Edward C. Malthouse, eds., *Medill on Media Engagement* (Cresskill: Hampton Press, 2010), 61–70.

40 Abe Peck and Edward C. Malthouse, eds., *Medill on Media Engagement* (Cresskill: Hampton Press, 2010).

41 See, for example, Georgia Christian, "How Does Progressive Profiling Work and What Are the Benefits?" *Advertising Age*, 21 April 2011 <http://www.btobonline.com/apps/pbcs.dll/article?AID=/20110421/EMAIL06/304219997/0/SEARCH>, accessed 12 May 2013; Jon VanZile, "Direct Marketers Need to Understand Their Customer's Buying Journey," *BtoB, Ad Age*, 4 March 2013 <http://adage.com/article/btob/direct-marketers-understand-customer-s-buying-journey/289311/>, accessed 31 May 2014; Matt Wesson, "Get More Data and Conversions with Progressive Profiling," Pardot, 21 March 2013 <http://www.pardot.com/forms/data-conversions-progressive-profiling/>, accessed 31 May 2014.

42 David Kirkpatrick, "B2B Marketing: 5 Privacy Factors to Consider When Using Marketing Automation," MarketingSherpa, 9 November 2011 <http://www.marketingsherpa.com/article/how-to/5-privacy-factors-to-consider>, accessed 31 May 2014.

43 Marcia R. Prior-Miller, "Research Review: Issues in Magazine Typology," in David Abrahamson, ed., *The American Magazine: Research Perspectives and Prospects* (Ames: Iowa State University Press, 1995), 3–23; see also, Marcia R. Prior-Miller, "Research Review: Issues in Magazine Typology," *Electronic Journal of Communication/La Revue Electronique de Communication* 4.2/4 (December 1994) <eric.ed.gov/?id=EJ494512>, accessed 30 May 2014.

44 *Architectural Digest*, also published by McGraw-Hill Construction, won the Jesse H. Neal Award for Best Single Issue of a Magazine for its September 2011 issue about 9/11, 10 years later. This coverage contributed to the magazine's winning that year's Grand Neal Award.

45 "Iraq: Will There Be Light?" *IEEE Spectrum*, 1 February 2006 <http://spectrum.ieee.org/energy/the-smarter-grid/iraq-will-there-be-light>, accessed 31 May 2014.

46 Scott Berinato, "Red Gold Rush: The Copper Theft Epidemic," CSO, 1 February 2007 <http://www.csoonline.com/article/221225/red-gold-rush-the-copper-theft-epidemic>, accessed 21 May 2013.

47 Deborah Dysart, "Narrative and Values: The Rhetoric of the Physician Assisted Suicide Debate," *New Jersey Journal of Communication* 8.2 (Fall 2000) <http://www.tandfonline.com/doi/abs/10.1080/15456870009367386#.UZxJX5VNzG4>, abstract accessed 21 May 2013.

48 Robert Chamblee and Dennis M. Sandler, "Business-to-Business Advertising: Which Layout Style Works Best?" *Journal of Advertising Research* 32.6 (November/December 1992): 39–46 <http://www.researchgate.net/publication/232600298_Business-to-business_advertising_Which_layout_style_works_best>, accessed 29 May 2014.

49 Christopher Benson and Charles Whitaker, "B2B: The Ultimate in Service Journalism," *Magazine Writing* (New York: Routledge, 2014), 275–284.

50 Pernilla Gluch and Ann-Charlotte Stenberg, "How Do Trade Media Influence Green Building Practice?" *Building Research & Information* 34.2 (2006) <http://www.tandfonline.com/doi/abs/10.1080/09613210500491613>, abstract accessed 24 January 2013.

51 Gluch and Stenberg, "How Do Trade Media Influence Green Building Practice?"

52 Philip M. Napoli, "The Media Trade Press as Technology Forecaster: A Case Study of the VCR's Impact on Broadcasting," *Journalism & Mass Communication Quarterly* 74.2 (Summer 1997) <http://jmq.sagepub.com/content/74/2/417.short>, abstract accessed 25 January 2013.

53 C. Ann Hollifield, "The Specialized Business Press and Industry-Related Political Communication: A Comparative Study," *Journalism & Mass Communication Quarterly* 74:4 (Winter 1997) <http://jmq.sagepub.com/content/74/4/757.short>, abstract accessed 24 January 2013.

54 Hollifield, "Specialized Business Press and Industry-Related Political Communication."

55 SISO has created a case study to spread the word on how events operate; it is available to universities via a PowerPoint and guest speakers, on request. The organization's URL is <http://www.siso.com>.

56 Markus Zinnbauer, "e-Newspaper: Consumer Demands on Attributes and Features," *JMM—The International Journal of Media Management* 5:2 (2003) <http://www.tandfonline.com/doi/abs/10.1080/14241270309390026?journalCode=hijm20#preview>, abstract accessed 12 May 2013.

57 David Lucking-Reiley and Daniel F. Spulber, "Business-to-Business Electronic Commerce," *Journal of Economic Perspectives* 15.1 (Winter 2001) <http://www.jstor.org/stable/2696539>, abstract accessed 29 May 2014.

58 Robert G. Hays and Ann E. Reisner, "Farm Journalists and Advertiser Influence: Pressures on Ethical Standards," *Journalism Quarterly* 68.1/2 (Spring/Summer, 1991) <http://jmq.sagepub.com/content/68/1-2/172.abstract>, abstract accessed 12 May 2013.

59 Paul W. Sullivan, "G.D. Crain Jr. and the Founding of 'Advertising Age,'" *Journalism History* 1.3 (1974): 94.

60 Sullivan, "G.D. Crain Jr. and the Founding of 'Advertising Age,'" 94.

61 Sullivan, "G.D. Crain Jr. and the Founding of 'Advertising Age,'" 95.

62 "ASBPE Ethics Advisories," ASBPE—American Society of Business Publication Editors <http://www.asbpe.org/ethics/asbpe-ethics-advisories-2>, accessed 14 January 2014.

63 Susan Caudill, Ed Caudill, and Michael W. Singletary, "'Journalist Wanted': Trade-Journal Ads as Indicators of Professional Values," *Journalism Quarterly* 64.2/3 (Summer/Autumn 1987) <http://www.eric.ed.gov/ERICWebPortal/search/detailmini.jsp?_nfpb=true&_&ERICExtSearch_SearchValue_0=EJ370125&ERICExtSearch_SearchType_0=no&accno=EJ370125>, abstract accessed 12 May 2013.

64 IDG, "IDG Total Portfolio," "Global Media Kit," IDG—International Data Group, 2014 <http://www.idg.com/www/home.nsf/BySection/Global_Media_Kit>, accessed 29 May 2014.

65 Jixiang Wang, "Scientific, Technical, Medical and Professional Publishing," in Robert E. Baensch, ed., *The Publishing Industry in China* (New Brunswick: Transaction Publishers, 2003), 71–75.

66 J. Ronald Milavsky, "Recent Journal and Trade Publication Treatments of Globalization in Mass Media Marketing and Social Change," *International Journal of Advertising* 12.1 (1993) <http://www.internationaljournalofadvertising.com/ArticleViewer.aspx?ID=5418>, abstract accessed 13 May 2013.

67 Milavsky, "Recent Journal and Trade Publication Treatments of Globalization."

68 Ulf Jonas Bjork, "'The Backbone of Our Business': American Films in Sweden, 1910–50," *Historical Journal of Film, Radio and Television* 15.2 (1995): 245–263.

69 Ulf Jonas Bjork, "'Have Gun, Will Travel': Swedish Television and American Westerns, 1959–1969," *Historical Journal of Film, Radio and Television* 21.2 (August 2001): 309–321.

70 Lynette S. McCullough and Ronald K. Taylor, "Humor in American, British, and German Ads," *Industrial Marketing Management* 22.1 (February 1993) <http://www.sciencedirect.com/science/article/pii/001985019390016Z>, abstract accessed 21 May 2013.

71 FIPP, "Home," FIPP Research Forum <http://www.fippresearchforum.com/Home.asp>, accessed 29 May 2014.

72 FIPP, "Home," Research Forum.

73 FIPP, "Home," Research Forum.

74 Roland B. Smith, "The Genesis of the Business Press in the United States," *Journal of Marketing* 19.2 (October 1954): 146–151.

75 Smith, "The Genesis of the Business Press in the United States," 146.

76 John Bidwell, "The *Engraver and Printer*, a Boston Trade Journal of the Eighteen Nineties," *Papers of the Bibliographical Society of America* 71 (January/March 1977): 29–48.

77 Laurel Brake, "Doing the Biz: Book-Trade and News-Trade Periodicals in the 1890s," *Media History* 4.1 (1998) <http://www.tandfonline.com/doi/abs/10.1080/13688809809357934?journalCode=cmeh20#.UZqDe5VNzG4>, abstract accessed 20 May 2013.

78 Donald B. Marti, "Agricultural Journalism and the Diffusion of Knowledge: The First Half-Century in America," *Agricultural History* 54.1 (January 1980) <http://www.jstor.org/discover/10.2307/3742591?uid=3

739560&uid=2129&uid=2&uid=70&uid=4&uid=3739256&sid=21102317316437>, abstract accessed 20 May 2013.

79 Stuart W. Shulman, "The Progressive Era Farm Press: A Primer on a Neglected Source of Journalism History," *Journalism History* 25.1 (Spring 1999) <http://www.questia.com/library/1P3-42962816/the-progressive-era-farm-press-a-primer-on-a-neglected>, abstract accessed 12 May 2013.

80 Stanley D. Brunn and Karl B. Raitz, "Regional Patterns of Farm Magazine Publication," *Economic Geography* 54.4 (October 1978) <http://www.jstor.org/discover/10.2307/143279?uid=3739560&uid=2129&uid=2&uid=70&uid=4&uid=3739256&sid=21102309397127>, abstract accessed 20 May 2013.

81 Joseph A. Coté, "Clarence Hamilton Poe: The Farmer's Voice, 1899–1964," *Agricultural History* 53.1 (January 1979) <http://www.jstor.org/discover/10.2307/3742857?uid=3739560&uid=2&uid=4&uid=3739256&sid=21102309582837>, abstract accessed 20 May 2013.

82 Sharienne Sweeney and C. Ann Hollifield, "Influence of Agricultural Trade Publications on the News Agendas of National Newspapers and News Magazines," *Journal of Applied Communications* 84.1 (2000): 23; see also, Sharienne Sweeney, "The Inter-Media Agenda Setting Influence of Trade Publications" (M.S. thesis, The Ohio State University, 1998).

83 Sweeney and Hollifield, "Influence of Agricultural Trade Publications," 23.

84 Jeff Rutenbeck, "The Triumph of News over Ideas in American Journalism: The Trade Journal Debate, 1872–1915," *Journal of Communication Inquiry* 18.1 (Winter 1994) <http://jci.sagepub.com/content/18/1/63.extract>, abstract accessed 20 May 2013.

85 Pama A. Mitchell, "The Response of the Broadcasting and Advertising Trade Press to Television Blacklisting Practices, 1950–1956," *Mass Comm Review* 16.1/2 (1989) <http://eric.ed.gov/?id=ED311487>, accessed 30 May 2014.

86 Schiller, "Informational Bypass," 104.

87 Endres, *Trade, Industrial, and Professional Periodicals*, 378.

88 Jean Russel Moss, "Walking the Tightrope: The Story of Nursing as Told by Nineteenth-Century Nursing Journals" (Ph.D. diss., The University of Iowa, 1987).

89 "Neal Awards," ABM—The Association of Business Information & Media Companies <http://www.abmassociation.com/abm/Neal_Awards2.asp>, accessed 30 May 2014.

90 "Azbee Awards," ASBPE—American Society of Business Publication Editors <http://www.asbpe.org/azbee-awards>, accessed 14 January 2014.

91 Kathleen L. Endres, "Ownership and Employment in Specialized Business Press," *Journalism Quarterly* 65.4 (Winter 1988) <http://connection.ebscohost.com/c/articles/14839741/ownership-employment-specialized-business-pressm>, abstract accessed 28 May 2013.

92 Richard van der Wurff, "Business Magazine Market Performance: Magazines for the Agricultural, Business Services, and Transportation Sectors in the Netherlands," *Journal of Media Economics* 18.2 (2005) <http://www.tandfonline.com/doi/abs/10.1207/s15327736me1802_5#.UxE_x_36Q4M>, abstract accessed 28 February 2014.

93 Yehouda Shenhav and Ely Weitz, "The Roots of Uncertainty in Organization Theory: A Historical Constructivist Analysis," *Organization* 7.3 (August 2000): 373–401.

94 "Business Information Network," ABM—The Association of Business Information & Media Companies <http://www.abmassociation.com/abm/Business_Information_Network.asp>, accessed 14 January 2014.

95 Mark W. Stuhlfaut, "Economic Concentration in Agricultural Magazine Publishing: 1993–2002," *Journal of Media Economics* 18.1 (2005) <http://www.tandfonline.com/doi/abs/10.1207/s15327736me1801_2#preview>, abstract accessed 21 May 2013.

96 ASBPE, Abe Peck, Bob LeBailly, Robin Sherman, with Mary Nesbitt, "Survey on Digital Skills and Strategies," (presentation by ASBPE—American Society of Business Publication Editors and Medill School and Media Management Center, Northwestern University, April 2010) <http://www.slideshare.net/asbpe/2010-0405asbpemedilldigitalskillsreport>, accessed 30 May 2014.

97 Dennis W. Jeffers, "A Descriptive Study of Perceived Impact of Gender on Employment Status, Type of Work, Industry Relationships, Working Environment and Job Satisfaction in Livestock Industry Magazines" (paper presented at the Annual Meeting, Association for Education in Journalism and Mass Communication, August 1987) <http://catalogue.nla.gov.au/Record/5480309>, abstract accessed 21 May 2013.

98 Jeffers, "A Descriptive Study of Perceived Impact of Gender on Employment Status."

99 Joseph Bernt, e-mail to author, 25 January 2013.

100 Anthony D. Hill, *Pages from the Harlem Renaissance: A Chronicle of Performance*, Studies in African and African-American Culture, vol. 6 (New York: Peter Lang, 1996) <http://www.peterlang.com/download/datasheet/46828/datasheet_69865.pdf>, abstract accessed 28 May 2013.

101 W. Dale Dannefer and Nicholas Poushinsky, "The C.B. Phenomenon, a Sociological Appraisal," *Journal of Popular Culture* 12.4 (1979) <http://onlinelibrary.wiley.com/doi/10.1111/j.0022-3840.1979.1204_611.x/abstract>, abstract accessed 21 May 2013.

102 Marcia R. Prior-Miller and Associates, "Bibliography of Published Research on Magazine and Journal Periodicals," 8th ed., research database (Ames: Iowa State University, last modified, 31 August 2012), MSWord file <mpm@iastate.edu gt;.

103 Marcia R. Prior-Miller, e-mail to author, 4 May 2013.

104 Prior-Miller, e-mail to author.

105 James C. Foust and Katherine A. Bradshaw, "Something for the Boys: Framing Images of Women in *Broadcasting* Magazine in the 1950s," *Journalism History* 33.2 (Summer 2007) <http://www.questia.com/library/1P3-1319083581/something-for-the-boys-framing-images-of-women-in>, abstract accessed 21 May 2013.

106 J.H. Bell and U.S. Pandey, "Gender-Role Stereotypes in Australian Farm Advertising," *Media Information Australia* 51 (February 1989) <http://search.informit.com.au/documentSummary;dn=207931994074409;res=IELLCC>, abstract accessed 21 May 2013.

107 Kathleen L. Endres, "'Help-Wanted Female': *Editor & Publisher* Frames a Civil Rights Issue," *Journalism & Mass Communication Quarterly* 81.1 (Spring 2004) <http://jmq.sagepub.com/content/81/1/7.abstract>, abstract accessed 21 May 2013.

108 *Folio:*, "Monetizing the Digital Revolution: Media Industry Benchmarks & Trends Study, Trends Study, Third Edition," Closed Survey <https://www.research.net/s.aspx?sm=HuPUyAZtUD4jVwk0hHQD-jg_3d_3d,Red7media.com>, accessed 29 May 2014.

109 Kantar Media SRDS, "Homepage," SRDS.com <www.srds.com>, accessed 30 May 2014.

Bibliography

"About ABM." ABM—The Association of Business Information & Media Companies <http://www.abmassociation.com/abm/About.asp>, accessed 14 January 2014.

Alterio, Michael Moran. "Print Advertising Down in August, but Select Verticals Show Life." ABM—The Association of Business Information & Media Companies, 5 December 2012 <http://www.abmassociation.com/News/2936/Print-ad-sales-continue-downward-trend>, accessed 25 January 2013.

"ASBPE Ethics Advisories." ASBPE—American Society of Business Publication Editors <http://www.asbpe.org/ethics/asbpe-ethics-advisories-2>, accessed 14 January 2014.

ASBPE; Peck, Abe; LeBailly, Bob; Sherman, Robin; with Nesbitt, Mary. "Survey on Digital Skills and Strategies." Presentation by ASBPE—American Society of Business Publication Editors and Medill School and Media Management Center, Northwestern University, April 2010 <http://www.slideshare.net/asbpe/2010-0405asbpemedilldigitalskillsreport>, accessed 30 May 2014.

"Azbee Awards." ASBPE—American Society of Business Publication Editors <http://www.asbpe.org/azbee-awards>, accessed 14 January 2014.

Bell, J.H. and Pandey, U.S. "Gender-Role Stereotypes in Australian Farm Advertising." *Media Information Australia* 51 (February 1989): 45–49 <http://search.informit.com.au/documentSummary;dn=207931994074409;res=IELLCC>, accessed 21 May 2013.

Benson, Christopher and Whitaker, Charles F. "B2B: The Ultimate in Service Journalism." *Magazine Writing*. New York: Routledge, 2014, 275–284.

Berinato, Scott. "Red Gold Rush: The Copper Theft Epidemic." CSO, 1 February 2007 <http://www.csoonline.com/article/221225/red-gold-rush-the-copper-theft-epidemic>, accessed 21 May 2013.

Bernhard, Jim. *Porcupine, Picayune, and Post: How Newspapers Get Their Names*. Columbia: University of Missouri Press, 2007.

Bidwell, John. "*The Engraver and Printer*, a Boston Trade Journal of the Eighteen Nineties." *Papers of the Bibliographical Society of America* 71 (January/March 1977): 29–48.

Bjork, Ulf Jonas. "'The Backbone of Our Business': American Films in Sweden, 1910–50." *Historical Journal of Film, Radio and Television* 15.2 (1995): 245–263 <http://www.tandfonline.com/doi/abs/10.1080/01439689500260151#.UZ0kj5VNzG4>, accessed 22 May 2013.

Bjork, Ulf Jonas. "'Have Gun, Will Travel': Swedish Television and American Westerns, 1959–1969." *Historical Journal of Film, Radio and Television* 21.2 (August 2001): 309–321.

Brake, Laurel. "Doing the Biz: Book-Trade and News-Trade Periodicals in the 1890s." *Media History* 4.1 (1998): 29–47 <http://www.tandfonline.com/doi/abs/10.1080/13688809809357934?journalCode=c-meh20#.UZqDe5VNzG4>, accessed 20 May 2013.

Brunn, Stanley D. and Raitz, Karl B. "Regional Patterns of Farm Magazine Publication." *Economic Geography* 54.4 (October 1978): 277–290 <http://www.jstor.org/discover/10.2307/143279?uid=3739560&uid=2129&uid=2&uid=70&uid=4&uid=3739256&sid=21102309397127>, accessed 20 May 2013.

"Business Information Network." ABM—The Association of Business Information & Media Companies <http://www.abmassociation.com/abm/Business_Information_Network.asp>, accessed 14 January 2014.

Caudill, Susan; Caudill, Ed; and Singletary, Michael W. "'Journalist Wanted': Trade-Journal Ads as Indicators of Professional Values." *Journalism Quarterly* 64.2/3 (Summer/Autumn 1987): 576–580, 633 <http://www.eric.ed.gov/ERICWebPortal/search/detailmini.jsp?_nfpb=true&_&ERICExtSearch_SearchValue_0=EJ370125&ERICExtSearch_SearchType_0=no&accno=EJ370125>, accessed 12 May 2013.

Chamblee, Robert and Sandler, Dennis M. "Business-to-Business Advertising: Which Layout Style Works Best?" *Journal of Advertising Research* 32.6 (November/December 1992): 39–46 <http://www.researchgate.net/publication/232600298_Business-to-business_advertising_Which_layout_style_works_best>, accessed 29 May 2014.

"*China Computerworld* Online." IDG International Data Group <http://careers.idg.com/www/IDGProducts.nsf/ByKey/People's-Republic-of-China_WebSite_China-Computerworld-Online>, accessed 29 May 2014.

Christian, Georgia. "How Does Progressive Profiling Work and What Are the Benefits?" *Advertising Age*, 21 April 2011 <http://www.btobonline.com/apps/pbcs.dll/article?AID=/20110421/EMAIL06 / 304219997/0/SEARCH>, accessed 12 May 2013.

Clinton, Patrick. *Guide to Writing for the Business Press*. Lincolnwood, IL: NTC Business Books, 1997.

"Conference Paper Abstracts." AEJMC—Association for Education in Journalism and Mass Communication <http://www.aejmc.org/home/scholarship/abstracts-archive/>, accessed 14 January 2014.

Coté, Joseph A. "Clarence Hamilton Poe: The Farmer's Voice, 1899–1964." *Agricultural History* 53.1 (January 1979): 30–41 <http://www.jstor.org/discover/10.2307/3742857?uid=3739560&uid=2&uid=4&uid=3739256&sid=21102309582837>, accessed 20 May 2013.

Dannefer, W. Dale and Poushinsky, Nicholas. "The C.B. Phenomenon, a Sociological Appraisal." *Journal of Popular Culture* 12.4 (Spring 1979): 611–619 <http://onlinelibrary.wiley.com/doi/10.1111/j.0022-3840.1979.1204_611.x/abstract>, accessed 21 May 2013.

Dysart, Deborah. "Narrative and Values: The Rhetoric of the Physician Assisted Suicide Debate." *New Jersey Journal of Communication* 8.2 (Fall 2000): 155–172 <http://www.tandfonline.com/doi/abs/10.1080/15456870009367386#.UZxJX5VNzG4>, accessed 21 May 2013.

Endres, Kathleen L. "'Help-Wanted Female': *Editor & Publisher* Frames a Civil Rights Issue." *Journalism & Mass Communication Quarterly* 81.1 (Spring 2004): 7–21 <http://jmq.sagepub.com/content/81/1/7.abstract>, accessed 21 May 2013.

Endres, Kathleen L. "Ownership and Employment in Specialized Business Press." *Journalism Quarterly* 65.4 (Winter 1988): 996–998 <http://connection.ebscohost.com/c/articles/14839741/ownership-employment-specialized-business-pressm>, accessed 28 May 2013.

Endres, Kathleen L. "Research Review: The Specialized Business Press." *Electronic Journal of Communication / La Revue Electronic de Communication* 4.2/4 (1994) <http://www.cios.org/EJCPUBLIC/004/2/004211.html>, accessed 12 May 2013.

Endres, Kathleen L. "Research Review: The Specialized Business Press." In Abrahamson, David, ed. *The American Magazine: Research Perspectives and Prospects*. Ames: Iowa State University Press, 1995, 72–83.

Endres, Kathleen L., ed. *Trade, Industrial, and Professional Periodicals of the United States*. Westport, CT and London: Greenwood Press, 1994.

FIPP. "Home." FIPP Research Forum <http://www.fippresearchforum.com/Home.asp>, accessed 29 May 2014.

Fisher, William, ed. *Business Journals of the United States*. Westport, CT: Greenwood Press, 1991.

Folio:. "Monetizing the Digital Revolution: Media Industry Benchmarks & Trends Study, Third Edition." Closed Survey <https://www.research.net/s.aspx?sm=HuPUyAZtUD4jVwk0hHQDjg_3d_3d,Red-7media.com>, accessed 29 May 2014.

Forsyth, David P. *The Business Press in America, 1750–1865*. Philadelphia: Chilton Books, 1964.

Foust, James C. and Bradshaw, Katherine A. "Something for the Boys: Framing Images of Women in *Broadcasting* Magazine in the 1950s." *Journalism History* 33.2 (Summer 2007): 93–100 <http://

www.questia.com/library/1P3–1319083581/something-for-the-boys-framing-images-of-women-in>, accessed 21 May 2013.

Freedman, Robert, ed. *Best Practices of the Business Press*. Dubuque, IA: Kendall/Hunt Publishing Company, 2004.

Gluch, Pernilla and Stenberg, Ann-Charlotte. "How Do Trade Media Influence Green Building Practice?" *Building Research & Information* 34.2 (2006): 104–117 <http://www.tandfonline.com/doi/abs/10.1080/09613210500491613>, accessed 24 January 2013.

Grunwald, Edgar A. *The Business Press Editor*. New York: New York University Press, 1988.

Gussow, Don. *The New Business Journalism: An Insider's Look at the Workings of America's Business Press*. San Diego: Harcourt Brace Jovanovich, 1984.

Harris, Mark. "A Shocking Truth." *IEEE Spectrum*, March 2012, 30–34, 57–58 <http://www.american-businessmedia.com/abm/C1A_Shocking_Truth.asp>, accessed 14 January 2014.

Hays, Robert G. and Reisner, Ann E. "Farm Journalists and Advertiser Influence: Pressures on Ethical Standards." *Journalism Quarterly* 68.1/2 (Spring/Summer, 1991): 172–178 <http://jmq.sagepub.com/content/68/1-2/172.abstract>, accessed 12 May 2013.

Hill, Anthony D. *Pages from the Harlem Renaissance: A Chronicle of Performance*. Studies in African and African-American Culture. Vol. 6. New York: Peter Lang, 1996 <http://www.peterlang.com/download/datasheet/46828/datasheet_69865.pdf>, accessed 28 May 2013.

Hollifield, C. Ann. "The Specialized Business Press and Industry-Related Political Communication: A Comparative Study." *Journalism & Mass Communication Quarterly* 74.4 (Winter 1997): 757–772 <http://jmq.sagepub.com/content/74/4/757.short>, accessed 24 January 2013.

IDG. "IDG Total Portfolio." "Global Media Kit," IDG—International Data Group, 2014 <http://www.idg.com/www/home.nsf/BySection/Global_Media_Kit>, accessed 29 May 2014.

"Iraq: Will There Be Light?" *IEEE Spectrum*, 1 February 2006 <http://spectrum.ieee.org/energy/the-smarter-grid/iraq-will-there-be-light>, accessed 31 May 2014.

Jeffers, Dennis W. "A Descriptive Study of Perceived Impact of Gender on Employment Status, Type of Work, Industry Relationships, Working Environment and Job Satisfaction in Livestock Industry Magazines." Paper presented at the Annual Meeting, Association for Education in Journalism and Mass Communication, August 1987 <http://catalogue.nla.gov.au/Record/5480309>, accessed 21 May 2013.

Kantar Media SRDS. "Homepage." SRDS.com <www.srds.com>, accessed 30 May 2014.

Kirkpatrick, David. "B2B Marketing: 5 Privacy Factors to Consider When Using Marketing Automation." MarketingSherpa, 9 November 2011 <http://www.marketingsherpa.com/article/how-to/5-privacy-factors-to-consider>, accessed 31 May 2014.

Lucking-Reiley, David and Spulber, Daniel F. "Business-to-Business Electronic Commerce." *Journal of Economic Perspectives* 15.1 (Winter 2001): 55–68 <http://www.jstor.org/stable/2696539>, accessed 29 May 2014.

Marino, Sal. *Business Magazine Publishing: Creative Ideas on Management, Editorial, Selling Space, Promotion . . . and Boosting Profits*. Lincolnwood, IL: NTC Business Books, 1992.

Marino, Sal. McAllister Top Management Fellowship winner speech given at the Medill School of Journalism, Northwestern University, Evanston, IL, 1985.

Marti, Donald B. "Agricultural Journalism and the Diffusion of Knowledge: The First Half-Century in America." *Agricultural History* 54.1 (January 1980): 28–37 <http://www.jstor.org/discover/10.2307/3742591?uid=3739560&uid=2129&uid=2&uid=70&uid=4&uid=3739256&sid=21102317316437>, accessed 20 May 2013.

McCullough, Lynette S. and Taylor, Ronald K. "Humor in American, British, and German Ads." *Industrial Marketing Management* 22.1 (February 1993): 17–28 <http://www.sciencedirect.com/science/article/pii/001985019390016Z>, accessed 21 May 2013.

McQuail, Denis. *McQuail's Mass Communication Theory*. 6th ed. London and Thousand Oaks, CA: Sage, 2010.

Milavsky, J. Ronald. "Recent Journal and Trade Publication Treatments of Globalization in Mass Media Marketing and Social Change." *International Journal of Advertising* 12.1 (1993): 45–56 <http://www.internationaljournalofadvertising.com/ArticleViewer.aspx?ID=5418>, accessed 13 May 2013.

Mitchell, Pama A. "The Response of the Broadcasting and Advertising Trade Press to Television Blacklisting Practices, 1950–1956." *Mass Comm Review* 16.1/2 (1989): 63–69 <http://eric.ed.gov/?id=ED311487>, accessed 30 May 2014.

Moss, Jean Russel. "Walking the Tightrope: The Story of Nursing as Told by Nineteenth-Century Nursing Journals." Ph.D. diss., The University of Iowa, 1987.

Mott, Frank Luther. *A History of American Magazines*. Vol. 1, *A History of American Magazines, 1741–1850*; Vol. 2, *A History of American Magazines, 1850–1865*; Vol. 3, *A History of American Magazines, 1865–1885*; Vol. 4, *A History of American Magazines, 1885–1905*; Vol. 5, *A History of American Magazines, 1905–1930*. New York: D. Appleton, 1930; Cambridge, MA: The Belknap Press, 1938, 1938, 1957; Cambridge, MA: Harvard University Press, 1968.

Napoli, Philip M. "The Media Trade Press as Technology Forecaster: A Case Study of the VCR's Impact on Broadcasting." *Journalism & Mass Communication Quarterly* 74.2 (Summer 1997): 417–430 <http://jmq.sagepub.com/content/74/2/417.short>, accessed 25 January 2013.

"Neal Awards." ABM—The Association of Business Information & Media Companies <http://www.abmassociation.com/abm/Neal_Awards2.asp>, accessed 30 May 2014.

Peck, Abe. "The Utilitarian Experience." In Peck, Abe and Malthouse, Edward C., eds. *Medill on Media Engagement*. Cresskill: Hampton Press, 2010, 61–70.

Peck, Abe and Malthouse, Edward C., eds. *Medill on Media Engagement*. Cresskill: Hampton Press, 2010.

Prior-Miller, Marcia R. "Research Review: Issues in Magazine Typology." *Electronic Journal of Communication/La Revue Electronique de Communication* 4.2/4 (December 1994) <eric.ed.gov/?id=EJ494512>, accessed 30 May 2014.

Prior-Miller, Marcia R. "Research Review: Issues in Magazine Typology." In Abrahamson, David. ed. *The American Magazine: Research Perspectives and Prospects*. Ames: Iowa State University Press, 1995, 3–23.

Prior-Miller, Marcia R. and Associates. "Bibliography of Published Research on Magazine and Journal Periodicals." 8th ed. Research database. Ames: Iowa State University, last modified, 31 August 2012, MSWord file <mpm@iastate.edu>.

Raphael, Todd. "Web Publications." In Freedman, Robert, ed. *Best Practices of the Business Press*. Dubuque, IA: Kendall/Hunt Publishing, 2004, 121–130.

Rutenbeck, Jeff. "The Triumph of News over Ideas in American Journalism: The Trade Journal Debate, 1872–1915." *Journal of Communication Inquiry* 18.1 (Winter 1994): 63–79 <http://jci.sagepub.com/content/18/1/63.extract>, accessed 20 May 2013.

Schiller, Dan. "Informational Bypass: Research Library Access to U.S. Telecommunications Periodicals." *Journal of Communication* 39.3 (September 1989): 104–109 <http://onlinelibrary.wiley.com/doi/10.1111/j.1460-2466.1989.tb01044.x/abstract>, accessed 20 May 2013.

Shenhav, Yehouda and Weitz, Ely. "The Roots of Uncertainty in Organization Theory: A Historical Constructivist Analysis." *Organization* 7.3 (August 2000): 373–401.

Shulman, Stuart W. "The Progressive Era Farm Press: A Primer on a Neglected Source of Journalism History." *Journalism History* 25.1 (Spring 1999): 26–35 <http://www.questia.com/library/1P3-42962816/the-progressive-era-farm-press-a-primer-on-a-neglected>, accessed 12 May 2013.

Smith, Roland B. "The Genesis of the Business Press in the United States." *Journal of Marketing* 19.2 (October 1954): 146–151.

SRDS Business Media Advertising Source. Part 1. Vol. 95. Des Plaines, IL: Kantar/SRDS/Standard Rate and Data Service, 2013.

Stuhlfaut, Mark W. "Economic Concentration in Agricultural Magazine Publishing: 1993–2002." *Journal of Media Economics* 18.1 (2005): 21–33 <http://www.tandfonline.com/doi/abs/10.1207/s15327736me1801_2#preview>, accessed 21 May 2013.

Sullivan, Paul W. "G.D. Crain Jr. and the Founding of 'Advertising Age.'" *Journalism History* 1.3 (1974): 94–95.

Sumner, David E. *The Magazine Century: American Magazines since 1900*. Mediating American History Series. New York: Peter Lang, 2010.

Sumner, David E. "Magazine-Related Articles in *Journalism Mass Communications Quarterly* 1990 to 2010." <http://davidabrahamson.com/WWW/MAG2/Sumner_JMCQ_Magazine_Bibliography.pdf>, accessed 02 June 2014.

Sweeney, Sharienne. "The Inter-Media Agenda Setting Influence of Trade Publications." M.S. thesis, The Ohio State University, 1998.

Sweeney, Sharienne and Hollifield, C. Ann. "Influence of Agricultural Trade Publications on the News Agendas of National Newspapers and News Magazines." *Journal of Applied Communications* 84.1 (2000): 23–45.

Ulrich's Periodicals Directory 2014. Vol. 1. 52nd ed. New Providence, NJ: ProQuest, 2013, s.v. "CIO Africa."

University of North Carolina at Chapel Hill School of Journalism and Mass Communication. "1500s–1800s: History of Business Journalism." <http://www.bizjournalismhistory.org/main_frame.htm>, accessed 29 May 2014.

van der Wurff, Richard. "Business Magazine Market Performance: Magazines for the Agricultural, Business Services, and Transportation Sectors in the Netherlands." *Journal of Media Economics* 18.2 (2005): 143–159 <http://www.tandfonline.com/doi/abs/10.1207/s15327736me1802_5?journalCode=hmec20#preview>, 28 February 2014.

VanZile, Jon. "Direct Marketers Need to Understand Their Customer's Buying Journey." *BtoB, Ad Age,* 4 March 2013 <http://adage.com/article/btob/direct-marketers-understand-customer-s-buying-journey/289311/>, accessed 31 May 2014.

Verdon, Dan, editor of *DVM Newsmagazine.* Speech given at the Medill School of Journalism, Northwestern University, Evanston, IL, 5 February 2009.

Walter, Gerry. "The Ideology of Success in Major American Farm Magazines, 1934–1991." *Journalism & Mass Communication Quarterly* 73.3 (Autumn 1996): 594–608.

Wang, Jixiang. "Scientific, Technical, Medical and Professional Publishing." In Baensch, Robert E., ed. *The Publishing Industry in China.* New Brunswick: Transaction Publishers, 2003, 67–84.

Wesson, Matt. "Get More Data and Conversions with Progressive Profiling." Pardot, 21 March 2013 <http://www.pardot.com/forms/data-conversions-progressive-profiling/>, accessed 31 May 2014.

Zinnbauer, Markus. "e-Newspaper: Consumer Demands on Attributes and Features." *JMM—The International Journal on Media Management* 5.2 (2003): 127–137 <http://www.tandfonline.com/doi/abs/10.1080/14241270309390026?journalCode=hijm20#preview>, accessed 12 May 2013.

Supplemental Resources: A B2B Resource Guide

A variety of media-analysis titles and organizations offer information on B2B media. These can trigger ideas and suggest trend lines for deeper academic exploration.

ABM <www.americanbusinessmedia.com> collects relevant research at <http://www.abmassociation.com/abm/Full_Research_Reports.asp>. The ABM/MPA Compensation Study is an annual report conducted by the Towers Watson consulting firm and is available to ABM members—including universities with associate memberships—at the above URL.

ABM *Vital Guide* e-newsletter aggregates e-media developments within and beyond B2B.

The ABM Website and the *ABM Connect* e-newsletter note research from ABM's various committees (audience development, editorial and content, marketing services, production / management technology, talent management) and councils (business information, digital media, postal).

Advertising Age reports on various media, including B2B. The *Ad Age Media Buzz* e-newsletter covers marketing developments.

BPA Worldwide, a leading audience assessment service, publishes performance audits that now convey reach across media.

Emediavitals, [sic] an "on-line magazine for Web and digital media experts," comments on emerging topics beyond print.

The *FIPP Vital Guide to emedia* newsletter provides case studies, reports and news items.

Folio: <http://www.foliomag.com> and the *Folio: Alert e-newsletter* monitor the magazine industry. *Folio:* surveys "Monetizing the Digital Revolution Media Industry Benchmarks and Trends Study" for how "consumer and business media and publishing companies are using digital to drive their businesses forward."[108] It also hosts the MediaNext conference (formerly the *Folio:* show) for B2B publishers.

Media Industry News offers several media newsletters, including *MINB2B,* hosts awards and conferences and collects white papers on industry issues <http://www.minonline.com/whitepapers.html>.

Scoutanalytics.com offers "analysis and observations of revenue models in the Cloud." An e-newsletter spotlights related research.

SRDS.com "is an on-line multimedia planning platform that connects media buyers with media sellers."[109] Its B2B coverage includes publication data and, via Kantar Media, research studies on categories such as B2B medical titles.

VSS/Veronis Suhler Stevenson is a major private investor firm in the B2B and IT space. Its annual report on growth or decline in numerous media sectors is an industry benchmark <http:www.vssforecast.com>. It also produces the VSS Communications Industry Historical Database.

7

ORGANIZATIONAL MAGAZINES

Addressing Captive or Cautious Audiences

Michael Heller and Michael Rowlinson

All magazines are organizational in the sense that they are produced by organizations, but organizational magazines are intended for employees of the organizations that produce them—and according to research on organizational magazines, they may inform, instruct, entertain or even provide collective meaning for employees. Organizational magazines may be supplied to and read by various parties outside the organization, such as customers or shareholders, but their primary audience is internal rather than external.[1] With the rise of the large-scale modern corporation, in both the private and public sectors, in the late-nineteenth and early twentieth century, the number of organizational magazines increased as they became institutionalized as a genre of communication.[2] Like other magazines, however, their continued existence is threatened by the digital revolution and the competing forms of media, with many organizations abolishing magazines and replacing them with executive blogs and podcasts as well as e-mail.[3]

This chapter focuses primarily on the large-scale business corporation as a setting for organizational magazines, but it is important to note that these publications exist in a variety of institutional environments. They can be found in local and central government, in hospitals, schools, universities, churches, sports clubs and associations, charities, trade unions, political parties and pressure groups. Yet in all these spaces their structures, functions, roles, meanings and historical development—areas which this chapter will deal with—have been broadly similar. Because of their proximity, however, to business organizations, to the extent that they have attracted the interest of academic researchers, it has come primarily from those within business and management. Organization theory and public relations, rather than the traditional spheres of journalism, media and communication studies, have been the main locus for the study of organizational magazines.

Literature Review and Method

This chapter surveys the research literature on organizational magazines primarily from a historical perspective, drawing on research that examines their emergence since the 1880s, in order to provide an historical context for considering current debates about the status of organizational magazines. Because organizational magazines are neither recognized widely as a genre of magazine, nor as a specific field of study, it is not always easy to identify them as an object of research. Of necessity it has been necessary to search an eclectic literature where organizational magazines are mentioned as part of more general studies, which means that inevitably the literature reviewed is partial and much may have been missed.

The chapter is organized in two parts. The first part, following this literature review, discusses internal communication to which organizational magazines belong. Following a brief definition of terms, there is a much longer survey of the history and genres of internal communication, which includes a review of the historical literature on the development of organizational magazines between 1880 and 1945, in relation to the rise of the modern corporation. Following JoAnne Yates's path-breaking historical study of communication in organizations,[4] organizational magazines have encountered growing interest from historians. The relationship between organizational magazines and organizational remembering is then considered, and it is argued that almost as soon as they appeared organizational magazines promulgated the invented traditions and heritage of twentieth-century corporate cultures.

The second part of the chapter then summarizes the literature on organizational magazines that emerged in the 1950s, primarily from American practitioners, with some input from public relations specialists. It should be noted that no continuation of this literature past the 1990s could be found in preparation for this chapter. Consequently the chapter returns to the literature on internal communications that has appeared since the beginning of the twenty-first century, highlighting themes for future research into this surprisingly neglected medium, especially for the emerging field of organizational history and the cultural history of organizations.[5] The primary themes of the chapter are the history, functions and meaning of organization magazines for both the institutions from which they emerged and, insofar as they can be inferred, for the organization members who read them.

Internal Communication

The public relations expert Liz Yeomans has defined *internal communication* as an organization's managed communication system where employees are regarded as a public or a stakeholder group.[6] In the United States it is usually referred to as "employee communication."[7] The area normally falls under the academic and professional remit of organization theory and public relations. While Yeomans's definition covers the main areas of internal communication, it needs qualification in two areas. The first is that the neat bifurcation between internal and external communication does not completely exist. Some internal communication is also meant for external consumption. Company magazines, for example, can be made available to external publics to demonstrate a caring and responsible organization or to divulge corporate identity.[8] In addition, internal communication is increasingly seen as an important form of marketing communication that enhances products, services and brands. Employees in this context are seen as brand ambassadors, an important source of word-of-mouth marketing. In addition, employees must understand and appreciate products and brands before marketing them to customers and consumers.[9] This is especially the case in service industries where employees are a core element of the product.

Yeoman's definition also lacks an appreciation of the extent to which there are multiple stakeholders within organizations, who may require different kinds of communication. This point is discussed from a corporate communication perspective by Mary Welch and Paul R. Jackson, who have developed an internal communication model that integrates both internal and external stakeholders.[10] Welch and Jackson distinguish between four internal stakeholders within the organization: senior or strategic managers, line managers, team colleagues and project group colleagues.[11] While team colleagues and project group colleagues' communication is two-way, line management communication to colleagues can be both one and two way, and strategic management communication is predominantly one way. In addition, the content of the communication will differ between the stakeholders. For example, line manager communication will focus on instruction, control and feedback, while project group communication will revolve around project information and discussion. Welch and Jackson's model is not exhaustive, as it makes no distinction, for example, between employees in the organization who are differentiated by factors such as role, skill, gender, ethnicity and location. However, its inclusion and acknowledgement of internal stakeholder groups reveals the complexity of internal communication.

Yeomans locates organizational magazines within the remit of internal communications,[12] but they are merely one in a complex array of communication tools and channels. This includes memos, e-mails, noticeboards, briefing groups, meetings, management conferences, speeches, intranets and social media.[13] The task of internal communication revolves around issues of what and how the organization communicates with its own members. The problem for researching the organizational magazine, however, is that most commentary and analysis focuses on internal communication as a whole and rarely focuses on the magazine. The increasing digitalization of communication has exacerbated this. Consequently, an important task for those studying organizational magazines is to ask what specific roles do these publications play within such a multiplicity of organizational communication? How do organizational magazines contribute to internal communication?

History and Genres

Organizational magazines can be seen as one of several written, internal genres of communication that increasingly replaced oral communication in the late nineteenth and early twentieth century.[14] Other genres of internal communication identified in Yates's extensive study of systematic management and communication in American business include the committee meeting, with its minutes, the report and the ubiquitous memorandum, as well as the filing cabinet replacing ledgers for storing information. Within a fairly short space of time organizational magazines became commonplace for large industrial employers in both Britain and the United States. The magazines were closely associated with the rise of welfare programs, providing a vehicle to inform employees about the welfare available, while clubhouses and sports activities in particular provided material for reporting that recreated a "family feeling" in large plants with increasingly impersonal management systems.[15]

In functional terms organizational magazines can be seen as "a form of downward communication, ultimately aimed at improving cooperation, control, and efficiency," albeit "indirectly rather than directly."[16] The extensive literature on welfare programs and scientific management associated with the new factory system that arose in the United States between 1880 and 1920 does not examine organizational magazines specifically.[17] However, this literature does cite contemporary sources from the early twentieth century, and on closer inspection these sources reveal an increasingly prevalent expectation that organizational magazines could facilitate more participatory, if not exactly democratic, forms of communication. Several surveys of welfare programs were published in the late nineteenth and early twentieth century, seemingly with the intention of publicizing the work of progressive companies, especially those manufacturing consumer products. Budgett Meakin's *Model Factories and Villages*, published in 1905, was one of the most extensive international surveys of welfare programs.[18] Meakin devoted several pages to a discussion of "Business Magazines," noting that they varied from

> the unaided production of the employees, not seen by the Heads until published, and in no way utilized to push the business,—to an elaborate advertising medium conducted as a business venture, but chronicling the social life of factory and "field force" at the same time, inspiring all with the feeling of a life-mission to provide the world with their particular products.[19]

As examples of "elaborate" magazines, Meakin cited Lever Brothers' *Progress* in Britain and the *N.C.R.*, produced by the American National Cash Register Company. Meakin described the *N.C.R.* as "still more pretentious, with an entirely new picture cover in colours each month."[20] Even though Meakin's survey was partly sponsored by the British cocoa and chocolate manufacturer Cadbury, which featured heavily in his book, along with N.C.R., it is difficult to resist the irony in his description of magazines as "elaborate," "inspiring," and "pretentious." Meakin's barely suppressed preference was obviously for the more "modest" publications produced by employees, as they were at Filene's Store in Boston or the Debenham and Freabody store in London.[21] Critique, it seems, has accompanied the organizational magazine since its origins.

Following on from Yates's research, the history of organizational magazines has received increasing attention from historians in the United Kingdom, the United States, Canada and Australia.[22] The business and public relations historian Michael Heller has mapped the history of the company magazine between 1880 and 1939 in the United Kingdom,[23] arguing that the organizational magazine was a product of the rise of the large-scale corporation. Business historians such as Alfred D. Chandler Jr., Leslie Hannah and John Francis Wilson[24] have charted how the large-scale corporation emerged in response to the growth of mass markets, a growth facilitated by urbanization, the growth of railways and mass communication. However, conventional business historians have tended to neglect communication within the modern corporation, seeing organizational magazines mainly as sources for research on organizations rather than as the focus for research in their own right. That is why Yates's research is so important, signaling a shift of focus toward corporate cultural communication, including organizational magazines, as an object for research in its own right.

The growth of large-scale organizations led to a break-down in organizational communication. This resulted in problems in areas such as organizational identity and organizational culture.[25] This was particularly marked in sectors such as banking and the railways, which had separate branches spread across wide geographic areas. It was also problematic for companies that had grown through merger and acquisition and had operations in disparate sectors. These large-scale organizations also faced challenges to their power and legitimacy from trade unionism. Finally, corporations were increasingly criticized by external publics, not only for the lack of any check on their power, but also for their soulless operations. This history has been carefully reconstructed by the American historian of public relations Roland Marchand in his landmark study *Creating the Corporate Soul*.[26] He has demonstrated how corporations in the United States suffered widespread criticism between 1890 and 1940 from a collection of groups, which included federal and state politicians, local government, trade unions, journalists and local business interests. Corporations were portrayed as monopolistic, antagonistic to local interests, un-American and soulless. This rhetoric was given teeth with the passing of the Sherman Antitrust Act (1890) and the Clayton Antitrust Act (1914). Big business was now vulnerable to being broken up by the federal government, and one of its first victims was John D. Rockefeller's Standard Oil.

Although by no means a panacea, organizational magazines could be perceived as part of the solution to these problems of the soulless corporation. They reconnected employees and provided a means of internal communication. They helped engender organizational culture and identity and hence provided organizational members with collective meaning, motivation and purpose. This was at the time commonly referred to as *esprit de corps*. Magazines also acted as powerful propaganda tools, a means for owners and senior management to influence and control their employees. Many publications emerged in the interwar period (1919–1939), possibly as a response to the resurgence of trade unionism and the economic problems of the period, although there is obviously a danger of lapsing into an overly economistic interpretation. In addition, organizational magazines became powerful public relations tools.[27] They rebutted the argument that organizations were soulless, bureaucratic machines, whose thankless employees were locked in a Kafkaesque nightmare. Images of smiling employees on company day trips or enjoying themselves in company-sponsored sports facilities helped to dispel this negative perception. In the words of Marchand, organizational magazines helped to provide these bodies with a corporate soul.[28]

Many of these themes were developed in a special, August 2008 edition on the company magazine published by the journal *Management & Organizational History*. As co-editor of the special issue, Michael Heller argued that company magazines emerged in two phases in Britain between 1880–1914 and 1914–1939.[29] In the first period they tended to be limited to a minority of the staff (predominantly clerical workers) and were initiated and written by the staff themselves rather than by management. In the second period company magazines became more professional and corporate. They were now targeted at all the employees, were funded and founded by management and were written by professional editors. In the same special issue the business historian Howard Cox demonstrated how in the interwar period the staff magazine of British American Tobacco, the *BAT Bulletin*, successfully created a corporate identity and culture in an organization that had been created through a merger of American and British tobacco companies.[30] What is interesting in Cox's account is that the culture and identity created at BAT came not from its founders or senior management but originated from its magazine, which was founded and written by its employees. It was bottom-up rather than top-down. The creation of corporate identity and corporate culture through company magazines in the interwar period was also explored by business historian Simon Phillips in his study of the British pharmacist Boots. Through its magazine Boots portrayed itself to its employees as a progressive company, which focused on care for the customers it served and for the towns where its branches were based.[31]

In addition to organizational identity and culture, other articles in the special edition focused on the role that company magazines played in enhancing managerial power. As labor historians, Greg Patmore and Jonathan Rees show how the Colorado Fuel and Iron Company, made infamous by the Ludlow massacre of 1914, used its company magazines as an instrument of managerial control and an anti-union device between 1915 and 1942.[32] Corporate welfare and joint consultative management-staff committees, underpinned by the company magazine, were used to integrate staff, stave off unions and generate public goodwill. The business historian and sociologist Bart Dredge's account of company magazines in the southern textile towns of South Carolina between 1880 and 1940 draws a similar picture.[33] Magazines were part of a wider strategy of corporate welfare and propaganda in an effort to control employees and prevent collective organization. Finally, health and safety historian Mike Esbester provided a highly original account of the role of the company magazine in the "Safety First" campaign of the Great Western Railway in Britain between 1913 and 1939.[34] Making use of Michel Foucault's theory of knowledge, discipline and power, Esbester argues that the campaign acted as an exercise in managerial authority by its attempts to control worker's behavior, attitudes and bodily movements. Rather than using overt discipline, management attempted, via the *Great Western Railway Magazine*, to persuade workers to control and discipline themselves and each other through appeals to "knowledge" and normative codes.[35] These case studies illustrate the variety of possible perspectives for conducting research on the history of organizational magazines, which had become institutionalized in Britain to the extent that a British Association of Industrial Editors was established in 1949.[36]

Organizational Memory

The proliferation of printed periodicals with a national circulation was central to Benedict Anderson's argument that nations were constructed as "imagined communities" through the creation of a shared national history.[37] It could be argued that organizational magazines played a similar role in the construction of twentieth-century "corporate cultures," as described by Terrence E. Deal and Allan A. Kennedy,[38] especially in relation to organizational remembering.[39] An example of this is provided from an organization studies perspective by Michael Rowlinson in his historical account of corporate culture at the British chocolate confectionery firm Cadbury,[40] which he likens to the "invented traditions" of nations described by the historians Eric Hobsbawm and Terence Ranger.[41] Almost from the outset one of the main themes for Cadbury's *Bournville Works Magazine* was the history of the company itself. Recollections of the early years of the firm were collected from longstanding employees for special issues of the *Bournville Works Magazine*, published in September and October 1909 to mark 30 years since the firm moved to a purpose-built factory on a greenfield site.[42] For the firm's centenary in 1931, a major, 300-page history was commissioned, *The Firm of Cadbury 1831–1931*,[43] and 4,450 copies of the book were given to employees with at least 10 years' service. However, a more modest work was also published by Cadbury: *A Century of Progress 1831–1931*, written by the full-time editor of the *Bournville Works Magazine*.[44] Some 180,000 copies were produced and distributed to customers in Britain, as well as being used by Cadbury's subsidiaries in Australia, New Zealand and Canada.[45] It is clear then, that the *Bournville Works Magazine*, in common with other organizational magazines, was a vehicle for constructing a reassuring image of the past as part of a corporate culture.[46]

The role of the organizational magazine in relation to corporate history and memory has become self-perpetuating, as can be seen again from the example of Cadbury. In 1990 Cadbury opened a highly successful visitor attraction, Cadbury World, featuring the Cadbury brands and celebrating the firm's Quaker heritage. Interviewed in 2001, the sales and marketing manager of Cadbury World was of the opinion that it would not have come into existence without the *Bournville Works Magazine*.[47] Thus the organizational magazine has largely become a historical source for organizational remembering, where once it was a primary channel of communication for memory itself. Deal and Kennedy attributed the declining legitimacy of the new corporate cultures of late twentieth-century America in part to their tendency to denigrate history.[48] Deal and Kennedy maintain that "Good companies . . . understand that it is from history that the symbolic glue congeals to hold a group of people together and bond them to their shared mythology and enabling purpose."[49] On the assumption that "Most companies—especially those that have been around for some time—have a rich history," they advise companies to mine their history, which includes "old mission statements, documents outlining corporate beliefs, oral history about the 'good old days,' and past traditions that have contributed to the company's success."[50] Deal and Kennedy's argument raises the question for further research of whether the historical component in corporate cultures may have declined for the more prosaic reason that organizational magazines, which were once a genre for remembering and communicating the past in organizations, have also been in decline.

Research and Analysis

Following the Second World War, as organizational magazines became widespread and normative, they began to receive attention from researchers and practitioners. This was assisted by the growing prestige of research on internal communication in the United States, where a series of studies appeared on the organizational magazine between the 1970s and 1990s. Broadly speaking, three areas of interest can be outlined: (1) the content of the organizational magazines, (2) research into employees' media consumption of these journals and newsletters, and (3) a normative critique of the organizational magazine. This section briefly summarizes the research in each area, in turn.

The business communication experts Phillip G. Clampitt, Jean M. Crevcoure and Robin L. Hartel's 1986 article stated that company magazines made their way into 75 million homes in the United States and Canada and had a circulation of 228 million, over three times the circulation of daily papers in both countries.[51] A 1988 survey confirmed this, showing that 90% of Fortune 500 firms produced "house organs."[52] Journalism and communication expert Peter Johansen estimated that in the United States there were 60,000 house organs with a circulation four times greater than daily newspapers.[53] Employee publications had also evolved in terms of format, size and shape. Employee communication specialists Joan Kampe and Lyn Christenson identified four different forms of the organization magazine.[54] These were short newsletters, newspapers, magazines and so-called magapapers, which were a hybrid of newspapers and magazines. A survey by the International Association of Business Communicators showed that 31.5% of such publications were magazines, 12.5% were newspapers, 8.5% were megapapers and 39.5% were newsletters. Another 8% were hybrids of these formats.[55] By 1999 the electronic magazine, or e-zine, accessed from intranets on computer terminals, could be added to this list. Clampitt, Crevcoure and Hartel's study of 53 publications showed that the average publication was issued on a monthly basis, was written primarily by the editor, had begun life in 1967, had a circulation of 3,000 copies, was 10 pages long, with 1 to 10 photos, cost 40 cents and was aimed at employees and their families.[56]

Organizational Magazine Content

The management communication expert C.J. Dover has argued that employee publications passed historically through three periods in the United States.[57] The first was the period before the Second World War, which was called the "entertainment" era. Here the organizational magazine focused on recreational activities and news about colleagues. The second, "information" era began in the 1940s. Magazines provided employees with news on company activities, growth, productivity, products and job opportunities. The third era, "interpretation and persuasion," originated in the 1950s, when the role of the magazine became that of explaining organizational events to employees and convincing them to accept senior management's strategic and industrial policies. Dover's taxonomies are in many respects ideal types, and several writers in the 1970s and 1980s have questioned whether most company magazines have progressed beyond the information era, with many, indeed, said to be still mired in the entertainment era.[58] Johansen argued that many magazines still focused on the three B's, of babies, bowling scores and birthdays, despite claims by many of their editors that their principal role was in providing information to their readers and focusing on hard, current organizational issues.[59] Such arguments were indeed borne out by content analysis and survey research. Clampitt, Crevcoure and Hartel's 1986 research showed that employee recognition, personnel changes and promotions, and company business projects were the three most common articles in employee publications.[60] While company business projects relate to the so-called information era, both employee recognition and personnel changes relate to the prior, entertainment period.

Articles in the 1970s and 1980s on what employees actually wanted from organizational magazines produced insightful data. Business communication experts David Bateman and Jeffrey Miller in 1981 published research from a Fortune 500 corporation that had surveyed employees' attitudes on what they considered to be the most important topics in their company magazine.[61] Based on their comparison of data from surveys conducted in 1974 and 1979, Bateman and Miller identified five interest clusters or topics. In descending order of perceived importance by employees, these were economic security, products/services, general company news, social news and societal news. In 1974 the five most important subjects in descending order were "new or improved corporate products," "fringe benefit information," "corporate sales," "all corporate products" and "features on my division or location's departments." As shown in Table 7.1, in 1979 they were "business trends affecting corporation," "fringe benefit information," "features on my division or location's departments," "corporate sales" and "how corporate products are used."[62] Differences in ranking were said to be due to the uncertain economic environment of the late 1970s.

Employee Consumption

The organizational communication theorists John V. Pavlik, Ikechukwu E. Nwosu and Diana G. Ettel's research on employee motivation for reading newsletters revealed that there was no relationship between integration in the company (both socially and professionally) or length of employment and overall newsletter readership.[63] From a survey of the employees of the

Table 7.1. Comparison of topic importance by time, 1974 versus 1979

Perceived Importance 1974 Rankings		1974 to 1979 Shift		Perceived Importance 1979 Rankings
New or improved corporate products	1	1/5	1	Business trends affecting corporation
Fringe benefit information	2	2/2	2	Fringe benefit information
Corporate sales	3	3/4	3	Features on my division or location's departments
All corporate products	4	4/5	4	Corporate sales
Features on my division or location's departments	5	5/3	5	How corporate products are used

Honeywell Corporation in the United States, they found there was, however, a correlation between career aspiration (i.e., wanting to get promoted) and newsletter readership.[64] It would appear that a desire to be more integrated in the organization acted as a motivation to read the newsletter, but once this occurred, its positive effects wore off. Pavlik, Nwosu and Ettel's research also found that different employees read the newsletter for different reasons. This was particularly affected by gender. Women placed greater emphasis on reading to keep track of their friends, while men were keener on keeping up with the company's business activities.[65]

Various Critiques

Research on content and employee motivation for reading laid the basis for the third area of interest—that of critiquing the organizational magazine. What employees wanted and what they received were clearly two different things. This provided support for the argument, which had always accompanied publications aimed at employees, that they were instruments of management propaganda. They were at best mere diversion, rather than important tools of internal communication.[66] This argument was given theoretical ammunition from Clampitt, Crevcoure and Hartel's research.[67] They argued that within organizational magazines there were three key stakeholders: employers, employees and editors. This could lead to three scenarios that were dependent on how these three groups interacted with each other. In the first, "collaboration,"[68] the three groups actively co-operate and try to maximize the value of the organizational magazine. In the second scenario, "capitulation,"[69] the magazine is used as a propaganda tool by management. Editors resign themselves to reproducing the views of management, and employees either passively accept such journalism or simply ignore it. In the third situation, "trivialization,"[70] the conflicting demands of these groups remain unresolved, and the magazine, in response, opts for a strategy of following a path of least resistance. The content of the organizational magazine is filled with material which will offend nobody, focusing on trivia and entertainment, the three deadly B's of babies, bowling scores and birthdays.[71] Content analysis certainly lent support to the final strategy of "trivialization."[72] In addition, research demonstrated that senior management censored staff editors' decisions concerning content of organizational magazines. As Peter Johansen wrote, "Things get to the point where editors simply censor themselves because they know what will not be approved."[73] Here is a clear indication of capitulation.

More prescriptive managerialist writers on organizational magazines have reacted in dismay to this scenario. The internal communication expert Roger D'Aprix, for example, has repeatedly argued that employee publications and internal communication in general should focus on integrating employees into their organizations.[74] This will both improve commitment and enhance both productivity and a sense of organizational well-being on the part of the employee. D'Aprix explains this with his mantra of the six basic questions that every employee has in relation to his or her position. The first three are "I" questions: "What's my job?" "How am I performing?" "Does anyone care how I am performing?" Once employees receive satisfactory answers, they then began to ask "we" questions: "As a work team, what are our objectives and how are we doing?" "How can we fit into the total picture?" "How can I help?"[75] For D'Aprix internal communication is fundamental to answering these questions. For this to happen, however, such communication has to be meaningful and relevant to employees and to the organization as a whole. It has to proactively deal with issues that affect the organization and its workers, such as strategy, globalization and employment policy, rather than trying to obfuscate them or deal with them on a reactive basis.[76] Senior management should use organizational magazines and other tools of internal communication to enter into meaningful two-way dialogues with employees for the good of all stakeholders within the organization. This argument has been echoed by other business communication commentators such as Peter Johansen and Stanley Peterfreund.[77]

Such analysis does not bode well and may account, to some degree, for the apparent decline of academic research and discussion on contemporary organizational magazines since the 1990s, even though there has been increasing interest in the organizational magazine as an historical phenomenon in its own right. However, one final article, aptly titled "Is the Employee Publication Extinct?," provided some grounds for hope.[78] Chief executive Gary Grates argued that employee publications were still very relevant to the organization at the turn of the twenty-first century and appreciated by employees and managers alike. Employees valued them because they enabled workers to feel connected to the company. In an era of globalization, where large corporations had employees scattered all over the world, this was highly important. In addition, employees were argued to value the publications' recognition of workers' efforts and achievements. People still liked seeing their names and pictures in print. Employee publications were valued by management because they were able, through their tone, to give the organization a personality. It should be noted, however, that Grates's article was lacking in hard evidence. Research is clearly needed to substantiate his claims for the employee publication in the twenty-first century. Furthermore, Grates has claimed that these magazines allowed senior management to explain policy, strategy and issues to employees. They acted as important discursive tools of communication. In relation to this, Grates argued that the employee publication had changed in response to instantaneous digital communication, such as e-mails and intranets. Rather than providing news and information, which was done far more efficiently by new media technology, the employee publication's role now was to explain, discuss and persuade.[79] Has the organizational magazine in the digital age of instant information finally achieved its goal of providing a platform for substantive communication? More research is clearly needed.

Future Research

While academic research on contemporary organizational magazines may have declined after the 1990s, the literature on internal communication in general continued to expand. An examination of some of the literature on internal communication therefore offers an indication of where future research into organizational magazines could lie and, indeed, suggests something of their contemporary role and importance. Two areas in particular can be considered: (1) the relationship between organizational cultural and internal communication; and (2) the role of internal communication during organizational change and restructuring.

Organizational culture can be defined as a system of values, beliefs and practices, which are shared by members of an organization.[80] There is a clear connection between organizational culture and internal communication. All communication is culturally constructed. How we communicate, what we communicate and the very symbols and linguistic structures we use are all influenced by culture. In addition, culture is carried and mediated by communication. Communication theorists Jill Fenton Taylor and John Carroll, for example, have noted that organizational identity, as a key manifestation of organizational culture, is sustained by institutions recounting narratives about themselves to both internal and external stakeholders.[81] Such institutional storytelling provides an important role in generating organizational meaning. One notable paper on this topic is public policy experts and theorists James L. Garnett, Justin Marlowe and Sanjay K. Pandey's research into communication and culture in relation to performance in the public sector.[82] They suggest that communication can either be a mediator or a moderator in the nexus between culture and performance. From a managerialist perspective, therefore, internal communication either directly conveys organizational culture and consequently has a direct impact on performance, or simply affects this impact but does not determine it. The role of organizational magazines in relation to internal communication, culture and organizational performance therefore represents a possible line for future research if the value of organizational magazines is to be demonstrated.[83]

A second area of interest is that of the relationship between internal communication and organizational change. Since the 1990s there has been a strong impetus for structural reorganization, which has often involved drastic changes for many individuals and their relationships with organizations. Terms such as re-engineering, delayering, outsourcing and off-shoring have become commonplace and feared ways of describing these changes. Many organizations have been "hollowed out,"[84] with their operations, including production, removed from the organization's core and headquarters to be outsourced and off-shored across the globe. Researchers have demonstrated that internal communication is important to the process of organizational change. Internal communication can explain the rationale for change, outline its pace and extent, and persuade organizational members that reform is necessary.

The organizational communication theorists Paul Nelissen and Martine van Selm, for example, studied a Dutch branch of a large international company that had undergone organizational change and made a number of workers redundant.[85] They surveyed surviving employees in order to understand the role of management communication in accommodating employees to the restructuring process. Nelissen and van Selm surveyed staff about attitudes during the change and retrospectively, that is, at a later point, after they had already occurred.[86] Negative views initially expressed toward the changes had become more positive over time. They also found that satisfaction with management communication tended to correlate with positive responses to the changes at both stages.[87] Competent internal communication was argued to assist the process of organization change. In this context, organizational change expert Stefanie C. Reissner's research on the importance of internal storytelling in clarifying and justifying organizational change emphasizes that the construction of narratives are vital during organizational change to explain "events and happenings."[88] Furthermore, in the absence of such narratives or in situations where experience does not match expectations, employees will begin to construct their own narratives. In relation to this, Reissner found three kinds of stories: those of the good old days; those of deception, taboo and silence; and those of influence.[89] The control of narrative, and an understanding of employee construction of their own stories, is clearly important for any company undergoing structural reorganization.

Research on organizational culture and change is certainly pertinent for considering the role of contemporary organizational magazines in internal communication. As this chapter has demonstrated, these themes are increasingly salient in historical research on company magazines. Historians, such as John Griffiths, Michael Heller, Howard Cox and Simon Phillips, have focused on the role of magazines in constructing and perpetuating organizational culture, identity and meaning.[90] Clearly organizational magazines have played an important role historically in explaining and justifying organizational change, but the effect of their continuation or demise in contemporary internal communication and organizational change remains under-researched.

When one thinks of magazines, those that originate from organizations hardly spring first to mind. Yet, as this chapter has argued, they have enjoyed a long history and an extensive circulation. While perhaps not as glamorous as other magazines, they have contributed a fundamental role in the development of corporations since the late nineteenth century. For those interested in large-scale organizations, their functions, their members, their impact and the work, products and services they provide, these magazines are a deserving area of study. They provide a vital insight into these bodies. As this chapter has suggested, organizational magazines can be seen as constituting organizational histories, cultures and identities, and not merely communicating them. This leads to the question of how organizational cultures were constituted before organizational magazines and how they are constituted and communicated in the absence of organizational magazines, given that they also provide an important hermeneutic framework of reference in which organizational actors see and interpret events. In addition, in a more prosaic but vital area, they divulge something of how organizations communicate and provide a forum of debate concerning how they should do so. They also reveal something about the versatility of the magazine and its ability to colonize myriad spaces. The success of the organizational magazine in the twentieth century owed something to the success of the magazine in general. The future of the two are clearly intertwined.

As this chapter has argued, there is scope for much more research on organizational magazines, and the recent interest in the history of the organizational magazine should not be taken to mean that as a medium it is bereft of a future. While organizational magazines may not have been ignored by professional bodies such as the International Association of Business Communicators, their contemporary significance, or even their demise, has been neglected by academic researchers in the opening years of the twenty-first century. As a result there is very little indication of how organizational magazines have been affected by the digital revolution in communications and how they have been replaced in organizations, if at all. While perhaps diminished, it is difficult to believe that they will completely disappear. Their continued role within internal communications precludes this. If scholars are interested in organizations and the communications which they produce, if topics such as globalization, organizational culture, organizational change and staff motivation continue to remain relevant and interesting, more academic engagement with organizational magazines must take place. Moreover, there may be larger lessons yet to be learned from the broader spectrum of organizational magazines earlier identified as found in government institutions at both the local and central level, in hospitals, schools, universities, churches, sports clubs and associations, charities, trade unions, political parties and pressure groups, as well as in the political, commercial and civic spheres.

Notes

1 Mary Welch and Paul R. Jackson, "Rethinking Internal Communication: A Stakeholder Approach," *Corporate Communications: An International Journal* 12.2 (2007): 177–198; Michael Heller, "British Company Magazines, 1878–1939: The Origins and Functions of House Journals in Large-Scale Organisations," *Media History* 15.2 (2009): 158–159.

2 JoAnne Yates, *Control through Communication: The Rise of System in American Management* (Baltimore: Johns Hopkins University Press, 1989).

3 From interviews with archivists at leading banks in London that have large holdings of historical organizational magazines, it is clear that many of these organizations not only do not produce magazines, but actively police the organization to prevent their being produced.

4 Yates, *Control through Communication.*

5 Charles Booth and Michael Rowlinson, "*Management and Organizational History*: Prospects," *Management & Organizational History* 1.1 (2006): 5–30.

6 Liz Yeomans, "Internal Communication," in Ralph Tench and Liz Yeomans, eds., *Exploring Public Relations*, 2nd ed. (Harlow, UK: FT Prentice Hall, 2009), 318.

7 Yeomans, "Internal Communication," 318.

8 Welch and Jackson, "Rethinking Internal Communication."

9 Richard J. Varey and Barbara R. Lewis, eds., *Internal Marketing: Directions for Management* (London: Routledge, 2000); Michael Heller, "Corporate Brand Building: Shell-Mex Ltd. in the Interwar Period," in Teresa da Silva Lopes and Paul Duguid, eds., *Trademarks, Brands, and Competitiveness* (London: Routledge, 2010), 197–200.

10 Welch and Jackson, "Rethinking Internal Communication."

11 Welch and Jackson, "Rethinking Internal Communication," 184–186.

12 Yeomans, "Internal Communication," 321.

13 Yeomans, "Internal Communication," 321.

14 Yates, *Control through Communication*, 5.

15 Yates, *Control through Communication*, 17; Roland Marchand, *Creating the Corporate Soul: The Rise of Public Relations and Corporate Imagery in American Big Business* (Berkeley: University of California Press, 1998).

16 Yates, *Control through Communication*, 17.

17 Daniel Nelson, *Managers and Workers: Origins of the Twentieth-Century Factory System in the United States, 1880–1920*, 2nd ed. (Madison: University of Wisconsin Press, 1995).

18 Budgett Meakin, *Model Factories and Villages: Ideal Conditions of Labour and Housing* (London: T. Fisher Unwin, 1905).

19 Meakin, *Model Factories and Villages*, 60.

20 Meakin, *Model Factories and Villages*, 60.

21 Meakin, *Model Factories and Villages*, 60–64.

22 John Griffiths, "'Give My Regards to Uncle Billy . . . ': The Rites and Rituals of Company Life at Lever Brothers, c.1900–c.1990," *Business History* 37.4 (October 1995): 25–45; John Griffiths, "Exploring Corporate Culture: The Potential of Company Magazines for the Business Historians," *Business Archives Sources and History* 78 (1999): 27–37; Peter Johansen, "'For Better, Higher and Nobler Things': Massey's Pioneering Employee Publication," *Journalism History* 27.3 (Fall 2001): 94–104.

23 Heller, "British Company Magazines," 143–166.

24 Alfred D. Chandler, Jr., *The Visible Hand: The Managerial Revolution in American Business* (Cambridge, MA: Belknap Press, 1977); Leslie Hannah, *The Rise of the Corporate Economy* (London: Methuen, 1976); John F. Wilson, *British Business History, 1720–1994* (Manchester: Manchester University Press, 1995).

25 Heller, "British Company Magazines."

26 Marchand, *Creating the Corporate Soul*.

27 Heller, "British Company Magazines"; Michael Heller, "Company Magazines 1880–1940: An Overview," *Management & Organizational History* 3.3/4 (August/November 2008): 179–196.

28 Marchand, *Creating the Corporate Soul*.

29 Heller, "Company Magazines 1880–1940."

30 Howard Cox, "Shaping a Corporate Identity from Below: The Role of the *BAT Bulletin*," *Management & Organizational History* 3.3/4 (August/November 2008): 197–215.

31 Simon Phillips, "'Chemists to the Nation': House Magazines, Locality and Health at Boots The Chemists 1919–1939," *Management & Organizational History* 3.3/4 (August/November 2008): 239–255. Editorial note: Phillips reports the official name of the company as being Boots The Chemists, with a capital T.

32 Greg Patmore and Jonathan Rees, "Employee Publications and Employee Representation Plans: The Case of Colorado Fuel and Iron, 1915–1942," *Management & Organizational History* 3.3/4 (August/November 2008): 257–272.

33 Bart Dredge, "Company Magazines and the Creation of Industrial Cooperation: A Case Study from the Southern Textile Industry, 1880–1940," *Management & Organizational History* 3.3/4 (August/November 2008): 273–288.

34 Mike Esbester, "Organizing Work: Company Magazines and the Discipline of Safety," *Management & Organizational History* 3.3/4 (August/November 2008): 217–237.

35 Esbester, "Organizing Work," 217–237.

36 Yeomans, "Internal Communication," 318.

37 Benedict Anderson, *Imagined Communities: Reflections on the Origin and Spread of Nationalism*, rev. ed. (London and New York: Verso, 2006).

38 Terrence E. Deal and Allan A. Kennedy, *The New Corporate Cultures: Revitalizing the Workplace after Downsizing, Mergers, and Reengineering* (New York: Perseus Books, 1999).

39 Michael Rowlinson, Charles Booth, Peter Clark, Agnès Delahaye, and Stephen Procter, "Social Remembering and Organizational Memory," *Organization Studies* 31.1 (January 2010): 69–87.

40 Michael Rowlinson and John Hassard, "The Invention of Corporate Culture: A History of the Histories of Cadbury," *Human Relations* 46.3 (March 1993): 299–326.

41 Eric Hobsbawm and Terence Ranger, eds., *The Invention of Tradition*, Canto ed. (Cambridge, UK: Cambridge University Press, 1992).

42 Rowlinson and Hassard, "The Invention of Corporate Culture," 299–326.

43 Iolo A. Williams, *The Firm of Cadbury, 1831–1931* (London: Constable and Co. Ltd., 1931).

44 T.B. Rogers, *A Century of Progress, 1831–1931: Cadbury Bournville* (Chicago: Hudson & Kearns, 1931).

45 Rowlinson and Hassard, "The Invention of Corporate Culture," 308.

46 Agnès Delahaye, Charles Booth, Peter Clark, Stephen Procter, and Michael Rowlinson, "The Genre of Corporate History," *Journal of Organizational Change Management* 22.1 (2009): 27–48.

47 Michael Rowlinson, "Public History Review Essay: Cadbury World," *Labour History Review* 67.1 (April 2002): 101–119; see also, Carl Chinn, *The Cadbury Story: A Short History* (Studley, UK: Brewin Books, 1998).

48 Deal and Kennedy, *The New Corporate Cultures.*

49 Deal and Kennedy, *The New Corporate Cultures,* 4.

50 Deal and Kennedy, *The New Corporate Cultures,* 206.

51 Phillip G. Clampitt, Jean M. Crevcoure, and Robin L. Hartel, "Exploratory Research on Employee Publications," *Journal of Business Communication* 23.3 (Summer 1986): 5.

52 Peter Johansen, "Where's the Meaning and the Hope? Trends in Employee Publications," *Journal of Popular Culture* 29.3 (Winter 1995): 129.

53 Johansen, "Where's the Meaning and the Hope?," 129.

54 Joan Kampe and Lyn Christenson, "Publications: What's in the Package," in Carol Reuss and Donn Silvis, eds., *Inside Organizational Communication,* 2nd ed. (London and New York: Longman, 1985), 129–144.

55 Kampe and Christenson, "Publications," 130–131.

56 Clampitt, Crevcoure, and Hartel, "Exploratory Research," 10.

57 C.J. Dover, "The Three Eras of Management Communication," in W. Charles Redding and George A. Sanborn, eds., *Business and Industrial Communication: A Source Book* (New York: Harper and Row, 1964), 61–65.

58 Stanley Peterfreund, "Employee Publications: Deadly but Not Dead Yet," *Public Relations Journal* 30.1 (January 1974): 20–21; Clampitt, Crevcoure, and Hartel, "Exploratory Research," 15–17; Johansen, "Where's the Meaning and the Hope?," 130–132.

59 Johansen, "Where's the Meaning and the Hope?"

60 Clampitt, Crevcoure, and Hartel, "Exploratory Research," 12–13.

61 David N. Bateman and Jeffrey Miller, "Employee Communication: Messages for the 1980s," *Journal of Business Communication* 18.3 (Summer 1981): 3–10.

62 Bateman and Miller, "Employee Communication," 4–5.

63 John V. Pavlik, Ikechukwu E. Nwosu, and Diana G. Ettel, "Why Employees Read Company Newsletters," *Public Relations Review* 8.3 (1982): 23–33.

64 Pavlik, Nwosu, and Ettel, "Why Employees Read Company Newsletters," 29.

65 Pavlik, Nwosu, and Ettel, "Why Employees Read Company Newsletters," 30.

66 Peterfreund, "Employee Publications," 20–23; David N. Bateman, "The Employees' Right to Know the Issues and the Corporations' Responsibility to Communicate," *Journal of Business Communication* 14.2 (Winter 1977): 3–9; Johansen, "Where's the Meaning and the Hope?"

67 Clampitt, Crevcoure, and Hartel, "Exploratory Research."

68 Clampitt, Crevcoure, and Hartel, "Exploratory Research," 6–7.

69 Clampitt, Crevcoure, and Hartel, "Exploratory Research," 7.

70 Clampitt, Crevcoure, and Hartel, "Exploratory Research," 7.

71 Clampitt, Crevcoure, and Hartel, "Exploratory Research," 6–8.

72 Bateman and Miller, "Employee Communication"; Clampitt, Crevcoure, and Hartel, "Exploratory Research"; Johansen, "Where's the Meaning and the Hope?"

73 Johansen, "Where's the Meaning and the Hope?," 134.

74 David Hoffman, "D'Aprix Discusses Communication Awareness," *IABC Communication World,* November 1985, 14–16; Roger D'Aprix, "Communicators in Contemporary Organizations," in Carol Reuss and Donn Silvis, eds., *Inside Organizational Communication,* 2nd ed. (London and New York: Longman, 1985), 15–29.

75 Hoffman, "D'Aprix Discusses Communication Awareness," 14–16.

76 D'Aprix, "Communicators in Contemporary Organizations," 15–29.

77 Johansen, "Where's the Meaning and the Hope?"; Peterfreund, "Employee Publications."

78 Gary Grates, "Is the Employee Publication Extinct?" *Communication World,* December 1999–January 2000, 27–30.

79 Grates, "Is the Employee Publication Extinct?," 29.

80 Mats Alvesson, *Understanding Organizational Culture* (London: Sage, 2002); Deal and Kennedy, *The New Corporate Cultures*; Edgar H. Schein, *Organizational Culture and Leadership,* 3rd ed. (London: Jossey-Bass, 2004).

81 Jill Fenton Taylor and John Carroll, "Corporate Cultural Narratives as the Performance of Organisational Meaning," *Qualitative Research Journal* 10.1 (2010): 28–39.

82 James L. Garnett, Justin Marlowe, and Sanjay K. Pandey, "Penetrating the Performance Predicament: Communication as a Mediator or Moderator of Organizational Culture's Impact on Public Organizational Performance," *Public Administration Review* 68.2 (March/April 2008): 266–281.

83 Garnett, Marlowe, and Pandey, "Penetrating the Performance Predicament," 274–277.

84 Richard Sennett, *The Corrosion of Character: The Personal Consequences of Work in the New Capitalism* (New York and London: W.W. Norton, 1999), 56.

85 Paul Nelissen and Martine van Selm, "Surviving Organizational Change: How Management Communication Helps Balance Mixed Feelings," *Corporate Communications: An International Journal* 13.3 (2008): 306–318.

86 Nelissen and van Selm, "Surviving Organizational Change."

87 Nelissen and van Selm, "Surviving Organizational Change," 314.

88 Stefanie C. Reissner, "Patterns of Stories of Organisational Change," *Journal of Organizational Change Management* 24.5 (2011): 593, 593–609.

89 Reissner, "Patterns of Stories of Organisational Change," 594.

90 Griffiths, " 'Give My Regards to Uncle Billy . . . ' "; Griffiths, "Exploring Corporate Culture"; Heller, "British Company Magazines"; Cox, "Shaping a Corporate Identity from Below"; Phillips, " 'Chemists to the Nation.' "

Bibliography

Alvesson, Mats. *Understanding Organizational Culture*. London: Sage, 2002.

Anderson, Benedict. *Imagined Communities: Reflections on the Origin and Spread of Nationalism*. Rev. ed. London and New York: Verso, 2006.

Bateman, David N. "The Employees' Right to Know the Issues and the Corporations' Responsibility to Communicate." *Journal of Business Communication* 14.2 (Winter 1977): 3–9.

Bateman, David N. and Miller, Jeffrey. "Employee Communication: Messages for the 1980s." *Journal of Business Communication* 18.3 (Summer 1981): 3–10.

Booth, Charles and Rowlinson, Michael. "*Management and Organizational History*: Prospects." *Management & Organizational History* 1.1 (2006): 5–30.

Chandler, Alfred D., Jr. *The Visible Hand: The Managerial Revolution in American Business*. Cambridge, MA: Belknap Press, 1977.

Chinn, Carl. *The Cadbury Story: A Short History*. Studley, UK: Brewin Books, 1998.

Clampitt, Phillip G.; Crevcoure, Jean M.; and Hartel, Robin L. "Exploratory Research on Employee Publications." *Journal of Business Communication* 23.3 (Summer 1986): 5–17.

Cox, Howard. "Shaping a Corporate Identity from Below: The Role of the BAT Bulletin." *Management & Organizational History* 3.3/4 (August/November 2008): 197–215.

D'Aprix, Roger. "Communicators in Contemporary Organizations." In Reuss, Carol and Silvis, Donn, eds. *Inside Organizational Communication*. 2nd ed. London and New York: Longman, 1985, 15–29.

Deal, Terrence E. and Kennedy, Allan A. *The New Corporate Cultures: Revitalizing the Workplace after Downsizing, Mergers, and Reengineering*. New York: Perseus Books, 1999.

Delahaye, Agnès; Booth, Charles; Clark, Peter; Procter, Stephen; and Rowlinson, Michael. "The Genre of Corporate History." *Journal of Organizational Change Management* 22.1 (2009): 27–48.

Dover, C.J. "The Three Eras of Management Communication." In Redding, W. Charles and Sanborn, George A., eds. *Business and Industrial Communication: A Source Book*. New York: Harper and Row, 1964, 61–65.

Dredge, Bart. "Company Magazines and the Creation of Industrial Cooperation: A Case Study from the Southern Textile Industry, 1880–1940." *Management & Organizational History* 3.3/4 (August/November 2008): 273–288.

Esbester, Mike. "Organizing Work: Company Magazines and the Discipline of Safety." *Management & Organizational History* 3.3/4 (August/November 2008): 217–237.

Garnett, James L.; Marlowe, Justin; and Pandey, Sanjay K. "Penetrating the Performance Predicament: Communication as a Mediator or Moderator of Organizational Culture's Impact on Public Organizational Performance." *Public Administration Review* 68.2 (March/April 2008): 266–281.

Grates, Gary. "Is the Employee Publication Extinct?" *Communication World*, December 1999–January 2000, 27–30.

Griffiths, John. "Exploring Corporate Culture: The Potential of Company Magazines for the Business Historians." *Business Archives: Sources and History* 78 (1999): 27–37.

Griffiths, John. "'Give My Regards to Uncle Billy . . .': The Rites and Rituals of Company Life at Lever Brothers, c.1900–c.1990." *Business History* 37.4 (October 1995): 25–45.

Hannah, Leslie. *The Rise of the Corporate Economy.* London: Methuen, 1976.

Heller, Michael. "British Company Magazines, 1878–1939: The Origins and Functions of House Journals in Large-Scale Organisations." *Media History* 15.2 (2009): 143–166.

Heller, Michael. "Company Magazines 1880–1940: An Overview." *Management & Organizational History* 3.3/4 (August/November 2008): 179–196.

Heller, Michael. "Corporate Brand Building: Shell-Mex Ltd. in the Interwar Period." In Lopes, Teresa da Silva and Duguid, Paul, eds. *Trademarks, Brands, and Competitiveness.* London: Routledge, 2010, 194–214.

Hobsbawm, Eric and Ranger, Terence, eds. *The Invention of Tradition.* Canto ed. Cambridge, UK: Cambridge University Press, 1992.

Hoffman, David. "D'Aprix Discusses Communication Awareness." *IABC Communication World,* November 1985, 14–16.

Johansen, Peter. "'For Better, Higher and Nobler Things': Massey's Pioneering Employee Publication." *Journalism History* 27.3 (Fall 2001): 94–104.

Johansen, Peter. "Where's the Meaning and the Hope? Trends in Employee Publications." *Journal of Popular Culture* 29.3 (Winter 1995): 129–138.

Kampe, Joan and Christenson, Lyn. "Publications: What's in the Package." In Reuss, Carol and Silvis, Donn, eds. *Inside Organizational Communication.* 2nd ed. London and New York: Longman, 1985, 129–144.

Marchand, Roland. *Creating the Corporate Soul: The Rise of Public Relations and Corporate Imagery in American Big Business.* Berkeley: University of California Press, 1998.

Meakin, Budgett. *Model Factories and Villages: Ideal Conditions of Labour and Housing.* London: T. Fisher Unwin, 1905.

Nelissen, Paul and van Selm, Martine. "Surviving Organizational Change: How Management Communication Helps Balance Mixed Feelings." *Corporate Communications: An International Journal* 13.3 (2008): 306–318.

Nelson, Daniel. *Managers and Workers: Origins of the Twentieth-Century Factory System in the United States, 1880–1920.* 2nd ed. Madison: University of Wisconsin Press, 1995.

Patmore, Greg and Rees, Jonathan. "Employee Publications and Employee Representation Plans: The Case of Colorado Fuel and Iron, 1915–1942." *Management & Organizational History* 3.3/4 (August/November 2008): 257–272.

Pavlik, John V.; Nwosu, Ikechukwu E.; and Ettel, Diana G. "Why Employees Read Company Newsletters." *Public Relations Review* 8.3 (1982): 23–33.

Peterfreund, Stanley. "Employee Publications: Deadly but Not Dead Yet." *Public Relations Journal* 30.1 (January 1974): 20–23.

Phillips, Simon. "'Chemists to the Nation': House Magazines, Locality and Health at Boots The Chemists 1919–1939." *Management & Organizational History* 3.3/4 (August/November 2008): 239–255.

Reissner, Stefanie C. "Patterns of Stories of Organisational Change." *Journal of Organizational Change Management* 24.5 (2011): 593–609.

Rogers, T.B. *A Century of Progress, 1831–1931: Cadbury Bournville.* Chicago: Hudson & Kearns, 1931.

Rowlinson, Michael. "Public History Review Essay: Cadbury World." *Labour History Review* 67.1 (April 2002): 101–119.

Rowlinson, Michael; Booth, Charles; Clark, Peter; Delahaye, Agnès; and Procter, Stephen. "Social Remembering and Organizational Memory." *Organization Studies* 31.1 (January 2010): 69–87.

Rowlinson, Michael and Hassard, John. "The Invention of Corporate Culture: A History of the Histories of Cadbury." *Human Relations* 46.3 (March 1993): 299–326.

Schein, Edgar H. *Organizational Culture and Leadership.* 3rd ed. London: Jossey-Bass, 2004.

Sennett, Richard. *The Corrosion of Character: The Personal Consequences of Work in the New Capitalism.* New York and London: W.W. Norton, 1999.

Taylor, Jill Fenton and Carroll, John. "Corporate Cultural Narratives as the Performance of Organisational Meaning." *Qualitative Research Journal* 10.1 (2010): 28–39.

Varey, Richard J. and Lewis, Barbara R., eds. *Internal Marketing: Directions for Management.* London: Routledge, 2000.

Welch, Mary and Jackson, Paul R. "Rethinking Internal Communication: A Stakeholder Approach." *Corporate Communications: An International Journal* 12.2 (2007): 177–198.

Williams, Iolo A. *The Firm of Cadbury, 1831–1931*. London: Constable and Co. Ltd., 1931.

Wilson, John F. *British Business History, 1720–1994*. Manchester: Manchester University Press, 1995.

Yates, JoAnne. *Control through Communication: The Rise of System in American Management*. Baltimore: Johns Hopkins University Press, 1989.

Yeomans, Liz. "Internal Communication." In Tench, Ralph and Yeomans, Liz, eds. *Exploring Public Relations*. 2nd ed. Harlow, UK: FT Prentice Hall, 2009, 316–337.

Supplemental Resources

Lewin, Kurt. "Frontiers in Group Dynamics: Concept, Method and Reality in Social Science; Social Equilibria and Social Change." *Human Relations* 1.5 (June 1947): 5–41.

Pascale, Richard Tanner and Athos, Anthony G. *The Art of Japanese Management: Applications for American Executives*. New York: Simon and Schuster, 1981.

Peters, Thomas J. and Waterman, Robert H., Jr. *In Search of Excellence: Lessons from America's Best Run Companies*. New York: Harper & Row, 1982.

Weick, Karl E. *Sensemaking in Organizations*. London: Sage, 1995.

8

INTERNATIONAL MAGAZINE PUBLISHING

The Transformative Power of Globalization

Leara D. Rhodes

Magazine publishing on national and international levels is changing as new technologies and economic instability have combined to encourage late twentieth and early twenty-first century publishers to expand their brands. Publishers' stabilizing strategies have included moving into new markets to reach new audiences, build circulation and increase advertising revenues, as well as using on-line or other digital technologies to strengthen reach and reduce costs. Magazine scholars have taken note of some of these changes and their effects on the medium; other changes wait to be examined. The growing interest among scholars in transnational and global inquiry has an additional dimension: the importance of a universal perspective for theory development.

This chapter surveys scholarship on international magazine publishing from 1990 to the present. Building on a 1995 review of research on international periodicals and publishing,[1] two core questions guide the current review: What kinds of studies have been done on international magazines in the almost two decades since, and what, if any, is their importance to advancing scholarship on magazines?

Literature Search and Method

Given the increased importance of international publishing, the search for the literature focused on identifying scholarly articles published between 1990 and the present. Thirteen sources were used to locate the studies on international publishing reviewed in this chapter. These included the AEJMC Web site for archival abstracts, *Communication Abstracts*, the *Journal of Applied Journalism and Media Studies*, David Sumner's survey of *Journalism & Mass Communication Quarterly*,[2] the *Online Journal of Communication and Media Technologies*, the *International Journal of Communication*, *Journal of African Cultural Studies*, JSTOR, the *European Journal of Marketing*, *Journal of Communication*, *Media International Australia*, *Journalism & Communication Monographs* and *Communication Monographs*. Keywords and phrases used to locate the articles were *magazines*, *magazines* and *international*, *on-line publications*, *international* and *magazine apps*, and *digital publications*.

A total of 60 studies were identified. Of these, 55 were scholarly articles, 4 were book chapters and 1, a book-length study. No studies of U.S. magazines' coverage of foreign events, people or issues were included. With the exception of a few comparative studies, only studies using magazines published outside the United States were included. Finally, only fully accessed articles were included in this review. Each study was examined to (1) determine the kinds of studies being conducted to advance scholarship in the magazine sector of international media and communication research and (2) establish whether the scholarship was driving or responding to industry decisions and developments. The review also looked for areas to be researched.

From reading the articles, several patterns, or themes, emerged. Scholars have conducted both cross-cultural and multi-country case studies, content, discourse and textual analyses, as well as multimodal analyses. Theoretical bases in the articles were dominated by *globalization theories* but also included *hybridity, glocalization, localization versus standardization, post-colonial, feminist* and *critical cultural* perspectives. A sizable section of the research focused on women's magazines in Asian countries, particularly related to advertising. To make sense of the variations of theories and methods and for the purposes of discussing the research, this chapter is divided according to the several dimensions of the periodical magazine: editorial content, advertising content, visuals and marketing.

Research on magazine editorial content focuses on the text of magazines and includes issues of identity and transmitting culture. Advertising research includes questions of gender, stereotypes and beauty ideals. Studies of visuals are divided into photos, covers and overall design. Marketing is subdivided into branding, expansion issues related to localization versus globalization and hybridity. Within each of these divisions the review includes discussions of theoretical approaches, methods and critiques. Finally, suggestions will be offered for how to advance scholarship related to magazines in the global market.

The studies used multiple methodologies and theoretical concepts; identifying studies as just editorial or just advertising was also difficult in some instances. Within the divisions suggested, approximately one-third of the 60 studies fall under editorial, one-third under advertising, and one-third under marketing. The visual component had the fewest, with only four studies.

International Magazine Publishing

International magazine and journal periodical publishing has a long history: At the most basic level are magazines published in the home country, that is, *indigenous* periodicals that are international to other nations. International publishers also use multiple strategies for reaching international audiences. Leonard Mogel has summarized these, noting that publishers target audiences outside the countries of titles' origins, selling *serial rights* for articles and book excerpts. Publishers also distribute magazines across national boundaries so that through *international distribution* one nation's magazines appear on newsstands in others, particularly in the world's most cosmopolitan cities, whether Bangkok, Copenhagen, Brasilia or New York City. A third strategy also has a long history: establishing companion titles in countries through franchises and international licensing,[3] or *transnational publishing*.

An emerging body of literature, identified through the search for this chapter, gives evidence that the convergence of Internet and digital technologies and an increasingly international economy have given new impetus to questions related to the last of the traditional strategies, transnational publishing. The growing interest in reaching international audiences triggers questions that are important not only for what is happening in industry but also scholarly inquiry. Business and trade publications regularly carry announcements of ways in which publishers are expanding, locating new markets in emerging countries, producing digital and on-line publications and entering into working partnerships with global advertising agencies. Scholars are researching how expansion and globalization are affecting publications in other local markets, including whether new markets are culturally aligned with the newly arrived foreign publications and the effects of introducing global advertising into new markets that constitute different countries and cultures.

Mature markets push publishers to become leaders in the global market.[4] Crain Communications' Ad Age Group, for example, has transformed its print product, *Advertising Age*, into a digital format, as it refocuses its international news resources. *Advertising Age*, in turn, has expanded its coverage of global news, trends and data. The iPad is being used to expand Time Inc.'s periodicals into India through magazine apps. Other publications, such as *National Geographic*, with its 37 language editions, are using multiple languages on their Web sites to appeal to other markets.[5]

David Machin and Sarah Niblock posit in their study of news providers that those who are providing multiplatform services, such as those available for Bloomberg News and *Foreign Affairs*, are flourishing despite the hugely challenging economic climate for journalism. These scholars suggest, based on their findings from linguistic analysis supported by interviews with journalists, that publishers are catering to a new kind of global audience: a professional readership that demands a different editorial strategy. Machin and Niblock suggest that the emphasis is on niche marketing that is more task than entertainment driven, and audiences enter through search engines, not because of branding. The authors conclude by raising questions about the continued efficacy of traditional models of journalism practice and notions of audience.[6]

Developing an audience through a digital periodical is another way to focus on international or global niche audiences. Susan Glasser reports that a digital publication, such as the on-line magazine *Foreign Policy*, publishes more original writing about international affairs than the *Washington Post* or *Newsweek*.[7] The resulting, expanded audience may point to the importance of international magazine publishing. Global media packaging also nurtures a kind of market synergy. Hachette early established itself as a leader in using this strategy, moving into many markets, including the United States.[8] The French publisher has agreements with Ford Motor Co., General Motors Corp., Benetton, Eastman Kodak Co., various Japanese automakers, L'Oreal and Hermes to link advertisers with magazines for global marketing. The goal is to expand products internationally to create a friendly context for the advertiser.[9]

Katherine T. Frith, Yang Feng and Lan Ye suggest the advertiser is the reason international women's magazines have expanded into China, driven by global brands in need of advertising vehicles for global products.[10] Kavita Karan and Yang Feng's findings from a study of international women's magazines in China also support this notion, from global and local perspectives. These researchers argue that almost all the literature on international women's magazines is based on the current expansion of Western global media.[11] Recent studies focus on how culture (often gender and beauty) is portrayed in advertisements placed in the new international magazines that are being introduced into emerging markets, as is discussed in a later section.

Research on the changing climate within a country when international magazines are introduced includes Leara Rhodes's study of magazines in Russia after the fall of the Soviet Union. In that case, the introduction of *Cosmopolitan* magazine caused a shift in the content of established Soviet magazines. The change was from a political model, where all magazines were run by the state, to a commodity model, where magazines were introduced that were based on economics and had no connection with the state, a unique concept for Russia at that time.[12]

Research on Editorial Content

The current research on editorial content in international magazines draws on perspectives that include framing, discourse analysis and textual analysis perspectives. The studies discussed in this section examine ways content shapes a message and may influence a culture. Studies used variations of hybridity theory to explain how local magazines adapt content to compete with international magazines that enter their markets. Scholars have looked at a variety of issues, from identity and gender to the environment.

Identity studies include Ole Jacob Madsen and Brita Ytre-Arne's examination of therapeutic ideals in Norwegian women's magazines. Madsen and Ytre-Arne conducted a qualitative content analysis of two magazines, *KK* and *Tara*, and found that the magazines' content supports the idea that empowered women learn how to take care of themselves.[13] Global or national identities are examined through critical cultural and gender perspectives in two studies. Loubna H. Skalli examined local Moroccan women's magazines and drew on a progression of theories, beginning with cultural imperialism, media globalization and hybridity, to explain how cultures have developed. Skalli cites Featherstone and his argument that cultures represent conduits for diverse cultural flows and exchanges between world regions through the help of various elements.[14] Skalli lists these elements as technologies of communications, national entrepreneurs, and transnational investors.[15] Martha Wörsching's findings from her study of *Der Spiegel* and the *Economist* suggest that discourses of nature and sport are conceived to assert a uniform, global hegemonic masculinity[16] and support the magazine industry's goal to expand brands and reach out to a global audience. Machin and Niblock, in researching Bloomberg using textual analysis and interviews, similarly identify how brands are reaching a new audience.[17]

Other identity studies are examined through a gender theory lens. One of the most in-depth studies is Fabienne Darling-Wolf and Andrew L. Mendelson's study of how a glocalized (global and local) *National Geographic* story, "The Samurai Way," resonated with Japanese readers. Darling-Wolf and Mendelson described the study goal thus:

> This investigation of the intersection between the means of production and the reception of the text aims at shedding a light on broad theoretical debates relating to processes of cross-cultural representation and influence, local interpretation, and cultural-identity formation in an increasingly global environment.[18]

Their textual analysis of the 2006 story, published in the Japanese edition of *National Geographic*, also included responses of 36 Japanese college students in six focus groups. The report of the discussion indicated the students saw the story more as history than culture and perceived a definite U.S. slant to the story. This study opens the debate on *hybridity*, for although hybridity suggests a blending of products, cultures ebb and flow, refusing to remain constant. This is an issue seldom considered in globalization studies. Tiffany J. Shoop, Catherine Luther and Carolynn McMahan, in their study of gender role changes between men and women in Japan, argue that these changes benefit mass media and advertisers by leading to increased sales of magazines.[19]

The impact of global and local forces in the portrayal of women's roles in women's magazines in China was the focus of Yang Feng and Kavita Karan's quantitative analysis of the editorial content of both local and international magazines. To locate globalization influences, they traced the changing depiction of women in the magazines, using six of the top selling magazines in China to include U.S., French, Japanese and local Chinese magazines. Four issues were randomly selected during a 12-month period from October 2006 to September 2007. Their results indicated that women's magazines in China tend both to reinforce traditional sex role stereotypes and to underline the pervasiveness of consumerism and the commercialization of gender.[20] Kopnina also studied representations of women, related to issues of sex, gender and authority. She examined the April 2005 issues of three international editions of *Vogue* (English, French and Russian) and analyzed political and social elements of text and images. Her study design, that is, examining the same brand of a magazine across different cultural markets, suggests an intriguing approach to exploring cultural differences and similarities.[21]

National Geographic was also the focus of Radhika Parameswaran's critique of gender and identity in the August 1999 millennium issue's narratives on globalization.[22] Basing her research on the insights of semiotic, feminist and Marxist critiques of consumer culture, Parameswaran used textual analysis to study multiple media texts and historical contexts that filter the magazine's imagery. The analysis draws from postcolonial theories of gender, Orientalism and nationalism to explore the disturbing ambivalence that permeates *National Geographic*'s stories on global culture. Critiquing discourses of gender, the author found that the magazine's interpretation of global culture was suffused with representations of femininity, masculinity and race that subtly echo the *Othering* modalities of Euro American colonial discourses. Parameswaran argues in her article on "Local Culture in Global Media" that *National Geographic*'s articulation of global culture addresses Asians only as modern consumers of global commodities and that the magazine maintains the invisibility of colonial history, labor and global production. Parameswaran concludes that the insights of postcolonial theories enable critics of globalization to challenge the subtle hegemony of modern neocolonial discursive regimes.[23] Victoria B. Korzeniowska also examined discourses of gender in a study of two French language magazines in Morocco—*Femmes du Maroc* and *Citadine*. She asked how Moroccan women portrayed in magazines reconcile the opposing attractions of tradition and modernity.[24] Again, this study challenges the definition of gender identity within a society.

A number of scholars have looked at international magazines' coverage of environmental issues. Their findings suggest that critiques of the kind of content found in magazines may actually produce changes in industry practices. William Tillinghast and Marie McCann studied the coverage of climate change in four newsmagazines, the *Economist* (United Kingdom), *Maclean's* (Canada), *Newsweek* (United States) and *U.S. News and World Report* (United States), during a 20-year period. Though the magazines did not change their coverage of climate change, the term *greenhouse effect* did change to *climate change*. The authors concluded from the analyses that the initially dominant political and scientific frame diminished over time while the ecological-meteorological frame virtually disappeared.[25]

The environment is also the central focus of Lyn McGaurr's study of the ways U.S. and U.K. journalists criticize forestry practices in travel articles about Australia's Tasmania. The study, based on articles published in newspapers and magazines, is included in this international magazine review because McGaurr uses cosmopolitan theory to place the discussion in a different context than the economic or cultural context so often found in travel writing. McGaurr described the study goal as an "example of how tourism, consumerism, activism and the media converge and overlap in our increasingly globalized world."[26]

Research on Advertising Content

Research on cross-national advertising in magazines is the fastest growing and most prolific area of research on international magazines. Much of the research identified for this review focuses on both women's magazines in Asia and the effects of localization versus standardization strategies. A number of the studies use globalization theory to understand advertising content. The literature reviewed in this section includes studies about gender, stereotypes and beauty ideals related to magazine advertising research.

Gender studies include Katherine Frith's work that uses globalization theory to understand how portrayals of gender roles in women's magazines may impact a local market in Asia. Frith analyzed the content of advertisements in *Her World* and *Female*, the international editions of *Harper's Bazaar* and *Elle*. She compared the products advertised, as well as the race, ethnicity and beauty types of models, to understand the kinds of messages given to women in Singapore. Frith drew on globalization theory to discuss how increased trade and improved communication technologies are bringing about increasing levels of global integration between cultures. Her findings suggest advertisers want to have a consistent look for their products when crossing borders.[27]

To identify some of the culture-specific, gender-based advertising strategies being used to target global market segments, Katharina M. Dallmann conducted a cross-national, empirical study of German and Japanese magazine advertising. She compared the statistical strength of four dimensions of advertisements: format, use of models, male and female role portrayal and value appeals.[28] She also found support for the advertising strategy of maintaining consistency. Though some studies evaluate the role advertisements play in culture, another approach is that used by researchers Emmanuella Plakoyiannaki and Yorgos Zotos, who argue the industry needs to adjust its communication practices to the changing role of women in society. These researchers used an integrative approach in their analysis of the content of a sample of 3,830 ads in 10 high-circulation U.K. magazines to question stereotypes in the ads. They found that advertisers used female stereotypes to promote products.[29]

Katherine Frith, Ping Shaw and Hong Cheng studied the beauty ideal to determine how it is constructed across cultures. From their examination of advertisements found in magazines of Singapore, Taiwan and the United States, they concluded that Asian advertisements focus on cosmetics and facial beauty products, but U.S. advertisements are dominated by clothing. The authors suggest that beauty is constructed in the United States in terms of the body, whereas in Asia beauty is constructed by a pretty face. They argued that feminist critiques of the sexual objectification of women in advertising may need to be considered within a historical, Western context of origin.[30]

Mariko Morimoto and Susan Chang explored the Western influences in a comparative study of the use of models from different racial or ethnic backgrounds in local Japanese magazines and three global fashion magazines launched in Japan: *Vogue*, *Marie Claire* and *Harper's Bazaar*. The results of their analysis of the content of advertising in the magazines suggest that Western models dominated both but for different products. Western models were featured in ads for beauty products, clothing and accessories, while a greater number of Asian models are used in ads for health aids, automobiles and travel.[31] Morimoto and Chang also drew on globalization theory, which they suggest explains the gradual decrease of national market boundaries resulting from the advancement of technologies and improved distribution of global brands. Additionally, these studies support the idea that markets must expand globally in order to grow.

Jaehee Jung and Yoon-Jung Lee also used content analysis to determine whether women are objectified in fashion and beauty advertisements in magazines of South Korea and the United States. Jung and Lee drew on the feminist objectification perspective because it asserts that women are frequently objectified as sex or beauty objects in the media, which can lead to physical self-objectification. By using content analysis, the authors did not aim to demonstrate social consequences of advertisements but merely to look at the differences or similarities of female models as they are portrayed in fashion and beauty magazines. The authors suggest that future research might include interviews of local consumers to obtain magazine readers' perspectives and probe the consequences of advertising portrayals of women. They also suggest cross-cultural studies of target reader characteristics, advertised brand images and visual image characteristics in consumer behavior and marketing areas.[32]

Research on the introduction of and competition between international and national magazines suggests international titles have changed the look and content of local women's magazines. Katherine Frith and Yang Feng used historical analysis and political economy theory in their case study to explore the shift in gender ideology in China resulting from a proliferation of women's magazines—both local and international—such as Chinese language versions of *Elle*, *Vogue*, *Cosmopolitan*, *Marie Claire* and *Harper's Bazaar*, and the Japanese magazines *Rayli*, *Mina*, *With* and *ViVi*. The study examined the increasing role advertising plays in shaping the content of women's magazines and the messages they aim at women in China.[33] Drawing on cultural hybridity theory to explain the relationship between global media and local culture, Frith and Feng argue that even though the local magazines are shifting from a state-owned model to a new model that allows global titles to form alliances with local magazines, a shift is also taking place in both economic ideology and gender ideology in China. Frith and Feng's study was designed to answer the question, "With the introduction of international women's magazines how has the 'Open Door Policy' and the free market mechanism changed the face of women's magazines in China?"[34] Frith and Feng's findings suggest that hybrid theory does not explain their findings because the magazines reflect and transmit consumer values that clearly serve the interests of global brands. The underlying emphasis was not on the liberalization of women but an over-emphasis on women as consumers.[35]

Combining research on beauty in advertising with the goal of determining the extent to which advertising copy and models are standardized, Michelle Nelson and Hye-Jin Paek analyzed the content of *Cosmopolitan* magazine advertising across product nationality (multinational, domestic) and category (beauty, other) in seven countries (Brazil, China, France, India, South Korea, Thailand and the United States). Their findings indicate local editions delivered more advertisements for multinational products than domestic across all countries except India.[36] This, Nelson and Paek suggest, is because multinational product advertisements tend to use more standardized strategies and tactics than do domestic product advertisements, although this propensity varies across countries. Advertisers are more likely to present beauty products (cosmetics, fashion) using standardized approaches than for other products (e.g., cars, food, household goods). The research examines only one kind of magazine and for one kind of audience, though Nelson and Paek suggest a global medium, such as *Cosmopolitan* magazine, offers international advertisers the opportunity to reach a shared consumer segment of women with varying degrees of standardization and that even in Asian countries some standardization is possible. By comparing advertising across local editions of the same transnational magazine from seven countries that vary in terms of geography, culture and sociopolitical systems, these researchers investigated the extent to which local versus global factors might contribute to distinct or homogenous sexualized gender images within advertising content.[37]

Nelson and Paek earlier investigated the standardization issue when they looked at how Western values of sexuality might transfer to other cultures. Within the study, the authors provided the following advertising guidelines and self-regulations that dictate what is sexy, sexist or indecent:

> For example, guidelines typically suggest the following criteria are inappropriate representations according to measures of taste and decency: (1) if the advertisement does not conform to standards of good taste and modesty; (2) if the advertisement uses sexual imagery or suggestiveness; (3) if the advertisement objectifies women or men by presenting them as decorative or attention-getting objects with little or no relevance to the product advertised; and (4) if the advertisement employs gender-role stereotypes or suggests violence.[38]

In one of the first multi-country studies to examine global advertising strategies for a transnational media brand, Nelson and Paek created the guidelines for the study as suggestions. The guidelines do not determine which advertisements are actually published in many countries because of different standards of taste, modesty and even sexual imagery based on national cultural values and social norms.[39] Nelson and Paek identify multiple factors that might predict the degree of sexuality in advertisements: localized factors, such as cultural values, political and economic systems and advertising elements, might explain differences in levels of sexuality in advertising content.

Research on Visual Content

Visuals are a dominant part of any magazine. In the two preceding sections, research on magazines has included visuals as part of larger questions. Kopnina, for example, included both text and visual images in her exploration of how women are represented in editorial content.[40] Studies of advertising content explored ways that advertisers standardize the presentation of their products as they reach across multiple national boundaries. However, in this section, the focus will be on studies in which scholars have looked specifically at visual presentation in international periodicals: in photos, covers and overall design.

The most powerful of the small sample of studies on magazine visuals is David Machin's discourse analysis of Getty bank images as a symbolic system.[41] Machin began by putting the issue of creating a symbolic system in a political and economic context. The Getty image bank was actively and intentionally created in 1995 by powerful global corporations and now contains a quarter of the world's $2 billion-a-year industry. Within their collection is the Eastman Kodak's image bank stock; the Visual Communications Group, with a collection of 10 million images; and the *National Geographic* image collection, which contains more than 10 million images. To use these data, Machin narrowed his research to focus only on the representations of women in global media, based on his larger analysis of Getty photos published in *Cosmopolitan* magazine that has 44 versions around the world. Machin writes that his methodology is distributed throughout the subsections of the article due to the density and size of the Getty collection, yet he fails to specify anything related to the images within *Cosmopolitan* magazine. Using the 44 editions appears to be just one way of choosing images for their generic concepts. He is more concerned with providing an argument that visual language becomes more homogenized, generic and limited in its iconography through the use of image banks in magazines. His study serves as a representative example of the way particular kinds of actors, actions, settings, moods, etc., tend to be seen around the world. Machin argues that the images, in reflecting consumer categories, show a stylized, harmonized corporate world of work, as well as commodified leisure and individualism, which is abstracted from politics and society.[42]

Magazine covers have become iconic as the face of the magazine. Andrea Pyka, Scott Fosdick and William Tillinghast examined covers of Germany's *Der Spiegel* to explore the magazine's visual framing of patriotism and national identity. Their analysis of cover contents showed an increase in presentation of patriotic and national identity visual symbols following key historical events: the building of the Berlin Wall, the reunification of Germany, the adoption of the Euro, and the 2006 World Cup.[43] The study suggests possible, similar examinations of other nations' magazines to determine whether they reflect political or sociological trends within the countries. Are latent messages being presented through magazine covers? If so, what are they? These studies might offer new understanding of socio-political issues within countries.

Design, suggests Patrick Roessler, offers yet another visual language that can be studied through globalization or at a global level.[44] Roessler characterizes the history of magazines—and particularly the history of magazine design in the twentieth century—as a mutual relationship through which different media outlets influence each other's visual appearance. His study focuses on the cross-national diffusion of graphic design between German and American magazines by taking the reader through the history of the German and American illustrated magazines from the 1920s into the 1950s. The explanatory framework for this dynamic is the migration of ideas passed along by global players, including publishers, international groups and individual artists and art directors. He shows that, "as a consequence, innovations in editorial content as well as in magazine layout traveled between national media systems, simulating an 'international language' of modern magazine visuals."[45] Finally, Bob D. Cutler, Rajshekhar G. Javalgi and M. Krishna Erramilli used globalization theory for their comparative analysis of advertising practices and visual appeals to identify ways those reflect cross-cultural similarities and differences between the United States, the United Kingdom, France, India and South Korea.[46]

The emphasis on globalization in many of the studies of international magazines suggests that other studies might build on Machin's study of Getty images and Roessler's tracking of design migration across international borders. Studies on cross-cultural reading of design might further explore the discussions and importance of localization versus standardization.

Marketing Issues

Research on marketing magazines described in this review section begins with studies related to branding. Studies of expansion of magazines and related localization versus globalization dimensions will lead to *glocalization* research. Finally studies related to hybridity will be reviewed. Branding studies include examinations of how companies extend their magazine brand—in the sense that their *title* is tied to the *brand*—into other markets. Among these are studies of magazines that may create "a *brand* as a set of representations and values that are not indissolubly tied to a specific product or products."[47] *Cosmopolitan* magazine is an example of a title that has its own branding philosophy. David Machin and Joanna Thornborrow argue that *Cosmopolitan* magazine builds its brand on *discourse* for women to have independence, power and fun.[48] To that end, Machin and Thornborrow studied 44 national versions of the November 2001 issue of the magazine. The authors chose texts and visuals for two domains of *female agency*, women at work and women's sexuality, and then compared these across the versions through the lens of multimodal discourse and globalization theory.[49] Their intent was to compare discourses about women in the magazine's versions published around the world. They found the messages were localized but still transmitted the Cosmo brand, creating a fantasy world through which "women act alone and rely on acts of seduction and social maneuverings rather than on intellect, to act in and on the world."[50]

Sexuality in magazines is accepted in some cultures but seen as a problem in others. Philip Kitley chose the legal case of *Playboy Indonesia* to study the reactions of conservative Islamist groups, which are concerned about the global spread of commercial media products and circulation of sexual imagery.[51] A professor at the University of Wollongong in Australia and also the cultural attaché in the Australian Embassy in Jakarta in the late 1980s, Kitley provides a legal analysis of the 2006 trial of *Playboy Indonesia*, a publication that is part of the international Playboy franchise. He examined the complaint before the South Jakarta District Court and the evidence that was presented by the prosecutor, along with the comments made by various expert witnesses. Kitley describes the prosecutor as having moved "quickly through the problems with pornography in the media to consideration of the transformation of the symbolic and moral character of the urban landscape under capitalism, and new media services and products."[52] Kitley reports that during the trial concerns were raised about the global spread of commercial media products and the circulation of sexual imagery from outside the existing culture. He asks a two-pronged question: Was the trial about "frustrated political ambitions and the interest some conservative Islamist groups had in reinstating the Jakarta Charter and establishing the rule of Sharia law,"[53] or was it also about a growing, worldwide concern about the character and content of the visual and cyber-spheres? Kitley's main research focus is with how media impact social, cultural and political change in Indonesia and Malaysia.

As studies further explore globalization issues, the term *glocalization* emerges. Coined by Japanese economists in the *Harvard Business Review* in the 1980s, the sociologist Roland Robertson is credited with popularizing the term.[54] The term indicates the blending of the local culture with a global culture, and the concept is used to explain how magazines adapt to competition and to expansion. David Machin and Theo van Leeuwen use critical discourse analysis to examine *Cosmopolitan* magazine's use of business agreements with other countries to produce a mixture of the original international brand with the local content: that is, a glocalization product.[55] In the cultural mélange that is glocalization, cultural influences and transformations create a complex flow that goes around the planet.[56]

Glocalization is also the focus of studies of the results of expanding a magazine brand into another market. Magazine publishers in the 1990s increasingly began going outside national boundaries by taking advantage of the decade's liberalization and open door policies through which developing countries allowed entrance of foreign titles. Katherine Frith suggests from her research that this has changed the content and structure of local magazines.[57] As previously discussed, Nelson and Paek also looked at the relationship between expansion and the brand in their study of advertising in *Cosmopolitan* magazine across seven countries. The findings from their content analysis suggest that standardization is used in global advertising strategies to keep *Cosmopolitan* magazine marketable.[58]

Standardization practices are also studied based on the tensions caused by the expansion of brands into new markets. In his case study of *For Him Magazine*, Gillian Doyle explored the economic and managerial challenges of global expansion through the magazine's licensing and franchising agreements.[59] Other expansion studies examine issues that include licensing agreements, joint ventures, co-publishing, copyright or translation rights sales and unconcealed capital. Several give extensive explanations of licensing and joint ventures.[60]

Glocalization has led scholars to compare local publications with international brands. From these studies, Hyun Sook Oh and Katherine Frith in South Korea,[61] Pin Li in China[62] and

Jinna Tay, from a case study of *WestEast* magazine in Hong Kong,[63] reached several conclusions about adaptation. Drawing on globalization theory, these researchers suggest that the local market is seen as behind and must catch up with the international market; therefore, the local publications must adapt to a more global marketing strategy. Shuang Li took a different approach in studying the tensions created by globalization in China. Li looked at how Chinese journalists working on international consumer magazines in China negotiate the cultural collision between commercialism and professionalism.[64] Finally, Mania Strube studied how four Western publishing houses entered the Chinese market. Strube offered a rationale as to why: "Home markets show high competition and saturation, so Western media companies expand their activities globally to attain new sources of revenue and diversify business risk."[65] The process is not an easy one. Magazine publishers entering China must establish Chinese-foreign cooperative enterprises or Chinese-foreign joint ventures with the Chinese investment ratio at least 51 percent.[66] Expansion also diversifies business risks. However, expansion into China includes high business risk, an unstable legal situation and missing infrastructures that require a unique entry strategy.[67]

As noted earlier, Doyle explored the economics and main managerial challenges associated with global expansion of media products. In his case study of *For Him Magazine*, Doyle examined how the brand was extended across additional media platforms.[68] Doyle concluded from his analysis that the brand had to be established in the home market before expanding. Additionally, expansion would best include international partners who could adapt the product for different local conditions. Finally, management would need to have consistent skill and success in managing these partnerships as well as the social and cultural changes that have spurred a demand for men's lifestyle magazines.[69] Oh and Frith also explored the effectiveness of licensing agreements to expanding products to other countries. They interviewed editors with international women's magazines in South Korea that are published via licensing agreements or joint ventures with local companies. These joint ventures were seen as giving local publishers more control, compared with foreign partners, than did licensing agreements.[70]

These expansion studies followed industry announcements about where publishers are expanding, as Western publishers have sought developing countries where magazines are still growing and where the Internet does not cost the publishers revenue.[71] Ives and Parekh described the expansions: Since 2007, Hearst has exported *Cosmopolitan*, *Harper's Bazaar* and *Esquire* to India, Vietnam, Spain, Australia, Romania, the Philippines and Dubai.[72] Magazine publishers have also focused on the BRIC countries, Brazil, Russia, India and China, which offer faster growth and less crowded markets. Tim Holmes has provided a brief statistical and discursive overview of expansion into the BRIC countries: Condé Nast operates in 24 markets; Hachette Filipacchi Media (HFM) publishes 260 titles in 41 countries.[73] Strube found that one-third of the magazines *HFM* publishes worldwide are based on its main brands, but the titles contain 70 percent localized content with editorial content commissioned by local editors.[74] Strube also found that Hearst publishes 152 titles in 36 languages, mostly through joint ventures in Asian markets.[75] Studies that discuss many of these issues include Pin Li's, which adds copyright or translation rights sales to joint investments and co-publishing to enter Asian markets. Li also uses globalization theory to examine international markets. Li concludes from the study findings that, based on a comparative review of locally produced magazines in China, all have foreign capital, advertising that appears in both the original United States, European and Chinese editions, or translation and copyright agreements.[76] Sheila Parry studied translation issues *Deutsche Post* encountered in producing the company's internal corporate magazine for different audiences within Germany. She asked, with the increase in globalization, how does a company ensure that a multinational workforce is connecting with business messages in the same way? Based on her findings, Parry suggests that communication is more than just translation among varied publics.[77]

Building on previous studies of expansion, Katherine Frith and Yang Feng found that expansion creates hybrids made up of local and foreign publications fusing or adapting to each other.[78]

The studies of hybridization in periodicals examine ways magazines serve both foreign and native readers, the availability of foreign capital for most profitable magazines and ways local publications emulate international magazines to create a friendly context for advertisers. These studies blend many theoretical approaches and combinations of terms: localization, internationalization, globalization, glocalization and hybridity. Many of the magazine titles combine these approaches and carry local content via global formats.[79] Machin and van Leeuwen even suggest that media conglomerates will continue to expand; thus, hybrids will be created as a global style:

> . . . Cosmopolitan style is a hybrid of different styles, chosen for the connotations they bring, for the way they help express the magazine's identity and values. Like the media styles of the 1920s and 1930s, this style has been quite deliberately designed. And although local versions adopt it in their own specific ways, overall it is a global style. The local languages may differ, but the identities and values conveyed by the style do not.[80]

Lessons from Transnational Publishing Research

Evidence from this body of studies, and specifically Frith's, suggests that international titles tend to divert local readers and advertisers away from local women's magazines.[81] This is underscored by Frith's finding that promotional gifts can be worth twice the cover price of the magazine in China.[82] This competition has impacted local magazines to the point that cooperative agreements with foreign publishers are taking up most of the advertising revenue. As a result, magazines for women published by Chinese publishers without foreign partners have all but disappeared. Those that have survived have changed their content into formats favored by transnational advertisers. The content or messages aimed at women have taken on a decidedly commercial form.[83] Tay argues that fashion magazines are the perfect medium to observe the twin synergies of adaptation and copying within the larger thesis of glocalization.[84]

In summary, globalization is defined by scholars in these media studies, mainly of Asia, as an extension of the transnational expansion of corporations, in which the corporate media giants play an enormous role in leading the world toward standardization of editorial and advertising content. The studies point to an erosion of local experience and knowledge due to transnational and transcultural influences. The globalization perspective predicts a cultural homogenization and imperialism, or both, of the world's values, beliefs, practices and lifestyles.[85] The increased traffic between global and local products and the resulting experiences are causing researchers to be more attentive to the emerging spaces in which these articulations take place.[86] Hybridity theory is thereby used as a conduit for studying diverse cultural flows and exchanges between world regions, through the help of various elements such as communication technologies, transnational corporations and national entrepreneurs.[87] Scholars like Boyd-Barrett have acknowledged the need to revise the definition of the cultural or media imperialism perspective to recognize how it has changed to include hybridity.[88] The studies that use globalization perspectives to explain hybridity support the idea that the goal of international magazines is to create consistent content across international editions. Two examples from Machin's study are Elle's promotion of the stylish, spirited and sexy reader and Cosmopolitan's fun, fearless, female reader.[89] Visual studies give evidence that global corporate storytelling is more than text and advertising; it is also the structure of design, layout and photos.

Globalization studies offer a particular set of discourses. Machin and Thornborrow suggest that Cosmopolitan also sells core values of independence, power and fun.[90] Machin and van Leeuwen examined Cosmopolitan for global schemas and local discourses and found the problem-solution discourse schema may be global and may occur in all the versions of the magazine; however, the content of the magazine allows for local variation in terms of the kinds of problems and solutions it can accommodate. "The schema is described as an interpretive framework which constructs social life as an individual struggle for survival in a world of risky and unstable relationships."[91] Other studies have shown the Internet's ability to build transnational communities in ways that publishers may only have begun to tap.[92] Consumerism has become a discourse with which women can and do signify their roles and identities across the globe.[93]

A key domain of contemporary globalization is also the exchange and spread of symbolic and cultural capital. Globalization is known for its interconnectedness, not just of goods, images and information, but also of people.[94] Roessler suggests that individuals who produce magazines serve as opinion leaders for concepts and stimulate the exchange of ideas and concepts.[95] Therefore, the most well recognized manifestation of interconnectedness is travel. For international magazines travel means tourism, which serves as both channel and agent of globalization. This is important because the strategies for airlines are therefore predicated on establishing global platforms and local adaptations, and inflight magazines are used to examine how travel acts as principal channels, context and agents of globalization.[96]

The review of the past, almost two decades' research on international magazines offers insight into new directions for this stream of study. Scholars' interests in editorial and advertising have focused largely on women's magazines. Their questions have explored the impact of globalization, glocalization and hybridity as those relate to beauty, identity and culture. *Cosmopolitan*, *Harper's Bazaar*, *Elle*, *Vogue* and *National Geographic* have dominated researchers' choices of magazines to study. The countries of magazines' origins were primarily the United States, United Kingdom, South Korea, Japan, China, Singapore and Brazil. Multiple studies used globalization theory for case studies, textual and discourse analyses as well as empirical content analysis.

Missing are studies on many areas of the world and kinds of magazines. From the search of the literature, few studies were found of magazines published in South America (with the exception of Brazil), Central America, Australia, India, African countries, Canada and the Middle East. Greater diversity of theories could also be used: critical, critical cultural and other theories of communication in organizations, cultural approaches to organizations, narrative analysis, postmodernism, semiotics and standpoint theory to suggest a few. Missing from the studies were also research on health issues, new technology and theme magazines (e.g., anniversary magazines, Caribbean and Brazilian carnival magazines) and milestone events, such as inaugurations of presidents, the British Queen's Diamond Jubilee and the Olympics. There are limited studies on editorial content and design. Other suggestions are discussed earlier in the chapter.

Gaps in the research may be based on lack of accessibility to magazine and journal archives, limited keywords for searches, language limitations on the part of the reviewer and the interdisciplinary study on magazines (e.g., fashion and textiles, graphic design, marketing, etc.). For example, the best way at present to locate articles on new technologies related to international magazines and on-line publications is to search in business or trade publications. There are vast opportunities to broaden the research and expand it around the world.

Notes

1 Leara Rhodes, "Research Review: An International Perspective on Magazines," in David Abrahamson, ed., *The American Magazine: Research Perspectives and Prospects* (Ames: Iowa State University Press, 1995), 159–171.

2 David E. Sumner, "Magazine-Related Articles in *Journalism Mass Communications Quarterly* 1990 to 2010," e-mail correspondence with David Abrahamson, 18 July 2012 <http://davidabrahamson.com/WWW/MAG2/Sumner_JMCQ_Magazine_Bibliography.pdf>, accessed 02 June 2014.

3 Leonard Mogel, "Serial Rights, Foreign Licensing, and Publishing," *The Magazine*, 4th ed. (Pittsburgh, PA: GATFPress, 1998), 147–151.

4 Scott Donaton, Bruce Crumley, and Raymond Serafin, "Hachette Signs Ford in Global Media Deal," *Advertising Age*, 10 February 1992, 3; Nat Ives, "Hearst Adds *Elle*, but New Global Footprint May Mean More in the Long Run," *Advertising Age*, 7 February 2011, 4.

5 Nat Ives and Rupal Parekh, "For Pubs, Going Global Comes with Challenges," *Advertising Age*, 14 June 2010, 17.

6 David Machin and Sarah Niblock, "The New Breed of Business Journalism for Niche Global News: The Case of Bloomberg News," *Journalism Studies* 11.6 (December 2010): 783.

7 Susan B. Glasser, "Creating a Go-To Digital Destination for Foreign Affairs Reporting and Commentary," *Neiman Reports*, Fall 2010, 55.

8 Donaton, Crumley, and Serafin, "Hachette Signs Ford," 1.

9 Donaton, Crumley, and Serafin, "Hachette Signs Ford," 1.

10 Katherine T. Frith, Yang Feng, and Lan Ye, "International Women's Magazines and Transnational Advertising in China" (paper presented at the Annual Meeting, Association for Education in Journalism and Mass Communication, August 2008).

11 Kavita Karan and Yang Feng, "International Women's Magazines in China: Global and Local Perspectives," *Chinese Journal of Communication* 2.3 (November 2009): 348–349.

12 Leara Rhodes, "Magazines in Capitalist Russia: Impact of Political and Economic Transitions" (paper presented at the Annual Meeting, Association for Education in Journalism and Mass Communication, August 1997).

13 Ole Jacob Madsen and Brita Ytre-Arne, "Me at My Best: Therapeutic Ideals in Norwegian Women's Magazines," *Communication, Culture & Critique* 5.1 (March 2012): 20–37.

14 Loubna H. Skalli, *Through a Local Prism: Gender, Globalization, and Identity in Moroccan Women's Magazines* (Lanham, MD: Lexington Books, 2006), 41, citing Mike Featherstone, "Global Culture: An Introduction," in Mike Featherstone, ed., *Global Culture: Nationalism, Globalization and Modernity* (London: Sage, 1990), 1.

15 Skalli, *Through a Local Prism*, 41.

16 Martha Wörsching, "Gender and Images of Nature and Sport in British and German News Magazines: The Global and the National in Images of Advertising," *International Journal of Media and Cultural Politics* 5.3 (2009): 217–232.

17 Machin and Niblock, "The New Breed of Business Journalism," 783–798.

18 Fabienne Darling-Wolf and Andrew L. Mendelson, "Seeing Themselves through the Lens of the Other: An Analysis of the Cross-Cultural Production and Negotiation of *National Geographic*'s 'The Samurai Way' Story," *Journalism & Communication Monographs* 10.3 (Autumn 2008): 288.

19 Tiffany J. Shoop, Catherine A. Luther, and Carolynn McMahan, "Advertisement Images of Men and Women in Culturally Diverging Societies: An Examination of Images in U.S. and Japanese Fashion Magazines," *Journal of International Business and Economics* 8.3 (September 2008): 29–41 <http://www.freepatentsonline.com/article/Journal-International-Business-Economics/190616968.html>, accessed 6 September 2013.

20 Yang Feng and Kavita Karan, "The Global and Local Influences in the Portrayal of Women's Roles: Content Analysis of Women's Magazines in China," *Journal of Media and Communication Studies* 3.2 (February 2011): 33–44.

21 Helen Kopnina, "Culture and Media: The Study of National Editions of a Fashion Magazine," *Studies in Communication Sciences* 7.1 (2007): 85–101.

22 Radhika Parameswaran, "Local Culture in Global Media: Excavating Colonial and Material Discourses in *National Geographic*," *Communication Theory* 12.3 (August 2002): 287–315.

23 Parameswaran, "Local Culture in Global Media," 287–315.

24 Victoria B. Korzeniowska, "Gender, Space and Identification in *Femmes du Maroc* and *Citadine*," *International Journal of Francophone Studies* 8.1 (April 2005), 3–22.

25 William Tillinghast and Marie McCann, "Climate Change in Four News Magazines: 1989–2009," *Online Journal of Communication and Media Technologies* 3.1 (January 2013): 22–48 <http://www.ojcmt.net/articles/31/312.pdf>, accessed 12 February 2013.

26 Lyn McGaurr, "Travel Journalism and Environmental Conflict: A Cosmopolitan Perspective," *Journalism Studies* 11.1 (February 2010): 53. For more on Cosmopolitan Theory, see Pankaj Ghemawat, "The Cosmopolitan Corporation," *Harvard Business Review*, May 2011, 92–99.

27 Katherine Frith, "Race and Ethnicity: A Comparison of Global and Local Women's Magazine Advertising in Singapore" (paper presented at the Annual Meeting, International Communication Association, June 2006), 1.

28 Katharina M. Dallmann, "Targeting Women in German and Japanese Magazine Advertising: A Difference-in-Differences Approach," *European Journal of Marketing* 35.11/12 (2001): 1320–1339.

29 Emmanuella Plakoyiannaki and Yorgos Zotos, "Female Role Stereotypes in Print Advertising: Identifying Associations with Magazine and Product Categories," *European Journal of Marketing* 43.11/12 (2009): 1411–1434.

30 Katherine Frith, Ping Shaw, and Hong Cheng, "The Construction of Beauty: A Cross-Cultural Analysis of Women's Magazine Advertising," *Journal of Communication* 55.1 (March 2005): 56–70 <http://onlinelibrary.wiley.com/doi/10.1111/j.1460-2466.2005.tb02658.x/pdf>, accessed 2 June 2014; see also, Hong Cheng and Katherine Toland Frith, "Going Global: An Analysis of Global Women's Magazine Ads in China" [on-line],

Media International Australia, Incorporating Culture & Policy Issue 119 (May 2006): 138–151 <http://search.informit.com.au/documentSummary;dn=009938041484775;res=IELLCC>, accessed 8 February 2013.

31 Mariko Morimoto and Susan Chang, "Western and Asian Models in Japanese Fashion Magazine Ads: The Relationship with Brand Origins and International Versus Domestic Magazines," *Journal of International Consumer Marketing* 21.3 (July 2009): 173–187.

32 Jaehee Jung and Yoon-Jung Lee, "Cross-Cultural Examination of Women's Fashion and Beauty Magazine Advertisements in the United States and South Korea," *Clothing & Textiles Research Journal* 24.4 (October 2009): 274–286.

33 Katherine Frith and Yang Feng, "Transnational Cultural Flows: An Analysis of Women's Magazines in China," *Chinese Journal of Communication* 2.2 (July 2009): 158.

34 Frith and Feng, "Transnational Cultural Flows," 170.

35 Frith and Feng, "Transnational Cultural Flows," 173.

36 Michelle R. Nelson and Hye-Jin Paek, "A Content Analysis of Advertising in a Global Magazine across Seven Countries: Implications for Global Advertising Strategies," *International Marketing Review* 24.1 (2007): 64.

37 See, for example, Kineta H. Hung, Stella Yiyan Li, and Russell W. Belk, "Glocal Understandings: Female Readers' Perceptions of the New Woman in Chinese Advertising," *Journal of International Business Studies* 38.6 (November 2007): 1034–1051 <http://dx.doi.org/10.1057/palgrave.jibs.8400303>, accessed 3 February 2013.

38 Michelle R. Nelson and Hye-Jin Paek, "Cross-Cultural Differences in Sexual Advertising Content in a Transnational Women's Magazine," *Sex Roles* 53.5/6 (September 2005): 371.

39 Nelson and Paek, "Cross-Cultural Differences in Sexual Advertising Content," 371.

40 Kopnina, "Culture and Media," 85–101.

41 David Machin, "Building the World's Visual Language: The Increasing Global Importance of Image Banks in Corporate Media," *Visual Communication* 3.3 (October 2004): 316–336.

42 Machin, "Building the World's Visual Language," 316–336.

43 Andrea Pyka, Scott Fosdick, and William Tillinghast, "Visual Framing of Patriotism and National Identity on the Covers of *Der Spiegel*" (paper presented at the Annual Meeting, Association for Education in Journalism and Mass Communication, August 2010).

44 Patrick Roessler, "Global Players, Émigrés, and *Zeitgeist*: Magazine Design and the Interrelation between the United States and Germany," *Journalism Studies* 8.4 (August 2007): 566–583.

45 Roessler, "Global Players, Émigrés, and *Zeitgeist*," 566.

46 Bob D. Cutler, Rajshekhar G. Javalgi, and M. Krishna Erramilli, "The Visual Components of Print Advertising: A Five-Country Cross-Cultural Analysis," *European Journal of Marketing* 26.4 (1992): 7–20.

47 David Machin and Joanna Thornborrow, "Branding and Discourse: The Case of *Cosmopolitan*," *Discourse & Society* 14.4 (2003): 454.

48 Machin and Thornborrow, "Branding and Discourse," 454.

49 Machin and Thornborrow, "Branding and Discourse," 453.

50 Machin and Thornborrow, "Branding and Discourse," 453.

51 Philip Kitley, "*Playboy Indonesia* and the Media: Commerce and the Islamic Public Sphere on Trial in Indonesia," *South East Asia Research* 16.1 (March 2008): 85; see also, Fang-Chih Irene Yang, "International Women's Magazines and the Production of Sexuality in Taiwan," *Journal of Popular Culture* 37.3 (February 2004): 505–530.

52 Kitley, "*Playboy Indonesia* and the Media," 85.

53 Kitley, "*Playboy Indonesia* and the Media," 85.

54 Roland Robertson, "Glocalization: Time-Space and Homogeneity-Heterogeneity," in Mike Featherstone, Scott Lash, and Roland Robertson, eds., *Global Modernities*, Theory, Culture & Society, ed. Mike Featherstone (London: Sage, 1995), 25–44.

55 David Machin and Theo van Leeuwen, "Global Schemas and Local Discourses in *Cosmopolitan*," *Journal of Sociolinguistics* 7.4 (November 2003): 493–512.

56 Machin and van Leeuwen, "Global Schemas," 493; David Machin and Theo van Leeuwen, "Language Style and Lifestyle: The Case of a Global Magazine," *Media, Culture & Society* 27.4 (July 2005): 577–600; Jinna Tay, "'Pigeon-Eyed Readers': The Adaptation and Formation of a Global Asian Fashion Magazine," *Continuum: Journal of Media & Cultural Studies* 23.2 (April 2009): 245–256.

57 Katherine Frith, "Global Media Texts and Consumption: The Study of International Magazines" (paper presented at the Annual Meeting, International Communication Association, 2009), 1; see also, Ives and Parekh, "For Pubs, Going Global Comes with Challenges," 17.

58 Nelson and Paek, "A Content Analysis of Advertising," 371.

59 Gillian Doyle, "Managing Global Expansion of Media Products and Brands: A Case Study of *FHM*," *International Journal on Media Management* 8.3 (2006): 105–115.

60 Doyle, "Managing Global Expansion," 105; Frith and Feng, "Transnational Cultural Flows," 158; Hyun Sook Oh and Katherine Frith, "Globalization and Localization in the Production Process of International Women's Magazines in Korea" (paper presented at the Annual Meeting, International Communication Association, May 2007), 1.

61 Oh and Frith, "Globalization and Localization," 1.

62 Pin Li, "International Cooperation and Globalization of the Magazine Industry in China," *Publishing Research Quarterly* 24.1 (March 2008): 59–63.

63 Tay, "'Pigeon-Eyed Readers,'" 245–256.

64 Shuang Li, "A New Generation of Lifestyle Magazine Journalism in China: The Professional Approach," *Journalism Practice* 6.1 (February 2012): 122–137.

65 Mania Strube, "Entering Emerging Media Markets: Analyzing the Case of the Chinese Magazine Market," *International Journal on Media Management* 12.3/4 (December 2010): 183.

66 Frith and Feng, "Transnational Cultural Flows," 163.

67 Strube, "Entering Emerging Media Markets," 184.

68 Doyle, "Managing Global Expansion," 105.

69 Doyle, "Managing Global Expansion," 113.

70 Oh and Frith, "Globalization and Localization," 1.

71 Ives and Parekh, "For Pubs, Going Global Comes with Challenges," 17.

72 Ives and Parekh, "For Pubs, Going Global Comes with Challenges," 17.

73 Tim Holmes and Liz Nice, "The International Perspective," *Magazine Journalism*, Journalism Studies: Key Texts Series (Los Angeles and London: Sage, 2012), 109–119.

74 Strube, "Entering Emerging Media Markets," 193.

75 Strube, "Entering Emerging Media Markets," 193.

76 Li, "International Cooperation and Globalization," 62.

77 Sheila Parry, "Finding a Global Voice for DP DHL's Internal Magazine," *Strategic Communication Management* 13.4 (June/July 2009): 24–27.

78 Frith and Feng, "Transnational Cultural Flows," 170.

79 Oh and Frith, "Globalization and Localization," 1.

80 Machin and van Leeuwen, "Language Style and Lifestyle," 598.

81 Frith, "Race and Ethnicity," 1.

82 Frith, "Race and Ethnicity," 1.

83 Frith and Feng, "Transnational Cultural Flows," 169.

84 Tay, "'Pigeon-Eyed Readers,'" 245.

85 Karan and Feng, "International Women's Magazines in China," 348.

86 Karan and Feng, "International Women's Magazines in China," 352.

87 Featherstone, as quoted in Skalli, *Through a Local Prism*, 41.

88 Oliver Boyd-Barrett, "Media Imperialism Reformulated," in Daya Kishan Thussu, ed., *Electronic Empires: Global Media and Local Resistance* (London: Arnold, 1998), 157–176.

89 Machin, "Building the World's Visual Language," 316–336.

90 Machin and Thornborrow, "Branding and Discourse," 453.

91 Machin and van Leeuwen, "Global Schemas," 493.

92 Machin, "Building the World's Visual Language," 316; Cheris Kramarae, "The Language and Nature of the Internet: The Meaning of Global," *New Media & Society* 1.1 (April 1999): 47–53; Machin and Niblock, "The New Breed of Business Journalism," 783–798.

93 Machin and Thornborrow, "Branding and Discourse," 453–471.

94 Crispin Thurlow and Adam Jaworski, "Communicating a Global Reach: Inflight Magazines as a Globalizing Genre in Tourism," *Journal of Sociolinguistics* 7.4 (November 2003): 579–606.

95 Roessler, "Global Players, Émigrés, and *Zeitgeist*," 566.

96 Thurlow and Jaworski, "Communicating a Global Reach," 580; see also, Leara Rhodes, "Inflight Magazines: Changing How Magazines Market to Travelers," *Journal of Magazine & New Media Research* 2.1 (Fall 1999): 1–22.

Bibliography

Boyd-Barrett, Oliver. "Media Imperialism Reformulated." In Thussu, Daya Kishan, ed. *Electronic Empires: Global Media and Local Resistance*. London: Arnold, 1998, 157–176.

Cheng, Hong and Frith, Katherine Toland. "Going Global: An Analysis of Global Women's Magazine Ads in China" [on-line]. *Media International Australia, Incorporating Culture & Policy* Issue 119 (May 2006): 138–151. <http://search.informit.com.au/documentSummary;dn=009938041484775;res=IELLCC>, accessed 8 February 2013.

Cutler, Bob D.; Javalgi, Rajshekhar G.; and Erramilli, M. Krishna. "The Visual Components of Print Advertising: A Five-Country Cross-Cultural Analysis." *European Journal of Marketing* 26.4 (1992): 7–20.

Dallmann, Katharina M. "Targeting Women in German and Japanese Magazine Advertising: A Difference-in-Differences Approach." *European Journal of Marketing* 35.11/12 (2001): 1320–1339.

Darling-Wolf, Fabienne and Mendelson, Andrew L. "Seeing Themselves through the Lens of the Other: An Analysis of the Cross-Cultural Production and Negotiation of *National Geographic*'s 'The Samurai Way' Story." *Journalism & Communication Monographs* 10.3 (Autumn 2008): 285–322.

Donaton, Scott; Crumley, Bruce; and Serafin, Raymond. "Hachette Signs Ford in Global Media Deal." *Advertising Age*, 10 February 1992, 3, 41.

Doyle, Gillian. "Managing Global Expansion of Media Products and Brands: A Case Study of *FHM*." *International Journal on Media Management* 8.3 (2006): 105–115.

Featherstone, Mike. "Global Culture: An Introduction." In Featherstone, Mike, ed. *Global Culture: Nationalism, Globalization and Modernity*. London: Sage, 1990, 1–14.

Feng, Yang and Karan, Kavita. "The Global and Local Influences in the Portrayal of Women's Roles: Content Analysis of Women's Magazines in China." *Journal of Media and Communication Studies* 3.2 (February 2011): 33–44.

Frith, Katherine. "Global Media Texts and Consumption: The Study of International Magazines." Paper presented at the Annual Meeting, International Communication Association, 2009.

Frith, Katherine. "Race and Ethnicity: A Comparison of Global and Local Women's Magazine Advertising in Singapore." Paper presented at the Annual Meeting, International Communication Association, June 2006.

Frith, Katherine and Feng, Yang. "Transnational Cultural Flows: An Analysis of Women's Magazines in China." *Chinese Journal of Communication* 2.2 (July 2009): 158–173.

Frith, Katherine T.; Feng, Yang; and Ye, Lan. "International Women's Magazines and Transnational Advertising in China." Paper presented at the Annual Meeting, Association for Education in Journalism and Mass Communication, August 2008.

Frith, Katherine; Shaw, Ping; and Cheng, Hong. "The Construction of Beauty: A Cross-Cultural Analysis of Women's Magazine Advertising." *Journal of Communication* 55.1 (March 2005): 56–70 <http://onlinelibrary.wiley.com/doi/10.1111/j.1460-2466.2005.tb02658.x/pdf>, accessed 2 June 2014.

Ghemawat, Pankaj. "The Cosmopolitan Corporation." *Harvard Business Review*, May 2011, 92–99.

Glasser, Susan B. "Creating a Go-To Digital Destination for Foreign Affairs Reporting and Commentary." *Neiman Reports*, Fall 2010, 55–57.

Holmes, Tim and Nice, Liz. "The International Perspective." *Magazine Journalism*. Journalism Studies: Key Texts Series. Los Angeles and London: Sage, 2012, 109–119.

Hung, Kineta H.; Li, Stella Yiyan; and Belk, Russell W. "Glocal Understandings: Female Readers' Perceptions of the New Woman in Chinese Advertising." *Journal of International Business Studies* 38.6 (November 2007): 1034–1051 <http://dx.doi.org/10.1057/palgrave.jibs.8400303>, accessed 3 February 2013.

Ives, Nat. "Hearst Adds *Elle*, but New Global Footprint May Mean More in the Long Run." *Advertising Age*, 7 February 2011, 4.

Ives, Nat and Parekh, Rupal. "For Pubs, Going Global Comes with Challenges." *Advertising Age*, 14 June 2010, 17.

Jung, Jaehee and Lee, Yoon-Jung. "Cross-Cultural Examination of Women's Fashion and Beauty Magazine Advertisements in the United States and South Korea." *Clothing & Textiles Research Journal* 27.4 (October 2009): 274–286.

Karan, Kavita and Feng, Yang. "International Women's Magazines in China: Global and Local Perspectives." *Chinese Journal of Communication* 2.3 (November 2009): 348–366.

Kitley, Philip. "*Playboy Indonesia* and the Media: Commerce and the Islamic Public Sphere on Trial in Indonesia." *South East Asia Research* 16.1 (March 2008): 85–116.

Kopnina, Helen. "Culture and Media: The Study of National Editions of a Fashion Magazine." *Studies in Communication Sciences* 7.1 (2007): 85–101.

Korzeniowska, Victoria B. "Gender, Space and Identification in *Femmes du Maroc* and *Citadine*." *International Journal of Francophone Studies* 8.1 (April 2005): 3–22.

Kramarae, Cheris. "The Language and Nature of the Internet: The Meaning of Global." *New Media & Society* 1.1 (April 1999): 47–53.

Li, Pin. "International Cooperation and Globalization of the Magazine Industry in China." *Publishing Research Quarterly* 24.1 (March 2008): 59–63.

Li, Shuang. "A New Generation of Lifestyle Magazine Journalism in China: The Professional Approach." *Journalism Practice* 6.1 (February 2012): 122–137.

Machin, David. "Building the World's Visual Language: The Increasing Global Importance of Image Banks in Corporate Media." *Visual Communication* 3.3 (October 2004): 316–336.

Machin, David and Niblock, Sarah. "The New Breed of Business Journalism for Niche Global News: The Case of Bloomberg News." *Journalism Studies* 11.6 (December 2010): 783–798.

Machin, David and Thornborrow. Joanna. "Branding and Discourse: The Case of *Cosmopolitan*." *Discourse & Society* 14.4 (2003): 453–471.

Machin, David and van Leeuwen, Theo. "Global Schemas and Local Discourses in *Cosmopolitan*." *Journal of Sociolinguistics* 7.4 (November 2003): 493–512.

Machin, David and van Leeuwen, Theo. "Language Style and Lifestyle: The Case of a Global Magazine." *Media, Culture & Society* 27.4 (July 2005): 577–600.

Madsen, Ole Jacob and Ytre-Arne, Brita. "Me at My Best: Therapeutic Ideals in Norwegian Women's Magazines." *Communication, Culture & Critique* 5.1 (March 2012): 20–37.

McGaurr, Lyn. "Travel Journalism and Environmental Conflict: A Cosmopolitan Perspective." *Journalism Studies* 11.1 (February 2010): 50–67.

Mogel, Leonard. "Serial Rights, Foreign Licensing, and Publishing." *The Magazine.* 4th ed. Pittsburgh, PA: GATF*Press*, 1998, 147–151.

Morimoto, Mariko and Chang, Susan. "Western and Asian Models in Japanese Fashion Magazine Ads: The Relationship with Brand Origins and International Versus Domestic Magazines." *Journal of International Consumer Marketing* 21.3 (July 2009): 173–187.

Nelson, Michelle R. and Paek, Hye-Jin. "A Content Analysis of Advertising in a Global Magazine across Seven Countries: Implications for Global Advertising Strategies." *International Marketing Review* 24.1 (2007): 64–86.

Nelson, Michelle R. and Paek, Hye-Jin. "Cross-Cultural Differences in Sexual Advertising Content in a Transnational Women's Magazine." *Sex Roles* 53.5/6 (September 2005): 371–383.

Oh, Hyun Sook and Frith, Katherine. "Globalization and Localization in the Production Process of International Women's Magazines in Korea." Paper presented at the Annual Meeting, International Communication Association, May 2007.

Parameswaran, Radhika. "Local Culture in Global Media: Excavating Colonial and Material Discourses in *National Geographic*." *Communication Theory* 12.3 (August 2002): 287–315.

Parry, Sheila. "Finding a Global Voice for DP DHL's Internal Magazine." *Strategic Communication Management* 13.4 (June/July 2009): 24–27.

Plakoyiannaki, Emmanuella and Zotos, Yorgos. "Female Role Stereotypes in Print Advertising: Identifying Associations with Magazine and Product Categories." *European Journal of Marketing* 43.11/12 (2009): 1411–1434.

Pyka, Andrea; Fosdick, Scott; and Tillinghast, William. "Visual Framing of Patriotism and National Identity on the Covers of *Der Spiegel*." Paper presented at the Annual Meeting, Association for Education in Journalism and Mass Communication, August 2010.

Rhodes, Leara. "Inflight Magazines: Changing How Magazines Market to Travelers." *Journal of Magazine & New Media Research* 2.1 (Fall 1999): 1–22.

Rhodes, Leara. "Magazines in Capitalist Russia: Impact of Political and Economic Transitions." Paper presented at the Annual Meeting, Association for Education in Journalism and Mass Communication, August 1997.

Rhodes, Leara. "Research Review: An International Perspective on Magazines." In Abrahamson, David, ed. *The American Magazine: Research Perspectives and Prospects.* Ames: Iowa State University Press, 1995, 159–171.

Robertson, Roland. "Glocalization: Time-Space and Homogeneity-Heterogeneity." In Featherstone, Mike; Lash, Scott; and Robertson, Roland, eds. *Global Modernities.* Theory, Culture & Society, ed. Mike Featherstone. London: Sage, 1995, 25–44.

Roessler, Patrick. "Global Players, Émigrés, and *Zeitgeist*: Magazine Design and the Interrelation between the United States and Germany." *Journalism Studies* 8.4 (August 2007): 566–583.

Shoop, Tiffany J.; Luther, Catherine A.; and McMahan, Carolynn. "Advertisement Images of Men and Women in Culturally Diverging Societies: An Examination of Images in U.S. and Japanese Fashion

Magazines." *Journal of International Business and Economics* 8.3 (September 2008): 29–41 <http://www.freepatentsonline.com/article/Journal-International-Business-Economics/190616968.html>, accessed 6 September 2013.

Skalli, Loubna H. *Through a Local Prism: Gender, Globalization, and Identity in Moroccan Women's Magazines*. Lanham, MD: Lexington Books, 2006.

Strube, Mania. "Entering Emerging Media Markets: Analyzing the Case of the Chinese Magazine Market." *International Journal on Media Management* 12.3/4 (December 2010): 183–204.

Sumner, David E. "Magazine-Related Articles in *Journalism Mass Communications Quarterly* 1990 to 2010." E-mail correspondence with David Abrahamson, 18 July 2012 <http://davidabrahamson.com/WWW/MAG2/Sumner_JMCQ_Magazine_Bibliography.pdf>, accessed 02 June 2014.

Tay, Jinna. "'Pigeon-Eyed Readers': The Adaptation and Formation of a Global Asian Fashion Magazine." *Continuum: Journal of Media & Cultural Studies* 23.2 (April 2009): 245–256.

Thurlow, Crispin and Jaworski, Adam. "Communicating a Global Reach: Inflight Magazines as a Globalizing Genre in Tourism." *Journal of Sociolinguistics* 7.4 (November 2003): 579–606.

Tillinghast, William and McCann, Marie. "Climate Change in Four News Magazines: 1989–2009." *Online Journal of Communication and Media Technologies* 3.1 (January 2013): 22–48 <http://www.ojcmt.net/articles/31/312.pdf>, accessed 12 February 2013.

Wörsching, Martha. "Gender and Images of Nature and Sport in British and German News Magazines: The Global and the National in Images of Advertising." *International Journal of Media and Cultural Politics* 5.3 (2009): 217–232.

Yang, Fang-Chih Irene. "International Women's Magazines and the Production of Sexuality in Taiwan." *Journal of Popular Culture* 37.3 (February 2004): 505–530.

Supplemental Resources

Chen, Peiqin. "Magazines: An Industry in Transition." In Scotton, James F. and Hachten, William A., eds. *New Media for a New China*. Oxford, UK: Wiley-Blackwell, 2010, 61–73.

Feng, Yang and Frith, Katherine. "The Growth of International Women's Magazines in China and the Role of Transnational Advertising." *Journal of Magazine & New Media Research* 10.1 (Fall 2008): 1–14. <http://aejmcmagazine.arizona.edu/Journal/Fall2008/FengFrith.pdf>, accessed 21 September 2013.

Frith, Katherine. "Globalising Women: How Global Women's Magazines in China and Singapore Transmit Consumer Culture" [on-line]. *Media International Australia, Incorporating Culture & Policy* Issue 133 (November 2009): 130–145.

Frith, Katherine Toland and Wesson, David. "A Comparison of Cultural Values in British and American Print Advertising: A Study of Magazines." *Journalism Quarterly* 68.1/2 (Spring/Summer 1991): 216–223.

Machin, David and van Leeuwen, Theo. "Global Media: Generic Homogeneity and Discursive Diversity." *Continuum: Journal of Media & Cultural Studies* 18.1 (March 2004): 99–120.

Macleod, Colin. "Adspend in G7 Countries." *International Journal of Advertising* 23.4 (2004): 534–536.

Miller, Laura. "There's More than *Manga*: Popular Nonfiction Books and Magazines." In Robertson, Jennifer, ed. *A Companion to the Anthropology of Japan*. Malden, MA: Blackwell Publishing, 2005, 314–326.

Morris, Pamela K. and Waldman, Jennifer A. "Culture and Metaphors in Advertising: France, Germany, Italy, the Netherlands, and the United States." *International Journal of Communication* 5 (2011): 942–968.

Mussey, Dagmar and Hall, Emma. "Global Highlight: *Vanity Fair* in Germany." *Advertising Age*, 26 February 2007, 36.

Rhodes, Leara D. "Magazines." In Thomas, Erwin K. and Carpenter, Brown H., eds. *Mass Media in 2025: Industries, Organizations, People and Nations*. Westport, CT: Greenwood Press, 2001, 39–49.

Part II

MAGAZINE PUBLISHING
The People and the Work

9

AUTOBIOGRAPHY AND BIOGRAPHY

Lives Well Lived in the Magazine World

Elizabeth Meyers Hendrickson

This chapter considers scholarly studies that focus on individuals whose professional contribution, taken as a whole, made magazines what they are today. The people who are the focus of this body of research are noteworthy individuals who gained distinction within various publishing cultures. As a result, a wide range of autobiographical and biographical attention has been devoted to learning how they lived, worked and shaped the field. From their experiences may come unique perspectives on the medium and insights for new generations of professionals.

A framework for research on the lives of people in the field might well be Manfred Kets de Vries's cross-disciplinary, *clinical paradigm* for studying the behavior of people in organizations. Kets de Vries approaches his consulting analyses by drawing on three premises. Simply stated, they are that "1. What you see isn't necessarily what you get. 2. All human behavior, no matter how irrational it appears, has a rationale," and "3. We're all products of our past."[1] The premises also apply to the lives described in autobiographies and biographies, each of which to some extent assumes the subject lived a life worth understanding.

This chapter begins with a description of the method used to identify the biographies and autobiographies that are included in the chapter. The subsequent analysis and discussion sections consider the thematic order of these studies, and concluding remarks offer suggestions for future research.

Literature Review and Method

The selection of autobiographies and biographies to include in this chapter involved a process of deduction. After consulting a bibliography for guidance,[2] the multidisciplinary database Academic Search Premiere was used, employing an author-determined standard search protocol in EBSCO Host. The guidelines consisted of a basic search of individuals' first and last names in quotation marks and, if pertinent, particular phrases regularly mentioned by or about the individuals. In the latter cases, the field option TX was selected and the phrase enclosed in quotation marks. A citation's inclusion depended on two broad criteria: The subject's name was included in either the title or abstract, and the research publication date was 1990 or later. The scholarship identified through the search offers research about magazine publishers, editors and contributors for well-known U.S. magazines and global brands, such as *Time*, the

New Yorker, Esquire and *Vogue*, who guided particular magazines or publishing genres in the twentieth-century magazine industry.

Since the early 1990s, myriad scholarly works have chronicled the lives and work of note-worthy magazine editors, publishers and other industry players. This research seldom appears in academic journals that focus on theory-based communication research. Instead, it is more often found within the pages of scholarly journals such as *American Periodicals, Feminist Media Studies, Journalism History, Literary Journalism Studies, American Journalism* and the *Journal of Magazine & New Media Research.* In addition, biographical information can be found in leading trade publications such as *Columbia Journalism Review* and *Nieman Reports.*

Five themes emerged from the sample of research: early innovators, entrepreneurs and lead-ers in their field; creators of journalistic form and distinctive design; shapers of lifestyle and celebrity culture; individuals seeking societal redirection; and conceptual and general study research. These categories span multiple time periods. Some studies cover individuals' life-times; others focus on an individual's relationship with another person or small group. The following sections examine each of these in turn.

Founding Publishers

Long before Rupert Murdoch's News Corporation became a global concern,[3] pioneering pub-lishers founded the companies that eventually dominated the national and international media industry. Representative among these publishing companies and the people who gave them their names include Time Inc. (Henry Luce), Condé Nast (Condé Nast), Johnson Pub-lishing (John F. Johnson), Hearst Magazines (William Randolph Hearst), Axel Springer AG (Axel Springer), Macfadden Publishing (Bernarr Macfadden) and Reader's Digest Association (Dewitt and Lila Wallace).

The last 20 years of scholarship on the life and work of William Randolph includes David Nasaw's biography, *The Chief: The Life of William Randolph Hearst,* which focuses primarily on Hearst's personal life.[4] Arthur Scherr was critical of Nasaw's work, as evidenced by the review published in *The Midwest Quarterly:*

> Nasaw makes efficient use of the small number of secondary works he cites, but ignores numerous relevant titles, such as Albert Fried's recent *FDR and His Enemies* (1999) and Betty H. Winfield's *FDR and the News Media* (1990). *The Chief* suffers from the use of excessive, frequently irrelevant quotations from Hearst's letters, a sign that Nasaw wished to tout the privileged access he had received to Hearst's papers. Surpris-ing in such a lengthy, scholarly work, *The Chief* lacks a bibliography.[5]

Kenneth Whyte's *The Uncrowned King: The Sensational Rise of William Randolph Hearst* is a com-prehensive examination of Hearst's first three years in New York City (beginning in 1896) as an ambitious idealist elbowing his way into the city's crowded and competitive media industry.[6]

Studies of entrepreneur Henry Luce, the man generally credited for creating *Time* magazine, expand the understanding of his legacy. Notable additions include three books on this U.S. publisher: Alan Brinkley's 2010 comprehensive description of Luce's private life, a feat made possible when the author became the first to access both Luce's family and personal corre-spondence; Jane S. McConnell's 1997 examination of Luce's challenging attempt to influence the commission on freedom of the press; and Daniel Marshall Haygood's 2009 analysis of Luce's anti-communist stance and its legacy.[7]

In the first years of the new millennium, Time, Inc. opened its vaults to new Yale graduate Isaiah Wilner, who as a student wrote for the *Yale Daily News,* as had Luce and his *Time* mag-azine co-founder, Briton Hadden.[8] In 2006, Wilner published a recounting of Luce and Had-den's rocky partnership that was cut short when Hadden died at age 31. The book posits that after Hadden's death, Luce betrayed his collaborator's will by buying up his stock and distributing it to his inner circle, thus guaranteeing Luce company control.[9] Carl Session Stepp's review of Wilner's book illustrates a culture that continues to be captivated by the human narrative behind one of the U.S. magazine industry's most prominent marques:

> In hundreds of Luce speeches examined by Wilner, Hadden's name is mentioned only four times. Luce's son, Henry III, could not recall his father ever bringing up Hadden in conversation. In 1963, at *Time*'s 40th anniversary celebration, Luce never spoke Hadden's name. Whatever the complexities of their relationship, Luce and Hadden clearly fed constructively on each other. Together they changed journalism. As *Time* itself might write, they proved again that better than one are two heads.[10]

An overview of magazine entrepreneur research should not be without mention of U.S. powerhouse publishers such as Condé Nast or Lila Acheson and Dewitt Wallace. It has been more than 30 years since Caroline Seebohm[11] published her biography of Condé Montrose Nast, but the magazine empire's 2001 hire of an official archivist has since produced The Condé Montrose Nast Collection, a trove split into three series based on content and scope: (1) Personalities, (2) CNP Memoranda and Research Files, and (3) Financial.[12] Recent biographical materials about the philanthropic and populist Wallaces also remain relatively lean, with a cluster of mid-1990 biographies, including an "insider's story" written by a former *Reader's Digest* managing editor, Peter Canning.[13]

Perhaps more notable is the detailed and absorbing autobiography of Katharine Graham,[14] which, as its title states, is a personal history written by the privileged, powerful and passionate woman who published *The Washington Post* during times of great American conflict that included the controversies surrounding the Pentagon Papers and Watergate era. Included are insights to her relationship with the New York City–based *Newsweek*, and Graham's own descriptions of her, at times, unsettling managerial involvement. She writes,

> I tried my best to learn what made the magazine work, but I often got quite depressed up there. I was constantly worried about perceived minor slights, or awkward encounters with people. I couldn't tell which were valid worries and which were not.[15]

John F. Kennedy Jr. contributed to the late-twentieth-century conflation of politics and popular culture by co-founding with businessman Michael J. Berman a glossy lifestyle magazine, *George*, in 1995. The tragedy of Kennedy's death in a 1999 plane crash and the shuttering of *George* little more than a year later inspired both book-length tributes[16] and scholarly analysis of national mourning.[17]

Also receiving scholarly mention were studies of lesser-known but equally captivating publishers, such as entrepreneur Axel Springer, whose Berlin-based namesake company currently publishes *Auto Bild, Computer Bild* and *Sports Bild*.[18] Gudrun Kruip, in his 1999 paper presented to the German Historical Institute in Washington, DC,[19] drew on the biography of Springer that he authored, *The 'World-View' of the Axel Springer Publishing Company: Journalism between Western Values and German Traditions of Thought*. The paper examined the cultural significance of Springer's West Germany newspaper empire during the 1950s and 1960s, with particular attention to Springer's negotiation of shifting German views and values. Wilbert Ubbens described Kruip's book research:

> The two newspapers, the books of speeches and memoirs of Axel Springer, his personal files and papers, and interviews with surviving managers of that period form the research material of this first programmatic study of the company. It is well-written and extensively documented.[20]

Also worthwhile are studies of entrepreneur Bernarr Macfadden, the eccentric and progressive creator of such niche publications as *Physical Culture* and *True Story*, who practiced the health and exercise regimens he passionately preached.[21] Mark Adams's 2009 popular press biography, *Mr. America: How Muscular Millionaire Bernarr Macfadden Transformed the Nation through Sex, Salad, and the Ultimate Starvation Diet*,[22] is one example. Another is Kathleen L. Endres's scholarly examination of the connection between Macfadden's *Physical Culture* and suffrage. Macfadden's conviction that women's empowerment can be strengthened by their own improved health regimen illustrates an entrepreneur who embraced both physical culture reform and feminist efforts.[23] Given Macfadden's propensity for embracing such then-unconventional philosophies, he is portrayed as a public reformer. In Macfadden's case, optimal personal health was the goal, rather than profit.

Innovators in Writing, Editing and Photography

Despite differences in feature content in magazines such as *Physical Culture* and *Time*, writers for mass publications tended to use standard writing structures and conventional forms that included that magazine's voice.[24] Others, including Lillian Ross, John Steinbeck and Ernest Hemingway, developed their own distinctive voices in the narrative essay form.[25] The postwar era set into motion literary journalism, a new style that, Norman Sims notes, focused primarily on ordinary lives, prioritized immersion reporting and narrative conventions that encourage personal voice, yet followed journalistic standards of accuracy.[26] In addition, magazine writers such as Tom Wolfe[27] and Gay Talese[28] used dialogues and scenes in ways similar to novel writing conventions, a style labeled "new journalism."[29]

This highlights scholarship about editors and writers at magazines noted for writing excellence and style. These include Hunter S. Thompson,[30] the *New Yorker*'s founding editor Harold Ross,[31] Dorothy Parker[32] and William Shawn,[33] *Esquire*'s tastemaker Harold Hayes,[34] *New York* magazine founder Clay Felker[35] and *Harper's Magazine* Willie Morris.[36] Persons interested in the literary influence of U.S. writer Hunter S. Thompson need not look further than the spring 2012 special issue of *Literary Journalism Studies*.[37] In the introduction to his article, scholar William McKeen wrote,

> The time has come to take Hunter S. Thompson seriously as a literary artist, and without the distraction of the overshadowing persona. There is no better time, since we mark with this issue the fortieth anniversary of the appearance of *Fear and Loathing in Las Vegas* in book form. The book was his undeniable masterpiece, perfect in a way that few books are.[38]

The journal's issue offers six original research articles that include studies of both Thompson's seminal *Fear and Loathing in Las Vegas* and his literary journalism contributions, along with a complete Thompson bibliography that McKeen compiled. McKeen's involvement with documenting early New Journalism practitioner Tom Wolfe is equally impressive, with his 1995 biography[39] of the white-suited author, as well as a personal Web site[40] offering a behind-the-scenes glimpse of the man who successfully combined journalism reporting with literary techniques.

Another central member of the new journalism era, indeed, the man who helped encourage and cultivate this style, is *Esquire* editor-in-chief Harold Hayes, whose influence is both chronicled and critiqued. Timothy Foote, in his *New York Times* review of Carol Polsgrove's book about *Esquire* during the 1960s, wrote,

> Ironically, it was not the gimmicks or provocative Hayes projects like "California Evil" (after the Charles Manson case) or "The Final Decline and Total Collapse of the American Avant-Garde" that made *Esquire* memorable. It was the writing. Ms. Pols-

grove does not make enough of the serious fiction that this mass-audience commercial magazine managed to keep publishing, or of the powerful essays like Rebecca West's remarkable reflections on "The New Meaning of Treason."[41]

Indeed, Hayes's guidance of writers was considerable, and it included *New York* magazine founder Clay Felker, who himself mentored a legion of enthusiastic and talented writers.[42]

Few magazines have weathered America's constantly evolving culture as has the *New Yorker*. Scholarship pertaining to the magazine's famously adroit editors, such as founder Harold Ross,[43] who as a member of the Algonquin Roundtable also edited and mentored such luminaries as Dorothy Parker and future editor-in-chief William Shawn, details both the public magic and the intensely personal staff relationships[44] of this dominant literary monthly, whose subscribers have been described as "less an audience than a tribe."[45] Also of interest is the magazine's role as nexus for American expatriate writers living in Paris, who included Gertrude Stein, Ernest Hemingway and Alice B. Toklas, all friends of the *New Yorker* longtime "Letter from Paris" columnist Janet Flanner.[46] In a 2002 study, Monica B. Pearl offers insight into Flanner's life, contrasting the writer's professional prose under nom de plume Genet with her personal letters, written from 1944 to 1975, to her "passionate friend," Natalia Danesi Murray.[47]

Finally, one must not overlook notable purveyors of distinct visual style, in this case, photographers Henri Cartier-Bresson and Walker Evans. Although their respective work was divergent in both subject and style (Cartier-Bresson's active "decisive moment" of the individual and Evan's documentarian-style focus on American culture), Cartier-Bresson cites Walker's work as a motivating factor for his own professional longevity.[48] Curator Agnès Sire in 2009 juxtaposed selected work from the photographers' catalogues and locates an underlying shared philosophy of using their respective cameras as tools for social criticism.[49]

Shapers of Culture

While current business media encourage managers to "be the brand,"[50] notable celebrity editors of the last 50 years helped shepherd to publication titles that supported their ideas and vision. Among the visionaries were Helen Gurley Brown (*Cosmopolitan*), Susan Taylor (*Essence*), Anna Wintour (*Vogue*) and Martha Stewart (*Martha Stewart Living*), who all set the bar for cultural currency and often pushed the limits of societal norms in the United States.

Former *Cosmopolitan* editor-in-chief Helen Gurley Brown, considered by many as the queen bee of promoting sexuality and power for middle-class women during her 1965 to 1997 reign at the magazine, penned her own story.[51] She is also the subject of several biographies.[52] Scholarly research includes Laurie Ouellette's analysis of Brown's perpetuation of a "girl-style American dream that promised transcendence from class roles as well as sexual ones."[53] Janet D. Hamlet's scholarly analysis of Susan L. Taylor's rhetoric in her monthly *Essence* column focuses on Taylor's cultural influence as a driving force behind African American women's empowerment.[54] Taylor was editor-in-chief of *Essence* from 1981 to 2000. Also insightful are Jerry Oppenheimer's unauthorized biographies of *Vogue* editor-in-chief Anna Wintour and *Martha Stewart Living*'s editor-in-chief Martha Stewart,[55] as well as research accompanying the women's significant cultural impact. Diana Crane's research yields an analysis of *Vogue* magazine's fashion photos and advertisements during Wintour's editorship.[56] Carol A. Stabile examined the gendered social discourse about Stewart during the scion's much-reported corporate scandal.[57]

The burgeoning celebrity magazine industry provided another dimension within the popular culture spectrum, which S. Elizabeth Bird describes in her scholarly analysis of tabloid history and its readers.[58] Jack Vitek provides similar insights in his biographical examination of *National Enquirer* creator Generoso Pope, Jr., a successful and complex businessman and editor.[59] Other key players in celebrity magazine publishing were former *Us Weekly* editor-in-chief Bonnie Fuller, whose newsstand success using celebrity gossip inspired both industry praise and derision,[60] and Tina Brown, the British editor behind the celebrity-infused transformations of *Vanity Fair*, the *New Yorker* and *Newsweek*.[61]

Purveyors of Change

Long before social media provided users with the platform to proclaim and share political opinions, magazines offered audiences a cultural continuum of outlets for news and opinion. The past two decades' research included studies of editors and writers of opinion magazines, which have more segmented, and often socially vocal, audiences. Victor Navasky, long-time editor-in-chief and publisher of the left-leaning *Nation* magazine, authored *A Matter of Opinion*.[62] The book of lively recollections about his experiences at the magazine earned him the 2005 George Polk Book Award.[63] Also notable is Bill Lueder's 1996 biography of Erwin Knoll, the iron-willed radical pacifist and longtime editor-in-chief of the decidedly leftist *Progressive* magazine.[64] Amanda Izzo's 2002 analysis of Ms. Magazine co-founder Gloria Steinem's personal papers from 1940 to 1997 can provide feminist and historical scholars new depth of understanding of this twentieth-century U.S. women's movement leader.[65]

Autobiographical work on the influential founder of the conservative *National Review*, William F. Buckley, Jr., included two books.[66] The second of these, his 2004 collected essays about his family and childhood, *Miles Gone By, A Literary Autobiography*, achieved *New York Times* bestseller status. Carl T. Bogus in his 2011 biography examined Buckley's role as America's conservative movement architect and described Buckley as having created a new-model conservative to include religious faith into the political equation.[67] Another important contribution is Nathan Abrams's 2010 nuanced assessment of *Commentary* magazine's long-time editor-in-chief Norman Podhoretz and his vast influence over neoconservative ideology and the George W. Bush administration's globalist foreign policy.[68] Abrams describes Podhoretz as an individual wholly opposed to totalitarianism and the book's goal, to provide accurate information about his politics.

> Through a case study of the neoconservative movement's leading thinker and magazine—Norman Podhoretz and *Commentary*—[the book] will argue that much of what has been said about neoconservatism over recent years is the product of willful distortion and exaggeration both by the neoconservatives themselves as well as many enemies and detractors.[69]

Historical and Genre Research

A review of scholarly biographical contributions from the last two decades is not complete without mentions of studies of clusters of magazines and the people who produced them. Some of these books cut a wide swath through U.S. publishing history. An example is Mary Ellen Zuckerman's examination of 200 years of the United States' popular women's magazines.[70] All published in the last 20 years, taken together, the work creates a rich blend of personalities and publications. Individually, they provide snapshots of the innovators and mold-breakers who shaped the industry.

Norberto Angeletti and Alberto Oliva's 2004 study of international perspectives on the magazine industry considers the success of eight different magazines in Europe and the United States.[71] Similarly, Richard Ohmann's 1996 work, *Selling Culture: Magazines, Markets, and Class at the Turn of the Century*, locates social problems within media texts. The book's pages offer ample visual examples of advertisements featured in early and mid-century magazines. Ohmann's postmodern critical approach contextualizes American culture as it relates to American magazine history.[72] George H. Douglas's examination of *Vanity Fair*, the *New Yorker*, *Life*, *Esquire* and the *Smart Set*[73] contextualizes the magazines' creators and content within American culture during the first half of the twentieth century.

Other contributions include Nancy A. Walker's study of American women's magazines from 1940 to 1960, in which she reassesses the texts cited by feminist critics as portraying women as dependent and passive.[74] Walker's findings indicate a more complex interplay between magazine and reader, and, as a result, Amy Beth Aronson writes that Walker's analysis "restores the reputation of tens of millions of women's magazine readers."[75] Also important is Roger Streitmatter's scholarly chronicle of America's post–WWII gay and lesbian press. The study includes interviews with many of the period's pioneering journalists of the gay and lesbian press.[76] Streitmatter articulates the book's perspective in his introduction:

> Some readers will cringe at my comparing the subjects of this work with . . . icons of American journalism. Certainly it is true that many of the women and men described in these pages are more accurately described as activists than journalists. And yet, as early as the mid-1950s, the lesbian and gay press was attracting professionals who had journalism degrees from the universities of Missouri and California, as well as some with experience on the *Kansas City Star* and the *San Francisco Chronicle*. For half a century, these and other talented and committed journalists have led one of the most important social movements of the twentieth century—in both their published words and their militant actions.[77]

Conclusion

This chapter's cited body of research illustrates the importance of biographical and autobiographical work that defines individuals and their journalistic contributions. As noted, this deeply contextual research seldom appears in academic journals that focus on theory-based communication research. However, if Kets de Vries's clinical paradigm[78] holds true, future conceptual research on media leadership and organizational power might well take note of this rich body of investigations into the personalities and people who shaped our media landscape and, as such, compare current media phenomena to a fascinating past. Such a comparison would allow emerging scholars to better locate the reasons and understandings of where the industry is now.

Notes

1 Manfred F.R. Kets de Vries, *The Leadership Mystique: A User's Manual for the Human Enterprise* (New York: Financial Times Prentice Hall, 2001), 8–9.

2 Marcia R. Prior-Miller and Associates, "Bibliography of Published Research on Magazine and Journal Periodicals," 8th ed., research database (Ames: Iowa State University, last modified, 31 August 2012), MSWord file <mpm@iastate.edu>; Sam G. Riley, ed., *American Magazine Journalists, 1900–1960, First Series* (Detroit: Gale Research, 1990).

3 Murdoch moved from his native Australia to Great Britain in 1968, and it was then News Corporation began purchasing non-Australian newspapers, thus becoming international in scope.

4 David Nasaw, *The Chief: The Life of William Randolph Hearst* (Boston: Houghton Mifflin, 2000).

5 Arthur Scherr, review of *The Chief: The Life of William Randolph Hearst*, by David Nasaw, *Midwest Quarterly* 45.3 (March 2004): 320.

6 Kenneth Whyte, *The Uncrowned King: The Sensational Rise of William Randolph Hearst* (Berkeley: Counterpoint, 2009).

7 Alan Brinkley, *The Publisher: Henry Luce and His American Century* (New York: Alfred A. Knopf, 2010); James L. Baughman, review of *The Publisher: Henry Luce and His American Century*, by Alan Brinkley, *Journal of American History* 97.4 (2011): 1167; Jane S. McConnell, "Choosing a Team for Democracy: Henry R. Luce and the Commission on Freedom of the Press," *American Journalism* 14.2 (Spring 1997): 148–163; Daniel Marshall Haygood, "Henry Luce's Anti-Communist Legacy: An Analysis of U.S. News Magazines' Coverage of China's Cultural Revolution," *Journalism History* 35.2 (Summer 2009): 98–105.

8 Isaiah Wilner, *The Man Time Forgot: A Tale of Genius, Betrayal, and the Creation of Time Magazine* (New York: HarperCollins, 2006).

9 Andrea Sachs, "Q & A: Isaiah Wilner," *Time*, 5 October 2006, 91; see also, Wilner, *The Man Time Forgot*, 225–260.

10 Carl Sessions Stepp, "Giving a Forgotten Visionary His Due," *American Journalism Review*, October/November 2006 <http://www.ajr.org/article.asp?id=4198,>, accessed 27 January 2014.

11 Caroline Seebohm, *The Man Who Was* Vogue: *The Life and Times of Condé Nast* (New York: Viking Press, 1982).

12 David E. Sumner, "A Visit to the Condé Nast Library and Archives," *Journal of Magazine & New Media Research* 10.2 (2009) <http://aejmcmagazine.arizona.edu/Journal/Spring2009/Sumner.pdf>, accessed 20 February 2014; "Condé Nast Heritage," *Condé Nast* <http://www.condenast.com/about-us/heritage>, accessed 12 March 2014.

13 Peter Canning, *American Dreamers: The Wallaces and* Reader's Digest: *An Insider's Story* (New York: Simon & Schuster, 1996); John Heidenry, *Theirs Was the Kingdom: Lila and DeWitt Wallace and the Story of the* Reader's Digest (New York: W.W. Norton, 1993).

14 Katharine Graham, *Personal History* (New York: Alfred A. Knopf, 1997).

15 Graham, *Personal History*, 345.

16 Robert T. Littell, *The Men We Became: My Friendship with John F. Kennedy, Jr.* (New York: St. Martin's Press, 2004); Richard Blow, *American Son: A Portrait of John F. Kennedy, Jr.* (New York: Henry Holt & Co., 2002).

17 Carolyn Kitch, "'A Death In The American Family': Myth, Memory, and National Values in the Media Mourning of John F. Kennedy Jr.," *Journalism & Mass Communication Quarterly* 79.2 (Summer 2002): 294–309.

18 Axel Springer, "Our Media," <http://www.axelspringer.de/en/media/index.html=, accessed 20 February 2014.

19 Gudrun Kruip, "Restricted Support: The Role of the Axel Springer Verlag in the Process of Westernization" (paper presented at American Impact on Western Europe: Americanization and Westernization in Transatlantic Perspective, Washington, DC: German Historical Institute, 25–27 March 1999) <http://webdoc.sub.gwdg.de/ebook/p/2005/ghi_12/www.ghi-dc.org/conpotweb/westernpapers/kruip.pdf=, accessed 22 July 2013.

20 Wilbert Ubbens, review of *The 'World-View' of the Axel Springer Publishing Company: Journalism between Western Values and German Traditions of Thought*, by Gudrun Kruip, *Communication Booknotes Quarterly* 31.1 (Winter 2000): 37–38.

21 Bruce M. Swain, "Bernarr Macfadden," in Sam G. Riley, ed., *American Magazine Journalists, 1900–1960, First Series*, Dictionary of Literary Biography, vol. 91 (Detroit: Gale Research, 1990), 205–215.

22 Mark Adams, *Mr. America: How Muscular Millionaire Bernarr Macfadden Transformed the Nation Through Sex, Salad, and the Ultimate Starvation Diet* (New York: HarperCollins Publishers, 2009).

23 Kathleen L. Endres, "The Feminism of Bernarr Macfadden: *Physical Culture* Magazine and the Empowerment of Women," *Media History Monographs* 13.2 (2011): 2–14 <http://facstaff.elon.edu/dcopeland/mhm/mhmjour13-2.pdf=, accessed 27 November 2012.

24 Edward Jay Friedlander and John Lee, *Feature Writing for Newspapers and Magazines: The Pursuit of Excellence*, 4th ed. (New York: Longman, 2000).

25 Mark Kramer, "Breakable Rules for Literary Journalists," in Norman Sims and Mark Kramer, eds., *Literary Journalism: A New Collection of the Best American Nonfiction* (New York: Ballantine Books, 1995), 21–34.

26 Norman Sims, "The Art of Literary Journalism," in Norman Sims and Mark Kramer, eds., *Literary Journalism: A New Collection of the Best American Nonfiction* (New York: Ballantine Books, 1995), 3–19.

27 See *New York* magazine's Tom Wolfe archive <http://nymag.com/nymag/tom-wolfe/>, accessed 31 January 2014.

28 Gay Talese, "Frank Sinatra Has a Cold," *Esquire*, April 1966 <http://www.esquire.com/features/esq1003-oct_sinatra_rev_=, accessed 20 June 2013.

29 Tom Wolfe, "The Birth of 'The New Journalism': Eyewitness Report by Tom Wolfe," *New York* Magazine, 14 February 1972 <http://nymag.com/news/media/47353/=, accessed 20 June 2013.

30 [Special Issue: Hunter S. Thompson] *Literary Journalism Studies* 4.1 (Spring 2012) <http://www.ialjs.org/?p=1495>, accessed 20 February 2014.

31 Thomas Kunkel, *Genius in Disguise: Harold Ross of the* New Yorker (New York: Random House, 1995); Renata Adler, *Gone: The Last Days of the* New Yorker (New York: Simon & Schuster, 1999); Thomas Kunkel, "Eighty-Two and Counting: The Continuing Excellence of the *New Yorker*," *American Journalism Review*, 1 April 2007 <http://www.highbeam.com/doc/1G1-162680245.html>, accessed 31 January 2013.

32 Kathleen M. Helal, "Celebrity, Femininity, Lingerie: Dorothy Parker's Autobiographical Monologues," *Women's Studies* 33.1 (January/February 2004): 77–102.

33 Lillian Ross, *Here but Not Here: My Life with William Shawn and the* New Yorker (New York: Random House, 1998).

34 Carol Polsgrove, *It Wasn't Pretty, Folks, but Didn't We Have Fun?* Esquire *in the Sixties* (New York: W.W. Norton, 1995); Dan Wakefield, "Harold Hayes and the New Journalism: *Esquire* Editor Encouraged a Generation of Writers to Experiment with Non-Fiction Techniques." *Nieman Reports*, Summer 1992, 32–35.

35 A. Kent MacDougall, "Clay Felker's *New York*," *Columbia Journalism Review* (March/April 1974), 36–47.

36 Berkley Hudson and Rebecca Townsend, "Unraveling the Webs of Intimacy and Influence: Willie Morris and *Harper's* Magazine, 1967–1971," *Literary Journalism Studies* 1.2 (2009): 63–78.

37 [Special Issue: Hunter S. Thompson] *Literary Journalism Studies*.

38 William McKeen, "The Two Sides of Hunter Thompson," [Special Issue: Hunter S. Thompson] *Literary Journalism Studies* 4.1 (Spring 2012): 7.

39 William McKeen, *Tom Wolfe* (New York: Twayne Publishers, 1995).

40 William McKeen, "The Wolfe Man," 2014 <http://www.williammckeen.com/Tom_Wolfe.html>, accessed 5 December 2012.

41 Timothy Foote, "There Goes (Varoom!) *Esquire* Magazine," *New York Times*, 13 August 1995, G9; see Polsgrove, *It Wasn't Pretty, Folks, but Didn't We Have Fun?*

42 MacDougall, "Clay Felker's *New York*."

43 Ross, *Here but Not Here*.

44 Ross, *Here but Not Here*.

45 Kunkel, "Eighty-Two and Counting."

46 Monica B. Pearl, "'What Strange Intimacy': Janet Flanner's Letters from Paris," *Journal of European Studies* 32.125/126 (September 2002): 303–318.

47 Pearl, "'What Strange Intimacy,'" 303.

48 Andrew Robinson, review of *Photographing America: Henri Cartier-Bresson and Walker Evans*, Agnès Sire, curator, *History Today* 59.11 (November 2009): 59.

49 Agnès Sire, curator, *Henri Cartier-Bresson/Walker Evans, Photographing America: 1929–1947* (London: Thames & Hudson, 2009).

50 Adrian Caddy, "Be the Brand," *Fast Company*, 19 December 2007 <http://www.fastcompany.com/73124/be-brand>, accessed 12 December 2012.

51 Helen Gurley Brown, *I'm Wild Again: Snippets from My Life and a Few Brazen Thoughts* (New York: St. Martin's Press, 2000).

52 Jennifer Scanlon, *Bad Girls Go Everywhere: The Life of Helen Gurley Brown* (New York and Oxford: Oxford University Press, 2009); James Landers, *The Improbable First Century of Cosmopolitan Magazine* (Columbia: University of Missouri Press, 2010).

53 Laurie Ouellette, "Inventing the Cosmo Girl: Class Identity and Girl-Style American Dreams," *Media, Culture & Society* 21.3 (May 1999): 360.

54 Janice D. Hamlet, "Assessing Womanist Thought: The Rhetoric of Susan L. Taylor," *Communication Quarterly* 48.4 (Fall 2000): 420–436.

55 Author Jerry Oppenheimer wrote both *Front Row: Anna Wintour, the Cool Life and Hot Times of Vogue's Editor-In-Chief* (New York: St. Martin's Press, 2005) and *Martha Stewart—Just Desserts: The Unauthorized Biography* (New York: William Morrow and Company, 1997).

56 Diana Crane, "Gender and Hegemony in Fashion Magazines: Women's Interpretations of Fashion Photographs," *Sociological Quarterly* 40.4 (August 1999): 541–563.

57 Carol A. Stabile, "Getting What She Deserved: The News Media, Martha Stewart, and Masculine Domination," *Feminist Media Studies* 4.3 (November 2004): 315–332.

58 S. Elizabeth Bird, *For Enquiring Minds: A Cultural Study of Supermarket Tabloids* (Knoxville: University of Tennessee Press, 1992).

59 Jack Vitek, *The Godfather of Tabloid: Generoso Pope Jr. and the National Enquirer* (Lexington: University Press of Kentucky, 2008).

60 Carl Swanson with Amy Larocca, "What Makes Bonnie Run?" *New York*, 14 July 2003 <http://nymag.com/nymetro/news/nedia/features/n_8946/>, accessed 29 January 2014; "Star Power: Bonnie Fuller and the Feminist Case for Celebrity Journalism," *Economist*, 5 August 2004 <http://www.economist.com/node/3062089>, accessed 11 November 2012.

61 Vanessa Grigoriadis, "What Does Tina Brown Have to Do to Get Some Attention?" *New York*, 10 June 2007 <http://nymag.com/news/features/33159/>, accessed 15 November 2012.

62 Victor S. Navasky, *A Matter of Opinion* (New York: Farrar, Straus and Giroux, 2005).

63 Macmillan Publishers, Victor S. Navasky, *A Matter of Opinion*, Winner of the 2005 George Polk Book Award <http://us.macmillan.com/amatterofopinion/VictorNavasky>, accessed 19 February 2014.

64 Bill Lueders, *An Enemy of the State: The Life of Erwin Knoll* (Monroe, ME: Common Courage Press, 1996).

65 Amanda Izzo, "Outrageous and Everyday: The Papers of Gloria Steinem," *Journal of Women's History* 14.2 (Summer 2002): 151–153; Jillian Klean Zwilling, "A Feminist Icon in Uncharted Territory: The Public Memory of Gloria Steinem" (paper presented at the Annual Meeting, International Communication Association, May, 2009).

66 William F. Buckley Jr., *Nearer, My God: An Autobiography of Faith* (New York: Doubleday, 1997); William F. Buckley Jr., *Miles Gone By: A Literary Autobiography* (Washington, DC: Regnery Publishing, Inc., 2004).

67 Carl T. Bogus, *Buckley: William F. Buckley Jr. and the Rise of American Conservatism* (New York: Bloomsbury Press, 2011).

68 Nathan Abrams, *Norman Podhoretz and* Commentary Magazine: *The Rise and Fall of the Neocons* (New York: Continuum: 2010).

69 Abrams, *Norman Podhoretz and* Commentary Magazine, 2.

70 Mary Ellen Zuckerman, *A History of Popular Women's Magazines in the United States, 1792–1995* (Westport, CT: Greenwood Press, 1998).

71 Norberto Angeletti and Alberto Oliva, *Magazines That Make History: Their Origins, Development, and Influence* (Barcelona: Editorial Sol 90 and Gainesville: University Press of Florida, 2004).

72 Richard Ohmann, *Selling Culture: Magazines, Markets, and Class at the Turn of the Century* (London and New York: Verso, 1996).

73 George H. Douglas, *The Smart Magazines: 50 Years of Literary Revelry and High Jinks at* Vanity Fair, *the* New Yorker, Life, Esquire, *and the* Smart Set (Hamden, CT: Archon Books, 1991).

74 Nancy A. Walker, *Shaping Our Mothers' World: American Women's Magazines* (Jackson: University Press of Mississippi, 2000).

75 Amy Beth Aronson, review of *Shaping Our Mothers' World: American Women's Magazines*, by Nancy A. Walker, *American Periodicals* 12 (2002): 209.

76 Rodger Streitmatter, *Unspeakable: The Rise of the Gay and Lesbian Press in America* (Boston: Faber & Faber, 1995).

77 Streitmatter, *Unspeakable*, xii.

78 Kets de Vries, *The Leadership Mystique*.

Bibliography

Abrams, Nathan. *Norman Podhoretz and* Commentary Magazine: *The Rise and Fall of the Neocons.* New York: Continuum, 2010.

Adams, Mark. *Mr. America: How Muscular Millionaire Bernarr Macfadden Transformed the Nation Through Sex, Salad, and the Ultimate Starvation Diet.* New York: HarperCollins Publishers, 2009.

Adler, Renata. *Gone: The Last Days of the* New Yorker. New York: Simon & Schuster, 1999.

Angeletti, Norberto and Oliva, Alberto. *Magazines that Make History: Their Origins, Development, and Influence.* Barcelona: Editorial Sol 90 and Gainesville: University Press of Florida, 2004.

Aronson, Amy Beth. Review of *Shaping Our Mothers' World: American Women's Magazines*, by Nancy A. Walker. *American Periodicals* 12 (2002): 209–212.

Axel Springer. "Our Media." <http://www.axelspringer.de/en/media/index.html>, accessed 20 February 2014.

Baughman, James L. Review of *The Publisher: Henry Luce and His American Century*, by Alan Brinkley. *Journal of American History* 97.4 (2011): 1167.

Bird, S. Elizabeth. *For Enquiring Minds: A Cultural Study of Supermarket Tabloids.* Knoxville: University of Tennessee Press, 1992.

Blow, Richard. *American Son: A Portrait of John F. Kennedy, Jr.* New York: Henry Holt & Co., 2002.

Bogus, Carl T. *Buckley: William F. Buckley Jr. and the Rise of American Conservatism.* New York: Bloomsbury Press, 2011.

Brinkley, Alan. *The Publisher: Henry Luce and His American Century.* New York: Alfred A. Knopf, 2010.

Brown, Helen Gurley. *I'm Wild Again: Snippets from My Life and a Few Brazen Thoughts.* New York: St. Martin's Press, 2000.

Buckley, William F., Jr. *Miles Gone By: A Literary Autobiography.* Washington, DC: Regnery Publishing, Inc., 2004.

Buckley, William F., Jr. *Nearer, My God: An Autobiography of Faith.* New York: Doubleday, 1997.

Caddy, Adrian. "Be the Brand." *Fast Company*, 19 December 2007. <http://www.fastcompany.com/73124/be-brand>, accessed 12 December 2012.

Canning, Peter. *American Dreamers: The Wallaces and* Reader's Digest: *An Insider's Story.* New York: Simon & Schuster, 1996.

"Condé Nast Heritage." *Condé Nast* <http://www.condenast.com/about-us/heritage>, accessed 12 March 2014.

Crane, Diana. "Gender and Hegemony in Fashion Magazines: Women's Interpretations of Fashion Photographs." *Sociological Quarterly* 40.4 (August 1999): 541–563.

Douglas, George H. *The Smart Magazines: 50 Years of Literary Revelry and High Jinks at* Vanity Fair, *the* New Yorker, Life, Esquire, *and the* Smart Set. Hamden, CT: Archon Books, 1991.

Endres, Kathleen L. "The Feminism of Bernarr Macfadden: *Physical Culture* Magazine and the Empowerment of Women." *Media History Monographs* 13.2 (2011): 2–14 <http://facstaff.elon.edu/dcopeland/mhm/mhmjour13-2.pdf>, accessed 27 November 2012.

Foote, Timothy. "There Goes (Varoom!) *Esquire* Magazine." *New York Times*, 13 August 1995, G9.

Friedlander, Edward J. and Lee, John. *Feature Writing for Newspapers and Magazines: The Pursuit of Excellence*. 4th ed. New York: Longman, 2000.

Graham, Katharine. *Personal History*. New York: Alfred A. Knopf, 1997.

Grigoriadis, Vanessa. "What Does Tina Brown Have to Do to Get Some Attention?" *New York*, 10 June 2007 <http://nymag.com/news/features/33159/>, accessed 15 November 2012.

Hamlet, Janice D. "Assessing Womanist Thought: The Rhetoric of Susan L. Taylor." *Communication Quarterly* 48.4 (Fall 2000): 420–436.

Haygood, Daniel Marshall. "Henry Luce's Anti-Communist Legacy: An Analysis of U.S. News Magazines' Coverage of China's Cultural Revolution." *Journalism History* 35.2 (Summer 2009): 98–105.

Heidenry, John. *Theirs Was the Kingdom: Lila and DeWitt Wallace and the Story of the* Reader's Digest. New York: W.W. Norton, 1993.

Helal, Kathleen M. "Celebrity, Femininity, Lingerie: Dorothy Parker's Autobiographical Monologues." *Women's Studies* 33.1 (January/February 2004): 77–102.

Hudson, Berkley and Townsend, Rebecca. "Unraveling the Webs of Intimacy and Influence: Willie Morris and *Harper's* Magazine, 1967–1971." *Literary Journalism Studies* 1.2 (2009): 63–78.

Izzo, Amanda. "Outrageous and Everyday: The Papers of Gloria Steinem." *Journal of Women's History* 14.2 (Summer 2002): 151–153.

Kets de Vries, Manfred F.R. *The Leadership Mystique: A User's Manual for the Human Enterprise*. New York: Financial Times Prentice Hall, 2001.

Kitch, Carolyn. "'A Death in the American Family': Myth, Memory, and National Values in the Media Mourning of John F. Kennedy Jr." *Journalism & Mass Communication Quarterly* 79.2 (Summer 2002): 294–309.

Klean Zwilling, Jillian. "A Feminist Icon in Uncharted Territory: The Public Memory of Gloria Steinem." Paper Presented at the Annual Meeting, International Communication Association, May 2009.

Kramer, Mark. "Breakable Rules for Literary Journalists." In Sims, Norman and Kramer, Mark, eds. *Literary Journalism: A New Collection of the Best American Nonfiction*. New York: Ballantine Books, 1995, 21–34.

Kruip, Gudrun. "Restricted Support: The Role of the Axel Springer Verlag in the Process of Westernization." Paper presented at Conference, American Impact on Western Europe: Americanization and Westernization in Transatlantic Perspective, Washington, DC: German Historical Institute, 25–27 March 1999 <http://webdoc.sub.gwdg.de/ebook/p/2005/ghi_12/www.ghi-dc.org/conpotweb/westernpapers/kruip.pdf>, accessed 22 July 2013.

Kunkel, Thomas. "Eighty-Two and Counting: The Continuing Excellence of the *New Yorker*." *American Journalism Review*, 1 April 2007 <http://www.highbeam.com/Doc/1G1-162680245.html>, accessed 31 January 2013.

Kunkel, Thomas. *Genius in Disguise: Harold Ross of the* New Yorker. New York: Random House, 1995.

Landers, James. *The Improbable First Century of* Cosmopolitan *Magazine*. Columbia: University of Missouri Press, 2010.

Littell, Robert T. *The Men We Became: My Friendship with John F. Kennedy, Jr*. New York: St. Martin's Press, 2004.

Lueders, Bill. *An Enemy of the State: The Life of Erwin Knoll*. Monroe, ME: Common Courage Press, 1996.

MacDougall, A. Kent. "Clay Felker's *New York*." *Columbia Journalism Review* (March/April 1974), 36–47.

Macmillan Publishers. Victor S. Navasky. A *Matter of Opinion*. Winner of the 2005 George Polk Book Award <http://us.macmillan.com/amatterofopinion/VictorNavasky>, accessed 19 February 2014.

McConnell, Jane S. "Choosing a Team for Democracy: Henry R. Luce and the Commission on Freedom of the Press." *American Journalism* 14.2 (Spring 1997): 148–163.

McKeen, William. *Tom Wolfe*. New York: Twayne Publishers, 1995.

McKeen, William. "The Two Sides of Hunter Thompson." [Special Issue: Hunter S. Thompson] *Literary Journalism Studies* 4.1 (Spring 2012): 7–18.

McKeen, William. "The Wolfe Man." 2014 <http://www.williammckeen.com/Tom_Wolfe.html>, accessed 5 December 2012.

Nasaw, David. *The Chief: The Life of William Randolph Hearst*. Boston: Houghton Mifflin, 2000.

Navasky, Victor S. *A Matter of Opinion*. New York: Farrar, Straus and Giroux, 2005.

New York Magazine. Archives: Tom Wolfe <http://nymag.com/nymag/tom-wolfe/>, accessed 31 January 2014.

Ohmann, Richard. *Selling Culture: Magazines, Markets, and Class at the Turn of the Century*. London and New York: Verso, 1996.

Oppenheimer, Jerry. *Front Row: Anna Wintour, the Cool Life and Hot Times of Vogue's Editor-In-Chief*. New York: St. Martin's Press, 2005.

Oppenheimer, Jerry. *Martha Stewart—Just Desserts: The Unauthorized Biography*. New York: William Morrow and Company, 1997.

Ouellette, Laurie. "Inventing the Cosmo Girl: Class Identity and Girl-Style American Dreams." *Media, Culture & Society* 21.3 (May 1999): 359–383.

Pearl, Monica B. "'What Strange Intimacy': Janet Flanner's Letters from Paris." *Journal of European Studies* 32.125/126 (September 2002): 303–318.

Polsgrove, Carol. *It Wasn't Pretty, Folks, but Didn't We Have Fun? Esquire in the Sixties*. New York: W.W. Norton, 1995.

Prior-Miller, Marcia R. and Associates. "Bibliography of Published Research on Magazine and Journal Periodicals." 8th ed. Research database. Ames: Iowa State University, last modified, 31 August 2012, MSWord file <mpm@iastate.edu>.

Riley, Sam G., ed. *American Magazine Journalists, 1900–1960*. First Series. Detroit: Gale Research, 1990.

Robinson, Andrew. Review of *Photographing America: Henri Cartier-Bresson and Walker Evans*, Agnès Sire, curator. *History Today* 59.11 (November 2009): 59.

Ross, Lillian. *Here but Not Here: My Life with William Shawn and the New Yorker*. New York: Random House, 1998.

Sachs, Andrea. "Q & A: Isaiah Wilner." *Time*, 5 October 2006, 91.

Scanlon, Jennifer. *Bad Girls Go Everywhere: The Life of Helen Gurley Brown*. New York and Oxford: Oxford University Press, 2009.

Scherr, Arthur. Review of *The Chief: The Life of William Randolph Hearst*, by David Nasaw. *Midwest Quarterly* 45.3 (March 2004): 319–321.

Seebohm, Caroline. *The Man Who Was Vogue: The Life and Times of Condé Nast*. New York: Viking Press, 1982.

Sims, Norman. "The Art of Literary Journalism." In Sims, Norman and Kramer, Mark, eds. *Literary Journalism: A New Collection of the Best American Nonfiction*. New York: Ballantine Books, 1995, 3–19.

Sire, Agnès, curator. *Henri Cartier-Bresson/Walker Evans: Photographing America 1929–1947*. London: Thames & Hudson, 2009.

[Special Issue: Hunter S. Thompson] *Literary Journalism Studies* 4.1 (Spring 2012) <http://www.ialjs.org/?p=1495>, accessed 20 February 2014.

Stabile, Carol A. "Getting What She Deserved: The News Media, Martha Stewart, and Masculine Domination." *Feminist Media Studies* 4.3 (November 2004): 315–332.

"Star Power: Bonnie Fuller and the Feminist Case for Celebrity Journalism." *Economist*, 5 August 2004. <http://www.economist.com/node/3062089>, accessed 11 November 2012.

Stepp, Carl Sessions. "Giving a Forgotten Visionary His Due." *American Journalism Review*, October/November 2006. <http://ajrarchive.org/article_printable.asp?id=4198>, accessed 27 January 2014.

Streitmatter, Rodger. *Unspeakable: The Rise of the Gay and Lesbian Press in America*. Boston: Faber and Faber, 1995.

Sumner, David E. "A Visit to the Condé Nast Library and Archives." *Journal of Magazine & New Media Research* 10.2 (2009) <http://aejmcmagazine.arizona.edu/journal/spring2009/Sumner.pdf>, accessed 20 February 2014.

Swain, Bruce M. "Bernarr Macfadden." In Riley, Sam G., ed. *American Magazine Journalists, 1900–1960, First Series*. Dictionary of Literary Biography. Vol. 91. Detroit: Gale Research, 1990, 205–215.

Swanson, Carl with Larocca, Amy. "What Makes Bonnie Run?" *New York*, 14 July 2003 <http://nymag.com/nymetro/news/media/features/n_8946/>, accessed 29 January 2014.

Talese, Gay. "Frank Sinatra Has a Cold." *Esquire*, April 1966 <http://www.esquire.com/features/esq1003-oct_sinatra_rev_>, accessed 20 June 2013.

Ubbens, Wilbert. Review of *The 'World-View' of the Axel Springer Publishing Company: Journalism between Western Values and German Traditions of Thought*, by Gudrun Kruip. *Communication Booknotes Quarterly* 31:1 (Winter 2000): 37–38.

Vitek, Jack. *The Godfather of Tabloid: Generoso Pope Jr. and the* National Enquirer. Lexington: University Press of Kentucky, 2008.

Wakefield, Dan. "Harold Hayes and the New Journalism: *Esquire* Editor Encouraged a Generation of Writers to Experiment with Non-Fiction Techniques." *Nieman Reports*, Summer 1992, 32–35.

Walker, Nancy A. *Shaping Our Mothers' World: American Women's Magazines*. Jackson: University Press of Mississippi, 2000.

Wilner, Isaiah. *The Man Time Forgot: A Tale of Genius, Betrayal, and the Creation of* Time *Magazine*. New York: HarperCollins, 2006.

Whyte, Kenneth. *The Uncrowned King: The Sensational Rise of William Randolph Hearst*. Berkeley: Counterpoint, 2009.

Wolfe, Tom. Archive. *New York* Magazine <http://nymag.com/nymag/tom-wolfe/>, accessed 20 June 2013.

Wolfe, Tom. "The Birth of 'The New Journalism': Eyewitness Report by Tom Wolfe." *New York* Magazine, 14 February 1972 <http://nymag.com/news/media/47353/>, accessed 20 June 2013.

Zuckerman, Mary Ellen. *A History of Popular Women's Magazines in the United States, 1792–1995*. Westport, CT: Greenwood Press, 1998.

Supplemental Resources

Edel, Leon. "Biography and the Science of Man." In Friedson, Anthony M. ed. *New Directions in Biography*. Honolulu: University Press of Hawaii, 1981, 1–11.

Gunn, Simon and Faire, Lucy. *Research Methods for History*. Edinburgh: Edinburgh University Press, 2012.

Kazanjian, Dodie. *Alex: The Life of Alexander Liberman*. New York: Knopf, 1993.

Kosner, Edward. *It's News to Me: The Making and Unmaking of an Editor*. New York: Thunder's Mouth Press, 2006.

Merrill, John C. "The Four Theories of the Press Four and a Half Decades Later: A Retrospective." *Journalism Studies* 3.1 (February 2002): 133–136.

Mirabella, Grace. *In and Out of Vogue: A Memoir*. New York: Doubleday, 1995.

Nord, David Paul. "Intellectual History, Social History, Cultural History . . . and Our History." *Journalism Quarterly* 67.4 (Winter 1990): 645–648.

Sweeney, Michael S. "'Delays and Vexation': Jack London and the Russo-Japanese War." *Journalism & Mass Communication Quarterly* 75.3 (Autumn 1998): 548–559.

10
EDITORIAL ROLES AND PRACTICES

Exploring the Creative Enterprise

Susan Greenberg

The individuals engaged in day-to-day acts of editing are often invisible to those outside the editorial process. Apart from a handful of stars, practitioners lack a public profile and there are no prizes for their work. This is partly because periodical editing is inherently collaborative. There is also a sense in which an awareness of process—what goes on behind the scenes—disrupts what Walter Benjamin called the "aura" of cultural artifacts.[1] However, editing is a very important part of what makes the magazine form distinctive. The orchestration carried out by editors, whatever their job title, is what provides the aesthetic unity needed to create a successful collective identity.[2] This aspect alone makes an understanding of the magazine vital to any broader, generic analysis of editing practice. Practices that evolved in a magazine setting have also been influential in other areas of publishing. This includes book editing and contemporary digital "curation," a term used since the late 1990s to describe the mediation of digital content.[3]

This chapter provides an overview of existing research that considers what magazine editors do, how editing has changed over time and why such a form of textual mediation—or its absence—might matter. It also aims to identify gaps in the literature and suggest possible areas of future scholarship. Because of the inherent invisibility and ubiquity of the role and the changing terminology over time,[4] the research has focused on the act rather than the person, across time, location and genre.

Defining Editing

The term *editing* is used to describe a wide range of editorial interventions. In a comparative study, editing has been broken down into three stages: *selection*, *shaping* and *linking*, considered within the context of a newly defined *poetics of editing*.[5] This draws on a long tradition of debate about the principles of the writing arts, laying the basis for an understanding of editing as the opening up of possibilities, rather than closing things down and as a collaborative conversation rather than a system of hierarchical control. As shown by the new challenges posed by on-line editing, that debate is set to continue.[6]

The generic analysis of editing as such is rare. Definitions are found chiefly in biographical narratives, teaching manuals or books giving practical advice, rather than in academic research literature. This absence was noted in a review of scholarship about magazine editing and editing practice, published in 1995, in which Lee Jolliffe said that research on the subject "has not been viewed as a body, its parts having been published at wide intervals in a disparate range of publications and made relatively inaccessible due to poor cataloguing and indexing."[7] The picture has changed only slightly since then.

The possible exception to the case described above is the field of scholarly editing, sometimes referred to as *bibliography*.[8] Here a substantial literature engages in debates about interpretive frameworks that are potentially relevant to other editorial media, although the focus here is primarily on texts of historical or literary significance rather than the everyday "process of acquiring and preparing texts for publication."[9] A snapshot of different stances is given in two international essay collections of the early 1990s, edited by Philip Cohen[10] and by George Bornstein and Ralph Williams,[11] while an up-to-date interpretation by an influential participant can be found in Jerome McGann's 2013 essay, "Philology in a New Key."[12]

A big picture view of editorial practices across Europe and North America can also be gained from the related field of book history, authoritatively summarized by David Finkelstein and Alistair McCleery's *Introduction to Book History*, which is supported by a comprehensive *Reader*.[13] Landmark concepts in the field include Don McKenzie's 1985 Panizzi Lecture, "Bibliography and the Sociology of Texts," which helped to open up debate in the contemporary period; Roger Darnton's "communications circuit," which places editorial production in the wider context of authorship and reader reception; and Pierre Bourdieu's analysis of social relationships at play in textual production.[14]

In the social sciences and cultural studies, the *selection* role of editing is commonly analyzed in terms of gatekeeping. The metaphor was first articulated by Kurt Lewin in 1943[15] to describe communication channels in general and was applied early on to the news industry, particularly the editorial decision-making process whereby news travels from the provider to the consumer through an editorial filter. The filter has variously been understood as based on personal experience,[16] commercial interests,[17] group culture[18] and other power structures. The metaphor gained new life from the 1990s in debates about the Internet, which is perceived as providing individuals with the power to bypass the gatekeeping of mainstream media. For some, the Internet is inherently a marker of democracy and anti-elitism,[19] while others identify a more positive role for the gatekeeping editor as a "potential force of cohesion in an increasingly fragmented society."[20]

A range of other general approaches to journalism practice have been mapped and analyzed by Barbie Zelizer.[21] A recent trend has been to draw on anthropology[22] and phenomenology[23] to provide a perspective that takes account of the personal experience of producers themselves. Individual case studies can also throw light on wider issues concerning editorial judgment and ethics; a notable example is Forde's 2008 detailed examination of Masson vs. *New Yorker*.[24] Sociological close-ups of the workplace provide insights into particular editing roles. Recent examples include Cynthia Ryan's study of a magazine launch in New York for breast cancer patients and survivors, which involved the development of a new reader community,[25] and Brian Moeran's analysis of the editing of an international fashion magazine, as a case study of the orchestration of cooperative networks.[26]

The literature considered to date relates to the *selection* function of editing. Works relating to *shaping* and *linking* are considered in the next section.

Literature of Advice

In some countries, aspects of media production now have a home in the academy rather than the workplace, and the *shaping* function is a substantive concern in writing-related disciplines such as journalism, composition and creative writing. However, by and large these subjects concern themselves chiefly with revision of one's own texts, rather than someone else's work. When attention turns to professional editing, its specific identity can become subsumed under broader categories, such as publishing or journalism, thereby contributing to its invisibility.

The full range of editing practices is perceived as difficult to teach because they depend so heavily on the subtle exercise of judgment. In Australia, for example, Katya Johanson notes the need for the teaching of editing to deal with a tendency of students to veer from one extreme to another in their responses to a text, from derogatory to placatory, rather than finding a middle ground of critical engagement.[27] With some exceptions,[28] the teaching of editing in the academy therefore appears to focus on micro-level interventions such as copyediting rather than more macro, structural editing.[29] Because authoring and editing share many core concerns, however, research can benefit from comparative work between the two. In one example of this approach, Jocelyne Bisaillon in Canada recommends the observation of professional editing as a way of extrapolating general principles of practice, which are transferable to the self-revision carried out by writers on their own texts.[30] For further study, an annotated 2003 bibliography provides a review of resources for the teaching of revising and editing. It is part of a series on textual production, led by Bruce Speck, which includes a bibliography on editing practice from 1960 to 1988 and 14 pages specifically on magazine editing.[31]

Books of advice written for a general public, although not scholarly literature, can provide a valuable resource. Examples include Gerald Gross's collection of essays,[32] general primers,[33] maxims[34] and manuals dedicated specifically to magazines.[35] Some guides explicitly put editing into a bigger frame, drawing out its full role in *linking* as well as selecting and shaping text. Michael Evans, for example, describes the different "layers" of magazine editing, from big-picture decisions about audience, design and "mission,"[36] down to fact-checking and grammar, placing equal importance on each.[37]

Normative manuals sometimes shade into personal accounts by editing practitioners. These also provide an important resource for scholarship, offering insights into practice and relationships, for example, between editors and authors. However, the biographical approach provides only a partial and fragmented picture. As with other areas of textual culture, the focus tends to be on famous names rather than everyday practice, books rather than periodicals and literary or political titles, rather than commercial ones. A cluster of publications has grown up, for example, around the *New Yorker* and other "smart set" magazines such as *Vanity Fair, Life*, and *Esquire*.[38] In political magazine publishing, a collection of essays edited by Victor Navasky and Evan Cornog takes the discussion up to the present day.[39] Examples relating not to the literary or political elite but to commercial titles include memoirs by Edward Bok, editor of the mass circulation magazine *Ladies' Home Journal* in turn-of-century New York, and Edgar A. Grunwald, who summed up a long career in business magazine publishing in a 1988 volume.[40]

Editing: A History

A historical approach provides an essential insight into how editing roles have changed over time, how magazine editing developed its own distinctive characteristics and how those qualities influenced other cultural forms. The historiography itself illustrates the shift in focus from the substantive content of magazines—and the way the content is *consumed* by the public—to the social and cultural processes of *production*. This new scrutiny has been aided by the digitization of many magazine and newspaper archives. Taken together, the shift in means and aims has created the conditions for an expanded study of editing as a distinctive material practice in its own right, which deserves greater attention.

A valuable example of the earlier, content-led approach is provided by a multi-volume study of American magazines by Frank Luther Mott, the first of which was published in the 1930s, the last in 1968.[41] Here, a perspective on editing can be gained from information about notable personalities and business conditions, including pay rates and employment levels.[42] In historical scholarship of the second kind, one can trace the ways in which textual authority was developed and maintained over time. Print correctors replaced scribes as sources of editorial quality control, adapting the regulated system of copying manuscripts from an exemplar. Anthony Grafton shows how early correctors in Europe assumed a wide range of editing roles extending far beyond proofing or copyediting, while Robert Ritter's study of "house style" defines editorial authority and takes the analysis into the modern era.[43]

A historical approach is helpful in showing how different media interacted with each other, over time and across different national cultures. In particular, the different editing styles of books and magazines were important mutual influences. The first periodicals were protean in nature. Magazines such as the *Spectator* and the *Gentleman's Magazine* appeared in early eighteenth-century Britain.[44] In "The Evolution of Editors," first published at the turn of the twentieth century, the prominent British magazine editor Leslie Stephen describes the early periodicals as being so miscellaneous, no editor was required; instead, informal collation was organized by the proprietor or groups of friends.[45]

It was not until the start of the nineteenth century that a new wave of titles—the *Westminster Review* and *Edinburgh Review* were both launched in 1802—began to define a specific style distinct from book culture. In particular, Francis Jeffrey, editor of the *Edinburgh Review* in Scotland, is credited as the man who "invented the trade of editorship. Before him an editor was a bookseller's drudge; he is now a distinguished functionary."[46] One of the features of the new magazine was the development of a distinctive collective identity or *persona*, conveyed in the selection of content, prose style and overall presentation. Dallas Liddle's analysis of British journalism provides a subtle, detailed picture of the evolution of magazine genres in the nineteenth century.[47]

The importance of understanding magazines as the outcome of many hands emerges clearly in accounts of practice in the Victorian period.[48] Serious British novelists, such as William Thackeray and Charles Dickens,[49] used their experience as magazine editors to inform their craft,[50] and magazine and book editing practice became mutually influential. For example, when magazine readership dropped after World War I, book publishing took on some of the magazine's editorial characteristics by offering cheap, disposable paperbacks with a strong collective identity defined by editors.[51]

Although the first magazine in the American colonies was published as early as 1741, and periodical growth took off on both sides of the Atlantic in the 1840s, British titles held sway over the U.S. market for a long time. As Mott notes, "It is not easy to realize now how large an American public the great English periodicals had before the Civil War. The *Edinburgh Review* was much more widely read in the United States than the *North American*."[52] Like British counterparts such as *Blackwood's*, early magazines in the United States were usually linked to book publishers and aimed at a relatively genteel audience. The main challenge to gentility, on both sides of the Atlantic, was the emergence of popular magazines from the 1830s onwards. As in Britain, recounts Mott, this came with the development of a distinct class of professional writers who were encouraged by higher pay, but the assertive writ of editors remained large:

> Under the system of anonymity, editors had plenary powers. It was a logical result of such a system that blue-pencilling should be unrestrained. Many American editors doubtless followed the lead of Jeffrey, of the *Edinburgh Review*, who is said to have regarded a young contributor "as supplying raw material which might be rather arbitrarily altered by the editor."[53]

Popular magazines in this period were often edited by women, who entered publishing in large numbers for the first time. Patricia Okker was one of the first scholars to map the field, listing more than 700 women magazine editors in mid-nineteenth-century America.[54] A collection of essays about the late nineteenth and early twentieth century, edited by Sharon Harris, considers opportunities for work experience for women editors, African-American and Native American experiences, campaigning magazine editors and the "subtle subversion" of mass market women's titles.[55] In the foreword, Ellen Gruber Garvey places the invisibility of women editors within the larger invisibility of collaborative editorial work. Garvey makes a claim for the contribution of editors of all kinds, including those involved in the less glamorous "housekeeping" role of copyediting, to the persuasive creation of an "imagined community" of readers in American society, and hence the maintenance of magazines' overall value.[56]

Around the turn of the twentieth century, gentility was also challenged in the United States by the new breed of modernist journals and *little magazines*. These competed among themselves and with other middlebrow titles, generating debate in new literary periodicals such as the *Nation*, the *New Republic*, the *New Yorker* and *Bookman*.[57] Garvey points to the earlier, innovative scholarship of Jane Marek in *Women Editing Modernism*,[58] which put the spotlight on the working relationships between women editors. These include self-taught figures such as Margaret Anderson and Jane Heap of the *Little Review* and Harriet Monroe and Alice Corbin Henderson of *Poetry* who, as Garvey puts it, "invented a new kind of magazine as they went along."[59]

By the early twentieth century, when the United States had begun to challenge the United Kingdom economically, the style and content of U.S. magazines started to diverge from their British counterparts and take the form described in the biographical and how-to literature cited earlier in this section. Their success also made them a new source of income for writers, who often made more from the serial rights than from book royalties.[60] At the same time, as in the United Kingdom, periodicals were a key influence on book publishing, encouraging a more pro-active approach by editors.[61] By the 1930s, the prospect of commercial, Americanization was a subject of debate in Britain. However, comparative research about national practices—both transatlantic and elsewhere—remains relatively unexplored.

The Digital Argument

By the end of the twentieth century, the global challenge to magazines had come from economic and technological changes that encode some editing features in automated interfaces and shift responsibility from in-house professionals to freelancers and ultimately readers.[62]

The distinctiveness of the magazine form continues to be influential in new, digital contexts, a precursor to social media in the way that it collates diverse material and encourages a conversation within a defined community—a literal form of *linking*. The Nieman Journalism Lab, for example, describes Henry Luce's *Time* magazine as "a fully fledged aggregator" *avant la lettre*,[63] while a history of the Web log genre points to Dennis Dutton's *Arts & Letters Daily* as an example of the aggregated blog-as-magazine, relying on editors to find thought-provoking articles.[64] Others draw analogies between digital orality in contemporary international media and eighteenth-century British coffee shop culture,[65] as well as explore and debate the continuities between magazine editing and new formats designed for mobile platforms.[66]

In this international debate, editing has also found itself at the center of more contentious arguments about the future in which self-publishing by the producer-consumer is defined *against* professional mediation.[67] Questions also arise about the potential limitations of "network editing,"[68] as well as the hidden role of institutions in supporting peer production.[69]

Conclusions

In 1995, Jolliffe, calling for more research about editing, recommended a comparative and contextual approach as a way of mapping a relatively uncharted field, making greater use of interviews, attitude surveys, content analysis, ethnography and semantic and rhetorical analysis.[70] Since then, one can note an increase in media scholarship across the board. This is encouraged in part by the entry of scholar-practitioners into the academy, noted recently in two U.K. studies,[71] among others, and the emergence of other practice-related fields such as the *digital humanities*.[72] In both cases, a shared impulse exists to fight on two fronts, challenging existing interpretive frameworks on the one hand and context-free practice on the other. The aim in both cases is also the same: to make room for an approach that recognizes the messy realities of practice. However, when it comes to specific research about the invisible editor, the process has only just begun. It is hoped that this chapter provides further encouragement for that effort.

Notes

1 Walter Benjamin, *Illuminations*, ed. with Introduction by Hannah Arendt, trans. Harry Zorn (London: Pimlico, 1999), 216.

2 Susan Greenberg, "When the Editor Disappears, Does Editing Disappear?" *Convergence: The International Journal of Research into New Media Technologies* 16.1 (February 2010): 9.

3 Susan Greenberg, "The Hidden Art of Editing: Theory, History and Identity" (Ph.D. diss., University College London, 2013), 156.

4 Greenberg, "Hidden Art of Editing," 13, 19.

5 Greenberg, "Hidden Art of Editing," 72.

6 Ben Smith, "What the Longform Backlash Is All About," *Journalism, Deliberated* (blog), 26 January 2014 <https://medium.com/journalism-deliberated/958f4e7691f5>, accessed 20 March 2014.

7 Lee Jolliffe, "Research Review: Magazine Editors and Editing Practices," in David Abrahamson, ed., *The American Magazine: Research Perspectives and Prospects* (Ames: Iowa State University Press, 1995), 52.

8 David Finkelstein and Alistair McCleery, *An Introduction to Book History*, 2nd ed. (London: Routledge, 2012), 7–27.

9 Bruce W. Speck, *Editing: An Annotated Bibliography* (Westport, CT: Greenwood Press, 1991), vii.

10 Philip Cohen, ed., *Devils and Angels: Textual Editing and Literary Theory* (Charlottesville: University Press of Virginia, 1991).

11 George Bornstein and Ralph G. Williams, eds., *Palimpsest: Editorial Theory in the Humanities* (Ann Arbor: University of Michigan Press, 1993).

12 Jerome McGann, "Philology in a New Key," *Critical Inquiry* 39.2 (Winter 2013): 327–346.

13 Finkelstein and McCleery, *Introduction to Book History*; David Finkelstein and Alistair McCleery, eds., *The Book History Reader*, 2nd ed. (London: Routledge, 2006).

14 Donald F. McKenzie, *Bibliography and the Sociology of Texts: The Panizzi Lectures 1985* (Cambridge: Cambridge University Press, 1999); Robert Darnton, "What Is the History of Books?" in *The Kiss of Lamourette: Reflections in Cultural History* (New York: W. W. Norton & Co., 1990), 107–135; Pierre Bourdieu, *The Field of Cultural Production: Essays on Art and Literature*, ed., Randal Johnson (Cambridge: Polity Press, 1993).

15 Kurt Lewin, *Field Theory in Social Science: Selected Theoretical Papers*, ed., Dorwin Cartwright (New York: Harper & Row, 1951): 143–153.

16 David Manning White, "The 'Gate Keeper': A Case Study in the Selection of News," *Journalism Quarterly* 27.4 (Fall 1950): 383–390.

17 Lewis Donohew, "Newspaper Gatekeepers and Forces in the News Channel," *Public Opinion Quarterly* 31.1 (Spring 1967): 61–68.

18 Steven E. Clayman and Ann Reisner, "Gatekeeping in Action: Editorial Conferences and Assessments of Newsworthiness," *American Sociological Review* 63.2 (April 1998): 178–199.

19 Jo Bardoel and Mark Deuze, "'Network Journalism': Converging Competencies of Old and New Media Professionals," *Australian Journalism Review* 23.2 (December 2001): 91–103; Axel Bruns, *Gatewatching: Collaborative Online News Production* (New York: Peter Lang, 2005).

20 Jane B. Singer, "Online Journalists: Foundations for Research into Their Changing Roles," *Journal of Computer-Mediated Communication* 4.1 (September 1998): n.p. <http://onlinelibrary.wiley.com/doi/10.1111/j.1083-6101.1998.tb00088.x/full>, accessed 12 May 2004.

21 Barbie Zelizer, *Taking Journalism Seriously: News and the Academy* (London: Sage, 2004).

22 Birgit Bräuchler and John Postill, eds., *Theorising Media and Practice*, Anthropology of Media, vol. 4 (New York: Berghahn Books, 2010).

23 Jane B. Singer and Ian Ashman, "'Comment Is Free, but Facts Are Sacred': User-Generated Content and Ethical Constructs at the *Guardian*," *Journal of Mass Media Ethics* 24.1 (January/March 2009): 3–21.

24 Kathy Roberts Forde, *Literary Journalism on Trial: Masson v. New Yorker and the First Amendment* (Amherst: University of Massachusetts Press, 2008).

25 Cynthia Ryan, "Struggling to Survive: A Study of Editorial Decision-Making Strategies at MAMM Magazine," *Journal of Business and Technical Communication* 19.3 (July 2005): 353–376.

26 Brian Moeran, "More Than Just a Fashion Magazine," *Current Sociology* 54.5 (September 2006): 725–744.

27 Katya Johanson, "Dead, Done For and Dangerous: Teaching Editing Students What Not to Do," *New Writing: The International Journal for the Practice and Theory of Creative Writing* 3.1 (April 2006): 50–51.

28 Leara Rhodes and Amber Roessner, "Teaching Magazine Publishing through Experiential Learning," *Journalism & Mass Communication Educator* 63 (Winter 2009): 304–316.

29 Susan Greenberg, *Editors Talk about Editing* (New York: Peter Lang, forthcoming).

30 Jocelyne Bisaillon, "Professional Editing Strategies Used by Six Editors," *Written Communication* 24.4 (October 2007): 295–322.

31 Bruce W. Speck, Dean A. Hinnen, and Kathleen Hinnen, *Teaching Revising and Editing: An Annotated Bibliography* (Westport, CT: Greenwood Press, 2003); Speck, *Editing*.

32 Gerald Gross, ed., *Editors on Editing: What Writers Need to Know About What Editors Do* (New York: Grove Press, 1993).

33 Scott Norton, *Developmental Editing: A Handbook for Freelancers, Authors, and Publishers* (Chicago: University of Chicago Press, 2009); Arthur Plotnik, *The Elements of Editing: A Modern Guide for Editors and Journalists* (New York: Macmillan, 1982); Carol Fisher Saller, *The Subversive Copy Editor: Advice from Chicago* (Chicago: University of Chicago Press, 2009).

34 John E. McIntyre, *The Old Editor Says: Maxims for Writing and Editing* (Baltimore, MA: Apprentice House, 2013).

35 Michael Robert Evans, *The Layers of Magazine Editing* (New York: Columbia University Press, 2004); Jenny McKay, *The Magazines Handbook*, 3rd ed. (London and New York: Routledge, 2013).

36 Evans, *Layers of Magazine Editing*, 40–63.

37 Evans, *Layers of Magazine Editing*.

38 George H. Douglas, *The Smart Magazines: 50 Years of Literary Revelry and High Jinks at* Vanity Fair, *the* New Yorker, Life, Esquire, *and the* Smart Set (Hamden, CT: Archon Books, 1991); Brendan Gill, *Here at the New Yorker* (New York: Random House, 1975); Philip Gourevitch, ed., *The Paris Review: Interviews*, vol. 4 (Edinburgh, UK: Canongate, 2009); Thomas Kunkel, ed., *Letters from the Editor: The* New Yorker's *Harold Ross* (New York: Modern Library, 2001); Ved Mehta, *Remembering Mr. Shawn's* New Yorker*: The Invisible Art of Editing* (Woodstock, NY: The Overlook Press, 1998).

39 Victor S. Navasky and Evan Cornog, eds., *The Art of Making Magazines: On Being an Editor and Other Views from the Industry* (New York: Columbia University Press, 2012).

40 Edward W. Bok, *A Man from Maine* (New York: C. Scribner's Sons, 1923); Edgar A. Grunwald, *The Business Press Editor* (New York: New York University Press, 1988).

41 Mott, Frank Luther. *A History of American Magazines*. Vol. 1, *A History of American Magazines, 1741–1850*; Vol. 2, *A History of American Magazines, 1850–1865*; Vol. 3, *A History of American Magazines, 1865–1885*; Vol. 4, *A History of American Magazines, 1885–1905*; Vol. 5, *A History of American Magazines, 1905–1930* (New York: D. Appleton, 1930; Cambridge, MA: The Belknap Press, 1938, 1938, 1957; Cambridge, MA: Harvard University Press, 1968).

42 For example, Mott, *History of American Magazines*, 1:495.

43 Anthony Grafton, *The Culture of Correction in Renaissance Europe* (London: British Library, 2011), 2–3; Robert Mark Ritter, "The Transformation of Authority in Print and the Rise of House Style" (D.Phil. diss., St. Anne's College, University of Oxford, 2010), ii, 98.

44 For example, Dallas Liddle, *The Dynamics of Genre: Journalism and the Practice of Literature in Mid-Victorian Britain* (Charlottesville: University of Virginia Press, 2009), 75; Robert L. Patten, "When Is a Book Not a Book?" *Biblion: The Bulletin of the New York Public Library* 4.2 (Spring 1996): 35–63.

45 Leslie Stephen, "The Evolution of Editors," *Studies of a Biographer*, vol. 1 (New York: G. P. Putnam's Sons, 1907), 35.

46 Walter Bagehot, "The First Edinburgh Reviewers," *National Review* 1 (October 1855): 276.

47 Liddle, *Dynamics of Genre*.

48 Laurel Brake, Aled Jones, and Lionel Madden, eds., *Investigating Victorian Journalism* (New York: St. Martin's Press, 1990).

49 Dickens edited magazines over several decades that included *Bentley's Miscellany*, *Household Words* and *All the Year Round*.

50 Liddle, *Dynamics of Genre*; Patten, "When Is a Book."

51 Allen Mikaelian, "Middlemen by Profession: Popular Fiction and the Rise of the In-House Book Editor" (M.A. diss., Institute of English Studies, University of London, 1997), 11.

52 Mott, *History of American Magazines*, 3:129. Unfortunately, Mott was in error in confusing describing "English" with "British"; the *Edinburgh Review*, based in Scotland, belongs to the latter category.

53 Mott, *History of American Magazines*, 3:26.

54 Patricia Okker, *Our Sister Editors: Sarah J. Hale and the Tradition of Nineteenth-Century American Women Editors* (Athens: University of Georgia Press, 1995).

55 Sharon M. Harris, ed., with a Foreword by Ellen Gruber Garvey, *Blue Pencils and Hidden Hands: Women Editing Periodicals, 1830–1910* (Boston: Northeastern University Press, 2004).

56 Ellen Gruber Garvey, "Foreword," in Sharon M. Harris, ed., *Blue Pencils and Hidden Hands: Women Editing Periodicals, 1830–1910* (Boston: Northeastern University Press, 2004), xi, xii, xiii.

57 Janice A. Radway, "Learned and Literary Print Cultures in an Age of Professionalization and Diversification," in Carl F. Kaestle, and Janice A. Radway, eds., *Print in Motion: The Expansion of Publishing and Reading*

in the United States, 1880–1940, A History of the Book in America, David D. Hall, ed., vol. 4 (Chapel Hill: University of North Carolina Press, 2009).

58 Jayne E. Marek, *Women Editing Modernism: "Little" Magazines and Literary History* (Lexington: University Press of Kentucky, 1995).

59 Garvey, "Foreword," xx.

60 James L. W. West, III, *American Authors and the Literary Marketplace since 1900* (Philadelphia: University of Pennsylvania Press, 1988).

61 Perhaps the most prominent example of this trend is Maxwell Perkins, celebrated for his role as editor of F. Scott Fitzgerald and Thomas Wolfe. The extensive literature on this canonical figure includes the following: Matthew J. Bruccoli and Judith S. Baughman, eds., *The Sons of Maxwell Perkins: Letters of F. Scott Fitzgerald, Ernest Hemingway, Thomas Wolfe, and Their Editor* (Columbia: University of South Carolina Press, 2004); A. Walton Litz, "Maxwell Perkins: The Editor as Critic," in Wm J. Howard, ed., *Editor, Author, and Publisher: Papers Given at the Editorial Conference, University of Toronto, November 1968* (Toronto: University of Toronto Press, 1969), 96–112; John Hall Wheelock, ed., *Editor to Author: The Letters of Maxwell E. Perkins*, Introduction by Marcia Davenport, 2nd ed. (New York: Charles Scribner Sons, 1979); A. Scott Berg, *Max Perkins, Editor of Genius* (New York: E.P. Dutton, 1978).

62 Greenberg, "When the Editor Disappears," 13.

63 David Skok, "Aggregation Is Deep in Journalism's DNA," *Nieman Journalism Lab*, 27 January 2012 <http://www.niemanlab.org/2012/01/david-skok-aggregation-is-deep-in-journalisms-dna/>, accessed 11 August 2012.

64 Rudolf Ammann, "Weblogs 1994–2000: A Genealogy" (Ph.D. diss., University College London, 2013), 168–169.

65 Geoffrey Nunberg, "Farewell to the Information Age," in Geoffrey Nunberg, ed., *The Future of the Book* (Berkeley: University of California Press, 1996), 132–133.

66 Susan Greenberg, "Slow Journalism in the Digital Fast Lane," in Richard Lance Keeble and John Tulloch, eds., *Global Literary Journalism: Exploring the Journalistic Imagination* (New York: Peter Lang, 2012), 381–393; see also, Ben Smith, "What the Longform Backlash Is All About."

67 Greenberg, "Hidden Art of Editing," 165–166.

68 John Jones, "Patterns of Revision in Online Writing: A Study of Wikipedia's Featured Articles," *Written Communication* 25.2 (April 2008): 285.

69 Daniel Kreiss, Megan Finn, and Fred Turner, "The Limits of Peer Production: Some Reminders from Max Weber for the Network Society," *New Media & Society* 13.2 (March 2011): 251.

70 Jolliffe, "Research Review," 64–65.

71 Susan Greenberg, "Theory and Practice in Journalism Education," *Journal of Media Practice* 8.3 (December 2007): 298–303; Tony Harcup, "Hackademics at the Chalkface: To What Extent Have Journalism Teachers Become Journalism Researchers?" *Journalism Practice* 5.1 (August 2011): 34–50 <http://dx.doi.org/DOI: 10.1080/17512786.2010.493333>, accessed 20 October 2010.

72 Claire Warwick, Melissa Terras, and Julianne Nyhan, *Digital Humanities in Practice* (London: Facet Books, 2012).

Bibliography

Ammann, Rudolf. "Weblogs 1994–2000: A Genealogy." Ph.D. diss., University College London, 2013.

Bagehot, Walter. "The First Edinburgh Reviewers." *National Review* 1 (October 1855): 276.

Bardoel, Jo and Deuze, Mark. "'Network Journalism': Converging Competencies of Old and New Media Professionals." *Australian Journalism Review* 23.2 (December 2001): 91–103.

Benjamin, Walter. *Illuminations*. Edited with Introduction by Hannah Arendt. Translated by Harry Zorn. London: Pimlico, 1999.

Berg, A. Scott. *Max Perkins, Editor of Genius*. New York: E.P. Dutton, 1978.

Bisaillon, Jocelyne. "Professional Editing Strategies Used by Six Editors." *Written Communication* 24.4 (October 2007): 295–322.

Bok, Edward W. *A Man from Maine*. New York: C. Scribner's Sons, 1923.

Bornstein, George and Williams, Ralph G., eds. *Palimpsest: Editorial Theory in the Humanities*. Ann Arbor: University of Michigan Press, 1993.

Bourdieu, Pierre. *The Field of Cultural Production: Essays on Art and Literature*. Edited by Randal Johnson. Cambridge: Polity Press, 1993.

Brake, Laurel; Jones, Aled; and Madden, Lionel, eds. *Investigating Victorian Journalism*. New York: St. Martin's Press, 1990.

Bräuchler, Birgit and Postill, John. eds. *Theorising Media and Practice*. Anthropology of Media. Vol. 4. New York: Berghahn Books, 2010.

Bruccoli, Matthew J. and Baughman, Judith S., eds. *The Sons of Maxwell Perkins: Letters of F. Scott Fitzgerald, Ernest Hemingway, Thomas Wolfe, and Their Editor*. Columbia: University of South Carolina Press, 2004.

Bruns, Axel. *Gatewatching: Collaborative Online News Production*. New York: Peter Lang, 2005.

Clayman, Steven E. and Reisner, Ann. "Gatekeeping in Action: Editorial Conferences and Assessments of Newsworthiness." *American Sociological Review* 63.2 (April 1998): 178–199.

Cohen, Philip, ed. *Devils and Angels: Textual Editing and Literary Theory*. Charlottesville: University Press of Virginia, 1991.

Darnton, Robert. "What Is the History of Books?" In *The Kiss of Lamourette: Reflections in Cultural History*. New York: W. W. Norton & Co., 1990, 107–135.

Donohew, Lewis. "Newspaper Gatekeepers and Forces in the News Channel." *Public Opinion Quarterly* 31.1 (Spring 1967): 61–68.

Douglas, George H. *The Smart Magazines: 50 Years of Literary Revelry and High Jinks at* Vanity Fair, *the* New Yorker, Life, Esquire, *and the* Smart Set. Hamden, CT: Archon Books, 1991.

Evans, Michael Robert. *The Layers of Magazine Editing*. New York: Columbia University Press, 2004.

Finkelstein, David and McCleery, Alistair, eds. *The Book History Reader*. 2nd ed. London: Routledge, 2006.

Finkelstein, David and McCleery, Alistair. *An Introduction to Book History*. 2nd ed. London: Routledge, 2012.

Forde, Kathy Roberts. Literary Journalism on Trial: *Masson v.* New Yorker *and the First Amendment*. Amherst: University of Massachusetts Press, 2008.

Garvey, Ellen Gruber. "Foreword." In Harris, Sharon M., ed. *Blue Pencils and Hidden Hands: Women Editing Periodicals, 1830–1910*. Boston: Northeastern University Press, 2004, xi–xxiii.

Gill, Brendan. *Here at the* New Yorker. New York: Random House, 1975.

Gourevitch, Philip, ed. *The Paris Review: Interviews*. Vol. 4. Edinburgh, UK: Canongate, 2009.

Grafton, Anthony. *The Culture of Correction in Renaissance Europe*. London: British Library, 2011.

Greenberg, Susan. *Editors Talk about Editing*. New York: Peter Lang, forthcoming.

Greenberg, Susan. "The Hidden Art of Editing: Theory, History and Identity." Ph.D. Diss., University College London, 2013.

Greenberg, Susan. "Slow Journalism in the Digital Fast Lane." In Keeble, Richard Lance and Tulloch, John, eds. *Global Literary Journalism: Exploring the Journalistic Imagination*. New York: Peter Lang, 2012, 381–393.

Greenberg, Susan. "Theory and Practice in Journalism Education." *Journal of Media Practice* 8.3 (December 2007): 298–303.

Greenberg, Susan. "When the Editor Disappears, Does Editing Disappear?" *Convergence: The International Journal of Research into New Media Technologies* 16.1 (February 2010): 7–21.

Gross, Gerald, ed. *Editors on Editing: What Writers Need to Know About What Editors Do*. New York: Grove Press, 1993.

Grunwald, Edgar A. *The Business Press Editor*. New York: New York University Press, 1988.

Harcup, Tony. "Hackademics at the Chalkface: To What Extent Have Journalism Teachers Become Journalism Researchers?" *Journalism Practice* 5.1 (August 2011): 34–50 <http://dx.doi.org/DOI: 10.1080/17512786.2010.493333>, accessed 20 October 2010.

Harris, Sharon M., ed. With a Foreword by Gruber Garvey, Ellen. *Blue Pencils and Hidden Hands: Women Editing Periodicals, 1830–1910*. Boston: Northeastern University Press, 2004.

Johanson, Katya. "Dead, Done For and Dangerous: Teaching Editing Students What Not to Do." *New Writing: The International Journal for the Practice and Theory of Creative Writing* 3.1 (April 2006): 47–55.

Jolliffe, Lee. "Research Review: Magazine Editors and Editing Practices." In Abrahamson, David, ed. *The American Magazine: Research Perspectives and Prospects*. Ames: Iowa State University Press, 1995, 51–71.

Jones, John. "Patterns of Revision in Online Writing: A Study of Wikipedia's Featured Articles." *Written Communication* 25.2 (April 2008): 262–289.

Kreiss, Daniel; Finn, Megan; and Turner, Fred. "The Limits of Peer Production: Some Reminders from Max Weber for the Network Society." *New Media & Society* 13.2 (March 2011): 243–259.

Kunkel, Thomas, ed. *Letters from the Editor: The* New Yorker's *Harold Ross*. New York: Modern Library, 2001.

Lewin, Kurt. *Field Theory in Social Science: Selected Theoretical Papers*. Edited by Dorwin Cartwright. New York: Harper & Row, 1951.

Liddle, Dallas. *The Dynamics of Genre: Journalism and the Practice of Literature in Mid-Victorian Britain*. Charlottesville: University of Virginia Press, 2009.

Litz, A. Walton. "Maxwell Perkins: The Editor as Critic." In Howard, Wm J. ed. *Editor, Author, and Publisher: Papers Given at the Editorial Conference, University of Toronto, November 1968*. Toronto: University of Toronto Press, 1969, 96–112.

Marek, Jayne E. *Women Editing Modernism: "Little" Magazines and Literary History*. Lexington: University Press of Kentucky, 1995.

McGann, Jerome. "Philology in a New Key." *Critical Inquiry* 39.2 (Winter 2013): 327–346.

McIntyre, John E. *The Old Editor Says: Maxims for Writing and Editing*. Baltimore, MA: Apprentice House, 2013.

McKay, Jenny. *The Magazines Handbook*. 3rd ed. London and New York: Routledge, 2013.

McKenzie, Donald F. *Bibliography and the Sociology of Texts: The Panizzi Lectures 1985*. Cambridge: Cambridge University Press, 1999.

Mehta, Ved. *Remembering Mr. Shawn's New Yorker: The Invisible Art of Editing*. Woodstock, NY: The Overlook Press, 1998.

Mikaelian, Allen. "Middlemen by Profession: Popular Fiction and the Rise of the In-House Book Editor." M.A. diss., Institute of English Studies, University of London, 1997.

Moeran, Brian. "More than Just a Fashion Magazine." *Current Sociology* 54.5 (September 2006): 725–744.

Mott, Frank Luther. *A History of American Magazines*. Vol. 1, *A History of American Magazines, 1741–1850*; Vol. 2, *A History of American Magazines, 1850–1865*; Vol. 3, *A History of American Magazines, 1865–1885*; Vol. 4, *A History of American Magazines, 1885–1905*; Vol. 5, *A History of American Magazines, 1905–1930*. New York: D. Appleton, 1930; Cambridge, MA: The Belknap Press, 1938, 1938, 1957; Cambridge, MA: Harvard University Press, 1968.

Navasky, Victor S. and Cornog, Evan, eds. *The Art of Making Magazines: On Being an Editor and Other Views from the Industry*. New York: Columbia University Press, 2012.

Norton, Scott. *Developmental Editing: A Handbook for Freelancers, Authors, and Publishers*. Chicago: University of Chicago Press, 2009.

Nunberg, Geoffrey. "Farewell to the Information Age." In Nunberg, Geoffrey, ed. *The Future of the Book*. Berkeley: University of California Press, 1996, 103–138.

Okker, Patricia. *Our Sister Editors: Sarah J. Hale and the Tradition of Nineteenth-Century American Women Editors*. Athens: University of Georgia Press, 1995.

Patten, Robert L. "When is a Book Not a Book?" *Biblion: The Bulletin of the New York Public Library* 4.2 (Spring 1996): 35–63.

Plotnik, Arthur. *The Elements of Editing: A Modern Guide for Editors and Journalists*. New York: Macmillan, 1982.

Radway, Janice A. "Learned and Literary Print Cultures in an Age of Professionalization and Diversification." In Kaestle, Carl F. and Radway, Janice A., eds. *Print in Motion: The Expansion of Publishing and Reading in the United States, 1880–1940*. A History of the Book in America, David D. Hall, ed. Vol. 4. Chapel Hill: University of North Carolina Press, 2009.

Rhodes, Leara and Roessner, Amber. "Teaching Magazine Publishing through Experiential Learning." *Journalism & Mass Communication Educator* 63 (Winter 2009): 304–316.

Ritter, Robert Mark. "The Transformation of Authority in Print and the Rise of House Style." D.Phil. diss., St. Anne's College, University of Oxford, 2010.

Ryan, Cynthia. "Struggling to Survive: A Study of Editorial Decision-Making Strategies at MAMM Magazine." *Journal of Business and Technical Communication* 19.3 (July 2005): 353–376.

Saller, Carol Fisher. *The Subversive Copy Editor: Advice from Chicago*. Chicago: University of Chicago Press, 2009.

Singer, Jane B. "Online Journalists: Foundations for Research into Their Changing Roles." *Journal of Computer-Mediated Communication* 4.1 (September 1998): n.p. <http://onlinelibrary.wiley.com/doi/10.1111/j.1083-6101.1998.tb00088.x/full >, accessed 12 May 2004.

Singer, Jane B. and Ashman, Ian. "'Comment Is Free, but Facts Are Sacred': User-Generated Content and Ethical Constructs at the *Guardian*." *Journal of Mass Media Ethics* 24.1 (January/March 2009): 3–21.

Skok, David. "Aggregation Is Deep in Journalism's DNA." *Nieman Journalism Lab*, 27 January 2012 <http://www.niemanlab.org/2012/01/david-skok-aggregation-is-deep-in-journalisms-dna/>, accessed 11 August 2012.

Smith, Ben. "What the Longform Backlash Is All About." *Journalism, Deliberated* (blog), 26 January 2014 <https://medium.com/journalism-deliberated/958f4e7691f5>, accessed 20 March 2014.

Speck, Bruce W. *Editing: An Annotated Bibliography*. Westport, CT: Greenwood Press, 1991.

Speck, Bruce W.; Hinnen, Dean A.; and Hinnen, Kathleen. *Teaching Revising and Editing: An Annotated Bibliography*. Westport, CT: Greenwood Press, 2003.

Stephen, Leslie. "The Evolution of Editors." *Studies of a Biographer*. Vol. 1. New York: G. P. Putnam's Sons, 1907, 35–68.

Warwick, Claire; Terras, Melissa; and Nyhan, Julianne. *Digital Humanities in Practice*. London: Facet Books, 2012.

West, James L. W., III, *American Authors and the Literary Marketplace since 1900*. Philadelphia: University of Pennsylvania Press, 1988.

Wheelock, John Hall, ed. *Editor to Author: The Letters of Maxwell E. Perkins*. Introduction by Marcia Davenport. 2nd ed. New York: Charles Scribner Sons, 1979.

White, David Manning. "The 'Gate Keeper': A Case Study in the Selection of News." *Journalism Quarterly* 27.4 (Fall 1950): 383–390.

Zelizer, Barbie. *Taking Journalism Seriously: News and the Academy*, London: Sage, 2004.

11

THE BUSINESS OF MAGAZINES

Advertising, Circulation and Content Issues

Sela Sar and Lulu Rodriguez

For most magazines, advertising is a primary source of revenue. This chapter focuses on the business side of magazines specifically related to advertising. First, the chapter describes the practice of magazine advertising, the cost and effects of readership and circulation rates, as well as the placement of advertisements in magazines. Second, it synthesizes the literature that has examined the content of magazine advertisements and summarizes the results of studies that have investigated portrayals of gender, race and ethnicity in magazine ads. The implications of these findings on the practice of magazine advertising also are discussed. Finally, the chapter suggests lines of inquiry about magazine advertising content that would assist media scholars in strengthening the body of literature in this area, help advertising practitioners handle the business aspects of the industry more effectively and add more value to magazine reading among audiences.

Method

To arrive at a synopsis of the effects on audiences of race, gender and ethnicity portrayals in magazine ads, a content analysis of scholarly research published over the last two decades, between 1993 and 2013, was conducted. Using the search terms *magazine ads, magazine advertising, magazine advertisements, magazine ad + gender, magazine ads + race,* and *magazine ads + gender, race and ethnicity, and print advertising,* a total of 68 articles in 16 peer-reviewed journals of international circulation were retrieved from the Academic Search Premier (EBSCO) database. The majority of these studies ($N = 39$) examined how men and women were depicted in magazine advertisements; differences in representation based on ethnicity were the second most studied topic ($N = 27$). Most studies examined the content of magazine advertisements in the United States. A few used content analysis to compare U.S., Korean, Japanese, and Chinese magazine advertisements. The 68 articles were full-length articles published in peer review journals over the period of 20 years; they did not include editorial essays and book reviews. Of the 68 articles found, 31 (45%) were published in the journal *Sex Roles* and 8 (11%) saw print in the *Journal of Business Ethics.* The remaining 14 journals, *International Marketing Review, International Journal of Research in Marketing, Journal of Marketing Communication, Journal of Advertising, International Journal of Advertising, Journal of Communication, Journal of Current Issues and Research in Advertising, Advances in Consumer Research,* the *Journal of Advertising Research, Marketing & Psychology, Journal of Consumer Psychology, Journalism and*

Mass Communication Quarterly, *Journal of Social Issue*, and *Journal of Black Studies*, each contributed 1 to 3 articles to the sample.

Studies that examined gender role portrayals mainly used content analysis (59, or 87%) as the research method to gather data. Some (7, or 10%) employed surveys and focus groups to determine consumer responses toward sex role stereotyping in advertisements. The experiment method was used in but a couple (2, or about 3%).

Circulation Rates and Advertising Placement

The medium's essential strength lies in the active way in which readers choose and use their magazines. Readers become deeply engaged with their titles so that, over time, a strong relationship—a bond of trust—grows. For many, reading a favorite magazine is like spending time with a friend. As such, readers commit to their magazines, sometimes reading a copy repeatedly. Such an intimacy benefits advertisers who understand the magazine environment can make readers receptive to the ads they place in them. In other words, the strong positive brand value of a magazine can transfer onto ads. The stronger the reader's affiliation with the magazine as a brand, the higher the level of endorsement the advertising receives from the magazine's personality.

Thus, a critical area of research in magazine advertising relates to the measurement of magazine audience and readership to understand how circulation rates impact cost and advertising effects. To do this, advertisers use methods such as those employed by the U.S. Standard Rate and Data Service (SRDS).[1]

Magazines for Advertising Placement

To make the most out of advertising investments, advertisers adopt circulation strategies (e.g., guaranteed circulation and pass-along readership) that aim at placing their pieces in magazines with high circulation or those that target product buyers or consumers with the desired demographic characteristics. This section discusses how advertisers arrive at these strategies.

The relationship between publishers and advertisers has always been crucial to the profitability and longevity of both parties. Ulrich Kaiser and Julian Wright describe magazines as constituting a two-sided market, referring to a system in which two distinct groups of users interact on a common platform, for which the structure of prices between the two sides (rather than just the total level of costs) matters.[2] On the one side, publishers depend on circulation rates and advertising revenues to survive. On the other side, advertisers rely on publishers to reach the increasingly segmented and fragmented consumer groups for the products and services they offer (e.g., women, men, teens, retirees and ethnic sub-populations). Thus, in this two-sided market, publishers sell magazines to readers and then sell readers to advertisers.[3]

This relationship between publishers and advertisers is becoming more complex as high circulation rates no longer translate in many cases to higher advertising rates.[4] Today, it is common to invest a large percentage of advertising dollars in two or three magazine leaders, leaving a small share for smaller publications. This has led magazines to expand circulation and readership by targeting specific demographic groups, but the practice has proven to be non-profitable or unsustainable in many cases. Thus, magazines tend to come and go.

Magazines have cost concerns similar to those of newspapers. Declining circulation rates and the rising cost of paper, delivery, marketing and overhead make it increasingly difficult for both magazines and newspapers to turn a profit despite a sharp increase in advertising revenues. Conversely, advertisers need to choose whether it is cost effective to place ads in magazines with limited circulation.[5] Counts vary substantially, but the *National Directory of Magazines* reported more than 7,300 consumer magazines in the United States in 2011,[6] many of which have limited and small circulation. Indeed, at the beginning of the second decade of the twenty-first century, more than two-thirds of U.S. magazine titles had fewer than 500,000 readers.[7] In such a competitive marketing arena, increasing and sustaining circulation become persistent challenges for publishers and, consequently, a major concern of advertisers, especially during periods of economic downturn. It is small wonder, therefore, that there is a growing list of magazines that have quit print under pressure from the recession and digital media.

It is estimated that five or more new magazines covering diverse topics are introduced to the market each week. Competing against long-running titles that regularly demonstrate editorial excellence, few of these upstarts are expected to survive. The downturn in print advertising, the increasingly specialized needs of core readers and the proliferation of other resources all work against sustainability.[8] Whether new or well-established, each publication has unique strengths, weaknesses, opportunities and threats to contend with. Major, venerable magazines, such as *Gourmet* (Condé Nast, 1941–2009), *Home* (Hachette Filipacchi, 1951–2008), *Teen* (Hearst Magazines, 1954–2008), *Southern Accents* (Time Inc., 1977–2009) and *Metropolitan Home* (Hachette Filipacchi, 1981–2009), have been knocked out of print due to many factors, but mostly for economic reasons.[9] Many start-up magazines, such as *Portfolio* (Condé Nast, 2007–2009), *Hallmark Magazine* (Hallmark Cards, 2006–2009) and *Wondertime* (Walt Disney Publishing, 2006–2009), were short-lived, buckling under the economic meltdown.[10]

To survive a rapidly evolving industry, magazines constantly adopt new formulas and formats. For example, *U.S. News & World Report* has been available only on-line since 2010.[11] *Life* magazine, once part and parcel of American life, now offers only special topic editions that are few and far between. Traditional women's magazines, a historically strong U.S. consumer magazine category, have experienced significant changes in the past decade in an attempt to fend off competition from new entrées to the women's lifestyle market, such as *O The Oprah Winfrey Magazine* (Hearst Corporation) and *Real Simple* (Time Inc.).[12] Magazines that flourish today have been successful at targeting audience niches with unique editorial offerings. These include *Women's Health* (Rodale), *Fast Company* (Mansuelo Ventures), *People Stylewatch* (Time Inc.) and *Every Day with Rachael Ray* (Reader's Digest Association), which have led advertising revenue growth in recent years.[13]

Circulations and Ad Rates

Advertising media planners do not buy magazines; they buy audiences. More specifically, they pay for access to current and potential consumers of their products and services. As such, measuring magazine readership is important to them. In the magazine industry, there are two distinct methods of measuring audience size: (1) paid circulation or rate base and (2) rate of readership.[14]

Major magazines hire outside companies (e.g., Verified Audit Circulation, BPA Worldwide, Circulation Audit Services) to conduct circulation audits.[15] The more common and reliable method these services use is determining *paid circulation*. Advertising rates—that is, the cost to purchase space in a given magazine—are based on the circulation a publisher promises to deliver, also known as the *guaranteed circulation* or the number of readers advertisers purchase. It also is referred to as the *rate base*, or the circulation on which advertising rates for a specific magazine are pegged.[16]

Readership combines paid circulation (subscribers and newsstand purchasers) with pass-along readers. For example, although *Elle* (Hatchette Filipacchi) has a paid circulation of 1.1 million, Mediamark Research Inc. (MRI) lists it as having 5.1 million readers. This means *Elle* has approximately 4.5 readers per copy (RPC).[17] The more general a publication's editorial content, the more likely it is to have a high pass-along readership. Advertisers pay close attention to the rate of readership because it goes above and beyond what paid circulation rates convey. The use of readership rate, rather than paid circulation, is rooted in the historical rivalry between magazines and television for audience attention.[18] Publishers want to project total readership, not just the number of people who purchase a copy off the newsstand or through subscriptions.

The value publishers and advertisers place on readership rate is dependent on their objectives and strategies.

Advertising media planners determine ad placement, advertising space options, costs and a magazine's circulation base using data generated by SRDS, a service that gathers and publishes information on the vast majority of consumer and business magazines as well as scholarly journals distributed in the United States and other countries.[19] In Europe, such a service is often provided by direct marketing firms (e.g., Hilite Direct Marketing Services in the United Kingdom) and consulting firms (e.g., Gesselschaft fur Informatiklosungen Media Solutions, Kirchner Communication and Marketing, Living Logic Media Solutions and Bairle Media Solutions in Germany). In many parts of Asia and the Pacific, advertising and public relations agencies often build campaigns based on the findings of their own research divisions, such as Media West China and Startcom Shanghai in China, TAM Media Research in India[20] and Fiji Media Holdings, Inc., in Japan.[21]

In regard to magazine sales in Europe, especially in France, Germany, Italy, Spain and the UK, magazine publishers have developed a new strategy to help increase magazine sales. As in the United States, many European countries are struggling with declining sales of magazines.[22] The new strategy is called the *non-price promotion sale*. The idea of these kinds of promotions is to assemble a value pack containing the magazine plus another product and to sell both at a price above the price of the magazine but below the sum of the expected price of the two products combined. For example, a particular magazine may be sold with a popular CD.[23]

Advertising media planners also use market research provided by companies such as the Alliance for Audited Media (formerly the Audit Bureau of Circulations or ABC),[24] Mediamark Inc. (MRI) and Simmons Market Research Bureau (SMRB) to determine magazine circulation and audience characteristics. Of these, AAM is the largest. It provides the publisher's statements or *pink sheets* that report data over six-month periods ending June 30 and December 31 each year, and the *white sheets* that show annual audit data indicated in the publisher's statements. AAM reports total national circulation as well as circulation figures by state, by county size and per issue during each six-month period.[25] It verifies circulation statements twice a year. AAM also conducts annual audits to substantiate or correct earlier reports. Audits are conducted by personally inspecting the publisher's records.

Advertisers also use syndicated databases (e.g., from MRI and SMRB) to help them better understand who the readers are, their interests and what they buy. To do this, MRI selects a sample of 26,000 respondents who are asked about their demographic characteristics, media use habits, lifestyle and product-purchase decisions through personal interviews, self-administered questionnaires or a combination of both. SMRB does the same by sampling more than 25,000 adults, including more than 7,500 Hispanic or Latino respondents. Both services collect data on several hundred magazines. Advertising and marketing personnel also use the Starch scores[26] to measure ad readership[27] and ad placement in magazines.[28]

Magazine Rate-Placement Relationships

Once advertisers have identified and verified magazine circulation rates, they next ascertain exactly where to place their ads in these magazines, also called *magazine placement*. In making decisions about placement, advertisers bank on the notion that readers tend to create a repertoire of magazines to meet different needs and moods, eventually developing a personal relationship with their publications and ensuring that reading takes place in a highly receptive frame of mind. Advertisers capitalize on this condition, aware that readers screen advertisements in much the same way that they screen editorial parts—looking for items that interest, intrigue, catch the eye, entertain or inform. Advertisers take maximum advantage of readers' active involvement by experimenting with creative formats such as gatefolds, textures, special papers, samples, sponsorship and advertisement features (also called *advertorials*) to create additional impact and interaction. Because the interpretation of a given advertisement can be influenced by the specific publication in which it appears, advertisers are able to target consumers with some degree of precision, a key strength of magazine advertising.[29]

Decisions about placement are aided by matching the product with the magazine environment to achieve maximum *match-up* or *congruity effect*.[30] This practice recognizes that an ad for men's razor blades, for example, probably would have little effect in a home and garden magazine; hair products for women probably would have little use in a fitness magazine that caters to men. Sporting goods advertisers place ads in athletics-related magazines to match the product with known audience interests.[31]

Ad placement also takes into consideration where ads should be positioned within a magazine issue. For example, British Petroleum and Exxon often place ads following articles about oil exploration or other energy-related topics.[32] Advertisers also place advertisements high in emotional appeal after articles that seek a strong emotional response. For instance, advertisements soliciting donations and other contributions to cancer research immediately follow articles on cancer survivors or breakthroughs in treating the disease.[33] This practice stems from the recognition that excitatory responses generated by one event can carry over to subsequent events, a phenomenon known as *excitation transfer*.[34]

To reach the most number of customers in the most cost effective way with the strongest impact, advertisers also conduct or commission research to ascertain that their ads are congruent with magazine content. Exploiting the match-up effects between advertising content and magazine content is one of the most widely used, current advertising placement strategies.[35]

Advertisement Content

Magazine ads live or die by the presentation of content. As such, the business side of magazines pays close attention to advertising content and how such content is delivered, a topic to which this section turns. Although the main goal of advertising may be to sell goods and services to consumers, it is also a major socializing agent that influences the development of ideals and norms. There are many aspects of advertising content that may be subjected to scrutiny, but this chapter focuses on three issues that have caused some controversy and public debate over time. These are the portrayals of (1) gender and gender roles; (2) sex and sexuality; and (3) race, ethnicity and ethnic groups in magazine ads and the impact of such portrayals on self-image, perceptions of identity, audience attitudes toward the products and services being promoted, and general consumer behavior, among other dependent variables.[36]

Portrayals of Gender and Gender Roles

How gender roles have been stereotyped has been a prominent topic in the literature since the 1970s[37] in the wake of the women's rights movement that ushered greater access to educational and employment opportunities,[38] economic independence, changing gender roles within the family[39] and a number of significant legal gains in court decisions pertaining to women's rights.[40] Gender-related studies have differentiated how men and women were shown in ads,[41] how they process information,[42] how spokespersons affect gender responses and effects[43] and how men and women respond to gendered advertising content.[44]

In general, scholars have documented how magazine ads show women in narrow roles (e.g., as those who perform domestic work and other traditional feminine occupations)[45] or as sex objects (e.g., female models were more likely to be suggestively clad than men or are displayed as embodiments of physical perfection).[46] Messages about women's position in the social structure depict them as subordinate to men.[47] Women were underrepresented in ads that promote expensive "masculine" products, while males were overrepresented in ads for non-domestic products.[48] Scholars have suggested that advertisements in predominantly male-oriented and more established publications tended to stereotype women more often than do those in publications for general readership.[49]

The findings of more recent studies add to the body of literature that conveys increasing bias toward the sexist depiction of women in print advertisements. For example, the results of a study by Emmanuella Plakoyiannaki and Yorgos Zotos[50] indicated that women in British magazine advertisements were mainly portrayed in decorative roles, supporting the notion of retro-sexism. The findings additionally suggested that female role stereotypes vary significantly across magazine genres; specifically, male-oriented magazines seemed to promote women in decorative and traditional roles, while general audience magazines used female depictions of women shown equal to men. Hedonic products also were found to be associated with models showing women in decorative roles.

There is empirical evidence from comparative studies indicating that sexism in advertising is a cross-cultural phenomenon and that Western advertising models are the trendsetters of sexual images in magazine advertising in many parts of the world. In their analysis of the content of 19 general interest Chinese magazines as well magazines that cater exclusively to men or women, Ying Huang and Dennis T. Lowry,[51] for instance, showed that female models were more likely to be shown in different levels of nudity than male models, and Western models were more likely to be shown in different levels of nudity than Chinese models, as they predicted. Chia-Wen Chi and Cecelia Baldwin[52] concluded that magazine ads in Taiwan and the United States displayed the inferior status of females in both cultures. By ignoring the growing strength of the female workforce universally, the authors argue that the print media in these two countries misrepresented female images as non-working in a majority of the portrayals in magazine advertisements. Surprisingly, advertising in the United States stereotyped men as working and women as non-working in even higher percentages than in Taiwan. The study also found that women were shown as inferior to men in the work they do. While men were portrayed as business and professional people, women were most likely to be portrayed in entertainment or sports or mid-level, non-professional roles regardless of country.

Studying advertising images, Roxanne Hovland, Carolynn McMahan, Guiohk Lee, Jang-Sun Hwang, and Juran Kim[53] explored implied gender roles in American and Korean magazine advertisements and found strong evidence that stereotypic depictions of women in American magazine advertisements are becoming less prevalent. Despite the profound differences in the two cultures, the contrast in depictions of women in American and Korean advertisements was not pronounced. With certain exceptions, the Korean advertisements offered fewer stereotypic images of women. Sexist images appeared more frequently in their sample of American magazine advertisements.

How do audiences respond to stereotypical content? Measuring the attitudes of young women to sexually objectified advertising, Amanda Zimmerman and John Dahlberg[54] found that their young and educated female respondents agreed that women were often portrayed as sex objects, but they were less offended by these portrayals than those who responded to the same questionnaire administered 17 years earlier. Results also show females' attitudes toward such ads have little effect on purchase intention, a highly significant change from the attitudes that prevailed in 1991.

Surveying a sample of advertisements from eight U.S. magazines aimed at men of varying social-demographic characteristics, Megan Vokey, Bruce Tefft, and Chris Tysiaczny[55] found that hyper-masculine depictions are highly prevalent in advertising (especially in ads that target young and low SES men). They found images and text that buttress toughness, violence, dangerousness and calloused attitudes toward women and sex—the four hallmarks of hyper-masculinity as an extreme form of masculine gender ideology—present in 56% of 527 advertisements they analyzed. As many find repeated exposure to advertisements depicting hyper-masculinity as not only acceptable but desirable and socially sanctioned, the authors worry about its contribution to harmful gender attitudes and beliefs. The finding that such depictions are most widespread in advertisements targeting young males heightens concerns that such advertising may play a strong role in the development and reinforcement of unhealthy beliefs about masculinity, including perpetuating violence against women, drug and alcohol abuse, dangerous driving, accidents, drop-out rates, medical mistrust and high-risk sexual behaviors.

To determine the emotions evoked by advertisements featuring female and male models in different sex roles, Orth and Holancova[56] exposed participants to selected stimuli showing female and male models in occupational and non-occupational settings in magazine advertisements for a cell phone service in the Czech Republic. Their results indicate that female and male consumers exhibited significantly different emotional and attitudinal reactions measured in terms of approval, surprise, attitude toward the ad, brand attitude and purchase intention. The participants responded most favorably to ads that exclusively portrayed their own gender. Females exhibited the least favorable reactions to advertisements featuring female models in roles superior to males. Regardless of gender, the participants' responses were significantly influenced by their attitude toward sex role portrayals.

Although there has been long standing consensus that gender stereotyping was alive and well in magazines, later studies have reported a diminishing trend. For instance, more recent studies showed that magazine advertisements have decreased the portrayals of women in more traditional occupations.[57] The general body of literature suggests that marketers should consider segmenting audiences by marital status and degree of employment to further reduce stereotypical representations.[58]

Portrayals of Sex and Sexuality

Critics consistently have raged against the way scantily clad, suggestively portrayed women are displayed to sell every type of product in magazines. The intensity with which advertisers continue to use sexual imagery to attract attention and for other purposes has led to a slew of studies that have examined the intended and unintended consequences of varying levels of sexual portrayals. Following up on their analysis of the use of sex in full-page or larger ads in six American consumer magazines from 1983–1993, Tom Reichert and Courtney Carpenter[59] report findings that indicate overall increases in sexual dress and intimate contact from 1983 to 2003. They also found that female models were more explicitly dressed in 2003 than 1993. In addition, sexual content continued to be more explicit and prevalent in women's and men's magazines compared to newsweeklies. The findings suggest that some kinds of sexual explicitness in advertising, despite becoming more pronounced as would be expected considering the habituation effect, have at least reached a temporary plateau perhaps in response to increasing public criticism of indecency in the media.

Later studies seem to bear this out. Julie M. Stankiewicz and Francine Rosselli[60] examined the depiction of women in 1,988 advertisements from 58 popular U.S. magazines and found that on average across magazines, one of two advertisements that featured women portrayed them as sex objects. The authors also note that men's, women's fashion, and female adolescent magazines were more likely to portray women as sex objects and as victims than news and business, special interest or women's non-fashion magazines. Since the early 1980s, researchers in marketing have applied Geert Hofstede's[61] cross-cultural typology in advertising research to study how advertising appeals differ between cultures. The model consists of four dimensions on which societies differ: individualism, power distance, uncertainty avoidance and masculinity. Studies that fall along these lines generally found an indirect way of expressing sex in Asian advertisements, while Western advertisements were more straightforward about it. For instance, Stella Lai Man So's[62] content analysis of advertisements from the top circulated women's magazines of Hong Kong and Australia revealed that Hong Kong advertisements contain more information cues, sexier and less emotional content compared to Australian advertisements.

Michelle R. Nelson and Hye-Jin Paek[63] examined the degrees of sexuality in advertising within *Cosmopolitan* magazine across seven countries (Brazil, China, France, India, South Korea, Thailand and the United States) and report that even within a transnational Western magazine, sex portrayal differs in degree and intensity. They found that the presence of Western models in ads, sexual freedom values and a less authoritarian political culture contribute to greater sexuality in magazine advertising.

In a rare examination of audience effects, Christian Dianoux and Zdenek Linhart[64] explored whether a print ad that uses nudity is more or less effective than an ad without nudity in the Czech Republic, Spain and France, all free-market economies with long advertising traditions. Their results indicate that nationality does not appear to influence preferences for advertisements with or without nudity, reinforcing previous findings that the value hierarchies of people from Belgium, the United Kingdom, Germany, the Netherlands and Spain do not differ significantly. However, differences emerged among the three countries in attitudes toward the ad. Regardless of nationality, women adopted a more negative attitude toward ads with nude imagery compared to men, suggesting that advertisers intending to use nude images should define their target market by gender even more so than in terms of the European country in which the advertising will appear.

In Indonesia where sex-related materials are taboo and advertisers are prohibited by law from using strong overt advertising, Catur Sugiarto and Virginie De Barnier[65] recommend that advertising should not only be interesting, but must also be convincing. The results of their experiment indicate that "mild" and "demure" sex appeal has a greater chance of getting a favorable response from Muslim consumers.

Portrayals of Race and Ethnicity

Ads also have been found to present racial groups in stereotypical ways, often leading scholars to infer that such representations have a profound bearing on how these groups are treated in society. A conspicuous example is the depiction of African Americans who are often relegated to three roles: as entertainers, athletes and servants.[66] Except for entertainers and athletes, they also were frequently portrayed as uneducated, low-status members of society.[67] Over the past decade, the body of literature suggests that African Americans were less blatantly stereotyped as servants or inferiors compared to the 1960s, although some concerns still remain.[68] The large number of Blacks in minor and background roles and the relative infrequency of their appearance in major roles suggested an unwelcome tokenism.[69] Further, the underrepresentation of African Americans in technical product categories seemed to sustain stereotypes related to educational and occupational status.[70]

Although there were fewer studies on the portrayals of Asian Americans, members of these ethnic groups also were often found to be depicted in positive albeit stereotypical ways: as technically competent, hardworking, serious and well assimilated.[71] Perhaps the most striking finding regarding racial portrayals was the consistently stereotypical portrayal of Asian Americans as an "all work, no play" group. The "model minority"[72] stereotype, which suggests that Asian Americans are hardworking, technologically savvy, business oriented, successful and well assimilated, is clearly reflected in advertising portrayals. They tended to be portrayed in ads that promote technology-related products in business and technical magazines and in business settings and relationships.[73] Following up on the portrayals of this *model minority*, Charles R. Taylor, Stacy Landreth and Hae-Kyong Bang[74] found that despite improved representation, stereotyped portrayals persist in that depictions of family and social contexts are seldom seen. Moreover, even magazines with high Asian American readership reflected the same stereotypes.

Lawrence Bowen and Jill Schmid argue that this one-sided portrayal neglects the family and social life of Asian Americans and encourages expectations of career success that put pressure on them to excel only in business and technological fields, thus blocking the development of rich social relationships or the achievement of self-actualization needs. To correct for these potential negative impacts, advertisers are urged to include Asian Americans in a variety of non-business settings and in personal relationships in advertisements for food, clothing, leisure activities and other nontechnical products.[75]

In 1990, Lee Jussim observed that Hispanics represented 9.0% of the U.S. population, but they were found in only 4.7% of the ads the author reviewed, making Hispanics the most underrepresented minority group in his study.[76] Research shows that advertising has tended to reinforce stereotypes of Hispanic Americans as well, portraying them as uneducated blue-collar workers with large, close-knit families who were yet to be assimilated into mainstream American culture.[77] To correct negative interpretations, Bowen and Schmid urge advertisers to portray Hispanic Americans more frequently and in settings, product use and relationships not determined by family orientation.[78] At 53 million as of July 2012, people of Hispanic origin make up the nation's largest ethnic or racial minority, constituting 17 percent of the nation's total population.[79] More studies are needed to determine whether advertisers in the U.S. context have responded to this call.

Contrary to earlier studies, however, Robin T. Peterson's[80] results no longer support the persistent finding that white Americans are more positively depicted in advertisements than are other ethnic groups. Rather, the reverse configuration appeared manifest in his analysis of a sample of magazine advertisements appearing in the 1994 to 2004 issues of 10 popular magazines in the United States.[81] The reasons for this relative under-representation and less favorable portrayal for whites than for the other groupings are not readily apparent, but might be traced to advertiser awareness of the relative economic success of Asian Americans and the rapidly expanding Hispanic and African American populations, which signal opportunities inherent in targeting these groups. The affluence of Asians, the potential marketing opportunities of an expanding Hispanic base, and the tenacity and resolve of various African American organizations and opinion leaders to exert social and legal pressure may be factors that are driving this strategy.

There are other reasons why marketers are showing more minority group models in magazine ads. Mainly, they are desirable targets because they tend to have more favorable attitudes toward advertising, and, in general, those with more favorable attitudes toward advertising find ads more acceptable, informative and enjoyable. Scholars have also suggested that positive attitudes toward advertising can lead to favorable attitudes toward the brand and, ultimately, to purchase. Members of minority groups also are more likely to be market mavens; that is, they diffuse information to others, are aware of new products earlier, provide information to other consumers across product categories, engage in general market information seeking, and exhibit general market interest and attentiveness. In this regard, Peterson's findings indicate that the socializing effects of advertising may be greater for members of minority groups than it is for Caucasians.[82]

In summary, the body of literature on gender portrayals indicates that advertising content still relies on old stereotypes of men and women, often in ways that diminish the effectiveness of ads or produce unintended negative results.[83] The same can be said of race and ethnic portrayals. A compendium of studies that analyzed advertising content indicates that African Americans are slightly underrepresented, Hispanic Americans are severely underrepresented, and Asian Americans are narrowly portrayed in ads that grace magazine pages.[84] However, when gender and ethnic or portrayals of both are matched or are congruent with publication content, these advertisements stand a good chance of reaching the target demographics. That said, it still behooves advertisers to portray less stereotypical models and scenarios regardless of magazine content.

Future Prospects

The literature review made clear that although the ways in which men, women and minorities are depicted in magazine advertisements are slowly moving away from stereotypes, there is still much work that needs to be done in this area. Beyond the portrayals of gender, race and ethnicity, there are other content aspects that beg for attention. For example, scholars can explore advertising appeals and their impact on different audience segments in terms of cognitions, attitudes and behavior. As magazines convert to the on-line mode, it is best to re-examine how such on-line versions influence people's information processing strategies. This line of inquiry subsumes the use of all types of visuals (moving or static) that are often the main elements of advertising pieces. As visuals play an increasing role in the presentation of content, studies that look at how their use can be optimized are in order. As the areas of exploration expand, the field will benefit considerably by moving beyond content analysis to closer examinations of audience effects.

Portrayals of women and men's roles as well as the disposition to the use of sex appeal strategies in advertising vary across cultures. For example, Alexander N. Ifezue observed that in southern African cultures, men appear not to pay close attention to the nutritional value of what they consume as gleaned from ads. His findings suggest that in that part of the world, advertising helps to strengthen the cultural predisposition to value men for what they think and women for what they look like.[85] Understanding cultural differences in the factors that make for effective gender advertising as well as the relevance of sex in advertising is an area of inquiry that demands scholars' attention.[86]

The predominance of content analysis as the method used to gather data precluded the application of theoretical frameworks that relate magazine content with psychological, sociological or cultural variables. Those that attempted to relate content to impact on audiences, such as consumers' body image, sexuality and spending habits, suggest strong cultivation effects, but were not particularly explicit in elucidating the paths of influence. Doing so will greatly illuminate the nature and intensity of advertising impacts.

Notes

1 *SRDS* is a leading provider of media rates (ad prices) and related data for advertisers in the United States. It lists advertising rates, editorial or programming content, circulation and other basic information (e.g., how many years in business and the name of the owner) for a broad range of media that sell advertising space (newspapers, magazines, billboards, radio, TV, direct markets, the Internet, on-line video and tablets). *SRDS* also contains selected demographic and market information for metropolitan areas and counties.

2 Ulrich Kaiser and Julian Wright, "Price Structure in Two-Sided Markets: Evidence from the Magazine Industry," *International Journal of Industrial Organization* 24.1 (January 2006): 1–28.

3 Vincent P. Norris, "Consumer Magazine Prices and the Mythical Advertising Subsidy," *Journalism Quarterly* 59.2 (Summer 1982): 205–211.

4 Daniel S. Diamond, "A Quantitative Approach to Magazine Advertisement Format Selection," *Journal of Marketing Research* 5.4 (November 1968): 376–386.

5 W. Ronald Lane, Karen Whitehill King, and Tom Reichert, "Using Magazines," *Kleppner's Advertising Procedure*, 18th ed. (Upper Saddle River, NJ: Prentice Hall/Pearson, 2011), 321.

6 *National Directory of Magazines*, "A Magazine for Everyone" 14 July 2011 <www.magazine.org/handbook_2010/2011>, accessed 12 November 2012.

7 Lane, King, and Reichert, "Using Magazines," 320–321.

8 Lane, King, and Reichert, "Using Magazines," 321–325.

9 Nat Ives, "The Last Page: A Guide to Magazines that Have Ceased Publication," *Ad Age Media News*, 15 December 2009 <http:adage.com/article/media/a-guide-magazines-ceased-publication/132779/>, accessed 1 March 2014.

10 Simon Dumeco, "Magazines Are Dead, or Why There's No Such Thing as a (Mere) Magazine Company Anymore," *Ad Age Media News*, 21 October 2012 <http://adage.com/article/the-media-guy/thing-a-mere-magazine-anymore/244851/>, accessed 9 July 2013.

11 Jeremy W. Peters, "*U.S. News & World Report* to Become Online Only," *New York Times*, 5 November 2010 <http:mediadecoder.blogs.nytimes.com/2010/11/05/u-s-news-to-cease-printing-become-online-only/?_r=0>, accessed 12 November 2012.

12 Aimee Deeken, "Service Upgrades," *Mediaweek*, 2 December 2012, 45–46f.

13 Nat Ives, "Magazines: The A-list," *Advertising Age*, 6 October 2008, 1.

14 Lane, King, and Reichert, "Using Magazines," 330–333.

15 In the United States, firms that provide audit services include the Verified Audit Circulation, Alliance for Audited Media and the Circulation Audit Bureau. Outside the United States, circulation audit services are provided by firms such as the International Federation of Audit Bureau of Circulations and BPA Worldwide.

16 Martin A. Koschat and William P. Putsis, Jr., "Audience Characteristics and Bundling: A Hedonic Analysis of Magazine Advertising Rates," *Journal of Marketing Research* 39.2 (May 2002): 262–273.

17 Adsprouts, "*Elle* Magazine Media Kit," *Adsprouts: Just Media Kits* <http://justmediakits.com/mediak it/1224-elle.html>, accessed 19 February 2014.

18 Diamond, "Quantitative Approach to Magazine Advertisement Format Selection," 376–386.

19 Paul Farris W. and Mark E. Parry, "Clarifying Some Ambiguities Regarding GRP and Average Frequency: A Comment on 'GRP: A Case of Mistaken Identity,'" *Journal of Advertising Research* 31.6 (December 1991): 75–77; Koschat and Putsis, "Audience Characteristics and Bundling," 265–266; Norris, "Consumer Magazine Prices," 206–207.

20 Shareen Pathak, "East Meets West in Nissan Social Media Bollywood Link," *Ad Age Media News*, 21, 9 April 2012 <http://adage.com/article/global-news/east-meets-west-nissan-social-media-bollywood-link/ 233980/>, accessed 9 July 2013.

21 Normandy Madden, "Dentsu Builds Media Offices across Asia," *Ad Age Media News*, 28 April 2012 <http:// adage.com/results?endeca=1&searchprop=AdAgeAll&return=endeca&search_offset=0&search_order_ by=score&search_phrase=Dentsu+media/>, accessed 9 July, 2013.

22 Mercedes Esteban-Bravo, José M. Múgica, and Jose M. Vidal-Sanz, "Magazine Sales Promotion: A Dynamic Response Analysis," *Journal of Advertising* 38.1 (Spring 2009): 137.

23 Esteban-Bravo, Múgica, and Vidal-Sanz, "Magazine Sales Promotion," 143.

24 The Audit Bureau of Circulations (ABC) became the Alliance for Audited Media (AAM) in late 2012. It is a tripartite membership organization of North America's leading advertisers, advertising agencies and content providers committed to providing independently verified data and information critical to evaluating and purchasing media, <http://www.auditbureau.org/>, accessed 15 March, 2013.

25 Koschat and Putsis, "Audience Characteristics and Bundling," 263–264.

26 The Starch scores measure press advertisement readership and are computed following an aided recall method. Respondents are taken through a publication page by page and asked a series of questions to determine whether they (1) remembered seeing or reading each ad, (2) accurately recalled the product or brand and the ad referred to, and (3) read more than half the copy. These three elements provide three corresponding scores of readership: (1) noted, (2) associated and (3) read most, <http://www.starchresearch.com/ services.html/>, accessed 17 February 2013.

27 Diamond, "Quantitative Approach to Magazine Advertisement Format Selection," 377–388; see also, Michal Galin, "Magazine Ads that Drove Readers to the Web: MRI Starch Picks the 10 Most Effective Print to Online Ads," *Advertising Age*, 18 December 2008. <adage.com/article/media/magazine-ads-drove-readers-web/133258/>, accessed 12 November 2012.

28 Bob M. Fennis and Arnold B. Bakker, "'Stay Tuned—We Will Be Back Right after These Messages': Need to Evaluate Moderates the Transfer of Irritation in Advertising," *Journal of Advertising* 30.3 (Fall 2001): 15–25.

29 Lee Sherman and John Deighton, "Banner Advertising: Measuring Effectiveness and Optimizing Placement," *Journal of Interactive Marketing* 15.2 (Spring 2001): 60–64.

30 Stephen R. McDaniel, "An Investigation of Match-Up Effects in Sport Sponsorship Advertising: The Implications of Consumer Advertising Schemas," *Psychology & Marketing* 16.2 (March 1999): 163–184.

31 McDaniel, "An Investigation of Match-Up Effects," 184.

32 Youjae Yi, "Contextual Priming Effects in Print Advertisements: The Moderating Role of Prior Knowledge," *Journal of Advertising* 22.1 (March 1993): 1–10.

33 Mahima Mathur and Amitava Chattopadhyay, "The Impact of Moods Generated by Television Programs on Responses to Advertising," *Psychology & Marketing* 8.1 (Spring 1991): 59–77.

34 Dolf Zillmann, "Excitation Transfer in Communication-Mediated Aggressive Behavior," *Journal of Experimental Social Psychology* 7.4 (July 1971): 419–434.

35 McDaniel, "An Investigation of Match-up Effects," 184.

36 Lori D. Wolin, "Gender Issues in Advertising—An Oversight Synthesis of Research: 1970–2002," *Journal of Advertising Research* 43.1 (March 2003): 111–129.

37 Michelle R. Nelson and Hye-Jin Paek, "Cross-Cultural Differences in Sexual Advertising Content in a Transnational Women's Magazine," *Sex Roles*, 53.5/6 (September 2005): 371–383.

38 Éric Charbonnier and Corinne Heckmann, "Women's Outcomes in Education and Employment: Strong Gains, but More to Do," *OECD EducationToday* (blog), 27 March 2012 <http://oecdeducationtoday.blog spot.com/2012/03/womens-outcomes-in-education-and.html>, accessed 6 September 2013; see also, Drew Faust, "Educate Women; Change the World," *Harvard Gazette*, 22 March 2013 <http://www.harvard.edu/ president/educate-women-change-world-ewha-womans-university>, accessed 27 February 2014; Douglas

Fugate, Philip J. Decker, and Joyce J. Brewer, "Women in Professional Selling: A Human Resource Management Perspective," *Journal of Personal Selling & Sales Management* 8.3 (November 1988): 33–41.

39 Sharon Jayson, "Family Life, Roles Changing as Couples Seek Balance," *USA Today*, 19 April 2009 <http:// usatoday30.usatoday.com/news/health/2009-04-18-families-conf_N.htm>, accessed 6 September 2013; see also, Fredric Neuman, "Changing Gender Roles in Marriage," *Fighting Fear* (blog), *Psychology Today*, 4 January 2013 <http://www.psychologytoday.com/blog/fighting-fear/201301/changing-gender-roles-in-mar riage>, accessed 6 September 2013; Michael L. Klassen, Cynthia R. Jasper, and Anne M. Schwartz, "Men and Women: Images of Their Relationships in Magazine Advertisements," *Journal of Advertising Research* 33.2 (March/April 1993): 30–39.

40 Richard Lee, "Botswana: Victory for Women's Rights in Botswana," *All Africa*, 3 September 2013 <http:// allafrica.com/stories/201309040359.html>, accessed 1 March 2014; see also, American Civil Liberties Union (ACLU) "ACLU Women's Rights Victories," 31 December 1996 <https://www.aclu.org/wom ens-rights/aclu-womens-rights-victories>, accessed 6 September 2013.

41 Jennifer Ford, "Fashion Advertising, Men's Magazines, and Sex in Advertising: A Critical-Interpretive Study" (Master's thesis, University of South Florida, 2008); see also, Anthony J. Vigorito and Timothy J. Curry, "Marketing Masculinity: Gender Identity and Popular Magazines," *Sex Roles* 39.1/2 (July 1988): 135–152; Kathleen Martin, "How Far Really? Some Marketers Are Ditching the Old Sex Role Stereotype, but Advertising Still has a Long Way to Go," *Marketing Magazine*, 2 July 2001, 13–14; Hong Cheng, "'Holding Up Half the Sky'?: A Socio-Cultural Comparison of Gender-Role Portrayals in Chinese and U.S. Advertising," *International Journal of Advertising* 16.4 (1997): 295–319.

42 Alexander N. Ifezue, "What Makes an Effective Advertising for a Man or a Woman?" *Journal of Communication* [*J Communication*, India] 1.1 (July 2010): 13–18.

43 James Lynch and Drue Schuler, "The Matchup Effect of Spokesperson and Product Congruency: A Schema Theory Interpretation," *Psychology & Marketing* 11.5 (September/October 1994): 417–445; see also, Matthew Tingchi Liu and James L. Brock, "Selecting a Female Athlete Endorser in China: The Effect of Attractiveness, Match-Up, and Consumer Gender Difference," *European Journal of Marketing* 45.7/8 (2011): 1214–1235.

44 Wolin, "Gender Issues in Advertising," 115; see also, Millward Brown, "Do Men and Women Respond Differently to Ads?" *WPP* <http://www.wpp.com/wpp/marketing/advertising/do-men-and-women-respond-differently-to-ads/#>, accessed 6 September 2013.

45 Emmanuella Plakoyiannaki and Yorgos Zotos, "Female Role Stereotypes in Print Advertising: Identifying Associations with Magazine and Product Categories," *European Journal of Marketing* 43.11/12 (2009): 1411–1434; see also, Julie M. Stankiewicz and Francine Rosselli, "Women as Sex Objects and Victims in Print Advertisements," *Sex Roles* 58.7/8 (April 2008): 579–589.

46 Plakoyiannaki and Zotos, "Female Role Stereotypes in Print Advertising," 1411–1434; see also, Stankiewicz and Rosselli, "Women as Sex Objects and Victims in Print Advertisements," 579–589.

47 Wolin, "Gender Issues in Advertising," 115; see also, Brown, "Do Men and Women Respond Differently to Ads?"

48 Plakoyiannaki and Zotos, "Female Role Stereotypes in Print Advertising," 1411–1434.

49 Wolin, "Gender Issues in Advertising," 115; see also, Brown, "Do Men and Women Respond Differently to Ads?"

50 Plakoyiannaki and Zotos, "Female Role Stereotypes in Print Advertising," 1411–1434.

51 Ying Huang and Dennis T. Lowry, "An Analysis of Nudity in Chinese Magazine Advertising: Examining Gender, Racial and Brand Differences," *Sex Roles* 66.7/8 (April 2012): 440–452; see also, Tiffany J. Shoop, Catherine A. Luther, and Carolynn McMahan, "Advertisement Images of Men and Women in Culturally Diverging Societies: An Examination of Images in U.S. and Japanese Fashion Magazines," *Journal of International Business and Economics* 8.3 (September 2008): 29–41 <http://www.freepatentsonline.com/article/ Journal-International-Business-Economics/190616968.html>, accessed 6 September 2013.

52 Chia-Wen Chi and Cecelia Baldwin, "Gender and Class Stereotypes: A Comparison of U.S. and Taiwanese Magazine Advertisements," in Marcia Texler Segal and Theresa A. Martinez, eds., *Intersections of Gender, Race, and Class: Readings for a Changing Landscape* (Los Angeles: Roxbury Publishing, 2007), 251–264; see also, Jae W. Hong, Aydin Muderrisoglu, and George M. Zinkhan, "Cultural Differences and Advertising Expression: A Comparative Content Analysis of Japanese and U.S. Magazine Advertising," *Journal of Advertising* 16.1 (July 1987): 55–62, 68.

53 Roxanne Hovland, Carolynn McMahan, Guiohk Lee, Jang-Sun Hwang, and Juran Kim, "Gender Role Portrayals in American and Korean Advertisements," *Sex Roles* 53.11/12 (December 2005): 887–899; see also, Klassen, Jasper, and Schwartz, "Men and Women," 34–35.

54 Amanda Zimmerman and John Dahlberg, "The Sexual Objectification of Women in Advertising: A Contemporary Cultural Perspective," *Journal of Advertising Research* 48.1 (March 2008): 71–79; see also, Ran

Wei and Jing Jiang, "New Media Advertising and Its Social Impact in China," in Hong Cheng and Kara Chan, eds., *Advertising and Chinese Society: Impacts and Issues* (Copenhagen: Copenhagen Business School Press, 2009), 245–263.

55 Megan Vokey, Bruce Tefft, and Chris Tysiaczny, "An Analysis of Hyper-Masculinity in Magazine Advertisements," *Sex Roles* 68.9/10 (May 2013): 562–576; Plakoyiannaki and Zotos, "Female Role Stereotypes in Print Advertising," 1411–1434.

56 Ulrich R. Orth and Denisa Holancova, "Men's and Women's Responses to Sex Role Portrayals in Advertisements," *International Journal of Research in Marketing* 21.1 (March 2004): 77–88; see also, Sela Sar and Kenneth O. Doyle, "A Comparative Content Analysis of Cambodian and Thai Print Advertisements," in Punam A. Keller and Dennis W. Rook, eds., *Advances in Consumer Research*, vol. 30 (Valdosta, GA: Association for Consumer Research, 2003), 223–229; see also, Abhijit Biswas, Janeen E. Olsen, and Valerie Carlet, "A Comparison of Print Advertisements from the United States and France," *Journal of Advertising* 21.4 (December 1992): 73–81.

57 Vokey, Tefft, and Tysiaczny, "An Analysis of Hyper Masculinity in Magazine Advertisements," 562–576; Orth and Holancova, "Men's and Women's Responses to Sex Role Portrayals."

58 Vokey, Tefft, and Tysiaczny, "An Analysis of Hyper-Masculinity in Magazine Advertisements," 576.

59 Tom Reichert and Courtney Carpenter, "An Update on Sex in Magazine Advertising: 1983 to 2003," *Journalism & Mass Communication Quarterly* 81.4 (Winter 2004): 823–837.

60 Stankiewicz and Rosselli, "Women as Sex Objects and Victims in Print Advertisements," 579–589; Bruce L. Stern, Dean M. Krugman, and Alan Resnik, "Magazine Advertising: An Analysis of Its Information Content," *Journal of Advertising Research* 21.2 (April 1981): 39–44; see also, Richard H. Kolbe and Paul J. Albanese, "Man to Man: A Content Analysis of Sole-Male Images in Male-Audience Magazines," *Journal of Advertising* 25.4 (Winter 1996): 1–20.

61 Geert Hofstede, *Culture's Consequences: International Differences in Work Related Values*, Abridged ed. (Beverly Hills, CA: Sage Publications, 1984), 136–194.

62 Stella Lai Man So, "A Comparative Content Analysis of Women's Magazine Advertisements from Hong Kong and Australia on Advertising Expressions," *Journal of Current Issues and Research in Advertising* 26.1 (Spring 2004): 47–58; see also, Sar and Doyle, "A Comparative Content Analysis of Cambodian and Thai Print Advertisements," 167.

63 Michelle R. Nelson and Hye-Jin Paek, "A Content Analysis of Advertising in a Global Magazine Across Seven Countries: Implications for Global Advertising Strategies," *International Marketing Review* 24.1 (2007): 64–86; Katherine Frith, Ping Shaw, and Hong Cheng, "The Construction of Beauty: A Cross-Cultural Analysis of Women's Magazine Advertising," *Journal of Communication* 55.1 (March 2005): 56–70; see also, Mee-Eun Kang, "The Portrayal of Women's Images in Magazine Advertisements: Goffman's Gender Analysis Revisited," *Sex Roles* 37.11/12 (December 1997): 979–996.

64 Christian Dianoux and Zdenek Linhart, "The Effectiveness of Female Nudity in Advertising in Three European Countries," *International Marketing Review* 27.5 (2010): 562–578.

65 Catur Sugiarto and Virginie De Barnier, "Sexually Appealing Ads Effectiveness on Indonesian Customers," *European Journal of Business and Management* 5.9 (2013): 125–135 <http://www.iiste.org/Journals/index.php/EJBM/article/view/5133>, accessed 27 September 2013.

66 Ronald E. Hall, "The Ball Curve: Calculated Racism and the Stereotype of African American Men," *Journal of Black Studies* 32.1 (September 2001): 104–119; see also, Dennis Rome, *Black Demons: The Media's Depiction of the African American Male Criminal Stereotype* (Westport, CT: Praeger, 2004); Avery Abernethy M. and George R. Franke, "The Information Content of Advertising: A Meta-Analysis," *Journal of Advertising* 25.2 (Summer 1996): 1–17; Kent A. Ono and Vincent N. Phan, *Asian Americans and the Media* (Malden, MA: Polity Press, 2009); Judy Cohen, "White Consumer Response to Asian Models in Advertising," *Journal of Consumer Marketing* 9.2 (Spring 1992): 17–27.

67 Lawrence Bowen and Jill Schmid, "Minority Presence and Portrayal in Mainstream Magazine Advertising: An Update," *Journalism & Mass Communication Quarterly* 74.1 (Spring 1997): 134–146.

68 Kimberly Wallace-Sanders, *Mammy: A Century of Race, Gender, and Southern Memory* (Ann Arbor: University of Michigan Press, 2008).

69 Helen A. Neville and Alex L. Pieterse, "Racism, White Supremacy, and Resistance Contextualizing Black American Experiences," in Helen A. Neville, Brendesha M. Tynes, and Shawn O. Utsey, eds., *Handbook of African American Psychology* (Los Angeles, CA: Sage, 2009), 159–272.

70 Ono and Phan, *Asian Americans and the Media*; see also, Cohen, "White Consumer Response," 17–27.

71 Cohen, "White Consumer Response," 17–27.

72 Charles R. Taylor, Stacy Landreth, and Hae-Kyong Bang, "Asian Americans in Magazine Advertising: Portrayals of the 'Model Minority.'" *Journal of Macromarketing* 25.2 (December 2005): 163–174.

73 Bowen and Schmid, "Minority Presence and Portrayal," 140.

74 Taylor, Landreth, and Bang, "Asian Americans in Magazine Advertising," 163–174.
75 Bowen and Schmid, "Minority Presence and Portrayal," 142.
76 Lee Jussim, "Social Reality and Social Problems: The Role of Expectancies," *Journal of Social Issues* 46.2 (Summer 1990): 9–34.
77 Cuong Nguyen Le, *Asian American Assimilation: Ethnicity, Immigration, and Socioeconomic Attainment* (New York: LFB Scholarly Publishing, 2007).
78 Bowen and Schmid, "Minority Presence and Portrayal," 144.
79 See also U.S. Census Bureau, "Hispanic Americans by the Numbers," *InfoPlease* <http://www.infoplease.com/spot/hhmcensus1.html>, accessed 5 September 2013.
80 Robin T. Peterson, "Consumer Magazine Advertisement Portrayal of Models by Race in the U.S.: An Assessment," *Journal of Marketing Communications* 13.3 (September 2007): 199–211.
81 The magazines examined include *Reader's Digest, Better Homes & Gardens, American Way, Esquire, Travel & Leisure, People, TV Guide, Cosmopolitan, Family Circle* and *Business Week*.
82 Peterson, "Consumer Magazine Advertisement Portrayal of Models by Race," 199–211.
83 Michael Inzlicht, Alexa M. Tullett, Lisa Legault, and Sonia K. Kang, "Lingering Effects: Stereotype Threat Hurts More than You Think," *Social Issues and Policy Review* 5.1 (December 2011): 227–256.
84 Helena Czepiec and J. Steven Kelly, "Analyzing Hispanic Roles in Advertising: A Portrait of an Emerging Subculture," *Current Issues & Research in Advertising* 6.1 (1983): 219–240.
85 Ifezue, "What Makes an Effective Advertising?" 13–18.
86 Kolbe and Albanese, "Man to Man," 18.

Bibliography

Abernethy, Avery M. and Franke, George R. "The Information Content of Advertising: A Meta-Analysis." *Journal of Advertising* 25.2 (Summer 1996): 1–17.

Adsprouts. "*Elle* Magazine Media Kit." *Adsprouts: Just Media Kits* <http://justmediakits.com/mediakit/1224-elle.html>, accessed 19 February 2014.

American Civil Liberties Union (ACLU). "ACLU Women's Rights Victories." 31 December 1996 <https://www.aclu.org/womens-rights/aclu-womens-rights-victories>, accessed 06 September 2013.

Biswas, Abhijit; Olsen, Janeen, E.; and Carlet, Valerie. "A Comparison of Print Advertisements from the United States and France." *Journal of Advertising* 21.4 (December 1992): 73–81.

Bowen, Lawrence and Schmid, Jill. "Minority Presence and Portrayal in Mainstream Magazine Advertising: An Update." *Journalism & Mass Communication Quarterly* 74.1 (Spring 1997): 134–146.

Brown, Millward. "Do Men and Women Respond Differently to Ads?" *WPP* <http://www.wpp.com/wpp/marketing/advertising/do-men-and-women-respond-differently-to-ads/#>, accessed 6 September 2013.

Charbonnier, Éric and Heckmann, Corinne. "Women's Outcomes in Education and Employment: Strong Gains, but More to Do." *OECD EducationToday* (blog), 27 March 2012 <http://oecdeducationtoday.blogspot.com/2012/03/womens-outcomes-in-education-and.html>, accessed 6 September 2013.

Cheng, Hong. "'Holding Up Half the Sky'?: A Socio-Cultural Comparison of Gender-Role Portrayals in Chinese and U.S. Advertising." *International Journal of Advertising* 16.4 (1997): 295–319.

Chi, Chia-Wen and Baldwin, Cecelia. "Gender and Class Stereotypes: A Comparison of U.S. and Taiwanese Magazine Advertisements." In Segal, Marcia Texler and Martinez, Theresa A., eds. *Intersections of Gender, Race, and Class: Readings for a Changing Landscape*. Los Angeles: Roxbury Publishing, 2007, 251–264.

Cohen, Judy. "White Consumer Response to Asian Models in Advertising." *Journal of Consumer Marketing* 9.2 (Spring 1992): 17–27.

Czepiec, Helena and Kelly, J. Steven. "Analyzing Hispanic Roles in Advertising: A Portrait of an Emerging Subculture." *Current Issues & Research in Advertising* 6.1 (1983): 219–240.

Deeken, Aimee. "Service Upgrades." *Mediaweek*, 2 December 2002, 45–46f.

Diamond, Daniel S. "A Quantitative Approach to Magazine Advertisement Format Selection." *Journal of Marketing Research* 5.4 (November 1968): 376–386.

Dianoux, Christian and Linhart, Zdenek. "The Effectiveness of Female Nudity in Advertising in Three European Countries." *International Marketing Review* 27.5 (2010): 562–578.

Dumeco, Simon. "Magazines Are Dead, or Why There's No Such Thing as a (Mere) Magazine Company Anymore." *Ad Age Media News*, 21 October 2012 <http://adage.com/article/the-media-guy/thing-a-mere-magazine-anymore/244851/>, accessed 9 July 2013.

Esteban-Bravo, Mercedes; Múgica, José M.; and Vidal-Sanz, Jose M. "Magazine Sales Promotion: A Dynamic Response Analysis." *Journal of Advertising* 38.1 (Spring 2009): 137–146.

Farris, Paul W. and Parry, Mark E. "Clarifying Some Ambiguities Regarding GRP and Average Frequency: A Comment on 'GRP: A Case of Mistaken Identity.'" *Journal of Advertising Research* 31.6 (December 1991): 75–77.

Faust, Drew. "Educate Women; Change the World." *Harvard Gazette*, 22 March 2013 <http://www.harvard.edu/president/educate-women-change-world-ewha-womans-university>, accessed 27 February 2014.

Fennis, Bob M. and Bakker, Arnold B. "'Stay Tuned—We Will Be Back Right after These Messages': Need to Evaluate Moderates the Transfer of Irritation in Advertising." *Journal of Advertising* 30.3 (Fall 2001): 15–25.

Ford, Jennifer. "Fashion Advertising, Men's Magazines, and Sex in Advertising: A Critical-Interpretive Study." Master's thesis, University of South Florida, 2008.

Frith, Katherine; Shaw, Ping; and Cheng, Hong. "The Construction of Beauty: A Cross-Cultural Analysis of Women's Magazine Advertising." *Journal of Communication* 55.1 (March 2005): 56–70.

Fugate, Douglas L.; Decker, Philip J.; and Brewer, Joyce J. "Women in Professional Selling: A Human Resource Management Perspective." *Journal of Personal Selling & Sales Management* 8.3 (November 1988): 33–41.

Galin, Michal. "Magazine Ads that Drove Readers to the Web: MRI Starch Picks the 10 Most Effective Print to Online Ads." *Advertising Age*. 18 December 2008 <adage.com/article/media/magazine-ads-drove-readers-web/133258/>, accessed 12 November 2012.

Hall, Ronald E. "The Ball Curve: Calculated Racism and the Stereotype of African American Men." *Journal of Black Studies* 32.1 (September 2001): 104–119.

Hofstede, Geert. *Culture's Consequences: International Differences in Work-Related Values.* Abridged ed. Beverly Hills, CA: Sage Publications, 1984.

Hong, Jae W.; Muderrisoglu, Aydin; and Zinkhan, George M. "Cultural Differences and Advertising Expression: A Comparative Content Analysis of Japanese and U.S. Magazine Advertising." *Journal of Advertising* 16.1 (July 1987): 55–62, 68.

Hovland, Roxanne; McMahan, Carolynn; Lee, Guiohk; Hwang, Jang-Sun; and Kim, Juran. "Gender Role Portrayals in American and Korean Advertisements." *Sex Roles* 53.11/12 (December 2005): 887–899.

Huang, Ying and Lowry, Dennis T. "An Analysis of Nudity in Chinese Magazine Advertising: Examining Gender, Racial and Brand Differences." *Sex Roles* 66.7/8 (April 2012): 440–452.

Ifezue, Alexander N. "What Makes an Effective Advertising for a Man or a Woman?" *Journal of Communication* [J Communication, India] 1.1 (July 2010): 13–18.

Inzlicht, Michael; Tullett, Alexa M.; Legault, Lisa; and Kang, Sonia K. "Lingering Effects: Stereotype Threat Hurts More than You Think." *Social Issues and Policy Review* 5.1 (December 2011): 227–256.

Ives, Nat. "The Last Page: A Guide to Magazines that Have Ceased Publication." *Ad Age Media News*, 15 December 2009 <http:adage.com/article/media/a-guide-magazines-ceased-publication/132779/>, accessed 1 March 2014.

Ives, Nat. "Magazines: The A-list." *Advertising Age*, 6 October 2008, 1.

Jayson, Sharon. "Family Life, Roles Changing as Couples Seek Balance." *USA Today*, 19 April 2009 <http://usatoday30.usatoday.com/news/health/2009-04-18-families-conf_N.htm>, accessed 06 September 2013.

Jussim, Lee. "Social Reality and Social Problems: The Role of Expectancies." *Journal of Social Issues* 46.2 (Summer 1990): 9–34.

Kaiser, Ulrich and Wright, Julian. "Price Structure in Two-Sided Markets: Evidence from the Magazine Industry." *International Journal of Industrial Organization* 24.1 (January 2006): 1–28.

Kang, Mee-Eun. "The Portrayal of Women's Images in Magazine Advertisements: Goffman's Gender Analysis Revisited." *Sex Roles* 37.11/12 (December 1997): 979–996.

Klassen, Michael L.; Jasper, Cynthia R.; and Schwartz, Anne M. "Men and Women: Images of Their Relationships in Magazine Advertisements." *Journal of Advertising Research* 33.2 (March/April 1993): 30–39.

Kolbe, Richard H. and Albanese, Paul J. "Man to Man: A Content Analysis of Sole-Male Images in Male-Audience Magazines." *Journal of Advertising* 25.4 (Winter 1996): 1–20.

Koschat, Martin A. and Putsis, William P., Jr. "Audience Characteristics and Bundling: A Hedonic Analysis of Magazine Advertising Rates." *Journal of Marketing Research* 39.2 (May 2002): 262–273.

Lane, W. Ronald; King, Karen Whitehill; and Reichert, Tom. "Using Magazines." *Kleppner's Advertising Procedure.* 18th ed. Upper Saddle River, NJ: Prentice Hall/Pearson, 2011, 319–355.

Le, Cuong Nguyen. *Asian American Assimilation: Ethnicity, Immigration, and Socioeconomic Attainment.* New York: LFB Scholarly Publishing, 2007.

Lee, Richard. "Botswana: Victory for Women's Rights in Botswana." *All Africa,* 3 September 2013 <http://allafrica.com/stories/201309040359.html>, accessed 1 March 2014.

Liu, Matthew Tingchi and Brock, James L. "Selecting a Female Athlete Endorser in China: The Effect of Attractiveness, Match-Up, and Consumer Gender Difference." *European Journal of Marketing* 45.7/8 (2011): 1214–1235.

Lynch, James and Schuler, Drue. "The Matchup Effect of Spokesperson and Product Congruency: A Schema Theory Interpretation." *Psychology & Marketing* 11.5 (September/October 1994): 417–445.

Madden, Normandy. "Dentsu Builds Media Offices across Asia," *Ad Age Media News,* 28 April 2012 <http://adage.com/results?endeca=1&searchprop=AdAgeAll&return=endeca&search_offset=0&search_order_by=score&search_phrase=Dentsu+media/>, accessed 9 July, 2013.

Martin, Kathleen. "How Far Really? Some Marketers Are Ditching the Old Sex Role Stereotypes, but Advertising Still Has a Long Way to Go." *Marketing Magazine,* 2 July 2001, 13–14.

Mathur, Mahima and Chattopadhyay, Amitava. "The Impact of Moods Generated by Television Programs on Responses to Advertising." *Psychology & Marketing* 8.1 (Spring 1991): 59–77.

McDaniel, Stephen R. "An Investigation of Match-Up Effects in Sport Sponsorship Advertising: The Implications of Consumer Advertising Schemas." *Psychology & Marketing* 16.2 (March 1999): 163–184.

National Directory of Magazines. "A Magazine for Everyone." 14 July 2011 <www.magazine.org/handbook_2010/2011>, accessed 12 November 2012.

Nelson, Michelle R. and Paek, Hye-Jin. "A Content Analysis of Advertising in a Global Magazine Across Seven Countries: Implications for Global Advertising Strategies." *International Marketing Review* 24.1 (2007): 64–86.

Nelson, Michelle R. and Paek, Hye-Jin. "Cross-Cultural Differences in Sexual Advertising Content in a Transnational Women's Magazine." *Sex Roles* 53.5/6 (September 2005): 371–383.

Neuman, Fredric. "Changing Gender Roles in Marriage." *Fighting Fear* (blog). *Psychology Today,* 4 January 2013 <http://www.psychologytoday.com/blog/fighting-fear/201301/changing-gender-roles-in-marriage>, accessed 6 September 2013.

Neville, Helen A. and Pieterse, Alex L. "Racism, White Supremacy, and Resistance: Contextualizing Black American Experiences." In Neville, Helen A.; Tynes, Brendesha M.; and Utsey, Shawn O., eds. *Handbook of African American Psychology.* Los Angeles, CA: Sage, 2009, 159–272.

Norris, Vincent P. "Consumer Magazine Prices and the Mythical Advertising Subsidy." *Journalism Quarterly* 59.2 (Summer 1982): 205–211.

Ono, Kent A. and Phan, Vincent N. *Asian Americans and the Media.* Malden, MA: Polity Press, 2009.

Orth, Ulrich R., and Holancova, Denisa. "Men's and Women's Responses to Sex Role Portrayals in Advertisements." *International Journal of Research in Marketing* 21.1 (March 2004): 77–88.

Pathak, Shareen. "East Meets West in Nissan Social Media Bollywood Link." *Ad Age Media News,* 21, 9 April 2012 < http://adage.com/article/global-news/east-meets-west-nissan-social-media-bollywood-link/233980/>, accessed 9 July 2013.

Peters, Jeremy W. "*U.S. News & World Report* to Become Online Only." *New York Times,* 5 November 2010 <http:mediadecoder.blogs.nytimes.com/2010/11/05/u-s-news-to-cease-printing-become-online-only/?_r=0>, accessed 12 November 2012.

Peterson, Robin T. "Consumer Magazine Advertisement Portrayal of Models by Race in the U.S.: An Assessment." *Journal of Marketing Communications* 13.3 (September 2007): 199–211.

Plakoyiannaki, Emmanuella and Zotos, Yorgos. "Female Role Stereotypes in Print Advertising: Identifying Associations with Magazine and Product Categories." *European Journal of Marketing* 43.11/12 (2009): 1411–1434.

Reichert, Tom and Carpenter, Courtney. "An Update on Sex in Magazine Advertising: 1983 to 2003." *Journalism & Mass Communication Quarterly* 81.4 (Winter 2004): 823–837.

Rome, Dennis. *Black Demons: The Media's Depiction of the African American Male Criminal Stereotype.* Westport, CT: Praeger, 2004.

Sar, Sela and Doyle, Kenneth O. "A Comparative Content Analysis of Cambodian and Thai Print Advertisements." In Keller, Punam A. and Rook, Dennis W., eds. *Advances in Consumer Research.* Vol. 30. Valdosta, GA: Association for Consumer Research, 2003, 223–229.

Sherman, Lee and Deighton, John. "Banner Advertising: Measuring Effectiveness and Optimizing Placement." *Journal of Interactive Marketing* 15.2 (Spring 2001): 60–64.

Shoop, Tiffany J.; Luther, Catherine A.; and McMahan, Carolynn. "Advertisement Images of Men and Women in Culturally Diverging Societies: An Examination of Images in U.S. and Japanese Fashion Magazines." *Journal of International Business and Economics* 8.3 (September 2008): 29–41 <http://www.freepatentsonline.com/article/Journal-International-Business-Economics/190616968.html>, accessed 6 September 2013.

So, Stella Lai Man. "A Comparative Content Analysis of Women's Magazine Advertisements from Hong Kong and Australia on Advertising Expressions." *Journal of Current Issues and Research in Advertising* 26.1 (Spring 2004): 47–58.

Stankiewicz, Julie M. and Rosselli, Francine. "Women as Sex Objects and Victims in Print Advertisements." *Sex Roles* 58.7/8 (April 2008): 579–589.

Stern, Bruce L.; Krugman, Dean M.; and Resnik, Alan. "Magazine Advertising: An Analysis of Its Information Content." *Journal of Advertising Research* 21.2 (April 1981): 39–44.

Sugiarto, Catur and De Barnier, Virginie. "Sexually Appealing Ads Effectiveness on Indonesian Customers." *European Journal of Business and Management* 5.9 (2013): 125–135 <http://www.iiste.org/Journals/index.php/EJBM/article/view/5133>, accessed 27 September 2013.

Taylor, Charles R.; Landreth, Stacy; and Bang, Hae-Kyong. "Asian Americans in Magazine Advertising: Portrayals of the 'Model Minority.'" *Journal of Macromarketing* 25.2 (December 2005): 163–174.

U.S. Census Bureau. "Hispanic Americans by the Numbers." *InfoPlease* <http://www.infoplease.com/spot/hhmcensus1.html>, accessed 5 September 2013.

Vigorito, Anthony J. and Curry, Timothy J. "Marketing Masculinity: Gender Identity and Popular Magazines." *Sex Roles* 39.1/2 (July 1988): 135–152.

Vokey, Megan; Tefft, Bruce; and Tysiaczny, Chris. "An Analysis of Hyper-Masculinity in Magazine Advertisements." *Sex Roles* 68.9/10 (May 2013): 562–576.

Wallace-Sanders, Kimberly. *Mammy: A Century of Race, Gender, and Southern Memory.* Ann Arbor: University of Michigan Press, 2008.

Wei, Ran and Jiang, Jing. "New Media Advertising and Its Social Impact in China." In Cheng, Hong and Chan, Kara, eds. *Advertising and Chinese Society: Impacts and Issues* Copenhagen: Copenhagen Business School Press, 2009, 245–263.

Wolin, Lori D. "Gender Issues in Advertising—An Oversight Synthesis of Research: 1970–2002." *Journal of Advertising Research* 43.1 (March 2003): 111–129.

Yi, Youjae. "Contextual Priming Effects in Print Advertisements: The Moderating Role of Prior Knowledge." *Journal of Advertising* 22.1 (March 1993): 1–10.

Zillmann, Dolf. "Excitation Transfer in Communication-Mediated Aggressive Behavior." *Journal of Experimental Social Psychology* 7.4 (July 1971): 419–434.

Zimmerman, Amanda and Dahlberg, John. "The Sexual Objectification of Women in Advertising: A Contemporary Cultural Perspective." *Journal of Advertising Research* 48.1 (March 2008): 71–79.

Supplemental Resources

Allan, Kenneth and Coltrane, Scott. "Gender Displaying Television Commercials: A Comparative Study of Television Commercials in the 1950s and 1980s." *Sex Roles* 35.3/4 (1996): 185–203.

Barry, Thomas E.; Gilly, Mary C.; and Doran, Lindley E. "Advertising to Women with Different Career Orientations." *Journal of Advertising Research* 25.2 (April/May1985): 26–35.

Bonham, Lorie. "Gender Images and Power in Magazine Advertisements: The Consciousness Scale Revisited." M.A. thesis, Georgia State University, 2005.

Busby, Linda J. and Leichty, Greg. "Feminism and Advertising in Traditional and Nontraditional Women's Magazines 1950s–1980s." *Journalism Quarterly* 70.2 (Summer 1993): 247–264.

Chen, Yongmin and He, Chuan. "Paid Placement: Advertising and Search on the Internet." NET Institute Working Paper No. 06–02 (September 2006): 1–29 <http://dx.doi.org/10.2139/ssrn.936472>, accessed 24 November 2012.

Endicott, R. Craig. "Top 300 Revenue a Record $32.5 Bil." *Advertising Age*, 20 September 2004 <http://adage.com/article/special-report-magazine-300/top-300-revenue-a-record-32-5-bil/100462/>, accessed 24 November 2012.

Ford, John B.; Voli, Patricia Kramer; Honeycutt, Earl D., Jr.; and Casey, Susan L. "Gender Role Portrayals in Japanese Advertising: A Magazine Content Analysis." *Journal of Advertising* 27.1 (Spring 1998): 113–124.

Hughes, Marie Adele and Garrett, Dennis E. "Intercoder Reliability Estimation Approaches in Marketing: A Generalizability Theory Framework for Quantitative Data." *Journal of Marketing Research* 27.2 (May 1990): 185–195.

Kilbourne, William E. "An Exploratory Study of the Effect of Sex Role Stereotyping on Attitudes toward Magazine Advertisements." *Journal of the Academy of Marketing Science* 14.4 (Winter 1986): 43–46.

Long, Michael. "Fonic Set for Exposure at Munich's Allianz Arena." *SportsPro*, 6 September 2013 <http://www.sportspromedia.com/news/fonic_set_for_exposure_at_munichs_allianz_arena>, accessed 05 September 2013.

Spiegler, Marc. "Hot Media Buy: The Farm Report." *American Demographics*, October 1995, 18–19.

Ukman, Lesa. *IEG's Complete Guide to Sponsorship: Everything You Need to Know about Sports, Arts, Event, Entertainment and Cause Marketing.* Chicago, IL: IEG, 1996.

12

MAGAZINE MANAGEMENT

Publishing as a Business

Hanna-Kaisa Ellonen
and Anette Johansson

Magazine management as a field of study lies within the area of Media Management and Economics (MME). MME research is producing a growing body of literature focusing on economic, management and business issues in the media industries, based largely on traditional concepts and theories in the two related disciplines of management and economics. Study of media management and economics has grown in stature since the 1990s pioneering works of Robert Picard and Alan Albarran. Several seminal books have been published in the 2000s, including the *Handbook of Media Management and Economics*[1] and Annet Aris and Jacques Bughin's *Managing Media Companies*.[2] The founding of three academic journals, namely the *Journal of Media Economics* (in 1988), the *International Journal of Media Management* (in 1999) and the *Journal of Media Business Studies* (in 2007), has established the field by providing industry-specific publication outlets for research on journalism and media-based business and economics.

This chapter comprises a review of the current research on the magazine industry, segmented in the following five categories: *media economics, management research, business modeling, innovation* and *brand management*. These categories reflect the main body of research related to magazines and magazine publishing from a business perspective. Research specific to magazine publishing is scarce by comparison with that in other media sectors, such as the newspaper industry. However, a strength is that the body of magazine-related research includes both global and digital studies, with theory and applications continuing to mature. Included in this review is management research that focuses on magazine publishers, as well as research in which magazine publishing is the empirical context for a larger theoretical approach.

Literature Review and Method

As the research on magazine management is scattered across different theoretical arenas, such as strategy, marketing, management and leadership, it was necessary to apply a broad approach to the literature review. The major sources of information used to identify the studies to be included in this review were the ABI Inform, EBSCO, Elsevier and Google Scholar electronic databases. A further search was also conducted for relevant refereed books, journal articles, conference contributions, edited volumes and working papers that were unavailable in electronic databases. The authors worked in parallel and used combined screening methods to make sure no relevant publications from 1990 to the present were excluded. These methods included (1) a traditional database search using all combinations of the keywords *magazine*, *publishing, journal, periodical* and *print industry*; (2) a library database search using the same keywords to find related books; (3) tracking and tracing relevant publications, based on the bibliographies of found articles and books; (4) reviewing the media management related journals, *Journal of Media Business Studies*, *International Journal of Media Management* and *Journal of Media Economics*; and (5) reviewing the main books in the fields of media economics and management[3] for magazine specific information.

Based on the searches, a list of material was drafted. Next, the authors scanned the abstracts of the journal articles and conference publications to exclude irrelevant studies. As this review focuses on *media economics, management research, business modeling, innovation* and *brand management*, studies not falling under these categories were excluded. Also excluded were studies focusing solely on trade magazines.

Media Economics

Within the media economics stream of literature, where research has traditionally focused on analyzing both *industry structure* and *competitive dynamics*, the key question since the 1990s has been, *How does the Internet affect the industry?* In the decade of the 1990s and early 2000s, the Internet was often referred to as a potentially disruptive technology in publishing, and industry professionals and media scholars expected that print and the Internet could not coexist as publications channels.[4] However, based on their analysis on competitive forces,[5] Hanna-Kaisa Ellonen, Ari Jantunen and Olli Kuivalainen found no observable major changes in the industry caused by the Internet.[6] It has not significantly changed the five forces that shape the nature and state of the competition, the competitive positions have not been challenged, and no publisher has gained a position from which to exercise market power. Hence, from this perspective, the Internet's impact on the industry level has been relatively marginal and has resulted mainly in increased rivalry among existing competitors. The Internet has thus not been disruptive. Magazine publishers have used it to extend and refine rather than to displace existing products and business models.

Nevertheless, the Internet has clearly affected how magazines are made: There is a shift from the pure print version to broader brand concepts. Magazines follow different strategies on-line, resulting in differences in the value and cost positions of the products. Thus, Web sites are a means of differentiation and of creating new value for customers.[7]

Joanna Barsh and her colleagues, Emily Kramer, David Maue and Neal Zuckerman, identified two types of magazine Web sites: *companion sites* aimed at supporting the print magazine and *destination sites* that pursue success as an independent service.[8] This classification of magazine Web sites has been adopted by several researchers in their empirical inquiries on the so-called cannibalization question. That is, do magazine Web sites cannibalize the readership of print magazines? Until now, the evidence is two-fold: Based on econometric studies conducted in Germany and the United States from the 1990s until 2001, the evidence shows that digital content either had no effect on or cannibalized print sales. Data from 2002 until 2012 suggest there is a positive relationship between Web site visits and circulation. Cannibalization effects also seem to vary across time, readership age and Internet adoption.[9]

It has been 10 years since the first studies on cannibalization, and many things have changed in the meantime. There is therefore a need for research that re-explores cannibalization's effects, in multiple markets and in the cases of mobile devices and paid content. It would also be valuable to analyze the current market structure and potential changes in competitive positioning in order to better understand how the development of Internet and mobile reading devices in particular have influenced the overall industry structure.

Management Research

Magazine professionals are seldom singled out as a specific group in the management literature but are rather included in the broader concept of journalists or creative professionals within the media industry. Aris and Bughin emphasize that "media business [is] a people business," and the prerequisites for motivating creative staff include entrepreneurial freedom, a great media brand, peer recognition and inspiring leadership.[10] The few studies that focus on magazine publishing can be categorized in two subsets: (1) managing what the organization has and does, i.e., its resources and capabilities, and (2) managing how the organization thinks, i.e., its decision-making.

In the first, researchers build on the resource-based view (RBV)[11] of the firm and investigate idiosyncratic relationships between and characteristics of *resources and capabilities* as a source of competitiveness. Sylvia Chan-Olmsted suggests categorizing resources as *property-based* and *knowledge-based* in research on media companies.[12] Ellonen, Jantunen and Kuivalainen found the main property-based resources of a magazine publisher include customer databases, brands and copyrights. Their research identified the important knowledge-based resources to be business and marketing skills, customer-relationship management, the ability to identify potential customers, and sales knowledge and skills. They also found the Internet does not seem to have changed the core competence of the magazine publisher. However, new resources are needed, such as technical skills and the ability to change.[13]

Continuing within the same stream of capability and resources research, some scholars have speculated on what exactly constitutes the core competence of magazine publishers. Helene Hafstrand suggested the strategic capabilities of a magazine publisher are located in human resource management, market knowledge and product development. She also maintains that capabilities, knowledge and routines within these functions accumulate over a long time, become embedded in the organization and thus cannot easily be replicated.[14] Along the same lines, Picard adds that the core competence of the magazine publisher lies in the selection, processing and packaging of content and thus in catching the look and feel of the concept—a notion that is linked to the concept-focused nature of the magazine product.[15] Also Ellonen notes that the core competence and strategic resources of a magazine publisher are not linked to content creation per se. It is rather the processes and structures that make it possible, as well as finding and keeping the right people.[16]

Several Scandinavian empirical studies have explored the roles of these different capabilities among magazine publishers who are actively developing new on-line services. First, researchers found that publishers tend to build on their strongest area, in terms of market and technology capabilities, and focus on leveraging those, rather than risk experimenting in an area in which they are weak.[17] Second, in another study researchers noted differences in the dynamic capability portfolios of four Scandinavian magazine publishers: Some publishers were better equipped than others with routines and processes that advance organizational change.[18] Third, it has been found that these change-advocating routines (i.e., dynamic capabilities) tend to have similar characteristics among different publishers.[19]

The second stream of magazine-specific studies deals with the question of how magazine organizations think, which in the management context relates to *managerial cognition and decision-making*.[20] Johansson, Ellonen and Jantunen found publishers tend to differ in terms of decision-making logic: Whereas some favor the traditional goal-means business logic, others are more entrepreneurial and willing to use the opportunities that arise without formal business planning.[21] Anette Johansson and Alexander McKelvie's research on key decision makers in the industry provides evidence that corporate culture, as opposed to individual expertise, strongly influences the decision-making approach used. An entrepreneurial culture that allows ideas to flourish thus seems to make managers more ready to deal with change.[22]

The next question is how to define the optimal decision-making logic for a situation. Research attention should also be paid to potential resistance: in other words, to leading and managing magazine professionals during times of change if they are not willing to change. Publisher capability development and management will no doubt remain on the research agenda in this industry and will grow in importance as magazine publishers are forced to innovate not only their products but also their business models.

Business Modeling

Research on the business models magazine publishers use concentrates on the firm's logic for creating and commercializing value.[23] Of the three general dimensions of the business model—economic, operational and strategic—magazine-related research focuses mostly on the economic aspect, that is, the revenue model. Charles P. Daly, Patrick Henry and Ellen Ryder describe the traditional commercial success of a magazine as a model which rests on the "three-legged stool" of editorial content, advertising and circulation: The shortcomings of any "leg" affect the others and the stability of the entire venture.[24] This mainstream revenue model remained largely untouched until the financial crisis of 2008, when it became evident that relying only on advertising, subscriptions and single-copy sales would not bring prosperity in the future. As Picard found from his research, although long-term contracts have a stabilizing effect on revenue sources, the financial performance of magazines is still highly cyclical. Picard concluded from his reviews that new business models need to focus less on advertising and more on capitalizing the core business: the production of editorial content.[25]

Lucy Küng describes the Internet as having brought one of the most significant changes in decades to the industry and hence contributing to the wholesale alteration of business models.[26] As the Internet presence of magazine publishers gradually increased during the first decade of the new millennium, the revenue models also became more elaborate. Publishers started to experiment with different types of revenue streams. John Gallaugher, Pat Auger and Anat BarNir found evidence of four revenue models of magazine Web site performance: (1) sales of on-line advertising, (2) subscriptions for on-line content, (3) selling subscriptions for the print publication and (4) content syndication with other on-line services. On-line business models have thus far showed little profit, however.[27] Florian Stahl, Marc-Frederic Schäfer and Wolfgang Mass studied sales of content on magazine and newspaper Web sites and concluded that cannibalization occurred when the same bundle of information goods was offered on-line and off-line at the same time. On the other hand, revenues from paid content were higher when the information was re-bundled on-line.[28]

Patrik Wikström and Hanna-Kaisa Ellonen incorporated the operational and strategic dimensions of the business model and presented results from a multiple case study of four Scandinavian magazine publishers. It seems that, although skillful in incorporating on-line innovations such as social-media features (e.g., feedback and voting functions), the magazine publishers were less successful in transforming them into revenue streams. Wikström and Ellonen also found that the reason for including social media in on-line platforms was unclear and rather mirrored a general fear of losing ground in the fierce competition, on-line as well as off-line.[29] Their findings substantiate the research of Olli Kuivalainen and his colleagues, who found that social media added to perceived consumer value.[30]

There are, nevertheless, magazine publishers who have achieved financial success in their on-line businesses, although academic researchers have not addressed the question. In fact, there is very little research in this area, and publishers are generally reluctant to share their financial data publicly. Thus there is little detailed knowledge of the revenue model in terms of both content and outcomes. Business-model research provides the opportunity to explore developments in magazine publishing in more detail.

Innovation

Innovation in magazine publishing is a highly pertinent and important research topic, for as more and more actors come into the industry, the competition becomes fiercer. New firms entering the magazine sector are providing similar editorial content to that in existing magazines. These players provide content for on-line communities, Web sites, smartphone applications and blogs that are not related to a magazine brand but still compete for the same audiences. These new firms have substantially increased the pressure on magazine publishers to innovate.

Despite the relevance of the topic, however, the number of published studies of the phenomenon is surprisingly small. Among the main contributions are Ellonen, Wikström and Jantunen's[31] study linking the different capabilities and resources[32] of magazine publishers with the type of innovative outcome and Johansson and McKelvie's[33] study exploring the determinants of decision-making behavior in the context of innovation projects. Both studies aim to enhance understanding of the innovation-related work that magazine publishing organizations engage in: the resources they possess, the routines they put into practice and the cognitive approach to decision-making.[34]

Ellonen and her colleagues used theories of dynamic capabilities to analyze the question and concluded that publishers with high levels of capabilities on all dimensions—that is, able to *sense* (market and technology needs and changes), *seize* (opportunities) and *reconfigure* (existing knowledge and resources for purposeful action)—create more niche innovations requiring knowledge of new markets or of new technology. On the other hand, those with weaker or less balanced capabilities produce more radical innovations incorporating knowledge of both. Hence, publishers appear to possess heterogeneous (i.e., different from each other) capabilities that are linked to the type of innovative output.[35] Hanna Silvennoinen and Ari Jantunen found support for these notions in their test of the impact of different types of dynamic capabilities on innovation radicalness among Finnish consumer magazines. They found that sensing and seizing capabilities had a positive effect, whereas no such effect was detected in the case of reconfiguring capabilities.[36]

Johansson and McKelvie's reported findings from a survey of 246 key decision makers in the Swedish magazine publishing industry, from which they sought to determine what triggers the cognitive approach to innovation, complements current research on entrepreneurial decision-making.[37] Johansson and McKelvie's results suggest that a corporate entrepreneurial culture has a stronger effect on decision-making behavior on the individual level than factors related to human capital, such as education and previous work experience. This implies that publishers who wish to foster an entrepreneurial mindset among their staff should consider elements related to the overall culture, such as the values they communicate and processes that support innovative efforts, rather than hiring the most experienced and talented individuals.[38]

Other interesting explorations of innovations in the industry include Rita Järventie-Thesleff, Mikko Villi and Johanna Moisander's comparative multiple case study of on-line and print publishing. Their cases revealed interesting differences in change-management practices, reflecting the need for prediction and efficiency on the print side while emphasizing adaptive and non-predictive skills on the on-line side. The authors conclude that organizations wishing to improve their *ambidextrous change-management skills*, in other words, managing exploitation as well as exploration, need to ease the tensions and conflicts between departments in order to encourage mutual learning.[39]

Magazine publishers are quickly adapting to the opportunities that new technology offers. Publishers' habit of constantly introducing new and creative content and keeping in close contact with their readers and users gives them a major advantage over the newspaper industry, for example, which has struggled considerably harder to adjust to the digital society. Interestingly, despite the growing use of Web sites, smartphones and other digital media, the time spent reading printed consumer magazines does not seem to decrease. This means that digital media are used as a complementary source of information and amusement.[40] For the future this may imply that even if printed content gradually moves on-line, the time spent consuming editorial content is not likely to decrease to any great extent. Thus, opportunities will arise for magazine publishers to reinvent their own industry and for researchers to explore this process further.

Brand Management

There has been a considerable amount of research on magazine brands and their role in guiding consumer behavior, which can be found within the media management literature and, to some extent, in the larger body of theory and research on brand-management.[41] Gillian Doyle maintains that segmentation is at the heart of consumer magazine publishing and that the magazine's brand is a major asset in terms of ensuring that the brand appeals to a particular segment or niche.[42] Ellonen, Jantunen and Kuivalainen note an ongoing switch from the print product toward a multidimensional brand concept and suggest that the magazine's brand is pivotal in combining the different dimensions (print, Web site, plus possible others). Their research specifically suggests that Web sites and prospective virtual communities and mobile services are new dimensions of the magazine's brand rather than merely new channels.[43] This underlines the emerging role of these complements to the print magazine, adding something new rather than simply distributing the journalistic content in a different way.

Correspondingly, magazine Web sites tend to be seen as *brand extensions* within the research on media management.[44] Several studies explore the connections between experiences of the magazine on the brand level, consumer behavior on the Web site and intentions to buy or subscribe to the print magazine: A study conducted in Finland of 867 visitors of a magazine Web site found that brand-level experiences affected consumer satisfaction, trust and loyalty on the Web site level.[45] This supports the basic argument that brands have a halo effect on-line. Another study, also in Finland, explored the effect from the opposite perspective: that is, the impact of the Web site on the brand or print magazine. Researchers found that the Web site complemented the print version in different ways. It facilitates both more frequent communication between the publisher and the magazine's readers on the one hand and consumer-initiated interaction among readers on the other. In both cases something is offered that cannot be obtained from the print magazine alone but is assumed to complement it.[46] Paweena Srisuwan and Stuart Barnes also found that enjoyment was an important factor on-line, especially for the younger audience, and hence vital for attracting loyal Web site visitors.[47]

Hanna-Kaisa Ellonen, Anssi Tarkiainen and Olli Kuivalainen explored the key question of whether active Web site visitors are more likely to buy or subscribe to the magazine in the future. They found that the impact of Web site activity on loyalty to the print magazine differed between subscribers and non-subscribers, indicating that Web site usage may substitute the print magazine among non-subscribers while subscribers remain faithful to both.[48] In a further study,[49] however, they noted that both the frequency of visits and the time spent on the Web site strengthened trust in the brand and consequently also affected the likelihood of buying the magazine in future or recommending it to friends.

Because of the Internet, magazines now have a two-way relationship with their readers.[50] The Internet provides a means for increasing customer engagement and for strengthening the customer relationship.[51] Several researchers have studied *brand communities*[52] on magazine Web sites.[53] It has been suggested that magazine brands are a natural context for such communities in that they target a specific audience that shares similar characteristics.[54] Magazine communities bring several benefits, including strengthening brand attachment[55] and obtaining customer input for new articles.[56] However, in a quantitative study of four Finnish magazines and 1,779 readers, no evidence was found that participation in brand communities enhanced trust in the brand and, consequently, loyalty to the print magazine.[57]

A majority of the studies of magazine brand management were conducted before 2008 on magazines that were considered pioneers in this area. However, as interactive features and social media applications are becoming the norm, researchers will face new questions: the value of social media applications for magazines and the relationship between mobile devices and the magazine brand, for example.

Conclusions

Media management and economics research that focuses on the dynamics of the magazine publishing industry is gradually beginning to develop several streams of inquiry. Researchers are building on each other's efforts and working together to examine innovation management, business modeling and brand management. The introduction of mobile devices continues to change consumer behavior and hence to challenge publishers' current knowledge.

Among the weaknesses of the literature are that research on magazine management is relatively scarce and is dispersed over a wide range of publication outlets. Consequently, there is no independent and established stream of literature on the subject. Magazine publishing tends to be included as one of the media sectors in contemporary MME books. However, there are rather few industry-specific literary works such as academic and management books as well as academic articles. It is also worth noting that magazine and journal periodical management and economics is seldom the focus or even the context of research in scholarly MME journals.

Of the active streams of research, the magazine-management stream is the most fragmented at present. More industry-focused research is needed to fill this gap. In Aris and Bughin's words,[58] magazine publishing is a people's business, and hence we need to know more about how to lead and manage creative individuals in these times of change.

Notes

1 Alan B. Albarran, Sylvia M. Chan-Olmsted, and Michael O. Wirth, eds., *Handbook of Media Management and Economics* (Mahwah, NJ: Lawrence Erlbaum Associates, 2006).

2 Annet Aris and Jacques Bughin, *Managing Media Companies: Harnessing Creative Value* (Chichester, UK: John Wiley & Sons, 2005).

3 European Media Management Education Association, "Seminal Reading on Media Management and Media Economics" <http://www.media-management.eu/member-directory/seminal-readings.html>, accessed 30 August 2013.

4 See, for example, Robert G. Picard, "Cash Cows or Entrecôte: Publishing Companies and Disruptive Technologies," *Trends in Communication* 11.2 (2003): 127–136; Bozena I. Mierzjewska and C. Ann Hollifield, "Theoretical Approaches in Media Management Research," in Alan B. Albarran, Sylvia M. Chan-Olmsted, and Michael O. Wirth, eds., *Handbook of Media Management and Economics* (Mahwah, NJ: Lawrence Erlbaum Associates, 2006), 37–66.

5 For further reading on the five competitive forces, see Michael Porter, *Competitive Advantage: Creating and Sustaining Superior Performance* (New York: Free Press, 1985).

6 Hanna-Kaisa Ellonen, Ari Jantunen, and Olli Kuivalainen, "The Strategic Impact of Internet on Magazine Publishing," *International Journal of Innovation and Technology Management* 5.3 (2008): 341–361.

7 Ellonen, Jantunen, and Kuivalainen, "The Strategic Impact of Internet on Magazine Publishing," 346–357.

8 Joanna Barsh, Emily E. Kramer, David Maue, and Neal Zuckerman, "Magazines' Home Companion," [Special Edition] *McKinsey Quarterly* 2 (Spring 2001): 82–91.

9 Ulrich Kaiser, "Magazines and Their Companion Websites: Competing Outlet Channels?" *Review of Marketing Science* 4.3 (August 2006): 1–24; Daniel H. Simon and Vrinda Kadiyali, "The Effect of a Magazine's Free Digital Content on Its Print Circulation: Cannibalization or Complementarity?" *Information Economics and Policy* 19.3/4 (October 2007): 344–361.

10 Aris and Bughin, *Managing Media Companies*, 382.

11 For further reading on the resource-based view, see, e.g., Jay Barney, "Firm Resources and Sustained Competitive Advantage," *Journal of Management* 17.1 (March 1991): 99–120; and Margaret Peteraf, "The Cornerstones of Competitive Advantage: A Resource-Based Perspective," *Strategic Management Journal* 14.3 (1993): 179–191.

12 Sylvia M. Chan-Olmsted, *Competitive Strategy for Media Firms: Strategic and Brand Management in Changing Media Markets* (Mahwah, NJ: Lawrence Erlbaum Associates, 2006), 30.

13 Ellonen, Jantunen, and Kuivalainen, "The Strategic Impact of Internet on Magazine Publishing," 346–357.

14 Helene Hafstrand, "Competitive Advantage in the Magazine Publishing Business—A Resource-Based Perspective" (paper presented at the 15th Nordic Conference on Media and Communication Research, Reykjavik, 10–13 August 2001).

15 Robert G. Picard, "Unique Characteristics and Business Dynamics of Media Products," *Journal of Media Business Studies* 2.2 (2005): 61–69.

16 Hanna-Kaisa Ellonen, "Exploring the Strategic Impact of Technological Change: Studies on the Role of Internet in Magazine Publishing" (Ph.D. thesis, Lappeenranta University of Technology, *Acta Universitatis Lappeenrantaensis*, No. 261, 2007), 64.

17 Vera Valanto, Miia Kosonen, and Hanna-Kaisa Ellonen, "Are Publishers Ready for Tomorrow? Publishers' Capabilities and Online Innovations," *International Journal of Innovation Management* 16.1 (February 2012): 1–18.

18 Hanna-Kaisa Ellonen, Patrik Wikström, and Ari Jantunen, "Linking Dynamic Capability Portfolios and Innovation Outcomes," *Technovation* 29.11 (2009): 753–762.

19 Ari Jantunen, Hanna-Kaisa Ellonen, and Anette Johansson, "Beyond Appearances—Do Dynamic Capabilities of Innovative Firms Actually Differ?" *European Management Journal* 30.2 (2012): 141–155; Anette Johansson, Hanna-Kaisa Ellonen, and Ari Jantunen, "Magazine Publishers Embracing New Media: Exploring Their Capabilities and Decision Making Logic," *Journal of Media Business Studies* 9.2 (Summer 2012): 97–114.

20 For more reading on decision-making logics, see, for example, Saras Sarasvathy, "Causation and Effectuation: Toward a Theoretical Shift from Economic Inevitability to Entrepreneurial Contingency," *Academy of Management Review* 26.2 (2001): 243–263.

21 Johansson, Ellonen, and Jantunen, "Magazine Publishers Embracing New Media," 105–112.

22 Anette Johansson and Alexander McKelvie, "Unpacking the Antecedents of Effectuation and Causation in a Corporate Context," *Frontiers of Entrepreneurship Research* 32.17 (2012): Article 1.

23 For more reading on business models, see Alexander Osterwalder, Yves Pigneur, and Christopher Tucci, "Clarifying Business Models: Origins, Present and Future of the Concept," *Communications of the Association for Information Systems* 15 (May 2005): 1–25; and Christopher Zott and Raphael Amit, "Business Model Design: An Activity System Perspective," *Long Range Planning* 43.2 (2010): 216–226.

24 Charles P. Daly, Patrick Henry, and Ellen Ryder, *The Magazine Publishing Industry* (Boston, MA: Allyn and Bacon, 1997), 12–13.

25 Robert G. Picard, *The Economics and Financing of Media Companies* (New York: Fordham University Press, 2002), 21–47.

26 Lucy Küng, *Strategic Management in the Media: Theory to Practice* (London: Sage Publications, 2008), 15–105.

27 John Gallaugher, Pat Auger, and Anat BarNir, "Revenue Streams and Digital Content Providers: An Empirical Investigation," *Innovation & Management* 38.7 (August 2001): 473–485.

28 Florian Stahl, Marc-Frederic Schäfer, and Wolfgang Mass, "Strategies for Selling Paid Content on Newspaper and Magazine Web Sites: An Empirical Analysis of Bundling and Splitting of News and Magazine Articles," *International Journal on Media Management* 6.1/2 (2004): 59–66.

29 Patrik Wikström and Hanna-Kaisa Ellonen, "The Impact of Social Media Features on Print Media Firms' Online Business Model," *Journal of Media Business Studies* 9.3 (2012): 63–80.

30 Olli Kuivalainen, Hanna-Kaisa Ellonen, and Liisa-Maija Sainio, "An Online Success Story: The Role of an Online Service in a Magazine Publisher's Business Model," *International Journal of E-Business Research* 3.3 (2007): 43–59.

31 Ellonen, Wikström, and Jantunen, "Linking Dynamic Capability Portfolios and Innovation Outcomes," 753–762.

32 For further reading on dynamic capabilities, see, for example, David J. Teece, "Explicating Dynamic Capabilities: The Nature and Microfoundations of (Sustainable) Enterprise Performance," *Strategic Management Journal* 28.13 (December 2007): 1319–1350.

33 Johansson and McKelvie, "Unpacking the Antecedents of Effectuation and Causation."

34 For further reading on entrepreneurial decision-making logic see, for example, Sarasvathy, "Causation and Effectuation," 243–263.

35 Ellonen, Wikström, and Jantunen, "Linking Dynamic Capability Portfolios and Innovation Outcomes," 753–762.

36 Hanna Silvennoinen and Ari Jantunen, "Dynamic Capabilities and Innovation in the Magazine Publishing Industry" (paper presented at the 23rd ISPIM Conference, Barcelona, Spain, 17–20 June 2012).

37 Sarasvathy, "Causation and Effectuation," 243–263.

38 Johansson and McKelvie, "Unpacking the Antecedents of Effectuation and Causation."

39 Rita Järventie-Thesleff, Mikko Villi, and Johanna Moisander, "Traditional and Online Publishing in Juxtaposition—A Comparison of Change Management Practices" (paper presented at EMMA Annual Conference, Budapest, 10–12 February 2012).

40 For international industry data, see FIPP—The Worldwide Magazine Media Association <http://www.fipp.com>, accessed 18 February 2013.

41 For more reading on brand management, see, for example, David A. Aaker, *Managing Brand Equity: Capitalizing on the Value of a Brand Name* (New York: Free Press, 1991).

42 Gillian Doyle, *Understanding Media Economics* (London: Sage Publications, Ltd., 2002), 137–140.

43 Ellonen, Jantunen, and Kuivalainen, "The Strategic Impact of Internet on Magazine Publishing," 346–357.

44 See, for example, Walter S. McDowell, "Issues in Marketing and Branding," in Alan B. Albarran, Sylvia M. Chan-Olmsted, and Michael O. Wirth, eds., *Handbook of Media Management and Economics* (Mahwah, NJ: Lawrence Erlbaum Associates, 2006), 229–250.

45 Marianne Horppu, Olli Kuivalainen, Anssi Tarkiainen, and Hanna-Kaisa Ellonen, "Online Satisfaction, Trust and Loyalty, and the Impact of the Offline Parent Brand," *Journal of Product and Brand Management* 17.6 (2008): 403–413.

46 Anssi Tarkiainen, Hanna-Kaisa Ellonen, and Olli Kuivalainen, "Complementing Consumer Magazine Brands with Internet Extensions?" *Internet Research* 19.4 (2009): 408–424.

47 Paweena Srisuwan and Stuart Barnes, "Predicting Online Channel Use for an Online and Print Magazine: A Case Study," *Internet Research* 18.3 (2008): 266–285.

48 Hanna-Kaisa Ellonen, Anssi Tarkiainen, and Olli Kuivalainen, "The Effect of Magazine Web Site Usage on Print Magazine Loyalty," *International Journal on Media Management* 12.1 (March 2010): 21–37.

49 Hanna-Kaisa Ellonen, Anssi Tarkiainen, and Olli Kuivalainen, "The Effect of Website Usage and Virtual Community Participation on Brand Relationships," *International Journal of Internet Marketing and Advertising* 6.1 (2010): 85–105.

50 Ellonen, Jantunen, and Kuivalainen, "The Strategic Impact of Internet on Magazine Publishing," 346–357.

51 Marko Ala-Fossi, Piet Bakker, Hanna-Kaisa Ellonen, Lucy Küng, Stephen Lax, Charo Sabada, and Richard van der Wurff, "The Impact of the Internet on the Business Models in the Media Industries—A Sector-by-Sector Analysis," in Lucy Küng, Robert G. Picard, and Ruth Towse, eds., *The Internet and the Mass Media* (Los Angeles, London: Sage Publications, 2008), 149–169.

52 For more reading on brand communities, see for example, Albert Muniz and Thomas O'Guinn, "Brand Community," *Journal of Consumer Research* 27.4 (2001): 412–432; and James McAlexander, John Schouten, and Harold Koenig, "Building Brand Community," *Journal of Marketing* 66.1 (2002): 38–54.

53 Tobias Johansson, "Lighting the Campfire: The Creation of a Community of Interest around a Media Company," *International Journal on Media Management* 4.1 (2002): 4–12; Laura Davidson, Lisa McNeill, and Shelagh Ferguson, "Magazine Communities: Brand Community Formation in Magazine Consumption," *International Journal of Sociology and Social Policy* 27.5/6 (2007): 208–220; and Hanna-Kaisa Ellonen, Miia Kosonen, and Kaisa Henttonen, "The Development of a Sense of Virtual Community," *International Journal of Web-Based Communities* 3.1 (2007): 114–130.

54 Ellonen, "Exploring the Strategic Impact of Technological Change," 55–62.

55 Davidson, McNeil, and Ferguson, "Magazine Communities," 208–220.

56 Hanna-Kaisa Ellonen and Olli Kuivalainen, "Exploring a Successful Magazine Web Site," *Management Research News* 31.5 (2008): 386–398.

57 Ellonen, Tarkiainen, and Kuivalainen, "The Effect of Website Usage and Virtual Community Participation on Brand Relationships," 85–105.

58 Aris and Bughin, *Managing Media Companies*, 397.

Bibliography

Aaker, David A. *Managing Brand Equity: Capitalizing on the Value of a Brand Name.* New York: Free Press, 1991.

Ala-Fossi, Marko; Bakker, Piet; Ellonen, Hanna-Kaisa; Küng, Lucy; Lax, Stephen; Sabada, Charo; and van der Wurff, Richard. "The Impact of the Internet on the Business Models in the Media Industries—A Sector-by-Sector Analysis." In Küng, Lucy; Picard, Robert G.; and Towse, Ruth, eds. *The Internet and the Mass Media.* Los Angeles, London: Sage Publications, 2008, 149–169.

Albarran, Alan B.; Chan-Olmsted, Sylvia M.; and Wirth, Michael O., eds. *Handbook of Media Management and Economics.* Mahwah, NJ: Lawrence Erlbaum Associates, 2006.

Aris, Annet and Bughin, Jacques. *Managing Media Companies: Harnessing Creative Value.* Chichester, UK: John Wiley & Sons, 2005.

Barney, Jay. "Firm Resources and Sustained Competitive Advantage." *Journal of Management* 17.1 (March 1991): 99–120.

Barsh, Joanna; Kramer, Emily E.; Maue, David; and Zuckerman, Neal. "Magazines' Home Companion." [Special Edition] *McKinsey Quarterly* 2 (Spring 2001): 82–91.

Chan-Olmsted, Sylvia M. *Competitive Strategy for Media Firms: Strategic and Brand Management in Changing Media Markets.* Mahwah, NJ: Lawrence Erlbaum Associates, 2006.

Daly, Charles P.; Henry, Patrick; and Ryder, Ellen. *The Magazine Publishing Industry.* Boston, MA: Allyn and Bacon, 1997.

Davidson, Laura; McNeill, Lisa; and Ferguson, Shelagh. "Magazine Communities: Brand Community Formation in Magazine Consumption." *International Journal of Sociology and Social Policy* 27.5/6 (2007): 208–220.

Doyle, Gillian. *Understanding Media Economics.* London: Sage Publications, Ltd., 2002.

Ellonen, Hanna-Kaisa. "Exploring the Strategic Impact of Technological Change: Studies on the Role of Internet in Magazine Publishing." Ph.D. thesis, Lappeenranta University of Technology. *Acta Universitatis Lappeenrantaensis.* No. 261, 2007.

Ellonen, Hanna-Kaisa; Jantunen, Ari; and Kuivalainen, Olli. "The Strategic Impact of Internet on Magazine Publishing." *International Journal of Innovation and Technology Management* 5.3 (2008): 341–361.

Ellonen, Hanna-Kaisa; Kosonen, Miia; and Henttonen, Kaisa. "The Development of a Sense of Virtual Community." *International Journal of Web-Based Communities* 3.1 (2007): 114–130.

Ellonen, Hanna-Kaisa and Kuivalainen, Olli. "Exploring a Successful Magazine Web Site." *Management Research News* 31.5 (2008): 386–398.

Ellonen, Hanna-Kaisa; Tarkiainen, Anssi; and Kuivalainen, Olli. "The Effect of Magazine Web Site Usage on Print Magazine Loyalty." *International Journal on Media Management* 12.1 (March 2010): 21–37.

Ellonen, Hanna-Kaisa; Tarkiainen, Anssi; and Kuivalainen, Olli. "The Effect of Website Usage and Virtual Community Participation on Brand Relationships." *International Journal of Internet Marketing and Advertising* 6.1 (2010): 85–105.

Ellonen, Hanna-Kaisa; Wikström, Patrik; and Jantunen, Ari. "Linking Dynamic Capability Portfolios and Innovation Outcomes." *Technovation* 29.11 (2009): 753–762.

European Media Management Education Association. "Seminal Reading on Media Management and Media Economics" <http://www.media-management.eu/member-directory/seminal-readings.html>, accessed 30 August 2013.

FIPP—The Worldwide Magazine Media Association <http://www.fipp.com>, accessed 18 February 2013.

Gallaugher, John; Auger, Pat; and BarNir, Anat. "Revenue Streams and Digital Content Providers: An Empirical Investigation." *Innovation & Management* 38.7 (August 2001): 473–485.

Hafstrand, Helene. "Competitive Advantage in the Magazine Publishing Business—A Resource-Based Perspective." Paper presented at the 15th Nordic Conference on Media and Communication Research, Reykjavik, 10–13 August 2001.

Horppu, Marianne; Kuivalainen, Olli; Tarkiainen, Anssi; and Ellonen, Hanna-Kaisa. "Online Satisfaction, Trust and Loyalty, and the Impact of the Offline Parent Brand." *Journal of Product and Brand Management* 17.6 (2008): 403–413.

Jantunen, Ari; Ellonen, Hanna-Kaisa; and Johansson, Anette. "Beyond Appearances—Do Dynamic Capabilities of Innovative Firms Actually Differ?" *European Management Journal* 30.2 (Summer 2012): 141–155.

Järventie-Thesleff, Rita; Villi, Mikko; and Moisander, Johanna. "Traditional and Online Publishing in Juxtaposition—A Comparison of Change Management Practices." Paper presented at EMMA Annual Conference, Budapest, 10–12 February 2012.

Johansson, Anette; Ellonen, Hanna-Kaisa; and Jantunen, Ari. "Magazine Publishers Embracing New Media: Exploring Their Capabilities and Decision Making Logic." *Journal of Media Business Studies* 9.2 (Summer 2012): 97–114.

Johansson, Anette and McKelvie, Alexander. "Unpacking the Antecedents of Effectuation and Causation in a Corporate Context." *Frontiers of Entrepreneurship Research* 32.17 (2012): Article 1.

Johansson, Tobias. "Lighting the Campfire: The Creation of a Community of Interest around a Media Company." *International Journal on Media Management* 4.1 (2002): 4–12.

Kaiser, Ulrich. "Magazines and Their Companion Websites: Competing Outlet Channels?" *Review of Marketing Science* 4.3 (August 2006): 1–24.

Kuivalainen, Olli; Ellonen, Hanna-Kaisa; and Sainio, Liisa-Maija. "An Online Success Story: The Role of an Online Service in a Magazine Publisher's Business Model." *International Journal of E-Business Research* 3.3 (2007): 43–59.

Küng, Lucy. *Strategic Management in the Media: Theory to Practice*. London: Sage Publications, 2008.

McAlexander, James; Schouten, John; and Koenig, Harold. "Building Brand Community." *Journal of Marketing* 66.1 (2002): 38–54.

McDowell, Walter S. "Issues in Marketing and Branding." In Albarran, Alan B.; Chan-Olmsted, Sylvia M.; and Wirth, Michael O., eds. *Handbook of Media Management and Economics*. Mahwah, NJ: Lawrence Erlbaum Associates, 2006, 229–250.

Mierzjewska, Bozena I. and Hollifield, C. Ann. "Theoretical Approaches in Media Management Research." In Albarran, Alan B.; Chan-Olmsted, Sylvia M.; and Wirth, Michael O., eds. *Handbook of Media Management and Economics*. Mahwah, NJ: Lawrence Erlbaum Associates, 2006, 37–66.

Muniz, Albert and O'Guinn, Thomas. "Brand Community." *Journal of Consumer Research* 27.4 (2001): 412–432.

Osterwalder, Alexander; Pigneur, Yves; and Tucci, Christopher. "Clarifying Business Models: Origins, Present and Future of the Concept." *Communications of the Association for Information Systems* 15 (May 2005): 1–25.

Peteraf, Margaret. "The Cornerstones of Competitive Advantage: A Resource-Based Perspective." *Strategic Management Journal* 14.3 (1993): 179–191.

Picard, Robert G. "Cash Cows or Entrecôte: Publishing Companies and Disruptive Technologies." *Trends in Communication* 11.2 (2003): 127–136.

Picard, Robert G. *The Economics and Financing of Media Companies.* New York: Fordham University Press, 2002.

Picard, Robert G. "Unique Characteristics and Business Dynamics of Media Products." *Journal of Media Business Studies* 2.2 (2005): 61–69.

Porter, Michael. *Competitive Advantage: Creating and Sustaining Superior Performance.* New York: Free Press, 1985.

Sarasvathy, Saras. "Causation and Effectuation: Toward a Theoretical Shift from Economic Inevitability to Entrepreneurial Contingency." *Academy of Management Review* 26.2 (2001): 243–263.

Silvennoinen, Hanna and Jantunen, Ari. "Dynamic Capabilities and Innovation in the Magazine Publishing Industry." Paper presented at the 23rd ISPIM Conference, Barcelona, Spain, 17–20 June 2012.

Simon, Daniel H. and Kadiyali, Vrinda. "The Effect of a Magazine's Free Digital Content on Its Print Circulation: Cannibalization or Complementarity?" *Information Economics and Policy* 19.3/4 (October 2007): 344–361.

Srisuwan, Paweena and Barnes, Stuart. "Predicting Online Channel Use for an Online and Print Magazine: A Case Study." *Internet Research* 18.3 (2008): 266–285.

Stahl, Florian; Schäfer, Marc-Frederic; and Mass, Wolfgang. "Strategies for Selling Paid Content on Newspaper and Magazine Web Sites: An Empirical Analysis of Bundling and Splitting of News and Magazine Articles." *International Journal on Media Management* 6.1/2 (2004): 59–66.

Tarkiainen, Anssi; Ellonen, Hanna-Kaisa; and Kuivalainen, Olli. "Complementing Consumer Magazine Brands with Internet Extensions?" *Internet Research* 19.4 (2009): 408–424.

Teece, David J. "Explicating Dynamic Capabilities: The Nature and Microfoundations of (Sustainable) Enterprise Performance." *Strategic Management Journal* 28.13 (December 2007): 1319–1350.

Valanto, Vera; Kosonen, Miia; and Ellonen, Hanna-Kaisa. "Are Publishers Ready for Tomorrow? Publishers' Capabilities and Online Innovations." *International Journal of Innovation Management* 16.1 (February 2012): 1–18.

Wikström, Patrik and Ellonen, Hanna-Kaisa. "The Impact of Social Media Features on Print Media Firms' Online Business Model." *Journal of Media Business Studies* 9.3 (2012): 63–80.

Zott, Christopher and Amit, Raphael. "Business Model Design: An Activity System Perspective." *Long Range Planning* 43.2 (2010): 216–226.

Part III

STUDIES IN CONTENT
Magazines as Textual Communication

13

GENDER, RACE AND ETHNICITY

Magazines and the Question of Self-Identity

Cheryl Renée Gooch

Among the most enduring questions raised by studies of magazine content and treatment of issues are the portrayals of women, men and people of diverse ethnic origins. Arguably one of the most prolific areas of study for contemporary scholars, research examines treatment and messages—both explicit and implicit—that appear in every dimension of the magazine form: editorial and advertising, verbal and visual. Contemporary research shows the issues are international, not just of concern to U.S. scholars and periodical content. Magazine studies by media scholars have used mostly established theoretical frameworks and approaches to inform research questions, often limiting the creation of knowledge and understanding of gender, race and ethnicity across broad, diverse sociocultural contexts. David Sumner posits that "a theoretical framework may not always be necessary or desirable in magazine research"[1] when seeking to construct models that predict behaviors of content producers or consumers. The research explored in this chapter indicates the need for diversified approaches to achieve more in-depth understanding of the human and sociological aspects of the issues under study. Armed with increasingly diverse theoretical perspectives and a growing body of empirical research, scholars examining gender, race and ethnicity are challenged to make sense of wide-ranging questions and measures as they plumb new aspects of the problems raised by periodical portrayals and assumptions about acceptable practices versus efforts to push the envelope.[2] This chapter explores and suggests improvements to approaches used to study the complexities of race, gender and ethnicity, and the question of self-identity in relation to magazines.

Literature Review and Method

As a woman of African descent who grew up during the era of civil rights and the Black cultural renaissance of the 1970s while participating in the desegregation of public schools, the author of this chapter has a lifelong interest in observing the role of mass media in documenting transformative social change. Gender, race and ethnicity and self-identity are complex, intersecting issues. For the purposes of this chapter, particular attention has been devoted to identifying media studies that explore these intersections and attempt to interpret the implications of findings for daily life issues and challenges.

Key search words and phrases for studies, both in media-based and related disciplines, included *gender, race, sexuality, ethnicity, portrayals,* and *women's, men's* and *magazines.* The search phrases yielded more than 50 studies informed by a range of theoretical perspectives, interpreting the effects or influence of mass media on identity, perspective and behavior. These issues have been explored in several related disciplines, including cultural studies, gender studies, psychology and sociology. The published studies explore the psycho-social implications of media effects and use.

The studies reviewed in this chapter are informed by a range of perspectives, including identity dissonance, social comparison and cultivation theoretical perspectives. Erving Goffman's pioneering study of gender depictions in magazine advertisements provides a relevant framework to explore how today's magazines convey messages about cultural norms and gender relations.[3] The identity dissonance framework, an elaboration of Leon Festinger's theory of cognitive dissonance, is evident in studies exploring gender identity dissonance experienced by readers of women's magazines who attempt to negotiate conflicting identities.[4] Carolyn Kitch's *Pages from the Past: History and Memory in American Magazines* provides consciously historical perspectives of how mass media, especially magazines, construct ideal body types and how cultural narratives perpetuate them.[5] Similarly, Herbert Blumer's symbolic interactionist perspective,[6] as applied to shared meanings of messages, informs recent media studies exploring identity issues associated with gender, race and ethnicity, as does the application of Albert Bandura's social learning theory's idea of modeling[7] to studying the influence of magazine advertisements on identity and behavior. Studies reviewed in the chapter address enduring questions raised by Nancy Signorielli and Michael Morgan,[8] and George Gerbner, Larry Gross, Michael Morgan and Nancy Signorielli[9] about the mass media's impact on the construction of reality and how frequent exposure to stereotypical portrayals of specific groups may cultivate audience beliefs about and expectations of those groups.

Researchers employing historical and cultural critical perspectives have contributed to the expanding body of literature from which magazine studies continue to draw. Jannette L. Dates and William Barlow's *Split Image: African Americans in the Mass Media* provides a historical framework for the on-going, complex relationship that segments of the African American community have with mediated racial depictions of them and their role in society.[10] In *Ladies' Pages: African American Women's Magazines and the Culture That Made Them,* Noliwe M. Rooks examines changing constructs of African American femininity and gender while exploring narrative strategies that African-American women's magazines use to confront or control cultural constructions of their targeted readers in relation to sex and sexuality.[11] Carolyn Kitch's *The Girl on the Magazine Cover: The Origins of Visual Stereotypes in American Mass Media,* which covers women's and men's imagery, challenges the outdated, even draconian, media definitions of gender that inform current debates about these issues and is a useful framework for exploring contemporary magazine content.[12]

Scholars who are critical of aspects of popular culture, advertising and cultural industries have provided informative frameworks for examining the impact and use of magazines in our multiracial, multi-gendered world. Ben Bagdikian's *New Media Monopoly* warned of the effects of corporate ownership and mass advertising on content, including pressure from advertisers on magazine editors.[13] Bagdikian's work informs the dominant, status quo themes that David Chison Oh addressed in a study of *Time's* coverage of Michelle Rhee, former chancellor of the District of Columbia Public Schools. Oh's study also reveals the magazine's use of "complementary objectivity."[14] Oh, buttressed by the work of Herbert Altschull and Theodore L. Glasser,[15] who have both argued that objectivity reproduces the dominant status quo, concludes that *Time's* purported impartial coverage promoted historical stereotypes of Asian Pacific Americans. Also, Sut Jhally's extensive critiques of commercial images and audience participation in the culture of consumerism provide insights into issues being explored by scholars of magazine studies across the globe.[16]

Theoretical Shifts

Media scholarship addressing gender, race and ethnicity reflects a shift toward exploring the complexities of identity. Rosalind Gill in *Gender and the Media*[17] examines the theoretical tools available for analyzing the often contradictory nature of contemporary gender representations while considering the impact of more complex theories of meaning to address questions raised by cultural politics. Analyzing gender in media texts, including magazines, Gill examines how representations of women and men are changing in the twenty-first century, partly in response to feminist, queer and anti-racist critique. She devotes a portion of her analysis to audience studies, noting the limitations of textual analysis in providing insight about how audiences consume and interpret media content. In the chapter "Gender in Magazines from *Cosmopolitan* to *Loaded*," Gill examines magazine discourses, ideological and thematic shifts in teen magazines, women's magazines and new constructions of masculinity in men's magazines.[18] Gill notes the need for researchers to be aware of divergent and even subversive interpretations made by readers of the content,[19] hence her emphasis on audience analysis and feminist cultural politics.

David Gauntlett, in his updated edition of *Media, Gender and Identity*, explores social theories and ideas about identity that offer broad, diverse perspectives on the role media play in the formation and negotiation of individual gender and sexual identities.[20] Gauntlett devotes two full chapters to men's and women's magazines. In "Men's Magazines and Modern Masculinities," he considers the ideas of manhood conveyed by the magazines and whether they are simply mainstream vehicles for old-fashioned attitudes and 'soft porn' pleasures or whether they offer new models of male identity to modern men.[21] In "Women's Magazines and Female Identities" he builds on earlier research on the history of women's magazines with their traditional emphasis on the home, beauty and finding a husband, to the success of the "independent and sexy" *Cosmopolitan* in the 1980s and 1990s.[22] In both chapters Gauntlett explores what these messages convey about gender and the possible impact of these messages on contemporary audiences. This work provides glimpses of new, creative methods being used to explore identities, an approach Gauntlett describes as the fluidity of identities and the decline of tradition.[23] He concludes that "popular ideas about the self in society have changed, so that identity is today seen as more fluid and transformable than ever before."[24]

In *Gender, Race, and Class in Media: A Critical Reader*, Gail Dines and Jean Humez present critical scholarship examining mass media as economic and cultural institutions that shape social and self- identities.[25] Several chapters in this volume provide insightful case studies that reflect changing theoretical approaches to analyzing the role of magazines in shaping gender, race and ethnic identities and how audiences and even the magazines are renegotiating or countering content. Chong-suk Han's "'Sexy Like a Girl and Horny Like a Boy': Contemporary Gay 'Western' Narratives about Gay Asian Men" includes an insightful discussion of how the now defunct *Noodle Magazine* attempted to offer alternative images of gay Asian men to those found in mainstream gay publications.[26] Han's study aims to contribute to literature on the intersection of race and sexuality and how such intersections inform the development of various identities among "multiply marginalized groups."[27] Barbara Mueller's "Reaching African American Consumers" criticizes the dearth of behavioral research on Black and ethnic consumers.[28] Citing the psychographics provided by special studies commissioned by *Essence* magazine, Mueller says the data show that, to successfully market to Black and ethnic consumers, advertisers need to tailor messages relevant to the daily lives of these consumers. This is a key point advocated by Gill and others for studies of audience and audience interpretations. Karen Goldman's "La Princesa Plastica: Hegemonic and Oppositional Representations of *Latinidad* in Hispanic Barbie" explores how *Pocho Magazine* and its accompanying Web site encourage people of Mexican heritage, including American assimilated Mexicans, to embrace their identity as one of "fluidity and hybridity,"[29] perspectives not usually offered in mainstream media.

Rebecca Lind's *Race/Gender/Class/Media 3.0: Considering Diversity across Content, Audiences, and Production* contains cultural and critical studies by scholars who investigate media content that represents limited ideas and images of marginalized social groups while unapologetically advocating for empowering the voices of these groups.[30] Sharing informed observations, as an Asian American woman, of *Audrey* magazine's representations of Asian American women to the public, Thuc Doan Nguyen finds that the magazine "reinforces the assimilationist ideal, showing a new generation of Asian America women that they should be just like women of their mother's generation and of their grandmother's generation before that."[31] Nguyen concludes that *Audrey* does not meet its stated goals of serving as a lifestyle magazine for Asian American women but instead reflects an American lifestyle. She calls for stronger advocacy of informed examinations of portrayals affecting regular Asian American women. In a similar culture-centered framework, Cindy S. Vincent's ethnographic study of the citizen-led *POOR Magazine* demonstrates how citizens' media and community education when applied to the magazine format helps articulate the voices of subjects historically ignored or misrepresented.[32]

Content and Textual Analytic Studies

Content and textual analytic studies point to useful knowledge that emerges from raising new, different questions while expanding assumptions about gender, race and identity. In one of the first studies to use social comparison theory as a framework to examine the male muscular body ideal and its possible effects on men, Cheryl Law and Magdala Peixoto Labre analyzed images of male bodies in the popular magazines *GQ*, *Rolling Stone* and *Sports Illustrated* from 1967 to 1997. They found that the featured male bodies increasingly conformed to the thin ideal of attractiveness, namely lean, muscular and V-shaped.[33] Noting the importance of studying body images as an indicator of how men compare themselves to sociocultural ideals of attractiveness, Joseph Schwartz and Julie L. Andsager found a similar trend toward thin muscularity in an analysis covering the four-decade period from 1967 to 2008 of images published in the *Advocate* and *Out*, the highest-circulation magazines targeted to gay men.[34]

Portrayal studies of women both in advertisements and editorial coverage, national and global, reveal an array of issues informing ideas of sexual and gender identity, fashion, beauty and social position. Analyzing U.S. magazine advertisements from 2003 as an extension of a study that assessed sex in advertising in 1983 and 1993, Tom Reichert and Courtney Carpenter found overall increases in sexualized dress, intimate contact and explicitly dressed female models.[35] Katherine Frith, Ping Shaw and Hong Cheng's cross-cultural analysis of ads from women's fashion and beauty magazines in Singapore and the United States found differences in the construction of beauty and suggests further study of the objectification of women within cultural contexts of origin.[36] Analyzing the growth of international women's magazines in China, Yang Feng and Katherine Frith compared the content of advertising in U.S.-inspired *Cosmopolitan China* with Japanese *Rayli Fashion and Beauty* and the local Chinese magazine *Women's Friend*.[37] Finding that Western-brands are more predominate in the international magazines than in local magazines and that the former feature mostly white models while the Japanese and local Chinese magazines use mostly Asian models, the authors question the continued prevalence of Western cultural imperialism.

Rhea Sengupta's study of the representations of Black, East Asian and white women in magazines for adolescent girls also considers the intersection of race and gender in advertising. The results of this study illustrate that traditional stereotypes persist while some new stereotypes are being formed. Designed to compare how white, Black and East Asian women were portrayed in advertisements found in fashion magazines directed at adolescent girls, the study gave evidence of a correlation between race and the kind of product advertised: Black women were prominent in clothing advertisements; East Asian women were prominent in advertisements for technology products.[38] Sengupta argues that these results illustrate that old stereotypes may still exist (white beauty ideal, hypersexual Black women), and some new stereotypes are being formed (technologically savvy East Asians). Presenting a theory of gender identity dissonance and examining the complexity of marketing gender identity dissonance to women, Sarah B. Crymble analyzed De Beer's right-hand ring advertising campaign featured in women's magazines from 1998 to 2006.[39] "Advertisements and information gathered from industry sources indicate that there is a conscious focus within the industry . . . towards the representation and [use] of feminine complexity and female gender identity dissonance to product marketing."[40]

Jennifer E. Millard and Peter R. Grant's examination of the portrayal of Black and white women in magazine advertisements and fashion spreads in *Cosmopolitan, Glamour* and *Vogue* targeted to predominately white Canadian women found prevalent incidences of explicitly sexual and submissive poses. Yet their findings reflect unanticipated responses from the study's respondents. Mostly white Canadian college students, many interpreted the submissive poses of Black models as more positive than negative and associated the models with intelligence and achievement.[41] Millard and Grant note the need for further research, both to replicate and explain the complexity of the findings and to examine whether other less educated and more biased segments of Canadian society would have similar interpretations. They recommend more in-depth, qualitative examination of how people form impressions of models in advertising and fashion industries.

Brian Moeran, from his innovative study of beauty in both ads and texts of international magazines, such as *Elle, Vogue* and *Marie Claire*, concludes that both editors and advertisers "adopt a 'technology of enchantment' as a means of exercising control over their readers."[42] Based on a content analysis of more than 700 issues of these titles published in France, Hong Kong, Japan, the United Kingdom and the United States, the finding that magazine and advertising language is imbued with a kind of "magical power" is buttressed by ethnographic interviews of editorial staff and readers of these magazines.[43]

Sheila M. Webb's textual analysis of Reiman magazines shows how the role of suburban, middle-class, white women is tied to traditional values, religion and presumed core American cultural values.[44] Employing in-depth interviews, close textual reading, narrative and rhetorical analysis, the study demonstrates how an imagined community is constructed and suggests how these magazines frame and build core values, binding readers into a community by voicing a shared lifestyle and self-image.[45] Juanita J. Covert and Travis L. Dixon, after investigating trends in the representation of women of color in mainstream women's magazines, identified the need for further study of the characteristics of these portrayals and recommend qualitative interviews or focus groups to provide additional understanding of how readers of color react psychologically and emotionally to these representations.[46]

Studies of popular magazine framing of texts and coverage continue to explore questions about girls' and women's self-perceptions and others' purported perceptions of them. Suchi P. Joshi, Peter Jochen and Patti M. Valkenburg extended the ambivalence concept to their content analysis of sexual, relationship and gender role texts and images in the teen girl magazine *Seventeen* from 1997 and 2007.[47] Their findings suggest scholars would do well to use the ambivalence concept, that is, messages about sex and sexuality that contradict each other, in analyses of other teen magazines and media in general, in discussing the ambivalent coverage of sex, relationships and gender roles in media.

Elizabeth A. Daniels's analysis of photos on covers and in feature stories in *YM, Teen Vogue, Teen People, Seventeen* and *CosmoGirl* magazines revealed that, overall, there were very few images of women engaged in sport or fitness activities in magazines that teen girls popularly read. When women were portrayed in a physical activity, they were engaged in fitness, rather than sport activities, a pattern consistent with the emphasis on women's physical and sexual attractiveness in U.S. society.[48] Ethnic minority magazines, such as *Ebony* and *Latina*, resemble mainstream magazines in their lack of images of women athletes. Daniels suggests both further exploration of on-line magazine ad formats and critiques of embedded messages of the images of overly thin, standard portrayal of females still prevalent in media.

Emma Bedor and Atsushi Tajima used textual analysis to examine *People* magazine's use of celebrity mothers' postpartum weight loss as a primary tool in assessing motherhood competency. They found an emerging fitness narrative in the popular medium that places the postpartum body among other anti-fat discourses demanding weight loss.[49] The study presents a preliminary examination of this trend through textual analysis but suggests that research further explore the effects such narratives have on readers. Bushra H. Rahman's analysis of news articles about politically engaged Muslim women in countries such as Pakistan, Indonesia, Bangladesh, Iran and Malaysia that appeared in *Time* and *Newsweek* between early 1979 and late 2002 revealed traces of gender stereotyping of such women leaders as celebrities estranged from other oppressed women.[50] Karen Grandy's preliminary study of the inclusion of women as feature profile subjects, interviewees and cover photo subjects in popular American and Canadian business magazines in 2010 suggests continued marginalization. The profile subject, interview and cover photo data suggest that women are considered to be less newsworthy than men, have less experience and expertise and are less able to attract popular business magazine readers.[51]

Content analyses of portrayals of racial groups in magazine ads as well as discourses about interracial relationships illustrate the use of cultivation effects, critical race frameworks and longitudinal studies in examining race content. Grounding their study in cultivation effects theory, Ki-Young Lee and Sung-Hee Joo's content analysis of popular magazines to identify the frequency and nature of Asian American portrayals in ads revealed that stereotypic "model minority" themes persist.[52] Such stereotypes, reflected and reinforced through advertising, may contribute to biased expectations and negative consequences for Asian Americans. Noting previous research that examined minorities' representation in advertising in mainstream media but not media popular with minority consumers, Silvia Knobloch-Westerwick and Brendon Coates also asked how advertisements contribute to the cultivation of perceptions of these groups. Their content analysis of models of African, Asian and Hispanic descent appearing in *Better Homes and Gardens, National Geographic* and *Good Housekeeping* advertisements showed that each ethnic group had its highest representation in ads in magazines popular with the respective groups.[53] Robin T. Peterson's study of the frequency of depictions of models of African, Asian, Hispanic and European descent in consumer magazine advertisements over a 10-year period found that minority group models were generally featured relative to their proportion in the total U.S. population and in a favorable manner, relative to white models.[54] Similarly, Thomas H. Stevenson's longitudinal study of the portrayal of African Americans in magazine advertisements suggests an increase in frequency and no negative stereotypes.[55] Catherine A. Luther and Jodi L. Rightler-McDaniels's discourse analysis of news stories about interracial marriages appearing in general audience magazines *Newsweek* and *Time* and in African-American–targeted magazines *Ebony* and *JET*, in the 40-year period between 1960 and 2011, revealed negative undertones.[56] The researchers concluded, based on their findings and analysis that drew on the *critical race theory* framework, that interracial relationships are rejected due to subtle racism and underlying efforts to maintain race-related subordination.

Critical Perspectives and Effects

Media studies addressing the intersections of gender, race and ethnicity offer a range of rhetorical, social scientific and critical or cultural perspectives that increasingly inform research questions. Recent critical analyses and effects studies of race, gender and ethnicity explore in meaningful depth the implications of these issues on social identity while challenging assumptions that have informed approaches to magazine research. Lisa Duke examined culture as a mitigating factor in adolescents' media uses and gratifications by interviewing middle-class African-American and white female readers of popular teen magazines.[57] Looking for their interpretations of the feminine ideal presented in these texts, the Black and white girls revealed different uses and gratifications in response to the content that reflected conflicting messages of beauty and racial bias that they found unappealing or offensive. Similarly, J. Robyn Goodman's study of how Latina and white women read and incorporate the thin body ideal featured in magazines found that the two groups negotiate differently the concepts of idealized body types.[58] The study considers how Latina women's exposure to Hispanic culture, which offers alternative feminine ideals, prompts them to resist the mediated ideal more than could white women.

Additional effects studies show that continuing exposure to thin ideal images in women's magazines is associated with preoccupation with ideal body types. Steven R. Thomsen's survey of college-age woman between 18 and 25 found health and fitness magazine reading was directly linked to body shape concerns, as well as indirectly linked to beliefs about men's thinness expectations and, to a lesser degree, expected future weight gain or loss.[59]

Building on studies demonstrating the association between exposure to media-disseminated thinness ideals and body image concerns among women, who at the same time assert that media effects on peers are greater than media effects on themselves, Stella C. Chia investigated the third-person effect in relation to college-age women in Singapore. Concerned with idealized body image and weight-loss, the respondents reported thinness, as portrayed in magazine ads, to be positively associated with their intention to lose weight and perceived the same ads to have a greater effect on their peers.[60] Stella C. Chia and Nainan Wen's investigation of college men's third-person perception in relation to body image factors among students of Chinese descent in Singapore found a positive relationship between the respondents' media exposure to idealized body images and their body dissatisfaction.[61]

Zhengjia Liu and Lulu Rodriguez's investigation of the impact of psychological and social motive for the use of fashion magazines among female college students in Shanghai, China, revealed desires to enhance current body image and prepare for future career roles as significant predictors of fashion magazine use. Their findings suggest that the desire to satisfy consumerist needs do not motivate students' fashion magazine use.[62] Liu and Rodriguez suggest future investigations adopt critical cultural approaches to understanding consumption habits.

Studies of male depictions, body images and sexual attitudes have increasingly critiqued findings within broader societal contexts, thus making much needed contributions to the study of men's magazines. Deana A. Rohlinger's study of male objectification in advertisements examined how activism and changing American values have influenced advertiser practices while positioning these sexualized images in larger social, political and economic contexts. The study suggests the erotic male has become a depiction that dominates mainstream conceptions of masculinity.[63] Exploring associations between reading Lad—a British term for men's magazines with more permissive content—and pornographic magazines and college males' attitudes and sexual beliefs, as well as impact on their sexual self-schema, Laramie D. Taylor's study suggests there are differences in the way these magazines are read or experienced. The results indicate a relationship between reading Lad magazines and endorsement of permissive sexual attitudes and expectations of greater sexual variety, while reading pornographic magazines is associated with permissive sexual attitudes.[64] As both kinds of magazines appeal to male sexual identity and beliefs consistent with the content, further investigation into the influence on the content on long-term attitudes, identities and behaviors of college males would be insightful. Donnalyn Pompper, Jorge Soto and Lauren Piel's lab study of male body image used both social comparison theory to examine how males use magazine images to benchmark the ideal male and a modified theory of magazines as standard bearers for the ideal man, based on the assumption that magazines set standards for both sexes. The multi-racial and generational respondents, while mostly cynical of magazine images of male bodies, expressed extreme dissatisfaction with their bodies and how the images constantly remind them of how they do not measure up.[65]

Conclusion

The last decade and a half's media scholarship addressing the intersections of gender, race and ethnicity in magazines reflects a range of rhetorical, social scientific and critical perspectives that inform old and new research questions. Behavioral scientists, overall, have been more assertive in examining issues of gender, race and ethnicity and the psycho-social implications of media effects and use. Their work prompts the question, "How much does or should research from neighboring disciplines tie into or inform media studies?"

Dines and Humez's *Gender, Race and Class in Media*, a well-regarded source of critical mass media scholarship, has addressed these issues within broad cultural, political and economic contexts not often used in traditional approaches.[66] Noting how both the media landscape and the cultural field of ethnic minorities have changed, Simon Cottle's *Ethnic Minorities and the Media: Changing Cultural Boundaries* addresses how such recent developments threaten to outpace the researcher's ability to map, understand and intervene in processes of change. The work raises some key questions about the principal forces of change that currently shape the field and inform the questions researchers ask and pursue when examining the mass media and treatment of ethnic minorities.[67] In a similar vein, examining how people of color fit into the fabric of America and how the media tell them and others how they fit, Clint C. Wilson, II, Félix Gutiérrez and Lena M. Chao's *Racism, Sexism, and the Media: The Rise of Class Communication in Multicultural America* illustrates the complexity of racial and ethnic identities.[68]

A recurring theme of some of the recent studies cited in this chapter is what Lind calls "the concept of intersectionality,"[69] that is, the acknowledgement of the variety of influences on self-identity. Some of the cited studies directly address the interaction of race, gender and class, while others, to varying extent, are informed by intersectionality, that is, how different aspects of identity combine or intersect. Clearly, there is a need for further research on and more provocative questions about the intersections of gender, race and ethnicity in magazines.

Notes

1 David E. Sumner, "Theory? Bah Humbug!" *Journal of Magazine & New Media Research* 10.1 (Fall 2008): 1–2 <http://aejmcmagazine.arizona.edu/Journal/Fall2008/SumnerColumn.pdf>, accessed 9 September 2012.

2 Papers presented at the annual meeting, Association for Education in Journalism and Mass Communication, between 2007 and 2013, reflect these diverse approaches. The magazine studies summarized in conference paper abstracts on the AEJMC Web site, <http://www.aejmc.org/home/scholarship/abstracts-archive/>, with links and access dates by year, follow:

- **2013**: Chingshan Jiang, "Development of Men's Magazines Industry in Taiwan"; Andrew Mendelson and Nancy Morris, "Examining the Lens on the World: Reader Negotiation of Identity through *National Geographic* Coverage of Puerto Rico"; Chelsea Reynolds, "'50 Ways to Seduce a Man' vs. 'The Better Sex Diet': A Content Analysis"; Yan Yan, "Men's Images in Women's Eyes." <http://www.aejmc.org/home/2013/06/mag-2013-abstracts/>, accessed 28 September 2013.
- 2012: Catherine Luther, "'More Trouble than the Good Lord Ever Intended': Representations of Interracial Marriage in U.S. News Magazines." <http://www.aejmc.org/home/2012/04/mag-2012-abstracts/>, accessed 12 August 2012.
- 2011: Yan Yan and Kim Bissell, "The Globalization of Beauty: An Examination of Messages about Ideal Beauty Communicated to Readers of Fashion and Beauty Magazines Published Worldwide"; Stacey Hust, Paula Adams, Emily Marett, Jessica Willoughby, Chunbo Ren, Ming Lei, Weina Ran, Cassie Norman, and Marie Louise Radanielina-Hita, "Establishing and Adhering to Sexual Consent: The Association between Reading Magazines and College Students' Sexual Consent Negotiation"; and Zhengjia Liu, Marcia R. Prior-Miller, and Jie Yan, "China's Editorial Strategies: Self-Schema-Persuasion Perspectives on Localization vs. Internationalization: A Case Study of *Elle*." <http://www.aejmc.org/home/2011/06/mag-2011-abstracts/>, accessed 12 August 2012.
- 2010: Ashley Furrow, "Photographic Images of Gender and Race Portrayed in *Sports Illustrated for Kids*, 2000–2009"; Zhengjia Liu, "Psychological and Sociological Motives for Fashion Magazine Use among Shanghai's Female College Students"; and Jingyi Luo, "The Growth of International Women's Magazine and Media Portrayal of Women in China." <http://www.aejmc.com/?p=1469>, accessed 12 August 2012.
- 2009: Katherine Eaves, "Unrealistic Expectations: Representations of Celebrity Motherhood in *People* Magazine"; Yang Feng and Kavita Karan, "Women's Roles Portrayed in Women's Magazines in China: An Analysis of Global and Local Influences"; Catherine Luther, "Japanese Fashion Magazines as Reflections of Gender-Related Societal Changes in Japan"; and Sheila Webb, "The Creation of Community

in Reiman Magazines—A Reader Reception Study." <http://www.aejmc.com/home/2011/03/mag-2009-abstracts/>, accessed 12 August 2012.

- 2008: Naeemah Clark,"Looking into the Past, Present and the Future: Frames of Presidential Spouses in Popular News Magazines"; Andrea Duke and Jennifer Greer, "Athlete as 'Model' or Athlete as 'Power'? Gender Stereotypes of Athletic Women in Magazine Photographs"; and Teresa Mastin and Shalane Walker, "Selected Black Magazines' Mental Health Coverage, 2000–2007." <http://www.aejmc.com/home/2011/03/2008-abstracts/>, accessed 12 August 2012.
- 2007: Anya Britzius and Carol Schwalbe, "Images of Subordination, Independence, and Sexual Overtones: A Comparison of Advertisements in *Seventeen* and *Girl's Life* Magazines"; Donnalyn Pompper, Jorge Soto, and Lauren Piel, "Male Body Image and Magazine Standards: Considering Dimensions of Age and Ethnicity"; Kate Reil, "The Changing Shape of Beauty: An Analysis of Non-Stereotypical Body Types in Women's Magazine Advertising"; Tracey Thomas, "A Comparison of Bust and Bitch: The Paradox of Alternative Magazines"; Yi Tian, "How the *Advocate* Covered AIDS: A Content Analysis of the Gay Magazine's AIDS Coverage, 1981–2006." <http://www.aejmc.com/home/2011/03/mag-2007-abstracts/>, accessed 12 August 2012.

3 Erving Goffman, *Gender Advertisements* (Cambridge, MA: Harvard University Press, 1979).

4 Leon Festinger, *A Theory of Cognitive Dissonance* (Stanford, CA: Stanford University Press, 1957); Sarah B. Crymble, "Contradiction Sells: Feminine Complexity and Gender Identity Dissonance in Magazine Advertising," *Journal of Communication Inquiry* 36.1 (January 2012): 62–84.

5 Carolyn Kitch, *Pages from the Past: History and Memory in American Magazines* (Chapel Hill: University of North Carolina Press, 2005).

6 Herbert Blumer, *Symbolic Interactionism: Perspective and Method* (Berkeley: University of California Press, 1986).

7 Albert Bandura, "Social Learning Theory of Aggression," *Journal of Communication* 28.3 (September 1978): 12–29.

8 Nancy Signorielli and Michael Morgan, *Cultivation Analysis: New Directions in Media Effects Research* (Newbury Park, CA: Sage, 1990).

9 George Gerbner, Larry Gross, Michael Morgan, and Nancy Signorielli, "The 'Mainstreaming' of America: Violence Profile No. 11," *Journal of Communication* 30.3 (Summer 1980): 10–29.

10 Jannette L. Dates and William Barlow, eds., *Split Image: African Americans in the Mass Media*, 2nd ed. (Washington, DC: Howard University Press, 1993).

11 Noliwe M. Rooks, *Ladies' Pages: African American Women's Magazines and the Culture That Made Them* (New Brunswick, NJ: Rutgers University Press, 2004), 5.

12 Carolyn Kitch, *The Girl on the Magazine Cover: The Origins of Visual Stereotypes in American Mass Media* (Chapel Hill and London: University of North Carolina Press, 2001).

13 Ben H. Bagdikian, *The New Media Monopoly* (Boston: Beacon Press, 2004).

14 David Chison Oh, "Complementary Objectivity and Ideology: Reifying White Capitalist Hierarchies in *Time* Magazine's Construction of Michelle Rhee," *Journal of Communication Inquiry* 34.2 (April 2010): 153.

15 J. Herbert Altschull, *Agents of Power: The Media and Public Policy* (White Plains, NY: Longman, 1995), 63–66; Theodore L. Glasser, "Objectivity and News Bias," in Elliot D. Cohen, ed., *Philosophical Issues in Journalism* (New York: Oxford University Press, 1992), 176–183.

16 Sut Jhally, *The Codes of Advertising: Fetishism and the Political Economy of Meaning in the Consumer Society* (New York: Routledge, Chapman and Hall, 1990).

17 Rosalind Gill, *Gender and the Media* (Cambridge, UK: Polity Press, 2007), 3–4.

18 Rosalind Gill, "Gender in Magazines from *Cosmopolitan* to *Loaded*," *Gender and the Media* (Cambridge, UK: Polity Press, 2007), 180–217.

19 Gill, *Gender and the Media*, 216–217.

20 David Gauntlett, *Media, Gender and Identity: An Introduction*, 2nd ed. (London: Routledge, 2008).

21 David Gauntlett, "Men's Magazines and Modern Masculinities," *Media, Gender and Identity: An Introduction*, 2nd ed. (London: Routledge, 2008), 164–189.

22 David Gauntlett, "Women's Magazines and Female Identities," *Media, Gender and Identity: An Introduction*, 2nd ed. (London: Routledge, 2008), 190.

23 Gauntlett, *Media, Gender and Identity*, 247.

24 Gauntlett, *Media, Gender and Identity*, 278.

25 Gail Dines and Jean M. Humez, eds., *Gender, Race, and Class in Media: A Critical Reader*, 3rd ed. (Thousand Oaks, CA: Sage, 2011).

26 Chong-suk Han, "'Sexy Like a Girl and Horny Like a Boy': Contemporary Gay 'Western' Narratives about Gay Asian Men," in Gail Dines and Jean M. Humez, eds., *Gender, Race, and Class in Media: A Critical Reader*, 3rd ed. (Thousand Oaks, CA: Sage, 2011), 163–170.

27 Han, "'Sexy Like a Girl and Horny Like a Boy,'" 163.

28 Barbara Mueller, "Reaching African American Consumers: African American Shopping Behavior," in Gail Dines and Jean M. Humez, eds., *Gender, Race, and Class in Media: A Critical Reader*, 3rd ed. (Thousand Oaks, CA: Sage, 2011), 213–220.

29 Karen Goldman,"La Princesa Plastica: Hegemonic and Oppositional Representations of *Latinidad* in Hispanic Barbie," in Gail Dines and Jean M. Humez, eds., *Gender, Race, and Class in Media: A Critical Reader*, 3rd ed. (Thousand Oaks, CA: Sage, 2011), 380.

30 Rebecca Ann Lind, ed., *Race/Gender/Class/Media 3.0: Considering Diversity across Content, Audiences, and Production*, 3rd ed. (New York: Pearson, 2013).

31 Thuc Doan Nguyen, "*AudreyMagazine.com*: Portrayals of Asian American Women Online by Asian American Women," in Rebecca Ann Lind, ed., *Race/Gender/Class/Media 3.0: Considering Diversity across Content, Audiences, and Production*, 3rd ed. (New York: Pearson, 2013), 270.

32 Cindy S. Vincent, "*POOR Magazine* and Civic Engagement through Community Media," in Rebecca Ann Lind, ed., Race/Gender/Class/Media 3.0: Considering Diversity across Content, Audiences, and Production, 3rd ed. (New York: Pearson, 2013), 316–322.

33 Cheryl Law and Magdala Peixoto Labre, "Cultural Standards of Attractiveness: A Thirty-Year Look at Changes in Male Images in Magazines," *Journalism & Mass Communication Quarterly* 79.3 (Autumn 2002): 697–711.

34 Joseph Schwartz and Julie L. Andsager, "Four Decades of Images in Gay Male-Targeted Magazines," *Journalism & Mass Communication Quarterly* 88.1 (Spring 2011): 76–98.

35 Tom Reichert and Courtney Carpenter, "An Update on Sex in Magazine Advertising: 1983 to 2003," *Journalism & Mass Communication Quarterly* 81.4 (Winter 2004): 823–837.

36 Katherine Frith, Ping Shaw, and Hong Cheng, "The Construction of Beauty: A Cross-Cultural Analysis of Women's Magazine Advertising," *Journal of Communication* 55.1 (March 2005): 56–70 <http://onlinelibrary.wiley.com/doi/10.1111/j.1460–2466.2005.tb02658.x/pdf>, accessed 2 June 2014.

37 Yang Feng and Katherine Frith, "The Growth of International Women's Magazines in China and the Role of Transnational Advertising," *Journal of Magazine & New Media Research* 10.1 (Fall 2008): 1–14. <http://aejmcmagazine.arizona.edu/Journal/Fall2008/FengFrith.pdf>, accessed 21 September 2013.

38 Rhea Sengupta, "Reading Representations of Black, East Asian, and White Women in Magazines for Adolescent Girls," *Sex Roles* 54.11/12 (June 2006): 799–808.

39 Crymble, "Contradiction Sells," 62–84.

40 Crymble, "Contradiction Sells," 62.

41 Jennifer E. Millard and Peter R. Grant, "The Stereotypes of Black and White Women in Fashion Magazine Photographs: The Pose of the Model and the Impression She Creates," *Sex Roles* 54.9/10 (May 2006): 659–673.

42 Brian Moeran, "The Portrayal of Beauty in Women's Fashion Magazines," *Fashion Theory: The Journal of Dress, Body & Culture* 14.4 (December 2010): 507.

43 Moeran, "The Portrayal of Beauty in Women's Fashion Magazines," 507.

44 Sheila M. Webb, "The Narrative of Core Traditional Values in Reiman Magazines," *Journalism & Mass Communication Quarterly* 83.4 (December 2006): 865–882.

45 Webb, "The Narrative of Core Traditional Values," 881.

46 Juanita J. Covert and Travis L. Dixon, "A Changing View: Representation and Effects of the Portrayal of Women of Color in Mainstream Women's Magazines," *Communication Research* 35.2 (April 2008): 232–256.

47 Suchi P. Joshi, Peter Jochen, and Patti M. Valkenburg, "Ambivalent Messages in *Seventeen* Magazine: A Content Analytic Comparison of 1997 and 2007," *Journal of Magazine & New Media Research* 12.1 (Fall 2010): 1–20 <http://aejmcmagazine.arizona.edu/Journal/Fall2010/JoshiPeterValkenburg.pdf>, accessed 19 September 2012.

48 Elizabeth A. Daniels, "The Indivisibility of Women Athletes in Magazines for Teen Girls," *Women in Sport & Physical Activity Journal* 18.2 (Fall 2009): 14–24.

49 Emma Bedor and Atsushi Tajima, "No Fat Moms! Celebrity Mothers' Weight-Loss Narratives in *People* Magazine," *Journal of Magazine & New Media Research* 13.2 (Summer 2012): 1–26 <http://aejmcmagazine.arizona.edu/Journal/Summer2012/BedorTajima.pdf>, accessed 10 August 2012.

50 Bushra H. Rahman, "Analysis of the Coverage of Muslim Political Women in *Time* and *Newsweek*," *Journal of Media Studies* 25.1 (January 2010): 50–65.

51 Karen Grandy, "The Glossy Ceiling: Coverage of Women in Canadian and American Business Magazines," *Journal of Magazine & New Media Research* 14.1 (Spring 2013): 1–20 <http://aejmcmagazine.arizona.edu/Journal/Summer2013/Grandy.pdf>, accessed 21 September 2013.

52 Ki-Young Lee and Sung-Hee Joo, "The Portrayal of Asian Americans in Mainstream Magazine Ads: An Update," *Journalism & Mass Communication Quarterly* 82.3 (Autumn 2005): 654, 664.

53 Silvia Knobloch-Westerwick and Brendon Coates, "Minority Models in Advertisements in Magazines Popular with Minorities," *Journalism & Mass Communication Quarterly* 83.3 (Autumn 2006): 596–614.

54 Robin T. Peterson, "Consumer Magazine Advertisement Portrayal of Models by Race in the U.S.: An Assessment," *Journal of Marketing Communications* 13.3 (September 2007): 199–211.

55 Thomas H. Stevenson, "Four Decades of African American Portrayals in Magazine Advertising," *Journal of Business & Economics Research* 7.3 (March 2009): 23–30.

56 Catherine A. Luther and Jodi L. Rightler-McDaniels, "'More Trouble than the Good Lord Ever Intended': Representations of Interracial Marriage in U.S. News-Oriented Magazines," *Journal of Magazine & New Media Research* 14.1 (Spring 2013): 1–30 <http://aejmcmagazine.arizona.edu/Journal/Summer2013/Luther. pdf>, accessed 21 September 2013. The authors define interracial as "Black/White."

57 Lisa Duke, "Black in a Blonde World: Race and Girls' Interpretations of the Feminine Ideal in Teen Magazines," *Journalism & Mass Communication Quarterly* 77.2 (Summer 2000): 367–392.

58 J. Robyn Goodman, "Flabless Is Fabulous: How Latina and Anglo Women Read and Incorporate the Excessively Thin Body Ideal into Everyday Experience," *Journalism & Mass Communication Quarterly* 79.3 (Autumn 2002): 712–727.

59 Steven R. Thomsen, "Health and Beauty Magazine Reading and Body Shape Concerns among a Group of College Women," *Journalism & Mass Communication Quarterly* 79.4 (Winter 2002): 988–1007.

60 Stella C. Chia, "Third-Person Perceptions about Idealized Body Image and Weight-Loss Behavior," *Journalism & Mass Communication Quarterly* 84.4 (Winter 2007): 677–694.

61 Stella C. Chia and Nainan Wen, "College Men's Third-Person Perceptions about Idealized Body Image and Consequent Behavior," *Sex Roles* 63.7/8 (October 2010): 542–555.

62 Zhengjia Liu and Lulu Rodriguez, "Psychological and Social Motives for Fashion Magazine Use among Shanghai's Female College Students," *Journal of Magazine & New Media Research* 13.2 (Summer 2012): 1–17 <http://aejmcmagazine.arizona.edu/Journal/Summer2012/LiuRodriguez.pdf>, accessed 19 September 2012.

63 Deana A. Rohlinger, "Eroticizing Men: Cultural Influences on Advertising and Male Objectification," *Sex Roles* 46.3/4 (February 2002): 61–74.

64 Laramie D. Taylor, "College Men, Their Magazines, and Sex," *Sex Roles* 55.9/10 (November 2006): 693–702.

65 Donnalyn Pompper, Jorge Soto, and Lauren Piel, "Male Body Image and Magazine Standards: Considering Dimensions of Age and Ethnicity," *Journalism & Mass Communication Quarterly* 84.3 (Autumn 2007): 537.

66 Dines and Humez, *Gender, Race, and Class in Media.*

67 Simon Cottle, *Ethnic Minorities and the Media: Changing Cultural Boundaries* (Philadelphia: Open University Press, 2000).

68 Clint C. Wilson, II, Félix Gutiérrez, and Lena M. Chao, *Racism, Sexism, and the Media: The Rise of Class Communication in Multicultural America*, 3rd ed. (Thousand Oaks, CA: Sage, 2003).

69 Lind, *Race/Gender/Class/Media*, 6.

Bibliography

Altschull, J. Herbert. *Agents of Power: The Media and Public Policy.* White Plains, NY: Longman, 1995.

Bagdikian, Ben H. *The New Media Monopoly.* Boston: Beacon Press, 2004.

Bandura, Albert. "Social Learning Theory of Aggression." *Journal of Communication* 28.3 (September 1978): 12–29.

Bedor, Emma and Tajima, Atsushi. "No Fat Moms! Celebrity Mothers' Weight-Loss Narratives in *People* Magazine." *Journal of Magazine & New Media Research* 13.2 (Summer 2012): 1–26 <http://aejmcmag azine.arizona.edu/Journal/Summer2012/BedorTajima.pdf>, accessed 10 August 2012.

Blumer, Herbert. *Symbolic Interactionism: Perspective and Method.* Berkeley: University of California Press, 1986.

Chia, Stella C. "Third-Person Perceptions about Idealized Body Image and Weight-Loss Behavior." *Journalism & Mass Communication Quarterly* 84.4 (Winter 2007): 677–694.

Chia, Stella C. and Wen, Nainan. "College Men's Third-Person Perceptions about Idealized Body Image and Consequent Behavior." *Sex Roles* 63.7/8 (October 2010): 542–555.

Cottle, Simon. *Ethnic Minorities and the Media: Changing Cultural Boundaries.* Philadelphia: Open University Press, 2000.

Covert, Juanita J. and Dixon, Travis L. "A Changing View: Representation and Effects of the Portrayal of Women of Color in Mainstream Women's Magazines." *Communication Research* 35.2 (April 2008): 232–256.

Crymble, Sarah B. "Contradiction Sells: Feminine Complexity and Gender Identity Dissonance in Magazine Advertising." *Journal of Communication Inquiry* 36.1 (January 2012): 62–84.

Daniels, Elizabeth A. "The Indivisibility of Women Athletes in Magazines for Teen Girls." *Women in Sport & Physical Activity Journal* 18.2 (Fall 2009): 14–24.

Dates, Jannette L. and Barlow, William, eds. *Split Image: African Americans in the Mass Media*. 2nd ed. Washington, DC: Howard University Press, 1993.

Dines, Gail and Humez, Jean M., eds. *Gender, Race, and Class in Media: A Critical Reader*. 3rd ed. Thousand Oaks, CA: Sage, 2011.

Duke, Lisa. "Black in a Blonde World: Race and Girls' Interpretations of the Feminine Ideal in Teen Magazines." *Journalism & Mass Communication Quarterly* 77.2 (Summer 2000): 367–392.

Feng, Yang and Frith, Katherine. "The Growth of International Women's Magazines in China and the Role of Transnational Advertising." *Journal of Magazine & New Media Research* 10.1 (Fall 2008): 1–14. <http://aejmcmagazine.arizona.edu/Journal/Fall2008/FengFrith.pdf>, accessed 21 September 2013.

Festinger, Leon. *A Theory of Cognitive Dissonance*. Stanford, CA: Stanford University Press, 1957.

Frith, Katherine; Shaw, Ping; and Cheng, Hong. "The Construction of Beauty: A Cross-Cultural Analysis of Women's Magazine Advertising." *Journal of Communication* 55.1 (March 2005): 56–70.

Gauntlett, David. *Media, Gender and Identity: An Introduction*. 2nd ed. London: Routledge, 2008.

Gauntlett, David. "Men's Magazines and Modern Masculinities." *Media, Gender and Identity: An Introduction*. 2nd ed. London and New York: Routledge, 2008, 164–189.

Gauntlett, David. "Women's Magazines and Female Identities." *Media, Gender and Identity: An Introduction*. 2nd ed. London and New York: Routledge, 2008, 190–222.

Gerbner, George; Gross, Larry; Morgan, Michael; and Signorielli, Nancy. "The 'Mainstreaming' of America: Violence Profile No. 11." *Journal of Communication* 30.3 (Summer 1980): 10–29.

Gill, Rosalind. *Gender and the Media*. Cambridge, UK: Polity Press, 2007.

Gill, Rosalind. "Gender in Magazines from *Cosmopolitan* to *Loaded*." *Gender and the Media*. Cambridge, UK: Polity Press, 2007, 180–217.

Glasser, Theodore L. "Objectivity and News Bias." In Cohen, Elliot D., ed. *Philosophical Issues in Journalism*. New York: Oxford University Press, 1992, 176–183.

Goffman, Erving. *Gender Advertisements*. Cambridge, MA: Harvard University Press, 1979.

Goldman, Karen. "La Princesa Plastica: Hegemonic and Oppositional Representations of *Latinidad* in Hispanic Barbie." In Dines, Gail and Humez, Jean M., eds. *Gender, Race, and Class in Media: A Critical Reader*. 3rd ed. Thousand Oaks, CA: Sage, 2011, 375–382.

Goodman, J. Robyn. "Flabless Is Fabulous: How Latina and Anglo Women Read and Incorporate the Excessively Thin Body Ideal into Everyday Experience." *Journalism & Mass Communication Quarterly* 79.3 (Autumn 2002): 712–727.

Grandy, Karen. "The Glossy Ceiling: Coverage of Women in Canadian and American Business Magazines." *Journal of Magazine & New Media Research* 14.1 (Spring 2013): 1–20 <http://aejmcmagazine.arizona.edu/Journal/Summer2013/Grandy.pdf>, accessed 21 September 2013.

Han, Chong-suk. "'Sexy Like a Girl and Horny Like a Boy': Contemporary Gay 'Western' Narratives about Gay Asian Men." In Dines, Gail and Humez, Jean M., eds. *Gender, Race, and Class in Media: A Critical Reader*. 3rd ed. Thousand Oaks, CA: Sage, 2011, 163–170.

Jhally, Sut. *The Codes of Advertising: Fetishism and the Political Economy of Meaning in the Consumer Society*. New York: Routledge, Chapman and Hall, 1990.

Joshi, Suchi P.; Peter, Jochen; and Valkenburg, Patti M. "Ambivalent Messages in *Seventeen* Magazine: A Content Analytic Comparison of 1997 and 2007." *Journal of Magazine & New Media Research* 12.1 (Fall 2010): 1–20 <http://aejmcmagazine.arizona.edu/Journal/Fall2010/JoshiPeterValkenburg.pdf >, accessed 19 September 2012.

Kitch, Carolyn. *The Girl on the Magazine Cover: The Origins of Visual Stereotypes in American Mass Media*. Chapel Hill and London: University of North Carolina Press, 2001.

Kitch, Carolyn. *Pages from the Past: History and Memory in American Magazines*. Chapel Hill: University of North Carolina Press, 2005.

Knobloch-Westerwick, Silvia and Coates, Brendon. "Minority Models in Advertisements in Magazines Popular with Minorities." *Journalism & Mass Communication Quarterly* 83.3 (Autumn 2006): 596–614.

Law, Cheryl and Labre, Magdala Peixoto. "Cultural Standards of Attractiveness: A Thirty-Year Look at Changes in Male Images in Magazines." *Journalism & Mass Communication Quarterly* 79.3 (Autumn 2002): 697–711.

Lee, Ki-Young and Joo, Sung-Hee. "The Portrayal of Asian Americans in Mainstream Magazine Ads: An Update." *Journalism & Mass Communication Quarterly* 82.3 (Autumn 2005): 654–671.

Lind, Rebecca Ann, ed. *Race/Gender/Class/Media 3.0: Considering Diversity across Content, Audiences, and Production*. 3rd ed. New York: Pearson, 2013.

Liu, Zhengjia and Rodriguez, Lulu. "Psychological and Social Motives for Fashion Magazine Use among Shanghai's Female College Students." *Journal of Magazine & New Media Research* 13.2 (Summer 2012): 1–17 <http://aejmcmagazine.arizona.edu/Journal/Summer2012/LiuRodriguez.pdf>, accessed 19 September 2012.

Luther, Catherine A. and Rightler-McDaniels, Jodi L. "'More Trouble than the Good Lord Ever Intended': Representations of Interracial Marriage in U.S. News-Oriented Magazines." *Journal of Magazine & New Media Research* 14.1 (Spring 2013): 1–30 <http://aejmcmagazine.arizona.edu/Journal/Summer2013/Luther.pdf>, accessed 21 September 2013.

Millard, Jennifer E. and Grant, Peter R. "The Stereotypes of Black and White Women in Fashion Magazine Photographs: The Pose of the Model and the Impression She Creates." *Sex Roles* 54.9/10 (May 2006): 659–673.

Moeran, Brian. "The Portrayal of Beauty in Women's Fashion Magazines." *Fashion Theory: The Journal of Dress, Body & Culture* 14.4 (December 2010): 491–510.

Mueller, Barbara. "Reaching African American Consumers: African American Shopping Behavior." In Dines, Gail and Humez, Jean M., eds. *Gender, Race, and Class in Media: A Critical Reader.* 3rd ed. Thousand Oaks, CA: Sage, 2011, 213–220.

Nguyen, Thuc Doan. "*AudreyMagazine.com*: Portrayals of Asian American Women Online by Asian American Women." In Lind, Rebecca Ann, ed. *Race/Gender/Class/Media 3.0: Considering Diversity across Content, Audiences, and Production.* 3rd ed. New York: Pearson, 2013, 269–273.

Oh, David Chison. "Complementary Objectivity and Ideology: Reifying White Capitalist Hierarchies in *Time* Magazine's Construction of Michelle Rhee." *Journal of Communication Inquiry* 34.2 (April 2010): 151–167.

Peterson, Robin T. "Consumer Magazine Advertisement Portrayal of Models by Race in the U.S.: An Assessment." *Journal of Marketing Communications* 13.3 (September 2007): 199–211.

Pompper, Donnalyn; Soto, Jorge; and Piel, Lauren. "Male Body Image and Magazine Standards: Considering Dimensions of Age and Ethnicity." *Journalism & Mass Communication Quarterly* 84.3 (Autumn 2007): 525–545.

Rahman, Bushra H. "Analysis of the Coverage of Muslim Political Women in *Time* and *Newsweek*." *Journal of Media Studies* 25.1 (January 2010): 50–65.

Reichert, Tom and Carpenter, Courtney. "An Update on Sex in Magazine Advertising: 1983 to 2003." *Journalism & Mass Communication Quarterly* 81.4 (Winter 2004): 823–837.

Rohlinger, Deana A. "Eroticizing Men: Cultural Influences on Advertising and Male Objectification." *Sex Roles* 46.3/4 (February 2002): 61–74.

Rooks, Noliwe M. *Ladies' Pages: African American Women's Magazines and the Culture That Made Them.* New Brunswick, NJ: Rutgers University Press, 2004.

Schwartz, Joseph and Andsager, Julie L. "Four Decades of Images in Gay Male-Targeted Magazines." *Journalism & Mass Communication Quarterly* 88.1 (Spring 2011): 76–98.

Sengupta, Rhea. "Reading Representations of Black, East Asian, and White Women in Magazines for Adolescent Girls." *Sex Roles* 54.11/12 (June 2006): 799–808.

Signorielli, Nancy and Morgan, Michael. *Cultivation Analysis: New Directions in Media Effects Research.* Newbury Park, CA: Sage, 1990.

Stevenson, Thomas H. "Four Decades of African American Portrayals in Magazine Advertising." *Journal of Business & Economics Research* 7.3 (March 2009): 23–30.

Sumner, David E. "Theory? Bah Humbug!" *Journal of Magazine & New Media Research* 10.1 (Fall 2008): 1–2 <http://aejmcmagazine.arizona.edu/Journal/Fall2008/SumnerColumn.pdf>, accessed 9 September 2012.

Taylor, Laramie D. "College Men, Their Magazines, and Sex." *Sex Roles* 55.9/10 (November 2006): 693–702.

Thomsen, Steven R. "Health and Beauty Magazine Reading and Body Shape Concerns among a Group of College Women." *Journalism & Mass Communication Quarterly* 79.4 (Winter 2002): 988–1007.

Vincent, Cindy S. "*POOR Magazine* and Civic Engagement through Community Media." In Lind, Rebecca Ann, ed. *Race/Gender/Class/Media 3.0: Considering Diversity across Content, Audiences, and Production.* 3rd ed. New York: Pearson, 2013, 316–322.

Webb, Sheila M. "The Narrative of Core Traditional Values in Reiman Magazines." *Journalism & Mass Communication Quarterly* 83.4 (Winter 2006): 865–882.

Wilson, Clint C., II; Gutiérrez, Félix; and Chao, Lena M. *Racism, Sexism, and the Media: The Rise of Class Communication in Multicultural America.* 3rd ed. Thousand Oaks, CA: Sage, 2003.

14

COVERING PUBLIC AFFAIRS

The Arena of the Newsmagazines

Isabel Soares

Without a proper focus, the expression *public affairs* can conjure a plethora of meanings, ranging from politics to international relations, war, public policies, urban questions, or health matters. Dictionary entries on public affairs vary greatly in the definitions they provide, from public relations to the relations between a company and the surrounding world, vaguely concluding that the term may be used to refer to public administration and even lobbying. More generally, public affairs is defined as "matters of general interest or concern, especially those dealing with current social or political issues."[1] There are also those who define it as "the *common knowledge* of mass politics,"[2] which points toward a closer connection between public affairs and the political arena.

Moreover, the *Journal of Public Affairs*, the specialized scholarly forum and disciplinary authority in public affairs, publishes articles on wide-ranging topics that include "government relations and lobbying, issues management, community relations, corporate social responsibility and political strategy and marketing."[3] Thus, far from establishing clear cut boundaries or encapsulating the concept of public affairs in a watertight definition, the journal's description allows for ample interpretation of the meaning of the field whose academic mouthpiece it intends to be. The journal publishes in a bifid stream of both academic and practice papers in the field. Given the multiplicity of topics it covers under its umbrella, the journal thereby provides a definition of public affairs in its broader sense(s), incorporating political and societal concerns.

All around the world, the media play a pivotal role in giving consistency to what society considers important, that is, concerns that are important to the public at large. Benedict Anderson's notion of imagined communities[4] can be thus cemented by what the press chooses to bring to public light, or not. Such communities, as defined by Anderson, are usually juxtaposed to what we commonly call nations. Thus, news reports are important not just in the delivery of information, they are tools for the construction of "particular images of self, community, and nation," which render the study of news as important as that of any social science.[5] Among the media, newsmagazines are for the public at large important complements to newspaper, broadcast and Internet sources of information on public affairs. Scrutinizing the abundant research on newsmagazines over the last 20-odd years gives evidence that the term public affairs also includes for these publications wide-ranging topics, as divergent as the economy, electoral campaigns, agriculture, poverty, diplomacy, conflict in all its forms, education and the educational system, domestic and international affairs.

This chapter seeks to circumscribe public affairs as portrayed by newsmagazines by conducting a qualitative meta-analysis of scholarly research on newsmagazine coverage of public affairs over the decades since 1990. Concomitantly, by studying patterns that emerge through examining what researchers have identified in discrete studies, this research seeks to discern what visions of the public sphere newsmagazines have portrayed as important for the shaping of society. The chapter develops in four sections. In the first, attention is placed on the kind of research previously carried out on newsmagazines. Second, the identification and assembling of the corpus of studies is characterized. A third section describes the analysis of published studies identified as focusing on public affairs and the means used to arrive at a more restricted meaning of this concept for the meta-analysis. The fourth part of the chapter concentrates on scholars' research on newsmagazines' selection and coverage of the content they present to the public. Basically the research question could be formulated as follows: What, topically, has the academy been studying on newsmagazines and public affairs since 1990? To answer to this question, a secondary analysis was conducted of scholarly work identified as published over the past 20 years, which focuses on newsmagazines as a vehicle of information to the broader public for content about public affairs. These steps shaped the backbone of this meta-research, from which conclusions are drawn and described. In the final section, attention also is given to future research on the depiction of public affairs in newsmagazines.

Literature Review

Trying to establish a connection between newsmagazine content on public affairs and academic research focusing very specifically on printed media and the topic of public affairs poses not only the questions of which newsmagazines have been studied and what definitions provided for the term public affairs, it also raises the question of the study of newsmagazines themselves. Indeed, when looking at scholarly interest in the printed media, it is easy to verify, as Tim Holmes observed, that there are "hundreds of books about newspapers, perhaps a couple of dozen about magazines; if you are in a good library."[6] When it comes to studies dealing specifically with newsmagazines, the scenario is even bleaker. Browsing through David E. Sumner's 2010 bibliographic compilation on American magazine research in *The Magazine Century: American Magazines since 1900* suggests a paucity of studies conducted on newsmagazines.[7] There are studies on certain newsmagazines, the ones credited to be more mainstream and disseminated, such as *Newsweek* or *Time*, but no overall study on newsmagazines per se. Probable explanations for this are that, as Holmes writes, generically "magazines are less easy to study than newspapers" because they "are highly diverse in subject matter and a great deal more emphasis is put on presentation, making them more complex to 'read' than newspapers."[8] This, however, is not a convincing justification when compared to gender studies and their correlation to women's magazines. The segmentation of the magazine market may also help account for a lesser interest in the study of newsmagazines. For, as Sumner clarifies about the growing popularity of tabloid and celebrity magazines compared with that of newsmagazines, "their combined circulation of 14.5 million is about 40 percent more than the combined 10 million circulation of ten leading news and opinion magazines: *Time, Newsweek, US News & World Report*, the *Economist*, the *Week, Harper's*, the *Atlantic*, the *New Republic*, the *Nation*, and *National Review*."[9] That is, the increase in niche-oriented magazines may have propelled a consequent interest in them, as opposed to more generalist magazines.

Undeniable is the fact that social scientists frequently resort to the media, namely the printed media, as both objects of study and as a document pool from which to interpret society. John T. Woolley writes that "political scientists have often used media reports—usually print media—as the basis for data on important aspects of politics and the policy process."[10] More particularly, "scholars drawing on data sets for measures of coups, riots, demonstrations, elections, and other political events . . . are utilizing data originally drawn from newspaper accounts."[11] The aim of this research follows a similar path. That is, to use newsmagazines to understand how public affairs have been perceived by journalists and concomitantly channeled to the public. However, to get such information this study will not be a primary analysis on the newsmagazines themselves, but a scrutiny of what scholars have identified and interpreted in newsmagazine content devoted to public affairs. That way, the research is enriched not only by discovering which public affairs topics are more often mediatized but also by perceiving which topical options have been elected by academics interested in the analysis of the link between public affairs and newsmagazine content.

Political science is not our ground of departure. Rather, and because public affairs is such a vast field and one of such diverse denominations, the study draws on the social sciences as a whole, to look at public affairs from the standpoint of political, international relations and sociological-related content. This is supported by the fact that the definitions of public affairs accessed prior to engaging in this study (see introduction) thematically point in that direction. These definitions guided the gathering of a corpus that could help gain a deeper knowledge of the research already carried out on public affairs topics transmitted by newsmagazines to broader audiences.

Method: Assembling a Corpus

A sample of studies was gathered to gain a more precise picture of which public affairs topics have been scrutinized in academic research on newsmagazines since the 1990s. Because, as Klaus Bruhn Jensen has observed, "the textual output of media has naturally been a central object of analysis in qualitative media studies, being the vehicles of cultural forms and historical worldviews,"[12] the operationalization of this research entailed collecting a corpus of scholarly articles on newsmagazines and public affairs published from 1990 to 2012.

Given the prolific use of the term public affairs, a preliminary search was conducted in Google Scholar by simply combining the terms *newsmagazines* and *public affairs* to check the nature of the titles that came up. This step showed articles relating to wide-ranging topics, such as agriculture, health and the environment, along with articles on international politics, war and other socioeconomic matters. The disparate array of themes led to a first decision to narrow the scope of investigation. Hence, discarded from the subsequent research were the topics outside the boundaries of social and political sciences. This pilot search was also instrumental in that it allowed for verification of which newsmagazines were being more often scrutinized in academic research. *Time* and *Newsweek* showed up more conspicuously. This was fundamental to composing a pool of terms to use in a next step of the research process, when research needed to be more consistent and formal.

An important caveat relates to the decision to limit research to English keywords, best exemplified by the word *newsmagazines*. On the one hand, English is today's lingua franca, but, on the other, this strategic decision, taken at the onset of this project, entails the handicap of creating blind zones of information by obliterating content in other languages. When the issue is newsmagazines and research is conducted in English alone, major world Indo-European languages, to use as an example only in the dominant languages of the so-called West,[13] will be inherently left out. Better put, a newsmagazine such as Brazilian *Veja*, with a circulation of more than one million copies,[14] will not be brought under consideration. The merit of this a priori decision was to limit the scale of research, but, much like a double-edged sword, the decision naturally omits a great proportion of what goes on in the world as far as newsmagazines are concerned.

After these initial decisions, the gathering of articles for analysis was conducted using JSTOR, ProQuest, EBSCOhost and Google Scholar search engines. Moreover, given their status as scholarly publications with a specific interest in journalism and communication, the on-line archives of *Journalism & Mass Communication Quarterly* and the *International Journal of Press/Politics* were also searched. Such options naturally reflect the paradox the researcher in social sciences faces when qualitative methodologies are used. Notwithstanding, as Jensen suggests,

> A . . . feature of qualitative research concerns the role of the researcher, who is defined emphatically as an *interpretative subject*. In one sense, all research depends on the human subject as a primary instrument. What distinguishes qualitative from quantitative projects in this regard is a global and continuous form of interpretation. . . . The qualitative ambition . . . has been for a single researcher to interpret "meaning in action."[15]

In this light, research trajectories are intrinsically dependent on the researcher's own choices established at the onset of the project. Ultimately, the same research could, and would, be conducted differently by two distinct *interpretative subjects*. Thus, after the first decisions were made, which fields were to be favored, where and through which means research would be conducted were determined, as follows.

The U.S. newsmagazines *Newsweek*[16] and *Time*[17] were chosen because of their international impact, high readership and years in business. Scholarly articles featuring either of these newsmagazines in the title or subject of the article were selected for the current analysis. In order to avoid the ambiguity created by the polysemic nature of the word *time*, it was not included as a search keyword on its own but always combined with other expressions being searched (e.g., "*Newsweek* and *Time*," or "*Time*, war"). Another keyword used at this initial stage was the noun *newsmagazines* itself.

The combination of the keywords (newsmagazines, *Newsweek*, *U.S. News & World Report* and *Time*) identified five articles in which *Newsweek*, *Time* and *U.S. News & World Report* were included in the titles of articles produced by scholars with an interest in newsmagazine content: Michael Griffin and Jongsoo Lee's "Picturing the Gulf War: Constructing an Image of War in *Time*, *Newsweek* and *U.S. News & World Report*," published in *Journalism & Mass Communication Quarterly* in Winter 1995[18]; Jack Lule's 1995 article, "Enduring Image of War: Myth and Ideology in a *Newsweek* Cover"[19]; Shahzad Ali and Khalid's 2008 "U.S. Mass Media and Muslim World: Portrayal of Muslim by *Newsweek* and *Time* (1991–2001)," published in the *European Journal of Scientific Research*[20]; Richard K. Popp and Andrew L. Mendelson's "'X'-ing out Enemies: *Time* Magazine, Visual Discourse, and the War in Iraq," published in *Journalism* in 2010[21]; and the article "U.S. Mass Media and Image of Afghanistan: Portrayal of Afghanistan by *Newsweek* and *Time*" by Ghulam Shabir, Shahzad Ali, and Zafar Iqbal, published in *South Asian Studies* in 2011.[22]

Other newsmagazines with only one or two occurrences in the search included the *Nation*, the *Economist* and Canada's *Maclean's*. These, however, were found not in the article titles but in the abstracts. The conclusion from this preliminary search was that the favored newsmagazines for academic research are *Time*, *Newsweek* and *U.S. News & World Report*. Because the articles analyzing the *Nation*, the *Economist* and *Maclean's* also focused on the other three newsmagazines, they were retained in this study. A preliminary conclusion is that *Time*, *Newsweek* and *U.S. News & World Report* are considered the mainstream newsmagazines over which academic research tends to concentrate.

The search also allowed verification of the more recurrent topics, which enabled furthering the search by means of different keywords. Consequently, in a second stage, searches also included additional keywords: *war*, *poverty*, *electoral campaigns* and *terrorism*, because they pointed in the direction of the contents that were showing up more frequently in the second search. That is, research was based on two fundamental stages. The first was to find out which newsmagazines figured more prominently in academic investigation. Bearing in mind English-speaking and widely international newsweeklies, the initial research keywords included *Newsweek* and *Time*. Because *U.S. News & World Report* showed up persistently whenever there were titles and abstracts of academic articles mentioning *Time* and *Newsweek*, it was included at this stage. The conclusions pointed to *Time*, *Newsweek* and *U.S. News & World Report* being the most recurrent newsmagazines being investigated by academics. For the second stage, a pilot analysis on the articles found in the first stage sought to identify the main topics of academic interest. Once the topical concerns became evident, adding new keywords enriched the search.

From these initial steps came an amalgamated total of 52 articles that constituted the raw material for the research. The articles were then grouped by topics, duplicates were discarded, and a closer reading of their respective abstracts helped locate those that fell outside the boundaries of subjects in the social and political sciences. Thus, articles on *body image*, *children* and *media ethics* were not kept. Also eliminated were articles in which the target newsmagazines were marginal to the study. This happened either because the study focused principally on other media, such as television or newspapers, and newsmagazines were just mentioned incidentally as a point to establish *apropos* comparisons that were neither determinant nor essential to the main subject of research, or because newsmagazines were used secondarily to corroborate findings and points of view. In the end 44 articles were determined to be worthy of treatment. The articles were (1) published within the time frame 1990–2012; (2) related primarily to *Newsweek*, *Time* and *U.S. News & World Report*; and (3) focused on issues determined to be public affairs, as defined for this study: societal issues relating primarily to war and war-related anxieties, terrorism, electoral campaigns, economic deprivation and mediatized court rulings. These are discussed further in the next section.

Analyzing the Corpus

After identifying the corpus of studies, the first concern was how to organize it topically to provide a clearer definition of what was understood by public affairs for the purposes of this research. This would also indicate which public affairs topics had been most frequently scrutinized and thus might be interpreted to reflect newsmagazines' perception of the most important public affairs to be brought to the public sphere.

A review of the articles' topics suggested two immediate findings that proved relevant to the subsequent analysis. On the one hand, it was possible to identify clear clusters of topics. On the other, a clear chronological division of pre- and post- 9/11 articles emerged when it came to issues related to international relations and diplomacy, war, terrorism and geopolitics. Hence, it was possible to organize the corpus into three broad categories (See Table 14.1). These were identified as War and International Relations, Pre-9/11; War and International Relations, Post-9/11; and Domestic Public Affairs. Because of its relative heterogeneous nature, the third category was subdivided into three subcategories: Socio-Political Concerns, Poverty and Unemployment Issues, and Supreme Court Rulings.

The categorization of the corpus provided a clearer definition for the study: Based on the review of the literature, the working definition of public affairs will henceforth be understood to be

> general interest issues related to conflict situations, including war and terrorism both at the national and international levels; matters of political and judicial public interest; and economic concerns related to individuals' welfare, namely socioeconomic deprivation and unemployment.

Taken as a whole, this definition suggests academics analyzing the news coverage of newsmagazines within the realm of public affairs have focused on the importance of risk for modern societies. That is, social threat or threats were at the core of scholarly interest in newsmagazine coverage in the 1990–2012 period.

Topics pertaining to the numerous perils impending on society concentrate more attention than topics of a more benign nature. Indeed, looking at the articles that were left outside the borders of the selection for our research, risk is also a recurring theme. Articles on body image, for instance, reflected the threat of anorexia, and health articles dealt frequently with disease

Table 14.1. Article topics by categories, authors and publication dates

War and International Relations, Pre-9/11 11 articles

Downing	1990	Griffin & Lee	1995
Simmons & Lowry	1990	Lule	1995
Entman	1991	Kenney	1995
Solomon	1992	Wall	1997
Gutierrez-Villalobos, Hertog & Rush	1994	Ramos, Ron & Thoms	2007
King & Wells	1994		

War and International Relations, Post-9/11 17 articles

Swain	2003	Shehata	2007
Kozol	2004	Ricchiardi	2008
Hutcheson, Domke, Billeaudeaux & Garland	2004	Friedman	2008
Deveau and Fouts	2005	Ali & Khalid	2008
Fried	2005	Porpora & Nikolaev	2008
Brooten	2005	Nikolaev	2009
Woods	2007	Harp, Loke & Bachmann	2010
Altheide	2007	Popp & Mendelson	2010
		Shabir, Ali & Iqbal	2011

Domestic Public Affairs in 3 subcategories 16 articles

Socio-Political Concerns 9 articles

Moriarty & Popovich	1991	Edwards	1998
Major	1992	Moldovan	2009
Buckman	1993	Bachechi	2010
Cramer	1994	Squires & Jackson	2010
Husselbee & Stempel	1997		

Poverty and Unemployment Issues 4 articles

Gilens	1996	Kanayama	2004
Clawson & Trice	2000	Dreier	2005

Supreme Court Rulings 3 articles

Bowles & Bromley	1992	Packer & Gower	1997
O'Callaghan & Dukes	1992		

and research funding matters. In other words, risk can be said to be a common denominator in the interest for the topical study of newsmagazines and their relation to public affairs.

Apropos to the selected studies is Ulrich Beck's observation, "If you distinguish between calculable and non-calculable threats, under the surface of risk calculation new kinds of *industrialized, decision-produced incalculability and threats* are spreading within the globalization of high risk industries, whether for warfare or welfare purposes."[23] In this light, it is safe to say that risk society is "a world risk society."[24]

The articles included for further analysis suggest that in a globalized society of risk(s), newsmagazines mirror social anxieties relating to the perils faced by the community of readers, be they threats to the individual or to the whole group. In order to understand better which public affairs matter to newsmagazines in the coverage of risk-related issues, scholars most often used qualitative methodologies, and such methodological choices are usually stated in the articles' abstracts. The analysis of data collection instruments used gave evidence that all articles in this study used content-based analysis, whether it was visual or discourse-based.

Indeed, five articles were based specifically on visual content analysis, either examining the covers of magazines, as in Lule's "Enduring Image of War: Myth and Ideology in a *Newsweek* Cover,"[25] or scrutinizing illustrations, as in "Images of War: Content Analysis of the Photo Coverage of the War in Kosovo" by Alexander Nikolaev.[26] In two instances, scholars used a mixed-methods approach. Adam Shehata combined qualitative and quantitative methods in "Facing the Muhammad Cartoons: Official Dominance and Event-Driven News in Swedish and American Elite Press."[27] And, in "Reducing Race: News Themes in the 2008 Primaries,"[28] Catherine R. Squires and Sarah J. Jackson used a model based on the frequency of determined words and phrases for a qualitative/quantitative research methodology. The conclusion is that when analyzing the intersection between newsmagazines and public affairs, scholars favored qualitative methodologies in the time period of this study.

Having determined which newsmagazines have been more frequently studied, which public affairs' topics have been preferred and which research methodologies have been used for study, it is also important to identify and detail the contents of each of the three identified topical clusters.

Describing Content

War and International Relations, Pre-9/11 formed the first identifiable cluster of public affairs topics (See Table 14.2). Although one of the articles, Howard Ramos, James Ron and Oskar N.T. Thoms's "Shaping the Northern Media's Human Rights Coverage, 1986–2000"[29] was published in 2007, the study focused on a pre-9/11 period. The other articles included in this cluster were published between 1990 and 1997, and their research contents focused on that time frame.

War and International Relations, Pre-9/11 Studies

Analysis showed that the First Gulf War (1990–1991) was the object of scrutiny in three of the articles. Erika G. King and Robert A. Wells pointed out that in a comparison between the First Gulf War and other instances of war, namely World War II and Vietnam, newsmagazines clearly favored the historical analogy of World War II rather than the war in Southeast Asia.[30] In "Picturing the Gulf War: Constructing an Image of War in *Time*, *Newsweek* and *U.S. News & World Report*," Michael Griffin and Jongsoo Lee's *leitmotif* for research was how the newsmagazines depicted the conflict, commonly known by its codename, Operation Desert Storm, through the pictures they chose to publish. Griffin and Lee found a very limited range of images in the pictorial coverage, with emphasis being placed on military weaponry and technology, not on ongoing military activities.[31] For "Enduring Image of War: Myth and Ideology in a *Newsweek* Cover,"[32] Lule focused on analyzing one image of the First Gulf War that made a cover of *Newsweek*.

Under the heading War and International Relations, Pre-9/11 there were three studies of the Persian Gulf War coverage and other research on newsmagazine coverage of international affairs throughout the globe. The latter included studies of issues that did not include direct U.S. intervention.

The pre-9/11 period was fertile in articles referring to countries undergoing political turmoil and conflict. Three articles focused on Africa. In "U.S. Media Discourse on South Africa: The

Table 14.2. Topical concerns in war and international relations, pre-9/11 by author and publication year

Article Topics	Author(s)	Publication Year
Persian Gulf War	King & Wells	1994
	Griffin & Lee	1995
	Lule	1995
Africa	Downing	1990
	Kenney	1995
	Wall	1997
Central America	Solomon	1992
	Gutierrez-Villalobos, Hertog & Rush	1994
Terrorism	Simmons & Lowry	1990
Downing of planes	Entman	1991
War and human rights	Ramos, Ron & Thoms	2007

Development of a Situation Model,"[33] John Downing analyzed the discursive treatment on South Africa in *Time* and *Newsweek*. In "Images of Africa in News Magazines: Is There a Black Perspective?,"[34] Keith Kenney compared *Newsweek* and *Emerge*'s 1989 through 2000 coverage of news of Africa of particular relevance to African-Americans. In "The Rwanda Crisis: An Analysis of News Magazine Coverage,"[35] Melissa Wall focused on American coverage of the crisis in Rwanda in 1994 in *Newsweek*, *Time* and *U.S. News & World Report*. Interest in Africa in this period reflects interest in several major events in Africa during the 1990s: the release of Nelson Mandela in February 1990 and the Rwandan Genocide in 1994. In fact, Heidi Mau and Carolyn Kitch say moments of such historic intensity provide newsweeklies with their "finest moments" and allow them to dig deeper into the hows and whys which are "too often missing from breaking news coverage."[36]

Countries where the United States played a role of either diplomatic or direct intervention included El Salvador and Panama in Central America. William S. Solomon analyzed the portrayal in *Time*, *Newsweek* and *U.S. News & World Report* of U.S. policy in El Salvador during the Salvadoran Civil War of 1989–1992.[37] There was also interest in Panama because of the U.S. invasion that put an end to internal turmoil and culminated in the deposition of General Manuel Noriega. Sonia Gutierrez-Villalobos, James K. Hertog and Ramona R. Rush concluded that the more mainstream newsmagazines *Time* and *Newsweek* offered little critique of the strategies pursued by President George H.W. Bush's administration in the invasion of that Central American country, whereas the *Nation* showed more opposition to the administration's policies.[38]

International terrorism, human rights in war-torn countries and the downing of planes produced other focuses of research on the coverage of international relations in the pre-9/11 period.[39] In the 1990–2001 period scholarship on newsmagazines and public affairs focused on war and international relations and issues triggered by events in the global arena. Events such as Mandela's release, the Persian Gulf War or the invasion of Panama, and Rwandan tribalism became historical landmarks.

War and International Relations, Post-9/11 Studies

The topical cluster War and International Relations, Post-9/11 shows a relative uniformity around one single theme (See Table 14.3). That is in a stark contrast to the multiplicity of topics around the same subject in the pre-9/11 period. Indeed, the dominant topic after the attacks on the World Trade Center is terrorism and terrorism-related issues, whose spinoffs coincide with events centered in the Muslim world that may have repercussions outside its religious and geographic borders. One of the most studied wars in the period was the war in Iraq sanctioned by the Bush administration in 2003 under the pretext of finding weapons of mass destruction, followed by the war in Afghanistan, which was part of the armed strategy to fight terrorism.[40]

The interest in globalized, mediatized terror might be explained by Bethami Dobkin's observation,

> It is easy to conceptualize media coverage of terrorism as a public action because both the news media and terrorists have audience-directed goals. Further, the violent nature of terrorism increases drama and therefore news value, making terrorist acts stand out against the routinized news treatment of crime and politically motivated violence.[41]

After the dramatic incidents of 11 September 2001, the debate around terrorism may have gained momentum because, as Naco writes,

> Terrorism's efficacy, like beauty, is in the eyes of the beholder in that those who commit political violence deliberately directed against civilians believe in the success of their deeds. . . . whenever [terrorists] strike, especially if they stage so-called terrorist spectaculars, their deeds assure them massive news coverage and the attention of the general public and governmental decision makers in their particular target societies.[42]

This means that the sheer "dramaturgical perspective of terrorism,"[43] or terror as entertainment, feeds the general public's interest in it. Similarly, by reflecting the public's concern and, in turn, shaping it, the media are responsible for a heightened awareness of terror. That is, "the forms on which our understanding of terrorism is based are constructed by both mass media and official discourse, or governmental rhetoric."[44]

After the shocking events perpetrated on the morning of 11 September 2001, when terror took the media by storm, scholarship on newsmagazines' coverage of the events reflected this orientation. Ali and Khalid's article, "U.S. Mass Media and Muslim World: Portrayal of Muslim by *Newsweek* and *Time* (1991–2001)," scrutinized how the two newsmagazines covered and portrayed 12 Islamic countries in the decade between 1991 and 2001. Although published in 2008, at a time when the war on terror was being fought by international armed forces in the Persian Gulf, Ali and Khalid's research reflected the attention devoted to the Muslim world in the aftermath of the events of 9/11.[45]

Terrorism, as stated previously, was at the core of much scholarship on newsmagazines' contents in the period starting with the 2001 attack on the United States. The coverage of terrorism was, in fact, the preferred topic under this umbrella: Studies included how the polemic Muhammad cartoons were framed by Swedish and American press as tolerance or intolerance toward the controversy[46]; how women are engaged in terrorist actions and how female suicide bombers have been depicted by U.S. media, namely *Newsweek*[47]; and both how the mass media cover terrorism and how it is defined by them.[48]

War in Iraq and Afghanistan were part of a concerted international strategy to fight terror in the aftermath of the attacks on the United States. Dobkin writes, "As public hysteria over terrorism mounts, so does support for direct military action in foreign conflicts. This raises the level of acceptable violence as retaliation."[49] That is, war was an expected outcome of that fight. War assumes special relevance in the topical cluster War and International Relations, Post-9/11. As seen in Table 14.3, of the seven articles referring specifically to war, five relate to the war in Iraq and the war in Afghanistan; only two look at the war in Kosovo.

Table 14.3. Topical concerns in war and international relations, post-9/11 by author and publication year

Article Topics	Author(s)	Publication Year
War in Iraq	Porpora & Nikolaev	2008
	Popp & Mendelson	2010
	Harp, Loke & Bachmann	2010
War in Afghanistan	Ricchiardi	2008
	Shabir, Ali & Iqbal	2011
War in Kosovo	Kozol	2004
	Nikolaev	2009
Terrorism	Fried	2005
	Woods	2007
	Altheide	2007
	Friedman	2008
Media and the Muslim world	Shehata	2007
	Ali & Khalid	2008
Revenge and patriotism after 9/11	Hutcheson, Domke, Billeaudeaux & Garland	2004
	Deveau & Fouts	2005
U.S. foreign policy	Brooten	2005
Africa	Swain	2003

Of the three articles about the war in Iraq, two take the controversy regarding American legitimacy to invade that country to the center of research. In "Voices of Dissent in the Iraq War: Moving from Deviance to Legitimacy,"[50] Dustin Harp, Jaime Loke and Ingrid Bachmann analyze *Time*'s coverage of those voices, whether coming from official sources, civilians or journalists who opposed the war. In "Moral Muting in U.S. Newspaper Op-Eds Debating the Attack on Iraq,"[51] Douglas Porpora and Alexander Nikolaev examine editorial and opinion pieces in both newspapers and newsmagazines to determine whether, in the debate concerning the American legitimacy to attack Iraq, moral muting, which they define as overlapping with mitigation but not being an exact synonym for it, was present in those pieces. Finally, Richard Popp and Andrew Mendelson debated *Time* and *Newsweek*'s graphic coverage of the death of al-Zarqawi, Al-Qaeda's leader in Iraq. Popp and Mendelson compared *Time*'s chosen cover, in which the leader's face was crossed out as a symbol of finality or elimination, with similar covers the newsmagazine printed to record the falls of Hitler and Saddam Hussein, to *Newsweek*'s, which registered the terrorist leader's death in a joint operation involving the Jordan secret services and American Special Forces.[52]

Newsweek and *Time*'s coverage was again targeted for analysis when the topic was the war in Afghanistan. Specifically, scholars looked at how the conflict was covered and which images were made public by these publications. Shabir, Ali and Iqbal concluded from their analysis of 20 articles published by the two newsmagazines that negative coverage represented the greatest percentage of those articles. That is, Afghanistan was regarded as a harbor for Taliban extremism and Al-Qaeda learning centers, and it was also depicted as a country economically dependent on opium poppy production.[53] In a second article, Sherry Ricchiardi discussed the press's apparent neglect of the war in Afghanistan when compared with the war going on in Iraq. Ricchiardi attributed the difference not only to a more aggressive and intensive struggle in Afghanistan than in the Gulf but also to the lack of infrastructures in the country and the greater dangers of abduction and death faced by Western journalists going there.[54]

At a time when America was so violently attacked and the toll claimed by terrorism was in the thousands of civilian casualties—which led to American troops being deployed to a war in the Middle East to safeguard its citizens from further attacks—scholarship also reflected on core notions of identity. When mass-mediated terrorism, which Nacos describes as "the centrality of media considerations in the calculus of political violence that is committed by non-state actors against civilians,"[55] figures prominently in the press, collective angst is also exorcized through the press.

How the press and newsmagazines depressurized panic after 9/11 was also worthy of academic study. John Hutcheson, David Domke, Andre Billeaudeaux and Philip Garland analyzed *Time* and *Newsweek*'s coverage to determine whether the magazines had somehow invigorated a patriotic sense in their readership by aligning with the official discourse emphasizing American virtues and resilience while demonizing terrorists. The authors concluded journalists had followed these nationalist themes in the weeks immediately after the attacks on New York City and Washington, DC.[56] In a different study, Vicki Deveau and Gregory Fouts examined the frequency of use of revenge words in U.S. and Canadian newsmagazines in the aftermath of the 9/11 terrorist acts to determine if there were any discernible differences between the incidents of using those words on either side of the border and if revenge was associated with justifications of evil. The researchers found that the U.S. magazine *Newsweek* presented evil justifications more often than did the Canadian edition of *Time* and Canadian *Maclean's*. However, they also found evidence that *Maclean's* used more revenge words than did either *Newsweek* or *Time*.[57]

The trauma represented by 9/11 and the clear shift it represents in the history of terrorist events focuses in this cluster's almost monothematic attention to terrorism and the war to fight it. Notwithstanding, another war quite remote from the Gulf was another recipient of scholarly attention.

The war in Kosovo lasted from 1998 to 1999. Although the conflict occurred in the pre-9/11 era, research on the war was being published well into the post-9/11 period. The reason is not clear, but may be a result of the war in the Middle East calling attention to another recent conflict in which international forces led by NATO were called into action. Both articles on the Kosovo war share the same methodological approach, visual content analysis. In the first, Alexander Nikolaev sought to verify whether the three major mainstream American newsmagazines accurately described the struggle opposing Albanian and Serbian communities. He concluded from the data that the magazines showed some bias against the Serbs.[58] In a second study that focused on the newsmagazines' photo coverage, Wendy Kozol gave evidence to suggest the three magazines preferred images of fleeing women and children, while not showing acts of torture and repression.[59] As was also true in the case of picturing the First Gulf War,[60] the findings of both Nikolaev and Kozol's studies lead to the conclusion that images of the actual acts of armed warfare are not presented to the public. Indeed, analyzing the scholarly inquiry into newsmagazines' pre- and post- 9/11 coverage of war suggests newsmagazines exercise a sort of self-censorship. They do not publish images of actual warfare horror to the public. Direct confrontation, torture and correlated situations derived from extreme conflict are neither much written about nor illustrated through pictures. Inversely, weaponry, refugees, explanations and justifications for war are preferred to the actual description of atrocities. Similarly, the analysis shows the killing of U.S. troops was also muted in the 1990 to 2012 coverage.

In the War and International Relations, Post-9/11 cluster, international relations outside the borders of the Middle East were almost eclipsed by intense attention being directed to terrorism and war. However, U.S. newsmagazines' coverage of U.S. foreign policy and America's protective role in besieged democracies was analyzed in Lisa Brooten's study of Burma and Nobel Peace Prize winner Aung San Suu Kyi. The study is an example of an analysis of the role of America, a mature democratic state, in its relationship with countries where democracies are feeble in a post–Cold War era. The newsmagazines in the analysis were again *Time, News-week* and *U.S. News & World Report.*[61]

Africa provided topical interest for three articles in the pre-9/11 cluster. However, in the post-9/11 period, only one study focused on Africa: Kristen Alley Swain's inquiry into U.S. and British newsmagazines' coverage of the AIDS drama in Sub-Saharan Africa. Swain sought to determine whether power status, as measured by Gross Domestic Product (GDP), population and military spending, among other indicators, contributed to the frequency of references to the countries in Western newsmagazines.[62]

Domestic Public Affairs Studies

The bulk of the corpus of research in this meta-analysis, a total of 28 articles, fell in the two clusters labeled pre- and post- 9/11 War and International Relations. The remaining 16 studies clustered into three subgroups that fell under the broader category Domestic Public Affairs (See Table 14.4).

Socio-Political Concerns. Socio-Political Concerns includes studies ranging from the coverage of mass murder and ethical issues raised when only a dim line separates the mediation of crime from entertainment,[63] to questions of meritocracy in U.S. politics and how leading newsmagazines reflect the still prevailing hierarchy of discrimination related to gender and ethnicity of political actors.[64] In this block of nine articles, the most prominent issues were related to elections and electoral campaigns.

Scholarly work on social-political concerns devotes careful attention to democratic processes of representation. Among these studies are several that pay particular attention to how newsmagazines cover electoral campaigns at both U.S. and international levels, using a comparative approach to contrast the coverage.[65] Another recurrent topic was analysis of press coverage of particular candidates, especially those whose profiles differed from white males, as in the cases of Colin Powell[66] and Hillary Clinton.[67] Finally, analyses of campaign coverage focused on newsmagazines' visual profiles of candidates and whether there was a relationship between the number of images and the amount of attention given to candidates' campaigns. Sandra Moriarty and Mark Popovich concluded that newsmagazines devote the same amount of attention to the candidates irrespective of the number of photos they publish.[68] Racial issues in electoral campaigns were also analyzed to determine whether there was a relationship between candidates' origins and newsmagazines' coverage of their campaigns. Catherine Squires and Sarah J. Jackson's data indicated that during the 2008 primaries newsmagazines did not so much put an emphasis on candidates' ethnicity but rather treated voters in terms of competing blocs arranged along a racial divide.[69]

Poverty and Unemployment Issues. In the second subgroup of studies, Poverty and Unemployment Issues, researchers looked at urban contexts and reflections of population rungs directly

Table 14.4. Topical summary of articles

Topic	Articles N
War and International Relations, Pre-9/11	11
War and International Relations, Post-9/11	17
Domestic Public Affairs	16
Socio-Political Concerns	9
Poverty and Unemployment Issues	4
Supreme Court Rulings	3
Total:	44

connected to ethnicity. Scholars here examined the role newsmagazines play in disseminating stereotypes: of the poor as gangsters, undeserving of welfare, living in derelict urban centers and mostly not white. Findings were consistent across the four studies, suggesting that newsmagazines perpetuate wrong images of the poor and accentuate the negatives of economic exclusion by connecting it with race and crime.[70]

Supreme Court Rulings. Studies in the third subcategory focused attention mainly on *Time*, *Newsweek* and *U.S. News & World Report*'s coverage of U.S. Supreme Court Rulings that affect citizens' lives. Articles in the period covered by this meta-study concentrated on a uniform theme: coverage of Supreme Court decisions related to the First Amendment. Scholars concluded that issues such as civil rights cases, media taxation and judicial personality tend to receive more coverage than what would be justified by the Supreme Court's caseload.[71]

Summarizing the research in the broad topic of domestic affairs suggests that scholarly interest in newsmagazine's coverage of modern society and mediated risk has tended to cast light on threats close to people's worries: judicial rulings affecting the liberties safeguarded by the First Amendment, economic opportunity and electoral campaigns as the hallmarks of democracy. These in turn suggest the blanket afforded by the expression *public affairs* has covered issues that are mostly associated with a society of danger(s), as Beck described. However, academic interest in this cluster also indicates the importance associated with the socializing role of the mass media. Audiences exposed to the media "learn and internalize some of the values, beliefs, and norms presented in media products."[72] Similarly, the media "mediate our relationship with various social institutions,"[73] such as the government, the judiciary, to name but a few. In a nutshell, newsmagazines' depiction of public affairs is none other than the exercise of a socializing role that provides communities with a sense of belonging, exactly what Anderson's views expressed at the beginning of this chapter presume: The media help in the creation of imagined communities.

Future Prospects

This meta-analysis showed that scholarly literature on newsmagazines and public affairs covers an eclectic range of subjects, with a common denominator of risk and the perilous nature of contemporary society. In this light, public affairs may be defined as issues that generate social anxiety. War was by far the topic most often scrutinized by scholars. In the post-9/11 era, war was mostly associated with the Middle East and the fight against terrorism. Terrorism itself, almost absent from research on public affairs coverage in newsmagazines in the 1990 to 2001, pre-9/11 setting, gained prominence in the aftermath of that traumatic event. However, issues associated with fear and anxiety are the main focus of research on newsmagazines' coverage of public affairs in general. Topics analyzed also focus on socioeconomic inequalities, elections and judicial decisions affecting the most basic civil liberties.

Future research might therefore be expected to similarly follow the emerging ebbs and flows as threats in the contemporary world are covered by newsweeklies. The functionings of democracy will continue to draw attention as will the newest wars and attacks on human lives. The magazine, as a "supple reflector of the social reality of its time,"[74] is inextricable from all and any of the manifold walks of life in society. Newsmagazines and their interest in public affairs do not constitute an exception and will likely go on mirroring the changes and evolution pertaining to the topics specifically highlighted for this research.

Scholarly attention to newsmagazines was dominated by the U.S. magazines *Time*, *Newsweek* and *U.S. News & World Report* through the time frame for this research, 1990 through 2012, as evidenced in the studies found in the literature search. Whether analyzed individually or in aggregate, the three titles are representative of what is understood by newsmagazines. What the future will bring is open to conjecture. *Newsweek* was for a time a solely on-line publication.[75] *U.S. News & World Report* also changed focus to "the business of selling 'essential information' defined not as news but, as data on which people base buying decisions."[76] Nevertheless, it does seem likely that scholarly interest on the content of newsmagazines will not wane, irrespective of further migrations to a digital format or shifts in purpose.

Indeed, if there were a fourth cluster for this research, it would be on literature about the future of newsmagazines. The challenges of the digital era concern news emporiums and members of the academy. The roads for research are wide and open. Electoral campaigns have now also been fought in Twitter; tablet applications provide new functionalities for the dissemination of news; blogs and Facebook allow for self-publishing content, and Web journalism is on the increase. Each of these raises questions for debate and study.[77] Newsmagazines have kept pace with modernity in the on-line era. The days of initial adaptation belong to the past, and new trials and transformations reflect the inexorable progress of technology and the broadening of communication alleys. If readership of print editions has declined, the same cannot be stated about the public accessing newsweeklies' on-line pages. Figures show that monthly Web traffic for 2010 was at 4.9 million for *Time* and 3.7 million for *Newsweek*.[78] If newsmagazines are here to stay, so too is research on them.

This research also suggests intriguing possibilities for analysis of other countries' newsmagazines' coverage of public affairs, which is indeed a limitation to this study. It would be interesting to see how established newsweeklies such as Canadian *Maclean's*, Britain's *New Statesman* or Germany's *Der Spiegel* cover the topics that fell into the categories scholars studied in U.S. newsmagazine contexts. Similarly worthy of attention would be to see how the Portuguese *Visão* and Brazilian *Veja* cater for a 200 million Lusophone audience on both sides of the Atlantic when the topic is public affairs. And the same could be said of New Delhi–based *India Today*, a newsmagazine with a circulation of more than one million copies and representative of the press from one of the fastest growing emergent economies in the world and, simultaneously, its largest democracy. Whether case studies for individual countries or languages or comparative analysis, research on the coverage of public affairs by newsmagazines is open to an almost infinite array of possibilities and will continue to be so in the future.

Notes

1 Dictionary.com, s.v. "Public Affairs" <http://dictionary.reference.com/browse/public+affairs>, accessed 27 December 2012.

2 W. Russell Neuman, Marion R. Just, and Ann N. Crigler, *Common Knowledge: News and the Construction of Political Meaning* (Chicago: University of Chicago Press, 1992), 3. Italics in the original.

3 See "*Journal of Public Affairs*: Description." Wiley <http://eu.wiley.com/WileyCDA/WileyTitle/productCd-PA.html>, accessed 27 December 2012.

4 Anderson defines *nation* as "an imagined political community—and imagined as both inherently limited and sovereign. . . . In fact, all communities larger than primordial villages of face-to-face contact . . . are imagined." Benedict Anderson, *Imagined Communities: Reflection on the Origin and Spread of Nationalism*, rev. ed. (London and New York: Verso, 2006), 6.

5 Michael Schudson, "News, Public, Nation," *American Historical Review* 107.2 (April 2002): 484.

6 Tim Holmes, "Mapping the Magazine: An Introduction," *Journalism Studies* 8.4 (August 2007): 510.

7 David E. Sumner, "A Bibliography of American Magazine History," *The Magazine Century: American Magazines since 1900*, Mediating American History Series (New York: Peter Lang, 2010), 225–234.

8 Holmes, "Mapping the Magazine," 511.

9 Sumner, "A Bibliography of American Magazine History," 12.

10 John T. Woolley, "Using Media-Based Data in Studies of Politics," *American Journal of Political Science* 44.1 (January 2000): 156.

11 Woolley, "Using Media-Based Data," 156.

12 Klaus Bruhn Jensen, "The Qualitative Research Process," in Klaus Bruhn Jensen, ed., *A Handbook of Media and Communication Research: Qualitative and Quantitative Methodologies* (London and New York: Routledge, 2002), 244.

13 The linguistic dominance of languages, such as Portuguese, Spanish and English, is accounted for by the colonial past of their respective European powers. As Nicholas Ostler elucidates, "English, Spanish, Portuguese and French, all owe their status to the colonial empires that came to dominate the earth in the second half of the second millennium AD. They are the languages of colonial populations that were able to grow massively in their new, transplanted, homes, adding the strength of immigrants to their natural increase; they were also able to spread at the expense of languages previously local to the colonized lands: in this way, languages of wider communication often ended up monopolising all the communication." Nicholas Ostler, *Empires of the Word: A Language History of the World* (New York and London: Harper Perennial, 2005), 531.

14 The actual figure for April 2013 indicates that *Veja* has a circulation of 1,191,803 copies and 917,193 subscribers. See "Tabela Circulação Geral," *IVC*, May 2013 <http://www.publiabril.com.br/tabelas-gerais/revistas/circulacao-geral/imprimir>, accessed 19 April 2013.

15 Jensen, "The Qualitative Research Process," 236. Italics in the original.

16 Founded in 1933, *Newsweek* had an estimate weekly readership of about 1.5 million since 2005. See Robert Daniel and Keach Hagey, "Turning a Page: *Newsweek* Ends Print Run," *Wall Street Journal*, 26 December 2012, B.3.

17 *Time*, founded in 1923, describes itself as the "world's largest weekly newsmagazine, with a domestic audience of more than 20 million and a global audience of more than 24 million," in "TimeInc: News/Business /Sports," TimeInc. <http://www.timeinc.com/brands/news-businessfinance.php>, accessed 13 January 2013.

18 Michael Griffin and Jongsoo Lee, "Picturing the Gulf War: Constructing an Image of War in *Time, Newsweek*, and *U.S. News & World Report*," *Journalism & Mass Communication Quarterly* 72.4 (Winter 1995): 813–825.

19 Jack Lule, "Enduring Image of War: Myth and Ideology in a *Newsweek* Cover," *Journal of Popular Culture* 29.1 (Summer 1995): 199–211.

20 Shahzad Ali and Khalid, "US Mass Media and Muslim World: Portrayal of Muslim by 'News Week' and 'Time' (1991–2001)," *European Journal of Scientific Research* 21.4 (August 2008): 554–580.

21 Richard K. Popp and Andrew L. Mendelson, "'X'-ing Out Enemies: *Time* Magazine, Visual Discourse, and the War in Iraq," *Journalism* 11.2 (April 2010): 203–221.

22 Ghulam Shabir, Shahzad Ali, and Zafar Iqbal, "U.S. Mass Media and Image of Afghanistan: Portrayal of Afghanistan by *Newsweek* and *Time*," *South Asian Studies* 26.1 (January/June 2011): 83–101.

23 Ulrich Beck, *Risk Society: Towards a New Modernity*, trans. Mark Ritter (London and Newbury Park, CA: Sage Publications, 1992), 22. Italics in the original.

24 Beck, *Risk Society*, 23.

25 Lule, "Enduring Image of War," 199–211.

26 Alexander G. Nikolaev, "Images of War: Content Analysis of the Photo Coverage of the War in Kosovo," *Critical Sociology* 35.1 (January 2009): 105–130. The five articles specifically concentrating on visual contents analysis are: Sandra E. Moriarty and Mark N. Popovich, "Newsmagazine Visuals and the 1988 Presidential Election," *Journalism Quarterly* 68.3 (Fall 1991): 371–380; Lule, "Enduring Image of War," 199–211; Griffin and Lee, "Picturing the Gulf War," 813–825; Nikolaev, "Images of War," 105–130; and Popp and Mendelson, "'X'-ing Out Enemies," 203–221.

27 Adam Shehata, "Facing the Muhammad Cartoons: Official Dominance and Event-Driven News in Swedish and American Elite Press," *International Journal of Press/Politics* 12.4 (October 2007): 131–153.

28 Catherine R. Squires and Sarah J. Jackson, "Reducing Race: News Themes in the 2008 Primaries," *International Journal of Press/Politics* 15.4 (October 2010): 375–400.

29 Howard Ramos, James Ron, and Oskar N.T. Thoms, "Shaping the Northern Media's Human Rights Coverage, 1986–2000," *Journal of Peace Research* 44.4 (July 2007): 385–406.

30 Erika G. King and Robert A. Wells, "American Newsmagazine Coverage of the Persian Gulf War: The Parallels of World War II and Vietnam," *Southeastern Political Review* 22.2 (June 1994): 341–367.

31 Griffin and Lee, "Picturing the Gulf War," 813–825.

32 Lule, "Enduring Image of War."

33 John D.H. Downing, "U.S. Media Discourse on South Africa: The Development of a Situation Model," *Discourse & Society* 1.1 (July 1990): 39–60.

34 Keith R. Kenney, "Images of Africa in News Magazines: Is There a Black Perspective?" *Gazette* 54.1 (August 1995): 61–85.

35 Melissa A. Wall, "The Rwanda Crisis: An Analysis of News Magazine Coverage," *International Communication Gazette* 59.2 (April 1997): 121–134.

36 Heidi Mau and Carolyn Kitch, "'No Longer Chasing Yesterday's Story': New Roles for Newsmagazines in the 21st Century," in Stuart Allen, ed., *Routledge Companion to News and Journalism*, rev. ed. (London and New York: Routledge/Taylor & Francis, 2012), 650.

37 William S. Solomon, "News Frames and Media Packages: Covering El Salvador," *Critical Studies in Mass Communication* 9.1 (March 1992): 56–74.

38 Sonia Gutierrez-Villalobos, James K. Hertog, and Ramona R. Rush, "Press Support for the U.S. Adminis-tration during the Panama Invasion: Analyses of Strategic and Tactical Critique in the Domestic Press," *Journalism Quarterly* 71.3 (Autumn 1994): 618–627.

39 Brian K. Simmons and David N. Lowry, "Terrorists in the News, as Reflected in Three News Magazines, 1980–1988," *Journalism Quarterly* 67.4 (Winter 1990): 692–696; Robert M. Entman, "Framing U.S. Cover-age of International News: Contrasts in Narratives of the KAL and Iran Air Incidents," *Journal of Communi-cation* 41.4 (Autumn 1991): 6–27; Ramos, Ron, and Thoms, "Shaping the Northern Media's Human Rights Coverage," 385–406.

40 Articles focusing on the war in Iraq include Douglas V. Porpora and Alexander Nikolaev, "Moral Muting in U.S. Newspaper Op-Eds Debating the Attack on Iraq," *Discourse & Communication* 2.2 (May 2008): 165–184; Dustin Harp, Jaime Loke, and Ingrid Bachmann, "Voices of Dissent in the Iraq War: Moving from Deviance to Legitimacy?" *Journalism & Mass Communication Quarterly* 87.3/4 (Autumn/Winter 2010): 467–483; Popp and Mendelson, "'X'-ing Out Enemies," 203–221.

41 Bethami A. Dobkin, *Tales of Terror: Television News and the Construction of the Terrorist Threat* (New York: Praeger, 1992), 36.

42 Brigitte L. Nacos, "Terrorism as Breaking News: Attack on America," *Political Science Quarterly* 118.1 (Spring 2003): 23.

43 Philip Schlesinger, *Media, State, and Nation: Political Violence and Collective Identities* (London, Thousand Oaks and New Delhi: Sage Publications, 1991), 22.

44 Dobkin, *Tales of Terror*, 2.

45 Ali and Khalid, "U.S. Mass Media and Muslim World," 554–580.

46 Shehata, "Facing the Muhammad Cartoons," 131–153.

47 Barbara Friedman, "Unlikely Warriors: How Four U.S. News Sources Explained Female Suicide Bombers," *Journalism & Mass Communication Quarterly* 85.4 (Winter 2008): 841–859.

48 Amy Fried, "Terrorism as a Context of Coverage before the Iraq War," *International Journal of Press/Politics* 10.3 (Summer 2005): 125–132; Joshua Woods, "What We Talk about When We Talk about Terrorism: Elite Press Coverage of Terrorism Risk from 1997 to 2005," *International Journal of Press/Politics* 12.3 (Summer 2007): 3–20; and David L. Altheide, "The Mass Media and Terrorism," *Discourse & Communication* 1.3 (August 2007): 287–308.

49 Dobkin, *Tales of Terror*, 38.

50 Harp, Loke, and Bachmann, "Voices of Dissent in the Iraq War," 467–483.

51 Porpora and Nikolaev, "Moral Muting in U.S. Newspaper Op-Eds," 165–184.

52 Popp and Mendelson, "'X'-ing Out Enemies," 203–221.

53 Shabir, Ali, and Iqbal, "U.S. Mass Media and Image of Afghanistan," 83–101.

54 Sherry Ricchiardi, "Offscreen," *American Journalism Review*, October/November 2008 <http://www.ajr.org/article.asp?id=4602>, accessed 14 January 2013.

55 Nacos, "Terrorism as Breaking News," 23.

56 John Hutcheson, David Domke, Andre Billeaudeaux, and Philip Garland, "U.S. National Identity, Political Elites, and a Patriotic Press Following September 11," *Political Communication* 21.1 (January/March 2004): 27–50.

57 Vicki Deveau and Gregory Fouts, "Revenge in U.S. and Canadian News Magazines Post 9/11," *Canadian Journal of Communication* 30.1 (2005): 99–109.

58 Nikolaev, "Images of War," 105–130.

59 Wendy Kozol, "Domesticating NATO's War in Kosovo/a: (In)Visible Bodies and the Dilemma of Photo-journalism," *Meridians: Feminism, Race, Transnationalism* 4.2 (2004): 1–38.

60 Griffin and Lee, "Picturing the Gulf War."

61 Lisa Brooten, "The Feminization of Democracy under Siege: The Media, 'The Lady' of Burma, and U.S. Foreign Policy," *NWSA Journal* [National Women's Studies Association Journal] 17.3 (Fall 2005): 134–156.

62 Kristen Alley Swain, "Proximity and Power Factors in Western Coverage of the Sub-Saharan AIDS Crisis," *Journalism & Mass Communication Quarterly* 80.1 (Spring 2003): 145–165.

63 Clayton E. Cramer, "Ethical Problems of Mass Murder Coverage in the Mass Media," *Journal of Mass Media Ethics* 9.1 (1994): 26–42.

64 Kimberly Bachechi, "Taking Care of Washington," *Journal of American Culture* 33.2 (June 2010): 126–138.

65 Ann Marie Major, "'Problematic' Situations in Press Coverage of the 1988 U.S. and French Elections," *Journalism Quarterly* 69.3 (Fall 1992): 600–611; Robert T. Buckman, "How Eight Weekly Newsmagazines Covered Elections in Six Countries," *Journalism Quarterly* 70.4 (Winter 1993): 780–792; and L. Paul Hus-selbee and Guido H. Stempel, III, "Contrast in U.S. Media Coverage of Two Major Canadian Elections," *Journalism & Mass Communication Quarterly* 74.3 (Autumn 1997): 591–601.

66 Janis L. Edwards, "The Very Model of a Modern Major (Media) Candidate: Colin Powell and the Rhetoric of Public Opinion," *Communication Quarterly* 46.2 (Spring 1998): 163–176.

67 Raluca Moldovan, "A Tale of Two Clintons: Media Bias in the Coverage of Hillary Clinton's 2008 Presidential Campaign," *Studia Universitatis Babeş-Bolyai, Studia Europaea* 54.2 (2009): 41–60.

68 Moriarty and Popovich, "Newsmagazine Visuals and the 1988 Presidential Election."

69 Squires and Jackson, "Reducing Race," 375–400.

70 Martin Gilens, "Race and Poverty in America: Public Misperceptions and the American News Media," *Public Opinion Quarterly* 60.4 (Winter 1996): 515–541; Rosalee A. Clawson and Rakuya Trice, "Poverty as We Know It: Media Portrayals of the Poor," *Public Opinion Quarterly* 64.1 (Spring 2000): 53–64; Peter Dreier, "How the Media Compound Urban Problems," *Journal of Urban Affairs* 27.2 (June 2005): 193–201; and Tomoko Kanayama, "Magazine Coverage of Welfare Recipients 1969–1996: Media Rituals and American Society," *Journal of American and Canadian Studies* 21 (March 2004): 83–113.

71 Jerome O'Callaghan and James O. Dukes, "Media Coverage of the Supreme Court's Caseload," *Journalism Quarterly* 69.1 (Spring 1992): 195–203; Dorothy A. Bowles and Rebekah V. Bromley, "Newsmagazine Coverage of the Supreme Court during the Reagan Administration," *Journalism Quarterly* 69.4 (Winter 1992): 948–959; and Cathy Packer and Karla K. Gower, "The Persistent Problem of Media Taxation: First Amendment Protection in the 1990s," *Journalism & Mass Communication Quarterly* 74.3 (Autumn 1997): 579–590.

72 David Crouteau and William Hoynes, *Media/Society: Industries, Images, and Audiences*, 2nd ed. (London: Thousand Oaks and New Delhi: Pine Forge Press, 2000), 15.

73 Crouteau and Hoynes, *Media/Society*, 16.

74 David Abrahamson, "The Future of Magazines: 2010–2020," *Journal of Magazine & New Media Research* 10.2 (Spring 2009): 1.

75 In 2013, *Newsweek* was published exclusively in an on-line format.

76 Mau and Kitch, "'No Longer Chasing Yesterday's Story,'" 652.

77 Michael Bromley and Heather Purdey, "Journo-Morphosis: Today's New Media and the Education and Training of Tomorrow's 'Cool' Journalists," *Convergence, the International Journal of Research into New Media Technologies* 4.4 (December 1998): 77–93; Carla Rodrigues Cardoso, "The Future of Newsmagazines," *Journalism Studies* 11.4 (August 2010): 577–586; Susan Greenberg, "When the Editor Disappears, Does Editing Disappear?" *Convergence: The International Journal of Research into New Media Technologies* 16.1 (February 2010): 7–21; Jodi Enda, "Campaign Coverage in the Time of Twitter," *American Journalism Review*, 25 August 2011 <http://www.ajr.org/article.asp?id=5134>, accessed 18 January 2013; and Caitlin Johnston, "Second Chance," *American Journalism Review*, April/May 2012 <http://ajr.org/Article.asp?id=5278>, accessed 18 January 2013.

78 Mau and Kitch, "'No Longer Chasing Yesterday's Story,'" 654.

Bibliography

Abrahamson, David. "The Future of Magazines, 2010–2020." *Journal of Magazine & New Media Research* 10.2 (Spring 2009): 1–3.

Ali, Shahzad and Khalid. "US Mass Media and Muslim World: Portrayal of Muslim by 'News Week' and 'Time' (1991–2001)." *European Journal of Scientific Research* 21.4 (August 2008): 554–580.

Altheide, David L. "The Mass Media and Terrorism." *Discourse & Communication* 1.3 (August 2007): 287–308.

Anderson, Benedict. *Imagined Communities: Reflections on the Origin and Spread of Nationalism*. Rev. ed. London and New York: Verso, 2006.

Bachechi, Kimberly. "Taking Care of Washington." *Journal of American Culture* 33.2 (June 2010): 126–138.

Beck, Ulrich. *Risk Society: Towards a New Modernity*. Translated by Mark Ritter. London and Newbury Park, CA: Sage Publications, 1992.

Bowles, Dorothy A. and Bromley, Rebekah V. "Newsmagazine Coverage of the Supreme Court during the Reagan Administration." *Journalism Quarterly* 69.4 (Winter 1992): 948–959.

Bromley, Michael and Purdey, Heather. "Journo-Morphosis: Today's New Media and the Education and Training of Tomorrow's 'Cool' Journalists." *Convergence, the International Journal of Research into New Media Technologies* 4.4 (December 1998): 77–93.

Brooten, Lisa. "The Feminization of Democracy under Siege: The Media, 'The Lady' of Burma, and U.S. Foreign Policy." *NWSA Journal* [*National Women's Studies Association Journal*] 17.3 (Fall 2005): 134–156.

Buckman, Robert T. "How Eight Weekly Newsmagazines Covered Elections in Six Countries." *Journalism Quarterly* 70.4 (Winter 1993): 780–792.

Cardoso, Carla Rodrigues. "The Future of Newsmagazines." *Journalism Studies* 11.4 (August 2010): 577–586.

Clawson, Rosalee A. and Trice, Rakuya. "Poverty as We Know It: Media Portrayals of the Poor." *Public Opinion Quarterly* 64.1 (Spring 2000): 53–64.

Cramer, Clayton E. "Ethical Problems of Mass Murder Coverage in the Mass Media." *Journal of Mass Media Ethics* 9.1 (1994): 26–42.

Crouteau, David and Hoynes, William. *Media/Society: Industries, Images, and Audiences.* 2nd ed. Thousand Oaks, London and New Delhi: Pine Forge Press, 2000.

Daniel, Robert and Hagey, Keach. "Turning a Page: *Newsweek* Ends Print Run." *Wall Street Journal*, 26 December 2012, B.3.

Deveau, Vicki and Fouts, Gregory. "Revenge in U.S. and Canadian News Magazines Post 9/11." *Canadian Journal of Communication* 30.1 (2005): 99–109.

Dictionary.com. s.v. "Public Affairs" <http://dictionary.reference.com/browse/public+affairs>, accessed 27 December 2012.

Dobkin, Bethami A. *Tales of Terror: Television News and the Construction of the Terrorist Threat.* New York: Praeger, 1992.

Downing, John D.H. "U.S. Media Discourse on South Africa: The Development of a Situation Model." *Discourse & Society* 1.1 (July 1990): 39–60.

Dreier, Peter. "How the Media Compound Urban Problems." *Journal of Urban Affairs* 27.2 (June 2005): 193–201.

Edwards, Janis L. "The Very Model of a Modern Major (Media) Candidate: Colin Powell and the Rhetoric of Public Opinion." *Communication Quarterly* 46.2 (Spring 1998): 163–176.

Enda, Jodi. "Campaign Coverage in the Time of Twitter." *American Journalism Review*, 25 August 2011 <http://www.ajr.org/article.asp?id=5134>, accessed 18 January 2013.

Entman, Robert M. "Framing U.S. Coverage of International News: Contrasts in Narratives of the KAL and Iran Air Incidents." *Journal of Communication* 41.4 (Autumn 1991): 6–27.

Fried, Amy. "Terrorism as a Context of Coverage before the Iraq War." *International Journal of Press/Politics* 10.3 (Summer 2005): 125–132.

Friedman, Barbara. "Unlikely Warriors: How Four U.S. News Sources Explained Female Suicide Bombers." *Journalism & Mass Communication Quarterly* 85.4 (Winter 2008): 841–859.

Gilens, Martin. "Race and Poverty in America: Public Misperceptions and the American News Media." *Public Opinion Quarterly* 60.4 (Winter 1996): 515–541.

Greenberg, Susan. "When the Editor Disappears, Does Editing Disappear?" *Convergence: The International Journal of Research into New Media Technologies* 16.1 (February 2010): 7–21.

Griffin, Michael and Lee, Jongsoo. "Picturing the Gulf War: Constructing an Image of War in *Time*, *Newsweek*, and *U.S. News & World Report*." *Journalism & Mass Communication Quarterly* 72.4 (Winter 1995): 813–825.

Gutierrez-Villalobos, Sonia; Hertog, James K.; and Rush, Ramona R. "Press Support for the U.S. Administration during the Panama Invasion: Analyses of Strategic and Tactical Critique in the Domestic Press." *Journalism Quarterly* 71.3 (Autumn 1994): 618–627.

Harp, Dustin; Loke, Jaime; and Bachmann, Ingrid. "Voices of Dissent in the Iraq War: Moving from Deviance to Legitimacy?" *Journalism & Mass Communication Quarterly* 87.3/4 (Autumn/Winter 2010): 467–483.

Holmes, Tim. "Mapping the Magazine: An Introduction." *Journalism Studies* 8.4 (August 2007): 510–521.

Husselbee, L. Paul and Stempel, Guido H., III. "Contrast in U.S. Media Coverage of Two Major Canadian Elections." *Journalism & Mass Communication Quarterly* 74.3 (Autumn 1997): 591–601.

Hutcheson, John; Domke, David; Billeaudeaux, Andre; and Garland, Philip. "U.S. National Identity, Political Elites, and a Patriotic Press Following September 11." *Political Communication* 21.1 (January/March 2004): 27–50.

Jensen, Klaus Bruhn. "The Qualitative Research Process." In Jensen, Klaus Bruhn, ed. *A Handbook of Media and Communication Research: Qualitative and Quantitative Methodologies.* London and New York: Routledge, 2002, 235–253.

Johnston, Caitlin. "Second Chance." *American Journalism Review*, April/May 2012 <http://ajr.org/Article.asp?id=5278>, accessed 18 January 2013.

"*Journal of Public Affairs*: Description." Wiley <http://eu.wiley.com/WileyCDA/WileyTitle/productCd-PA.html>, accessed 27 December 2012.

Kanayama, Tomoko. "Magazine Coverage of Welfare Recipients 1969–1996: Media Rituals and American Society." *Journal of American and Canadian Studies* 21 (March 2004): 83–113.

Kenney, Keith R. "Images of Africa in News Magazines: Is There a Black Perspective?" *Gazette* 54.1 (August 1995): 61–85.

King, Erika G. and Wells, Robert A. "American Newsmagazine Coverage of the Persian Gulf War: The Parallels of World War II and Vietnam." *Southeastern Political Review* 22.2 (June 1994): 341–367.

Kozol, Wendy. "Domesticating NATO's War in Kosovo/a: (In)Visible Bodies and the Dilemma of Photojournalism." *Meridians: Feminism, Race, Transnationalism* 4.2 (2004): 1–38.

Lule, Jack. "Enduring Image of War: Myth and Ideology in a *Newsweek* Cover." *Journal of Popular Culture* 29.1 (Summer 1995): 199–211.

Major, Ann Marie. "'Problematic' Situations in Press Coverage of the 1988 U.S. and French Elections." *Journalism Quarterly* 69.3 (Fall 1992): 600–611.

Mau, Heidi and Kitch, Carolyn. "'No Longer Chasing Yesterday's Story': New Roles for Newsmagazines in the 21st Century." In Allen, Stuart, ed. *Routledge Companion to News and Journalism*. Rev. ed. London and New York: Routledge/Taylor & Francis, 2012, 649–660.

Moldovan, Raluca. "A Tale of Two Clintons: Media Bias in the Coverage of Hillary Clinton's 2008 Presidential Campaign." *Studia Universitatis Babeş-Bolyai, Studia Europaea* 54.2 (2009): 41–60.

Moriarty, Sandra E. and Popovich, Mark N. "Newsmagazine Visuals and the 1988 Presidential Election." *Journalism Quarterly* 68.3 (Fall 1991): 371–380.

Nacos, Brigitte L. "Terrorism as Breaking News: Attack on America." *Political Science Quarterly* 118.1 (Spring 2003): 23–52.

Neuman, W. Russell; Just, Marion R.; and Crigler, Ann N. *Common Knowledge: News and the Construction of Political Meaning*. Chicago: University of Chicago Press, 1992.

Nikolaev, Alexander G. "Images of War: Content Analysis of the Photo Coverage of the War in Kosovo." *Critical Sociology* 35.1 (January 2009): 105–130.

O'Callaghan, Jerome and Dukes, James O. "Media Coverage of the Supreme Court's Caseload." *Journalism Quarterly* 69.1 (Spring 1992): 195–203.

Ostler, Nicholas. *Empires of the Word: A Language History of the World*. New York and London: Harper Perennial, 2005.

Packer, Cathy and Gower, Karla K. "The Persistent Problem of Media Taxation: First Amendment Protection in the 1990s." *Journalism & Mass Communication Quarterly* 74.3 (Autumn 1997): 579–590.

Popp, Richard K. and Mendelson, Andrew L. "'X'-ing Out Enemies: *Time* Magazine, Visual Discourse, and the War in Iraq." *Journalism* 11.2 (April 2010): 203–221.

Porpora, Douglas V. and Nikolaev, Alexander. "Moral Muting in U.S. Newspaper Op-Eds Debating the Attack on Iraq." *Discourse & Communication* 2.2 (May 2008): 165–184.

Ramos, Howard; Ron, James; and Thoms, Oskar N.T. "Shaping the Northern Media's Human Rights Coverage, 1986–2000." *Journal of Peace Research* 44.4 (July 2007): 385–406.

Ricchiardi, Sherry. "Offscreen." *American Journalism Review*, October/November 2008 <http://www.ajr.org/article.asp?id=4602>, accessed 14 January 2013.

Schlesinger, Philip. *Media, State, and Nation: Political Violence and Collective Identities*. London, Thousand Oaks and New Delhi: Sage Publications, 1991.

Schudson, Michael. "News, Public, Nation." *American Historical Review* 107.2 (April 2002): 481–495.

Shabir, Ghulam; Ali, Shahzad; and Iqbal, Zafar. "U.S. Mass Media and Image of Afghanistan: Portrayal of Afghanistan by *Newsweek* and *Time*." *South Asian Studies* 26.1 (January/June 2011): 83–101.

Shehata, Adam. "Facing the Muhammad Cartoons: Official Dominance and Event-Driven News in Swedish and American Elite Press." *International Journal of Press/Politics* 12.4 (October 2007): 131–153.

Simmons, Brian K. and Lowry, David N. "Terrorists in the News, as Reflected in Three News Magazines, 1980–1988." *Journalism Quarterly* 67.4 (Winter 1990): 692–696.

Solomon, William S. "News Frames and Media Packages: Covering El Salvador." *Critical Studies in Mass Communication* 9.1 (March 1992): 56–74.

Squires, Catherine R. and Jackson, Sarah J. "Reducing Race: News Themes in the 2008 Primaries." *International Journal of Press/Politics* 15.4 (October 2010): 375–400.

Sumner, David E. "A Bibliography of American Magazine History." *The Magazine Century: American Magazines since 1900*. Mediating American History Series. New York: Peter Lang, 2010, 225–234.

Swain, Kristen Alley. "Proximity and Power Factors in Western Coverage of the Sub-Saharan AIDS Crisis." *Journalism & Mass Communication Quarterly* 80.1 (Spring 2003): 145–165.

"Tabela Circulação Geral." *IVC*, May 2013 <http://www.publiabril.com.br/tabelas-gerais/revistas/circula cao-geral/imprimir>, accessed 19 April 2013.

"TimeInc.: News/Business/Sports." TimeInc. <http://www.timeinc.com/brands/news-businessfinance. php>, accessed 13 January 2013.

Wall, Melissa A. "The Rwanda Crisis: An Analysis of News Magazine Coverage." *International Communication Gazette* 59.2 (April 1997): 121–134.

Woods, Joshua. "What We Talk About When We Talk About Terrorism: Elite Press Coverage of Terrorism Risk from 1997 to 2005." *International Journal of Press/Politics* 12.3 (Summer 2007): 3–20.

Woolley, John T. "Using Media-Based Data in Studies of Politics." *American Journal of Political Science* 44.1 (January 2000): 156–173.

15

BUSINESS JOURNALISM IN MAGAZINES

Wrestling with Economic Issues

Dane S. Claussen

President Calvin Coolidge once said, "The business of America is business."[1] This is no less true in its magazine industry than anywhere else—from the size of the industry, the amount of business news in consumer publications and the number of business-to-business and professional magazines that add up to the thousands.

The only characteristic about business or economics journalism that is different from other beats is that many U.S. journalists have long internalized public criticisms of business journalism, their own reservations about it or both. As a result, they view writing about business as difficult, boring or irrelevant. As the business-oriented magazine the *Economist* put it in 2004, business journalism in the booming 1990s was

> . . . really about getting rich, [but] watching share prices crumble was less fun, and being misled by bulls was more costly than being misled by bears. . . . The reality of business—a tough, often tedious slog—and of investing may not be compelling enough for television.[2]

That seriously covering business is tedious resulted in a bias among business journalists toward only good news and easily reported stories. What helped business journalism, nonetheless, to improve overall in the 1990s was merely how much of it there was. As business journalism professor Chris Roush recounts about that time, "With more reporters focused on writing about the economy and the business world, previously uncovered issues now received some scrutiny. In addition, new strategies for covering business helped reader comprehension."[3]

Some scholars studied business, financial and economic news during the past 25 years and systematically gathered evidence about it using social scientific, historical and other qualitative research methodologies. This chapter attempts to organize and summarize this literature in two primary ways: the first by aspect of magazine industry and content (such as news-editorial, advertising, etc.) and the second by kind of audience (and, therefore, function of magazines).

Literature Review and Method

A literature review of scholarly research into magazine coverage of business, finance and the economy must necessarily be systematic, thorough, creative and persistent, because such research is fairly minimal compared with other areas, such as magazine coverage of women's issues, sports or magazine portrayal of African-Americans. Researchers must take into account that coverage can be of entire industries, individual corporations, individual executives or other workers, job functions (such as sales people or manufacturing plant managers), trade associations, laws and regulations on business, public attitudes toward everything from capitalism generally to individual news events (such as a corporate merger that might prompt monopoly and antitrust concerns) and more. Researchers also must decide whether to allow any flexibility in a literature review that many would argue should be exclusively limited to theory and data driven, double-blind refereed articles in academic journals. This is possible, and certainly ideal, in conducting literature reviews in most areas of social science and science. However, on the topic of magazine coverage of business and economics, much of the most insightful analysis, especially on specific subjects, is by scholars writing non-refereed books or by the best journalists critiquing their fellow journalists.

This chapter cites refereed scholarly journal articles, relevant high-quality books by professors and journalists and carefully chosen articles from both the best newspapers and professional journalism magazines. Theories driving scholarly research are noted when studies were disseminated through scholarly communication journals or conferences or published by communication scholars in other disciplines' journals. Theories and research methods are not noted when cited studies were conducted by scholars in other disciplines and published in those other disciplines' journals. Most published scholarly research and trade press articles cited here were located by using search terms such as *business, economics, economy, financial* and *finance* in the Communication & Mass Media Complete database (an EBSCO product). All books cited here were located using similar search terms on the Library of Congress on-line catalog and the Amazon.com Web site. Some articles were located through reading the end notes and bibliographies of articles and books already located.

Covering Business News

The most critical question about magazine coverage of business, financial and economic news is whether magazines that should be getting the major stories are covering them and doing it well. Although magazines can be scrutinized for how they covered several major stories over the past 20-plus years, they can also be criticized for the stories they failed to cover. Three stand out: (1) the Enron story, (2) the dot com story and (3) the events and trends leading up to what is now called the Great Recession, which started in 2007, and the Global Financial Crisis of 2008.

The rise and fall of Enron, the Houston, Texas, energy, commodities and services company, is one story which, as it was and was not covered, was embarrassing to U.S. news media, as viewed by business leaders and the public alike. No mass communication scholars have published research on news coverage of Enron by magazines or any other media, even though the professional journalism magazine *Nieman Reports* analyzed Enron coverage in great depth.[4] One would think there are lessons to be learned from the entire U.S. journalism profession's failure to understand why Enron's financial statements made no sense. That revenues were always higher and always growing more quickly than cash flow should have been a red flag to journalists, that is, if they brought to their analyses an understanding of corporate finance or backgrounds in brokering mergers and acquisitions, as would this author. Unfortunately, the problems at Enron was not the only major story U.S. business journalists missed in the last 25 years.

The second missed story (among many others) was the *dot com bubble* and the inevitable *dot.bombs* of the late 1990s. In this case, Internet-related start-up companies were obtaining venture capital, frequently going public and, most, going bankrupt when or after their stock prices collapsed. U.S. magazine scholars have also not published research on these journalistic failures, although these embarrassments have also been well documented by professional articles and books published for the mass market. For instance, journalist Howard Kurtz's 2000 book,

The Fortune Tellers,[5] is a devastating portrait of not only banking and financial companies, but also of news media, including magazines, that cover business.

By the time the Great Recession started several years after Enron's problems came to light, two camps had formed. In sum, one camp claimed that U.S. business journalists had done their job on the Great Recession and Global Financial Crisis (aspects of which included the housing bubble, bank deregulation, lax regulatory enforcement and new financial instruments, among others), but that no one was listening or reading. Another camp granted that not all U.S. business journalists totally failed, but that the majority had failed the majority of the time.

An example from the first camp is Roush's late 2008 *American Journalism Review* article, "Unheeded Warnings,"[6] which followed his 2006 textbook that also cheerleads for business journalism, *Profits and Losses: Business Journalism and Its Role in Society*.[7] Arguably also in this first camp is journalist Michael M. Lewis, who in his 2009 book, *Panic: The Story of Modern Financial Insanity*,[8] provides a collection of writings on major financial and economics events back to the 1987 stock market crash.

In the second camp are those such as Dean Starkman, whose *Columbia Journalism Review* articles, "Red Ink Rising: How the Press Missed a Sea Change in the Credit-Card Industry" (March/April 2008) and "Power Problem: The Business Press Did Everything but Take on the Institutions That Brought Down the Financial System" (May/June 2009),[9] and Columbia University scholar Anya Schiffrin's 2011 book, *Bad News: How America's Business Press Missed the Story of the Century*,[10] were more convincing. And even a very few journalists have admitted their own and others' incompetence: For example, Floyd Norris, chief financial correspondent of the *New York Times*, confessed, "I did not take the time to understand the intricacies of collateralized debt obligations," and "I think we were all too willing to assume [Federal Reserve Chairman] Alan Greenspan knew what he was talking about. It seems pretty clear to me now that Greenspan worshipped free markets but didn't understand them."[11] Martha M. Hamilton, former *Washington Post* columnist, admitted,

> In the twenty-five years after the Reagan Revolution, journalists got so accustomed to deregulation that we didn't look hard enough at all the issues and problems it obscured. We used to joke that we didn't need an antitrust reporter anymore because there was no such thing as antitrust.[12]

Serving the General Public

One can gauge how news media serve consumers—and, thus, the general public—by whether they respond to perceived needs of consumers, which also are business opportunities for corporations, as they occur. Magazines, newspapers and television have for decades provided consumers with news and information about personal and family finances, covering everything from credit card interest rates to saving for their children's college education to shopping for airfares.[13] Over the past 40 years, several periods of significant growth in personal finance magazines have occurred, starting with 1972's landmark launch of *Money*. So many were started during the 1980s and 1990s that there was too much competition; *Individual Investor, Your Money* and *Family Money* closed in 2001, while in 2002 *Mutual Funds* folded and *Worth* declared bankruptcy.

It is in this area of scrutinizing one particular magazine or group of magazines for their coverage of one story or one kind of story that researchers of U.S. magazines' business news have been most active. The specific research hypotheses have been diverse, ranging from examining sexism in news coverage to accuracy to other areas of journalistic performance (including, but not limited to, ethics). Examples of these studies follow.

News sources. Shannon E. Martin's 1991 article on news sources was based on a study that found science magazines did not use expert sources more often or even publish more stories than news and business magazines about the 1989 *cold fusion* controversy.[14] Steven L. McShane's 1995 article on source biases showed through content analysis that U.S. and

Canadian business magazine journalists relied heavily on senior corporate executives and not on government officials or other company employees. He also found that women employees were significantly underrepresented, as were sources in the U.S. Midwest and U.S. Southwest relative to the U.S. Mid-Atlantic region; Canadian magazines overwhelmingly used Ontario sources.[15]

Henk Pander Maat's 2007 genre analysis investigated how advertising-like text in press releases is dealt with. Maat's "corpus analysis" found that air travel magazines generally retained that language when they used the press releases (and Dutch newspaper journalists generally did not retain promotional language from a variety of corporate press releases).[16] Maria E. Len-Ríos, Amanda Hinnant and Sun-A. Park, for their 2009 sociology of journalism article, analyzed how health journalists view public relations practitioners and how they use PR materials. Results of their survey and depth interviews showed that health journalists are "least accepting" of material from businesses and federal government agencies, and magazine and TV journalists use health public relations materials more than newspaper and freelance health journalists.[17]

News content. Magazine researchers have been particularly interested in the last 20 years in how magazines have been covering corporate mergers and acquisitions, both in the media industry and throughout the economy. Sanghee Kweon's 2000 article on both framing and, more especially, source bias investigated M&A coverage based on type of merger, relevant government policy and journalistic frame. A content analysis of three newsmagazines showed that mergers and acquisitions (especially media industry) were generally covered favorably, with almost two-thirds of coverage being thematic and about one-third episodic.[18] Bryan Greenberg's 2001 refereed paper also found newsmagazine M&A coverage to be favorable, with stories often framing M&A as driven by personalities, not public interest.[19] Jaemin Jung's 2002 journalistic performance article showed, through content analysis, that Time Inc. magazines favored their parent company's mergers, although there were differences in how newsmagazines and business magazines framed the three mergers (with Warner Communications, then Turner Broadcasting, then America Online).[20]

The globalization of business, including the media business, also has been the focus of substantial academic research during the past 20 years. Charles Mayo and Yorgo Pasadeos's 1991 research showed that about one-sixth of all 1964 to 1988 articles in *Business Week, Forbes* and *Fortune* were about international, even global, news, and the number of such stories increased, even while their length decreased. The study also suggested that Western Europe was over-represented and Latin America under-represented, relative to trade levels.[21] Majia Holmer Nadesan's 2001 critical analysis indicated that *Fortune* reflected corporate executives' views on an information-based economy and its relationship to globalization, omitting alternative, especially dissenting, opinion.[22] David Machin and Sarah Niblock, in their 2010 news globalization article, argued, via interview evidence and a methodology variously called linguistic analysis, textual analysis and discourse analysis, that Bloomberg and business-to-business magazines are increasingly writing news for a "global professional readership" rather than for various local markets. They concluded that this raised questions about both models of journalism and concepts of audience.[23]

Other studies on business and economics news in U.S. magazines have been diverse, with no obvious long-term research agendas or other trends. Gary L. Clark, Peter F. Kaminski and Gene Brown concluded in their 1990 article that while trade journals vary substantially in readability, individual journals' news, editorial and advertising content are generally written at about the same readability levels.[24] C. Ann Hollifield's 1997 mobilization model study found, through content analysis, that trade publications published expert industry and technical information on the National Information Infrastructure but were less likely than non-industry media to cover social implications.[25] Scott R. Meier's 2000 sociology of journalism and media ethics research found, through secondary analysis of survey data, that editors and reporters read trade publications, such as *Editor & Publisher* magazine, but do not rely on them for ethics advice.[26]

Joe Bob Hester and Rhonda Gibson's 2003 agenda-setting theory study found through content analysis that U.S. print and broadcast news media usually framed economic news negatively, which can become a self-fulfilling prophecy of the economy.[27] James S. Miller's 2003 critical and historical analysis interpreted how *Fortune* magazine idealized the U.S. corporate executive as "objective, disinterested, and . . . a-historical" and constructed a "Professional Managerial Class" identity.[28] Karen M. Rowley and David D. Kurpius's journalistic performance work showed by textual analysis that *Forbes* and *Fortune* magazines hardly cover black-owned businesses; *Black Enterprise* magazine covers them a lot.[29] Sherianne Shuler's 2003 feminist theory study used rhetorical analysis to document how *Fortune* magazine perpetuated familiar stereotypes of women in organizations even while ostensibly showing the glass ceiling being shattered.[30]

Daniel Riffe, Stephen Lacy and Miron Varouhakis's 2008 media dependency research showed from survey data that one-third to one-half of U.S. users nationwide consult the Internet at least weekly for information on health, science or business or all of these, valuing the Internet more than magazines, books or friends and families as a source of in-depth information.[31] María Enriqueta Cortés de los Ríos's 2010 axiological linguistics, cognitive semantics and image schemas article interpreted the *Economist* magazine's covers to show how the economy is often framed as a natural, rather than manmade, institution or system. For example, the 6 December 2008 *Economist* cover headline, "Where have all your savings gone?," was run above the image of a man looking into a black hole in the ground; the scholar called this an "apocalyptic metaphor."[32]

Studies on business or economics news in magazines outside the United States also have been diverse and also scarce. Karen Grandy's 2013 feminist theory research showed through a content analysis that Canadian magazine articles about women in business were much more likely to mention whether they were parents or not, as opposed to men in business,[33] while Einat Lachover's 2013 feminist theory study qualitatively examined feminist discourse in Israeli women's business magazines.[34] Bohai Zhang's 2008 interpretive essay traced the development of business-to-business magazines in China.[35]

Agricultural news. Three studies about agricultural industry publications also have been published in the last 20 years. Gerry Walter's 1996 historical research shows how farm magazines from 1934 to 1991 consistently covered farmers with larger than average farms (an "ideology of success") and framed those farmers to "promote conventional, commercial agrarian values of production, efficiency, and expansion."[36] Karen Grandy's 2010 feminist theory study documented through framing analysis how a female corporate executive was subject to myriad manifestations of gender stereotyping in magazine coverage of her.[37]

Serving Workplace and Government Communities

Investors, large and small. Stock analysts, brokers, pension fund managers and other large investors are, or at least should be, pleased with the amount of news and information typically available to them. These market players long were subscribing to magazines such as *Forbes* and *Fortune*, newspapers such as the *Wall Street Journal* and the *New York Times*, specialized newsletters and, since 1981, increasingly Bloomberg L.P.'s financial and economic data, available on a leased Bloomberg computer terminal. Bloomberg in 1990 launched its wire service, and later the company also moved into television, radio and other businesses and bought *BusinessWeek* magazine.

The Internet allowed all news media to disseminate more business news and information than they ever had. Magazines jumped in and metro daily newspapers supposedly started writing business news with more analysis. "*Fortune* and *Business Week* . . . both added on-line Web sites and beefed up their technology coverage overall,"[38] Roush observed.

Howard Kurtz, author of five books on news media, which he covered for the *Washington Post* from 1990 to 2010, has been even more critical of business journalism, both generally and specifically with regard to typical, small investors. In his 2000 book, *The Fortune Tellers*, Kurtz repeatedly criticizes journalists, especially but not only on cable television,[39] for using nonobjective sources about business news. Kurtz also labeled as "ephemeral advice" such articles as the 18 January 1999 *New York* magazine cover story, "Secrets of the Stock Stars,"[40] and *Smart-Money* magazine's "Best and Worst Mutual Funds."[41] The hype problem was longstanding:

> *Money* magazine had run its annual cover story on a dozen hot stocks in 1992. A year later, only one of the previous year's dozen had made the list. And by '95, not one of *Money*'s previous 40 recommendations had made the cut. Each month, each week, the media needed something new to sell, and Wall Street operators were only too happy to comply.[42]

Despite the mushrooming of investing advice in magazines and, yet, sharp criticism of business news and advice in those magazines, magazine industry scholars have done almost no research in the past 25 years on the performance of business magazines for investors. One exception was Mark S. Johnson, whose framing theory-driven study focused on magazine and newspaper coverage of store closings during 1990 to 1996. His content analysis gave evidence that news media generally attributed cause-effect relationships to store closings and that reasons given sometimes were and sometimes were not consistent with official corporate explanations.[43]

Rank-and-file employees. Typical workers at companies that might be covered by the news media surely could expect that their company's major news be covered, rather than ignored. They might expect news media to also cover their competitors and the industry as a whole, not only individual companies. Workers who belong to unions also could expect that their unions be covered because a single union can represent up to hundreds of thousands of workers, negotiate multi-year contracts, call for strikes, etc. Indeed, some industries get covered well, especially industries that are large, tend toward oligopoly and are considered important by journalists, politicians and the financial sector. But most U.S. workers will go years or decades without seeing their employers covered by any journalist. Labor union coverage, once a staple of business sections, especially at metro dailies, has been cut back dramatically, if not eliminated. Moreover, almost all coverage of organized labor in U.S. news media is negative, as scholarly studies have repeatedly shown.[44] Some U.S. news media—including numerous magazines, plus the *New York Times*, the *Wall Street Journal* and other media—also provide valuable advice on career planning, performing one's job better, managing one's boss, and other useful topics. But U.S. news media do a poor job of covering unemployment or trends in jobs and job training, making noteworthy the minimal good coverage of these topics.[45]

Mass communication scholars also have conducted minimal research on how magazines' business news serves the country's workers. One exception to this was Eric Freedman's 2004 article in which he showed how, as Congress in 1993 was considering the North American Free Trade Agreement (NAFTA), unions used magazines for articles that criticized NAFTA and directed union members to take political action to defeat it as if their jobs were at stake, but downplayed NAFTA's other characteristics, such as its de-emphasis on environmental issues.[46]

Managers and executives. One major way that business news organizations can best serve consumers is to change as events and trends occur in the business world or among competing news organizations. For example, the growth of the *Wall Street Journal* over the past 60 years is well documented. Other U.S. business news media have also attempted, within their resources, to grow and adapt, usually disproportionately serving perceived needs of executives and major investors over other audience members.[47] However, as the business world became more complex, it has become increasingly difficult for the news media, with their reporters who usually do not have experience in the industries they are covering and may not know much about business or economics generally,[48] to provide the kind of analysis and detail that corporate executives need. In any case, the value of business news in magazines to business executives has not been studied by magazine researchers in the last 25 years.

Politicians and regulators. While journalists do not work for government, business and economics journalism has a role to play in helping to communicate to elected and appointed political leaders and government bureaucrats information, ideas, and opinions that they need to know from and for various constituencies. Government action that affects business ranges from major Congressional legislation, such as financial sector reforms passed in 2010, to congressional hearings, to state legislation or regulation, down to formal or informal investigations by regulators that may or may not result in fines or indictments. Sometimes government beats journalists, sometimes journalists beat government. For instance, Greg Miller found in 2003 that in more than 260 cases of corporate accounting fraud, almost one-third of them were reported by news media before either the involved corporation or the Securities and Exchange Commission announced investigations. Miller wrote, "In each of these articles, it is the reporter making the case for accounting impropriety based on analysis of public and private information. No other information intermediaries (i.e., analysts, auditors, or the legal system) are cited."[49] In another example, in 2010, a Bloomberg investigation showed that by using "transfer pricing," by which the sale of an item is attributed to the country in which it was manufactured rather than to where it was sold if the manufacturing country's tax rates are lower, Forest Laboratories alone had saved $60 billion in U.S. income taxes. Bloomberg reported that all U.S. corporations have a trillion dollars in profits parked off-shore, most from transfer pricing, saving on a 35% U.S. corporate tax rate.[50] News media also need to report on executives' incompetence as well as criminality. For example, the *New York Times* media critic David Carr wrote in late 2009, "now it has become clear that the titans who were wielding those obscure [financial] tools have no idea what they were doing—even less an idea than the journalists in some cases."[51] In any case, the value of business news in magazines to politicians and regulators, or both, has not been studied by magazine researchers.

Moving Beyond Complex and Boring

Even if business and investing themselves are not always a Roush's *slog* to cover, then it certainly must be understood that reading or writing about business and investing also can be that way at least for some people. Thus, the journalist has two tasks here: staying interested and focused when reading, interviewing and writing about business news and trying to make such news as interesting as possible while meeting the highest professional journalism standards.

Kurtz, explaining news coverage of "dot bombs," wrote, "Net companies were sexy and fascinating to journalists, compared to, say, the Exxon-Mobil merger, which was important but dull."[52] Business journalists have been advised more than once, "Dare to be dull"—an old admonition among both business investors and television journalists—but as media critic David Carr admits, "Nobody is going to read, let alone aspire to, magazines called *Middled, Outsourced, Left Behind* and *Clobbered.*"[53] In any case, the readability (both technically speaking and as narrative storytelling) of business news in magazines has not been studied by magazine researchers in the last 25 years, except by Clark, Kaminski and Brown, whose research was previously noted.

An intriguing question, especially to track over time with both job market, magazine industry and general economic trends, is whether business journalists sought out that beat, and even if they did not, whether they enjoy covering it. Anecdotal evidence suggests that TV, wire service and weekly magazine journalists in the last 20 years have placed great emphasis on being first with news and have been overall rather pro-business, whether they enjoyed it or not. Historically, business journalists at metropolitan daily newspapers had often burned out on more important beats, and their quality varies dramatically.[54] This also seems true at industry and professional magazines, where even, or perhaps especially, media industry publications such as *Editor & Publisher* or *Broadcasting & Cable* were primarily cheerleaders for their industries.[55] This might not improve: Hundreds of young journalists work in business journalism, not always by choice or by qualification, while senior business journalists have moved on.[56]

Evidence for business journalists' lack of sufficient preparation is not merely circumstantial. Roush has observed, "A number of these [business] journalists . . . were unprepared to cover the top business stories of the time [1990s], such as the savings and loan scandal of the late 1980s and early 1990s, hostile takeovers [of corporations], the rise in mergers and acquisitions, and the excesses of Wall Street. In addition, business journalists were 'blindsided by globalization. . .'" Worse, Roush added, "these shortcomings were not readily apparent to those practicing the craft or those reading business coverage."[57] Roush[58] and Claussen[59] have called for more business education in U.S. journalism and communication schools, but the education and training levels of magazines' business journalists have not otherwise been studied.

Advertiser Influence

Although advertiser pressure on magazine editors has been a frequent topic of magazine industry publications and convention sessions, mass communication scholars have conducted few studies of it in the last 25 years. One exception to this was a 1991 media performance, ethics study by Robert G. Hays and Ann E. Reisner, who found that 62% of farm journalists surveyed reported receiving pressure from advertisers (and half the total said keeping their distance from advertisers was challenging), while about half also said that advertising had literally been withdrawn on occasion.[60] In 1993, Dennis M. Sandler and Eugene Secunda published their own media performance study (also with obvious ethics implications) on magazine industry professionals' positions on where news and editorial content "ends" and advertising "begins,"[61] a frequent topic at magazine industry conventions and in criticism of magazines.

Magazine History

If one area of scholarly research on magazine coverage of business and economics has made substantial progress in the last 20 to 25 years, that is the history of magazines. Mary M. Cronin's 1993 historical article showed how content differences in newspaper industry magazines during 1884–1917 could be correlated with their relative popularity and success levels.[62] Joey Senat's 1997 history paper documented the newspaper industry's main trade publication's sexist language and references to women during 1967 to 1974 and suggested that the newspaper industry itself was therefore discouraged from modernizing.[63] Kevin S. Reilly's 1999 historical article discusses the founding years of a major new business magazine, *Fortune*, with competition during the Great Depression.[64] Stuart W. Shulman's 1999 historical research proposes that early twentieth century, Progressive Era agricultural magazines and newspapers are fruitful sources for studying media history, as are other specialized media.[65]

Gib Prettyman's 2001 critical article recounts, through literary analysis, how the lavishly illustrated *Harper's Weekly* newsmagazine was an obvious cheerleader for the country's industrialization in the nineteenth century.[66] Keith Massie and Stephen D. Perry's 2002 historical research connects a major early figure in the U.S. radio industry, Hugo Gernsback, with radio industry magazines.[67] Kathleen L. Endres's 2004 framing theory article documented, through textual analysis, *Editor & Publisher* magazine's opposition to Title VII (primarily on First Amendment grounds) and its trivialization of its supporters.[68] Scott Fosdick and Sooyoung Cho's 2005 article explained how the entertainment industry magazine *Variety*, founded in 1906, became business news–oriented by 1937.[69] Kevin Stoker and Brad L. Rawlins's 2005 historical research threw new light on very early U.S. public relations, when it was still called "publicity."[70] Douglas B. Ward's 2005 historical article documents how *Country Gentleman* and other Curtis Publishing Company magazines during 1910 to 1930 framed rural consumers as voluminous and valuable, thus also boosting advertising revenue of the Philadelphia-based publisher.[71]

Andrew L. Yarrow's 2006 historical article traced the dramatic rise in business magazines in the 20 years following World War II and argues that they made business news more central to the American culture and society.[72] Karen Miller Russell and Carl O. Bishop's 2009 historical research traces changes in print media's early, 1865 to 1904 coverage of what is today called public relations, with a focus on Ivy Lee's Declaration of Principles and how previous misunderstanding of this history has skewed public relations theory.[73] Marc Poitras and Daniel Sutter's 2009 article provides evidence that advertiser boycotts was not a detectable reason for the decline in muckraking journalism by U.S. magazines in the twentieth century's second decade.[74] Elizabeth Hewitt's 2010 interpretive article is based on a literary analysis of early business magazines.[75] Roei Davidson's 2012 critical theory article showed, through textual analysis, how personal finance magazines' emergence after World War II can be correlated with a shift from corporate liberalism to neoliberalism and individual investors taking relatively more advice from magazines rather than finance professionals.[76] Karen Miller Russell and Margot Opdycke Lamme's 2013 historical article explored how the U.S. business community was slow to respond to the Civil Rights movement and that public relations practitioners' involvement in that response seems to have been minimal despite being blamed for businesses' unsuccessful initiatives.[77]

Conclusion

Professional, industry and trade, corporate and other magazines not primarily for consumers account for the majority of magazines published in the United States. Collectively, they are a large industry themselves and serve a wide variety of purposes for a huge audience. Business and economics news composes an important part of the content of consumer magazines. All of this is ripe for study by magazine scholars, business and economics researchers, historians and others. Yet there is no risk to concluding that scholarly study of business and economic news in U.S. magazines has barely scratched the surface, if that. Perhaps the next 25 years will see more such research than the last 25 years.

Notes

1 Cultural Dictionary, Dictionary.com, LLC, *American Heritage New Dictionary of Cultural Literacy*, 3rd ed. (New York: Houghton Mifflin, 2005) <http://dictionary.reference.com/browse/The+business+of+America+is+business>, accessed 26 March 2014.

2 Chris Roush, *Profits and Losses: Business Journalism and Its Role in Society* (Oak Park, IL: Marion Street Press, 2006), 130.

3 Roush, *Profits and Losses*, 153.

4 Peter Behr, "Looking for Answers in the Enron Story: 'Start with a Pretty Straightforward Question,'" *Nieman Reports*, Summer 2002, 8–9; Paul E. Steiger, "Not Every Journalist 'Missed' the Enron Story," *Nieman Reports*, Summer 2002, 10–12.

5 Howard Kurtz, *The Fortune Tellers: Inside Wall Street's Game of Money, Media, and Manipulation* (New York: Free Press, 2000).

6 Chris Roush, "Unheeded Warnings," *American Journalism Review*, December 2008/January 2009, 34–39.

7 Roush, *Profits and Losses*.

8 Michael M. Lewis, ed., *Panic: The Story of Modern Financial Insanity* (New York: W.W. Norton & Company, 2009).

9 Dean Starkman, "Red Ink Rising: How the Press Missed a Sea Change in the Credit-Card Industry," *Columbia Journalism Review*, March/April 2008, 14–16; and Dean Starkman, "Power Problem: The Business Press Did Everything but Take on the Institutions That Brought Down the Financial System," *Columbia Journalism Review*, May/June 2009, 24–30. See also, Dean Starkman, *The Financial Crisis and the Disappearance of Investigative Journalism* (New York: Columbia University Press, 2014).

10 Anya Schiffrin, ed., *Bad News: How America's Business Press Missed the Story of the Century* (New York: New Press, 2011).

11 Floyd Norris, quoted in Martha M. Hamilton, "What We Learned in the Meltdown: Financial Journalists Saw Some Trees but Not the Forest. Now What?" *Columbia Journalism Review*, January/February 2009, 38.

12 Hamilton, "What We Learned in the Meltdown," 39.

13 Roush, *Profits and Losses*, 61.

14 Shannon E. Martin, "Using Expert Sources in Breaking Science Stories: A Comparison of Magazine Types," *Journalism Quarterly* 68.1/2 (Spring/Summer 1991): 179–187.

15 Steven L. McShane, "Occupational, Gender, and Geographic Representation of Information Sources in U.S. and Canadian Business Magazines," *Journalism & Mass Communication Quarterly* 72.1 (Spring 1995): 190–204.

16 Henk Pander Maat, "How Promotional Language in Press Releases Is Dealt with by Journalists: Genre Mixing or Genre Conflict?" *Journal of Business Communication* 44.1 (January 2007): 59–95.

17 María E. Len-Ríos, Amanda Hinnant, and Sun-A. Park, "Understanding How Health Journalists Judge Public Relations Sources: A Rules Theory Approach," *Public Relations Review* 35.1 (March 2009): 61–63.

18 Sanghee Kweon, "A Framing Analysis: How Did Three U.S. News Magazines Frame about Mergers or Acquisitions?" *International Journal on Media Management* 2.3/4 (Autumn/Winter 2000): 165–176.

19 Bryan Greenberg, "Different Voices, Same Script: How Newsmagazines Cover Media Consolidation Issues" (paper presented at the Annual Meeting, Association for Education in Journalism and Mass Communication, August 2001).

20 Jaemin Jung, "How Magazines Covered Media Companies' Mergers: The Case of the Evolution of Time Inc.," *Journalism & Mass Communication Quarterly* 79.3 (Autumn 2002): 681–696.

21 Charles Mayo and Yorgo Pasadeos, "Changes in the International Focus of U.S. Business Magazines, 1964–1988," *Journalism Quarterly* 68.3 (Fall 1991): 509–514.

22 Majia Holmer Nadesan, "*Fortune* on Globalization and the New Economy: Manifest Destiny in a Technological Age," *Management Communication Quarterly* 14.3 (February 2001): 498–506.

23 David Machin and Sarah Niblock, "The New Breed of Business Journalism for Niche Global News: The Case of Bloomberg News," *Journalism Studies* 11.6 (December 2010): 783–798, 783.

24 Gary L. Clark, Peter F. Kaminski, and Gene Brown, "The Readability of Advertisements and Articles in Trade Journals," *Industrial Marketing Management* 19.3 (August 1990): 251–260.

25 C. Ann Hollifield, "The Specialized Business Press and Industry-Related Political Communication: A Comparative Study," *Journalism & Mass Communication Quarterly* 74.4 (Winter 1997): 757–772.

26 Scott R. Maier, "Do Trade Publications Affect Ethical Sensitivity in Newsrooms?" *Newspaper Research Journal* 21.1 (Winter 2000): 41–50.

27 Joe Bob Hester and Rhonda Gibson, "The Economy and Second-Level Agenda Setting: A Time-Series Analysis of Economic News and Public Opinion about the Economy," *Journalism & Mass Communication Quarterly* 80.1 (Spring 2003): 73–90.

28 James S. Miller, "White-Collar Excavations: *Fortune* Magazine and the Invention of the Industrial Folk," *American Periodicals* 13 (2003): 102–103.

29 Karen M. Rowley and David D. Kurpius, "Separate and Still Unequal: A Comparative Study of Blacks in Business Magazines," *Howard Journal of Communications* 14.4 (October/December 2003): 245–255.

30 Sherianne Shuler, "Breaking Through the Glass Ceiling without Breaking a Nail: Women Executives in *Fortune* Magazine's 'Power 50' List," *American Communication Journal* 6.2 (Winter 2003): 1.

31 Daniel Riffe, Stephen Lacy, and Miron Varouhakis, "Media System Dependency Theory and Using the Internet for In-Depth, Specialized Information," *Web Journal of Mass Communication Research* 11 (January 2008): 1–14.

32 María Enriqueta Cortés de los Ríos, "Cognitive Devices to Communicate the Economic Crisis: An Analysis through Covers in the *Economist*," *Ibérica* 20 (Fall 2010): 81–106.

33 Karen Grandy, "Mother Load: Parental-Status References in Canadian Business Magazines," *Canadian Journal of Communication* 38.2 (2013): 245–254.

34 Einat Lachover, "Influential Women: Feminist Discourse in Women's Business Magazines—The Case of Israel," *Communication, Culture & Critique* 6.1 (March 2013): 121–141.

35 Bohai Zhang, "The Development of Business-to-Business Magazines in China," *Publishing Research Quarterly* 24.1 (March 2008): 54–58.

36 Gerry Walter, "The Ideology of Success in Major American Farm Magazines, 1934–1991," *Journalism & Mass Communication Quarterly* 73.3 (Autumn 1996): 594.

37 Karen Grandy, "Busy Bee, Tough Mom, Farmer's Daughter: The Canadian Business Press Portrayal of Annette Verschuren," *Canadian Journal of Communication* 35.1 (2010): 49–62.

38 Roush, *Profits and Losses*, 188.

39 Kurtz, *The Fortune Tellers*, 32–33.

40 Alex Williams, "Secrets of the Stock Stars," *New York*, 18 January 1999 <http://nymag.com/nymetro/news/bizfinance/biz/features/1026/>, accessed 29 November 2013, quoted in Kurtz, *The Fortune Tellers*, xx.

41 Cover, *SmartMoney*, February 1999, quoted in Kurtz, *The Fortune Tellers*, xx.

42 Kurtz, *The Fortune Tellers*, xx.

43 Mark S. Johnson, "Causes and Consequences of U.S. Chain Store Closings: Attributions in the Media," *Psychology & Marketing* 17.8 (August 2000): 721–743.

44 Jon Bekken, "The Invisible Enemy: Representing Labour in a Corporate Media Order," *Javnost-The Public* 12.1 (2005): 71–84; Deepa Kumar, *Outside the Box: Corporate Media, Globalization, and the UPS Strike* (Urbana: University of Illinois Press, 2007); and Christopher R. Martin, *Framed!: Labor and the Corporate Media* (Ithaca, NY: ILR Press/Cornell University Press, 2004).

45 Holly Yeager, "Jobs, Jobs, Jobs? As Press Coverage Falters, the Washington Conversation Keeps Shifting," *The Audit* (blog), *Columbia Journalism Review*, 18 May 2010 <http://www.cjr.org/the_audit/shifting_the_washington_conversation_to_jobs_again.php>, accessed 29 November 2013; and Holly Yeager, "Crook on Broken 'Labour' Markets, Bartlett Notices That We're Getting Old, *WSJ* Notices Fannie and Freddie," *The Audit* (blog), *Columbia Journalism Review*, 24 May 2010 <http://www.cjr.org/the_audit/audit_dc_notes_crook_on_broken.php>, accessed 29 November 2013.

46 Eric Freedman, "Union Magazines' Coverage of the NAFTA Controversy before Congressional Approval," *Journal of Labor Research* 25.2 (Spring 2004): 301–313.

47 See generally, Roush, *Profits and Losses*.

48 Richard Sine, "Who's Taking Care of Business? Editors Have a Hard Time Finding Qualified Applicants for Business Desk Jobs," *American Journalism Review*, August/September 2004, 20–21.

49 Greg Miller, cited in Roush, "Unheeded Warnings," 37.

50 Ryan Chittum, "Bloomberg Investigates a 'Double Irish' Corporate Tax Scheme," *The Audit* (blog), *Columbia Journalism Review*, 24 May 2010 <http://www.cjr.org/the_audit/bloomberg_investigates_a_doubl.php>, accessed 29 November 2013.

51 David Carr, "Business Is a Beat Deflated," *New York Times*, 2 November 2009, B1.

52 Kurtz, *The Fortune Tellers*, xxii.

53 Carr, "Business Is a Beat Deflated," B1.

54 Gregory J. Millman, "No Longer Just Gray: Business Journalism Takes Off," *Financial Executive*, October 2006, 23.

55 Dane S. Claussen, "*Broadcasting & Cable Magazine*: Serving Readers and/or Advertisers?" in Ginger R. Carter, ed., *Proceedings of the Southeast Colloquium* (Milledgeville, GA: Georgia College and State University, 1998).

56 Dean Starkman, "Ouryay Eatbay Just Ewblay Upyay: Ten Fundamentals for the Business Press Now," *The Audit* (blog), *Columbia Journalism Review*, 29 September 2008 <http://www.cjr.org/the_audit/ouryay_eatbay_just_ewblay_upya.php>, accessed 29 November 2013.

57 Roush, *Profits and Losses*, 152, citing *New York Times* business reporter Diana Henriques, "Business Reporting: Behind the Curve," *Columbia Journalism Review*, November/December 2000, 18; see also, Roush, *Profits and Losses*, 227–228, for survey and poll results on lack of confidence in U.S. business journalists and journalism by U.S. corporate executives.

58 Chris Roush, "The Need for More Business Education in Mass Communication Schools," *Journalism & Mass Communication Educator* 61.2 (Summer 2006): 195–204.

59 Dane S. Claussen, "'They're in for a Rude Awakening,'" *Journalism & Mass Communication Educator* 63.2 (Summer 2008): 103–106.

60 Robert G. Hays and Ann E. Reisner, "Farm Journalists and Advertiser Influence: Pressures on Ethical Standards," *Journalism Quarterly* 68.1/2 (Spring/Summer 1991): 172.

61 Dennis M. Sandler and Eugene Secunda, "Point of View: Blurred Boundaries—Where Does Editorial End and Advertising Begin?" *Journal of Advertising Research* 33.3 (May/June 1993): 73–80.

62 Mary M. Cronin, "Trade Press Roles in Promoting Journalistic Professionalism, 1884–1917," *Journal of Mass Media Ethics* 8.4 (Winter 1993): 227–238.

63 Joey Senat, "From Pretty Blondes and Perky Girls to Competent Journalists: *Editor & Publisher*'s Evolving Depiction of Women from 1967–74" (paper presented at the Annual Meeting, Association for Education in Journalism and Mass Communication, 1997).

64 Kevin S. Reilly, "Dilettantes at the Gate: *Fortune* Magazine and the Cultural Politics of Business Journalism in the 1930s," *Business & Economic History* 28.2 (Winter 1999): 213.

65 Stuart W. Shulman, "The Progressive Era Farm Press: A Primer on a Neglected Source of Journalism History," *Journalism History* 25.1 (Spring 1999): 26–35.

66 Gib Prettyman, "*Harper's Weekly* and the Spectacle of Industrialization," *American Periodicals* 11 (2001): 24–48.

67 Keith Massie and Stephen D. Perry, "Hugo Gernsback and Radio Magazines: An Influential Intersection in Broadcast History," *Journal of Radio Studies* 9.2 (2002): 264–281.

68 Kathleen L. Endres, "'Help-Wanted Female': *Editor & Publisher* Frames a Civil Rights Issue," *Journalism & Mass Communication Quarterly* 81.1 (Spring 2004): 7–21.

69 Scott Fosdick and Sooyoung Cho, "No Business Like Show Business: Tracking Commodification Over a Century of *Variety*," *Journal of Magazine & New Media Research* (Spring 2005): 1–14.

70 Kevin Stoker and Brad L. Rawlins, "The 'Light' of Publicity in the Progressive Era: From Searchlight to Flashlight," *Journalism History* 30.4 (Winter 2005): 177–188.

71 Douglas B. Ward, "From Barbarian Farmers to Yeoman Consumers: Curtis Publishing Company and the Search for Rural America, 1910–1930," *American Journalism* 22.4 (Fall 2005): 47–67.

72 Andrew L. Yarrow, "The Big Postwar Story: Abundance and the Rise of Economic Journalism," *Journalism History* 32.2 (Summer 2006): 58–76.

73 Karen Miller Russell and Carl O. Bishop, "Understanding Ivy Lee's Declaration of Principles: U.S. Newspaper and Magazine Coverage of Publicity and Press Agentry, 1865–1904," *Public Relations Review* 35.2 (June 2009): 91–101.

74 Marc Poitras and Daniel Sutter, "Advertiser Pressure and Control of the News: The Decline of Muckraking Revisited," *Journal of Economic Behavior & Organization* 72.3 (December 2009): 944–958.

75 Elizabeth Hewitt, "Romances of Real Life; or, the Nineteenth-Century American Business Magazine," *American Periodicals* 20.1 (2010): 1–22.

76 Roei Davidson, "The Emergence of Popular Personal Finance Magazines and the Risk Shift in American Society," *Media, Culture & Society* 34.1 (January 2012): 3–20.

77 Karen Miller Russell and Margot Opdycke Lamme, "Public Relations and Business Responses to the Civil Rights Movement," *Public Relations Review* 39.1 (March 2013): 63–73.

Bibliography

Behr, Peter. "Looking for Answers in the Enron Story: 'Start with a Pretty Straightforward Question.'" *Nieman Reports*, Summer 2002, 8–9.

Bekken, Jon. "The Invisible Enemy: Representing Labour in a Corporate Media Order." *Javnost-The Public* 12.1 (2005): 71–84.

Carr, David. "Business Is a Beat Deflated." *New York Times*, 2 November 2009, B1.

Chittum, Ryan. "Bloomberg Investigates a 'Double Irish' Corporate Tax Scheme." *The Audit* (blog). *Columbia Journalism Review*, 24 May 2010 <http://www.cjr.org/the_audit/bloomberg_investigates_a_doubl.php>, accessed 29 November 2013.

Clark, Gary L.; Kaminski, Peter F.; and Brown, Gene. "The Readability of Advertisements and Articles in Trade Journals." *Industrial Marketing Management* 19.3 (August 1990): 251–260.

Claussen, Dane S. "*Broadcasting & Cable Magazine*: Serving Readers and/or Advertisers?" In Carter, Ginger R., ed. *Proceedings of the Southeast Colloquium*. Milledgeville, GA: George College and State University, 1998.

Claussen, Dane S. "'They're in for a Rude Awakening.'" *Journalism & Mass Communication Educator* 63.2 (Summer 2008): 103–106.

Cronin, Mary M. "Trade Press Roles in Promoting Journalistic Professionalism, 1884–1917." *Journal of Mass Media Ethics* 8.4 (Winter 1993): 227–238.

Cultural Dictionary. Dictionary.com, LLC. *American Heritage New Dictionary of Cultural Literacy*, 3rd ed. New York: Houghton Mifflin, 2005 <http://dictionary.reference.com/browse/The+business+of+America+is+business>, accessed 26 March 2014.

Davidson, Roei. "The Emergence of Popular Personal Finance Magazines and the Risk Shift in American Society." *Media, Culture & Society* 34.1 (January 2012): 3–20.

de los Ríos, María Enriqueta Cortés. "Cognitive Devices to Communicate the Economic Crisis: An Analysis through Covers in the *Economist*." *Ibérica* 20 (Fall 2010): 81–106.

Endres, Kathleen L. "'Help-Wanted Female': *Editor & Publisher* Frames a Civil Rights Issue." *Journalism & Mass Communication Quarterly* 81.1 (Spring 2004): 7–21.

Fosdick, Scott and Cho, Sooyoung. "No Business Like Show Business: Tracking Commodification Over a Century of *Variety*." *Journal of Magazine & New Media Research* (Spring 2005): 1–14.

Freedman, Eric. "Union Magazines' Coverage of the NAFTA Controversy before Congressional Approval." *Journal of Labor Research* 25.2 (Spring 2004): 301–313.

Grandy, Karen. "Busy Bee, Tough Mom, Farmer's Daughter: The Canadian Business Press Portrayal of Annette Verschuren." *Canadian Journal of Communication* 35.1 (2010): 49–62.

Grandy, Karen. "Mother Load: Parental-Status References in Canadian Business Magazines." *Canadian Journal of Communication* 38.2 (2013): 245–254.

Greenberg, Bryan. "Different Voices, Same Script: How Newsmagazines Cover Media Consolidation Issues." Paper presented at the Annual Meeting, Association for Education in Journalism and Mass Communication, August 2001.

Hamilton, Martha M. "What We Learned in the Meltdown: Financial Journalists Saw Some Trees but Not the Forest. Now What?" *Columbia Journalism Review*, January/February 2009, 36–39.

Hays, Robert G. and Reisner, Ann E. "Farm Journalists and Advertiser Influence: Pressures on Ethical Standards." *Journalism Quarterly* 68.1/2 (Spring/Summer 1991): 172–178.

Henriques, Diana. "Business Reporting: Behind the Curve," *Columbia Journalism Review*, November/December 2000, 18.

Hester, Joe Bob and Gibson, Rhonda. "The Economy and Second-Level Agenda Setting: A Time-Series Analysis of Economic News and Public Opinion about the Economy." *Journalism & Mass Communication Quarterly* 80.1 (Spring 2003): 73–90.

Hewitt, Elizabeth. "Romances of Real Life; Or, the Nineteenth-Century American Business Magazine." *American Periodicals* 20.1 (2010): 1–22.

Hollifield, C. Ann. "The Specialized Business Press and Industry-Related Political Communication: A Comparative Study." *Journalism & Mass Communication Quarterly* 74.4 (Winter 1997): 757–772.

Johnson, Mark S. "Causes and Consequences of U.S. Chain Store Closings: Attributions in the Media." *Psychology & Marketing* 17.8 (August 2000): 721–743.

Jung, Jaemin. "How Magazines Covered Media Companies' Mergers: The Case of the Evolution of Time Inc." *Journalism & Mass Communication Quarterly* 79.3 (Autumn 2002): 681–696.

Kumar, Deepa. *Outside the Box: Corporate Media, Globalization, and the UPS Strike*. Urbana: University of Illinois Press, 2007.

Kurtz, Howard. *The Fortune Tellers: Inside Wall Street's Game of Money, Media, and Manipulation*. New York: Free Press, 2000.

Kweon, Sanghee. "A Framing Analysis: How Did Three U.S. News Magazines Frame about Mergers or Acquisitions?" *International Journal on Media Management* 2.3/4 (Autumn/Winter 2000): 165–176.

Lachover, Einat. "Influential Women: Feminist Discourse in Women's Business Magazines—The Case of Israel." *Communication, Culture & Critique* 6.1 (March 2013): 121–141.

Len-Ríos, María E.; Hinnant, Amanda; and Park, Sun-A. "Understanding How Health Journalists Judge Public Relations Sources: A Rules Theory Approach." *Public Relations Review* 35.1 (March 2009): 56–65.

Lewis, Michael M., ed. *Panic: The Story of Modern Financial Insanity*. New York: W.W. Norton & Company, 2009.

Maat, Henk Pander. "How Promotional Language in Press Releases Is Dealt with by Journalists: Genre Mixing or Genre Conflict?" *Journal of Business Communication* 44.1 (January 2007): 59–95.

Machin, David and Niblock, Sarah. "The New Breed of Business Journalism for Niche Global News: The Case of Bloomberg News." *Journalism Studies* 11.6 (December 2010): 783–798.

Maier, Scott R. "Do Trade Publications Affect Ethical Sensitivity in Newsrooms?" *Newspaper Research Journal* 21.1 (Winter 2000): 41–50.

Martin, Christopher R. *Framed!: Labor and the Corporate Media*. Ithaca, NY: ILR Press/Cornell University Press, 2004.

Martin, Shannon E. "Using Expert Sources in Breaking Science Stories: A Comparison of Magazine Types." *Journalism Quarterly* 68.1/2 (Spring/Summer 1991): 179–187.

Massie, Keith and Perry, Stephen D. "Hugo Gernsback and Radio Magazines: An Influential Intersection in Broadcast History." *Journal of Radio Studies* 9.2 (2002): 264–281.

Mayo, Charles and Pasadeos, Yorgo. "Changes in the International Focus of U.S. Business Magazines, 1964–1988." *Journalism Quarterly* 68.3 (Fall 1991): 509–514.

McShane, Steven L. "Occupational, Gender, and Geographic Representation of Information Sources in U.S. and Canadian Business Magazines." *Journalism & Mass Communication Quarterly* 72.1 (Spring 1995): 190–204.

Miller, James S. "White-Collar Excavations: *Fortune* Magazine and the Invention of the Industrial Folk." *American Periodicals* 13 (2003): 84–104.

Millman, Gregory J. "No Longer Just Gray: Business Journalism Takes Off." *Financial Executive*, October 2006, 18–23.

Nadesan, Majia Holmer. "*Fortune* on Globalization and the New Economy: Manifest Destiny in a Technological Age." *Management Communication Quarterly* 14.3 (February 2001): 498–506.

Poitras, Marc and Sutter, Daniel. "Advertiser Pressure and Control of the News: The Decline of Muckraking Revisited." *Journal of Economic Behavior & Organization* 72.3 (December 2009): 944–958.

Prettyman, Gib. "*Harper's Weekly* and the Spectacle of Industrialization." *American Periodicals* 11 (2001): 24–48.

Reilly, Kevin S. "Dilettantes at the Gate: *Fortune* Magazine and the Cultural Politics of Business Journalism in the 1930s." *Business & Economic History* 28.2 (Winter 1999): 213–222.

Riffe, Daniel; Lacy, Stephen; and Varouhakis, Miron. "Media System Dependency Theory and Using the Internet for In-Depth, Specialized Information." *Web Journal of Mass Communication Research* 11 (January 2008): 1–14.

Roush, Chris. "The Need for More Business Education in Mass Communication Schools." *Journalism & Mass Communication Educator* 61.2 (Summer 2006): 196–204.

Roush, Chris. *Profits and Losses: Business Journalism and Its Role in Society.* Oak Park, IL: Marion Street Press, 2006.

Roush, Chris. "Unheeded Warnings." *American Journalism Review*, December 2008/January 2009, 34–39.

Rowley, Karen M. and Kurpius, David D. "Separate and Still Unequal: A Comparative Study of Blacks in Business Magazines." *Howard Journal of Communications* 14.4 (October/December 2003): 245–255.

Russell, Karen Miller and Bishop, Carl O. "Understanding Ivy Lee's Declaration of Principles: U.S. Newspaper and Magazine Coverage of Publicity and Press Agentry, 1865–1904." *Public Relations Review* 35.2 (June 2009): 91–101.

Russell, Karen Miller and Lamme, Margot Opdycke. "Public Relations and Business Responses to the Civil Rights Movement." *Public Relations Review* 39.1 (March 2013): 63–73.

Sandler, Dennis M. and Secunda, Eugene. "Point of View: Blurred Boundaries—Where Does Editorial End and Advertising Begin?" *Journal of Advertising Research* 33.3 (May/June 1993): 73–80.

Schiffrin, Anya, ed. *Bad News: How America's Business Press Missed the Story of the Century.* New York: New Press, 2011.

Senat, Joey. "From Pretty Blondes and Perky Girls to Competent Journalists: *Editor & Publisher's* Evolving Depiction of Women from 1967–74." Paper presented at the Annual Meeting, Association for Education in Journalism and Mass Communication, Chicago, 30 July–2 August 1997.

Shuler, Sherianne. "Breaking Through the Glass Ceiling without Breaking a Nail: Women Executives in *Fortune* Magazine's 'Power 50' List." *American Communication Journal* 6.2 (Winter 2003): Unpaginated.

Shulman, Stuart W. "The Progressive Era Farm Press: A Primer on a Neglected Source of Journalism History." *Journalism History* 25.1 (Spring 1999): 26–35.

Sine, Richard. "Who's Taking Care of Business? Editors Have a Hard Time Finding Qualified Applicants for Business Desk Jobs." *American Journalism Review*, August/September 2004, 20–21.

Starkman, Dean. *The Financial Crisis and the Disappearance of Investigative Journalism.* New York: Columbia University Press, 2014.

Starkman, Dean. "Ouryay Eatbay Just Ewblay Upyay: Ten Fundamentals for the Business Press Now." *The Audit* (blog). *Columbia Journalism Review*, 29 September 2008 <http://www.cjr.org/the_audit/ouryay_eatbay_just_ewblay_upya.php>, accessed 29 November 2013.

Starkman, Dean. "Power Problem: The Business Press Did Everything but Take On the Institutions that Brought Down the Financial System." *Columbia Journalism Review*, May/June 2009, 24–30.

Starkman, Dean. "Red Ink Rising: How the Press Missed a Sea Change in the Credit-Card Industry." *Columbia Journalism Review*, March/April 2008, 14–16.

Steiger, Paul E. "Not Every Journalist 'Missed' the Enron Story." *Nieman Reports*, Summer 2002, 10–12.

Stoker, Kevin and Rawlins, Brad L. "The 'Light' of Publicity in the Progressive Era: From Searchlight to Flashlight." *Journalism History* 30.4 (Winter 2005): 177–188.

Walter, Gerry. "The Ideology of Success in Major American Farm Magazines, 1934–1991." *Journalism & Mass Communication Quarterly* 73.3 (Autumn 1996): 594–608.

Ward, Douglas B. "From Barbarian Farmers to Yeoman Consumers: Curtis Publishing Company and the Search for Rural America, 1910–1930." *American Journalism* 22.4 (Fall 2005): 47–67.

Williams, Alex. "Secrets of the Stock Stars." *New York*, 18 January 1999 <http://nymag.com/nymetro/news/bizfinance/biz/features/1026/>, accessed 29 November 2013.

Yarrow, Andrew L. "The Big Postwar Story: Abundance and the Rise of Economic Journalism." *Journalism History* 32.2 (Summer 2006): 58–76.

Yeager, Holly. "Crook on Broken 'Labour' Markets, Bartlett Notices That We're Getting Old, *WSJ* Notices Fannie and Freddie." *The Audit* (blog). *Columbia Journalism Review*, 24 May 2010 <http://www.cjr.org/the_audit/audit_dc_notes_crook_on_broken.php>, accessed 29 November 2013.

Yeager, Holly. "Jobs, Jobs, Jobs? As Press Coverage Falters, the Washington Conversation Keeps Shifting." *The Audit* (blog). *Columbia Journalism Review*, 18 May 2010 <http://www.cjr.org/the_audit/shift ing_the_washington_conversation_to_jobs_again.php>, accessed 29 November 2013.

Zhang, Bohai. "The Development of Business-to-Business Magazines in China." *Publishing Research Quarterly* 24.1 (March 2008): 54–58.

Supplemental Resources

Endres, Kathleen L., ed. *Trade, Industrial, and Professional Periodicals of the United States*. Westport, CT and London: Greenwood Press, 1994.

Riley, Sam G., ed. *Corporate Magazines of the United States*. Westport, CT: Greenwood Press, 1992.

Zullow, Harold M. "Pessimistic Rumination in Popular Songs and Newsmagazines Predict Economic Recession via Decreased Consumer Optimism and Spending." *Journal of Economic Psychology* 12.3 (September 1991): 501–526.

16
SOCIETAL CONSIDERATIONS

Uses and Gratifications of Magazines

Vincent F. Filak

Research regarding consumer magazines has often fallen into two primary areas: cultural criticism and effects research. In both cases, the primary approach to understanding what magazines are and how they integrate themselves into the lives of readers is to assess what is in the pages of the magazine and then ascertain the negative outcomes associated with consuming that content. Although many of the studies performed on these magazines relate to the objectification of women or the heavy reliance on "fixing" women,[1] the role of male consumers,[2] gays and lesbians,[3] teens and even senior citizens, the research has trod the same formulaic path. Even this author's research has taken various magazines to task for the consumer-based and stereotypically negative content they put forth.[4]

If scholarship pertaining to magazines is to begin and end in repeatedly demonstrating that they are self-absorbed and vapid publications, researchers run the risk of creating shallow scholarship on these supposedly shallow publications. Clearly there has to be more to the glossy-print format than a series of advertisements that attempt to engender false crises in order to offer product-based solutions.

One key aspect of magazines that has been under-researched is the social function of these periodicals.[5] Over the past three decades, niche publications have seen massive growth in terms of circulation and titles. In addition, traditional publishers within the men's, women's, parents' and other magazine groups have followed the lead of food manufacturers by extending their brand lines,[6] finely dicing each market niche and then placing a well-targeted title in it. In creating *Teen Vogue* and *Teen Cosmo*, for example, the publishers of *Vogue* and *Cosmopolitan* sought to reach for younger consumers with interests akin to their adult female counterparts. The publishers were also able to grasp an audience that would likely transition from one magazine to the next as readers transition from one stage of life to the next. Given what is known regarding branding and marketing, this is a logical approach to *growing* consumers over time.[7]

Yet, as already noted, research has demonstrated that these magazines are often unremarkable in their content, which tends to offer product-based solutions or overly simplify the real problems of readers, offering little more than repetitive answers to well-worn topics. In short, how many times before oversaturating the market can a magazine promise to provide a reader with ways to get a good man, lose those stubborn 10 pounds, ask a boy out on a date for the first time, apply subtle eye shadow, eat out on a budget or have amazing sex? Instead of examining this question, perhaps it would behoove researchers to use an audience-centric approach to scholarship to take a deeper look at what readers seek from these publications.

This chapter attempts to examine research conducted on consumer magazines and, to a lesser extent, trade publications through a readjusted focus of an active audience seeking to obtain specific things from their reading habits. This reexamination of previous research will allow for a more nuanced approach to understanding media use as well as offer some opportunities to reconsider what has previously been published in regard to magazines. In addition, this chapter offers an overarching theoretical perspective that may shed light on the intricate and distinctive needs of individuals who read magazines.

Drawing primarily from a uses and gratifications approach, this chapter helps to create a more complete understanding of how and why individuals use these publications, despite criticism that content might be shallow and repetitive. By understanding how active consumers evaluate themselves, their reading choices and their media-based needs, it may be possible to ascertain why some of the most criticized magazines continue to have value to their readers.

Literature Review and Method

While uses and gratifications research and magazine research have each yielded large quantities of scholarship, the intersection of the two has been limited. An electronic search of five academic databases[8] returned a total of 37 studies that included *uses and gratifications* and *magazine* or *magazines* or *periodical* or *periodicals* since 1990.[9] After replications and improperly captured items were removed, this number shrank to 18.[10]

The articles were examined for the focus of their topic, and three dominant areas emerged. One set of studies (5 of the 18) examined the information-seeking behaviors of individuals who used magazines to gain knowledge on important personal topics, such as health, or societal topics, such as the environment.[11] A second and more expected category (5 of the 18) is the focus on women-related magazines and topics through the lens of uses and gratifications theory. This area included studies on things such as reasons women read certain magazines and the impact the magazines have on women based on the gratifications they seek and obtain.[12] The third major area (5 of the 18) looked at magazines as a subset of traditional media during comparative analyses of traditional and digital media. In the majority of these studies, magazines were not singled out but were mentioned as part of a larger whole and viewed as being a traditional niche medium.[13]

Given the extremely limited set of data from which conclusions can be drawn, it makes little sense to dissect this series of articles in hopes of reaching any meaningful conclusions. To that end, magazine-effects research and UAG scholarship first are examined independently; then the value of future intersections of the theory and the medium is explored, using the few examples identified as available within the literature.

Effects-Based Research and Criticism

Much of the research pertaining to magazines takes an effects-based approach or engages in critical review to outline the impacts and the socio-cultural values associated with the publications. For instance, feminist scholars have taken various magazines to task for their sexualization of women and beauty[14] while ignoring or minimizing sexual risks[15] and other concerns pertaining to oversimplification of women and women's issues.

Angela McRobbie found that the teen magazine *Jackie!* treated sexual relationships between boys and girls as the primary focal point of its content,[16] while Diane T. Prusank noted that these magazines portray girls as being responsible for managing romantic relationships.[17] Furthermore, she argues that young girls are introduced to a mediated sense of self that requires them to act in certain ways to maintain normal inter-gender relationships. Magdala Peixoto Labre and Kim Walsh-Childers, from their broader look at the Web sites associated with these magazines, concluded that the sites promoted beauty as a requirement for young women. In addition, the sites took on the role of "friend" in offering ways to solve appearance deficits through the purchase and application of beauty products.[18]

In taking a health-based view, Jean Chow found that teen magazines create and promote models who attained an idealized version of perfection.[19] In order to become healthy, the content implied, teens were required to attain specific beauty attributes, maintain an overly thin body type and seek male attention. Chow noted that healthcare providers needed to understand the impact these images could have on young women and find ways to counterbalance these social demands. In a similar study, Elaine Bell Kaplan and Leslie Cole found that the emphasis on sexuality and femininity in these magazines cut across racial and cultural divides. These authors also state that young women who turn to these magazines are provided a very narrow view of these topics. Thus, the readers should find other ways to gain control over their own sense of self.[20]

Image control is a constant theme within niche consumer magazines. Jason A. Saucier and Sandra L. Caron's study of four magazines that targeted gay men (the *Advocate, Genre, Instinct* and *Out!*) assessed what types of images are dominant within their pages.[21] The authors noted that their results mimicked those of studies on women's magazines: high levels of physical objectification, focus on specific body parts and a high degree of importance placed on having the right body type. The stereotype perpetuated within these magazines, Saucier and Caron noted, was that gay men should be "young, hairless, Caucasian, interested in popular culture/entertainment and, of course, they should like to travel."[22] Joseph Schwartz and Julie L. Andsager also found that the *Advocate* and *Out!* magazines used images of men with high levels of muscle tone and low levels of body fat, leading to concerns pertaining to body image for readers.[23]

Gay and other niche publications have also received criticism for stereotyping their readers via content. A study that examined the 25 years in which the *Advocate* moved from a gay-rights local newspaper to a dominant magazine in the gay community showed that the publication created a "dominant gay habitus" for its readers.[24] Author Katherine Sender noted that the increasing need to appeal to advertisers marginalized lesbians and bisexual women, provided a sense that gay men were wealthy consumers and proposed that lifestyle was to be valued over sexuality.

In parenting magazines, similar concerns have emerged regarding stereotypes. Jennifer M. Greve Spees and Toni Schindler Zimmerman studied the messages and approaches presented by the publication and found problematic patterns in gender biases.[25] The authors noted that traditional gender myths, including the importance of beauty to girls and the value of athletics for boys, were prominent. In addition, although the magazines were supposedly geared toward all parents, the majority of the material was written for mothers. A similar study of *Parents, Parenting* and *Baby Years* magazines revealed that fathers were almost universally ignored and that the visuals and voices within the magazines furthered gendered stereotypes.[26]

Uses and Gratifications Research

Uses and gratifications theory takes a different approach to understanding media than do most of the theories scholars apply to analyses of magazine content and the impact that content has on the publication's readership. While most theoretical approaches seek to understand what media do to people, UAG theory attempts to understand what people do with media.[27] Within this perspective, scholars have posited that certain biological and psychological needs are innate to the human condition. Individuals faced with these needs will seek out sources to satisfy those needs, and, when those sources are located, individuals will repeatedly return to them when the needs reemerge.

Researchers have outlined several key assumptions pertaining to UAG and media use: (1) The audience is active, (2) media use is goal directed, (3) media consumption satisfies a wide range of needs, (4) people can articulate why they are using media and (5) gratification can be obtained through the use of media.[28] These assumptions provide a picture of a more engaged and aware audience that understands what it is seeing and what it wants from its media experiences. They also indicate that not all media satisfy all needs and that people know where to go to satisfy the needs they have at any point in time.

Unlike many other theories, the uses and gratifications approach lacks a concrete set of mutually agreed upon variables, known within the theory as *needs*; however, several kinds of needs have emerged as part of media studies, including *passage of time* (boredom relief, escapism, entertainment), *relational needs* (personal relationships, parasocial relationships, social utility), *personal identity* (self-awareness, downward social comparison) and *informational needs* (surveillance, knowledge gain) to name a few.[29]

The UAG approach has been used to study television,[30] telephones,[31] instant messaging[32] and the Internet.[33] In each case, the needs vary based on the medium and even the kind of material. For example, Cynthia Frisby noted that reality-television experienced mood improvement that suggested they engaged in downward social comparison while watching.[34] Study participants noted they felt better when they were able to project themselves as being superior to the "actors" on the show. On the other hand, Robert Abelman, David Atkin and Michael Rand's work could be interpreted to suggest that viewers of scripted television shows were likely to watch for companionship, escapism and entertainment needs.[35]

Given the array of magazines available to readers and magazines' reliance on hyper-specialized niche targeting, the limited number of studies on the intersection of UAG theory and these publications suggests that researchers could do much more to mine this rich vein of scholarship. That said, what has been published has yielded some quality outcomes that support the continued use of this perspective.

Gregg A. Payne, Jessica J.H. Severn and David M. Dozier examined differentiated gratification-seeking based on "magazine type."[36] The authors studied the needs associated with consumer and trade magazines in order to assess why individuals read each of them. The authors found that consumer magazines were primarily used as a diversion and that trade magazines were also used to satisfy the needs for diversion but also surveillance and interaction. In a similar fashion, Nandan Dixit examined why people read a special interest computer magazine. The author found that individuals sought to satisfy information and guidance needs as opposed to entertainment or utility needs.[37] Wayne M. Towers noted that individuals sought and obtained different types of gratifications from news and general circulation magazines.[38] By using a discriminant analysis, Towers argued that interaction and surveillance motives were key for the use of newsmagazines but diversion predicted the use of consumer magazines. Quint Randle found that the Web was superior to print magazines in terms of satisfying niche-based needs. In addition, Randle noted that magazines were still viewed as important in satisfying affective and self-oriented uses.[39]

In sum, this research suggests that individuals seek specific kinds of media to satisfy a wide range of needs. In actively pursuing these media, the readers are goal-driven in their approach and will continue to return to those media that best satiate those needs. The media can provide a wide array of gratifications, even within a specific media format, and individuals can satisfy multiple needs through one form of media. Furthermore, magazines' niche approach to content as well as their high level of individual consistency can create opportunities for individuals to form patterns of gratification-seeking to meet those needs. In order to more fully value the social function and inherent value of magazines, it might be worthwhile to examine what magazines do and what they are through this UAG lens.

Social Function and Value

The use of magazines is by no means an obligatory social function. Individuals are not forcibly compelled to read general interest magazines to avoid some sort of reprisal, nor is there evidence to suggest they feel required to keep up on the latest trends in fashion or culture for fear of being shunned. Instead, as suggested by uses and gratifications, consuming this content is based on choice, desire and free will, as the magazines offer an opportunity to fulfill a psychological or socio-cultural need.

Joke Hermes labeled magazines as "easy to put down," noting that they failed to demand any effort from readers.[40] Hermes argued that due to the lack of high-quality content, they lacked meaning and value for readers. In reframing the issue in terms of need-satisfaction, it becomes clear that these publications can still gratify the needs of readers. Payne, Severn and Dozier's work provided evidence that readers saw consumer magazines as a way to pass time, relax and be happy.[41] Towers also found that readers of these magazines used them to gratify basic diversion needs.[42] Chow stated that Hermes does not note whether "anything is ever a diversion,"[43] but this does raise the issue of the degree to which readers of any publication must be engaged in higher-order thinking in order for the material to be of merit. Even McRobbie tempered her critical approach to content of this nature when she later wrote, "the superficial does not necessarily represent a decline into the meaninglessness or valuelessness in culture."[44] The diversion gratifications serve to ameliorate boredom or to mentally decompress. For lack of a better term, they are a small serving of brain candy.

This content can also have merit beyond its ability to help readers bide time if it can create an opportunity for individuals of like-minded interests to coalesce. John Battelle, the co-founder of *Wired* magazine, captured the underlying essence of magazines by noting that successful publishers attempt to gather individuals who have similar interests as part of a collective. "The fundamental purpose of a magazine is to bring together a market and a market is a community."[45]

Broader scholarly research into group-based ideology and behavior has revealed that human beings seek like-minded others who are able to establish patterns of norms and values for that group.[46] This allows people to not only feel comfortable in their place within the group, but also enjoy a sense of comfort from the group's approach to those norms and values. It is through content that reflects these norms and values that individuals can gratify social identity and relational needs. Jan Whitt found from her study of lesbian magazines from 1947 to 1994 that the purpose of these publications was to provide readers with social connections to lesbian communities and give them support systems as they dealt with problems associated with homophobia. Although the publications were tied to politically active groups, Whitt argued that the main purpose of the magazines was to help readers gain a stronger sense of self and create a bond of togetherness.[47]

The codifying of these norms and values within the pages of the publication can lead to repetition, which media critics are quick to point to as a negative aspect of the form.[48] In this criticism, scholars ignore several key values of magazines and the general concept of social niches. First, if magazines are to gratify specific needs, they are required to assess the needs to which their niche is most directly attached. In other words, they must understand what draws individuals to pick up the magazine. A fashion magazine, for example, may gratify a surveillance need for readers who want to know what clothing lines will be coming out in the fall. A woodworker's magazine may satisfy a knowledge-gain need by teaching readers how to restore a piece of furniture properly. These niche publications satisfy niche interests. Colleen P. Labbe and Rosanne W. Fortner found in a review of subscribers to *E/The Environmental Magazine* that subscribers saw the publication as an important source of reliable environmental information.[49] Uses and gratifications theory combined with social identity theory would argue that the readers, who saw the magazine's readership as a generally homogenized group, used the information in the magazine to satisfy surveillance needs and to reinforce what they believed regarding the environment. If this magazine failed to meet these needs, the readership would likely drop off as individuals would seek other sources of need-satisfaction, given that the need remains while the source of gratification has failed to satisfy it.

Second, and perhaps more importantly, many of these magazines do not need to evolve beyond this level of repetition because their audience block continues to shift over time.

Magazines tend to target specific groups with specific needs, such as teen girls who are looking to understand their place in a new social order or parents who are raising children for the first time. The gratifications these magazines are attempting to satisfy are informational and relational needs for new members of these societal niches. Kaplan and Cole's study of why young women read *Seventeen* revealed that participants in their research said the magazine would "tell them something about 'what it is like being a teenage girl.'"[50] Kirsi Lumme-Sandt noted that 50+, a magazine aimed at senior citizens, offered advice on how to continue to live their lives and also how to reshape their sense of self as they felt the need. In both cases, readers of the magazines are seeking to better understand their current status within a demographic or socio-cultural role.[51]

Once individuals gain mastery over their roles or their roles change, they might leave the magazines behind. For example, first-time parents are likely faced with a wide array of concerns, ranging from fussy eaters to children who need to be toilet trained. Given their limited experience in this role, parents turn to parenting magazines for suggestions on how to deal with these issues. The parents will likely attempt to solve their problems via some of the options espoused in the magazine while rejecting others, for a variety of reasons. Once the parents have met with success in their efforts, they will no longer need the magazine. If they have a second child, they may return to the parenting magazines for pointers and more recent additions to the knowledge base. Even if experienced parents do not return, new parents will be added to the circulation roll each day as they seek to master these challenges associated with their personal identity. In this way, criticizing magazines for printing repetitive content is akin to criticizing a university for publishing a freshman orientation guide each year.

Researchers have also stated that this repetitive content has yielded deleterious consequences for readers. Kaplan and Cole argue that *Seventeen* sends a message to young girls that they gain self-worth by valuing femininity and beauty.[52] Other researchers have leveled similar criticisms, noting that the magazines in this genre focus on beauty, fashion and sex as the dominant aspects of young women's lives.[53] Research into women's magazines has also led to concerns regarding gendered self-concept,[54] body-image concerns,[55] warped versions of masculinity[56] and domestic violence.[57]

Obviously, these issues merit study and are of great concern to society at large; however, this approach to magazines is myopic when it incorrectly intimates that magazines will affect readers in a uniform fashion and without their consent. Lumme-Sandt noted that the elderly are often erroneously viewed as being passive victims of stereotyping. In her study of 50+, she found that aging is "an individualized project," and thus readers of the magazine were able to both reflect on who they were and seek answers as to who they might become.[58] In their study of *Seventeen*, Kaplan and Cole's interviews with young readers revealed that although some participants sought specific gratifications ("I want to read stuff on boys"), not all participants were equally engaged at that level ("It has a lot of girl and guy stuff and I'm not into all that stuff.").[59] Additionally, some participants saw ways the magazine gratified their relational needs, noting that its tips on fashion and style would help them associate with other people interested in similar topics. Other readers rejected the magazine because it failed to gratify their self-identity interests ("It just isn't part of me, where I come from. It's, like, for white people.").[60] Other research into ethnic and teen magazines also revealed that black teens saw the magazines as lacking socialization value for themselves but were able to use them to gratify social comparison and surveillance interests in regard to observing and critiquing white beauty culture.[61]

In Chow's study of adolescent perceptions of popular teen magazines, members of her focus groups actively rejected the idealized images they saw ("Who has a body like that? Nobody!") and were able to critique the images ("Their eyes and their teeth and everything look so perfectly pearly white. Like you know, they're too clean and neat and perfect, you know, and regulated"). In addition, the study participants appeared to be able to derive social comparison gratification even though they saw themselves as failing to measure up to the idealized images they were viewing ("That chick at the bottom still looks like a bimbo." "[They] look like ditsies to me").[62] Merja Mahrt also noted that some readers of women's magazines disagree with the values espoused within the publications. These readers view the magazine as a negotiable text, in which they can project their own sense of identity upon the publication. Furthermore, some individuals chose to engage in selective exposure based on the need to find reinforcement of their own personal values.[63]

Discussion and Analysis

The purpose of this chapter was to examine the research on magazines from a broader social standpoint and offer some discussion pertaining to the inherent value of what is often viewed as meaningless content. A deeper look at magazines from a more audience-centric approach reveals that readers actively select content that either supports their current suppositions or offers them additional levels of need-satisfaction in a variety of ways.

The uses and gratifications approach allows us to better examine what people are doing with these publications and why they use them. In many cases, the magazines are exactly what critics have noted they are: easily putdownable; however, in terms of gratification, this simple use of brain candy can have value nonetheless. Individuals often have a need to simply pass time in a doctor's office or relieve boredom as they are standing in line at a store. Magazines that satisfy those needs are not attempting to be more than that: a simple pleasure, a way to escape or an entertainment opportunity. From a broader theoretical and social standpoint, these are important and valuable needs. Criticizing magazines of that nature for not being something else is akin to criticizing an apple for not being a banana.

Magazines also offer information to niches that continue to regenerate their audiences. The content in these publications can appear repetitive to scholars and long-time readers. Those criticisms are valid, but social identity and uses and gratifications theories point to magazines' having a limited shelf-life and a constantly changing audience that fits within their niches. The magazines that offer information on a topic that is repetitive can be doing so to reach new and secondary audiences to satisfy their needs for knowledge gain.

The first time a parent faces a night without sleep or can't get a child to eat, advice is welcome, whether it is the latest in child sociology or a well-worn, tried-and-true remedy. Publishers of these types of material provide this material because they understand that people who read these magazines have limited experience with these issues. In other words, many parents read parenting magazines because they are new at parenting and don't know what to do or what to expect. The same is true for older citizens who read plus-50 magazines[64] or teens who read teen magazines.

In reexamining research conducted on various magazines and niches, it is also clear that people see value in these publications far beyond the content itself. In offering people opportunities to receive information in communal ways, magazine publishers are providing readers with opportunities to gain social utility and forge relationships with others of similar interests. As John Battelle noted, magazines allow for the creation of communities based on a set of norms and values germane to that community.[65] To that end, readers are able to engage in a broader examination of self and others via this media conduit.

The studies of gay and lesbian publications showed that the magazines meshed with the social identities of the readers. Whitt described the lesbian magazines she studied as "a labor from the heart," noting that the women who founded and sustained these magazines often did so on limited budgets and with tiny levels of readership.[66] However, the ability to find others who were like them and to create a safe space in which important issues could be discussed outweighed the importance of any financial gain for them.

Given the limited amount of scholarship that looks at this broader approach to evaluating magazines, it is difficult to ascertain to what degree the positives outweigh the negatives. That said, a more holistic approach to understanding why readers actively seek and use magazines should be considered in any study of these publications. Readers actively select what they want to read and have a reason behind those choices. In examining what needs these publications satisfy, perhaps critics could offer a viable option that both gratifies the readers and sidesteps the concerns generally associated with the magazines. In addition, perhaps publishers could better understand the audience needs and offer additional material that both satisfies the needs of the readers and also improves the quality of the publication. Either way, this broader view is an opening gambit to what should hopefully be a broader discussion of how best to view magazines from a larger social standpoint.

Notes

1 Mary C. Martin and James W. Gentry, "Stuck in the Model Trap: The Effects of Beautiful Models in Ads on Female Pre-Adolescents and Adolescents," *Journal of Advertising* 26.2 (Summer 1997): 19–33.

2 Kenon Breazeale, "In Spite of Women: *Esquire* Magazine and the Construction of the Male Consumer," *Signs: Journal of Women in Culture and Society* 20.1 (Autumn 1994): 1–22.

3 Joseph Schwartz and Julie L. Andsager, "Four Decades of Images in Gay Male-Targeted Magazines," *Journalism & Mass Communication Quarterly* 88.1 (Spring 2011): 76–98; Katherine Sender, "Gay Readers, Consumers, and a Dominant Gay Habitus: 25 Years of *The Advocate* Magazine," *Journal of Communication* 51.1 (March 2001): 73–99.

4 Vincent F. Filak, "Marriage, Magazines and Makeup Tips: A Comparative Content Analysis of *Brides* Magazine and *Glamour* Magazine" (paper presented at the Annual Meeting, Association of Education in Journalism and Mass Communication, August 2002), 17.

5 Juanne N. Clarke, "The Paradoxical Portrayal of the Risk of Sexually Transmitted Infections and Sexuality in U.S. Magazines *Glamour* and *Cosmopolitan* 2000–2007," *Health, Risk & Society* 12.6 (December 2010): 560–574; Magdala Peixoto Labre and Kim Walsh-Childers, "Friendly Advice? Beauty Messages in Web Sites of Teen Magazines," *Mass Communication and Society* 6.4 (Fall 2003): 379–396.

6 Lisa M. Guidone, "The Magazine at the Millennium: Integrating the Internet," *Publishing Research Quarterly* 16.2 (Summer 2000): 14–33.

7 For example, *Teen Vogue* listed the various ways in which lipstick was used to accentuate certain characteristics (see "London Bloggers Show Off Their Bold Lip Looks" <http://www.teenvogue.com/beauty/makeup/2013–08/blogger-statement-lipstick/?slide=1>, accessed 9 September 2013), while a similar article ran via the Beauty Staple section of the *Vogue* Web site (see "Kate Foley's Bright Lipstick" <http://www.vogue.com/vogue-daily/article/beauty-staple-kate-foleys-bright-lipstick/#1>, accessed 9 September 2013). Other similar parallels can be found throughout the paired sites, as they look at fashion, cosmetics, exercises and more.

8 The databases included in this search were Academic Search Complete, Communication & Mass Media complete, ERIC, PsychINFO and SocINDEX. These databases were selected based on their inclusion of full-text versions of scholarly articles, their overall completeness in terms of field coverage and the author's familiarity with the databases' quality.

9 The year 1990 was used as the cutoff for this examination as it was the target date established for this book. Additional research revealed other work on uses and gratifications and magazines, with many of those pieces being cited in other portions of this chapter.

10 An example of a repetition would be a conference paper that was filed twice, once with each of the search engines. An example of an improperly captured item would be when a conference program listing was returned as a case.

11 Studies in this category mainly centered on healthcare concerns and include J. David Johnson and Hendrika Meischke, "A Comprehensive Model of Cancer-Related Information Seeking Applied to Magazines," *Human Communication Research* 19.3 (March 1993): 343–367. An exception is Colleen P. Labbe and Rosanne W. Fortner, "Perceptions of the Concerned Reader: An Analysis of the Subscribers of E/*The Environmental Magazine*," *Journal of Environmental Education* 32.3 (March 2001): 41–46.

12 See, for example, Fan Hu and Mena Wang, "Beauty and Fashion Magazines and College-Age Women's Appearance-Related Concerns" (paper presented at the Annual Meeting, International Communication Association, May 2009), 23; Lisa Duke, "Black in a Blonde World: Race and Girls' Interpretations of the Feminine Ideal in Teen Magazines," *Journalism & Mass Communication Quarterly* 77.2 (Summer 2000): 367–392.

13 Examples include Antonio La Pastina and Brian Quick, "An Exploration of Internet and Traditional Media Uses in the Rio Grande Valley" (paper presented at the Annual Meeting, International Communication

Association, May 2004), 30; Barbara K. Kaye and Thomas J. Johnson, "From Here to Obscurity? Media Substitution Theory and Traditional Media in an On-Line World," *Journal of the American Society for Information Science & Technology* 54.3 (February 2003): 260–273.

14 See, for example, Kathryn McMahon, "The *Cosmopolitan* Ideology and Management of Desire," *Journal of Sex Research* 27.3 (August 1990): 381–396.

15 Clarke, "The Paradoxical Portrayal of the Risk."

16 Angela McRobbie, "Jackie: An Ideology of Adolescent Femininity," in Bernard Waites, Tony Bennett, and Graham Martin, eds., *Popular Culture: Past and Present* (London: Open University Press, 1982), 263–283.

17 Diane T. Prusank, "Masculinities in Teen Magazines: The Good, the Bad, and the Ugly," *Journal of Men's Studies* 15.2 (Spring 2007): 160–177.

18 Labre and Walsh-Childers, "Friendly Advice?," 393–394.

19 Jean Chow, "Adolescents' Perceptions of Popular Teen Magazines," *Journal of Advanced Nursing* 48.2 (October 2004): 132–139.

20 Elaine Bell Kaplan and Leslie Cole, "'I Want to Read Stuff on Boys': White, Latina, and Black Girls Reading *Seventeen* Magazine and Encountering Adolescence," *Adolescence* 38.149 (Spring 2003): 141–159.

21 Jason A. Saucier and Sandra L. Caron, "An Investigation of Content and Media Images in Gay Men's Magazines," *Journal of Homosexuality* 55.3 (July 2008): 504–523.

22 Saucier and Caron, "An Investigation of Content and Media Images," 522.

23 Schwartz and Andsager, "Four Decades of Images."

24 Sender, "Gay Readers."

25 Jennifer M. Greve Spees and Toni Schindler Zimmerman, "Gender Messages in Parenting Magazines: A Content Analysis," *Journal of Feminist Family Therapy* 14.3/4 (Fall/Winter 2002): 73–100.

26 Jane Sunderland, "'Parenting' or 'Mothering'?: The Case of Modern Childcare Magazines," *Discourse & Society* 17.4 (July 2006): 503–527.

27 Elihu Katz, Jay G. Blumler, and Michael Gurevitch, "Uses and Gratifications Research," *Public Opinion Quarterly* 37.4 (Winter 1973): 509–523.

28 Philip Palmgreen, Lawrence A. Wenner, and Karl Erik Rosengren, "Uses and Gratifications Research: The Past Ten Years," in Karl Erik Rosengren, Lawrence A. Wenner and Philip Palmgreen, eds., *Media Gratifications Research* (London: Sage, 1985), 11–37.

29 See Katz, Blumler, and Gurevitch, "Uses and Gratifications Research"; Thomas E. Ruggiero, "Uses and Gratifications Theory in the 21st Century," *Mass Communication and Society* 3.1 (Winter 2000): 3–37, for a more complete overview.

30 Alan M. Rubin, "Television Uses and Gratifications: The Interactions of Viewing Patterns and Motivations," *Journal of Broadcasting* 27.1 (Winter 1983): 37–51.

31 Garrett J. O'Keefe and Barbara K. Sulanowski, "More Than Just Talk: Uses, Gratifications, and the Telephone," *Journalism & Mass Communication Quarterly* 72.4 (Winter 1995): 922–933.

32 Louis Leung, "College Student Motives for Chatting on ICQ," *New Media & Society* 3.4 (December 2001): 483–500.

33 Barbara K. Kaye and Thomas J. Johnson, "Online and in the Know: Uses and Gratifications of the Web for Political Information," *Journal of Broadcasting & Electronic Media* 46.1 (March 2002): 54–71.

34 Cynthia Frisby, "Getting Real with Reality TV," *USA Today* (Magazine), September 2004, 50–54.

35 Robert Abelman, David Atkin, and Michael Rand, "What Viewers Watch When They Watch TV: Affiliation Change as Case Study," *Journal of Broadcasting & Electronic Media* 41.3 (Summer 1997): 360–379.

36 Gregg A. Payne, Jessica J. H. Severn, and David M. Dozier, "Uses and Gratifications Motives as Indicators of Magazine Readership," *Journalism Quarterly* 65.4 (Winter 1988): 909–913, 959.

37 Nandan Dixit, "A Case Study of Uses and Gratification that People Seek from a Special Interest Computer Magazine" (Master's thesis, San Jose State University, 1987), 75.

38 Wayne M. Towers, "Uses and Gratifications of Magazine Readers: A Cross-Media Comparison," *Mass Comm Review* 13.1/2/3 (1986): 44–51.

39 Quint Randle, "Gratification Niches of Monthly Print Magazines and the World Wide Web among a Group of Special-Interest Magazine Subscribers," *Journal of Computer-Mediated Communication* 8.4 (July 2003): Unpaginated [Open Access Journal, ICA].

40 Joke Hermes, *Reading Women's Magazines: An Analysis of Everyday Media Use* (Cambridge, UK: Polity Press, 1995), 64.

41 Payne, Severn, and Dozier, "Uses and Gratifications Motives," 912–913.

42 Towers, "Uses and Gratifications of Magazine Readers."

43 Hermes, *Reading Women's Magazines*, n.p., quoted in Chow, "Adolescents' Perceptions of Popular Teen Magazines," 137.

44 Angela McRobbie, *Postmodernism and Popular Culture* (Florence, KY: Routledge, 1994), 4.

45 Guidone, quoting John Battelle in "The Magazine at the Millennium," 15.

46 See Henri Tajfel and John C. Turner, "The Social Identity Theory of Intergroup Behavior," in Stephen Worchel and William G. Austin, eds., *The Psychology of Intergroup Relations*, 2nd ed. (Chicago: Nelson-Hall Publishers, 1986), 7–24, for a more complete review.

47 Jan Whitt, "A 'Labor from the Heart': Lesbian Magazines from 1947–1994," *Journal of Lesbian Studies* 5.1/2 (March 2001): 229–251.

48 See Dawn H. Currie, *Girl Talk: Adolescent Magazines and Their Readers* (Toronto: University of Toronto Press, 1999) for an extended examination of this issue as it pertains to girls' magazines.

49 Labbe and Fortner, "Perceptions of the Concerned Reader," 41–46.

50 Kaplan and Cole, "'I Want to Read Stuff on Boys,'" 146.

51 Kirsi Lumme-Sandt, "Images of Ageing in a 50+ Magazine," *Journal of Aging Studies* 25.1 (January 2011): 45–51.

52 Kaplan and Cole, "'I Want to Read Stuff on Boys,'" 157–158.

53 Labre and Walsh-Childers, "Friendly Advice?" 396; McRobbie, "Jackie."

54 Sarah B. Crymble, "Contradiction Sells: Feminine Complexity and Gender Identity Dissonance in Magazine Advertising," *Journal of Communication Inquiry* 36.1 (January 2012): 62–84.

55 Brett Silverstein, Lauren Perdue, Barbara Peterson, and Eileen Kelly, "The Role of the Mass Media in Promoting a Thin Standard of Bodily Attractiveness for Women," *Sex Roles* 14.9/10 (May 1986): 519–532.

56 Prusank, "Masculinities in Teen Magazines."

57 Pamela Hill Nettleton, "Domestic Violence in Men's and Women's Magazines: Women Are Guilty of Choosing the Wrong Men, Men Are Not Guilty of Hitting Women," *Women's Studies in Communication* 34.2 (Summer 2011): 139–160.

58 Lumme-Sandt, "Images of Ageing," 50. See also John A. Cutter, "Specialty Magazines and the Older Reader," in [Images of Aging in Media and Marketing] theme issue, *Generations* 25.3 (Fall 2001): 13–15.

59 Kaplan and Cole, "'I Want to Read Stuff on Boys,'" 148.

60 Kaplan and Cole, "'I Want to Read Stuff on Boys,'" 154.

61 Duke, "Black in a Blonde World," 367–392.

62 Chow, "Adolescents' Perceptions of Popular Teen Magazines," 135.

63 Merja Mahrt, "The Attractiveness of Magazines as 'Open' and 'Closed' Texts: Values of Women's Magazines and Their Readers," *Mass Communication and Society* 15.6 (November/December 2012): 852–874.

64 Cutter, "Specialty Magazines and the Older Reader."

65 Guidone, quoting John Battelle in "The Magazine at the Millennium," 15.

66 Whitt, "A 'Labor from the Heart."

Bibliography

Abelman, Robert; Atkin, David; and Rand, Michael. "What Viewers Watch When They Watch TV: Affiliation Change as Case Study." *Journal of Broadcasting & Electronic Media* 41.3 (Summer 1997): 360–379.

Breazeale, Kenon. "In Spite of Women: *Esquire* Magazine and the Construction of the Male Consumer." *Signs: Journal of Women in Culture and Society* 20.1 (Autumn 1994): 1–22.

Chow, Jean. "Adolescents' Perceptions of Popular Teen Magazines." *Journal of Advanced Nursing* 48.2 (October 2004): 132–139.

Clarke, Juanne N. "The Paradoxical Portrayal of the Risk of Sexually Transmitted Infections and Sexuality in U.S. Magazines *Glamour* and *Cosmopolitan* 2000–2007." *Health, Risk & Society* 12.6 (December 2010): 560–574.

Crymble, Sarah B. "Contradiction Sells: Feminine Complexity and Gender Identity Dissonance in Magazine Advertising." *Journal of Communication Inquiry* 36.1 (January 2012): 62–84.

Currie, Dawn H. *Girl Talk: Adolescent Magazines and Their Readers.* Toronto: University of Toronto Press, 1999.

Cutter, John A. "Specialty Magazines and the Older Reader." [Theme Issue: Images of Aging in Media and Marketing]. *Generations* 25.3 (Fall 2001): 13–15.

Dixit, Nandan. "A Case Study of Uses and Gratification that People Seek from a Special Interest Computer Magazine." Master's thesis, San Jose State University, 1987.

Duke, Lisa. "Black in a Blonde World: Race and Girls' Interpretations of the Feminine Ideal in Teen Magazines." *Journalism & Mass Communication Quarterly* 77.2 (Summer 2000): 367–392.

Filak, Vincent F. "Marriage, Magazines and Makeup Tips: A Comparative Content Analysis of *Brides* Magazine and *Glamour* Magazine." Paper presented at the Annual Meeting, Association of Education in Journalism and Mass Communication, August 2002.

Frisby, Cynthia. "Getting Real with Reality TV." *USA Today* (Magazine), September 2004, 50–54.

Guidone, Lisa M. "The Magazine at the Millennium: Integrating the Internet." *Publishing Research Quarterly* 16.2 (Summer 2000): 14–33.

Hermes, Joke. *Reading Women's Magazines: An Analysis of Everyday Media Use.* Cambridge, UK: Polity Press, 1995.

Hu, Fan and Wang, Mena. "Beauty and Fashion Magazines and College-Age Women's Appearance-Related Concerns." Paper presented at the Annual Meeting, International Communication Association, May 2009.

Johnson, J. David and Meischke, Hendrika. "A Comprehensive Model of Cancer-Related Information Seeking Applied to Magazines." *Human Communication Research* 19.3 (March 1993): 343–367.

Kaplan, Elaine Bell and Cole, Leslie. "'I Want to Read Stuff on Boys': White, Latina, and Black Girls Reading *Seventeen* Magazine and Encountering Adolescence." *Adolescence* 38.149 (Spring 2003): 141–159.

Katz, Elihu; Blumler, Jay G.; and Gurevitch, Michael. "Uses and Gratifications Research." *Public Opinion Quarterly* 37.4 (Winter 1973): 509–523.

Kaye, Barbara K. and Johnson, Thomas J. "From Here to Obscurity? Media Substitution Theory and Traditional Media in an On-Line World." *Journal of the American Society for Information Science & Technology* 54.3 (February 2003): 260–273.

Kaye, Barbara K. and Johnson, Thomas J. "Online and in the Know: Uses and Gratifications of the Web for Political Information." *Journal of Broadcasting & Electronic Media* 46.1 (March 2002): 54–71.

La Pastina, Antonio and Quick, Brian. "An Exploration of Internet and Traditional Media Uses in the Rio Grande Valley." Paper presented at the Annual Meeting, International Communication Association, May 2004.

Labbe, Colleen P. and Fortner, Rosanne W. "Perceptions of the Concerned Reader: An Analysis of the Subscribers of *E/The Environmental Magazine*." *Journal of Environmental Education* 32.3 (March 2001): 41–46.

Labre, Magdala Peixoto and Walsh-Childers, Kim. "Friendly Advice? Beauty Messages in Web Sites of Teen Magazines." *Mass Communication and Society* 6.4 (Fall 2003): 379–396.

Leung, Louis. "College Student Motives for Chatting on ICQ." *New Media & Society* 3.4 (December 2001): 483–500.

Lumme-Sandt, Kirsi. "Images of Ageing in a 50+ Magazine." *Journal of Aging Studies* 25.1 (January 2011): 45–51.

Mahrt, Merja. "The Attractiveness of Magazines as 'Open' and 'Closed' Texts: Values of Women's Magazines and Their Readers." *Mass Communication and Society* 15.6 (November/December 2012): 852–874.

Martin, Mary C. and Gentry, James W. "Stuck in the Model Trap: The Effects of Beautiful Models in Ads on Female Pre-Adolescents and Adolescents." *Journal of Advertising* 26.2 (Summer 1997): 19–33.

McMahon, Kathryn. "The *Cosmopolitan* Ideology and Management of Desire." *Journal of Sex Research* 27.3 (August 1990): 381–396.

McRobbie, Angela. "Jackie: An Ideology of Adolescent Femininity." In Waites, Bernard; Bennett, Tony; and Martin, Graham, eds. *Popular Culture: Past and Present*. London: Open University Press, 1982, 263–283.

McRobbie, Angela. *Postmodernism and Popular Culture*. Florence, KY: Routledge, 1994.

Nettleton, Pamela Hill. "Domestic Violence in Men's and Women's Magazines: Women Are Guilty of Choosing the Wrong Men, Men Are Not Guilty of Hitting Women." *Women's Studies in Communication* 34.2 (Summer 2011): 139–160.

O'Keefe, Garrett J. and Sulanowski, Barbara K. "More Than Just Talk: Uses, Gratifications, and the Telephone." *Journalism & Mass Communication Quarterly* 72.4 (Winter 1995): 922–933.

Palmgreen, Philip; Wenner, Lawrence A.; and Rosengren, Karl Erik. "Uses and Gratifications Research: The Past Ten Years." In Rosengren, Karl Erik; Wenner, Lawrence A.; and Palmgreen, Philip, eds. *Media Gratifications Research*. London: Sage, 1985, 11–37.

Payne, Gregg A.; Severn, Jessica J. H.; and Dozier, David M. "Uses and Gratifications Motives as Indicators of Magazine Readership." *Journalism Quarterly* 65.4 (Winter 1988): 909–913, 959.

Prusank, Diane T. "Masculinities in Teen Magazines: The Good, the Bad, and the Ugly." *Journal of Men's Studies* 15.2 (Spring 2007): 160–177.

Randle, Quint. "Gratification Niches of Monthly Print Magazines and the World Wide Web among a Group of Special-Interest Magazine Subscribers." *Journal of Computer-Mediated Communication* 8.4 (July 2003): Unpaginated [Open Access Journal, ICA].

Rubin, Alan M. "Television Uses and Gratifications: The Interactions of Viewing Patterns and Motivations." *Journal of Broadcasting* 27.1 (Winter 1983): 37–51.

Ruggiero, Thomas E. "Uses and Gratifications Theory in the 21st Century." *Mass Communication and Society* 3.1 (Winter 2000): 3–37.

Saucier, Jason A. and Caron, Sandra L. "An Investigation of Content and Media Images in Gay Men's Magazines." *Journal of Homosexuality* 55.3 (July 2008): 504–523.

Schwartz, Joseph and Andsager, Julie L. "Four Decades of Images in Gay Male-Targeted Magazines." *Journalism & Mass Communication Quarterly* 88.1 (Spring 2011): 76–98.

Sender, Katherine. "Gay Readers, Consumers, and a Dominant Gay Habitus: 25 Years of *The Advocate* Magazine." *Journal of Communication* 51.1 (March 2001): 73–99.

Silverstein, Brett; Perdue, Lauren; Peterson, Barbara; and Kelly, Eileen. "The Role of the Mass Media in Promoting a Thin Standard of Bodily Attractiveness for Women." *Sex Roles* 14.9/10 (May 1986): 519–532.

Spees, Jennifer M. Greve and Zimmerman, Toni Schindler. "Gender Messages in Parenting Magazines: A Content Analysis." *Journal of Feminist Family Therapy* 14.3/4 (Fall/Winter 2002): 73–100.

Sunderland, Jane. "'Parenting' or 'Mothering'?: The Case of Modern Childcare Magazines." *Discourse & Society* 17.4 (July 2006): 503–527.

Tajfel, Henri and Turner, John C. "The Social Identity Theory of Intergroup Behavior." In Worchel, Stephen and Austin, William G., eds. *The Psychology of Intergroup Relations*, 2nd ed. Chicago: Nelson-Hall Publishers, 1986, 7–24.

Towers, Wayne M. "Uses and Gratifications of Magazine Readers: A Cross-Media Comparison." *Mass Comm Review* 13.1/2/3 (1986): 44–51.

Whitt, Jan. "A 'Labor from the Heart': Lesbian Magazines from 1947–1994." *Journal of Lesbian Studies* 5.1/2 (March 2001): 229–251.

17
CREATING CONSUMER LIFESTYLES

Esteem and Enjoyment, Influence and Appetite

Yanick Rice Lamb

The U.S. edition of *Vogue* magazine is a bible of consumptive behavior. Its pages, which may range from as few as 130 to more than 900 per issue, are filled with the gospel of Editor-in-Chief Anna Wintour on everything from fashion to politics. While many magazines place five or more cover lines to gain attention on newsstands, *Vogue* used only three on the cover of its annual Power Issue in March 2009. That is all the world's leading fashion magazine needed with its iconic cover girl and a main cover line that boldly stated, "Michelle Obama: The First Lady the World's Been Waiting For." The other two cover lines read, "Spring Fashion Special: Every Look That Matters" and "Super Powers! Queen Rania of Jordan, Carla Bruni-Sarkozy, Melinda Gates."

It is the perfect combination. Obama is wearing a sleeveless magenta silk dress by one of her favorite designers, Jason Wu, in a portrait that strategically showcases her much-debated toned arms,[1] shot by one of *Vogue*'s principal photographers, Annie Leibovitz,[2] at one of the nation's landmark hotels, the Hay-Adams in Washington, DC, for what *Vogue* describes as a "historic sitting" just before the first inauguration of the first black president of the United States.[3] As Sammye Johnson and Patricia Prijatel note in *The Magazine from Cover to Cover*, "Magazines are lively and engaging societal resources, affecting the world around them and, in turn, being affected themselves by that world."[4] A prime example of the interdependency Johnson and Prijatel describe is the U.S. edition of *Vogue*'s consumerist approach to its 2009 Power Issue, which was published at one of the twenty-first century's most pivotal times in international politics and economics. This chapter examines such interdependency by examining scholarly research on consumerism and lifestyles as reflected in contemporary magazines that subscribe to a consumerist philosophy and are marketed to the general public.

Defining Consumerism

"Mass culture shapes habitual audiences, around common needs or interests, and it is made for profit," wrote Richard M. Ohmann in *Selling Culture: Magazines, Markets and Class at the Turn of the Century*, which focused on the two decades spanning 1890 to 1910.[5] A key vehicle for shaping these audiences was the consumer magazine, which focuses on common needs or interests to make a profit. This chapter examines consumer magazines through a research review and historical analysis. It explores research focusing on the interplay between magazines and consumer lifestyles—how magazines cover and often influence consumer lifestyles, as well as how consumer lifestyles influence the content in magazines. A common thread in the literature is how readers increasingly came to be viewed and valued as consumers, particularly as potential buyers of the products and services advertised in magazines. In the process, magazines stimulated consumptive behavior by playing to the needs and wants of consumers. These consumer magazines help to create and feed reader appetites for esteem and enjoyment—whether readers aspire to the lifestyles featured in the publications and whether they can afford to obtain or maintain them.

Richard Campbell, Christopher R. Martin and Bettina Fabos have noted that throughout their existence magazines have served as agenda setters and change agents, dating back to London's *Review* in 1704 and the U.S. colonies' early 1740s firsts: Andrew Bradford's *American Magazine* and Benjamin Franklin's *General Magazine and Historical Chronicle*.[6] With the growth of advertising in their pages during the Industrial Revolution and the evolving visual appeal of the editorial pages, magazines fueled desires for certain products, services and lifestyles, nurturing a culture of consumerism.[7] Thus magazines began to take on a greater role in shaping who readers are, what readers do, where readers go, why readers take action, when readers do it (as in right now!) and how readers think.

By the twenty-first century, magazine scholar David E. Sumner could describe consumer magazines as "those that anyone can subscribe to or purchase at newsstands."[8] Similarly, Johnson and Prijatel wrote, "Consumer magazines are created primarily for popular consumption. They are sold on the newsstand or by subscription and are marketed like any other consumer product. They usually contain advertising; readers are important to advertisers because of their potential as consumers."[9] They are small as a category, but mighty in their individual reach as general or special-interest magazines, such as *Vanity Fair* or *Vogue*, respectively. They can be hybrids, such as *Lucky*, a fashion "magalog"[10] that is part magazine and part catalog, offering "consumerism at its most raw."[11]

Consumerism can be so raw in fact that some have likened the relationship between women and advertisers to that of sheep to wolves.[12] "Yet that is not exactly what happened," Amy Beth Aronson wrote in *Taking Liberties: Early American Women's Magazines and Their Readers*.[13] "Nevertheless," Aronson said, "the consensus remains that mass-market women's magazines into the present day have betrayed and co-opted unsuspecting readers, and have done so with near-perfect efficiency—expertly, single-mindedly and without the slightest conflict, undertow, or fear of failure."[14]

Bourgeois or Low-Brow Artifacts

This section examines the symbolic aspect of magazines as artifacts and the evolution of their intellectual and literary content from the Antebellum period in the United States to the early twenty-first century. During this time, magazines have served as symbols of social mobility and literacy, as Daniel A. Clark evidenced in his *Creating the College Man: American Mass Magazines and Middle-Class Manhood, 1890–1915*.[15] Sharing and debating the information in a magazine is a time-honored tradition that has expanded with the growth of technology, morphing in new directions through social media, particularly among readers between the ages of 18 and 34 years, as reported in a 2012 study by the MPA—The Association of Magazine Media.[16] In addition to *sharing* what they are reading, many people have treated magazines as artifacts, *showing* others what they are reading by displaying covers electronically or placing new and old issues alongside coffee-table books.[17] Since *Ebony*'s debut in 1945, for example, living room displays of the magazine have taken on an air of racial pride over positive news about African Americans, for a change or another first to tout.[18]

During the Antebellum era, variously defined as the period falling between 1781 and 1860, U.S. residents were split on "whether the democratization of reading represented growth or decline," wrote Isabelle Lehuu in *Carnival on the Page: Popular Print Media in Antebellum America*.[19] In this examination of ephemeral printed matter and reading habits, Lehuu describes a "circus atmosphere" of sensationalism, exuberance and burlesque that infiltrated the America's print culture of magazines, newspapers and books.[20] "Cultural values embodied in newspapers and magazines appeared intertwined with or opposed to their market value," Lehuu wrote. "Popularization was entangled in a process of commodification. The second quarter of the nineteenth century witnessed the coming together of commerce and culture."[21]

> The public taste for lowbrow printed artifacts did not go unchallenged. Indeed, a highbrow critique attempted to curtail popular reading, which, unlike the traditional activity long encouraged by a Protestant and republican culture, had become controversial in the age of abundance and boundlessness. The reformer's elitist call for fasting and discipline in the midst of carnival was matched only by the contempt of European travelers, who did not fail to critique the outpouring of print in nineteenth-century America.[22]

Ohmann in *Selling Culture* describes Daniel Lerner's modernization theory of mass culture as evolving from urbanization to literacy to media participation, and then electoral participation. "Modernity is primarily a state or mind," he quotes Lerner as saying.[23] Ohmann also refers to historian Richard Brown's analysis of attitudes and how communication vehicles, such as magazines, came to be viewed as necessities.[24]

During the twentieth century, some of the best writers in elite magazines of the era offered the thinking man or woman a mix of in-depth journalism, criticism, literature and humor, said Campbell, Martin and Fabos. The modern-day list of elite magazines maintaining such content includes the *New Yorker, Harper's, Vanity Fair* and *Atlantic Monthly*.[25] These magazines, however, are in the minority. In *The Magazine Century: American Magazines Since 1900*, David E. Sumner wrote,

> The intellectual and literary content of magazines declined as they reached wider and wider audiences. Toward the end of the century, the content of mass market magazines had become increasingly focused on celebrities, sex, lifestyle and very individualized leisure pursuits.[26]

This change resulted as magazines became cheaper to purchase because of technological advances and the growing role of advertising as a revenue source—two factors that form what Sumner calls the popularization of content theory.[27] "Between 1900 and 2000, magazines generally became a *business enterprise* instead of a *literary enterprise*,"[28] Sumner wrote. "In the early 1900s, magazines looked like small versions of books. At the end of the century, magazines looked like television screens."[29] Ironically, key drivers of the magazine industry's decline in intellectual and literary content were employed as strategies to breathe life into one of the leading newsmagazines, *Newsweek*. However, attempts to make the 80-year-old magazine trendier and more lifestyle oriented might have contributed to its demise as a print publication in 2012. *Newsweek* lacked the deep-pocketed and strong parent of its chief rival, *Time*, and circulation had fallen more than 50 percent from 3.3 million in 1991 to 1.5 million in 2012.[30] In late 2013, *Newsweek*'s third owner in as many years announced that it would resume weekly publication with a subscription-based business model in 2014.[31]

Shaping Gender, Cultural and Social Issues

The ebb and flow of the magazine's role as change agent has often influenced public opinion. As a leading mass medium, the magazine and its pages and covers have drawn attention to gender, race, ethnicity, politics and social issues. In the process, they have promoted the image of a well-rounded person as someone who is knowledgeable and potentially concerned about the world. "Change only happens when the messages magazines present find a receptive ear in society," Johnson and Prijatel note. "Conversely, those messages may not be heard without the help of magazines."[32] Some early consumer articles came in the form of muckraking, even at leading women's magazines.[33] Articles on corrupted food, for example, drew attention to matters of home and hearth. They helped to place Victorian women at the head of the "national household,"[34] fighting for change. The push for the purity of household and food products led to the creation of the *Good Housekeeping* Testing Institute in 1901.[35]

"Magazines set the public agenda by their emphasis on the major as well as the minor," wrote Johnson and Prijatel, with issues ranging from *Ladies Home Journal's* crusades against harmful additives in medicine (major) to *Playboy's* Playmate picks (minor).[36] The former could be considered a precursor to consumer tips in magazines such as *Health* or *WebMD*, while the latter likely spawned images of scantily clad women in *Maxim* or the rap magazine *XXL*—an area for potential research.

In shaping the public agenda, magazines have also shaped gender roles and expectations for women, as well as men. For example, Daniel Clark argues that fiction and nonfiction articles, advertising and opinion pieces in magazines helped to foster the acceptance of college education for men during the early 1900s.[37] "Mass magazines formed the principal cultural forum where the perception of college was re-crafted and worked into the cultural horizon of the plain middle-class businessman," Clark wrote. "The college man often received the stereotype of a drinking and gambling sport—either the nouveau-riche brat or an elitist snob."[38] In either case, Clark said, the male college student was criticized as being lazy, arrogant, unsuitable for business and lower than a self-made man.[39]

Clark shows that, from 1902 to 1905, the image of the male college student began improving "with the rising interest in college life and its reinterpretation in the magazines and with businessmen warming to the idea of college education for their sons (future executives) as the years progressed."[40] In addition, Clark cites growing competition for some jobs from immigrants and women, making college another way in which to set men apart.[41] Carolyn Kitch also makes reference to the "extensive public discourse on the role of men in American society" during this era that was marked by rising immigration and advances for women rising from the suffrage movement:[42]

> During the 1910s, Americans' hopes for, and anxieties about, changing gender roles were frequently debated in magazine and newspaper articles. These concerns also provided a recurrent theme for visual communication. The specter of a world in which domineering and destructive women emasculated weak and powerless men inspired a distinctive motif that ran through various forms of popular culture: the pairing of large (though usually beautiful) women and little, often tiny, men. While this motif was always presented as a joke, it never was only a joke.[43]

Many women's magazines, however, focused on an image opposite to what Kitch described; that is, they portrayed an image of men holding power over women. Even some of the decision-makers of magazine content were men, Amy Beth Aronson wrote, with male editors at top magazines such as the *Delineator, Woman's Home Companion, Ladies' Home Journal* and *Good Housekeeping* for most of the twentieth century. "A focus on women's interests as housewives, mothers and consumers bolstered advertising potential and perhaps their own sense of themselves as professionals, as bosses—and indeed as men,"[44] Aronson said.

The advertising potential of women's interests has been a key driver of the magazine industry. Long before consumerism took off, women's magazines dominated publishing. In 1825, roughly 100 magazines existed overall. By 1830, Philadelphia had 24 women's magazines and New England had 38.[45] In Britain and in the United States, Kathryn Fraser noted, "The gendering of magazine audiences had been present since the late 18th century; the gendering of consumption had not."[46] This meant a heavier focus on home, beauty, fashion, parenting, shopping and, for a time, sewing patterns. In addition to catering to women's needs—perceived or not—national advertisers provided revenue to help bring down the cost of buying magazines, which in turn fueled the growth of the audience. "Simply put," Fraser wrote, "the history of the woman's magazine is also the history of the construction of the woman as a consumer."[47] This history includes The Big Six: the *Delineator, Woman's Home Companion, Pictorial Review, Ladies' Home Journal, Good Housekeeping* and *McCall's*.[48]

The Big Six eventually became known as the Seven Sisters, including the latter three magazines plus *Redbook, Better Homes & Gardens, Family Circle* and *Woman's Day*. Their name was a reference to the alma maters of many editors, which included Seven Sister colleges such as Radcliffe and Vassar. These leading women's magazines eventually reinvented themselves "as feminists and others questioned their relevance and historical focus on homemaking especially during the women's movement of the 1960s and 1970s."[49] In June 1980, *Savvy*, a career-oriented women's magazine, made its debut. Its cover lines included, "False Grit. You Don't Have to Be Macho to Get Ahead" and "How to Get the Title You Deserve."[50] Jerry Oppenheimer wrote,

> This new breed of magazine was targeting a seemingly untapped and lucrative market: ambitious Reagan-era women armed with MBAs who were entering the worlds of business, finance and government and needed straight talk on everything from buying the best spreadsheet software to choosing the most appropriate wide-shouldered pinstripe pantsuit, then in fashion, to wear to an important meeting.[51]

Christine E. Crouse-Dick has noted that newer magazines, such as *Real Simple*, which was founded in 2000, are reframing domestic themes and the conventional notion that the home is a man's castle. Although writers emphasize the home as a woman's personal sanctuary, they still relegate her to a separate sphere and limit her domain to the home.[52]

Just as women's rights influenced magazines, so did civil rights. Peggy A. Lewis, in her doctoral dissertation, argues that leaders of the Civil Rights Movement counted on society's growing sense of social consciousness and morality as they strategized on media coverage to support their cause. Lewis noted that a 1963 cover of *Life* featured the grieving family of slain civil rights leader Medgar Evers. The same year, *Newsweek* ran a special issue of "The Negro in America." A decade earlier, *Jet* magazine published what has been described as one of the most dramatic photos in 1955, after Mamie Till insisted on an open casket for her son, Emmett.[53] Till wanted the world to see how his body was mangled for allegedly whistling at a white woman, both Lewis and Craig Flournoy noted.[54]

In addition to covering discrimination, ethnic audience-targeted magazines, such as *Essence, Ebony* and *Latina*, help readers celebrate who they are and what makes them unique. The magazines' positive messages are often similar to the tagline of *Asian Woman: The Magazine for the Woman Who Wants the World*. The late John H. Johnson, in his autobiography, described his philosophy for *Ebony*, the magazine he created as his answer to *Life* and *Look* magazines. "We wanted to emphasize the positive aspects of black life," Johnson wrote. "We wanted to highlight achievements and make blacks proud of themselves. We wanted to create a windbreak that would let them get away from 'the problem' for a few moments and say, 'Here are some blacks who are making it. And if they can make it, I can make it, too.'"[55] Johnson also explained his approach to showcasing aspirational lifestyles. "We were going places we had never been before and doing things we'd never done before, and we wanted to see that."[56]

By presenting lifestyles of the rich and famous as well as the common man and woman, magazines like *Ebony* attempt to counter stereotypes and offset the under-representation of their target audiences in general-market publications. Ki-Young Lee and Sung-Hee Joo, in looking at this question, found from their analysis of the content of 1,843 magazine ads that 2.6% of the ads contained at least one Hispanic person; 8.3%, one Asian American; and 17.5%, one African American.[57] From the findings of the content analysis, the researchers concluded that portrayals of minority groups in the media may affect beliefs and attitudes toward the groups, as well as the treatment they receive. Lee and Joo also argued that seemingly positive portrayals of, for example, Asian Americans as the industrious "model minority," could be detrimental in terms of over-generalizing, setting a hard-to-reach bar and creating stereotypes of being anti-social workaholics.

Consumption Practices

Before the 1930s, Johnson and Prijatel write, researchers saw audiences as a "faceless blob."[58] By the 1970s, they and magazine staffs recognized readers as individuals and paid more attention to the uses readers made of their magazines and the gratifications they sought. Drawing on findings of researchers at the University of Pennsylvania and the Hebrew University of Jerusalem, Johnson and Prijatel identified five consumer needs met by magazines: (1) Cognitive: "They tell us what's going on in our world and what that means to us"; (2) Affective: "Magazines are great dream machines, and readers know that, using magazines for vicarious experiences"; (3) Personal: "They reinforce our values, provide us with psychological reassurance and self-understanding, and give us a chance to explore reality"; (4) Social: "We use the media to help us fit in with our society"; and (5) Tension Release: "Readers often head for magazines for escape and diversion."[59]

Vogue exemplifies the Yin Yang of consumer magazines and their audiences. In its 2009 Power Issue, for example, *Vogue* demonstrates how its content is influenced by politics and how it uses politics to influence the fashion sense of its readers, along the lines of Quint Randle's findings on gratifications. Randle found that roughly half the respondents in a survey on magazines and their use of Web sites gave the following as gratifications, among others: to find products through ads, to make buying decisions, to improve the quality of my lifestyle, to live out a fantasy, to feel important, to relax and to feel good.[60]

Vogue's editor in chief, Anna Wintour, also speaks to the magazine's recognition of the interplay between the larger political, economic and global issues in the world and the audience the magazine serves. She wrote,

> There's no doubt that we live in the toughest and most trying of times: wars in Afghanistan, Iraq and Gaza; a global economic recession of historic proportion; and a planet whose physical and biological health grows more imperiled by the day. Those are the facts, and we are forced to face them whether we like it or not.[61]

In her "however" mode, Wintour cautioned that "it is critical that we not exchange one bubble—that of euphoric consumerism—for another, that of funeral pessimism." She counted the collective blessings of "drive and talent" and dedicated the Power Issue to the "spirit of clearheaded, forward-looking realism." The opening of the second paragraph sums up the *raison d'etre* of the Power Issue and perhaps even *Vogue* itself, while capturing the essence of how deeply magazines have shaped consumptive behavior and consumer lifestyles throughout history:

> Before we come to the world leaders, let's talk about the clothes. A word in defense of the fashion industry, if I may: When people stop shopping, other people lose their jobs. So there is no moral high ground to be gained by abstaining from felicity. That said, shopping differently is a wise response to the current landscape. Our editors have been thinking about the one or two (or three) items that a woman can buy and wear multiple times a week and for years to come. This is the season to buy a single, perfect pair of shoes, or a khaki jacket that sneaks you through to next fall. It's a time to sharpen your personal aesthetic and discover your innermost notions about your style, and a perfect moment to dwell on value and values: how garments are made, where

they are made, and why they cost what they cost. A Fendi python bag in a classic shape made in Italy? The high price tag makes sense. An organic seersucker suit from a company based in upstate New York? Worth every penny.[62]

The Fendi bag in question "makes sense" at $5,740.[63] The aspirational reader, who is more likely to look for a lower-priced knockoff, can still find something affordable in *Vogue*'s "Index Checklist: 100+ Under $100." [64] She can mark khaki's comeback and sneak "through to next fall"[65] in a Gap blazer for $58.[66]

Magazines as Meta-Commodities

Magazines have multiple roles. They serve as sources of enjoyment, providing images and information to intrigue readers from cover to cover. In addition, magazines serve as things to be enjoyed, in and of themselves. Helen Kopnina discussed these varied roles when she wrote in *Dialectical Anthropology*, "Beyond the surface level of brand advertisements and industry information, [magazines] are cultural objects that reflect the cultural *zeitgeist* both visually and textually. . . . As cultural media objects, they narrate dominant cultural trends."[67]

At the same time, magazines are commodities that convey information about products, not only through advertising, but also on the editorial pages in many cases. Advertising largely pays the bill to keep magazines afloat, and Campbell, Martin and Fabos argue this growing dependency has downsides.[68] The researchers describe a contradiction in this relationship. "Contemporary commercial magazines provide essential information about politics, society and culture, thus helping us think about ourselves as participants in a democracy. Unfortunately, however, these magazines have often identified their readers as consumers first and citizens second."[69] In their analysis of media and culture, the authors point out that "Controversial content sometimes has difficulty finding its way into print. More and more, magazines define their readers merely as viewers of displayed products and purchasers of material goods."[70]

The American Society of Magazine Editors (ASME) in its code of ethics tries to prevent its members from going too far. ASME advises members to avoid compromising the reader experience. The code states, in part, "Editors and publishers should avoid positioning advertisements near editorial pages that discuss or show the same or similar products sold by the advertiser (a rule of thumb used by many magazines is, the reader must turn the page at least twice between related ad and edit)."[71] However, while some readers complain about wading through advertisements, other readers view ads as part of the magazine experience.[72] This is an opportunity for more research, especially with the growth in native advertising, which blurs the lines even more than traditional advertorials—ads that look similar to editorial content but are commonly labeled as being promotional items.

In *Vogue*'s March 2009 Power Issue, readers must flip through nearly 60 pages of ads to find the magazine's table of contents. These front-of-the-book advertisements might be called prime real estate for advertisers such as Ralph Lauren, Balenciaga, Alberta Ferretti, Chanel, Miu Miu, Oscar de la Renta, Escada, Moschino, Sephora and Juicy Couture, to name a few. The second contents page is on page 110, opposite a pricey, six-panel gatefold Prada ad that is printed on heavier card stock.[73] Two dozen more ad pages and the reader finally reaches the third and last page of the table of contents, on page 136. This page marks the beginning of the issue's editorial well. However, for less fortunate and less prosperous magazines, it would have been the end of the entire issue.[74] These gaps are even more pronounced in the 2013 Power Issue, which featured Beyonce on the cover and had a record-setting 610 pages. Yet, with its focus on politics and historic timing, the 2009 Power Issue provided more striking examples of consumerism than the 2013 issue featuring a mega-celebrity like Beyonce, who was already strongly associated with consumerism, as well as her own product lines.

Magazines and Self-Making

Consumers often seek reinvention through magazines. That is where some readers learn how to be: how to be better versions of themselves or how to be like the people who run or make magazines or appear on the pages. The cult of personality is legendary with eponymous magazines such as *Lear's, Jane, Rosie* or *O the Oprah Magazine*. Added to this list can be publishers, editors and the magazines they led or continue to lead, such as Ruth Whitney of *Glamour*, Hugh Hefner of *Playboy*, Susan Taylor of *Essence*, Tina Brown of *Vanity Fair* and, most notably, Anna Wintour of *Vogue*, who is said to have also inspired *The Devil Wears Prada*, a film that grossed $326.5 million worldwide, as reported in Box Office Mojo.[75]

Magazines such as *Seventeen* can plant the seeds of consumerism in their readers at an early age:

> Teena writes her favorite magazine for the tip-off on the clothes she wears, the food she eats, the lipstick she wields, the room she bunks in, the budget she keeps, the boy she has a crush on. *Seventeen* seems to have all the answers—that's why like Teena, smart advertisers use *Seventeen*.[76]

Here, too, there is a downside. Concern about body image transcends the teenage years. Much has been written about how extreme concern can lead to eating disorders among girls and women in Western cultures.[77] Less, but some attention has also been paid to the effects on men of mediated lean, muscular male images: the ideal, V-shaped torso "featuring a broad chest tapering to a narrow waist."[78] In their three-decade review of magazines such as *Sports Illustrated*, GQ and *Rolling Stone*, researchers Cheryl Law and Magdala Peixoto Labre found these images to be more prevalent in the years between 1967 to 1997. "Social comparison theory suggests that a discrepancy between desired and perceived muscularity could lead men to engage in behaviors designed to increase muscle mass," Law and Labre wrote. Attempts to achieve such a cultural ideal contribute to body dissatisfaction, obsessive bodybuilding and weight control, anabolic steroid use and consumption of untested supplements.[79] Eating disorders have increased among men, who are outnumbered by women 1 million to 7 million, respectively.[80]

Future Outlook

This review of the literature suggests consumptive behavior and the appeal of consumptive lifestyles are stronger than ever. The question is where and how consumers will feed their passions. Print-based media—magazines, newspapers and books—have been criticized for allowing others to circulate and promote their eulogies so extensively. Is print really dead? Will claims of the demise of print media become a self-fulfilling prophecy? The magazine industry maintains that print is not dead; it is different.[81] This difference is reflected in the renaming of magazine associations. For example, the MPA is no longer the Magazine Publishers of America. It is the Association of Magazine Media. Its new name reflects today's difference. MPA, as it is still known, continues to proclaim the power of print, in print campaigns, promotional videos with magazine executives and even a Valentine's Day graphic distributed on Twitter in 2014. The latter campaign goes beyond print to incorporate smartphones, tablets, the Internet, Cupid and a heart. It asks: "What are 91% of adults doing? They're reading magazine media!"[82]

"The rise in readership and advertiser investment in our brands from print to tablets and beyond proves that Magazine Media is an industry rife with opportunities for growth in the new media age," said Mary G. Berner, president and CEO of MPA—The Association of Magazine Media. "I'm optimistic that publishers' experimentation and innovations for their print and digital products will continue to be rewarded."[83] From spring 2012 to spring 2013, print readership rose 2 percent. The increase for tablet audiences was 73 percent.[84]

The magazine is now a meta-commodity in various mobile forms, from tablets to smartphones. As consumptive devices in tablet form, many digital magazines are taking advantage of the sharp resolution, multimedia features and appeal of tapping, pinching, swiping and zooming, as Yanick Rice Lamb wrote in "All the News That Fits on Tablets: An Analysis of News Consumption and Best Practices."[85] As with printed magazines, consumers are now reading tablet editions on planes, in bed or at the beach. A third of Americans now own tablets—a great source of hope for publishers.[86] And MPA claims that advertisers are following tablet readers. iPad advertising units rose 24.5 percent between 2012 and 2013. The increase was 7 percent among magazines that measure iPad and print advertising, Berner said. The Publishers Information Bureau (PIB), which is maintained by MPA, reported that overall print advertising was 0.4 percent to 0.5 percent higher for the first two quarters of 2013.[87]

Consumers who want to bypass advertising are less able to avoid it as GPS technology and other interactive methods to tailor messages to reader habits expand. Those who are receptive to advertising will likely become more engaged because ads are increasingly more interactive with greater immersive experiences.[88]

Consumptive behavior and lifestyle engagement are poised to grow, with more magazine content on mobile devices as well as greater opportunities for e-commerce, allowing impulse buyers to purchase goods and services on the spot. Instead of simply poring over recipes, readers can watch food demonstrations. They can view mini-Westerns and other scenic videos with fashion shoots. They can upload photos to preview makeup and hairstyles.[89] They can work out with trainers, watch flowers bloom, go behind the scenes, or see a celebrity wink at them on a cover, or view two or three alternate versions from the same cover photo shoot. Much of what they see on the screen they can immediately purchase. Magazines such as *Esquire* and the *Atlantic* are experimenting with tablet editions that come out more frequently than the replica version for the print issue, but less often than what they offer on the Web.[90]

With more applications, or apps, specialization is likely to increase. Magazines have a greater ability to create customized content, special issues or projects, digital storytelling, an article at a time and tailored consumer offerings, depending on magazine budgets and readers' willingness to pay. *Wired* magazine was creating a feature called Vision Quest, "an immersive digital experience that mashes up text, imagery, animation and video to retell a print magazine story."[91] The shelter magazine, *Domino*, described as *Lucky* for the home, has been resurrected as a quarterly under an e-commerce arrangement.[92] Unfazed by *Domino*'s history and the deaths of *Metropolitan Home* and *House & Garden*, a Houston interior designer set a fall 2013 launch for a quarterly home furnishings magazine called *Milieu*.[93] As Sumner noted, magazines increasingly focus on celebrities, sex, lifestyle and very individualized leisure pursuits. Although celebrity magazines account for 25 percent of consumer magazine sales, the category is threatened by the ability of social media to spread celebrity news long before publications can go to press.

Samir Husni, director of the Magazine Innovation Center at the Meek School of Journalism and New Media at the University of Mississippi, has pointed out that magazines exist for every interest and age group, in all sizes and formats. Husni said 10,000 print magazines currently exist, compared to 2,000 in 1980, and 870 new titles filled retail newsstands in 2012. He added, "I'm seeing no signs of a slowdown."[94]

It is a new digital world; there's always something new to explore and research.

Notes

1 Imaeyen Ibanga, "Obama's Choice to Bare Arms Causes Uproar," ABC News, 2 March 2009 <http://abcnews.go.com/GMA/story?id=6986019>, accessed 15 December 2013.
2 *Vogue*, "Photographers: Annie Leibovitz," Voguepedia <http://www.vogue.com/voguepedia/Annie_Leibovitz>, accessed 15 December 2013.
3 First Cover and "Cover Look: First Blush," *Vogue*, March 2009, First Cover, 136.

4 Sammye Johnson and Patricia Prijatel, *The Magazine from Cover to Cover*, 3rd ed. (New York and London: Oxford University Press, 2013), 97.

5 Richard M. Ohmann, *Selling Culture: Magazines, Markets and Class at the Turn of the Century* (London and New York: Verso, 1996), 14.

6 Richard Campbell, Christopher R. Martin, and Bettina Fabos, "Magazines," *Media and Culture: Mass Communication in a Digital Age*, 9th ed. (Boston: Bedford/St. Martin's, 2014), 316–317.

7 Campbell, Martin, and Fabos, "Magazines," 316–317.

8 David E. Sumner, *The Magazine Century: American Magazines since 1900*, Mediating American History Series (New York: Peter Lang, 2010), vii.

9 Johnson and Prijatel, *The Magazine from Cover to Cover*, 2013:11.

10 Sammye Johnson and Patricia Prijatel, *The Magazine from Cover to Cover*, 2nd ed. (New York and London: Oxford University Press, 2007), 15.

11 Johnson and Prijatel, *The Magazine from Cover to Cover*, 2007:15.

12 Amy Beth Aronson, *Taking Liberties: Early American Women's Magazines and Their Readers* (Westport, CT: Praeger, 2002), 155–156.

13 Aronson, *Taking Liberties*, 156.

14 Aronson, *Taking Liberties*, 157.

15 Daniel A. Clark, *Creating the College Man: American Mass Magazines and Middle-Class Manhood, 1890–1915* (Madison: University of Wisconsin Press, 2010), 156.

16 MPA—The Association of Magazine Media, "Magazine Media Readers Are Social," April 2012, 4, 9 <http://www.magazine.org/sites/default/files/SOCIAL-f5%20website.pdf>, accessed 8 January 2014.

17 Mik Stroyberg, "Social Sharing: The New Coffee Table Magazine Spread," *Adam Sherk* (blog), 4 December 2012 <http://www.adamsherk.com/publishing/mik-stroyberg-social-sharing-the-new-coffee-table-magazine-spread/>, accessed 15 December 2013.

18 Don Terry, "An Icon Fades," *Columbia Journalism Review*, 16 March 2010 <http://www.cjr.org/feature/an_icon_fades_1.php?page=all>, accessed 15 December 2013; John H. Johnson, with Lerone Bennett, Jr., *Succeeding Against the Odds: The Autobiography of a Great American Businessman* (New York: Amistad, 1992), 156–159.

19 Isabelle Lehuu, *Carnival on the Page: Popular Print Media in Antebellum America* (Chapel Hill: University of North Carolina Press, 2000), 158.

20 Lehuu, *Carnival on the Page*, 9.

21 Lehuu, *Carnival on the Page*, 159.

22 Lehuu, *Carnival on the Page*, 157.

23 Ohmann, *Selling Culture*, 38–41.

24 Ohmann, *Selling Culture*, 38–41.

25 Campbell, Martin, and Fabos, "Magazines," 333.

26 Sumner, *The Magazine Century*, 5.

27 Sumner, *The Magazine Century*, 5.

28 Sumner, *The Magazine Century*, 9. Emphasis in the original.

29 Sumner, *The Magazine Century*, 11.

30 Christine Haughney and David Carr, "At *Newsweek*, Ending Print and a Blend of Two Styles," *Media Decoder* (blog), *New York Times*, 18 October 2012 <http://mediadecoder.blogs.nytimes.com/2012/10/18/newsweek-will-cease-print-publication-at-end-of-year/?ref=newsweekinc>, accessed 15 December 2013.

31 Christine Haughney, "*Newsweek* Plans Return to Print," *New York Times*, 3 December 2013 <http://www.nytimes.com/2013/12/04/business/media/newsweek-plans-return-to-print.html>, accessed 15 December 2013.

32 Johnson and Prijatel, *The Magazine from Cover to Cover*, 2013:98.

33 Johnson and Prijatel, *The Magazine from Cover to Cover*, 2013:101.

34 Johnson and Prijatel, *The Magazine from Cover to Cover*, 2013:101.

35 Johnson and Prijatel, *The Magazine from Cover to Cover*, 2013:101.

36 Johnson and Prijatel, *The Magazine from Cover to Cover*, 2013:101–124.

37 Clark, *Creating the College Man*, 156.

38 Clark, *Creating the College Man*, 156.

39 Clark, *Creating the College Man*, 156.

40 Clark, *Creating the College Man*, 156.

41 Clark, *Creating the College Man*, 156–157.

42 Carolyn Kitch, "Destructive Women and Little Men: Masculinity, the New Woman, and Power in 1910s Popular Media," *Journal of Magazine & New Media Research* 1.1 (Spring 1999): 1–2.

43 Kitch, "Destructive Women and Little Men," 2.

44 Aronson, *Taking Liberties*, 158.

45 Aronson, *Taking Liberties*, 2.

46 Kathryn Fraser, "The Makeover and Other Consumerist Narratives" (Ph.D. diss., McGill University, 2002), 45.

47 Fraser, "The Makeover and Other Consumerist Narratives," 45.

48 Fraser, "The Makeover and Other Consumerist Narratives," 43–45.

49 Yanick Rice Lamb and Kendra Desrosiers, "The Seven Sisters and Their Siblings Go Digital: An Analysis of Women's Magazine Content on Websites, iPads and Cell Phones," in Kehbuma Langmia, Tia C.M. Tyree, Pamela O'Brien, and Ingrid Sturgis, eds., *Social Media: Pedagogy and Practice* (Lanham, MD: University of America Press Inc., 2014), 129.

50 Jerry Oppenheimer, *Front Row: Anna Wintour, The Cool Life and Hot Times of* Vogue's *Editor in Chief* (New York: St. Martin's Press, 2005), 160.

51 Oppenheimer, *Front Row*, 158.

52 Christine E. Crouse-Dick, "Reframing the Domestic Angel: *Real Simple* Magazine's Repackaging of the Victorian-Era 'Angel in the House' Narrative," *Communication Studies* 63.4 (September/October 2012): 441.

53 Peggy A. Lewis, "Preaching, Praying and Strategic Media Planning: From Montgomery to Selma, How the Civil Rights Movement Forced Journalists to Do Their Job" (Ph.D. diss., Howard University, 2013).

54 Craig Flournoy, "Covering a Mississippi Murder Trial: The Emmett Till Lynching" (paper presented at the Annual Meeting, Association for Education in Journalism and Mass Communication, August 2005).

55 Johnson with Bennett, *Succeeding Against the Odds*, 156–157.

56 Johnson with Bennett, *Succeeding Against the Odds*, 156.

57 Ki-Young Lee and Sung-Hee Joo, "The Portrayal of Asian Americans in Mainstream Magazine Ads: An Update," *Journalism & Mass Communication Quarterly* 82.3 (Autumn 2005): 659.

58 Johnson and Prijatel, *The Magazine from Cover to Cover*, 2013:8.

59 Johnson and Prijatel, *The Magazine from Cover to Cover*, 2013:8; see Elihu Katz, Michael Gurevitch, and Hadassah Haas, "On the Use of the Mass Media for Important Things," *American Sociological Review* 38.2 (April 1973): 164–181.

60 Quint Randle, "Gratification Niches of Monthly Print Magazines and the World Wide Web among a Group of Special-Interest Magazine Subscribers," *Journal of Computer-Mediated Communication* 8.4 (July 2003): Unpaginated [Open Access Journal, ICA].

61 Anna Wintour, "Letter from the Editor: Vision Quests," *Vogue*, March 2009, 170.

62 Wintour, "Letter from the Editor," 170, 178.

63 Wintour, "Letter from the Editor," 178, 413.

64 "Index Checklist: 100+ Under $100," *Vogue*, March 2009, 502.

65 Wintour, "Letter from the Editor," 178.

66 "Index Checklist," 502.

67 Helen Kopnina, "The World According to *Vogue*: The Role of Culture(s) in International Fashion Magazines," *Dialectical Anthropology* 31.4 (June 2007): 369.

68 Campbell, Martin, and Fabos, "Magazines," 341.

69 Campbell, Martin, and Fabos, "Magazines," 340.

70 Campbell, Martin, and Fabos, "Magazines," 341.

71 "Editorial Guidelines: ASME Guidelines for Editors and Publishers," Updated May 2014, American Society of Magazine Editors <http://www.magazine.org/asme/editorial-guidelines>, accessed 26 May 2014.

72 Jeremy W. Peters, "Advertisement or *Vogue* Feature? You Decide," *Media Decoder* (blog), *New York Times*, 8 September 2010 <http://mediadecoder.blogs.nytimes.com/2010/09/08/advertisement-or-vogue-feature-you-decide/?_php=true&_type=blogs&_r=0>, accessed 15 December 2013.

73 *Vogue*, March 2009, 110.

74 *Vogue*, March 2009, 136.

75 "Devil Wears Prada, The," Box Office Mojo <http://www.boxofficemojo.com/movies/?id=devilwearsprada.htm>, accessed 1 August 2013.

76 Carley Moore, "Invasion of the Everygirl: *Seventeen* Magazine, 'Traumarama!' and the Girl Writer," *Journal of Popular Culture* 44.6 (December 2011): 1252.

77 Daniel Clay, Vivian L. Vignoles, and Helga Dittmar, "Body Image and Self-Esteem among Adolescent Girls: Testing the Influence of Sociocultural Factors," *Journal of Research on Adolescence* 15.4 (2005): 451–477.

78 Cheryl Law and Magdala Peixoto Labre, "Cultural Standards of Attractiveness: A Thirty-Year Look at Changes in Male Images in Magazines," *Journalism & Mass Communication Quarterly* 79.3 (Autumn 2002): 697.

79 Law and Labre, "Cultural Standards of Attractiveness," 699.

80 Law and Labre, "Cultural Standards of Attractiveness," 698.

81 Yanick Rice Lamb, "All the News That Fits on Tablets: An Analysis of News Consumption and Best Practices" (paper presented at the Annual Meeting, Association for Education in Journalism and Mass Communication, August 2013), 3.

82 MPA—The Association of Magazine Media, Twitter Infographic, 13 February 2014, 7:24 a.m. <https://twitter.com/mpamagmedia/status/433984949876584448/photo/1>, accessed 16 February 2014.

83 "Magazine Media Brands See Advertising, Readership Growth during the First Half of 2013," MPA—The Association of Magazine Media, 9 July 2013 <http://www.magazine.org/mpa/magazine-media-brands-see-advertising-readership-growth-during-first-half-2013#sthash.CJJc7Gor.dpuf>, accessed 1 August 2013.

84 "Magazine Media Brands See Advertising, Readership Growth."

85 Lamb, "All the News That Fits on Tablets," 3.

86 Jane Sasseen, Kenny Olmstead, and Amy Mitchell, "Digital: As Mobile Grows Rapidly, the Pressures on News Intensify," The State of the News Media 2013: An Annual Report on American Journalism, Washington, DC: Pew Research Center <http://stateofthemedia.org/2013/digital-as-mobile-grows-rapidly-the-pressures-on-news-intensify/>, accessed 1 August 2013.

87 "Magazine Media Brands See Advertising, Readership Growth."

88 Lamb, "All the News That Fits on Tablets," 27.

89 Lamb and Desrosiers, "The Seven Sisters and Their Siblings Go Digital," 135–139.

90 Lamb, "All the News That Fits on Tablets," 4.

91 Caysey Welton, "Wired Reveals Its Future Digital Content Strategy with 'Vision Quest,'" Folio:, 28 August 2013 <http://www.foliomag.com/2013/wired-reveals-its-future-digital-content-strategy-vision-quest#.Uh-SRaUyu5e>, accessed 28 May 2014.

92 Erik Maza, "Project Décor Revising Domino Brand," Women's Wear Daily, 29 August 2013 <http://www.wwd.com/media-news/fashion-memopad/playing-dominoes-7103095>, accessed 28 May 2014.

93 Julie Lasky, "A New Home Décor Magazine, but Why?" New York Times, 28 August 2013 <http://www.nytimes.com/2013/08/29/garden/a-new-home-decor-magazine-but-why.html?_r=0>, accessed 28 May 2014.

94 Samir Husni, as quoted in Karlene Lukovitz, "Perception vs. Reality: Print's Power in a Digital Age," MPA—The Association of Magazine Media, 14 June 2013 <http://www.magazine.org/node/25206>, accessed 10 October 2013.

Bibliography

Aronson, Amy Beth. Taking Liberties: Early American Women's Magazines and Their Readers. Westport, CT: Praeger, 2002.

Campbell, Richard; Martin, Christopher R.; and Fabos, Bettina. "Magazines." Media and Culture: Mass Communication in a Digital Age. 9th ed. Boston: Bedford/St. Martin's, 2014, 312–343.

Clark, Daniel A. Creating the College Man: American Mass Magazines and Middle-Class Manhood, 1890–1915. Madison: University of Wisconsin Press, 2010.

Clay, Daniel; Vignoles, Vivian L.; and Dittmar, Helga. "Body Image and Self-Esteem among Adolescent Girls: Testing the Influence of Sociocultural Factors." Journal of Research on Adolescence 15.4 (2005): 451–477.

Crouse-Dick, Christine E. "Reframing the Domestic Angel: Real Simple Magazine's Repackaging of the Victorian-Era 'Angel in the House' Narrative." Communication Studies 63.4 (September/October 2012): 441–456.

"Devil Wears Prada, The." Box Office Mojo <http://www.boxofficemojo.com/movies/?id=devilwearsprada.htm>, accessed 1 August 2013.

"Editorial Guidelines: ASME Guidelines for Editors and Publishers." Updated May 2014. American Society of Magazine Editors <http://www.magazine.org/asme/editorial-guidelines>, accessed 26 May 2014.

First Cover, and "Cover Look: First Blush," Vogue, March 2009, First Cover, 136.

Flournoy, Craig. "Covering a Mississippi Murder Trial: The Emmett Till Lynching." Paper presented at the Annual Meeting, Association for Education in Journalism and Mass Communication, August 2005.

Fraser, Kathryn. "The Makeover and Other Consumerist Narratives." Ph.D. diss., McGill University, 2002.

Haughney, Christine. "Newsweek Plans Return to Print." New York Times, 3 December 2013 <http://www.nytimes.com/2013/12/04/business/media/newsweek-plans-return-to-print.html>, accessed 15 December 2013.

Haughney, Christine and Carr, David. "At Newsweek, Ending Print and a Blend of Two Styles." Media Decoder (blog). New York Times, 18 October 2012 <http://mediadecoder.blogs.nytimes.

com/2012/10/18/newsweek-will-cease-print-publication-at-end-of-year/?ref=newsweekinc>, accessed 15 December 2013.

Ibanga, Imaeyen. "Obama's Choice to Bare Arms Causes Uproar." ABC News, 2 March 2009 <http://abcnews.go.com/GMA/story?id=6986019>, accessed 15 December 2013.

"Index Checklist: 100+ Under $100," Vogue. March 2009, 502.

Johnson, John H., with Bennett, Lerone, Jr. Succeeding Against the Odds: The Autobiography of a Great American Businessman. New York: Amistad, 1992.

Johnson, Sammye and Prijatel, Patricia. The Magazine from Cover to Cover. 2nd ed. New York and London: Oxford University Press, 2007.

Johnson, Sammye and Prijatel, Patricia. The Magazine from Cover to Cover. 3rd ed. New York and London: Oxford University Press, 2013.

Katz, Elihu; Gurevitch, Michael; and Haas, Hadassah. "On the Use of the Mass Media for Important Things." American Sociological Review 38.2 (April 1973): 164–181.

Kitch, Carolyn. "Destructive Women and Little Men: Masculinity, the New Woman, and Power in 1910s Popular Media." Journal of Magazine & New Media Research 1.1 (Spring 1999): 1–15.

Kopnina, Helen. "The World According to Vogue: The Role of Culture(s) in International Fashion Magazines." Dialectical Anthropology 31.4 (December 2007): 363–381.

Lamb, Yanick Rice. "All the News That Fits on Tablets: An Analysis of News Consumption and Best Practices." Paper presented at the Annual Meeting, Association of Education in Journalism and Mass Communication, August 2013.

Lamb, Yanick Rice and Desrosiers, Kendra. "The Seven Sisters and Their Siblings Go Digital: An Analysis of Women's Magazine Content on Websites, iPads and Cell Phones." In Langmia, Kehbuma; Tyree, Tia C.M.; O'Brien, Pamela; and Sturgis, Ingrid, eds. Social Media: Pedagogy and Practice. Lanham, MD: University of America Press Inc., 2014.

Lasky, Julie. "A New Home Décor Magazine, but Why?" New York Times, 28 August 2013 <http://www.nytimes.com/2013/08/29/garden/a-new-home-decor-magazine-but-why.html?_r=0>, accessed 28 May 2014.

Law, Cheryl and Labre, Magdala Peixoto. "Cultural Standards of Attractiveness: A Thirty-Year Look at Changes in Male Images in Magazines." Journalism & Mass Communication Quarterly 79.3 (Autumn 2002): 697–711.

Lee, Ki-Young and Joo, Sung-Hee. "The Portrayal of Asian Americans in Mainstream Magazine Ads: An Update." Journalism & Mass Communication Quarterly 82.3 (Autumn 2005): 654–671.

Lehuu, Isabelle. Carnival on the Page: Popular Print Media in Antebellum America. Chapel Hill: University of North Carolina Press, 2000.

Lewis, Peggy A. "Preaching, Praying and Strategic Media Planning: From Montgomery to Selma, How the Civil Rights Movement Forced Journalists to Do Their Job." Ph.D. diss., Howard University, 2013.

Lukovitz, Karlene. "Perception vs. Reality: Print's Power in a Digital Age." MPA—The Association of Magazine Media, 14 June 2013 <http://www.magazine.org/node/25206>, accessed 10 October 2013.

"Magazine Media Brands See Advertising, Readership Growth during the First Half of 2013." MPA—The Association of Magazine Media, 9 July 2013 <http://www.magazine.org/mpa/magazine-media-brands-see-advertising-readership-growth-during-first-half-2013#sthash.CJJc7Gor.dpuf>, accessed 1 August 2013.

Maza, Erik. "Project Décor Reviving Domino Brand." Women's Wear Daily, 29 August 2013 <http://www.wwd.com/media-news/fashion-memopad/playing-dominoes-7103095>, 28 May 2014.

Moore, Carley. "Invasion of the Everygirl: Seventeen Magazine, 'Traumarama!' and the Girl Writer." Journal of Popular Culture 44.6 (December 2011): 1248–1267.

MPA—The Association of Magazine Media. "Magazine Media Readers Are Social." April 2012, 4, 9 <http://www.magazine.org/sites/default/files/SOCIAL-f5%20website.pdf>, accessed 8 January 2014.

MPA—The Association of Magazine Media. Twitter Infographic, 13 February 2014, 7:24 a.m. <https://twitter.com/mpamagmedia/status/433984949876584448/photo/1>, accessed 16 February 2014.

Ohmann, Richard M. Selling Culture: Magazines, Markets and Class at the Turn of the Century. London and New York: Verso, 1996.

Oppenheimer, Jerry. Front Row: Anna Wintour, The Cool Life and Hot Times of Vogue's Editor in Chief. New York: St. Martin's Press, 2005.

Peters, Jeremy W. "Advertisement or Vogue Feature? You Decide." Media Decoder (blog). New York Times, 8 September 2010 <http://mediadecoder.blogs.nytimes.com/2010/09/08/advertisement-or-vogue-feature-you-decide/?_php=true&_type=blogs&_r=0>, accessed 15 December 2013.

Randle, Quint. "Gratification Niches of Monthly Print Magazines and the World Wide Web among a Group of Special-Interest Magazine Subscribers." *Journal of Computer-Mediated Communication* 8.4 (July 2003): Unpaginated [Open Access Journal, ICA].

Sasseen, Jane; Olmstead, Kenny; and Mitchell, Amy. "Digital: As Mobile Grows Rapidly, the Pressures on News Intensify." *The State of the News Media 2013: An Annual Report on American Journalism*. Washington, DC: Pew Research Center <http://stateofthemedia.org/2013/digital-as-mobile-grows-rapidly-the-pressures-on-news-intensify/>, accessed 1 August 2013.

Stroyberg, Mik. "Social Sharing: The New Coffee Table Magazine Spread." *Adam Sherk* (blog), 4 December 2012 <http://www.adamsherk.com/publishing/mik-stroyberg-social-sharing-the-new-coffee-table-magazine-spread/>, accessed 15 December 2013.

Sumner, David E. *The Magazine Century: American Magazines since 1900*. Mediating American History Series. New York: Peter Lang, 2010.

Terry, Don. "An Icon Fades." *Columbia Journalism Review*, 16 March 2010 <http://www.cjr.org/feature/an_icon_fades_1.php?page=all>, accessed 15 December 2013.

Vogue. "Photographers: Annie Leibovitz." Voguepedia <http://www.vogue.com/voguepedia/Annie_Leibovitz>, accessed 15 December 2013.

Welton, Caysey. "*Wired* Reveals Its Future Digital Content Strategy with 'Vision Quest.'" *Folio*, 28 May 2013 <http://www.foliomag.com/2013/wired-reveals-its-future-digital-content-strategy-vision-quest#.Uh-SRaUyu5e>, accessed 28 May 2014.

Wintour, Anna. "Letter from the Editor: Vision Quests." *Vogue*, March 2009, 170, 178, 192.

18

MAGAZINES AND POPULAR CULTURE

Exceptional People, an Exceptional Medium

Elizabeth Crisp Crawford

"Media texts do not present messages about our culture; they ARE culture."[1] In this statement Lana Rakow emphasizes the cultural significance of mediated messages. Rakow's perspective reinforces ideas originally presented by French sociologist and philosopher Pierre Bourdieu, who argues that mediated messages serve as a powerful cultural reinforcement, generating symbolic and cultural capital that helps establish societal norms.[2] One such culture is *celebrity culture*, which Imogene Tyler and Bruce Bennett argue "is disseminated across such a vast range" of contemporary popular communication media that its boundaries are challenging to define. Moreover, they suggest that journalistic commentary and gossip extend the exceptional "personae" of celebrity into ordinary social exchanges and practices,[3] giving the portrayal of celebrities exceptional power over audiences and society as a whole, both nationally and internationally. Although journalistic media share a number of common characteristics, magazines are distinct from other forms of media. David Abrahamson describes magazines, unlike newspapers, broadcast media and on-line media, as having a distinct and powerful role both as a product of social and cultural movements and as a catalyst for social change—what Abrahamson calls "magazine exceptionalism."[4]

This chapter reviews the scholarly literature on magazine coverage and creation of celebrity and popular culture within the framework of exceptionalism. The chapter also argues the magazine form itself is exceptional, as are the sports, entertainment and music celebrities who are covered. Drawing on research that suggests the medium provides a potent combination of celebrity and exceptionalism that allows its content to influence readers and society in a unique and powerful way, the chapter explores the concepts of exceptionalism, magazines, celebrity culture, and symbolic and cultural capital, and thereby reviews the research literature thematically.

Literature and Method

Diverse academic disciplines explore the influence of celebrity on media audiences, as evidenced by a review of the relevant literature, which included books and other literature that span a vast array of scholarship. Literature for this chapter was gathered from scholarship in American and British cultural studies, popular culture, American and British social psychology, psychology, human communication studies, public health, criminal justice, mass communication, education, consumer research and gender studies. Because media and celebrity are becoming increasingly global phenomena, the research for this paper included international journals and, specifically, British scholarship. One limitation on the scope of the research for this chapter is that only periodicals published in English were reviewed. In addition to scholarly work, a variety of magazines were also used to provide examples for the sections in the chapters. Preference was given to recent research, especially articles published after 1990.

Relevant scholarly works were located using a variety of Internet search engines and databases, including Google Scholar, EBSCO Academic Search Premier, JSTOR and Communication and Mass Media Complete. Keywords and phrases used in the searches included *magazines and celebrity, celebrity and journalism, celebrity and body image, celebrity romance* and *celebrity and criminal justice*. The themes that emerged from a review of the literature on celebrity culture include the influence of celebrity and magazines on society's view of success and notoriety; beauty, health and identity; and sex roles and romantic relationships. Within the context of these overarching themes, the observed patterns of influence of sports, entertainment and music celebrities are examined in light of Bourdieu's definitions of capital and the concept of magazine exceptionalism.

Magazine Exceptionalism

The magazine possesses qualities that differentiate it from other media forms. Newspapers differ from magazines because they are published more frequently than other print media, often daily, and are often intended for a local or community audience. In addition, when compared with magazines, newspaper articles tend to be brief and fact-driven. On the other hand, broadcast media reach a wide audience and, Abrahamson argues, respond to social trends instead of instigating them and tend to cover a variety of current events in a more cursory manner.[5] Magazines are unique because they are feature driven. Instead of covering a wide range of stories, magazines are published periodically, focus on fewer items and discuss them in greater depth. The depth of coverage that magazines provide includes more visual content, including photographs and other images. The magazine cover is, for the celebrity, the most desirable spot, giving the celebrity more enduring visual prominence than television, the Internet or newspapers can provide. Readers keep magazines for longer periods of time than other media, and magazines are typically passed from person to person instead of discarded.[6] For these reasons, magazines have more *permanence* than other media. The magazine feature and form provides a spotlight for celebrity that illuminates the individual more completely than can other media.

Although it is difficult to pinpoint one single reason for the influence of magazines, Abrahamson identifies a couple of distinguishing factors that play a role in establishing the magazine's exceptional status. First, magazines have very little *journalistic distance*, which Abrahamson defines as the "ideational and figurative distance between the producer and consumer of a media form."[7] Secondly, magazine editorial content is often created by journalists and read by its audience as *a call to action*. Magazine editorial is not intended to simply inform an audience. Magazine content satisfies the reader's appetite for information and interest in a particular outcome. This desire could be what attracts audiences to magazines in the first place.[8]

The Power of Celebritude

What is celebrity and why is it important to the magazine form? The concept of *celebrity* has fostered a growing literature that is split on the costs and benefits. Nick Couldry and Tim Markham point out that media coverage results in celebrities serving as role models for millions of people, especially the young. Feature-length celebrity narratives found in magazines, they argue, invite the public to observe struggles over identity, sexuality, giving birth and other issues and are a source of public fascination.[9] Graeme Turner observed that audiences that consume and invest in celebrity tend to describe it as an innate or "natural" quality, which is possessed only by some extraordinary individuals and "discovered" by industry talent scouts. For the popular press, the fanzines, the television and movie industries, the defining qualities of the celebrity are both natural and magical.[10]

Journalists writing for the popular press praise celebrities for their "star quality" and "charisma."[11] Drawing on the work of scholars who have studied celebrity from a critical perspective, Turner believes modern celebrity to be indicative of a troubling cultural shift "that privileges the momentary, the visual and the sensational over the enduring, the written and the rational."[12] Todd Gitlin suggests that although "the flow of images" through modern households "seems unremarkable" to people who have ready access to them, the multitude of new images and sounds that enter homes through various media would be startling to people from impoverished backgrounds or from earlier times.[13] Moreover, Gitlin says, most of the faces people see, they encounter in mediated form.[14] Gitlin draws further on the work of Raymond Williams, who has noted that the continual flow of mediated images creates a culture of drama in habitual experience.[15]

However, other literature in cultural and media studies focuses on celebrity as the product of a variety of cultural and economic factors. For instance, Turner says celebrity can be viewed as the product of "the commodification of the individual celebrity through promotion, publicity, and advertising." Involving celebrities in the processes through which cultural identity is negotiated and formed, and, most importantly, he writes, "the representational processes employed by the media in their treatment of prominent individuals," gives celebrities exceptional influence.[16] Noting the work of Daniel J. Boorstin, Turner suggests that the combination of these factors formed the celebrity industry as it exists today.[17]

Boorstin wrote, *The celebrity is a person who is well-known for his well-knownness.*"[18] Further, the celebrity is made by "all of us who willingly read about him, who like to see him on television, who buy recordings of his voice, and talk about him to our friends."[19] Boorstin argues that celebrities develop a capacity for fame not by achieving great things but by differentiating their own personalities from others in the public arena. For this reason, a celebrity is defined as a well-publicized person instead of a person who has achieved greatness.[20] Indeed, these icons are manufactured by public relations professionals who make news happen and the audiences that willingly read about the *pseudo-events* and celebrities.[21] Therefore, while heroes are distinguished by the virtues of their character, celebrities become famous through the generated publicity that focuses on the trivial aspects of their personalities that form a type of brand or trademark.[22] Consequently, a long negative tradition of celebrity views celebrities and the mediated events constructed around them as *pseudo-personalities* and *pseudo-events* attaining importance by virtue of the magnitude of the media coverage instead of its significance.[23] However, some scholars and human research subjects have made a case "that celebrity culture is an essential component of public debate about the issues that require public resolution."[24] Celebrity could serve "as part of an increasing personalization of politics . . . or as part of the broader" democratic narrative "that includes a wider section of" the population.[25] It can also be argued that the proliferation of celebrity culture has placed celebritude at the center of public and civic discourse.

Jessica Evans defines *celebritisation* as "the process in which a person is turned into a celebrity, . . . the process in which a celebrity is fabricated," and a process that has become increasingly democratic. This theoretical "process is of considerable [cultural], social and even political significance."[26] Celebrities come from a variety of social and economic backgrounds and represent individuals who are not often represented in the political system. Evans suggests celebrity culture can create a form of social leveling.[27] The idea that celebrity culture is democratic is based on two central arguments. The first is that because celebrities can come from almost any background, celebrity provides visibility to marginal groups, such as minorities and the poor and working class. The second indication that the media have been democratized is audience participation in the selection of celebrities. The increase in the number of audience voting opportunities in reality television, game shows and news allows for commentary and selection by the average viewer at home, fostering a DIY celebrity culture.[28] However, Tyler and Bennett argue that even though the process has an appearance of being more democratic, other forces may be at work.[29]

While the magazine form and participatory media, such as blogs, blur the distinctions between the producers and audiences of content about celebrities, Tyler and Bennett concluded from their research that it is not clear that the widening of participation is indicative of social leveling.[30] Douglas E. Allen and Paul F. Anderson argue that one of Bourdieu's contributions to class theory and research was establishing the role that non-economic factors—such as symbolic (social status and reputation) and cultural (education, skills, taste) capital—play in creating and maintaining class distinctions. Bourdieu also rejects the idea, they argue, that "'tastes,' (that is, consumer preferences) are the result of innate individualistic choices of the human intellect." Instead, taste becomes a "social weapon" that defines and differentiates those of high social class from low social class.[31] Therefore, the previous research suggests that the media one consumes, the celebrities one follows and emulates, and the other consumer choices one makes indicate one's social class. Tyler and Bennett argue that the social classification process is central to celebrity narratives in magazines.[32] Social class is often cited euphemistically in magazines through references to individuals, such as Jade Goody and Britney Spears, being *real* or *ordinary* people. These class distinctions are further systemized through the distinctions between A-list, B-list and Z-list celebrities.[33]

Celebrity culture cannot be differentiated from the media, such as magazines, that serve as the engines of celebrity culture and publicity. As the magazines through which celebrity images and gossip proliferate become more central to the popularity and social function of popular forms of the medium, the exceptional nature of the magazine and the celebrity become more interconnected. Magazines increasingly appear to be depending on celebrities to provide content for their features. Celebrities increasingly depend on magazines to fuel their celebrity status, which may include product consumption, including sales of tickets for movies, sporting events or other celebrity-related goods.[34]

Audience Involvement with Celebrity

William J. Brown, Michael D. Basil and Mihai C. Bocarnea point out that media effects research shows that audience members "who become psychologically involved with popular media," such as magazines, "are susceptible to their influence. . . . The level of audience involvement is an important predictor of attitudinal and behavioral changes that result from exposure to media personae."[35] Mark R. Levy found that people who are repeatedly exposed to media stars often develop a sense of kinship or closeness with them.[36] These *parasocial relationships* are created when audience members view celebrities or other media personalities as friends or look to them for comfort. Parasocial relationships can influence how audience members interpret mediated events and have been found to be particularly important among young adults. Susan Boon and Christine Lomore learned from their 2001 study of celebrity influence that 90% of the 194 young adults surveyed reported a strong "attraction to an idol celebrity at some point in their lives. . . ."[37] Although celebrity attachments can have negative effects, parasocial relationships can also be interpreted as part of normal identity development.[38] Research in parasocial interaction generally supports the idea that audience members who become involved with a particular celebrity will be more likely to use media, such as magazines, to see that person and find out additional information about him or her. People who closely follow celebrities are also more likely to adopt the celebrity's attitudes and beliefs about social issues.[39]

Celebrity parasocial relationships have been shown to influence audience attitudes in a variety of instances. For example, Tony Walter observed that, in Britain, reality star Jade Goody's death from cervical cancer increased cancer awareness among young women.[40] American audiences formed a strong parasocial relationship with basketball star "Magic" Johnson that helped increase HIV awareness among heterosexual adults.[41] Fans who developed a parasocial relationship with baseball star Mark McGwire were more likely to be concerned about child abuse, a cause McGwire championed, and to consider taking androstenedione, the muscle-enhancing drug that McGwire used.[42] Likewise, people who identified with Princess Diana were more likely to have a negative view of the press and perhaps blame the news media for her death.[43]

Research on Magazines and Celebrity

A variety of scholarly studies in a number of fields—including mass communication, sociology, critical and cultural, studies, and public health—have looked at the relationship of celebrity journalism and its influence on readers and society. The research has explored magazine coverage of celebrity success and notoriety,[44] the celebrity image as it relates to health and beauty,[45] and celebrity romance and relationships.[46] In addition to analyzing magazine coverage of these topics, the research on celebrity journalism has also examined the influence that magazine editorial has had on society at large.[47] Although the research spans a breadth of subjects, it is evident that the power of celebrity combines with the exceptional magazine form to influence our culture in profound ways. In addition to shaping our culture, the narratives in magazines reveal subtle aspects of our cultural norms, values and practices that might otherwise go unnoticed.

Narratives on Success and Notoriety

Celebrities are perceived to be exceptional because they possess a quality or characteristic that makes them superior to or different from the average person. Boorstin argues that stakeholders who cultivate celebrity, such as public relations professionals or press secretaries and other marketing professionals, promote an individual's exceptional quality to an interested audience.[48] This exceptional quality inspires admirers to learn about and emulate celebrities. The characteristic could be a talent or ability that audiences value, such as athleticism or musicianship; a physical characteristic, such as beauty or strength; or the mere possession of exceptional wealth or social status.

Through its coverage, magazine editorial informs an audience about the nature of success, including the material possessions, glamorous lifestyle and fame that accompany it. Chris Rojek writes, "Although God-like qualities are often attributed to celebrities, the modern meaning of the term *celebrity* actually derives from the fall of the gods and the rise of democratic governments and secular societies."[49] Glamour and notoriety are often thought to be opposites. Rojek observes that glamour is associated with positive recognition, and notoriety is associated with negative public recognition.[50] Notoriety is a sub-category of celebrity culture that is becoming increasingly important.[51] When a celebrity fails to maintain societal standards for success, magazines tell the stories of failure and notoriety. The stories of celebrity success and notoriety reinforce the accepted standards for ethics and morality. A variety of research explores how magazines cover stories of acquiring fame and social status and later falling from grace.

Stories of Notoriety and Redemption

Most celebrities prefer positive fame to notoriety or infamy. Circumstances such as failed relationships and substance abuse can cause the once glamorous to become notorious. For instance, Elizabeth Taylor, Richard Burton, Judy Garland, Frank Sinatra, Jennifer Lopez and Larry King experienced difficulties establishing permanent relationships and marriages. The patterns of marriage and divorce they established led to notoriety.[52] Others can become notorious through addiction and substance abuse and receive redemption and compassion through their battle to become substance free. Elizabeth Taylor, Robert Downy Jr., Drew Barrymore and Ozzy Osbourne juxtaposed their idealized status with the public face of vulnerability and addiction. Confession can play a key role in re-acquiring a positive celebrity image.[53]

However, some celebrities or *celetoids* are famous for a compressed amount of time, often due to infamy or notoriety. Rojek argues, they "are the accessories of cultures organized around mass communications and staged authenticity."[54] Instead of achieving celebrity through a special talent or skill, the celetoid status is granted to an individual because of some sort of sensational or staged occurrence. The goal of sensationalism, says Rojek, is "to generate public interest with the object of galvanizing public attention."[55] Hence, *ordinary people*, such as Nadya Suleman, who became the infamous "Octomom" through in vitro fertilization; Luciana Morad, the mother of one of Mick Jagger's illegitimate children; and a variety of reality stars, became famous at the behest of mass media executives seeking higher program ratings or increased circulation for their publications.[56] As Boorstin suggests, society is in the process of degrading all celebrity into notoriety.[57] Therefore, the celetoids are becoming more and more like other celebrities.

As a British celetoid, Jade Goody did not possess many of the extraordinary attributes that usually accompany celebrity, but she was eventually admired for her candor and openness. However, before that, she had attracted significant media criticism and notoriety for her behavior on *Celebrity Big Brother 5*, when she made derogatory and racist remarks toward fellow housemate and Bollywood actress Shillipa Shetty. When one compares Shetty and Goody, one sees a contrast between celebrity virtue and vice. Shetty represents all of the beauty and class a glamorous celebrity should possess. Goody represents celebrity notoriety that is characterized by spectacle and criticism instead of admiration. To redeem herself and her tarnished public reputation from allegations of racism, Goody in mid-2008 appeared in the Indian version of *Big Brother*, *Bigg Boss*. Two days into the show, Goody was informed that she had cervical cancer. Walter argues that in Jade Goody's last days and death, the notorious Goody was redeemed. She turned around public opinion, especially among working class women, by demonstrating that she was still in control of her own fate. In the final weeks of her fight with cervical cancer, she signed media contracts with popular media venues and celebrity magazines to support her children's education, and she raised awareness of smear testing.[58]

Clive Seale identifies differences in how the media portray male and female heroism in the face of cancer, emphasizing women's skills in the area of emotional labor and self-transformation, while cancer in men is depicted as a test of pre-existing character.[59] Goody's determination to tell her story, both mundane and fearful, regularly broke through in the magazine *OK!* Walter described the coverage of her death as a mesh of "autographical fear and journalistic heroism."[60]

Although Jade's story was of heroism in the face of dying, it was even more of redemption through dying. Redemption narratives typically appear after tragedies, such as the Oklahoma City bombing[61] and September 11,[62] or after a celebrity successfully bids for public forgiveness. Redemption narratives are also found in post-mortem constructions of celebrities' lives. The Goody redemption story is unique because a celetoid story rarely reaches the redemption phase. Carolyn Kitch and Janice Hume found that celebrity redemption stories are told in a "remarkably uniform narrative, that draws moral lessons from a star's life difficulties" but, in the end, the celebrity, or even the celetoid, can be celebrated.[63]

Pack Journalism and Criminal Justice

Many celebrities' legal troubles are being given increasing coverage in the media. Richard L. Fox, Robert W. Van Sickel and Thomas L. Steiger call this phenomenon *tabloid justice*.[64] Robert Downey Jr. was sentenced to three years in prison for parole violations on drug and weapons charges.[65] Charlie Sheen was involved in a variety of domestic abuse incidents, including a 1997 battery conviction and a variety of restraining orders and other assault charges.[66] American football star O.J. Simpson was tried in criminal court and convicted in civil trial for the deaths of his ex-wife Nicole Brown Simpson and restaurant waiter Ronald Goldman.[67] Winona Ryder was convicted of felony grand theft in 2002 and sentenced to three years of probation and 480 hours of community service.[68] It would seem that celebrities on trial would receive more sympathy than their non-celebrity counterparts; however, that assumption is not always true. A study using rape as an example of a criminal offense found that white male, celebrity defendants are perceived more positively than white male, non-celebrity defendants and that black male, celebrity defendants fare worse than black male, non-celebrity defendants.[69]

A substantial body of research focuses on Michael Jackson and his dealings with the criminal justice system. In many ways, Jackson should fit the celebrity ideal. He attained his celebrity through an exceptional musical talent that allowed him to achieve beyond his working class background. However, the many scandals that plagued Jackson's career, including charges of sexual molestation, overshadowed his musical success and philanthropic interests. Jackson's public persona is a combination of superstar, genius, suspected sexual deviant and self-mutilating plastic surgery patient. His popular music, international fame and outlandish behavior and personal appearances placed him in an incomparable and exceptional position, distinguishing him from the rest of the society.[70]

Magazines and other mass media that cover celebrity and celebrity scandal are often plagued by *pack journalism*. Gerald Mark Breen and Jonathan Matusitz define *pack journalism* as "a collection of behavior and conditions by which substantial groups of reporters from diverse and typically large media outlets collaborate in the same physical surroundings to cover the same story."[71] *Pack journalism* also involves a variety of ethical issues, such as the loss of independent reporting, and it can undermine the justice system.[72]

Breen and Matusitz conclude that the journalists who reported on the 1993 Michael Jackson sexual molestation case assisted Jackson in a variety of unethical ways, as demonstrated by his full acquittal in spite of the numerous charges that were brought against him. On the other hand, Breen and Matusitz found evidence that the journalists, acting as a pack, "maintained a clear pattern of demonizing" the prosecution and characterized the case against Jackson as being "weak, unsubstantial, and malicious."[73] The irony here is that sometimes celebrity magazines work in concert to create stories that are all surprisingly similar, making their coverage less than one would expect from an exceptional medium.

Although pack journalism might help certain celebrities escape criminal conviction, it can also feed a celebrity's notoriety or infamy. Jackson is arguably not remembered for his musical talent. And, although Jackson was affiliated with a variety of humanitarian causes in his life, he is not remembered for his initiatives, which Hilde van den Bulk and Koen Panis note included AIDS, cancer, children's welfare and famine.[74] In other cases, scandalous stories about a celebrity's private life are not detrimental to and can be countered by activism, as is the case with celebrities such as Angelina Jolie and Bono who overcame scandals through their philanthropic work. But this was not the case with Michael Jackson. Van den Bulk and Panis argue that gaining an understanding of this seeming contradiction could be achieved through the concept of *consistency*. Many of Jackson's charitable contributions related to children. The narratives of child abuse and child philanthropy were inconsistent.[75] Therefore, the media found it difficult to mask the story of child abuse with the stories of child philanthropy. Because he was thought to be a pedophile, Jackson's philanthropic work would be viewed with suspicion.

Jack Levin, James Alan Fox and Jason Mazaik have observed that "throughout much of the American history of celebrity, stardom was typically bestowed on those regarded as paragons of virtue," because of some exceptional talent or ability.[76] However, in their analysis of *People* magazine covers, they found that from the 1970s to the start of the twenty-first century, celebrity status has been granted based upon what these scholars call the "'accomplishments' of rapists, child abusers, drug addicts and murderers." Celebrity criminals who are featured in magazines "entertained the masses with their spectacularly bizarre and criminal behavior. Former *People* magazine editor Richard Stolley may have recognized this shift . . . when he suggested in 1977, 'We haven't changed the concept of magazine, we're just expanding the concept of 'star.' "[77]

The Celebrity Image: Beauty, Health and Identity

Athletes and entertainment celebrities as featured in magazines often set physical standards that are unattainable. Although these standards are gendered, the research suggests they influence readers of both sexes as they strive to meet the perceived norm and judge others according to expectations they see in the magazines. This section discusses the findings of research on the influence of these messages on vulnerable populations, such as teens and young adults.

In his book, *Understanding Celebrity*, Turner suggests that more empirical work needs to focus on the construction of celebrity because, "Modern celebrity, then, is a product of media representation: understanding it demands close attention to the representational repertoires and patterns employed in this discursive regime."[78] And, in the case of the magazine, much of this representation is visual in nature. However, the visual representations of celebrities profoundly influence societal standards of beauty and create ideals that can be difficult for readers to attain.

Disordered Admiration and the Feminine Image

The literature gives strong support to the findings of John Maltby, David C. Giles, Louise Barber and Lynn E. McCutcheon who observed that "in recent years, there has been considerable research on the association between the mass media and eating disorders," specifically among adolescent women.[79] These scholars also found a growing belief in the field of health psychology "that media representations may play an important role in shaping heath beliefs and behaviors."[80] Research has shown that comparing oneself with thin images and idealizing those images predicts body dissatisfaction and a desire for thinness.[81]

In addition, reading magazines has been a consistent predictor of body images and eating disorders in women. Kristen Harrison and Joanne Cantor found that magazine reading was related to an increased desire to be thin.[82] Kristen Harrison found that increased exposure to thin bodies in magazines was also related to increased symptoms of eating disorders among adolescent girls.[83] Likewise, interpersonal attraction to thin media personalities is an important aspect of the relationship between consuming media that depict and promote thinness and disordered eating. Attraction to thin media personalities also influences disordered eating beyond the influence of mere media exposure.[84]

Celebrity worship can have harmful effects on an individual's mental and physical health. Lynn E. McCutcheon, Rense Lange and James Houran found that celebrity worship can take on two forms, *pathological* and *non-pathological*. The non-pathological form of celebrity worship suggests a deep admiration and an intense interest in the individual celebrity. The pathological form of celebrity worship can lead to unhealthy behaviors such as stalking, *erotomania* (a deluded feeling that the celebrity is in love with his or her admirer), and inappropriate correspondence with the celebrity. In either case, celebrity worship can impede an individual's ability to form healthy relationships with others because the admirer can become overly absorbed with or addicted to the celebrity.[85] Another compounding factor to this issue is that celebrity worship can be related to poor body image among adolescent females. However, the research suggests that the relationship between poor body image and celebrity worship tends to disappear once females reach adulthood.[86]

Celebrity and the Masculine Image

When compared with the research on women, far less study has been given to the impact of magazines and celebrity on men's body image. Men have traditionally been thought to be more impervious than women to the pressures to meet societal expectations regarding physical appearance. However, research over the past few decades suggests men have become increasingly concerned with body image. Geoffrey H. Cohane and Harrison G. Pope, Jr., found that body image disturbance exists among men; however, dysmorphia is usually linked to trying to be muscular rather than thin.[87] Sociocultural standards measure masculine beauty by strength and muscularity, or a *mesomorphic* (average build) instead of an *ectomorphic* (thin) or *endomorphic* (fat) body shape. Law and Labre concluded that during the last two decades of the twentieth century, idealized images of naked or half-naked men began to be featured extensively in men's magazines, such as *Men's Health* and *Men's Fitness*.[88] Law and Labre also noted the growing popularity of celebrities such as The Rock (the WWF wrestling star), Arnold Schwarzenegger and Sylvester Stallone reinforced the growing popularity of the idealized masculine form.[89] Men's magazines have been publishing more articles that focus on body image.[90]

Traditionally, popular culture producers promoted a traditional hegemonic masculinity in magazines, including men's lifestyle magazines. From their review of the literature, Guy Cafri and J. Kevin Thompson found that idealizing muscular images can be associated with body dissatisfaction and promotes steroid abuse.[91] However, they note that this body of research also indicates that men are interested in enhancing their physical appearance.[92] Pompper, drawing on Deborah Schooler and Monique L. Ward's research, noted that "Dissonance results when a man's real body is compared to a sanitized body free of hair, sweat, and odor such as those depicted by bare-chested magazine images."[93] Pompper also summarized MacKinnon's work, observing, "Such trends reflect how emergent gender and sexuality discourses shape masculinities and make them visible . . ."[94]

Mohmin Rahman, in his study of British soccer star David Beckham, described Beckham's unique celebrity status as "evident not only in those [British] magazines which have paid for the privilege of access" but also in celebrity weeklies circulated in the United Kingdom, such as *Heat*. However, media coverage of Beckham coupled respect "with a sense of ridicule." Beckham was praised for his athletic physique but was also portrayed as being consumed with his own physical beauty. "This gentle undercurrent becomes stronger when linked to Beckham's fashion icon status." Mohmin Rahman argues that "ridicule undercuts the celebrity credentials of extravagance and glamour with an implication of tackiness and vulgarity."[95]

Additionally, Rahman argues that Beckham's sexuality was anchored in his hetero-family, his masculine status or both. However, his heterosexual and star athlete roles conflicted with his vanity, grooming and gay icon status. Periodicals covering Beckham used a form of gender role ridicule termed *queering*. For instance, Rahman described the queering of Beckham in the following example from the weekly magazine, *Heat*:

> An example from *Heat* (20–26th July 2002) has the cover byline: "Phwoar! Another new look for Becks" with a trail for a story on pages 18–20 which has a photograph of Beckham with his nail varnish highlighted and the text, "David sported a new blonde barnet and a fitted black suit, and despite the controversy caused by his pink nail varnish he still managed to look macho and absolutely beautiful." This [example] demonstrates some feminization of Beckham but is counterbalanced by the very masculine anchor of "macho."[96]

Likewise, Rahman points out that the June 2002 GQ magazine also played on Beckham's gender and sexuality by publishing a cover photo of Beckham lying down, bare-chested but wearing a suit and hat, a ring and nail polish showing on one hand. The other hand was under the waistband of his slacks.[97] Therefore, the magazine coverage of Beckham played on his metrosexual fashion sense and appeared to market his image to a gay audience in spite of the fact that Beckham was not a homosexual but, rather, more accurately, a *metrosexual*. Aldrich defines the metrosexual as a heterosexual who "is nevertheless 'in touch' with his feminine side."[98]

Rahman points out that in the world of male sports celebrities, Beckham was thought to be exceptional. Beckham is one of the few British soccer players, known in the United Kingdom as footballers, to achieve full celebrity status. "He transgresses the discipline and work ethic associated with sporting bodies."[99] Magazine images of Beckham pushed the boundaries of the construction of respectable images of sporting bodies. Rahman argues that the deliberate sexualization of Beckham's body "derives its power from the 'danger' this presents to sporting masculinity and heterosexual masculinity. Thus we need 'family, fatherhood' *and* 'football' to anchor the 'queer' Beckham."[100] Beckham serves as an example of how the magazine form and celebrity are changing traditional masculine norms. Rahman has argued that Beckham is "a 'post modern' or 'hybrid celebrity'" for whom the media have given the ability to transcend traditional gender norms and represent a variety of different things to various fan groups.[101]

Celebrity Romance and Sex Research

Magazines and celebrities define sex roles in powerful ways. In addition to setting standards for femininity and masculinity, magazine editorial explores the interplay between the two sexes within the context of celebrity romance. The lessons to be learned from magazines are especially poignant when it comes to narratives about celebrity romance, adultery and domestic abuse.

Magazine Discourse on Domestic Violence

Popular magazines are an important source of public information about relationships. Summarizing and building on the existing body of research, Nettleton found from her research that when explaining domestic violence, the discourse in men's and women's magazines tends to blame women as choosing the wrong men, but suggests that men are not responsible for hitting women. Men's magazines are tolerant of violence. Women's magazines present an assumption that women bear the responsibility for preventing violence for both sexes. Furthermore, the narratives of women's magazines imply that women are responsible for every facet of domestic abuse, including identifying and avoiding potentially violent men, understanding the legal system and serving as advocates for abused women and activists against domestic violence. Men's magazines position violence against women as "something other men would understand."[102]

Rothman and colleagues summarize other research, the results of which suggest that media coverage tends to "perpetuate patriarchal myths that reinforce the subordination of women to men" in a number of ways:

> by minimizing the illegality [of domestic abuse] by referring to it as a "crime of passion," implicating victims in the crime (i.e., "victim-blaming"), attributing violence perpetration to psychopathology rather than social forces that support misogyny, and depicting domestic abuse as "natural" or ordinary.[103]

"The literature also suggests that the media have ignored larger structural factors [such as] race, class and gender in a manner that facilitates domestic violence by supporting patriarchal ideals."[104] Further, the research finds that "media are one of the most powerful influences in shaping public perceptions about crime and victimization."[105]

Nettleton suggests that "magazine coverage of exceptional cases of violence, such as stories about sports or music celebrities who beat their [partners]," rarely serves to educate the public about domestic violence as a social issue. Instead, the coverage "demonizes a few, troubled men."[106] Other research suggests that both magazine and newspaper coverage obscures the abuser's wrongdoing and places the blame on the battered victim.[107] Pamela Hill Nettleton reported *Rolling Stone's* coverage of rock musician Tommy Lee's attacking his wife, Pamela

Anderson, when Lee was unable to find a frying pan. Lee described his loss of control as reasonable; in response to Lee's fury, Anderson said, "Calm down. You're scaring me." Anderson's fear was reported as feeding Lee's rage, and Lee's description and evaluation of the incident remained unquestioned: Anderson's fear was portrayed as triggering the escalation of violence.[108]

In their study of the media coverage of the Chris Brown and Robyn (Rihanna) Fenty[109] domestic abuse incident, Rothman and colleagues found that some magazine coverage seemed to suggest Rihanna was responsible. "Some [articles] stated directly that she may be the responsible party, whereas others contained references to speculation that she gave Chris Brown a sexually transmitted infection (STI), hit him first, or expressed jealousy."[110] Celebrity tabloid magazines, such as *Star* magazine, seemed to imply that Rihanna "had it coming" by focusing on what made Brown angry.[111] One of the subheads accompanying a photo of Rihanna featured on the cover of the 2 March 2009 edition of *Star* magazine read, "What made Chris snap."[112] In the immediate aftermath, many U.S. teens expressed the opinion that Brown was innocent, in spite of Brown's public apology on 19 February 2009 and "the unauthorized release of a graphic photo of Rihanna's injured face."[113] The Boston Health Commission published survey results showing that 46% of a convenience sample of 200 young people believed that Rihanna was responsible for the violence, while 52% believed that both were to blame.[114]

Likewise, Nettleton found that domestic abuse by star athletes is often excused when covered in *Sports Illustrated*. Nettleton quoted one athlete who said, "Should a man still be held accountable for an incident that, though troubling, seems isolated? Not if the incident is truly isolated."[115] Nettleton described a *Sports Illustrated* feature on Roy Tarpley, in which domestic violence was "equated to a traffic ticket and then excused because of Tarpley's athletic performance." In another article, a *Sports Illustrated* writer excused Riddick Bowe of any blame for domestic abuse.[116]

The public's exposure to violence in the media is a social concern because it can increase the likelihood of domestic violence. Research that supports the idea that exposure to violence "affects dating violence behavior, both as perpetrator and victim," suggests that media exposure is "a potential pathway to dating violence."[117] Studies using media effects approaches and Bandura's Social Learning Theory suggest that "viewing examples of negative interactions in relationships or dating violence . . . has the potential to shape attitudes and behavior about what is normal and acceptable."[118] Jennifer A. Manganello proposed a conceptual model based on Steele and Brown's five-aspect model for media's influence on victimization and dating abuse perpetration. Manganello's model identifies three primary ways media exposure influences relational abuse: through (1) the selection of the media vehicle, (2) interpretation of the media story, and (3) application of the media to the media consumers' own lives.[119]

Celebrity Sex, Romance and Scandal

An interesting outcome of the combination of exceptional people with an exceptional medium is that sometimes the mundane becomes exceptional. This is suggested by magazine coverage of celebrities and sex. While "scandalous" celebrity sex stories rely upon and reproduce traditional assumptions of gendered sexuality, Gamson suggests there are reasons to doubt that the communication of sexual values is the stories' primary cultural contribution. He argues that, as in other public discussions, sexuality takes its place in these morality tales more as a vehicle or symbol than a topic. The sexual activity that is covered is usually surprisingly banal or ordinary. Moreover, when sex scandals are being covered, the scandalous element itself is "the least important" element in the story.[120]

Gamson gives one example of how the scandalous element of a sex scandal can be secondary to other elements: the coverage of British actor Hugh Grant's 1995 arrest for "lewd conduct" with a prostitute.[121] Gamson points out that Grant's arrest did not trigger any moral outrage. Most coverage referred to the sex with the prostitute only as "a sex act." The journalistic storytelling focused instead on gossip about problems in Grant's relationship with actress and model Elizabeth Hurley. Most media coverage of the scandal initially tried to answer questions about why Grant solicited sex from a street hooker when he was a desirable celebrity who could easily have any girl he wanted. A variety of explanations were offered, such as "sexual compulsion, the desire for uncomplicated sex, male piggishness, British innocence, the lures of the Hollywood playground, [and] the pressures of fame." However, the Grant sex scandal story was ultimately played out in the media as a story of betrayal and forgiveness. The incongruence between Grant's image as a shy, suave actor and the circumstances surrounding his arrest created additional drama. Gamson suggests celebrity image management played an important role. A headline on the cover of *People* magazine read, "Bizarre arrest tarnishes the image of Hollywood's most charming leading man." Gamson found that many celebrity movie goers felt that by tarnishing their image of him, Grant had cheated on them just as much as he had cheated on Hurley.[122]

Likewise, Erin Meyers points to the magazine coverage of Britney Spears as being marked by the contrast between the wholesome celebrity image audiences wanted from Spears and her social class and sexuality. When she started her pop music career at age 15, Spears was a veteran of the *Mickey Mouse Club*. Her image personified youth and innocence. As Spears became a legal adult, however, Meyers describes her image as having become increasingly sexualized, both in her public performances "and in celebrity media coverage of her exploits." The latter included "alleged heavy partying" and a Las Vegas wedding and marriage that lasted a mere 55 hours.[123] Then, when Spears and backup dancer Kevin Federline began dating, magazines reported that Federline left Shar Jackson, his then-pregnant girlfriend with whom he had already fathered a child, to start a relationship with Spears. Most of the magazine coverage of their relationship focused on Spears "as a trashy home wrecker" and Federline "as a cheating cad"[124] rather than someone who gave true love and was monogamous. An interesting aspect of the shift in Spears's public image was the conflict in media coverage and Spears's self-reports of her activities. While the celebrity media criticized her for becoming increasingly trashy and hypersexual, compared with her initial public image, Spears maintained that she was simply blossoming into womanhood and, as such, was merely staying true to herself and what she wanted, instead of what her audience and the public supposedly wanted from her.[125]

Meyers suggests one way Spears tried to manage her public image was allowing *People* magazine exclusive, official interviews. After getting married in a surprise, secret ceremony, Britney and Kevin Federline gave *People* an exclusive interview and the rights to their wedding photos for its 4 October 2005 edition. And, Meyers argues, Spears's self-created image relied on the idea that she was "the girl next door or just like the average person" and her presentation of her relationship and marriage to Kevin Federline helped "solidify this image."[126] Like the Grant sex scandal narrative, the Spears-Federline narrative focused on resolving an incongruent public image rather than the actual details of the celebrity romance.

María Lamuedra points out that in media coverage of celebrity romance, even the absence of scandal or other problems can attract media attention. She described former Spice Girl Victoria Beckham and British football star David Beckham as having enjoyed a happy and relatively scandal-free, romantic relationship that started with dating and resulted in marriage. Yet the British celebrity magazine *Now* centered on trivial matters in the Beckhams' relationship to create celebrity drama. Lamuedra observed that Victoria Beckham was portrayed as an insecure woman who needed constant reassurance from her husband. Stories generated from gossip about the couple speculated about whether David Beckham would tire of his wife because of her insecurity and self-obsession. Thus the narratives on the Beckhams' relationship speculated about whether their happiness was temporary.[127] Lamuedra compared the Beckham coverage with that of Tom Cruise and Katie Holmes: once a happy couple but now their relationship seemed to be in trouble. Would the same thing happen to the Beckhams? The magazine's coverage of the Beckhams' relatively happy marriage had escapist and entertainment value. However, it was still not portrayed as an ideal romance.

The body of research exploring magazine journalism and celebrity often covers topics that point to the media's cynicism in its portrayal of romance,[128] perhaps because of the many famous people who have failed romantic relationships.[129] In addition, the positive coverage of the Beckhams' relationship could be seen as the synthesis of escapism. However, cynicism is evident in the implication that there is no safe path to happiness in celebrity romance. Not even money, glamour and love can guarantee a lasting and happy marriage. Although the research has focused a great deal of attention on the negative aspects of celebrity relationships, scholars could also study healthy celebrity relationships and positive coverage. This type of research might provide some positive guidance for journalists instead of their focusing on the negative issues.

Society, Social Class and Celebrity Research

After considering multiple examples of the coverage of exceptional people in an exceptional medium, the magazine, a next question is how celebrity narratives retold in magazines inform their audiences and the population? Why are these stories powerful? What do they tell about society? Bourdieu argues that individuals can possess capital, or accumulated labor or effort, in three primary areas: *economic, cultural* and *social. Economic capital* is made up of an individual's wealth, usually measured in money and property. *Cultural capital* is an individual's competence, skill or learning. And *social capital* is made up of "social obligations" or expectations and "connections" that individuals are compelled to satisfy because of their membership in a particular social group.[130]

One might assume that celebrities would possess each of the three forms of capital: economic, social and cultural. However, from the analysis of the literature, it seems that celebrity narratives found in magazines often point to a deficiency in one or more of the forms. Therefore, through celebrity narratives readers learn about the inherent structure of the social world as expressed through the various forms of capital that are possessed, lost or gained.

The Role of Economic Capital

Economic capital is present in most celebrity narratives. However, unless a celebrity gains his or her status from a heinous or notorious act, as did Oklahoma City bomber Timothy McVeigh, most celebrities possess economic capital or will acquire it. However, the fact that most celebrities possess wealth demonstrates the value that society places on their status, or social capital; or their abilities and learning, that is, their cultural capital. Of course, personal finances can occasionally enter into celebrity narratives. For instance, Jade Goody allowed magazine journalists to cover her last days so she could earn money to support her sons after her death. Michael Jackson's dwindling finances that resulted in his reduced ability to support his Neverland Ranch seemed to accentuate Jackson's status as a troubled star. Thus it can be argued that economic capital is a contributing element to magazine coverage of celebrities. However, it appears to be either subordinate to or a complement to other forms of celebrity capital.

The Role of Cultural Capital

Most celebrities who come to fame do so not by being born into a famous family, but rather because they have cultural capital: an exceptional talent, virtue or ability (musical, athletic, intellectual) that allowed their mobility into the celebrity caste. For instance, Robyn "Rihanna" Fenty, Britney Spears, Tommy Lee, Michael Jackson and Victoria Beckham rose to fame through their exceptional musical ability. Beauty, as in the cases of Pamela Anderson and Elizabeth Hurley, can also be a form of cultural capital that can translate into celebrity status and become a focus of media attention. However, a reality star, such as Jade Goody, can rise without cultural capital. This new kind of star exists because of the social capital generated through popularity or notoriety fed by the media industry to create reality stars.

The Role of Social Capital

As evidenced by their renown and public admiration, most celebrities have a large degree of social capital. In fact, having the status of celebrity means that one has been accepted for membership into the elite group of the famous. However, there are various rites that indicate the level of stardom one has attained. For instance, winning or being nominated for awards, being selected for sponsorships or socializing with the elite can all indicate or contribute to one's social capital. This level of celebrity capital is evident in one's ranking as an A-list, B-list, or Z-list star. Many stories about celebrity scandal relate to some sort of violation of expectations the audience has for a member of celebrity society. Romantic relationships can be of particular importance because they initiate new members into the celebrity class.

Maintaining proper weight is equated with social status and a positive celebrity image. Therefore, magazine audiences witness the rewards and punishments associated with weight and not maintaining the celebrity-thin ideal that is expected of those who rise to fame. Celebrity is also an image-related profession. Celebrities must maintain a certain appearance to remain free of scandal and maintain their social status. Weight plays an especially important role for female stars. Celebrities such as Jessica Simpson, Sarah Ferguson, Kirstie Alley, Carnie Wilson and Wynona Judd have all been featured on the covers of magazines because of their weight issues. In their battle to lose weight, celebrities have joined diet and exercise programs and even undergone surgery.

Male celebrities are not immune from the social pressures of fame and maintaining a proper image. For instance, magazines present the *mesomorphic* muscular build as the ideal for men. In addition to maintaining the ideal body shape, men are pressured to uphold the ideal of masculine behavior and will face ridicule if they are not sufficiently masculine. David Beckham received extensive magazine coverage because his public persona did not subscribe to the masculine norm. However, as noted, some magazine coverage of Beckham's personal style bordered on ridicule.

Although a large body of the research covered in this chapter focuses on implicit messages about social class, cultural norms and violations of expectations contained in celebrity dialogues, other research discussed in this chapter focuses on the influence these messages have on audience members. Because celebrities attract media attention and are of high social standing, audience members take cues from celebrities. Traditionally, these cues have related to fashion, standards for beauty and other matters of personal taste. However, the limited empirical research on audience effects has found that emulating celebrities has led to more negative and disordered behavior among audience members, such as body *dysmorphia* and unhealthy *parasocial relationships*. Therefore, research suggests the power of celebrity extends beyond simply giving cues about social class, social expectations and class mobility. It can affect the physical and mental health of the readers and fans.

Future Research

Although a growing body of research has examined celebrity journalism and magazines, more research remains to be done. Critical and cultural scholars have studied the attributes of celebrity and the traits that make celebrities influential. Less research has focused on the influence of the magazine as a vehicle of this influence. Likewise, more research needs to focus on the effects that celebrities and their behavior have on magazine audiences.

There are a variety of areas where future research can be done on magazine coverage of exceptional people. A body of research has explored democratization of celebrity through the emergence of the reality star; however, the nature of celebrity and media coverage of celebrity continues to change with the emergence of new media. More research could focus on magazine content on the Internet.[131] Scholarly research has also focused on the negative influence of celebrity on body image. However, very little research explores the influence of magazine coverage of celebrities on other negative behaviors. For instance, there is little academic research on the relationship between magazine coverage of celebrities' criminal behavior or drug abuse and audience behavior.[132] In addition, although the research looks at how celebrity culture reflects social and cultural norms and values, there is little research that looks at how celebrity culture might be shaping or changing these norms and values. Likewise, more research could explore how magazine coverage of the extravagances associated with the celebrity lifestyle could be increasing materialism among audience members and resulting in increased consumer spending and debt. Little scholarly attention has been to the *celebritization* process and the motives of the individuals who create celebrities. More research could explore how celebrity is used as a marketing tool for the magazine industry. For instance, the magazine industry uses celebrities to market its publications, and celebrities use the publicity that magazines provide to promote themselves and their interests, such as their films and albums.

Scholarly research has explored magazine coverage of celebrities and their stories. More research remains to be done to uncover the influence of these celebrity stories on magazine readers' attitudes and behaviors. In addition, future research should study the individuals and institutions that produce fame by marketing celebrities and their stories to magazines.

Conclusion

The exceptional nature of magazines and periodicals combined with the exceptional nature of celebrity status profoundly shape contemporary magazine journalism. Events that are not normally newsworthy are featured in magazine editorial content and headlines because of celebrity involvement. The powerful combination of magazines and celebrity can create both positive and negative outcomes. Media coverage of celebrities has the ability to create awareness for social causes and issues that merit the public's attention. Likewise, the tendency for magazine journalists and audiences to idolize celebrities can result in unethical journalistic practices. These practices can lead the public to minimize the severity of crimes that celebrities commit or, in the worst cases, emulate their negative behavior. Although celebrity journalism in magazines shares many news values with other media, the magazine is unique in its presentation of narrative. More than other media, magazine narratives join the public dialogue on morality, sexuality and social class. Some magazines encourage social progress, and others encourage conformity to the established norms. News about celebrities provides readers with a venue for social commentary that is unique in its nature and format. Rather than just presenting factual stories, magazines work with the reader to help them understand society and current events. This practice gives the reader a unique view of current cultural norms and where these norms may shift in the future.

Notes

1 Lana Rakow, "Feminists, Media, Freed Speech," *Feminist Media Studies* 1.1 (2001): 42.
2 Pierre Bourdieu, *Outline of a Theory of Practice*, trans. Richard Nice (Cambridge, UK and New York: Cambridge University Press, 1977), 183–184; 159–197.
3 Imogen Tyler and Bruce Bennett, "'Celebrity Chav': Fame, Femininity and Social Class," *European Journal of Cultural Studies* 13.3 (2010): 376–377.
4 David Abrahamson, "Magazine Exceptionalism: The Concept, the Criteria, the Challenge," *Journalism Studies* 8.4 (2007): 667–670.
5 Abrahamson, "Magazine Exceptionalism," 667.
6 PPA Marketing, "The Case for Consumer Magazines," Powerpoint Presentation, PowerShow.com <http://www.powershow.com/view1/1e5ce9-MzY5M/Mixed_Media_Planning_powerpoint_ppt_presentation>, accessed 7 April 2014.
7 Abrahamson, "Magazine Exceptionalism," 669.

8 Abrahamson, "Magazine Exceptionalism," 670.

9 Nick Couldry and Tim Markham, "Celebrity Culture and Public Connection: Bridge or Chasm?" *International Journal of Cultural Studies* 10.4 (December 2007): 403–421.

10 Graeme Turner, "Understanding Celebrity," *Understanding Celebrity* (London: Sage, 2004), 4.

11 Turner, "Understanding Celebrity," 4.

12 Turner, "Understanding Celebrity," 4. See Todd Gitlin, "Supersaturation, or, the Media Torrent and Disposable Feeling," *Media Unlimited: How the Torrent of Images and Sounds Overwhelms Our Lives* (New York: Metropolitan Books / Henry Holt & Co., 2007), 12–70; Richard Schickel, *Intimate Strangers: The Culture of Celebrity* (New York: Doubleday, 1985).

13 Gitlin, "Supersaturation," 14.

14 Gitlin, "Supersaturation," 14.

15 Gitlin, "Supersaturation," 15, citing Raymond Williams, "Drama in a Dramatised Society," in Alan O'Connor, ed., *Raymond Williams on Television* (Toronto: Between the Lines, 1989), 3–5.

16 Turner, "Understanding Celebrity," 4.

17 Turner, "Understanding Celebrity," 5; Daniel J. Boorstin, "From Hero to Celebrity: The Human Pseudo-Event," *The Image: A Guide to Pseudo-Events in America* (New York: Vintage Books, 1992), 45–76.

18 Boorstin, "From Hero to Celebrity," 57 (italics in original).

19 Boorstin, "From Hero to Celebrity," 58.

20 Boorstin, "From Hero to Celebrity," 57–61.

21 Daniel J. Boorstin, "From News Gathering to News Making: A Flood of Pseudo-Events," *The Image: A Guide to Pseudo-Events in America* (New York: Vintage Books, 1992), 10–11; Boorstin, "From Hero to Celebrity," 57–61.

22 Boorstin, "From Hero to Celebrity," 61.

23 Boorstin, "From Hero to Celebrity," 64–65.

24 Couldry and Markham, "Celebrity Culture and Public Connection," 404.

25 Couldry and Markham, "Celebrity Culture and Public Connection," 404.

26 Jessica Evans, "Celebrity, Media and History," in Jessica Evans and David Hesmondhalgh, eds., *Understanding Media: Inside Celebrity* (Maidenhead, UK: Open University Press, 2005), 12–14, 37.

27 Evans, "Celebrity, Media and History," 12–55.

28 Evans, "Celebrity, Media and History," 14; Tyler and Bennett, "'Celebrity Chav,'" 378–379.

29 Tyler and Bennett, "'Celebrity Chav,'" 387–390.

30 Tyler and Bennett, "'Celebrity Chav,'" 378.

31 Douglas E. Allen and Paul F. Anderson, "Consumption and Social Stratification: Bourdieu's Distinction," *Advances in Consumer Research* 21.1 (1994): 70, citing Pierre Bourdieu, *Distinction: A Social Critique of the Judgment of Taste*, trans. Richard Nice (Cambridge, MA: Harvard University Press, 1984); see also, Pierre Bourdieu, "The Forms of Capital," in John G. Richardson, ed., *Handbook of Theory and Research for the Sociology of Education* (New York: Greenwood Press, 1986), 241–258.

32 Tyler and Bennett, "'Celebrity Chav,'" 376.

33 Tyler and Bennett, "'Celebrity Chav,'" 377.

34 Julianne Treme, "Effects of Celebrity Media Exposure on Box-Office Performance," *Journal of Media Economics* 23.1 (2010): 5.

35 William J. Brown, Michael D. Basil, and Mihai C. Bocarnea, "Social Influence of an International Celebrity: Responses to the Death of Princess Diana," *Journal of Communication* 53.4 (December 2003): 589.

36 Mark R. Levy, "Watching TV News as Para-Social Interaction," *Journal of Broadcasting* 23.1 (1979):78–79.

37 Susan D. Boon and Christine D. Lomore, "Admirer-Celebrity Relationships among Young Adults: Explaining Perceptions of Celebrity Influence on Identity," *Human Communication Research* 27.3 (July 2001): 439.

38 Lynn E. McCutcheon, Rense Lange, and James Houran, "Conceptualization and Measurement of Celebrity Worship," *British Journal of Psychology* 93.1 (2002): 68.

39 Brown, Basil, and Bocarnea, "Social Influence of an International Celebrity," 601.

40 Tony Walter, "Jade and the Journalists: Media Coverage of a Young British Celebrity Dying of Cancer," *Social Science and Medicine* 71.5 (2010): 856.

41 William J. Brown and Michael D. Basil, "Media Celebrities and Public Health: Responses to 'Magic' Johnson's HIV Disclosure and Its Impact on AIDS Risk and High-Risk Behaviors," *Health Communication* 7.4 (1995): 358–361, 364.

42 William J. Brown, Michael D. Basil, and Mihai C. Bocarnea, "The Influence of Famous Athletes on Health Beliefs and Practices: Mark McGwire, Child Abuse Prevention, and Androstenedione," *Journal of Health Communication* 8.1 (2003): 53.

43 Brown, Basil, and Bocarnea, "Social Influence of an International Celebrity," 600.

44 Walter, "Jade and the Journalists," 853–860; Chris Rojek, "Celebrity and Celetoids," *Celebrity* (London: Reaktion Books Ltd., 2001), 9–49.

45 John Maltby, David C. Giles, Louise Barber, and Lynn E. McCutcheon, "Intense-Personal Celebrity Worship and Body Image: Evidence of a Link among Female Adolescents," *British Journal of Health Psychology* 10.1 (2005): 17–32; Kristen Harrison, "The Body Electric: Thin-Ideal Media and Eating Disorders in Adolescents," *Journal of Communication* 50.3 (Summer 2000): 119–143; Kristen Harrison and Joanne Cantor, "The Relationship between Media Consumption and Eating Disorders," *Journal of Communication* 47.1 (1997): 40–67; Geoffrey H. Cohane and Harrison G. Pope, Jr., "Body Image in Boys: A Review of the Literature," *International Journal of Eating Disorders* 29.4 (2001): 373–379; Cheryl Law and Magdala Peixoto Labre, "Cultural Standards of Attractiveness: A Thirty-Year Look at Changes in Male Images in Magazines," *Journalism & Mass Communication Quarterly* 79.3 (Autumn 2002): 697; Jane Gordon, "The Fears Aroused by a Fine Physique: Modern Men Face the Same Media Pressure to be Perfect that Women Have Long Endured," *Daily Telegraph* (London, UK), 12 June 1996, 19; Robert Aldrich, "Homosexuality and the City: An Historical Overview," *Urban Studies* 41.9 (August 2004): 1733; Donnalyn Pompper, "Masculinities, the Metrosexual, and Media Images: Across Dimensions of Age and Ethnicity" [Special Issue, Fiction, Fashion, and Function: Gendered Experiences of Women's and Men's Body Image], *Sex Roles* 63.9 (2010): 682–696.

46 María Lamuedra Graván, "Comparative Study of Magazine Romantic Fiction, True Life Stories and Celebrity Stories: Utopia, Closure and Reader's Participation" (paper presented at Mapping the Magazine Conference, UK, 2008); Pamela Hill Nettleton, "Domestic Violence in Men's and Women's Magazines: Women Are Guilty of Choosing the Wrong Men, Men Are Not Guilty of Hitting Women," *Women's Studies in Communication* 34.2 (Summer 2011): 139–160; Emily F. Rothman, Anita Nagaswaran, Renee M. Johnson, Kelley M. Adams, Juliane Scrivens, and Allyson Baughman, "U.S. Tabloid Magazine Coverage of a Celebrity Dating Abuse Incident: Rihanna and Chris Brown," *Journal of Health Communication: International Perspectives* 17.6 (2012): 733–744; Kimberly A. Maxwell, John Huxford, Catherine Borum, and Robert Hornik, "Covering Domestic Violence: How the O.J. Simpson Case Shaped Reporting of Domestic Violence in the News Media," *Journalism & Mass Communication Quarterly* 77.2 (Summer 2000): 258–272; Michelle L. Meloy and Susan L. Miller, "Words that Wound: Print Media's Presentation of Gendered Violence," in Drew Humphries, ed., *Women, Violence and the Media* (Hanover, NH: University Press of New England, 2009), 29–56; Elizabeth Stanko, *Intimate Intrusions: Women's Experience of Male Violence* (London: Routledge & Kegan Paul, 1985).

47 Brown, Basil, and Bocarnea, "Social Influence of an International Celebrity," 593–600; Gitlin, "Supersaturation," 14–15; Couldry and Markham, "Celebrity Culture and Public Connection," 403–421; Boon and Lomore, "Admirer-Celebrity Relationships among Young Adults," 439; McCutcheon, Lange, and Houran, "Conceptualization and Measurement of Celebrity Worship," 67–87; Evans, "Celebrity, Media and History," 12–55; Joshua Gamson, "Normal Sins: Sex Scandal Narratives as Institutional Morality Tales," *Social Problems* 48.2 (May 2001): 185–205.

48 Boorstin, "From Hero to Celebrity," 45.

49 Rojek, "Celebrity and Celetoids," 9.

50 Rojek, "Celebrity and Celetoids," 10.

51 Rojek, "Celebrity and Celetoids," 10.

52 Rojek, "Celebrity and Celetoids," 12.

53 Chris Rojek, "Celebrity and Religion," *Celebrity* (London: Reaktion Books, 2001), 88–89.

54 Rojek, "Celebrity and Celetoids," 20–21.

55 Rojek, "Celebrity and Religion," 18.

56 Rojek, "Celebrity and Celetoids," 18.

57 Boorstin, "From Hero to Celebrity," 48.

58 Walter, "Jade and the Journalists," 853–860.

59 Clive Seale, "Cancer Heroics: A Study of News Reports with Particular Reference to Gender," *Sociology* 36.1 (2002): 123.

60 Walter, "Jade and the Journalists," 855.

61 Edward Tabor Linenthal, *The Unfinished Bombing: Oklahoma City in American Memory* (New York: Oxford University Press, 2001), 239–241.

62 Carolyn Kitch, "'Mourning in America': Ritual, Redemption, and Recovery in News Narrative after September 11," *Journalism Studies* 4.2 (2003): 222.

63 Carolyn Kitch and Janice Hume, *Journalism in a Culture of Grief* (New York: Routledge, 2008), 77.

64 Richard L. Fox, Robert W. Van Sickel, and Thomas L. Steiger, *Tabloid Justice: Criminal Justice in an Age of Media Frenzy* (Boulder, CO: Lynne Rienner Publishers, 2007), 6.

65 Monte Morin, "Robert Downy Jr. Gets 3 Years in Prison," *Los Angeles Times*, 6 August 1999 <http://articles.latimes.com/1999/aug/06/local/me-63303>, accessed 8 October 2013.

66 Sheila Marikar, "Charlie Sheen's Long List of Legal Woes," *ABC NEWS*, 9 March 2011, 1–2 <http://abcnews.go.com/Entertainment/charlie-sheens-long-list-legal-woes/story?id=13075771>, accessed [8 Octo-

ber 2013]; see also, "Charlie Sheen: 'It's Not an Act,'" *People*, 2 March 2011 <http://www.people.com/people/article/0,,20470054,00.html>, accessed 9 October 2013.

67 CNN Library, "O.J. Simpson Fast Facts," CNN.com, 13 August 2013 <http://www.cnn.com/2013/04/12/us/o-j-simpson-fast-facts/index.html>, accessed 9 October 2013; see also, "The People vs. Simpson," *People Magazine*, 10 October 1994 <http://www.people.com/people/archive/article/0,,20104089,00.html>, accessed 9 October 2013.

68 Bootie Cosgrove-Mather and Angela Watercutter, "Reduced Charges for Winona Ryder," *CBS News*, 18 June 2004 <http://www.cbsnews.com/8301-207_162-624887.html>, accessed 7 April 2014; see also, C. Young, "Winona Ryder Busted for Shoplifting," *People*, 14 December 2001 <http://www.people.com/people/article/0,,623102,00.html>, accessed 10 October 2013.

69 Jennifer L. Knight, Traci A. Giuliano, and Monica G. Sanchez-Ross, "Famous or Infamous? The Influence of Celebrity Status and Race on Perceptions of Responsibility for Rape," *Basic and Applied Social Psychology* 23.3 (September 2001): 186.

70 Bob Jones and Stacy Brown, *Michael Jackson: The Man behind the Mask* (New York: Select Books, 2005), 4–9.

71 Gerald Mark Breen and Jonathan Matusitz, "Communicating the Negative Aspects of Pack Journalism to Media Reporters," *Global Media Journal* 7.12 (Spring 2008): 2.

72 Breen and Matusitz, "Communicating the Negative Aspects of Pack Journalism," 2, 5.

73 Breen and Matusitz, "Communicating the Negative Aspects of Pack Journalism," 5.

74 Hilde Van den Bulck and Koen Panis, "Michael as He Is Not Remembered: Jackson's 'Forgotten' Celebrity Activism," *Celebrity Studies* 1.2 (2010): 242–243.

75 Van den Bulck and Panis, "Michael as He Is Not Remembered," 243.

76 Jack Levin, James Alan Fox, and Jason Mazaik, "Blurring Fame and Infamy: A Content Analysis of Cover-Story Trends in *People* Magazine," *Internet Journal of Criminology* (2005): 12 <http://www.internetjournalofcriminology.com/index.html>, accessed 7 February 2015.

77 Levin, Fox, and Mazaik, "Blurring Fame and Infamy," citing Richard Stolley, as quoted in Joshua Gamson, *Claims to Fame: Celebrity in Contemporary America* (Berkeley: University of California, 1994), 43.

78 Turner, "Understanding Celebrity," 8.

79 Maltby, Giles, Barber, and McCutcheon, "Intense-Personal Celebrity Worship and Body Image," 18; see also, Harrison, "The Body Electric," 119–143; Harrison and Cantor, "The Relationship between Media Consumption and Eating Disorders," 40–67; Cohane and Pope, "Body Image in Boys," 373–379; Law and Labre, "Cultural Standards of Attractiveness," 697; Gordon, "The Fears Aroused by a Fine Physique," 19; Aldrich, "Homosexuality and the City," 1733; Pompper, "Masculinities, the Metrosexual, and Media Images," 682–696.

80 Maltby, Giles, Barber, and McCutcheon, "Intense-Personal Celebrity Worship," 18.

81 Renée A. Botta, "The Mirror of Television: A Comparison of Black and White Adolescents' Body Image," *Journal of Communication* 50.3 (Summer 2000): 152.

82 Harrison and Cantor, "The Relationship between Media Consumption and Eating Disorders," 54–55.

83 Harrison, "The Body Electric," 131, 135.

84 Harrison, "The Body Electric," 120; Harrison and Cantor, "The Relationship between Media Consumption and Eating Disorders," 41.

85 McCutcheon, Lange, and Houran, "Conceptualization and Measurement of Celebrity Worship," 68–69.

86 Maltby, Giles, Barber, and McCutcheon, "Intense-Personal Celebrity Worship and Body Image," 28.

87 Cohane and Pope, "Body Image in Boys," 378; Richard A. Leit, James J. Gray, and Harrison G. Pope, Jr., "The Media's Representation of the Ideal Male Body: A Cause for Muscle Dysmorphia?" *International Journal of Eating Disorders* 31.3 (April 2002): 334–338.

88 Law and Labre, "Cultural Standards of Attractiveness," 697.

89 Law and Labre, "Cultural Standards of Attractiveness," 697–698; see also, Harrison G. Pope, Jr., Katharine A. Phillips and Roberto Olivardia, *The Adonis Complex: The Secret Crisis of Male Body Obsession* (New York: Free Press, 2000).

90 Law and Labre, "Cultural Standards of Attractiveness," 697; Gordon, "The Fears Aroused by a Fine Physique," 19.

91 Guy Cafri and J. Kevin Thompson, "Measuring Male Body Image: A Review of the Current Methodology," *Psychology of Men and Masculinity* 5.1 (2004): 25.

92 Cafri and Thompson, "Measuring Male Body Image," 21.

93 Pompper, "Masculinities, the Metrosexual, and Media Images," 684, citing Deborah Schooler and L. Monique Ward, "Average Joes: Men's Relationships with Media, Real Bodies, and Sexuality," *Psychology of Men & Masculinity* 7.1 (2006): 28.

94 Pompper, "Masculinities, the Metrosexual, and Media Images," 684, citing Kenneth MacKinnon, *Representing Men: Maleness and Masculinity in the Media* (New York: Oxford University Press, 2003); see also Donnalyn

Pompper, Jorge Soto, and Lauren Piel, "Male Body Image and Magazine Standards: Considering Dimensions of Age and Ethnicity," *Journalism & Mass Communication Quarterly* 84.3 (Autumn 2007): 525–545.

95 Mohmin Rahman, "Is Straight the New Queer? David Beckham and the Dialectics of Celebrity," *M/C Journal* 7.5 (2004): 2.

96 Rahman, "Is Straight the New Queer?" 2.

97 Rahman, "Is Straight the New Queer?" 2.

98 Aldrich, "Homosexuality and the City," 1733; see also, Pompper, "Masculinities, the Metrosexual, and Media Images," 682–696.

99 Rahman, "Is Straight the New Queer?" 3; Garry Whannel, *Media Sport Stars: Masculinities and Moralities* (London: Routledge, 2002), 212.

100 Rahman, "Is Straight the New Queer?" 3 (italics in original).

101 Rahman, "Is Straight the New Queer?" 3.

102 Nettleton, "Domestic Violence in Men's and Women's Magazines," 147–148, 149.

103 Rothman, Nagaswaran, Johnson, Adams, Scrivens, and Baughman, "U.S. Tabloid Magazine Coverage of a Celebrity Dating Abuse Incident," 734.

104 Maxwell, Huxford, Borum, and Hornik, "Covering Domestic Violence," 260.

105 Meloy and Miller, "Words that Wound," 29.

106 Nettleton, "Domestic Violence in Men's and Women's Magazines," 144; see also Stanko, *Intimate Intrusions*.

107 Maxwell, Huxford, Borum, and Hornik, "Covering Domestic Violence," 259.

108 Nettleton, "Domestic Violence in Men's and Women's Magazines," 149, citing Neil Strauss, "The Ballad of Pamela Anderson and Tommy Lee," *Rolling Stone*, 10 May 2001, 4 <http://www.rollingstone.com/music/news/the-ballad-of-pamela-anderson-tommy-lee-20010510>, accessed 17 September 2013.

109 Robyn (Rihanna) Fenty is known in her celebrity status as "Rihanna," as used in this account.

110 Rothman, Nagaswaran, Johnson, Adams, Scrivens, and Baughman, "U.S. Tabloid Magazine Coverage of a Celebrity Dating Abuse Incident," 739.

111 Celebitchy. "*Star* Magazine Seems to Suggest that Rihanna Had It Coming," *Cele|bitchy*, 25 February 2009 <http://www.celebitchy.com/38419/star_magazine_seems_to_suggest_rihanna_had_it_coming/>, accessed 2 October 2013.

112 "*Star* Magazine Seems to Suggest That Rihanna Had It Coming," *Star* Magazine [print edition], 2 March 2009, Front Cover.

113 Rothman, Nagaswaran, Johnson, Adams, and Baughman, "U.S. Tabloid Magazine Coverage of a Celebrity Dating Abuse Incident: Rihanna and Chris Brown," 735.

114 Boston Public Health Commission, News Release 03–12–2009, "Public Health Commission Surveys Youths on Dating Violence," 12 March 2009 <http://www.bphc.org/Newsroom/Pages/TopStoriesView.aspx?ID=60>, accessed 2 October 2013.

115 Nettleton, "Domestic Violence in Men's and Women's Magazines," 149, citing Karl Taro Greenfeld, "A Life after Wide Right," *Sports Illustrated*, 12 July 2004, 140.

116 Nettleton, "Domestic Violence in Men's and Women's Magazines," 149.

117 Jennifer A. Manganello, "Teens, Dating Violence, and Media Use: A Review of the Literature and Conceptual Model for Future Research," *Trauma, Violence & Abuse* 9.1 (January 2008): 9.

118 Manganello, "Teens, Dating Violence, and Media Use," 9; see also, Christine Wekerle and David A. Wolfe, "Dating Violence in Mid-Adolescence: Theory, Significance, and Emerging Prevention Initiatives," *Clinical Psychology Review* 19.4 (June 1999): 435–456; Ximena B. Arriaga and Vangie A. Foshee, "Adolescent Dating Violence: Do Adolescents Follow in Their Friends,' Or Their Parents,' Footsteps?," *Journal of Interpersonal Violence* 19.2 (February 2004): 162–184.

119 Manganello, "Teens, Dating Violence, and Media Use," 8; see also Jeanne R. Steele and Jane D. Brown, "Adolescent Room Culture: Studying Media in the Context of Everyday Life," *Journal of Youth and Adolescence* 24.5 (1995): 551–576.

120 Gamson, "Normal Sins," 186, quoting Michael Schudson, "Sex Scandals," in *Our National Passion: 200 Years of Sex in America*, Sally Banes, Sheldon Frank, and Tem Horwitz, eds. (Chicago: Follett Publishing, 1976), 51.

121 Gamson, "Normal Sins," 191.

122 Gamson, "Normal Sins," 191–193.

123 Erin Meyers, "'Can You Handle My Truth?': Authenticity and the Celebrity Star Image," *Journal of Popular Culture* 42.5 (2009): 899–900.

124 Meyers, "'Can You Handle My Truth?'" 903.

125 Meyers, "'Can You Handle My Truth?'" 901–902.

126 Meyers, "'Can You Handle My Truth?'" 901.

127 Lamuedra, "Comparative Study of Magazine Romantic Fiction," 11.

128 Meyers, "'Can You Handle My Truth?'" 890–907; Gamson, "Normal Sins," 185–205; Nettleton, "Domestic Violence in Men's and Women's Magazines," 139–160.
129 Rojek, "Celebrity and Celetoids," 12–13.
130 Bourdieu, "The Forms of Capital," 242–243ff.
131 P. David Marshall, "New Media–New Self: The Changing Power of Celebrity," in P. David Marshall, ed., *The Celebrity Culture Reader* (London: Routledge, 2006), 634–644.
132 Lorraine Sheridan, Adrian North, John Maltby, and Raphael Gillett, "Celebrity Worship, Addiction and Criminality," *Psychology, Crime & Law* 13.6 (2007): 559–571.

Bibliography

Abrahamson, David. "Magazine Exceptionalism: The Concept, the Criteria, the Challenge." *Journalism Studies* 8.4 (2007): 667–670.

Aldrich, Robert. "Homosexuality and the City: An Historical Overview." *Urban Studies* 41.9 (August 2004): 1719–1737.

Allen, Douglas E. and Anderson, Paul F. "Consumption and Social Stratification: Bourdieu's Distinction." *Advances in Consumer Research* 21.1 (1994): 70–74.

Arriaga, Ximena B. and Foshee, Vangie A. "Adolescent Dating Violence: Do Adolescents Follow in Their Friends,' Or Their Parents,' Footsteps?" *Journal of Interpersonal Violence* 19.2 (February 2004): 162–184.

Boon, Susan D. and Lomore, Christine D. "Admirer-Celebrity Relationships among Young Adults: Explaining Perceptions of Celebrity Influence on Identity." *Human Communication Research* 27.3 (July 2001): 432–465.

Boorstin, Daniel J. "From Hero to Celebrity: The Human Pseudo-Event." *The Image: A Guide to Pseudo-Events in America.* New York: Vintage Books, 1992, 45–76.

Boorstin, Daniel J. "From News Gathering to News Making: A Flood of Pseudo-Events." *The Image: A Guide to Pseudo-Events in America.* New York: Vintage Books, 1992, 7–44.

Boston Public Health Commission. News Release 03–12–2009, "Public Health Commission Surveys Youths on Dating Violence." 12 March 2009 <http://www.bphc.org/Newsroom/Pages/TopStories View.aspx?ID=60>, accessed 2 October 2013.

Botta, Renée A. "The Mirror of Television: A Comparison of Black and White Adolescents' Body Image." *Journal of Communication* 50.3 (Summer 2000): 144–159.

Bourdieu, Pierre. *Distinction: A Social Critique of the Judgment of Taste.* Translated by Richard Nice. Cambridge, MA: Harvard University Press, 1984.

Bourdieu, Pierre. "The Forms of Capital." In Richardson, John G., ed. *Handbook of Theory and Research for the Sociology of Education.* New York: Greenwood Press, 1986, 241–258.

Bourdieu, Pierre. *Outline of a Theory of Practice.* Translated by Richard Nice. Cambridge, UK and New York: Cambridge University Press, 1977.

Breen, Gerald-Mark and Matusitz, Jonathan. "Communicating the Negative Aspects of Pack Journalism to Media Reporters." *Global Media Journal* 7.12 (Spring 2008): 1–7.

Brown, William J. and Basil, Michael D. "Media Celebrities and Public Health: Responses to 'Magic' Johnson's HIV Disclosure and Its Impact on AIDS Risk and High-Risk Behaviors." *Health Communication* 7.4 (1995): 345–370.

Brown, William J.; Basil, Michael D.; and Bocarnea, Mihai C. "The Influence of Famous Athletes on Health Beliefs and Practices: Mark McGwire, Child Abuse Prevention, and Androstenedione." *Journal of Health Communication* 8.1 (2003): 41–57.

Brown, William J.; Basil, Michael D.; and Bocarnea, Mihai C. "Social Influence of an International Celebrity: Responses to the Death of Princess Diana." *Journal of Communication* 53.4 (December 2003): 587–605.

Cafri, Guy and Thompson, J. Kevin. "Measuring Male Body Image: A Review of the Current Methodology." *Psychology of Men & Masculinity* 5.1 (2004): 18–29.

Celebitchy. "*Star* Magazine Seems to Suggest that Rihanna Had It Coming." *Cele | bitchy*, 25 February 2009 <http://www.celebitchy.com/38419/star_magazine_seems_to_suggest_rihanna_had_it_coming/>, accessed 2 October 2013.

"Charlie Sheen: 'It's Not an Act.'" *People*, 2 March 2011, <http://www.people.com/people/article/0,,20470054,00.html>, accessed 9 October 2013.

CNN Library. "O.J. Simpson Fast Facts." CNN.com, 13 August 2013 <http://www.cnn.com/2013/04/12/us/o-j-simpson-fast-facts/index.html>, accessed 9 October 2013.

Cohane, Geoffrey H. and Pope, Harrison G., Jr. "Body Image in Boys: A Review of the Literature." *International Journal of Eating Disorders* 29.4 (2001): 373–379.

Cosgrove-Mather, Bootie and Watercutter, Angela. "Reduced Charges for Winona Ryder." *CBS News*, 18 June 2004 <http://www.cbsnews.com/news/reduced-charges-for-winona-ryder/>, accessed 7 April 2014.

Couldry, Nick and Markham, Tim. "Celebrity Culture and Public Connection: Bridge or Chasm?" *International Journal of Cultural Studies* 10.4 (December 2007): 403–421.

Evans, Jessica. "Celebrity, Media and History." In Evans, Jessica and Hesmondhalgh, David, eds. *Understanding Media: Inside Celebrity*. Maidenhead, UK: Open University Press, 2005, 12–55.

Fox, Richard L.; Van Sickel, Robert W.; and Steiger, Thomas L. *Tabloid Justice: Criminal Justice in an Age of Media Frenzy*. Boulder, CO: Lynne Rienner Publishers, 2007.

Gamson, Joshua. *Claims to Fame: Celebrity in Contemporary America*. Berkeley: University of California, 1994.

Gamson, Joshua. "Normal Sins: Sex Scandal Narratives as Institutional Morality Tales." *Social Problems* 48.2 (May 2001): 185–205.

Gitlin, Todd. "Supersaturation, or, the Media Torrent and Disposable Feeling." *Media Unlimited: How the Torrent of Images and Sounds Overwhelms Our Lives*. New York: Metropolitan Books / Henry Holt & Co. 2007, 12–70.

Gordon, Jane. "The Fears Aroused by a Fine Physique: Modern Men Face the Same Media Pressure to be Perfect that Women Have Long Endured." *The Daily Telegraph* (London, UK), 12 June 1996, 19.

Greenfeld, Karl Taro. "A Life after Wide Right." *Sports Illustrated*, 12 July 2004, 140.

Harrison, Kristen. "The Body Electric: Thin-Ideal Media and Eating Disorders in Adolescents." *Journal of Communication* 50.3 (Summer 2000): 119–143.

Harrison, Kristen and Cantor, Joanne. "The Relationship between Media Consumption and Eating Disorders." *Journal of Communication* 47.1 (1997): 40–67.

Jones, Bob and Brown, Stacy. *Michael Jackson: The Man behind the Mask*. New York: Select Books, 2005.

Kitch, Carolyn. "'Mourning in America': Ritual, Redemption, and Recovery in News Narrative after September 11." *Journalism Studies* 4.2 (2003): 213–224.

Kitch, Carolyn and Hume, Janice. *Journalism in a Culture of Grief*. New York: Routledge, 2008.

Knight, Jennifer L.; Giuliano, Traci A.; and Sanchez-Ross, Monica G. "Famous or Infamous? The Influence of Celebrity Status and Race on Perceptions of Responsibility for Rape." *Basic and Applied Social Psychology* 23.3 (September 2001): 183–190.

Lamuedra, María Graván. "Comparative Study of Magazine Romantic Fiction, True Life Stories and Celebrity Stories: Utopia, Closure and Reader's Participation." Paper presented at Mapping the Magazine Conference, UK, 2008.

Law, Cheryl and Labre, Magdala Peixoto. "Cultural Standards of Attractiveness: A Thirty-Year Look at Changes in Male Images in Magazines." *Journalism & Mass Communication Quarterly* 79.3 (Autumn 2002): 697–711.

Leit, Richard A.; Gray, James J.; and Pope, Harrison G., Jr. "The Media's Representation of the Ideal Male Body: A Cause for Muscle Dysmorphia?" *International Journal of Eating Disorders* 31.3 (April 2002): 334–338.

Levin, Jack; Fox, James Alan; and Mazaik, Jason. "Blurring Fame and Infamy: A Content Analysis of Cover-Story Trends in *People* Magazine." *Internet Journal of Criminology* (2005): 1–17 <http://www.internetjournalofcriminology.com/index.html>, accessed 7 February 2015.

Levy, Mark R. "Watching TV News as Para-Social Interaction." *Journal of Broadcasting* 23.1 (1979): 69–80.

Linenthal, Edward Tabor. *The Unfinished Bombing: Oklahoma City in American Memory*. New York: Oxford University Press, 2001.

MacKinnon, Kenneth. *Representing Men: Maleness and Masculinity in the Media*. New York: Oxford University Press, 2003.

Maltby, John; Giles, David C.; Barber, Louise; and McCutcheon, Lynn E. "Intense-Personal Celebrity Worship and Body Image: Evidence of a Link among Female Adolescents." *British Journal of Health Psychology* 10.1 (2005): 17–32.

Manganello, Jennifer A. "Teens, Dating Violence, and Media Use: A Review of the Literature and Conceptual Model for Future Research." *Trauma, Violence & Abuse* 9.1 (January 2008): 3–18.

Marikar, Sheila. "Charlie Sheen's Long List of Legal Woes." *ABC NEWS*, 9 March 2011, 1–2 <http://abcnews.go.com/Entertainment/charlie-sheens-long-list-legal-woes/story?id=13075771>, accessed 8 October 2013.

Marshall, P. David. "New Media–New Self: The Changing Power of Celebrity." In Marshall, P. David, ed. *The Celebrity Culture Reader.* London: Routledge, 2006, 634–644.

Maxwell, Kimberly A.; Huxford, John; Borum, Catherine; and Hornik, Robert. "Covering Domestic Violence: How the O.J. Simpson Case Shaped Reporting of Domestic Violence in the News Media." *Journalism & Mass Communication Quarterly* 77.2 (Summer 2000): 258–272.

McCutcheon, Lynn E.; Lange, Rense; and Houran, James. "Conceptualization and Measurement of Celebrity Worship." *British Journal of Psychology* 93.1 (2002): 67–87.

Meloy, Michelle L. and Miller, Susan L. "Words that Wound: Print Media's Presentation of Gendered Violence." In Humphries, Drew, ed. *Women, Violence and the Media.* Hanover, NH: University Press of New England, 2009, 29–56.

Meyers, Erin. "'Can You Handle My Truth?': Authenticity and the Celebrity Star Image." *Journal of Popular Culture* 42.5 (2009): 890–907.

Morin, Monte. "Robert Downy Jr. Gets 3 Years in Prison." *Los Angeles Times*, 6 August 1999 <http://articles.latimes.com/1999/aug/06/local/me-63303>, accessed 8 October 2013.

Nettleton, Pamela Hill. "Domestic Violence in Men's and Women's Magazines: Women Are Guilty of Choosing the Wrong Men, Men Are Not Guilty of Hitting Women." *Women's Studies in Communication* 34.2 (Summer 2011): 139–160.

"The People vs. Simpson." *People Magazine*, 10 October 1994 <http://www.people.com/people/archive/article/0,,20104089,00.html>, accessed 9 October 2013.

Pompper, Donnalyn. "Masculinities, the Metrosexual, and Media Images: Across Dimensions of Age and Ethnicity." [Special Issue, Fiction, Fashion, and Function: Gendered Experiences of Women's and Men's Body Image] *Sex Roles* 63.9 (2010): 682–696.

Pompper, Donnalyn; Soto, Jorge; and Piel, Lauren. "Male Body Image and Magazine Standards: Considering Dimensions of Age and Ethnicity." *Journalism & Mass Communication Quarterly* 84.3 (Autumn 2007): 525–545.

Pope, Harrison G., Jr.; Phillips, Katharine A.; and Olivardia, Roberto. *The Adonis Complex: The Secret Crisis of Male Body Obsession.* New York: Free Press, 2000.

PPA Marketing. "The Case for Consumer Magazines," Powerpoint Presentation. PowerShow.com <http://www.powershow.com/view1/1e5ce9-MzY5M/Mixed_Media_Planning_powerpoint_ppt_presentation>, accessed 7 April 2014.

Rahman, Mohmin. "Is Straight the New Queer? David Beckham and the Dialectics of Celebrity." *M/C Journal* 7.5 (November 2004): Unpaginated.

Rakow, Lana. "Feminists, Media, Freed Speech." *Feminist Media Studies* 1.1 (2001): 41–44.

Rojek, Chris. "Celebrity and Celetoids." *Celebrity.* London: Reaktion Books, 2001, 9–49.

Rojek, Chris. "Celebrity and Religion." *Celebrity.* London: Reaktion Books, 2001, 51–99.

Rothman, Emily F.; Nagaswaran, Anita; Johnson, Renee M.; Adams, Kelley M.; Scrivens, Juliane; and Baughman, Allyson. "U.S. Tabloid Magazine Coverage of a Celebrity Dating Abuse Incident: Rihanna and Chris Brown." *Journal of Health Communication: International Perspectives* 17.6 (2012): 733–744.

Schickel, Richard. *Intimate Strangers: The Culture of Celebrity.* New York: Doubleday, 1985.

Schooler, Deborah and Ward, L. Monique. "Average Joes: Men's Relationships with Media, Real Bodies, and Sexuality." *Psychology of Men & Masculinity* 7.1 (2006): 27–41.

Schudson, Michael. "Sex Scandals." In *Our National Passion: 200 Years of Sex in America.* Banes, Sally; Frank, Sheldon; and Horwitz, Tem, eds. Chicago: Follett Publishing, 1976, 41–57.

Seale, Clive. "Cancer Heroics: A Study of News Reports with Particular Reference to Gender." *Sociology* 36.1 (2002): 107–126.

Sheridan, Lorraine; North, Adrian; Maltby, John; and Gillett, Raphael. "Celebrity Worship, Addiction and Criminality." *Psychology, Crime & Law* 13.6 (December 2007): 559–571.

Stanko, Elizabeth. *Intimate Intrusions: Women's Experience of Male Violence.* London: Routledge & Kegan Paul, 1985.

"*Star* Magazine Seems to Suggest that Rihanna Had It Coming." *Star* Magazine [print edition], 2 March 2009, Front Cover.

Steele, Jeanne R. and Brown, Jane D. "Adolescent Room Culture: Studying Media in the Context of Everyday Life." *Journal of Youth and Adolescence* 24.5 (1995): 551–576.

Strauss, Neil. "The Ballad of Pamela Anderson and Tommy Lee." *Rolling Stone*, 10 May 2001, 1–5 <http://www.rollingstone.com/music/news/the-ballad-of-pamela-anderson-tommy-lee-20010510>, accessed 17 September 2013.

Treme, Julianne. "Effects of Celebrity Media Exposure on Box-Office Performance." *Journal of Media Economics* 23.1 (2010): 5–16.

Turner, Graeme. "Understanding Celebrity." *Understanding Celebrity*. London: Sage, 2004, 3–27.

Tyler, Imogen and Bennett, Bruce. "'Celebrity Chav': Fame, Femininity and Social Class." *European Journal of Cultural Studies* 13.3 (2010): 375–393.

Van den Bulck, Hilde and Panis, Koen. "Michael as He Is Not Remembered: Jackson's 'Forgotten' Celebrity Activism." *Celebrity Studies* 1.2 (2010): 242–244.

Walter, Tony. "Jade and the Journalists: Media Coverage of a Young British Celebrity Dying of Cancer." *Social Science and Medicine* 71.5 (2010): 853–860.

Wekerle, Christine and Wolfe, David A. "Dating Violence in Mid-Adolescence: Theory, Significance, and Emerging Prevention Initiatives." *Clinical Psychology Review* 19.4 (June 1999): 435–456.

Whannel, Garry. *Media Sport Stars: Masculinities and Moralities*. London: Routledge, 2002.

Williams, Raymond. "Drama in a Dramatised Society." In O'Connor, Alan, ed. *Raymond Williams on Television*. Toronto: Between the Lines, 1989, 3–5.

Young, C. "Winona Ryder Busted for Shoplifting." *People*, 14 December 2001 <http://www.people.com/people/article/0,,623102,00.html>, accessed 10 October 2013.

Supplemental Resources

Boorstin, Daniel J. *The Image, or, What Happened to the American Dream*. New York: Atheneum, 1962.

Hartley, John. *Uses of Television*. London and New York: Routledge, 1999.

19

RELIGIOUS MAGAZINES

Keeping the Faith

Ken Waters

For centuries religious publications in the English-speaking world have played an important role in periodical publishing, helping believers define their faith and share common interests and dialogue about their relationship to mainstream culture. Through news and feature articles, editorials and commentaries, these typically small-circulation magazines aimed at educated, but non-scholarly audiences have entered into national debates about slavery, prohibition, personal piety, doctrine and theology, science, abortion, gay marriage and a variety of other human and civil rights issues. Despite their longevity, "Writings on the American religious press are far from numerous or satisfactory. To a great extent this field still awaits exploration by secular and church historians."[1] Church historian Martin Marty once referred to U.S. Protestant publications as vibrant, but invisible.[2] Heather Hendershot notes, "[M]any [Christian] films, books, videos, magazines and other cultural products have until now received only scant scholarly attention. . . ."[3] These observations about the paucity of scholarly attention to religious publications pertain only to North American magazines. Much less research has been conducted on religious publications in other parts of the world.

Method

The number of religious publications worldwide, and the potential readership, is unknown. Data gathered from the Web sites of the prominent religious press associations indicate the number of publications worldwide easily exceeds 1,000, although no definitive list of international religious publications exists.[4] The estimate derives from the fact that the Web sites of the Catholic Press Association in North America list more than 600 members, the Evangelical Press Association lists more than 300 member publications, and the Australasian Press Association lists 82 publications. This estimate does not include publications in the United Kingdom, Europe, Africa and Asia, and only one source could be found that listed magazines, all Christian, existing internationally.[5] An exhaustive Google keyword search for *religious trade associations*, *religious press associations* and related terms failed to find a definitive database of religious publications. To identify scholarly research and theorizing about religious publications, the author consulted eight electronic databases and did extensive Internet searching, using a variety of keywords such as *religious publications*, *religious magazines* and *magazines and religion*, while also searching for articles using the names of dozens of religious magazines known to the author.[6] In addition to academic journals such as *Journalism & Mass Communication Quarterly* and *Journalism & Communication Monographs* (formerly *Journalism Monographs*), case studies about individual religious magazines and essays exploring cultural, historical and social issues within religious groups are mainly published in specialized journals such as *Journal of*

Communication and Religion, Journal of Media and Religion, Journal of Religion and Popular Culture and *Sociology of Religion*. The majority of the studies are descriptive, using historical or critical methodologies, or both. A few employed quantitative content analysis or surveys of religious magazine editors. Recently, scholars have studied religious magazines as a reflection of James Carey's communication as culture theory, in which these publications help readers form tribal identity and culture.[7] Other research has used theories of uses and gratification,[8] moral authority[9] and racial formation theory.[10]

Research emerging from this review points to four issues that could impact the future of the religious magazine form. These include the role religious magazines play in fostering dialogue with readers in ways that indirectly impact the larger culture; the manner in which religious magazines have helped readers formulate a unique tribal identity; the role that changing demographics may play in determining whether those publications will remain relevant and economically viable; and how the Internet is and will change both the content and form of religious magazines, perhaps increasing their usefulness or leading to their demise.[11]

Religious Dialogue and Identity

Descriptive and analytical studies of magazines associated with religious movements or denominations dominate published scholarly research. The premise of this research as applied to North American Christianity is summed up in the following statement: "When a theological, social, or political movement begins within American Christendom, it inevitably spawns a magazine or newspaper."[12] In similar fashion, the growth of Eastern religions, Islam and Mormonism has also spawned publications explaining those movements' boundaries and threats to their members. Scholars note that since the eighteenth century, "popular periodicals have been a major means of promoting personal religious commitment and of nurturing individual piety while advancing causes of denominations, new religious movements, and agencies calling for social reform."[13]

This use of periodicals to promote religious commitment and advocacy dominates past research, with a few studies examining the publishing landscape from the standpoint of the editors.[14] What this research shows is that the editorial foci and purposes of religious publications have changed little since *Christian History*, the first religious magazine in North America, was published from 1743 to 1745. That magazine presented reprints of noted sermons, religious news and even the movement of goods into ports along the eastern coast of the Colonies.[15] Another early magazine, *Christian Scholars and Farmers*, captured the editorial mission of a number of the early Colonial publications. Its three-fold purpose was "to promote religion, to diffuse useful knowledge, and to help farmers in their work."[16] Encouragement to believers to remain steady in the faith dominated the editorial intent of most early publications. "Religious magazines described their contents as 'edifying,' an idea which occurs so often the conclusion is inescapable that editors thought of the moral and spiritual benefiting of readers as their *raison d'être*."[17]

Historical studies have also noted the utility of religious magazines in helping immigrants bridge the gap between their former culture and that of their new surroundings. These non-English language publications included *Ein Geistliches Magazien* (A Religious Magazine) in the early eighteenth century.[18] Later, newspapers helped newly arrived Jewish immigrants navigate the difficult transition from Europe to America, and Spanish, Korean, Chinese and other language publications perform the same service today.[19]

By the early 1800s, enterprising ministers began publishing periodicals focusing on the targeted needs of readers. The most prominent African American magazine, the *Christian Recorder*, debuted in 1852 in Philadelphia as an organ of the African Methodist Episcopal

Church. Its editorial purpose was to provide a "program of 'racial uplift' that sought to raise the masses to its own social and cultural level as well as to theorize issues of black nationality."[20] The publication's various editors encouraged Black literacy, and its pages were often filled with lively debates over critical issues such as the African Emigration Movement.[21] Frederick G. Detweiler wrote, "This paper was looked upon by the slave holders of the South and proslavery people of the North as a very dangerous document or sheet, and was watched with a critical eye. It could not be circulated in the slave-holding states."[22] The *Recorder* still presents denominational news and identity-building information for African Americans today.

An enduring part of the American mindset is that of personal freedom. In a religious context, that meant anyone with a complaint against his or her denomination or church was free to split off and start a competing religious endeavor. Prominent among these were the founding and growth of the Church of Jesus Christ of Latter Day Saints (Mormons), started by Joseph Smith in 1830, and the founding of the Restoration Movement by a disgruntled Presbyterian Alexander Campbell and frustrated Baptist Barton Stone. Gaylord P. Albaugh claims that nearly 600 religious publications were printed during the first 100 years of the American Experiment. The largest number, 360, appeared between 1820 and 1829.[23] After that apex in the early Republic, Protestant influence on mainstream culture waned amidst the influx of immigrants from Eastern Europe, many of whom were Catholic and Jewish. Later the Scientific and Industrial revolutions with their focus on reason rather than faith undermined the intellectual appeal of religious belief.

In the early twentieth century, established denominational leaders within the Methodist, Lutheran and Presbyterian denominations sought through their seminaries and colleges to find ways to accommodate evolution and scientific explanations for life with biblical teaching. In 1917 an existing Disciples of Christ publication renamed itself the *Christian Century*, hoping to bridge denominational lines to unite believers desiring to accommodate the discoveries of science. This proved effective in 1923 when religious and mainstream papers descended on a small town in Tennessee to witness the trial of John Scopes. While the trial itself focused on whether Scopes had violated the law by teaching evolution, national reporting on the trial set an agenda of vigorous discussion about the Protestant faith.[24] Voices such as *Christian Century* were pitted against the more conservative Protestants who called themselves fundamentalists. Fundamentalists felt no need to accommodate science or evolution, preferring to continue to believe the Bible was the literal word of God. While Scopes was found guilty, the cultural verdict was that fundamentalists were backwards, illiterate believers out of touch with modern society. Church historians note that after the trial, the outpouring of ridicule caused conservative Protestants to retreat from engagement with the larger culture, even to the extent of retreating from voting.[25] The fundamentalist movement was not a denomination with a headquarters or leadership. Its believers, numbering in the millions, found newspapers and magazines, coupled with newly established Bible colleges, to be the main source of identity formation. Its publications went by names such as *Christian Beacon*,[26] *Christian Fundamentalist*, *King's Business* and *Sword of the Lord*.[27] In these periodicals believers could find solace in their doctrines and theology and read stories of likeminded believers battling infidelity found in mainstream culture.

This role performed in part by fundamentalist magazines is important because out of this movement a focus on evangelizing the *lost* gave rise to young preachers like the Rev. Billy Graham. Following World War II, Graham and his colleagues, who were associated with a high school outreach called Youth for Christ, began holding large crusades to preach to their peers, many of whom were young men shell-shocked by the horrors of war. "This new evangelistic thrust prompted moderate Fundamentalists to restore the movement's public image," noted *Moody Monthly* at the time.[28] Two influential evangelical publications arose from Graham's ministries. *Decision* magazine became the mouthpiece of his crusades, reaching hundreds of thousands of people with news about how faith in Christ was changing the hearts of people. While Graham was a product of the fundamentalist movement that began in the early twentieth century, several church historians refer to his ministry's influence as ushering in what they commonly refer to as the evangelical movement, a reformed fundamentalism stressing a return to social advocacy on the part of conservative Christians.[29] In 1956, feeling the need to better define that evangelical movement, Graham convinced donors to subsidize the start-up of *Christianity Today*. Recent studies credit the magazine with serving a key role in helping readers define their relationship to historic Protestant beliefs while challenging them to play an active role in confronting social justice and poverty around the world.[30] During the late twentieth century, more politically conservative groups within this evangelical movement pushed back against changing social mores, the legalization of abortion and the growth of government welfare programs by forming what became known as the Religious Right. Religious magazines such as *Christianity Today*, *WORLD*, *Sojourners* and others provided more nuanced, intellectual forums for pastors and denominational leaders to civilly discuss the challenges they faced in accommodating or confronting the changing cultural undercurrents.[31]

Less than a decade after Graham founded *Christianity Today*, the Catholic Church worldwide began a series of welcomed and feared changes as Pope John XXIII called leaders to the Vatican to renew the church and its focus on worship and concern for justice. Vatican II revolutionized the Catholic Church, and North Americans relied heavily on Catholic publications to help them process the enormity of change facing the church. The primary question of what it means to be a Catholic was one that publications such as *U.S. Catholic*, *Commonweal*, the *National Catholic Reporter* (formerly a diocesan newspaper) and *America* tried to answer for believers. The strength of these publications was that they were published outside a web of approval and occasional censorship from local bishops. In keeping with the questioning spirit of the times, Denise P. Ferguson notes that these independent magazines "challenged church positions on celibacy of priests, birth control and abortion, the role of women in the church, the priest shortage, and the clergy sex abuse scandals."[32] Indeed, she claims the *National Catholic Reporter* first published a story on sexual abuse by priests in 1985, but the national furor over numerous incidents did not reach mainstream readers until seven years later when the *Boston Globe* published the first of its investigative stories."[33] Even as they called into question actions of church leaders, these publications played a key role in helping explain to jittery church members the changes in worship from Latin and a renewed emphasis on advocating for the poor.

Jewish publications first appeared in the 1840s and aimed at helping with the "diffusion of knowledge on Jewish literature and religion."[34] Later publications, such as *Commentary*, attempted to redefine what it meant to be a Jew after the horrors of the Holocaust. While its political leanings have changed over the years, the publication's first editor, Elliott Cohen, directed the publication at Jewish intellectuals. "*Commentary* showed Jews how to weave the strands of Jewishness into the texture of American life."[35] The magazine was the first to publish the diaries of Anne Frank in a two-part series and has been a staunch defender of Israel.[36]

This summary of historical research shows a religious press in the colonies and early Republic assuming all who lived in the emerging nation held to a Protestant worldview and how that Protestant worldview was losing ascendency to the rise of modernism, industrialism, multiculturalism and a variety of other social changes. By the early twentieth century, religious publications focused on educating and encouraging tribal groupings of readers rather than the larger society. Secular mass media—the plethora of metropolitan newspapers, national magazines and electronic media—pushed both religion and religious publications to the margins of the public sphere. "Today all social institutions, including the church and the state, must submit themselves to the conditions of the mediated public realm in order to exist in the public sphere."[37]

In the absence of religious conversation in mainstream media, sociologists studying religious magazines have noted these periodicals help individuals with identity formation. Lester R. Kurtz summarized this truth when he wrote, "The beliefs of a religious tradition never stand in isolation, either from one another or from the life of the community."[38] Quentin J. Schultze suggested these periodicals help believers form their own identity and "engage clergy and lay members of churches in vigorous conversations about important events, ideas, and artistic expressions that are shaping culture far beyond the boundaries of the ecclesiastical channels."[39] He argues these publications provide collective ways of knowing and interpreting the world through the eyes of faith. Throughout America's history, he contends, religious publications have fostered a rhetoric of communication and discernment as these dialogues unfold. "In the United States, the religious press has been one of the most important vehicles for bringing people of faith into a shared public space to converse about the broader society."[40]

While helping readers negotiate their identity as members of a religious group, religious publications have indirectly influenced mainstream culture. Schultze notes that these periodicals serve a valuable mediation role between religious beliefs and mainstream culture, between what he calls "the tribe's transcendent metanarrative and the wider culture's sub narratives of immanent meaning and significance."[41] Put another way, "religious periodicals can press for forms of rhetorical discernment that engage the tribe in the broader conversations about the nature of the good life in contemporary society."[42] This has been the most important role religious magazines have played in the lives of its readers and, by extension, the culture in general.

Methods, theories and scholarly assumptions about religious media in North America may not be easily applied to religious publications from other cultures. In an analysis of religious media usage and gratification in Kuwait, Al-Kandari suggests uses and gratification theory must be altered to include both "individual-religious and social-religious gratifications," as the identity of a Muslim is linked to both her relationship with Allah and society.[43] A person's religious identity in Islam is intricately linked to his community. Even the state is subject to Allah. Scholars are already arguing that any analysis of non-Western press activity must rely on a broadened understanding of the role of culture and politics, as long-standing assumptions based on ideas like the Four Theories of the Press are insufficient.[44] Future research on religious magazines must be sensitive to these scholarly realities.

Social Concerns

Concern for social justice and good works toward others is a prominent theme in many religious publications. Religious publications have encouraged advocacy on behalf of the poor, activism for human rights and analyses of political and social issues. This section details research on how magazines have communicated to readers about these important topics. Within Christian denominations in North America, there is often a symbiotic relationship between a cause and a magazine created to further educate people about that cause. In the 1930s, for instance, Catholic convert Dorothy Day founded the Catholic Worker's movement, a communist-inspired group advocating for an end to hunger and oppression in the United States. Within a year of the group's founding, the *Catholic Worker* began its influential run as a religious publication aimed mainly at Catholic believers. The publication gradually moderated its radical social positions and became a voice of reason, uniting Catholic radicals strongly opposed to the Vietnam War and continued abuses of capitalism, while keeping ties open with the established Catholic Church.[45]

After World War II, the growing missionary movement encouraged individuals to take a message of Christian peace throughout the world. As they did, though, faith-based people recognized that many in the world were too ill or distracted by poverty or oppression to hear and process a religious message. A more practical approach, they noted, called for believers to meet peoples' physical and emotional needs first. Two magazines exemplify the rush of religious believers to publish magazines with these editorial themes. In 1950, an associate of Billy Graham named Bob Pierce substituted for Graham in giving a series of evangelical crusades on mainland China. Pierce was so stricken by the poverty around him, and the plight of orphans and women in particular, that he returned to the United States vowing to help. He began raising funds in churches to send to China and later to Korea as the war there created hundreds of thousands of orphans and refugees. Eventually Pierce, a pioneer in the use of visual media to communicate the emotion of human tragedy, founded an organization called World Vision to funnel funds to Asian orphans and widows. In 1952, he started publishing *World Vision* magazine. For the past 60 years, this magazine has touted the success the organization and its partner agencies have achieved, thanks to the generosity of its individual and corporate donors. *World Vision*, distributed to some 400,000 U.S. households, has tried to encourage individuals to take an active role in providing resources to eradicate poverty and injustice while also lobbying government leaders to provide more international aid.[46]

Sojourners magazine and its editor Jim Wallis gained national visibility in recent years as an evangelical progressive who has advised President Barack Obama on social issues.[47] Wallis began his magazine in 1972 to challenge evangelicals to take an active involvement in opposing the Vietnam War and nuclear arms build-ups and channeling their funds and advocacy into programs to help the poor, even if those programs were run by the government. The magazine's content focuses on analysis of public policy decisions and proposals and profiles of people living out their commitments as peacemakers in the world's toughest places.[48]

Both *World Vision* and *Sojourners* were at the forefront of Protestant magazines sounding the alarm about the AIDS crisis in Africa. Researchers have found evidence to suggest the magazines may have indirectly influenced the large American offensive against HIV and AIDS launched under the George W. Bush administration.[49]

Not all religious magazines with a social justice focus have kept sufficient readership to survive financially. In a 2011 study that included the fate of magazines reaching members of the progressive evangelicals, David R. Swartz listed eight publications focused on social justice issues during the 1970s.[50] Today only two of those publications exist. He cites "identity politics" as a partial explanation for the demise of the movement and its publications, as disparate groups of evangelicals identified more closely with their race, gender, or both, and thus struggled to reach unity because of differing ways to ameliorate centuries of what they felt were oppressive viewpoints from a largely male and white dominance of American evangelicalism.[51] A book-length case study of the influential journal *Christianity and Crisis* further illuminates the issues that confronted the attempts among Protestants to unite their evangelistic and social justice foci.[52]

The role of women in the leadership of male-dominated religious groups remains a continual topic of study for scholars. Therese L. Leuck's case study of a missionary publication from the nineteenth century argues that Christian feminism began before the movement toward universal suffrage and role of women in ministry.[53] Janet M. Cramer uses post-colonial theory to show how three women's missionary periodicals marginalized non-white women in their crusade to recruit single female missionaries.[54] The role of women in the Mormon Church has been the topic of several studies about women. Lisa Olsen Tait asserts that the *Young Women's Journal* was as an attempt to help young Mormon women understand their identity in the emerging church as the magazine provided

> a public female space, the sisterly editorial voice, and the dialogism—sometimes dissonant—of the magazine form. At the core of the *Young Woman's Journal* was a specific generational voice, addressing itself to the 'girls' in response to the pressures and transitions registering in Mormondom during a pivotal decade.[55]

In analyzing a group of Mormon periodicals from 1897 to 1999, Laura Vance notes that women and men are often equals in the battle to create or defend a new religion. As the religion gains acceptance, however, women tend to be marginalized. She shows how this theory works itself out in the changing content of Mormon magazines during this nearly 100-year period. Today, Mormon magazines usually parrot the official viewpoints of their leaders that women should work outside the home only under unusual circumstances, such as the loss of a spouse.[56] The official magazine of the Mormon Church, *Ensign*, was outspoken in its opposition to the Equal Rights Amendment and, more recently, has forcefully set forth the church's opposition to gay marriage.[57] Helen M. Sterk analyzed 10 years of articles appearing in the *Journal of Communication and Religion* and found the number of articles studying the intersection of faith and feminism sorely lacking.[58]

Recent social issues such as race and religion,[59] homosexuality and gay marriage,[60] and the relationship between religious belief and care for the environment[61] have only recent attracted scholarly attention.

Changing Demographics

Religious magazine editors, always working with limited budgets and the threat of extinction, face even greater headwinds in the future. All of these concerns are areas where scholars of the future need to focus their attention.

An Increasingly Multicultural Environment

Throughout the world, people are on the move. Immigration resulting from globalization and refugees brings not only new ethnic groups into receptive countries, but new religious expressions as well. In the United States, 70 percent of Americans are still white, and this group forms the primary readers of most Protestant and Roman Catholic publications. But recent census data say 52 million Latinos live in the United States, a 48 percent increase since the year 2000. The majority of this growth comes from birth, not immigration.[62] Likewise, the Asian American population is growing as a percentage, with approximately 18.2 million people residing in the United States. Asian American Christians (42 percent), primarily Koreans, comprise the largest religious affiliation, while 26 percent express no affiliation.[63] Protestant editors look ahead to a future with fewer potential readers as these populations are unlikely to begin reading magazines that have historically been edited to white Protestants. Non-Christian expressions of religion in North America are growing, and magazines catering to those religious expressions are growing.[64]

The Rise of the "Nones"

Perhaps more concerning to editors of religious publications and scholars is the declining number of Americans professing any sort of religious belief. From 2007 to 2012, the number of Americans identifying themselves as Christian declined from 78 percent to 73 percent.[65] White Protestants declined from 53 percent to 48 percent of the population, with evangelicals and mainline Protestants both losing about 3 percentage points. Black Protestants meanwhile, have held steady at 8 percent of the population. "Other" religions have grown from 4 percent to 6 percent of the population, while the most noteworthy number is that of people who consider themselves unaffiliated or "none." This category has grown from 15 to nearly 20 percent of the overall population from 2007 to 2012. The growth of those professing no religious affiliation is most noteworthy among younger generations. Twenty-nine percent of Americans say they have never gone to church, a 4 percent increase since 2003.

Internet Challenges

The Internet may pose the biggest challenge to the future of religious magazines. While evangelicals have a history of embracing new technologies and have not been afraid to experiment with differing ways to ensure economic viability on the Web, the challenges are daunting. Future researchers would do well to consider emerging trends in how religious publications are adapting to the Web. Several studies may be useful. One is to analyze the growth of *Relevant*, which began as an on-line Web site for young adults and teens to converse around topics of interest. Only later did it also publish a hard copy magazine. Another trend is the use of the Web to create international religious magazines. Headquartered in Washington DC, the on-line *Christian Post*, for example, boasts a wide variety of news, commentary and bloggers discussing international and national events from a Christian worldview. Another fruitful area of study is the success of existing publications that have moved on-line and created a *brand* rather than magazine Web sites. Christian publications *Christianity Today*, *Sojourners*, *WORLD* and *Relevant* all feature a Web presence with daily updates and a variety of blogs that never appear in their print editions. Will this multimedia approach to religious communication actually increase the reach and influence of these publications? Initial evidence says yes; the issue, then, will be achieving financial viability in this new environment. Finally, the Internet is not available in all households. Will lack of access serve as a deterrent to the consumption of religious magazines?

Another fruitful area for international scholars of religious magazines is presented in a recent study by Hamid Abdollahyan, who surveyed younger Iranian students. He found traditional religious media in Iran furthered the religious beliefs of those surveyed, yet found Internet users with access to the broader world of religious ideas reflected a more global mode of behavior "that challenges their religious identity."[66]

A closely related area of research is economic survival. Most religious publications survive with limited or no advertising revenue, and subscription revenue usually doesn't cover the entire operation of editorial salaries, design, printing, marketing and subscription fulfillment. Thus, subsidies from organizations or grants from foundations, even individual gifts, have kept some magazines afloat.[67] In recent years, once thriving general interest publications such as *Moody Monthly* and *Christian Herald* failed to remain financially viable and were discontinued, while denominationally sponsored publications such as *DisciplesWorld* and the *United Methodist Reporter* met the same fate.[68]

Future Research Possibilities

Fruitful research can continue to be conducted in topic areas such as how personal and corporate identity is shaped by religious publications and how those publications help readers negotiate the seeming dichotomy between personal piety and social action. Yet shifts in methodology, context and application are necessary. More theory building is also necessary. Some suggested areas follow:

First, while research on religious periodicals may be slim, most of that research is focused on North American magazines. For internationally focused scholars, the role of religious publications in identity construction and social action within world religions other than Christianity and Judaism is a ripe field of study. Second, researchers in North America and Europe might pay more attention to the interrelationship between religious groups where Christianity once had a hegemonic presence. How do Muslim, Buddhist and Hindu publications, not to mention non-traditional religious expressions, define themselves as outsiders within the larger culture? And how might the content of long-standing Christian publications change as readers encounter a more globalized and multi-cultural world?

A third area of research might compare the culture and political organization of nation-states with the presence of religious publications. In Islam, there is no separation between church and state. Thus there may not be explicitly religious publications at all, given that any media in a Muslim state must be subservient to the Islamic religion. All of what Westerners call mainstream media are therefore religious. The sociology of religion and its effect upon the presence or absence of religious magazines is thus an area that at present is unexplored outside of the North American context. Fourth, again, from a sociological standpoint, why are there few studies of religious publications in Europe? Do religious publications exist, and if so, what purposes do they serve?

Fifth, applied research is also needed. Religious publications may arise to support a denomination or cause, but these publications are not immune to economic and technological struggles. Are there case studies in how religious magazines have achieved economic stability that might be instructive to other religious publications? Sixth, the Internet not only serves to diffuse religious belief, but it also provides anyone with a computer the opportunity to start a religious e-zine. How might content of on-line only publications differ from more traditional print publications? Seventh, as print magazines migrate to the Web, how are they engaging new audiences? What types of paywalls and other methods for monetizing Web site content are print magazines using? Further research should also consider whether or how magazines are not only moving to multiple delivery platforms for content, but how the content is changed through the creation of sites where news and commentary are continuously updated. Are magazines moving to create something closer to a communication brand than a magazine? Will there be a resulting move toward a new definition for the term *magazine*?

These are only a few of the fruitful areas of future research in the area of religious magazines. Throughout history humans have sought answers to the big questions of life outside their own existence, namely through religious explanations. As long as this human impulse continues, people will continue to seek answers through mediated content. How magazines and their content negotiate today's cultural and technological challenges, as well as those in the future, should continue to engage scholars for decades to come.

Notes

1 Nelson R. Burr, *A Critical Bibliography of Religion in America*, Religion in American Life, eds. James Ward Smith and A. Leland Jamison, vol. 4 (Princeton, NJ: Princeton University Press, 1961), 952.

2 Martin E. Marty, "The Protestant Press: Limitations and Possibilities," in Martin E. Marty, John G. Deedy, Jr., David Wolf Silverman, and Robert Lekachman, eds., *The Religious Press in America* (New York: Holt, Rinehart and Winston, 1963), 9.

3 Heather Hendershot, *Shaking the World for Jesus: Media and Conservative Evangelical Culture* (Chicago: University of Chicago Press, 2004), 6.

4 Denise P. Ferguson, "The Independent Catholic Press and Vatican II," in Diane H. Winston, ed., *The Oxford Handbook of Religion and the American News Media* (New York: Oxford University Press, 2012), 509; "Directory," Evangelical Press Association <http://www.evangelicalpress.com/member-list>, accessed 29 November 2013; "Welcome to ARPA!" The Australasian Religious Press Association <http://www.arpanews.org>, accessed 29 November 2013.

5 See "About Mission Training International." Mission Training International <http://mti.org>, accessed 30 November 2013.

6 Databases searched include Academic Search Complete, American Periodicals Series Online, ATLA Religion Database, Communication & Mass Communication Complete, Dissertations and Theses, JSTOR and Pro Quest Religion.

7 Quentin J. Schultze, "Leading the Tribes out of Exile: The Religious Press Discerns Broadcasting," *Christianity and the Mass Media in America: Toward a Democratic Accommodation* (East Lansing: Michigan State University Press, 2003), 89–138.

8 Ali A.J. Al-Kandari, "Predicting the Clash of Civilizations: The Use and Impact of Religious Media in Kuwait," *Journal of Media and Religion* 10.4 (2011): 206–223.

9 Jeremy N. Thomas and Daniel V.A. Olson, "Evangelical Elites' Changing Responses to Homosexuality 1960–2009," *Sociology of Religion* 73.3 (2012): 239–272.

10 Antony W. Alumkal, "American Evangelicalism in the Post-Civil Rights Era: A Racial Formation Theory Analysis," *Sociology of Religion* 65.3 (Fall 2004): 195–213.

11 See, for instance, Nat Ives, "Magazines Shape Up for Digital Future," *Advertising Age*, 17 April 2006 <http://adage.com/article/media/magazines-shape-digital-future/108620>, accessed 28 November 2013; Graydon Carter, "Print Is Dying . . . Really?" *Brandweek*, 29 March 2010, 37; and Mark Hooper, "Who Says Print Is Dead?" *Guardian*, 3 June 2012 <http://www.theguardian.com/media/2012/jun/03/who-says-print-is-dead/print>, accessed 28 November 2013.

12 Charles Austin, "The History and Role of the Protestant Press," in Benjamin J. Hubbard, ed., *Reporting Religion: Facts and Faith* (Sonoma, CA: Polebridge Press, 1990), 108.

13 P. Mark Fackler and Charles H. Lippy, eds., *Popular Religious Magazines of the United States* (Westport, CT: Greenwood Press, 1995), xvii.

14 See, for instance, Roberta J. Moore, "The Beginning and Development of Protestant Journalism in the United States, 1743–1850" (Ph.D. diss., Syracuse University, 1968); Barbara Straus Reed, "The Antebellum Jewish Press: Origins, Problems, Functions," *Journalism Monographs* 139 (June 1993): 1–42; Marvin Olasky, *Telling the Truth: How to Revitalize Christian Journalism* (Wheaton, IL: Crossway Books, 1996). Studies examining magazines from the editors' standpoint include Ken Waters, "Vibrant, but Invisible: A Study of Contemporary Religious Periodicals," *Journalism & Mass Communication Quarterly* 78.2 (Summer 2001): 307–320; and Douglas J. Trouten, "The Development of Professionalization in the Evangelical Press Association" (M.A. thesis, University of Minnesota, 1999).

15 Moore, "The Beginning and Development of Protestant Journalism," 19.

16 Nathan O. Hatch, *The Democratization of American Christianity* (New Haven, CT: Yale University Press, 1989), 8.

17 Moore, "The Beginning and Development of Protestant Journalism," 7.

18 Ken Waters, "The Evangelical Press," in Diane H. Winston, ed., *The Oxford Handbook of Religion and the American News Media* (New York: Oxford University Press, 2012), 553.

19 Reed, "The Antebellum Jewish Press," 7–9.

20 Carla L. Peterson, *"Doers of the Word": African-American Women Speakers and Writers in the North (1830–1880)* (New York: Oxford University Press, 1995), 11. See also, Mitch Kachun, "Interrogating the Silences: Julia C. Collins, 19th-Century Black Readers and Writers, and the *Christian Recorder*," *African American Review* 40.4 (Winter 2006): 649–659; and Dennis C. Dickerson and Robert H. Reid, Jr., "*Christian Recorder*," in P. Mark Fackler and Charles H. Lippy, eds., *Popular Religious Magazines of the United States* (Westport, CT: Greenwood Press, 1995), 162–167.

21 Gilbert Anthony Williams, "The Role of the *Christian Recorder* in the African Emigration Movement, 1854–1902," *Journalism Monographs* 111 (April 1989); see also, Gilbert Anthony Williams, "The A.M.E. *Christian Recorder*: A Forum for the Social Ideas of Black Americans, 1854–1902" (Ph.D. diss., University of Illinois, 1979).

22 Frederick G. Detweiler, *The Negro Press in the United States* (Chicago: University of Chicago Press, 1922), 42.

23 Gaylord P. Albaugh, *History and Annotated Bibliography of American Religious Periodicals and Newspapers Established from 1730 through 1830* (Worcester, MA: American Antiquarian Society, 1994), quoted in Marcia Bolton Rivers, "Old, New, Borrowed, Read: The Powers and Problems of American Protestant Periodicals— Then and Now" (Capstone research paper presented to Northeastern Seminary, 22 July 2004), 6.

24 Elesha Coffman, "The Measure of a Magazine: Assessing the Influence of the *Christian Century*," *Religion and American Culture: A Journal of Interpretation* 22.1 (Winter 2012): 53–82.

25 See, for instance, George M. Marsden, *Fundamentalism and American Culture: The Shaping of Twentieth-Century Evangelicalism: 1870–1925*, 2nd ed. (New York: Oxford University Press, 2006).

26 Thomas Ferris, "*Christian Beacon*," in Ronald Lora and William Henry Longton, eds., *The Conservative Press in Twentieth-Century America* (Westport, CT: Greenwood Press, 1999), 141–153; and Ruotsila Markku, "Carl McIntire and the Fundamentalist Origins of the Christian Right," *Church History* 81.2 (June 2012): 378–407.

27 See for instance, W. Russell Congleton, "*Sword of the Lord*," in P. Mark Fackler and Charles H. Lippy, eds., *Popular Religious Magazines of the United States* (Westport, CT: Greenwood Press, 1995), 457–462.

28 Joel A. Carpenter, "*Moody Monthly*, 1900-," in Ronald Lora and William Henry Longton, eds., *The Conservative Press in Twentieth-Century America* (Westport, CT: Greenwood Press, 1999), 107.

29 Curtis J. Evans, "White Evangelical Protestant Responses to the Civil Rights Movement," *Harvard Theological Review* 102.2 (April 2009): 245–273.

30 Phyllis Elaine Alsdurf, "*Christianity Today* Magazine and Late Twentieth Century Evangelicalism" (Ph.D. diss., University of Minnesota, 2004), 68–100. See also Mark G. Toulouse, "*Christianity Today* and American Public Life: A Case Study," *Journal of Church and State* 35.2 (Spring 1993): 241–284; Thomas and Olson, "Evangelical Elites' Changing Responses to Homosexuality," 239–272.

31 See Ken Waters, "Evangelical Magazines," in Robert H. Woods, Jr., ed., *Evangelical Christians and Popular Culture: Pop Goes the Gospel*, vol. 3 (Santa Barbara, CA: Praeger, 2013), 195–211; and Ken Waters, "Pursuing New Periodicals in Print and Online," in Quentin J. Schultze and Robert H. Woods, Jr., eds., *Understanding Evangelical Media: The Changing Face of Christian Communication* (Downers Grove, IL: IVP Academic, 2008), 71–84.

32 Ferguson, "The Independent Catholic Press and Vatican II," 518.

33 Ferguson, "The Independent Catholic Press and Vatican II," 518.

34 Quoted in Jonathan D. Sarna, "The American Jewish Press," in Diane H. Winston, ed., *The Oxford Handbook of Religion and the American News Media* (New York: Oxford University Press, 2012), 539.

35 Edward Alexander, review of *Running Commentary: The Contentious Magazine that Transformed the Jewish Left into the Neoconservative Right*," by Benjamin Balint, in *Modern Judaism* 31.1 (February 2011): 104.

36 Alexander, review of *Running Commentary*, 105.

37 Stewart M. Hoover, "Mass Media and Religious Pluralism," in Philip Lee, ed., *The Democratization of Communication* (Cardiff: University of Wales Press, 1995), 190.

38 Lester R. Kurtz, *Gods in the Global Village: The World's Religions in Sociological Perspective*, 2nd ed., Sociology for a New Century (Thousand Oaks, CA: Pine Forge Press, 2007), 12.

39 Schultze, "Leading the Tribes out of Exile," 90–91.

40 Schultze, "Leading the Tribes out of Exile," 100.

41 Schultze, quoting Mary Patrice Thaman in "Leading the Tribes out of Exile," 93.

42 Schultze, "Leading the Tribes out of Exile," 102.

43 Al-Kandari, "Predicting the Clash of Civilizations," 210.

44 Jaifei Yin, "Beyond the Four Theories of the Press: A New Model for the Asian and the World Press," *Journalism & Communication Monographs* 10.1 (Spring 2008): 3–62.

45 Sarah Ann Mehltretter, "Dorothy Day, the Catholic Workers, and Moderation in Religious Protest during the Vietnam War," *Journal of Communication and Religion* 32.1 (March 2009): 1–32. See also, Nancy L. Roberts, "Journalism for Justice: Dorothy Day and the *Catholic Worker*," *Journalism History* 10.1/2 (Spring/ Summer 1983): 2–9.

46 Ken Waters, "*World Vision*," in P. Mark Fackler and Charles H. Lippy, eds., *Popular Religious Magazines of the United States* (Westport, CT: Greenwood Press, 1995), 537–542; and John Robert Hamilton, "An Historical Study of Bob Pierce and World Vision's Development of the Evangelical Social Action Film" (Ph.D. diss., University of Southern California, 1980), 7.

47 Dan Gilgoff, "Evangelical Minister Jim Wallis Is in Demand in Obama's Washington," *U.S. News*, 31 March 2009 <http://www.usnews.com/news/religion/articles/2009/03/31/evangelical-minister-jim-wallis-is-in-demand-in-obamas-washington>, accessed 28 November 2013.

48 See Bohn David Lattin and Steve Underhill, "*The Soul of Politics*: The Reverend Jim Wallis's Attempt to Transcend the Religious/Secular Left and the Religious Right," *Journal of Communication and Religion* 29.2 (November 2006): 205–223; and David R. Swartz, "Identity Politics and the Fragmenting of the 1970s Evangelical Left," *Religion and American Culture: A Journal of Interpretation* 21.1 (Winter 2011): 81–120.

49 Elizabeth Smith, Josh Fleer, and Ken Waters, "Deviating from the Pack: How Religious Publications Frame the AIDS in Africa Crisis" (Unpublished paper, Pepperdine University, 2004).

50 Swartz, "Identity Politics and the Fragmenting of the 1970s Evangelical Left," 81–120.

51 Swartz, "Identity Politics and the Fragmenting of the 1970s Evangelical Left," 82.

52 Mark Hulsether, *Building a Protestant Left*: Christianity and Crisis *Magazine, 1941–1993* (Knoxville: University of Tennessee Press, 1999); see also, Peter Steinfels, "Influential Christian Journal Prints Last Issue," *New York Times*, 4 April 1993 <http://www.nytimes.com/1993/04/04/us/influential-christian-journal-prints-last-issue.html>, accessed 29 November 2013.

53 Therese L. Lueck, "Women's Moral Reform Periodicals of the 19th Century: A Cultural Feminist Analysis of the *Advocate*," *American Journalism* 16.3 (Summer 1999): 37–52.

54 Janet M. Cramer, "White Womanhood and Religion: Colonial Discourse in the U.S. Women's Missionary Press, 1869–1904," *Howard Journal of Communications* 14.4 (2003): 209–224.

55 Lisa Olsen Tait, "The *Young Woman's Journal*: Gender and Generations in a Mormon Women's Magazine," *American Periodicals* 22.1 (2012): 53.

56 Laura Vance, "Evolution of Ideals for Women in Mormon Periodicals, 1897–1999," *Sociology of Religion* 63.1 (Spring 2002): 96.

57 Vance, "Evolution of Ideals for Women in Mormon Periodicals," 110.

58 Helen M. Sterk, "Faith, Feminism and Scholarship: *The Journal of Communication and Religion*, 1999–2009," [Special Issue], *Journal of Communication and Religion* 33.2 (November 2010): 206–216; see also, Helen M. Sterk, "How Rhetoric Becomes Real: Religious Sources of Gender Identity," *Journal of Communication and Religion* 12.2 (September 1989): 24–33.

59 John M. Giggie, "The African American Religious Press," in Diane H. Winston, ed., *The Oxford Handbook of Religion and the American News Media* (New York: Oxford University Press, 2012), 580–591; David A. Hollinger, "After Cloven Tongues of Fire: Ecumenical Protestantism and the Modern American Encounter with Diversity," *Journal of American History* 98.1 (June 2011): 21–48; Gregory A. Prince, "'Let the Truth Heal': The Making of *Nobody Knows: The Untold Story of Black Mormons*," *Dialogue: A Journal of Mormon Thought* 42.3 (Fall 2009): 74–100.

60 Thomas and Olson, "Evangelical Elites' Changing Responses to Homosexuality 1960–2009," 239–272.

61 Raymond E. Grizzle, Paul E. Rothrock, and Christopher Barrett, "Evangelicals and Environmentalism: Past, Present, and Future," *Trinity Journal* 19.1 (Spring 1998): 3–27.

62 Suro, Roberto and Associates, "Changing Faiths: Latinos and the Transformation of American Religion," *Pew Forum on Religion & Public Life*. Washington, DC: Pew Research Center, March 2007 <http://www.pewforum.org/uploadedfiles/Topics/Demographics/hispanics-religion-07-final-mar08.pdf>, accessed 8 July 2013; see also, Stephen Ceasar, "Hispanic Population Tops 50 Million in U.S.," *Los Angeles Times*, 24 March 2011 <http://articles.latimes.com/2011/mar/24/nation/la-na-census-hispanic-20110325>, accessed 8 July 2013.

63 "Asian Americans: A Mosaic of Faiths," Pew Research: Religion and Public Life Project, PewForum.org, 19 July 2012 <http://www.pewforum.org/Asian-Americans-A-Mosaic-of-Faiths.aspx>, accessed 15 June 2013.

64 See Faiza Hirji, "One Nation, Many Voices: The Muslim Press in the United States," in Diane H. Winston, ed., *The Oxford Handbook of Religion and the American News Media* (New York: Oxford University Press, 2012), 565–578; and Mohammad A. Siddiqi, "Muslim Media: Present Status and Future Directions," *Gazette* 47.1 (February 1991): 19–31.

65 "'Nones on the Rise,'" Pew Research: Religion and Public Life Project, 9 October 2012 <http://www.pewforum.org/2012/10/09/nones-on-the-rise>, accessed 15 June 2013.

66 Hamid Abdollahyan, "Gender and Generations Modes of Religiosity: Locality versus Globality of Iranian Media," *Journal of Media and Religion* 7.1/2 (2008): 4.

67 Waters, "Vibrant, but Invisible," 301.

68 "*DisciplesWorld* Magazine, Website to Cease Publishing; Non-Profit to Dissolve," *DisciplesWorld*, 16 December 2009 <http://www.disciplesworldmagazine.com/node/7486>, accessed 29 November 2013; Michael Gryboski, "United Methodist Publication '*Reporter*' Founded in 1840s to Close," *Christian Post*, 17 May 2013 <http://www.christianpost.com/news/united-methodist-publication-reporter-founded-in-1840s-to-close-96140/>, accessed 29 November 2013; and Todd Hertz and Stan Guthrie, "Moody Closes Magazine, Restructures Aviation Program," *Christianity Today*, 1 February 2003 <http://www.christianitytoday.com/ct/2003/februaryweb-only/2–24–21.0.html>, accessed 29 November 2013.

Bibliography

Abdollahyan, Hamid. "Gender and Generations Modes of Religiosity: Locality versus Globality of Iranian Media." *Journal of Media and Religion* 7.1/2 (2008): 4–33.

"About Mission Training International." Mission Training International <http://mti.org>, accessed 30 November 2013.

Albaugh, Gaylord P. *History and Annotated Bibliography of American Religious Periodicals and Newspapers Established from 1730 through 1830.* Worcester, MA: American Antiquarian Society, 1994.

Alexander, Edward. Review of *Running Commentary: The Contentious Magazine that Transformed the Jewish Left into the Neoconservative Right*, by Benjamin Balint. In *Modern Judaism* 31.1 (February 2011): 103–108.

Al-Kandari, Ali A.J. "Predicting the Clash of Civilizations: The Use and Impact of Religious Media in Kuwait." *Journal of Media and Religion* 10.4 (2011): 206–223.

Alsdurf, Phyllis Elaine. "*Christianity Today* Magazine and Late Twentieth-Century Evangelism." Ph.D. diss., University of Minnesota, 2004.

Alumkal, Antony W. "American Evangelicalism in the Post-Civil Rights Era: A Racial Formation Theory Analysis." *Sociology of Religion* 65.3 (Fall 2004): 195–213.

"Asian Americans: A Mosaic of Faiths." Pew Research: Religion and Public Life Project. PewForum. org, 19 July 2012 <http://www.pewforum.org/Asian-Americans-A-Mosaic-of-Faiths.aspx>, accessed 15 June 2013.

Austin, Charles. "The History and Role of the Protestant Press." In Hubbard, Benjamin J., ed. *Reporting Religion: Facts and Faith*. Sonoma, CA: Polebridge Press, 1990, 108–117.

Burr, Nelson R. *A Critical Bibliography of Religion in America*. Religion in American Life. Edited by James Ward Smith and A. Leland Jamison. Vol. 4. Princeton, NJ: Princeton University Press, 1961.

Carpenter, Joel A. "*Moody Monthly*, 1900-." In Lora, Ronald and Longton, William Henry, eds. *The Conservative Press in Twentieth-Century America*. Westport, CT: Greenwood Press, 1999, 103–111.

Carter, Graydon. "Print Is Dying . . . Really?" *Brandweek*, 29 March 2010, 37.

Ceasar, Stephen. "Hispanic Population Tops 50 Million in U.S." *Los Angeles Times*, 24 March 2011 <http://articles.latimes.com/2011/mar/24/nation/la-na-census-hispanic-20110325>, accessed 8 July 2013.

Coffman, Elesha. "The Measure of a Magazine: Assessing the Influence of the *Christian Century*." *Religion and American Culture: A Journal of Interpretation* 22.1 (Winter 2012): 53–82.

Congleton, W. Russell. "*Sword of the Lord*." In Fackler, P. Mark and Lippy, Charles H., eds. *Popular Religious Magazines of the United States*. Westport, CT: Greenwood Press, 1995, 457–462.

Cramer, Janet M. "White Womanhood and Religion: Colonial Discourse in the U.S. Women's Missionary Press, 1869–1904." *Howard Journal of Communications* 14.4 (2003): 209–224.

Detweiler, Frederick G. *The Negro Press in the United States*. Chicago: University of Chicago Press, 1922.

Dickerson, Dennis C. and Reid, Robert H., Jr. "*Christian Recorder*." In Fackler, P. Mark and Lippy, Charles H., eds. *Popular Religious Magazines of the United States*. Westport, CT: Greenwood Press, 1995, 162–167.

"Directory." Evangelical Press Association <http://www.evangelicalpress.com/member-list>, accessed 29 November 2013.

"*DisciplesWorld* Magazine, Website to Cease Publishing; Non-Profit to Dissolve." *DisciplesWorld*, 16 December 2009 <http://www.disciplesworldmagazine.com/node/7486>, accessed 28 November 2013.

Evans, Curtis J. "White Evangelical Protestant Responses to the Civil Rights Movement." *Harvard Theological Review* 102.2 (April 2009): 245–273.

Fackler, P. Mark and Lippy, Charles H., eds. *Popular Religious Magazines of the United States*. Westport, CT: Greenwood Press, 1995.

Ferguson, Denise P. "The Independent Catholic Press and Vatican II." In Winston, Diane H., ed. *The Oxford Handbook of Religion and the American News Media*. New York: Oxford University Press, 2012, 509–522.

Ferris, Thomas. "*Christian Beacon*." In Lora, Ronald and Longton, William Henry, eds. *The Conservative Press in Twentieth-Century America*. Westport, CT: Greenwood Press, 1999, 141–153.

Giggie, John M. "The African American Religious Press." In Winston, Diane H., ed. *The Oxford Handbook of Religion and the American News Media*. New York: Oxford University Press, 2012, 579–592.

Gilgoff, Dan. "Evangelical Minister Jim Wallis Is in Demand in Obama's Washington." *U.S. News*, 31 March 2009 <http://www.usnews.com/news/religion/articles/2009/03/31/evangelical-minister-jim-wallis-is-in-demand-in-obamas-washington>, accessed 28 November 2013.

Grizzle, Raymond E.; Rothrock, Paul E.; and Barrett, Christopher B. "Evangelicals and Environmentalism: Past, Present, and Future." *Trinity Journal* 19.1 (Spring 1998): 3–27.

Gryboski, Michael. "United Methodist Publication '*Reporter*' Founded in 1840s to Close." *Christian Post*, 17 May 2013 <http://www.christianpost.com/news/united-methodist-publication-reporter-founded-in-1840s-to-close-96140/>, accessed 29 November 2013.

Hamilton, John Robert. "An Historical Study of Bob Pierce and World Vision's Development of the Evangelical Social Action Film." Ph.D. diss., University of Southern California, 1980.

Hatch, Nathan O. *The Democratization of American Christianity*. New Haven, CT: Yale University Press, 1989.

Hendershot, Heather. *Shaking the World for Jesus: Media and Conservative Evangelical Culture*. Chicago: University of Chicago Press, 2004.

Hertz, Todd and Guthrie, Stan. "Moody Closes Magazine, Restructures Aviation Program." *Christianity Today*, 1 February 2003 <http://www.christianitytoday.com/ct/2003/februaryweb-only/2–24–21.0.html>, accessed 29 November 2013.

Hirji, Faiza. "One Nation, Many Voices: The Muslim Press in the United States." In Winston, Diane H., ed. *The Oxford Handbook of Religion and the American News Media*. New York: Oxford University Press, 2012, 565–578.

Hollinger, David A. "After Cloven Tongues of Fire: Ecumenical Protestantism and the Modern American Encounter with Diversity." *Journal of American History* 98.1 (June 2011): 21–48.

Hooper, Mark. "Who Says Print Is Dead?" *Guardian*, 3 June 2012 <http://www.theguardian.com/media/2012/jun/03/who-says-print-is-dead/print>, accessed 28 November 2013.

Hoover, Stewart M. "Mass Media and Religious Pluralism." In Lee, Philip, ed. *The Democratization of Communication*. Cardiff: University of Wales Press, 1995, 185–198.

Hulsether, Mark. *Building a Protestant Left: Christianity and Crisis Magazine, 1941–1993*. Knoxville: University of Tennessee Press, 1999.

Ives, Nat. "Magazines Shape Up for Digital Future." *Advertising Age*, 17 April 2006 <http://adage.com/article/media/magazines-shape-digital-future/108620>, accessed 28 November 2013.

Kachun, Mitch. "Interrogating the Silences: Julia C. Collins, 19th-Century Black Readers and Writers, and the *Christian Recorder*." *African American Review* 40.4 (Winter 2006): 649–659.

Kurtz, Lester R. *Gods in the Global Village: The World's Religions in Sociological Perspective.* 2nd ed. Sociology for a New Century. Thousand Oaks, CA: Pine Forge Press, 2007.

Lattin, Bohn David and Underhill, Steve. "*The Soul of Politics*: The Reverend Jim Wallis's Attempt to Transcend the Religious/Secular Left and the Religious Right." *Journal of Communication and Religion* 29.2 (November 2006): 205–223.

Lueck, Therese L. "Women's Moral Reform Periodicals of the 19th Century: A Cultural Feminist Analysis of the *Advocate.*" *American Journalism* 16.3 (Summer 1999): 37–52.

Markku, Ruotsila. "Carl McIntire and the Fundamentalist Origins of the Christian Right." *Church History* 81.2 (June 2012): 378–407.

Marsden, George M. *Fundamentalism and American Culture: The Shaping of Twentieth-Century Evangelicalism: 1870–1925.* 2nd ed. New York: Oxford University Press, 2006.

Marty, Martin E. "The Protestant Press: Limitations and Possibilities." In Marty, Martin E.; Deedy, John G., Jr.; Silverman, David Wolf; and Lekachman, Robert, eds. *The Religious Press in America.* New York: Holt, Rinehart and Winston, 1963, 3–63.

Mehltretter, Sarah Ann. "Dorothy Day, the Catholic Workers, and Moderation in Religious Protest during the Vietnam War." *Journal of Communication and Religion* 32.1 (March 2009): 1–32.

Moore, Roberta J. "The Beginning and Development of Protestant Journalism in the United States, 1743–1850." Ph.D. diss., Syracuse University, 1968.

"'Nones' on the Rise." Pew Research: Religion and Public Life Project, 9 October 2012 <http://www.pewforum.org/2012/10/09/nones-on-the-rise>, accessed 15 June 2013.

Olasky, Marvin. *Telling the Truth: How to Revitalize Christian Journalism.* Wheaton, IL: Crossway Books, 1996.

Peterson, Carla L. *"Doers of the Word": African-American Women Speakers and Writers in the North (1830–1880).* New York: Oxford University Press, 1995.

Prince, Gregory A. "'Let the Truth Heal': The Making of *Nobody Knows: The Untold Story of Black Mormons.*" *Dialogue: A Journal of Mormon Thought* 42.3 (Fall 2009): 74–100.

Reed, Barbara Straus. "The Antebellum Jewish Press: Origins, Problems, Functions." *Journalism Monographs* 139 (June 1993): 1–42.

Rivers, Marcia Bolton. "Old, New, Borrowed, Read: The Powers and Problems of American Protestant Periodicals—Then and Now." Capstone research paper presented to Northeastern Seminary, 22 July 2004.

Roberts, Nancy L. "Journalism for Justice: Dorothy Day and the *Catholic Worker.*" *Journalism History* 10.1/2 (Spring/Summer 1983): 2–9.

Sarna, Jonathan D. "The American Jewish Press." In Winston, Diane H. ed. *The Oxford Handbook of Religion and the American News Media.* New York: Oxford University Press, 2012, 537–550.

Schultze, Quentin J. "Leading the Tribes out of Exile: The Religious Press Discerns Broadcasting." *Christianity and the Mass Media in America: Toward a Democratic Accommodation.* East Lansing: Michigan State University Press, 2003, 89–138.

Siddiqi, Mohammad A. "Muslim Media: Present Status and Future Directions." *Gazette* 47.1 (February 1991): 19–31.

Smith, Elizabeth; Fleer, Josh; and Waters, Ken. "Deviating from the Pack: How Religious Publications Frame the AIDS in Africa Crisis." Unpublished paper, Pepperdine University, 2004.

Steinfels, Peter. "Influential Christian Journal Prints Last Issue." *New York Times,* 4 April 1993 <http://www.nytimes.com/1993/04/04/us/influential-christian-journal-prints-last-issue.html>, accessed 29 November 2013.

Sterk, Helen M. "Faith, Feminism and Scholarship: The Journal of Communication and Religion, 1999–2009." [Special Issue]. *Journal of Communication and Religion* 33.2 (November 2010): 206–216.

Sterk, Helen M. "How Rhetoric Becomes Real: Religious Sources of Gender Identity." *Journal of Communication and Religion* 12.2 (September 1989): 24–33.

Suro, Roberto and Associates. "Changing Faiths: Latinos and the Transformation of American Religion." *Pew Forum on Religion & Public Life.* Washington, DC: Pew Research Center, March 2007 <http://www.pewforum.org/uploadedfiles/Topics/Demographics/hispanics-religion-07-final-mar08.pdf>, accessed 8 July 2013.

Swartz, David R. "Identity Politics and the Fragmenting of the 1970s Evangelical Left." *Religion and American Culture: A Journal of Interpretation* 21.1 (Winter 2011): 81–120.

Tait, Lisa Olsen. "The *Young Woman's Journal*: Gender and Generations in a Mormon Women's Magazine." *American Periodicals* 22.1 (2012): 51–71.

Thomas, Jeremy N. and Olson, Daniel, V.A. "Evangelical Elites' Changing Responses to Homosexuality 1960–2009." *Sociology of Religion* 73.3 (2012): 239–272.

Toulouse, Mark G. "*Christianity Today* and American Public Life: A Case Study." *Journal of Church and State* 35.2 (Spring 1993): 241–284.

Trouten, Douglas J. "The Development of Professionalization in the Evangelical Press Association." M.A. thesis, University of Minnesota, 1999.

Vance, Laura. "Evolution of Ideals for Women in Mormon Periodicals, 1897–1999." *Sociology of Religion* 63.1 (Spring 2002): 91–112.

Waters, Ken. "Evangelical Magazines." In Woods, Robert H., Jr., ed. *Evangelical Christians and Popular Culture: Pop Goes the Gospel*. Vol. 3. Santa Barbara, CA: Praeger, 2013, 195–211.

Waters, Ken. "The Evangelical Press." In Winston, Diane H. ed. *The Oxford Handbook of Religion and the American News Media*. New York: Oxford University Press, 2012, 551–564.

Waters, Ken. "Pursuing New Periodicals in Print and Online." In Schultze, Quentin J. and Woods, Robert H., Jr., eds. *Understanding Evangelical Media: The Changing Face of Christian Communication*. Downers Grove, IL: IVP Academic, 2008, 71–84.

Waters, Ken. "Vibrant, but Invisible: A Study of Contemporary Religious Periodicals." *Journalism & Mass Communication Quarterly* 78.2 (Summer 2001): 307–320.

Waters, Ken. "*World Vision*." In Fackler, P. Mark and Lippy, Charles H., eds. *Popular Religious Magazines of the United States*. Westport, CT: Greenwood Press, 1995, 537–542.

"Welcome to ARPA!" The Australasian Religious Press Association <http://www.arpanews.org>, accessed 29 November 2013.

Williams, Gilbert Anthony. "The A.M.E. *Christian Recorder*: A Forum for the Social Ideas of Black Americans, 1854–1902." Ph.D. diss., University of Illinois, 1979.

Williams, Gilbert Anthony. "The Role of the *Christian Recorder* in the African Emigration Movement, 1854–1902." *Journalism Monographs* 111 (April 1989).

Yin, Jaifei. "Beyond the Four Theories of the Press: A New Model for the Asian and the World Press." *Journalism & Communication Monographs* 10.1 (Spring 2008): 3–62.

Supplemental Resources

"Growth of the Nonreligious." Pew Research: Religion and Public Life Project, PewForum.org, 2 July 2013 <http://www.pewforum.org/growth-of-the-nonreligious-many-say-trend-is-bad-for-american-society.aspx>, accessed 8 July 2013.

Hubbard, Benjamin J., ed. *Reporting Religion: Facts and Faith*. Sonoma, CA: Polebridge Press, 1990.

Lee, Philip, ed. *The Democratization of Communication*. Cardiff: University of Wales Press, 1995.

Lora, Ronald and Longton, William Henry, eds. *The Conservative Press in Twentieth-Century America*. Westport, CT: Greenwood Press, 1999.

Marty, Martin E.; Deedy, John G., Jr.; Silverman, David Wolf; and Lekachman, Robert. *The Religious Press in America*. New York: Holt, Rinehart and Winston, 1963.

Schultze, Quentin J. *Christianity and the Mass Media in America: Toward a Democratic Accommodation*. East Lansing: Michigan State University Press, 2003.

Schultze, Quentin J. and Woods, Robert H., Jr., eds. *Understanding Evangelical Media: The Changing Face of Christian Communication*. Downers Grove, IL: IVP Academic, 2008.

Winston, Diane H., ed. *The Oxford Handbook of Religion and the American News Media*. New York: Oxford University Press, 2012.

Woods, Robert H., Jr., ed. *Evangelical Christians and Popular Culture: Pop Goes the Gospel*. Santa Barbara, CA: Praeger, 2013.

20
COVERING SCIENCE AND TECHNOLOGY

Opportunities for Greater Scope and New Methods

Lulu Rodriguez and Michael F. Dahlstrom

This chapter provides an overview of the state of research regarding magazine coverage of science- and technology-related topics and issues. International in scope, it surveys empirical and cultural works that examine how science and technology topics have been discussed, presented and portrayed in popular and special magazines that target general or niche audiences. It also canvasses works that analyze the impact of these portrayals on individuals and societies. From a synthesis of findings and observations, suggestions for further investigation are offered and challenges and opportunities for expansion are drawn.

Overview and Method

To survey the current research landscape regarding magazine coverage of science- and technology-related topics and issues, a content analysis of studies published in refereed journals over the last 20 years was conducted. An electronic search of five databases[1] for articles examined science and technology topics discussed in magazines from 1 January 1992 to 30 December 2012. The articles were collected by first using the global search term *magazine*. A secondary sweep was conducted by combining the term *magazine* with *science* and *technology*. Another search was done by pairing the term *magazine* with *health, energy, environment, innovation* and *risk*. These three steps combined produced 83 such studies—hereafter referred to as *science and technology magazine research*—retrieved from 64 journal titles (Tables 20.1, 20.2) from five article indexes and databases. This scant body of work over two decades indicates the topic has yet to capture the attention of scholars or emerge as a research priority.

The unit of analysis was the complete article. Each article was coded for the journal where it saw print, year of publication, the science topic discussed, the method(s) used to gather data, whether the study adopted a qualitative or quantitative approach, the presence of a theoretical framework, the theory tested, the extent to which the study advanced theory, the dependent variables examined, whether the article discussed the implications of the ascendancy of the on-line medium on the magazine industry and the magazines' effects on audiences.[2]

Only a handful of articles were released from 1996 to 2006, averaging about three per year. The watershed periods were 2007 and 2010, which saw the publication of 13 and 15 articles, respectively (Table 20.1). The publishing momentum, however, was not sustained in the years 2011 and 2012. As shown in Table 20.2, most of the articles were found in the *Journal of Health Communication: International Perspectives* (6) and *Health Communication* (4).

Table 20.1. Sample characteristics, articles by year of publication (N=83)

Year of publication	Frequency	Percent of total
1996	2	2.4
1997	2	2.4
1998	2	2.4
1999	6	7.2
2000	1	1.2
2001	4	4.8
2002	2	2.4
2003	1	1.2
2004	4	4.8
2005	2	2.4
2006	5	6.0
2007	13	15.7
2008	8	9.6
2009	3	3.6
2010	15	18.1
2011	7	8.4
2012	6	7.2
Totals	83	100

Table 20.2. Sample characteristics, articles by journal title (N=83)

Journals	Frequency	Percent of total
AIDS Care	1	1.2
Administration and Policy in Mental Health	1	1.2
American Journal of Health Promotion	1	1.2
American Journal of Human Genetics	1	1.2
Area	2	2.4
BioScience	1	1.2
Canadian Journal of Public Health	1	1.2
Child and Family Social Work	1	1.2
Culture, Health & Sexuality	1	1.2
Communication Studies	1	1.2
Educational Gerontology	1	1.2
European Eating Disorders Review	1	1.2
European Journal of Epidemiology	1	1.2
European Journal of Oncology Nursing	1	1.2
Health Communication	4	4.8
Health Expectations	1	1.2
Health, Risk & Society	1	1.2

Journals	Frequency	Percent of total
History of Education	1	1.2
Howard Journal of Communications	1	1.2
Interdisciplinary Science Reviews	1	1.2
International Journal of Geographical Information Science	1	1.2
International Journal of Life Cycle Assessment	1	1.2
International Journal of Nonprofit and Voluntary Sector Marketing	1	1.2
International Journal of Qualitative Studies in Education	1	1.2
Journal of Alternative and Complementary Medicine	1	1.2
Journal of Applied Communication Research	1	1.2
Journal of Cancer Education	1	1.2
Journal of Chemical Education	1	1.2
Journal of Communication	1	1.2
Journal of Community Health	1	1.2
Journal of Documentation	1	1.2
Journal of Gender Studies	1	1.2
Journal of General Internal Medicine	1	1.2
Journals of Gerontology Series B: Psychological Sciences and Social Sciences	1	1.2
Journal of Health Communication: International Perspectives	6	7.2
Journal of Historical Geography	1	1.2
Journal of Hospitality & Leisure Marketing	1	1.2
Journal of Nutrition Education	3	3.6
Journal of Popular Culture	1	1.2
Journal of Structural Chemistry	1	1.2
Journalism & Mass Communication Quarterly	3	3.6
Journalism Studies	1	1.2
Midwifery	1	1.2
Nutrition & Dietetics	1	1.2
Philosophical Magazine	1	1.2
Preventing Chronic Disease: Public Health Research, Practice, and Policy	1	1.2
Preventive Medicine	1	1.2
Psycho-Oncology	1	1.2
Public Relations Review	1	1.2
Public Understanding of Science	2	2.4
Research Evaluation	1	1.2
Scandinavian Journal of Caring Sciences	1	1.2
Scandinavian Journal of Educational Research	1	1.2
Science & Education	1	1.2
Science & Technology Libraries	1	1.2

(Continued)

Table 20.2. Continued

Journals	Frequency	Percent of total
Science of Health Promotion	1	1.2
Scientometrics	1	1.2
Sex Roles	2	2.4
Social Science & Medicine	3	3.6
Sociological Inquiry	1	1.2
Sociological Spectrum	1	1.2
Sociology of Health & Illness	2	2.4
Women & Health	2	2.4
Women's Studies International Forum	1	1.2
Totals: 64 Titles	83	100

Table 20.3. Sample characteristics, articles by topic (*N*=83)

Science and related themes	Frequency	Percent of total
Environment	7	8.4
Health	57	68.7
Popularizing science	6	7.2
Social science	3	3.6
Technology	3	3.6
Other	7	8.4
Totals	83	100

Close to 70% of the 83 articles collected investigated topics that pertain to health issues (Table 20.3), followed by the environment (8.4%) and the popularization of science topics (7.2%). A large majority of the studies (74.7%) employed content analysis as the data gathering method, with an almost even split between those that employed a qualitative approach (e.g., case studies, discourse analysis and network analysis) and quantitative methods (Table 20.4). Six (7.2%) applied the cultural approach, four (4.8%) adopted a historical stance, two employed experimental designs (2.4%) and only one (1.2%) gathered data through a survey. None used longitudinal designs. The preponderance of health topics and the overwhelming use of content analysis suggest wide swaths of topical domains that could be explored using more diverse methods of inquiry.

Only 37.3% of the sample, or 31 of the 83 studies, indicated a theoretical framework (Table 20.4). Of those that did, 10 were anchored on framing as the theoretical foundation (12%) and three or 3.6% applied the health belief model and variants of the protection motivation theory. Close to 70%, or 58 of the 83 articles, examined general interest magazines, while the rest explored publications that were devoted to science (18.1%) and health (1.2%). Science magazines are those that publish news, opinions and reports about science mainly for a non-expert audience. Within the sample, articles investigated science magazines such as *Popular Science* (U.S.); *Focus, Quark, T3, Jack,* and *Explora* (Italy); *Forskning och Framsteg* (Research and Progress) and *Illustrerad Vetenskap* (Illustrated Science), both from Sweden, and *Ibérica* (Spain). Health magazines, on the other hand, are those that contain articles about fitness, nutrition, healthy eating and lifestyles, weight loss, and general wellness. In the sample, articles

Table 20.4. Sample characteristics, articles by method (N=83)

Method(s)	Frequency	Percent of total
Content analysis	62	74.7
Critical-cultural	6	7.2
Experiment	2	2.4
Historical	4	4.8
Survey	2	2.4
Other	7	8.4
Totals	100	83
Approach		
Quantitative	35	42.2
Qualitative	35	42.2
Combination	12	14.4
Other	1	1.2
Totals	83	100
Theory		
Present	31	37.3
Absent	52	62.6
Totals	83	100

Table 20.5. Sample characteristics, studied magazines by country of origin (N=83)

Place of publication of magazines examined	Frequency	Percent of total
Australia	6	7.2
Belgium	3	3.6
Canada	4	4.8
Canada and United States	7	8.4
Finland	1	1.2
France	1	1.2
Germany	2	2.4
Greece	1	1.2
Italy	2	2.4
Mexico	1	1.2
Netherlands	1	1.2
Spain	4	4.8
Sub-Saharan Africa, East Africa, Central Africa	1	1.2
Sweden	1	1.2
Uganda	1	1.2
United Kingdom	6	7.2
United States	41	49.4
Totals	83	100

analyzed the content of health magazines such as *Men's Health, Shape, Prevention, Muscle and Fitness, Cure, Caring4Cancer* and *Living with Cancer Health Monitor* (U.S.). Table 20.5 gives a summary of the countries of origin for the magazines scholars chose to study.

Although the period under analysis saw an increasing number of publications with on-line counterparts, the articles examined for this chapter were drawn only from print magazine editions. Data for on-line counterparts were not collected.

Major Research Themes

A more detailed examination of the major themes within science and technology magazine research, including the questions explored, the methods used and theoretical frameworks advanced, was conducted. Most of the studies discussed themes related to health, the environment and the popularization of science, except for four that were the sole representatives of their own themes, that of psychology, sociology, and the representations of age and death.

The Health Theme

Science and technology magazine research had a sharp focus on health, a theme that remained dominant over the entire time period of the study. The most common kind of health study is issue-focused, selecting a particular health issue and using content analysis to explore how it is presented. Breast cancer was the most common issue examined,[3] but the range of health issues covered was wide, including breast implants,[4] childhood cancer,[5] cardiovascular health,[6] depression and mental health,[7] HIV-AIDS and other sexually-transmitted infections,[8] eating disorders and obesity,[9] Alzheimer's[10] and chronic diseases in general.[11] Studies also analyzed the depiction of health-related practices such as infant feeding,[12] tobacco use,[13] hysterectomy,[14] prostate and colon cancer screening[15] and general cancer experiences.[16] Other health-related topics examined included genetics,[17] complementary and alternative medicine,[18] sexuality and sexual desire,[19] dietary supplements[20] and weight loss and nutrition.[21]

Most of these issue-focused studies examine general interest magazines instead of specialized science or health magazines, and it is common for the studies to focus on a subset of general interest magazines aimed at a specific target audience, such as African Americans,[22] teenage girls[23] or older adults.[24] The content analyzed is almost completely dominated by editorial text, with comparatively few exploring the associated visuals[25] or advertisements.[26]

The outcomes of these issue-focused studies generally fall along a continuum of complexity of content evaluation. At the low end, the analysis is confined to a general description of how the heath issue was presented with little evaluation of the content's appropriateness to target audiences. For example, Juanne N. Clarke and Adele Gawley analyzed the coverage of depression in high circulating magazines in the United States and Canada over a 25-year period and conclude that the disease was increasingly framed as a bio-medical problem.[27] At the high end, the study evaluates whether the coverage cleaves close to real world scenarios or the adequacy or accuracy of information provided relative to the prescribed action a reader should take to address the health issue. For example, Mira L. Katz and her colleagues analyzed the coverage of three kinds of cancer in high-circulating magazines and note the absence of content that will enable readers to address the issue, such as the relative importance of cancer risk factors, when to stop screening and uncertainties associated with screening tests.[28] While some of these studies on the high end of the continuum consider the coverage to be of nominal quality,[29] the general consensus is that magazine coverage of most health issues does not provide adequate or sufficiently accurate information to readers.

The content analysis modes used varied across quantitative and qualitative designs, in both cases with the usual caveats. The quantitative analyses assume that the surface meaning of content is easily recoverable and that the frequency of occurrence of a coded construct is representative of its importance. Qualitative content analyses require close reading to find deeper, cultural meanings, such as the link between eating disorders and feminine power[30] or the construction of an ideal male as being able to maintain his own health,[31] but at the cost of reliability and generalizability.

Taken together, these issue-focused studies provide a descriptive scattershot of coverage regarding health issues important to society, but the literature has yet to synthesize these findings into larger patterns generalizable beyond the specific health issue under investigation. A few studies do move in this direction, either comparing coverage between different kinds of magazines[32] or from different time periods,[33] but an underlying framework linking these findings remains underdeveloped. In fact, with few exceptions,[34] these issue-focused studies generally lack theoretical grounding to offer generalizability or predictive power.

Moving beyond issue-focused studies, health themes within science and technology magazine research become more diverse. Some studies treat health as a general topic and examine its relation to larger cultural values, such as powerless language[35] and feminine responsibility.[36] Other studies use health as a context to examine other constructs, such as the moderators and mediators of advertisement effects,[37] or approaches related to magazines, such as entertainment-education.[38] These results are difficult to generalize but suggest that magazines can play an influential role in how health issues become integrated into society.

The idiosyncrasies of health coverage within science and technology magazine research may best be understood in contrast to the next two dominant, but much less covered, themes present in the literature: the environment and the popularization of science.

The Environment and the Popularization of Science Themes

Themes related to the environment and the popularization of science in magazine research are more recent, appear most frequently after 2006 and are more diverse in their focus, design and method.

Studies examining environmental themes usually analyzed magazines with science and science-related focuses rather than magazines of general interest. In contrast to the issue-specific focus of the health theme, the environment is usually treated more inclusively, eschewing specifics such as recycling or climate change for broader concepts, such as environmental advocacy.[39] Historical perspectives also become more frequent, such as using magazine coverage to track the cultural meaning assigned to nature over time.[40] The results are too varied to generalize but again suggest a role for magazines in constructing a social definition for and public understanding of the environment and issues related to it.

Studies examining the popularization of science through (or via) magazines also tend to focus more on science-related than general interest magazines but often treat the magazine more as a context within which to examine the techniques used to popularize science. For instance, metaphor[41] and narrative[42] have received attention as techniques of popularization. Similar to what was found within the environmental theme, historical perspectives are also more common within the popularization of science theme, using magazine coverage to track the popularization of the periodic table,[43] the representations of science in nineteenth-century Britain or the portrayals of technology in popular Italian techno-scientific magazines published in the early to mid-2000s.[44]

The varied approaches in both the environment and the popularization of science themes do not lead to generalizations about the methods used beyond noting that both quantitative and qualitative traditions are present. Much like the health theme, these themes also generally lack theoretical grounding that could allow greater explanatory power from study findings. Part of this is undoubtedly due to the smaller number of studies exhibiting these themes. The more varied approaches at least suggest new questions of interest and vantage points with which to examine science and technology magazine research.

Considering the search uncovered only 83 science and technology magazine studies in 20 years of literature across 64 international journals, it is clear that this area is in its formative stage. The studies reviewed here have done much to provide initial points of understanding of how magazines covered issues related to science and technology. The field is therefore well positioned to make some significant steps to synthesize existing findings and develop theoretical explanations as to the role of magazines in the communication of science and technology.

Inferred Audience Effects

The sample, which consisted mainly of studies that employed comprehensive content and discourse analyses, offered revealing overviews of key dimensions of magazine coverage. Content analyses, however, inherently preclude examinations of the impact of coverage on target and unintended audiences. Even though 63.8% or 62 of the 83 studies analyzed magazines of relatively high circulation figures (often described as "popular" or "mass circulation" magazines) across critical time periods, they cannot make claims about the coverage's level of pragmatic influence on, or reflection of, their audiences. At the most, such studies can only infer, by reason of the size of their audiences, that magazines had significant influence over public understanding and opinion, attitudes, experiences of stigmatization (in the case of those who suffer from specific ailments) and individual or social action.

In the absence of systematic examinations of audience effects, authors often speculate on the implications of content analysis findings, particularly in studies of health issues, primarily on how readers see the feasibility of proposed solutions to health concerns, which range from individual prevention behaviors to national policy and government or institutional response. While others contend that the emphasis on disease risk factors that are within the control of the individual affirms the power of the active citizen,[45] some find that the pattern of giving greater stress to individual responsibility serves to undermine the potential for societal-level reforms. For example, Phil Brown and his colleagues, coding for the causes of breast cancer discussed in periodicals, highlighted frequent references to individual responsibility for diet, age at birth of first child and other personal behaviors and attributes to the disregard of possible environmental antecedents.[46] They worry that scant attention to corporate and governmental responsibility may hold back scientific and activist pursuits of environmental causes of cancer and foster an over-reliance on personal responsibility for preventing diseases and other social pathologies.

Although acknowledging that health-related information gleaned from magazines can have implications for health promotion, scholars lament the inadequacy and timing of coverage. Several works cite inaccuracies and inconsistencies in reporting and storytelling, which were presumed to have a bearing on the quality and efficacy of institutional or individual response.[47] Women's magazines, in particular, were seen as espousing what is considered to be socially acceptable, individual ways of dealing with personal issues, specifically pointing to a person's responsibility to avert health threats.[48] Consequently, in much the same way that Sandra Berns argues the need for more diverse representations to expand conventional understandings in the judicial systems,[49] Hoffman-Goetz and MacDonald point to ways that common modes of discourse in magazines tend to marginalize feminist and sociological explanations, playing into the medical field's dominant epidemiological paradigm that assigns the duty of controlling the spread of diseases and unhealthy practices particularly to women.[50] Scholars studying the portrayals of health issues in magazines circulated in the developing world, particularly in Sub-Saharan Africa, also critique that national policies often fail to take people's belief structures into account, which renders such policies insufficient to engage with the gendered nature of some diseases and their relation to social inequities. Magazine coverage, they contend, replicates this lack of sensitivity to gender- and class-based concerns.[51]

A number of studies assume behavioral effects of magazine exposure. For example, Clarke posits probable practical consequences of media portrayals on the actions of parents and the ways in which they approach clinicians regarding the health of their children suffering from depression.[52] Possible links between idealized, polarized and biased portrayal of children with cancer and their documented experiences of stigma also are inferred.[53] Kyle J. Tobler and his team were concerned that an overemphasis on the coverage of breast cancer and the conspicuous lack of coverage of other cancers (e.g., lung, cervical, prostate and colon) might influence risk perceptions and, indirectly, cancer control behaviors.[54] Following the conventional tenets of cultivation theory, Silvia Mondini and colleagues conclude that Italian magazines parlay notions of ideal feminine beauty that contribute to increasing rates of eating disorders.[55] In addition, Annie Lang and Narine S. Yegiyan have indicated that a surprising number of messages about health might create "boomerang effects" in terms of prescribed practices.[56] A few have suggested that the enormous variation in the type of health-related information given to people with different socioeconomic backgrounds affects their level of participation in decision-making in clinical encounters.[57] Some worried that a focus on optimistic treatment might have a counterproductive impact on audiences' perceived survival rate or fatality risk, level of anxiety and motivations to implement preventive behaviors.[58] Other scholars posit that widespread coverage of emerging nationwide environmental initiatives with the potential to climb up the national news agenda, including campaigns to curb the use of agricultural pesticides and the presence of chemicals in cosmetics and household products, might stimulate collective action.[59]

Authors generally acknowledge that many magazines are commercial products, the content of which responds to editorial policy, audience wishes and advertising demands, among other influences. Thus, content—and the shaping of content—are hypothesized to have important implications for audience cognitions. For example, Ann M. Henderson reported qualitative findings indicating that the human interest angle, often expressed through personal narratives, statistics and celebrity accounts, engages attention and shapes understanding of stories describing genetic risks.[60]

There are studies that conclude with speculations that magazine coverage tends to support the maintenance of prevailing ideologies, attitudes and beliefs, including the value of heterosexual marriage and patriarchy, thus reinforcing existing power relations. For example, Laurie Hoffman-Goetz found that magazines read predominantly by African-American women emphasize religious beliefs in cancer survival while presenting mixed attitudes toward European-American medical institutions. She conjectures that such a discourse has a strong tendency to shape women's attitudes about survival from cancer.[61] In another work, Ashley M. Fandrich and Stephenson J. Beck postulate that "powerless" language, a linguistic marker for women's discourse, influences how media consumers perceive the believability and trustworthiness of news sources.[62] In these ways, magazines are presumed to serve as vehicles for the intensification of existing trends and social norms underlying gender roles.

Following cultivation axioms, researchers also evaluated the depiction of specific groups (e.g., males, the elderly and single-parent families) to determine whether magazine representations captured realities, created or reinforced stereotypes, or fostered a homogenized view of these social segments.[63] Such studies generally argue that their findings lend support to the notion that media images contribute to society's perception of these groups.

Studies that explored magazine coverage of scientific and technological breakthroughs were found to display favorable valence toward science and technology, especially in the early stages of coverage.[64] Vasilia Christidou's team for example, found that the most frequently employed metaphors in popular science magazines published in Greece describe the nature and the evolution of space science and astronomy, genetics and biotechnology, the natural sciences and engineering and informatics, representing them as activities that extend the frontiers of knowledge. The authors suggest that the social representations evoked by these metaphors contribute to the cultural authority of these scientific fields, hence playing a significant role in the maintenance of the social autonomy and integrity of the techno-scientific profession.[65]

Magazines are a popular cultural source of diverse exhortations for the achievement of health and well-being made possible in large part by advances in science and technology. Nonetheless, there is a dearth of literature that offers empirical and validated evidence of the link between exposure to magazines and audience members' cognitions, attitudes or behavior.

Future Directions

After examining the past 20 years of international research on magazine coverage of science and technology, a few trends emerge: health dominates as the theme and content analysis dominates as the method used. Effects on audiences are often inferred, but rarely tested and the inclusion of a theoretical foundation remains less than desired. Based on the broad commitments of societies to the scientific and technological enterprise and the attendant value of information dispersed through magazines, there are five considerations and future directions scholars should take to tap the potentials of the medium to enhance popular discourse about science and technology.

Diversifying the Inquiry

There are two clear areas that would benefit from diversification. The first is in the *conceptualization of science* itself.[66] Existing research focuses predominantly on the subsection of health with a handful of disjointed studies investigating other areas of science. However, science is a complex construct, involving not only specific fields such as chemistry or biology, but also the issues involved when science and society interact, such as risk,[67] uncertainty,[68] expertise or perceptions thereof and public science literacy.[69] This multifaceted conceptualization of what counts as science can be seen in the acronyms used to describe it. Contemporary university programs increasingly combine science, technology, engineering and mathematics (STEM) when grouping science-related fields as academic units. The science communication-related division of the Association for Education in Journalism and Communication (AEJMC) combines science, health, the environment and risk (ComSHER) when conceptualizing science. Focusing so heavily on health coverage overlooks the diversity within science and hinders an accurate understanding of its intersection with the medium. The blossoming of newer areas of research within this very broad domain, such as the environment and the popularization of science themes, is a promising trend. A few studies have also explored other topics such as depictions of the atomic bomb,[70] radioactivity[71] and intelligent design.[72]

The dominance of health, however, is not surprising and is likely an appropriate place to begin study. The science subsection most relevant to a general audience, and therefore most likely to be covered by general interest magazines, would likely be health. Therefore, how health is presented in magazines and evaluations of the coverage's accuracy or adequacy is an important topic to investigate. Yet, the infrequency with which the research questions themselves have deviated from this question of presentation may itself be an artifact of the second area ripe for diversification, the focus on inquiry.

The second area that would benefit from diversification is the *inquiry* itself. This refers to data gathering methods beyond content analysis, including attempts to uncover long-term effects through longitudinal designs, stronger measures of causality through experiments and surveys that provide evidence for audience media consumption habits and preferences. Within existing science and technology magazine research, there is almost a complete focus on the content of magazines, but very little on the downstream effects of content on audiences or the upstream organizational factors that lead to such content.

The paucity of studies that attempt to understand the impact of magazines' coverage of science and technology on audiences demands greater attention. Considering consumers' need for information and the decisions they make about what sources of information to use, given the expanding array of possibilities, more audience-oriented questions are in order. What kinds of information do people *want* magazines to provide and to what extent do magazines satisfy their information needs? Does reading magazine content increase or decrease people's perceived susceptibility to a disease, and if so, do those changes in perceived susceptibility influence adoption of preventive behaviors? Or does the coverage simply remind people of their greatest fears, leading to fear control responses that may ultimately put them at greater risk? These questions are critical, considering changing consumption patterns, information delivery systems and increased fragmentation of audiences brought about by advances in communication technology. Communicating updated research results to magazine editors might help them do a better job of meeting readers' needs.

Content analysis findings inevitably lead to questions that examine why magazines portray science and technology topics the way they do. This line of inquiry calls for an examination of journalistic routines and practices to answer questions such as the following: Why do magazine editors make the choices they make about which science and technology topics do and do not receive coverage? Have there been drastic changes to conventional gatekeeping processes? Why are some information items emphasized more often than others (e.g., individual- as opposed to system-level responses to health threats; controllable vs. uncontrollable health risk factors)? Specific to the coverage of diseases, what assumptions do writers and editors make about readers' knowledge about risks, diagnosis, treatment and survival? What motivates them to include and exclude various kinds of information? Such studies could also examine the influence of other factors in the creation or modification of content, including cultural, social-structural or organizational variables, the ideological leanings of magazine staff members, or perceived audience demand and need for specific kinds of information.

Justifying the Medium

The call for increased diversity in science communication-related inquiry could apply to media beyond magazines. Thus, the second consideration addresses the need to justify why magazines as a medium are worthy of study. Of the studies examined, authors variously justify selecting magazines as the medium of study because they are important sources of science-related information, they transmit and preserve cultural trends, or they offer a way to capture how science-related constructs are perceived within society. While true, these justifications are not unique to magazines; the same could be said about many other forms of media. A recent study reports that television is the medium from which most people get their science information,[73] which heightens the need to justify why scholarly inquiry on magazine coverage of science and technology is relevant.

Magazines have many unique, medium-related factors, and future studies should do more to leverage these differences. One obvious way magazines differ from other media is in the predominance of visuals over text. Surprisingly, only a handful of the examined studies considered the visuals in magazines as carrying relevant meaning.[74] Yet visuals are known to be easier to comprehend and lead to different audience effects than text. Overlooking the influence of visuals may be handicapping critical insights to what magazines are actually contributing beyond other media. Magazines also differ from other media in the actions they require of their audiences. With the exception of those with controlled circulations, magazines are read by those who had to actively select the magazine from many niche titles. This implies audiences with higher interest in the topic, greater background knowledge and more motivation to seek and learn information. Such audience members contrast the more passive television, radio or even general news consumers who make choices based more on medium than on content. Audience studies could examine if the activity of the audience intersects with either the expectation for certain kinds of science content or the effects of it.

Finally, justifying the medium does not need to be done *a priori* but can become the focus of inquiry itself. Comparative studies contrasting the coverage of science and technology or its effects between magazines and other forms of media could both provide evidence as to how magazines differ as a medium as well as discover new factors on which to justify future studies.

Incorporating Theory

While the frequencies, themes and methods within science and technology magazine studies are clear from analyzing the 83 studies published between 1992 and 2010, theoretical explanations of the results are not. Almost two-thirds of the examined studies had no theoretical foundation that attempts to explain the findings. The literature, therefore, offers scattered data points relevant to science and technology coverage. A greater incorporation of theory into this research could help causally explain and predict data beyond the instances already studied.

Take framing studies in new directions. The array of studies that examined how specific diseases have been framed or portrayed in magazines points to *new directions for framing research*. Studies that employed frame analysis primarily detected the presence (or absence) of discrete information items (e.g., discussions of technical risk assessment, assignment of responsibility, individual and societal actions, or both, to mitigate a health threat), but disregarded how a topic has been discursively presented or contextualized to purposively influence audience beliefs, attitudes and practices. Popular discourse about science and technology will be expanded profitably by considering a broader array of meta-perspectives or holistic frames. Of the 27 framing studies analyzed, a great majority limited the scope to the analysis of content or media frames.[75] Future efforts could delve into how audiences interpret magazine frames and whether the differences in tone of coverage across issues affect people's behavior, knowledge and attitudes.

More *contextualized frames* also are necessary. One that is already in use, albeit in an oversimplified form, is the interrelationship of health and the evolution of medical science and technology.[76] Another frame casts the challenges of diseases as myriad opportunities for political engagement—from grassroots organizing[77] to activities within established parties, from environmentalism to pressuring particular industries (food, chemical, etc.) for reforms[78] and from fighting for more federal funding for basic research[79] to working for better screening and treatment for the disadvantaged.[80] Such messages have the ability to encourage people to understand the broad range of ways to work for and expect a healthier future.

Apply theories from science and risk communication. While framing can be applied to most topics and media, there are areas of interest unique to science and technology with related theories or general frameworks that could be employed to better understand science and technology as it is covered in magazines. These areas generally address the interaction of science within society and include topics such as risk communication, presentation of uncertainty, perceptions of expertise, societal role of science communication[81] and dimensions of science literacy.

Taking risk communication as an example, there exist many theories that attempt to explain how individuals come to form judgments when presented with risk information, using factors such as information insufficiency,[82] fear[83] or cultural worldviews.[84] Magazine studies could apply any of these theories to, for instance, either predict or explain the response of readers to specific health coverage. The benefit of such theoretical application is that results can be generalized beyond specific health issues and provide predictive power in new contexts. Additionally, many of these theories have been tested using text-based communication. It is entirely possible that the unique attributes of magazines offer significant extensions of existing theory, further enhancing the utility of science and technology magazine research.

Suggesting Ways of Improving Performance

Seventy of the 83 studies analyzed for this chapter stopped at description or critique, rarely offering recommendations about how the findings can be applied to improve magazine performance. A notable exception is Brigitta R. Brunner and Larissa R. Brunner Huber's work that investigates the types and quality of health information reported in *Glamour* and *Men's Health* magazines, suggesting, among others, that health experts, public information officers and journalists can offer readers more information about harm, costs and insurance coverage to make educated health care decisions.[85] Although magazines are assigned special roles in communicating about diseases, the findings indicate that these publications are not disseminating very accurate information in relation to scientific and medical literature. The results of the present analysis suggest room for improvement in the information magazines are providing their readers and the way such information is presented.

For example, there is a need to compare the pattern of disease coverage in magazines to medical indicators of disease origin and spread because such indicators provide an objective measure of population burden and are often a basis of national policy formation and allocation of resources.[86] This means comparing information disseminated through magazines against science-based standards or "real world" indicators following the conventional ways of testing cultivation effects.[87] Stories could also direct readers to credible information sources using appropriate contact information to enhance the quality and value of health communication in the popular media. The translation of scientific research for popular consumption can be accompanied by the development of public vocabularies that recognize the ways in which science and technology exert influence on human outcomes without portraying those factors either simplistically or as all-powerful. By doing so, magazines can be more valuable instruments for enhancing scientific literacy.

Considering the Digital Future

The digital future of magazines is a prominent topic within general magazine research[88] but has yet to become a significant focus when considering coverage of science and technology within magazines. Many of the same trends that are impacting the medium itself should be addressed in a science and technology context. Will general interest magazines remain an appropriate pool of content to analyze for health coverage if audiences continue to be fragmented? Will readers expect different kinds of science-related information from on-line magazines than print, based on differences in uses and gratifications?

Additionally, there are considerations regarding the move from print to digital magazines that are unique to science and technology contexts. Will the greater participatory nature of on-line magazines lead to a rejection of the top-down Public Understanding of Science model or for the more bottom-up Public Engagement in Science and Technology model?[89] How might interactive graphics compare to static visuals in the communication of complex scientific and technical concepts? How will the digital divide influence the kind and depth of science knowledge different audiences bring to different platforms?

Notes

1 The following databases were searched: (1) ABI/Inform (Proquest), which contains full-text trade and scholarly articles; (2) ComAbstracts, which compiles abstracts of selected articles from more than 50 communication journals. Its companion database, ComIndex, provides citations to articles from 80 communication journals dating back to 1970; (3) Current Contents Connect, which compiles abstracts and tables of content of journals, books and conference proceedings; (4) Expanded Academic ASAP, a source for full-text scholarly articles from the sciences and the humanities; and (5) PsychInfo, which provides citations and abstracts and some full texts from the disciplines of psychology, sociology, anthropology, education, journalism and mass communication. PsychInfo indexes journal articles from 1872 to the present and books and book chapters dated 1987 to the present.

2 To check inter-coder reliability, two coders analyzed half of the total sample according to the coding scheme. Using the formula from Robert C. North, Ole R. Holsti, M. George Zaninovich, and Dina A. Zinnes, *Content Analysis: A Handbook with Applications for the Study of International Crisis* (Evanston, IL:

Northwestern University Press, 1963, p. 49), the following inter-coder reliability scores were obtained: research method applied (97.4%); science topic discussed (96.8%); theory tested (97.1%); qualitative or quantitative approach (96.2%); whether the study advanced theory (91%); the dependent variables examined (94.2%); and whether the article discussed the implications of the ascendancy of the on-line medium on the magazine industry and the magazines' effects on audiences (93.6%).

3 Studies that examined magazine coverage of breast cancer include Julie L. Andsager and Angela Powers, "Social or Economic Concerns: How News and Women's Magazines Framed Breast Cancer in the 1990s," *Journalism & Mass Communication Quarterly* 76.3 (Autumn 1999): 531–550; Charles K. Atkin, Sandi W. Smith, Courtnay McFeters, and Vanessa Ferguson, "A Comprehensive Analysis of Breast Cancer News Coverage in Leading Media Outlets Focusing on Environmental Risks and Prevention," *Journal of Health Communication* 13.1 (January/February 2008): 3–19; Deena Blanchard, Joel Erblich, Guy H. Montgomery, and Dana H. Bovbjerg, "Read All about It: The Over-Representation of Breast Cancer in Popular Magazines," *Preventive Medicine* 35.4 (October 2002): 343–348; Phil Brown, Stephen M. Zavestoski, Sabrina McCormick, Joshua Mandelbaum, and Theo Luebke, "Print Media Coverage of Environmental Causation of Breast Cancer," *Sociology of Health & Illness* 23.6 (2001): 747–775; Christina Marino and Karen K. Gerlach, "An Analysis of Breast Cancer Coverage in Selected Women's Magazines, 1987–1995," *American Journal of Health Promotion* 13.3 (January/February 1999): 163–170; Susan McKay and Frances Bonner, "Educating Readers: Breast Cancer in Australian Women's Magazines," *International Journal of Qualitative Studies in Education* 17.4 (July/August 2004): 517–535; Kyle J. Tobler, Philip K. Wilson, and Peter G. Napolitano, "Frequency of Breast Cancer, Lung Cancer, and Tobacco Use Articles in Women's Magazines from 1987 to 2003," *Journal of Cancer Education* 24.1 (2009): 36–39; Kim Walsh-Childers, Heather Edwards, and Stephen Grobmyer, "Covering Women's Greatest Health Fear: Breast Cancer Information in Consumer Magazines," *Health Communication* 26.3 (April/May 2011): 209–220; Kim Walsh-Childers, Heather M. Edwards, and Stephen Grobmyer, "*Essence, Ebony* and O: Breast Cancer Coverage in Black Magazines," *Howard Journal of Communications* 23.2 (April/June 2012): 136–156; Lesley Wilkes, Janice Withnall, Rebecca Harris, Kate White, Barbara Beale, Jane Hobson, Marsha Durhan, and Linda Kristjanson, "Stories about Breast Cancer in Australian Women's Magazines: Information Sources for Risk, Early Detection and Treatment," *European Journal of Oncology Nursing* 5.2 (June 2001): 80–88.

4 Julie Andsager and Angela Powers, "Framing Women's Health with a Sense-Making Approach: Magazine Coverage of Breast Cancer and Implants," *Health Communication* 13.2 (2001): 163–185.

5 Juanne N. Clarke, "Portrayal of Childhood Cancer in English Language Magazines in North America: 1970–2001," *Journal of Health Communication* 10.7 (October/November 2005): 593–607.

6 Juanne N. Clarke, Gudrun van Amerom, and Jeannine Binns, "Gender and Heart Disease in Mass Print Media: 1991, 1996, 2001," *Women and Health* 45.1 (2007): 17–35; Juanne N. Clarke, and Jeannine Binns, "The Portrayal of Heart Disease in Mass Print Magazines, 1991–2001," *Health Communication* 19.1 (2006): 39–48; Carolyn M. Edy, "Women's Magazine Coverage of Heart Disease Risk Factors: *Good Housekeeping* Magazine, 1997 to 2007," *Women & Health* 50.2 (March 2010): 176–194; Melanie B. Turner, Amanda M. Vader, and Scott T. Walters, "An Analysis of Cardiovascular Health Information in Popular Young Women's Magazines: What Messages Are Women Receiving?" *American Journal of Health Promotion* 22.3 (January/February 2008): 183–186.

7 Juanne N. Clarke and Adele Gawley, "The Triumph of Pharmaceuticals: The Portrayal of Depression from 1980 to 2005," *Administration & Policy in Mental Health & Mental Health Services Research* 36.2 (2009): 91–101; Juanne N. Clarke, "Childhood Depression and Mass Print Magazines in the USA and Canada: 1983–2008," *Child and Family Social Work* 16.1 (February 2011): 52–60; Daniela B. Friedman, James N. Laditka, Sarah B. Laditka, and Anna E. Mathews, "Cognitive Health Messages in Popular Women's and Men's Magazines, 2006–2007," *Preventing Chronic Disease* 7.2 (March 2010): 1–10.

8 Juanne N. Clarke, "The Paradoxical Portrayal of the Risk of Sexually Transmitted Infections and Sexuality in US Magazines *Glamour* and *Cosmopolitan* 2000–2007," *Health, Risk & Society* 12.6 (December 2010): 560–574; Juanne N. Clarke, Lianne McLellan, and Laurie Hoffman-Goetz, "The Portrayal of HIV/AIDS in Two Popular African American Magazines," *Journal of Health Communication* 11.5 (July/August 2006): 495–507; Satya Krishnan, Tracy Durrah, and Karen Winkler, "Coverage of AIDS in Popular African American Magazines," *Health Communication* 9.3 (1997): 273–288.

9 Silvia Mondini, Angela Favaro, and Paolo Santonastaso, "Eating Disorders and the Ideal of Feminine Beauty in Italian Newspapers and Magazines," *European Eating Disorders Review* 4.2 (June 1996): 112–120; Kally Whitehead and Tim Kurz, "Saints, Sinners and Standards of Femininity: Discursive Constructions of Anorexia Nervosa and Obesity in Women's Magazines," *Journal of Gender Studies* 17.4 (December 2008): 345–358.

10 Juanne N. Clarke, "The Case of the Missing Person: Alzheimer's Disease in Mass Print Magazines 1991–2001," *Health Communication* 19.3 (2006): 269–276.

11 Francisco J. Mercado-Martinez, Leticia Robles-Silva, Nora Moreno-Leal, and Claudia Franco-Almazan, "Inconsistent Journalism: The Coverage of Chronic Diseases in the Mexican Press," *Journal of Health Communication* 6.3 (July/September 2001): 235–247.

12 Ann M. Henderson, "Mixed Messages about the Meanings of Breast-Feeding Representations in the Australian Press and Popular Magazines," *Midwifery* 15.1 (March 1999): 24–31.

13 Laurie Hoffman-Goetz, Karen K. Gerlach, Christina Marino, and Sherry L. Mills, "Cancer Coverage and Tobacco Advertising in African-American Women's Popular Magazines," *Journal of Community Health* 22.4 (August 1997): 261–270; Tobler, Wilson, and Napolitano, "Frequency of Breast Cancer, Lung Cancer, and Tobacco Use Articles."

14 Kaisa Nykanen, Tarja Suominen, and Merja Nikkonen, "Representations of Hysterectomy as a Transition Process in Finnish Women's and Health Magazines," *Scandinavian Journal of Caring Sciences* 25.3 (September 2011): 608–616.

15 Mira L. Katz, Stacey Sheridan, Michael Pignone, Carmen Lewis, Jamila Battle, Claudia Gollop, and Michael O'Malley, "Prostate and Colon Cancer Screening Messages in Popular Magazines," *Journal of General Internal Medicine* 19.8 (August 2004): 843–848.

16 Laurie Hoffman-Goetz, "Cancer Experiences of African-American Women as Portrayed in Popular Mass Magazines," *Psycho-Oncology* 8.1 (January/February 1999): 36–45; Laurie Hoffman-Goetz and Megan MacDonald, "Cancer Coverage in Mass-Circulating Canadian Women's Magazines," *Canadian Journal of Public Health* 90.1 (January/February 1999): 55–59.

17 Celeste M. Condit, Nneka Ofulue, and Kristine M. Sheedy, "Determinism and Mass Media Portrayals of Genetics," *American Journal of Human Genetics* 62.4 (April 1998): 979–984.

18 Juanne N. Clarke, Amy Romagnoli, Cristal Sargent, and Gudrun van Amerom, "The Portrayal of Complementary and Alternative Medicine in Mass Print Magazines since 1980," *Journal of Alternative and Complementary Medicine* 16.1 (January 2010): 125–130.

19 Juanne N. Clarke, "Women's Work, Worry and Fear: The Portrayal of Sexuality and Sexual Health in U.S. Magazines for Teenage and Middle-Aged Women, 2000–2007," *Culture, Health & Sexuality* 11:4 (May 2009): 415–429; Suchi P. Joshi, Jochen Peter, and Patti M. Valkenburg, "Scripts of Sexual Desire and Danger in U.S. and Dutch Teen Girl Magazines: A Cross-National Content Analysis," *Sex Roles* 64. 7/8 (April 2011): 463–474.

20 Ruth Kava, Kathleen A. Meister, Elizabeth M. Whelan, Alicia M. Lukachko, and Christina Mirabile, "Dietary Supplement Safety Information in Magazines Popular among Older Readers," *Journal of Health Communication* 7.1 (January/February 2002): 13–23.

21 Mary Korinis, Mary K. Korslund, Gabriella Belli, Joyce M. Donohue, and Janet M. Johnson, "Comparison of Calcium and Weight Loss Information in Teen-Focused Versus Women's Magazines over Two 4-Year Periods (1986–1989 and 1991–1994)," *Journal of Nutrition Education* 30.3 (May 1998): 149–154.

22 Walsh-Childers, Edwards, and Grobmyer, "*Essence, Ebony* & O, 136–156."

23 Joshi, Peter, and Valkenburg, "Scripts of Sexual Desire and Danger."

24 Kava, Meister, Whelan, Lukachko, and Mirabile, "Dietary Supplement Safety Information in Magazines."

25 Eva-Marie Kessler and Clemens Schwender, "Giving Dementia a Face? The Portrayal of Older People with Dementia in German Weekly News Magazines between the Years 2000 and 2009," *Journals of Gerontology, Series B: Psychological Sciences and Social Sciences* 67B.2 (March 2012): 261–270. See also Selene G. Phillips, Lindsay J. Della, and Steve H. Sohn, "What Does Cancer Treatment Look Like in Consumer Cancer Magazines? An Exploratory Analysis of Photographic Content in Consumer Cancer Magazines," *Journal of Health Communication* 16.4 (April 2011): 416–430.

26 Patricia A. Aloise-Young, Michael D. Slater, and Courtney C. Cruickshank, "Mediators and Moderators of Magazine Advertisement Effects on Adolescent Cigarette Smoking," *Journal of Health Communication* 11.3 (April/May 2006): 281–300; Jan M. Hill and Kathy L. Radimer, "Health and Nutrition Messages in Food Advertisements: A Comparative Content Analysis of Young and Mature Australian Women's Magazines," *Journal of Nutrition Education* 28.6 (November 1996): 313–320; Yongjun Sung and Heidi J. Hennink-Kaminski, "The Master Settlement Agreement and Visual Imagery of Cigarette Advertising in Two Popular Young Magazines," *Journalism and Mass Communication Quarterly* 85.2 (Summer 2008): 331–352; Peter Williams, Linda Tapsell, Sandra Jones, and Kellie McConville, "Health Claims for Food Made in Australian Magazine Advertisements," *Nutrition & Dietetics* 64.4 (December 2007): 234–240.

27 Clarke and Gawley, "The Triumph of Pharmaceuticals."

28 Katz, Sheridan, Pignone, Lewis, Battle, Gollop, and O'Malley, "Prostate and Colon Cancer Screening Messages."

29 Edy, "Women's Magazine Coverage of Heart Disease Risk Factors"; Turner, Vader, and Walters, "An Analysis of Cardiovascular Health Information."

30 Whitehead and Kurz, "Saints, Sinners and Standards of Femininity."

31 Paul Crawshaw, "Governing the Healthy Male Citizen: Men, Masculinity and Popular Health in *Men's Health* Magazine," *Social Science & Medicine* 65.8 (October 2007): 1606–1618.

32 Andsager and Powers, "Framing Women's Health"; Clarke, "Portrayal of Childhood Cancer."

33 Korinis, Korslund, Belli, Donohue, and Johnson, "Comparison of Calcium and Weight Loss Information"; Krishnan, Durrah, and Winkler, "Coverage of AIDS in Popular African American Magazines."

34 Aloise-Young, Slater, and Cruickshank, "Mediators and Moderators of Magazine Advertisement Effects"; Elizabeth A. Gill and Austin S. Babrow, "To Hope or to Know: Coping with Uncertainty and Ambivalence in Women's Magazine Breast Cancer Articles," *Journal of Applied Communication Research* 35.2 (May 2007): 133–155; Beth Potter, Judy Sheeshka, and Ruta Valaitis, "Content Analysis of Infant Feeding Messages in a Canadian Women's Magazine, 1945 to 1995," *Journal of Nutrition Education* 32.4 (July/August 2000): 196–203.

35 Ashley M. Fandrich and Stephenson J. Beck, "Powerless Language in Health Media: The Influence of Biological Sex and Magazine Type on Health Language," *Communication Studies* 63.1 (January/March 2012): 36–53.

36 Stephannie C. Roy, "'Taking Charge of Your Health': Discourses of Responsibility in English-Canadian Women's Magazines," *Sociology of Health & Illness* 30.3 (April 2008), 463–477.

37 Aloise-Young, Slater, and Cruickshank, "Mediators and Moderators of Magazine Advertisement Effects."

38 Marjolein Gysels, Robert Pool, and Stella Nyanzi, "The Adventures of the Randy Professor and Angela the Sugar Mummy: Sex in Fictional Serials in Ugandan Popular Magazines," *AIDS Care* 17.8 (November 2005): 967–977.

39 Denise Bortree, Lee Ahern, Xue Dou, and Alexandra Nutter Smith, "Framing Environmental Advocacy: A Study of 30 Years of Advertising in *National Geographic Magazine*," *International Journal of Nonprofit and Voluntary Sector Marketing* 17.2 (May 2012): 77–91; Robin T. Peterson, "The Utilization of Ecological Themes in State and Local Government Tourism Magazine Commercials: An Assessment, *Journal of Hospitality & Leisure Marketing* 6.4 (2000): 5–16.

40 Christopher W. Podeschi, "The Culture of Nature and the Rise of Modern Environmentalism: The View through General Audience Magazines, 1945–1980," *Sociological Spectrum* 27.3 (March 2007): 299–331.

41 Vasilia Christidou, Kostas Dimopoulos, and Vasilis Koulaidis, "Constructing Social Representations of Science and Technology: The Role of Metaphors in the Press and the Popular Scientific Magazines," *Public Understanding of Science* 13.4 (October 2004): 347–362; Niklas Pramling and Roger Säljö, "Scientific Knowledge, Popularisation, and the Use of Metaphors: Modern Genetics in Popular Science Magazines," *Scandinavian Journal of Educational Research* 51.3 (July 2007): 275–295.

42 James Mussell, "Nineteenth-Century Popular Science Magazines: Narrative and the Problem of Historical Materiality," *Journalism Studies* 8.4 (August 2007): 656–666.

43 Peter Weinberger, "The *Philosophical Magazine* and the Periodic Table of Elements," *Philosophical Magazine* 92.13 (May 2012): 1727–1732.

44 Geoffrey Cantor, Sally Shuttleworth, and Jonathan R. Topham, "Representations of Science in the Nineteenth Century Periodical Press," *Interdisciplinary Science Reviews* 28.3 (September 2003): 161–168; Oscar Ricci, "Technology for Everyone: Representations of Technology in Popular Italian Scientific Magazines," *Public Understanding of Science* 19.5 (September 2010): 578–589.

45 Sarah Nettleton, "Governing the Risky Self: How to Become Healthy, Wealthy and Wise," in Alan Petersen and Robin Bunton, eds. *Foucault: Health and Medicine* (London: Routledge, 1997), 207–222.

46 Brown, Zavestoski, McCormick, Mandelbaum, and Luebke, "Print Media Coverage of Environmental Causation of Breast Cancer."

47 Krishnan, Durrah, and Winkler, "Coverage of AIDS in Popular African American Magazines"; Kava, Meister, Whelan, Lukachko, and Mirabile, "Dietary Supplement Safety Information in Magazines."

48 Hoffman-Goetz and MacDonald, "Cancer Coverage in Mass-Circulating Canadian Women's Magazines."

49 Sandra A. Berns, "To Speak as a Judge/Woman: A Different Voice," *To Speak as a Judge: Difference, Voice, and Power* (Aldershot, England and Brookfield, VT: Ashgate/Dartmouth, 1999), 210.

50 Hoffman-Goetz and MacDonald, "Cancer Coverage in Mass-Circulating Canadian Women's Magazines."

51 Cornelius B. Pratt, Louisa Ha, and Charlotte A. Pratt, "Setting the Public Health Agenda on Major Diseases in Sub-Saharan Africa: African Popular Magazines and Medical Journals, 1981–1997," *Journal of Communication* 52.4 (December 2002): 889–904.

52 Clarke, "Childhood Depression and Mass Print Magazines."

53 Clarke, "Portrayal of Childhood Cancer."

54 Tobler, Wilson, and Napolitano, "Frequency of Breast Cancer."

55 Mondini, Favaro, and Santonastaso, "Eating Disorders and the Ideal of Feminine Beauty."

56 Annie Lang and Narine S. Yegiyan, "Understanding the Interactive Effects of Emotional Appeal and Claim Strength in Health Messages," *Journal of Broadcasting and Electronic Media* 52.3 (September 2008): 432–447.

57 Karen S. Dobias, Cheryl A. Moyer, Sarah E. McAchran, Steven J. Katz, and Seema S. Sonnad, "Mammography Messages in Popular Media: Implications for Patient Expectations and Shared Clinical Decision-Making," *Health Expectations* 4.2 (June 2001): 131–139; Clarke, van Amerom, and Binns, "Gender and Heart Disease."

58 Atkin, Smith, McFeters, and Ferguson, "A Comprehensive Analysis of Breast Cancer News Coverage."

59 Robert J. Griffin, Sharon Dunwoody, and Kurt Neuwirth, "Proposed Model of the Relationship of Risk Information Seeking and Processing to the Development of Preventive Behaviors," *Environmental Research* 80.2 (February 1999): S230–S245.

60 Henderson, "Mixed Messages about the Meanings of Breast-Feeding Representations."

61 Hoffman-Goetz, "Cancer Experiences of African-American Women."

62 Fandrich and Beck, "Powerless Language."

63 Crawshaw, "Governing the Healthy Male Citizen"; Kessler and Schwender, "Giving Dementia a Face?"; Kava, Meister, Whelan, Lukachko, and Mirabile, "Dietary Supplement Safety Information in Magazines"; Margaret L. Usdansky, "The Emergence of a Social Problem: Single-Parent Families in U.S. Popular Magazines and Social Science Journals, 1900–1998," *Sociological Inquiry* 78.1 (February 2008): 74–96.

64 An example is Néstor Herran's study, "'Science to the Glory of God': The Popular Science Magazine *Ibérica* and Its Coverage of Radioactivity, 1914–1936," *Science & Education* 21.3 (March 2012): 335–353.

65 Christidou, Dimopoulos, and Koulaidis, "Constructing Social Representations of Science and Technology," 359.

66 Thomas Gieryn, "Boundaries of Science," in Sheila Jasanoff, Gerald E. Markle, James C. Petersen, and Trevor Pinch, *Handbook of Science and Technology Studies*, rev. ed. (London: Sage, 1995), 393–443.

67 Paul Slovic, Melissa L. Finucane, Ellen Peters, and Donald G. MacGregor, "Risk as Analysis and Risk as Feelings: Some Thoughts about Affect, Reason, Risk, and Rationality," *Risk Analysis* 24.2 (April 2004): 311–322; Tom R. Tyler and Fay Lomax Cook, "The Mass Media and Judgments of Risk: Distinguishing Impact on Personal and Societal Level Judgments," *Journal of Personality and Social Psychology* 47.4 (October 1984): 693–708.

68 Julia B. Corbett and Jessica L. Durfee, "Testing Public (Un)certainty of Science: Media Representations of Global Warming," *Science Communication* 26.2 (December 2004): 129–151; Sharon Dunwoody, "Scientists, Journalists, and the Meaning of Uncertainty," in Sharon M. Friedman, Sharon Dunwoody, and Carol L. Rogers, eds. *Communicating Uncertainty: Media Coverage of New and Controversial Science* (Mahwah, NJ: Lawrence Erlbaum Associates, 1999), 59–79; Branden B. Johnson, "Further Notes on Public Response to Uncertainty in Risks and Science," *Risk Analysis* 23.4 (2003): 781–789.

69 Jon D. Miller, "Public Understanding of, and Attitudes toward, Scientific Research: What We Know and What We Need to Know," *Public Understanding of Science* 13.3 (July 2004): 273–294; Pablo Briñol and Richard E. Petty, "Source Factors in Persuasion: A Self-Validation Approach," *European Review of Social Psychology* 20 (2009): 49–96; Matthew C. Nisbet and Dietram A. Scheufele, "What's Next for Science Communication? Promising Directions and Lingering Distractions," *American Journal of Botany* 96.10 (October 2009): 1767–1778.

70 Scott C. Zeman, "'Taking Hell's Measurements': *Popular Science* and *Popular Mechanics* Magazines and the Atomic Bomb from Hiroshima to Bikini," *Journal of Popular Culture* 41.4 (August 2008): 695–711.

71 Herran, "'Science to the Glory of God.'"

72 Jason Rosenhouse and Glenn Branch, "Media Coverage of 'Intelligent Design,'" *Bioscience* 56.3 (March 2006): 247–252.

73 John B. Horrigan, *The Internet as a Resource for News and Information about Science* (Washington, DC: Pew Internet and American Life Project, 2006), 5.

74 Examples are Kessler and Schwender, "Giving Dementia a Face?"; Phillips, Della, and Sohn, "What Does Cancer Treatment Look Like?"; Sung and Hennink-Kaminski, "The Master Settlement Agreement and Visual Imagery."

75 Examples are Whitehead and Kurz, "Saints, Sinners and Standards of Femininity"; Walsh-Childers, Edwards, and Grobmyer, "Covering Women's Greatest Health Fear"; Turner, Vader, and Walters, "An Analysis of Cardiovascular Health Information"; Susan McKay and Frances Bonner, "Telling Stories: Breast Cancer Pathographies in Australian Women's Magazines," *Women's Studies International Forum* 22.5 (September/October 1999): 563–571; Marino and Gerlach, "An Analysis of Breast Cancer Coverage."

76 An example is Condit, Ofulue, and Sheedy, "Determinism and Mass Media Portrayals of Genetics," which examined whether the introduction of substantial coverage of medical genetics in the mass media from the late 1970s to the late 1990s represents an increase in biological determinism in public discourse.

77 Bortree, Ahern, Dou, and Nutter Smith, "Framing Environmental Advocacy."

78 Griffin, Dunwoody, and Neuwirth, "Proposed Model of the Relationship of Risk Information Seeking and Processing."

79 Podeschi, "The Culture of Nature and the Rise of Modern Environmentalism."

80 Suzy Gattuso, Simone Fullagar, and Ilena Young, "Speaking of Women's 'Nameless Misery': The Every-day Construction of Depression in Australian Women's Magazines," *Social Science & Medicine* 61.8 (October 2005): 1640–1648.

81 Michael F. Dahlstrom and Shirley S. Ho, "Ethical Considerations of Using Narrative to Communicate Science," *Science Communication* 34.5 (October 2012): 592–617; Edna F. Einsiedel, "Public Participation and Dialogue: A Research Review," in Massimiano Bucchi and Brian Trench, eds., *Handbook of Public Communication of Science and Technology* (New York: Routledge, 2008), 173–184.

82 Griffin, Dunwoody, and Neuwirth, "Proposed Model of the Relationship of Risk Information Seeking and Processing."

83 Kim Witte, "Putting the Fear Back into Fear Appeals—The Extended Parallel Process Model," *Communication Monographs* 59.4 (December 1992): 329–349.

84 Mary Douglas and Aaron Wildavsky, *Risk and Culture: An Essay on the Selection of Technical and Environmental Dangers* (Berkeley: University of California Press, 1982).

85 Brigitta R. Brunner and Larissa R. Brunner Huber, "101 Ways to Improve Health Reporting: A Comparison of the Types and Quality of Health Information in Men's and Women's Magazines," *Public Relations Review* 36.1 (March 2010): 84–86.

86 Ross C. Brownson, Patricia Hartge, Jonathan M. Samet, and Roberta B. Ness, "From Epidemiology to Policy: Toward More Effective Practice," *Annals of Epidemiology* 20.6 (June 2010): 409–411.

87 Ronald Weitzer and Charis E. Kubrin, "Breaking News: How Local TV News and Real-World Conditions Affect Fear of Crime," *Justice Quarterly* 21.3 (September 2004): 497–520.

88 Examples are Carla Rodrigues Cardoso, "The Future of Newsmagazines," *Journalism Studies* 11.4 (April 2010): 577–586; Giulio Lizzi, Lorenzo Cantoni, and Alessandro Inversini, "When a Magazine Goes Online: A Case Study in the Tourism Field," in Rob Law, Matthias Fuchs, and Francesco Ricci, eds., *Information and Communication Technologies in Tourism 2011: Proceedings of the International Conference, 26–28 January 2011* (Vienna, Austria: Springer-Verlag, 2011), 355–366; Brita Ytre-Arne, "'I Want to Hold It in My Hands': Readers' Experiences of the Phenomenological Differences between Women's Magazines Online and in Print," *Media Culture & Society* 33.3 (April 2011): 467–477.

89 David Dickson, "Weaving a Social Web—The Internet Promises to Revolutionize Public Engagement with Science and Technology," *Nature* 414.6864 (6 December 2001): 587.

Bibliography

Aloise-Young, Patricia A.; Slater, Michael D.; and Cruickshank, Courtney C. "Mediators and Moderators of Magazine Advertisement Effects on Adolescent Cigarette Smoking." *Journal of Health Communication* 11.3 (April/May 2006): 281–300.

Andsager, Julie L. and Powers, Angela. "Framing Women's Health with a Sense-Making Approach: Magazine Coverage of Breast Cancer and Implants." *Health Communication* 13.2 (2001): 163–185.

Andsager, Julie L. and Powers, Angela. "Social or Economic Concerns: How News and Women's Magazines Framed Breast Cancer in the 1990s." *Journalism & Mass Communication Quarterly* 76.3 (Autumn 1999): 531–550.

Atkin, Charles K.; Smith, Sandi W.; McFeters, Courtnay; and Ferguson, Vanessa. "A Comprehensive Analysis of Breast Cancer News Coverage in Leading Media Outlets Focusing on Environmental Risks and Prevention." *Journal of Health Communication* 13.1 (January/February 2008): 3–19.

Berns, Sandra A. "To Speak as a Judge/Woman: A Different Voice." *To Speak as a Judge: Difference, Voice, and Power.* Aldershot, England and Brookfield, VT: Ashgate/Dartmouth, 1999, 193–213.

Blanchard, Deena; Erblich, Joel; Montgomery, Guy H.; and Bovbjerg, Dana H. "Read All About It: The Over-Representation of Breast Cancer in Popular Magazines." *Preventive Medicine* 35.4 (October 2002): 343–348.

Bortree, Denise; Ahern, Lee; Dou, Xue; and Nutter Smith, Alexandra. "Framing Environmental Advocacy: A Study of 30 Years of Advertising in *National Geographic Magazine*." *International Journal of Nonprofit and Voluntary Sector Marketing* 17.2 (May 2012): 77–91.

Briñol, Pablo and Petty, Richard E. "Source Factors in Persuasion: A Self-Validation Approach." *European Review of Social Psychology* 20 (2009): 49–96.

Brown, Phil; Zavestoski, Stephen M.; McCormick, Sabrina; Mandelbaum, Joshua; and Luebke, Theo. "Print Media Coverage of Environmental Causation of Breast Cancer." *Sociology of Health & Illness* 23.6 (2001): 747–775.

Brownson, Ross C.; Hartge, Patricia; Samet, Jonathan M.; and Ness, Roberta B. "From Epidemiology to Policy: Toward More Effective Practice." *Annals of Epidemiology* 20.6 (June 2010): 409–411.

Brunner, Brigitta R. and Brunner Huber, Larissa R. "101 Ways to Improve Health Reporting: A Comparison of the Types and Quality of Health Information in Men's and Women's Magazines." *Public Relations Review* 36.1 (March 2010): 84–86.

Cantor, Geoffrey; Shuttleworth, Sally; and Topham, Jonathan R. "Representations of Science in the Nineteenth Century Periodical Press." *Interdisciplinary Science Reviews* 28.3 (September 2003): 161–168.

Cardoso, Carla Rodrigues. "The Future of Newsmagazines." *Journalism Studies* 11.4 (April 2010): 577–586.

Christidou, Vasilia; Dimopoulos, Kostas; and Koulaidis, Vasilis. "Constructing Social Representations of Science and Technology: The Role of Metaphors in the Press and the Popular Scientific Magazines." *Public Understanding of Science* 13.4 (October 2004): 347–362.

Clarke, Juanne N. "The Case of the Missing Person: Alzheimer's Disease in Mass Print Magazines 1991–2001." *Health Communication* 19.3 (2006): 269–276.

Clarke, Juanne N. "Childhood Depression and Mass Print Magazines in the USA and Canada: 1983–2008." *Child and Family Social Work* 16.1 (February 2011): 52–60.

Clarke, Juanne N. "The Paradoxical Portrayal of the Risk of Sexually Transmitted Infections and Sexuality in U.S. Magazines *Glamour* and *Cosmopolitan* 2000–2007." *Health, Risk & Society* 12.6 (December 2010): 560–574.

Clarke, Juanne N. "Portrayal of Childhood Cancer in English Language Magazines in North America: 1970–2001." *Journal of Health Communication* 10.7 (October/November 2005): 593–607.

Clarke, Juanne N. "Women's Work, Worry and Fear: The Portrayal of Sexuality and Sexual Health in U.S. Magazines for Teenage and Middle-Aged Women, 2000–2007." *Culture, Health & Sexuality* 11.4 (May 2009): 415–429.

Clarke, Juanne N. and Binns, Jeannine. "The Portrayal of Heart Disease in Mass Print Magazines, 1991–2001." *Health Communication* 19.1 (2006): 39–48.

Clarke, Juanne N. and Gawley, Adele. "The Triumph of Pharmaceuticals: The Portrayal of Depression from 1980 to 2005." *Administration & Policy in Mental Health & Mental Health Services Research* 36.2 (March 2009): 91–101.

Clarke, Juanne N.; McLellan, Lianne; and Hoffman-Goetz, Laurie. "The Portrayal of HIV/AIDS in Two Popular African American Magazines." *Journal of Health Communication* 11.5 (July/August 2006): 495–507.

Clarke, Juanne N.; Romagnoli, Amy; Sargent, Cristal; and van Amerom, Gudrun. "The Portrayal of Complementary and Alternative Medicine in Mass Print Magazines since 1980." *Journal of Alternative and Complementary Medicine* 16.1 (January 2010): 125–130.

Clarke, Juanne N.; van Amerom, Gudrun; and Binns, Jeannine. "Gender and Heart Disease in Mass Print Media: 1991, 1996, 2001." *Women & Health* 45.1 (2007): 17–35.

Condit, Celeste M.; Ofulue, Nneka; and Sheedy, Kristine M. "Determinism and Mass Media Portrayals of Genetics." *American Journal of Human Genetics* 62.4 (April 1998): 979–984.

Corbett, Julia B. and Durfee, Jessica L. "Testing Public (Un)certainty of Science: Media Representations of Global Warming." *Science Communication* 26.2 (December 2004): 129–151.

Crawshaw, Paul. "Governing the Healthy Male Citizen: Men, Masculinity and Popular Health in *Men's Health* Magazine." *Social Science & Medicine* 65.8 (October 2007): 1606–1618.

Dahlstrom, Michael F. and Ho, Shirley S. "Ethical Considerations of Using Narrative to Communicate Science." *Science Communication* 34.5 (October 2012): 592–617.

Dickson, David. "Weaving a Social Web—The Internet Promises to Revolutionize Public Engagement with Science and Technology." *Nature* 414.6864 (6 December 2001): 587.

Dobias, Karen S.; Moyer, Cheryl A.; McAchran, Sarah E.; Katz, Steven J.; and Sonnad, Seema S. "Mammography Messages in Popular Media: Implications for Patient Expectations and Shared Clinical Decision-Making." *Health Expectations* 4.2 (June 2001): 131–139.

Douglas, Mary and Wildavsky, Aaron. *Risk and Culture: An Essay on the Selection of Technical and Environmental Dangers.* Berkeley: University of California Press, 1982.

Dunwoody, Sharon. "Scientists, Journalists, and the Meaning of Uncertainty." In Friedman; Sharon M.; Dunwoody, Sharon; and Rogers, Carol L., eds. *Communicating Uncertainty: Media Coverage of New and Controversial Science.* Mahwah, NJ: Lawrence Erlbaum Associates, 1999, 59–79.

Edy, Carolyn M. "Women's Magazine Coverage of Heart Disease Risk Factors: *Good Housekeeping* Magazine, 1997 to 2007." *Women & Health* 50.2 (March 2010): 176–194.

Einsiedel, Edna F. "Public Participation and Dialogue: A Research Review." In Bucchi, Massimiano and Trench, Brian, eds. *Handbook of Public Communication of Science and Technology*. New York: Routledge, 2008, 173–184.

Fandrich, Ashley M. and Beck, Stephenson J. "Powerless Language in Health Media: The Influence of Biological Sex and Magazine Type on Health Language." *Communication Studies* 63.1 (January/March 2012): 36–53.

Friedman, Daniela B.; Laditka, James N.; Laditka, Sarah B.; and Mathews, Anna E. "Cognitive Health Messages in Popular Women's and Men's Magazines, 2006–2007." *Preventing Chronic Disease* 7.2 (March 2010): 1–10.

Gattuso, Suzy; Fullagar, Simone; and Young, Ilena. "Speaking of Women's 'Nameless Misery': The Everyday Construction of Depression in Australian Women's Magazines." *Social Science & Medicine* 61.8 (October 2005): 1640–1648.

Gieryn, Thomas. "Boundaries of Science." In Jasanoff, Sheila; Markle, Gerald E.; Petersen, James C.; and Pinch, Trevor. *Handbook of Science and Technology Studies*. Rev. ed. London: Sage, 1995, 393–443.

Gill, Elizabeth A. and Babrow, Austin S. "To Hope or to Know: Coping with Uncertainty and Ambivalence in Women's Magazine Breast Cancer Articles." *Journal of Applied Communication Research* 35.2 (May 2007): 133–155.

Griffin, Robert J.; Dunwoody, Sharon; and Neuwirth, Kurt. "Proposed Model of the Relationship of Risk Information Seeking and Processing to the Development of Preventive Behaviors." *Environmental Research* 80.2 (February 1999): S230–S245.

Gysels, Marjolein; Pool, Robert; and Nyanzi, Stella. "The Adventures of the Randy Professor and Angela the Sugar Mummy: Sex in Fictional Serials in Ugandan Popular Magazines." *AIDS Care* 17.8 (November 2005): 967–977.

Henderson, Ann M. "Mixed Messages about the Meanings of Breast-Feeding Representations in the Australian Press and Popular Magazines." *Midwifery* 15.1 (March 1999): 24–31.

Herran, Néstor. "'Science to the Glory of God': The Popular Science Magazine *Ibérica* and Its Coverage of Radioactivity, 1914–1936." *Science & Education* 21.3 (March 2012): 335–353.

Hill, Jan M. and Radimer, Kathy L. "Health and Nutrition Messages in Food Advertisements: A Comparative Content Analysis of Young and Mature Australian Women's Magazines." *Journal of Nutrition Education* 28.6 (November 1996): 313–320.

Hoffman-Goetz, Laurie. "Cancer Experiences of African-American Women as Portrayed in Popular Mass Magazines." *Psycho-Oncology* 8.1 (January/February 1999): 36–45.

Hoffman-Goetz, Laurie; Gerlach, Karen K.; Marino, Christina; and Mills, Sherry L. "Cancer Coverage and Tobacco Advertising in African-American Women's Popular Magazines." *Journal of Community Health* 22.4 (August 1997): 261–270.

Hoffman-Goetz, Laurie and MacDonald, Megan. "Cancer Coverage in Mass-Circulating Canadian Women's Magazines." *Canadian Journal of Public Health* 90.1 (January/February 1999): 55–59.

Horrigan, John B. *The Internet as a Resource for News and Information about Science*. Washington, DC: Pew Internet and American Life Project, 2006.

Johnson, Branden B. "Further Notes on Public Response to Uncertainty in Risks and Science." *Risk Analysis* 23.4 (2003): 781–789.

Joshi, Suchi P.; Peter, Jochen; and Valkenburg, Patti M. "Scripts of Sexual Desire and Danger in U.S. and Dutch Teen Girl Magazines: A Cross-National Content Analysis." *Sex Roles* 64.7/8 (April 2011): 463–474.

Katz, Mira L.; Sheridan, Stacey; Pignone, Michael; Lewis, Carmen; Battle, Jamila; Gollop, Claudia; and O'Malley, Michael. "Prostate and Colon Cancer Screening Messages in Popular Magazines." *Journal of General Internal Medicine* 19.8 (August 2004): 843–848.

Kava, Ruth; Meister, Kathleen A.; Whelan, Elizabeth M.; Lukachko, Alicia M.; and Mirabile, Christina. "Dietary Supplement Safety Information in Magazines Popular among Older Readers." *Journal of Health Communication* 7.1 (January/February 2002): 13–23.

Kessler, Eva-Marie and Schwender, Clemens. "Giving Dementia a Face? The Portrayal of Older People with Dementia in German Weekly News Magazines between the Years 2000 and 2009." *Journals of Gerontology, Series B: Psychological Sciences and Social Sciences* 67B.2 (March 2012): 261–270.

Korinis, Mary; Korslund, Mary K.; Belli, Gabriella; Donohue, Joyce M.; and Johnson, Janet M. "Comparison of Calcium and Weight Loss Information in Teen-Focused Versus Women's Magazines over Two 4-Year Periods (1986–1989 and 1991–1994)," *Journal of Nutrition Education* 30.3 (May 1998): 149–154.

Krishnan, Satya P.; Durrah, Tracy; and Winkler, Karen. "Coverage of AIDS in Popular African American Magazines." *Health Communication* 9.3 (1997): 273–288.

Lang, Annie and Yegiyan, Narine S. "Understanding the Interactive Effects of Emotional Appeal and Claim Strength in Health Messages." *Journal of Broadcasting and Electronic Media* 52.3 (September 2008): 432–447.

Lizzi, Giulio; Cantoni, Lorenzo; and Inversini, Alessandro. "When a Magazine Goes Online: A Case Study in the Tourism Field." In Law, Rob; Fuchs, Matthias; and Ricci, Francesco, eds. *Information and Communication Technologies in Tourism 2011: Proceedings of the International Conference*. 26–28 January 2011, Vienna, Austria: Springer-Verlag, 2011, 355–366.

Marino, Christina and Gerlach, Karen K. "An Analysis of Breast Cancer Coverage in Selected Women's Magazines, 1987–1995." *American Journal of Health Promotion* 13.3 (January/February 1999): 163–170.

McKay, Susan and Bonner, Frances. "Educating Readers: Breast Cancer in Australian Women's Magazines." *International Journal of Qualitative Studies in Education* 17.4 (July/August 2004): 517–535.

McKay, Susan and Bonner, Frances. "Telling Stories: Breast Cancer Pathographies in Australian Women's Magazines." *Women's Studies International Forum* 22.5 (September/October 1999): 563–571.

Mercado-Martinez, Francisco J.; Robles-Silva, Leticia; Moreno-Leal, Nora; and Franco-Almazan, Claudia. "Inconsistent Journalism: The Coverage of Chronic Diseases in the Mexican Press." *Journal of Health Communication* 6.3 (July/September 2001): 235–247.

Miller, Jon D. "Public Understanding of, and Attitudes toward, Scientific Research: What We Know and What We Need to Know." *Public Understanding of Science* 13.3 (July 2004): 273–294.

Mondini, Silvia; Favaro, Angela; and Santonastaso, Paolo. "Eating Disorders and the Ideal of Feminine Beauty in Italian Newspapers and Magazines." *European Eating Disorders Review* 4.2 (June 1996): 112–120.

Mussell, James. "Nineteenth-Century Popular Science Magazines: Narrative and the Problem of Historical Materiality." *Journalism Studies* 8.4 (August 2007): 656–666.

Nettleton, Sarah. "Governing the Risky Self: How to Become Healthy, Wealthy and Wise." In Petersen, Alan and Bunton, Robin, eds. *Foucault, Health and Medicine*. London: Routledge, 1997, 207–222.

Nisbet, Matthew C. and Scheufele, Dietram A. "What's Next for Science Communication? Promising Directions and Lingering Distractions." *American Journal of Botany* 96.10 (October 2009): 1767–1778.

North, Robert C.; Holsti, Ole R.; Zaninovich, M. George; and Zinnes, Dina A. *Content Analysis: A Handbook with Applications for the Study of International Crisis*. Evanston, IL: Northwestern University Press, 1963.

Nykanen, Kaisa; Suominen, Tarja; and Nikkonen, Merja. "Representations of Hysterectomy as a Transition Process in Finnish Women's and Health Magazines." *Scandinavian Journal of Caring Sciences* 25.3 (September 2011): 608–616.

Peterson, Robin T. "The Utilization of Ecological Themes in State and Local Government Tourism Magazine Commercials: An Assessment." *Journal of Hospitality & Leisure Marketing* 6.4 (2000): 5–16.

Phillips, Selene G.; Della, Lindsay J.; and Sohn, Steve H. "What Does Cancer Treatment Look Like in Consumer Cancer Magazines? An Exploratory Analysis of Photographic Content in Consumer Cancer Magazines." *Journal of Health Communication* 16.4 (April 2011): 416–430.

Podeschi, Christopher W. "The Culture of Nature and the Rise of Modern Environmentalism: The View through General Audience Magazines, 1945–1980." *Sociological Spectrum* 27.3 (March 2007): 299–331.

Potter, Beth; Sheeshka, Judy; and Valaitis, Ruta. "Content Analysis of Infant Feeding Messages in a Canadian Women's Magazine, 1945 to 1995." *Journal of Nutrition Education* 32.4 (July/August 2000): 196–203.

Pramling, Niklas and Säljö, Roger. "Scientific Knowledge, Popularisation, and the Use of Metaphors: Modern Genetics in Popular Science Magazines." *Scandinavian Journal of Educational Research* 51.3 (July 2007): 275–295.

Pratt, Cornelius B.; Ha, Louisa; and Pratt, Charlotte A. "Setting the Public Health Agenda on Major Diseases in Sub-Saharan Africa: African Popular Magazines and Medical Journals, 1981–1997." *Journal of Communication* 52.4 (December 2002): 889–904.

Ricci, Oscar. "Technology for Everyone: Representations of Technology in Popular Italian Scientific Magazines." *Public Understanding of Science* 19.5 (September 2010): 578–589.

Rosenhouse, Jason and Branch, Glenn. "Media Coverage of 'Intelligent Design.'" *BioScience* 56.3 (March 2006): 247–252.

Roy, Stephannie C. "'Taking Charge of Your Health': Discourses of Responsibility in English-Canadian Women's Magazines." *Sociology of Health & Illness* 30.3 (April 2008): 463–477.

Slovic, Paul; Finucane, Melissa L.; Peters, Ellen; and MacGregor, Donald G. "Risk as Analysis and Risk as Feelings: Some Thoughts about Affect, Reason, Risk, and Rationality." *Risk Analysis* 24.2 (April 2004): 311–322.

Sung, Yongjun and Hennink-Kaminski, Heidi J. "The Master Settlement Agreement and Visual Imagery of Cigarette Advertising in Two Popular Youth Magazines." *Journalism & Mass Communication Quarterly* 85.2 (Summer 2008): 331–352.

Tobler, Kyle J.; Wilson, Philip K.; and Napolitano, Peter G. "Frequency of Breast Cancer, Lung Cancer, and Tobacco Use Articles in Women's Magazines from 1987 to 2003." *Journal of Cancer Education* 24.1 (March 2009): 36–39.

Turner, Melanie B.; Vader, Amanda M.; and Walters, Scott T. "An Analysis of Cardiovascular Health Information in Popular Young Women's Magazines: What Messages are Women Receiving?" *American Journal of Health Promotion* 22.3 (January/February 2008): 183–186.

Tyler, Tom R. and Cook, Fay Lomax. "The Mass Media and Judgments of Risk: Distinguishing Impact on Personal and Societal Level Judgments." *Journal of Personality and Social Psychology* 47.4 (October 1984): 693–708.

Usdansky, Margaret L. "The Emergence of a Social Problem: Single-Parent Families in U.S. Popular Magazines and Social Science Journals, 1900–1998." *Sociological Inquiry* 78.1 (February 2008): 74–96.

Walsh-Childers, Kim; Edwards, Heather; and Grobmyer, Stephen. "Covering Women's Greatest Health Fear: Breast Cancer Information in Consumer Magazines." *Health Communication* 26.3 (April/May 2011): 209–220.

Walsh-Childers, Kim; Edwards, Heather M.; and Grobmyer, Stephen. "*Essence, Ebony* and O: Breast Cancer Coverage in Black Magazines." *Howard Journal of Communications* 23.2 (April/June 2012): 136–156.

Weinberger, Peter. "The *Philosophical Magazine* and the Periodic Table of Elements." *Philosophical Magazine* 92.13 (May 2012): 1727–1732.

Weitzer, Ronald and Kubrin, Charis E. "Breaking News: How Local TV News and Real-World Conditions Affect Fear of Crime." *Justice Quarterly* 21.3 (September 2004): 497–520.

Whitehead, Kally and Kurz, Tim. "Saints, Sinners and Standards of Femininity: Discursive Constructions of Anorexia Nervosa and Obesity in Women's Magazines." *Journal of Gender Studies* 17.4 (December 2008): 345–358.

Wilkes, Lesley; Withnall, Janice; Harris, Rebecca; White, Kate; Beale, Barbara; Hobson, Jane; Durham, Marsha; and Kristjanson, Linda. "Stories about Breast Cancer in Australian Women's Magazines: Information Sources for Risk, Early Detection and Treatment." *European Journal of Oncology Nursing* 5.2 (June 2001): 80–88.

Williams, Peter; Tapsell, Linda; Jones, Sandra; and McConville, Kellie. "Health Claims for Food Made in Australian Magazine Advertisements." *Nutrition & Dietetics* 64.4 (December 2007): 234–240.

Witte, Kim. "Putting the Fear Back into Fear Appeals—The Extended Parallel Process Model." *Communication Monographs* 59.4 (December 1992): 329–349.

Ytre-Arne, Brita. "'I Want to Hold It in My Hands': Readers' Experiences of the Phenomenological Differences between Women's Magazines Online and in Print." *Media, Culture & Society* 33.3 (April 2011): 467–477.

Zeman, Scott C. "'Taking Hell's Measurements': *Popular Science* and *Popular Mechanics* Magazines and the Atomic Bomb from Hiroshima to Bikini." *Journal of Popular Culture* 41.4 (August 2008): 695–711.

21

MAGAZINES AND THE VISUAL ARTS

The Ideal Showcase

Sheila M. Webb

This chapter discusses the state of research *on* art magazines, on art *in* magazines, and on magazines as an *art form* since 2000, and it focuses mainly on studies done on periodicals produced in the United States. Because magazines constitute an ideal venue to showcase art, the multi-faceted dimensions of the periodical provide a rich avenue for research. The subject offers provocative opportunities to investigate the creation of taste publics and to consider how cultural awareness impacts social positioning[1]; to consider issues of standard setting and the attendant discussion of art as an exclusively elite venue versus one that is considered available to all; to investigate how visuals may express political agendas; to explore the relationship between consumer culture and art practice; to conduct archival work on specific titles and their editors; to expand on work done on the contradictory role of magazines in art reception and art criticism—to both promote art and to provide space for critiques of such promotions; to discuss how artists exploit publicity and counter-publicity via art journals; or to analyze the expressive possibilities artists themselves find in the magazine form.

The art periodical also affords the opportunity to explore the relationship between the historical development of art periodicals and technology. For example, the British *Burlington Magazine* premiered in 1903, just when it was possible to print high-quality photogravures, and the large-format, glossy pages of *Life* magazine furnished a prime 1930s showcase in the United States for art and photography with its launch in 1936.

Further, research suggests the history and reach of magazines is intimately connected to the development of visuals. Richard Ohmann argues magazines became the first national mass medium,[2] and this reach was driven in part by the increasing ability to print visuals. Cynthia Lee Patterson gives evidence that in the mid-nineteenth century, with galleries and museums not widely available, readers interested in art depended on magazines to inform them about fine art.[3] Later in the century, with the emerging consumer culture, magazines such as *Scribner's* participated in the expansion of the magazine industry by satisfying the sharply increasing demand for pictorials, thereby, as Page Stevens Knox shows, profiting in the process.[4] Sheila Webb writes that in the twentieth century, magazines functioned as printed art galleries that one could peruse. Magazines such as *Life* offered taste education to its middle-class audience with the express purpose of informing its readership on the import of movements, artists and events.[5]

The concept of a tie between magazines and art is elucidated by the work of German philosopher Walter Benjamin, who argued that the reproducibility of art changed both its nature and its reception. Magazines' reproductions of art caused fine art to become something that was affordable, accessible and "designed for reproducibility."[6] Benjamin's analysis of twinned aspects of modern media—technical reproducibility and a new chance for a collective experience—is worth more exploration in the magazine form, as work previously off limits, that is, fine art, became accessible. One example of such an audience response is a letter from a working girl to *Life* magazine in 1938, thanking the editors for providing large reproductions of paintings, as she did not have time to visit galleries.

> . . . thank you for the excellent taste you displayed in publishing photographs of fine art. It is very difficult for me, as a working girl, and for many other people in my position to find sufficient time to visit art galleries as much as we would like to. But now that you are planning to give us reproductions (and in beautiful colors), I cannot help but express my sincerest gratification.[7]

Drawing on these points, this chapter explores scholars' work that looks at art magazines, art *in* magazines and magazines as an *art form*. Within these three approaches, the following themes were identified: the theme of modernism, a natural outcome of the confluence of art and the growth of mass media; research on little magazines, which is tied to the theme of modernism; research on specific art movements, such as surrealism, and how they were conveyed or expressed via magazines; research on gender and class; biographical and historical examinations of particular magazines and their editors; analyses of art magazines of the 1960s and 1970s as embodying a new expressive form; and research on the role of covers in defining either a magazine's audience or in reflecting an era.

The State of the Research

In the past, magazine scholars lamented the dearth of peer-reviewed inquiry on the magazine form and argued for magazines' place in media and communication research, one rich for social and cultural commentary.[8] This situation was reassessed in 2008 when the Magazine Division of the Association for Education in Journalism and Mass Communication sponsored a panel devoted to ascertaining the state of magazine research since the 1995 publication of *The American Magazine: Research Perspectives and Prospects*.[9] Members of the panel proposed the following appraisal: the field was still unfulfilled, with potential avenues for research not yet explored. Further, the field was being transformed by new scholarship and by technological developments, such as on-line magazines. A number of insights expressed at the panel provide grounding for some of the findings of this chapter, which treats scholarship on visual art published since 2000.

Panelist Carolyn Kitch noted that certain topics dominate magazine studies—among them biographies and histories of companies. This theme was also found in the current review of published scholarly research on art and magazines. One thread in the findings for this chapter was a focus on influential magazines, in particular the *Burlington Magazine*, with attention for the most part on the role of editors, accompanied at times by an examination of how such magazines fit into discourse on art and its role in society. One complaint Kitch voiced was the tendency to view magazines as a "window" into history rather than as a worthy topic on their own.[10] However, many of the studies examined in this chapter do attempt to place magazines within a cultural construct. For example, Gwen Allen, rather than approaching art magazines of the 1960s as a form of historical archive, assesses how art magazines influenced both theory and practice of art in a particular time and place.[11]

Also on the 2008 panel, historian Joe Bernt described the importance of historical studies of magazines to the study of American culture; he also noted the connection to class.[12] One example described here that embodies Bernt's call is Patterson's examination of illustrated magazines of the 1840s.[13] For Bernt, the time period of magazines' ascendance—the two decades on either side of the turn of the twentieth century—was instrumental in codifying the U.S. concept of modern frameworks, as well as what has been called "middlebrow culture."[14]

This remains a very promising area that has not been fully explored. The role of magazines in portraying and even performing class distinctions is ripe for study. Two recent works that treat class include Rachel Lynn Schreiber's examination of the portrayal of women's roles in cover illustrations of the *Masses* in the second decade of the twentieth century[15] and Isadora Anderson Helfgott's study of the role of art in magazines during a time of labor strife in the 1930s.[16]

Panelist David Abrahamson described magazines as an "art form, not just a delivery system." Further, he suggested that magazines, traditionally thought of as "mirrors," can also be considered as "catalysts."[17] Although Abrahamson's remarks were meant to describe how magazines could successfully meet the challenge of on-line presence, his insight might also apply to recent scholarship that covers historical challenges to the traditional magazine form in a variety of ways: magazines that became the outlet and voice of art movements, such as Dada[18]; artists, such as Ed Ruscha,[19] who used magazines to further their work; artists who created magazines as an art form in itself, as seen in, for example, *Aspen* magazine[20]; art magazines that were founded as a distinct challenge to traditional art magazines, such as *Avalanche* and *Bomb*[21]; and artists and publishers who used magazines to challenge not only magazines as a form but also to push back against the perceived restrictions of the art world, as seen in the tumult of the art scene in Los Angeles in the 1970s.[22]

Method

This chapter treats scholarship on the visual arts only, as a distinct area of scholarship. Thus, the chapter does not address periodicals that cover architecture, the performing or musical arts. Comics and cartoons, illustrations and graphic design also constitute separate research areas, so, with a few exceptions, are not covered here. Further, this chapter focuses on U.S. publications, as very few studies were found on foreign publications. For the same reason, the chapter eschews research on zines and on-line art magazines.

To identify recent research, the author investigated the following sources, looking at material published from January 2000 through 2013. Using the search terms *art in magazines*; *art coverage + magazines*; *magazines cover art*; *art + magazines*; *fine art + journalism*; *fine art + art magazines + journalism*, the following databases were searched: Communication and Mass Media Complete, JSTOR, EBSCO and ProQuest Dissertation and Theses. Individual searches were also done of the archives of the following journals: *American Historical Review, Art History, American Periodicals, American Quarterly, Journal of American History, Journal of Design History, Journal of Modern Periodical Studies, Journal of Magazine & New Media Research, Journal of the Society of Architectural Historians, Oxford Art Journal, Sociological Perspectives, Sociological Quarterly, Studies in Art Education* and *Visual Arts Research*. Individual examinations were made of the following art magazines: *Art Bulletin, Art in America, Art Forum, ARTnews, Burlington Magazine, Winterthur Portfolio* and *Women's Art Journal*.

In this thorough search for research on art and magazines, both in databases and in numerous individual titles, 29 works done in the realm of art were found. Most take a historical approach, some a critical-cultural studies approach; some studies combine the two. One can speculate as to why there is not more done. If journalism and mass communication journals do indeed view magazines as a specific niche, focusing on an esoteric subject reduces the possibilities of scholarly publication even further. Art may seem to be a rarefied field, one that journalism and mass communication scholars are not trained in or feel equipped to discuss. Art historians are more likely to write for journals in their field and to focus on artists and movements as opposed to researching how either might have been framed in the media.

Yet this field offers a rich resource for not only journalism and mass communication scholars but for cultural historians as well. A 2010 issue of *American Periodicals* devoted to visual culture pointed out the possibilities. Calling the topic a "vexed" one, editor Janice Simon noted the historical link between the success of magazines and their increasing number of images, as well as the huge range of visuals to be explored, from cartoons to ads. She also proposed areas of investigation—how visuals relate to text, the political messages they convey or the implicit cultural messages they carry.[23] Also in *American Periodicals*, Judith Yaross Lee earlier noted the delimiting influence of research traditions—historians of journalism focus mainly on editorial processes as opposed to more literary or cultural topics—and called for a more "holistic" approach.[24]

Themes

Themes identified for this chapter include the critical theme of modernism (Table 21.1). This is a logical pairing, as the ability of magazines to print visuals and the growth of modernism occurred at the same time. Further, magazines championed modernism, so the connection was integral to conveying the new cultural movement. Among these were the Little Magazines,

Table 21.1. Summary of themes and approaches by kind of publication[1]

Themes	Publication Title or Kind by Chapter Mention Order	Approach	Study Author/s	N = 29
Modernism				7
• Little Magazines				
	American Periodicals	Art *in* Magazine	Churchill and McKible (2005)	
	Book	Art *in* Magazines	Scholes and Wulfman (2010)	
	Modern Periodical Studies	Art *in* Magazines	Scholes (2011)	
• Art World				
	American Art	Art *in* Magazines	Masteller (1997)	
	Ph.D. Dissertation	Art *in* Magazines	Cottrell (2002)	
• Fashion/Avant-Garde				
	American Periodicals	Art *in* Magazines	Crawforth (2004)	
	Fashion Theory	Art *in* Magazines	Söll (2009)	
Class and Gender				6
	Book	Art *in* Magazines	Patterson (2010)	
	Ph.D. Dissertation	Art *in* Magazines	Knox (2012)	
	Ph.D. Dissertation	Art *in* Magazines	Helfgott (2006)	
	American Periodicals	Art *in* Magazines	Langa (2011)	
	Ph.D. Dissertation	Art *in* Magazines	Slater (2005)	
	Ph.D. Dissertation	Art *in* Magazines	Schreiber (2008)	
Magazines and Their Editors				7
	Ph.D. Dissertation	Art *in* Magazines	Yahr (2012)	
	Ph.D. Dissertation	On Art Magazines	Houser (2011)	
	Burlington Magazine	On Art Magazines	Santori (2003)	
	Burlington Magazine	On Art Magazines	Elam (2003)	
	Burlington Magazine	On Art Magazines	Rhodes (2004)	
	Book Review	Art *in* Magazines	Wilson (2006)	
	American Journalism	Art *in* Magazines	Webb (2010)	

Themes	Publication Title or Kind by Chapter Mention Order	Approach	Study Author/s	N = 29
The Magazine as Art Strategy				7
	Modern Periodical Studies	Magazines *as* Art	Hage (2011)	
	Ph.D. Dissertation	Magazines *as* Art	Allen (2004)	
	Book	Magazines *as* Art	Allen (2011)	
	Art Journal	Magazines *as* Art	Allen (2005)	
	M.A. Thesis	Magazines *as* Art	Weiner (2011)	
	Ph.D. Dissertation	Magazines *as* Art	Allan (2004)	
	New Art Publications	Magazines *as* Art	McClister (2006)	
Covers				2
	Ph.D. Dissertation	Art *in* Magazines	Knopf (2011)	
	Book	Art *in* Magazines	Kitch (2001)	

[1] Dissertations provide primary art in magazines scholarship; *Modern Periodical Studies* and *American Periodicals* also actively support research on art in magazines.

which were also connected to the theme of modernism. Another thread is research on specific art movements. Some of the research described here deals with class and gender. Other research treats specific magazines with a focus on the role of editors rather than an analysis of art. Provocative research includes examination of challenges to the art establishment—e.g., galleries, museums, art criticism, mainstream art periodicals and commercialism—by artists who created their own magazines. Finally, research on the role of covers in defining either a magazine's audience or in expressing an era provides another thread.

Very little work has been done on the art magazines themselves. These would be a rich venue in which to explore more fully the role of magazines in fostering movements or the work of particular artists, in establishing standards for taste, in partnering with museums and the federal government to promote art, and in identifying the ties between the magazines and the advertisements they carry.

Modernism

Historians, sociologists and cultural scholars have long been attracted to the issue of modernity. Recently, the meaning of the term has shifted from a concept of the avant-garde toward a more comprehensive exploration. Marshall Berman applies the term to convey multiple meanings: "modernization," which references innovations in science, politics and economics that took social form; "modernity," which addresses the impact that modernization had on daily life; and "modernism," which identifies the way art responded to these changes.[25] Berman's third definition is useful in assessing the intimate connection between modernism and magazines, both in form and in content. The concept offers a rich research topic for magazine scholars.

Little Magazines

A number of works published since 2000 show how intimately tied the *little magazines* were to the concept of modernism. A special 2005 issue of *American Periodicals* examined the critical role little magazines performed in modernism's development. They were, in Suzanne Churchill and Adam McKible's words, the "center of American modernism in the early decades of the twentieth century . . . considered vital by the men and women who were busy shaping the nation's cultural and political landscape."[26]

In *Modernism in the Magazines: An Introduction*, Robert Scholes and Clifford Wulfman outline the research possibilities for academics. They describe magazines as central to the development of modernism and advocate for more exploration of such periodicals. Their approach takes advantage of recent perspectives, that is, to not view magazines as vehicles of data, but rather as multivocal texts. Although the concept of modernism in little magazines typically considers literature, especially the role of Ezra Pound, Scholes and Wulfman devote a chapter to the visual arts, which they describe as having benefited from the "cultural space" where "challenging new modes of literature and visual art could appear side by side with less challenging works, thus instigating an important dialog about which works were best suited for the modern world."[27] This area of scholarship was enhanced by the founding of the *Journal of Modern Periodical Studies* in 2010. Writing in the journal on the coverage of fine art in *Scribner's Monthly* in the early 1900s, Scholes addresses the lack of knowledge about how modern art was covered in the larger magazines of the era. Scholes describes the mixed response to modern art and, through a description of reproduced art and the accompanying commentary in *Scribner's*, traces the transition from initial resistance to acceptance.[28]

Art World

Another work that examines the acceptance of modernism in the early twentieth century as promulgated in magazines focuses on the sculptures of Brancusi. Richard Masteller argues that during a time of conflicting versions of modernism, an investigation of how three magazines covered the influential sculptor shows how each played a role in "selling versions of modernism to readers beyond the circle of the avant-garde."[29] Masteller describes the disparity of the coverage of Brancusi in the *Little Review*, *Vanity Fair* and the *Dial*. Ezra Pound in the *Little Review* discussed form, *Vanity Fair* domesticated the radical sculptor through a personality profile, and the *Dial* published a poem that interacted with feelings elicited by Brancusi's work.[30] Masteller's approach offers a fresh way to investigate the debates over modernism and, in so doing, illustrates how the definition of the art movement was evolving. The next study in this category moves into the interwar period and looks at how dealers, collectors, educators and museums mainstreamed modern art. When the center of the art world shifted from Paris to New York, Camille Cottrell argues, these constituencies viewed the future of American art as married to modernism and so drew together to promote modern art as "a visual symbol of independence and intellectual freedom."[31] Each of these multidisciplinary works exploits the lively debates about modernism, art and culture and comprises a primary area of research in this chapter.

Fashion Art

Modern art was considered by both its practitioners and its critics as a disruptive force. One way in which these transgressive genres were domesticated was in fashion magazines. Hannah Crawforth documents the ways surrealist artists exploited fascination with the fashionable world in their work for *Vogue* and *Harper's Bazaar* during the 1930s and 1940s.[32] Crawforth posits that a connection existed between surrealism, which highlighted the process of construction, and the magazine form, which itself was "perishable and ephemeral."[33] The editor of *Vogue* wrote, "we like to give you fantasy . . . side by side with common sense."[34] Crawforth offers an important insight: Rather than being a one-way street, in which artists showcased surrealism in magazines, artists working for fashion magazines influenced surrealism. Through this mutual process, she wrote, "the notions of mass-production and consequent disposability inherent in the fashion magazine as a form, would be rapidly assimilated into the process of surrealism."[35] Further, this example of a fine art being incorporated into magazines raises questions about how such journals mediate between the elite and the reader, in the process, killing off the "exclusivity of the more select group."[36]

Vogue's tying of the avant-garde to fashion is also explored by Änne Söll in provocative research on photographer Cecil Beaton's use of Jackson Pollock's paintings in a fashion shoot in 1951.[37] Like Crawforth, Söll addresses the connection among the elite, art and fashion and notes that Vogue had long covered fine art.[38] In posing models in front of Pollock's drip paintings, Beaton showed the avant-garde environment that women who purchase haute couture inhabit; the models' presence, in a sense, legitimated Abstract Expressionism.[39] In Söll's analysis, Pollock's aggressive style symbolized American authenticity and power. Rather than being a backdrop for the more "feminine" realm of fashion, Pollock's work asserts authenticity yet still functions as "an aesthetic environment that enters a mutually reinforcing, aesthetically reproductive and identity fostering relationship with the model as a representative of the American elite."[40]

Class and Gender

Richard Ohmann's Selling Culture: Magazines, Markets, and Class at the Turn of the Century tied the emergence of the professional class to the growth of magazines. Ohmann's theoretical perspective suggests a framework for describing the ways in which magazines functioned as educators to the rising middle class while at the same time creating taste publics.[41] This perspective is embodied in a number of recent studies. Because magazines brought reproduced engravings of original art into middle class homes, Cynthia Lee Patterson regards the 1840s illustrated monthlies, called the Philadelphia pictorials, as prime actors in the commodification and democratization of art in the United States. Patterson views these periodicals as one element, along with salons and societies, that helped serve the growing middle class. Patterson explores both technological and social developments, paying attention also to how the evaluation and purchase of American art served as a marker of upward social mobility.[42]

The 1870s brought a burgeoning of the middle class. Knox argues that Scribner's Monthly exploited the growing desire for pictorials and, in the process, advanced improvements in both technology and critical commentary, thus helping educate the nation on art during America's Gilded Age. Occurring as it did during the time of tremendous growth in the last decades of the nineteenth century, this development is credited to the magazine's influential editor, Richard Watson Gilder. Knox argues that in Scribner's pages, art began to function as art in its own right, as opposed to being mere illustration. In Knox's view, Scribner's thus changed the way "Americans looked at, valued and understood images, and actively participated in the forging of a national art."[43]

An inherent conflict exists between art, a form that traditionally honored exclusivity, and a democratic society, which honors equality. Given this, some scholars have pondered "whether and how art serves democracy and whether and how democracy serves art."[44] Historian A. Joan Saab describes the attempts in the 1930s to create art that was peculiarly "American," the competing agendas of left-wing activists and those who advocated access to commercial goods, and the role of institutions, the government, and artists in debating the uses and definition of art.[45] In a dissertation that examines this theme, Isadora Anderson Helfgott looks at how fine art was popularized during the 1930s, at the search to encourage new audiences for art and at debates over who would define what fine art was. Helfgott argues that expanding channels—instituted by left-wing artists who viewed art as a tool for change—were institutionalized by museums and collectors.[46] Another work that examines the use of visuals in the 1930s is Helen Langa's research on the New Masses, a magazine devoted to the visual arts. The magazine's focus makes it unique in Langa's view. Her examination shows the conflict between politics—in this case left-wing—and issues of avant-garde practice, as the editors rejected modernism and called for art by workers. Further, artists were expected to emphasize "recognizable themes of class struggle."[47]

Few studies were found that explore gender, which would seem like a fruitful topic, especially given the interest in gender shown in other areas of magazine scholarship, in the work of art historians and cultural studies. One study examines cultural changes at the turn of the nineteenth century through the lens of gender by examining the cultural construction of the "ideal American girl." [48] David Slater calls the 10-cent magazine "the internal combustion engine that revolutionized the way Americans consumed culture" but posits that such magazines, full of pictures, "provided the spark that set the machine in motion."[49] In his discussion of this concept, Slater traces the imagery of the ideal woman, from the Gibson Girl to the flapper, and ties these portrayals to the cultural moment, whether it was fear of immigrants, an insistence on gentility or a fear of women's sexuality.[50]

Rachel Lynn Schreiber gauged the disjuncture between socialist artists' experiments with new forms of visual imagery in the early 1900s to promote their views with their simultaneous depictions of women that conformed to traditional stereotypes.[51] This was a period of great tumult that included the fight for women's suffrage and protests for labor rights. Although this research views such depictions as a window into history, in this case, the tensions of the period are also conveyed. Schreiber makes the case that illustrations "distill" ideas and elucidate "the affective significance of historical events."[52] She describes artwork published in the *Masses* as "aesthetically more daring and modern than the conventional magazines of its day."[53] Her research adds to work done on the *Masses* in two ways: Schreiber focuses on gender, and she compares the *Masses'* coverage to that in the mainstream press.[54] She shows that the *Masses* joined a working class subject with a modernist form. Thus, even though Schreiber examines cartoons and not art per se, her research is included here because it fits the themes of this chapter.

Magazines and Their Editors

Seven studies treat specific publications. Of these, several investigate the role of an influential editor in bringing new, innovative work to the attention of readers. Jayme Alyson Yahr focuses her attention on the nineteenth century in her description of the interaction among an editor, his publication and the artists he promoted.[55] Yahr describes how, through the pages of the *Century Illustrated Monthly Magazine*, editor Richard Watson Gilder championed the work of contemporary artists and a more up-to-date abstract style. Yahr views Gilder's activity as instrumental in helping establish a modern style of art practice in the period. This included his role in forming the Society for American Artists, a new group of artists devoted to modern art practice. Thus, this close examination of a magazine at the turn of the twentieth century provides an in-depth view of the role an editor can play in nourishing a movement: in this case, one that expressed and promulgated modernism.

Craig Houser studied the relationship between academia and the art world. In his examination of the College Art Association's publications that included the *Art Bulletin*, Houser makes the case that the publications functioned far beyond providing a forum for ideas, serving also to establish the authority of particular art historians. He also describes the uneasy alliance between an academic organization and those in the field, and he documents the antagonism between the art historians who took over the journals from the educators who had founded them. His archival work thus sheds light on the development of prestige and hierarchy within the field of art education.[56]

Art historian Wanda Corn pointed out that art historians focused until around 1980 on examining careers, describing styles and showing influences, at the expense of exploring iconography. However, as in other disciplines, including communication and magazine scholarship, U.S. scholars in the 1980s began to use interdisciplinary approaches and to incorporate literary and critical theory. Corn writes that instead of "problem-oriented scholarship," researchers began to examine how cultural and social forces shaped art, which allowed scholars to move beyond viewing history as background and instead toward presenting art, the artist and history as intertwined.[57]

Three studies that focus on the British *Burlington Magazine* afford the opportunity to examine the growth of art journals at the early stage.[58] Founded in 1903 by connoisseurs and art historians, early articles in *Burlington Magazine* can inform the reader of comparable trends in U.S. scholarship in art history as they dovetail with aspects of the growth of magazine scholarship. Flaminia Gennari Santori discusses the development of the art establishment and its relationship to magazines by looking at the "Art in America," *Burlington Magazine* section that lasted from 1905 to 1910. Santori describes its editors' struggle to define what art coverage should consist of. Of note is the simultaneous growth of fine art museums and the debate around whether the responsibility of American museums was to be popular or to focus on aesthetic values. Santori found that the editors tried to influence the role of museums in the period and also asserted their responsibility to educate collectors to "embrace new territories."[59] Her detailed discussion of the contributions of various editors shows insight into the history of a new medium—the art journal. In 1912, the section became the independent magazine *Art in America*, which is still published today.

Caroline Elam looked at the founding of the *Burlington Magazine*, the critical role of editor Roger Fry and the journal's early mission: to be devoted to amateurs, to focus on the art of the past and to establish information of "solid and permanent value."[60] The 2003 issue commemorating the *Burlington Magazine*'s first-century included Colin Rhodes's article on the framing of the *primitive* in this prestigious journal. Rhodes reviewed the articles published during the journal's first 30 years that analyzed the influx of Japanese, Chinese, Peruvian and African art into the European market. Initially making the case that, as collectibles, such objects need not aspire to be *high art*, the magazine moved to demonstrate the value of such new, stylistic influences on European art. Rhodes wrote that the "reappraisal and admittance of tribal objects . . . was made possible by shifts in the language of criticism of contemporary European modernist art itself." He noted that writers in the journal "authenticated" tribal art through its influence on modern art, and vice versa.[61] This close reading of all articles on *primitive* art shows how a journal framed the value and meaning of such influences on the contemporary art scene. Thus, these articles, written about the *Burlington Magazine* appearing in the *Burlington Magazine*, show trends in recent scholarship in an art journal examining itself.

No doubt due to its reach, its large audience, its numerous titles, and its titles' range and popularity, the U.S. company Time Inc. has garnered the interest of scholars. Researchers describe the active role that Time Inc. took in educating its middle-class audience and using its magazines to nurture specific artists and critical viewpoints. The decades between the 1930s Depression and the growth of leisure culture in the 1960s have attracted particular attention. For example, in his book on *Fortune*, Michael Augspurger examined the magazine's coverage and analysis of art from the 1930s to the 1950s, a period in which *Fortune* not only showcased artwork but also commissioned surveys and sponsored roundtables on art.[62] Augspurger approached *Fortune*'s coverage as one factor in the formation of the professional class that became decidedly "middlebrow."[63]

Sheila Webb's research positions the first decade of *Life* within the cultural milieu of the 1930s.[64] *Life* was one example of what Vanessa R. Schwartz and Jeannene M. Przyblyski describe as the "explosion of image-making [that] made visual experience and visual literacy important elements in the rubric of modernity."[65] Webb argues that *Life* can be viewed as the very embodiment of modernity as it pioneered a new way of reaching and influencing an audience through the photo-essay, an innovative marriage of text and images. The new pictorial became one actor among others in the cultural landscape, one of what Terry Smith calls the several "agencies of transformation"[66] that declared the value of modernity and worked to educate the public in modern taste standards. Webb describes *Life*, the new Museum of Modern Art and the Works Progress Administration as "important actors in pushing middle class Americans toward understanding and embracing the new" as "all three shared the belief that art was integral to creating modern society."[67] Saab suggests this period offers the chance to "interrogate the uses of art as both cultural capital and a critical form of communication in the creation of democratic communities."[68] *Life*, MoMa and the WPA believed they were engaged in the "lofty goal of producing knowledge; all three viewed this knowledge as tied to the ideals of democracy."[69] In her analysis of *Life*'s approach, Webb examined the ways the magazine domesticated modern art through a variety of approaches: telling the life story of an artist, highlighting investment opportunities and examining in minute detail all aspects of art production. This analysis of *Life*'s art coverage in the interwar period describes the role a media giant played in attempting to devise taste standards, identify class boundaries and codify what was considered worthy.

The Magazine as Art Strategy

Much of the research described here focuses on two important historical periods: the second decade of the twentieth century, which was a period in which consumer culture was consolidated, aspects of modernism were debated and magazines became a mass medium suited to appeal to the growing professional class; and the 1930s, interwar period, which was a time of great social upheaval that embraced the growing use of visuals and saw the codification of art magazines and the art world. The 1960s and 1970s are decades that are equally ripe for analysis. A number of works examine artists' rejection of establishment periodicals by creating their own. A brief history will set the stage for this development. The first art magazine in the United States dates to the mid-1850s. With the growth of art schools, the opening of great museums to the public and the ability to reproduce artwork, art magazines began to flourish around the turn of the twentieth century. During this period, some artists produced independent projects that explored the magazine as form, as opposed to the commercial periodicals. Emily Hage describes Tristan Tzara's *Dada* in this way—as a publication that played a role in the Dada movement. She approaches the magazine's pages as functioning as "primary sites of Dada activity."[70]

By the mid-1960s, three publications numbered among the most important mainstream periodicals in the United States: *ARTnews* (1902–), *Arts* (1913–1992) and *Art in America* (1913–).[71] These periodicals began to pay great attention to how they showcased art. Among trends of the time was what Stanley T. Lewis found to be "art periodicals . . . being designed to be 'seen' rather than 'read.'"[72] Gwen Allen argues that this signaled a redefinition of the art magazine, as magazines began to be conceived of as a primary way for the public to receive art.[73] John Walker called this a "conflation of art and the art periodical"[74] that offered new possibilities.

Allen's innovative work on how magazines became both challenges to the art establishment as well as art expressions in their own right has appeared in both books and articles. In her introduction to a recent book on artists' magazines, Allen writes that the earlier artist magazines, such as *Dada*, functioned as a means to an end, that is "vehicles for defining artistic agendas and circulating ideas, rather than works of art in themselves."[75] Allen cites Clive Phillpot, who noted that artists of the 1960s evidenced an entirely different attitude toward periodicals and art,[76] as they experimented with radical departures that broke away from the static page, creating 3-dimensional pages that explored typography, allowed the reader to draw on the pages, etc. These experiments were deliberately viewed as oppositional to the mainstream press.

In writing on this period and within this changing context, Allen notes that magazines helped establish what art critic Arthur Danto called "the artworld,"[77] that is, discourse around art that becomes a shared language. During the 1960s, the art magazine became more important than galleries or museums to an artist's career, and magazines played a critical role in providing the imprimatur for new movements.[78] In fact, a common phrase at the time was "A reproduction in an art magazine is worth two one-man shows."[79] *Artforum* serves as Allen's example of the mainstream press; *Aspen*, as a multimedia experiment which violates the format; and

Avalanche, as a venue founded to give artists a way to communicate directly with each other or with the public via interviews. Allen offers an example of magazine research thoroughly grounded in a theoretical perspective, in her case, of how magazines function in the public sphere, and deals with works deliberately designed to elicit a certain reception, a topic too often unexplored.

Just as Allen compared the above three models of practice in the 1960s, so Camille Mary Weiner compares three artist-driven periodicals from the 1970s and finds each intimately connected to postmodern practice in Los Angeles, in this case, of conceptual and performance art. Weiner views each magazine as providing an *alternative space* that allowed artists and audience to interact in a space outside the institutional art system at the same time they pioneered a new medium—the art periodical as art expression.[80] Both of these pieces express the excitement and boundary-breaking aspects of the 1960s and 1970s, the dialogue around commercial vs. independent expression and the radical reframing of discourse around artistic practice.

Ken Allan regards earlier models, such as Tzara's *Dada*, as laying the groundwork for conceptual art of the 1970s and magazines in which published artist projects were not reproductions of art works but were designed specifically to be works in their own right in printed form. Further, such works were meant to challenge the very concept of the magazine by altering the viewer's experience. In finding not disruptive breaks in these conceptual pieces, but rather continuation based on precedence, Allan offers a perspective different from Allen or Phillpot's on such avant-garde movements. At the same time, Ken Allan trains his eye on a current area of investigation, that is, audience reception.[81]

On the East Coast of the United States, growing out of New York City's SoHo alternative art scene, *Avalanche* was launched to provide artists the space to interact directly with the public. Allen describes *Avalanche*'s innovations as tied to the desire to document performance and conceptual art of the time. *Avalanche* perfected a type of *anti-criticism*, one far different from that used by mainstream periodicals in which criticism functioned as a form of advertising. Allen places *Avalanche* historically, tying the magazine to reception of art of the time: It served as a "physical support" for art, which was itself "dematerialized"[82] in the form of performances or earthworks. Allen credits *Avalanche* with providing an alternative space to question elite art practice and art reception.[83]

Although *Avalanche* was published only 13 times, another alternative magazine devoted to provide a new and fresh venue for artists to reach the public is still thriving. *Bomb*, the subject of a profile by Nell McClister in *New Art Publications*, premiered in 1981. *Bomb* reacted to the crisis of art criticism in the 1970s, when critics like Clement Greenberg were viewed as collaborating with the commercialization of the art world and when the "critic's voice was considered more important than the artist's."[84]

Covers: On the Face of It

Scholars have examined magazine covers from a variety of perspectives: for the light they shed on political figures, for their role in creating the design of a magazine and for the way they reach and retain an audience.[85] Two studies published since 2000 examine *the art* on covers, focusing on periods that were able to exploit the growing ability to print illustrations in print media. Both deal with eras of great political upheaval and place the imagery in their historical settings. June Knopf views covers as a form of visual history that illuminates the 1890 to 1920 Progressive Era. Her contribution is in her choice of subject, as she argues that cover art served to sanction the incursion of technology into people's lives and, secondly, that these images served as propaganda to foster support for World War I.[86]

In her book on images of women on covers, Carolyn Kitch focuses mainly on the first three decades of the twentieth century—again, the timeframe in which magazines became a mass medium and played a role in the formation of consumer culture. Kitch establishes links between various cover portrayals of women (such as the Gibson girl and the flapper), shifting social patterns (such as the growth of domesticity, the display of wealth and status, issues of masculinity and propaganda to support entry into World War I) and the connection to ideology, such as racial purity and imperialism.[87]

Future Research

This discussion describes recent scholarship surrounding magazines and visual art. Although some of the research hues to an older approach, such as examining editors alone or treating periodicals as windows into history, most studies take a more interdisciplinary approach and convey the complex relationship between art practice and the surrounding culture. This chapter point to gaps that suggest areas for further scholarship. More investigation of specific art journals could explore the integral role that art journals play in providing information about art trends, the relationship of journals to commercialization and advertisers, or the complex dance to set standards among art periodicals and museums, art historians, artists and connoisseurs. Most of the work described here treats U.S. periodicals. Attention could be paid to the increasingly global aspect of the art world, as artists, galleries, dealers and museums expand their reach abroad, respond to global developments and pioneer new ways to collaborate.

Although magazine scholarship outside the parameters of this chapter treats gender fully, gender was not found as a focus in the studies identified for this review. Yet investigations of gender offer a fruitful avenue for further research, both in terms of portrayals of women in art and in terms of hearing from women artists. For example, the challenges to the traditional art establishment in the mid-1980s by the Guerrilla Girls and the founding of the National Museum of Women in the Arts could be placed in an updated context. Issues of class, identity, ethnicity and race, the latter of which is rarely touched upon in the work described in this chapter, deserve more attention.[88]

In studies published since 2000, research stops at art of the 1980s. Developments in the 1990s and early 2000s deserve the same careful eye as, for example, artists' periodicals of the 1960s have received. The art field has exploded in the last 20 years, and many exciting developments provide rich veins for exploration. Only a few examples include outsider art, street art, digital art and the increasing connections between art and craft, street art and digital art. New magazine forms that provide new avenues for artists at the same time they challenge the print periodical in profound ways, such as zines and on-line magazines, are mainly unexplored in research since 2000. The hope and expectation is that in laying out both current practice and future possibilities, magazine, cultural and art history scholars will begin to exploit more fully the rich opportunities this chapter outlines, be it *on* art magazines, on art *in* magazines, or on magazines *as* art.

Notes

1 Pierre Bourdieu, *Distinction: A Social Critique of the Judgment of Taste*, trans. Richard Nice (Cambridge, MA: Harvard University Press, 1984).

2 Richard Ohmann, *Selling Culture: Magazines, Markets, and Class at the Turn of the Century* (London and New York: Verso, 1996), vii.

3 Cynthia Lee Patterson, *Art for the Middle Classes: America's Illustrated Magazines of the 1840s* (Jackson: University Press of Mississippi, 2010), 3–17, 160–168.

4 Page Stevens Knox, "*Scribner's Monthly*, 1870–1881: Illustrating a New American Art World" (Ph.D. diss., Columbia University, 2012).

5 Sheila Webb, "Art Commentary for the Middlebrow: Promoting Modernism and Modern Art through Popular Culture—How *Life* Magazine Brought 'The New' into Middle-Class Homes," *American Journalism* 27.3 (2010): 115–150.

6 Walter Benjamin, "The Work of Art in the Age of Mechanical Reproduction," *Illuminations: Essays and Reflections*, ed. Hannah Arendt, trans., Harry Zohn (New York: Schocken Books, 1968), 224.

7 From "Letters to the Editors," *Life*, 10 January 1938, 4, as quoted in Webb, "Art Commentary for the Middlebrow," 127.

8 See Sammye Johnson, "Overview of Research into the Magazine Form: The Relationship of Academic Scholarship to the Magazine Industry" (Keynote address, Mapping the Magazine 2 International Conference, Cardiff University, Cardiff, Wales, 15 September 2005); see also, David E. Sumner, "Letter from Our Division Head: Revisiting an Old Question," *Magazine Matter*, Spring 2000, 1.

9 Scott Fosdick, "The State of Magazine Research in 2008," *Journal of Magazine & New Media Research* 10.1 (Fall 2008): 1–4; David Abrahamson, ed., *The American Magazine: Research Perspectives and Prospects* (Ames: Iowa State University Press, 1995).

10 Carolyn Kitch, as quoted in Fosdick, "The State of Magazine Research in 2008," 3.

11 Gwen L. Allen, "From Specific Medium to Mass Media: The Art Magazine the 1960s and Early 1970s" (Ph.D. diss., Stanford University, 2004).

12 Joe Bernt, as quoted in Fosdick, "The State of Magazine Research in 2008," 2.

13 Patterson, *Art for the Middle Classes.*

14 Bernt, as quoted in Fosdick, "The State of Magazine Research in 2008," 2.

15 Rachel Lynn Schreiber, "Constructive Images: Gender in the Political Cartoons of the *Masses* (1911–1917)" (Ph.D. diss., Johns Hopkins University, 2008).

16 Isadora Anderson Helfgott, "Art and the Struggle for the American Soul: The Pursuit of a Popular Audience for Art in America from the Depression to World War II" (Ph.D. diss., Harvard University, 2006).

17 David Abrahamson, as quoted in Fosdick, "The State of Magazine Research in 2008," 2.

18 Emily Hage, "The Magazine as Strategy: Tristan Tzara's *Dada* and the Seminal Role of Dada Art Journals in the Dada Movement," *Journal of Modern Periodical Studies* 2.1 (2011): 33–53.

19 Alexandra K. Schwartz, "Designing Ed Ruscha: The Invention of the Los Angeles Artist 1960–1980 (Ph.D. diss., University of Michigan, 2004).

20 Gwen L. Allen, "Against Criticism: The Artist Interview in *Avalanche* Magazine, 1970–76." *Art Journal* 64.3 (Fall 2005): 50–61.

21 Allen, "From Specific Medium to Mass Media"; and Nell McClister, "*Bomb* Magazine: Celebrating 25 Years," *New Art Publications* no. 96 (Summer 2006): 22–23.

22 Camille Mary Weiner, "Artists as Authors: Three Los Angeles Art Periodicals of the 1970s" (Master's Thesis, University of California, 2011).

23 Janice Simon, "Introduction: American Periodicals and Visual Culture," *American Periodicals* 20.2 (2010): 117–119.

24 Judith Yaross Lee, "From the Field: The Future of *American Periodicals* and American Periodical Research," *American Periodicals* 15.2 (2005): 197, 198.

25 Marshall Berman, *All That Is Solid Melts into Air: The Experience of Modernity* (London: Verso, 1983), 16–17.

26 Suzanne W. Churchill and Adam McKible, "Little Magazines and Modernism: An Introduction," *American Periodicals* 15.1 (2005): 4.

27 Robert Scholes and Clifford Wulfman, *Modernism in the Magazines: An Introduction* (New Haven: Yale University Press, 2010), 74.

28 Robert Scholes, "Modernist Art in a 'Quality' Magazine, 1908–1922," *The Journal of Modern Periodical Studies* 2.2 (2011): 135, 154.

29 Richard N. Masteller, "Using Brancusi: Three Writers, Three Magazines, Three Versions of Modernism," *American Art* 11.1 (Spring 1997): 47.

30 Masteller, "Using Brancusi," 47–67.

31 Camille Cottrell, "The Mainstreaming of Modern Art in America" (Ph.D. diss., The University of Georgia, 2002), 2.

32 Hannah Crawforth, "Surrealism and the Fashion Magazine," *American Periodicals* 14.2 (2004): 212–246.

33 Crawforth, "Surrealism and the Fashion Magazine," 214.

34 Edna Woolman Chase, as quoted in Crawforth, "Surrealism and the Fashion Magazine," 215.

35 Crawforth, "Surrealism and the Fashion Magazine," 219.

36 Crawforth, "Surrealism and the Fashion Magazine," 231.

37 Änne Söll, "Pollock in *Vogue*: American Fashion and Avant-Garde Art in Cecil Beaton's 1951 Photographs," *Fashion Theory* 13.1 (2009): 29–50.

38 Änne Söll, "Pollock in *Vogue*," 40.

39 Änne Söll, "Pollock in *Vogue*," 39.

40 Änne Söll, "Pollock in *Vogue*," 45.

41 Ohmann, *Selling Culture*, 118–174.

42 Patterson, *Art for the Middle Classes.*

43 Knox, "*Scribner's Monthly*."

44 Arthur M. Melzer, Jerry Weinberger, and M. Richard Zinman, eds., *Democracy and the Arts* (Ithaca, NY: Cornell University Press, 1999), 3.

45 A. Joan Saab, *For the Millions: American Art and Culture between the Wars* (Philadelphia: University of Pennsylvania Press, 2004), 7–8.

46 Helfgott, "Art and the Struggle for the American Soul."

47 Helen Langa, "'At Least Half the Pages Will Consist of Pictures': *New Masses* and Politicized Visual Art," *American Periodicals* 21.1 (2011): 24–49.

48 David Jeremiah Slater, "The American Girl, Her Life and Times: An Ideal and Its Creators, 1890–1930" (Ph.D. diss., University of Minnesota, 2005).

49 Slater, "The American Girl," 10.

50 Slater, "The American Girl," 12–39.

51 Schreiber, "Constructive Images."

52 Schreiber, "Constructive Images," ii.

53 Schreiber, "Constructive Images," 1.

54 Schreiber, "Constructive Images," 9.

55 Jayme Alyson Yahr, "The Art of the *Century*: Richard Watson Gilder, the Gilder Circle, and the Rise of American Modernism" (Ph.D. diss., University of Washington, 2012).

56 Craig Houser, "The Politics of Scholarship: College Art Association and the Uneasy Relationship between Art and Art History 1911–1945" (Ph.D. diss., City University of New York, 2011).

57 Wanda M. Corn, "Coming of Age: Historical Scholarship in American Art," *Art Bulletin*, June 1988, 193, 200.

58 The *Burlington Magazine* is a monthly nonprofit, scholarly journal that publishes on art history, from ancient to current practice. Editor Richard Shone described the articles as not peer-read in the common sense, but assessed by multiple outside readers and members of its consultative committee. Some articles are commissions to long-standing contributors. Correspondence with author (November 2013).

59 Flaminia Gennari Santori, "Holmes, Fry, Jaccaci and the 'Art in America' Section of the *Burlington Magazine*, 1905–10," [Centenary Issue], *Burlington Magazine* 145.1200 (March 2003): 161.

60 Quoted in Caroline Elam, "'A More and More Important Work': Roger Fry and the *Burlington Magazine*," [Centenary Issue], *Burlington Magazine* 145.1200 (March 2003): 145.

61 Colin Rhodes, "*Burlington* Primitive: Non-European Art in the *Burlington Magazine* before 1930," *Burlington Magazine* 146.1211 (February 2004): 99, 102.

62 Michael Augspurger, *An Economy of Abundant Beauty*: Fortune *Magazine and Depression America* (Ithaca, NY: Cornell University Press, 2004).

63 Christopher P. Wilson, review of *An Economy of Abundant Beauty*: Fortune *Magazine and Depression America*, by Michael Augspurger, *American Historical Review* 111.3 (June 2006): 856.

64 Webb, "Art Commentary for the Middlebrow," 115–150.

65 Vanessa R. Schwartz and Jeannene M. Przyblyski, eds., *The Nineteenth-Century Visual Culture Reader* (New York: Routledge, 2004), 9. See also Benjamin, "The Work of Art in the Age of Mechanical Reproduction," 219–253.

66 Terry Smith, *Making the Modern: Industry, Art, and Design in America* (Chicago: University of Chicago Press, 1993), 161.

67 Webb, "Art Commentary for the Middlebrow," 115.

68 Saab, *For the Millions*, 12.

69 Webb, "Art Commentary for the Middlebrow," 115–116. See Saab, *For the Millions*, 2, 14.

70 Hage, "The Magazine as Strategy," 33.

71 Allen, "From Specific Medium to Mass Media," 14. See also John A. Walker, "Periodicals since 1945," in Trevor Fawcett and Clive Phillpot, eds., *The Art Press: Two Centuries of Art Magazines* (London: The Art Book Company, 1976), 45–52.

72 Stanley T. Lewis, "Periodicals in the Visual Arts," *Library Trends* 10.3 (1962): 334.

73 Allen, "From Specific Medium to Mass Media," 17.

74 Walker, "Periodicals since 1945," 52.

75 Gwen L. Allen, *Artists' Magazines: An Alternative Space for Art* (Cambridge: MIT Press, 2011), 3.

76 Clive Phillpot, "Art Magazines and Magazine Art," *Artforum*, February 1980, 52.

77 Arthur Danto, "The Artworld," in Steven Henry Madoff, ed., *Pop Art: A Critical History* (Berkeley: University of California Press, 1997), 275, 269–278.

78 John A. Walker, "Internal Memorandum," *Studio International*, 193.983 (September/October, 1976): 113.

79 Quoted in Allen, "Against Criticism," 51.

80 Weiner, "Artists as Authors."

81 Ken Allan, "Conceptual Art Magazine Projects and Their Precedents" (Ph.D. diss., University of Toronto, 2004).

82 Allen, "Against Criticism," 52.

83 Allen, "Against Criticism," 61.

84 McClister, "*Bomb* Magazine," 22.

85 See Sammye Johnson and Patricia Prijatel, *The Magazine from Cover to Cover*, 3rd ed. (New York and London: Oxford University Press, 2013), 275–283.

86 June S. Knopf, "Images of Change: Magazine Cover Art of the Tumultuous Late Progressive Era" (D.Litt., Drew University, 2011), 1–435.

87 Carolyn Kitch, *The Girl on the Magazine Cover: The Origins of Visual Stereotypes in American Mass Media* (Chapel Hill and London: University of North Carolina Press, 2001).

88 One exception is Krys Verrall's article on a single issue of *artscanada* that covered a 1967 intercontinental phone "roundtable" discussion among seven men involved in the various arts of the meaning of the word "black" and constituting a "rare intersection between elite art and racial politics." See Krys Verrall, "*artscanada*'s 'Black' Issue: 1960s Contemporary Art and African Liberation Movements," *Canadian Journal of Communication* 36.4 (2011): 539.

Bibliography

Abrahamson, David, ed. *The American Magazine: Research Perspectives and Prospects*. Ames: Iowa State University Press, 1995.

Allan, Ken. "Conceptual Art Magazine Projects and Their Precedents." Ph.D. diss., University of Toronto, 2004.

Allen, Gwen L. "Against Criticism: The Artist Interview in *Avalanche* Magazine, 1970–76." *Art Journal* 64.3 (Fall 2005): 50–61.

Allen, Gwen L. *Artists' Magazines: An Alternative Space for Art*. Cambridge: MIT Press, 2011.

Allen, Gwen L. "From Specific Medium to Mass Media: The Art Magazine in the 1960s and Early 1970s." Ph.D. diss., Stanford University, 2004.

Augspurger, Michael. *An Economy of Abundant Beauty: Fortune Magazine and Depression America*. Ithaca, NY: Cornell University Press, 2004.

Benjamin, Walter. "The Work of Art in the Age of Mechanical Reproduction," *Illuminations: Essays and Reflections*. Edited by Hannah Arendt. Translated by Harry Zohn. New York: Schocken Books, 1968, 217–251.

Berman, Marshall. *All That Is Solid Melts into Air: The Experience of Modernity*. London: Verso, 1983.

Bourdieu, Pierre. *Distinction: A Social Critique of the Judgment of Taste*. Translated by Richard Nice. Cambridge, MA: Harvard University Press, 1984.

Churchill, Suzanne W. and McKible, Adam. "Little Magazines and Modernism: An Introduction." *American Periodicals* 15.1 (2005): 1–5.

Corn, Wanda M. "Coming of Age: Historical Scholarship in American Art." *Art Bulletin*, June 1988, 188–207.

Cottrell, Camille. "The Mainstreaming of Modern Art in America." Ph.D. diss., University of Georgia, 2002.

Crawforth, Hannah. "Surrealism and the Fashion Magazine." *American Periodicals* 14.2 (2004): 212–246.

Danto, Arthur. "The Artworld." In Madoff, Steven Henry, ed. *Pop Art: A Critical History*. Berkeley: University of California Press, 1997, 269–278.

Elam, Caroline. "'A More and More Important Work': Roger Fry and the *Burlington Magazine*." [Centenary Issue]. *Burlington Magazine* 145.1200 (March 2003): 142–152.

Fosdick, Scott. "The State of Magazine Research in 2008." *Journal of Magazine & New Media Research* 10.1 (Fall 2008): 1–4.

Hage, Emily. "The Magazine as Strategy: Tristan Tzara's *Dada* and the Seminal Role of Dada Art Journals in the Dada Movement." *Journal of Modern Periodical Studies* 2.1 (2011): 33–53.

Helfgott, Isadora Anderson. "Art and the Struggle for the American Soul: The Pursuit of a Popular Audience for Art in America from the Depression to World War II." Ph.D. diss., Harvard University, 2006.

Houser, Craig. "The Politics of Scholarship: College Art Association and the Uneasy Relationship between Art and Art History 1911–1945." Ph.D. diss., City University of New York, 2011.

Johnson, Sammye. "Overview of Research into the Magazine Form: The Relationship of Academic Scholarship to the Magazine Industry." Keynote Address, Mapping the Magazine 2 International Conference, Cardiff University, Cardiff, Wales, 15 September 2005.

Johnson, Sammye and Prijatel, Patricia. *The Magazine from Cover to Cover*. 3rd ed. New York and London: Oxford University Press, 2013.

Kitch, Carolyn. *The Girl on the Magazine Cover: The Origins of Visual Stereotypes in American Mass Media*. Chapel Hill and London: University of North Carolina Press, 2001.

Knopf, June S. "Images of Change: Magazine Cover Art of the Tumultuous Late Progressive Era." D.Litt., diss., Drew University, 2011.

Knox, Page Stevens. "*Scribner's Monthly*, 1870–1881: Illustrating a New American Art World." Ph.D. diss., Columbia University, 2012.

Langa, Helen. "'At Least Half the Pages Will Consist of Pictures': *New Masses* and Politicized Visual Art." *American Periodicals* 21.1 (2011): 24–49.

Lee, Judith Yaross. "From the Field: The Future of *American Periodicals* and American Periodicals Research." *American Periodicals* 15.2 (2005): 196–201.

Lewis, Stanley T. "Periodicals in the Visual Arts." *Library Trends* 10.3 (1962): 330–352.

Masteller, Richard N. "Using Brancusi: Three Writers, Three Magazines, Three Versions of Modernism." *American Art* 11.1 (Spring 1997): 46–67.

McClister, Nell. "*Bomb* Magazine, Celebrating 25 Years." *New Art Publications* No. 96 (Summer 2006): 22–23.

Melzer, Arthur M.; Weinberger, Jerry; and Zinman, M. Richard, eds. *Democracy and the Arts*. Ithaca, NY: Cornell University Press, 1999.

Ohmann, Richard. *Selling Culture: Magazines, Markets, and Class at the Turn of the Century*. London and New York: Verso, 1996.

Patterson, Cynthia Lee. *Art for the Middle Classes: America's Illustrated Magazines of the 1840s*. Jackson: University Press of Mississippi, 2010.

Phillpot, Clive. "Art Magazines and Magazine Art." *Artforum*, February 1980, 52–54.

Rhodes, Colin. "*Burlington* Primitive: Non-European Art in the *Burlington Magazine* before 1930." *Burlington Magazine* 146.1211 (February 2004): 98–104.

Saab, A. Joan. *For the Millions: American Art and Culture between the Wars*. Philadelphia: University of Pennsylvania Press, 2004.

Santori, Flaminia Gennari. "Holmes, Fry, Jaccaci and the 'Art in America' Section of the *Burlington Magazine*, 1905–10." [Centenary Issue] *Burlington Magazine* 145.1200 (March 2003): 153–163.

Scholes, Robert. "Modernist Art in a 'Quality' Magazine, 1908–1922." *Journal of Modern Periodical Studies* 2.2 (2011): 135–164.

Scholes, Robert and Wulfman, Clifford. *Modernism in the Magazines: An Introduction*. New Haven: Yale University Press, 2010.

Schreiber, Rachel Lynn. "Constructive Images: Gender in the Political Cartoons of the *Masses* (1911–1917)." Ph.D. diss., Johns Hopkins University, 2008.

Schwartz, Alexandra K. "Designing Ed Ruscha: The Invention of the Los Angeles Artist 1960–1980." Ph.D. diss., University of Michigan, 2004.

Schwartz, Vanessa R. and Przyblyski, Jeannene M., eds. *The Nineteenth-Century Visual Culture Reader*. New York: Routledge, 2004.

Simon, Janice. "Introduction: American Periodicals and Visual Culture." *American Periodicals* 20.2 (2010): 117–119.

Slater, David Jeremiah. "The American Girl, Her Life and Times: An Ideal and Its Creators, 1890–1930." Ph.D. diss., University of Minnesota, 2005.

Smith, Terry. *Making the Modern: Industry, Art, and Design in America*. Chicago: University of Chicago Press, 1993.

Söll, Änne. "Pollock in *Vogue*: American Fashion and Avant-Garde Art in Cecil Beaton's 1951 Photographs." *Fashion Theory* 13.1 (2009): 29–50.

Sumner, David E. "Letter from Our Division Head: Revisiting an Old Question." *Magazine Matter*, Spring 2000, 1.

Verrall, Krys. "*artscanada*'s 'Black' Issue: 1960s Contemporary Art and African Liberation Movements." *Canadian Journal of Communication* 36.4 (2011): 539–558.

Walker, John A. "Internal Memorandum." *Studio International* 192.983 (September/October 1976): 113–118.

Walker, John A. "Periodicals since 1945." In Fawcett, Trevor and Phillpot, Clive, eds. *The Art Press: Two Centuries of Art Magazines*. London: The Art Book Company, 1976, 45–52.

Webb, Sheila. "Art Commentary for the Middlebrow: Promoting Modernism and Modern Art through Popular Culture—How *Life* Magazine Brought 'The New' into Middle-Class Homes." *American Journalism* 27.3 (2010): 115–150.

Weiner, Camille Mary. "Artists as Authors: Three Los Angeles Art Periodicals of the 1970s." Master's thesis, University of Southern California, 2011.

Wilson, Christopher P. Review of *An Economy of Abundant Beauty*: Fortune *Magazine and Depression America*, by Michael Augspurger. *American Historical Review* 111.3 (June 2006): 856.

Yahr, Jayme Alyson. "The Art of the *Century*: Richard Watson Gilder, the Gilder Circle, and the Rise of American Modernism." Ph.D. diss., University of Washington, 2012.

Supplemental Resources

Editorial. "The *Burlington Magazine*, March 1903–February 2004." *Burlington Magazine* 146.1211 (February 2004): 75.

Marquis, Alice G. *Hopes and Ashes: The Birth of Modern Times, 1929–1939*. New York: The Free Press, 1986.

Wheeler, Britta B. "The Institutionalization of an American Avant-Garde: Performance Art as Democratic Culture, 1970–2000." *Sociological Perspectives* 46.4 (Winter 2003): 491–512.

22

LITERARY JOURNALISM

Journalism Aspiring to Be Literature

Miles Maguire

After Tom Wolfe discovered in the mid-1960s what he went on to call "The New Journalism," he described how this innovative mode of reporting had taken form outside the dominant media culture of daily newspapers, emerging instead at periodicals such as *New York* and *Esquire*. Articles published in these magazines had marked "the sudden arrival of this new style of journalism, from out of nowhere,"[1] Wolfe wrote. "All of a sudden there was some sort of artistic excitement in journalism, and that was a new thing in itself."[2] Wolfe was certainly correct about the role of magazines in nurturing a style of journalism that mixed fact-based reporting with the use of a range of literary devices, but he was wrong in arguing that this phenomenon was unprecedented.

Right from the start, Wolfe acknowledged that he didn't know how this style had evolved. Scholars and critics would soon set the record straight: that what Wolfe had observed could scarcely be described as new. Just how far back the American antecedents of New Journalism could be traced was demonstrated in 2000, when John C. Hartsock published *A History of American Literary Journalism: The Emergence of a Modern Narrative Form*. There Hartsock cited a precedent from 1855, when *Putnam's Monthly Magazine* published Henry David Thoreau's four sketches of Cape Cod, narratives that carried many of the distinctive marks that Wolfe would attribute, more than a century later, to his New Journalism.[3]

Hartsock's book, the first full-length treatment of the evolution of literary journalism in the United States, was one of a number of factors that came together around the turn of the twenty-first century to raise the profile of the genre and clearly establish the form as a legitimate subject for substantive critical analysis. Some of these factors were changes in professional practice that put greater emphasis on interpretive and explanatory reporting; others came out of the growing application of alternative approaches, including those enabled by new technology. But much of this impetus derived from a rapidly expanding body of scholarship, including re-publication of seminal works, such as Norman Sims's *Literary Journalism in the Twentieth Century*.[4] Further establishing the study of literary (or narrative) journalism on the larger scholarly agenda was the 2006 founding and subsequent growth of the International Association for Literary Journalism Studies (IALJS) and its journal, *Literary Journalism Studies*. This chapter reviews the themes and theories that have informed the recent research, much of which derives from and deals with the form's essentially hybrid character.

Definitional Studies

Even proponents and practitioners of *literary journalism* struggle to find the right words to describe it and differ over whether to classify it as a style or an approach to writing or a philosophy of writing and reporting. The phrase "literary journalism" is "roughly accurate," says Mark Kramer, because it combines the essential qualities of the form, the "arts of style and narrative construction" along with a focus on the immediacy of current events.[5] But the "discipline"[6] of literary journalism, to use the term preferred by John S. Bak, founding president of IALJS, over alternatives such as genre or form, has been defined so broadly that it takes in long-established categories such as travel writing and memoir while also including more experimental approaches that borrow from fields such as anthropology.

In his introduction to a 2011 collection of essays on literary journalism, Bak noted that "nearly every book on literary journalism over the last twenty-five years at least has begun with an introduction that defines or characterizes 'literary journalism.'"[7] But these efforts have not yielded any universally accepted criteria, a situation that many scholars have come to accept as essentially inevitable and not necessarily problematic. Sims has argued that "written definitions of literary journalism are, at best, abstractions."[8] In the inaugural issue of *Literary Journalism Studies*, founding editor Hartsock provided a range of terms that might be used to describe works in this form, such as "literary journalism, narrative journalism, literary reportage, reportage literature, literary nonfiction, creative nonfiction, the Chinese *bagao wenxue* or the Russian *ocherk*," and added one of his own devising, "narra-descriptive journalism."[9]

For Bak and many other scholars, efforts to establish a definition of literary journalism are unlikely to succeed simply because the field itself is dynamically innovative. But the lack of definitional consensus can be seen as key to a set of interrelated problems, including a relative lack of theoretical scaffolding to help support criticism and scholarship of literary journalism. In the realm of literary studies, the role of critical theory is well established, and schools of critical thought are so numerous that they have been grouped into categories that facilitate the examination both of the relationships between different theories and of the assumptions that these theories invoke.[10] The scholarship of literary journalism, by contrast, is not nearly so advanced with respect to theory development and application.

In addition to inhibiting the growth of theory, the lack of consensus on an appropriate definition for literary journalism creates further complications, which can be conceptualized as horizontal and vertical. On the horizontal plane the problem that remains is the question of what must be included and what should be excluded from the study of literary journalism. D. G. Myers argues that if almost anything that bears the marks of narrative and poetic language can be considered literary journalism, then perhaps nothing truly is.[11] Similarly the inclusivity of the field can make it difficult to develop the kind of meaningful distinctions that allow for critical comparisons between different works or kinds of work.

The vertical problem gets to the issue of quality and whether some forms, or some examples, of literary journalism can be judged to be superior as compared to others. The problem of defining quality in the wider world of journalism has remained elusive,[12] and so it is not surprising that articulations of criteria by which to judge literary journalism are similarly hard to find. Sims has pointed to *New Yorker* writer Joseph Mitchell as a singularly successful literary journalist who has provided a standard of achievement that can be used to distinguish the highest forms of literary journalism. This standard implies a crossing over from purely observational journalism into a sphere of creative activity wherein the journalist establishes an authorial presence, similar to that of a great poet or playwright, in part by investing subjects with a symbolic resonance without adding to or altering the record of events. In this way literary journalism differs from traditional journalism not so much in its use of artistic techniques but in its embrace of ambiguity, what Sims calls "the edge of uncertainty,"[13] which is exactly the opposite goal of objective reporting with its emphasis on fixed and verifiable facts.

As a practical matter, the lack of a widely accepted framework for the field may be a limiting factor that has contributed to a narrowness of focus, which scholars are still working to enlarge. Thomas B. Connery noted that much of the early scholarship in the field tended to focus on just a handful of writers, including Tom Wolfe, Norman Mailer, Joan Didion and Truman Capote.[14] Only in recent years have scholars responded to calls by Connery and others[15] to study lesser-known writers, especially women and minorities. A notable example of this trend is Jan Whitt's *Settling the Borderland: Other Voices in Literary Journalism*.[16]

Although the larger definitional issues remain unresolved, scholars have been more successful in defining, or at least describing, national traditions of literary journalism. Two recent books, both collections of scholarly essays, have argued for literary journalism as an international phenomenon, albeit with particular local characteristics. *Literary Journalism across the Globe: Journalistic Traditions and Transnational Influences* considers examples of literary journalism found in, among other places, Australia,[17] China,[18] Finland,[19] New Zealand,[20] Poland,[21] Portugal[22] and Slovenia.[23] *Global Literary Journalism: Exploring the Journalistic Imagination* adds to the mix with essays on writers in India,[24] the Middle East,[25] Norway[26] and Sweden.[27]

While it has a special relationship with the magazine form, literary journalism can also be found in other print venues, such as newspapers and books, as well as in other media, and the scholarship reflects the cross-media use. Cindy Royal and James W. Tankard, Jr., for example, looked at an example of newspaper literary journalism that had a companion Internet site, arguing that the World Wide Web's ability to integrate text, images, sound, video and interactivity could lead to further innovations in storytelling.[28] As Susan Greenberg has noted, digital media, both in the more established forms such as blogging and in still-evolving manifestations enabled by mobile platforms, represent both a challenge and opportunity for narrative, long-form journalism. The still expanding on-line environment can bring new attention to literary journalism while also adding to the overload of information that can make it harder for readers to engage with the form.[29] Part of this process is driven by sites that rely on what is called *aggregation and curation*, an Internet-era term that describes a technology-powered form of the long-established editorial process of culling and tailoring information.

Process Research

Like jazz music, literary journalism evolves by borrowing from and combining previously known modes and methods, finding new ways of expression that can seem strikingly original but that can also be traced to earlier styles. The recurring apparent newness of literary journalism is reflected in the scholarship. For example, Barbara Lounsberry, writing in 1990, identified "exhaustive research"[30] as one of the defining qualities of literary journalism. Fifteen years later, Robert S. Boynton argued that a new form of New Journalism had more recently emerged, distinguished in much the same way that Lounsberry had defined an earlier group of writers—by the fact that its practitioners engaged in extensive reporting.[31]

A widely used term for the kind of intensive research that Boynton described is *immersion journalism*, and numerous studies have examined the reporting methods of literary journalists who have used variations of this technique. These range from Richard Critchfield, who consciously based his methods on the work of anthropologist Oscar Lewis,[32] to Hunter S. Thompson, whose "gonzo" method of reporting entailed engaging with his subjects on their own psychotropic terms.[33]

In a critical anthology published in 1997, Ben Yagoda provided a useful roadmap for considering different approaches to writing literary journalism.[34] His first category was *narrative*, which he subdivided by identifying two models, either the novel or the film. In both cases the reporter assembles a vast amount of information and then presents it either with the kind of omniscience that might be found in a novel or, alternatively, allows it to unfold the way it would appear in a film or play. The second category consists of *first-person accounts*, where the reporter stands in the foreground. The third category, where the emphasis is on *style*, is the broadest, including works that are distinctive because of the writer's skill in establishing a voice, experimenting with structure or producing high-quality prose.

Literary journalists make the claim that their use of specialized techniques allows them, and their readers, access to an understanding of reality—a form of truth—that is not available through traditional means of fact gathering and article construction. But by consciously crossing the bounds of mainstream practice, literary journalists expose themselves to a range of ethical issues that arise as the consequence of the methods used for both reporting and writing.

A landmark study of the ethical issues associated with the practice of literary journalism can be found in Kathy Roberts Forde's *Literary Journalism on Trial: Masson v. New Yorker and the First Amendment*,[35] an account of a libel case that threw a harsh light on the way the magazine went about constructing supposedly direct quotes. The case raised questions about acceptable practice in literary journalism and specifically whether in pursuit of a larger truth certain smaller truths, that is, specific factual details, may be sacrificed. "In the literary report, 'truth' and 'reality' have generally been thought to inhere in the interpretation of facts, often through narrative," Forde writes. "The whole literary report, some of its historical practitioners would aver, is true, even if some facts are not, at least as they might be assessed by an 'objective' journalist."[36]

While journalism scholars and critics concern themselves with the ethical issues involved in the practice of narrative nonfiction, cultural and literary scholars often take a far different approach. Phyllis Frus, for example, went so far as to argue against a distinction between fiction and reporting, in part because of the important role of the reader in judging the credibility of a text.[37] In Daniel W. Lehman's words, "any literary text, whether fiction or nonfiction, even one's own memory of events, is arbitrated or 'crafted' in important ways, rendering impossible the simple equation of 'actuality' with nonfiction."[38] Indeed Robert Alexander has shown how literary journalists frequently, whether consciously or unconsciously, have been drawn to writing about persons who in important ways correspond with themselves, to the point "where the journalist and subject are one."[39]

Authorial Studies

One of the most fertile areas of literary journalism research has been the examination of the work of individual practitioners. The range of writers who have published works of literary journalism in magazines is vast and diverse. Expressly biographical work addressing the arc of individual careers has been published in a variety forms, including full-length works, special journal issues and individual articles. The lives and careers of some literary journalists were intertwined, at least for a time, and these connections are described in books, such as *Gellhorn: A Twentieth-Century Life*, which examines the work of Martha Gellhorn, who was a foreign correspondent for *Collier's* magazine when she met and later married Ernest Hemingway.[40] Other literary journalists, such as Rachel Carson, worked in a more solitary fashion. Her story has been told in several recent biographies, including William Souder's 2012 *On a Farther Shore: The Life and Legacy of Rachel Carson*.[41]

The spring 2012 issue of *Literary Journalism Studies* marked the fortieth anniversary of the publication in book form of Hunter Thompson's *Fear and Loathing in Las Vegas* by publishing seven articles on Thompson. It was guest-edited by William McKeen, himself the author of two biographies of the gonzo journalist, and included a bibliography of Thompson's published work.[42] Articles covered such topics as the development of the gonzo style as well as the way it has influenced writers in different cultures and eras.

Edd Applegate's 1996 *Literary Journalism: A Biographical Dictionary of Writers and Editors*[43] provides synoptic information on individual writers. Similar information can be found in edited collections, such as Norman Sims and Mark Kramer's *Literary Journalism*. Particularly useful insights about the reporting and writing processes involved in literary journalism appear in several volumes that are based largely on interviews or presentations by practitioners. Boynton's *The New New Journalism* is based on interviews with writers, while Mark Kramer and Wendy Call's *Telling True Stories* is based almost entirely on material from the annual Nieman Conference on Narrative Journalism at Harvard University. The latter book includes sections on many of the same issues that concern scholars and critics, including ethics, story structure and genre distinctions.[44]

These works could be considered primary sources because they rely so heavily on the journalists' own words. Secondary works, which similarly focus on individual journalists but consist primarily of critical considerations by scholars, make up much of the foundational scholarship on literary journalism. For example, in his *Literary Journalism in the Twentieth Century*, Sims includes a chapter he wrote dealing primarily with Joseph Mitchell.[45] Some of the scholarship in this area is comparative, with an emphasis on similarities and differences in cultural production. That same volume includes Shelley Fisher Fishkin's essay considering the work of W.E.B. Du Bois, James Agee, Tillie Olsen and Gloria Anzaldúa, "stories of people who were dismissed and devalued because they had the 'wrong' race, class, gender, ethnicity, or sexual preference."[46] Thomas B. Connery's 1992 collection, *A Sourcebook of American Literary Journalism: Representative Writers in an Emerging Genre*, contains nearly three dozen essays on individual writers as well as summary descriptions of the contributions of other important figures.[47]

The IALJS journal regularly features studies of individual literary journalists, some of which also highlight distinctive modes of work. Roberta S. Maguire, for example, described how the African-American cultural critic Albert Murray used his book-length literary journalism to challenge the approaches and presuppositions that white journalists, such as Norman Mailer, had incorporated in writings that had appeared in magazines and elsewhere.[48]

Media Effects

Given the reformist impulse of much literary journalism, scholars have frequently examined the form and its effect on socio-cultural change. Narrative has been an important ingredient in the muckraking style of U.S. journalism, both as it emerged in magazines of the early twentieth century, such as *Collier's* and *McClure's*, as well as in later manifestations in publications like *Mother Jones*, *Ramparts* and the *Nation*.[49] While literary journalism is frequently associated with progressive political advocacy, one scholar notes that the form's leftward tilt is not a universal phenomenon and may be mostly evident in the Northern Hemisphere. "In the South (or the developing world), however, a fair amount of literary journalism tends to perceive reality from a rightist point of view," says David Abrahamson.[50]

Several scholars have described the ways that literary journalism has been employed in Latin America in the face of authoritarian regimes and extreme political turmoil. Pablo Calvi argues that Anglo American literary journalism has been driven by market considerations, while Latin American narratives are more deeply involved in politics, in a way that forces a reexamination of the standard demarcations between fact and fiction, truth and falsehood. Writes Calvi: "Latin American nonfiction, therefore, oscillates between the 'official story' of the regime, which is a false account, and the seemingly 'fictionalized' account of a story that contradicts the official statements in unveiling a different 'truth' of what happened."[51]

In the cultural sphere, literary journalism has likewise documented and contributed to changing beliefs and expectations. In a 2009 study Dallas Liddle makes the case, for example, that Victorian literature as a whole and individual writers as well were directly influenced by the genres that were employed in the periodicals of the time and to a greater degree than has been previously acknowledged.[52] Connery has similarly shown that narrative journalism was a key factor in the broad social shift toward realism that began in late nineteenth-century America.[53] By focusing on the biographies of literary figures who also worked as journalists at magazines and newspapers, Doug Underwood argued for a "hybrid form of scholarship that mirrors the hybrid nature of much journalistically influenced literature."[54]

The form is fluid, and writers have used it across a wide range of topics and occasions because of its ability to convey information in a way that traditional approaches cannot. In the first Iraq War, for example, newsmagazines such as *Time* and *Newsweek* were fully capable of bringing readers the basics of the conflict: accountings of casualties and descriptions of strategies. But it took coverage in places like *Esquire* by journalists like John Sack to bring "the palpable sense of fear, confusion, exhilaration and exasperation that surely lies at the epicenter of human conflict," as shown in a 2012 study by J. Keith Saliba and Ted Geltner.[55]

In yet another manifestation of the paradoxical nature of the form, literary journalism does not necessarily depend on moments of intense conflict or high drama to reach its full effect. In fact, many of the most accomplished practitioners of literary journalism have focused on the ordinary. Sims provides a catalog of distinguished writers whose work celebrates "the journalism of everyday life,"[56] including Daniel Defoe, Mark Twain, Lefcadio Hearn, George Ade, Finley Peter Dunne, John Reed, James Agee, Joseph Mitchell, Ted Conover and John McPhee. Scholars have been more recently urged to look not only at ordinary topics but at forms of publication that might be considered ordinary and yet could yield examples of literary journalism. Nancy Roberts suggests that examples of literary journalism might be found in a range of places, citing the possibilities of "household magazines and newspapers; letters, memoirs, and diaries; epistolary journalism; religious tracts; travel writing; and social movement, muckraking and African American periodicals."[57]

While unusually successful in illuminating cultural issues and trends and in dramatizing conflicts involving individual figures, literary journalism has been less often focused on the kind of group and organizational complexities that have come to define so much of contemporary life in advanced Western societies. John J. Pauly, who has long argued for a greater recognition of the political contributions and potential of literary journalism,[58] believes that the form could do more to "assert its relevance to public life" but not without first wrestling with issues both technical and theoretical.[59]

Intersections

It is an understatement to say that magazines have played a preeminent role in the development of literary journalism, even if that role has perhaps diminished in recent years. Writers such as Thompson may have become better known for their book-length works, but magazines were often their launching pads, either for showcasing shorter pieces of literary journalism or by commissioning articles that were later turned into books. Sims points out that before beginning his campaign on behalf of New Journalism, Wolfe had published a parody of *New Yorker* editor William Shawn, which may have served to obscure the role of that magazine in promoting literary journalism and the role of Shawn himself in nurturing the form.[60] Yagoda notes that between 1962 and 1964, Shawn "published a series of articles that, in their social and political reporting and impact, are probably unmatched in the history of magazines."[61] Some of these pieces, such as the serialized version of Carson's *Silent Spring*, are claimed as literary journalism, and other pieces incorporate to a lesser or greater extent the techniques of the form. In 1965 Shawn's *New Yorker* printed one of the most significant examples of what came to be called the nonfiction novel, Truman Capote's "In Cold Blood."[62]

Other figures have also played a connecting role, linking writers and publications and even different forms of media in a similar sensibility. Bill Reynolds, for example, has documented the contributions of Bill Hedley, a Canadian-born writer and editor who saw New Journalism "as a way of thinking—a state of mind—for conveying what has been called the 'aesthetics of experience.'"[63] Hedley contributed to such publications as *Esquire* in the United States and *Maclean's* in Canada but achieved his greatest financial success by writing the original script for the hit movie *Flashdance*.

Because of their longer publication cycles and larger news holes, magazines made a natural fit with long-form narrative, an increasingly popular term that is often applied to literary journalism. More recently, as Jim Collins has pointed out, the rise of celebrity journalism, focusing on short features of famous persons, as well as the ongoing domination of the magazine industry by niche publications with vertical orientations, has forced writers to work harder for assignments.[64]

Although literary journalism is, naturally enough, associated with print, it is a mistake to assume a limited future for the form in the multimedia environment. Some magazine publishers have formed partnerships with Web sites that promote the form, and publishers have turned to the Web as a new distribution channel for narratives that would be considered long-form without necessarily being book-length.[65] The ability of literary journalism to connect across non-print media platforms is not a new phenomenon, however, as scholars have shown, for example, how the impact of John Hersey's "Hiroshima" article was greatly amplified because of radio broadcasts.[66]

Another place where literary journalism continues to forge new connections is the classroom. Frequently referred to as "creative nonfiction," it is increasingly seen as a fertile area of study both as literature and as a mode of teaching composition.[67] Lee Gutkind has pointed out that "students can earn undergraduate degrees, MFA degrees and PhDs" in the form.[68] But the form can also present acute ethical challenges for instructors because of its frequent focus on personal history, often traumatic. "Much has been written in mainstream media about ethical transgression purporting to the veracity of memoir texts but little theory has been produced within academia in addressing the ethical and pedagogical tensions constellating the supervision of life writing on trauma, and how to navigate these," writes Sue Joseph in describing some of her experiences in overseeing creative projects.[69]

Ongoing and Future Research

It has been more than two decades since Lounsberry described "the artistry of nonfiction [as] the great unexplored territory of contemporary criticism."[70] Since then scholars have focused a great deal of energy and attention toward fact-based works of narrative,[71] but much work remains to be done. In 1995 Connery cataloged a long list of potential research topics, some of which have been entered into but none of which have been exhausted.[72] In 2009 Sims identified half a dozen areas where the scholarship of literary journalism could fruitfully be pursued, including historical, cultural and international aspects of the form.[73] While progress has been made, it has been uneven. As Alice Donat Trindade has noted, for example, the field has been less successful in attracting Asian and African scholars.[74]

Given the innovative and even experimental nature of much of literary journalism, it is impossible to predict the future of the form and thus also foolhardy to try to foresee what direction research and criticism will take. But it is possible to sense that the scholarship has matured and is ready to emerge into a new phase, one in which less attention may be paid to extending boundary lines or claiming individual writers for literary journalism while more energy is directed to bringing new methodologies to bear and erecting the kinds of theoretical frameworks that will allow for deeper consideration and appreciation of the works themselves.

Notes

1 Tom Wolfe, *The New Journalism*, With an Anthology edited by Tom Wolfe and E. W. Johnson, eds. (New York: Harper & Row, 1973), 25.

2 Wolfe, *The New Journalism*, 23.

3 John C. Hartsock, *A History of American Literary Journalism: The Emergence of a Modern Narrative Form* (Amherst: University of Massachusetts Press, 2000), 129.

4 Norman Sims, *Literary Journalism in the Twentieth Century* (New York: Oxford University Press, 1990, and Evanston, IL: Northwestern University Press, 2008).

5 Mark Kramer, "Breakable Rules for Literary Journalists," in Norman Sims and Mark Kramer, eds., *Literary Journalism: A New Collection of the Best American Nonfiction* (New York: Ballantine Books, 1995), 21.

6 John S. Bak, "Introduction," in John S. Bak and Bill Reynolds, eds., *Literary Journalism across the Globe: Journalistic Traditions and Transnational Influences* (Amherst: University of Massachusetts Press, 2011), 18.

7 Bak, "Introduction," 7.

8 Norman Sims, "A True Story," in *True Stories: A Century of Literary Journalism* (Evanston, IL: Northwestern University Press, 2007), 24.

9 John C. Hartsock, "Note from the Editor," *Literary Journalism Studies* 1.1 (Spring 2009): 5.

10 David H. Richter, "Introduction," in David H. Richter, ed., *The Critical Tradition: Classic Texts and Contemporary Trends*, 3rd ed. (Boston: Bedford/St. Martin's, 2007), 2.

11 David G. Myers, "The Decline and Fall of Literary Journalism," *Literary Commentary* (blog), *Commentary*, 8 June 2012 <http://www.commentarymagazine.com/2012/06/08/literary-journalism-then-now/>, accessed 6 January 2014.

12 Ivor Shapiro, "Evaluating Journalism: Towards an Assessment Framework for the Practice of Journalism," *Journalism Practice* 4.2 (April 2010): 143–162.

13 Norman Sims, "The Bomb," in *True Stories: A Century of Literary Journalism* (Evanston, IL: Northwestern University Press, 2007), 185–186.

14 Thomas B. Connery, "Research Review: Magazines and Literary Journalism, An Embarrassment of Riches," in David Abrahamson, ed., *The American Magazine: Research Perspectives and Prospects* (Ames: Iowa State University Press, 1995), 208.

15 See, for example, Barbara Lounsberry, *The Art of Fact: Contemporary Artists of Nonfiction* (New York: Greenwood Press, 1990).

16 Jan Whitt, *Settling the Borderland: Other Voices in Literary Journalism* (Lanham, MD: University Press of America, 2008).

17 Willa McDonald, "Creditable or Reprehensible? The Literary Journalism of Helen Garner," in John S. Bak and Bill Reynolds, eds., *Literary Journalism across the Globe: Journalistic Traditions and Transnational Influences* (Amherst: University of Massachusetts Press, 2011), 260–275.

18 Peiqin Chen, "Social Movements and Chinese Literary Reportage," in John S. Bak and Bill Reynolds, eds., *Literary Journalism across the Globe: Journalistic Traditions and Transnational Influences* (Amherst: University of Massachusetts Press, 2011), 148–161.

19 Maria Lassila-Merisalo, "Literary Journalism in Twentieth-Century Finland," in John S. Bak and Bill Reynolds, eds., *Literary Journalism across the Globe: Journalistic Traditions and Transnational Influences* (Amherst: University of Massachusetts Press, 2011), 184–207.

20 Nikki Hessell, "Riding the Rails with Robin Hyde: Literary Journalism in 1930s New Zealand," in John S. Bak and Bill Reynolds, eds., *Literary Journalism across the Globe: Journalistic Traditions and Transnational Influences* (Amherst: University of Massachusetts Press, 2011), 211–224.

21 Soenke Zehle, "Ryszard Kapuściński and the Borders of Documentarism: Toward Exposure without Assumption," in John S. Bak and Bill Reynolds, eds., *Literary Journalism across the Globe: Journalistic Traditions and Transnational Influences* (Amherst: University of Massachusetts Press, 2011), 276–294.

22 Isabel Soares, "Literary Journalism's Magnetic Pull: Britain's 'New' Journalism and the Portuguese at the Fin-de-Siècle," in John S. Bak and Bill Reynolds, eds., *Literary Journalism across the Globe: Journalistic Traditions and Transnational Influences* (Amherst: University of Massachusetts Press, 2011), 118–133.

23 Sonja Merljak Zdovc, "Željko Kozinc, the Subversive Reporter: Literary Journalism in Slovenia," in John S. Bak and Bill Reynolds, eds., *Literary Journalism across the Globe: Journalistic Traditions and Transnational Influences* (Amherst: University of Massachusetts Press, 2011), 238–259.

24 Jane Chapman, "From India's Big Dams to Jungle Guerillas: Arundhati Roy and the Literary Polemics of Global versus Local," in Richard Lance Keeble and John Tulloch, eds., *Global Literary Journalism: Exploring the Journalistic Imagination* (New York: Peter Lang, 2012), 317–331.

25 David Abrahamson and Ibrahim N. Abusharif, "Literary Journalism in the Middle East: The Paradox of Arab Exceptionalism," in Richard Lance Keeble and John Tulloch, eds., *Global Literary Journalism: Exploring the Journalistic Imagination* (New York: Peter Lang, 2012), 23–38.

26 Jenny McKay, "Åsne Seierstad and the Bookseller of Kabul," in Richard Lance Keeble and John Tulloch, eds., *Global Literary Journalism: Exploring the Journalistic Imagination* (New York: Peter Lang, 2012), 175–190.

27 Anna Hoyles, "Pickled Herrings and Politics: The Early Journalism of Moa Martinson," in Richard Lance Keeble and John Tulloch, eds., *Global Literary Journalism: Exploring the Journalistic Imagination* (New York: Peter Lang, 2012), 72–88.

28 Cindy Royal and James W. Tankard, Jr. "Literary Journalism Techniques Create Compelling *Blackhawk Down* Web Site," *Newspaper Research Journal* 25.4 (Fall 2004): 88.

29 Susan Greenberg, "Slow Journalism in the Digital Fast Lane," in Richard Lance Keeble and John Tulloch, eds., *Global Literary Journalism: Exploring the Journalistic Imagination* (New York: Peter Lang, 2012), 381–393.

30 Lounsberry, *The Art of Fact*, xiii.

31 Robert S. Boynton, ed., *The New New Journalism: Conversations with America's Best Nonfiction Writers on Their Craft* (New York: Vintage Books, 2005), xxvii.

32 Miles Maguire, "Richard Critchfield: 'Genius' Journalism and the Fallacy of Verification," *Literary Journalism Studies* 1.2 (Fall 2009): 9–21.

33 See, for example, Jennifer M. Russell, "'A Savage Place!': Hunter S. Thompson and His Pleasure Dome," *Literary Journalism Studies* 4.1 (Spring 2012): 37–50.

34 Ben Yagoda, "Preface," in Kevin Kerrane and Ben Yagoda, eds., *The Art of Fact: A Historical Anthology of Literary Journalism* (New York: Scribner, 1997), 13–16.

35 Kathy Roberts Forde, *Literary Journalism on Trial: Masson v. New Yorker and the First Amendment* (Amherst: University of Massachusetts Press, 2008).

36 Forde, *Literary Journalism on Trial*, 206–207.

37 Phyllis Frus, *The Politics and Poetics of Journalistic Narrative: The Timely and the Timeless* (New York: Cambridge University Press, 1994), x.

38 Daniel W. Lehman, *Matters of Fact: Reading Nonfiction over the Edge* (Columbus: Ohio State University Press, 1997), 7

39 Robert Alexander, "'My Story Is Always Escaping into Other People': Subjectivity, Objectivity, and the Double in American Literary Journalism," *Literary Journalism Studies* 1.1 (Spring 2009): 57–66.

40 Caroline Moorehead, *Gellhorn: A Twentieth-Century Life* (New York: Henry Holt, 2003). See also Janet Groth, *The Receptionist: An Education at the New Yorker* (Chapel Hill, NC: Algonquin Books of Chapel Hill, 2012) for an account of Joseph Mitchell's relationship with a coworker.

41 William Souder, *On a Farther Shore: The Life and Legacy of Rachel Carson* (New York: Crown, 2012).

42 William McKeen, "A Hunter S. Thompson Bibliography," [Special Issue: Hunter S. Thompson], *Literary Journalism Studies* 4.1 (Spring 2012): 117–124.

43 Edd Applegate, ed., *Literary Journalism: A Biographical Dictionary of Writers and Editors* (Westport, CT: Greenwood Press, 1996).

44 Mark Kramer and Wendy Call, eds., *Telling True Stories: A Nonfiction Writers' Guide from the Nieman Foundation at Harvard University* (New York: Plume, 2007).

45 Norman Sims, "Joseph Mitchell and the *New Yorker* Nonfiction Writers," in Norman Sims, ed., *Literary Journalism in the Twentieth Century* (New York: Oxford University Press, 1990, and Evanston, IL: Northwestern University Press, 2008), 82–109.

46 Shelley Fisher Fishkin, "The Borderlands of Culture: Writing by W.E.B. Du Bois, James Agee, Tillie Olsen, and Gloria Anzaldúa," in Norman Sims, ed., *Literary Journalism in the Twentieth Century* (New York: Oxford University Press, 1990, and Evanston, IL: Northwestern University Press, 2008), 133–182.

47 Thomas B. Connery, ed., *A Sourcebook of American Literary Journalism: Representative Writers in an Emerging Genre* (New York: Greenwood Press, 1992).

48 Roberta S. Maguire, "Riffing on Hemingway and Burke, Responding to Mailer and Wolfe: Albert Murray's 'Anti-Journalism,'" *Literary Journalism Studies* 2.2 (Fall 2010): 9–26.

49 James L. Aucoin, "Journalistic Moral Engagement: Narrative Strategies in American Muckraking," *Journalism* 8.5 (October 2007): 559–572.

50 David Abrahamson, "The Counter-Coriolis Effect: Contemporary Literary Journalism in a Shrinking World," in John S. Bak and Bill Reynolds, eds., *Literary Journalism across the Globe: Journalistic Traditions and Transnational Influences* (Amherst: University of Massachusetts Press, 2011), 81.

51 Pablo Calvi, "Latin America's Own 'New Journalism,'" *Literary Journalism Studies* 2.2 (Fall 2010): 78.

52 Dallas Liddle, *The Dynamics of Genre: Journalism and the Practice of Literature in Mid-Victorian Britain* (Charlottesville: University of Virginia Press, 2009).

53 Thomas B. Connery, *Journalism and Realism: Rendering American Life* (Evanston, IL: Northwestern University Press, 2011).

54 Doug Underwood, *Journalism and the Novel: Truth and Fiction, 1700–2000* (Cambridge: Cambridge University Press, 2008): 13.

55 J. Keith Saliba and Ted Geltner, "Literary War Journalism: Framing and the Creation of Meaning," *Journal of Magazine & New Media Research* 13.2 (Summer 2012): 15.

56 Norman Sims, "New Generations," in *True Stories: A Century of Literary Journalism* (Evanston, IL: Northwestern University Press, 2007), 287.

57 Nancy L. Roberts, "Firing the Canon: The Historical Search for Literary Journalism's Missing Links," *Literary Journalism Studies* 4.2 (Fall 2012): 82.

58 John J. Pauly, "The Politics of the New Journalism," in Norman Sims, *Literary Journalism in the Twentieth Century* (New York: Oxford University Press, 1990, and Evanston, IL: Northwestern University Press, 2008), 110–129.

59 John J. Pauly, "Literary Journalism and the Drama of Civic Life: Keynote Address, IALJS, Brussels, Belgium, May 13, 2011," *Literary Journalism Studies* 3.2 (Fall 2011): 79.

60 Norman Sims, "Tourist in a Strange Land: Tom Wolfe and the New Journalists," *True Stories: A Century of Literary Journalism* (Evanston, IL: Northwestern University Press, 2007), 231–235.

61 Ben Yagoda, *About Town: The New Yorker and the World It Made* (New York: Scribner, 2000), 313.

62 Yagoda, *About Town*, 314.

63 Bill Reynolds, "Recovering the Peculiar Life and Times of Tom Hedley and of Canadian New Journalism," *Literary Journalism Studies* 1.1 (Spring 2009): 79–104.

64 Jim Collins, "Making It as a Freelancer," in Mark Kramer and Wendy Call, eds., *Telling True Stories: A Nonfiction Writers' Guide from the Nieman Foundation at Harvard University* (New York: Plume, 2007), 264–268.

65 Michael Meyer, "Going to Great Lengths," *Columbia Journalism Review*, November/December 2012, 16–17.

66 See Kathy Roberts Forde, "Profit and Public Interest: A Publication History of John Hersey's 'Hiroshima,'" *Journalism & Mass Communication Quarterly* 88.3 (Autumn 2011): 562–579; and Kathy Roberts Forde and Matthew W. Ross, "Radio and Civic Courage in the Communications Circuit of John Hersey's 'Hiroshima,'" *Literary Journalism Studies* 3.2 (Fall 2011): 31–53.

67 Douglas Hesse, "The Place of Creative Nonfiction," *College English* 65.3 (January 2003): 237–241.

68 Lee Gutkind, *You Can't Make This Stuff Up: The Complete Guide to Writing Creative Nonfiction—from Memoir to Literary Journalism and Everything in Between* (Boston: Da Capo Press, 2012), 9–10.

69 Sue Joseph, "Supervising Life-Writing of Trauma in a Tertiary Setting," *Text* 15.2 (October 2011) <http://textjournal.com.au/oct11/joseph.htm>, accessed 13 January 2013.

70 Lounsberry, *The Art of Fact*, xi.

71 See, for example, Miles Maguire and Roberta S. Maguire, "Building a Bibliography for the Study of Literary Journalism," *Literary Journalism Studies* 3.2 (Fall 2011): 123–125; Miles Maguire and Roberta S. Maguire, "Selected Bibliography of Scholarship and Criticism, Examining Literary Journalism: New Additions," *Literary Journalism Studies* 3.2 (Fall 2011): 126–127; see also, International Association for Literary Journalism Studies, "*Literary Journalism Studies* Selected Bibliography of Scholarship and Criticism," *Literary Journalism Studies* Updated 1 March 2012 <http://www.davidabrahamson.com/WWW/IALJS/LJS_Biblio_v120301.pdf>, accessed 17 January 2013.

72 Connery, "Research Review."

73 Norman Sims, "The Problem and the Promise of Literary Journalism Studies," *Literary Journalism Studies* 1.1 (Spring 2009): 7–16.

74 Alice Donat Trindade, "What Will the Future Bring?" *Literary Journalism Studies* 4.2 (Fall 2012): 101–105.

Bibliography

Abrahamson, David. "The Counter-Coriolis Effect: Contemporary Literary Journalism in a Shrinking World." In Bak, John S. and Reynolds, Bill, eds. *Literary Journalism across the Globe: Journalistic Traditions and Transnational Influences.* Amherst: University of Massachusetts Press, 2011, 79–84.

Abrahamson, David and Abusharif, Ibrahim N. "Literary Journalism in the Middle East: The Paradox of Arab Exceptionalism." In Keeble, Richard Lance and Tulloch, John, eds. *Global Literary Journalism: Exploring the Journalistic Imagination.* New York: Peter Lang, 2012, 23–38.

Alexander, Robert. "'My Story Is Always Escaping into Other People': Subjectivity, Objectivity, and the Double in American Literary Journalism." *Literary Journalism Studies* 1.1 (Spring 2009): 57–66.

Applegate, Edd, ed. *Literary Journalism: A Biographical Dictionary of Writers and Editors.* Westport, CT: Greenwood Press, 1996.

Aucoin, James L. "Journalistic Moral Engagement: Narrative Strategies in American Muckraking." *Journalism* 8.5 (October 2007): 559–572.

Bak, John S. "Introduction." In Bak, John S. and Reynolds, Bill, eds. *Literary Journalism across the Globe: Journalistic Traditions and Transnational Influences.* Amherst: University of Massachusetts Press, 2011, 1–20.

Boynton, Robert S., ed. *The New New Journalism: Conversations with America's Best Nonfiction Writers on Their Craft.* New York: Vintage Books, 2005.

Calvi, Pablo. "Latin America's Own 'New Journalism.'" *Literary Journalism Studies* 2.2 (Fall 2010): 63–83.

Chapman, Jane. "From India's Big Dams to Jungle Guerillas: Arundhati Roy and the Literary Polemics of Global versus Local." In Keeble, Richard Lance and Tulloch, John, eds. *Global Literary Journalism: Exploring the Journalistic Imagination.* New York: Peter Lang, 2012, 317–331.

Chen, Peiqin. "Social Movements and Chinese Literary Reportage." In Bak, John S. and Reynolds, Bill, eds. *Literary Journalism across the Globe: Journalistic Traditions and Transnational Influences.* Amherst: University of Massachusetts Press, 2011, 148–161.

Collins, Jim. "Making It as a Freelancer." In Kramer, Mark and Call, Wendy, eds. *Telling True Stories: A Nonfiction Writers' Guide from the Nieman Foundation at Harvard University*. New York: Plume, 2007, 264–268.

Connery, Thomas B. *Journalism and Realism: Rendering American Life*. Evanston, IL: Northwestern University Press, 2011.

Connery, Thomas B. "Research Review: Magazines and Literary Journalism, An Embarrassment of Riches." In Abrahamson, David, ed. *The American Magazine: Research Perspectives and Prospects*. Ames: Iowa State University Press, 1995, 207–216.

Connery, Thomas B., ed. *A Sourcebook of American Literary Journalism: Representative Writers in an Emerging Genre*. New York: Greenwood Press, 1992.

Fishkin, Shelley Fisher. "The Borderlands of Culture: Writing by W.E.B. Du Bois, James Agee, Tillie Olsen, and Gloria Anzaldúa." In Sims, Norman, ed. *Literary Journalism in the Twentieth Century*. New York: Oxford University Press, 1990, and Evanston, IL: Northwestern University Press, 2008, 133–182.

Forde, Kathy Roberts. *Literary Journalism on Trial: Masson v.* New Yorker *and the First Amendment*. Amherst: University of Massachusetts Press, 2008.

Forde, Kathy Roberts. "Profit and Public Interest: A Publication History of John Hersey's 'Hiroshima.'" *Journalism & Mass Communication Quarterly* 88.3 (Autumn 2011): 562–579.

Forde, Kathy Roberts and Ross, Matthew W. "Radio and Civic Courage in the Communications Circuit of John Hersey's 'Hiroshima.'" *Literary Journalism Studies* 3.2 (Fall 2011): 31–53.

Frus, Phyllis. *The Politics and Poetics of Journalistic Narrative: The Timely and the Timeless*. New York: Cambridge University Press, 1994.

Greenberg, Susan. "Slow Journalism in the Digital Fast Lane." In Keeble, Richard Lance and Tulloch, John, eds. *Global Literary Journalism: Exploring the Journalistic Imagination*. New York: Peter Lang, 2012, 381–393.

Groth, Janet. *The Receptionist: An Education at the* New Yorker. Chapel Hill, NC: Algonquin Books of Chapel Hill, 2012.

Gutkind, Lee. *You Can't Make This Stuff Up: The Complete Guide to Writing Creative Nonfiction—from Memoir to Literary Journalism and Everything in Between*. Boston: Da Capo Press, 2012.

Hartsock, John C. *A History of American Literary Journalism: The Emergence of a Modern Narrative Form*. Amherst: University of Massachusetts Press, 2000.

Hartsock, John C. "Note from the Editor." *Literary Journalism Studies* 1.1 (Spring 2009): 5.

Hesse, Douglas. "The Place of Creative Nonfiction." *College English* 65.3 (January 2003): 237–241.

Hessell, Nikki. "Riding the Rails with Robin Hyde: Literary Journalism in 1930s New Zealand." In Bak, John S. and Reynolds, Bill, eds. *Literary Journalism across the Globe: Journalistic Traditions and Transnational Influences*. Amherst: University of Massachusetts Press, 2011, 211–224.

Hoyles, Anna. "Pickled Herrings and Politics: The Early Journalism of Moa Martinson." In Keeble, Richard Lance and Tulloch, John, eds. *Global Literary Journalism: Exploring the Journalistic Imagination*. New York: Peter Lang, 2012, 72–88.

International Association for Literary Journalism Studies, "*Literary Journalism Studies* Selected Bibliography of Scholarship and Criticism." *Literary Journalism Studies* Updated 1 March 2012 <http://www.davidabrahamson.com/WWW/IALJS/LJS_Biblio_v120301.pdf>, accessed 17 January 2013.

Joseph, Sue. "Supervising Life-Writing of Trauma in a Tertiary Setting." *Text* 15.2 (October 2011) <http://textjournal.com.au/oct11/joseph.htm>, accessed 13 January 2013.

Kramer, Mark. "Breakable Rules for Literary Journalists." In Sims, Norman and Kramer, Mark, eds. *Literary Journalism: A New Collection of the Best American Nonfiction*. New York: Ballantine Books, 1995, 21–34.

Kramer, Mark and Call, Wendy, eds. *Telling True Stories: A Nonfiction Writers' Guide from the Nieman Foundation at Harvard University*. New York: Plume, 2007.

Lassila-Merisalo, Maria. "Literary Journalism in Twentieth-Century Finland." In Bak, John S. and Reynolds, Bill, eds. *Literary Journalism across the Globe: Journalistic Traditions and Transnational Influences*. Amherst: University of Massachusetts Press, 2011, 184–207.

Lehman, Daniel W. *Matters of Fact: Reading Nonfiction over the Edge*. Columbus: Ohio State University Press, 1997.

Liddle, Dallas. *The Dynamics of Genre: Journalism and the Practice of Literature in Mid-Victorian Britain*. Charlottesville: University of Virginia Press, 2009.

Lounsberry, Barbara. *The Art of Fact: Contemporary Artists of Nonfiction*. New York: Greenwood Press, 1990.

Maguire, Miles. "Richard Critchfield: 'Genius' Journalism and the Fallacy of Verification." *Literary Journalism Studies* 1.2 (Fall 2009): 9–21.

Maguire, Miles and Maguire, Roberta S. "Building a Bibliography for the Study of Literary Journalism." *Literary Journalism Studies* 3.2 (Fall 2011): 123–125.

Maguire, Miles and Maguire, Roberta S. "Selected Bibliography of Scholarship and Criticism, Examining Literary Journalism: New Additions." *Literary Journalism Studies* 3.2 (Fall 2011): 126–127.

Maguire, Roberta S. "Riffing on Hemingway and Burke, Responding to Mailer and Wolfe: Albert Murray's 'Anti-Journalism.'" *Literary Journalism Studies* 2.2 (Fall 2010): 9–26.

McDonald, Willa. "Creditable or Reprehensible? The Literary Journalism of Helen Garner." In Bak, John S. and Reynolds, Bill, eds. *Literary Journalism across the Globe: Journalistic Traditions and Transnational Influences.* Amherst: University of Massachusetts Press, 2011, 260–275.

McKay, Jenny. "Åsne Seierstad and the Bookseller of Kabul." In Keeble, Richard Lance and Tulloch, John, eds. *Global Literary Journalism: Exploring the Journalistic Imagination.* New York: Peter Lang, 2012, 175–190.

McKeen, William. "A Hunter S. Thompson Bibliography." [Special Issue: Hunter S. Thompson]. *Literary Journalism Studies* 4.1 (Spring 2012): 117–124.

Meyer, Michael. "Going to Great Lengths." *Columbia Journalism Review*, November/December 2012, 16–17.

Moorehead, Caroline. *Gellhorn: A Twentieth-Century Life.* New York: Henry Holt, 2003.

Myers, David G. "The Decline and Fall of Literary Journalism." *Literary Commentary* (Blog). *Commentary*, 8 June 2012 <http://www.commentarymagazine.com/2012/06/08/literary-journalism-then-now/>, accessed 6 January 2014.

Pauly, John J. "Literary Journalism and the Drama of Civic Life: Keynote Address, IALJS, Brussels, Belgium, May 13, 2011." *Literary Journalism Studies* 3.2 (Fall 2011): 73–82.

Pauly, John J. "The Politics of the New Journalism." In Sims, Norman. *Literary Journalism in the Twentieth Century.* New York: Oxford University Press, 1990, and Evanston, IL: Northwestern University Press, 2008, 110–129.

Reynolds, Bill. "Recovering the Peculiar Life and Times of Tom Hedley and of Canadian New Journalism." *Literary Journalism Studies* 1.1 (Spring 2009): 79–104.

Richter, David H. "Introduction." In Richter, David H., ed. *The Critical Tradition: Classic Texts and Contemporary Trends.* 3rd ed. Boston: Bedford/St. Martin's, 2007, 1–22.

Roberts, Nancy L. "Firing the Canon: The Historical Search for Literary Journalism's Missing Links." *Literary Journalism Studies* 4.2 (Fall 2012): 81–93.

Royal, Cindy and Tankard, James W., Jr. "Literary Journalism Techniques Create Compelling *Blackhawk Down* Web Site." *Newspaper Research Journal* 25.4 (Fall 2004): 82–88.

Russell, Jennifer M. "'A Savage Place!': Hunter S. Thompson and His Pleasure Dome." *Literary Journalism Studies* 4.1 (Spring 2012): 37–50.

Saliba, J. Keith and Geltner, Ted. "Literary War Journalism: Framing and the Creation of Meaning." *Journal of Magazine & New Media Research* 13.2 (Summer 2012): 1–19.

Shapiro, Ivor. "Evaluating Journalism: Towards an Assessment Framework for the Practice of Journalism." *Journalism Practice* 4.2 (April 2010): 143–162.

Sims, Norman. "The Bomb." In *True Stories: A Century of Literary Journalism.* Evanston, IL: Northwestern University Press, 2007, 163–199.

Sims, Norman. "Joseph Mitchell and the *New Yorker* Nonfiction Writers." In Norman Sims, ed. *Literary Journalism in the Twentieth Century.* New York: Oxford University Press, 1990, and Evanston, IL: Northwestern University Press, 2008, 82–109.

Sims, Norman. *Literary Journalism in the Twentieth Century.* New York: Oxford University Press, 1990, and Evanston, IL: Northwestern University Press, 2008.

Sims, Norman. "New Generations." In *True Stories: A Century of Literary Journalism.* Evanston, IL: Northwestern University Press, 2007, 279–317.

Sims, Norman. "The Problem and the Promise of Literary Journalism Studies." *Literary Journalism Studies* 1.1 (Spring 2009): 7–16.

Sims, Norman. "Tourist in a Strange Land: Tom Wolfe and the New Journalists." *True Stories: A Century of Literary Journalism.* Evanston, IL: Northwestern University Press, 2007, 219–262.

Sims, Norman. "A True Story." In *True Stories: A Century of Literary Journalism.* Evanston, IL: Northwestern University Press, 2007, 1–24.

Soares, Isabel. "Literary Journalism's Magnetic Pull: Britain's 'New' Journalism and the Portuguese at the Fin-de-Siècle." In Bak, John S. and Reynolds, Bill, eds. *Literary Journalism across the Globe: Journalistic Traditions and Transnational Influences*. Amherst: University of Massachusetts Press, 2011, 118–133.

Souder, William. *On a Farther Shore: The Life and Legacy of Rachel Carson*. New York: Crown, 2012.

Trindade, Alice Donat. "What Will the Future Bring?" *Literary Journalism Studies* 4.2 (Fall 2012): 101–105.

Underwood, Doug. *Journalism and the Novel: Truth and Fiction, 1700–2000*. Cambridge: Cambridge University Press, 2008.

Whitt, Jan. *Settling the Borderland: Other Voices in Literary Journalism*. Lanham, MD: University Press of America, 2008.

Wolfe, Tom. *The New Journalism*. With an Anthology edited by Wolfe, Tom and Johnson, E.W., eds. New York: Harper & Row, 1973.

Yagoda, Ben. *About Town: The* New Yorker *and the World It Made*. New York: Scribner, 2000.

Yagoda, Ben. "Preface." In Kerrane, Kevin and Yagoda, Ben, eds. *The Art of Fact: A Historical Anthology of Literary Journalism*. New York: Scribner, 1997, 13–16.

Zdovc, Sonja Merljak. "Željko Kozinc, the Subversive Reporter: Literary Journalism in Slovenia." In Bak, John S. and Reynolds, Bill, eds. *Literary Journalism across the Globe: Journalistic Traditions and Transnational Influences*. Amherst: University of Massachusetts Press, 2011, 238–259.

Zehle, Soenke. "Ryszard Kapuściński and the Borders of Documentarism: Toward Exposure without Assumption." In Bak, John S. and Reynolds, Bill, eds. *Literary Journalism across the Globe: Journalistic Traditions and Transnational Influences*. Amherst: University of Massachusetts Press, 2011, 276–294.

Part IV

STUDIES IN PRESENTATION
Magazines as Visual Communication

23

THE MAGAZINE COVER

The Craft of Identity and Impact

Ted Spiker

The magazine cover is the beachfront mansion, the penthouse condo, the thousand-acre western ranch: It is the most valuable piece of real estate for any magazine. Like no other medium, magazines rely on this singular page to do two crucial things: one, send a message about the personality and voice of the magazine and two, sell issues. As Steve Cohn wrote, "You probably don't associate magazine covers with the Liberty Bell, Grand Canyon or Pike's Peak, but the great covers—like our national monuments—are American treasures."[1]

As such a visible part of the media landscape, magazine covers can make a lasting impression on readers no matter their perspective. While some readers of U.S. magazines may adore the more than 300 covers that Norman Rockwell drew for *Saturday Evening Post*,[2] others may prefer *Esquire*'s cover showing Andy Warhol drowning in a Campbell's can of tomato soup.[3] The cover of *Rolling Stone* featuring Yoko Ono and a naked John Lennon[4] (voted in 2005 as the best magazine cover of the past 40 years)[5] may be framed in the living rooms of music fans, while sports fanatics may have chosen to do the same with a wordless cover of *Sports Illustrated* on which the U.S. Olympic ice hockey team celebrates its miracle on ice.[6] International readers may remember any number of visually striking covers from *Stern*, a popular German magazine that features covers that "draw you in, making you linger, curious to discover more,"[7] such as one depicting a skull on the front of a plane[8] to depict terrorism or one showing Jimmy Carter and Leonid Breshnev covered in icicles to depict the cold war.[9]

Of course, magazine covers can make readers laugh, cry or cry laughing, as might the *New York* cover that identified the brain of former New York governor Eliot Spitzer as existing below his waist (Figure 23.1).[10] Of all the verbs that a magazine cover can incite, perhaps the most important one is to *sell*. Magazine covers "aim to catch the eye of the passer-by and to tantalize the onlooker with the promise of fascinating content within," wrote Andrew Losowsky.[11] Author Steve Taylor added,

> Magazine covers can be breathtaking, beautiful, confrontational, resonant, heartbreaking, stimulating, irritating and uplifting. At their best, they come together as a kind of spontaneous street level exhibition, publicly displaying the work of some of our best creative talent, featuring what is most admirable and dismissible about the modern world, communicating the people and events that shape our culture.[12]

As the media environment has changed with the introduction of digital technology and more competition for readers' attention, the magazine cover, too, is changing. Still, the magazine cover—equal parts art, editorial and marketing—remains a unique page in the media landscape, with editors facing both challenges and opportunities to create a magazine cover with an image, a message, or both, that stands above the day-to-day barrage of information from all forms of media.

Figure 23.1. New York's 2008 Eliot Spitzer cover. Used by permission.

   This chapter aims to address scholarly and industry literature that explores the importance of the magazine cover, both culturally and economically. What is the magazine cover's role in the media landscape, and what impacts do its messages have on its viewers and buyers?

Literature Review

To research the literature on magazine covers, this author used a number of popular-press and academic search tools. These included a bibliography compiled by one of this book's editors,[13] the archives of the *Journal of Magazine & New Media Research*, books about magazine covers in the author's collection, academic databases via OneSearch through the University of Florida library system and consumer-oriented search engines, such as Google and Amazon. Because magazine covers have a mainstream popularity and some magazines, such as *Sports Illustrated* and the *New Yorker*, sell replications of their covers as artwork, it was deemed important to include non-scholarly work as representative of industry trends and interests. From these searches were identified books on magazine covers, popular and trade press articles and scholarly research. These will be described in turn.

Books about magazine covers most typically take three different approaches. First are books that focus on a single magazine title or artist. For example, *Vogue*,[14] *Sports Illustrated*[15] and the *New Yorker*[16] all have published books showcasing their covers. Other books feature the 332 covers drawn by Norman Rockwell[17] and the controversial covers of *Esquire* designed by George Lois.[18] These books tend to be what are sometimes called *coffee-table books*—large-scale, hardback books with large images, which reinforce the notion that these magazines value their covers not just as vehicles through which to sell magazines, but as cultural icons and pieces of artwork. Second are books that serve a similar purpose of showcasing beautiful or important covers, or both, but from various titles. Both *Front Page*[19] and *100 Years of Magazine Covers*[20] act as this kind of gallery of global covers, with accompanying text to provide some historical and cultural context for many of the covers, as well as to describe their significance. A select few books take a specific, scholarly angle on magazine covers. A notable example is Carolyn Kitch's *The Girl on the Magazine Cover*, which examines the origins of visual stereotypes as they pertain to the magazine cover.[21]

Magazine covers are also a popular topic of discussion and analysis in the trade and popular press. Such publications as *Folio:*, which covers the magazine industry, often run articles that address cover trends and issues. Various mainstream publications, such as the *New York Times* and the *Washington Post*, have or have had media beat reporters who write about magazine covers when relevant. For example, Peter Carlson, who for a number of years wrote about the magazine world for the *Washington Post*, called the magazine cover line the "American haiku—a tiny work of art that carries tons of wisdom in a few well-chosen words."[22] In the same article, he wrote,

> You see a lot of cover lines in the magazine-reviewer business, and I have amassed a collection that I hope will one day serve as the basis for the long-awaited Norton Anthology of Magazine Cover Lines. It ranges from the ludicrous (*American Health*'s "Dreams Decoded: Solve Your Problems While You Sleep") to the laughable (*Spin*'s "King Pins: The Secret Pathos of Pro Bowling"), from the pugnacious (*Mirabella*'s "The Joy of Kicking Ass") to the perverse (the *Hustler* Inflation Index: A Consumer's Guide to Blow-Up Dolls").[23]

With the advent and explosion of digital media, many media-centric Web sites focus on magazine covers either exclusively or as part of their overall examination of the media industry. For example, the site Coverjunkie.com is devoted to showcasing excellent covers, while Gawker.com, which thrives on media gossip, often comments on covers it deems notable. In 2012, Britain's *Daily Mail* featured a controversial cover on *Dazed & Confused* magazine, in which female rapper Azealia Banks is pictured blowing up a red condom and holding it up to her mouth as if she were smoking a cigarette.[24] Author Fehintola Betiku reported that the cover had been "banned in no less than seven countries."[25] In addition, the digital media world enables organizations to have a role in presenting magazine covers to the masses. The Society of Publication Design, for example, highlights a cover of the day on Spd.org. The American Society of Magazine Editors has featured galleries of magazine covers, such as the display of 100 covers that had some tie to the events of 11 September 2001.[26]

In terms of scholarly research, historically very little has been written about the subject. Sammye Johnson, in a review of issues of *Journalism Quarterly* from 1924 to 1985, found no articles that directly addressed magazine covers.[27] Johnson also studied later issues of *Journalism & Mass Communication Quarterly* and six other journals, including *Journalism History*, "for research about covers. We found none."[28] Thus, Johnson in 2002 concluded there is not a lot of research published in journals about magazine covers.[29] With the advent of the

Journal of Magazine & New Media Research in 1999, more research has been published about covers. Some of these studies focus on one particular magazine, such as David Sumner's study of 2,128 *Life* magazine covers.[30] David W. Scott and Daniel A. Stout, in their close-text analysis of religion as depicted on the cover of *Time* magazine, found that "*Time* covers embrace private religious practice, are skeptical of institutions, lack a common code of symbols, and synthesize religion with art, entertainment and scientific information."[31]

Gerald Grow, from his historical research on magazine cover lines, wrote that early magazine covers resembled those of books, but that has changed over time.[32] During the 1980s, he wrote, it seemed that magazines were trying to place entire tables of contents on the cover, and for most magazines at the turn of the twenty-first century, cover lines were as important as cover art. "A powerful picture is rarely enough for magazine covers of this period."[33]

Sumner, as cited by Johnson, attributes the lack of research to the fact that designing magazine covers is more art than science, thus making them difficult to study using content analysis.[34] That doesn't mean magazine covers have not been studied. Some researchers use the magazine cover as a vehicle to study larger cultural issues. For example, Donnalyn Pompper, Suekyung Lee and Shana Lerner used the cover of *Rolling Stone* "as a measure for examining the 1960s social equality movement in terms of representations of gender and ethnicity over time."[35] Mia Foley Sypeck, James J. Gray and Anthony H. Ahrens studied cover models of *Cosmopolitan*, *Glamour*, *Mademoiselle* and *Vogue* to determine how the ideal female body size has changed over the years.[36] Still, the potential for scholarly study of the magazine cover remains largely untapped. Johnson concludes, "As both historical artifacts and marketing tools, magazine covers deserve closer study."[37]

With ample dimensions to study, the magazine cover can serve as a rich area for exploration. The design, editorial and business tactics used—combined with the cultural significance that some covers have—can lead to robust research possibilities. Scholars have the opportunity not only to continue to study magazine cover messages and media effects, that is, the impact that covers have on their viewers and buyers, but also to bridge the gap between industry and academia by doing more research that has business ramifications (of what sells and *why*, for example).

Though the research on magazine covers is limited, the cover remains the most prominent page of any magazine. That begs multiple questions: What is the cover's role? What is its cultural and historical significance? And, as the cover continues to be re-defined in an ever-increasing digital world, what is its future?

Cover Principles and Economics

In many ways, a magazine cover serves as a kind of media wrapping paper—a promise of a gift in the form of content inside. While coming in different colors and styles, the magazine cover ultimately must be the first, but certainly not the only force that drives potential buyers to open up and see what is inside. Sammye Johnson and Patricia Prijatel divide magazine cover design and content strategies into five categories: *poster* (one image and logo with no cover lines); *one theme, one image* (a few words to help identify the subject of the image); *multi-theme, one image* (cover lines for several stories with one dominant image); *multi-theme, multi-image* (a collage-type approach); *all-typographic* (no photographs or illustrations).[38] Tactics used for covers have changed over the years, but some industry observers agree that creating a magazine cover that attracts newsstand browsers to buy or subscribers to read is more art than science. "Though cover trends may be fascinating to observe, one has to bear in mind that there are no hard rules to live by," wrote Sarah Gonser.[39] Andrew Losowsky noted, however, that in some countries magazines are sold in places where browsing is not permitted, thus placing more importance on brand loyalty than impulse buying.[40]

Losowsky wrote, "Many people say that the quality of magazine covers—and indeed of magazines—has declined greatly in the last half century. In many respects, both positive and negative, today's magazine marketplace is certainly not what it was 50 years ago."[41] That notion is perhaps reinforced by statistics on the sell-through rate of magazines—that is, the percentage of magazines sold on the newsstand. Alex Kuczynski, citing Magazine Publishers of America statistics published in the *New York Times*, reported the sell-through rate in the United States has been declining over the decades—65 percent in 1973, 48 percent in 1988 and 35 percent in 2000.[42] Covers from a half century ago, such as those from the U.S. magazine *Esquire* in the 1960s, were thought of as more intellectual, artistic and controversial,[43] while today's covers are more conformist. Many covers in similar niche areas use the same tactics (one model with lots of cover lines in women's magazines, for example).

Some estimate that in today's world, creating, styling and shooting a magazine cover may cost $100,000.[44] "The irony is that mainstream magazines," Losowsky said, "in searching for cover images that will stand out from their rivals, so often end up looking identical."[45] David Crowley, a professor in Britain's Royal College of Art, observed that areas where competition is the greatest (e.g., women's magazines) is where the pressure on the cover is also the highest. "It can make the sale in a market where readers often have little brand loyalty."[46] Katharine Seelye wrote about the newsstand,

> The escalating numbers reflect a new reality for monthly magazines as they struggle against hot-selling, celebrity-crazed weeklies and the Internet to maintain their traditional roles as guideposts in an aspirational society and as glossy vehicles for advertisers, particularly those in the multibillion-dollar cosmetics and fashion industries.[47]

Magazine editors analyze sell-through rates to try to determine what factors might have prompted one cover to sell better than another. While there's no formula, and editors today use focus groups and on-line testing of mock covers to try to guess what cover of several may sell best, editors seem to agree that several factors do make a difference—namely sex, celebrity and large numbers written in big type because they stand out on the clutter of the newsstand and are a function of service magazines.[48] Still, Gonser said, cover lines are the deciding "buy factors," and they can account for "as much as 90 percent of a cover's impact," even over the dominant image, colors or design.[49] For those cover lines, Gonser noted, editors say they "stick to the 80 percent rules—80 percent of your cover lines should appeal to 80 percent of your readers—but they also recommend gambling with the remaining 20 percent."[50]

These statistics provide an opportunity for communication scholars to work closely with industry executives. Industry organizations have researched the data on such hard numbers as issue sales and ad revenue to see trends in growth and decline. Industry editors have certainly used a number of techniques to test their covers to try to predict sales. Scholars could use both qualitative and quantitative research methods to help identify what factors contribute to *why* certain covers may sell better or worse than others, especially in an increasingly competitive marketplace.

Content and Cultural Significance

While the economics of newsstand sales is the driving force behind many magazine covers, the other role a cover serves is as a piece of content itself—that is, *What does it say?* In an environment of fleeting images, video and audio, the magazine cover stops time, reminds readers of influential moments in history and acts as a barometer for what is important in the world. The magazine cover, Steve Taylor said, performs "a very significant series of social and cultural functions."[51] One of the innovators of cover design was George Lois, who, Taylor wrote, "brought an all-out, grab-by-the-eyeballs approach to *Esquire* during his 1960s tenure as art director."[52] Taylor's description pointed to Lois's 1965 cover that showed quadrants of four faces—Bob Dylan, Malcolm X, Fidel Castro and John F. Kennedy.[53] The cultural significance of magazine covers manifests itself in a number of different areas: in serving as a sort of visual history book, but also in providing singular images that can represent a mood or a movement.

Recording History

From photos of various U.S.-involved wars on the covers of *Life* to the modern-day covers of international newsweeklies, magazine covers depict the world's major events with photos or words—or both—that attempt to capture complex situations, lives and events on one lasting page. One of the more famous war covers in the United States came from the Vietnam War, when *Life* featured a photograph of a Vietcong prisoner with tape over his eyes and mouth.[54] Through its war covers, "*Life* conveyed another essential aspect of this war: America's belief, still as strong today if not stronger, that quantitative and qualitative superiority of arms was essential to crush the enemy and spare soldiers' lives," wrote Stéphane Duperray, Raphaële Vidaling and their colleagues.[55] *Paris Match*, which was re-named in 1949 after French press magnate Jean Prouvost bought *Match* in 1936 and changed its format to follow *Life*'s model, began using powerful war imagery on its cover. Business success followed, with a print run of 1.8 million in 1958.[56]

Words can also play a prominent role. In 1966, *Esquire* ran an all-black cover with white type that read, "Oh My God—We Hit a Little Girl," for a 33,000-word story by war correspondent John Sack.[57] ASME, when naming the cover in 2005 as the eighth best of the last 40 years, said the story and the cover that represented it "helped change the public perception of the Vietnam War."[58] In 2009, *Time* ran a cover of an 18-year-old Afghan woman whose nose and ears had been sliced off in 2009 under orders from a local Taliban commander. The image was also significant. Rod Nordland wrote,

> Reaction to the *Time* cover has become something of an Internet litmus test about attitudes toward the war, and what America's responsibility is in Afghanistan. Critics of the American presence in Afghanistan call it "emotional blackmail" and even "war porn," while those who fear the consequences of abandoning Afghanistan see it as a powerful appeal to conscience.[59]

After 11 September 2001, American magazines were faced with the challenge of trying to depict on their covers an unprecedented situation in an uncertain and emotional time. Covers published in 2011 and for subsequent anniversary issues portrayed what this author identified as the changing moods in the United States: terror, sorrow, pride and hope. Initial covers, such as those from *Time* that featured a black border instead of its traditional, red border,[60] featured news-style photos.

> The most dominant portrayal of terror came in some visual form of the World Trade Center towers being attacked, or of them burning, or of individuals being covered by debris. The images of mass destruction seemed to be the most representative symbol for those magazines that wanted to capture the terror of September 11.[61]

Later covers featured a variety of themes, such as a *Newsweek* cover of firefighters raising an American flag amidst debris[62] or Art Speigelman's two-tone black illustration of the Twin Towers on the *New Yorker*.[63]

Celebrating Life and Death

Magazines have long used celebrities as cover subjects, but not only for their mass appeal. In theory, the more famous—or infamous—the celebrity, the greater is the potential for newsstand sales. With the unexpected deaths of prominent people (e.g., Michael Jackson, Whitney Houston), magazines can experience an economic advantage, as some regular issues have sold remarkable numbers immediately after the news broke. Commemorative issues have also sold well. The five top events that triggered a run on the newsstand in recent years included two celebrity deaths: the Oklahoma City bombing of 1995; Princess Diana's death in 1997; John F. Kennedy Jr.'s death in 1999; the September 11 attacks of 2001; and the election of Barack Obama as president in 2008.[64]

When Michael Jackson died in 2009, "a slew of news, music and celebrity magazines rushed to publish commemorative issues—or, at least, feature Jackson as the cover story," wrote Jason Fell.[65] Fell quoted one executive, John Harrington, who predicted that these commemorative issues would be virtual sell-outs or have better sell-through rates than 75 percent, which is well above industry averages.[66] In memoriam and commemorative issues serve a different purpose than other media, not only in content but also the power of the cover image. Crowley wrote, "Although magazines operate at a different tempo from the mainstream news press, they can offer seasoned reflection and commentary on affairs rather than report the drama of events as they unfold."[67] Johnson and Prijatel wrote, "Far from being exploitative, tribute issues generally accentuate the positive and play down the negative in individuals' lives."[68] This also provides an opportunity for researchers to look at the psychology of buyers in the aftermath of tragedy— whether large-scale or personal—as it relates to magazine covers. What role do (or can) covers play in the grieving process?

Shaping Cultural Values

Though magazine covers are often heralded for their cultural importance, they are also the subject of criticism. The single page acts as a showcase for people, leading researchers to analyze portrayals of body image or gender representation. A growing body of research examines the effects on readers' body image, health and other aspects of life of unrealistic and altered images of models and celebrities as portrayed on the covers of magazines. Two such studies used magazine covers as a means to study gender and body image issues, respectively. Erin Hatton and Mary Nell Trautner, from a longitudinal content analysis of images of men and women on more than 1,000 covers of *Rolling Stone* published from 1967 to 2009, found that in the 1960s, 11% of men and 44% of women on the covers were sexualized. In the 2000s, 17% of men and 83% of women were sexualized.[69] They wrote,

> We argue, however, that the intensity of their sexualization suggests that "sexual object" may indeed be the only appropriate label. The accumulation of sexualized attributes in these images leaves little room for observers to interpret them in any other way than as instruments of sexual pleasure and visual possession for a heterosexual male audience. Such images do not show women as sexually agentic musicians and actors; rather, they show female actors and musicians as ready and available for sex.[70]

It is also interesting to note that the subject of sexualization is of interest even in respect to the covers of medical journals. Jocalyn Clark looked at 50 covers of the *Journal of the American Medical Association* in the late 1990s. Reporting the results in her *British Medical Journal* article, "Babes and Boobs? Analysis of JAMA Cover Art," Clark wrote that 74% of the covers depicting humans "presented stereotyped sex images—that is, women were predominantly positioned as 'objects' of desire and men as (powerful, strong) 'subjects.'" Of the 15 covers depicting women, 12 included babies and 6 showed nudity.[71] Carolyn Kitch, in *The Girl on the Magazine Cover*, wrote,

> The face of a woman could represent both a specific type of female beauty and a "style" that conveyed model attributes—youth, innocence, sophistication, modernity,

upward mobility. . . . In 1915, when Irving Berlin wrote a song about a young man pining away for the ideal "girl," his title located her where most Americans would expect to find her—on the magazine cover. Her various permutations were the first mass media stereotypes.[72]

Some argue that today's covers perpetuate and reinforce these stereotypes about body shape and size. Ellen McCracken wrote, "Most covers try to create an idealized reader-image of the group advertisers seek to reach . . . There is often an implied male presence, communicated through the woman's facial expression, make-up, body pose and clothing, as well as through the camera angle, lighting and color."[73] These images are often found on the covers of women's magazines, as well as men's. Amy R. Malkin, Kimberlie Wornian and Joan C. Chrisler found "94% of the covers of women's magazines showed a thin female in excellent shape."[74] McCracken also said, "The covers that use the photo of a glamorous woman to represent physical perfection rely on readers' personal sense of inferiority, especially about their physical appearance."[75]

Deliberate Fun, Deliberate Seriousness

Controversial magazine covers can fall into all kinds of categories. Some controversies are somewhat playful. For example, there is the *Sports Illustrated* Jinx: a theory that if an athlete appears on the cover of the magazine, bad luck is to follow. In fact, the magazine did its own study of the *SI* Jinx. Of 2,456 covers that *Sports Illustrated* had published up until the point the study began in 2002, 913 featured "a person who, or a team that, suffered some verifiable misfortune that conformed to our definition—a Jinx rate of 37.2%."[76] Those misfortunes were defined as such things as a bad loss, a blunder or bad play, an injury and even death.[77]

Some controversies are a bit more serious, such as those created by body distortion and digital manipulation. Some magazines have received backlash for doctoring photos, as when *Men's Fitness* featured a photo of tennis player Andy Roddick with arms that did not appear to be Roddick's[78] and *Redbook* combined two separate shots of Julia Roberts, one of her body and one of her head.[79] "It's known as airbrushing, or digital manipulation. At magazines, it's standard practice to zap a zit, or brighten those baby blues," Donna Freydkin wrote. "But, as those who do the tweaking point out, there's a huge difference between eradicating stretch marks and cutting body parts from two separate photos and fusing them together into a composite shot."[80] This, too, could be a rich area of research: to study editors and art directors and readers' attitudes to learn where they see the ethical lines of altering a cover image. How does the cover image differ from a news photograph? Do readers consider the cover more of an advertisement for the magazine, so they have more tolerance or acceptance for altered images?

Perhaps the more important controversies surrounding covers involve the subjects and images that are featured to portray societal issues. Michael Barthel credits George Lois of *Esquire*, who once featured Muhammad Ali posing as an arrow-stricken St. Sebastian,[81] as one of the innovators of the controversial cover.[82] "The only reason I got away with those covers was because they were selling," Lois said in a 2007 interview with Jandos Rothstein.[83] A big year for controversial covers was 2012. *Newsweek* featured a photo of President Barack Obama with a rainbow-colored halo over his head and the cover line "The First Gay President."[84] Another controversial magazine cover that year was *Time* magazine's, featuring a woman breastfeeding a toddler who was standing on a chair. The cover line read, "Are You Mom Enough?"[85] Britain's *Spectator* came under fire for its cover on Olympic censorship. Ironically, the magazine's editor Fraser Nelson was told the magazine might be banned for sale. "The issue appears to be over the unauthorized use of the Olympic rings, which the IOC (the International Olympic Committee) is notoriously litigious about," wrote Adam Taylor.[86]

Controversial covers are important not only for the issues about which they might provoke thought and discussion, but also because of the economics of magazine sales in a digital age. Magazine expert Samir Husni, interviewed by Rene Lynch, said,

> Not a day goes by without someone rambling on about the decline of the traditional media and the rise of digital. But *Time*'s cover proves that print can still be king if it steals from digital's playbook—by becoming the conversation starters (not the followers), choosing relevant, edgy subjects and then tackling them in a visually arresting way.[87]

Barthel said magazine covers have increasingly become controversial, partly because of this emphasis on digital. "On the Web, where media outlets no longer control their own space and a personal blog appears with equal weight beside an international publication on Twitter and Facebook, controversy is a much more successful strategy to get people on a particular page," Barthel wrote.[88] He argued that when clicks matter, publications cannot resist sensationalistic images. "A cover that goes viral does more for a publication than any individual story could."[89]

What are the long-lasting effects of controversial covers? Even if readers do not like or buy them, do they actually have a positive long-term impact, such as increased brand exposure through the coverage of such controversies? This would seem to be a needed area for research, especially in an era in which more and more magazine covers seem to be getting attention for controversial images or words. On its March 2013 issue, *Philadelphia* magazine ran a controversial, text-only cover that read, "In a city that is largely poor and segregated, white people have become afraid to say anything at all about race. Here's what's not being said. Being White in Philly."[90] Though the cover and accompanying story were blasted on social media and Web sites,[91] it would be interesting to study both the immediate and long-term effects of such high-profile covers.

The Future

Even with examples of provocative covers, it can be argued that the majority of magazine covers have become stale and safe—a place far away from the George Lois–created covers of *Esquire* of the 1960s. In fact, in 2007 Lois told Rothstein,

> Readers don't think about covers now because magazines have Nicole Kidman on the cover. That's the assignment, case closed. That's not an assignment—that's ridiculous. The way you solve it is you get a terrific photographer, and he does bullshit. Annie Liebovitz takes a picture of someone with a thumb up his ass. Who cares?[92]

Others would argue that magazines need to have more of a point-of-view. Jon Friedman said magazines ask too many questions, rather than taking a stance. "Magazines probably feel more secure by laying out the facts and letting readers decide. I, as a devoted magazine reader, would prefer it if the publishing biz presented a point of view on the covers."[93] This, of course, presents an interesting relationship between the so-called safe and standard covers that readers have become accustomed to seeing on the newsstand and the dashes of controversial ones that were perhaps more standard in the 1960s and that get a lot of attention when they break the current-day, newsstand norms. One notable exception is *Bloomberg Businessweek*, which has gained attention for its point-of-view and artistic covers. These include (1) covers that feature images with sexual innuendo, such as one about hedge funds with an upward-pointing arrow that originates at a man's waist[94]; (2) all-type covers, such as one with the text reading "How to Sell Drugs: 1- Hire a doctor on Craigslist, 2- Order opioids, but not too many, 3- Rake it in"[95]; and (3) covers that have heavy illustrations, such as one that shows a black, red and white drawing for a story about "Coke in Africa."[96]

No matter what subjects will be featured on magazine covers—celebrities, current issues or service journalism that aims to help readers improve their lives—magazine editors will be faced with economic realities of a competitive media environment. They will have to find, pick and use covers that can help sell their product and generate revenue.

One question that may emerge from this reality is the use of advertising on the cover. Though the magazine cover is essentially a marketing tool for the magazine itself, the cover has generally been a place where no outside ads appear. Ads on covers violate the rules of the American Society of Magazine Editors, which require a separation between editorial and advertising space.[97] It should be noted that business-to-business magazines often use advertising on their covers, and some people have argued that perhaps ASME should relax its guidelines. Jeffrey L. Seglin wrote in *Folio:*,

> Are the covers of consumer magazines sacred? I don't believe so. No more than the front page of newspaper sections are off limits from clearly-defined advertisements placed among the news or feature articles. There's always an outcry when another major newspaper starts engaging in the practice that seems to quickly die down when readers recognize that these advertisements are distinct from and don't influence the editorial . . . If magazines want to explore new models for generating income, they should be encouraged to do so as creatively as possible. But they'd be wise to make sure that whatever they do doesn't violate a trust with their readers.[98]

In the summer of 2014 *Time* magazine took a step in what many considered a wrong direction when it ran an almost invisible sentence at the bottom of the address label on the front cover suggesting that readers turn to a specific page inside to see a specific display ad.[99] The line, however, is blurry when advertisers may provide props or clothing for models who pose for the cover. "As long as the products used serve the magazine's editorial and design purpose and the advertiser does not pay for placement, most editors see this as serving both the readers and advertisers," Johnson and Prijatel wrote. "Critics, however, see this as being dangerously close to the ethical line."[100] Abe Sauer addressed the question when he wrote about *GQ*'s 2011 cover featuring a photo of actress Mila Kunis sipping a coffee drink in which "the fat green straw held by marine pin-up Mila Kunis is recognizable to pretty much anyone who has been to a Starbucks."[101] *Forbes* was critical of a magazine cover used by *Newsweek* featuring then Alaska governor Sarah Palin in a sweatshirt with the logo of a local gym. "It seems probably, therefore, that she's getting something for her endorsements—perhaps free personal training," wrote Jeff Bercovici, who noted that the issue is more with Palin herself than with *Newsweek*, since it didn't appear the magazine was financially benefitting from the logo appearing on the cover.[102]

What might be most interesting to ask is what the magazine cover of the future will look like. In recent years, *Esquire* has served as a leader in experimentation (i.e., a battery-powered e-ink cover that flashed).[103] *Esquire* and *Popular Science* have both used what has been called *augmented reality* on their covers, as well. Stephanie Clifford wrote, "[Augmented reality] combines a real image with a virtual one, and viewers can adjust the real image to change the virtual one. To kick start the technology, the providers ask viewers to hold up a trigger image—the cover, in this case—to a Webcam."[104] The introduction of tablets provides the opportunity for magazines to add motion to their singular images. The tablet may provide the richest area for future research as the role of the magazine cover shifts from being not only a driver of newsstand sales, but also a driver of digital traffic.

Despite changes that will inevitably come in reader habits, new technology and new ideas, the magazine cover will likely remain one of the most powerful visual and verbal tools a magazine can use to produce revenue and send a message. Losowsky wrote,

> The evolution of magazine covers is a mirror of the changes in magazines themselves. No matter whom you're talking to, and however much things have moved on, the

essence of the medium remains the same. The iconography and the celebrities are different now, but magazine covers exist, today as they always have, to say the same three words: "Pick me up."[105]

Notes

1 Steve Cohn, ed., *The Most Intriguing and Top-Selling Magazine Covers* (Rockville, MD: Access Intelligence LLC, 2010), 3.

2 Sammye Johnson and Patricia Prijatel, *The Magazine from Cover to Cover*, 2nd ed. (New York and London: Oxford University Press, 2007), insert between 254 and 255.

3 *Esquire*, May 1969; see also, Johnson and Prijatel, *The Magazine from Cover to Cover*, insert between 254 and 255.

4 *Rolling Stone*, 22 January 1981.

5 "ASME's Top 40 Magazine Covers of the Last 40 Years," American Society of Magazine Editors <http://www.magazine.org/asme/magazine-cover-contests/asmes-top-40-magazine-covers-last-40-years>, accessed 1 January 2013.

6 *Sports Illustrated*, 3 March 1980.

7 Stéphane Duperray and Raphaële Vidaling with Cécile Amara, Agnieszka Ples, and Alain-Xavier Wurst, *Front Page: Covers of the Twentieth Century* (London: Weidenfeld & Nicolson, 2003), 72.

8 *Stern*, 21 April 1988.

9 *Stern*, 15 February 1979.

10 *New York*, 24 March 2008.

11 Andrew Losowsky, ed., *We Love Magazines* (Luxembourg: Editions Mike Koedinger SA, 2007), 34.

12 Steve Taylor, *100 Years of Magazine Covers* (London: Black Dog Publishing, 2006), 15.

13 Marcia R. Prior-Miller and Associates, "Bibliography of Published Research on Magazine and Journal Periodicals," 8th ed., research database (Ames: Iowa State University, last modified, 31 August 2012), MSWord file <mpm@iastate.edu>.

14 Dodie Kazanjian, *Vogue: The Covers* (New York, Abrams, 2011).

15 Editors of *Sports Illustrated*, *Sports Illustrated: The Covers* (New York: *Sports Illustrated* Books, 2010).

16 John Updike, "Foreword," *Complete Book of Covers from the* New Yorker, *1925–1989* (New York: Knopf, 1989).

17 Christopher Finch, *Norman Rockwell: 332 Magazine Covers* (New York: Abbeville Press/Random House Publishers, 1979).

18 George Lois, *Covering the '60s: George Lois, the* Esquire *Era* (New York: Monacelli Press, 1996).

19 Duperray, Vidaling, Amara, Ples, and Wurst, *Front Page: Covers of the Twentieth Century*.

20 Taylor, *100 Years of Magazine Covers*.

21 Carolyn Kitch, *The Girl on the Magazine Cover: The Origins of Visual Stereotypes in American Mass Media* (Chapel Hill and London: University of North Carolina Press, 2001).

22 Peter Carlson, "Magazine Tease a Rare Art Form," *Sun Sentinel*, 12 November 1997 <http://articles.sun-sentinel.com/1997–11–12/lifestyle/9711110381_1_orgasm-national-magazine-award-outdoor-life>, accessed 22 February 2013.

23 Carlson, "Magazine Tease a Rare Art Form."

24 Fehintola Betiku, "Hip-Hop Wild Child Azealia Banks Blows Up a Condom on Controversial Magazine Cover That's Been Banned in Seven Countries," *Mail Online*, 16 August 2012 <http://www.dailymail.co.uk/tvshowbiz/article-2189047/Azealia-Banks-controversial-magazine-cover-thats-banned-seven-countries.html>, accessed 1 March 2013.

25 Betiku, "Hip-Hop Wild Child."

26 Ted Spiker, "9/11 Magazine Covers," American Society of Magazine Editors <http://www.magazine.org/asme/magazine-cover-contests/9/11-magazine-covers>, accessed 11 September 2011.

27 Sammye Johnson, "The Art and Science of Magazine Cover Research," *Journal of Magazine & New Media Research* 5.1 (Fall 2002): 3.

28 Johnson, "The Art and Science of Magazine Cover Research," 4.

29 Johnson, "The Art and Science of Magazine Cover Research," 4.

30 David E. Sumner, "Sixty-Four Years of *Life*: What Did Its 2,128 Covers Cover?" *Journal of Magazine & New Media Research* 5.1 (Fall 2002): 1–16.

31 David W. Scott and Daniel A. Stout, "Religion on *Time*: Personal Spiritual Quests and Religious Institutions on the Cover of a Popular News Magazine," *Journal of Magazine & New Media Research* 8.1 (Spring 2006): 11.

32 Gerald Grow, "Magazine Covers and Cover Lines: An Illustrated History," *Journal of Magazine & New Media Research* 5.1 (Fall 2002): 1–19.

33 Grow, "Magazine Covers and Cover Lines," 1–19.

34 David Sumner, as quoted in Johnson, "The Art and Science of Magazine Cover Research," 5.

35 Donnalyn Pompper, Suekyung Lee, and Shana Lerner, "Gauging Outcomes of the 1960s Social Equality Movements: Nearly Four Decades of Gender and Ethnicity on the Cover of the *Rolling Stone* Magazine," *Journal of Popular Culture* 42.2 (2009): 273.

36 Mia Foley Sypeck, James J. Gray, and Anthony H. Ahrens, "No Longer Just a Pretty Face: Fashion Magazines' Depictions of Ideal Female Beauty from 1959 to 1999," *International Journal of Eating Disorders* 36.3 (2004): 343.

37 Johnson, "The Art and Science of Magazine Cover Research," 7.

38 Johnson and Prijatel, *The Magazine from Cover to Cover*, 284–287.

39 Sarah Gonser, "Revising the Cover Story," *Folio:*, 1 March 2003, 20.

40 Losowsky, *We Love Magazines*, 35.

41 Losowsky, *We Love Magazines*, 37.

42 Alex Kuczynski, "How Magazines Stimulate Newsstand Sales," *New York Times*, 18 June 2001, C2.

43 Duperray, Vidaling, Amara, Ples, and Wurst, *Front Page: Covers of the Twentieth Century*, 28.

44 Losowsky, *We Love Magazines*, 41.

45 Losowsky, *We Love Magazines*, 41.

46 David Crowley, *Magazine Covers* (London: Michael Beazley, 2003), 8.

47 Katharine Q. Seelye, "Lurid Numbers on Glossy Pages! (Magazines Exploit What Sells)," *New York Times*, 10 February 2006, A1(L).

48 Seelye, "Lurid Numbers on Glossy Pages!" A1(L).

49 Gonser, "Revising the Cover Story," 20.

50 Gonser, "Revising the Cover Story," 20.

51 Taylor, *100 Years of Magazine Covers*, 9.

52 Taylor, *100 Years of Magazine Covers*, 43.

53 *Esquire*, September 1965.

54 *Life*, 26 November 1965.

55 Duperray, Vidaling, Amara, Ples, and Wurst, *Front Page: Covers of the Twentieth Century*, 121.

56 Duperray, Vidaling, Amara, Ples, and Wurst, *Front Page: Covers of the Twentieth Century*, 54–55.

57 *Esquire*, October 1966.

58 "ASME's Top 40 Magazine Covers of the Last 40 Years."

59 Rod Nordland, "Portrait of Pain Ignites a Debate Over the Afghan War," *New York Times*, 5 August 2010, A6(L).

60 *Time*, 14 September 2001.

61 Ted Spiker, "Cover Coverage: How U.S. Magazine Covers Captured the Emotions of the September 11 Attack—and How Editors and Art Directors Decided on Those Themes," *Journal of Magazine & New Media Research* 5.2 (Spring 2003): 6.

62 *Newsweek*, 24 September 2001.

63 *New Yorker*, 24 September 2001.

64 Cohn, *Most Intriguing and Top-Selling Magazine Covers*, 16.

65 Jason Fell, "Michael Jackson's Death Spurs 'Biggest Newsstand Push' since Election," *Folio:*, 10 July 2009 <http://www.foliomag.com/2009/michael-jackson-death-spurs-biggest-newsstand-push-elections>, accessed 1 January 2013.

66 Fell, "Michael Jackson's Death."

67 Crowley, *Magazine Covers*, 58.

68 Johnson and Prijatel, *The Magazine from Cover to Cover*, 236.

69 Erin Hatton and Mary Nell Trautner, "Equal Opportunity Objectification? The Sexualization of Men and Women on the Cover of *Rolling Stone*," *Sexuality & Culture* 15.3 (September 2011): 266.

70 Hatton and Trautner, "Equal Opportunity Objectification?" 273.

71 Jocalyn P. Clark, "Babes and Boobs? Analysis of JAMA Cover Art," *BMJ: British Medical Journal* 319.7225 (18–25 December 1999): 1603.

72 Kitch, *The Girl on the Magazine Cover*, 5.

73 Ellen McCracken, *Decoding Women's Magazines: From Mademoiselle to Ms.* (New York: St. Martin's Press, 1993), 20.

74 Amy R. Malkin, Kimberlie Wornian, and Joan C. Chrisler, "Women and Weight: Gendered Messages on Magazine Covers," *Sex Roles* 40.7/8 (April 1999): 651.

75 McCracken, *Decoding Women's Magazines*, 36.

76 Alexander Wolff, "That Old Black Magic," *Sports Illustrated*, 21 January 2002, unpaginated <http://sportsillustrated.cnn.com/vault/article/magazine/MAG1024790/index.htm>, accessed 18 September 2012.

77 Wolff, "That Old Black Magic," unpaginated.

78 *Men's Fitness*, May 2007.
79 *Redbook*, July 2003.
80 Donna Freydkin, "Doctored Cover Photos Add Up to Controversy," *USA Today*, 17 June 2003, 3D.
81 *Esquire*, April 1968.
82 Michael Barthel, "Magazines: Hey, Look at Us!" *Salon.com*, 23 August 2012 <http://www.salon.com/2012/08/23/magazines_hey_look_at_us/>, accessed 27 August 2012.
83 Lois, as quoted in Jandos Rothstein, *Designing Magazines: Inside Periodical Design, Redesign, and Branding* (New York: Allworth Press, 2007), 101.
84 *Newsweek*, 21 May 2012.
85 *Time*, 21 May 2012.
86 Adam Taylor, "The Cover of this British Magazine about Olympic Censorship Could Be Banned Due to Olympic Censorship," *Business Insider*, 11 July 2012 <http://www.businessinsider.com/spectator-cover-olympic-censorship-2012-7>, accessed 4 March 2013.
87 Samir Husni, as quoted in Rene Lynch, *Time* Magazine Breastfeeding Cover: A Shocking 'Stroke of Genius,'" *Los Angeles Times*, 11 May 2012 <http://articles.latimes.com/2012/may/11/nation/la-na-nn-time-magazine-breastfeeding-cover-20120511>, accessed 2 January 2014.
88 Barthel, "Magazines: Hey, Look at Us!"
89 Barthel, "Magazines: Hey, Look at Us!"
90 *Philadelphia*, March 2013.
91 Christine Haughney, "A Magazine Article on Race Sets Off an Outcry," *Media Decoder* (blog), *New York Times*, 24 March 2013 <http://mediadecoder.blogs.nytimes.com/2013/03/24/being-white-in-philly-article-brings-an-outcry/?_r=0>, accessed 2 January 2014.
92 Lois, as quoted in Rothstein, *Designing Magazines*, 99.
93 Jon Friedman, "Magazines Have Questionable Covers," CBS.MarketWatch.com, 18 June 2004 <http://www.marketwatch.com/story/magazine-covers-should-answer-not-ask-questions>, accessed 18 June 2004.
94 *Bloomberg Businessweek*, 13 July 2013.
95 *Bloomberg Businessweek*, 6 August 2012.
96 *Bloomberg Businessweek*, 11 January 2010.
97 Stephanie Clifford, "Magazine Cover Ads, Subtle and Less So," *New York Times*, 12 June 2009, B3.
98 Jeffrey L. Seglin, "ASME is Really, Really Mad about Ads on Covers—and You Should Be, Too," *Folio:*, 17 April 2009 <http://www.foliomag.com/2009/asme-really-really-mad-about-ads-covers-and-you-should-be-too#.UT00lFfAHTo>, accessed 1 March 2013.
99 Arti Patel, "Time Inc.'s Cover Ads Cause Stir, But No Backlash," *Folio:*, 22 May 2014 <http://www.foliomag.com/2014/time-inc-s-cover-ads-cause-stir-no-backlash?hq_e=el&hq_m=2886693&hq_l=7&hq_v=289ee2c2f2#.U38ssyhuJU1>, accessed 22 May 2014.
100 Johnson and Prijatel, *The Magazine from Cover to Cover*, 51.
101 Abe Sauer, "Straw Poll: Is GQ's Mila Kunis Cover a Stealth Starbucks Product Placement?" *BrandChannel*, 13 July 2011 <http://www.brandchannel.com/home/post/2011/07/13/GQ-Starbucks-Cover-Plays-With-Mag-Guidelines.aspx>, accessed 1 March 2013.
102 Jeff Bercovici, "Did Sarah Palin Use *Newsweek* for Product Placement?" *Forbes.com*, 11 July 2011 <http://www.forbes.com/sites/jeffbercovici/2011/07/11/did-sarah-palin-use-newsweek-for-product-placement>, accessed 1 March 2013.
103 *Esquire*, October 2008.
104 Clifford, "Magazine Cover Ads," B3.
105 Losowsky, *We Love Magazines*, 42.

Bibliography

"ASME's Top 40 Magazine Covers of the Last 40 Years." American Society of Magazine Editors <http://www.magazine.org/asme/magazine-cover-contests/asmes-top-40-magazine-covers-last-40-years>, accessed 1 January 2013.

Barthel, Michael. "Magazines: Hey, Look at Us!" *Salon.com*, 23 August 2012 <http://www.salon.com/2012/08/23/magazines_hey_look_at_us/>, accessed 27 August 2012.

Bercovici, Jeff. "Did Sarah Palin Use *Newsweek* for Product Placement?" *Forbes*, 11 July 2011 <http://www.forbes.com/sites/jeffbercovici/2011/07/11/did-sarah-palin-use-newsweek-for-product-placement>, accessed 1 March 2013.

Betiku, Fehintola. "Hip-Hop Wild Child Azealia Banks Blows Up a Condom on Controversial Magazine Cover That's Been Banned in Seven Countries." *Mail Online*, 16 August 2012 <http://www.

dailymail.co.uk/tvshowbiz/article-2189047/Azealia-Banks-controversial-magazine-cover-thats-banned-seven-countries.html>, accessed 1 March 2013.

Carlson, Peter. "Magazine Tease a Rare Art Form." *Sun Sentinel*, 12 November 1997 <http://articles.sun-sentinel.com/1997–11–12/lifestyle/9711110381_1_orgasm-national-magazine-award-outdoor-life>, accessed 22 February 2013.

Clark, Jocalyn P. "Babes and Boobs? Analysis of JAMA Cover Art." *BMJ: British Medical Journal* 319.7225 (18–25 December 1999): 1603–1604.

Clifford, Stephanie. "Magazine Cover Ads, Subtle and Less So." *New York Times*, 12 June 2009, B3.

Cohn, Steve, ed. *The Most Intriguing and Top-Selling Magazine Covers*. Rockville, MD: Access Intelligence LLC, 2010.

Crowley, David. *Magazine Covers*. London: Mitchell Beazley, 2003.

Duperray, Stéphane and Vidaling, Raphaële, with Amara, Cécile; Ples, Agnieszka; and Wurst, Alain-Xavier. *Front Page: Covers of the Twentieth Century*. London: Weidenfeld & Nicolson, 2003.

Editors of *Sports Illustrated*. Sports Illustrated: *The Covers*. New York: *Sports Illustrated* Books, 2010.

Fell, Jason. "Michael Jackson's Death Spurs 'Biggest Newsstand Push' since Election." *Folio:*, 10 July 2009 <http://www.foliomag.com/2009/michael-jackson-death-spurs-biggest-newsstand-push-elections>, accessed 1 January 2013.

Finch, Christopher. *Norman Rockwell: 332 Magazine Covers*. New York: Abbeville Press/Random House Publishers, 1979.

Freydkin, Donna. "Doctored Cover Photos Add Up to Controversy." *USA Today*, 17 June 2003, 3D.

Friedman, Jon. "Magazines Have Questionable Covers." CBS.MarketWatch.com, 18 June 2004 <http://www.marketwatch.com/story/magazine-covers-should-answer-not-ask-questions>, accessed 18 June 2004.

Gonser, Sarah. "Revising the Cover Story." *Folio:*, 1 March 2003, 20.

Grow, Gerald. "Magazine Covers and Cover Lines: An Illustrated History." *Journal of Magazine & New Media Research* 5.1 (Fall 2002): 1–19.

Hatton, Erin and Trautner, Mary Nell. "Equal Opportunity Objectification? The Sexualization of Men and Women on the Cover of *Rolling Stone*." *Sexuality & Culture* 15.3 (September 2011): 256–278.

Haughney, Christine. "A Magazine Article on Race Sets Off an Outcry." *Media Decoder* (blog). *New York Times*, 24 March 2013 <http://mediadecoder.blogs.nytimes.com/2013/03/24/being-white-in-philly-article-brings-an-outcry/?_r=0>, accessed 2 January 2013.

Johnson, Sammye. "The Art and Science of Magazine Cover Research." *Journal of Magazine & New Media Research* 5.1 (Fall 2002): 1–10.

Johnson, Sammye and Prijatel, Patricia. *The Magazine from Cover to Cover*. 2nd ed. New York and London: Oxford University Press, 2007.

Kazanjian, Dodie. Vogue: *The Covers*. New York: Abrams, 2011.

Kitch, Carolyn. *The Girl on the Magazine Cover: The Origins of Visual Stereotypes in American Mass Media*. Chapel Hill and London: University of North Carolina Press, 2001.

Kuczynski, Alex. "How Magazines Stimulate Newsstand Sales." *New York Times*, 18 June 2001, C1–C2.

Lois, George. *Covering the '60s: George Lois, the* Esquire *Era*. New York: The Monacelli Press, 1996.

Losowsky, Andrew, ed. *We Love Magazines*. Luxembourg: Editions Mike Koedinger SA, 2007.

Lynch, Rene. "*Time* Magazine Breastfeeding Cover: A Shocking 'Stroke of Genius.'" *Los Angeles Times*, 11 May 2012 <http://articles.latimes.com/2012/may/11/nation/la-na-nn-time-magazine-breastfeeding-cover-20120511>, accessed 2 January 2014.

Malkin, Amy R.; Wornian, Kimberlie; and Chrisler, Joan C. "Women and Weight: Gendered Messages on Magazine Covers." *Sex Roles* 40.7/8 (April 1999): 647–655.

McCracken, Ellen. *Decoding Women's Magazines*: From *Mademoiselle* to *Ms.* New York: St. Martin's Press, 1993.

Nordland, Rod. "Portrait of Pain Ignites a Debate Over the Afghan War." *New York Times*, 5 August 2010, A6(L).

Patel, Arti. "Time Inc.'s Cover Ads Cause Stir, But No Backlash." *Folio:*, 22 May 2014 <http://www.foliomag.com/2014/time-inc-s-cover-ads-cause-stir-no-backlash?hq_e=el&hq_m=2886693&hq_l=7&hq_v=289ee2c2f2#.U38ssyhuJU1>, accessed 22 May 2014.

Pompper, Donnalyn; Lee, Suekyung; and Lerner, Shana. "Gauging Outcomes of the 1960s Social Equality Movements: Nearly Four Decades of Gender and Ethnicity on the Cover of the *Rolling Stone* Magazine." *Journal of Popular Culture* 42.2 (2009): 273–290.

Prior-Miller, Marcia R. and Associates. "Bibliography of Published Research on Magazine and Journal Periodicals." 8th ed. Research database. Ames: Iowa State University, last modified, 31 August 2012, MSWord file <mpm@iastate.edu>.

Rothstein, Jandos. *Designing Magazines: Inside Periodical Design, Redesign, and Branding.* New York: Allworth Press, 2007.

Sauer, Abe. "Straw Poll: Is GQ's Mila Kunis Cover a Stealth Starbucks Product Placement?" *Brand Channel*, 13 July 2011 <http://www.brandchannel.com/home/post/2011/07/13/GQ-Starbucks-Cover-Plays-With-Mag-Guidelines.aspx>, accessed 1 March 2013.

Scott, David W. and Stout, Daniel A. "Religion on *Time*: Personal Spiritual Quests and Religious Institutions on the Cover of a Popular News Magazine." *Journal of Magazine & New Media Research* 8.1 (Spring 2006): 1–17.

Seelye, Katharine Q. "Lurid Numbers on Glossy Pages! (Magazines Exploit What Sells)." *New York Times*, 10 February 2006, A1(L).

Seglin, Jeffrey L. "ASME is Really, Really Mad about Ads on Covers—and You Should Be, Too." *Folio:*, 17 April 2009 <http://www.foliomag.com/2009/asme-really-really-mad-about-ads-covers-and-you-should-be-too#.UT00lFfAHTo>, accessed 1 March 2013.

Spiker, Ted. "Cover Coverage: How U.S. Magazine Covers Captured the Emotions of the September 11 Attack—and How Editors and Art Directors Decided on Those Themes." *Journal of Magazine & New Media Research* 5.2 (Spring 2003): 1–18.

Spiker, Ted. "9/11 Magazine Covers." American Society of Magazine Editors <http://www.magazine.org/asme/magazine-cover-contests/9/11-magazine-covers>, accessed 11 September 2011.

Sumner, David E. "Sixty-Four Years of *Life*: What Did Its 2,128 Covers Cover?" *Journal of Magazine & New Media Research* 5.1 (Fall 2002): 1–16.

Sypeck, Mia Foley; Gray, James J.; and Ahrens, Anthony H. "No Longer Just a Pretty Face: Fashion Magazines' Depictions of Ideal Female Beauty from 1959 to 1999." *International Journal of Eating Disorders* 36.3 (2004): 342–347.

Taylor, Adam. "The Cover of this British Magazine about Olympic Censorship Could Be Banned Due to Olympic Censorship." *Business Insider*, 11 July 2012 <http://www.businessinsider.com/spectator-cover-olympic-censorship-2012-7>, accessed 4 March 2013.

Taylor, Steve. *100 Years of Magazine Covers.* London: Black Dog Publishing, 2006.

Updike, John. "Foreword." *Complete Book of Covers from the* New Yorker, *1925–1989.* New York: Knopf, 1989.

Wolff, Alexander. "That Old Black Magic." *Sports Illustrated*, 21 January 2002, Unpaginated <http://sportsillustrated.cnn.com/vault/article/magazine/MAG1024790/index.htm>, accessed 18 September 2012.

24

MAGAZINE DESIGN

Defining the Visual Architecture

Carol Holstead

The intimate experience that magazines offer readers is as much visual as textual. A magazine expresses its personality through its visual style—its symbiotic use of type, art and photos, colors and space. A magazine is, in essence, branded by its design. And yet, scholarly journals, the design press and graphic design books include little on magazine design compared to the design of other media. William Owen, in the preface to the only book that comprehensively covers magazine design history, *Modern Magazine Design*, writes that graphic design books have neglected magazine design history.

> That the design of this ubiquitous print medium has been given no systematic history or critique is something of an anomaly, . . . Yet despite the important part that magazines have played as laboratories of experiment, especially in the development of modern design principles and visual expression, the technical, journalistic and artistic evolution of magazine design has received only the marginal treatment that general graphic design histories can provide.[1]

This chapter examines the scholarly study of magazine design, which falls into three overlapping areas: theoretical, applied (research that focuses on the use of specific elements of design such as color) and historical. Magazine design, as well as graphic design, is defined as the purposeful combination of type, images, color and space to express a message[2] or what Gunther Kress and Theo van Leeuwen call "visual grammar": how elements within an image or a design combine to make a larger statement.[3]

Literature Review and Method

Scholars have studied magazine advertising, covers and the use of photographs and illustrations in magazines but have not much explored magazine design, which became apparent in the search for scholarly articles on magazine design for this chapter. The specific focus here is to review what scholars have written since 1990 about the design of magazines—in other words, the use of the elements of design (photos, illustrations, text, type and space) in combination to create magazines. Photographs and illustrations are specifically addressed in other chapters.

A search of library databases, the tables of contents of design journals, design industry publications and the Internet turned up only 12 articles, one thesis and one dissertation on magazine design. The terms and combinations of terms used in the search were as follows: *magazine design, magazine layout, magazine graphic design, magazine typography, magazine gestalt, magazine design branding, magazines and framing, magazine design and theory* and *magazine design history.* Databases searched included the Design and Applied Art Index, Academic Search Complete,

ProQuest Research Library and Google Scholar. When articles surfaced in specific journals, tables of content since 1990 for those journals were reviewed. The journals included the *Journal of Visual Literacy, Design Issues, Design Studies, International Journal of Design, Journal of Design History* and *Journal of Media & Cultural Studies.* Bibliographies of articles were also reviewed for relevant scholarship from 1990 and earlier.

Design industry periodicals that focus on graphic communication in all forms—print and digital—of publications and advertising were also searched, including *Eye, Graphis, Communication Arts* and *Print.* These address magazine design but in commentary, interviews with art directors, and stories and photos about the design of individual magazines.

A Google database search found about two dozen books written specifically about magazine design; the books tend to take one of two directions: They present and discuss examples or offer instruction. Magazines are included in the content of many more books about design, typography and visual communication. The prolific design writer Steven Heller has authored or co-authored roughly 150 books on design, including two specifically about magazine design: *Magazines Inside and Out* and *Merz to Émigré and Beyond: Progressive Magazine Design of the Twentieth Century.*[4] Many books dating back 50 or more years are instructive in nature. An Amazon search identified 583 books that focus on the techniques of graphic design. Textbooks such as William Ryan and Theodore Conover's *Graphics Communications Today*[5] cover history, theory and the how-to of designing everything from newsletters to ads to magazines. Scholars have speculated that the neglect of graphic design as a subject of study relates to how children are educated: In their early years, children draw and write, but eventually art is dropped in favor of writing, which continues through college. As a result, people focus more on text than images or design.[6]

Scholarly articles on design apply such theories as visual framing, gestalt, semiotics and rhetoric to information design and photography. These theories have not often been used to study magazine design but offer opportunities for research. As a result, research most closely connected to magazines was also reviewed in the chapter. Scholarly articles on magazine design tended to be disconnected. They rarely referenced each other; writers were more likely to build on their own research than others,' which made linking research within the chapter challenging.

Magazine Design Theory

Rune Pettersson has summarized the nature of scholarship on information design, saying it is "interdisciplinary and encompasses influences and facts from more than 50 areas of research," including art and aesthetics, language, communication, information and cognition.[7] In the works covered here, scholars applied multiple theories to graphic design, as well as magazine design, including semiotics, rhetoric, gestalt and visual framing.

Semiotic Theory

Semiotics, the study of signs, is commonly used to analyze text and images for their meaning[8] and provides the base for Kress and van Leeuwen's theory of the grammar of visual language. Their theory helps explain all kinds of visual representations, from oil paintings to magazine layouts.[9] Kress and van Leeuwen identify three elements: One is *narrative*, a path for the viewer to take when reading an image. Another is *modality*, or cues within an image—color, for example—that a viewer uses to determine its truth (e.g., full color typically equals more truth). Most directly applicable to magazine design is *composition*, which can be used to evaluate single photos, as well as designs that combine text, images and other graphic elements in print or on screen. Applied to a magazine spread, the grammar of composition might help determine how to arrange text and photos to emphasize what is most important.[10] Layout of page elements using size, weight and contrast also creates meaning.

Paul Cleveland incorporates Kress and van Leeuwen's theory of visual grammar, as well as the theories and works of about 80 scholars in his doctoral thesis, which explored the factors that influence magazines' evolving design.[11] His thesis draws on research in a variety of disciplines, including art, design, neurology, psychology and technology. The subjects of his study were two titles: the *Face*, a culture magazine; and the *Australian Women's Weekly*. Cleveland sought principally to do two things: first, quantify style changes over 16 years as those occurred in the *Face* and the *Australian Women's Weekly* and, second, determine how readers reacted to the magazines' design over the 16 years of the study. The goal was to learn how and when magazines should redesign.[12]

In the first part of the study, Cleveland quantified changes in 10 stylistic elements (i.e., white space, color and grids) in the magazines. The elements were derived from Kress and van Leeuwen's theories of visual grammar.[13] Cleveland developed a different means of measurement for each element. For example, he mapped changes in the color palettes in the two magazines by scanning images and computer analyzing color usage.[14] He then determined the *visual power* of each magazine as it evolved. The concept of visual power also derives from Kress and van Leeuwen's theory of visual grammar and is a result of a magazine's *arousal potential*, which is its ability to provide pleasure to readers.[15] In the second part of Cleveland's study, respondents looked at covers and spreads from the magazines and rated attributes related to arousal potential to evaluate how that information might be used to keep the magazines visually stimulating.[16] The study revealed that when readers become habituated to a magazine's design, it becomes less visually stimulating; it loses its visual power. A redesign can revive a magazine's visual power.[17] Cleveland also determined that technology has influenced how magazines deploy visual power by making altering and layering text and photos easier. He argued that the novelty of these effects increased arousal potential and visual power in magazines.[18]

Cleveland expanded his study of the visual power of magazine layouts in a subsequent paper. He offered a new assessment of the data from his earlier study where respondents rated style attributes in the *Face* and the *Australian Women's Weekly*. He believes designers who understand visual power can gauge how well a layout, or, say, a magazine cover will attract and keep the attention of its intended audience. From his case study of the visual power of the *Face* and the *Australian Women's Weekly*, Cleveland reported findings that showed the opposite of Russell N. Baird's original model of visual power. Baird had concluded that messages not focused on reader interests needed more visual power to get attention.[19] But Cleveland found that the *Face*, the magazine with the greatest focus on audience interests, also had the most visual power. Readers of the *Face* also had a narrower age range than the *Australian Women's Weekly*, which also had less visual power.[20] These results led Cleveland to conclude that the more homogeneous a magazine's audience, the more risks it can take with its design.[21]

In research that also relies in part on semiotic theory, Veronika Koller argues that visual metaphors are a persuasive element in business magazines. She defines the *visual metaphor* as "the representation of an abstract concept through a concrete visual image that bears some analogy to that concept."[22] Koller used visual grammar theory in her analysis of the ways *Fortune*, *Business Week* and the *Economist* employed metaphors in story illustrations. She found that war, sports and games metaphors were used most frequently—which, she argued, connected the predominantly male readership to the content of these business magazines.[23] Koller also found that the way images were integrated into the page layouts of these magazines heightened their effectiveness, or *salience*, a component of composition in Kress and van Leeuwen's visual grammar. A design element's salience is essentially its ability to attract attention. In a magazine layout salience is affected both by placement and whether the image is in a frame (in other words, boxed) or unframed. For example, an image at the center of a page with text wrapped around it would be highly salient because it is imbedded in the text.[24] *Fortune* and *Business Week* both showed a more salient use of metaphor in design than the more conservatively designed *Economist*.[25]

Koller and Cleveland are the only scholars to have published theoretical research on magazine design. However, in a 1990 study that is relevant to magazines, Robert Craig used semiotic theory to explore the ideological aspects of newspaper design. Craig noted that late in the nineteenth century, newspaper design began to evolve from a format that was primarily typographic—newspapers looked like books—to one that was more complex and included illustrations.[26] Craig added that a boom in manufacturing and the development of brand products made companies more competitive, and they put pressure on newspapers to make advertisements more attention getting. As a result, Craig wrote, advertising became more pictorial and had more and larger type. This change in the ideology of advertising design led to radical changes in all of print design.[27] Craig described the process: Newspapers themselves became more competitive, and they adopted the visual code of advertising, particularly use of big display type, to attract attention. The press oriented itself toward a "capitalist-dominated ideology" of selling news and products.[28]

Craig argues that the "functional" aspects of design—essentially creating a layout—are rooted in ideology. In newspapers, the purpose of design is to package news: to make the paper identifiable and attractive, and to sort the news hierarchically for the reader. In other words, the ideology of newspaper design is to promote the news. So while designers may work using functionalist principles, they also operate ideologically.[29] They are trying to persuade readers, using the conventions of advertising design. These conventions denote how to process a layout (e.g., Look from this photo to this headline.) and connote meaning (e.g., This is what's most important; read this first.).[30] Craig argued these conventions are semiotic codes of design.[31]

Craig's research raises questions that might be fruitfully explored with magazines. Magazine design follows these design codes as well and is, arguably, even more persuasive: A magazine is branded by its design, by its use of typefaces and color and photos and space. (A comparison of the U.S. magazines *Real Simple* versus *Esquire*, for example, evidences that one is modular, and the other is more textured.) It could be argued—another opportunity for scholarly inquiry— the best magazine layouts connote meaning and denote how to process them.

In addition to semiotic theory, researchers have applied other theories to other forms of media that have implications for magazine design.

Gestalt Theory

The functional conventions of design are related to *gestalt theory*, a theory that has its roots in Gestalt psychology. Developed by Austrian and German psychologists in the late 1800s and early 1900s,[32] gestalt theory is based on the idea that the brain is self-organizing: It processes the whole of what the eyes see before perceiving the individual parts. When readers of English look at the word "whole," for example, they see the whole word instantly, not the individual letters.[33] Lisa Graham describes the impact gestalt theory had on graphic design after György Képes and Rudolph Arnheim codified the principles in the 1940s and 1950s, and the principles became a standard in design education. Képes's 1944 book, *Language of Vision*, was the first to discuss the *laws of visual organization*. In two later books, Arnheim applied the gestalt principles to the ways "humans perceive and process visual information."[34] Researchers have applied gestalt theory in a variety of disciplines, from architecture to musicology.[35] In visual communications, gestalt can help explain how and why a layout works or does not. Gestalt visual principles are useful partly because they are easy to understand, but they also are enormously powerful.

Graham proposes that the gestalt principles—*figure/ground, proximity, closure, similarity* and *continuation*—apply to interactive media design. Drawing from Képes's and Arnheim's works, she explains the principles and shows how they relate to the design of interactive media. For example, proximity is the principle of spatial placement: Képes explained that when items are situated together, they will be perceived as a unit.[36] In print design, if a title and subtitle are placed together, a reader understands intuitively that the two are related. The same holds true in interactive media design. So, for example, a list of hyperlinks placed between two columns of text on a Web site would disrupt a reader's intuitive ability to know that one text column continues from the other.[37] A second example: The principle of similarity says that items that look similar—same size, shape or color—are perceived as a unit. Graham applies this principle to interactive designs, suggesting "keeping text, links, and animated elements similar increases the tendency of the reader to believe the objects belong together either physically or conceptually."[38]

Gestalt is not without controversy in the design field. In her 2011 essay, Julia Moszkowicz writes, "Many of the gestalt applications to graphic design from the 1930s onward are viewed (by those in design practice and education) as outmoded."[39] Moszkowicz cites designer and educator Ellen Lupton as one critic of gestalt, saying Lupton perceives gestalt principles as being too scientific, too divorced from human experience, culture and socio-economic conditions, to be useful to design. In other words, gestalt promotes design without cultural context.[40] Moszkowicz argues in her essay that this is reductive thinking. She reviews the primary texts on Gestalt psychology (principally those written by Max Wertheimer and Kurt Koffka[41]) and gestalt visual theory (principally those written by Képes and Roy Berhens[42]), and concludes gestalt principles as practiced in design are, in fact, embedded in culture and human experience because they arise from people's need to organize their thinking as a way to solve problems and reduce stress. "At a time when graphic design is engaging actively with the notions of interactivity and audience participation, Gestalt theory offers productive ways of thinking about possible structures for orchestrating positive human experiences."[43]

Scholars have not applied gestalt visual theory to the design of magazines; however, magazines, arguably, embody gestalt design principles in the way they organize and express information visually. This would seem to offer an opportunity for researchers. Gestalt is a practical tool for designers: Used consciously, it can, at the least, help designers create layouts that are accessible and usable. Gestalt tells a designer how to group type and lay out art and photos so they will move a reader's eyes logically through a page. Applying gestalt theory helps designers create sensible layouts. At its best, gestalt theory can, for example, inspire plastic use of type—where type is shaped to look like what it says, a process that relies on the gestalt principles of both proximity and continuation (The eye follows a line or curve.[44]) and the merging of type and art so that a design becomes a metaphor for a story's subject (see Figure 24.1).

Figure 24.1. "Sea Greens," *Nature Conservancy* magazine. Used by permission.

When used this way, gestalt principles not only organize information so it is consistent with the way people process visuals, but also create meaning, which is consistent with Moszkowicz's view of gestalt visual theory's therapeutic benefits.[45]

Rhetorical Theory

Like gestalt, *rhetoric* has also influenced graphic design, although perhaps in a less direct way. A number of researchers have written about rhetoric and design, mostly as a model for making decisions about persuasive communications, such as advertisements. Gui Bonsiepe was, in 1965, the first to connect rhetorical analysis to visual communications, in this case to advertising.[46] In 1984, Hanno Ehses expanded rhetoric's visual application to other media: "Because all human communication is, in one way or another, infiltrated rhetorically, design for visual or verbal communication cannot be exempt from that fact."[47]

Inspired by Robin Kinross's essay, "The Rhetoric of Neutrality,"[48] Bárbara Emanuel posits in her (author's note: beautifully designed) master's thesis that nothing in graphic design is neutral, or without intention: "Every decision designers make during the process of creation influences the perception and reaction to the content."[49] She goes on to explain the rhetorical nature of designing information graphics and maps and choosing typography. Emanuel supports her explanations with illustrations that show how, say, two newspaper front pages covering the same topics but designed in different ways can communicate very different messages. Front pages from the day after the Haitian earthquake, 14 January 2010, show how a newspaper's photo selection and type sizing influenced the impact of the story.[50] Emanuel also provides a guide to the practical use of design elements to amplify a design's rhetorical message. She ties her guidelines to other visual theories, drawing on framing and the gestalt principles, as well as rhetorical principles such as *reduction*, which is paring a design of all but its essential elements: for example, using only type, or only black-and-white photos, rather than color.[51]

Cristina de Almeida argues that the rhetorical process in design is consistent with the phases of message development in classic rhetoric: *invention* (discovery of the idea and selecting material to support it) and *disposition* (the actual arranging or designing of the message or artifact).[52] De Almeida proposes a rhetorical strategy for design built on the classic process. It starts with identifying the archetypal model most appropriate to a message, for example, *summation*, or reducing a message to a symbol such as a logo.[53] The next step is to determine what *expressive pattern* is most appropriate to the message, for example, advertising or announcing something.[54] The final step is to decide which *graphic medium* is most appropriate to the expression, for example, a billboard or a print advertisement in a magazine.[55] De Almeida argues that in her model designers are essential from the outset, and when they have greater *authorship* over the development of a message, instead of just executing a design, a message is more likely to succeed.[56]

Rhetorical theory might offer a useful lens to examine the design of magazines, as well as the authorship of their designers. Art directors have had authorship at magazines since the late 1920s, starting when Condé Nast hired M.F. Agha to design *Vogue* and *Vanity Fair* in 1928,[57] Henry Luce hired T.M. Cleland to design *Fortune* in 1930[58] and Carmel Snow hired Alexey Brodovitch to design *Harper's Bazaar* in 1934.[59] Authorship is evident today in the design of such magazines as *Real Simple*, where editors and designers storyboard articles so each element, from titles to captions to art, adds new information.[60]

Frame Theory

Frame theory is another tool researchers might use to study magazine design. Research that uses frame theory has focused mostly on media texts. However, since 2000, researchers have used framing to study images either within text or standing alone. For example, Nicole E. Smith in 2006 analyzed newsmagazine photos about stem cell research and identified four themes as news frames: science, politics, medicine and religion.[61]

Lulu Rodriguez and Daniela Dimitrova review visual framing techniques and methods used in previous studies and propose a four-tiered model for identifying and analyzing visual frames. The first level of their *semiotic theory of visual frames* is *denotative* analysis, essentially answering the question, "Who or what is being depicted here?"[62] The second is *stylistic-semiotic* analysis, examining photos for their social meanings using framing devices such as social distance, the distance of the subject in a photo, and visual modality—that is, the use of such elements as color and detail to enhance realism.[63] This level of analysis comprises the theories of multiple scholars, including Gunther Kress and Theo van Leeuwen, Edward Hall and Philip Bell.[64] The third level is *connotative* analysis, examining the ideas an image expresses through its depiction of symbols, such as a cross, or through visual metaphors—for example, the use of an American flag in a news image to represent patriotism.[65] The fourth level is *ideological* analysis. At this level, researchers are looking to answer such questions as, "What interests are being served by these representations? Whose voices are being heard? What ideas dominate?" This level looks at how news images are used to shape public consciousness and historical memory.[66] Given that magazines strive to create a synthesis between images, type and space, these framing levels would seem to offer tools for analysis not just of images, but how they work within the often seamless whole of a magazine layout.

Applied Research

Information design is a craft, and Rune Pettersson writes that much of the research in information design focuses on the practical application of design principles.[67] Comparatively few scholars have done formal research on applied design, especially in magazines. Applied scholarly research typically uses theory to explain the process—how or why design decisions were made—and the outcomes or other dimensions.

Researchers Larry Burriss and Don McComb examined newsmagazines' use of color to identify political parties. They write that color also conveys mood and meaning, although the meanings associated with different colors vary from culture to culture (for example, in imperial China, yellow was the color of the emperor, while in the West it represents cowardice), and a specific color may have no fixed meaning even within one culture (in the West, green variously connotes nature and envy).[68] Nevertheless, Burriss and McComb's quantitative study reveals that in newsmagazines blue tends to be associated with the Republican Party and red with the Democratic Party. The researchers tested their theory by recording the colors of all the politically related infographics published in *Newsweek*, *U.S. News and World Report* and *Time* during the presidential election years between 1980 and 1996.[69] The overall results, while perhaps not statistically significant, the researchers said, showed red used more often to represent Democrats and blue more often to represent Republicans. Color association varied across magazines, though *Time* consistently used blue for Republican infographics and red for Democratic infographics, *Newsweek* used red for both, and *U.S. News and World Report* was more likely to use red for Republicans and blue for Democrats. Historically, red has been associated with the Communist party and blue with patriotism and loyalty.[70] When the study was published in 2001, *Time* was the most conservative magazine among the three.[71]

Australian scholar Douglas Booth also has examined color in magazine design, looking at how color, among other elements, communicates the *affects* of surfing in *Tracks: The Surfers' Bible*, Australia's leading surfing title. In his study of how *Tracks* represents gender,[72] Booth asserts that a magazine's physical form—its design, size and photos, type and colors—expresses its cultural orientation as much as its text. This is especially true of *Tracks* because surfing is a visual culture. Photographs are the principal attraction for readers; they create fantasy and show the sport in action.[73] Booth analyzed the use of photos on covers and how the photos portrayed the *affect* of surfers—facial expressions, form and "stoke": basically the anticipation and thrill of surfing. He then looked at how the affects on the cover were reinforced inside the magazine through use of fragmented type (broken lines, mixed typefaces) and color. He found that grays and deep blues signified treacherous conditions; light blues, greens and yellows signified bliss.[74] While *Tracks* is oriented toward young male surfers, Booth concluded that both text and design are less about gender than about sport. "Time after time gender disappears under mountains of collapsing water or deep inside cylindrical waves. . . ."[75]

Paul Cleveland's interest in magazine design includes theory and process. Drawing on the semiotic theories of Kress and van Leeuwen[76]; the eye track theories of Alfred Yarbus[77]; the work of two neuroscientists, Laurent Itti and Christof Koch[78]; and equations developed by mathematician George Birkhoff,[79] Cleveland created a means for producing computer-generated layouts consistent with a magazine's style. To produce these automated layouts, he developed a *Style Attribution Index* that accounts for all the variables in a design, including a grid, art and photos, graphics, type and space, scaled from simple to complex, light to dark, weak to powerful. He based these calibrations on the work of researchers from several disciplines, including anthropology, computer science, neuroscience, mathematics and visual communications.

He started by using Kress and van Leeuwen's semiotic theories of type and design, particularly as they relate to salience, the degree to which the subjects of an image or the arrangement of type and graphic elements attract the reader's attention.[80] He then determined salience with the eye track theories of Yarbus. A Russian psychologist, Yarbus was the first to study gaze. He published a seminal book on the subject in 1967, *Eye Movements and Vision*.[81] Cleveland also incorporated a computer model invented by Itti and Koch that simulates visual attention and can predict the path a viewer's eye will take through an image.[82] He applied an equation developed by Birkhoff in 1933 that measures aesthetics to compute the structure of grids of varied complexity.[83] Cleveland tested his model using attributes of 1950s magazine layouts to show that his system can create designs consistent with a particular style. Cleveland's thinking is that designers could use automated layouts to design simpler parts of magazines such as departments. He also believes an automated system capable of producing varied layouts that fit within a magazine's particular style has more potential to arouse attention than formulaic templates.[84]

Historical Research

Historical research on magazines tends to be scholarly or descriptive, although the lines between are blurry. Virtually all the historical articles and books on magazines offer some narrative or a chronology related to their subjects. The scholarly articles also offer analysis. Two books on magazine design, William Owen's *Modern Magazine Design* and Jeremy Aynsley and Kate Forde's *Design and the Modern Magazine*, both blend narrative with analysis, although Aynsley and Forde's book has more scholarly intentions.[85]

Design and the Modern Magazine is a collection of historical essays and part of an ongoing series, Studies in Design, produced by graduate students and faculty at the Royal College of Art and the Victoria & Albert Museum in London. The essays focus on the magazine as a designed object, its relationship with consumers and the ways magazines promoted design ideals to readers in their content and by example. The section covering the magazine as designed object deals most directly with the visual components of magazines—type, art and their relationship on the page. Marie-Louise Bowallius examines design changes in the *Woman's Home Companion* from 1923 to 1933.[86] Bowallius offers historical context and discusses the magazine's format, design, color usage and advertising.[87] Aynsley examines the relationship between typefaces, magazines and fashion in the 1920s, a topic, he writes, not previously covered.[88] "[Lucian] Bernhard's Fashion and [A.M.] Cassandre's Bifur are just two examples of typefaces from this period that offer new perspectives on the relationship between fashion and typography and their interconnectedness as they appeared on the pages of magazines."[89] Emily King examines the design of

Britain's *Time Out* covers from 1970 to 1981. The piece is based on interviews King had with Pearce Marchbank, "the most significant designer of *Time Out* during the 1970s,"[90] and with Tony Elliott, *Time Out*'s founder.[91]

Owen's *Modern Magazine Design* is the only history of magazine design in the twentieth century, when improved printing technologies made it easier to set type and reproduce photos.[92] His book is both descriptive and discursive: He connects art movements, such as the Bauhaus and Dadaism, and historical events, such as the world wars, to the evolution of magazine design in the United States, Europe and Russia. The book, which by count has about 230 illustrations, is in two chronological parts. Part one starts with the early weekly magazines, such as the *London Illustrated News*,[93] and then goes on to cover photojournalism magazines, the history and influence of the first art directors in America, the New York School (designers who were the students of the first art directors and designed major consumer magazines between 1945 and 1968[94]), the revival of magazine design in Europe in the 1950s and American magazine design after 1968, when the underground and independent press were most open to design innovation.[95] Part two of the book focuses on magazine design between about 1985 and 1990, the year before the book's publication. The second part is more topical, covering layout, covers, and photography and illustration. The last chapter looks ahead to digital design and the ways computers were likely to influence design style, which already had become more layered and less linear, what Owen refers to as a "new aesthetic."[96] The book even anticipates electronic magazines, although on-line and not as portable publications.[97]

Scholarly articles published during this period reflect diverse interests, from the design of nineteenth-century illustrated magazines to the development of punk fanzines and a do-it-yourself aesthetic.

Illustrations in nineteenth-century newsmagazines have long been of interest to art historians; however, only Tom Gretton's 2010 study puts them in the context of the design of the magazines in which they appeared.[98] Gretton found that the newsmagazines that featured illustrations basically commodified the work and also influenced the development of a genre of art. Printed from woodcuts, where an image is etched into a block of wood, some illustrations were created by illustrators, many by fine artists.[99] Gretton analyzed the way these illustrations were used within the pages of four prominent London and Paris newsweeklies, showing how magazine design evolved to accommodate art and text. He examined 60 years of the serial archives of *L'Illustration*, *Le Monde Illustrè*, the *Illustrated London News* and the *Graphic*, charting the number of illustrations in each and their layouts.[100] Gretton found that around 1840, these magazines placed an emphasis on using a lot of photos, but over time they ran fewer but larger illustrations, up to whole page size by 1860. Between 1850 and 1870, most pages were laid out symmetrically, using three columns. By 1870, they were using more full-page illustrations, sometimes running them horizontally, next to full pages of text. By 1890, they were running some images across spreads.[101] Gretton observed that a consistent challenge was accommodating text and images on one page. Designers typically placed the art and then put text in the empty spaces, frequently wrapping text around the art, which often diminished its importance.[102] Gretton noted the invention of the photomechanical process for printing pictures that at the end of the nineteenth century lessened the artistic value of the illustrations in the magazines he studied.[103]

Photography is the focus of Katarina Romanenko's exploration into its use in post-1917 Soviet periodicals, where photos represented truth and realism, which legitimized them over illustration. Romanenko argues that in 1930s Russia, photos and the women's periodicals that featured them extensively were a tool the government employed to promote its domestic agenda and bring "culture" closer to the masses.[104] She notes that *culture* in Soviet terms included art and literature, but also manners and personal hygiene. Women were a key target of Soviet propaganda because they were resistant to change and were responsible for childrearing and domestic life. Lenin endorsed photography over art, and the status of illustration, and illustrators, slipped in Soviet periodicals. Romanenko found that photomontage, the combination of photos with graphic elements, drew on the strengths of photography and illustration.[105] She wrote that Soviet photomontage typically combined images unified by one subject, or parts of separate images into one image. It was often applied to groups of portraits. Complex montages that combined graphic elements, such as lines and type, with photos required artistic training, but the advantage of montage was that it could mask technical imperfections in photos and printing.[106]

Just as Romanenko showed that photomontages represented political and artistic shifts in Soviet magazines, Craig Buckley found that photos and their integration in layout in the Austrian magazine *Bau* represented a shift in architectural design thinking in the mid-to-late 1960s.[107] *Bau* looked back at the work of seminal architects, but also advocated a radical expansion of the definition of architecture, mostly through manifestos. One particularly influential manifesto was "Alles ist Architektur" (Everything Is Architecture), written by Hans Hollein, one of the magazine's editors. Published in the 1968 edition of *Bau*, the manifesto had one page of text followed by 27 full-bleed pages of images designed to elucidate the argument.[108] The images, everything from buildings to people to objects, unfolded as a way of saying that architects must think not only in terms of structures but also environments.[109] Photos were laid out both symmetrically and asymmetrically into a photomontage in which the layout itself and the order and juxtaposition of images created a visual metaphor for a changing ideal of architecture.[110] Buckley's article includes photos of 16 pages from the magazine with a detailed discussion of the design to illustrate Hollein's premise.[111]

Illustrated magazines also are at the center of Patrick Roessler's study of the crosspollination of German and American popular news and entertainment magazines between the late 1920s and 1950.[112] Roessler argues that the influence they had on each other's editorial concepts and design gave rise to a common visual language, one that featured photography and photomontage. The popular illustrated German weekly, *BIZ* (*Berliner Illustrirte Zeitung*), which was started after World War I, emphasized photojournalism and hired an artistic adviser to select photos and create photo stories. In the United States, Henry Luce saw an opportunity to capitalize on Americans' interest in movie-related weeklies. He created his interpretation of *BIZ*, *Life* magazine, hiring former *BIZ* editor Kurt Korff to help develop *Life*'s editorial concept and format. Korff participated in "secret planning sessions," making suggestions about type, layout and photographers.[113] *Der Querschnitt*, a magazine founded in 1924 for the intellectual elite in Weimar, Germany, was inspired in part by American niche magazines. The magazine was also a design innovator. Its editor introduced a "confrontational" spread design, in which the juxtaposition of seemingly unrelated photos created insight.

> For example, the promotional photo of a countess from Paris resting on her sofa bed was paralleled by a snapshot of a reclining polar bear from the London Zoo; or two Nazi members are confronted with the comedians Pat and Patachon, who were famous for their dullness.[114]

Roessler points out that before the Nazis, Germany was a trendsetter in illustrated magazines; after Nazi rule, American illustrated magazines became design leaders, and this exchange of influences occurred largely because of the migration of designers and art directors to the United States.[115]

Teal Triggs, a design professor in London, has explored the postmodern design of the British punk music fanzines of the 1970s. Triggs writes that the design of punk fanzines reflected the rebellious, underground culture of which they were a part. Triggs references Stephen Duncombe, an American academic who has written about "zines, saying punk fanzines" "chaotic" design contributed to the development of a *graphic language of resistance* to authority.[116] In describing this graphic language of resistance, Triggs draws on the semiotic theory of Kress and van Leeuwen, who observed,

. . . a shift taking place in the "era of late modernity" from a dominance of "mono-modality," a singular communication mode, to "multimodality" which embraces a "variety of materials and to cross the boundaries between the various art, design and performance disciplines.[117]

Triggs describes the design evolution of punk fanzines, whose cut-and-paste construction exemplified the do-it-yourself (DIY) ethos of punk musicians. Punk fanzines were designed with photocopied album covers and images ripped off from other publications, typewritten texts that included typos, strikeouts and handwritten graffiti texts. They featured collages and low-value production—the magazines were printed on photocopiers and stapled.[118] Triggs found that, over time, punk fanzines all began to share this aesthetic, which "went some way to establish a set of commonly used principles and a way of creating a distinctive graphic language, which ultimately mirrored the particular aesthetic of punk music."[119]

Holstead's study of magazines in the 1990s operated from the premise that publications had lost their historical footing, which was reflected in their design. She found that prominent designers, particularly those who were part of magazine design's "golden age" from 1945 to around 1968, lamented the busy, seemingly uncontrolled design of magazines in the 1990s, which they blamed on designers' exuberant use of the computer, still a novel tool. They also criticized magazines' apparent lack of historical reference.[120] Women's magazines especially went crazy with colors and typefaces, both easy to change with a computer design program. For example, one cover of *Woman's Day* from 1994 featured 10 sell lines printed in or on top of six spot colors over a photo, with two more, smaller photos printed on top of that photo.[121] The attitude seemed to be "We can! So we will!" There were exceptions, of course. *Elle*, for example, appeared inspired by midcentury modernism's modular, clean layouts, and *Harper's Bazaar* by its influential midcentury art directors, Alexey Brodovitch and Henry Wolf.[122]

Since then technology has moved at a furious pace, but the design of many magazines seems to have regained its historical footing, while capitalizing on what design programs can do that people could not, at least not easily, 50 years ago. Take *Real Simple*, for example: Its design clearly reflects the Bauhaus's modular, minimalist aesthetic, but it is able to make ample use of images with dropout backgrounds in such departments as Problem Solvers of the Month.

Apart from scholarly works, historical articles about magazine design sometimes surface in design trade publications such as *Graphis*, *Communication Arts* and *Print*. Patricia Prijatel's history of a magazine that lived for one year, from 1950 to 1951, offers a good example. Prijatel describes *Flair* as an inventively, lavishly designed magazine that tested the limits of printing technology. *Flair* was a magazine for readers interested in travel, art and culture. Magazine publisher and editor Mike Cowles and his wife, advertising director Fleur Cowles, founded it. Among its marvels included die-cut and embossed covers, new logo designs for every issue, removable booklets bound into its pages, and experimental and traditional artworks printed on heavy stock and suitable for framing.

> A trip through *Flair*'s pages is a trip through the imagination of artists, designers, and writers who were given the challenge to create a magazine unlike any other the world had seen. They did. It's as lively a collection of color, art, paper, and design innovations ever bound between covers.[123]

The expense of producing such innovations, however, became crushing. By the time the magazine folded, it had cost the publisher close to $2.5 million (in 1950s dollars) before taxes.[124]

The value of historical research in magazine design is that looking back can help designers, educators and change-makers look forward. Estelle Ellis, one of the founders of *Seventeen*, which launched in 1944, said in 1993, "Design on the basis of what you know and understand, but don't underestimate looking back to what was great in an earlier time. You drive with a rearview mirror. You have to design the same way."[125]

Articles reviewed in this section open a window to future research. Roessler's study of the trans-Atlantic influence of magazine design could be further explored. For example, some of the earliest art directors in America immigrated, including M.F. Agha and Alexey Brodovitch. Agha had worked in Germany and France before Condé Nast hired him to design its flagship magazines, *Vanity Fair* and *Vogue*. Brodovitch was a Russian counter-revolutionary who fled to Europe and immigrated to the United States in 1931. Brodovitch art directed *Harper's Bazaar* for 24 years. There he pioneered fashion photography and the use of the magazine spread. As

Figure 24.2. Cover, *Ripped & Torn* magazine. Used by permission.

403

a teacher and mentor, he influenced the work of the most celebrated magazine designers of the mid-twentieth century, and his work still resonates in today's magazines.[126]

Romanenko's research on photomontage in Soviet magazines could be the basis for study of photomontage in modern magazines.[127] Owen writes that photomontage has been used since the invention of photography. Not only was it foundational to Constructivism (the rational, orderly approach to design invented in Russia in the 1920s), it proliferated as a technique of Dadism (an anarchical approach to art and design—disorder instead of order—invented by the Swiss in the 1920s).[128] Modern magazines have made frequent use of montage, for example, the collages of fragmented fashion images in American *Vogue*.

The DIY punk fanzines and their language of resistance that were the subject of Trigg's study also present ideas for research in how this aesthetic has influenced modern magazines. Owen writes that in the late 1980s, Japanese, European and American magazines all exhibited a "new disorder and a resurgence of experimentation in multi-layered collage, parallel texts, iconoclastic typography, and novel combinations of page components."[129] In a sense, they were co-opting punk fanzines' language of resistance. David Carson is one designer who applied the chaotic DIY aesthetic to two culture magazines, *Ray Gun* and *Transworld Skateboarding*, in the late 1980s and 1990s (see Figure 24.2).

Conclusion

This chapter set out to review the scholarly research on magazine design since 1990. What resulted was the discovery that there was surprisingly little—12 articles and one book. They fell into three overlapping categories: those with a theoretical base, those that focused on applied design (the actual use of design elements and the process of design) and those that were historical. The articles were diverse and somewhat disconnected. Theoretical researchers in magazines tended to reference the same core theories (for example, semiotics) but did not refer to each other's work on unrelated topics. One researcher, Paul Cleveland, an Australian designer and teacher who has written three articles about magazine design, builds on his own work. Only two scholars have done theory-based research on magazine design: Cleveland, as noted, and Veronika Koller, who writes about how business magazines use visual metaphors in illustrations within the context of their pages. Koller references Kress and van Leeuwen's semiotic theory in her work, as does Cleveland in his studies of the *visual power* of magazines.

The section on applied research includes one article about color use in newsmagazines and another about the ways color and other design techniques communicate the psychological *affects* of surfing in the Australian *Tracks: The Surfers' Bible* (a study the author, Douglas Booth, undertook in part to see if the magazine had a male bias). Also included is a study by Cleveland in which he develops a means for magazines to create automated layouts consistent with a particular publication's style.

Most of the scholarly work on magazine design is historical, comprising five articles and one book. The articles cover a range of topics: illustrations in nineteenth-century newsmagazines; photomontage in Soviet women's periodicals after 1917; the use of photos in the 1968 issue of the Austrian magazine *Bau* to represent a shift in ideological thinking about architecture; the cross-pollination of German and American magazines between the late 1920s and 1950; the visual *language of resistance* expressed in the design of British punk fanzines; and the apparent loss of historical footing in the design of magazines in the 1990s. Two books also are reviewed: a scholarly collection of essays about magazines with some focus on design and a book that is a detailed history of magazine design during the twentieth century.

An unexpected discovery from the literature search for this chapter was the amount of theoretical research done on graphic design that is relevant to magazine design. This includes gestalt theory, rhetorical theory and framing theory. Six articles are included here, although more could be mined. These other theories and articles present possibilities for research in magazines.

Magazines have not received the scholarly attention devoted more generally to information design, but the theories and practices of design are timeless, interconnected and point the way to future research as magazines evolve into new digital forms. A knowledge of history and an understanding of traditional design practices and theories will help magazine designers imagine the future and offer a mother lode of possibilities for research.

Notes

1 William Owen, *Modern Magazine Design* (New York: Rizzoli, 1991), 6.
2 Rune Pettersson, "Research in Information Design," *Journal of Visual Literacy* 26.1 (Spring 2006): 80.
3 Gunther Kress and Theo van Leeuwen, *Reading Images: The Grammar of Visual Design*, 2nd ed. (London and New York: Routledge, 2006), 16; see also, William Ryan and Theodore Conover, *Graphic Communications Today*, 4th ed. (Clifton Park, NY: Thomson/Delmar Learning, 2004), 1.
4 Steven Heller, "Books: Authored/Edited/Coauthored," Hellerbooks.com <http://www.hellerbooks.com/docs/books.html>, accessed 21 June 2013; see also, Steven Heller, *Merz to Émigré and Beyond: Avant-Garde Magazine Design of the Twentieth Century* (London: Phaidon Press) and Steven Heller and Teresa Fernandes, *Magazines Inside and Out* (Glen Cove, NY: PBC International, 1997).
5 Ryan and Conover, *Graphic Communications Today*.
6 Robert Craig, "Ideological Aspects of Publication Design," *Design Issues* 6.2 (Spring 1990): 18; see also, Rune Pettersson, "Research in Information Design," 77.
7 Pettersson, "Research in Information Design," 78.
8 Ryan and Conover, *Graphic Communications Today*, 25.
9 Kress and van Leeuwen, *Reading Images*, 3.
10 Kress and van Leeuwen, *Reading Images*, 201.
11 Paul Cleveland, "The Effect of Technology on the Development of Magazine Visual Design Style" (Ph.D. diss., Queensland College of Art, Griffith University, 2004), bibliography, 350.
12 Cleveland, "The Effect of Technology," abstract, 3.
13 Cleveland, "The Effect of Technology," 116.
14 Cleveland, "The Effect of Technology," 129.
15 Cleveland, "The Effect of Technology," 202.
16 Cleveland, "The Effect of Technology," 202.
17 Cleveland, "The Effect of Technology," 222.
18 Cleveland, "The Effect of Technology," 227.
19 Paul Cleveland, "How Much Visual Power Can a Magazine Take?" *Design Studies* 26.3 (May 2005): 291.
20 Cleveland, "How Much Visual Power Can a Magazine Take?" 303.
21 Cleveland, "How Much Visual Power Can a Magazine Take?" 272.
22 Veronika Koller, "Designing Cognition: Visual Metaphor as a Design Feature in Business Magazines," *Information Design Journal + Document Design* 13.2 (2005): 138.
23 Koller, "Designing Cognition," 148.
24 Koller, "Designing Cognition," 143.
25 Koller, "Designing Cognition," 144–145.
26 Craig, "Ideological Aspects of Publication Design," 18.
27 Craig, "Ideological Aspects of Publication Design," 19.
28 Craig, "Ideological Aspects of Publication Design," 19–20.
29 Craig, "Ideological Aspects of Publication Design," 22.
30 Craig, "Ideological Aspects of Publication Design," 26–27.
31 Craig, "Ideological Aspects of Publication Design," 23.
32 Lisa Graham, "Gestalt Theory in Interactive Media Design," *Journal of Humanities & Social Sciences* 2.1 (2008): 1.
33 Graham, "Gestalt Theory in Interactive Media Design," 4.
34 Graham, "Gestalt Theory in Interactive Media Design," 2; see also, György Képes, *Language of Vision* (Chicago: Paul Theobald, 1944. Reissued: New York: Dover Publications, 1995); Rudolph Arnheim, *Art and Visual Perception: A Psychology of the Creative Eye* (Berkeley: University of California Press, 1954, revised 1974); Rudolph Arnheim, *Visual Thinking* (Berkeley: University of California Press, 1969).
35 Graham, "Gestalt Theory in Interactive Media Design," 1.
36 Graham, "Gestalt Theory in Interactive Media Design," 4.
37 Graham, "Gestalt Theory in Interactive Media Design," 6.
38 Graham, "Gestalt Theory in Interactive Media Design," 4–9.
39 Julia Moszkowicz, "Gestalt and Graphic Design: An Exploration of the Humanistic and Therapeutic Effects of Visual Organization," *Design Issues* 27.4 (Autumn 2011): 56.

40 Moszkowicz, "Gestalt and Graphic Design," 57; see also, Ellen Lupton, "Visual Dictionary," in Ellen Lupton and J. Abbott Miller, eds, *The ABC's of [Triangle, Square, Circle]: The Bauhaus and Design Theory* (London: Princeton Architectural Press, 1993), 22–33.

41 Moszkowicz, "Gestalt and Graphic Design," 61–64.

42 Moszkowicz, "Gestalt and Graphic Design," 60.

43 Moszkowicz, "Gestalt and Graphic Design," 57.

44 Graham, "Gestalt Theory in Interactive Media Design," 10.

45 Moszkowicz, "Gestalt and Graphic Design," 57.

46 Gui Bonsiepe, "Visual/Verbal Rhetoric," presented at a conference led by Tomas Maldonado in Stuttgart, Germany, in 1965, is published in Michael Bierut, Jessica Helfand, Steven Heller, and Rick Poynor, eds., *Looking Closer 3: Classic Writings on Graphic Design* (New York: Allworth, 1999), 167.

47 Hanno H.J. Ehses, "Representing Macbeth: A Case Study in Visual Rhetoric," *Design Issues* 1.1 (Spring 1984): 54.

48 Bárbara Emanuel, "Rhetoric in Graphic Design" (M.A. thesis, Hochschule Anhalt, Anhalt University of Applied Sciences, Dessau, Germany, 2010), 20; see, Robin Kinross, "The Rhetoric of Neutrality," *Design Issues* 2.2 (Autumn 1985): 18–30.

49 Emanuel, "Rhetoric in Graphic Design," 10.

50 Emanuel, "Rhetoric in Graphic Design," 133.

51 Emanuel, "Rhetoric in Graphic Design," 145.

52 Cristina de Almeida, "The Rhetorical Genre in Graphic Design: Its Relationship to Design Authorship and Implications of Design Education," *Journal of Visual Literacy* 28.2 (Autumn 2009): 194.

53 de Almeida, "The Rhetorical Genre," 189.

54 de Almeida, "The Rhetorical Genre," 191.

55 de Almeida, "The Rhetorical Genre," 189–193.

56 de Almeida, "The Rhetorical Genre," 188.

57 Owen, *Modern Magazine Design*, 48.

58 Owen, *Modern Magazine Design*, 44.

59 Owen, *Modern Magazine Design*, 49.

60 Vanessa Holden, interview with author, 13 June 2005, New York, personal interview.

61 Nicole E. Smith, "Stem Cell Research: Visual Framing of the Ethical Debate in *Time* and *Newsweek*" (paper presented to the Annual Meeting, Association for Education in Journalism and Mass Communication, August 2006).

62 Lulu Rodriguez and Daniela V. Dimitrova, "The Levels of Visual Framing," *Journal of Visual Literacy* 30.1 (Spring 2011): 53.

63 Rodriguez and Dimitrova, "The Levels of Visual Framing," 54.

64 Rodriguez and Dimitrova, "The Levels of Visual Framing," 55; see also, Philip Bell, "Content Analysis of Visual Images," in Theo van Leeuwen and Jewitt Carey, eds, *Handbook of Visual Analysis* (Thousand Oaks, CA: Sage Publications, 2001), 10–34; Edward T. Hall, *The Hidden Dimension* (New York: Doubleday, 1969); Kress and van Leeuwen, *Reading Images*.

65 Rodriguez and Dimitrova, "The Levels of Visual Framing," 56.

66 Rodriguez and Dimitrova, "The Levels of Visual Framing," 57.

67 Pettersson, "Research in Information Design," 77.

68 Larry L. Burriss and Don McComb, "Use of Color in Three News Magazines to Identify Political Parties," *Journal of Visual Literacy* 21.2 (Autumn 2001): 168, 170.

69 Burriss and McComb, "Use of Color in Three News Magazines," 172.

70 Burriss and McComb, "Use of Color in Three News Magazines," 169, 174.

71 Burriss and McComb, "Use of Color in Three News Magazines," 174.

72 Douglas Booth, "(Re)reading the *Surfers' Bible*: The Affects of *Tracks*," *Continuum: Journal of Media & Cultural Studies* 22.1 (February 2008): 17.

73 Booth, "(Re)reading the *Surfers' Bible*," 22.

74 Booth, "(Re)reading the *Surfers' Bible*," 24–25.

75 Booth, "(Re)reading the *Surfers' Bible*," 31.

76 Paul Cleveland, "Style Based Automated Graphic Layouts," *Design Studies* 31 (January 2009): 3.

77 Cleveland, "Style Based Automated Graphic Layouts," 9.

78 Cleveland, "Style Based Automated Graphic Layouts," 11.

79 Cleveland, "Style Based Automated Graphic Layouts," 13.

80 Cleveland, "Style Based Automated Graphic Layouts," 12; Kress and van Leeuwen, *Reading Images*, 201.

81 Cleveland, "Style Based Automated Graphic Layouts," 11; see also, Alfred L. Yarbus, *Eye Movements and Vision*, trans. Basil Haigh, trans. ed. Lorrin A. Riggs (New York: Plenum, 1967).

82 Cleveland, "Style Based Automated Graphic Layouts," 11.

83 Cleveland, "Style Based Automated Graphic Layouts," 13.

84 Cleveland, "Style Based Automated Graphic Layouts," 11–23.

85 Owen, *Modern Magazine Design*; Jeremy Aynsley and Kate Forde, *Design and the Modern Magazine* (Manchester and New York: Manchester University Press, 2007), 2.

86 Marie-Louise Bowallius, "Advertising and the Use of Colour in *Woman's Home Companion*, 1923–33," in Jeremy Aynsley and Kate Forde, eds., *Design and the Modern Magazine* (Manchester and New York: Manchester University Press, 2007), 18.

87 Bowallius, "Advertising and the Use of Colour in *Woman's Home Companion*," 24–32.

88 Jeremy Aynsley, "Fashioning Graphics in the 1920s: Typefaces, Magazines and Fashion," in Jeremy Aynsley and Kate Forde, eds., *Design and the Modern Magazine* (Manchester and New York: Manchester University Press, 2007), 38.

89 Aynsley, "Fashioning Graphics in the 1920s," 52.

90 Emily King, "*Time Out* Cover Design, 1970–81," in Jeremy Aynsley and Kate Forde, eds., *Design and the Modern Magazine* (Manchester and New York: Manchester University Press, 2007), 56.

91 King, "*Time Out* Cover Design, 1970–81," 56–72.

92 Owen, *Modern Magazine Design*, 12.

93 Owen, *Modern Magazine Design*, 16.

94 Owen, *Modern Magazine Design*, 56.

95 Owen, *Modern Magazine Design*, 102.

96 Owen, *Modern Magazine Design*, 229.

97 Owen, *Modern Magazine Design*, 230.

98 Tom Gretton, "The Pragmatics of Page Design in Nineteenth-Century General-Interest Weekly Illustrated News Magazines in London and Paris," *Art History* 33.4 (September 2010): 706.

99 Gretton, "Pragmatics of Page Design," 682.

100 Gretton, "Pragmatics of Page Design," 685.

101 Gretton, "Pragmatics of Page Design," 687–699.

102 Gretton, "Pragmatics of Page Design," 704.

103 Gretton, "Pragmatics of Page Design," 707.

104 Katerina Romanenko, "Photomontage for the Masses: The Soviet Periodical Press of the 1930s," *Design Issues* 26.1 (Winter 2010): 29.

105 Romanenko, "Photomontage for the Masses," 30–32.

106 Romanenko, "Photomontage for the Masses," 36–37.

107 Craig Buckley, "From Absolute to Everything: Taking Possession in 'Alles Ist Architektur,'" *Grey Room* 28 (Summer 2007): 109.

108 Buckley, "From Absolute to Everything," 109.

109 Buckley, "From Absolute to Everything," 112.

110 Buckley, "From Absolute to Everything," 109.

111 Buckley, "From Absolute to Everything," 109–118.

112 Patrick Roessler, "Global Players, Émigrés, and *Zeitgeist*: Magazine Design and the Interrelation between the United States and Germany," *Journalism Studies* 8.4 (August 2007): 568, 579.

113 Roessler, "Global Players, Émigrés, and *Zeitgeist*," 571.

114 Roessler, "Global Players, Émigrés, and *Zeitgeist*," 574.

115 Roessler, "Global Players, Émigrés, and *Zeitgeist*," 579.

116 Teal Triggs, "Scissors and Glue: Punk Fanzines and the Creation of a DIY Aesthetic," *Journal of Design History* 19.1 (2006): 70.

117 Triggs, "Scissors and Glue," 73.

118 Triggs, "Scissors and Glue," 70–72, 76.

119 Triggs, "Scissors and Glue," 76.

120 Carol E. Holstead, "What's Old Is New: The Need for Historical Inspiration in Contemporary Magazine Design," *American Periodicals* 7 (1997): 74–75.

121 Holstead, "What's Old Is New," 79.

122 Holstead, "What's Old Is New," 81.

123 Patricia Prijatel, "Fleur's Folly," *Print*, March/April 1995, 99.

124 Prijatel, "Fleur's Folly," 99–108, 110.

125 Estelle Ellis, interview with author, 19 March 1994, New York, phone interview.

126 Owen, *Modern Magazine Design*, 44–48.

127 Romanenko, "Photomontage for the Masses."

128 Owen, *Modern Magazine Design*, 25.

129 Owen, *Modern Magazine Design*, 130.

Bibliography

Arnheim, Rudolph. *Art and Visual Perception: A Psychology of the Creative Eye.* Berkeley: University of California Press, 1954, revised 1974.

Arnheim, Rudolph. *Visual Thinking.* Berkeley: University of California Press, 1969.

Aynsley, Jeremy. "Fashioning Graphics in the 1920s: Typefaces, Magazines and Fashion." In Aynsley, Jeremy and Forde, Kate, eds. *Design and the Modern Magazine.* Manchester and New York: Manchester University Press, 2007, 37–55.

Aynsley, Jeremy and Forde, Kate. *Design and the Modern Magazine.* Manchester and New York: Manchester University Press, 2007.

Bell, Philip. "Content Analysis of Visual Images." In van Leeuwen, Theo and Carey, Jewitt eds. *Handbook of Visual Analysis.* Thousand Oaks, CA: Sage Publications, 2001, 10–34.

Bonsiepe, Gui. "Visual/Verbal Rhetoric." In Bierut, Michael; Helfand, Jessica; Heller, Steven; and Poynor, Rick. eds. *Looking Closer 3: Classic Writings on Graphic Design.* New York: Allworth, 1999, 167–173.

Booth, Douglas. "(Re)reading the *Surfers' Bible*: The Affects of *Tracks*." *Continuum: Journal of Media & Cultural Studies* 22.1 (February 2008): 17–35.

Bowallius, Marie-Louise. "Advertising and the Use of Colour in *Woman's Home Companion*, 1923–33." In Aynsley, Jeremy and Forde, Kate, eds. *Design and the Modern Magazine.* Manchester and New York: Manchester University Press, 2007, 18–36.

Buckley, Craig. "From Absolute to Everything: Taking Possession in 'Alles Ist Architektur.'" *Grey Room* 28 (Summer 2007): 109–122.

Burriss, Larry L. and McComb, Don. "Use of Color in Three News Magazines to Identify Political Parties." *Journal of Visual Literacy* 21.2 (Autumn 2001): 167–176.

Cleveland, Paul. "The Effect of Technology on the Development of Magazine Visual Design Style." Ph.D. diss., Queensland College of Art, Griffith University, 2004.

Cleveland, Paul. "How Much Visual Power Can a Magazine Take?" *Design Studies* 26.3 (May 2005): 271–317.

Cleveland, Paul. "Style Based Automated Graphic Layouts." *Design Studies* 31.1 (January 2009): 3–25.

Craig, Robert. "Ideological Aspects of Publication Design." *Design Issues* 6.2 (Spring 1990): 18–27.

de Almeida, Cristina. "The Rhetorical Genre in Graphic Design: Its Relationship to Design Authorship and Implications to Design Education." *Journal of Visual Literacy* 28.2 (Autumn 2009): 186–198.

Ehses, Hanno H.J. "Representing Macbeth: A Case Study in Visual Rhetoric." *Design Issues* 1.1 (Spring 1984): 53–63.

Ellis, Estelle. Interview with author, 19 March 1994, New York. Phone interview.

Emanuel, Bárbara. "Rhetoric in Graphic Design." M.A. thesis, Hochschule Anhalt, Anhalt University of Applied Sciences, Dessau, Germany, 2010.

Graham, Lisa. "Gestalt Theory in Interactive Media Design." *Journal of Humanities & Social Sciences* 2.1 (2008): 1–12.

Gretton, Tom. "The Pragmatics of Page Design in Nineteenth-Century General-Interest Weekly Illustrated News Magazines in London and Paris." *Art History* 33.4 (September 2010): 680–709.

Hall, Edward T. *The Hidden Dimension.* New York: Doubleday, 1969.

Heller, Steven. "Books: Authored/Edited/Coauthored." Hellerbooks.com <http://www.hellerbooks.com/docs/books.html>, accessed 21 June 2013.

Heller, Steven. *Merz to Émigré and Beyond: Avant-Garde Magazine Design of the Twentieth Century.* London: Phaidon Press, 2003.

Heller, Steven and Fernandes, Teresa. *Magazines Inside and Out.* Glen Cove, NY: PBC International, 1997.

Holden, Vanessa. Interview with author, 13 June 2005, New York. Personal interview.

Holstead, Carol E. "What's Old Is New: The Need for Historical Inspiration in Contemporary Magazine Design." *American Periodicals* 7 (1997): 73–86.

Képes, György. *Language of Vision.* Chicago: Paul Theobald, 1944. Reissued: New York: Dover Publications, 1995.

King, Emily. "*Time Out* Cover Design, 1970–1981." In Aynsley, Jeremy and Forde, Kate, eds. *Design and the Modern Magazine.* Manchester and New York: Manchester University Press, 2007, 56–74.

Kinross, Robin. "The Rhetoric of Neutrality." *Design Issues* 2.2 (Autumn 1985): 18–30.

Koller, Veronika. "Designing Cognition: Visual Metaphor as a Design Feature in Business Magazines." *Information Design Journal + Document Design* 13.2 (2005): 136–150.

Kress, Gunther and van Leeuwen, Theo. *Reading Images: The Grammar of Visual Design.* 2nd ed. London and New York: Routledge, 2006.

Lupton, Ellen. "Visual Dictionary." In Lupton, Ellen and Miller, J. Abbott, eds. *The ABC's of [Triangle, Square, Circle]: The Bauhaus and Design Theory.* London: Princeton Architectural Press, 1993.

Moszkowicz, Julia. "Gestalt and Graphic Design: An Exploration of the Humanistic and Therapeutic Effects of Visual Organization." *Design Issues* 27.4 (Autumn 2011): 56–67.

Owen, William. *Modern Magazine Design.* New York: Rizzoli, 1991.

Pettersson, Rune. "Research in Information Design." *Journal of Visual Literacy* 26.1 (Spring 2006): 77–88.

Prijatel, Patricia. "Fleur's Folly?" *Print*, March/April 1995, 99–108, 110.

Rodriguez, Lulu and Dimitrova, Daniela V. "The Levels of Visual Framing." *Journal of Visual Literacy* 30.1 (Spring 2011): 48–65.

Roessler, Patrick. "Global Players, Émigrés, and *Zeitgeist*: Magazine Design and the Interrelation between the United States and Germany." *Journalism Studies* 8.4 (August 2007): 566–583.

Romanenko, Katerina. "Photomontage for the Masses: The Soviet Periodical Press of the 1930s." *Design Issues* 26.1 (Winter 2010): 29–39.

Ryan, William and Conover, Theodore. *Graphic Communications Today.* 4th ed. Clifton Park, NY: Thomson/Delmar Learning, 2004.

Smith, Nicole E. "Stem Cell Research: Visual Framing of the Ethical Debate in *Time* and *Newsweek*." Paper presented to the Annual Meeting, Association for Education in Journalism and Mass Communication, August 2006.

Triggs, Teal. "Scissors and Glue: Punk Fanzines and the Creation of a DIY Aesthetic." *Journal of Design History* 19.1 (2006): 69–83.

Yarbus, Alfred L. *Eye Movements and Vision.* Translated by Basil Haigh. Translation edited by Lorrin A. Riggs. New York: Plenum, 1967.

25
PHOTOGRAPHY AND ILLUSTRATION

The Power and Promise of the Image

Berkley Hudson and Elizabeth A. Lance

In the years after about 1990, scholars brought to light three unrelated insights about the nature of magazine photographs and illustrations: (1) In the late nineteenth and early twentieth centuries, magazines published two kinds of images to complement stories: photographs to assert evidentiary realism and hand-drawn illustrations to suggest the artistic realm[1]; (2) French photojournalist Janine Niépce—a descendent of one of the earliest inventors of photography—provided an in-depth look into the twentieth century lives of ordinary French women and the French women's movement[2]; and (3) in the era of emerging digital technologies that allowed manipulation of photographs on newsmagazine covers, an infamous picture of celebrity and accused murderer O.J. Simpson created mistrust among readers.[3]

These narrow examples hint at recent scholarship published about magazine photographs and illustrations. Visual research on magazines is shot through books, journals and encyclopedias and is detailed at conferences worldwide. Beyond that, plentiful non-academic writing—in *Aperture*, for example—reveals research gaps about documentary, art, fashion and journalistic photography and illustrations in both print magazines and on-line. This chapter focuses on scholarship about underlying principles of visual communication and on some, but not all, studies, including those about the Web and how images are delivered when integrated with text on-line.

Literature Review and Method

Compared to other media, the magazine form has always offered readers a visual vitality, from the early days of wood engravings to today's digital images. The flexibility of magazines has yielded an unmatched degree of illustrative expansiveness through the use of photography and illustration. The movement from analog to digital has increased the torrent of images.

The last two decades saw many research gaps filled about magazine photography and illustrations. This represented an important shift. In the 1980s, academics acknowledged the inadequacy of theory and methods to cope with a flood of images. Victor Burgin maintained in 1980 that a theory of photography "does not yet exist."[4] Alan Trachtenberg wrote, "A *formal* criticism, a set of analyses and arguments that attempts to delineate a general character of the medium, has yet to emerge. The canons of art history, of connoisseurship, are not likely to provide the necessary model."[5] Instead, he said, the model may grow from "the more venturesome and intellectually aggressive work of *cultural* critics" such as Walter Benjamin or Roland Barthes. Theorizing is essential, Trachtenberg wrote, because photography "must be recognized as exercising a powerful kind of persuasion as a carrier of ideological messages in everyday life."[6]

Addressing the onslaught of images—a trickle when compared to what the Internet would spawn by the twenty-first century—Burgin in 1994 wrote,

> We are . . . bombarded by pictures not only of hopelessly unattainable images of idealized identities, but also of images of past and present suffering, images of destruction, of bodies quite literally in pieces. We ourselves are 'torn' in the process, not only emotionally and morally but in the fragmentary act of looking itself.[7]

By 1999, Jessica Evans and Stuart Hall sounded a similar theme: "'Visual culture' has been somewhat overlooked in the . . . expansion of cultural and media studies."[8]

Nonetheless, a review of the literature reveals that a visual, scholarly expansion has occurred in the last two to three decades. In part, this can be found in *American Journalism*, *American Periodicals*, *Journalism & Communication Monographs* and *Journalism History*. One of the earliest expressions of the visual expansion of scholarship came in 1977 when the journal *History of Photography* was born with an emphasis on nineteenth and early twentieth-century photography. *Visual Anthropology Review* started in 1985. Nine years later *Visual Communication Quarterly* arrived. Two other visual journals were founded in 2002: *Journal of Visual Culture* and *Visual Communication*.

Because this chapter does not allow for an in-depth discussion of the more than 300 books, articles and encyclopedia entries that have been identified and reviewed, some exemplars can highlight the substantial recent research about photography and illustration in magazines. The scholarship discussed here broadly includes *historical research*, *biographical studies*, *cultural communication*, *women as subject and photographer*, *agenda setting and gatekeeping* and *ethics and digital photojournalism*. By addressing these, the chapter suggests by reference the pathways in academy-magazine industry relations: how scholars could help magazines and their creators, producers and consumers and how magazines could help scholars who study issues surrounding creation, production and consumption.

Historical Research

A range of historical scholarship has dealt with photography and illustration, using both quantitative and qualitative approaches.[9] These include studies of the so-called Golden Age of consumer and trade magazines of the late nineteenth and early twentieth centuries.[10] Visual research has centered on longstanding magazines, such as *Scientific American* and *Harper's*,[11] and today's stalwarts of eye candy, such as *Cosmopolitan* and *Esquire*.[12] In addition, there increasingly have been studies of cartooning.[13]

Photography

Among the signal books is Alan Trachtenberg's *Reading American Photographs: Images as History, Mathew Brady to Walker Evans*. Trachtenberg has provided a template for thinking deeply about the visual.[14] Likewise, so has Susan Sontag in her *Regarding the Pain of Others*.[15] Bonnie Brennen and Hanno Hardt highlight how magazine photographs shape what and how we remember.[16] Photographic historian Mary Panzer in 2005 published a book that teased from curatorial legend John Szarkowski the comment to Panzer that, although he could be wrong, he believed that by 1955 photojournalism had been "on its last legs."[17] Panzer's book, *Things as They Are: Photojournalism in Context Since 1955*, disputes that. As evidence, the book offers 120 magazine picture stories made by a who's who of photographers.[18] Maria Pelizzari, in her review of the book, said, "Illustrated magazines still have a life, as they reinvent their layouts and messages for the contemporary visual culture, continuing to build a fragmentary, subjective, evocative archive of our visual history."[19]

Steidl in 2001 published a similar compendium, *Kiosk: A History of Photojournalism*, in German and English. With a dual, U.S. and European focus, the book reproduced facsimile spreads by photographers, such as Walker Evans and Robert Doisneau, from *Vogue, Life*, the [London] *Sunday Times Magazine, Look, Collier's, Picture Post, Match* and German serials, including *Berliner Illustrierte Zeitung* and *Die Woche*.[20]

Evocative of Walter Benjamin's predictions about photography in the age of mechanical reproduction, scholars have considered cultural history. With his concept of "unconscious optics," Benjamin highlighted photography as a doorway into the psychological and sociological realms of photograph, photographer and viewer. A full century after the medium's creation, Benjamin explained it this way: "The enlargement of a snapshot does not simply render more precise what in any case was visible, though unclear: it reveals entirely new structural formations of the subject. . . . The camera introduces us to unconscious optics as does psychoanalysis to unconscious impulses."[21] Peter Buse explored the dynamic of industrial uses of photography and aesthetics at Polaroid. The tensions between those poles were manifest in Polaroid's publications, its relationship with photographer Ansel Adams and *Aperture*.[22]

As much as any other scholar in recent years, Carolyn Kitch has contributed to our understanding of the visual representation of women and girls. She has marshaled evidence from *Rolling Stone, Ladies' Home Journal, Reader's Digest* and *Black Enterprise* to show the origins of stereotypes and how magazines influence memory and identity.[23]

Drawing from magazines in the United States and South Korea, Mim-Sun Kim analyzed the content of 400 photographs of magazine models and determined that models in advertisements in *Time, Newsweek* and *Good Housekeeping* and *Shin-Dong-Ah, Wol-Gan-Chason* and *Yeo-Sung-Jung-Ang* evidenced cultural differences via nonverbal cues. Indeed, Kim concluded from comparing the two countries' ads that international companies should tread lightly when developing standardized global ad campaigns.[24] In other ways, too, fashion magazine photography dating from the 1940s has received attention.[25]

As with research in other fields of mass communication, considerable work has brought to light African Americans' visual representation and, for example, how publications such as the *Crisis* became a site of contest over what constituted the proper image of African Americans.[26] Other examples include research about "brown diamond" models in periodicals, such as *Ebony*, that visually helped to define middle-class African American femininity.[27]

Tucked away in corners of *History of Photography* are insights into work practices and editing strategies, including this reference to famine photography of the late nineteenth century: "[T]he isolating of figures from their surroundings, the focus on the worst cases of suffering, the recurring depictions of women and children—can be found repeatedly in the many famine images, whether etchings or photographs, reproduced in serial publications."[28] *History of Photography* often contains analyses of photographers, such as Alfred Stieglitz and the Photo-Secession group, whose work appeared in the *Craftsman*.[29]

Representative of the innovative visual approaches scholars now are taking, Erik Palmer closely assessed magazine photographer Richard Avedon and "interrogate[d] the circumstances under which a photographic sequence might qualify as a pictorial metaphor." The detailed 2010 study drew from 16 Avedon books with 1,402 images and tested the claim "that Avedon's control of the selection, sequencing, and graphic design of his images comprised a self-aware means for construction and communication of knowledge."[30]

Cartoons

More so than prior to 1990, cartooning has received notice in the past decade and a half. For example, Martin Kuhn studied the late-nineteenth-century combining of art nouveau style with social and political satire in newspaper and magazine cartoons. Civil War–era illustrations of soldiers and draft riots in *Harper's Weekly* and *Leslie's Illustrated Newspaper*—both known for supporting Union involvement in the war—provided evidence of divergent views on the military draft.[31] Chris Lamb referenced Thomas Nast of *Harper's Weekly* and Joseph Keppler of *Puck* and how their biting cartoons captured the public imagination in the nineteenth century.[32] Additional research by Harlen Makemson has centered on Nast and Keppler's vilification of 1880s candidates.[33] The title of a 2009 study sums up a short-lived, Ohio cartoon magazine (1889–1891): "The *Light* that Failed: The History of an Unknown Magazine that Published the Work of a Galaxy of Emerging Stars."[34] Anne Magnussen's semiotics research into 1980s comics in an Argentinian magazine, in an era of the "disappearances" of political opponents, represented the expansion of cartooning scholarship.[35]

Illustrations

Although not as prominent as would be ideal, much research has centered on illustrations.[36] Four keystone, nineteenth-century magazines—*Harper's Weekly*, *Harper's Monthly*, *Scientific American* (Figure 25.1) and *Scribner's Monthly*—"used this new visual language [of illustrations] to posit their products as important commodities in the modern world."[37] Magazine readers were not only treated to illustrations of how factories made shoes, canned goods or sewing machines but were also provided illustrations of how magazines were made.[38] *Godey's*, *Graham's*, *Peterson's* and *Sartain's Union* commissioned illustrators to create images even before assigning a writer to fashion the text to accompany an illustration.[39] Using the work of Henry James, Amy Tucker drew from 120 illustrations to outline how magazines educated the tastes of nineteenth- and early twentieth-century readers.[40]

Helen Langa considered the unique status of the leftist *New Masses* in its use of reproductions of fine art, political cartoons and illustrations and how these combined with written text to deliver messages about social justice.[41] On the conservative end, iconic artist Norman Rockwell was the subject of Susan Herbst's *Political Communication* study that assessed his pictures in the *Saturday Evening Post* as the data set for public opinion analysis.[42] In a review of 1920s German popular press, Sherwin Simmons highlighted how photo-montages, collages and photo-caricature were used in advertisements, the illustrated press and humor magazines.[43] Meanwhile, research in Canada showed that *Chatelaine*, a women's magazine similar to *Ladies' Home Journal*, published illustrations in the 1920s and 1930s that "promoted maternal feminism" and created its visual appeal with "upbeat covers, illustrations, craft projects, and decorative features to be removed and manipulated or displayed."[44]

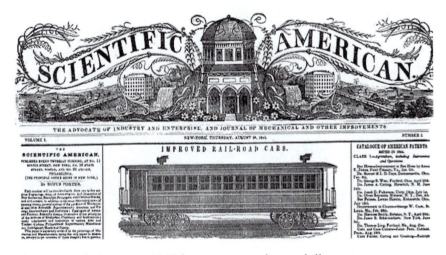

Figure 25.1. Scientific American, 1845 first issue nameplate and illustration.

A fuller portrait of the depictions of Native Americans emerged from John Coward's scholarship. He has argued that the pictorial journalism of nineteenth-century *Harper's Weekly* illustrator Theodore Davis contributed to public understanding of Native Americans and of the wars involving them.[45] A photograph of a sad Blackfoot Indian, "The Mourner," inspired another study.[46] In addition, research into 1870s illustrations of Chinese immigrant workers revealed that in some cases the pictures surprisingly were free of stereotypes.[47]

A fascinating subset of illustrations is that of World War II and Cold War era cartography in *Fortune* and *Life*. As a result of the "air age," that included the development of everything from helium balloons and zeppelins to rockets and satellites, sophisticated insights from global space allowed for more precise cartographic illustrations, presaging the twenty-first century's Google maps and global position systems.[48]

Biographical Studies

As rich as the Old Testament begats is the list of magazine photographers whose lives could be studied. Academics have highlighted elite photographers such as Diane Arbus, Margaret Bourke-White, Robert Capa, Dorothea Lange, Susan Mieseles, Peter Magubane and Mary Ellen Mark.[49] A far shorter list occurs with research on illustrators. Many an article, essay and book, however, has discussed photographer Walker Evans (Figure 25.2), whose images continue to be reprised. Evans contributed to what might be described as one of the least and the most successful magazine projects. *Fortune* in 1936 commissioned Evans and writer James Agee to document the Great Depression. *Fortune* then declined to print their story and photographs, but in 1941 Houghton Mifflin published them as *Let Us Now Praise Famous Men*. Initially, the book was a flop. Yet within two decades it captured public imagination, selling steadily ever since. Vibrant and haunting, Evans's photographs form a central statement about three Alabama sharecropper families. Later, from 1945 to 1965, with the title of Special Photographic Editor, Evans worked for *Fortune*. In the 1960s *Harper's Bazaar* published New York subway passenger photographs that Evans surreptitiously made in the 1930s and 1940s.[50] Other photographers who have received attention include Associated Press photographer Henry

Figure 25.2. Twentieth-century photographer Walker Evans.

D. Burroughs, whose work was featured on covers of *Life* and *Look*,[51] and longtime *Life* photographer Gordon Parks, the first African American to work for *Life*.[52] Also in extraordinary ways, Charles Moore's photographs of the civil rights movement, including ones in *Life*, riveted the world.[53]

Scholars have analyzed the work of war photojournalists who died in global conflicts. Dickey Chapelle, a "short, chain-smoking, gravel-voiced" photojournalist, was the first female correspondent to die in combat in Vietnam. Over the years, she worked for a half-dozen magazines, including *National Geographic*.[54] Two other photojournalists were in their thirties when they died during the 1980s political turmoil that tore through the heart of Central America. Richard Cross and John Hoagland were, David Levi Strauss asserted, "idealists who believed strongly in what they were doing."[55] Nominated for a Pulitzer for his Associated Press photographs of the Sandinista Revolution, Cross also worked for United Press International and Gamma-Liason. So did Hoagland. *Time, Newsweek*, the *Economist* and *U.S. News & World Report*, along with the *New York Times* and the *Los Angeles Times*, regularly published their photographs. Another noted war photographer was Carl Mydans.[56] In addition, Claude Cookman has detailed the 1960s work of Gilles Caron in the African ethnic violence in Biafra and the student rebellions of Paris. Cookman argued that Caron's "humanistic vision helped persuade western readers that the Biafrans were not merely pitiable, but deserving of help; that his thorough approach detailed the multiple dimensions of this complex political and humanitarian crisis."[57] Cookman also has researched Margaret Bourke-White,[58] who achieved many "firsts" and has received considerable attention as a woman magazine photojournalist. In his study of *National Geographic*'s senior editor Carolyn Bennett Patterson (1921–2003), Glenn Smith asserted that Patterson's "experiences were indicative of the successes and struggles of other women journalists and editors." She was known for her "groundbreaking work as editor of the *Geographic* legends, the captions that accompany the magazine's illustrations."[59]

History of Photography dutifully has recorded the passing of magazine photographers. Obituaries for Thomas Abercrombie of *National Geographic*[60] and Loomis Dean of *Life*[61] are examples of two of the many the journal has published in the last two decades, beginning with volume 14 in 1990.

Although few articles with a biographical focus can be found about illustrators, *American Periodicals* excellently filled a gap by profiling illustrator Albert Alexander Smith (1896–1940). Rhonda Reymond's study explored Smith as an African American illustrator "and ultimately his negotiation, revealed in his art, between overlapping and competing stratagems of selfhood open to African Americans in the 1920s."[62] His illustrations appeared in magazines such as *The Crisis* (National Association for Advancement of Colored People) and *Opportunity* (Congress of Racial Equality).

Cultural Communication

Photography throughout the years has both helped to define social and political struggles and been an outlet for cultures to define themselves in magazines. These include race, gender and identity studies and the theories buttressing them. Likewise, cultural communication research includes collective memory and nostalgia studies. In gender studies, a 1992 research anthology related to the construction of masculinity in the media included depictions in advertisements, comic books and magazines in general,[63] but few mass communication scholars have followed up. Researchers in Norway analyzed images and text in Norwegian forestry trade magazines, finding that the construction of masculinity had shifted from "macho-man" to a masculinity based on organizational skill and heavy machinery.[64] In a different vein, Arran Stibbe[65] and Paul Crawshaw[66] both analyzed the construction of masculinity in *Men's Health* through the discourse of text and images. Their findings diverge. Stibbe suggested a masculinity was constructed, in part visually, through behaviors that contradict good health, including drinking beer, eating convenience foods, and racking up sexual conquests. Crawshaw, on the other hand, suggested an ideal masculinity based on an improved lifestyle through individual choice.

Race and ethnicity scholars have centered on images created as early as the Civil War in the United States and as recently as the late twentieth and early twenty-first century wars in Iraq and Afghanistan. On 21 July 2008, a controversial *New Yorker* cover depicted then-candidate Barack Obama in a turban and *jellabiya* and fist-bumping with prospective First Lady Michelle Obama, who wore an Afro hairdo and carried an assault rifle. Shown as radical Islamists, they have taken over the White House where Osama bin Laden's portrait is above a fireplace. Below, the American flag burns. Related to this, Jasmine Cobb argued the United States had not truly entered a "post-racial" society even with the ascendency of African American Obama as presidential candidate.[67] Shawn Smith reiterates this fallacy of post-racialism in her discussion of covers featuring Obama, including a stylized 2008 *Time* cover that depicted his face as half-white and half-black.[68]

Following Foucault and Lacan, scholars have expanded on the concept of the gaze. Catherine Lutz and Jane Collins in *Reading National Geographic* used qualitative and quantitative techniques to assess the "intersection of gazes."[69] Their research inspired subsequent work, but was also critiqued. One reviewer suggested, "Ultimately, however, the history of the National Geographic Society and its monthly is more complicated than they allow."[70] In her *National Geographic* analysis, Tamar Rothenberg focused on the magazine's "strategies of innocence" as a method of reifying Western hegemony for the magazine's American readership.[71]

Researchers have broadened the idea of the gaze to include group, family and community photographs that represent not only an individual gaze but also a collective gaze. Leslie Tonkonow, referencing Barthes, speaks about this dynamic when she considers group portraiture as a *tableau vivant*, a living tableau that functions as if it were a primitive theatrical event, especially in fashion magazines.[72] In an engaging article on contemporary British life, John Hartley argued that innovative photographer Corinne Day presented her representations to the reading public not through photojournalism but through fashion photography in fashion magazines, creating a "national cultural imaginary."[73] Hartley asserted that photojournalism worked itself out of a job because of the medium's ubiquity. It no longer needed specialty publications and was instead incorporated into other periodical forms as they became more visual.[74] Okechukwu Nwafor made a similar argument about representations of contemporary life in Nigeria through fashion magazines.[75] In another tack, David Campbell took issue with photographic portrayals of famine in the *New York Times Magazine* but stopped short of a condemnation of reductionist and possibly racist stereotypes.[76]

The review of the literature identified several well-executed empirical studies on media representation, but those, unfortunately, do not include visual journalism in their analyses. In a special section, "Images and Stereotypes," in *Journalism & Mass Communication Quarterly*, for example, Angie Chuang and Robin Chin Roemer used key words from the visual lexicon, including *portrayal*, *representations* and *images*, in their inquiry on immigrant Muslims, but the study did not use visual materials as a unit of analysis.[77] Certainly not every study about representation needs to be visually rooted. That said, researchers are encouraged to identify areas of visual analysis that would complement text-based work. Together, scholarship on textual representation and visual representation can provide a more complete understanding of meaning-making in today's media landscape, particularly in strongly visual media, such as the magazine.

Women as Subject and Photographer

As gender studies have become more established in mass communication research in recent decades, scholars have used qualitative as well as quantitative approaches to focus on women as a subject and as photographers, in and for magazines. This section summarizes a few key studies in which scholars analyzed women as depicted in advertising and on magazine covers, or as photographers or editors working to produce images.

416

Woman as Subject

Women often are featured prominently—and provocatively—on covers of men's and women's magazines. As Carolyn Kitch has discussed in her account of the origins of visual stereotypes, cover images of women are intended to convey an ideal to help "form individual magazines' editorial identities."[78] This ideal for several decades was represented in illustration and later in photography, but the cover's role has not changed. Ellen McCracken similarly characterized the magazine cover as a "window to the future self" of readers.[79] McCracken argued that covers conjoin the "everyday and the extraordinary" through a combination of "visual images and headlines . . . [to] offer a complex semiotic system, communicating primary and secondary meanings, through language, photographs, images, color, and placement."[80]

In an ethnographic analysis of *Maxim* and other men's magazines in the 1990s and 2000s, Jacqueline Lambiase found that continued commodification of women's bodies on covers plays to a narrowly constructed, macho culture audience.[81] Sexualized magazine covers also served as the locus for an experiment to predict consumer responses. Tom Reichert and Shuhua Zhou discovered that the more sexualized covers predicted magazine interest and purchase intention, more sexual arousal and positive social comparison.[82] Perhaps not surprisingly, a content analysis of four decades of *Rolling Stone* covers revealed that men appeared three times as frequently as women, and women were more than twice as likely to be pictured nude or partially nude. More telling, though, was the finding that the number of women on *Rolling Stone* covers *has* increased over time, beginning an upward trend in the late 1990s after *Maxim* was first published.[83]

The striking and controversial image of the "Afghan Girl" on a 1985 cover of *National Geographic* was the subject of a visual rhetorical analysis, from which Rae Lynn Schwartz-DuPre identified six signifiers that constrained the possible interpretation of the image to reinforce the "universal victim category." Schwartz-DuPre argued this universal victim category would lead American readers to have sympathy for Afghanis and want to provide aid, with significant implications for foreign policy.[84]

Of course, women also appear frequently in advertising. In one of the earliest studies of advertisements in men's magazines, a team of researchers, using Goffman's frame analysis, found that although *Playboy* included more images of traditional representations of women's gender roles than did *Ms.* magazine, in the late 1980s this trend shifted to include greater numbers of advertisements that depicted men and women in equal roles.[85]

In another application of Goffman, Mee-Eun Kang found that images of women in magazine advertisements in 1991 had not changed significantly from those in Goffman's 1979 analysis: The 1991 advertisements continued to use traditional women stereotypes.[86] Though a final study employing Goffman did not reveal anything new about advertising portrayals of men and women, its most important contribution was methodological. Philip Bell and Marko Milic suggested that semiotic analysis can increase reliability and replicability when investigating representation, which, they argued, provides social and ideological significance.[87] Amy Aronson contextualized women's magazines by revisiting Naomi Wolf's *Beauty Myth*, arguing that advertisers were more likely to contest the *Beauty Myth* with campaigns featuring photographs of strong women than were the magazine's editorial pages that feature "fashion spreads with models whose rib cages were visible even from the distance of the runway."[88] Interestingly, C. Zoe Smith, Keith Greenwood and Hun Shik Kim concluded that various pairings of Pulitzer- and Pictures of the Year–winning photographs (many published in newsmagazines) reflected the world around us, although they did not include gender as an analysis category. Greenwood had included gender in an earlier study with a focus on Iran.[89]

Women in Combat

In an image study of female Israeli soldiers in American and Israeli magazines, Eva Berger and Dorit Naaman argued that the depictions followed dominant narrative frames for women in photographs: *direct gaze, taken from below, image taken out of context.* This worked to minimize the violence these women might face in their roles as combat soldiers because of the dual threat of women serving in combat: one, the threat to traditional notions of femininity, and two, the threat to core beliefs about the "masculine order of the military establishment."[90]

Images in eighteen newspapers and three magazines, including Web sites, became the data set for a content analysis by Susan Keith and Carol B. Schwalbe. Though the images that appeared in magazines were not distinguished from those in the newspapers, overall, Keith and Schwalbe found that women appeared in fewer than one-fifth of war-related images. Iraqi women appeared less frequently than U.S. women. The authors attributed this to news routines and to Orientalism[91]—defined by Edward Said as "a Western style for dominating, restructuring, and having authority over the Orient."[92]

Women in Politics

Although the title of her 1997 study refers to the "making of an image," Betty Winfield principally focused not on photographs or illustrations, but on verbal descriptions in two paragraphs devoted to the visual aspects of covering Hillary Rodham Clinton. They described television and still photographic conventions used while photographing the First Lady that portrayed her as dynamic and policy-oriented. In shooting an image for *Parade Magazine*, famed photographer Eddie Adams relied on traditional tropes, using a "typical First Lady pose: a seated position, hands in her lap, a pot of flowers behind her and a body leaned into the arm of the sofa."[93] In a qualitative content analysis of political women in the Swedish press, Åsa Kroon Lundell and Mats Ekström argued that gendering of women happens in a more complex manner than had been previously addressed. They argued this was because men dominate the press and visual culture in Sweden; that the press typecast women into princess, mad woman or witch; and that gendering depends upon the media relations between the political figure and the press.[94]

Woman as Photographer

A case study of a *New York Times Magazine* that featured 23 women photographers challenged the notion that by featuring the work of exclusively women photographers, readers would see a different perspective on women and power. Kimberly Sultze's findings suggested that was not the case. Instead, exclusively featuring the work of women photographers in the editorial content ignored mechanisms of magazine production that led to specific content, including advertising and the gatekeeping of editorial decision-making.[95] From her study, Sultze discovered "a persistent and recurring message. . . . women who are powerful should not call attention to it— that is, unless the source of their 'power' happens to be physical beauty and attractiveness."[96]

Claude Cookman made a contribution to the literature on *woman as subject and woman as photographer* in his research on photojournalist Janine Niépce, adding to our understanding of the woman photographer as insider. Niépce photographed ordinary French women, in contrast to most male photographers of her time who "[had] the habit of photographing beautiful women posing as models of high fashion, but rarely in the process of doing laundry."[97] As a magazine photographer, Niépce provided the only photographic lens through which the French women's movement could be seen from 1947 through 1968.[98] Dolores Flamiano investigated another overlooked woman photojournalist, Hansel Mieth, who, working for *Life* from the 1930s to 1950s, brought a humanistic touch to coverage of interned Japanese-Americans.[99]

In common, these photographers had a predilection to photograph social movements. Niépce's work reflected her desire to capture changes in tradition. Mieth was informed by her work as a migrant laborer in California after her immigration from Germany. If, as Niépce argued, men were busy shooting fashionable young women and women were shooting social movements, these two research projects offer a mandate for scholars to unearth other women magazine photographers obscured by the passage of time. Not only could future research reveal the history of the woman magazine photographer, but also an alternative view of social movements and the oppressed, enriching the understanding of social responsibility and photojournalism.

Agenda Setting and Gatekeeping

Photography can carry a bias and point of view. Photographers and editors who want their images to convey strong messages help to set the public and private agenda, bringing social and political issues to the fore. In an interview with then-incoming *National Geographic* Director of Photography Kent Kobersteen, Pete Souza provided insights into gatekeeping at one of the world's best-known publications for photography. Kobersteen described a multi-party process of crafting a visual story that included the photographer and Kobersteen himself, as well as the picture editor, the writer, the editor and other magazine managers. In other words, at *Geographic*, newsroom culture and routines influenced the photographic selection more than other gatekeeping factors.[100] Loup Langton provided a view of a slightly different process in his analysis at a newsmagazine. He described a more hierarchical culture, defined by top newsmagazine editors dictating what is news and how it is presented.[101] Further, because most newsmagazines are not as visually oriented as *Geographic* and most section editors come from writing, rather than a visual background, "words are generally favored over images."[102]

Other studies have centered on the problems editors and photographers face when they decide which photos are suitable. David Machin examined the role stock photo agencies play in transforming the visual language of magazines and newspapers.[103] He argued that the high technical quality of stock images contributes to their mass appeal and that the best-selling images reflect consumerist values, "removing reality from the image to create a harmonized world."[104] Machin further argued the market-oriented nature of the stock world shapes the work of photographers to come: "Photographers, in order to survive, will have to produce images that fit . . . these categories."[105]

Patrick Rössler and his colleagues undertook an empirical analysis of magazine photographs that led them to suggest a new theoretical approach to gatekeeping and magazine photography.[106] Rather than rely on a news value theory that is based on the text alone to understand how editors and journalists choose content, the authors urged researchers to consider a distinct news value theory for news photographs that is based not only on the communicator, but also on the message receiver as well. In a similar vein, David L. Perlmutter and Gretchen Wagner suggested adding icon analysis to better understand the role of news photographs, whether they appear in a newsmagazine or a newspaper. In their analysis of the photograph "a death in Genoa," from the 2001 G8 protests, they suggested an image functioned to represent the entire story of the death of the protestor by focusing on the moment of his provocative actions, rather than the moment the police force shot him or its aftermath. The latter photographs existed, but Western publications chose not to run them.[107]

In a meta-analysis of visual framing, Lulu Rodriguez and Daniela V. Dimitrova offered a four-tiered model for researchers to use.[108] They argue that visuals can be identified as *denotative* systems, *stylistic-semiotic* systems, *connotative* systems and *ideological* representations. This approach, they suggest, can help researchers by adding both "conceptual clarity and methodological rigor"[109] to visual framing scholarship.

Finally, magazines' photographic coverage of war has been an important research area, from the vulnerability of combatants and non-combatants to addressing the range of human responses, from compassion to atrocity. Research has considered the degree to which photographers have become involved with troops, long before the word "embedded" became part of the cultural lexicon.[110] Andrew Mendelson and C. Zoe Smith examined the relationship *Life* photographers had with the military during World War II, finding that despite the restrictions placed upon them, photographers had a fair amount of freedom.[111] That said, the censorship guidelines amounted to more than 200 pages, updated daily; running afoul of any of these guidelines could cost photographers their accreditation. Ultimately, though, the photographers and military were concerned with winning the war. The work of *Life*'s photographers reflected that.

In research about U.S. military conflicts in Libya, Panama and Grenada, Entman found that *Time* magazine opted not to include images of civilian deaths because, he argued, "to show as many pictures of dead civilians' bodies as of heroic U.S. armed forces would seem inappropriate to the elite consensus and reported mood of public celebration."[112] In a content analysis of 1,100 images from three newsmagazines,[113] Michael Griffin and Jongsoo Lee found that the scope of images presented was limited, and images of military weaponry and technology dominated. There were few images of loss of human life, political activity, cultural contexts or historical or geopolitical factors. Two separate studies of the recent wars in Afghanistan and Iraq showed similar trends: Magazine readers were not likely to see images of human casualties, enemy troops, Iraqi civilians or war-related activity in the United States,[114] and magazine photographers restricted themselves to the dominant narrative offered by the official government discourse.[115]

Finally, as noted earlier, Greenwood and Smith examined photographs from the Pictures of the Year competition, many of which first appeared in newsmagazines. They found that the award-winning photographs tended to depict Third World countries as war-torn and hostile and concluded the choices spoke to the values of contest judges who were themselves accomplished photographers and photo editors.[116]

Ethics and Digital Photojournalism

Closely related to issues of agenda setting and gatekeeping are questions surrounding ethics. Research in this area has highlighted photographers' and editors' treatment of images. The rise of digital technology has increased competition within photojournalism and added new ethical complications.[117] With the ability to *doctor photos* now a basic skill, studies have examined examples of photojournalistic tampering. Some have examined the ethics of showing details that subjects and audience consider private. Other studies have focused on the use of images in print advertising. In particular, these studies encompass illustration and ethics because of how images have been perceived when placed next to actual news photos. This section will look at selected examples of this research.

Scholars have addressed, if not at length at least in brief, a long list of ethical *faux pas* and digital manipulations in magazines: the *National Geographic*'s case of "shifting" the Egyptian pyramids to make a better-looking cover photograph in 1982,[118] *Time*'s changing the shadings of police booking photographs of celebrity O.J. Simpson when he was accused of murder in 1994; *TV Guide*'s putting television icon Oprah Winfrey's head on top of actress Ann-Margret's body, and *Chic* magazine's misrepresentation of its sexually-related purposes in obtaining the photograph of a swimsuit-wearing woman feeding a pig that was a performer at an amusement park.[119] Another ethical concern that has been studied relates to privacy and the paparazzi working for tabloids and celebrity magazines. One photographer said that celebrities "know the more they're in the magazines the more they get endorsements. . . . We're actually making them more money."[120]

In recent years considerable research has focused on the broader digital universe encompassing photography as well as the practice of digital manipulation, although much of the research has not centered on magazines.[121] However, in 2001 Edgar Shaohua Huang empirically examined the degree to which readers trust digital photography in newspapers and magazines.[122] Ten years prior, Christopher Harris interviewed newsmagazine photography editors about their opinions on manipulation.[123] Referencing examples from multiple magazines, Loup Langton tackled historical and contemporary ethical questions such as those that arose from images of Iraqi prisoners of war who were tormented by their soldier-captors from the United States. These images included a notable one of a hooded and robed prisoner with his arms outstretched and with wires attached to his body. The picture was among many not made by a photojournalist that were originally published in the *New Yorker*.[124] Beyond that, Langton also addressed how *People* and *Time* editors made cover selections based on the fact that not many readers of the magazines in the early 1990s were people of color.[125] Quoting Michael Carlebach, Langton said this approach of audience-influence was not new: In the early twentieth century, magazines "altered [photographs] in order to make them more palatable to the public or enhance their effect."[126]

Scholars such as Paul Martin Lester have explored how visual stereotypes can be harmful. In his book Lester quoted Dona Swartz, who wrote that visuals in parenting magazines "present hollow stereotypes . . . of blissful, predominantly Anglo, dual-parent childrearing."[127] Julianne H. Newton in her 2001 book, *The Burden of Visual Truth: The Role of Photojournalism in Mediating Reality*, detailed the layers of how individuals caught in the maelstrom of public events lose privacy and become public icons as part of "the ambiguous flow of relationships involving a media image of a real person."[128] Newton looked longitudinally at the photographing of Kim Phuc, who burst into the global media consciousness in 1972 when she was nine years old. Associated Press photographer Nick Ut won a Pulitzer Prize for the picture he took of her running naked and screaming in pain on a road in South Vietnam after napalm had burned her.[129]

Conclusion

Although barriers to research on photography and illustrations in magazines still exist, digitization now makes scholarship easier. Compare searching through the decades of the entire digital runs now available of *Life* magazine, the *New Yorker* or *Harper's* to what Frank Luther Mott undertook in the early and mid-twentieth century to produce his five volumes of *A History of American Magazines*.[130] However, even with nimble digital tools, it is not unusual to find a study on *Rolling Stone*, for example, that details the intertwined relationship between the Beatles and the alternative magazine, yet essentially ignores the photographs and illustrations of Annie Leibovitz and cartoonist Ralph Steadman.[131]

Even though he was not specifically discussing magazines, photographic historian Geoffrey Batchen raised an essential question about global digital context, its pervasive influence and the conundrum of how to engage in visual scholarship. He set this stage: In January 2012, Eastman Kodak went bankrupt while Facebook became a publicly traded company worth $100 billion. Three million photographs were being uploaded onto Facebook daily, for a total of 140 billion images on the site. The White House was releasing its official photographs onto Flickr. Batchen asked: "How can anyone examine a representative sample of contemporary photographic practice in the face of such overwhelming statistics?"[132] To that we would say the following: The original Arabic source of the word *magazine* suggests "a storehouse." Today, that means an ever-expanding storehouse, on-line and in print—ripe for further research, ripe for theoretical expansion and practical insights.[133]

Notes

1 Micheal Brown, "The Popular Art of American Magazine Illustration 1885–1917," *Journalism History* 24.3 (Autumn 1998): 94.

2 Claude Cookman, "Janine Niépce's Coverage of French Women's Lives and Struggle for Equal Rights," *Visual Communication Quarterly* 13.4 (2006): 202–223.

3 Gyong Ho Kim and Anna R. Paddon, "Digital Manipulation as New Form of Evidence of Actual Malice in Libel and False Light Cases," *Communications & the Law* 21.3 (September 1999): 57.

4 Victor Burgin, ed., *Thinking Photography* (London: Macmillan, 1982), 1.

5 Alan Trachtenberg, ed., *Classic Essays on Photography* (New Haven: Leete's Island Books, 1980), xiii. Trachtenberg's emphasis.

6 Trachtenberg, *Classic Essays on Photography*, xiii. Trachtenberg's emphasis.

7 Victor Burgin, "Paranoiac Space," in Lucien Taylor, ed., *Visualizing Theory: Selected Essays from V.A.R. 1990–1994* (New York and London: Routledge, 1994), 232.

8 Jessica Evans and Stuart Hall, eds., *Visual Culture: The Reader* (London, Thousand Oaks and New Delhi: Sage Publications, 1999), 1.

9 Berkley Hudson, "Photojournalists," *Encyclopedia of Journalism* (Thousand Oaks, CA: Sage Publications, 2009).

10 Amanda Hinnant and Berkley Hudson, "The Magazine Revolution, 1880–1920," in Christine Bold, ed., *The Oxford History of U.S. Popular Print Culture: 1860–1920*, vol. 6 (New York: Oxford University Press, 2012), 113–131.

11 Vanessa Meikle Schulman, "'Making the Magazine': Visuality, Managerial Capitalism, and the Mass Production of Periodicals, 1865–1890," *American Periodicals* 22.1 (2012): 1–28.

12 David Machin and Joanna Thornborrow, "Branding and Discourse: The Case of *Cosmopolitan*," *Discourse & Society* 14.4 (2003): 453–471; Richard H. Kolbe and Paul J. Albanese, "Man to Man: A Content Analysis of Sole-Male Images in Male-Audience Magazines," *Journal of Advertising* 25.4 (Winter 1996): 1–20.

13 Martin Kuhn, "Drawing Civil War Soldiers," *Journalism History* 32.2 (Summer 2006): 96–105; Chris Lamb, *Drawn to Extremes: The Use and Abuse of Editorial Cartoons* (New York: Columbia University Press, 2004); Anne Magnussen, "Imagining the Dictatorship, Argentina 1981 to 1982," *Visual Communication* 5.3 (October 2006): 323–344; Harlen Makemson, "One Misdeed Evokes Another: How Political Cartoonists Used 'Scandal Intertextuality' against Presidential Candidate James G. Blaine," *Media History Monographs* 7.2 (2004/2005): 1–20.

14 Alan Trachtenberg, *Reading American Photographs: Images as History, Mathew Brady to Walker Evans* (New York: Hill and Wang, 1989).

15 Susan Sontag, *Regarding the Pain of Others* (New York: Farrar, Straus and Giroux, 2003).

16 Bonnie Brennen and Hanno Hardt, eds., *Picturing the Past: Media, History, and Photography* (Urbana: University of Illinois Press, 1999); see also, Bonnie S. Brennen, "From Headline Shooter to Picture Snatcher: The Construction of Photojournalists in American Film, 1928–39," *Journalism* 5.4 (November 2004): 423–439.

17 Mary Panzer, *Things as They Are: Photojournalism in Context since 1955* (New York: Aperture, 2005), 9.

18 Panzer, *Things as They Are*.

19 Maria Antonella Pelizzari, "Photojournalism as Contemporary Artefact," Review of *Things as They Are: Photojournalism in Context since 1955*, by Mary Panzer, *History of Photography* 31.3 (Autumn 2007): 311.

20 Robert Lebeck and Bodo von Dewitz, *Kiosk: A History of Photojournalism* (Göttingen: Steidl, 2001); see also Anne H. Hoy, *The Book of Photography: The History, the Technique, the Art, the Future* (Washington, DC: National Geographic Society, 2005).

21 Walter Benjamin, *Illuminations*, ed. with Introduction by Hannah Arendt, trans. Harry Zorn (London: Pimlico, 1999), 229–230.

22 Peter Buse, "Polaroid, *Aperture* and Ansel Adams: Rethinking the Industry-Aesthetics Divide," *History of Photography* 33.4 (November 2009): 354–369. See also, Peter Buse, "The Polaroid Image as Photo-Object," *Journal of Visual Culture* 9.2 (August 2009): 189–207.

23 Carolyn Kitch, *The Girl on the Magazine Cover: The Origins of Visual Stereotypes in American Mass Media* (Chapel Hill and London: University of North Carolina Press, 2001); Carolyn Kitch, *Pages from the Past: History and Memory in American Magazines* (Chapel Hill: University of North Carolina Press, 2005).

24 Mim-Sun Kim, "A Comparative Analysis of Nonverbal Expressions as Portrayed by Korean and American Print-Media Advertising," *Howard Journal of Communications* 3.3/4 (Winter/Spring 1992): 317–339.

25 Antje Krause-Wahl, "Between Studio and Catwalk—Artists in Fashion Magazines," *Fashion Theory: The Journal of Dress, Body & Culture* 13.1 (March 2009): 7–27; Philip Charrier, "On Diane Arbus: Establishing a Revisionist Framework of Analysis," *History of Photography* 36.4 (November 2012): 422–438.

26 Megan E. Williams, "The *Crisis* Cover Girl: Lena Horne, the NAACP, and Representations of African American Femininity, 1941–1945," *American Periodicals* 16.2 (2006): 200–218.

27 Laila Haidarali, "Polishing Brown Diamonds: African American Women, Popular Magazines, and the Advent of Modeling in Early Postwar America," *Journal of Women's History* 17.1 (2005): 10–37.

28 Deborah Hutton, "Raja Deen Dayal and Sons: Photographing Hyderabad's Famine Relief Efforts," *History of Photography* 31.3 (2007): 263; Joyce Tsai, "*Der Kuckuck* and the Problem of Workers' Photography in Austria," *History of Photography* 29.3 (2005): 275–286.

29 Christian A. Peterson, "American Arts and Crafts: The Photograph Beautiful, 1895–1915," *History of Photography* 16.3 (Autumn 1992): 189–232.

30 Erik Palmer, "How to Read Richard Avedon," *Visual Communication Quarterly* 17.3 (July/September 2010): 147, 149.

31 Kuhn, "Drawing Civil War Soldiers."

32 Lamb, *Drawn to Extremes*, 51.

33 Makemson, "One Misdeed Evokes Another."

34 Richard Samuel West, "The *Light* that Failed: The History of an Unknown Magazine that Published the Work of a Galaxy of Emerging Stars," *American Periodicals* 19.2 (September 2009): 189–212.

35 Magnussen, "Imagining the Dictatorship."

36 Brown, "The Popular Art of American Magazine Illustration 1885–1917," 94.

37 Schulman, "'Making the Magazine,'" 2.

38 Schulman, "'Making the Magazine.'"

39 Cynthia Patterson, "'Illustration of a Picture': Nineteenth-Century Writers and the Philadelphia Pictorials," *American Periodicals* 19.2 (2009): 136–164.

40 Amy Tucker, *The Illustration of the Master: Henry James and the Magazine Revolution* (Stanford, CA: Stanford University Press, 2010).

41 Helen Langa, "'At Least Half the Pages Will Consist of Pictures': *New Masses* and Politicized Visual Art," *American Periodicals* 21.1 (2011): 24–49.

42 Susan Herbst, "Illustrator, American Icon, and Public Opinion Theorist: Norman Rockwell in Democracy," *Political Communication* 21.1 (2004): 1–25.

43 Sherwin Simmons, "Photo-Caricature in the German Popular Press, 1920," *History of Photography* 20.3 (Autumn 1996): 258–264.

44 Jaleen Grove, "A Castle of One's Own: Interactivity in *Chatelaine Magazine*, 1928–35," *Journal of Canadian Studies/Revue d'études canadiennes* 45.3 (Fall 2011): 166.

45 John M. Coward, "Making Images on the Indian Frontier," *Journalism History* 36.3 (Fall 2010): 150–159; see also, John M. Coward, "Making Sense of Savagery: Native American Cartoons in *The Daily Graphic*," *Visual Communication Quarterly* 19.4 (December 2012): 200–215; John M. Coward, "Promoting the Progressive Indian: Lee Harkins and *The American Indian Magazine*," *American Journalism* 14.1 (1997): 3–18.

46 Janet Dewan, "The Mourner: 'Red Man's Memories,'" *History of Photography* 15.2 (Summer 1991): 135–139.

47 Mary M. Cronin and William E. Huntzicker, "Popular Chinese Images and 'the Coming Man' of 1870: Racial Representations of Chinese," *Journalism History* 38.2 (Summer 2012): 86–99.

48 Timothy Barney, "Richard Edes Harrison and the Cartographic Perspective of Modern Internationalism," *Rhetoric & Public Affairs* 15.3 (Fall 2012): 397–433.

49 Darren Newbury, "Johannesburg Lunch-Hour 1951–1963," *Journalism Studies* 8.4 (August 2007): 584–594; Charrier, "On Diane Arbus: Establishing a Revisionist Framework of Analysis."

50 James R. Mellow, *Walker Evans* (New York: Basic Books, 1999).

51 Henry D. Burroughs, *Close-Ups of History: Three Decades through the Lens of an AP Photographer*, ed., with Introduction by Margaret Wohlgemuth Burroughs (Columbia: University of Missouri Press, 2007).

52 "Obituaries: Gordon Parks (1912–2006)," *History of Photography* 30.3 (Autumn 2006): 283–284.

53 John Kaplan, "The *Life* Magazine Civil Rights Photography of Charles Moore 1958–1965," *Journalism History* 25.4 (Winter 1999/2000): 126.

54 Zoe Smith, "Dickey Chapelle: Pioneer in Combat," *Visual Communication Quarterly* 1.2 (April 1994): 5.

55 David Levi Strauss, *Between the Eyes: Essays on Photography and Politics* (New York: Aperture, 2003), 12.

56 Darwin Marable, "Carl Mydans: An Interview," *History of Photography* 26.1 (2002): 47–52.

57 Claude Cookman, "Gilles Caron's Coverage of the Crisis in Biafra," *Visual Communication Quarterly* 15.4 (2008): 227; Claude Cookman, "Gilles Caron and the May 1968 Rebellion in Paris," *History of Photography* 31.3 (Autumn 2007): 239–259.

58 Claude Cookman, "*Life* Visits 'Middletown': Trying to Repair America's Social Contract with Margaret Bourke-White's Photographs," *Visual Communication Quarterly* 18.4 (October/December 2011): 204–222.

59 Glenn D. Smith, Jr., "'You Can Do Anything': The Agendas of Carolyn Bennett Patterson, *National Geographic's* First Woman Senior Editor," *Journalism History* 37.4 (Winter 2012): 190.

60 "Obituaries: Thomas J. Abercrombie (1931–2006)," *History of Photography* 30.3 (Autumn 2006): 283.

61 "Obituaries: Loomis Dean (1917–2005)," *History of Photography* 30.2 (Summer 2006): 185.

62 Rhonda L. Reymond, "Looking In: Albert A. Smith's Use of *Repoussoir* in Cover Illustrations for the *Crisis* and *Opportunity*," *American Periodicals* 20.2 (2010): 216.

63 Steve Craig, ed., *Men, Masculinity, and the Media*, Research on Men and Masculinities Series, edited by Michael S. Kimmel, vol. 1 (Newbury, CA: Sage Publications, 1992).

64 Berit Brandth and Marit S. Haugen, "From Lumberjack to Business Manager: Masculinity in the Norwegian Forestry Press," *Journal of Rural Studies* 16.3 (2000): 343.

65 Arran Stibbe, "Health and the Social Construction of Masculinity in *Men's Health* Magazine," *Men and Masculinities* 7.1 (July 2004): 31–51.

66 Paul Crawshaw, "Governing the Healthy Male Citizen: Men, Masculinity and Popular Health in *Men's Health* Magazine," *Social Science & Medicine* 65.8 (October 2007): 1606–1618.

67 Jasmine Nichole Cobb, "No We Can't!: Postracialism and the Popular Appearance of a Rhetorical Fiction," *Communication Studies* 62.4 (September/October 2011): 406.

68 Shawn Michelle Smith, "Obama's Whiteness," *Journal of Visual Culture* 8.2 (August 2009): 129–133.

69 Catherine A. Lutz and Jane L. Collins, *Reading* National Geographic (Chicago and London: University of Chicago Press, 1993), 187–216.

70 Susan Schulten, "The Perils of *Reading National Geographic*," *Reviews in American History* 23.3 (1995): 521.

71 Tamar Y. Rothenberg, *Presenting America's World: Strategies of Innocence in* National Geographic Magazine, *1888–1945* (Aldershot, UK and Burlington, VT: Ashgate, 2007).

72 Leslie Tonkonow, *Multiple Exposure: The Group Portrait in Photography* (New York: Independent Curators, 1995), 10.

73 John Hartley, "Documenting Kate Moss," *Journalism Studies* 8.4 (2007): 555.

74 Hartley, "Documenting Kate Moss," 555–565.

75 Okechukwu Nwafor, "Of *Mutuality* and *Copying*: Fashioning *Aso Ebi* through Fashion Magazines in Lagos," *Fashion Theory: The Journal of Dress, Body & Culture* 16.4 (December 2012): 493–520.

76 David Campbell, "The Iconography of Famine," in Geoffrey Batchen, Mick Gidley, Nancy K. Miller, and Jay Prosser, eds., *Picturing Atrocity: Photography in Crisis* (London, UK: Reaktion Books, 2012), 79–91.

77 Angie Chuang and Robin Chin Roemer, "The Immigrant Muslim American at the Boundary of Insider and Outsider: Representations of Faisal Shahzad as 'Homegrown' Terrorist," *Journalism & Mass Communication Quarterly* 90.1 (Spring 2013): 89–107.

78 Kitch, *The Girl on the Magazine Cover*, 5.

79 Ellen McCracken, *Decoding Women's Magazines: From* Mademoiselle *to* Ms. (Basingstoke, UK: Macmillan, 1993), 14.

80 McCracken, *Decoding Women's Magazines*, 13.

81 Jacqueline Lambiase, "Promoting Sexy Images: Case Study Scrutinizes *Maxim's* Cover Formula for Building Quick Circulation and Challenging Competitors," *Journal of Promotion Management* 13.1/2 (2007): 111.

82 Tom Reichert and Shuhua Zhou, "Consumer Responses to Sexual Magazine Covers on a Men's Magazine," *Journal of Promotion Management* 13.1/2 (January 2007): 127.

83 Jacqueline Lambiase and Tom Reichert, "Sex and the Marketing of Contemporary Consumer Magazines: How Men's Magazines Sexualized Their Covers to Compete with *Maxim*," in Tom Reichert and Jacqueline Lambiase, eds., *Sex in Consumer Culture: The Erotic Content of Media and Marketing* (Mahwah, NJ: Lawrence Erlbaum Associates, 2006), 69.

84 Rae Lynn Schwartz-DuPre, "Portraying the Political: *National Geographic's* 1985 Afghan Girl and a U.S. Alibi for Aid," *Critical Studies in Media Communication* 27.4 (October 2010): 351.

85 Michael L. Klassen, Cynthia R. Jasper, and Anne M. Schwartz, "Men and Women: Images of Their Relationships in Magazine Advertisements," *Journal of Advertising Research* 33.2 (March/April 1993): 30–39.

86 Mee-Eun Kang, "The Portrayal of Women's Images in Magazine Advertisements: Goffman's Gender Analysis Revisited," *Sex Roles* 37.11/12 (December 1997): 979–996.

87 Philip Bell and Marko Milic, "Goffman's Gender Advertisements Revisited: Combining Content Analysis with Semiotic Analysis," *Visual Communication* 1.2 (June 2002): 203–222.

88 Amy Beth Aronson, "Still Reading Women's Magazines: Reconsidering the Tradition a Half Century after *The Feminine Mystique*," *American Journalism* 27.2 (Spring 2010): 46.

89 Keith Greenwood and C. Zoe Smith, "How the World Looks to Us," *Journalism Practice* 1.1 (January 2007): 82–101; Hun Shik Kim and C. Zoe Smith, "Sixty Years of Showing the World to America: Pulitzer Prize Photographs, 1942–2002," *International Communication Gazette* 67.4 (August 2005): 307–323; and Keith Greenwood, "Picturing Defiance: Visions of Democracy in Iran," *International Communication Gazette* 74.7 (November 2012): 619–635.

90 Eva Berger and Dorit Naaman, "Combat Cuties: Photographs of Israeli Women Soldiers in the Press since the 2006 Lebanon War," *Media, War & Conflict* 4.3 (December 2011): 282.

91 Susan Keith and Carol B. Schwalbe, "Women and Visual Depictions of the U.S.-Iraq War in Print and Online Media," *Visual Communication Quarterly* 17.1 (January/March 2010): 4–17.

92 Edward Said, *Orientalism* (New York: Vintage Books, 1979), 3.

93 Berry Houchin Winfield, "The Making of an Image: Hillary Rodham Clinton and American Journalists," *Political Communication* 14 (1997): 245.

94 Åsa Kroon Lundell and Mats Ekström, "The Complex Visual Gendering of Political Women in the Press," *Journalism Studies* 9.6 (2008): 891–910.

95 Kimberly Sultze, "Women, Power, and Photography in the *New York Times Magazine*," *Journal of Communication Inquiry* 27.3 (July 2003): 274.

96 Sultze, "Women, Power, and Photography in the *New York Times Magazine*," 287.

97 Cookman, "Janine Niépce's Coverage of French Women's Lives," 203.

98 Cookman, "Janine Niépce's Coverage of French Women's Lives," 202–223.

99 Dolores Flamiano, "Too Human for Life: Hansel Mieth's Photographs of Heart Mountain Internment Camp," *Visual Communication Quarterly* 11.3/4 (Summer/Autumn 2004): 4–17.

100 Pete Souza, "Kent Kobersteen: The New Director of Photography at *National Geographic*," *Visual Communication Quarterly* 5.3 (Summer 1998): 3–8.

101 Loup Langton, *Photojournalism and Today's News: Creating Visual Reality* (Chichester, UK: Wiley-Blackwell), 2009.

102 Langton, *Photojournalism and Today's News*, 96.

103 David Machin, "Building the World's Visual Language: The Increasing Global Importance of Image Banks in Corporate Media," *Visual Communication* 3.3 (October 2004): 316–336.

104 Machin, "Building the World's Visual Language," 335.

105 Machin, "Building the World's Visual Language," 335.

106 Patrick Rössler, Jana Bomhoff, Josef Ferdinand Haschke, Jan Kersten, and Rüdiger Müller, "Selection and Impact of Press Photography: An Empirical Study on the Basis of Photo News Factors," *Communications: The European Journal of Communication Research* 36.4 (November 2011): 415–439.

107 David D. Perlmutter and Gretchen L. Wagner, "The Anatomy of a Photojournalistic Icon: Marginalization of Dissent in the Selection and Framing of 'a Death in Genoa,'" *Visual Communication* 3.1 (February 2004): 91–108.

108 Lulu Rodriguez and Daniela V. Dimitrova, "The Levels of Visual Framing," *Journal of Visual Literacy* 30.1 (Spring 2011): 48–65.

109 Rodriguez and Dimitrova, "The Levels of Visual Framing," 61.

110 Michael Pfau, Michel Haigh, Mitchell Gettle, Michael Donnelly, Gregory Scott, Dana Warr, and Elaine Wittenberg, "Embedding Journalists in Military Combat Units: Impact on Newspaper Story Frames and Tone," *Journalism & Mass Communication Quarterly* 81.1 (Spring 2004): 74–88.

111 Andrew Mendelson, and C. Zoe Smith, "Part of the Team: *Life* Photographers and Their Symbiotic Relationship with the Military during World War II," *American Journalism* 12.3 (1995): 276–289.

112 Robert M. Entman, *Projections of Power: Framing News, Public Opinion, and U.S. Foreign Policy* (Chicago: University of Chicago Press, 2004), 60.

113 Michael Griffin and Jongsoo Lee, "Picturing the Gulf War: Constructing an Image of War in *Time, Newsweek*, and *U.S. News & World Report*," *Journalism & Mass Communication Quarterly* 72.4 (Winter 1995): 813–825.

114 Susan Keith, Carol B. Schwalbe, and B. William Silcock, "Visualizing Cross-Media Coverage: Picturing War across Platforms during the U.S.-Led Invasion of Iraq," *Atlantic Journal of Communication* 17.1 (January/March 2009): 1–18.

115 Michael Griffin, "Picturing America's 'War on Terrorism' in Afghanistan and Iraq: Photographic Motifs as News Frames," *Journalism* 5.4 (November 2004): 381–402.

116 Greenwood and Smith, "How the World Looks to Us," 82–101.

117 Shiela Reaves, "Digital Alteration of Photographs in Consumer Magazines," *Journal of Mass Media Ethics* 6.3 (September 1991): 175.

118 Edwin Martin, "On Photographic Manipulation," *Journal of Mass Media Ethics* 6.3 (1991): 160.

119 Kim and Paddon, "Digital Manipulation as New Form of Evidence of Actual Malice," 57–73.

120 Ray Murray, "Stalking the Paparazzi: A View from a Different Angle," *Visual Communication Quarterly* 18.1 (January 2011): 12.

121 Paul Cobley and Nick Haeffner, "Digital Cameras and Domestic Photography: Communication, Agency and Structure," *Visual Communication* 8.2 (May 2009): 123–146; Edgar Shaohua Huang, "Where Do You Draw the Line?" *Visual Communication Quarterly* 7.4 (2000): 4–16; Susan Murray, "Digital Images, Photo-Sharing, and Our Shifting Notions of Everyday Aesthetics," *Journal of Visual Culture* 7.2 (2008): 147–163.

122 Edgar Shaohua Huang, "Readers' Perception of Digital Alteration in Photojournalism," *Journalism & Communication Monographs* 3.3 (Autumn 2001): 147–182.

123 Christopher R. Harris, "Digitization and Manipulation of News Photographs," *Journal of Mass Media Ethics* 6.3 (1991): 164.

124 Langton, *Photojournalism and Today's News*.

125 Langton, *Photojournalism and Today's News*, 128.

126 Langton, *Photojournalism and Today's News*, 142.

127 Paul Martin Lester, *Images that Injure: Pictorial Stereotypes in the Media* (Westport, CT: Praeger, 1996), 77.

128 Julianne H. Newton, *The Burden of Visual Truth: The Role of Photojournalism in Mediating Reality* (Mahwah, NJ: Lawrence Erlbaum, 2001), 149.

129 Newton, *Burden of Visual Truth*, 148–172.

130 See, for example, Frank Luther Mott, A *History of American Magazines 1850–1865*, vol. 2 (Cambridge, MA: The Belknap Press, 1938).

131 Michael R. Frontani, "'Beatlepeople': Gramsci, the Beatles, and *Rolling Stone* Magazine," *American Journalism* 19.3 (2002): 39–45.

132 Geoffrey Batchen, "Observing by Watching: Joachim Schmid and the Art of Exchange," *Aperture*, Spring 2013, 46.

133 Acknowledgments: The authors thank University of Missouri Discovery Fellows Andrew Beasley, Shelby Rees and Zachary Reger, along with research assistants Christopher Long and Yan F. Wu.

Bibliography

Aronson, Amy Beth. "Still Reading Women's Magazines: Reconsidering the Tradition a Half Century after *The Feminine Mystique*." *American Journalism* 27.2 (Spring 2010): 31–61.

Barney, Timothy. "Richard Edes Harrison and the Cartographic Perspective of Modern Internationalism." *Rhetoric & Public Affairs* 15.3 (Fall 2012): 397–433.

Batchen, Geoffrey. "Observing by Watching: Joachim Schmid and the Art of Exchange." *Aperture*, Spring 2013, 46–49.

Bell, Philip and Milic, Marko. "Goffman's Gender Advertisements Revisited: Combining Content Analysis with Semiotic Analysis." *Visual Communication* 1.2 (June 2002): 203–222.

Benjamin, Walter. *Illuminations*. Edited with Introduction by Hannah Arendt. Translated by Harry Zorn. London: Pimlico, 1999.

Berger, Eva and Naaman, Dorit. "Combat Cuties: Photographs of Israeli Women Soldiers in the Press since the 2006 Lebanon War." *Media, War & Conflict* 4.3 (December 2011): 269–286.

Brandth, Berit and Haugen, Marit S. "From Lumberjack to Business Manager: Masculinity in the Norwegian Forestry Press." *Journal of Rural Studies* 16.3 (2000): 343–355.

Brennen, Bonnie S. "From Headline Shooter to Picture Snatcher: The Construction of Photojournalists in American Film, 1928–39." *Journalism* 5.4 (November 2004): 423–439.

Brennen, Bonnie and Hardt, Hanno, eds. *Picturing the Past: Media, History, and Photography*. Urbana: University of Illinois Press, 1999.

Brown, Micheal. "The Popular Art of American Magazine Illustration 1885–1917." *Journalism History* 24.3 (Autumn 1998): 94–103. Editor's Note: Article carries name spelled as Micheal; correct spelling is Michael).

Burgin, Victor. "Paranoiac Space." In Taylor, Lucien, ed. *Visualizing Theory: Selected Essays from V.A.R., 1990–1994*. New York and London: Routledge, 1994, 230–241.

Burgin, Victor, ed. *Thinking Photography*. London: Macmillan, 1982.

Burroughs, Henry D. *Close-Ups of History: Three Decades through the Lens of an AP Photographer*. Edited with Introduction by Margaret Wohlgemuth Burroughs. Columbia: University of Missouri Press, 2007.

Buse, Peter. "Polaroid, *Aperture* and Ansel Adams: Rethinking the Industry-Aesthetics Divide." *History of Photography* 33.4 (November 2009): 354–369.

Buse, Peter. "The Polaroid Image as Photo-Object." *Journal of Visual Culture* 9.2 (August 2009): 189–207.

Campbell, David. "The Iconography of Famine." In Batchen, Geoffrey; Gidley, Mick; Miller, Nancy K.; and Prosser, Jay, eds. *Picturing Atrocity: Photography in Crisis*. London: Reaktion Books, 2012, 79–91.

Charrier, Philip. "On Diane Arbus: Establishing a Revisionist Framework of Analysis." *History of Photography* 36.4 (November 2012): 422–438.

Chuang, Angie and Roemer, Robin Chin. "The Immigrant Muslim American at the Boundary of Insider and Outsider: Representations of Faisal Shahzad as 'Homegrown' Terrorist." *Journalism & Mass Communication Quarterly* 90.1 (Spring 2013): 89–107.

Cobb, Jasmine Nichole. "No We Can't!: Postracialism and the Popular Appearance of a Rhetorical Fiction." *Communication Studies* 62.4 (September/October 2011): 406–421.

Cobley, Paul and Haeffner, Nick. "Digital Cameras and Domestic Photography: Communication, Agency and Structure." *Visual Communication* 8.2 (May 2009): 123–146.

Cookman, Claude. "Gilles Caron and the May 1968 Rebellion in Paris." *History of Photography* 31.3 (Autumn 2007): 239–259.

Cookman, Claude. "Gilles Caron's Coverage of the Crisis in Biafra." *Visual Communication Quarterly* 15.4 (2008): 226–242.

Cookman, Claude. "Janine Niépce's Coverage of French Women's Lives and Struggle for Equal Rights." *Visual Communication Quarterly* 13.4 (2006): 202–223.

Cookman, Claude. "*Life* Visits 'Middletown': Trying to Repair America's Social Contract with Margaret Bourke-White's Photographs." *Visual Communication Quarterly* 18.4 (October/December 2011): 204–222.

Coward, John M. "Making Images on the Indian Frontier." *Journalism History* 36.3 (Fall 2010): 150–159.

Coward, John M. "Making Sense of Savagery: Native American Cartoons in *The Daily Graphic*." *Visual Communication Quarterly* 19.4 (December 2012): 200–215.

Coward, John M. "Promoting the Progressive Indian: Lee Harkins and *The American Indian Magazine*." *American Journalism* 14.1 (1997): 3–18.

Craig, Steve, ed. *Men, Masculinity, and the Media*. Research on Men and Masculinities Series. Edited by Michael S. Kimmel. Vol. 1. Newbury, CA: Sage Publications, 1992.

Crawshaw, Paul. "Governing the Healthy Male Citizen: Men, Masculinity and Popular Health in *Men's Health* Magazine." *Social Science & Medicine* 65.8 (October 2007): 1606–1618.

Cronin, Mary M. and Huntzicker, William E. "Popular Chinese Images and 'the Coming Man' of 1870: Racial Representations of Chinese." *Journalism History* 38.2 (Summer 2012): 86–99.

Dewan, Janet. "The Mourner: 'Red Man's Memories.'" *History of Photography* 15.2 (Summer 1991): 135–139.

Entman, Robert M. *Projections of Power: Framing News, Public Opinion, and U.S. Foreign Policy*. Chicago: University of Chicago Press, 2004.

Evans, Jessica and Hall, Stuart, eds. *Visual Culture: The Reader*. London, Thousand Oaks and New Delhi: Sage Publications, 1999.

Flamiano, Dolores. "Too Human for Life: Hansel Mieth's Photographs of Heart Mountain Internment Camp." *Visual Communication Quarterly* 11.3/4 (Summer/Autumn 2004): 4–17.

Frontani, Michael R. "'Beatlepeople': Gramsci, the Beatles, and *Rolling Stone* Magazine." *American Journalism* 19.3 (2002): 39–61.

Greenwood, Keith. "Picturing Defiance: Visions of Democracy in Iran." *International Communication Gazette* 74.7 (November 2012): 619–635.

Greenwood, Keith and Smith, C. Zoe. "How the World Looks to Us." *Journalism Practice* 1.1 (January 2007): 82–101.

Griffin, Michael. "Picturing America's 'War on Terrorism' in Afghanistan and Iraq: Photographic Motifs as News Frames." *Journalism* 5.4 (November 2004): 381–402.

Griffin, Michael and Lee, Jongsoo. "Picturing the Gulf War: Constructing an Image of War in *Time, Newsweek*, and *U.S. News & World Report*." *Journalism & Mass Communication Quarterly* 72.4 (Winter 1995): 813–825.

Grove, Jaleen. "A Castle of One's Own: Interactivity in *Chatelaine Magazine*, 1928–35." *Journal of Canadian Studies/Revue d'études canadiennes* 45.3 (Fall 2011): 167–194.

Haidarali, Laila. "Polishing Brown Diamonds: African American Women, Popular Magazines, and the Advent of Modeling in Early Postwar America." *Journal of Women's History* 17.1 (2005): 10–37.

Harris, Christopher R. "Digitization and Manipulation of News Photographs." *Journal of Mass Media Ethics* 6.3 (1991): 164–174.

Hartley, John. "Documenting Kate Moss." *Journalism Studies* 8.4 (2007): 555–565.

Herbst, Susan. "Illustrator, American Icon, and Public Opinion Theorist: Norman Rockwell in Democracy." *Political Communication* 21.1 (2004): 1–25.

Hinnant, Amanda and Hudson, Berkley. "The Magazine Revolution, 1880–1920." In Christine Bold, ed. *The Oxford History of U.S. Popular Print Culture: 1860–1920*. Vol. 6. New York: Oxford University Press, 2012, 113–131.

Hoy, Anne H. *The Book of Photography: The History, the Technique, the Art, the Future*. Washington, DC: National Geographic Society, 2005.

Huang, Edgar Shaohua. "Readers' Perception of Digital Alteration in Photojournalism." *Journalism & Communication Monographs* 3.3 (Autumn 2001): 147–182.

Huang, Edgar Shaohua. "Where Do You Draw the Line?" *Visual Communication Quarterly* 7.4 (2000): 4–16.

Hudson, Berkley. "Photojournalists." *Encyclopedia of Journalism*. Thousand Oaks, CA: Sage Publications, 2009.

Hutton, Deborah. "Raja Deen Dayal and Sons: Photographing Hyderabad's Famine Relief Efforts." *History of Photography* 31.3 (2007): 260–275.

Kang, Mee-Eun. "The Portrayal of Women's Images in Magazine Advertisements: Goffman's Gender Analysis Revisited." *Sex Roles* 37.11/12 (December 1997): 979–996.

Kaplan, John. "The *Life* Magazine Civil Rights Photography of Charles Moore 1958–1965." *Journalism History* 25.4 (Winter 1999/2000): 126–139.

Keith, Susan and Schwalbe, Carol B. "Women and Visual Depictions of the U.S.-Iraq War in Print and Online Media." *Visual Communication Quarterly* 17.1 (January/March 2010): 4–17.

Keith, Susan; Schwalbe, Carol B.; and Silcock, B. William. "Visualizing Cross-Media Coverage: Picturing War across Platforms during the U.S.-Led Invasion of Iraq." *Atlantic Journal of Communication* 17.1 (January/March 2009): 1–18.

Kim, Gyong Ho and Paddon, Anna R. "Digital Manipulation as New Form of Evidence of Actual Malice in Libel and False Light Cases." *Communications & the Law* 21.3 (September 1999): 57–73.

Kim, Hun Shik and Smith, C. Zoe. "Sixty Years of Showing the World to America: Pulitzer Prize Photographs, 1942–2002." *International Communication Gazette* 67.4 (August 2005): 307–323.

Kim, Mim-Sun. "A Comparative Analysis of Nonverbal Expressions as Portrayed by Korean and American Print-Media Advertising." *Howard Journal of Communications* 3.3/4 (Winter/Spring 1992): 317–339.

Kitch, Carolyn. *The Girl on the Magazine Cover: The Origins of Visual Stereotypes in American Mass Media.* Chapel Hill and London: University of North Carolina Press, 2001.

Kitch, Carolyn. *Pages from the Past: History and Memory in American Magazines.* Chapel Hill: University of North Carolina Press, 2005.

Klassen, Michael L.; Jasper, Cynthia R.; and Schwartz, Anne M. "Men and Women: Images of Their Relationships in Magazine Advertisements." *Journal of Advertising Research* 33.2 (March/April 1993): 30–39.

Kolbe, Richard H. and Albanese, Paul J. "Man to Man: A Content Analysis of Sole-Male Images in Male-Audience Magazines." *Journal of Advertising* 25.4 (Winter 1996): 1–20.

Krause-Wahl, Antje. "Between Studio and Catwalk—Artists in Fashion Magazines." *Fashion Theory: The Journal of Dress, Body & Culture* 13.1 (March 2009): 7–27.

Kuhn, Martin. "Drawing Civil War Soldiers." *Journalism History* 32.2 (Summer 2006): 96–105.

Lamb, Chris. *Drawn to Extremes: The Use and Abuse of Editorial Cartoons.* New York: Columbia University Press, 2004.

Lambiase, Jacqueline. "Promoting Sexy Images: Case Study Scrutinizes *Maxim*'s Cover Formula for Building Quick Circulation and Challenging Competitors." *Journal of Promotion Management* 13.1/2 (2007): 111–125.

Lambiase, Jacqueline and Reichert, Tom. "Sex and the Marketing of Contemporary Consumer Magazines: How Men's Magazines Sexualized Their Covers to Compete with *Maxim*." In Reichert, Tom and Lambiase, Jacqueline, eds. *Sex in Consumer Culture: The Erotic Content of Media and Marketing.* Mahwah, NJ: Lawrence Erlbaum Associates, 2006, 67–86.

Langa, Helen. "'At Least Half the Pages Will Consist of Pictures': *New Masses* and Politicized Visual Art." *American Periodicals* 21.1 (2011): 24–49.

Langton, Loup. *Photojournalism and Today's News: Creating Visual Reality.* Chichester, UK: Wiley-Blackwell, 2009.

Lebeck, Robert and von Dewitz, Bodo. *Kiosk: A History of Photojournalism.* Göttingen: Steidl, 2001.

Lester, Paul Martin. *Images that Injure: Pictorial Stereotypes in the Media.* Westport, CT: Praeger, 1996.

Lundell, Åsa Kroon and Ekström, Mats. "The Complex Visual Gendering of Political Women in the Press." *Journalism Studies* 9.6 (2008): 891–910.

Lutz, Catherine A. and Collins, Jane L. *Reading National Geographic.* Chicago and London: University of Chicago Press, 1993.

Machin, David. "Building the World's Visual Language: The Increasing Global Importance of Image Banks in Corporate Media." *Visual Communication* 3.3 (October 2004): 316–336.

Machin, David and Thornborrow, Joanna. "Branding and Discourse: The Case of *Cosmopolitan*." *Discourse & Society* 14.4 (2003): 453–471.

Magnussen, Anne. "Imagining the Dictatorship, Argentina 1981 to 1982." *Visual Communication* 5.3 (October 2006): 323–344.

Makemson, Harlen. "One Misdeed Evokes Another: How Political Cartoonists Used 'Scandal Intertextuality' against Presidential Candidate James G. Blaine." *Media History Monographs* 7.2 (2004/2005): 1–20.

Marable, Darwin. "Carl Mydans: An Interview." *History of Photography* 26.1 (2002): 47–52.

Martin, Edwin. "On Photographic Manipulation." *Journal of Mass Media Ethics* 6.3 (1991): 156–163.

McCracken, Ellen. *Decoding Women's Magazines: From Mademoiselle to Ms.* Basingstoke, UK: Macmillan, 1993.

Mellow, James R. *Walker Evans.* New York: Basic Books, 1999.

Mendelson, Andrew and Smith, C. Zoe. "Part of the Team: *Life* Photographers and Their Symbiotic Relationship with the Military during World War II." *American Journalism* 12.3 (1995): 276–289.

Mott, Frank Luther. *A History of American Magazines 1850–1865*. Vol. 2. Cambridge, MA: The Belknap Press, 1938.

Murray, Ray. "Stalking the Paparazzi: A View from a Different Angle." *Visual Communication Quarterly* 18.1 (January 2011): 4–17.

Murray, Susan. "Digital Images, Photo-Sharing, and Our Shifting Notions of Everyday Aesthetics." *Journal of Visual Culture* 7.2 (2008): 147–163.

Newbury, Darren. "Johannesburg Lunch-Hour 1951–1963." *Journalism Studies* 8.4 (August 2007): 584–594.

Newton, Julianne H. *The Burden of Visual Truth: The Role of Photojournalism in Mediating Reality*. Mahwah, NJ: Lawrence Erlbaum, 2001.

Nwafor, Okechukwu. "Of *Mutuality* and *Copying*: Fashioning *Aso Ebi* through Fashion Magazines in Lagos." *Fashion Theory: The Journal of Dress, Body & Culture* 16.4 (December 2012): 493–520.

"Obituaries: Gordon Parks (1912–2006)." *History of Photography* 30.3 (Autumn 2006): 283–284.

"Obituaries: Loomis Dean (1917–2005)." *History of Photography* 30.2 (Summer 2006): 185.

"Obituaries: Thomas J. Abercrombie (1931–2006)." *History of Photography* 30.3 (Autumn 2006): 283.

Palmer, Erik. "How to Read Richard Avedon." *Visual Communication Quarterly* 17.3 (July/September 2010): 147–161.

Panzer, Mary. *Things as They Are: Photojournalism in Context since 1955*. New York: Aperture, 2005.

Patterson, Cynthia. "'Illustration of a Picture': Nineteenth-Century Writers and the Philadelphia Pictorials." *American Periodicals* 19.2 (2009): 136–164.

Pelizzari, Maria Antonella. "Photojournalism as Contemporary Artefact." Review of *Things as They Are: Photojournalism in Context since 1955*, by Mary Panzer. *History of Photography* 31.3 (Autumn 2007): 309–311.

Perlmutter, David D. and Wagner, Gretchen L. "The Anatomy of a Photojournalistic Icon: Marginalization of Dissent in the Selection and Framing of 'a Death in Genoa.'" *Visual Communication* 3.1 (February 2004): 91–108.

Peterson, Christian A. "American Arts and Crafts: The Photograph Beautiful, 1895–1915." *History of Photography* 16.3 (Autumn 1992): 189–232.

Pfau, Michael; Haigh, Michel; Gettle, Mitchell; Donnelly, Michael; Scott, Gregory; Warr, Dana; and Wittenberg, Elaine. "Embedding Journalists in Military Combat Units: Impact on Newspaper Story Frames and Tone." *Journalism & Mass Communication Quarterly* 81.1 (Spring 2004): 74–88.

Reaves, Shiela. "Digital Alteration of Photographs in Consumer Magazines." *Journal of Mass Media Ethics* 6.3 (September 1991): 175–181.

Reichert, Tom and Zhou, Shuhua. "Consumer Responses to Sexual Magazine Covers on a Men's Magazine." *Journal of Promotion Management* 13.1/2 (January 2007): 127–144.

Reymond, Rhonda L. "Looking In: Albert A. Smith's Use of *Repoussoir* in Cover Illustrations for the *Crisis* and *Opportunity*." *American Periodicals* 20.2 (2010): 216–240.

Rodriguez, Lulu and Dimitrova, Daniela V. "The Levels of Visual Framing." *Journal of Visual Literacy* 30.1 (Spring 2011): 48–65.

Rössler, Patrick; Bomhoff, Jana; Haschke, Josef Ferdinand; Kersten, Jan; and Müller, Rüdiger. "Selection and Impact of Press Photography: An Empirical Study on the Basis of Photo News Factors." *Communications: The European Journal of Communication Research* 36.4 (November 2011): 415–439.

Rothenberg, Tamar Y. *Presenting America's World: Strategies of Innocence in* National Geographic *Magazine, 1888–1945*. Aldershot, UK and Burlington, VT: Ashgate, 2007.

Said, Edward. *Orientalism*. New York: Vintage Books, 1979.

Schulman, Vanessa Meikle. "'Making the Magazine': Visuality, Managerial Capitalism, and the Mass Production of Periodicals, 1865–1890." *American Periodicals* 22.1 (2012): 1–28.

Schulten, Susan. "The Perils of *Reading National Geographic*." *Reviews in American History* 23.3 (1995): 521–527.

Schwartz-DuPre, Rae Lynn. "Portraying the Political: *National Geographic*'s 1985 Afghan Girl and a U.S. Alibi for Aid." *Critical Studies in Media Communication* 27.4 (October 2010): 336–356.

Simmons, Sherwin. "Photo-Caricature in the German Popular Press, 1920." *History of Photography* 20.3 (Autumn 1996): 258–264.

Smith, Glenn D., Jr. "'You Can Do Anything': The Agendas of Carolyn Bennett Patterson, *National Geographic*'s First Woman Senior Editor." *Journalism History* 37.4 (Winter 2012): 190–206.

Smith, Shawn Michelle. "Obama's Whiteness." *Journal of Visual Culture* 8.2 (August 2009): 129–133.

Smith, Zoe. "Dickey Chapelle: Pioneer in Combat." *Visual Communication Quarterly* 1.2 (April 1994): 4–9.

Sontag, Susan. *Regarding the Pain of Others*. New York: Farrar, Straus and Giroux, 2003.

Souza, Pete. "Kent Kobersteen: The New Director of Photography at *National Geographic*." *Visual Communication Quarterly* 5.3 (Summer 1998): 3–8.

Stibbe, Arran. "Health and the Social Construction of Masculinity in *Men's Health* Magazine." *Men and Masculinities* 7.1 (July 2004): 31–51.

Strauss, David Levi. *Between the Eyes: Essays on Photography and Politics*. New York: Aperture, 2003.

Sultze, Kimberly. "Women, Power, and Photography in the *New York Times Magazine*." *Journal of Communication Inquiry* 27.3 (July 2003): 274.

Tonkonow, Leslie. *Multiple Exposure: The Group Portrait in Photography*. New York: Independent Curators, 1995.

Trachtenberg, Alan, ed. *Classic Essays on Photography*. New Haven: Leete's Island Books, 1980.

Trachtenberg, Alan. *Reading American Photographs: Images as History, Mathew Brady to Walker Evans*. New York: Hill and Wang, 1989.

Tsai, Joyce. "*Der Kuckuck* and the Problem of Workers' Photography in Austria." *History of Photography* 29.3 (2005): 275–286.

Tucker, Amy. *The Illustration of the Master: Henry James and the Magazine Revolution*. Stanford, CA: Stanford University Press, 2010.

West, Richard Samuel. "The *Light* that Failed: The History of an Unknown Magazine that Published the Work of a Galaxy of Emerging Stars." *American Periodicals* 19.2 (September 2009): 189–212.

Williams, Megan E. "The *Crisis* Cover Girl: Lena Horne, the NAACP, and Representations of African American Femininity, 1941–1945." *American Periodicals* 16.2 (2006): 200–218.

Winfield, Berry Houchin. "The Making of an Image: Hillary Rodham Clinton and American Journalists." *Political Communication* 14 (1997): 241–253.

26
INFOGRAPHICS AND INTERACTIVITY

A Nexus of Magazine Art and Science

Carol B. Schwalbe

Information graphics, or infographics, have long been a staple of magazines. In the 1980s *National Geographic, Newsweek, Time, U.S. News & World Report* and other magazines led the way in turning mountains of quantitative data into clear, concise visuals that readers could easily and quickly understand. Today, locator maps, charts, diagrams and other infographics help readers find archaeological sites, view the ups-and-downs of house prices and visualize what happens after clicking the Google search button. In recent years, technological advances on-line have helped make the public comfortable with and even hungry for data.[1] Interactivity has exploded as a storytelling tool that allows viewers to interact with data—from simply clicking through a slideshow to exploring a virtual re-creation of the Sistine Chapel.

Literature Review and Method

The goal of this chapter is to summarize the scholarly literature on both static and interactive infographics. The chapter begins with a discussion of the similarities and differences between *infographics* and *data visualizations*. The next section looks back to the 1980s and the influence of British graphic designer Nigel Holmes, whose colorful, whimsical infographics in *Time* magazine helped spark the graphics craze. Another pioneer in information design, Yale statistician Edward Tufte, advocated clear, precise content without decorations that obscure meaning. The next part introduces Tufte's guidelines for preventing misleading or inaccurate displays of data, along with the findings of other scholars who identified common errors in media graphics. It is followed by a summary of research on how infographics can help readers understand and recall information. Drawing on the literature about information visualization, the next section considers how human cognitive processes underlie effective techniques for representing abstract data that the mind can process and understand. The chapter ends with an examination of interactive infographics as a storytelling tool and suggestions for further research.

Various combinations of the following keywords and phrases, used alone or with the word *magazine*, led to the relevant literature: *data visualization, Edward Tufte, graphics, infographics, information(al) graphics, interactivity, information visualization, international, Nigel Holmes, reader recall, reader understanding* and *visualization*. In addition, the references in articles often led to other pertinent studies.

Defining Terms

The terms *infographics* and *data visualizations* are sometimes used interchangeably because both are graphic visual representations that analyze and communicate statistical data and complex information. Some academics and designers, however, draw a sharp line between the two terms, determined by how much the material is edited.[2] The term *infographics* refers to edited information that is generally presented as charts, graphs and maps. These graphics appeal to the general readers of magazines and newspapers.[3] *Data visualizations* are usually more interactive, allowing viewers to explore, manipulate unedited data and discover their own story. These graphics appeal to experts and specialized readers, such as sports fans, who enjoy mining complex data.[4]

Alberto Cairo envisions infographics and data visualizations along a continuum. "All graphics present data and allow a certain degree of exploration of those same data," he wrote in *The Functional Art: An Introduction to Information Graphics and Visualization*.[5] Now an educator, the former infographics designer and editor emphasizes the importance of designing graphics that are both beautiful and understandable. Cairo stresses that knowledge of how the brain processes information and creates visual images is key to effective communication. The quality of a graphic depends on how well the brain extracts meaning from the information presented and how easily the viewer understands it. The goal of the graphic designer is to anticipate what the brain will do and arrange compositions accordingly. Red grabs attention, for example, so Cairo suggests using red to highlight important words. Because the brain has difficulty comparing the area inside circles, he advises against using bubble charts.

With the practitioner in mind, British data visualization architect Andy Kirk, in his book *Data Visualization: A Successful Design Process*, lays out a flexible approach to finding "the best path through the minefield of design choices."[6] As does Cairo, Kirk emphasizes that an informative graphic is much more than a nice-looking illustration with numbers on it. He points out that designers must shape, organize and analyze the data in a meaningful way. They must then make sure the data visualization works (function) before making it beautiful (form). A recommendation for melding function (quantitative precision) and form (artistic values) resulted from an experiment in which German cartography students used the same information as graphic designers working for *ZEITmagazin* to depict eBay sales in Germany.[7] The student mapmakers focused on the technical rather than the artistic aspects, leading to the conclusion that collaboration would benefit both cartographers and graphic designers.

Information Design Pioneers

Infographics became popular in the 1980s as the *Sunday Times* (U.K.), *Time*, *National Geographic*, *USA Today* and other publications increasingly used charts, graphs and maps to condense enormous amounts of information and help readers understand complicated issues. This popularity was spurred by factors such as the proliferation of Apple computers, innovations in graphics software, positive reader reaction and the hiring of more graphic designers and editors.[8]

A major influence on modern information design is Nigel Holmes, a British graphic designer hired by *Time* in 1977 to create "explanation graphics" (Figure 26.1). *Time*'s editors at first dismissed his illustrative charts, but they proved to be popular with the magazine's readers.[9] Holmes eventually moved into a new position as the magazine's graphics director—a post he held for 16 years. His colorful, humorous pictorial explanations of complex subjects blended information with visual cues to the subject and its meaning. Although some academics and imitators criticized Holmes for oversimplifying complex data, he helped shape *Time*'s graphic style by combining functionality with eye appeal. Holmes's playful pictorial approach enlivens his recent book, *The Lonely Planet Book of Everything: A Visual Guide to Travel and the World*.[10] True to form, his step-by-step graphics explain a wide range of difficult concepts with clarity and humor. In a biography titled *Nigel Holmes: On Information Design*, art director Steven Heller introduces readers to Holmes's career, motivation and philosophy of information design—from the role of truth to communicating with an audience and developing a signature style.[11]

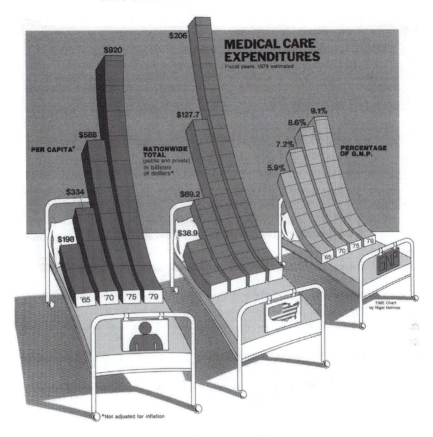

Figure 26.1. Holmes, Medical Care Expenditures. Used by permission.

Holmes's explanation graphics helped spark the graphics craze popularized by *USA Today* after its 1982 launch. Its short articles, bright colors, large photos and flashy infographics revolutionized newspapers' dull gray pages by making them more interesting and appealing to a wide audience. Graphic artist George Rorick transformed visual weather coverage in *USA Today* by changing the tiny, black-and-white weather map into a colorful, full-page map with explanatory drawings.[12] By the late 1990s, *USA Today*–style graphics were appearing in magazines and other newspapers as well.

Holmes's populist appeal at *Time* contrasted with the academic approach of Edward Tufte, now professor emeritus at Yale. A statistician and public policy expert, Tufte followed a simple, spare approach to infographics. As did Holmes, he exerted enormous influence on the field of data visualization, including serving as a consultant for *Newsweek*. Tufte broke new ground in 1983 when he self-published *The Visual Display of Quantitative Information*, which contends that infographics are compromised more by poor and inadvertently misleading presentation than by faulty information.[13] Updated in 2001, the book is still a much-thumbed reference for those who create and edit graphics. The first section reviews graphical practices over the last 200 years, while the second section sets forth both a language for discussing data graphics and a theory for improving the visual display of quantitative information.[14] In his second book, *Envisioning Information*, Tufte argues that excellence in data visualization comes from communicating complex ideas with clarity, precision and accuracy rather than relying on what is trendy.[15] The most effective way to display information depends on the nature of the data, the audience and the medium. Examples in the book reflect Tufte's philosophy of designing graphics that make complex information clear and accessible through the interplay of words, numbers and graphics. Tufte's third book, *Visual Explanations: Images and Quantities, Evidence and Narrative*, turns to design strategies for displaying dynamic data—information that changes over time.[16] His fourth book, *Beautiful Evidence*, introduces *sparklines*.[17] These small, simple line graphs pack a lot of information, such as fluctuating temperatures or housing prices, in the space occupied by just a few words.

The contrast between Tufte's spare approach and Holmes's whimsical touch plays out today between business analyst Stephen Few and infographic artist David McCandless. In his quarterly *Visual Business Intelligence* newsletter, Few points to examples of McCandless's data visualizations that Few argues lack substance, obfuscate data or impede understanding. Few claims that McCandless "has to [Few's] knowledge never produced an effective data visualization."[18]

The two men's books also reflect the differences in their approaches. Few's *Show Me the Numbers: Designing Tables and Graphs to Enlighten* is a primer on visual perception and statistics that takes a practical approach to designing clear, simple charts and tables.[19] By contrast, McCandless's *Information Is Beautiful* (Figure 26.2) presents creative ways of transforming data into fun, colorful infographics.[20] Another McCandless book, *The Visual Miscellaneum: A Colorful Guide to the World's Most Consequential Trivia*, approaches data visualizations as an art.[21] In the book McCandless takes information from publicly available but not always reliable sources, such as Google and Wikipedia, and makes it tangible by creatively revealing connections between facts and beliefs, such as ideas about creation. Examples of McCandless's graphics also appear on his Web site, Information Is Beautiful.[22]

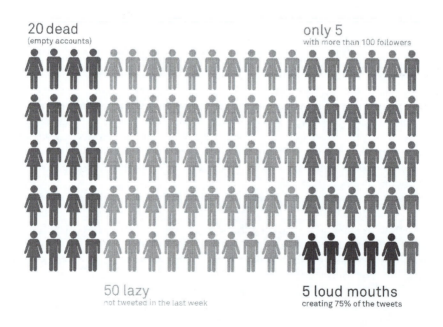

Let's Not Get Too Excited...
If the Twitter community was 100 people...

20 dead
(empty accounts)

only 5
with more than 100 followers

50 lazy
not tweeted in the last week

5 loud mouths
creating 75% of the tweets

by Loudmouth David McCandless @mccandelish // informationisbeautiful.net // @infobeautiful // v1.4 Aug 09
source: sysomos.com/insidetwitter/ [via rohitbhargava.typepad.com]

Figure 26.2. Courtesy of David McCandless, InformationisBeautiful.net. Used by permission.

Standards of Accuracy

In his writings about data visualization, Tufte identified common errors in media graphics and developed guidelines to prevent misleading or inaccurate displays of data. He charged that errors result more often from incompetence (a lack of statistical training, poor data, incorrect analysis, human perception and poor design) than intent (a need to exaggerate the data, deliberate distortion and visual tricks).[23] Tufte set forth guidelines for creating data-driven infographics that accurately reflect the facts (Figures 26.3 and 26.4). The *lie factor*, for example, measures the honesty of graphical displays by comparing the ratio of the size of the effect shown in a graphic to the actual size of the effect in the data.[24]

Tufte urged designers to avoid pretty but meaningless eye-candy or, as he put it, *chartjunk*—visual decorations and flourishes such as distracting patterns, saturated colors, shading, 3-D or unnecessary grid lines that do not represent the data or aid understanding:

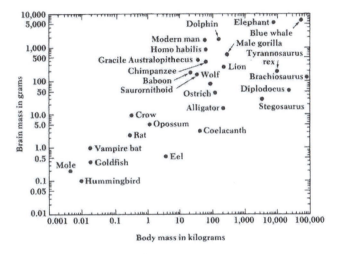

Figure 26.3. "Evolution1." Edward Tufte, *Beautiful Evidence* (Graphics Press), p. 118. Reprinted by permission.

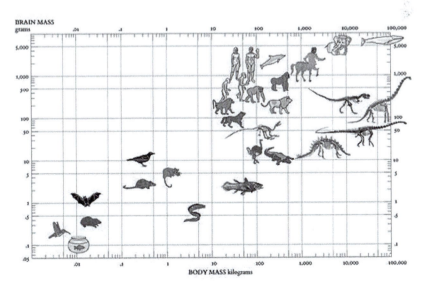

Figure 26.4. "Evolution2." Edward Tufte, *Beautiful Evidence* (Graphics Press), p. 212. Reprinted by permission.

Fortunately most chartjunk does not involve artistic considerations. It is simply conventional graphic paraphernalia routinely added to every display that passes by: overbusy grid lines and excess ticks, redundant representations of the simplest data, the debris of computer plotting, and many of the devices generating design variation.[25]

An experiment conducted by Scott Bateman and his colleagues, however, brought into question Tufte's minimalist approach.[26] Study participants thought the embellished, Holmes-style charts were more attractive than the plain, Tufte-style charts and were also easier to remember several weeks later. Stephen Few pointed out methodological shortcomings in the Bateman study design, including the size and composition of the study group (20 university students) and the "extreme examples of chartjunk" shown to the participants.[27]

James W. Tankard, Jr., pointed out that Tufte's admonitions against visual decorations might be too severe for newspaper infographics, which strive to find a balance between being accurate and clear on the one hand and entertaining and attention-getting on the other.[28] Tankard acknowledged that infographics can help readers understand data, but they can also mislead if not used correctly. He urged journalists to bring as much accuracy to visual data as they would to the same information presented in words. Prabu David emphasized the differences between the audiences served: Data analysts, such as Tufte, publish infographics in academic journals with homogenous audiences, while mass media practitioners, such as Holmes, serve a diverse readership and produce infographics that compete for attention with other items on a page.[29]

Statistical representations can be used to distort, inflate, sensationalize, oversimplify or manipulate in order to serve personal biases, warned journalist Darrell Huff in *How to Lie with Statistics*.[30] Huff used examples from *Time* and *Newsweek* to illustrate statistical pitfalls. Matthew Reavy also examined the nation's two top newsmagazines to see if graphical errors tended to err on the side of understatement or exaggeration.[31] Three times as many graphical errors appeared in *Time*, which had been influenced by Holmes, as in *Newsweek*, where Tufte served as a consultant. About 14% of the 152 *Time* graphics examined in the study tended toward exaggeration, compared with only 1% of the 95 studied in *Newsweek*. The graphics departments at both magazines strove for accuracy, but *Time* emphasized "visual appeal," while *Newsweek*'s approach favored "simplicity and straightforward presentation."[32]

Reader Understanding and Recall

The 1990s saw an increase in scholarly research about how infographics help readers understand and recall information in accompanying stories. Steve Pasternack and Sandra H. Utt found that people tend to look at large, flashy graphics before reading the article. The researchers, therefore, proposed that graphics not repeat the same information that appears in the text.[33] Experiments conducted by Jeffrey L. Griffin and Robert L. Stevenson, however, indicated that reader recall and retention are enhanced by repeating content from the text in locator maps or sidebars[34] and in complex, "how graphics" that depict an unfolding news event or a complicated process.[35] Griffin and Stevenson also observed that attractive maps and graphics capture readers' attention and that repeating geographical information in both the text and on a map enhances understanding.[36] Another of their experiments indicated that readers retain more statistical information when it is presented as an infographic as well as in text.[37] In an experiment with graphic forms common to magazines and newspapers, James D. Kelly found that readers process tables and graphs more efficiently than text but suggested that response time is a more reliable measure than recall.[38]

With the emergence of interactive graphics on-line, scholars began to compare content comprehension and recall of information on print-based Web sites versus multimedia Web sites. Leigh Talbert Berry conducted an experiment in which 84 undergraduates were shown two versions of the same Web site—one with animated visuals, audio and video; the other without any multimedia.[39] The presence of multimedia did not appear to affect Internet news readers' comprehension and recall. On the other hand, a pilot study by Val Pipps and her colleagues revealed that students' recall was significantly higher after reading either text only or shortened text with photos and captions than after looking at videos or animated graphics.[40] Bartosz W. Wojdynski observed that interacting with information displayed in graphics could lead to a more positive attitude toward the content but did not improve users' recall of numerical information.[41] A 2013 article in *Scientific American* summarizes two decades of research that indicates people have better comprehension and recall of text read on paper than on a screen.[42] The article, however, does not address graphics or multimedia.

Visual Perception

Infographics are part of the interdisciplinary field called *information visualization*—the study of computer-supported, interactive representations of abstract data to help amplify the human mind's ability to process and understand information.[43] This research helps develop ways to transform data into effective infographics that readers can understand and recall. The brain interprets visuals more quickly than text because reading words requires a linear logic, while visuals elicit an instant response.[44] Vision is the dominant human sense, with about half of the human brain related directly or indirectly to visual functions.[45] The principles for designing infographics are rooted in visual perception: "Visual representations and interaction techniques take advantage of the human eye's broad bandwidth pathway into the mind to allow users to see, explore, and understand large amounts of information at once."[46]

Information visualization studies draw from many fields, including graphic design, journalism, computer science, cognitive science and psychology. Stuart K. Card, Jock D. Mackinlay and Ben Shneiderman's 1999 volume, *Readings in Information Visualization: Using Vision to Think*, is the first compilation of classic research articles in the field.[47] James J. Thomas and Kristin A. Cook's 2005 edited volume of research, *Illuminating the Path: The Research and Development Agenda for Visual Analytics*, provides insights about more recent tools and techniques for synthesizing and analyzing massive amounts of data that are often ambiguous and contradictory.[48]

Robert Spence's *Information Visualization: Design for Interaction* links the theoretical and the practical.[49] Spence, a British professor of information engineering, provides an overview of visualization issues and techniques that hinge on three key concepts: representation, presentation and interaction. The examples in his book help illustrate the concepts and theories developed by researchers. Colin Ware, an expert in both computer science and the psychology of perception, has written two recent books that distill research on visual thinking, cognition and attention, then apply the findings to data visualization. *Visual Thinking for Design* translates scientific research into ways that designers can present data to facilitate the viewers' thinking process.[50] In *Information Visualization: Perception for Design*, Ware also derives effective techniques from research in psychology and neuropsychology and offers principles for improving the clarity, usefulness and persuasiveness of data visualizations.[51] The book focuses on perceptual issues as they relate to information design, including how visual perception is highly contextual and why it is important in design.

Well-designed infographics make it easier for viewers to relate to and process data, especially in an age of information overload. The process of visualizing information can reveal unexpected insights that might otherwise be overlooked, as data journalist David McCandless explained in a TED talk: "There's something almost quite magical about visual information. It's effortless. It literally pours in. If you're navigating a dense information jungle, coming across a beautiful graphic or lovely data visualization, it's a relief. It's like coming across a clearing in the jungle."[52]

Peter Aldhous, San Francisco bureau chief for *New Scientist* magazine, gained such insights when he downloaded publicly available information about earthquakes and fatalities from the Internet, crunched the data and created an interactive graphic. It showed that the high fatality rates of the 2010 Haiti earthquake resulted not from the seismic force but from urban over-crowding and poorly built houses.[53]

Interactive Storytelling Tools

The World Wide Web and social media have kindled a widespread resurgence of interest in infographics with the additional dimension of interactivity as a storytelling tool. Print info-graphics are generally static, linear and supplementary to the text, which conveys the story line and provides additional details or evidence. Interactive graphics, however, are dynamic and tell a complete nonlinear story that is often enhanced by movement, sound or both. Web graphics can be easily updated and allow users to interact with data. Computer scientist Ben Shneiderman proposes layering or sequencing information so readers can control the presenta-tion with buttons or sliders. Start broad, Shneiderman advises: "Overview first, zoom and filter, then details-on-demand."[54]

Alberto Cairo identifies three kinds of interactions: instruction, manipulation and explora-tion.[55] Users, for example, can simply instruct the graphic by clicking through a linear slide-show. In other cases, users can change an infographic by manipulating multiple variables, such as the time range, ZIP code and amount of donations in an interactive map about campaign finances. The third type of interaction—exploration—is exemplified by video games, such as World of Warcraft, which allow users to complete increasingly complex tasks.

Just as magazines led the way in modern information design, they are now at the forefront of reader interaction on Web sites and tablets. The *Economist, Time, Vanity Fair, Sports Illus-trated* and *Wired* were among the first magazines to launch iPad applications.[56] A number of print magazines now offer tablet versions that feature interactive elements, including dynamic infographics, audio pieces, photo galleries and videos. The fingertip control of a touch screen seems natural because it resembles the feel of a print magazine.

Data journalists and digital storytellers are increasingly integrating complex interactive graphics into their narratives. Although most scholars have focused on digital storytelling and interactive content in on-line newspapers, their findings also apply to interactive graphics designed for on-line magazines. Interactivity and storytelling are key elements in both media. Jennifer George-Palilonis and Mary Spillman proposed standard definitions and a theoretical model for studying the effectiveness of interactive graphics and their storytelling potential in on-line newspapers.[57] Palilonis and Spillman also examined the storytelling importance and cost effectiveness of interactive graphics as they competed with social media, news curation and the development of applications for news editors' time and enthusiasm.[58] The researchers conducted both a national survey and interviews, which revealed that editors value interactive graphics as a storytelling tool but do not give them prime space on Web sites. In *Data Visualiza-tion: A Successful Design Process*, Andy Kirk cautioned designers to use interactivity only after careful planning, because sometimes the most effective visualizations are static.[59] Edward Segel and Jeffrey Heer identified seven basic genres of narrative visualization that can be combined with interactivity across a spectrum of visual storytelling experiences—from author driven to reader driven.[60] These genres vary mainly in the number of frames (distinct visual scenes in time and space) and structure (the ordering of visual elements). Different genres suit different kinds of stories and audiences. The most common genre for static visualizations that Segel and Heer identified is the *magazine style*, which could be as simple as an image set in a page of text. The researchers suggest the magazine style could be enriched with interactive visualizations.

Opportunities for Research

Infographics lie at the nexus of journalism, graphic design, visual communication, cognitive science and computer science. Nonetheless, much of the research is somewhat dated. First, new research could include basic work surveying the current state of magazine graphics, both static and interactive, in the United States and other countries. After that, researchers could explore more specialized areas. A comparison of tone in magazine graphics compared with graphics in other media, for example, might reveal whether playfulness translates into reader attention and retention. Rapidly evolving tools and technologies provide opportunities for research about interactivity, viewer engagement and the potential for complex storytelling. Jennifer George-Palilonis and Mary Spillman propose further studies of interactive graphics, including their placement on Web sites, effect on reader understanding and appeal to younger audiences.[61] The new devices on which readers view infographics, such as smartphones and tablets, call for research into how people consume visual information. On these small but ever-present platforms, do graphics possessing Tuftean precision or Holmesean flair better aid reader understanding and recall?

The accuracy of both still and interactive magazine graphics is fertile ground as well. Does the desire for eye-catching graphics overshadow the importance of representing data accurately, resulting in information distortion and misleading readers? Also worth exploring is the use of prompts in interactive, nonlinear storytelling. Are readers who are knowledgeable about a subject more accepting of *low-coherence narratives* (i.e., less linear)? Are low-knowledge readers more responsive to such stories with the use of simple prompts that fill in their knowledge gaps?

Another fruitful area of research is the role of magazines in the development of modern information design. Researchers could compare the impact of Holmes and Tufte on magazine infographics, for example, or study the evolution of static and interactive graphics in specific publications around the world. Are there cultural differences in both presentation style and reader reception? Looking forward, scholars could examine design strategies for narrative visualization and the potential for new, richer approaches to magazine storytelling.

Notes

1 Joshua Yaffa, "The Information Sage," *Washington Monthly*, May/June 2011 <http://www.washington monthly.com/magazine/mayjune_2011/features/the_information_sage029137.php?page=all>, accessed 13 January 2014.

2 Max Gadney, David McCandless, Edward Tufte, and Nigel Holmes, "You Are Here," *Eye*, Winter 2012 <http://www.eyemagazine.com/feature/article/you-are-here>, accessed 15 March 2013.

3 Gadney, McCandless, Tufte, and Holmes, "You Are Here."

4 Gadney, McCandless, Tufte, and Holmes, "You Are Here."

5 Alberto Cairo, *The Functional Art: An Introduction to Information Graphics and Visualization* (Berkeley, CA: New Riders, 2013), xvi.

6 Andy Kirk, *Data Visualization: A Successful Design Process* (Birmingham, UK: Packt Publishing, 2012), 20.

7 Gertrud Schaab, Peter Freckmann, Ralph Stegmaier, and Sigrid Ortwein, "Visualizing Germany via Maps in a Magazine: 'Fancy' Graphic Design as Compared to 'Proper' Cartography" (paper presented at the 24th International Cartographic Conference (ICC 2009), Santiago, Chile, November 2009).

8 Sandra H. Utt and Steve Pasternack, "Infographics Today: Using Qualitative Devices to Display Quantitative Information," *Newspaper Research Journal* 14.3/4 (Summer/Fall 1993): 146–157.

9 Nigel Holmes, "Crashing through the Type," *Eye*, Winter 2012 <http://www.eyemagazine.com/feature/article/crashing-through-the-type>, accessed 12 March 2013.

10 Nigel Holmes, *The Lonely Planet Book of Everything: A Visual Guide to Travel and the World* (Victoria, AUS: Lonely Planet, 2012).

11 Steven Heller, *Nigel Holmes: On Information Design* (New York: Jorge Pinto Books, 2006).

12 Natalie Pompilio, "Graphics Evolution," *American Journalism Review*, April/May 2004, 9–10 <http://ajrarchive.org/article.asp?id=3642>, accessed 13 January 2014.

13 Edward R. Tufte, *The Visual Display of Quantitative Information* (Cheshire, CT: Graphics Press, 1983).

14 Edward R. Tufte, *The Visual Display of Quantitative Information*, 2nd ed. (Cheshire, CT: Graphics Press, 2001).

15 Edward R. Tufte, *Envisioning Information* (Cheshire, CT: Graphics Press, 1990).

16 Edward R. Tufte, *Visual Explanations: Images and Quantities, Evidence and Narrative* (Cheshire, CT: Graphics Press, 1997).

17 Edward R. Tufte, *Beautiful Evidence* (Cheshire, CT: Graphics Press, 2006).

18 Stephen Few, "Does GE Think We're Stupid?" *Visual Business Intelligence* (blog), 21 June 2011 <http://www.perceptualedge.com/blog/?p=995>, accessed 26 May 2013.

19 Stephen Few, *Show Me the Numbers: Designing Tables and Graphs to Enlighten*, 2nd ed. (Burlingame, CA: Analytics Press, 2012).

20 David McCandless, *Information Is Beautiful*, 2nd ed. (London: Collins, 2012).

21 David McCandless, *The Visual Miscellaneum: A Colorful Guide to the World's Most Consequential Trivia* (New York: HarperCollins Publisher, 2009), 46–47.

22 David McCandless, Information Is Beautiful.net <http://www.informationisbeautiful.net/>, accessed 23 May 2013.

23 Tufte, *Envisioning Information*.

24 Tufte, *Envisioning Information*, 57.

25 Tufte, *Visual Display of Quantitative Information*, 107.

26 Scott Bateman, Regan L. Mandryk, Carl Gutwin, Aaron Genest, David McDine, and Christopher Brooks, "Useful Junk? The Effects of Visual Embellishment on Comprehension and Memorability of Charts," in *Proceedings of the SIGCHI Conference on Human Factors in Computing Systems*. New York: Association for Computing Machinery, 2010, 2573–2582.

27 Stephen Few, "The Chartjunk Debate: Close Examination of Recent Findings," *Visual Business Intelligence Newsletter*, April/May/June 2011, 4 <http://www.perceptualedge.com/articles/visual_business_intelligence/the_chartjunk_debate.pdf>, accessed 28 May 2013.

28 James W. Tankard, Jr., "Quantitative Graphics in Newspapers," *Journalism Quarterly* 64.2/3 (Summer/Fall 1987): 406–415.

29 Prabu David, "Accuracy of Visual Perception of Quantitative Graphics: An Exploratory Study," *Journalism Quarterly* 69.2 (Summer 1992): 273–292.

30 Darrell Huff, *How to Lie with Statistics* (New York: W.W. Norton, 1993).

31 Matthew Reavy, "Rules and the Real World: An Examination of Information Graphics in *Time* and *Newsweek*," *Visual Communication Quarterly* 10.4 (Autumn 2003): 4–10.

32 Reavy, "Rules and the Real World," 9.

33 Steve Pasternack and Sandra H. Utt, "Reader Use and Understanding of Newspaper Infographics," *Newspaper Research Journal* 11.2 (Spring 1990): 28–41.

34 Jeffrey L. Griffin and Robert L. Stevenson, "Influence of Text and Graphics in Increasing Understanding of Foreign News Context," *Newspaper Research Journal* 13.1/2 (Winter/Spring 1992): 84–99.

35 Jeffrey L. Griffin and Robert L. Stevenson, "The Effectiveness of 'How Graphics' and Text in Presenting the News," *Visual Communication Quarterly* 1.2 (Spring 1994): 10–11, 16.

36 Jeffrey L. Griffin and Robert L. Stevenson, "The Effectiveness of Locator Maps in Increasing Reader Understanding of the Geography of Foreign News," *Journalism Quarterly* 71.4 (Winter 1994): 937–946.

37 Jeffrey L. Griffin and Robert L. Stevenson, "The Influence of Statistical Graphics on Newspaper Reader Knowledge Gain" (paper presented at the Annual Meeting, Association for Education in Journalism and Mass Communication, August 1992).

38 James D. Kelly, "The Effects of Display Format and Data Density on Time Spent Reading Statistics in Text, Tables and Graphs," *Journalism Quarterly* 70.1 (Spring 1993): 140–149.

39 Leigh Talbert Berry, "Comprehension and Recall of Internet News: A Quantitative Study of Web Page Design," *Journal of Magazine & New Media Research* 3.2 (Fall 2000): 1–26.

40 Val Pipps, Heather Walter, Kathleen Endres, and Patrick Tabatcher, "Information Recall of Internet News: Does Design Make a Difference? A Pilot Study," *Journal of Magazine & New Media Research* 11.1 (Fall 2009): 1–20.

41 Bartosz W. Wojdynski, "Graphical Depictions of Quantitative Data: Can Interactivity Affect Recall and Attitudes?" (paper presented at the Annual Meeting, Association for Education in Journalism and Mass Communication, August 2010).

42 Ferris Jabr, "Why the Brain Prefers Paper," *Scientific American*, November 2013, 48–53.

43 Stuart K. Card, Jock D. Mackinlay, and Ben Shneiderman, eds., *Readings in Information Visualization: Using Vision to Think* (San Diego: Academic Press, 1999).

44 Stephen Few, "Data Visualization for Human Perception," in Mads Soegaard and Rikke Friis Dam, eds., *The Encyclopedia of Human-Computer Interaction*, 2nd ed. (Aarhus, DNK: The Interaction Design Foundation, 2013).

45 Bhavin R. Sheth, Jitendra Sharma, S. Chenchal Rao, and Mriganka Sur, "Orientation Maps of Subjective Contours in Visual Cortex," *Science* [New Series] 274.5295 (20 December 1996): 2110–2115.

46 James J. Thomas and Kristin A. Cook, eds., *Illuminating the Path: The Research and Development Agenda for Visual Analytics* (Los Alamitos, CA: IEEE, 2005), 30.

47 Card, Mackinlay, and Shneiderman, *Readings in Information Visualization*.

48 Thomas and Cook, *Illuminating the Path*.

49 Robert Spence, *Information Visualization: Design for Interaction*, 2nd ed. (Harlow, UK: Pearson Education Limited, 2007).

50 Colin Ware, *Visual Thinking for Design* (Burlington, MA: Morgan Kaufmann, 2008).

51 Colin Ware, *Information Visualization: Perception for Design*, 3rd ed. (Waltham, MA: Morgan Kaufmann, 2012).

52 David McCandless, "The Beauty of Data Visualization" (talk presented at TEDGlobal 2010 Conference, filmed July 2010, TED video, 17:56) <http://www.ted.com/talks/david_mccandless_the_beauty_of_data_visualization.html>, accessed 22 May 2013.

53 Alex Williams, "How a Science Journalist Created a Data Visualization to Show the Magnitude of the Haiti Earthquake," *Readwrite.com*, 12 January 2011 <http://readwrite.com/2011/01/12/how-a-science-journalist-creat>, accessed 24 May 2013.

54 Ben Shneiderman, "The Eyes Have It: A Task by Data Type Taxonomy for Information Visualizations," in *Proceedings of the IEEE Symposium on Visual Languages* (Los Alamitos, CA: IEEE Computer Society Press, 1996), 336.

55 Cairo, *The Functional Art*.

56 "Loving Touch: Magazines and CDs Get Luxurious," *Economist*, 8 April 2010 <http://www.economist.com/node/15871885>, accessed 26 May 2013.

57 Jennifer George-Palilonis and Mary Spillman, "Interactive Graphics Development: A Framework for Studying Innovative Visual Story Forms," *Visual Communication Quarterly* 18.3 (2011): 167–177.

58 Jennifer George-Palilonis and Mary Spillman, "Storytelling with Interactive Graphics: An Analysis of Editors' Attitudes and Practices," *Visual Communication Quarterly* 20.1 (2013): 20–27.

59 Kirk, *Data Visualization*, 107.

60 Edward Segel and Jeffrey Heer, "Narrative Visualization: Telling Stories with Data," *IEEE Transactions on Visualization and Computer Graphics* 16.6 (November/December 2010): 1139–1148.

61 George-Palilonis and Spillman, "Storytelling with Interactive Graphics," 26.

Bibliography

Bateman, Scott; Mandryk, Regan L.; Gutwin, Carl; Genest, Aaron; McDine, David; and Brooks, Christopher. "Useful Junk? The Effects of Visual Embellishment on Comprehension and Memorability of Charts." In *Proceedings of the SIGCHI Conference on Human Factors in Computing Systems*. New York: Association for Computing Machinery, 2010, 2573–2582.

Berry, Leigh Talbert. "Comprehension and Recall of Internet News: A Quantitative Study of Web Page Design." *Journal of Magazine & New Media Research* 3.2 (Fall 2000): 1–26.

Cairo, Alberto. *The Functional Art: An Introduction to Information Graphics and Visualization*. Berkeley, CA: New Riders, 2013.

Card, Stuart K.; Mackinlay, Jock D.; and Shneiderman, Ben, eds. *Readings in Information Visualization: Using Vision to Think*. San Diego: Academic Press, 1999.

David, Prabu. "Accuracy of Visual Perception of Quantitative Graphics: An Exploratory Study." *Journalism Quarterly* 69.2 (Summer 1992): 273–292.

Few, Stephen. "The Chartjunk Debate: A Close Examination of Recent Findings." *Visual Business Intelligence Newsletter*, April/May/June 2011, 1–11 <http://www.perceptualedge.com/articles/visual_business_intelligence/the_chartjunk_debate.pdf>, accessed 28 May 2013.

Few, Stephen. "Data Visualization for Human Perception." In Soegaard, Mads and Dam, Rikke Friis, eds. *The Encyclopedia of Human-Computer Interaction*. 2nd ed. Aarhus, DNK: The Interaction Design Foundation, 2013.

Few, Stephen. "Does GE Think We're Stupid?" *Visual Business Intelligence* (blog), 21 June 2011 <http://www.perceptualedge.com/blog/?p=995>, accessed 26 May 2013.

Few, Stephen. *Show Me the Numbers: Designing Tables and Graphs to Enlighten*. 2nd ed. Burlingame, CA: Analytics Press, 2012.

Gadney, Max; McCandless, David; Tufte, Edward; and Holmes, Nigel. "You Are Here." *Eye*, Winter 2012 <http://www.eyemagazine.com/feature/article/you-are-here>, accessed 15 March 2013.

George-Palilonis, Jennifer and Spillman, Mary. "Interactive Graphics Development: A Framework for Studying Innovative Visual Story Forms." *Visual Communication Quarterly* 18.3 (2011): 167–177.

George-Palilonis, Jennifer and Spillman, Mary. "Storytelling with Interactive Graphics: An Analysis of Editors' Attitudes and Practices." *Visual Communication Quarterly* 20.1 (2013): 20–27.

Griffin, Jeffrey L. and Stevenson, Robert L. "The Effectiveness of 'How Graphics' and Text in Presenting the News." *Visual Communication Quarterly* 1.2 (Spring 1994): 10–11, 16.

Griffin, Jeffrey L. and Stevenson, Robert L. "The Effectiveness of Locator Maps in Increasing Reader Understanding of the Geography of Foreign News." *Journalism Quarterly* 71.4 (Winter 1994): 937–946.

Griffin, Jeffrey L. and Stevenson, Robert L. "The Influence of Statistical Graphics on Newspaper Reader Knowledge Gain." Paper presented at the Annual Meeting, Association for Education in Journalism and Mass Communication, August 1992.

Griffin, Jeffrey L. and Stevenson, Robert L. "Influence of Text and Graphics in Increasing Understanding of Foreign News Context." *Newspaper Research Journal* 13.1/2 (Winter/Spring 1992): 84–99.

Heller, Steven. *Nigel Holmes: On Information Design*. New York: Jorge Pinto Books, 2006.

Holmes, Nigel. "Crashing through the Type." *Eye*, Winter 2012 <http://www.eyemagazine.com/feature/article/crashing-through-the-type>, accessed 12 March 2013.

Holmes, Nigel. *The Lonely Planet Book of Everything: A Visual Guide to Travel and the World*. Victoria, AUS: Lonely Planet, 2012.

Huff, Darrell. *How to Lie with Statistics*. New York: W.W. Norton, 1993.

Jabr, Ferris. "Why the Brain Prefers Paper." *Scientific American*, November 2013, 48–53.

Kelly, James D. "The Effects of Display Format and Data Density on Time Spent Reading Statistics in Text, Tables and Graphs." *Journalism Quarterly* 70.1 (Spring 1993): 140–149.

Kirk, Andy. *Data Visualization: A Successful Design Process*. Birmingham, UK: Packt Publishing, 2012.

"Loving Touch: Magazines and CDs Get Luxurious." *Economist*, 8 April 2010 <http://www.economist.com/node/15871885>, accessed 26 May 2013.

McCandless, David. "The Beauty of Data Visualization." Talk presented at TEDGlobal 2010 Conference. Filmed July 2010. TED video, 17:56 <http://www.ted.com/talks/david_mccandless_the_beauty_of_data_visualization.html>, accessed 22 May 2013.

McCandless, David. *Information Is Beautiful*. 2nd ed. London: Collins, 2012.

McCandless, David. Information Is Beautiful.net <http://www.informationisbeautiful.net/>, accessed 23 May 2013.

McCandless, David. *The Visual Miscellaneum: A Colorful Guide to the World's Most Consequential Trivia*. New York: HarperCollins Publishers, 2009.

Pasternack, Steve and Utt, Sandra H. "Reader Use and Understanding of Newspaper Infographics." *Newspaper Research Journal* 11.2 (Spring 1990): 28–41.

Pipps, Val; Walter, Heather; Endres, Kathleen; and Tabatcher, Patrick. "Information Recall of Internet News: Does Design Make a Difference? A Pilot Study." *Journal of Magazine & New Media Research* 11.1 (Fall 2009): 1–20.

Pompilio, Natalie. "Graphics Evolution." *American Journalism Review*, April/May 2004, 9–10 <http://ajrarchive.org/article.asp?id=3642>, accessed 13 January 2014.

Reavy, Matthew. "Rules and the Real World: An Examination of Information Graphics in *Time* and *Newsweek*." *Visual Communication Quarterly* 10.4 (Autumn 2003): 4–10.

Schaab, Gertrud; Freckmann, Peter; Stegmaier, Ralph; and Ortwein, Sigrid. "Visualizing Germany via Maps in a Magazine: 'Fancy' Graphic Design as Compared to 'Proper' Cartography." Paper presented at the 24th International Cartographic Conference (ICC 2009). Santiago, Chile, November 2009.

Segel, Edward and Heer, Jeffrey. "Narrative Visualization: Telling Stories with Data." *IEEE Transactions on Visualization and Computer Graphics* 16.6 (November/December 2010): 1139–1148.

Sheth, Bhavin R.; Sharma, Jitendra; Rao, S. Chenchal; and Sur, Mriganka. "Orientation Maps of Subjective Contours in Visual Cortex." *Science* [New Series] 274.5295 (20 December 1996): 2110–2115.

Shneiderman, Ben. "The Eyes Have It: A Task by Data Type Taxonomy for Information Visualizations." In *Proceedings of the IEEE Symposium on Visual Languages*. Los Alamitos, CA: IEEE Computer Society Press, 1996, 336–343.

Spence, Robert. *Information Visualization: Design for Interaction*. 2nd ed. Harlow, UK: Pearson Education Limited, 2007.

Tankard, James W., Jr. "Quantitative Graphics in Newspapers." *Journalism Quarterly* 64.2/3 (Summer/Fall 1987): 406–415.

Thomas, James J. and Cook, Kristin A., eds. *Illuminating the Path: The Research and Development Agenda for Visual Analytics*. Los Alamitos, CA: IEEE, 2005.

Tufte, Edward R. *Beautiful Evidence*. Cheshire, CT: Graphics Press, 2006.

Tufte, Edward R. *Envisioning Information*. Cheshire, CT: Graphics Press, 1990.

Tufte, Edward R. *The Visual Display of Quantitative Information*. Cheshire, CT: Graphics Press, 1983.

Tufte, Edward R. *The Visual Display of Quantitative Information.* 2nd ed. Cheshire, CT: Graphics Press, 2001.

Tufte, Edward R. *Visual Explanations: Images and Quantities, Evidence and Narrative.* Cheshire, CT: Graphics Press, 1997.

Utt, Sandra H. and Pasternack, Steve. "Infographics Today: Using Qualitative Devices to Display Quantitative Information." *Newspaper Research Journal* 14.3/4 (Summer/Fall 1993): 146–157.

Ware, Colin. *Information Visualization: Perception for Design.* 3rd ed. Waltham, MA: Morgan Kaufmann, 2012.

Ware, Colin. *Visual Thinking for Design.* Burlington, MA: Morgan Kaufmann, 2008.

Williams, Alex. "How a Science Journalist Created a Data Visualization to Show the Magnitude of the Haiti Earthquake." *Readwrite.com*, 12 January 2011 <http://readwrite.com/2011/01/12/how-a-science-journalist-creat>, accessed 24 May 2013.

Wojdynski, Bartosz W. "Graphical Depictions of Quantitative Data: Can Interactivity Affect Recall and Attitudes?" Paper presented at the Annual Meeting, Association for Education in Journalism and Mass Communication, August 2010.

Yaffa, Joshua. "The Information Sage." *Washington Monthly*, May/June 2011 <http://www.washington monthly.com/magazine/mayjune_2011/features/the_information_sage029137.php?page=all>, accessed 13 January 2014.

Part V

PEDAGOGICAL AND CURRICULAR PERSPECTIVES

27

MAGAZINE JOURNALISM EDUCATION

The Challenge of Assessing Outcomes

Elliot King

Reviewing the current research associated with magazine journalism education immediately raises two major problems. First, magazines represent a small slice of journalism education. Secondly, investigating the literature of fields of study in the contemporary university in the United States leads to mentions of the fierce, ongoing debate stimulated by efforts to measure curricular effectiveness in higher education. As an example of the first challenge, in 2010, David Cuillier and Carole B. Schwalbe published a content analysis of 253 Great Ideas for Teaching Awards (GIFT) presented from 2000 to 2009 by the Association for Education in Journalism and Mass Communication (AEJMC).[1] From a decade of reports on teaching, the authors culled experiences that reflect the elements of effective pedagogy that foster learning. These peer-reviewed reports contain ideas that spark excitement in either the students, the teachers or both. The factors that Cuillier and Schwalbe identified included *incremental learning, motivation, relevance, higher learning*, that is, an appeal to creativity and critical thinking, and *appropriateness* for a range of learners.[2] Theoretically, at least, classroom activities that incorporate those characteristics have a better chance of enabling students to achieve the course learning objectives or minimally be enthusiastic about the learning experience.

As a part of the study, the authors reviewed both the area of the field and the subject areas being taught in which awards were given. Thirteen categories were listed for course structure and sequence, ranging from Sports Journalism, in which one award was given, to the catchall Could Apply to All, in which 64 awards were placed.[3] Magazines were not a category in the list. Of course this does not mean instructors teaching magazine articles writing, magazine design and production and related courses do not provide exciting classroom experiences for their students. For those familiar with the way magazine courses are often taught, it would appear that courses that focus on magazines typically incorporate many if not all of the features represented in effective pedagogy. Conversations with magazine editors as well as judges for the annual magazine contest sponsored by the AEJMC would suggest that magazine courses frequently are hands-on, incremental and focused on creativity and critical thinking. A more plausible explanation for the omission of magazines as a category in the GIFT Awards is that the omission reflects the general state of magazine education in the academy. The largest number of AEJMC's GIFT Awards, 106, fell into the Print Journalism subject area. Before the emergence of the World Wide Web blurred distinctions, magazines were clearly a subset of print journalism, so the awards in the print journalism category could reflect experience in classes in which magazines were the focus. Magazines do appear but in the authors' analysis of specific courses, or *topic area of focus*, which won awards. Magazines represented a little more than 1%, for a total of 3 of the 253 awards.[4]

That the exploration of magazine pedagogy is not specifically identified in the analysis of journalism and mass communication education in general is only part of the problem of understanding the contours of education about this publication format. The second serious challenge is that measuring teaching effectiveness has recently emerged as a critical debate in U.S. higher education. This is true in general and particularly in identifying and measuring learning outcomes.[5] Peter Brooks summarizes the concerns of multiple scholars who have observed that not only are there few good studies demonstrating that students are achieving specific learning outcomes through the university education, there are also no commonly agreed upon measures that could be used in those kinds of studies.[6]

This chapter explores three broad topics associated with the relationship of magazine pedagogy to journalism and mass communication education in general, as described in the literature. First, it explores several broad trends that have provided the context for magazine education over the past 20 years or so. It then looks at the literature associated with teaching students about magazines specifically and at magazine education, both within the larger contexts of print media education and journalism and mass communication education, which extends beyond teaching professional skills.[7] Finally, it explores the pedagogical relationship between magazine education and the emergence of digital media and on-line journalism, also as evidenced in the literature.

Literature Review and Method

In the mid-1990s, a review of research into the pedagogy of magazine education found that very little research had actually been conducted in the area.[8] In the intervening two decades or so, that situation has not largely changed. There continues to be comparatively little systematic inquiry into how the academy teaches magazine-oriented skills, concepts and working, or *operational theory*.[9] The lack of research is not surprising. Magazine education has always been a small slice of overall journalism education, and that slice, given the new developments in journalism generally and journalism education specifically, is getting smaller. The most comprehensive compilation of research into magazines to date is *The American Magazine: Research Perspectives and Prospects*, and the most comprehensive literature review of pedagogy devoted to magazine education appeared in that volume.[10] That review served as the starting point for this study. ERIC and other research databases then were searched, using terms such as *magazine education*, *magazine pedagogy* and *journalism pedagogy*.

The most prominent academic journal for research in journalism and mass communication education is *Journalism and Mass Communication Educator*. Every issue from 1995 forward was reviewed. The *Journal of Magazine & New Media Research*, an international, peer-reviewed electronic journal, was founded in 1999. Because it is the official journal of the Magazine Division of the AEJMC, every issue was reviewed. Beyond that, general searches using a wide range of search terms were conducted using major academic databases, including ProQuest, JStor and Lexis/Nexis.

Pedagogical Contexts

Several major trends have provided the context for magazine education since the early 1990s. First, the faculty of academic departments in which journalism programs reside often include members whose primary qualification for teaching is professional experience alongside those whose primary qualification is holding a Ph.D. While many faculty members today have both professional experience and a Ph.D., the different backgrounds faculty members bring with them can lead to different opinions as to where the emphasis of journalism education should be placed.[11] Secondly, one steady feature of magazine pedagogy has been to teach students how to write for, design and produce magazines. Therefore, it could be expected that the general health of the magazine industry would have some impact both on the popularity of magazine coursework among students as well as on the resources that journalism programs would be prepared to invest in magazine education. Finally, while magazine educators were early to embrace the changes in publishing brought about by the development of the Web, the relationship between publishing magazine-like content on-line and in print is not clear.

The U.S. magazine industry has been hard hit over the past 10 years by economic stresses and shifts triggered by the advent and maturing of the Internet. And not just the magazine industry: All traditional media sectors and media industries worldwide have been impacted. In the second half of the first decade of the 2000s, the print magazine industry witnessed the demise of hundreds of magazines. For example, *Crain's New York Business* reported that in 2008 more than 500 magazines went out of business.[12] While the rate of closures slowed, nearly 400 magazines closed in 2009.[13]

The magazine industry fell into the abyss for three inter-related reasons. First, the recession that hit in 2008 put pressure on advertising budgets overall.[14] Secondly, new advertising opportunities such as those offered by relatively new, on-line services, such as Google, raised doubts about the effectiveness of print advertising in general.[15] Finally, magazines were under pressure to invest their own resources in new on-line ventures.[16] The cessation of long-term national publications, such as *Newsweek*, and the spectacular flameouts of high-profile new ventures, such as *Talk*, spread a pallor of disillusionment on the industry itself.[17]

However, the years since 2008 were not all gloom and doom for the magazine industry. Industry analyst Samir Husni reported that in 2012 nearly 250 print magazines started publishing on a regular basis, the best year since 2007.[18] Moreover, during this period when the traditional magazine industry had to navigate rocky economic waters, the emergence of digital media platforms was on center stage and generating quite a bit of excitement. The relationship between magazines and on-line publishing has been evident since the Web first exploded as a mass public medium in the 1990s, with e-zines being one of the early prominent Web publishing genres. E-zines were largely the electronic progeny of small, self-published periodicals such as fanzines, sometimes called zines, or 'zines.[19] Nonetheless, faculty teaching in magazine courses quickly staked a claim to the scholarly exploration of "new media" when the Magazine Division of the Association for Education in Journalism and Mass Communication launched the on-line *Journal of Magazine & New Media Research*.[20] Tellingly, the journal was "born" digital and continued not to be published in a print format.

Although many magazine editors embraced e-zines and publishing on the Internet, the skill sets required for new media, or digital, publishing and traditional print magazine publishing emerged as clearly quite distinct. The pedagogy used in one area may not be universally appropriate in the other. Implementing on-line media curricula absorbed a lot of journalism and mass communication educators' attention following the turn of the twenty-first century. The conflux of factors—faculty priorities, the state of the industry and the demands of new media— have had an impact on magazine education in both enrollments and the number of courses available to students. Lee B. Becker, Tudor Vlad and Paris Desnoes's 2010 survey of 480 journalism programs in the United States found that while programs were still more often than not organized along traditional media industry lines, increasingly skills were being taught across media platforms. Their data also showed the demand for new courses, both from administrators and students, was in the area of new media.[21] A similar survey conducted two years earlier found that only 6.7% of all students enrolled in mass communication and journalism programs were in news/editorial or print journalism sequences, a drop of nearly 25% from a year earlier, when 8.9% of the respondents were in print journalism sequences. Another 14% or so of the respondents were enrolled in journalism programs that did not differentiate between different media formats. And while journalism as a whole held its own as a percentage of students within mass communication and journalism programs over the past 20 years, the survey data suggest that print journalism and news/editorial as specialty areas were slipping.[22] Courses devoted to magazine education were already a small percentage within the overall category of print journalism. The 1989 enrollment survey showed that only 47 schools offered dedicated magazine sequences compared to 242 news/editorial programs.[23] A 2012 compilation by David Sumner, a member of the AEJMC Magazine Division, suggested that number had fallen to perhaps as few as 19.[24]

These long-term trends appear not to auger well for magazine journalism education. The magazine industry itself is in a major transformation as dramatic as the one that saw many of the large, national, general-interest magazines fail in the 1950s, 1960s and 1970s. The Internet has provided a compelling new publishing platform that has captured the attention and resources of many journalism and mass communication programs. Despite these challenges, however, magazine journalism education remains a vibrant if perhaps small element in journalism education overall. The best evidence of its continuing vitality is the annual student magazine contest sponsored by the Magazine Division of the AEJMC. In 2012, the contest received 240 entries from students from at least 20 universities. This compares reasonably well to the 2005 contest, which had 251 entries from at least 17 schools.[25] Moreover, the skills at the center of magazine education—strong writing, editing and publication design— are valued across the journalism curriculum.[26] Interestingly, in the course offerings for the 19 schools with dedicated magazine journalism sequences listed on the AEJMC Magazine Division Web site, not one has a course in the history and development or cultural impact of magazines, and only six have courses that are management or publishing oriented. The overwhelming majority of the courses offered are in writing and editing followed by design and production.[27]

Magazine Pedagogy

Research into the pedagogy associated with magazine journalism is sparse and has been sparse for the past 40 years. In part, that reflects the state of research into journalism education generally. The primary journal in the area, *Journalism and Mass Communication Educator*, originally published reports about individual classroom experience. Over time, the focus shifted to research methods more associated with the social sciences. For some readers, the early focus on case studies and small samples lacked scientific rigor. On the other hand, Kate L. Peirce and Gilbert D. Martinez conclude the later approach has not produced results with direct applicability.[28] As this section shows, there are published studies that have yielded interesting and useful insights; however, the study of the pedagogy associated with magazine journalism still awaits researchers with a compelling research theory and method that will lead to outcomes that are rigorous and can have an impact on the field.

A sign of the state of research into magazine pedagogy is the deliberations of a panel session held at the 2008 convention of the AEJMC in Chicago, Illinois. The panel gathered together many of the top scholars in magazine journalism, whose presentations were later bundled into a report called "The State of Magazine Research in 2008."[29] The panel participants offered a plethora of astute observations. David Abrahamson noted that magazines were "second-class citizens" in the journalism academy and that scholarly inquiry into magazines was "dazed and confused." Joe Bernt agreed that magazines were "under-taught and under-researched." Carolyn Kitch countered what she felt was an "insidious assumption" that magazines were not on the cutting edge of media developments or media scholarship and, at the same time, lamented the narrow scope of topics associated with magazine research. Primarily, she noted, research into magazines explores biographies, institutional histories, covers and women's magazines. And the studies on women's magazines generally focus on body image, she added. Interestingly, not one of the panelists nor anybody who participated in the discussion that followed reflected on the research concerning magazine education and pedagogy.

Perhaps the most comprehensive article to directly address pedagogical issues in maga-zine journalism education over the past two decades is Leara Rhodes and Amber Roessner's exploration of experiential learning as it can be applied to magazine publishing.[30] Rhodes and Roessner interviewed 16 instructors who teach magazine publishing classes to examine course design and pedagogical approach in one class in which 15 students create a new magazine from concept to publication in one semester. While the courses were extremely diverse, Rhodes and Roessner found that courses of this type generally fall into one of four categories. In the *individual prototype model*, each student or a small team of students conducts research into a prospective market, develops a business plan and creates a prototype of a magazine that is pre-sented either to the class or outside experts.

The second, *magazine launch model*, follows basically the same trajectory, but the magazine produced is a finished product ready to be launched and not simply a prototype. Rhodes and Roessner found that instructors who use this model believe that it is a strong example of expe-riential learning as students become familiar with all the roles needing to be filled to actually launch a magazine. As one instructor reported, the magazine launch model is quintessentially learning by doing. In the third approach, *existing magazine model*, students create content for an existing magazine such as an alumni or student-focused publication. And in *a variation of the existing magazine model*, students take copy produced in other magazine-oriented courses, such as article writing, and produce an ongoing magazine, often one that circulates on campus.[31]

In addition to the specific magazine-focused and business oriented skills that students are supposed to learn in these hands-on experiences, they also learn general professional skills, such as how to manage their time and collaborate with others. In short, these courses to vary-ing degrees attempt to simulate what students may find in the magazine industry, should they ultimately find a job there. The role of the instructor is to serve as mentor and coach, providing guidance and background material.[32]

Rhodes and Roessner concluded that all the approaches have strengths and weaknesses. They all provide the kind of experiential learning environments that progressive educators have advocated and that can accommodate students with different learning styles. But for all the strengths of the article, Rhodes and Roessner leave unasked basic questions: What are the specific learning aims of the courses? How do those learning objectives fit into overall curriculum, both at the departmental and university level, and how are the students assessed to determine if the learning goals have been achieved? At the bottom line, however, given the state of pedagogical research in magazine journalism education, simply having an idea about what is going on in different departments offering sequences in magazine production is a major accomplishment.

Perhaps one of the reasons the literature does not provide insights into how and if magazine educators have explicitly examined the learning goals of their classes is that, as is true in many journalism and mass communication education courses, the implicit learning goal is to prepare students for life as a professional journalist, in this specific case, in the magazine industry. The experiential classes touch on more of the roles involved in publishing a magazine, with the launch and prototype models including, for example, conducting a market analysis. As noted earlier, one of the long-term tensions in journalism education has been whether classroom ped-agogy should be (or should still be, given the state of the industry) so oriented to professional skills training.[33] But even in the pre-professional skills camp, Thomas Dickson and Wanda Brandon note there are major tensions between what journalism educators think journalism students should learn and what industry professionals believe they should learn in their uni-versity educations.[34]

Carolyn Lepre and Glen Bleske in 2005 surveyed magazine editors and educators to explore and analyze attitudes about the set of skills job applicants should have. The results were eye opening. Educators rated 18 of the 23 skills, educational experiences and courses higher than did editors. While both groups found that writing, editing, reporting and proofing skills were essential for all students, editors devalued internships, magazine publishing classes, class stories

451

and working on a student magazine or the school newspaper. Editors were also less interested in advertising and, somewhat surprisingly, Web design and the publishing process. Neither group valued media theory very highly. For educators, it was at the bottom of the list (which perhaps demonstrates the esteem in which media theory is held by educators teaching these pre-professional skills courses).[35] The gap in the perceived value of hands-on and experiential courses in magazine journalism education between editors and educators is surprising because a similar survey of broadcast education found otherwise, with broadcasters highly valuing "experience" as the essential key to getting a first job.[36]

While magazine editors in 2005 downplayed the importance of skills such as Web design, the burgeoning of computer-based design technology had an impact on magazine education. In the analysis of the curricula of 19 specialized magazine sequences conducted by Sumner, one-third had a course in magazine design or magazine design and production.[37] The introduction of computer-based design raised important issues as early as the 1990s. How much class time should be spent teaching the technology itself and how much should be devoted to teaching the principles of design? Though not specifically aimed at magazine education, Michael O'Donnell addressed this challenge in 1995 when he vigorously argued that computer-based design instruction (he called it desktop publishing) should be incorporated in publication design courses.[38] His argument was that computer-based design provided a hands-on way to teach visual communication.

Computer graphics courses quickly became commonplace in journalism education and, Claude Cookman contended, provided a valuable educational experience in their own right, independent of pre-professional skills training.[39] Carefully conceived and based on sound educational theory, computer-based designed courses improve students' cognitive skills, Cookman wrote. Cognitive, or pre-professional, design is not just skills-oriented. In one of the most provocative articles directed specifically at magazine educators, Gigi Durham, drawing on the radical pedagogical theory of Paolo Freire, strongly advocated the idea that magazine design rests on ideological underpinnings. Durham stated that "consumer magazine design, in particular, perpetuates hegemonies of race, class and gender in its portrayal of marginalized societal groups" and that educators bring "students to an awareness of the role of magazine designers as agents of ideology."[40]

Durham's article is particularly refreshing for insisting that magazine educators, particularly magazine designers, move past a focus on technical skills and self-consciously examine their own assumptions. She attacks the idea that magazine design is value free or that educators can rely on intuition, based on their professional experience, to teach students. Design classes should begin, she argues, with designers critically reflecting on the imagined audience for the magazine and then asking themselves a series of questions: Who is included in that audience and who is excluded? What are the stereotypes associated with that audience and associated with those who are not included? How can those stereotypes be challenged? In this way, she contends, the mechanics of design are linked not to a sterile aesthetic sense but to politics and culture and the role design professionals can play in creating a more socially just world or offering a critique of the current power structure. Durham's essay—she was working on incorporating multiculturalism into her magazine design course at the University of Texas when she wrote the article but does not report on her experience in the class—is one of the few to explore, at least theoretically, the link between magazines and the society at large.

Social theory with its concern for power structures is not the only possible larger context for publication design. As a counterpoint to Durham's position, Renita Coleman and Jan Colbert proposed teaching strategies geared to incorporate ideas about creativity in general into the journalism design curriculum.[41] The authors argue that there is a well-developed literature about creativity, and students can be taught to be creative. Moreover, creativity is not the result of a mystical or inchoate process but stems from the use of certain techniques and cultivating certain attitudes of mind. As generally taught, the authors contend, two ideological obstacles stand in the way of introducing a conscious and self-aware approach to being creative in publication design classes. The first is the privileging of form over function. Design is taught to adhere to certain aesthetic standards rather than being driven by its journalistic function or what it is supposed to communicate. In classrooms in which creativity is at the foreground, they believe form should play a secondary role to the content. Design also requires a visual concept that tells the story visually. By focusing on content and concept, instructors can then incorporate strategies that foster creativity into their classrooms. They suggested specific strategies, such as incorporating active learning exercises and promoting the awareness of creativity. The authors tested their ideas, applying them to a magazine design class and using a newspaper design class as a control group. They found that visual communication classes in general enhance students' creative skills with or without formal creativity training.

Taken as a whole, the studies that explore magazine journalism pedagogy are not explicitly bound together by a common theory. Neither do they build on each other. But they do implicitly reflect the use of hands-on methods for teaching about magazine production and suggest that the wider literature on experiential education could be a fruitful paradigm within which to conduct this research.

Journalism and Mass Communication Education

As the previous section suggests, the research literature specifically aimed at magazine pedagogy is not robust. Neither is it recent (the discussion about publication design took place in the late 1990s). However, magazine education can be considered one aspect of print publication and sometimes is related to news/editorial sequences in some fashion. Moreover, magazines can be implicated in other curricular concerns such as ethics, law and history as well as general courses about writing, editing and proofreading. Consequently, research conducted in those more general areas can be relevant to magazine educators.

Mark Massé, who in three articles since the late 1990s has investigated educators' attitudes toward writing instruction, has perhaps spearheaded the most sustained exploration of the teaching of writing in journalism curricula. In his first article written in 1998, Massé identified two general approaches to teaching media writing.[42] The first was a top-down approach in which instructors conceive of themselves as editors, and the focus is on the finished product. Instructors in this model provide detailed critiques and extract severe penalties for errors in grammar and other infractions that others may deem trivial, Massé reported. In the second model, instructors see themselves as coaches, guiding students through the process of generating ideas and selecting topics as well as with the writing and revision processes. The focus is on helping students not only learn to write but to discover what they want to write about. Massé noted the difference between the two approaches to writing is sometimes summarized as product versus process. Massé set out to determine which approach journalism educators found more conducive to teaching writing across media platforms. The preference, he argued, would shape what was considered good writing in the classroom. Moreover, good writing skills are essential in all media industries, and the way writing is taught could have an impact on cognitive development. In other words, instructors' attitudes toward how writing should be taught matters.[43]

In 1997, Massé and his colleague Mark Popovich surveyed 16 journalism faculty at Ball State University to determine their attitudes toward the teaching of writing.[44] Magazine educators were included in that group. The survey was structured as a series of 47 statements that respondents ranked in terms of agreeing or disagreeing. The result was that nine of the faculty tended more toward a process orientation and seven leaned to a product orientation. Massé and Popovich concluded that journalism faculty should engage in an open dialogue about these differing orientations to the teaching of writing to create a more unified approach to writing for their students. Massé and Popovich's study was grounded in research about English composition and composition pedagogy. The authors noted that there was a paucity of research specifically into the pedagogy of media writing and suggested that media writing could be a topic for fruitful inquiry.[45]

In 2004, Massé and Popovich conducted a national survey of faculty teaching media writing.[46] The objective was two-fold. First, they sought to determine the demographics of faculty teaching media writing and their attitudes toward pedagogy, and they hoped to gain insight into faculty members' practices and available resources. More importantly, in light of the changes going on in journalism at the time, particularly the growth of on-line journalism, the authors wanted to learn if a more integrated paradigm for teaching media writing had emerged. In this article, the authors made clear their preference for an approach to media writing that combined an *editor/product* orientation with a *coach/process* orientation.[47] Interestingly, their survey of more than 400 instructors of media writing courses showed that two distinct approaches could still be identified, with about half the respondents in each camp. Regardless of their orientation, however, the activities each group actually assigned in class and the techniques they used differed very little. The largest gap was in how instructors presented themselves to their students. One group described themselves most often as editors, and the other described themselves more often as coaches. In fact, instructors who saw themselves as coaches gave low rankings to several of the activities generally associated with the instructor-as-coach model. Massé and Popovich concluded that most media writing instruction still followed the older editor/product orientation, or paradigm.[48] In another national survey conducted five years later, the authors largely found the same results and, given the rapidly changing professional environment, concluded that journalism educators were largely resistant to curricular reform, particularly those teaching in accredited programs.[49]

Writing is one skill that magazine education shares with other areas of journalism education. Copyediting and proofreading are others. In this review of the literature, not one article was located that explored the pedagogical issues associated with teaching copyediting. Interestingly, in a study that focused on the ways journalism educators learned to teach generally, Peirce and Martinez noted that the articles they found in *Journalism and Mass Communication Educator* were generally not helpful to faculty who wanted to learn how to teach copyediting.[50] Proofreading was the subject of research by Patty Wharton-Michael, who investigated whether trying to proofread material on-line as opposed to on paper led to additional errors.[51] Wharton-Michael noted that studies conducted by the American Society of Newspaper Editors demonstrated that textual errors hurt the credibility of publications. She also cited previous studies that explored the accuracy of proofreading on screen versus on paper. The results are mixed. The studies showed that in some situations proofing from paper was more effective; in other studies proofing from paper was not more effective than proofing on-line. Her study, in which communications students in a university in the northeastern United States participated, suggested that proofreading on the screen leads to more textual errors being missed, while students' familiarity with a subject was the critical factor in students' ability to identify factual errors.

Digital Journalism Emerges

This author has concluded that the most dramatic impact on journalism education over the past 20 years has been the emergence of the Internet and the World Wide Web.[52] Journalism and communication programs have had to respond to this powerful new platform that requires skills many faculty did not learn either in the professional world or in their academic experiences. Interestingly, as noted earlier, magazine pedagogy is largely skill based, so it is not surprising that there is not a large body of research.[53] In fact, very little research has been conducted into the other skills areas associated with journalism in general. The teaching of copyediting, interviewing, writing and other essential areas of the skills associated with journalism all have generated very little research interest. This is not the situation with the emergence of on-line journalism and digital media in general. The impact of on-line media and the related issue of convergence, or the integration of different kinds of media through computer-based platforms, was first felt in the mid- to late 1990s and then hit the academy like a tsunami wave in the 2000s. Digital media and convergence raised a whole raft of questions, including who is doing it, where does it fit into the curriculum, what impact will it have on the rest of journalism education, and how are people doing it? Lastly, what pedagogical techniques work and why?

The relationship between education about on-line journalism and magazine journalism education is ambiguous. As a clear integration of both visual and textual content, Web-based media appear a lot like magazines, even when they integrate video. (This is in contrast to newspapers, which originally were largely print only, or broadcast, which did not often use still images.) Text e-zines and blogs also have similarities to magazines. The magazine industry made an early substantial investment in Web-based publishing, perhaps most notably Time-Warner's disastrous investment in the Pathfinder Web portal in which the company spent $15 million a year for five years on a technologically flawed Web site only to shut it down.[54] As recently as the first half of 2013, very few Web sites of top magazine brands were in the top 100 of the most viewed Web sites, as reported by the Web analytics service Alexa. *People* magazine was the 199th most viewed Web site; Time.com was not in the top 500, and Cosmopolitan.com was not in the top 1,000.[55]

On the other hand, Web sites are clearly not digital magazines—that is, publications that adhere to the conventions of magazines but reside on the Web. The skills to create an effective Web site are not the same as the skills needed to create a successful magazine. The writing is different. The headlines are different. The mix of graphics, text and video is different. The use of links is different. The aesthetics are different. The publishing process is different. The job classifications and organizational hierarchy are different. And for courses that call for doing market research and audience analysis, the economics of Web publishing and magazine publishing are different, as are the audiences. In light of these differences, journalism educators have realized that on-line journalism reflects a new and unique genre. In one of the first systematic looks at the emergence of on-line journalism and the need for the academy to incorporate it into the curriculum, Lewis A. Friedland and Sheila Webb reported a three-year effort to incorporate multimedia journalism into the instruction at the University of Wisconsin School of Journalism.[56] Friedland and Webb set the stage for an ongoing theme in the examination of the role of digital media in the journalism curriculum when they observed that on-line journalism had dramatically destabilized the existing media industry and had had a dramatic impact on all media, including newspapers, magazines and broadcasting. The lines that demarcated traditional media were being blurred, and that, in and of itself, put pressure on journalism curricula that were organized along lines that mirrored the media industry. Finally, these industry changes were having a profound impact on the understanding of what is news and the ways in which journalism should be taught. Though in retrospect still in its infancy, the Internet and particularly the Web were already clearly seen as being a major disruptive force in journalism, to which both the industry and the academy would have to respond expeditiously. Since neither was known for rapid innovation, the challenges would be immense.[57]

After defining what they called "multimedia" journalism and delineating the difference from traditional media, Friedland and Webb reported that the School of Journalism at the University of Wisconsin began experimenting with on-line journalism in the summer of 1993 because the faculty recognized the media were, in fact, converging.[58] Using internal and external grants but relying on existing technology, the school launched a newsmagazine, *ONline Wisconsin*, which the authors believe was the third news journal on the Web, following the *Raleigh News and Observer*'s *Nando* and the *San Jose Mercury News*'s *Mercury Center*.[59] The authors describe their efforts to discover the right mix of content for the publication, the links they established with other news sources as they came onto the Web and the struggles in teaching students new technologies, such as HTML. They provide details that include their computer server and software platform. Finally, they noted that their students were getting good jobs with good companies.[60]

ONline Wisconsin is no longer on-line, but the Friedlander and Webb article put down a marker in what has become a two-decade process of incorporating digital media in journalism curricula. Perhaps what is most significant in terms of magazine education is that *ONline Wisconsin* was originally conceived to be a newsmagazine, even though it soon became apparent that an on-line journal's boundaries were quite different from traditional magazines.

From that starting point, two major underlying questions informed the pedagogical research into digital media in the journalism curricula: How should digital media fit into the curriculum, and what skills should students acquire? Everette E. Dennis and a number of scholars addressed the first question in 2003 by offering their personal opinions about the issues,[61] and Jeremy Sarachan, approximately six years later, surveyed 110 programs in North America to identify curriculum choices, technology tools and other trends associated with teaching convergence.[62] A report, "Learning Reconsidered: Education in the Digital Age—Communication, Convergence and the Curriculum," gives the results of the panel discussion of the application of technology to journalism or communication education that included Dennis, John Pavlik, Everett Rogers and Philip Meyer, among others.[63] Dennis and his colleagues observed that although the information age and digital revolution evolved over a 30-year period, when it finally burst into prominence in the 1990s, journalism educators were unprepared. Faculty representing different orientations in journalism education—i.e., skills-based educators versus those who cast a broader, perhaps more academic, net—found themselves talking past each other.[64] Philip Meyer opined that while the digital revolution opened the possibility of journalism becoming additionally more professionalized, the academy was moving more to a craft-orientation, toward new skills acquisition and very narrowly focused classes.[65] Overall, the panelists laid out many of the questions journalism educators faced. How much time should be spent acquiring technical skills? Should there be a separate sequence for digital media? How much focus should be on the larger social questions the Internet raised?

Sarachan provides some of the answers programs found over the next half decade.[66] He found that most programs added specific skills-oriented courses, such as Web design and multimedia newsgathering and storytelling. Courses in convergence journalism were at the top of the priority list to be added to the curriculum in the short term. Some programs offered separate theory classes for new media, while others incorporated theory into their skills-based classes. Sarachan concluded that academic units were systematically incorporating convergence technology into their curricula through a variety of avenues.[67] In short, the literature suggests that perhaps more slowly—or perhaps too haphazardly or too narrowly—than some observers would have liked, journalism educators have responded to the emergence of convergence. Though there is little published work on precisely how new media education has had an impact on education for other media forms, there has been some work on what new media skills students should learn. For example, in the magazine capstone course at Loyola University Maryland, students frequently build a companion Web site to the magazine prototype they develop. There seems to be a growing recognition that journalism education should be wider than just the acquisition of a specific skill set.[68] But, as always, one of the primary implicit or explicit learning objectives in journalism education is providing students with the skills to get a first job.

To explore the question of what employers want, Serena Carpenter conducted a quantitative analysis of on-line media help-wanted advertising.[69] She found that on-line news media professionals basically want students to have the same set of skills that traditional news media professionals want. Students should be able to write well, work under deadline and edit copy. They should have broad-based knowledge and know about the world outside the world of journalism. Additionally, they should possess the specific technical skills needed to do specific tasks. However, specific technical skills, such as knowing HTML (which was the most common technical skill required at the time of the survey), were in much less demand than solid writing skills.[70]

The most challenging aspect of digital media is that they touch on all the traditional communication platforms and genres. Digital media do not exist alongside magazines, for example, but are intrinsically intertwined with magazines in multiple ways. Many newspapers and magazines, ranging from the *Christian Science Monitor* to *Newsweek*, are going to all on-line formats. By going on-line, did *Newsweek* stop being a magazine? Did the skills students need to work at *Newsweek* change? Should magazine educators only be concerned with the skills needed to work at an on-line magazine, or must they also educate their students about the implications of magazines going completely on-line or existing in hybrid print and on-line formats? These are not rhetorical questions. They are among the issues magazine scholars and educators must face as they deal with the ongoing growth of digital platforms.

Conclusion

The research on magazine pedagogy over the past 20 years is limited. The studies reviewed in this article are generally based on small sample sets, case studies or surveys. They reflect to some degree the change in the way that research into journalism education generally has been conducted. But the context for research into pedagogy has changed. Higher education is under enormous pressure to create concrete measures by which its performance can be judged. The demand for accountability and assessment is filtering down to the course level. Programs and professors need to be able to articulate the learning goals of their courses and develop credible tools to determine if students have achieved those goals.

Magazine educators can participate in that process of defining learning goals, which could be a very healthy process overall. On the basis of the small body of research that has emerged, there is evidence that magazine pedagogy incorporates many of the best practices associated with the literature on effective teaching as well as aiding cognitive development and creativity. The hardest step to establishing a needed research agenda, however, may be the first step. Other than the implicit goal of preparing students for their first jobs, magazine educators, and journalism educators in general, have published little systematic research on articulating overall learning aims and objectives or learning aims and objectives of individual courses associated with magazine education. Research is needed to answer a series of very basic questions. What, besides perhaps being prepared for entry-level jobs, should students in magazine curricula or studying journalism generally know and be able to do when they graduate and why? What measures can be used to determine if magazine educators are effectively meeting their desired educational outcomes? What are those desired educational outcomes? Research could be conducted to determine how programmatic learning objectives could guide the development of individual course aims.

As long as magazines remain a viable medium—and there is no reason to think they will not—magazine education will hold an important place in journalism education. However, because the community of educators is relatively small, it may be too much to expect a specialized body of research to emerge that focuses the pedagogical issues involved in magazine education. Nonetheless, because of the defined focus, magazine educators are well positioned to participate in, and even lead, the wider conversations and research in the assessment and accountability that are so critical to the ongoing success of higher education in general and journalism and mass communication education specifically.

Notes

1 David Cuillier and Carol B. Schwalbe, "GIFTed Teaching: A Content Analysis of 253 Great Ideas for Teaching Awards in Journalism and Mass Communication Education," *Journalism & Mass Communication Educator* 65.1 (Spring 2010): 22–39.
2 Cuillier and Schwalbe, "GIFTed Teaching," 25.
3 Cuillier and Schwalbe, "GIFTed Teaching," 29.
4 Cuillier and Schwalbe, "GIFTed Teaching," 29.

5 ACEJMC, "2. Curriculum and Instruction," ACEJMC *Accrediting Standards*, Accrediting Council on Education in Journalism and Mass Communications <http://www2.ku.edu/~acejmc/PROGRAM/STANDARDS.SHTML#std2>, accessed 2 June 2014.

6 Peter Brooks, "Outcomes, Testing, Learning: What's at Stake?" *Social Research* 79.3 (Fall 2012): 601–611.

7 ACEJMC, "2. Curriculum and Instruction."

8 Elliot King, "Research Review: Issues in Magazine Journalism Education," in David Abrahamson, ed., *The American Magazine: Research Perspectives and Prospects* (Ames: Iowa State University Press, 1995), 122–133.

9 Denis McQuail, *McQuail's Mass Communication Theory*, 6th ed. (London and Thousand Oaks, CA: Sage, 2010), 14.

10 King, "Research Review," 122–133.

11 Thomas V. Dickson and Ralph L. Sellmeyer, "Green Eyeshades vs. Chi Squares Revisited: Editors' and JMC Administrators' Perceptions of Major Issues in Journalism Education" (paper presented at the Annual Meeting, Association for Education in Journalism and Mass Communication, August 1992) <http://eric.ed.gov/?id=ED349564>, accessed 2 June 2014.

12 Matthew Flamm, "525 Magazines Died in 2008," *Crain's New York Business*, 6 February 2009 <http://www.crainsnewyork.com/article/20090206/FREE/902069972>, accessed 20 December 2012.

13 "367 Magazines Closed in 2009 So Far," *Magazine Death Pool: "Who Will Be Next?"* (blog), 14 December 2009 <http://www.magazinedeathpool.com/magazine_death_pool/2009/12/367-magazines-closed-in-2009-so-far.html>, accessed 2 June 2014.

14 "Nothing to Shout About," *Economist*, 30 July 2009 <http://www.economist.com/node/14140373>, accessed 20 December 2012.

15 Will Oremus, "Google Has Officially Eaten the Newspaper Industry," *Future Tense* (blog), *Slate.com*, 12 November 2012 <http://www.slate.com/blogs/future_tense/2012/11/12/google_ad_revenue_tops_entire_us_print_media_industry_chart.html>, accessed 2 June 2014.

16 Bill Mickey, "How Revenue Models Are Evolving for Online-Only Publishers," *Folio:*, 17 December 2012 <http://www.foliomag.com/2012/how-revenue-models-are-evolving-online-only-publishers#.Ut2yjtLnbDc>, accessed 2 June 2014.

17 Christine Haughney and David Carr, "At *Newsweek*, Ending Print and a Blend of Two Styles," *Media Decoder* (blog), *New York Times*, 18 October 2012 <http://mediadecoder.blogs.nytimes.com/2012/10/18/newsweek-will-cease-print-publication-at-end-of-year/?_php=true&_type=blogs&_r=0>, accessed 2 June 2014; Alessandra Stanley, "Talk Ends and Spin Begins: Tina Brown Has No Regrets," *New York Times*, 20 January 2002 <http://www.nytimes.com/2002/01/20/us/talk-ends-and-spin-begins-tina-brown-has-no-regrets.html>, accessed 2 June 2014.

18 Samir Husni, "'*Recoil*' and '*Highlights Hello*' Top My List of Most Notable Launches of 2012: New Magazines Wrap-Up; Mr. Magazine Style," *Mr. Magazine* (blog), 29 December 2012 <https://mrmagazine.wordpress.com/2012/12/29/recoil-and-highlights-hello-top-my-list-of-most-notable-launches-of-2012-new-magazines-wrap-up-mr-magazine-style/>, accessed 2 June 2014.

19 Fred Wright, "The History and Characteristics of Zines," *Zine and E-Zine Resource Guide* <http://www.zinebook.com/resource/wright1.html>, accessed 20 December 2012.

20 AEJMC Magazine Division, "About the Journal," *Journal of Magazine & New Media Research* <http://aejmcmagazine.arizona.edu/journal.html>, accessed 2 June 2014.

21 Lee B. Becker, Tudor Vlad, and Paris Desnoes, "Enrollments Decline Slightly and the Student Body Becomes More Diverse," *Journalism & Mass Communication Educator* 65.3/4 (Autumn/Winter 2010): 224–249.

22 Lee B. Becker, Tudor Vlad, and Devora Olin, "2008 Enrollment Report: Slow Rate of Growth May Signal Weakening of Demand," *Journalism & Mass Communication Educator* 64.3 (Autumn 2009): 232–257.

23 Lee B. Becker, "Enrollments Increase in 1989, but Graduation Rates Drop," *Journalism Educator* 45.3 (Autumn 1990): 4–15.

24 David Sumner, "Undergraduate Magazine Programs and Courses at U.S. Universities" <http://aejmcmagazine.arizona.edu/Students/magazine_programs.pdf>, accessed 2 June 2014.

25 Contest summary available at AEJMC Magazine Division, "AEJMC Magazine Division Student Contest," 2012 <http://aejmcmagazine.arizona.edu/students.html>, accessed 2 June 2014.

26 Robin Blom and Lucinda D. Davenport, "Searching for the Core of Journalism Education: Program Directors Disagree on Curriculum Priorities," *Journalism & Mass Communication Educator* 67.1 (Spring 2012): 70–86.

27 Sumner, "Undergraduate Magazine Programs."

28 Kate L. Peirce and Gilbert D. Martinez, "How We Learn to Teach: Trial by Fire, by the Seat of Our Pants and Other (More Scientific) Methods," *Journalism & Mass Communication Educator* 67.2 (Summer 2012): 134–144.

29 Scott Fosdick, "The State of Magazine Research in 2008," *Journal of Magazine & New Media Research* 10.1 (Fall 2008): 1–4.

30 Leara Rhodes and Amber Roessner, "Teaching Magazine Publishing through Experiential Learning," *Journalism & Mass Communication Educator* 63.4 (Winter 2009): 304–316.

31 Rhodes and Roessner, "Teaching Magazine Publishing," 304–316.

32 Rhodes and Roessner, "Teaching Magazine Publishing," 304–316.

33 Elliot King, "The Role of Journalism History, and the Academy, in the Development of Core Knowledge in Journalism Education," *Journalism & Mass Communication Educator* 63.2 (Summer 2008): 166–178.

34 Thomas V. Dickson and Wanda Brandon, "The Gap between Educators and Professional Journalists," *Journalism & Mass Communication Educator* 55.3 (Autumn 2000): 50–67.

35 Carolyn Lepre and Glen L. Bleske, "Little Common Ground for Magazine Editors and Professors Surveyed on Journalism Curriculum," *Journalism & Mass Communication Educator* 60.2 (Summer 2005): 190–200.

36 Sonya Forte Duhé and Lee Ann Zukowski, "Radio-TV Journalism Curriculum: First Jobs and Career Preparation," *Journalism & Mass Communication Educator* 52.1 (Spring 1997): 4–15.

37 Sumner, "Undergraduate Magazine Programs."

38 Michael O'Donnell, "Teaching Publication Design with Desktop Technology," *Journalism Educator* 49.4 (Winter 1995): 47.

39 Claude Cookman, "A Computer-Based Graphics Course and Students' Cognitive Skills," *Journalism & Mass Communication Educator* 53.3 (Autumn 1998): 37–49.

40 Meenakshi Gigi Durham, "Revolutionizing the Teaching of Magazine Design," *Journalism & Mass Communication Educator* 53.1 (Spring 1998): 23.

41 Renita Coleman and Jan Colbert, "Grounding the Teaching of Design in Creativity," *Journalism & Mass Communication Educator* 56.2 (Summer 2001): 4–24.

42 Mark H. Massé and Mark N. Popovich, "Assessing Faculty Attitudes toward the Teaching of Writing," *Journalism & Mass Communication Educator* 53.3 (August 1998): 50–64.

43 Massé and Popovich, "Assessing Faculty," 50–64.

44 Massé and Popovich, "Assessing Faculty," 50–64.

45 Massé and Popovich, "Assessing Faculty," 50–64.

46 Mark H. Massé and Mark N. Popovich, "The National Media Writing Faculty Study," *Journalism & Mass Communication Educator* 59.3 (Autumn 2004): 214–238.

47 Massé and Popovich, "National Media Writing Faculty Study," 214–238.

48 Massé and Popovich, "National Media Writing Faculty Study," 214–238.

49 Mark H. Massé and Mark N. Popovich, "Accredited and Nonaccredited Media Writing Programs Are Stagnant, Resistant to Curricular Reform, and Similar," *Journalism & Mass Communication Educator* 62.2 (Summer 2007): 142–160.

50 Peirce and Martinez, "How We Learn to Teach," 134–144.

51 Patty Wharton-Michael, "Print vs. Computer Screen: Effects of Medium on Proofreading Accuracy," *Journalism & Mass Communication Educator* 63.1 (Spring 2008): 28–41.

52 Elliot King, *Free for All: The Internet's Transformation of Journalism* (Evanston, IL: Northwestern University Press, 2010).

53 King, "Research Review," 122–133.

54 Marc Gunther, "The Push to Create Original Magazines in Cyberspace: The Pioneers Have a Long Road Ahead—and Millions of Dollars Are at Stake," *Philly.com*, 9 August 1995 <http://articles.philly.com/1995-08–09/entertainment/25711011_1_internet-access-cyberspace-web-sites>, accessed 2 June 2014.

55 "The Top 500 Sites on the Web," Alexa <http://www.alexa.com/topsites>, accessed 2 June 2014.

56 Lewis A. Friedland and Sheila Webb, "Incorporating Online Publishing into the Curriculum," *Journalism & Mass Communication Educator* 51.3 (Autumn 1996): 54–65.

57 Jon Katz, "Online or Not, Newspapers Suck," *Wired*, September 1994 <http://www.wired.com/wired/archive/2.09/news.suck.html>, accessed 2 January 2013.

58 Friedland and Webb, "Incorporating Online Publishing," 54–65.

59 Friedland and Webb, "Incorporating Online Publishing," 54–65.

60 Friedland and Webb, "Incorporating Online Publishing," 54–65.

61 Everette E. Dennis, Philip Meyer, S. Shyam Sundar, Larry Pryor, Everett M. Rogers, Helen L. Chen, and John Pavlik, "Learning Reconsidered: Education in the Digital Age—Communications, Convergence and the Curriculum," *Journalism & Mass Communication Educator* 60.1 (Winter 2003): 292–317.

62 Jeremy Sarachan, "The Path Already Taken: Technological and Pedagogical Practices in Convergence Education," *Journalism & Mass Communication Educator* 66.2 (Summer 2011): 160–174.

63 Dennis, Meyer, Sundar, Pryor, Rogers, Chen, and Pavlik, "Learning Reconsidered," 292–317.

64 Dennis, Meyer, Sundar, Pryor, Rogers, Chen, and Pavlik, "Learning Reconsidered," 292–317.

65 Dennis, Meyer, Sundar, Pryor, Rogers, Chen, and Pavlik, "Learning Reconsidered," 292–317.

66 Sarachan, "The Path Already Taken," 160–174.

67 Sarachan, "The Path Already Taken," 160–174.

68 Hugo de Burgh, "Skills Are Not Enough: The Case for Journalism as an Academic Discipline," *Journalism* 4.1 (February 2003): 95–112.

69 Serena Carpenter, "An Application of the Theory of Expertise: Teaching Broad and Skill Knowledge Areas to Prepare Journalists for Change," *Journalism & Mass Communication Educator* 64.3 (Autumn 2009): 287–304.

70 Carpenter, "An Application of the Theory of Expertise," 287–304.

Bibliography

ACEJMC. "2. Curriculum and Instruction." *ACEJMC Accrediting Standards*. Accrediting Council on Education in Journalism and Mass Communications <http://www2.ku.edu/~acejmc/PROGRAM/STANDARDS.SHTML#std2>, accessed 2 June 2014.

AEJMC Magazine Division. "About the Journal." *Journal of Magazine & New Media Research* <http://aejmcmagazine.arizona.edu/journal.html>, accessed 2 June 2014.

AEJMC Magazine Division. "AEJMC Magazine Division Student Contest." 2012 <http://aejmcmagazine.arizona.edu/students.html>, accessed 2 June 2014.

Becker, Lee B. "Enrollments Increase in 1989, but Graduation Rates Drop." *Journalism Educator* 45.3 (Autumn 1990): 4–15.

Becker, Lee B.; Vlad, Tudor; and Desnoes, Paris. "Enrollments Decline Slightly and the Student Body Becomes More Diverse." *Journalism & Mass Communication Educator* 65.3/4 (Autumn/Winter 2010): 224–249.

Becker, Lee B.; Vlad, Tudor; and Olin, Devora. "2008 Enrollment Report: Slow Rate of Growth May Signal Weakening of Demand." *Journalism & Mass Communication Educator* 64.3 (Autumn 2009): 232–257.

Blom, Robin and Davenport, Lucinda D. "Searching for the Core of Journalism Education: Program Directors Disagree on Curriculum Priorities." *Journalism & Mass Communication Educator* 67.1 (Spring 2012): 70–86.

Brooks, Peter. "Outcomes, Testing, Learning: What's at Stake?" *Social Research* 79.3 (Fall 2012): 601–611.

Carpenter, Serena. "An Application of the Theory of Expertise: Teaching Broad and Skill Knowledge Areas to Prepare Journalists for Change." *Journalism & Mass Communication Educator* 64.3 (Autumn 2009): 287–304.

Coleman, Renita and Colbert, Jan. "Grounding the Teaching of Design in Creativity." *Journalism & Mass Communication Educator* 56.2 (Summer 2001): 4–24.

Cookman, Claude. "A Computer-Based Graphics Course and Students' Cognitive Skills." *Journalism & Mass Communication Educator* 53.3 (Autumn 1998): 37–49.

Cuillier, David and Schwalbe, Carol B. "GIFTed Teaching: A Content Analysis of 253 Great Ideas for Teaching Awards in Journalism and Mass Communication Education." *Journalism & Mass Communication Educator* 65.1 (Spring 2010): 22–39.

de Burgh, Hugo. "Skills Are Not Enough: The Case for Journalism as an Academic Discipline." *Journalism* 4.1 (February 2003): 95–112.

Dennis, Everette E.; Meyer, Philip; Sundar, S. Shyam; Pryor, Larry; Rogers, Everett M.; Chen, Helen L.; and Pavlik, John. "Learning Reconsidered: Education in the Digital Age—Communications, Convergence and the Curriculum." *Journalism & Mass Communication Educator* 57.4 (Winter 2003): 292–317.

Dickson, Thomas V. and Sellmeyer, Ralph L. "Green Eyeshades vs. Chi Squares Revisited: Editors' and JMC Administrators' Perceptions of Major Issues in Journalism Education." Paper presented at the Annual Meeting, Association for Education in Journalism and Mass Communication, August 1992 <http://eric.ed.gov/?id=ED349564>, accessed 2 June 2014.

Dickson, Thomas V. and Brandon, Wanda. "The Gap between Educators and Professional Journalists." *Journalism & Mass Communication Educator* 55.3 (Autumn 2000): 50–67.

Duhé, Sonya Forte and Zukowski, Lee Ann. "Radio-TV Journalism Curriculum: First Jobs and Career Preparation." *Journalism & Mass Communication Educator* 52.1 (Spring 1997): 4–15.

Durham, Meenakshi Gigi. "Revolutionizing the Teaching of Magazine Design." *Journalism & Mass Communication Educator* 53.1 (Spring 1998): 23–32.

Flamm, Matthew. "525 Magazines Died in 2008." *Crain's New York Business*, 6 February 2009 <http://www.crainsnewyork.com/article/20090206/FREE/902069972>, accessed 20 December 2012.

Fosdick, Scott. "The State of Magazine Research in 2008." *Journal of Magazine & New Media Research* 10.1 (Fall 2008): 1–4.

Friedland, Lewis A. and Webb, Sheila. "Incorporating Online Publishing into the Curriculum." *Journalism & Mass Communication Educator* 51.3 (Autumn 1996): 54–65.

Gunther, Marc. "The Push to Create Original Magazines in Cyberspace: The Pioneers Have a Long Road Ahead—and Millions of Dollars Are at Stake." *Philly*.com, 9 August 1995 <http://articles. philly.com/1995–08–09/entertainment/25711011_1_internet-access-cyberspace-web-sites>, accessed 2 June 2014.

Haughney, Christine and Carr, David. "At *Newsweek*, Ending Print and a Blend of Two Styles." *Media Decoder* (blog). *New York Times*, 18 October 2012 <http://mediadecoder.blogs.nytimes.com/ 2012/10/18/newsweek-will-cease-print-publication-at-end-of-year/?ref=newsweekinc>, accessed 15 December 2013.

Husni, Samir. "'*Recoil*' and '*Highlights Hello*' Top My List of Most Notable Launches of 2012: New Magazines Wrap-Up; Mr. Magazine Style." *Mr. Magazine* (blog), 29 December 2012 <https:// mrmagazine.wordpress.com/2012/12/29/recoil-and-highlights-hello-top-my-list-of-most-notable-launches-of-2012-new-magazines-wrap-up-mr-magazine-style/>, accessed 2 June 2014.

Katz, Jon. "Online or Not, Newspapers Suck." *Wired*, September 1994 <http://www.wired.com/wired/ archive/2.09/news.suck.html>, accessed 2 January 2013.

King, Elliot. *Free for All: The Internet's Transformation of Journalism*. Evanston, IL: Northwestern University Press, 2010.

King, Elliot. "Research Review: Issues in Magazine Journalism Education." In Abrahamson, David, ed. *The American Magazine: Research Perspectives and Prospects*. Ames: Iowa State University Press, 1995, 122–133.

King, Elliot. "The Role of Journalism History, and the Academy, in the Development of Core Knowledge in Journalism Education." *Journalism & Mass Communication Educator* 63.2 (Summer 2008): 166–178.

Lepre, Carolyn and Bleske, Glen L. "Little Common Ground for Magazine Editors and Professors Surveyed on Journalism Curriculum." *Journalism & Mass Communication Educator* 60.2 (Summer 2005): 190–200.

Massé, Mark H. and Popovich, Mark N. "Accredited and Nonaccredited Media Writing Programs Are Stagnant, Resistant to Curricular Reform, and Similar." *Journalism & Mass Communication Educator* 62.2 (Summer 2007): 142–160.

Massé, Mark H. and Popovich, Mark N. "Assessing Faculty Attitudes toward the Teaching of Writing." *Journalism & Mass Communication Educator* 53.3 (August 1998): 50–64.

Massé, Mark H. and Popovich, Mark N. "The National Media Writing Faculty Study." *Journalism & Mass Communication Educator* 59.3 (Autumn 2004): 214–238.

McQuail, Denis. *McQuail's Mass Communication Theory*. 6th ed. London and Thousand Oaks, CA: Sage, 2010.

Mickey, Bill. "How Revenue Models Are Evolving for Online-Only Publishers." *Folio:*, 17 December 2012 <http://www.foliomag.com/2012/how-revenue-models-are-evolving-online-only-publishers#. Ut2yjtLnbDc>, accessed 2 June 2014.

"Nothing to Shout About." *Economist*, 30 July 2009 <http://www.economist.com/node/14140373>, accessed 20 December 2012.

O'Donnell, Michael. "Teaching Publication Design with Desktop Technology." *Journalism Educator* 49.4 (Winter 1995): 47–56.

Oremus, Will. "Google Has Officially Eaten the Newspaper Industry." *Future Tense* (blog), *Slate.com*, 12 November 2012 <http://www.slate.com/blogs/future_tense/2012/11/12/google_ad_revenue_tops_ entire_us_print_media_industry_chart.html>, accessed 2 June 2014.

Peirce, Kate L. and Martinez, Gilbert D. "How We Learn to Teach: Trial by Fire, by the Seat of Our Pants and Other (More Scientific) Methods." *Journalism & Mass Communication Educator* 67.2 (Summer 2012): 134–144.

Rhodes, Leara and Roessner, Amber. "Teaching Magazine Publishing through Experiential Learning." *Journalism & Mass Communication Educator* 63.4 (Winter 2009): 304–316.

Sarachan, Jeremy. "The Path Already Taken: Technological and Pedagogical Practices in Convergence Education." *Journalism & Mass Communication Educator* 66.2 (Summer 2011): 160–174.

Stanley, Alessandra. "Talk Ends and Spin Begins: Tina Brown Has No Regrets." *New York Times*, 20 January 2002 <http://www.nytimes.com/2002/01/20/us/talk-ends-and-spin-begins-tina-brown-has-no-regrets.html>, accessed 2 June 2014.

Sumner, David. "Undergraduate Magazine Programs and Courses at U.S. Universities." <http://aejmcmagazine.arizona.edu/Students/magazine_programs.pdf>, accessed 2 June 2014.

"367 Magazines Closed in 2009 So Far." *Magazine Death Pool: "Who Will Be Next?"* (blog),14 December 2009 <http://www.magazinedeathpool.com/magazine_death_pool/2009/12/367-magazines-closed-in-2009-so-far.html>, accessed 2 June 2014.

"Top 500 Sites on the Web, The." Alexa <http://www.alexa.com/topsites>, accessed 2 June 2014.

Wharton-Michael, Patty. "Print vs. Computer Screen: Effects of Medium on Proofreading Accuracy." *Journalism & Mass Communication Educator* 63.1 (Spring 2008): 28–41.

Wright, Fred. "The History and Characteristics of Zines." *Zine & E-Zine Resource Guide* <http://www.zinebook.com/resource/wright1.html>, accessed 20 December 2012.

28

TEACHING MAGAZINE WRITING

The Long- and Short-Form of It

Kim Martin Long

Books abound with advice and instruction on how to write journalism—news or features, short or long form—so one wonders how new ones could possibly be justified. The field is changing rapidly, however, in the digital landscape. For example, a staple of American newsmagazines, *Newsweek* went out of print for the whole of 2013. Publishers' catalogs, therefore, list new and forthcoming titles such as *Feature and Magazine Writing: Action, Angle and Anecdotes*, 3rd ed.[1]; *Feature Writing: Telling the Story*, 2nd ed.[2] and scores of titles looking at how to write news stories, such as *Writing and Reporting News: A Coaching Method*[3] and *Journalism Next: A Practical Guide to Digital Reporting and Publishing*.[4] Most of these, however, do not offer much in the way of ground-breaking ideas, although the newer books do incorporate advice on writing for the new technologies in what is called cross-platform, multimodal journalism, or convergent journalism. The *Kemsley Manual of Journalism*,[5] first published in 1950 as a guide for journalists working in the British Kemsley Newspapers group, for example, provides advice on writing almost identical to that found in James Glen Stovall's 2012 *Writing for the Mass Media*.[6] In many ways, then, the series of books written by Harold Evans under the title *Editing and Design: A Five-Volume Manual of English, Typography and Layout*[7] (1972–1978) remain the benchmark for *traditional* journalistic writing. William Blundell's 1988 book, *The Art and Craft of Feature Writing*,[8] likewise, remains a staple, with specific strategies and helpful information for long-form writers.

Literature Review and Method

This chapter's primary goal is to survey resources for writing journalism, specifically magazine journalism, that have been produced roughly over the last 25 years and are still relevant today. The purpose, then, is to introduce some valuable resources for writing magazine journalism in these various forms and to recommend some areas in which future research should focus. The overall goal is that teachers, scholars, practicing journalists and students, in English-speaking countries and beyond, will find the information helpful as they teach, study or practice writing for magazines.

Reviewing the literature for what has been written on teaching magazine writing can be challenging because so few books and articles deal solely with this subject. Surveying the field thus began with simple Web searches, using the following key words and phrases: *teaching magazine writing, long-form journalism, short form journalism, feature writing* and *writing for magazines*. Next was a review of publishers' Web sites, specifically those who publish extensively in the field of journalism education and scholarship, such as Sage, Routledge/Taylor and Francis, or

Pearson/Allyn & Bacon. Also consulted were journals in the field, such as *Journalism & Mass Communication Quarterly*, the *Journal of Magazine & New Media Research* and *Journalism & Mass Communication Educator*. References cited in some of the books discussed in the chapter were examined, as were syllabi from faculty in selected journalism schools, to see what sources they have consulted. Personal contacts were also made with a few journalism professors who specialize in the magazine.[9]

As noted earlier, the bulk of what has been published in the last few decades on the topic has simply offered elegant or slightly updated or snappy variations of some of the same information. Some of those variations, however, are important in the context of magazine journalism, either because they offer specialized guidance for feature writers, or they offer specifically magazine-oriented advice and solutions. Jenny McKay's *The Magazines Handbook*[10] provides advice for magazine writing in general, and Vicky Hay offers solid advice for feature writers in *The Essential Feature*.[11] Books or journals dedicated solely to magazine writing are still rare. Those that do exist tend to look backwards toward a golden age of literary journalism, when a talented writer could be commissioned to supply 10,000 words of narrative prose and a long deadline in which to do it, or they explore the histories of niche magazine publishing, such as periodicals aimed at ethnic or socially marginalized groups (such as Rodger Streitmatter's *Unspeakable: The Rise of the Gay and Lesbian Press in America*,[12] Alan and Barbara Nourie's *American Mass-Market Magazines*[13] or the special issue of *American Periodicals* devoted to immigrant periodicals[14]).

Magazine journalism has evolved and changed in the last couple of decades in many substantive ways. Opportunities still exist to publish long-form journalism, but they are increasingly likely to look more like the *Atavist* rather than *Esquire*, and they could appear in a purely on-line venue rather than in print. Today magazine journalists need to be able to write catchy shorts, but these need to be creatively searchable on the Web rather than based on a traditional news pyramid. Journalists also need to be able to plan, if not execute, graphics and multimedia to embed in their work. Books—both text and professional—provide the extant body of *working theory* on how to write journalism, whether news or features, short or long form, for magazines and other print media in hard copy and on-line. These texts may not meet all the criteria for "working theory"[15] or "operational theory"[16] so capably articulated in the series of books that make up *McQuail's Mass Communication Theory*,[17] but they do contain the major portion of the current corpus of knowledge.

Drawing on the extant body of literature, then, the topics for this chapter roughly fall into these categories: (1) *Writing long form*: To identify existing work concerned with long-form writing that is worth carrying forward; (2) *Magazine-specific writing*: To identify existing sources specifically focused on writing for magazines that is considered successful and rewarding by readers; (3) *Short form, cross-platform and convergence*: To identify and evaluate existing research centered on issues related to the creation and presentation of content for cross-platforms or for a multimodal magazine (print, Web, app, social media, video, audio); (4) *Scholarly needs and areas of inquiry*: To identify gaps in the literature, both in the working theory and in the scholarly work.

Long-Form Writing

Finding a working theory or operational definition of long form is difficult, but most sources indicate long-form writing is that which deals with a subject in an extended and fully developed way. Matthew Ricketson has perhaps gone the furthest in nailing down a definition in his 2012 book *Australian Journalism Today*. He lists six elements of long-form journalism: that (1) its subject is actual events and people; (2) it concerns current issues; (3) it is the result of extensive research; (4) it uses a narrative approach; (5) it explores complex implications of an event or issue; and (6) it has an impact of some kind.[18] He claims that long form is needed "for conveying emotion, atmosphere and context" in a story.[19] He also asserts that "the more pronounced the emphasis on speed and shouting evident in the 24-hour news cycle, the more pronounced is the need—and the thirst—for long-form journalism," which allows for reflection.[20] Benjamin Ball's notable article on digital long form expands Ricketson's definition to include photography and media.[21] The on-line magazine-blog *Editia* from the University of Canberra, Australia, is devoted to long-form writing and can be a good source for current conversations on longer journalism.[22]

Word count to define long-form journalism is not as important as the careful treatment of a complex or engaging subject, although some sources still try to describe long form in terms of word count. Ricketson says that "magazine features range between two and ten thousand words, occasionally longer."[23] In his chapter, "The New Appreciation of Long-form Journalism in a Short-form World,"[24] Ricketson becomes the champion for book-length, long-form journalism and cites award-winning works (usually just classified as nonfiction) in both Australia and America.

> The examples given above, not to mention many others, show that what is being offered in book-length journalism is fresh information, more information, and information set in context and information [where] meaning has been mined and shaped into a narrative that fully engages readers' minds and emotions.[25]

Despite the rise of digital journalism, the sound byte and rumoured, shorter attention spans,[26] work on long-form writing, formerly the standard in journalism, is still very much alive, as Ricketson reminds us. Some quality books have been produced lately, and some others deserve to be reconsidered. Of the newer books, David Sumner and Holly Miller's *Feature and Magazine Writing* is among the most widely used by journalism instructors, according to a brief examination of course syllabi.[27] First published in 2005 and updated in 2009 and 2013, the book is divided into six parts: (a) Reading, writing and relevance; (b) Taking your articles to the freelance market; (c) Adding action and anecdotes; (d) Different formats, different results; (e) Exploring digital opportunities; and (f) Preparing the final draft.

As Sumner and Miller note,

> The new mobile, digital environment meant writers could abandon chunks for a more integrated, multimedia approach to storytelling. Video and audio files were no longer ancillaries to the written text. Now these elements could be embedded within a narrative, replacing the written word where it was most appropriate. Storytellers could use each media element as part of the one interactive, long-form digital story that could be experienced in both linear and nonlinear fashion. Since readers used these devices more like books and magazines, storytellers had to worry less about getting a point across as quickly as possible.
>
> This also meant the magazine world was no longer the domain only of writers and editors.[28]

The authors discuss the need to be part of an interdisciplinary team: "Writers can take heart, however, because the story remains at the heart of this new form, and the written word remains integral to the long-form process."[29] In the chapter on "Long-Form Digital Storytelling,"[30] Sumner and Miller provide some helpful heuristics for the writer new to the digital magazine world, such as "keep your navigation simple."[31] In this chapter the new tools of the digital age are compared with grammar as a subject to be understood by journalists. Sumner and Miller call this "the literacy of the digital age."[32] In the concluding chapter, the authors firmly assert that the magazine industry is surviving. "Magazines remain stronger and more resilient than newspapers . . . [because] they have found more ways to capitalize on digital media."[33] Sumner and Miller state that more magazines got off the ground than closed in 2011, and they encourage would-be writers not to despair. Good writers get jobs, they say, and the magazine industry thrives beyond the dream jobs at *Cosmopolitan* or *Rolling Stone*.

Friedlander and Lee's *Feature Writing: The Pursuit of Excellence*, now in its seventh edition,[34] also offers updated advice for the long-form writer, whether newspaper or magazine, but the book contains separate chapters on researching, interviewing and marketing the magazine article. The authors note that the "magazine article has its own character" from a newspaper feature: "Two of the most apparent differences in the magazine article are the leisurely approach to subject material and the fact that writers frequently take a subjective stand on what they are writing."[35] Friedlander and Lee explain that revealing the author's point of view is liberating but fraught with responsibility. They provide advice for the freelance writer about how to write a magazine article that speaks to its audience and market and delivers what it intends, as does Katie McCabe's Pulitzer Prize–winning, 1989 article from the *Washingtonian* magazine.[36] Providing other examples of award-winning articles throughout *Feature Writing*, Friedlander and Lee demonstrate how to write a quality long-form piece. The new seventh edition updates material, taking into account the technologies that continue to change the landscape of magazine writing. The authors totally revised their examination of Internet-assisted research and explore the on-line magazine market for freelance writers. The book also examines the future of print and electronic journalism in light of current trends in newspaper closings. Overall, it serves as a comprehensive text for feature writing.

An older but still relevant book, Vicky Hay's 1990 *The Essential Feature*, goes from defining what a feature is, a "hybrid that requires you to combine a reporter's skills with a storyteller's art," to selling it, developing it, researching and interviewing, and organizing it.[37] She discusses the "journalist as storyteller"[38] and reviews the techniques of fiction, such as point of view and characterization, to incorporate into feature articles. Hay's annotated samples of published articles are instructive, such as this one for a personal experience story by Marguerite Reiss: "Reiss never lets up on the specific, grueling description. Consider the in-depth interviewing required to elicit these details!"[39] The book's final chapters on law and ethics, editors and free-lancing round out this comprehensive guide that still communicates relevance to writers today.

Another older but still relevant book is Betsy Graham's *Magazine Article Writing*, which has valuable advice for the long-form writer. First published in 1980 and updated in 1992, the book provides nuts-and-bolts advice in a conversational style: "In the process of matching your topic to a targeted audience, you engage in a tentative try-it-on process, testing an article idea for a specific magazine and trying another combination if it doesn't fit."[40] The book includes the expected chapters on understanding the market as a freelancer, interviewing and legal issues, but it also instructs writers to start as good readers, using a careful and analytical method: "You may learn the effectiveness of rhythm, whether it comes from the emphatic repetition of words, from the repetition of structure in parallelism, or from the repeated sounds in alliteration."[41] Graham's book, like many others in the later twentieth century,[42] capitalized on the emerging discipline that was journalism and mass communication and offered would-be professional writers solid advice and quality examples to move their craft forward.

Another text often cited by others or appearing in syllabi is Matthew Ricketson's *Writing Feature Stories: How to Research and Write Newspaper and Magazine Articles*, which proclaims that feature writing is fun, hard work and important.[43] The Australian journalist includes routine chapters on generating ideas, planning and gathering, organizing, and writing strong leads and closes, but he also includes chapters on wordcraft, editing and working with editors and literary journalism. He writes,

> It is important to understand that the act of storytelling frames the world in a particular way and portrays people through a particular lens. But all this does not mean journalists should give up trying to find out what is going on in the world and striving to make sense of it and communicating it as widely and strongly as possible.[44]

Carla Johnson's textbook *21st Century Feature Writing* includes many samples from professionals and students, focuses on entry-level writing and contains a chapter on writing for the Internet that explains the techniques of linear and non-linear writing.[45] Daniel Reimold's *Journalism of Ideas: Brainstorming, Developing, and Selling Stories in the Digital Age* takes a fresh approach to the expected content of a primer, with chapters called "Timely Ideas," "Trendy Ideas" and "Criminal Ideas."[46] Each chapter includes an exercise called "Ideas Online," in which Reimold directs students to look at on-line archives, features and images to get ideas for stories. Rather than including an obligatory section on writing with and for the Internet, this text is written clearly with the multimodal in mind. Three Australian journalists—Stephen Tanner, Holly Kasinger and Nick Richardson focus on the long-form essay or creative nonfiction in *Feature Writing: Telling the Story*.[47] The authors use a step-by-step approach to help writers learn to write or improve their storytelling in the long-form essay or creative nonfiction, heavily emphasizing the new literary journalism, with instruction on dialogue. Jane Johnston wrote, "This boundary blurring approach, which we also saw in Ricketson, is part of a wider move within journalism education and practice, which now operates within expanded frameworks and contexts." She calls the book a "balanced mix of practice and theory, illustration and technique."[48] Overall, for long-form writing, the resources are fairly rich, with information about technology updates and some bells and whistles to add to the basics.

Still other books on writing, such as Charles H. Harrison's *How to Write for Magazines: Consumer, Trade, and Web*, focus on genre-specific magazines, providing advice for directing one's work toward these specific kinds of publications.[49] In most of the textbooks aimed at writing for magazines, discussed earlier, in fact, sections or chapters are devoted to specific genres.

One of the most exciting developments in magazine writing and research over the last 25 years or so has been the rise (or resurgence, actually) of narrative nonfiction, also called creative nonfiction or literary journalism, among other terms. Many standard texts, such as the *Journalist's Craft: A Guide to Writing Better Stories*,[50] include chapters or sections on narrative nonfiction. In this text, an entire chapter, "Writing Nonfiction Narrative,"[51] is devoted to using nonfiction narrative and storytelling to relate the news. In Mark Bowden's chapter, the author of *Blackhawk Down* explains that telling stories "means approaching reporting with a storyteller's mind, looking for anecdote and setting, finding characters, scenes and dialogue, and identifying a beginning, middle, and end."[52] Nancy M. Hamilton's *Uncovering the Secrets of Magazine Writing: A Step-by-Step Guide to Writing Creative Nonfiction for Print and Internet Publication* keeps nonfiction narrative at the center of the book while providing a hands-on education in all aspects of the magazine industry, the writing process and ethics.[53] Angela Phillips, however, in *Good Writing for Journalists*,[54] collects what she considers to be good writing in various categories. Phillips annotates the stories with instructional analysis and observation. For instance, in a section on writing an introduction, she comments on a piece in the *Guardian* about a railway construction site: "This descriptive introduction is slow for a British newspaper, but *Guardian* style tends to favor literary introductions, and, as the story has already been summarized in the stand-first, there is time to linger."[55] Continuing with her commentary, she then notes, "This was the killer fact. Something important that surprises us and hooks us into the action."[56] This kind of back and forth between the original news story and Phillips's annotations force the reader to see what the writer wrote and helps illustrate how to construct writing that people will want to read.

Jack Hart, in *Storycraft: The Complete Guide to Writing Narrative Nonfiction*,[57] also uses the coaching method, as he has practiced for some time at the *Oregonian*, mentoring many Pulitzer Prize-winning writers and collecting examples of good narrative nonfiction, what he calls "the literature of our time."[58] He relates the editors' perspectives in his book, how they worked with writers to bring the pieces to life, an aspect of writing that is often ignored. As he says, one must learn "enough about story theory to avoid the fatal error of forcing narrative onto inappropriate material," but one does not need to have a great deal of writing experience to produce quality narrative nonfiction, only a "determination to master the craft."[59] The periodical

Literary Journalism Studies is building a bibliography on scholarly work in this area, which is growing steadily.[60] Literary journalism has crossed the boundaries of English, communication and journalism departments as good writers seek to tell the truth with all the tools of good storytelling. While this is certainly not "new journalism," as it was called in the 1960s and 1970s—because writers like Daniel Defoe, Charles Dickens and Mark Twain employed literary techniques in their journalism[61]—literary journalism has brought writers and readers together in appreciation of a good story.[62] Scholars have no problems finding good books and articles on aspects of magazine writing, publishing and impact; however, general studies on writing for the magazine do not seem to be doing anything very new.[63]

Although not specifically for magazine writers, Paula LaRocque's 2003 *Book on Writing: The Ultimate Guide to Writing Well* is a valuable source for any writer.[64] Drawing upon her decades of work with the *Dallas Morning News* and in classrooms, LaRocque has written a useful and straightforward guide on writing. In addition to general writing skills, the book, divided into three sections, provides a section on good storytelling and a handbook on grammar and usage. LaRocque's casual and humorous style makes this a very readable guide even if one is not a grammar geek. As she explains in the introduction,

> Accuracy aside, simplicity, clarity, and brevity are the most important criteria for all writing . . . A CEO given to dense, pretentious, and undisciplined writing once said that following these guidelines would damage his "style." Perhaps unreadable writing could be called a "style," but it's not a style worth cultivating.[65]

Throughout the guide she hammers home her points with example after example, like a funny schoolmarm. Her advice applies, not just to writing for long form or for magazine-specific journalism but the next category as well—emerging media.

Short Form and Media Convergence

The most obvious change in writing for magazines over the last 25 years has been the need to learn how to write across many platforms for perhaps different audiences—those who want traditional print-style delivery, those who want short blurbs, and those who want embedded video, audio and graphics, even incorporating social media into the mix so that the magazine is no longer a one-way method of communication. Bob Britten notes the following in the introduction to the December 2013 issue of the *Journal of Magazine & New Media Research*:

> Traditionally, a magazine presented itself as a place for users to go to get the information they sought; the assumption is the magazine is a source for content. What the introduction of social media suggests is that the magazine may become a source for connection, a reliable nexus of the threads of information that are now everywhere.[66]

Convergent media have certainly complicated and invigorated the magazine landscape. Thorsten Quandt and Jane Singer, in an essay appearing in the *Handbook of Journalism Studies*, define convergence as "the blurring of boundaries between fixed and mobile communications; broadcast, telephone, mobile and home networks; media, information and communication; and, most notably, telecommunications, media and information technology."[67] Rather than focusing on the changes in the context of technology driving the convergence, they prefer to see the technology as a tool of the journalist to be more effective in getting out content in various ways to various audiences. They discuss the need for journalists to take a "content pool"[68] and disseminate it in various ways. They diagram the former methods of collecting content, where journalists research independently, and contrast that with convergence's communities of journalists contributing content while media organizations distribute it through broadcast, on-line and print. "This broadening of the media space through user and community participation represents a form of convergence that is likely to be an even greater challenge to journalists than the one posed by the need to master new tools and techniques."[69]

Nisha Chittal asks in a Poynter *MediaWire* article, "Are long and short form writing mutually exclusive?"[70] After interviewing noted writers of both types, she concludes,

> What all of this suggests is that long form and short form writing are, at the end of the day, mutually exclusive for writers to create simultaneously. Writers can't do both at the same time–something has to give. Writers have to alternate between long form and short form or phase them in and out. Creating original and truly exceptional and valuable content, whether long form or short form, demands a journalist's complete focus—excelling at both simultaneously is near impossible."[71]

Nevertheless, students who can do all of the above tend to get the jobs first.

Stephen Quinn and Vincent Filak's *Convergent Journalism, an Introduction*[72] provides a good overview of the aspects of the new convergent journalism. A series of essays by their Ball State University colleagues introduces the reader to the concept and the details of the new convergent platforms. Quinn says that, if the job of media is to get as many people as possible to look at media products, then "[c]onvergence increases an organization's chances of reaching the largest number of eyeballs."[73] Chapters cover all aspects of convergent journalism, from digital photography and video to writing for the Internet and advertising. As Filak reminds readers, though, "technology and toys can't save you."[74] He cites a 2002 University of South Florida study that found good writing was still the number one skill journalists need to be hired.[75]

Eugenia Siapera and Andreas Veglis's 2012 book, the *Handbook of Global Online Journalism*, traces the evolution of journalism through the on-line explosion. As Siapera and Veglis note, journalists were at first reluctant to embrace the on-line world, unsure of where it would take them; however, they soon became enthusiasts.[76] Magazines and newspapers both now have cross-platform presences, or they die. Divided into sections labeled Theories, Politics, Production, Practices, Contents, and Global Contexts, the book of essays covers a wide landscape of convergent media. Authored by the Infotendencias Group in Spain, the first essay lays out the various aspects of the theory of convergent media, noting that the theory refers to four different manifestations of convergence: (1) platforms, (2) the business, (3) the profession, and (4) multimedia.[77] The Infotendencias Group claims that in "any of its forms, convergence is a key factor of today's media industry. However, we are in front of a complex phenomenon, to some extent erratic."[78]

Textbooks, on the other hand, such as *Principles of Convergent Journalism*[79] and *All the News: Writing and Reporting for Convergent Media*,[80] stick to the nuts-and-bolts of showing emerging journalists how to navigate across different platforms, using technology and the principles of good writing to reach wider audiences. Janet Kolodzy's *Practicing Convergence Journalism: An Introduction to Cross-Media Storytelling* has this goal: to "organize and coordinate the story building blocks in which the planning, reporting, producing and distributing of journalism involve cross-media and multimedia thinking and execution."[81] Kolodzy also stresses the importance of distributing the news to diverse audiences with various needs and time to absorb it, audiences who demand video, audio, and graphics. She explains that today's audience ultimately controls the journalistic experience they receive. As Kolodzy demonstrates, using "words, visuals and sound in several combinations provides modern journalists a broader range of journalistic storytelling tools" than their predecessors.[82] In the chapter "The Multimedia Story: How to Help Audiences Get What They Want and Need,"[83] Kolodzy talks about "Search Engine Optimization" and "Social Media Optimization" and how these new ways of finding information are changing the ways that journalists conduct research. Convergence journalists know how to use the new media to get the story out. Kolodzy reminds readers that despite the new technologies, when writing spot or breaking news, the "basic tenets of journalism hold true: gather the information (using available reporting tools and skills) and deliver it in the best way to serve the audience (using the best templates for writing live news).[84]

A new edition of the *Routledge Handbook of Multimodal Analysis*, edited by Carey Jewitt, may be the most comprehensive guide available to multimodal publishing.

> The handbook takes a broad look at multimodality and engages with how a variety of other theoretical approaches have looked at multimodal communication and representation, including visual studies, anthropology, conversation analysis, socio-cultural theory, sociolinguistics, new literacy studies, multimodal corpora studies, critical discourse, semiotics and eye-tracking.[85]

The second edition includes additional chapters on recent developments in theory and methodology, multimodal research on digitally mediated texts and interaction between writer and audience. Essentially, this handbook attempts to keep up with the rapidly evolving field.

To focus solely on short-form writing, several new books help writers do the often difficult task of *writing short*. Roy Peter Clark's 2013 book *How to Write Short: Word Craft for Fast Times* provides a detailed look at the importance of short-form writing (Tweets, press releases, memos, T-shirt slogans, cards, titles and subtitles, sales pitches, even self-descriptions and tattoos), as well as step-by-step advice. Clark's chapter titles instruct: for example, "Write in the Margin," "Embrace the Lyric" and "Join the Six-Word Discipline."[86] His examples are memorable and his advice valuable.

Although older, Dom Sagolla's 2009 book *140 Characters: A Style Guide for the Short Form* remains valuable for learning the discipline it takes to write the short form, especially Twitter posts. Five sections, "Lead," "Value," "Master," "Evolve" and "Accelerate," contain chapters also titled with imperative verbs: "Simplify," "Mention," "Avoid," etc.[87] The advice is straightforward and practical, and his style is anything but stuffy. He instructs writers of the short form to try different platforms, collect good writing, experiment with style and voice and take risks. The skills he teaches (primarily with Twitter examples) are transferable across a number of platforms, audiences and occasions.

Finally, there are many books on writing for the Web in general and on specific short forms, such as titles and subtitles. Lynda Felder's 2012 book, *Writing for the Web: Creating Compelling Web Content Using Words, Pictures and Sound*,[88] provides help in integrating the word with picture and sound and provides a good refresher on the basics of good writing, style and grammar. Craig Baehr and Bob Schaller's *Writing for the Internet: A Guide to Real Communication in Virtual Space* contains a more theoretical approach than Felder's book, containing substantial chapters on "New Media Theory"[89] and "Cognitive and Psychological Aspects of Online Writing."[90] Although more academic in nature, the book also contains many practical tips, such as information on how to "chunk content,"[91] which is a technique related to putting together logical elements of content to make digital content easier to navigate. Baehr and Schaller also provide advice on digital copyright issues. Kenneth Kobré's *Videojournalism: Multimedia Storytelling*[92] focuses on short-form journalism for the Web. As the preface explains, "Videojournalism is a new field that has grown out of print photojournalism, slideshows that combine sound and pictures, public radio, documentary filmmaking, and the best of television news features."[93] This 2012 book provides a wealth of practical tips for today's short-form writer who needs to combine writing, audio and video, as well as providing a crash course on cameras, shooting, editing, ethics and the law. Finding good sources for short-form writing, however, is still much more difficult in general than finding information on long-form feature writing.[94]

Research on Magazines and Writing

In addition to books about long- and short-form writing, other resources have dealt more broadly with magazine history and writing for magazines. With the rise of cultural studies in the late twentieth century came scholarly works that explored magazines written for specific populations (African Americans, gay and lesbian, immigrants, for example). The journal *American Periodicals*, first published in 1991, continues to publish work on the history and culture of the American magazine and newspaper. The official publication of the Research Society for American Periodicals, the journal has provided a forum for scholarly considerations of everything from magazine covers and illustrations to literary and historical figures in the magazines to particular magazines and their influence on American culture. A good example of the latter is an article in the first issue by Robert Scholnick, which underscored the influence of *Scribner's Monthly* in the post–Civil War era.[95] A more recent article by Karin J. Bohleke examines the Americanization of French fashion in the pages of *Godey's* and *Peterson's*.[96] Scholars can find a wealth of scholarly reconsiderations of magazines, as well as book reviews and bibliographies, in the journal.[97]

Other scholarly works have looked at magazines in general, their historical and cultural impacts, such as David Sumner's *The Magazine Century: American Magazines since 1900*[98] and Amy Janello and Brennon Jones's tribute to the industry, *The American Magazine*.[99] David Abrahamson has done much to move the reconsideration of the magazine's historical and cultural influences in America in *Magazine-Made America*[100] and has moved forward periodical research in *The American Magazine: Research Perspectives and Prospects*.[101] These works, as with the journal *American Periodicals*, are good sources for bibliographical work and histories of the magazine.

Small by comparison with the number of academics whose scholarly contributions focus on literary, cultural and social-scientific perspectives for systematic study of the magazine form on other dimensions, there is, nonetheless, a small cluster of scholars who have broken ground by conducting empirical studies of writing and the interaction of writer, editor and audience (e.g., Ann B. Schierhorn and Kathleen L. Endres[102]). Some scholarly journals (*Journalism Practice*, for example) are also starting to publish an emerging body of work that examines how magazines may be able to co-create content with their readers. A complex process that provides insights into audience engagement, this requires magazine journalists firstly to revise assumptions about their own role and perhaps adjust their perspectives as they research and write. Examinations of the changing landscape of the magazine, blurring of boundaries between genres and between writer and reader and the effect of platforms and the multimodal magazine may provide insights into how emerging magazine journalists can take their craft into the twenty-first century, ensuring that the magazine form thrives, rather than just survives.

Future Areas of Inquiry

The rapid pace of change in the magazine world, as described in this chapter, suggests a need for scholarly attention to the moving target—to assess the impacts of the cross-platform approach on the subject, the writer and the reader. Has convergence, which really seems like divergence because of the splitting out of journalism from the single source, single writer paradigm of the past, caused the subject to be captured more fully or in more depth? Or has the subject gotten lost, reduced, iconized or otherwise fractured? Has the writer lost the discipline of the prolonged study of the article or the feature in the need for speed and the ease to find information digitally? Has the reader become impatient, demanding quick answers, in the world of apps like "Soundhound" (what is that song?), push notifications on the SmartPhone (they will send me anything that is really important), and Search Engine Optimization (if it is not in the first few hits, it must not be important). Social scientists may be looking at some of the impacts of these phenomena on human behavior,[103] but are journalism scholars looking at them closely enough to see how they are impacting quality journalism?[104] How to write the new short form well is also a subject just now being explored. It could use more analysis and scholarly attention, given the difficulty in finding serious studies on the subject.

A need may exist to look at journalism and mass communication curriculum and pedagogy, both accredited and unaccredited programs, to see if the changes are being taught adequately to emerging journalists. Are students coming out of programs ready to handle the multimodal demands they encounter in the job market, not just in using the technology but in knowing when to use what effectively?[105] Are they getting a strong foundation in good writing and in communicating an idea, in addition to using social media? Do schools have enough hands-on, experiential learning built into the curriculum so that graduates can find jobs and be successful in entry-level positions? Are students getting a strong liberal arts education so that they can think critically and communicate interpersonally, outside text messaging? How must journalism programs in high school be strengthened so that the best and brightest want to go into the field? Too often, it seems, journalism classes are taught by English teachers who need a full schedule, so it is not surprising that what the education students may be getting is not motivating them to pursue a career in magazine writing.

One may look at Marcia Prior-Miller's comprehensive bibliography,[106] always in progress, at Iowa State University to discover some areas that could use more scholarly attention. Scholarly work on the impacts of digital media, for instance, is rare and old, or not yet captured, with only two articles on the subject since 2004 in the 2012 bibliography.[107] More analyses of curriculum and pedagogy are warranted, in addition to the occasional journal article. Updated studies or texts on how to write for magazines, short or long form, incorporating the need for multimodal communication would be welcomed—books that do not repeat everything said about writing since Kemsley in 1950. In general scholarly works about writing for magazines, analyses of cross-platform writing and multimodal expectations of journalists and writing for a global audience would contribute to the field. Full-length works of this nature in the twenty-first century are rare.

A spate of scholarly works appeared in the 1990s and early 2000s, but scholarly publication on writing for magazines has slowed down. Perhaps this is a result of shrinking university presses, but it may be because things are changing so fast. As Mark Briggs says in *Journalism Next*, getting a book to print before the technology is obsolete has been a challenge.[108] As he encourages young journalists, the fact that the road ahead is uncertain with all of the new technologies makes the field especially exciting right now.[109] Still, Twitter, Facebook, crowd-sourcing, database mining and similar technologies and methods promise to be around for a while. How have readers' comments and participation in a magazine story on-line changed what we see as the story? How has non-linear reading of a magazine on an iPad changed the perception of the magazine as a whole? Are we in a post-McLuhan world, or is the medium still the message? Has good software replaced good writing? These and scores of other questions are left to be explored more fully. Books such as Aamidor, Kuypers and Weisinger's 2013 *Media Smackdown: Deconstructing the News and the Future of Journalism*, in which the authors posit that journalism is in crisis due to the economic downturn of 2008 and the new technologies,[110]and the new edition of the *Routledge Handbook of Multimodal Analysis* by Carey Jewitt,[111] discussed earlier, are starting to address some of these issues. The field for scholarly work in these areas is fertile indeed.

Notes

1 David Sumner and Holly G. Miller, *Feature and Magazine Writing: Action, Angle, and Anecdotes*, 3rd ed. (Malden, MA and Chichester, UK: Wiley-Blackwell, 2013).

2 Stephen Tanner, Molly Kasinger, and Nick Richardson, *Feature Writing: Telling the Story* (New York and Melbourne, AUS: Oxford University Press, 2009). A second edition of the book was published in 2012.

3 Carole Rich, *Writing and Reporting News: A Coaching Method*, 7th ed. (Boston: Cengage Learning, 2013).

4 Mark Briggs, *Journalism Next: A Practical Guide to Digital Reporting and Publishing*, 2nd ed. (Los Angeles: CQ Press, 2013).

5 Viscount Kemsley, *The Kemsley Manual of Journalism* (London: Cassell, 1950).

6 James Glen Stovall, *Writing for the Mass Media*, 8th ed. (Knoxville: University of Tennessee Press, 2012).

7 Harold Evans, *Editing and Design: A Five-Volume Manual of English, Typography and Layout* (New York: Holt, Rinehart and Winston, 1972–1978).

8 William E. Blundell, *The Art and Craft of Feature Writing: Based on the* Wall Street Journal *Guide* (New York: Plume, 1988). Portions of the book were reprinted from William E. Blundell, *Storytelling Step-by-Step: A Guide to Better Feature Writing* (New York: Dow Jones, 1986).

9 Special thanks to Mary Kay Blakely from the University of Missouri and Matthew Ricketson from the University of Canberra.

10 Jenny McKay, *The Magazines Handbook*, 3rd ed. (London and New York: Routledge, 2013).

11 Vicky Hay, *The Essential Feature: Writing for Magazines and Newspapers* (New York and Chichester, UK: Columbia University Press, 1990).

12 Rodger Streitmatter, *Unspeakable: The Rise of the Gay and Lesbian Press in America* (Boston: Faber and Faber, 1995).

13 Alan Nourie and Barbara Nourie, eds., *American Mass-Market Magazines* (Westport, CT: Greenwood Press, 1990).

14 "Special Issue: Immigrant Periodicals," *American Periodicals* 19.1 (Spring 2009).

15 In the first two editions of this book, the term "working theory" is used. See Denis McQuail, *Mass Communication Theory: An Introduction* (London and Beverly Hills, CA: Sage, 1983); Denis McQuail, *Mass Communication Theory: An Introduction*, 2nd ed. (London and Newbury Park, CA: Sage, 1987).

16 McQuail uses "operational theory" in subsequent editions. See Denis McQuail, *Mass Communication Theory: An Introduction*, 3rd ed. (London and Thousand Oaks, CA: 1994); Denis McQuail, *McQuail's Mass Communication Theory*, 4th ed. (London and Thousand Oaks, CA: Sage, 2000); Denis McQuail, *McQuail's Mass Communication Theory*, 5th ed. (London and Thousand Oaks, CA: Sage, 2005); Denis McQuail, *McQuail's Mass Communication Theory*, 6th ed. (London and Thousand Oaks, CA: Sage, 2010).

17 McQuail, *McQuail's Mass Communication Theory*, 6th ed.

18 Matthew Ricketson, "The New Appreciation of Long-Form Journalism in a Short-Form World," in Matthew Ricketson, ed., *Australian Journalism Today* (South Yarra, AUS: Palgrave Macmillan, 2012), 220–222.

19 Ricketson, "The New Appreciation of Long-Form," 218.

20 Ricketson, "The New Appreciation of Long-Form," 219.

21 Benjamin Ball, "Long-Form as Moral Category?" *Axon: Creative Explorations* 3.1 (March 2013) <http://www.axonjournal.com.au/issue-4/long-form-moral-category>, accessed 4 February 2014.

22 Founded and published by Charlotte Harper; see Charlotte Harper, "What Is Longform Journalism?" *Editia*, 28 August 2012 <http://editia.com/what-is-longform-journalism/>, accessed 2 February 2014.

23 Matthew Ricketson, *Writing Feature Stories: How to Research and Write Newspaper and Magazine Articles* (Crows Nest, AUS: Allen & Unwin, 2004), 4.

24 Ricketson, "The New Appreciation of Long-Form," 217–233.

25 Ricketson, "The New Appreciation of Long-Form," 230.

26 Naomi Sharp, "The Future of Longform," *Columbia Journalism Review*, 9 December 2013 <http://www.cjr.org/behind_the_news/longform_conference.php?page=all>, accessed 3 February 2014.

27 Sumner and Miller, *Feature and Magazine Writing*.

28 David E. Sumner and Holly G. Miller, "Long-Form Digital Storytelling," *Feature and Magazine Writing: Action, Angle, and Anecdotes*, 3rd ed. (Malden, MA and Chichester, UK: Wiley-Blackwell, 2013), 267.

29 Sumner and Miller, "Long-Form Digital Storytelling," 267.

30 Sumner and Miller, "Long-Form Digital Storytelling," 265–276.

31 Sumner and Miller, "Long-Form Digital Storytelling," 270.

32 Sumner and Miller, "Long-Form Digital Storytelling," 273.

33 Sumner and Miller, *Feature and Magazine Writing*, 299–300.

34 Edward Jay Friedlander and John Lee, *Feature Writing: The Pursuit of Excellence*, 7th ed. (Boston: Allyn & Bacon, 2011).

35 Friedlander and Lee, *Feature Writing*, 64.

36 Katie McCabe, "Like Something the Lord Made," *Washingtonian*, August 1989, 108–111, 226–233, as published in Friedlander and Lee, *Feature Writing*, 76–87. Originally published in the *Washingtonian*, August 1989. Reprinted in Friedlander and Lee by permission of the author.

37 Hay, *The Essential Feature*, 8.

38 Hay, *The Essential Feature*, 77–97.

39 Hay, *The Essential Feature*, 200; Marguerite Reiss, "Nightmare Hunt," reprinted in Hay, 199–201. Originally published in *Outdoor Life* in 1985, the version that Hay uses was published by *Reader's Digest* in 1986. The article was also reprinted as Marguerite Reiss, "Nightmare Hunt," in Larry Mueller and Marguerite Reiss, *Bear Attacks of the Century: True Stories of Courage and Survival* (Guilford, CT: Lyons Press, 2005), 103–112.

40 Betsy P. Graham, *Magazine Article Writing*, 2nd ed. (Fort Worth: Harcourt Brace Jovanovich, 1993), 33.

41 Graham, *Magazine Article Writing*, 8.

42 For other examples of books on feature and magazine writing, see Marcia R. Prior-Miller and Associates, "Bibliography of Published Research on Magazine and Journal Periodicals," 8th ed., research database (Ames: Iowa State University, last modified, 31 August 2012), MSWord file <mpm@iastate.edu>.

43 Ricketson, *Writing Feature Stories*.

44 Ricketson, *Writing Feature Stories*, 237.

45 Carla Johnson, *21st Century Feature Writing* (Boston: Pearson, 2004).

46 Daniel Reimold, *Journalism of Ideas: Brainstorming, Developing, and Selling Stories in the Digital Age* (New York and London: Routledge, 2013), 61–75, 76–83, and 84–98.

47 Tanner, Kasinger, and Richardson, *Feature Writing*.

48 Jane Johnston, "Changing Journalistic Environments," review of *Feature Writing: Telling the Story*, 2nd ed., by Stephen Tanner, Molly Kasinger, and Nick Richardson, in *Text* 13.1 (April 2009) <http://www.textjournal.com.au/april09/johnston_rev.htm>, accessed 26 November 2013.

49 Charles H. Harrison, *How to Write for Magazines: Consumer, Trade, and Web* (Boston: Allyn & Bacon, 2002).

50 Dennis Jackson and John Sweeney, eds., *The Journalist's Craft: A Guide to Writing Better Stories* (New York: Allworth Press, 2002).

51 Jackson and Sweeney, *The Journalist's Craft*, 55–90.

52 Mark Bowden, "Nonfiction Storytelling," in Dennis Jackson and John Sweeney, eds., *The Journalist's Craft: A Guide to Writing Better Stories* (New York: Allworth Press, 2002), 62–63.

53 Nancy M. Hamilton, *Uncovering the Secrets of Magazine Writing: A Step-by-Step Guide to Writing Creative Nonfiction for Print and Internet Publication* (Boston: Pearson, 2005).

54 Angela Phillips, *Good Writing for Journalists* (London: Sage, 2007).

55 Phillips, *Good Writing for Journalists*, 132.

56 Phillips, *Good Writing for Journalists*, 133.

57 Jack Hart, *Storycraft: The Complete Guide to Writing Narrative Nonfiction* (Chicago: University of Chicago Press, 2011).

58 Jack Hart, "A Note from Jack Hart," *Storycraft: The Complete Guide to Writing Narrative Nonfiction* (Chicago: University of Chicago Press, 2011) <http://www.press.uchicago.edu/books/hart/index.html>, accessed 30 November 2013.

59 Hart, *Storycraft*, iv.

60 For a link to the journal, which links to the extensive bibliography managed by Miles Maguire and Roberta S. Maguire, see "Building a Bibliography for the Study of Literary Journalism," *Literary Journalism Studies* 3.2 (Fall 2011): 123–124, "IALJS Homepage," International Association for Literary Journalism Studies <http://www.ialjs.org>, accessed 28 November 2013.

61 For history of literary journalists, see Edd Applegate, *Literary Journalism: A Biographical Dictionary of Writers and Editors* (Westport, CT: Greenwood Press, 1996).

62 For a good history of the genre in the twentieth century, see Norman Sims, *True Stories: A Century of Literary Journalism* (Evanston, IL: Northwestern University Press, 2007).

63 See Christopher D. Benson and Charles F. Whitaker, *Magazine Writing* (New York: Routledge, 2014), a forthcoming book that appears to cover mostly common ground with an obligatory chapter on writing for the new media.

64 Paula LaRocque, *The Book on Writing: The Ultimate Guide to Writing Well* (Arlington, TX: Grey and Guvnor Press, 2003).

65 LaRocque, *The Book on Writing*, 4.

66 Bob Britten, "Losing Control: Using Social Media to Engage and Connect," *Journal of Magazine & New Media Research* 14.2 (Fall 2013): 3.

67 Thorsten Quandt and Jane B. Singer, "Convergence and Cross-Platform Content Production," in Karin Wahl-Jorgensen and Thomas Hanitzsch, eds., *Handbook of Journalism Studies*, International Communication Association (ICA) Handbook Series, ed. Robert T. Craig (New York and London: Routledge, 2009), 131.

68 Quandt and Singer, "Convergence and Cross-Platform Content Production," 131–132.

69 Quandt and Singer, "Convergence and Cross-Platform Content Production," 132.

70 Nisha Chittal, "Are Long and Short Form Writing Mutually Exclusive?" *MediaWire*, Poynter.org, 16 December 2011 <http://www.poynter.org/latest-news/making-sense-of-news/156361/are-long-and-short-form-writing-mutually-exclusive/>, accessed 1 December 2013.

71 Nisha Chittal, "Are Long and Short Form Writing Mutually Exclusive?"

72 Stephen Quinn and Vincent Filak F., eds., *Convergent Journalism: An Introduction* (Burlington, MA and Oxford, UK: Focal Press, 2005).

73 Stephen Quinn, "What Is Convergence and How Will It Affect My Life?" in Stephen Quinn and Vincent Filak F., eds., *Convergent Journalism: An Introduction* (Burlington, MA and Oxford, UK: Focal Press, 2005), 8.

74 Vincent F. Filak, "Words: The Foundation Stone of Journalism," in Stephen Quinn and Vincent F. Filak, eds., *Convergent Journalism: An Introduction* (Burlington, MA and Oxford, UK: Focal Press, 2005), 39–52. The study referenced is David Bulla, "Media Convergence: Industry Practices and Implications for Education" (paper presented at the Annual Meeting, Association for Education in Journalism and Mass Communication, August 2002).

75 Filak, "Words," 40.

76 Eugenia Siapera and Andreas Veglis, "Introduction: The Evolution of Online Journalism," in Eugenia Siapera and Andreas Veglis, eds., *The Handbook of Global Online Journalism* (Chichester, UK: Wiley-Blackwell, 2012), 1.

77 Infotendencias Group, "Media Convergence," in Eugenia Siapera and Andreas Veglis, eds., *The Handbook of Global Online Journalism* (Chichester, UK: Wiley-Blackwell, 2012), 21–37.

78 Infotendencias Group, "Media Convergence," 35.

79 Jeffrey S. Wilkinson, August E. Grant, and Douglas J. Fisher, *Principles of Convergent Journalism* (New York: Oxford University Press, 2013).

80 Thom Lieb, *All the News: Writing and Reporting for Convergent Media* (Boston: Pearson, 2009).

81 Janet Kolodzy, *Practicing Convergence Journalism: An Introduction to Cross-Media Storytelling* (New York: Routledge, 2013), x.

82 Kolodzy, *Practicing Convergence Journalism*, 26.

83 Janet Kolodzy, "The Multimedia Story: How to Help Audiences Get What They Want and Need," *Practicing Convergence Journalism: An Introduction to Cross-Media Storytelling* (New York: Routledge, 2013), 133–147.

84 Kolodzy, *Practicing Convergence Journalism*, 61.

85 Carey Jewitt, ed., *The Routledge Handbook of Multimodal Analysis*, 2nd ed. (London: Routledge, 2013), as described on publisher Web site, Routledge.com <www.routledge.com/books/details/9780415519748/>, accessed 25 May 2014.

86 Roy Peter Clark, *How to Write Short: Word Craft for Fast Times* (New York: Little, Brown, 2013).

87 Dom Sagolla, *140 Characters: A Style Guide for the Short Form* (Hoboken, NJ: John Wiley & Sons, 2009).

88 Lynda Felder, *Writing for the Web: Creating Compelling Web Content Using Words, Pictures and Sound* (Berkeley, CA: New Riders Press, 2012).

89 Craig Baehr and Bob Schaller, "New Media Theory," *Writing for the Internet: A Guide to Real Communication in Virtual Space* (Santa Barbara, CA: Greenwood Press, 2010), 15–32.

90 Craig Baehr and Bob Schaller, "Cognitive and Psychological Aspects of Online Writing," *Writing for the Internet: A Guide to Real Communication in Virtual Space* (Santa Barbara, CA: Greenwood Press, 2010), 187–198.

91 Craig Baehr and Bob Schaller, "Chunking and Hyperlinking," *Writing for the Internet: A Guide to Real Communication in Virtual Space* (Santa Barbara, CA: Greenwood Press, 2010), 111–124.

92 Kenneth Kobré, *Videojournalism: Multimedia Storytelling* (Waltham, MA and Oxford, UK: Focal Press, 2012).

93 Kobré, *Videojournalism*, iv.

94 This statement is based on the author's own experience at searching for sources on writing for short-form venues.

95 Robert J. Scholnick, "*Scribner's Monthly* and the 'Pictorial Representation of Life and Truth' in Post-Civil War America," *American Periodicals* 1.1 (Fall 1991): 46–69.

96 Karin J. Bohleke, "Americanizing French Fashion Plates: *Godey's* and *Peterson's* Cultural and Socio-Economic Translation of *Les Modes Parisiennes*," *American Periodicals* 20.2 (2010): 120–155.

97 "About RSAP," Research Society for American Periodicals <http://www.periodicalresearch.org>, accessed 22 May 2014.

98 David E. Sumner, *The Magazine Century: American Magazines Since 1900*, Mediating American History Series (New York: Peter Lang, 2010).

99 Amy Janello and Brennon Jones, *The American Magazine* (New York: Abrams and Magazine Publishers Association, 1991).

100 David Abrahamson, *Magazine-Made America: The Cultural Transformation of the Postwar Periodical* (Cresskill, NJ: Hampton Press, 1996).

101 David Abrahamson, *The American Magazine: Research Perspectives and Prospects* (Ames: Iowa State University Press, 1995).

102 Ann B. Schierhorn and Kathleen L. Endres, "Magazine Writing Instruction and the Composition Revolution," *Journalism Educator* 47.2 (Summer 1992): 57–64; Kathleen L. Endres and Ann B. Schierhorn,

"New Technology and the Writer/Editor Relationship: Shifting Electronic Realities," *Journalism & Mass Communication Quarterly* 72.2 (Summer 1995): 448–457.

103 Jakob D. Jensen, Jennifer K. Bernat, Kari M. Wilson, and Julie Goonewardene, for example, look at the effects of the new media in "The Delay Hypothesis: The Manifestation of Media Effects over Time," *Human Communication Research* 37.1 (October 2011): 509–528.

104 The fall 2013 issue of *Journal of Magazine & New Media Research* is devoted entirely to social media and their impact on audiences, including millennials.

105 For an examination of some of these issues, see Laura Castañeda, Sheila Murphy, and Heather Jane Hether, "Teaching Print, Broadcast, and Online Journalism Concurrently: A Case Study Assessing a Convergence Curriculum," *Journalism & Mass Communication Educator* 60.1 (Spring 2005): 57–70.

106 See Prior-Miller and Associates, "Bibliography of Published Research on Magazine and Journal Periodicals."

107 Jensen, Bernat, Wilson, and Goonewardene, "The Delay Hypothesis," 509–528; Robert LaRose, "The Problem of Media Habits," *Communication Theory* 20.2 (May 2010): 194–222.

108 Briggs, *Journalism Next*, 8.

109 Briggs, *Journalism Next*, 8.

110 Abe Aamidor, Jim A. Kuypers, and Susan Wiesinger, *Media Smackdown: Deconstructing the News and the Future of Journalism* (New York: Peter Lang, 2013).

111 Jewitt, *Routledge Handbook of Multimodal Analysis*.

Bibliography

Aamidor, Abe; Kuypers, Jim A.; and Wiesinger, Susan. *Media Smackdown: Deconstructing the News and the Future of Journalism*. New York: Peter Lang, 2013.

"About RSAP." Research Society for American Periodicals <http://www.periodicalresearch.org>, accessed 22 May 2014.

Abrahamson, David. *The American Magazine: Research Perspectives and Prospects*. Ames: Iowa State University Press, 1995.

Abrahamson, David. *Magazine-Made America: The Cultural Transformation of the Postwar Periodical*. Cresskill, NJ: Hampton Press, 1996.

Applegate, Edd. *Literary Journalism: A Biographical Dictionary of Writers and Editors*. Westport, CT: Greenwood Press, 1996.

Baehr, Craig and Schaller, Bob. "Chunking and Hyperlinking." *Writing for the Internet: A Guide to Real Communication in Virtual Space*. Santa Barbara, CA: Greenwood Press, 2010, 111–124.

Baehr, Craig and Schaller, Bob. "Cognitive and Psychological Aspects of Online Writing." *Writing for the Internet: A Guide to Real Communication in Virtual Space*. Santa Barbara, CA: Greenwood Press, 2010, 187–198.

Baehr, Craig and Schaller, Bob. "New Media Theory." *Writing for the Internet: A Guide to Real Communication in Virtual Space*. Santa Barbara, CA: Greenwood Press, 2010, 15–32.

Ball, Benjamin. "Long-Form as Moral Category?" *Axon: Creative Explorations* 3.1 (March 2013) <http://www.axonjournal.com.au/issue-4/long-form-moral-category>, accessed 4 February 2014.

Benson, Christopher D. and Whitaker, Charles F. *Magazine Writing*. New York: Routledge, 2014.

Blundell, William E. *The Art and Craft of Feature Writing: Based on the Wall Street Journal Guide*. New York: Plume, 1988.

Blundell, William E. *Storytelling Step-by-Step: A Guide to Better Feature Writing*. New York: Dow Jones, 1986.

Bohleke, Karin J. "Americanizing French Fashion Plates: *Godey's* and *Peterson's* Cultural and Socio-Economic Translation of *Les Modes Parisiennes*." *American Periodicals* 20.2 (2010): 120–155.

Bowden, Mark. "Nonfiction Storytelling." In Jackson, Dennis and Sweeney, John, eds. *The Journalist's Craft: A Guide to Writing Better Stories*. New York: Allworth, 2002, 59–78.

Briggs, Mark. *Journalism Next: A Practical Guide to Digital Reporting and Publishing*. 2nd ed. Los Angeles: CQ Press, 2013.

Britten, Bob. "Losing Control: Using Social Media to Engage and Connect." *Journal of Magazine & New Media Research* 14.2 (Fall 2013): 1–3.

Bulla, David. "Media Convergence: Industry Practices and Implications for Education." Paper presented at the Annual Meeting, Association for Education in Journalism and Mass Communication, August 2002.

Castañeda, Laura; Murphy, Sheila; and Hether, Heather Jane. "Teaching Print, Broadcast, and Online Journalism Concurrently: A Case Study Assessing a Convergence Curriculum." *Journalism & Mass Communication Educator* 60.1 (Spring 2005): 57–70.

Chittal, Nisha. "Are Long and Short Form Writing Mutually Exclusive?" *MediaWire*. Poynter.org, 16 December 2011 <http://www.poynter.org/latest-news/making-sense-of-news/156361/are-long-and-short-form-writing-mutually-exclusive/>, accessed 1 December 2013.

Clark, Roy Peter. *How to Write Short: Word Craft for Fast Times*. New York: Little, Brown, 2013.

Endres, Kathleen L. and Schierhorn, Ann B. "New Technology and the Writer/Editor Relationship: Shifting Electronic Realities." *Journalism & Mass Communication Quarterly* 72.2 (Summer 1995): 448–457.

Evans, Harold. *Editing and Design: A Five-Volume Manual of English, Typography and Layout*. New York: Holt, Rinehart and Winston, 1972–1978.

Felder, Lynda. *Writing for the Web: Creating Compelling Web Content Using Words, Pictures and Sound*. Berkeley, CA: New Riders Press, 2012.

Filak, Vincent F. "Words: The Foundation Stone of Journalism." In Quinn, Stephen and Filak, Vincent F., eds. *Convergent Journalism: An Introduction*. Burlington, MA and Oxford, UK: Focal Press, 2005, 39–52.

Friedlander, Edward Jay and Lee, John. *Feature Writing: The Pursuit of Excellence*. 7th ed. Boston: Allyn & Bacon, 2011.

Graham, Betsy P. *Magazine Article Writing*. 2nd ed. Fort Worth: Harcourt Brace Jovanovich, 1993.

Hamilton, Nancy M. *Uncovering the Secrets of Magazine Writing: A Step-by-Step Guide to Writing Creative Nonfiction for Print and Internet Publication*. Boston: Pearson, 2005.

Harper, Charlotte. "What Is Longform Journalism?" *Editia*, 28 August 2012 <http://editia.com/what-is-longform-journalism/>, accessed 2 February 2014.

Harrison, Charles H. *How to Write for Magazines: Consumer, Trade, and Web*. Boston: Allyn & Bacon, 2002.

Hart, Jack. "A Note from Jack Hart." *Storycraft: The Complete Guide to Writing Narrative Nonfiction*. Chicago: University of Chicago Press, 2011 <http://www.press.uchicago.edu/books/hart/index.html>, accessed 30 November 2013.

Hart, Jack. *Storycraft: The Complete Guide to Writing Narrative Nonfiction*. Chicago: University of Chicago Press, 2011.

Hay, Vicky. *The Essential Feature: Writing for Magazines and Newspapers*. New York and Chichester, UK: Columbia University Press, 1990.

"IALJS Homepage." International Association for Literary Journalism Studies <http://www.ialjs.org>, accessed 28 November 2013.

Infotendencias Group. "Media Convergence." In Siapera, Eugenia and Veglis, Andreas, eds. *The Handbook of Global Online Journalism*. Chichester, UK: Wiley-Blackwell, 2012, 21–37.

Jackson, Dennis and Sweeney, John, eds. *The Journalist's Craft: A Guide to Writing Better Stories*. New York: Allworth Press, 2002.

Janello, Amy and Jones, Brennon. *The American Magazine*. New York: Abrams and Magazine Publishers of America, 1991.

Jensen, Jakob D.; Bernat, Jennifer K.; Wilson, Kari M.; and Goonewardene, Julie. "The Delay Hypothesis: The Manifestation of Media Effects over Time." *Human Communication Research* 37.1 (October 2011): 509–528.

Jewitt, Carey, ed. *The Routledge Handbook of Multimodal Analysis*. 2nd ed. London: Routledge, 2013.

Johnson, Carla. *21st Century Feature Writing*. Boston: Pearson, 2004.

Johnston, Jane. "Changing Journalistic Environments." Review of *Feature Writing: Telling the Story*, 2nd ed., by Stephen Tanner, Molly Kasinger, and Nick Richardson. In *Text* 13.1 (April 2009) <http://www.textjournal.com.au/april09/johnston_rev.htm>, accessed 26 November 2013.

Kemsley, Viscount. *The Kemsley Manual of Journalism*. London: Cassell, 1950.

Kobré, Kenneth. *Videojournalism: Multimedia Storytelling*. Waltham, MA and Oxford, UK: Focal Press, 2012.

Kolodzy, Janet. "The Multimedia Story: How to Help Audiences Get What They Want and Need." *Practicing Convergence Journalism: An Introduction to Cross-Media Storytelling*. New York: Routledge, 2013, 133–147.

Kolodzy, Janet. *Practicing Convergence Journalism: An Introduction to Cross-Media Storytelling*. New York: Routledge, 2013.

LaRocque, Paula. *The Book on Writing: The Ultimate Guide to Writing Well.* Arlington, TX: Grey and Guvnor Press, 2003.

LaRose, Robert. "The Problem of Media Habits." *Communication Theory* 20.2 (May 2010): 194–222.

Lieb, Thom. *All the News: Writing and Reporting for Convergent Media.* Boston: Pearson, 2009.

Maguire, Miles and Maguire, Roberta S. "Building a Bibliography for the Study of Literary Journalism." *Literary Journalism Studies* 3.2 (Fall 2011): 123–124.

McCabe, Katie. "Like Something the Lord Made." *Washingtonian*, August 1989, 108–111, 226–233.

McKay, Jenny. *The Magazines Handbook.* 3rd ed. London and New York: Routledge, 2013.

McQuail, Denis. *Mass Communication Theory: An Introduction.* London and Beverly Hills, CA: Sage, 1st ed., 1983; 2nd ed., Newbury Park: 1987; 3rd ed. Thousand Oaks, 1994.

McQuail, Denis. *McQuail's Mass Communication Theory.* London and Thousand Oaks, CA: Sage, 4th ed., 2000; 5th ed., 2005; 6th ed., 2010.

Nourie, Alan and Nourie, Barbara, eds. *American Mass-Market Magazines.* Westport, CT: Greenwood Press, 1990.

Phillips, Angela. *Good Writing for Journalists.* London: Sage, 2007.

Prior-Miller, Marcia R. and Associates. "Bibliography of Published Research on Magazine and Journal Periodicals." 8th ed. Research database. Ames: Iowa State University, last modified, 31 August 2012, MSWord file <mpm@iastate.edu>.

Quandt, Thorsten and Singer, Jane B. "Convergence and Cross-Platform Content Production." In Wahl-Jorgensen, Karin and Hanitzsch, Thomas, eds. *Handbook of Journalism Studies.* International Communication Association (ICA) Handbook Series, ed. Robert T. Craig. New York and London: Routledge, 2009, 130–144.

Quinn, Stephen. "What Is Convergence and How Will It Affect My Life?" In Quinn, Stephen and Filak, Vincent F., eds. *Convergent Journalism: An Introduction.* Burlington, MA and Oxford, UK: Focal Press, 2005, 3–19.

Quinn, Stephen and Filak, Vincent F., eds. *Convergent Journalism: An Introduction.* Burlington, MA and Oxford, UK: Focal Press, 2005.

Reimold, Daniel. *Journalism of Ideas: Brainstorming, Developing, and Selling Stories in the Digital Age.* New York and London: Routledge, 2013.

Reiss, Marguerite. "Nightmare Hunt." In Mueller, Larry and Reiss, Marguerite. *Bear Attacks of the Century: True Stories of Courage and Survival.* Guilford, CT: Lyons Press, 2005, 103–112.

Rich, Carole. *Writing and Reporting News: A Coaching Method.* 7th ed. Boston: Cengage Learning, 2013.

Ricketson, Matthew. "The New Appreciation of Long-Form Journalism in a Short-Form World." In Ricketson, Matthew, ed. *Australian Journalism Today.* South Yarra, AUS: Palgrave Macmillan, 2012, 217–233.

Ricketson, Matthew. *Writing Feature Stories: How to Research and Write Newspaper and Magazine Articles.* Crows Nest, AUS: Allen & Unwin, 2004.

Sagolla, Dom. *140 Characters: A Style Guide for the Short Form.* Hoboken, NJ: John Wiley & Sons, 2009.

Schierhorn, Ann B. and Endres, Kathleen L. "Magazine Writing Instruction and the Composition Revolution." *Journalism Educator* 47.2 (Summer 1992): 57–64.

Scholnick, Robert J. "*Scribner's Monthly* and the 'Pictorial Representation of Life and Truth' in Post-Civil War America." *American Periodicals* 1.1 (Fall 1991): 46–69.

Sharp, Naomi. "The Future of Longform." *Columbia Journalism Review*, 9 December 2013 <http://www.cjr.org/behind_the_news/longform_conference.php?page=all>, accessed 3 February 2014.

Siapera, Eugenia and Veglis, Andreas. "Introduction: The Evolution of Online Journalism." In Siapera, Eugenia and Veglis, Andreas, eds. *The Handbook of Global Online Journalism*, Chichester, UK: Wiley-Blackwell, 2012, 1.

Sims, Norman. *True Stories: A Century of Literary Journalism.* Evanston, IL: Northwestern University Press, 2007.

"Special Issue: Immigrant Periodicals." *American Periodicals* 19.1 (Spring 2009).

Stovall, James Glen. *Writing for the Mass Media.* 8th ed. Knoxville: University of Tennessee Press, 2012.

Streitmatter, Rodger. *Unspeakable: The Rise of the Gay and Lesbian Press in America.* Boston: Faber and Faber, 1995.

Sumner, David E. *The Magazine Century: American Magazines since 1900.* Mediating American History Series. New York: Peter Lang, 2010.

Sumner, David E. and Miller, Holly G. *Feature and Magazine Writing: Action, Angle, and Anecdotes.* 3rd ed. Malden, MA and Chichester, UK: Wiley-Blackwell, 2013.

Sumner, David E. and Miller, Holly G. "Long-Form Digital Storytelling." *Feature and Magazine Writing: Action, Angle, and Anecdotes*. 3rd ed. Malden, MA and Chichester, UK: Wiley-Blackwell, 2013, 265–276.

Tanner, Stephen; Kasinger, Molly; and Richardson, Nick. *Feature Writing: Telling the Story*. New York and Melbourne, AUS: Oxford University Press, 2009.

Wilkinson, Jeffrey S.; Grant, August E.; and Fisher, Douglas J. *Principles of Convergent Journalism*. New York: Oxford University Press, 2013.

29
TEACHING MAGAZINE EDITING
Part Art, Part Science, All Craft
Bill Reynolds

In late 2010, Alexis C. Madrigal, senior editor at the *Atlantic* magazine, posted on his blog a document titled, "The 12 Timeless Rules for Making a Good Publication."[1] He professed not to know the origin of the document, but guessed it had been formulated sometime in the 1950s. Presumably, the sheet of paper he was looking at—tacked on an *Atlantic* office wall in the Watergate building in Washington, DC—had made the journey from Boston, which until 2005 had been the home of the *Atlantic* for 148 years (and known as the *Atlantic Monthly*). Among the timeless advice offered were three nuggets: "Don't over-edit"; "Follow the news. Remember that timeliness means being on time, not before the time"; and "Quick decisions—except in poetry."

William Whitworth, editor of the *Atlantic Monthly*, 1980–1999, once admitted to a *Boston Globe* reporter that, yes, an editor ought to set the vision for the magazine, yet he would do well also to pay attention to his handpicked writers' ideas. "In my experience," Whitworth said in 1995, "when you assign a story, instead of letting the writer come up with the idea, two things happen. You're not happy and the writer's not happy with the result."[2] Whitworth's opinion is contrary to the commonly held belief that editors, not writers, know what is best for a publication's readers. Editors maintain the identity of the publication and choose writers accordingly. Here is a typical example of this line of reasoning: "Most ideas for articles and other content come from staff members, especially including the editor himself/herself, who ought to know better than anyone else what readers want, what she wants for the readers and what the magazine should have in it."[3]

Furthermore, the classic conception of the successful magazine is one where the publisher and editor work in tandem and in a top-down hierarchy to incubate the harmonious, well-oiled machine that will pay heed to reader needs and thus attract advertisers:

> The editor moves forward by developing the book's personality, a singularity that becomes a magnet for readers. An editor builds an environment and choreographs the movements of necessary editorial elements that will cause a reader to consider the publication his own. The editor designs the blend of the predictable and the surprising, of the constant and the dynamic, of the continuing and the innovative so that the reader will be both comfortable and stimulated in the reading.[4]

Peter Jacobi wrote this job description in 1990, and much has happened since then. Magazines are still around and the advice still applies, so far as it goes, but the readers—the audience—have fragmented because of the proliferation of choice on the Web. Consider the explosion of on-line magazines, short-book publishers and applications that make it easy to store stories for later reading—a personalized selection of which resides on most everyone's computer: *Epic Magazine*, Medium, *Grantland*, the *Awl*, *n+1*, *Rookie*, the *Rumpus*, *This Recording*, *Oxford American*, the *Believer*, *Longreads*, *Longform*, *Narrative*, McSweeney's, Give Me Something to Read, the Browser, Pocket, Read It Later, the *Quarterly*, the *Atavist*, Byliner and *Hazlitt*.

Early in 2013, this author interviewed the editor-in-chief of *Hazlitt*, Christopher Frey. *Hazlitt*, a start-up on-line publication that went live in August 2013, is based in Toronto and financed by Random House Canada. It is so named in honor of the English journalist and essayist William Hazlitt, whose works from the early nineteenth century have enjoyed a revival over the past two decades. Specifically, with regard to the game of editing, Frey's view of a magazine's worth would be at home in Whitworth's belief territory, but he came to his new project at a distinct twenty-first century angle.

> There is so much noise out there. Readers follow voices, people they like. In the magazine universe there is the magazine's identity—a *Toronto Life* story, a *Walrus* story, an *Atlantic* story—and the editors erect the scaffolding and protect this identity. Now the writers are the identity of the publication. The people are the scaffolding.[5]

Further, Frey argues that, although he wouldn't hire a writer solely on the basis of her Twitter following, he wouldn't ignore her self-built popularity, either. "If we like her ideas," he says, "having 20,000 Twitter followers is helpful in bringing readers to us."[6]

Between Whitworth's belief in choosing the writers appropriate to his publication and then having the courage to allow them the freedom to pursue their ideas and Frey's assertion that writers are not only the scaffolding of today's publications but also increasingly are their own brands, there would seem to be a change in blueprints in the past generation, perhaps leading to a de-centering of the magazine editing process itself.

Meanwhile, as the digital revolution hypnotizes eyeballs for greater periods of time away from cellulose to virtual products, publishers continue to push out how-to manuals for prospective magazine editors and writers. The purpose of this chapter is not to offer any prognostication on what might happen to magazine editing in the next 10 to 20 years—no one can predict the future in such an unstable universe—but rather to interrogate the recent changes that have affected the editing of magazines and attempt to separate what is timeless from what is timely, if not urgent.

The traditional journalism program offered students a course in newspaper-style copyediting and considered the pedagogical task complete. However, many recognize that laying a foundation of the micro-level editing skills of copyediting and shaping manuscripts ("pencil-editing") is not sufficient. Also needed are macro-level conceptualization skills ("idea editing"), as well as the ability for long-range planning and execution of a unique combination of the verbal and the visual. It is this larger view of editing that magazine specialists have brought to the educational mix. This chapter explores some contributions to the body of knowledge about teaching both the editing craft and larger editing management skills but also attempts to explore, briefly, how standards of craft might be maintained in an era of steep declines in display advertising revenues and significant reductions in circulation numbers.

The time frame chosen for this review is rooted in the date of publication of *The American Magazine: Research Perspectives and Prospects*, that is, 1995. This period is then extended backward two years in order to allow the review to cover two full decades. One advantage of this extension is that, in 1993, magazines were not yet part of digital culture. This peg sets up a powerful contrast with today's profound differences. The review's purview is the culture of editing and includes various textbooks on editing and writing, magazine articles about the craft of editing and scholarly articles on magazine editing, a number of which are provided for reference but not included in the discussion.

New Realities Outpace Textbooks

The editing craft encompasses many forms, including packaging a collection of articles under one concept; marrying display copy writing with text, photography and illustration; feature assignment editing; researching (or fact-checking); copyediting and proofreading. This chapter focuses on the first three in this list. Packaging editorial is an art unto itself. Feature assignments may be edited for newspapers or magazines or the Internet, and platforms have their own special methodologies. Magazine editing, usually the most rigorous of the group, has its own set of rules and principles that govern structure, itself an art form that requires some discussion. Two significant changes in the past 20 years have been the rise of importance in art direction and, since the late 1980s arrival of personal computers, the concomitant rise in general knowledge of design, typeface and presentation. Magazines and newspapers have never looked better.

The sixth edition of J. William Click and Russell N. Baird's *Magazine Editing and Production*[7] is 20 years old, yet much of its detail on building and running a magazine still applies. What it does not contain, of course, is any inkling of the changes occurring since editors and writers began to communicate using e-mails in the mid- to late 1990s. Their introduction to coming revolution was captured in the statement, "Computers and software programs have made in-house desktop prepress commonplace, and this edition reflects that."[8] Social media and Internet 2.0 began to revolutionize first the way readers consumed magazines in the mid-2000s, and then readers' and writers' ability to assert on-line autonomy outside the control of the editors' vision of the magazine. "The selection of content tests editors' mettle more than any other single task," the authors argue. "As they apply their knowledge of reader interests to the evaluation of manuscripts, editors must also apply their professional and technical skills. These skills are needed for their visualization of the final product that might emerge from the raw material they are evaluating."[9] Click and Baird want the reader to understand the complex relation between words and art on the magazine page. Editors look at a writer's manuscript and imagine how to sell the story to their readers, what kind of display copy will best attract the eye, how to frame the opening double-page spread (if the piece is to become a major feature or the cover story) and whether or not to use photography or illustration (being mindful which art form most generally suits the editorial staff's idea of the magazine's identity). All of these considerations still apply, but complications have been added courtesy of presenting the same material on the Web—whether, for example, to duplicate the magazine layout on-line, or to enrich the text with sound files, video and various links that would have the reader vacate the page.

Fast-forward 15 years and arrive at the ninth edition of another how-to book, Brian S. Brooks and James L. Pinson's *The Art of Editing in the Age of Convergence*.[10] Already, despite so many revisions, the word "convergence" in the subtitle suggests the book's near-instant obsolescence. (Perhaps *disruption* would have been a trendier word for the book's subtitle. But then, it wasn't a trend word in 2009, when the book was being revised.) In the preface, the authors rightly point to crucial issues that affect journalism, such as "greater ownership concentration,"[11] but what they really mean when they say convergence is multimedia platform journalism or adapting journalism teaching to the demands of the digital newsroom. This adaption simply means that instead of being satisfied with an adjunct newsroom for on-line reporting outside the traditional newsroom (where the *real* reporting is supposed to take place), in the social media era this hierarchy has disappeared. Convergence indeed happened in the newsroom: There is now one newsroom—not the room where the *real* journalists work and then, to pay lip-service to on-line journalism, the room off to the side which media executives thought they could bankroll at relative low cost, in that closet-sized space over there, where the technologically savvy toil. That era, which was the old era of convergence, is long gone. No, in the current newsroom, the editors send a reporter to court or to a major accident and the first thing she does is snap a photo and send it back for uploading onto the Web site. She'll tweet, she'll report, she'll interview, and she'll file using her thumbs and pressing *Send* on her iPhone. The file will be edited quickly and posted. Updates come next. A more traditionally reported story may or may not appear the next day. So, although Brooks and Pinson help readers through these endless changes, their advice is necessarily out of date. Technology is moving too fast for the textbook world to codify it.

There are other issues with this kind of manual as well, specifically to do with feature editing. Brooks and Pinson say, with a mild macho newsroom inflection, features are sometimes referred to as "soft-news stories" or "fluff pieces."[12] They say hard news stories are written in past tense while features are written in present tense,[13] not generally the case with newspaper features. They emphasize, in three bulleted points,[14] that a feature editor's main jobs are to make sure the names are spelled right, the photo matches the headline and the headline and underline relay the essence of the story to the scanning reader. And how is this different from Page One editing? Worse, the chapter on magazine editing is titled "Editing Magazines and Newsletters,"[15] lumping the two media together as if they were equivalent—an insult to magazine editors everywhere. The advice—for instance, "Magazines tend to have articles that are longer and less objective than newspaper articles"[16]—suggests that not only is the book out of date, its advice tends to be either obvious or, more troubling, inaccurate for most mainstream magazine editing. More to the editing point, in the revised version of *Editing for Today's Newsroom*, Carl Sessions Stepp makes clear that he cares not at all that 19 years and countless technological changes have come and gone since the first edition. His imperative, now more than ever, reads, "Editing is the essential difference between excellence and mediocrity in journalism."[17]

Although the emphasis in Stepp's book is on "today's newsroom," as opposed to the magazine boardroom, much of the advice offered on the practice of editing talks up to readers from any concentration. Stepp says as much at the beginning: "The book is intended primarily for advanced students of editing,"[18] or professional journalists making the leap to the editing desk. Much advice applies to the day-to-day worries of production and the management of writers, and there is some emphasis on the editor's evolving role in increasingly corporate media environments: "The editor's role is to grow in understanding the corporate culture as well as the news side, in order to have an informed, powerful voice representing the newsroom, asserting its interests, and sustaining the commitment to social responsibility and to reasonable corporate success."[19] This would be the prevailing view in the twenty-first century: Editors must, now more than they ever have, play nice with the business side but try to do so honorably—meaning, give away as little editorial integrity as possible.

Michael Robert Evans, in *The Layers of Magazine Editing*, tries to capture the entirety of the magazine experience, from conceiving a title that readers would want to buy to the usual tips on grammar and fact checking for magazines.[20] The volume is useful for those who want to understand the kind of alchemy an editor must perform in order to encourage and cultivate writers as people, not simply producers of words to be edited. Evans emphasizes the editing life as much as the editing itself, providing a fuller picture of the role. The book is a holistic primer that, in chatty patter, lays down the principles of editing for magazines.[21] In sections with subtitles written in magazine display writing style, such as "The plan's the thing" (about the need to think of story ideas several months in advance) and "Hands Off!" (which explores exactly what it implies: Read first, then edit), Evans's advice is simple and confident. "Changes should be made only after you understand the entire manuscript,"[22] he declares, and, "Trends are not predictors."[23] Unusually, he makes a plea for editors to take a course in symbolic logic, which would help them to spot weak argument structures.[24] Evans offers interview quotes from many working editors about craft and maintains a conversational tone throughout—although phrases such as "in the midst of the muddy morass of mediocre magazines"[25] tend to undercut the seriousness of his enterprise.

For a British take on the business of editing magazines, freelancing for magazines and managing magazines, Jenny McKay's *The Magazines Handbook*, 2nd ed.,[26] and John Morrish's *Magazine Editing: How to Develop and Manage a Successful Publication*, 2nd ed.,[27] offer many of the same kinds of tips as North American books but are targeted more precisely to the U.K. market. In fact, some advice seems to be peculiar to that market. "There are no minimum qualifications for journalists," McKay writes, "so in theory you could get a job without a GCSE or an A level or a Scottish Advanced Higher."[28] McKay's basic, crisp prose informs magazine neophytes how to break into the business. Along a path studded with routine information—the difference between features and news, how to pitch ideas, how to send in copy, etc.—she relates stories about her early infatuation with magazines and spotlights success stories such as John McKie, who ascended from nothing to edit a biweekly pop music journal.[29] McKay's advice is solidly aimed at the generalist. Hers is a primer on U.K. magazines for writers, editors and anyone else who might see themselves working in the field, not editing in particular. Morrish's slant is editing, of course. The subtitle, with its succession of business-oriented words—"develop," "manage," "successful"—is a clue that his take will be more about how to make money. "Editors," he declares, "must be managers and leaders in a publishing business."[30]

Books for Editors on Writing

There are recent texts in the area of editing and writing targeted to interested consumers as well as those in educational institutions. Theodore Cheney's *Writing Creative Nonfiction*[31] has been especially useful for its detailed coverage of the various types of structure for feature writing. Cheney begins at the beginning, with the oldest form of structure known—the sun rises; the sun sets—that is, *chronology*. He discusses other popular ways of telling a story, including *in medias res*, or starting the story with a scene culled from somewhere in the middle, doing so precisely because of its power to grab readers' attention, and otherwise the story follows a chronological pattern. Other major structure forms would include the *parallel narrative*, wherein two or more stories are told over the same time frame but never intersect; the *convergent narrative*, where two characters start far apart but eventually meet, with the narrative switching back and forth; and, of course, the one favored by John McPhee and many of the long-form writers interviewed by Robert S. Boynton for his book, *The New New Journalism*,[32] that is, *the process story*.

In a similar vein, although the focus is more on long newspaper features, not magazine-style narratives, Jack Hart's *Storycraft*, issued in 2011, may prove invaluable to both writers and editors. Sections are headed in no-nonsense fashion—Structure, Point of View, Voice and Style, Character, Scene, Action, Dialogue, and so on. No cute turns of phrase for Hart. For instance, when giving advice about scene-writing, he does not waste time: "The importance of action suggests you should get moving right out of the blocks. *Something* should happen in the first line of your narrative."[33] Hart writes like a writer's coach, but his exhortations are a refresher for editors.

Writers' Perspectives on Editing

The Pulitzer Prize-winning author John McPhee[34] lately has been looking at his relation to the editing process, in memoir fashion, in the pages of the *New Yorker*. In "Structure," he describes the not-inconsiderable influence that Olive McKee, his high school English teacher, had on him in the 1940s. McKee insisted students write three pieces per week. "We could write anything we wanted to, but each composition had to be accompanied by a structural outline, which she told us we had to do first."[35]

In "Progression,"[36] McPhee discusses an article structure he christened "ABC/D," his long apprenticeship writing profiles for *Time* and the *New Yorker*, and his attempts to break the bonds of this standard magazine feature straightjacket: Why settle for ABC/D? Why not a double profile? After all, 1 + 1 = 2.6. McPhee, in his usual sprawling style, connects Swedish massage, magazine article structure, the genesis of Edgar Allan Poe's "The Raven," a boys' camp in Vermont and the environmental movement, among other subjects.

In "Editors and Publisher," an ode to *New Yorker* editor William Shawn and publisher Roger W. Straus, Jr., McPhee mentions that his great uncle was also in the publishing business, selling book boards—the board that made hardcover books hard—to John C. Winston's publishing company. Winston "claimed to have published more Bibles than anyone else in the world, and at the other end of their list was my grandfather's specialty, the hardcover equivalent of the newspaper extra. In 1912, he published a quickie on the Titanic."[37] We have come around to McPhee's grandfather's way of making money. The Sunday *New York Times* published John Branch's deep, lengthy reportage, "Avalanche," in its own section on 23 December 2012—a "newspaper extra," to be sure—and teamed up with long-form Web publisher Byliner to republish the piece under the title, "Snow Fall: The Avalanche at Tunnel Creek," the same month.[38]

McPhee seems to be surveying his vast, enviable corpus, looking to dispense twilight insight. In the spirit of looking backward in order to look forward, in 1995 I was invited to be a temporary faculty member at the Banff Publishing Workshop, held at The Banff Centre, Banff, Alberta, Canada. The workshop was designed for young magazine professionals in their first five years on the job. The goal was to place each participant in an unfamiliar role at an equally unfamiliar magazine. When I was a participant, eight years before, in 1987, I was the editor of a small monthly music and arts publication. The program's directors stuck me in a group whose goal was to build a new business magazine in two weeks, and I was to be its art director. This fish-out-of-water training was a superb experience, not without its palpitations, and augmented by the many longtime magazine professionals who came to spend a day or two and offer advice. One such man was a publishing executive. He talked about the future, and the future envisioned at that point was jack in to an ATM-like machine and download the newspaper onto a flimsy, pliable computer. The future was coming, and print would be gone by 2012–2015. The future would undermine the way we conceive of magazine making.

New Approaches Lie Ahead

The publishing executive was not far off. In 2013, new models being financed by Silicon Valley are currently being tested in the marketplace. Two such models are the *Atavist* and Byliner. The former is located in Brooklyn, the latter in San Francisco. They are different. The *Atavist* sells features as long reads managed in one sitting. It also provides multimedia with each download. There may be music, maps, films and other intrusions into the text. Byliner is the more purist gambit. It focuses on recreating a classic long-form magazine reading experience, albeit in digital form. It is also building a database of long-form work by many of its writers. It seeks to become a destination place for serious long-form readers. A subscription service that encompasses both its growing archive and its growing collection of original work is forthcoming.

The digital format would seem to suggest a faster pace and an ability to tighten the time between editing and publishing. Yet, according to *Atavist* executive editor Charles Homans, whose previous editing jobs include stints at *Foreign Policy* and *Washington Monthly*, the commitment to deep editing is alive and well. "I get to spend a lot more time on each story I edit here than I did at my previous editing jobs," he wrote in an e-mail, "which was part of why I took this gig."[39] To name two of his recent editing jobs, Homans says he worked closely with author Deborah Blum on *Angel Killer*, a gruesome tale of child kidnapping and cannibalism, and with author Mary Cueddhe on *Agent Zapata*, an anatomy of the killing of a U.S. Immigration and Customs Enforcement officer. Homans believes editing at the *Atavist* can remain craft-conscious because, although the company began as a publisher, it now produces considerable revenues through its proprietary publishing software. "We're not a pure editorial venture," Homans wrote, "so our editorial work is not (yet) under as much pressure to produce revenue as I suspect other folks in this space are under."[40]

At Byliner, the long-form investigative and literary journalism comes in bite-sized form as well. Editorial director and cofounder Mark Bryant believes the entire point of building a site like Byliner is to bring long-form magazine writing into the digital age. He says the editing process at Byliner remains close to the magazine process. "We're marrying a group of old-school, highly craft-conscious editors to new technology, a new delivery system."[41] That sounds like a mission statement—and a goal. Certainly the idea of investing in editing goes against the prevailing winds of cost cutting and outsourcing, and Bryant knows this:

> We talk about publishing in that space between magazine and books, for the most part focusing between five thousand and thirty thousand words, narrative that can be read in a single sitting. It was clear to us when we were starting Byliner that, as editors and writers, there were fewer and fewer opportunities for writers to publish the kind of ambitious work that got them into the business in the first place. Magazines have been experiencing declining ad revenues and so they've been unable to publish the kind of material they normally would.[42]

And thus the aperture opens for the likes of the *Atavist* and Byliner. In the real world of editing long-form for the digital realm, however, there have been deviations. With Jon Krakauer's *Three Cups of Deceit*, the first Byliner Original, both Bryant and Krakauer fiddled with copy until hours before making the book available on-line.[43] Partly this has to do with the nature of digital publishing, and partly this has to do with the lengthy work history between Bryant and Krakauer. The editor and writer had worked together at *Outside* magazine, and Bryant was the editor who suggested to Krakauer that he cover the story of a young man named Christopher McCandless, who had starved to death in Alaska. The result, "Death of an Innocent," from 1993, became one of Krakauer's best-known pieces. He expanded it to book form, *Into the Wild*, in 1996, and the book graduated to the film screen with a Sean Penn-directed adaptation in 2007. With this history, the two men were confident they could add new material right up to deadline, but, as Bryant points out, "I had been working on *Three Cups of Deceit* for weeks, through various drafts."[44]

Bryant had a similar editing experience with another early Byliner Original, William Vollman's *Into the Forbidden Zone*, which covered the aftermath of the Tohoku earthquake and tsunami in March 2011 and the meltdown of the Fukushima I Nuclear Power Plant. That is to say, both author and writer worked closely on the final draft right up to going live. "But again," says Bryant, "that was the end of a long process. Bill's story was reported quickly—he's so prolific—because we wanted this piece, and he wanted this piece, to be the first narrative about the earthquake and the subsequent meltdown. He was working very quickly, and so were we, probably editing in haste, more like editing for a weekly rather than a monthly. But it wasn't an overnight edit. It was quick, but not that quick."[45]

Christopher Frey at *Hazlitt* said working on shorter deadlines actually might be a good thing for long-form writing. To his way of thinking, now that writing is firmly into the digital age, and with all due respect, etc., etc., to craft consciousness, magazine pieces are too often over-edited. "Or they're edited late in the process, even at the proofing stage, and it's usually because there is a perceived need to 'hot it up' and create some kind of controversy, something to sell on the cover." In an echo of William Whitworth's comment about his vision for the *Atlantic*, Frey continues, saying, "It is the writer who was out there getting the story and who knew better than anyone in the editorial boardroom what the story really was."[46] It must be pointed out, however, that ongoing tours of the *Hazlitt* Web site suggest that what Frey is aiming for is his magazine's namesake's preferred form of writing, the essay, and showcasing mostly established writers to give their learned opinions on a wide array of topics—which is not the same animal as the deeply reported long-form feature.

The People Who Edit

As for the beloved *Atlantic*, there was former editor William Whitworth's vision for the 1990s and now there is current editor James Bennet's vision for the 2010s. Digital reality squats over a large segment of that vision, as the *Atlantic* retooled itself in the past seven years to become an Internet publishing success story.[47] As Lee Jolliffe has pointed out,[48] examining the process of editing from the consumer magazine perspective can be a reductive exercise, devolving into a variation of the "Great Man" theory, which is to say that too much emphasis is placed on the career of one person—the editor—in order to explain how a magazine works or is successful. Scanning backward, Jolliffe found that some editors have enjoyed more prominence than others as biographical subjects, thus erecting subjective scholarly monuments to worthy editors at the expense of a bird's eye view of the editing perimeter as a whole. Nonetheless, it could be argued that some editors require more attention than others. For instance, no understanding of 1960s and 1970s American magazine culture can be without mention of the indelible accomplishments of a Harold Hayes, who, as editor of *Esquire*, presided over its golden age, 1963–1973; or a Clay Felker, who in 1968 founded *New York*, the prototype for all succeeding city magazines. Their visions guided their respective magazines to previously unknown heights.

In that context, it might be wise not only to applaud Bennet and the *Atlantic*, but also to pay attention to, and end this discussion with, David Remnick, one of the major editors of the past two decades. Remnick has directed the *New Yorker* since 1998 and is therefore somewhat equipped to pronounce on this volatile decade and a half. In addition, he presides over the magazine that many believe embodies the spirit of long-form magazine editing. Looking both forward and back, he must continue to appease his readers who still want their weekly *New Yorker* fix through the post. Yet, increasingly, he must also cater to readers who get everything, and are used to getting everything, including the entire archives dating back to 1925, on-line. In a Big Think conversation conducted in February 2012, he addressed this issue by highlighting the power of long-form writing and its ability to grip readers:

> My idea of the *New Yorker*, as long as I'm there, is that we are not going to change who we are, no matter what the delivery systems are, no matter what the means of reading us are. We are about reading: long-form journalism, analysis, humor, fiction, poetry, a sense of delight, a sense of seriousness when it's appropriate.[49]

He added, "This is a formula that took a long, long time to develop, and people want what we do."[50]

Notes

1 Alexis C. Madrigal, "The 12 Timeless Rules for Making a Good Publication," *Atlantic*, 11 November 2010 <http://www.theatlantic.com/technology/archive/2010/11/the-12-timeless-rules-for-making-a-good-publication/66444/>, accessed 25 February 2013.

2 M.R. Montgomery, "He Rules the *Atlantic* without Making Waves," *Boston Globe*, 7 March 1995, 55.

3 Benton Rain Patterson and Coleman E.P. Patterson, *The Editor-in-Chief: A Practical Management Guide for Magazine Editors* (Ames: Iowa State University Press, 1997), 44.

4 Peter Jacobi, "The Art of Editing: It's the Editor's Job to Bring the Publication to Life, and by So Doing, Serve the Reader's Need—Issue, after Issue, after Issue," *Folio*, July 1990, 102.

5 Christopher Frey, editor-in-chief of Hazlitt.com, interview by author, 28 January 2013.

6 Frey, Interview.

7 J. William Click and Russell N. Baird, *Magazine Editing and Production*, 6th ed. (Madison, WI: WCB Brown & Benchmark, 1994).

8 Click and Baird, *Magazine Editing and Production*, ix.

9 Click and Baird, *Magazine Editing and Production*, 99.

10 Brian S. Brooks and James L. Pinson, *The Art of Editing in the Age of Convergence*, 9th ed. (Boston: Pearson, 2009).

11 Brooks and Pinson, *The Art of Editing*, xiii.

12 Brooks and Pinson, *The Art of Editing*, 59.

13 Brooks and Pinson, *The Art of Editing*, 60.

14 Brooks and Pinson, *The Art of Editing*, 60.

15 Brooks and Pinson, *The Art of Editing*, 318.

16 Brooks and Pinson, *The Art of Editing*, 319.

17 Carl Sessions Stepp, *Editing for Today's Newsroom: A Guide for Success in a Changing Profession*, 2nd ed. (New York: Routledge, 2008), xi.

18 Stepp, *Editing for Today's Newsroom*, ix.

19 Stepp, *Editing for Today's Newsroom*, 41.

20 Michael Robert Evans, *The Layers of Magazine Editing* (New York: Columbia University Press, 2004).

21 Dane S. Claussen, "Review of *The Layers of Magazine Editing* by Michael Robert Evans," *Journalism & Mass Communication Quarterly* 82.1 (Spring 2005): 221–222. Claussen considers chapters six through nine essential, the other 12 chapters padding: "There, in chapters 6, 7, 8, and 9, Evans goes into great detail about exactly how to assign and monitor high-quality articles and how to give them a first reading, a second reading, and so on, going from the big questions of whether the writer gave the editor what he or she promised and whether the story makes sense and fits the goal and tone of the magazine, down to rewriting leads and so on," 221.

22 Evans, *The Layers of Magazine Editing*, 134.

23 Evans, *The Layers of Magazine Editing*, 146.

24 Evans, *The Layers of Magazine Editing*, 150.

25 Evans, *The Layers of Magazine Editing*, 4.

26 Jenny McKay, *The Magazines Handbook*, 2nd ed. (London and New York: Routledge, 2006).

27 John Morrish, *Magazine Editing: How to Develop and Manage a Successful Publication*, 2nd ed. (London and New York: Routledge, 2003).

28 McKay, *The Magazines Handbook*, 13.

29 McKay, *The Magazines Handbook*, 25.

30 Morrish, *Magazine Editing*, 219.

31 Theodore A. Rees Cheney, *Writing Creative Nonfiction: Fiction Techniques for Crafting Great Nonfiction* (Berkeley, CA: Ten Speed Press, 2001).

32 Robert S. Boynton, ed., *The New New Journalism: Conversations with America's Best Nonfiction Writers about Their Craft* (New York: Vintage Books, 2005). Boynton's essay, "The New New Journalism, Circa 2011," which discusses the effect of social media on long-form nonfiction, was published by Byliner, 15 September 2011 <https://www.byliner.com/robert-s-boynton/stories/the-new-new-journalism-circa-2011>, accessed 27 March 2013.

33 Jack Hart, *Storycraft: The Complete Guide to Writing Narrative Nonfiction* (Chicago: University of Chicago Press, 2011), 108.

34 McPhee won a Pulitzer Prize in the General Nonfiction category for his book, *Annals of the Former World*, *New York Times*, 13 April 1999.

35 John McPhee, "Structure: Beyond the Picnic-Table Crisis," *New Yorker*, 14 January 2013, 46.

36 John McPhee, "Progression," *New Yorker*, 14 November 2011, 39.

37 John McPhee, "Editors and Publisher," *New Yorker*, 2 July 2012, 38.

38 A 13 December 2012 press release, issued by Business Wire, announced that "digital startup" Byliner and the *New York Times* would collaborate on a line of e-books. See "The New York Times Launches E-Book Programs," Business Wire, 13 December 2012. <http://www.businesswire.com/news/home/20121213006180/en/York-Times-Launches-E-Book-Programs#.VMryz010wy4>, accessed 29 January 2015.

39 Charles Homans, executive editor of the *Atavist*, e-mail interview by author, 13 February 2013.

40 Homans, E-mail interview.

41 Mark Bryant, co-founder and editor-in-chief of Byliner, interview by author, 26 February 2013.

42 Sarah Lacy, "Byliner Launches with a Splash, Aims to Disrupt Long-Form Journalism," *TechCrunch.com*, 19 April 2011 <http://techcrunch.com/2011/04/19/byliner-launches-with-a-splash-aims-to-disrupt-long-form-journalism/>, accessed 25 February 2013. Lacy reported, "Authors will spend a few months—not years—writing, and Byliner will invest in real editing of the piece. That's something traditional publishers no longer do, and most writers I know yearn for. Great writers can always benefit from great editors, and great editors are disappearing from journalism and publishing."

43 Mallary Jean Tenore, "Byliner CEO Excited About 'Opportunity to Discover Some Great Writers,'" *MediaWire*, Poynter.org, 21 June 2011 <http://www.poynter.org/latest-news/top-stories/136421/byliner-ceo-were-really-excited-about-the-opportunity-to-discover-great-writers/>, accessed 2 December 2013.

44 Bryant, Interview.

45 Bryant, Interview.

46 Frey, Interview.

47 Jeremy W. Peters, "Web Focus Helps Revitalize the *Atlantic*," *New York Times*, 13 December 2010, B1. The *Atlantic* has managed to grow revenue through Web traffic, but it has also, using the *Atlantic* "brand," successfully branched into the conference game.

48 Lee Jolliffe, "Research Review: Magazine Editors and Editing Practices," in David Abrahamson, ed., *The American Magazine: Research Perspectives and Prospects* (Ames: Iowa State University Press, 1995), 54.

49 David Remnick, "Big Think Interview with David Remnick," BigThink.com, 22 April 2010 <http://bigth ink.com/videos/big-think-interview-with-david-remnick>, accessed 2 December 2013.

50 Remnick, "Big Think Interview with David Remnick."

Bibliography

Boynton, Robert S. "The New New Journalism, Circa 2011." Byliner, 15 September 2011 <https://www.byliner.com/robert-s-boynton/stories/the-new-new-journalism-circa-2011>, accessed 27 March 2013.

Boynton, Robert S., ed. *The New New Journalism: Conversations with America's Best Nonfiction Writers about Their Craft.* New York: Vintage Books, 2005.

Brooks, Brian S. and Pinson, James L. *The Art of Editing in the Age of Convergence.* 9th ed. Boston: Pearson, 2009.

Bryant, Mark, co-founder and editor-in-chief of Byliner. Interview by author. 26 February 2013.

Cheney, Theodore A. Rees. *Writing Creative Nonfiction: Fiction Techniques for Crafting Great Nonfiction.* Berkeley, CA: Ten Speed Press, 2001.

Claussen, Dane S. "Review of *The Layers of Magazine Editing* by Michael Robert Evans." *Journalism & Mass Communication Quarterly* 82.1 (Spring 2005): 221–222.

Click, J. William and Baird, Russell N. *Magazine Editing and Production.* 6th ed. Madison, WI: WCB Brown & Benchmark, 1994.

Evans, Michael Robert. *The Layers of Magazine Editing.* New York: Columbia University Press, 2004.

Frey, Christopher, editor-in-chief of Hazlitt.com. Interview by author, 28 January 2013.

Hart, Jack. *Storycraft: The Complete Guide to Writing Narrative Nonfiction.* Chicago: University of Chicago Press, 2011.

Homans, Charles, executive editor of the *Atavist.* E-mail interview by author, 13 February 2013.

Jacobi, Peter. "The Art of Editing: It's the Editor's Job to Bring the Publication to Life, and by So Doing, Serve the Reader's Need—Issue, after Issue, after Issue." *Folio:,* July 1990, 102.

Jolliffe, Lee. "Research Review: Magazine Editors and Editing Practices." In Abrahamson, David, ed. *The American Magazine: Research Perspectives and Prospects.* Ames: Iowa State University Press, 1995, 51–71.

Lacy, Sarah. "Byliner Launches with a Splash, Aims to Disrupt Long-Form Journalism." *TechCrunch.com,* 19 April 2011 <http://techcrunch.com/2011/04/19/byliner-launches-with-a-splash-aims-to-disrupt-long-form-journalism/>, accessed 25 February 2013.

Madrigal, Alexis C. "The 12 Timeless Rules for Making a Good Publication." *Atlantic,* 11 November 2010 <http://www.theatlantic.com/technology/archive/2010/11/the-12-timeless-rules-for-making-a-good-publication/66444/>, accessed 25 February 2013.

McKay, Jenny. *The Magazines Handbook.* 2nd ed. London and New York: Routledge, 2006.

McPhee, John. "Editors and Publisher." *New Yorker,* 2 July 2012, 32–38.

McPhee, John. "Progression." *New Yorker,* 14 November 2011, 36–41.

McPhee, John. "Structure: Beyond the Picnic-Table Crisis." *New Yorker,* 14 January 2013, 46–51.

Montgomery, M.R. "He Rules the *Atlantic* without Making Waves." *Boston Globe,* 7 March 1995, 55.

Morrish, John. *Magazine Editing: How to Develop and Manage a Successful Publication.* 2nd ed. London and New York: Routledge, 2003.

"The New York Times Launches E-Book Programs," Business Wire, 13 December 2012 <http://www.businesswire.com/news/home/20121213006180/en/York-Times-Launches-E-Book-Programs#.VMryz010wy4>, accessed 29 January 2015.

Patterson, Benton Rain and Patterson, Coleman E.P. *The Editor-in-Chief: A Practical Management Guide for Magazine Editors.* Ames: Iowa State University Press, 1997.

Peters, Jeremy W. "Web Focus Helps Revitalize the *Atlantic.*" *New York Times,* 13 December 2010, B1.

Remnick, David. "Big Think Interview with David Remnick." BigThink.com, 22 April 2010 <http://bigthink.com/videos/big-think-interview-with-david-remnick>, accessed 2 December 2013.

Stepp, Carl Sessions. *Editing for Today's Newsroom: A Guide for Success in a Changing Profession.* 2nd ed. New York: Routledge, 2008.

Tenore, Mallary Jean. "Byliner CEO Excited About 'Opportunity to Discover Some Great Writers.'" *MediaWire.* Poynter.org, 21 June 2011 <http://www.poynter.org/latest-news/top-stories/136421/byliner-ceo-were-really-excited-about-the-opportunity-to-discover-great-writers/>, 12 May 2014.

Supplemental Resources

Abrahamson, David, ed. *The American Magazine: Research Perspectives and Prospects*. Ames: Iowa State University Press, 1995.

Abrahamson, David. *Magazine-Made America: The Cultural Transformation of the Postwar Periodical*. Cresskill, NJ: Hampton Press, 1996.

Abrahamson, David. "Teaching Literary Journalism: A Diverted Pyramid?" *Journalism & Mass Communication Educator* 60.4 (Winter 2006): 430–434.

Abrahamson, David and Eddy, Nathan. Review of *Magazines That Make History: Their Origins, Development and Influence*. In *Journalism & Mass Communication Educator* 60.4 (Winter 2006): 441–443.

Applegate, Edd, ed. *Literary Journalism: A Biographical Dictionary of Writers and Editors*. Westport, CT: Greenwood Press, 1996.

Boers, Raoul; Ercan, Esra; Rinsdorf, Lars; and Vaaggan, Robert W. "From Convergence to Connectivism: Teaching Journalism 2.0." *On-line Journal of Communication and Media Technologies* 2.4 (October 2012): 52–64.

Bridges, Bill. "Teach Editing—If You Can." *Thinking Classroom*, July 2006, 45–46.

Carr, David. "Maturing as Publisher and Platform." *New York Times*, 21 May 2012, B1(L).

Clifford, Stephanie. "Making It Look Easy at the *New Yorker*." *New York Times*, 5 April 2010, B1.

Connery, Thomas B. "Research Review: Magazines and Literary Journalism, an Embarrassment of Riches." *Electronic Journal of Communication/La Revue Electronique de Communication* 4 (December 1994): 1–12.

Daglas, Cristina. "Point of View: Examining the Magazine Industry Standard." Master's thesis, University of Missouri-Columbia, May 2009.

Dale, Carolyn and Pilgrim, Tim. *Fearless Editing: Crafting Words and Images for Print, Web, and Public Relations*. Boston: Pearson Education, 2005.

Endres, Kathleen L. and Schierhorn, Ann B. "New Technology and the Writer/Editor Relationship: Shifting Electronic Realities." *Journalism & Mass Communication Quarterly* 72.2 (Summer 1995): 448–457.

Flaherty, Francis. *The Elements of Story: Field Notes on Nonfiction Writing*. New York: Harper Perennial, 2009.

Fry, Don and Clark, Roy Peter. "Return of the Narrative: the Rebirth of Writing in America's Newsrooms." *Quill*, May 1994, 27–28.

Greenberg, Susan. "When the Editor Disappears, Does Editing Disappear?" *Convergence: The International Journal of Research into New Media Technologies* 16.1 (February 2010): 7–21.

Greenberg, Susan and Phelps, Christopher. "Poetics of Fact." *Times Higher Education*, 15 August 2010, 36.

Harrigan, Jane T. and Dunlap, Karen Brown. *The Editorial Eye*. 2nd ed. Boston: Bedford / St. Martin's, 2003.

Hart, Jack. *Storycraft: The Complete Guide to Writing Narrative Nonfiction*. Chicago: University of Chicago Press, 2011.

Hart, Jack. *A Writer's Coach: An Editor's Guide to Words That Work*. New York: Pantheon Books, 2006.

Kamiya, Gary. "Let Us Now Praise Editors: They May Be Invisible and Their Art Unsung. But in the Age of Blogging, Editors Are Needed More Than Ever." *Salon.com*, 24 July 2007 <http://www.salon.com/2007/07/24/editing/>, accessed 25 February 2013.

Kramer, Mark. "Narrative Journalism Comes of Age." *Nieman Reports*, Fall 2000, 5–8.

Kramer, Mark and Call, Wendy, eds. *Telling True Stories: A Nonfiction Writers' Guide from the Nieman Foundation at Harvard University*. New York: Plume, 2007.

Langewiesche, William, author of Byliner e-book, *Finding the Devil*. Interview by author. 14 February 2013.

Lepre, Carolyn and Bleske, Glen L. "Little Common Ground for Magazine Editors and Professors Surveyed on Journalism Curriculum." *Journalism & Mass Communication Educator* 60.2 (Summer 2005): 190–200.

Lounsberry, Barbara. *The Art of Fact: Contemporary Artists of Nonfiction*. Santa Barbara, CA: Praeger, 1990.

Macfarlane, John. "Editing a Magazine Is Like Conducting an Orchestra." *Toronto Life*, July 2006, 19.

Meyer, Michael. "Going to Great Lengths." *Columbia Journalism Review*, November/December 2012, 16–17.

Owen, Laura Hazard. "The Rise of E-Singles: It's a Long Story." *Business Week*, 31 December 2012, 1.

Quart, Alissa. "The Long Tale." *Columbia Journalism Review*, 20 September 2011 <http://www.cjr.org/reports/the_long_tale.php?page=all>, accessed 25 February 2013.

Remnick, David. "Barbara Epstein: The Talk of the Town." *New Yorker*, 3 July 2006, 27.

Reynolds, Bill. "Adventures in Long-Form Magazine Editing." *J-Source*, 28 July 2009 <http://j-source.ca/article/adventures-long-form-magazine-editing>, accessed 25 February 2013.

Reynolds, Bill. "The Missing Link in Literary Journalism." *Literary Journalism: The Newsletter of the International Association for Literary Journalism Studies*, Winter 2013, 1, 10.

Rose, Rebecca. "You've Come a Long Way . . . Are Women Still Being Passed Over for the Top Magazine Editing Jobs? Or Are They Just Too Smart to Take It?" *Ryerson Review of Journalism*, Spring 2008 <http://www.rrj.ca/m4126/>, accessed 24 February 2013.

Saller, Carol Fisher. *The Subversive Copy Editor: Advice from Chicago*. Chicago: University of Chicago Press, 2009.

Schierhorn, Ann B. and Endres, Kathleen L. "Magazine Writing Instruction and the Composition Revolution." *Journalism Educator* 47.2 (Summer 1992): 57–64.

Sims, Norman. "Writing Literary History . . . *The Promised Land*, and *The Big Test*, an Interview with Author . . . Nicholas Lemann." *Literary Journalism Studies* 3.1 (Spring 2011): 9–31.

Tayman, John. "It's a Long Article. It's a Short Book. No, It's a Byliner E-Book." *Nieman Reports*, Winter 2011, 38.

Tenore, Mallary Jean. "How Technology Is Renewing Attention to Long-Form Journalism." *MediaWire*. Poynter.org, 4 March 2011 <http://www.poynter.org/latest-news/top-stories/104962/how-technology-is-renewing-attention-to-long-form-journalism/>, accessed 25 February 2013.

Ulin, David L. "Literary Journalism Finds New Platforms: Byliner, the *Atavist* and *Virginia Quarterly Review* Take the Form into the Future." *Los Angeles Times*, 15 May 2011 <latimes.com/entertainment/news/books/la-ca-david-ulin-20110515,0,3634450.story>, accessed 25 February 2013.

Wolman, David. "Journalism Done the *Atavist* Way." *Nieman Reports*, Winter 2011, 36–38.

Wood, Gaby. "The Quiet American." *Observer*, 9 September 2006.

Woods, Stuart. "Random House of Canada Launches On-line Magazine as Part of Digital Overhaul." *Quill & Quire*, 23 August 2012 <http://www.quillandquire.com/digital-publishing-and-technology/2012/08/23/random-house-of-canada-launches-online-magazine-as-part-of-digital-overhaul/>, accessed 25 April 2014.

30
TEACHING MAGAZINE RESEARCH

Explicating Theory and Methods

Carolyn Ringer Lepre

The number of degrees granted from journalism and mass communication undergraduate programs showed modest increases in recent years across the United States and, despite a lagging economy, even larger increases were seen at the graduate level.[1] The most recent, 2012 study of graduate programs reported more than 5,390 master's degrees were granted in the 2011–2012 school year; in 2008 only 4,079 students were graduated. A total of 276 doctoral degrees were granted in the 2011–2012 school year, compared to 226 doctoral graduates in 2008.[2] The number of U.S. colleges and universities offering master's and doctoral degrees has also increased. In their 2012 Enrollment Report, Lee Becker, Tudor Vlad, Holly Simpson and Konrad Kalpen reported that the number of master's programs had grown substantially from 12 years earlier—from 176 to 217—as well as an increase in the number of doctoral degree granting programs, from 40 to 50.[3] No comparable data on student enrollments in international graduate programs were found. However, the increase in media and mass communication research being done across the globe suggests similar increases in the graduate student population in media and mass communication programs are occurring worldwide. Despite this growth, U.S. scholars have long debated the make-up of the "ideal" mass communication graduate curriculum. In particular, educators have contemplated the issue of the focus of the mass communication master's program. For it is a program's overall emphasis on either professional practice, teaching and research, or both that guides curricular decisions. These discussions have special meaning for those interested in the magazine form, both from a research perspective and for those in the professoriate who wish to further enhance the study of magazines in the future.

Graduate education is traditionally, and in many disciplinary fields continues to be, synonymous with teaching students how to do theory-based research that adds to the discipline or field's body of knowledge. When that is true, graduate programs are structured to ensure students' immersion in research, both formally and informally, inside and outside the classroom. However, a number of factors have contributed to enlarging the definitions and scope of graduate education at both master's and doctoral levels in the United States over the past century. Among those is the linking of skills for professional practice with post-baccalaureate, higher-level conceptual knowledge. The linked areas of journalism, media and mass communication are on the growing list of fields in which that is occurring.

This chapter seeks to examine the current curricular trends in mass communication graduate education and how the magazine scholar fits into the larger picture. Mass communication graduate education, including the current structure of master's and doctoral curricula in the United States and what curricular trends might be forthcoming, is discussed. Through an examination of trends in theory and research and a discussion of educational trends, suggestions are made for what students need to learn to be productive researchers on the magazine form. Educational and communication research is also discussed and suggestions presented for future research.

Literature Review and Method

To answer these questions, the literature on journalism and mass communication graduate education published in communication and education journals and presented at communication or education conferences between 1990 and 2013 was reviewed. The current review suggests a pattern similar to Elliot King's 1995 finding. Research on magazines and magazine journalism education being published in top journalism and mass communication journals is limited.[4] Since 1990, only 80 articles, approximately 5 percent of the total 1,372 articles published in *Journalism & Mass Communication Quarterly*, have examined magazines.[5] Only 10 articles of the total 728 published in *Journalism & Mass Communication Educator* during the same period have explored magazine education. None have specifically addressed magazine graduate education.[6] Existing research on magazines is increasingly diverse as scholars draw on theoretical perspectives and methods from a rich plethora of fields. Preparing coming generations of scholars who want to focus on the magazine form may thus require a curriculum that reflects this diversity while simultaneously building on each program's unique strengths.

Because there were so few articles published or presented on this topic in the years selected for this chapter, each article was read. As with any form of research, the chapter research grew organically once it began. The original question, "What do students need to learn in graduate school to be productive researchers on the magazine form?" led from a search on mass communication graduate education to mass communication research trends, to mass communication theory trends, to a larger discussion on the purpose of higher education in general. With each article read, new ideas emerged, as did new sources and paths of inquiry.

While the majority of the existing articles discuss various perspectives on mass communication master's programs, some researchers have delved into the doctoral discussion as well. Pivotal articles referenced in this chapter include John Soloski's "On Defining the Nature of Graduate Education,"[7] published in a special issue of *Journalism Educator* in 1994 and offering insights into curricular trends. Elliot King's "Issues in Magazine Journalism Education"[8] in David Abrahamson's 1995 anthology, *The American Magazine: Research Perspectives and Prospects*, offered a place to begin this chapter, as it left off discussing the state of journalism and magazine journalism education in the early 1990s. Finally, for understanding the basic state of master's curricula at the start of the time period being studied here, Joey Senat and Elinor Kelley Grusin's "Seeking a Theoretical Framework for Master's Programs in the 1990s"[9] was critical.

Graduate Education in Journalism and Mass Communication

Journalism Educator in 1994 devoted an entire special issue to the topic of mass communication graduate education. In this critical issue, noted scholar of journalism and mass communication education John Soloski argues that the topic of mass communication graduate education has been ignored for too long and that the need for evaluation of programs is vital to better prepare students for their chosen careers.[10] He notes the ongoing skills versus theory debate that wages in many circles in graduate schools across the United States. If a unit offers a professional master's program, even if the program is side-by-side with a theoretical teaching and research program, criticism abounds. From within the academy, the professional programs run the risk of being seen as technical programs and the professors being seen as practitioners not scholars.[11] Alternatively, from the non-academic professionals' perspective, professors are frequently viewed as out of date and out of touch.[12]

Soloski is not alone in his characterization of this problem. Canadian journalism educator Marc Edge has noted that when social scientific research on mass communication began to take hold in the 1940s, universities, in order to encourage a stronger research agenda, pushed faculty to publish, or perish.[13] Edge wrote that "soon the battle lines were drawn in many journalism schools, with the 'green eyeshades' from the newsroom arguing for more skills training on one side and the 'chi squares' with their slide rules pondering theoretical questions on the other."[14] This characterization of the battle between skills versus theory is ongoing.[15] While some researchers have characterized this discussion as an attempt to find a balance between "the need for practical knowledge and training with theoretical framework of the field of study,"[16] others suggest that research is needed to evaluate whether journalism and mass communication programs that continue to attempt a balance are out of date and no longer meet the needs and interests of contemporary students.[17]

Trends in Doctoral Education

It is also important to examine the scholarship on mass communication doctoral curricula. The large issue at hand, again, invites the question Soloski asks: "Is there a body of knowledge being taught in doctoral programs that defines our field?"[18] To date, though the question has been asked, no studies were found of the question. Similarly, there are few studies of mass communication doctoral programs, their curricula, goals, student learning objectives or theoretical groundwork. Such analytical study would not have as its purpose regulation of curricula or coursework, but, Soloski argues, "to see if there is a shared knowledge base in our field and, if so, we should expect all our doctoral students to master this knowledge base."[19] Orlando L. Taylor, in his National Communication Association (NCA) president's letter in a 1999 issue of *Spectra*, wrote that a colleague once asked him a question that continues to occupy his thinking: " . . . exactly what is the *discipline* of communication?"[20] Taylor said the colleague noted that communication has no theory unique to itself, all have been borrowed from other "pure" academic disciplines, such as psychology, sociology or philosophy, and that communication therefore seemed more of a profession than a discipline.[21] Several years later, James L. Applegate, in his NCA president's letter in *Spectra*, considered communication graduate education reform, again asking the question, what is it that we are trying to do in communication doctoral programs?[22] Taylor and Applegate both call for an evaluation of graduate curricula content and purpose: What are we teaching students, and what do we want new Ph.D.'s to be able to do with this new degree?

Soloski argues that a doctoral program is "the training of students to be researchers" and therefore must, along with the study of research methodologies, include a strong foundation in theory. He noted a doctoral degree should also be interdisciplinary, with students required to take courses in the conceptual areas in which they intend to work or do research. Pamela Shoemaker criticizes mass communication research for being methodologically strong, but theoretically weak.[23] Perhaps this stands to reason. One of the only commonalities Jean Briggs and Charles Fleming found in graduate curricula is that research methods courses were more likely to be offered than theory courses.[24] Soloski argues that mass communication research focuses on problems that are too narrow and lack theoretical depth.[25] He suggests that communication faculty need to spend more time teaching graduate students to consider how to form research questions rather than how to use research methods.[26] Associate Dean of Graduate Studies Esther Thorson described the move at the University of Missouri-Columbia to create a culture of research and theory entwined with professional practice.[27] Though their graduate students took separate courses in these subjects, doctoral students were "expected to become theorists and skilled methodologists and tell us how their work might be applied to the 'real world' of journalism. We theorists believed research could be applied."[28]

In 2008 the Association for Education in Journalism and Mass Communication (AEJMC) Board of Directors charged the Standing Committee on Teaching to evaluate the status of

Mass Communication doctoral programs.[29] After exploring what schools were doing currently, the committee issued suggestions for improvement based on student-learning outcomes. Their overarching question: "How can we better prepare future faculty who may one day teach in journalism and mass communication programs?"[30] Their top two recommendations to better prepare students to do research was almost head-shakingly simple: have them do more research, and have them take additional theory or methods classes, or both.[31]

Interdisciplinarity

Craig Trumbo has observed a trend toward researchers engaging in interdisciplinary work.[32] This section discusses the literature that investigates curricular interdisciplinarity. Trumbo argues that graduate students should be trained and educated in a variety of methods and theories.[33] He also argues that curricula should be built so students can take courses from a variety of disciplines and take advantage of learning from a wider perspective.[34] The notion of curriculum flexibility is not new. George Sorensen in 1973 argued that graduate students in journalism and mass communication would benefit from an interdisciplinary approach—an argument that stems from the field's roots.[35] Communication has long borrowed both theory and methods from other social scientific fields, such as sociology, political science, marketing and psychology. Public policy scholar Susan Herbst has written, "Early media studies were open and wide ranging. There was a wonderful disrespect (or disinterest?) in disciplinary constraints, as pioneers sought to understand the American communication environment."[36]

The history of the field shows that sociology is the parent of journalism and mass communication research in terms of perspective, theory and methodology; many of the major theories used in communication research developed from sociological paradigms.[37] The very nature of the mass communication field and its ability to draw from multiple perspectives lends to open debates over research approaches. While the "quantitative" versus "qualitative" argument is perhaps the most commonly cited clashing point, the former stemming from a social scientific approach and the latter from an interpretative humanistic approach,[38] the discussion of an interdisciplinary approach goes beyond methodology. In other words, a researcher can have an interdisciplinary perspective and draw from a wide range of theories drawn from a wide range of disciplines, no matter what his or her chosen methods might be.

Herbst argues that in order to keep building the communication field, communication researchers need to remain open to the perspectives of other disciplines.[39] She suggests that those in the discipline of communication "circled the wagons" a bit in the late twentieth century and transitioned from conducting wide-ranging, interdisciplinary study to a more focused, isolated perspective.[40] Schools and departments were structured so graduate students and professors could work together on common goals. One primary goal was to strengthen the field of communication and assist the discipline in gaining the legitimacy of other established disciplines on campuses. Herbst notes that at the same time that communication was looking inward, there was a movement toward interdisciplinarity across all fields.[41] What began in the natural sciences soon moved to the liberal arts and social sciences until "interdisciplinarity became the mantra across the academy"[42] and part of virtually every strategic plan. Communication must also turn around, she argues, and embrace its interdisciplinary roots once again. She suggests, among other things, that communication scholars, and graduate students in particular, should be encouraged to publish in the best non-communication journals, not just to learn from other disciplines, but to contribute to them.[43]

Trends in Theory and Research

Looking toward the future of mass communication graduate programs and envisioning what the landscape will look like for those studying the magazine form, reviewing the current state of mass communication research makes sense. This section examines, in brief, the literature on journalism and mass communication research trends, which encompasses research done on the magazine form.

Researchers Tsan-Kuo Chang and Zixue Tai set out to discover, through an investigation of the most common citations and co-citations in *Journalism & Mass Communication Quarterly* articles, more about the journalism-related mass communication "invisible college" and what trends might emerge as to the creation of theory and methods.[44] They found some theoretical and methodological convergence in contemporary journalism-related studies, but most references were cited only once. They speculated that there may be a number of reasons for this, among them that many journalism-related articles attract little scholarly attention, especially once they are more than a few years old. The authors argue that instead of the literature building into strong theoretical discoveries, as occurs in other social science fields, these studies are "piecemeal contributions."[45] Nils Gleditsch drew similar conclusions in his study of peacemaking research, noting that much of the work done by any scholar today could be criticized as "self-indulgent enterprise with little object beyond narrow careerism."[46] Rasha Kamhawi and David Weaver concluded from their study of the research trends in major mass communication journals during the 1980 to 1999 time period that published communication research articles are often "one-shot studies without a theoretical trail."[47] Consensus on theory and method is important in the social sciences, Chang and Tai urge, as without this "intellectual and collegial enterprise," disciplinary development may be constrained.[48]

David Abrahamson in 1995 observed that magazine scholarship was quite fragmented.[49] He wrote, "In the absence of any overarching intellectual structure, many researchers have often pursued their studies in relative isolation. As a result, they have often produced what might be characterized as 'brilliant fragments'—worthy research of clear merit, but, it might be argued, occasionally unconnected to any larger framework."[50] Several reasons for this fragmentation in magazine scholarship have been offered. While other media have drawn a great deal of research attention, in particular newspapers and television, magazines have been the subject of far less study. In his study of 20 years of scholarship published in *Journalism Quarterly* up to 1983, Peter Gerlach found that a mere 6 percent of the total number of articles focused on magazine research.[51] More than half the articles were content analyses, with few focused on historical, economic or social topics, or on effects or audience analysis. Abrahamson had found that scholarship on magazine research in *Communication Abstracts* accounted for less than 1 percent of the content, while newspaper research represented more than 5 percent and television research more than 20 percent.[52]

Why is there so little research in studying magazines beyond the content analyses? One reason is that magazine research is not taught by universities, and few graduate programs offer coursework in magazine publishing. Gerlach in 1987 found that some researchers thought there is no need for academic researchers to do process and effect research because it was being done by the magazine industry itself.[53] Others were more specific about the reasons for the fragmentation of study on the magazine form, citing a lack of funding opportunities, few systematic studies on the medium and too much published research that was anecdotal, descriptive, on minor topics or limited in scope.[54]

Since the seventeenth century, "invisible colleges" have drawn together networks of like-minded researchers who "constitute intellectual groups that have developed a specific way of thinking and doing research"[55] and who share a "specific common interest or goal," wrote Chang and Tai.[56] The single researcher never works alone. It is within the "invisible college" that the scholar thrives and grows, and within this "invisible college" a discipline's knowledge and theoretical foundation emerges.[57] This research community, "both at the individual and collective levels, [has] for years been the driving force that advances the field's knowledge through such venues as graduate seminars, paper presentations, and publications."[58]

Within the journalism and mass communication "invisible college," Chang and Tai discovered that the most common trend in research indicates that there is scholarly effort to merge the social construction of reality perspective with framing analysis through a variety of approaches. Communication scholar David Weaver agrees that there has been a growing interest among researchers toward studying how people construct meaning from various messages and on framing.[59] He also noted a growing trend for the increased specialization within the field of communication, such as interpersonal, intercultural, political, health, popular, feminist and mass. This increased field specialization, he argues, leads to increased specialization in research. C. So and J. Chan found that the most commonly used theories were not "core concepts" or grand theories, but "middle range" theories and concepts within various specialty fields.[60] These include agenda-setting in political communication, diffusion theory in intercultural communication and uses and gratifications in mass communication. Jennings Bryant and Dorina Miron found the eight most popular theories in the twenty-first century, as used in research published in six major journalism and mass communication journals, were framing, agenda setting, cultivation, mediation models/theories, third-person effects, uses and gratifications, social cognitive/learning and selective exposure.[61]

Master's Program Models

This section discusses current models for journalism and communication master's programs, beginning with a look at the curricular differences between professional programs and theory and research-based programs. Next, the paradigms by which academics evaluate master's programs and from which curricula are created are reviewed. Finally, research on master's program curricula that examines commonalities in courses is reviewed, and implications for journalism master's programs and those students who wish to study the magazine form are discussed.

In 1995 Elliot King, building on Peter Gerlach's findings that very little academically oriented research on magazines had been published in *Journalism Quarterly* from 1964 to 1983, searched for and identified fewer than 20 people who had published on magazine journalism education in *Journalism Educator* since 1985.[62] The current review of the literature published from 1990 to 2012 echoes his findings, with comparatively few studies published on magazine journalism education and none specific to graduate magazine journalism education. However, literature does exist that examines journalism and communication graduate education more generally.

Two curricular paradigms have been defined by education scholars and can assist in analyzing and understanding mass communication master's programs.[63] Each paradigm, which William Schubert, based on the work of Thomas Kuhn, defines as "a loosely connected set of ideas, values and conduct of inquiry, the ways in which data are interpreted and the way the world may be viewed,"[64] is reflected in the master's programs in the United States. Professional programs, such as the master's program at Columbia University,[65] represent the "practical inquiry paradigm,"[66] which focuses on problem-centered, skills-based, situational learning instead of more abstract, theory-based study and "the handing down of generalized, published knowledge."[67] "Teaching-research programs,"[68] such as that at the University of Central Florida,[69] represent a perennial analytic paradigm, which seeks theory- and research-based education for its own sake.[70] UCF's Web site notes that their master's program "focuses on theoretical and applied perspectives of mass communication theory and research."[71]

Programs with a dual focus exhibit elements from each paradigm, sometimes in separate tracks, sometimes in combination, as the paradigms are not mutually exclusive and can "flow from one to the other."[72] For instance, the Master of Arts in Mass Communication—Journalism program at the University of Florida "combines study of academic literature on the societal role and effects of mass communication in general and journalism in particular with courses designed to improve students' practice of the journalism craft."[73] Other universities offer dual programs in the form of separate tracks: one master's program that is more theoretically based, one more focused on professional training.

Graduate curricula can be examined using these paradigms. Scholars Joey Senat and Elinor Kelley Grusin suggest that when analyzing a curriculum, the paradigms are evidenced in different ways: in core courses, electives and track requirements, such as the inclusion of a thesis or a comprehensive exam.[74] Senat and Grusin state that educators who are involved in graduate curriculum development must know and clearly understand their program's mission first and then allow it to guide the structure of the curriculum.[75]

In 1994, two separate studies were published by two research teams who examined the makeup of master's curricula to look for commonalities. Jean Briggs and Charles Fleming found that research methods was the most commonly offered core course (see Table 30.1), followed by theory of communication, and ethics/law.[76] Senat and Grusin analyzed 135 master's journalism and mass communication programs and found that 60%, or 81, self-reported as having a dual-focus—professional emphasis as well as research-teaching.[77] Just over a quarter, 28%, or 38, reported a professional emphasis; just under 12%, or 16, had a research-teaching program only.[78] Of the 127 schools listing core courses, a research methods course was required most frequently, by 70% of the programs (see Table 30.1). A mass communication theory course was required at 54% of the programs. Although Senat and Grusin found only 22%, or 27.9 of the 127 programs, required a law course, they reported 16, or 13% of the programs, included a core ethics course. This and other, far less frequently offered courses included an introduction to graduate studies (15%), media and society (12%), reporting (12%) and administration/ management (6%). In addition, 73% of the programs offered at least one graduate-level skills course. Senat and Grusin commented on the lack of consensus in the curricula studied and questioned whether journalism educators are able to build a body of knowledge when they cannot seem to agree on the intellectual content of their master's programs. However, Senat and Grusin also noted that there is diversity in the curricula because the programs studied must serve a varied clientele, from journalism students, including those studying magazine journalism, to those in advertising, public relations and other related fields.

The core question this chapter seeks to answer is what students need to learn to be productive researchers of the magazine form. A crucial foundation would appear to be a research methods course of some kind; some would argue a theory course as well. While studies to date on general programs may not agree on a specific set of courses that form the basis of what makes up a body of knowledge for all mass communication master's students to study, there is

Table 30.1. Comparison of master's program required courses, by study

Course	Briggs & Fleming, 1994 Programs Requiring (N = 102)		Senat & Grusin, 1994 Programs Requiring (N = 127)	
	n	%	n	%
Research Methods	81	70	89	70
Theory of Communications	63	62	68	54
Law	31	31	28	22
Ethics	(law/ethics combined)	N/A	16	13
Introduction to Graduate Study	0	0	19	15
Media and Society	23	23	15	12
Reporting	21	21	15	12
Administration / Management	N/A	N/A	8	6

consistency that a research methods course is important. This question takes on an interesting direction when master's programs become specialized.

Professors Linda Aldoory and Elizabeth Toth explored the question of how general journalism and mass communication programs compare with specialized programs when, in 2000, they studied 26 public relations master's programs in the United States, seeking to examine whether a specialized program would show a more focused curriculum.[79] They used the Commission of Graduate Education in Public Relations' recommended master's degree curriculum as a benchmark for the comparison.[80] The striking pattern they found across all programs was a lack of consistency. For instance, no required course was common to all. Other inconsistencies included the number of available public relations courses, which kinds of public relations courses were offered (the subjects of courses, skill-based versus theory) and whether there is a thesis option.

There were some consistencies. Nineteen of the 26 programs required a general communication research methods course and a communication theory course ($n = 19$). The most common public relations core course was a public relations theory course ($n = 14$), followed by courses in public relations campaigns and public relations management. Fewer than half of the 26 master's programs included specialized public relations research methods or public relations writing courses. The authors concluded that although these are specialized public relations master's programs, a lack of consensus and great curricular diversity still exists. They speculated that these programs, many of which were tracks in larger journalism and mass communication graduate programs, were still evolving or that the schools are confronted with "real, practical problems" in securing resources and expert faculty to teach specialized courses.[81]

Aldoory and Toth's research is particularly applicable to the question of how to enrich curricular content for students wanting to specialize in a particular area of communication. Briggs and Fleming observed a trend toward specialization in master's programs.[82] Though Briggs and Fleming found wide differences in the structure of master's programs,[83] with some offering only general programs in mass communication with no choice of specialty, they found that the majority of programs required, or had as an option, the choice of a specialty. Of the 102 programs Briggs and Fleming examined, the most common specialties offered were journalism/ news editorial (55%), public relations (42%), broadcast (40%) and advertising (32%).[84] Only 17%, or roughly 5, of the 26 programs Aldoory and Toth examined offered a magazine specialty, whether writing or publishing or both. No studies were found of graduate level offerings that focus on the unique theoretical and methodological questions posed for studying the wide range of magazines.

Master's Curricula: Where to Now?

Ultimately, Senat and Grusin argue that master's programs often suffer from trying to do too much.[85] Almost a decade later, Hon, Fitzpatrick and Hall concurred, stating that public relations programs, in particular, in an effort "to cast the widest net," try to "do it all."[86] They suggest that, in an effort to provide both pre-professional training and an academic training ground for doctoral programs, schools and their faculty find themselves overextended. Thus, Hon, Fitzpatrick and Hall argue that the diverse education and strong foundation the faculty seek to provide suffer from a lack of resources and an understanding of what the master's degree really means and what planners want their programs to accomplish. After all, if the program's faculty do not understand the program's overall purpose, it is difficult to articulate it to a prospective student and even more difficult for that student to make an informed choice.[87]

As with any debate over education, there are varying viewpoints on the appropriate direction to go. Soloski argues that professional training cannot dominate the graduate curriculum and that coursework should not be structured solely for the convenience of the faculty.[88] While he acknowledges that in a professional program educating students to be professionally competent is key, he makes clear that the first priority should always be to enable students to become critical thinkers. He argues that a master's program, whether the focus is professional, theoretical or both, must have conceptual courses such as media law, journalism history, visual communication, popular culture and international communication—and be included in the core courses students must take. That is, a master's program must have a strong academic presence. He also argues that conceptual coursework in other disciplines should be required or strongly encouraged.[89]

Not all educators agree with this perspective. Discipline specialization is a common trend in U.S. master's programs. While no research was found that sought to determine courses that might be appropriate for students desiring to pursue scholarship on the magazine form, it might again be useful to look at the study of a master's program in a related field of specialization to look for parallels. In one such example, the University of Florida formed a Public Relations Task Force to review the public relations master's curriculum.[90] The task force was charged with defining the student learning objectives, developed by the task force in consultation with the dean, which included, "to understand the conceptual foundations of public relations; to achieve professional competence/mastery in public relations; and to develop the expertise and skills required to understand, conduct and analyze public relations research."[91] After concluding their review, the task force reported there was a need to differentiate between master's programs that are pre-professional and those that are research focused. The curriculum for each program should be different, offering each audience a specific set of courses to meet their specific needs. For instance, students bound for doctoral programs would be advised to take mass communication theory and research courses, while pre-professional students would take a specially designed "public relations theories" course and a "public relations research" course. The task force argued that no one set of courses was appropriate for all. Attempting to create a common core was leading to student dissatisfaction and curricula that appropriately served few. Therefore, the task force's recommendation was to revise the existing curriculum to a dual-focus curriculum paradigm.

Some may view studying magazine journalism as strongly pre-professional, much like public relations. This perspective might argue a master's degree in journalism should, thus, have two distinct tracks: one that focuses on intense skills training and practice for those who will be seeking a job in industry after graduation and one that focuses on theory and research for those who plan on pursuing a doctorate or a career in research. The argument against trying to do both is certainly persuasive. With a limited number of credits, giving the master's student seeking a research degree depth of knowledge rather than a skim of the surface or a survey of skills courses is appropriate. Alternatively, it could be argued that students who are changing careers do not need research methods or mass communication theory as part of their coursework. As is true of public relations programs, study of journalism at the master's level is warranted as the numbers of students enrolling continues to climb and colleges and universities continue to wrestle with the question of how to educate this growing population of students.

Implications for Graduate Education

So what does this matter to the student who wishes to be the magazine researcher? In 2010, there were more than 1,798 doctoral students enrolled in 49 doctoral programs.[92] It seems logical to assume that the vast majority of these doctoral students wished to enroll in a program that would advance their understanding of mass communication and allow them time to practice conducting a specific kind of research on an intense level and to hone their area of specialty within the larger mass communication discipline. No program can be strong in all areas of theory and research, if one holds to the tenet that strength is measured by having faculty members who are active researchers in a particular area. Soloski argued that real doctoral program strength comes when these same active researchers teach what they research, thereby providing the depth of instruction required at the doctoral level.[93] Programs must identify areas of strength, build on those areas and ensure that potential master's and doctoral students know what the areas are. Students whose needs or research interests do not match a program's strengths should not be admitted.[94]

But if programs are different, and curricula are so varied, as the studies discussed here have shown, how is a student who wants to study magazines to know where to study? One answer might be for students to look outward from communication and to other disciplines for methodological and theoretical grounding. Studies show that many programs require, allow or encourage students to take courses outside their units.[95] By going outside their program walls, students have the opportunity to explore their chosen field from alternate perspectives and gain insight into mass communication issues through a wider lens. Graduate students interested in researching the magazine form would be well served by taking courses in any number of related areas. A student interested in discovering how useful women's magazines are at communicating health risks to minority populations might benefit by taking courses in public health.[96] Or students interested in seeing how conservatism is framed in a national consumer magazine could benefit from courses in political science and social psychology.[97] Certainly, there are numerous examples that show how magazine research could evolve through interdisciplinary connections.

As research continues in the twenty-first century, Weaver notes that many theories, such as agenda-setting and framing, have lasting value because "they offer ways to think about the processes and effects of communication that are more generally applicable than descriptions of specific experiences and anecdotes."[98] But he urges scholars to consider how theory has changed and how they might build and change existing theories in the future to better suit the changing media landscape. At a minimum, he argues, media research needs to be a "three-legged stool"[99] and should be concerned with sources, messages, and audiences jointly if scholars are to learn all they can about the communication process. Triangulation of methods might mean combining a magazine content analysis with survey data from the magazine's audience and interviews or observations of the magazine's editors and writers.[100] With these combined approaches, results can make greater contributions to the field of knowledge.

Conclusion

Senat and Grusin note that students seeking engineering, sociology or psychology degrees have a general idea of what the program will involve, regardless of school attended.[101] Not so in the field of journalism and mass communication. Students can be assured of having a "less certain grasp" of what their course of study will involve and what the end goal might be from program to program, school to school.[102] Each program seems so different. Different core courses. Different electives. Some with skills courses. Some without. The process can be complex to navigate. It would be difficult to find another discipline that offers graduate degrees where the ambiguity is as widespread. Even when systematic study is done, the recommendations are decidedly vague, as evidenced the 2008 AEJMC study of mass communication doctoral programs. Perhaps this kind of simplicity—and flexibility—is preferable; it offers individualized experience. But the alternative argument, presented in earlier sections of this chapter, that some common body of knowledge would offer a foundation for the discipline, is a persuasive one.

Ample opportunities exist for future research on this subject. To begin, of the studies cited in this chapter that analyze curricula, most are more than 10 years old, and none specifically examine journalism or magazine journalism master's programs. Several studies should be replicated, including those by Senat and Grusin[103] and Briggs and Fleming.[104] An in-depth analysis of mass communication doctoral education curricula should be undertaken to see what might be in common in the curricula and in student learning objectives. Beyond looking at the curriculum, a valuable resource would be the graduate students and current magazine faculty themselves. What do young, mid-career and mature career scholars see as needs in graduate curricular offerings and emphases? Where did current faculty receive their best training for their current research agendas? What are felt needs in the current status of magazine research and the training of magazine researchers? With so many good questions left to be asked, it is hoped, then, that this chapter should best serve to trigger discussion and lead to new inquiry.

Notes

1 Lee B. Becker, Tudor Vlad, and Devora Olin, "2008 Enrollment Report: Slow Rate of Growth May Signal Weakening of Demand," *Journalism & Mass Communication Educator* 64.3 (Autumn 2009): 232–257; Lee B. Becker, Tudor Vlad, David Sholla, and Konrad Kalpen, "Doctoral Programs in Communication: Updated Report for 2009–2010 Graduates, A Supplemental Report," 9 August 2012 <http://www.grady.uga.edu/annualsurveys/Doctoral_Survey/Doctoral_2010/DOCTO2010COMBINED.pdf>, accessed 8 March 2014; Tudor Vlad, Lee B. Becker, Holly Simpson, and Konrad Kalpen, "Annual Survey of Journalism and Mass Communication Enrollments," <http://www.grady.uga.edu/annualsurveys/Enrollment_Survey/Enrollment_2012/Enroll12Merged.pdf>, accessed 8 March 2014.

2 Becker, Vlad, Simpson, and Kalpen, "Annual Survey of Journalism and Mass Communication Enrollments."

3 Becker, Vlad, Simpson, and Kalpen, "Annual Survey of Journalism and Mass Communication Enrollments."

4 Elliot King, "Research Review: Issues in Magazine Journalism Education," in David Abrahamson, ed., *The American Magazine: Research Perspectives and Prospects* (Ames: Iowa State University Press, 1995), 123.

5 Data are based on an issue-by-issue examination of the 1,372 articles in *Journalism Quarterly* and *Journalism and Mass Communication Quarterly* published from Spring 1990 to Winter 2012. Using the on-line library database Communication & Mass Media Complete, each issue was retrieved and the article titles skimmed for relevant marker words, which included "magazine," a similar term or specific magazine title.

6 Data are based on an issue-by-issue examination of the 728 articles in *Journalism Educator* and *Journalism and Mass Communication Educator* from Spring 1990 to Winter 2012. Using the on-line library database Communication & Mass Media Complete, each issue was retrieved and the article titles skimmed for relevant marker words, which included things like "magazine," a similar term or specific magazine title.

7 John Soloski, "On Defining the Nature of Graduate Education," *Journalism Educator* 49.2 (Summer 1994): 4–11.

8 King, "Issues in Magazine Journalism Education," 122–133.

9 Joey Senat and Elinor Kelley Grusin, "Seeking a Theoretical Framework for Master's Programs in the 1990s," *Journalism Educator* 49.2 (Summer 1994): 18–28.

10 Soloski, "On Defining the Nature of Graduate Education," 4–11.

11 Soloski, "On Defining the Nature of Graduate Education," 4.

12 Soloski, "On Defining the Nature of Graduate Education," 4.

13 Marc Edge, "Professionalism versus Pragmatism," *Media*, Fall/Winter 2003, 10–12.

14 Edge, "Professionalism versus Pragmatism," 10.

15 Linda Childers Hon, Kathy R. Fitzpatrick, and Margarete Rooney Hall, "Searching for the 'Ideal' Graduate Public Relations Curriculum," *Journalism & Mass Communication Educator* 59.2 (Summer 2004): 126–142.

16 Senat and Grusin, "Seeking a Theoretical Framework for Master's Programs," 19.

17 Hon, Fitzpatrick, and Hall, "Searching for the 'Ideal' Graduate Public Relations Curriculum," 126–142.

18 Soloski, "On Defining the Nature of Graduate Education," 9.

19 Soloski, "On Defining the Nature of Graduate Education," 9.

20 Orlando L. Taylor, "What Is the Discipline of Communication?" *Spectra*, April 1999, 2, 12. Emphasis in original.

21 Taylor, "What Is the Discipline of Communication?" 2.

22 James L. Applegate, "Engaged Graduate Education: Skating to Where the Puck Will Be," *Spectra*, September 2001, 2–5.

23 Pamela J. Shoemaker, "Communication in Crisis: Theory, Curricula, and Power," *Journal of Communication* 43.4 (Autumn 1993): 146–153.

24 Jean E. Briggs and Charles A. Fleming, "A Survey of Master's Programs Documents Diversity," *Journalism Educator* 49.2 (Summer 1994): 12–17.

25 Soloski, "On Defining the Nature of Graduate Education," 4–11.

26 Soloski, "On Defining the Nature of Graduate Education," 4–11.

27 Esther Thorson, "Reconceptualizing the Influence of the News Industry on Journalism Graduate Education," *Journalism & Mass Communication Educator* 60.1 (Spring 2005): 17–22.

28 Thorson, "Reconceptualizing the Influence of the News Industry on Journalism Graduate Education," 18.

29 William G. Christ and Sheri J. Broyles, "Graduate Education at AEJMC Schools: A Benchmark Study," *Journalism & Mass Communication Educator* 62.4 (Winter 2008): 376–401.

30 Christ and Broyles, "Graduate Education at AEJMC Schools," 376.

31 Christ and Broyles, "Graduate Education at AEJMC Schools," 395.

32 Craig W. Trumbo, "Research Methods in Mass Communication Research: A Census of Eight Journals 1990–2000," *Journalism & Mass Communication Quarterly* 81.2 (Summer 2004): 417–436; see also, Roger Cooper, W. James Potter, and Michel Dupagne, "A Status Report on Methods Used in Mass Communication Research," *Journalism Educator* 48.4 (Winter 1994): 54–61.

33 Trumbo, "Research Methods in Mass Communication Research," 417–436.

34 Trumbo, "Research Methods in Mass Communication Research," 417–436; Susan Herbst, "Disciplines, Intersections, and the Future of Communication Research," *Journal of Communication* 58.4 (December 2008): 604.

35 George Sorensen, "Interdisciplinary Master's Program Serves Campus Well," *Journalism Educator* 28.3 (October 1973): 36–38.

36 Herbst, "Disciplines, Intersections, and the Future of Communication Research," 604.

37 Amy Shirong Lu, "The Characteristics of Introductory Research Methods Courses in Mass Communication Doctoral Programs," *Journalism & Mass Communication Educator* 62.3 (Autumn 2007): 289–304; William Paisley, "The Convergence of Communication and Information Science," in Hendrik Edelman, ed., *Libraries and Information Science in the Electronic Age* (Philadelphia, PA: ISI Press, 1986), 122–153.

38 Lu, "The Characteristics of Introductory Research Methods Courses," 289–304.

39 Herbst, "Disciplines, Intersections, and the Future of Communication Research," 605.

40 Herbst, "Disciplines, Intersections, and the Future of Communication Research," 603–614.

41 Herbst, "Disciplines, Intersections, and the Future of Communication Research," 605.

42 Herbst, "Disciplines, Intersections, and the Future of Communication Research," 605.

43 Herbst, "Disciplines, Intersections, and the Future of Communication Research," 612.

44 Tsan-Kuo Chang and Zixue Tai, "Mass Communication Research and the Invisible College Revisited: The Changing Landscape and Emerging Fronts in Journalism-Related Studies," *Journalism & Mass Communication Quarterly* 82.3 (Autumn 2005): 672–694.

45 Chang and Tai, "Mass Communication Research and the Invisible College," 687.

46 Nils Petter Gleditsch, "The Most-Cited Articles in JPR," *Journal of Peace Research* 30.4 (November 1993): 445–449.

47 Rasha Kamhawi and David Weaver, "Mass Communication Research Trends from 1980 to 1999," *Journalism & Mass Communication Quarterly* 80.1 (Spring 2003): 20.

48 Chang and Tai, "Mass Communication Research and the Invisible College," 687.

49 David Abrahamson, "Brilliant Fragments: The Scholarly Engagement with the American Magazine," in David Abrahamson, ed., *The American Magazine: Research Perspectives and Prospects* (Ames: Iowa State University Press, 1995): xvii–xxi.

50 Abrahamson, "Brilliant Fragments," xviii.

51 Peter Gerlach, "Research about Magazines Appearing in *Journalism Quarterly*," *Journalism Quarterly* 64:1 (Spring 1987): 178–182.

52 Abrahamson, "Brilliant Fragments," xviii.

53 Gerlach, "Research about Magazines Appearing in *Journalism Quarterly*," 181.

54 Gerlach, "Research about Magazines Appearing in *Journalism Quarterly*," 181.

55 Chang and Tai, "Mass Communication Research and the Invisible College," 672.

56 Chang and Tai, "Mass Communication Research and the Invisible College," 673.

57 Chang and Tai, "Mass Communication Research and the Invisible College," 672–694.

58 Chang and Tai, "Mass Communication Research and the Invisible College," 673.

59 David H. Weaver, "Mass Communication Research at the End of the 20th Century: Looking Back and Ahead," in Kenneth W.Y. Leung, James Kenny, and Paul S.N. Lee, eds., *Global Trends in Communication Education and Research* (Cresskill, NJ: Hampton Press, 2006), 1–16.

60 C.Y.K. So and J.M. Chan, "Evaluating and Conceptualizing the Field of Communication: A Survey of the Core Scholars" (paper presented at the Annual Meeting, Association for Education in Journalism and Mass Communication, August 1991).

61 Jennings Bryant and Dorina Miron, "Theory and Research in Mass Communication," *Journal of Communication* 54.4 (December 2004): 662–704.

62 King, "Issues in Magazine Journalism Education," 123.

63 Senat and Grusin, "Seeking a Theoretical Framework for Master's Programs," 18–28.

64 William H. Schubert, *Curriculum: Perspective, Paradigm, and Possibility* (New York: Macmillan Publishers, 1986), 414, citing Thomas S. Kuhn, *The Structure of Scientific Revolutions* (Chicago: University of Chicago Press, 1962).

65 Columbia University <http://www.journalism.columbia.edu/>, accessed 19 June 2013.
66 Schubert, *Curriculum: Perspective, Paradigm, and Possibility.*
67 Senat and Grusin, "Seeking a Theoretical Framework for Master's Programs," 21.
68 Schubert, *Curriculum: Perspective, Paradigm, and Possibility.*
69 University of Central Florida graduate catalog <http://www.graduatecatalog.ucf.edu/programs/program.aspx?id=1468&tid=326>, accessed 19 June 2013.
70 Senat and Grusin, "Seeking a Theoretical Framework for Master's Programs," 18–28.
71 University of Central Florida graduate catalog, <http://www.graduatecatalog.ucf.edu/programs/program.aspx?id=1468&tid=326>, accessed 19 June 2013.
72 Schubert, *Curriculum: Perspective, Paradigm, and Possibility.*
73 University of Florida Master of Arts in Mass Communication-Journalism Web catalog, <http://www.jou.ufl.edu/academics/masters/mamc-journalism/>, accessed 19 June 2013.
74 Senat and Grusin, "Seeking a Theoretical Framework for Master's Programs," 18–28.
75 Senat and Grusin, "Seeking a Theoretical Framework for Master's Programs," 27.
76 Briggs and Fleming, "A Survey of Master's Programs," 12–17.
77 Senat and Grusin, "Seeking a Theoretical Framework for Master's Programs," 22.
78 Senat and Grusin, "Seeking a Theoretical Framework for Master's Programs," 22.
79 Linda Aldoory and Elizabeth L. Toth, "An Exploratory Look at Graduate Public Relations Education," *Public Relations Review* 26.1 (Spring 2000): 115.
80 Aldoory and Toth, "An Exploratory Look at Graduate Public Relations Education," 115.
81 Aldoory and Toth, "An Exploratory Look at Graduate Public Relations Education," 115.
82 Briggs and Fleming, "A Survey of Master's Programs," 12–17.
83 Briggs and Fleming, "A Survey of Master's Programs," 12–17.
84 Briggs and Fleming, "A Survey of Master's Programs," 12–17.
85 Senat and Grusin, "Seeking a Theoretical Framework for Master's Programs," 18–28.
86 Hon, Fitzpatrick, and Hall, "Searching for the 'Ideal' Graduate Public Relations Curriculum," 130.
87 Hon, Fitzpatrick, and Hall, "Searching for the 'Ideal' Graduate Public Relations Curriculum," 126–142.
88 Soloski, "On Defining the Nature of Graduate Education," 9.
89 Soloski, "On Defining the Nature of Graduate Education," 10.
90 Hon, Fitzpatrick, and Hall, "Searching for the 'Ideal' Graduate Public Relations Curriculum," 126–142.
91 Hon, Fitzpatrick, and Hall, "Searching for the 'Ideal' Graduate Public Relations Curriculum," 127.
92 Becker, Vlad, Sholla, and Kalpen, "Doctoral Programs in Communication."
93 Soloski, "On Defining the Nature of Graduate Education," 4–11.
94 Soloski, "On Defining the Nature of Graduate Education," 4–11.
95 Senat and Grusin, "Seeking a Theoretical Framework for Master's Programs," 18–28.
96 Crystal Y. Lumpkins, Glen T. Cameron, and Cynthia M. Frisby, "Spreading the Gospel of Good Health: Assessing Mass Women's Magazines as Communication Vehicles to Combat Health Disparities among African Americans," *Journal of Media and Religion* 11.2 (Summer 2012): 78–90.
97 Susan Currie Sivek, "Editing Conservatism: How *National Review* Magazine Framed and Mobilized a Political Movement," *Mass Communication and Society* 11.3 (Autumn 2008): 248–274.
98 Weaver, "Mass Communication Research at the End of the 20th Century."
99 Weaver, "Mass Communication Research at the End of the 20th Century," 8.
100 For a review of triangulation, see, for example, Roger D. Wimmer and Joseph R. Dominick, *Mass Media Research: An Introduction*, 9th ed. (Boston, MA: Cengage Wadsworth Learning, 2011).
101 Senat and Grusin, "Seeking a Theoretical Framework for Master's Programs," 18–28.
102 Senat and Grusin, "Seeking a Theoretical Framework for Master's Programs," 26.
103 Senat and Grusin, "Seeking a Theoretical Framework for Master's Programs," 18–28.
104 Briggs and Fleming, "A Survey of Master's Programs," 12–17.

Bibliography

Abrahamson, David. "Brilliant Fragments: The Scholarly Engagement with the American Magazine." In David Abrahamson., ed. *The American Magazine: Research Perspectives and Prospects*. Ames: Iowa State University Press, 1995, xvii–xxi.

Aldoory, Linda and Toth, Elizabeth L. "An Exploratory Look at Graduate Public Relations Education." *Public Relations Review* 26.1 (Spring 2000): 115–125.

Applegate, James L. "Engaged Graduate Education: Skating to Where the Puck Will Be." *Spectra*, September 2001, 2–5.

Becker, Lee B.; Vlad, Tudor; and Olin, Devora. "2008 Enrollment Report: Slow Rate of Growth May Signal Weakening of Demand." *Journalism & Mass Communication Educator* 64.3 (Autumn 2009): 232–257.

Becker, Lee B.; Vlad, Tudor; Sholla, David; and Kalpen, Konrad. "Doctoral Programs in Communication: Updated Report for 2009–2010 Graduates, A Supplemental Report." 8 August 2010 <http://www.grady.uga.edu/annualsurveys/Doctoral_Survey/Doctoral_2010/DOCTO2010COMBINED.pdf>, accessed 8 March 2014.

Briggs, Jean E. and Fleming, Charles A. "A Survey of Master's Programs Documents Diversity." *Journalism Educator* 49.2 (Summer 1994): 12–17.

Bryant, Jennings and Miron, Dorina. "Theory and Research in Mass Communication." *Journal of Communication* 54.4 (December 2004): 662–704.

Chang, Tsan-Kuo and Tai, Zixue. "Mass Communication Research and the Invisible College Revisited: The Changing Landscape and Emerging Fronts in Journalism-Related Studies." *Journalism & Mass Communication Quarterly* 82.3 (Autumn 2005): 672–694.

Christ, William G. and Broyles, Sheri J. "Graduate Education at AEJMC Schools: A Benchmark Study." *Journalism & Mass Communication Educator* 62.4 (Winter 2008): 376–401.

Cooper, Roger; Potter, W. James; and Dupagne, Michel. "A Status Report on Methods Used in Mass Communication Research." *Journalism Educator* 48.4 (Winter 1994): 54–61.

Edge, Marc. "Professionalism versus Pragmatism." *Media*, Fall/Winter 2003, 10–12.

Gerlach, Peter. "Research about Magazines Appearing in *Journalism Quarterly*." *Journalism Quarterly* 64.1 (Spring 1987): 178–182.

Gleditsch, Nils Petter. "The Most-Cited Articles in JPR." *Journal of Peace Research* 30.4 (November 1993): 445–449.

Herbst, Susan. "Disciplines, Intersections, and the Future of Communication Research." *Journal of Communication* 58.4 (December 2008): 603–614.

Hon, Linda Childers; Fitzpatrick, Kathy R.; and Hall, Margarete Rooney. "Searching for the 'Ideal' Graduate Public Relations Curriculum." *Journalism & Mass Communication Educator* 59.2 (Summer 2004): 126–142.

Kamhawi, Rasha and Weaver, David. "Mass Communication Research Trends from 1980 to 1999." *Journalism & Mass Communication Quarterly* 80.1 (Spring 2003): 7–27.

King, Elliot. "Research Review: Issues in Magazine Journalism Education." In Abrahamson, David, ed. *The American Magazine: Research Perspectives and Prospects*. Ames: Iowa State University Press, 1995, 122–133.

Kuhn, Thomas S. *The Structure of Scientific Revolutions*. Chicago: University of Chicago Press, 1962.

Lu, Amy Shirong. "The Characteristics of Introductory Research Methods Courses in Mass Communication Doctoral Programs." *Journalism & Mass Communication Educator* 62.3 (Autumn 2007): 289–304.

Lumpkins, Crystal Y.; Cameron, Glen T.; and Frisby, Cynthia M. "Spreading the Gospel of Good Health: Assessing Mass Women's Magazines as Communication Vehicles to Combat Health Disparities among African Americans." *Journal of Media and Religion* 11.2 (Summer 2012): 78–90.

Paisley, William. "The Convergence of Communication and Information Science." In Edelman, Hendrik, ed. *Libraries and Information Science in the Electronic Age*. Philadelphia, PA: ISI Press, 1986, 122–153.

Schubert, William H. *Curriculum: Perspective, Paradigm, and Possibility*. New York: Macmillan Publishers, 1986.

Senat, Joey and Grusin, Elinor Kelley. "Seeking a Theoretical Framework for Master's Programs in the 1990s." *Journalism Educator* 49.2 (Summer 1994): 18–28.

Shoemaker, Pamela J. "Communication in Crisis: Theory, Curricula, and Power." *Journal of Communication* 43.4 (Autumn 1993): 146–153.

Sivek, Susan Currie. "Editing Conservatism: How *National Review* Magazine Framed and Mobilized a Political Movement." *Mass Communication and Society* 11.3 (Autumn 2008): 248–274.

So, C.Y.K. and Chan, J.M. "Evaluating and Conceptualizing the Field of Communication: A Survey of the Core Scholars." Paper presented at the Annual Meeting, Association for Education in Journalism and Mass Communication, August 1991.

Soloski, John. "On Defining the Nature of Graduate Education." *Journalism Educator* 49.2 (Summer 1994): 4–11.

Sorensen, George. "Interdisciplinary Master's Program Serves Campus Well." *Journalism Educator* 28.3 (October 1973): 36–38.

Taylor, Orlando L. "What is the Discipline of Communication?" *Spectra*, April 1999, 2, 12.

Thorson, Esther. "Reconceptualizing the Influence of the News Industry on Journalism Graduate Education." *Journalism & Mass Communication Educator* 60.1 (Spring 2005): 17–22.

Trumbo, Craig W. "Research Methods in Mass Communication Research: A Census of Eight Journals 1990–2000." *Journalism & Mass Communication Quarterly* 81.2 (Summer 2004): 417–436.

Vlad, Tudor; Becker, Lee B.; Simpson, Holly; and Kalpen, Konrad. "Annual Survey of Journalism and Mass Communication Enrollments" <http://www.grady.uga.edu/annualsurveys/Enrollment_Survey/Enrollment_2012/Enroll12Merged.pdf>, accessed 8 March 2014.

Weaver, David H. "Mass Communication Research at the End of the 20th Century: Looking Back and Ahead." In Leung, Kenneth W.Y.; Kenny, James; and Lee, Paul S.N., eds. *Global Trends in Communication Education and Research.* Cresskill, NJ: Hampton Press, 2006, 1–16.

Wimmer, Roger D. and Dominick, Joseph R. *Mass Media Research: An Introduction.* 9th ed. Boston, MA: Cengage Wadsworth Learning, 2011.

Part VI

THE FUTURE OF THE MAGAZINE FORM

31

MAGAZINES AND SUSTAINABILITY

Environmental and Sociocultural Impacts

Helen Kopnina

The pros and cons of paper (print) versus digital publications in relation to environmental sustainability have been summarized on the Green Technology weblog entry titled "Paper or Digital: Which Format Is Better for the Environment" where a blogger who identified himself as Green Dude wrote,

> Main selling points . . . of eReaders is that they are greener than print. . . . [A] common view held by consumers . . . is that going digital means going green and saving trees. Many are in for a rude awakening. . . . [S]ubjected to "cradle-to-cradle" life cycle analysis, eReading is not nearly as green as many naively assume it is. . . . Digital devices require a constant flow of electrons that predominately come from the combustion of coal, and at the end of their all-too-short useful lives electronics have become the single largest stream of toxic waste created by man.[1]

The blog post question reflects on the complexity of choice that sustainability-minded consumers ponder in relation to the transition from printed to digital media.

The primary purpose of this chapter is to provide insights into the body of scholarly literature on the question of magazines and sustainability—in both production and editorial content. The chapter also discusses production-side issues related to business decision-making and policy, as well as editorial-side considerations within publishing organizations. Drawing on recent literature on the environmental impact of both information and communication technologies, with the Internet on the one hand and digitalization of media on the other, this chapter identifies a number of important effects of new magazine production and issues of sustainability with a primary focus on reviewing the emerging body of scholarly literature that relates to the question. The sociological and anthropological literature is examined, and Cradle to Cradle (C2C) theory is introduced, in order to lead to the discussion of research rising from these perspectives as well as methods being used to explore these questions.

The Problem

Digital technologies and products such as e-magazines are essential to the measurement, modeling and communication of environmental processes, while also having a major role in improving the productivity of capital and natural resources. The optimization of processes

509

through digitalization of media has often benefited the environment because of improvements in resource efficiency—such as reducing the use of printed paper—but also because efficient processes tend to be relatively less polluting.[2] On the other hand, as prominent sociologist of globalization Saskia Sassen reflected, the "virtual economy" of digital products needs to be seen as intimately linked to the real, material economy.[3] While some observers have celebrated the beginning of the "paperless office," Matthews[4] shows that the ecological damage caused by manufacturing materials used for digital technology is growing across several environmental domains, such as energy consumption, water use and emissions of acids, metals, volatile organic compounds, chlorinated solvents and other substances.

Conservation psychologists make a distinction between different types of impacts of environmentally significant behavior, depending on the extent to which human behavior changes the availability of natural resources or alters the structure and dynamics of ecosystems.[5] *Direct environment effects* related to production of paper for print versions of magazines, for example, would be those that result from clearing forests, or, in the case of digital technology, from disposing of electronic waste, which directly or proximally cause environmental change. Other behavior is indirectly environmentally significant by shaping the context in which choices are made that cause direct environmental change.[6] Behaviors that affect international development policies concerned with forests, raw material prices on world markets, national environmental and tax policies, individual savings and pension funds that are invested in more or less environmentally friendly projects can have greater environmental impact indirectly than behaviors that directly change the environment.

The next area, *indirect impacts*, is related to the effect of digital technology on de-materialization of production processes, as well as changes in distribution channels and transportation.[7] The *structural and behavioral impacts* section examines research that focuses on the stimulation of structural change and growth in the economy through impacts on life styles and value systems that are partially promoted by the content of magazine articles, partly through actual life-style changes.

Both the perception and the reality of the relationship between new media and environment, including interdisciplinary perspectives, is explored in the section on *social and cultural impacts*. *Future impacts* addresses alternatives, with particular emphasis on the Cradle to Cradle model of production.[8]

Direct Impacts: Production Technologies and Environment

The effects of production of magazines are associated with resource use and pollution that are related to the production of infrastructure and devices, from the failed dream of the paperless office to hardware electricity consumption and electronic waste disposal. The current debate about digital technologies and the environment is characterized by contrasting optimistic and pessimistic assessments.[9] Environmental optimists consider the effects of digitalization of magazines to be positive because "information" is generally considered to be distinct from material and energy, acting as a substitute for the use of resources such as paper. The digital world was seen as virtually "weightless."[10]

By contrast, environmental pessimists demonstrate that digital technology is far from weightless. Don Carli[11] reports a growing recognition that digital media technology uses significant amounts of energy from coal-fired power plants, which are making a significant contribution to global warming. Greenpeace[12] cites The Climate Group's "Smart 2020: Enabling the Low Carbon Economy in the Information Age," which reports that by 2020 data centers will demand many times more electricity than is currently required. Production of machinery associated with digital technology involves mining, extraction and production of materials needed for maintaining digital technology. These include rare metals used for production of e-readers or mobile phones, as well as energy needed to run this technology such as electrical batteries for computers.[13] Electronic waste produced by digital technologies counts for another serious environmental factor.[14] Digital technology is now integrated in many ordinary consumer and commodity products, with the result that many of these devices and components are energy-consuming, have short life cycles and are composed of toxic materials.[15]

However, statistics for timber used for paper production and consumption in general and magazine production in particular are also disconcerting.[16] Paper produced from forests can negatively affect the environment in a number of ways: through the actual timber consumption, both from virgin and planted forests; through limited CO_2 reduction provided by these forests; and through space used for production of timber. Waste products from paper can be recycled; however, recycled materials still require energy for transportation and the actual process of recycling, producing lower grade paper and in fact causing down-cycling, which entails turning valuable raw material (such as wood) into less or smaller material (such as printing paper) and even a less valuable material after recycling (low grade toilet paper).[17] Down-cycling is illustrated by the case of electronic waste:

> Encouraging recycling is often proposed as a way to lower the embodied energy of products. Unfortunately, this does not work for micro-electronics (or nanomaterials). In the case of conventional manufacturing methods, the energy requirements of the manufacturing process (1 to 10 MJ per kilogram) are small compared to the energy required to produce the materials themselves. For instance, producing 1 kilogram of plastic out of crude oil requires 62 to 108 MJ of energy, while a typical mix of virgin and recycled aluminum requires 219 MJ. To make a fair comparison, you have to multiply the energy requirement of the manufacturing process by three (1 megajoule of electricity requires 3 megajoules of energy) but even then (with 3 to 30 MJ/kg) conventional manufacturing processes appear to be quite benign compared to materials extraction and primary processing . . . Recycling is not a solution for energy consumption if all your energy use is concentrated in the process itself.[18]

In some countries, such as the Netherlands, (paper) waste is burned and used for generating electricity. However, this process eliminates the valuable material—trees and paper—for one-time energy consumption.

Direct impacts of magazine production can be environmentally harmful because different production methods include both various types of resources being consumed and different kinds of pollution being produced. Definitive comparative studies of threats and benefits of electronic production of magazines in comparison to paper copies still need to be expanded. Suffice it to say that the direct impact of both digital and paper technologies is large and environmentally damaging.

Indirect Impacts: Production Technologies, Content and Environment

Since indirect environmental impacts can be more significant than direct ones, particular attention needs to be paid to both production and content impacts. In relation to production, indirect impacts are related to the effect of digital technology on paper-less magazines and changes in distribution channels and transportation.[19]

Negative indirect effects on environment include falling prices for resource inputs, proliferation of "intelligent" devices, and partial substitution.[20] For example, according to MIT researcher Timothy Gutowski,[21] manufacturing one kilogram of plastic or metal parts requires as much electricity as operating a flat screen television for 1 to 10 hours. In addition to considering the way digital media can create new possibilities for a better world, we also need to consider the less obvious impacts of the purchased energy, embodied energy, dark content and e-waste associated with the growing use of digital media.[22] Last, but not least, as De Decker[23] has noted, the energy-intensive nature of digital technology is not due only to energy-intensive manufacturing processes; equally as important is the extremely short lifecycle of most gadgets. A majority of computers and other electronic devices are replaced after only after a couple of years, while they are still perfectly workable devices. Addressing technological obsolescence would be the most powerful approach to reducing the ecological footprint of digital technology.[24]

Another indirect effect has to do with content and how printed or digital media actually inform the reader. For example, if we assume that on-line, open access journals have larger readership than traditional print versions, the author of this article would hope that her ideas about the relationship between forms of production and environment would be widely disseminated and thus inform readers as to the best choices. Another example would include dissemination of information which could mislead the readers as to the most sustainable choices. The following section explains how providing information on how "green" a particular form of production is could have a large effect on readers' evaluation and choice of the less environmentally damaging methods of production.

Structural and Behavioral Impacts

Structural and behavioral impacts of both print and digital technology focus on the stimulation of structural change within society and growth in the economy. Impacts on value systems are partially promoted by the content of magazine articles, partly through actual lifestyle changes. Both structural factors—such as the power and ideology of neo-liberal capitalist political systems and consumer-based responsibility for environmental protection—can limit efforts at sustainability. The material saturation level is hardly sustainable, due to high material demands for houses, transportation and consumer items, yet many (Western) consumers feel entitled to the negative spiral of globally increasing needs for resources. Depletion is not likely to cease. In the case of wealthier societies or consumers, scholars have warned of a "rebound effect"[25] in which "green" items are purchased to appease the wealthier consumer's conscience, contributing to resource depletion and waste.[26]

In line with the rebound effect theory, scholars have noted contradictions inherent in the oxymoronic term "green consumption."[27] Wilk notes that there may even be a "moral rebound effect," where reiterating the message creates guilt, which "drives the continuing bulimic cycle of binge and purge so characteristic of contemporary consumer culture."[28] In the case of e-magazines this might imply that while consumers might *think* they are being more environmentally responsible by reading e-magazines rather than paper, they may actually be discounting the environmental impact of digital technology. Similarly, reading a printed magazine advertised to be produced from 70% sustainable paper might lull the reader into overlooking the fact that the other 30% could come from virgin forests. Thus the reader accepts the "sustainability" of the whole without questioning the source of a part.

On the other hand, digital media can have a far-reaching effect of being able to reach the greater number of interested and responsible readers and thus better inform them of certain environmental choices and options. Open access books and articles tend to be distributed and read much more speedily and widely than those published by a traditional press. Because the content of magazines can have a significant influence in informing the reader about negative environmental effects, as well as suggesting informed ways to move forward, more efficient distribution of the media, such as digital technology, can have a large behavioral impact upon the readers.

Social and Cultural Impacts

Both the perception and the reality of the relationship between new media and environment can be examined in the light of insights from research in ecological sociology and environmental anthropology. Sociologists Ulrich Beck[29] and Anthony Giddens[30] developed the concept of *risk society*, linking issues of sustainability to trends in thinking about modernity and popular discourse, in particular the growing environmental concerns. While the perception of risks of climate change, industrialization and the like may be socially "manufactured," influenced by the media or simply imagined, scientific and technical experts also disagree about which production process or product is more harmful, as well as how such processes and products can be improved.

Environmental sociologists William Catton, Jr., and Riley Dunlap[31] have argued that environmental risks are partially a result of the process of socialization. However, they have also emphasized the need to explicitly address the reality of environmental risks as well as anthropocentric bias in perception of environmental problems. In their much cited article, "What environmental sociologists have in common (Whether concerned with 'built' or 'natural' environments)," Dunlap and Catton[32] assert that social scientists tend to underplay environmental problems and to subordinate conservation to social and economic interests. Similarly, environmental anthropologists Helen Kopnina and Eleanor Shoreman-Ouimet[33] have argued that anthropology historically tended to focus on cultural variables and cultural interpretations of environment, rather than seeking solutions to environmental issues that occur globally.

Anthropocentric bias in sociology,[34] anthropology[35] and even in the scholarship of education for sustainable development[36] indicates that members of the social science community tend to view issues such as depletion of natural resources and pollution in strictly instrumental terms—as something that negatively affects humans and can be solved by a technological fix. In anthropocentric thought, humans are largely in control of the surrounding world, and problems arising from modern living can be taken care of through technological development and by adjusting of certain social structures.[37]

In the case of paper versus e-magazines, the implications of this anthropocentrism can be described as two-fold. First, anthropocentrism manifests itself through dominant social and cultural norms and values of neo-liberal capitalist industrialist societies that view human welfare, material satisfaction, and consumption as something to be aspired to; and second, these values are internalized by ourselves, the social scientists of culture or media. In the first case viewing any object—be it e-magazine or paper—as "resource" can already be problematic. Resources such as metals used for digital technology or timber used for making paper support the "economic capture" approach to natural resources, in turn commodifying or putting a price on "product" without consideration of its intrinsic value. Many anthropologists question how "resource use" translates into global discourses, criticizing the very idea of converting "nature" or "wilderness" into "natural resources" or "ecosystem services," the way powerful Western institutions such as the World Bank or the United Nations do.[38]

It is worrying that the non-economic value of what is actually used to make either paper or digital magazines is rarely acknowledged. Concerns about protecting forest or wilderness area, which is being mined for valuable metals used for computer technology, are not necessarily contingent solely on social interests. For example, planted forests could, when harvested, perhaps better satisfy the economic need. Due to such extractive activities, extinction of some species of plants and animals could conceivably come to pass without jeopardizing the survival of the humans. People might be materially sustained by monocultures of cultivated plant and animal species, as well as minerals and other 'resources' made to yield services and products required for human life.[39] It is thus questionable whether a purely economic approach to environmental protection is adequate to address the environmental impact of both print and digital technology.

Future Impacts: Cradle to Cradle Framework

As an alternative to present models of either paper or material production, the Cradle to Cradle model of production deserves special consideration. William McDonough and Michael Braungart, in *Cradle to Cradle: Remaking the Way We Make Things*,[40] conceptualize sustainability differently from the mainstream idea of eco-efficiency. The Cradle to Cradle framework provides an ideological and technical framework that seeks to create industrial systems that are not just efficient but are essentially waste free. McDonough and Braungart ask us not just to contemplate minimizing the damage, but to imagine how contemporary waste might no longer exist.

The Cradle to Cradle approach is an argument that being less bad is not good enough. Continuing to use a system that generates massive amounts of waste in the endless spiral of production and consumption, the authors argue, will only prolong the bad system. The familiar reduce, reuse, recycle and regulate adage serves to maintain cradle-to-grave production rather than stimulating fundamental change toward eco-*effectiveness*.

McDonough and Braungart suggest that every product can be designed from the outset so that after its lifetime is over, the product will continue to live while providing nourishment for something new: that is, by becoming a nutrient within either a biological or technological cycle. Cradle to Cradle theory identifies three key design principles, which inform human design from a Cradle to Cradle perspective: (a) waste equals food; (b) use current solar income, and (c) celebrate diversity. These three principles are deduced from the intelligence of natural systems as explained below.

Waste equals food. Waste does not exist in nature because the processes of each organism contribute to the health of the whole ecosystem. A fruit tree's blossoms fall to the ground and decompose into food for other living things. Bacteria and fungi feed on the organic waste of both the trees and the animals that eat the tree's fruit, depositing nutrients in the soil in a form ready for the tree to use for growth. One organism's waste is food for another, and nutrients flow indefinitely in cycles of birth, decay and rebirth. In other words, *waste equals food*.

Understanding these regenerative systems allows engineers and designers to recognize that all materials can be designed as nutrients that flow through natural or designed metabolisms. While nature's nutrient cycles comprise the biological metabolism, the technical metabolism is designed to mirror them. It is considered a closed-loop system in which valuable, high-tech synthetics and mineral resources circulate in cycles of production, use, recovery and remanufacture.

Within this cradle-to-cradle framework, designers and engineers can use scientific assessments to select safe materials and optimize products and services, creating closed-loop material flows that are inherently benign and sustaining. Materials designed as biological nutrients, such as textiles and packaging made from natural fibers, can biodegrade safely and restore soil after use.

Use current solar income. Living things thrive on the energy of the sun. Trees and plants manufacture food from sunlight, an elegant, effective system that uses the earth's unrivaled and continuous source of energy income. Despite recent precedent, human energy systems can be nearly as effective. Cradle-to-cradle systems—from buildings to manufacturing processes—tap into current solar income by using direct solar energy collection or passive solar processes, such as day-lighting, which makes effective use of natural light. Wind power—thermal flows fueled by sunlight—can also be tapped.

Celebrate diversity. The celebrating diversity maxim does not necessarily refer to the popular idea of cultural or social diversity, but to respect of diversity in natural systems. From a holistic perspective, natural systems thrive on diversity. Healthy ecosystems are complex communities of living things, each of which has developed a unique response to its surroundings that works in concert with other organisms to sustain the system. Each organism fits in its place, and in each system the fittest thrive. Needless to say, long-term perspective is needed, because the introduction of an invasive species can enhance diversity for the immediate term while virtually destroying that diversity over time.

This idea is similar to that of biomimicry, inspired by Janine M. Benyus in her 1997 book, *Biomimicry: Innovation Inspired by Nature*. Biomimicry, a relatively new science, studies nature's designs and processes, imitating these models to solve human problems in the human sphere.[41]

As do bionics and biomimicry, C2C takes nature's diversity as a prototype for many models for human designs, tailoring designs to maximize their positive effects in order to "fit" within local natural systems and enhance the local landscape where possible. McDonough and Braungart have designed a number of urban areas and buildings. For each they have taken into account local climate, materials, and both human and ecological needs.

In short, by modeling human designs on nature's operating system—generating materials that are "food" for biological or industrial systems, tapping the energy of the sun and celebrating diversity, cradle-to-cradle design creates a new paradigm for industry, one in which human activity generates a wide spectrum of ecological, social and economic value.

In relation to magazines, the C2C approach can suggest practical applications of these principles, similar to other designs that those ascribing to C2C principles have used. The Melcher group, for example, which produces DuraBooks, advertises the books as good for the environment:

> Made in such a way to be upcyclable, the synthetic "paper" can be melted down and reused in perpetuity, thus sparing trees and reducing toxins in the earth's ecosystem. DuraBooks are also nontoxic and child safety tested.
>
> William McDonough, recognized by *Time* magazine in 1999 as a "Hero for the Planet," states "Unlike the paper with which we are familiar, [the DuraBook] does not use any wood pulp or cotton fiber but is made from plastic resins and inorganic fillers. This material . . . is a prototype for the book as a 'technical nutrient,' that is, as a product that can be broken down and circulated indefinitely in industrial cycles—made and remade as 'paper' or other products."[42]

Such designs still need to be carefully evaluated, but their potential to contribute true alternatives to either paper or digital publications can be profound. The issues to consider will be the entire supply chain used for production of alternative materials, economy of scale and possibility of mass production and its consequences—not just for niche markets of concerned readers, but globally.

Conclusions

Scholars' research agendas include the full range of communication-related questions, from magazine management and economics, to content of periodicals for the spectrum of periodicals for the general public, the work force, and organizations whose explicit goals focus on industry-related questions. The questions that are needed foci of future research for both scholars and researchers, industry professionals and practice, include those that relate to direct and indirect environmental impacts of print or digital technologies, as well as socio-economic and behavioral impacts of alternative technologies.

This section suggests research that exists, as well as that which is needed to build the bridges between what is known and what is not. This will support both the scholarly endeavor and the practicing professional in editorial and business decision-making roles. The strengths and weaknesses of different technologies call for urgent research into both what and how magazines are being produced and what, content-wise, is actually written about these strengths and weaknesses in the magazines themselves. The present chapter is limited to outlining a number of directions which both the scholar and a media executive could explore in order to ascertain the challenges, opportunities and choices presented by new and alternative technologies. Both direct and indirect environmental impacts of magazine production technology and content need to be further investigated before informed choices can be made.

The cradle-to-cradle framework offers scholars and practitioners alike a vision for moving away from the established anthropocentric theoretical paradigm and from an unsustainable cycle of production and waste in practice. In order for the scholarly agenda to move forward, and for optimal industry applications, the cradle-to-cradle framework has the impressive strategic potential to move the industry from current state-of-the-art technology, which is hardly sustainable in the long term, toward truly innovative solutions for the future of magazines.

Notes

1 Green Dude, "Paper or Digital: Which Format is Better for the Environment," Green Techno Log.com (blog), 25 February 2010 <http://greentechnolog.com/2010/02/paper_or_digital_which_ format_is_ better_for_the_ en.html>, accessed 30 October 2012.

2 Frans Berkhout and Julia Hertin, "De-materialising and Re-materialising: Digital Technologies and the Environment," *Futures* 36.8 (2004): 903–920.

3 Saskia Sassen, "Digital Networks and the State: Some Governance Questions," *Theory, Culture and Society* 17.4 (August 2000): 19.

4 H. Scott Matthews, "The Environmental Implications of the Growth of the Information and Communications Technology Sector" (paper presented to the Environment Directorate, OECD, Paris, 2001).

5 Paul C. Stern, "Toward a Coherent Theory of Environmentally Significant Behavior," *Journal of Social Issues* 56.3 (Fall/September 2000): 407–424.

6 Andrew P. Vayda, "Causal Explanation for Environmental Anthropologists," in Helen Kopnina and Eleanor Shoreman-Ouimet, eds., *Environmental Anthropology: Future Trends*, Routledge Studies in Anthropology Series (New York and Oxford: Routledge, 2013).

7 Berkhout and Hertin, "De-materialising and Re-materialising," 903–920.

8 William McDonough and Michael Braungart, eds., *Cradle to Cradle: Remaking the Way We Make Things* (New York: North Point Press, 2002).

9 Berkhout and Hertin, "De-materialising and Re-materialising," 903–920.

10 Kevin Kelly, "New Rules for the New Economy," *Wired*, 5.09 September 1997 <http://www.wired.com/wired/archive/5.09/newrules.html>, accessed 30 November 2012; Diane Coyle, *The Weightless World: Strategies for Managing the Digital Economy* (Cambridge, MA: MIT Press, 1998).

11 Don Carli, "Is Digital Media Worse for the Environment Than Print?" *Media Shift*, 31 March 2010 <http://www.pbs.org/mediashift/2010/03>, accessed 3 December 2012.

12 Greenpeace, *Dirty Data Timeline*, 29 May 2012 citing the Climate Group, "Smart 2020: Enabling the Low Carbon Economy in the Information Age," Greenpeace.org <http://www.greenpeace.org/international/en/campaigns/climate-change/cool-it/The-Dirty-Data-timeline/>, accessed 30 October 2012.

13 Matthews, "Environmental Implications."

14 Jacob Park and Nigel Roome, *The Ecology of the New Economy—Sustainable Transformation of Global Information, Communications and Electronics Industries* (Sheffield, UK: Greenleaf Publishing, 2002); Lorenz M. Hilty and Thomas F. Ruddy, "Towards a Sustainable Information Society," *Informatik/Informatique* 4 (August 2000): 2–9.

15 Commission of the European Communities (CEC), Proposal for a Directive of the European Parliament and the Council on Waste Electrical and Electronic Equipment and on Restriction of the Use of Certain Hazardous Substances in Electrical and Electronic Equipment (Brussels, 13 June 2000): 347.

16 WWF, "Deforestation," The World Wide Fund for Nature, 2012 <http://wwf.panda.org/about_our_earth/about_forests/deforestation/>, accessed 30 November 2012.

17 McDonough and Braungart, *Cradle to Cradle*.

18 Kris De Decker, "The Monster Footprint of Digital Technology," Vincent Grosjean, ed., *Low Tech Magazine*, 16 June 2009 <http://www.lowtechmagazine.com/2009/06/embodied-energy-of-digital-technology.html June 16, 2009>, accessed 30 November 2012.

19 Berkhout and Hertin, "De-materialising and Re-materialising," 903–920.

20 Berkhout and Hertin, "De-materialising and Re-materialising," 903–920.

21 Quoted in Carli, "Is Digital Media Worse for the Environment Than Print?"

22 Carli, "Is Digital Media Worse for the Environment Than Print?"

23 De Decker, "The Monster Footprint."

24 De Decker, "The Monster Footprint."

25 Lorna A. Greening, David L. Greene, and Carmen Difiglio, "Energy Efficiency and Consumption—The Rebound Effect—A Survey," *Energy Policy* 28.6/7 (2000): 389–401.

26 Kersty Hobson, "Competing Discourses of Sustainable Consumption: Does the 'Rationalisation of Lifestyles' Make Sense?" *Environmental Politics* 11.2 (Summer 2002): 95–120.

27 John Connolly and Andrea Prothero, "Green Consumption: Life-Politics, Risk and Contradictions," *Journal of Consumer Culture* 8.1 (March 2008): 117; Richard Wilk, "Consumption Embedded in Culture and Language: Implications for Finding Sustainability," *Sustainability: Science, Practice and Policy* 6.2 (Fall 2010):

38–48; Helen Kopnina, 'What Is (Responsible) Consumption? Discussing Environment and Consumption with Children from Different Socioeconomic Backgrounds in the Netherlands.' *The Environmentalist* 31.3 (September 2011): 216–226.

28 Wilk, "Consumption Embedded in Culture and Language," 40.

29 Ulrich Beck, *Risk Society: Towards a New Modernity*, trans. Mark Ritter (London and Newbury Park, CA: Sage Publications, 1992).

30 Anthony Giddens, *The Politics of Climate Change* (Cambridge, UK: Polity Press, 2009).

31 William R. Catton, Jr. and Riley E. Dunlap, "Environmental Sociology: A New Paradigm," *The American Sociologist* 13.1 (1978): 41–49.

32 Riley E. Dunlap and William R. Catton, Jr., "What Environmental Sociologists Have in Common (Whether Concerned with 'Built' or 'Natural' Environments)," *Sociological Inquiry* 53.2/3 (April 1983): 113–135.

33 Helen Kopnina and Eleanor Shoreman-Ouimet, *Environmental Anthropology: Future Trends*, Routledge Studies in Anthropology Series (New York and Oxford: Routledge, 2013); see also, Helen Kopnina and Eleanor Shoreman-Ouimet, *Environmental Anthropology Today* (New York and Oxford: Routledge, 2011).

34 Dunlap and Catton, "What Environmental Sociologists Have in Common."

35 Helen Kopnina, "The Lorax Complex: Deep Ecology, Ecocentrism and Exclusion," *Journal of Integrative Environmental Sciences* 9.4 (December 2012): 235–254 <http://dx.doi.org/10.1080/1943815X.2012.742914>, accessed 31 January 2015; Helen Kopnina, 'Toward Conservational Anthropology: Addressing Anthropocentric Bias in Anthropology," *Dialectical Anthropology* 36.1/2 (2012): 127–146.

36 Helen Kopnina, "Education for Sustainable Development (ESD): The Turn Away from 'Environment' in Environmental Education." *Environmental Education Research* 18.5 (2012): 699–717.

37 Carina Lundmark, "The New Ecological Paradigm Revisited: Anchoring the NEP Scale in Environmental Ethics," *Environmental Education Research* 13.3 (July 2007): 329–347.

38 Vandana Shiva, *Monocultures of the Mind: Biodiversity and Biotechnology* (London, UK; Atlantic Highlands, NJ: Zed Books, 1993); David Mosse, Cultivating Development: An Ethnography of Aid Policy and Practice (London and Ann Arbor, MI: Pluto Press, 2005).

39 Eileen Crist, "Limits-to-Growth and the Biodiversity Crisis," Wild Earth, Spring 2003, 62–65.

40 McDonough and Braungart, *Cradle to Cradle*.

41 Janine M. Benyus, *Biomimicry: Innovation Inspired by Nature* (New York: Morrow, 1997).

42 "DuraBooks: A Revolutionary New Concept," Melcher Media <http://www.melcher.com/about-us/>, accessed 15 May 2014.

Bibliography

Beck, Ulrich. *Risk Society: Towards a New Modernity*. Translated by Mark Ritter. London and Newbury Park, CA: Sage Publications, 1992.

Benyus, Janine M. *Biomimicry: Innovation Inspired by Nature*. New York: Morrow, 1997.

Berkhout, Frans and Hertin, Julia. "De-Materialising and Re-Materialising: Digital Technologies and the Environment." *Futures* 36.8 (2004): 903–920.

Carli, Don. "Is Digital Media Worse for the Environment Than Print?" *MediaShift*, 31 March 2010 <http://www.pbs.org/mediashift/2010/03>, accessed 3 December 2012.

Catton, William R., Jr., and Dunlap, Riley E. "Environmental Sociology: A New Paradigm." *The American Sociologist* 13.1 (1978): 41–49.

Commission of the European Communities (CEC). Proposal for a Directive of the European Parliament and the Council on Waste Electrical and Electronic Equipment and on Restriction of the Use of Certain Hazardous Substances in Electrical and Electronic Equipment. Brussels, 13 June 2000.

Connolly, John and Prothero, Andrea. "Green Consumption: Life-Politics, Risk and Contradictions." *Journal of Consumer Culture* 8.1 (March 2008): 117–145.

Coyle, Diane. *The Weightless World: Strategies for Managing the Digital Economy*. Cambridge, MA: MIT Press, 1998.

Crist, Eileen. "Limits-to-Growth and the Biodiversity Crisis." *Wild Earth*, Spring 2003, 62–65.

De Decker, Kris. "The Monster Footprint of Digital Technology." Grosjean, Vincent, ed. *Low Tech Magazine*. 16 June 2009 <http://www.lowtechmagazine.com/2009/06/embodied-energy-of-digital-technology.html>, accessed 5 November 2012.

Dunlap, Riley E. and Catton, William R., Jr. "What Environmental Sociologists Have in Common (Whether Concerned with 'Built' or 'Natural' Environments)." *Sociological Inquiry* 53.2/3 (April 1983): 113–135.

"DuraBooks: A Revolutionary New Concept." Melcher Media <http://www.melcher.com/about-us/>, accessed 15 May 2014.

Giddens, Anthony. *The Politics of Climate Change*. Cambridge, UK: Polity Press, 2009.

Green Dude. "Paper or Digital: Which Format is Better for the Environment" Green Techno Log.com (blog), 25 February 2010 <http://www.greentechnolog.com/2010/02/paper_or_ digital_which_format_is_better_for_the_en.html>, accessed 30 October 2012.

Greening, Lorna A.; Greene, David L.; and Difiglio, Carmen. "Energy Efficiency and Consumption—The Rebound Effect—A Survey." *Energy Policy* 28.6/7 (2000): 389–401.

Greenpeace. *Dirty Data Timeline*. 29 May 2012 citing The Climate Group. "Smart 2020: Enabling the Low Carbon Economy in the Information Age." Greenpeace.org <http://www.greenpeace.org/international/en/campaigns/climate-change/cool-it/The-Dirty-Data-timeline/>, accessed 30 October 2012.

Hilty, Lorenz M. and Ruddy, Thomas F. "Towards a Sustainable Information Society." *Informatik/Informatique* 4 (August 2000): 2–9.

Hobson, Kersty. "Competing Discourses of Sustainable Consumption: Does the 'Rationalisation of Lifestyles' Make Sense?" *Environmental Politics* 11.2 (Summer 2002): 95–120.

Kelly, Kevin. "New Rules for the New Economy." *Wired*, 5.09 September 1997 <http://www.wired.com/wired/archive/5.09/newrules.html>, accessed 30 November 2012.

Kopnina, Helen. "Education for Sustainable Development (ESD): The Turn Away from 'Environment' in Environmental Education?" *Environmental Education Research* 18.5 (2012): 699–717.

Kopnina, Helen. "The Lorax Complex: Deep Ecology, Ecocentrism and Exclusion." *Journal of Integrative Environmental Sciences* 9.4 (December 2012): 235–254 <http://dx.doi.org/10.1080/1943815X.2012.742914>, accessed 31 January 2015.

Kopnina, Helen. "Toward Conservational Anthropology: Addressing Anthropocentric Bias in Anthropology." *Dialectical Anthropology* 36.1/2 (2012): 127–146.

Kopnina, Helen. "What Is (Responsible) Consumption? Discussing Environment and Consumption with Children from Different Socioeconomic Backgrounds in the Netherlands." *The Environmentalist* 31.3 (September 2011): 216–226.

Kopnina, Helen and Shoreman-Ouimet, Eleanor. *Environmental Anthropology: Future Trends*. Routledge Studies in Anthropology Series. New York and Oxford: Routledge, 2013.

Kopnina, Helen and Shoreman-Ouimet, Eleanor. *Environmental Anthropology Today*. New York and Oxford: Routledge, 2011.

Lundmark, Carina. "The New Ecological Paradigm Revisited: Anchoring the NEP Scale in Environmental Ethics." *Environmental Education Research* 13.3 (July 2007): 329–347.

Matthews, H. Scott. "The Environmental Implications of the Growth of the Information and Communications Technology Sector." Paper presented to the Environment Directorate, OECD, Paris, 2001.

McDonough, William and Braungart, Michael, eds. *Cradle to Cradle: Remaking the Way We Make Things*. New York: North Point Press, 2002.

Mosse, David. *Cultivating Development: An Ethnography of Aid Policy and Practice*. London and Ann Arbor, MI: Pluto Press. 2005.

Park, Jacob and Roome, Nigel. *The Ecology of the New Economy—Sustainable Transformation of Global Information, Communications and Electronics Industries*. Sheffield, UK: Greenleaf Publishing, 2002.

Sassen, Saskia. "Digital Networks and the State: Some Governance Questions." *Theory, Culture & Society* 17.4 (August 2000): 19–33.

Shiva, Vandana. *Monocultures of the Mind: Biodiversity and Biotechnology*. London, UK; Atlantic Highlands, NJ: Zed Books, 1993.

Stern, Paul C. "Toward a Coherent Theory of Environmentally Significant Behavior." *Journal of Social Issues* 56.3 (Fall/Sept. 2000): 407–424.

Vayda, Andrew P. "Causal Explanation for Environmental Anthropologists." In Kopnina, Helen and Shoreman-Ouimet, Eleanor, eds. *Environmental Anthropology: Future Trends*. Routledge Studies in Anthropology Series. New York and Oxford: Routledge, 2013.

Wilk, Richard. "Consumption Embedded in Culture and Language: Implications for Finding Sustainability." *Sustainability: Science, Practice and Policy* 6.2 (2010): 38–48.

WWF. "Deforestation." The World Wide Fund for Nature. 2012 <http://wwf.panda.org/about_our_earth/about_forests/deforestation/>, accessed 30 November 2012.

32
THE CHANGING MAGAZINE AUDIENCE

Enriching the Reader Relationship

Rachel Davis Mersey

Tina Brown said it: "We have reached a tipping point at which we can most efficiently and effectively reach our readers in all-digital format."[1] Her comment was in reference to *Newsweek*'s final print issue, 31 December 2012, and the magazine's transition—perhaps better called the brand's transition (now Newsweek Global)—to e-readers, tablet devices and the Web.

At the 2012 American Magazine Conference, Forbes, Inc.'s Chief Revenue Officer Meredith Levien said half the company's revenue would be derived from its digital businesses.[2] Notably, *Forbes'* print revenue income was also rising commensurate with a 12.5 percent increase in advertising pages.[3] Erik Sass of *MediaDailyNews* called it "the *tipping point*."[4]

A year earlier, Affinity's American Magazine Study found that 15 magazines had reached what Affinity called "the audience tipping point": The size of the digital audiences had exceeded the print audiences. The 15 were *Barron's*, *ESPN the Magazine*, *Fast Company*, *Food Network Magazine*, *Forbes*, *Fortune*, *Harvard Business Review*, *MacWorld*, *Money*, *New York Magazine*, *Sporting News*, the *Atlantic*, the *Economist*, *WebMD the Magazine* and *Wired*.[5]

The assumption of many magazine practitioners and academics is that such tipping point changes in the industry, although all digitally related, are really marks of changes among the audiences of magazines. In fact, it is easy to find evidence that the behaviors, attitudes and needs of individuals have evolved in this digital age.[6] However, an unusual aspect of the magazine world, as opposed to other pockets of journalism, is that magazine journalists craft their products for their audiences.[7] This is part of what differentiates magazines from newspapers. It may, in fact, be the reason many magazines weathered the digital storm, which has been damaging to newspapers. Magazines and their audiences rise and fall together; the tipping points of the former married with those of the latter. This simpatico evolution is at the heart of magazine journalists' communication, whether print or digital.

Therefore to discuss what is known about the changing magazine audience requires focusing on the *relationship* between magazines and their audiences. This chapter briefly examines the broad literature regarding magazine audiences but primarily focuses on the seminal literature related to social identity theory (SIT). The reason for this attention to SIT is that it provides a psychological framework for understanding the relationship between magazines and their audiences, transcending the evolutions in technology that have dominated recent conversations among media practitioners and researchers. Essential to this is examining how the magazine-audience relationship is undergoing radical transformation and how magazines are adapting and, in some cases, thriving.

Audience Uses and Gratifications

The preponderance of early scholarly work on magazine audiences relied on the uses and gratifications framework, which emerged in the 1940s.[8] Although it is clear there is a longer history, research from the 1960s and 1970s is most often cited as the root of uses and gratifications.[9] Elihu Katz, Jay Blumler and Michael Gurevitch summarize the uses and gratifications approach:

> (1) the social and psychological origins of (2) needs, which generate (3) expectations of (4) the mass media or other sources, which lead to (5) differential patterns of media exposure resulting in (6) need gratifications and (7) other consequences, perhaps mostly unintended ones.[10]

The essential point is that this approach casts media consumption as a purposeful activity motivated by people's varying needs and interests.

Uses and gratifications studies specific to magazines have been limited by comparison to other media, such as television and newspapers. In 1988, Gregg Payne, Jessica Severn and David Dozier, relying on the earlier work by Wayne Towers and Barbara Hartung, examined the gratification differences between readers of consumer and trade magazines.[11] Payne, Severn and Dozier focused on three motivations: interaction, surveillance and diversion.[12] They "operationalized interaction usage as preparation for anticipated conversations with others, or for other interpersonal activities in the larger social order; surveillance as media attendance aimed at obtaining information about the world; and diversion as relaxing, escaping or passing time with entertainment material."[13] Payne and his team found that the content of a magazine is predictive of readers' uses of that magazine.

Other uses and gratifications research has focused on magazine readership as the dependent variable. Jack McLeod and Lee Becker found in an experimental study that individuals who were given advance notice that they would be tested about the current situation in Pakistan or asked to write an essay on U.S. aid to Pakistan made greater use of public affairs magazines in the waiting room than did those in the control group.[14] In addition, the two test groups (quiz takers versus essay writers) differed in the type of information they remembered from the magazines.

The entirety of what is known through the lens of uses and gratifications about magazine audiences is not learned from the literature about magazine audiences alone. From survey research on the rise of use of new audio technologies among young people, Alan Albarran and a research team at the University of North Texas, for example, found that "the gratifications formerly served by terrestrial radio are being met more positively by the MP3 player, and also through streaming media."[15] Albarran and his team's work provides an example of what might be called *the substitution effect*. Audiences will choose media that best serve their needs. Dalton State College's Kristin Barton, from survey research on competition-based reality television, identified *personal utility* as a new gratification.[16] Barton found personal utility to be a four-item factor: (1) The television shows make me feel less lonely; (2) They are different than anything else on TV; (3) They help me forget about my problems; and (4) They help me relax.[17] Her explanation, "Reality programming may begin catering more and more to niche groups and subgroups for ratings. In this, viewers may no longer be watching them as much for social utility, but to obtain gratifications on an individual or specialized level."[18] Barton's research advanced scholars' understanding of the breadth of gratifications media may serve.

This body of uses and gratifications research also frames the audience as actively seeking media content. Advancing this work, scholars have brought additional theoretical frameworks to bear on uses and gratifications to better understand motivations for audience media use.

Magazine Media-Identity Relationship

Researchers have traced the relationship between magazines and audiences, relying on the construct of identity as the primary driver of audience media selection and engagement as described by social identity theory.[19] Social identity theory argues that individuals have both personal identities *and* social identities. Henri Tajfel, the seminal author in this area, writes, "We shall understand social identity as that part of an individual's self-concept, which derives from his knowledge of his membership of a social group (or groups) together with the emotional significance attached to that membership."[20] Specifically, media scholars' studies show that media use helps individuals both construct and maintain social identities in a process that is best thought of as inextricably intertwined.[21] This segment of the chapter examines *audience* and *social identities* as separate constructs. The next section explores their *interconnection*.

Identity construction or, as Kate Peirce has called it, *socialization*, is perhaps best understood in reference to young people.[22] Media communicate messages—just as parents, teachers and peers do—that help, for example, a young woman think about who she is or who she wants to be. She learns what to wear, say, do, read, watch, buy, eat or not eat as a part of constructing how she presents herself to others and how she understands to which groups she belongs or aspires to join. As a part of the literature on young people, media use and identity, Anda Rožukalne of Riga Stradinš University in Latvia examined media use patterns in the country from 2007 to 2010.[23] Rožukalne concluded, "Media use and media devices can show one's status in society, help find an identity and belonging to a certain social group."[24] That is, people learn how to navigate the complex social world in part from media sources.

A related side note to this half of the relationship between media and identity—how people understand media use and social learning—has led to scholars and policy makers' concern about the malevolent effects of media.[25] Multiple media effects studies have looked at the relationship between media and social cues given young women.[26] Relying on much of the work in this area, researchers Stacy Smith and Amy Granados reviewed and summarized the literature on sex-role stereotyping:

> Taken as a whole, sex-role stereotyping on television or in film can contribute to a series of outcomes. Such portrayals can skew perceptions, attitudes, and beliefs about males and females' personality characteristics, social behaviors, and occupations. There is also some preliminary evidence to cautiously suggest that media exposure may be cultivating distorted schemas for romance and unattainable ideals for beauty and thinness.[27]

That is, media messages may be unrealistic. So-called reality television with all its careful cast selection, pre-production planning and drama-inducing editing has not helped the real world emerge any more honestly, and magazines have been just as guilty as television. A glance at any newsstand and women's magazines' airbrushed covers is evidence of the latter.

In addition to identifying boundaries for social identity, media play a more complex role. Jake Harwood argues that individuals use media to maintain or manage their social identities and group memberships in the most satisfying ways possible.[28] To test this thesis, Harwood merges the understanding of social identity theory with the uses and gratifications approach: "Social identity gratifications are one determinant of media choices."[29] In his early social identity theory research, which focused on television viewing, Harwood wrote,

> Individuals seek out particular messages which support their social identities (i.e., provide positive social comparisons with outgroups), and avoid messages which do not support their identities. Viewing media messages featuring individuals who we

identify as being 'in-group' members will be one way in which positive social comparisons can be achieved.[30]

As Harwood found occurs in television viewing, so, too, a young woman is likely to select from among all the magazines for young women—*American Cheerleader, Girls' Life, Muslim Girl, Seventeen, Tiger Beat* and *Teen Vogue*, for example—to read the titles that make her feel as positive as possible about the social self or selves she is developing.

The *identity construction* construct is not exclusive to young people. In research on older adults and magazine advertisements funded by the U.K. Economic and Social Research Council, Angie Williams and her co-investigators constructed a scheme to examine the presentation of older adults in an age-targeted magazine as opposed to a general readership magazine.[31] They concluded, "Positive images of old age are therefore deemed essential, especially for older media users to enhance their in-group identity."[32] The basic tenet from social identity theory is supported by Williams's research: People will consume media that make them feel good about themselves.

What about the situations where the too thin, extraordinarily beautiful models are on the covers and pages of the teen magazines girls are reading? This cannot make an average teen feel too positive about who she is. This is, in part, true. The psychological mechanism embedded in social identity theory argues that people will either adjust their interpretation of the media to better suit a positive sense of self ("I'm not like that overly thin model, I'm smarter and more focused on my success as a soccer player"), or they will change their social selves to meet the media ideal. How and why people engage in these psychological processes is beyond the scope of this chapter, but researchers have observed several aspects in the media context.

Merja Mahrt of Heinrich Heine University in Germany has examined the reinforcement relationship between women and women's magazines with specific attention to the reader's agency, or active role.[33] She argues that both selective exposure (choosing to consume certain magazines) and selective perception (seeing what a reader wants to see in those magazines) are at play. Given that a magazine on whose values readers tend to agree (e.g., *Libelle*) showed about the same level of congruence between readers' personal values and perceived magazine values as the least consensually rated title (*Elle*), the gratification of reinforcing one's values by the choice of a magazine may even follow a parabolic curve: Both open and closed magazines can provide their readers with the possibility of recognizing their own values in the published contents, albeit due to different mechanisms.[34] Mahrt's observation about "open" texts—that is, those that allow ample room for interpretation—is at the heart of the relationship between media and people's social selves.[35]

The processes of construction and maintenance are almost indistinguishable from each other in complex media–social identity relationships. Sarah Crymble explains in her study of DeBeers' right-hand ring campaign, media—and she argues specifically print magazine advertisements—"are an essential locality for exploring the embodiment and management of identities, and how the process of identification is marked by conflicting desires and representations."[36] Construction and maintenance of identities are intertwined concepts, and magazines are a ready player.

Crymble points to the U.S.-based DeBeers' campaign's polysemic nature, framing traditional marriage ("Your left hand says you're taken") and female empowerment ("Your right hand says you can take over") as oppositional.[37] Most important to this discussion, however, is Crymble's discussion of identity management, which highlights one of the cruxes of social identity theory—people will see in media that which makes them feel positively about their social identities:

> One of the ways in which these ads address and attempt to manage anxiety associated with the negative connotations of single and couplehood is by utilizing older models in their campaign. By featuring women in their 30s and 40s, with all the markers of

wealth and sophistication, the ads are able to target women who may be wrestling with the derogatory connotations of being either longtime single or longtime married, offering them ways to reinvigorate their lives by bringing more meanings and identities into play. In addition, another equally relevant interpretation would be that this campaign is trying to capitalize on women's desire to display a symbol that overtly reflects their retention of valued characteristics associated with an identity that is abdicated upon marriage (as marriage, more and more, occurs far later in life for women these days).[38]

While Crymble's focus is on magazine advertisements that have a more direct marketing tone in their attempt to influence purchasing, the principles of her study, the findings of which reinforce social identity theory, are applicable to magazine texts as wholes. Attention to the media–identity relationship in texts has emerged in some of the literature on magazines, such as that on *Latina* and *Details*. Katynka Zazueta Martínez's investigation of *Latina* uses textual analysis and interviews with the magazine's editorial staff, leading her to conclude the magazine makes "a strong investment in constructing, validating, and celebrating the Latinidad of both the celebrities [featured in] and readers of the magazine."[39] Similarly, Jimmy Draper examines *Details* magazine's use of gayness to construct a unique straight-identity on the basis of the argument that there are a multitude of straight masculine identities.[40] He argues that with its unique flavor of "gayness," *Details*—a men's book—is able to differentiate itself from its competitors. Martínez and Draper are addressing the niches in the consumer magazine market (women's books for Martínez and men's books for Draper) as prototypical examples of what social identity theory researchers call in-group and out-group.

When the concepts of in-group and out-group are examined more closely, selective exposure emerges as a prominent issue in media studies.[41] Specific to magazines, Silvia Knobloch-Westerwick and Matthias Hastall found in their study of age and on-line newsmagazine use that young adults concentrated their reading on individuals in their age bracket and showed a preference for positive news about such individuals.[42] On the other hand, older readers were more likely to focus on negative news about young people.[43]

The Changing Magazine Marketplace

The media have undergone fairly radical transformations. They have come through the emergence of the Web and continue to deal with its impact in the marketplace. Although tablets and other mobile devices are still in their infancy, audiences now have more access to more media in more places than ever before. In June 2013 Nielsen reported that three in five, or about 60 percent, of mobile subscribers in the United States had smartphones.[44] Northwestern University in Qatar's (NU-Q) eight-nation survey study found that mobile penetration is even greater in the Middle East. In the countries NU-Q studied, about 70 percent of people use smartphones and 22 percent use tablets.[45]

Frank Gillett of Forrester Research's business technology future team summarizes the tablet landscape and its expected changes:

> Tablets aren't the most powerful computing gadgets. But they are the most convenient.
>
> They're bigger than the tiny screen of a smartphone, even the big ones sporting nearly 5-inch screens.
>
> They have longer battery life and always-on capabilities better than any PC—and will continue to be better at that than any ultrathin/book/Air laptop. That makes them very handy for carrying around and using frequently, casually, and intermittently even where there isn't a flat surface or a chair on which to use a laptop.
>
> And tablets are very good for information consumption, an activity that many of us do a lot of. Content creation apps are appearing on tablets. They'll get a lot better

as developers get used to building for touch-first interfaces, taking advantage of voice input, and adding motion gestures.

They're even better for sharing and working in groups. There's no barrier of a vertical screen, no distracting keyboard clatter, and it just feels natural to pass over a tablet, like a piece of paper, compared to spinning around a laptop.

All these reasons add up to our prediction that tablets will become the preferred, primary device for millions of people around the world. . . . Note that there will still be lots of personal computers sold and in use—in fact our casual estimate is that there will be 2 billion PCs in use by 2016, despite growing tablet sales. That's because tablets only partially cannibalize PCs. Eventually tablets will slow laptop sales but increase sales of desktop PCs. That's because many people, especially information workers, will still need conventional PCs for any intensely creative work at a desk that requires a large display or significant processing power.[46]

If tablets are to become dominant, how do magazines ensure they are successful multi-dimensional, multi-platform products that serve their audiences across platforms? Forward-thinking magazine publishers and staffs are fundamentally rethinking what they do and reframing what they do, from producing magazines to creating and sustaining relationships with their audiences, which are evolving.

Audience members may read a magazine. But readers might also—or instead—follow a magazine writer on Twitter or Facebook, or they might watch the brand's television extension or its YouTube channel, or they might read books published under the brand's title, or they might attend branded events. There are multiple examples of magazines engaging in relationship-building and maintenance in these ways. Previously mentioned was Peirce's work on the role women's books play in helping craft different identities. Recognizing this is a cyclical relationship and the roles of women—and women themselves—are changing, publishers have introduced shifts in editorial content and redesigns in the women's service sector of the marketplace. In March 2012 *Glamour* and *Harper's Bazaar* unveiled major redesigns.[47]

Emma Bazilian of *Adweek* explained the changes among the large-circulation women's books:

> So, in the past year, *Good Housekeeping, Redbook, Family Circle, Ladies' Home Journal* and *Woman's Day*—all facing long-term advertising and newsstand sales declines—further downplayed their bread-and-butter housecleaning, parenting and relationship advice in favor of fashion, beauty, shopping and entertaining.
>
> While service titles indulge readers with style and home decor and put stars like Lauren Conrad on their covers, looking too much like fashion and beauty titles risks alienating loyal readers.
>
> Avoiding that trap means delivering the content in a way their readers expect. So instead of serving up fashion trends, *Woman's Day* gives women tips on dressing for their body type and saving money by shopping their closets. Unlike the typical fashion magazine, it also shows women of varying sizes and ethnicities.
>
> *Redbook*, rather than confining plus-size style tips to their own page as fashion books often do, sprinkles them prominently throughout the style department.
>
> Meanwhile, *Better Homes and Gardens'* beauty writers are foregoing long pieces and going straight to action steps, said Gayle Butler, editor in chief of *BHG* as well as executive vp/executive creative content director at parent company Meredith's National Media Group.[48]

Reinvention has occurred not only among the women's books, but also men's. After being named one of the "twelve major brands that will disappear" in 2009,[49] *Esquire* introduced a new voice and circulation rebounded. "Somewhere on the continuum between dude and dandy, the magazine has found a sweet spot," said David Carr of the *New York Times*. "*Esquire* looks and feels like something a bunch of guys put together for a bunch of other guys, not a glossy widget produced by a big corporation."[50]

Some magazines are increasing the inclusion of community members' voices alongside staff- or freelancer-written content. In 2012, *Lucky* magazine launched Lucky Community, a user-generated, on-line section. "[*Lucky*] is saying, let's not create the content ourselves, but let's go out to the community and find the most engaging producers of content and invite them to syndicate their content with us," explained Larry Levy, CEO of Appinions, which works with magazine and non-magazine companies (including *Lucky*) to identify, analyze, monitor and engage influential audience members across social media.[51]

Beyond introducing new content, magazines with strong relationships with their audiences are also able to capitalize on their existing content in new ways with people's regular use of second screens. For example, there has been a robust market of back issue sales on tablets, a marketplace that was nearly dormant with hard copy requests from readers and fulfillment being fairly cumbersome. Tablets have made the process almost frictionless. In early 2012, Hearst reported that 10 to 15 percent of the volume of digital sales was single issues and 30 percent of those were back issues.[52] Users are in control of selecting magazines—new or old—that are relevant to them.

The principle of the audience having control—people building what they want with magazine content—is pronounced on social networking sites like Pinterest, which has received attention for attracting design-savvy women.[53] *Real Simple* reported that Pinterest sent more traffic to its Web site than did Facebook. Facebook was considered a near-monolith in the social referral space. Pin-it buttons are now commonplace accompaniments to editorial content and advertisements.[54] However, this is not a lesson in creating content and leaving it for consumers to create community. Creating relationship with readers and potential readers requires more thoughtfulness. As Keith Pollack, editorial director of Elle.com, said,

> What works for Facebook isn't necessarily working for Tumblr, and what works for Tumblr isn't necessarily working for Pinterest. . . . With each one of these platforms, it's just a completely different behavior and different need, and we try to approach each one with different objectives.[55]

Magazines that are thoughtful in how they build and maintain relationships with audiences across platforms will succeed in creating communities and serving them.

Transformative Scenarios

As has been suggested throughout this chapter, magazines are operating in a media world that is being transformed at what may be an increasing pace. Emerging digital forms of delivery and the platform preferences audiences are manifesting are causing magazine publishers and staffs to think about relationships with their audiences, which are at the core of social identity theory, in entirely new ways. President of the Precision Media Group Robert Sacks has asserted that magazines should become luxury products. "Readers of free content don't have any skin or investment in the game and can come and go as they please without personal loss, while a reader [who] has paid dearly for the product will cherish each word and the experiences that they deliver," he said. "If printed magazines are going to have a future, it will be as a luxury item and will not be considered a luxury item till the public pays for more than its current perceived value."[56]

Chris Anderson, previously of the *Economist* and *Wired*, where he was editor-in-chief, and author of *The Long Tail: Why the Future of Business Is Selling Less of More*, espouses what he calls a freemium business model.[57] He argues that bandwidth, storage and processing are so ubiquitous that they are too plentiful to measure for payment. Companies must pair revenue-generating products with predominately free services. The following appears on Anderson's *Freemium Business Model* Web site: "The Rock group Nine Inch Nails is a great example of adaption product. In conjunction with the free album 'Ghost I-IV,' fans could buy a range of other products—ranging from the extended $5 download, to a $300 limited edition super deluxe box edition."[58] Anderson's assertion is that this model will be forced upon companies as they become digital and, specifically, that these companies should focus on revenue models that give most of their content away for free but charge for premium services or access.[59]

What is important about these approaches is that they are predicated on a magazine knowing its audience and serving it well. For the purpose of charging more—a lot more by Sacks' suggestion—a magazine must craft a product its audience really wants or needs. To charge only for premium services, a la Anderson, a magazine must know what portion of its product or products has added value. The audience relationship remains key, despite the whirlwind of surrounding change. Some magazines have been particularly successful thus far in navigating with their audience as their north star, exemplifying the best of social identity theory in practice. Two examples are the *Economist* and Politico.

The *Economist* has been a standout performer in the digital space. As global managing director and publisher of the *Economist Online*, Nick Blunden explained its general approach: "Publishers with strong brands need to look at the activity on-line and see that, yes, there is a role for real-time buying and ad exchanges but realize that we also have a responsibility to make sure that we are telling the right story about how valuable our audiences are within the context of our content."[60] In 2013 the *Economist* became the first magazine to set a digital rate base, setting it at 50,000.[61] This follows an April 2012 report from the magazine that it had 48,000 digital subscriptions, which is about 6 percent of its total circulation. The *Economist* audience is wealthy (average household net worth is more than $1.6 million) and connected (87 percent use the Internet for business) executives (25 percent are C-Suite).[62] Therefore it is not particularly surprising that the *Economist* is working to reach its audience digitally. What is especially important is how the magazine captures the essence of this audience for editorial and advertising purposes. It is summarized in its "ideas are the currency of the modern economy" campaign:

> Are you an ideas person?
> We all live in the knowledge economy.
> We get paid—and promoted—for the strength of our ideas.
> Management techniques and balancing budgets are important but it is creativity and brainpower that bring the top jobs.
> It's about ideas.[63]

The *Economist* is serving its elite audience with content, the correct delivery channels and providing a community of like-minded "ideas" people.

Unlike the *Economist*, exemplars in the magazine marketplace are not just making successful transitions with their audiences from print to digital, they are also standout magazines that are responding to their audiences, where they are and with relevant content. The on-line-first brand Politico has been one of the most facile examples. In early 2013 the on-line political journalism Web site Politico announced it had 1,000 subscribers to its Pro News service. As Anderson has suggested, Politico gives much of its content away for free. This service offers value-added personalization.[64] *Folio:*'s Bill Mickey explains,

> At the core of the [Pro News] service is the "whiteboard alert system," bursts of information—an important announcement, scoop or quote—sent throughout the day to subscribers' smartphones. And the underlying tech allows subscribers to tag their preferences so they receive only the content they want to.[65]

"The idea is to make people's lives easier," said Politico executive editor Jim VandeHei.[66] To this end, Politico was launching an afternoon newsletter (it already had a first-thing in the morning version) and a quarterly policy magazine to better serve its audience.[67]

Conclusion

For all the discussion of audience's changing behaviors, attitudes and needs, there is no evidence that people are turning away from content that has value for them. There is reason to know they are becoming more selective and perhaps, putting it bluntly, more demanding. People no longer wade through piles of information—or long articles—looking for a tidbit of relevance. They require value at the outset, creating opportunities for magazines that assert their editorial tone in service to the social identities of their audience members: Make me smarter; make me leaner; make me a better mother; make me a better leader; make me rich; make me feel rich. The current challenge for magazines is to determine their value propositions and, once they do, to realize that the relationships they have with their audiences are in constant evolution. The *Economist* and Politico are outstanding transformative examples, but the audience is outpacing many other titles.

This chapter has provided a discussion of what researchers know about social identity and how it might be applied to the craft of *transformative* magazine making. Each magazine has its own social identity. Thus magazines should invest human and financial resources in understanding their audiences. They should research audience attitudes, needs and behaviors, and then incorporate what they learn into decisions about content, presentation and delivery methods: that is, every contact point with the audience.

Social identity theory, as discussed throughout this chapter, remains at the foundation of understanding the relationships between magazines and their audiences. From this basis, there is a continued need for scholarly research that focuses on magazines, in print and in digital formats. To add the most value to the literature and to the practice of magazine making, researchers should stretch beyond descriptive studies of magazine–audience relationships to conduct experiments on how to strengthen those relationships. The richness of magazines in the modern media marketplace is their relationships with their audiences, relationships that must be fostered if magazines are to have a future.

Notes

1 Tina Brown in Tina Brown and Baba Shetty, "A Turn of the Page for *Newsweek*," *Daily Beast*, 18 October 2012 <http://www.thedailybeast.com/articles/2012/10/18/a-turn-of-the-page-for-newsweek.html>, accessed 5 September 2013.

2 Erik Sass, "'*Forbes*' Reports 50% of Revs from Digital," *MediaDailyNews*, MediaPost, 17 October 2012 <http://www.mediapost.com/publications/article/185400/forbes-reports-50-of-revs-from-digital.html#ax zz2NT0PUyM2>, accessed 14 March 2013.

3 Sass, "'*Forbes*' Reports 50% of Revs."

4 Meredith Levien, as quoted in Sass, "'*Forbes*' Reports 50% of Revs." Emphasis added.

5 "The Audience Tipping Point," AffinityResearch.net, 19 December 2011 <http://www.affinityresearch.net/images/Tipping_Point.pdf>, accessed 14 March 2013.

6 Mark Challinor, "Lessons for Newsmedia Companies from Around the Mobile Industry," INMA—International News Media Association, 19 February 2012 <http://www.inma.org/blogs/mobile-tablets/post.cfm/lessons-for-newsmedia-companies-from-around-the-mobile-industry>, accessed 7 December 2013; Sean Coughlan, "Young People 'Prefer to Read on Screen,'" BBC, 16 May 2013 <http://www.bbc.co.uk/news/education-22540408>, accessed 7 December 2013; Nat Ives, "Time Inc. CEO Laura Lang: Why We Changed Our Minds About the iPad," *Ad Age*, 14 June 2012 <http://adage.com/article/media/time-ceo-laura-lang-selling-ipad-subs/235381/>, accessed 19 May 2014; Helen Leggatt, "Digital Magazine Readers Want More Personalized Ads," *BizReport*, 7 February 2012 <http://www.bizreport.com/2012/02/digital-magazine-readers-want-more-personalized-ads.html>, accessed 7 December 2013; T.J. Raphael, "Condé Nast: Print

Isn't Dead for the Young, Yet," *Audience Development*, 30 May 2012 <http://www.audiencedevelopment.com/2012/cond+nast+print+isn+t+dead+young+yet#.UqO30WTF37A>, accessed 7 December 2013; Jeff John Roberts, "Hearst: Women Finally Embracing Online Magazines Thanks to 7-Inch Screens," *Gigaom* (blog), 12 February 2013 <gigaom.com/2013/02/12/women-finally-embracing-online-magazine-thanks-to-7-inch-screens-hearst-president/>, accessed 20 May 2014; Melissa Tabeek, "*NY Times*: Consumer Now at Media's Center," *NetNewsCheck*, 27 March 2012 <http://www.netnewscheck.com/article/17769/ny-times-consumer-now-at-medias-center>, accessed 7 December 2013.

7 Rachel Davis Mersey, "The Identity Experience," in Abe Peck and Edward C. Malthouse, eds., *Medill on Media Engagement* (New York: Hampton Press, 2010), 81–93.

8 Bernard Berelson, "What 'Missing the Newspaper' Means," in Paul F. Lazarsfeld and Frank N. Stanton, eds., *Communications Research, 1948–1949* (New York: Harper & Brothers, 1949), 111–128; Herta Herzog, "Why Do People Like a Program? Professor Quiz—A Gratification Study," in Paul F. Lazarsfeld, ed. *Radio and the Printed Page* (New York: Duell, Sloan & Pearce, 1940), 67–93; Herta Herzog, "What Do We Really Know About Daytime Serial Listeners?" in Paul F. Lazarsfeld and Frank N. Stanton, eds., *Radio Research, 1942–1943* (New York: Duell, Sloan & Pearce, 1944), 3–33. For a detailed history of uses and gratifications research, see Thomas E. Ruggiero, "Uses and Gratifications Theory in the 21st Century," *Mass Communication & Society* 3.1 (Winter 2000): 3–37.

9 Denis McQuail, *McQuail's Mass Communication Theory*, 6th ed. (London and Thousand Oaks, CA: Sage, 2010). See also, Werner J. Severin and James W. Tankard, Jr., *Communication Theories: Origins, Methods, and Uses in the Mass Media*, 5th ed. (New York: Addison Wesley Longman, 2000).

10 Elihu Katz, Jay G. Blumler, and Michael Gurevitch, "Utilization of Mass Communication by the Individual," in Jay G. Blumler and Elihu Katz, eds., *The Uses of Mass Communications: Current Perspectives on Gratifications Research* (Beverly Hills, CA: Sage, 1974), 20.

11 Gregg A. Payne, Jessica J.H. Severn, and David M. Dozier, "Uses and Gratifications Motives as Indicators of Magazine Readership," *Journalism Quarterly* 65.4 (Winter 1988): 909–913, 959; Wayne M. Towers and Barbara Hartung, "Explaining Magazine Readership with Uses and Gratifications Research" (paper presented at the Annual Meeting, Association for Education in Journalism and Mass Communication, 1983).

12 Payne, Severn, and Dozier, "Uses and Gratifications Motives as Indicators of Magazine Readership."

13 Payne, Severn, and Dozier, "Uses and Gratifications Motives as Indicators of Magazine Readership," 910.

14 Jack M. McLeod and Lee B. Becker, "The Uses and Gratifications Approach," in Dan D. Nimmo and Keith R. Sanders, eds., *Handbook of Political Communication* (Beverly Hills, CA: Sage, 1981), 67–99.

15 Alan B. Albarran, Tonya Anderson, Ligia Garcia Bejar, Anna L. Bussart, Elizabeth Daggett, Sarah Gibson, Matt Gorman, Danny Greer, Miao Guo, Jennifer L. Horst, Tania Khalaf, John Phillip Lay, Michael McCracken, Bill Mott, and Heather Way, "'What Happened to Our Audience?' Radio and New Technology Uses and Gratifications among Young Adult Users," *Journal of Radio Studies* 14.2 (November 2007): 99.

16 Kristin M. Barton, "Reality Television Programming and Diverging Gratifications: The Influence of Content on Gratifications Obtained," *Journal of Broadcasting & Electronic Media* 53.3 (September 2009): 460–476.

17 Barton, "Reality Television Programming and Diverging Gratifications," 466.

18 Barton, "Reality Television Programming and Diverging Gratifications," 474.

19 Gail E. Coover, "Television and Social Identity: Race Representation as 'White' Accommodation," *Journal of Broadcasting & Electronic Media* 45.3 (Summer 2001): 413–431; Yuki Fujioka, "Emotional TV Viewing and Minority Audience: How Mexican Americans Process and Evaluate TV News about In-Group Members," *Communication Research* 32.5 (October 2005): 566–593; Jake Harwood, "Viewing Age: Lifespan Identity and Television Viewing Choices," *Journal of Broadcasting & Electronic Media* 41.2 (Spring 1997): 203–213; Jake Harwood, "Age Identification, Social Identity Gratifications, and Television Viewing," *Journal of Broadcasting & Electronic Media* 43.1 (Winter 1999): 123–136; Rachel Davis Mersey, *Can Journalism Be Saved? Rediscovering America's Appetite for News* (Santa Barbara, CA: Praeger, 2010); Mersey, "The Identity Experience"; Thomas E. Ruggiero and Kenneth C.C. Yang, "Latino Ethnic Identity, Linguistic Acculturation, and Spanish Language Media Preference" (paper presented at the Annual Meeting, International Communication Association, May 2009).

20 Henri Tajfel, "Social Identity and Intergroup Behaviour," *Social Science Information* 13.2 (April 1974): 69.

21 See note 19.

22 Kate Peirce, "A Feminist Theoretical Perspective on the Socialization of Teenage Girls through *Seventeen* Magazine," *Sex Roles* 23.9/10 (November 1990): 491–500.

23 Anda Rožukalne, "Young People as a Media Audience: From Content to Usage Processes," *Central European Journal of Communication* 5.1 (2012): 105–120.

24 Rozukalne, "Young People as a Media Audience," 117.

25 See, for example, Brita Ytre-Arne, "Positioning the Self: Identity and Women's Magazine Reading," *Feminist Media Studies* 14.2 (May 2014): 237–252; Sherrie A. Inness, "Pretty Tough: The Cult of Femininity in Women's Magazines," in Cynthia Carter and Linda Steiner, eds., *Critical Readings: Media and Gender*,

Issues in Cultural and Media Studies, Allan Stuart, ed. (Maidenhead, UK: Open University Press, 2004), 123–142; Angela McRobbie, "Young Women and Consumer Culture: An Intervention," *Cultural Studies* 22.5 (September 2008): 531–550.

26 See note 25.

27 Stacy L. Smith and Amy D. Granados, "Content Patterns and Effects Surrounding Sex-Role Stereotyping on Television and Film," in Jennings Bryant and Mary Beth Oliver, eds., *Media Effects: Advances in Theory and Research*, 3rd ed. (New York: Routledge, 2009), 342–361.

28 Harwood, "Viewing Age," 203–213.

29 Harwood, "Viewing Age," 204.

30 Harwood, "Viewing Age." See also, Harwood, "Age Identification, Social Identity Gratifications, and Television Viewing"; Jake Harwood, "Age Identity and Television Viewing Preferences," *Communication Reports* 12.2 (Summer 1999): 85–90.

31 Angie Williams, Virpi Ylänne, Paul Mark Wadleigh, and Chin-Hui Chen, "Portrayals of Older Adults in UK Magazine Advertisements: Relevance of Target Audience," *Communications: The European Journal of Communication Research* 35.1 (March 2010): 1–27.

32 Williams, Ylänne, Wadleigh, and Chen, "Portrayals of Older Adults," 2.

33 Merja Mahrt, "The Attractiveness of Magazines as 'Open' and 'Closed' Texts: Values of Women's Magazines and Their Readers," *Mass Communication & Society* 15.6 (November/December 2012): 852–874.

34 Mahrt, "The Attractiveness of Magazines," 871.

35 Mahrt, "The Attractiveness of Magazines."

36 Sarah B. Crymble, "Contradiction Sells: Feminine Complexity and Gender Identity Dissonance in Magazine Advertising," *Journal of Communication Inquiry* 36.1 (January 2012): 64.

37 Crymble, "Contradiction Sells," 72.

38 Crymble, "Contradiction Sells," 76.

39 Katynka Zazueta Martínez, "*Latina* Magazine and the Invocation of a Panethnic Family: Latino Identity as It Is Informed by Celebrities and *Papis Chulos*," *Communication Review* 7.2 (2004): 155.

40 Jimmy Draper, "'Gay or Not?!': Gay Men, Straight Masculinities, and the Construction of the *Details* Audience," *Critical Studies in Media Communication* 27.4 (October 2010): 357–375.

41 Dana E. Mastro, "A Social Identity Approach to Understanding the Impact of Television Messages," *Communication Monographs* 70.2 (June 2003): 98–113; Jake Harwood and Lisa Sparks, "Social Identity and Health: An Intergroup Communication Approach to Cancer," *Health Communication* 15.2 (2003): 145–159; Thomas A. Morton and Julie M. Duck, "Social Identity and Media Dependency in the Gay Community: The Prediction of Safe Sex Attitudes," *Communication Research* 27.4 (August 2000): 438–460; J. Gerard Power, Sheila T. Murphy, and Gail Coover, "Priming Prejudice: How Stereotypes and Counter-Stereotypes Influence Attribution of Responsibility and Credibility among Ingroups and Outgroups," *Human Communication Research* 23.1 (September 1996): 36–58; Vincent Price, "Social Identification and Public Opinion: Effects of Communicating Group Conflict," *Public Opinion Quarterly* 53.2 (Summer 1989): 197–224.

42 Silvia Knobloch-Westerwick and Matthias R. Hastall, "Please Your Self: Social Identity Effects on Selective Exposure to News About In- and Out-Groups," *Journal of Communication* 60.3 (September 2010): 515–535.

43 Knobloch-Westerwick and Hastall, "Please Your Self."

44 Nielsen, "Mobile Majority: U.S. Smartphone Ownership Tops 60%," Nielsen, 6 June 2013 <http://www.nielsen.com/us/en/newswire/2013/mobile-majority—u-s—smartphone-ownership-tops-60-.html>, accessed 7 December 2013.

45 Everette E. Dennis, Justin D. Martin, and Robb Wood, *Media Use in the Middle East: An Eight-Nation Survey* (Doha: Northwestern University in Qatar, 2013). The eight nations: Bahrain, Egypt, Jordan, Lebanon, Qatar, Saudi Arabia, Tunisia and the United Arab Emirates.

46 Frank Gillett, "Why Tablets Will Become Our Primary Computing Device," *Frank Gillett's Blog*, 23 April 2012 <http://blogs.forrester.com/frank_gillett/12–04–23-why_tablets_will_become_our_primary_computing_device>, accessed 26 March 2013.

47 Eric Wilson, "Fashion Changes, and So Do the Magazines," *New York Times*, 1 February 2012 <http://www.nytimes.com/2012/02/02/fashion/fashion-changes-and-so-do-the-magazines.html>, accessed 29 April 2013.

48 Emma Bazilian, "Women's Service Mags Trade Housekeeping for Style," *Adweek*, 11 March 2013 <http://www.adweek.com/news/press/womens-service-mags-trade-housekeeping-style-147815>, accessed 11 March 2013.

49 Douglas A. McIntyre, "Twelve Major Brands That Will Disappear," 24/7 Wall St., 15 April 2009 <http://247wallst.com/2009/04/15/twelve-major-brands-that-will-disappear/>, accessed 28 April 2013.

50 David Carr, "How *Esquire* Survived Publishing's Dark Days," *New York Times*, 22 January 2012 <http://www.nytimes.com/2012/01/23/business/media/how-esquire-survived-publishings-dark-days.html?pagewanted=all&_r=0>, accessed 28 April 2013.

51 Levy, as quoted in Lucia Moses, "'*Lucky*' Mag's Technology Solution," *Adweek*, 16 July 2012 <http://www.adweek.com/news/press/lucky-mags-technology-solution-141910>, accessed 6 September 2013.

52 Lucia Moses, "Tablets Helping Publishers Sell Back Issues," *Adweek*, 9 January 2012 <http://www.adweek.com/news/press/tablets-helping-publishers-sell-back-issues-137387>, accessed 26 April 2013.

53 Melissa Pitts, "4 Reasons Pinterest Wins with Women (and Facebook Loses)," *Forbes*, 10 April 2012 <http://www.forbes.com/sites/gyro/2012/04/10/4-reasons-pinterest-wins-with-women-and-facebook-loses/>, accessed 7 December 2013.

54 Rupal Parekh, "Many Magazines Racing to Capitalize on Pinterest," *Ad Age*, 2 April 2012 <http://adage.com/article/media/magazines-racing-capitalize-pinterest/233865/>, accessed 28 April 2013.

55 Pollock as quoted in Parekh, "Many Magazines Racing."

56 Robert M. Sacks, "The Bleeding Edge," *Publishing Executive*, September 2012 <http://www.pubexec.com/article/bosacks-why-magazine-publishers-need-think-more-like-razor-companies#>, accessed 26 March 2013.

57 Freemium, "Information for Business Owners," *Freemium Business Model* <http://freemiumbusinessmodel.com/>, accessed 7 December 2013.

58 "Adapting the Business Model," *Freemium Business Model* <http://freemiumbusinessmodel.com/adapting-the-business-model/>, accessed 7 December 2013.

59 *Freemium Business Model.*

60 Nick Blunden as quoted in Carla Rover, "Inside the *Economist*'s Digital Strategy," *Digiday*, 17 January 2012 <http://www.digiday.com/publishers/inside-the-economists-digital-strategy/>, accessed 27 March 2013.

61 Lucia Moses, "'The *Economist*' Sets Digital Rate Base: Claims a First in the Magazine World," *Adweek*, 25 September 2012 <http://www.adweek.com/news/press/economist-sets-digital-rate-base-143969>, accessed 28 March 2013.

62 Audience Profile: Demographics, Economist Group, 2013 <http://www.economistgroupmedia.com/research/audience-profile/demographics>, accessed 29 April 2013.

63 Audience Profile: Overview, "Are You an Ideas Person?" Economist Group (2013) <http://www.economistgroupmedia.com/research/audience-profile/>, accessed 29 April 2013.

64 Bill Mickey, "Politico Plans Print Magazine Launch as It Passes 1,000 Pro Subscriber Mark," *Folio:*, 12 March 2013 <http://www.foliomag.com/2013/politico-plans-print-magazine-launch-it-passes-1–000-pro-subscriber-mark#.UVJJyI6wnTC>, accessed 27 March 2013.

65 Mickey, "Politico Plans Print Magazine."

66 Jim VandeHei as quoted in Mickey, "Politico Plans Print Magazine."

67 Mickey, "Politico Plans Print Magazine."

Bibliography

"Adapting the Business Model." *Freemium Business Model* <http://freemiumbusinessmodel.com/adapting-the-business-model/>, accessed 7 December 2013.

Albarran, Alan B.; Anderson, Tonya; Garcia Bejar, Ligia; Bussart, Anna L.; Daggett, Elizabeth; Gibson, Sarah; Gorman, Matt; Greer, Danny; Guo, Miao; Horst, Jennifer L.; Khalaf, Tania; Lay, John Phillip; McCracken, Michael; Mott, Bill; and Way, Heather. "'What Happened to Our Audience?' Radio and New Technology Uses and Gratifications among Young Adult Users." *Journal of Radio Studies* 14.2 (November 2007): 92–101.

Audience Profile: Demographics. Economist Group, 2013 <http://www.economistgroupmedia.com/research/audience-profile/demographics>, accessed 29 April 2013.

Audience Profile: Overview: "Are You an Ideas Person?" Economist Group, 2013 <http://www.economistgroupmedia.com/research/audience-profile/>, accessed 29 April 2013.

"Audience Tipping Point, The." AffinityResearch.net, 19 December 2011 <http://www.affinityresearch.net/images/Tipping_Point.pdf>, accessed 14 March 2013.

Barton, Kristin M. "Reality Television Programming and Diverging Gratifications: The Influence of Content on Gratifications Obtained." *Journal of Broadcasting & Electronic Media* 53.3 (September 2009): 460–476.

Bazilian, Emma. "Women's Service Mags Trade Housekeeping for Style." *Adweek*, 11 March 2013 <http://www.adweek.com/news/press/womens-service-mags-trade-housekeeping-style-147815>, accessed 11 March 2013.

Berelson, Bernard. "What 'Missing the Newspaper' Means." In Lazarsfeld, Paul F. and Stanton, Frank N., eds. *Communications Research, 1948–1949*. New York: Harper & Brothers, 1949, 111–128.

Brown, Tina and Shetty, Baba. "A Turn of the Page for *Newsweek*." *Daily Beast*, 18 October 2012 <http://www.thedailybeast.com/articles/2012/10/18/a-turn-of-the-page-for-newsweek.html>, accessed 5 September 2013.

Carr, David. "How *Esquire* Survived Publishing's Dark Days." *New York Times*, 22 January 2012 <http://www.nytimes.com/2012/01/23/business/media/how-esquire-survived-publishings-dark-days.html?pagewanted=all&_r=0>, accessed 28 April 2013.

Challinor, Mark. "Lessons for Newsmedia Companies from Around the Mobile Industry." INMA—International News Media Association, 19 February 2012 <http://www.inma.org/blogs/mobile-tablets/post.cfm/lessons-for-newsmedia-companies-from-around-the-mobile-industry>, accessed 7 December 2013.

Coover, Gail E. "Television and Social Identity: Race Representation as 'White' Accommodation." *Journal of Broadcasting & Electronic Media* 45.3 (Summer 2001): 413–431.

Coughlan, Sean. "Young People 'Prefer to Read on Screen.'" BBC, 16 May 2013 <http://www.bbc.co.uk/news/education-22540408>, accessed 7 December 2013.

Crymble, Sarah B. "Contradiction Sells: Feminine Complexity and Gender Identity Dissonance in Magazine Advertising." *Journal of Communication Inquiry* 36.1 (January 2012): 62–84.

Dennis, Everette E.; Martin, Justin D.; and Wood, Robb. *Media Use in the Middle East: An Eight-Nation Survey*. Doha: Northwestern University in Qatar, 2013.

Draper, Jimmy. "'Gay or Not?!': Gay Men, Straight Masculinities, and the Construction of the *Details* Audience." *Critical Studies in Media Communication* 27.4 (October 2010): 357–375.

Freemium. "Information for Business Owners." *Freemium Business Model* <http://freemiumbusinessmodel.com/>, accessed 7 December 2013.

Fujioka, Yuki. "Emotional TV Viewing and Minority Audience: How Mexican Americans Process and Evaluate TV News about In-Group Members." *Communication Research* 32.5 (October 2005): 566–593.

Gillett, Frank. "Why Tablets Will Become Our Primary Computing Device." *Frank Gillett's Blog*, 23 April 2012 <http://blogs.forrester.com/frank_gillett/12-04-23-why_tablets_will_become_our_primary_computing_device>, accessed 26 March 2013.

Harwood, Jake. "Age Identification, Social Identity Gratifications, and Television Viewing." *Journal of Broadcasting & Electronic Media* 43.1 (Winter 1999): 123–136.

Harwood, Jake. "Age Identity and Television Viewing Preferences." *Communication Reports* 12.2 (Summer 1999): 85–90.

Harwood, Jake. "Viewing Age: Lifespan Identity and Television Viewing Choices." *Journal of Broadcasting & Electronic Media* 41.2 (Spring 1997): 203–213.

Harwood, Jake and Sparks, Lisa. "Social Identity and Health: An Intergroup Communication Approach to Cancer." *Health Communication* 15.2 (2003): 145–159.

Herzog, Herta. "What Do We Really Know About Daytime Serial Listeners?" In Lazarsfeld, Paul F. and Stanton, Frank N., eds. *Radio Research, 1942–1943*. New York: Duell, Sloan & Pearce, 1944, 3–33.

Herzog, Herta. "Why Do People Like a Program? Professor Quiz—A Gratification Study." In Lazarsfeld, Paul F. ed. *Radio and the Printed Page*. New York: Duell, Sloan & Pearce, 1940, 67–93.

Inness, Sherrie A. "Pretty Tough: The Cult of Femininity in Women's Magazines." In Carter, Cynthia and Steiner, Linda, eds. *Critical Readings: Media and Gender*. Issues in Cultural and Media Studies. Allan Stuart, ed. Maidenhead, UK: Open University Press, 2004, 123–142.

Ives, Nat. "Time Inc. CEO Laura Lang: Why We Changed Our Minds About the iPad." *Ad Age*, 14 June 2012 <http://adage.com/article/media/time-ceo-laura-lang-selling-ipad-subs/235381/>, accessed 19 May 2014.

Katz, Elihu; Blumler, Jay G.; and Gurevitch, Michael. "Utilization of Mass Communication by the Individual." In Blumler, Jay G. and Katz, Elihu, eds. *The Uses of Mass Communications: Current Perspectives on Gratifications Research*. Beverly Hills, CA: Sage, 1974, 19–31.

Knobloch-Westerwick, Silvia and Hastall, Matthias R. "Please Your Self: Social Identity Effects on Selective Exposure to News About In- and Out-Groups." *Journal of Communication* 60.3 (September 2010): 515–535.

Leggatt, Helen. "Digital Magazine Readers Want More Personalized Ads." *BizReport*, 7 February 2012 <http://www.bizreport.com/2012/02/digital-magazine-readers-want-more-personalized-ads.html>, accessed 7 December 2013.

Mahrt, Merja. "The Attractiveness of Magazines as 'Open' and 'Closed' Texts: Values of Women's Magazines and Their Readers." *Mass Communication & Society* 15.6 (November/December 2012): 852–874.

Martínez, Katynka Zazueta. "*Latina* Magazine and the Invocation of a Panethnic Family: Latino Identity as It Is Informed by Celebrities and *Papis Chulos*." *Communication Review* 7.2 (2004): 155–174.

Mastro, Dana E. "A Social Identity Approach to Understanding the Impact of Television Messages." *Communication Monographs* 70.2 (June 2003): 98–113.

McIntyre, Douglas A. "Twelve Major Brands that Will Disappear." 24/7 Wall St., 15 April 2009 <http://247wallst.com/2009/04/15/twelve-major-brands-that-will-disappear/>, accessed 28 April 2013.

McLeod, Jack M. and Becker, Lee B. "The Uses and Gratifications Approach." In Nimmo, Dan D. and Sanders, Keith R., eds. Handbook of Political Communication. Beverly Hills, CA: Sage, 1981, 67–99.

McQuail, Denis. McQuail's Mass Communication Theory. 6th ed. London and Thousand Oaks, CA: Sage, 2010.

McRobbie, Angela. "Young Women and Consumer Culture: An Intervention." Cultural Studies 22.5 (September 2008): 531–550.

Mersey, Rachel Davis. Can Journalism Be Saved? Rediscovering America's Appetite for News. Santa Barbara, CA: Praeger, 2010.

Mersey, Rachel Davis. "The Identity Experience." In Peck, Abe and Malthouse, Edward C., eds. Medill on Media Engagement. New York: Hampton Press, 2010, 81–93.

Mickey, Bill. "Politico Plans Print Magazine Launch as It Passes 1,000 Pro Subscriber Mark." Folio:, 12 March 2013 <http://www.foliomag.com/2013/politico-plans-print-magazine-launch-it-passes-1-000-pro-subscriber-mark#.UVJJyI6wnTC>, accessed 27 March 2013.

Morton, Thomas A. and Duck, Julie M. "Social Identity and Media Dependency in the Gay Community: The Prediction of Safe Sex Attitudes." Communication Research 27.4 (August 2000): 438–460.

Moses, Lucia. "'The Economist' Sets Digital Rate Base: Claims a First in the Magazine World." Adweek, 25 September 2012 <http://www.adweek.com/news/press/economist-sets-digital-rate-base-143969>, accessed 28 March 2013.

Moses, Lucia. "'Lucky' Mag's Technology Solution." Adweek, 16 July 2012 <http://www.adweek.com/news/press/lucky-mags-technology-solution-141910>, accessed 6 September 2013.

Moses, Lucia. "Tablets Helping Publishers Sell Back Issues." Adweek, 9 January 2012 <http://www.adweek.com/news/press/tablets-helping-publishers-sell-back-issues-137387>, accessed 26 April 2013.

Nielsen. "Mobile Majority: U.S. Smartphone Ownership Tops 60%." Nielsen, 6 June 2013 <http://www.nielsen.com/us/en/newswire/2013/mobile-majority—u-s—smartphone-ownership-tops-60-.html>, accessed 7 December 2013.

Parekh, Rupal. "Many Magazines Racing to Capitalize on Pinterest." Ad Age, 2 April 2012 <http://adage.com/article/media/magazines-racing-capitalize-pinterest/233865/>, accessed 28 April 2013.

Payne, Gregg A.; Severn, Jessica J.H.; and Dozier, David M. "Uses and Gratifications Motives as Indicators of Magazine Readership." Journalism Quarterly 65.4 (Winter 1988): 909–913, 959.

Peirce, Kate. "A Feminist Theoretical Perspective on the Socialization of Teenage Girls through Seventeen Magazine." Sex Roles 23.9/10 (November 1990): 491–500.

Pitts, Melissa. "4 Reasons Pinterest Wins with Women (and Facebook Loses)." Forbes, 10 April 2012 <http://www.forbes.com/sites/gyro/2012/04/10/4-reasons-pinterest-wins-with-women-and-facebook-loses/>, accessed 7 December 2013.

Power, J. Gerard; Murphy, Sheila T.; and Coover, Gail. "Priming Prejudice: How Stereotypes and Counter-Stereotypes Influence Attribution of Responsibility and Credibility among Ingroups and Outgroups." Human Communication Research 23.1 (September 1996): 36–58.

Price, Vincent. "Social Identification and Public Opinion: Effects of Communicating Group Conflict." Public Opinion Quarterly 53.2 (Summer 1989): 197–224.

Raphael, T.J. "Condé Nast: Print Isn't Dead for the Young, Yet." Audience Development, 30 May 2012 <http://www.audiencedevelopment.com/2012/cond+nast+print+isn+t+dead+young+yet#.UqO30WTF37A>, accessed 7 December 2013.

Roberts, Jeff John. "Hearst: Women Finally Embracing Online Magazines Thanks to 7-Inch Screens." Gigaom (blog), 12 February 2013 <gigaom.com/2013/02/12/women-finally-embracing-online-magazine-thanks-to-7-inch-screens-hearst-president/>, accessed 20 May 2014.

Rover, Carla. "Inside the Economist's Digital Strategy." Digiday, 17 January 2012 <http://www.digiday.com/publishers/inside-the-economists-digital-strategy/>, accessed 27 March 2013.

Rožukalne, Anda. "Young People as a Media Audience: From Content to Usage Processes." Central European Journal of Communication 5.1 (2012): 105–120.

Ruggiero, Thomas E. "Uses and Gratifications Theory in the 21st Century." Mass Communication & Society 3.1 (Winter 2000): 3–37.

Ruggiero, Thomas E. and Yang, Kenneth C.C. "Latino Ethnic Identity, Linguistic Acculturation, and Spanish Language Media Preference." Paper presented at the Annual Meeting, International Communication Association, May 2009.

Sacks, Robert M. "The Bleeding Edge." *Publishing Executive*, September 2012 <http://www.pubexec. com/article/bosacks-why-magazine-publishers-need-think-more-like-razor-companies#>, accessed 26 March 2013.

Sass, Erik. "'*Forbes*' Reports 50% of Revs from Digital." *MediaDailyNews*. MediaPost, 17 October 2012 <http://www.mediapost.com/publications/article/185400/forbes-reports-50-of-revs-from-digital. html#axzz2NT0PUyM2>, accessed 14 March 2013.

Severin, Werner J. and Tankard, James W., Jr. *Communication Theories: Origins, Methods, and Uses in the Mass Media*. 5th ed. New York: Addison Wesley Longman, 2000.

Smith, Stacy L. and Granados, Amy D. "Content Patterns and Effects Surrounding Sex-Role Stereotyping on Television and Film." In Bryant, Jennings and Oliver, Mary Beth, eds. *Media Effects: Advances in Theory and Research*. 3rd ed. New York: Routledge, 2009, 342–361.

Tabeek, Melissa. "*NY Times*: Consumer Now at Media's Center." *NetNewsCheck*, 27 March 2012 <http://www.netnewscheck.com/article/17769/ny-times-consumer-now-at-medias-center>, accessed 7 December 2013.

Tajfel, Henri. "Social Identity and Intergroup Behaviour." *Social Science Information* 13.2 (April 1974): 65–93.

Towers, Wayne M. and Hartung, Barbara. "Explaining Magazine Readership with Uses and Gratifications Research." Paper presented at the Annual Meeting, Association for Education in Journalism and Mass Communication, 1983.

Williams, Angie; Ylänne, Virpi; Wadleigh, Paul Mark; and Chen, Chin-Hui. "Portrayals of Older Adults in UK Magazine Advertisements: Relevance of Target Audience." *Communications: The European Journal of Communication Research* 35.1 (March 2010): 1–27.

Wilson, Eric. "Fashion Changes, and So Do the Magazines." *New York Times*, 1 February 2012 <http:// www.nytimes.com/2012/02/02/fashion/fashion-changes-and-so-do-the-magazines.html>, accessed 29 April 2013.

Ytre-Arne, Brita. "Positioning the Self: Identity and Women's Magazine Reading." *Feminist Media Studies* 14.2 (May 2014): 237–252.

33

DIGITAL TRANSFORMATION, PRINT CONTINUITY

Magazine as Art Form Rather Than Platform

David Abrahamson

Some future historians may maintain that it was the advent of the World Wide Web in the mid-1990s that marked the true dawn of the Digital Age. Yet this would be almost 30 years after the birth of the Internet, with the invention in the late 1960s of packet-switching networks by ARPANET in the United States and the United Kingdom's National Physical Laboratory. Certainly a number of the historical scholars who will subscribe to this school of thought are likely to be media historians because the disruptions fostered by the Web have clearly had profound implications for all media—indeed, across the entire information ecosystem. And while it can be argued that the world of magazines has suffered somewhat less from the paradigm tremors than other media, for many magazine professionals that may, at best, be lukewarm comfort.

Since the mid-1990s, existing magazines have experimented with using the Web as a companion to the print product, as well as with the various demands and opportunities offered by a range of delivery platforms: desktop, laptop, tablet, mobile, wearable, etc. In addition, new business models are being tested, of which the most important result may be the impact on both the editorial processes and product. Moreover, Web-only publications—*destination sites*, in the argot of the day—have emerged that explicitly lay claim to the magazine form. With all this technological change, perhaps the most telling questions come easily to mind: What indeed lies ahead? How will digital technology shape the magazine and journal periodical? Will the print medium co-exist with the digital and, if so, in what form? Or will digital replace paper as the Internet replaced telegraph wire? Or stranger still, might some further new technology emerge that would express all the advantages of digital yet somehow retain the tactile benefits of paper?

Magazine as Art Form

These are certainly pressing questions. However, before addressing them, there might be value in examining what is unique about the magazine form—for doing so might lead to clues about what lies over the horizon. It was Victor Navasky, long-time editor of the *Nation*, who captured one of the central truisms of the form. Magazines, he said, are "an art form, not just a delivery method."[1] The nature of the art form can be explicated through a variety of lenses. Continuing the photographic metaphor, one can, for example, further examine magazines' focus and depth of field. Again, it was Navasky calling on the wisdom of the seventeenth-century Englishman Francis Bacon:

> At the loftiest level, one might think of magazines as what Francis Bacon, the philosopher . . . meant when he referred to as "the middle axiom". . . . Magazines as a genre do not specialize in abstract generalities; nor, at the other extreme, do they present raw, undigested experience. Rather, their comparative advantage is in dealing with the in-between or netherworld—the middle region, inhabited, according to Bacon, by "the solid and living axioms on which depend the affairs and fortunes of men."[2]

Bacon derived his "middle axiom" almost a century before the magazine form as we know it evolved, but it can easily be applied for comparative purposes. Magazines fall in what may be considered a "privileged position"[3]—more detailed and interpretive than newspapers and somewhat less reflective yet more accessible than books. As an art form, magazines have a certain binary quality that serves to secure them a special place in their readers' lives. The combination of what Lori Cole called "ephemerality and periodicity"[4] has an almost seductive effect. Given that they are experienced periodically, magazines strive to be a loyalty-producing editorial blend of the *expected*—that which is looked forward to by the readers—and the *unexpected*—the piquant surprise, perhaps even exceeding the readers' expectations. Because the structural elements of a magazine's table of contents do not change greatly from issue to issue, the editorial structure itself serves as the constant, and what fills it in each issue is the surprise.[5]

Other observers have attempted to explicate magazines' essential nature. Christopher Phin, editor of the United Kingdom's *Macformat* magazine, offered an arguable yet interesting list of attributes to define the magazine form. In his view a magazine was

> a point of coalescence for passion; something that makes one feel cooler/smarter/more interesting; a treat; something that informs inspires and enriches one's life; something made by someone else who one trusts; a curated thing, which is to say knowledge refined; a finite thing; something for a quiet half-hour; or for the toilet; something one buys that might increase in value; has a cover; is regular so that one can subscribe to; something one can lose; and something that is hard and expensive to produce.[6]

Responding to Phin, Alan Rutter, whose somewhat improbable title at Condé Nast International was "editorial tools subject matter expert," added few additional attributes, suggesting that a magazine was a collection of linked stories; designed; an experience, not a commodity; collaborative; and shareable.[7]

One of the fascinating things about the magazine form is that it can be regarded from a range of perspectives, from finely granular to sweepingly societal. Considering the magazine's cultural role, Tim Holmes offered, "If culture is the stories we tell about ourselves, then magazines are prime examples of cultural resource. They are full of stories which we tell about ourselves, . . . which we accept as being about *ourselves*."[8] In a similar but perhaps more expansive vein, Abrahamson noted,

> The magazine form . . . has a unique and powerful role both as a product of its social and cultural moment and as a catalyst for social change. As a result, periodicals can perhaps be usefully understood to lie on a continuum of function, ranging in both intent and effect from the reflective to the transformative. It might also be suggested that magazines can serve, in both professional and scholarly research, as singularly useful markers of the sociocultural reality.[9]

In any consideration of the magazine form, it is hard to improve on the oft-quoted phrase offered by George Washington in a 1788 letter to Matthew Carey, editor of the *American Museum*. Magazines were, Washington wrote, "such easy vehicles of knowledge."[10] It must be added, however, that the letter was actually a note of condolence to Carey when the *American Museum* ceased publication.

Platform Evolution

Skeptics about the future of the magazine form, particularly printed on paper, are far from elusive. Dismal predictions are the currency of the realm. "Magazines, as we know them, are dying," wrote David Renard, author of a book published in 2006, appropriately titled *The Last Magazine*.[11] "Without a doubt," wrote Nick Hampshire in a contributed chapter in the same volume, "within a few decades we will look back on paper-based publications, as we now look back on parchment scrolls, and say, 'How quaint.'"[12] Opinions like these appear to be most fervently held by those moved by what David Nye called "technological sublime"[13]—a sense of wonder and awe in the presence of new technologies, along with the belief that technological advances are uniformly beneficial and, more significantly, ultimately irresistible.

Clearly, the digital revolution has provided new delivery platforms such as the desktop computer, the tablet, the smart phone and the wearable optical head-mounted display, which many magazine publishers are learning how to embrace. Further, most observers are quite certain that alternative means of digital delivery will continue to emerge. Which is part of the on-going problem. In a study of the diffusion of digital technology within the magazine publishing industry in the early 1990s, Stephen Driver and Andrew Gillespie wrote that "technical horizons can draw attention away from . . . [the fact] that the existing technologies may well be intermediate or hybrid systems."[14] The volatility of the technological environment presents a huge challenge for both the producer and consumer because it distorts, even violates, the implicit *magazine-reader social contract*. Addressing this issue of instability, Holmes wrote,

> So rather than an inability or unwillingness to keep up, the biggest problems for magazines has been that the physical expression of technology keeps changing, and each change is not only like starting all over again, it brings in its wake new challenges for modes of production, methods of distribution and means of making money.[15]

With Apple's release of its first version of the iPad in April 2010, there was a substantial body of professional opinion that expected the new device to be particularly suited to the magazine market. However, despite the commitment of substantial resources by a few prominent publishers to finding ways to display their magazines on tablets, the results were not encouraging. One of the major stumbling blocks involved the issues of *physicality* and *materiality*. Perhaps the concepts were not as well understood as they could have been. In a seminal article on the subject, Joy Enriquez wrote,

> Digital devices such as tablet computers . . . have failed to overtake the periodical's primary medium—paper. . . . Whether it is thumbing through pages, marking the margins with handwritten notes [or] displaying a collection on a coffee table . . . this essentially means that the physical attributes of a particular medium plays a part in how humans interact with it. . . . In an information-saturated society where the economy is increasingly based on knowledge, the physicality and materiality of media cannot be ignored.[16]

Even worse, it was not long before an even more problematic outcome emerged. It was soon discovered that even people who owned and used tablet computers did not find them notably useful when reading magazine content. Reviewing a 2013 study, "How American Adults Consume Magazines on Tablets,"[17] Deborah Corn wrote,

> Here's the real news: Three-fourths of U.S. tablet users *do not* prefer digital magazines to print magazines. . . . Isn't that a bit like people with Blu-Ray players preferring to watch VHS tapes? . . . Despite all the hype about iPads and Kindles, U.S. magazine publishers are . . . generally wondering when their tablet investments will pay off.[18]

Setting aside for the moment whether the printed magazine will survive, surely the magazine industry would be well-advised to find a fitting delivery system—one comfortably favored by its readers—in the brave new digital world. Perhaps the most promising emerging opportunity for magazines will be *flexible screen* technology, which promises to mimic the tactility and portability of printed paper in a booklet of electronic pages that display downloaded content. With development funded by the U.S. Department of Defense since the mid-2000s, *digital paper* does indeed show promise. "The e-paper technologies being developed today will give us paper-thin, full-color flexible displays that will rival the print quality of paper," wrote Nick Hampshire. "Such displays will have all the necessary electronics integrated into the display, with reader units having several pages bound together much like a current book or magazine, with the binding housing the power supply, data storage and communications circuitry."[19]

What made the concept of electronic paper feasible was a technology called *electrophoretic* screens. The key to their success was the fact they consume only a fraction of the power of liquid crystal displays. Moreover, in many aspects their performance was surprisingly similar to that of the conventional printed page:

> Unlike an LCD, this [electrophoretic] image does not require backlighting. Instead, the user relies on reflected light, as he would if he were reading a sheet of printed paper. Moreover . . . this means the image remains on the screen without drawing power. A further dose of electricity is required only when the image changes; when a user "turns" to the next page, for example. Not only does this mean that electrophoretic displays are cheaper to run, the lack of constant refreshment makes them more comfortable to read—as comfortable, it is claimed, as printed paper.[20]

It has been suggested that flexible displays may appear in the marketplace by 2020, but a note of caution is called for: This prediction refers only to the screen technology. The other necessary components will no doubt require further development. "The display panel itself is only a small part of the battle," said Nicholas Colaneri, director of the Flexible Electronics and Display Center at Arizona State University. "All the ancillary electronics, the power, transistors and circuitry are all things today that are not yet fully flexible at large scales."[21]

The Editorial Vineyards

Regardless of what technology prevails in the future, the advent of the digital age has, in a number of ways, transformed the nature of magazine content. On-line presentation means (1) the removal of the space limitations formerly imposed by costly printing and distribution; (2) the new display architectures required by new display formats; (3) the added value offered by the availability of hyperlinks to further information, as well as archival materials; and (4) the promise of reader interactivity.[22] Driven by the new technologies, the magazine industry is also undergoing transformations in the working processes through which magazines are editorially produced, altering not only required skill sets but also the working relationships within the editorial enterprise.

Perhaps the most affected of those relationships is one of the most important: the one between the creator and the consumer, the writer and the reader. The late William Zinsser, author of 18 books, including the million seller *On Writing Well*, and one of the world's authorities on putting pen to paper, captured the thrill of the reach of the Web. Reacting, at age 88 in 2011, to a pleasure of 16,000 hits on one of his weekly on-line columns for the *American Scholar*, he wrote, "Yikes! There are real people out there. Real people reading real articles. On that day my umbilical cord to Mother Paper was snipped."[23]

Not everyone, however, has been quite so sanguine. For some there was a dark side to the new digital realities of the magazine editing profession. James Truman, once called the "crown prince" of the Condé Nast magazine publishing empire, was no doubt expressing the view of other workers in the magazine editorial vineyards when he offered the following *cri de coeur*:

> I also felt in some fundamental sense that the problems magazines faced didn't and don't have editorial solutions. So in a sense I could bring my very best game, and it wouldn't make much difference to what inevitably was going to occur when this business for publishers was almost overnight unwound. . . . It is in some fundamental way over. . . . I have an analogy. I think magazines are going to be somewhat like department stores. They'll stay in business, but you'll wonder why, since you get everything in them from other places, usually with a better customer experience.[24]

Economic Issues

Reduced to essentials, there were two key economic questions facing the magazine industry as the digital age proceeded. They reflected the two distinct yet interrelated revenue streams, *advertising* and *circulation*, which have been the financial life's blood of the industry for more than 100 years. The first question was whether the advertising-based business model—invented in the 1890s and profitably omnipresent through the end of the twentieth century—would continue to flourish in the future. The median cost-per-thousand CPM for a one-time, one-page advertisement in an American consumer magazine in the late 2010s was approximately $150; that is, $150 for every thousand paid readers, i.e., those who had purchased the magazine. In comparison, the average equivalent on the Web was less than half a cent. And even if one moved beyond mere impressions to a metric that might be an indication of interest on the part of the viewer—cost-per-click—the 2015 average was only $1.58, yielding a CPM of only $12.[25]

Once one did the arithmetic and saw that the average on-line advertising revenue potential was only a small fraction of that in print, it was easy to understand why on-line advertising produced such diminished revenue returns for a publication. And one integral aspect of this circumstance, the fact that in 2017 readers rarely paid for on-line content, also clearly affected the advertising revenue equation. A print magazine with its paid readership did not have to prove to advertisers that the readers were interested in the content—and therefore in the accompanying advertisements. The fact that readers cared enough to purchase the magazine amply demonstrated their interest and commitment, which was why advertisers were on average willing to pay $150 for every thousand of them. In contrast, since on-line content was typically free to viewers, it was logical that advertisers were only willing to pay rates reduced by more than one order of magnitude.

Which led to the second essential question: Given a possible decline in circulation revenue, would it be possible for magazines, in the face of a generalized public expectation for free on-line content, to erect pay-walls that would produce a revenue stream from their on-line readership? In 2017 there was not yet a definitive answer to the question, but other issues related to circulation were matters of some debate. For example, did a companion Web site cannibalize a magazine's print circulation? "On average, a magazine's print circulation declines about 3–4% when it offers a Web site," wrote Daniel H. Simon and Vrinda Kadiyali in 2007. "However, the effect varies with the type of digital content offered. Offering digital access to the entire contents of the current print magazine reduces print sales by about 9%. We find no evidence that digital content complements print magazines."[26] Five years later, however, a study by Ulrich Kaiser and Hans Christian Kongsted produced contradictory results:

> [Our] econometric analysis finds some support for the widespread belief that the Internet cannibalizes print media. On average, a 1% increase in companion Web site traffic is associated with a weakly significant decrease in total print circulation by 0.15%. . . . [We] do not find any statistically significant relationship between Web site visits and subscriptions.[27]

To be sure, it was quickly apparent to everyone in the magazine industry that the Web showed great promise on the expense side of the ledger. Approximately half of all costs in print magazine publishing are accounted for in a category typically called *manufacturing and distribution*. This includes the tangible costs of buying paper, ink, printing and postage. The on-line world, however, is free of such tangibles. As Erik Brynjolfsson and Andrew McAfee observed, "Two of the well-understood and unique economic properties of digital information [are that] such information is *non-rival*, and it has *close to zero marginal cost of reproduction*. In everyday language, we might say that digital information is not 'used up' when it gets used, and it is extremely cheap to make another copy of a digitized resource."[28]

But no matter how far expenses could be reduced in the on-line business environment, the issue of revenue continued to be problematic. In 2014 the Tow Center for Digital Journalism at Columbia University produced a study that included a fairly definitive explication of the business models worth examining in the search for financial support for magazine-like journalism on-line. Paraphrasing the list, the following models were discussed: (1) *Á la carte*—stories are sold individually, readers have to pay each time; (2) *subscription*—readers pay monthly or annually; (3) A mix of *á la carte and subscription*; (4) *donation*—readers decide what to pay; (5) *external media funding*—movie studios, in exchange for first refusal rights, to option a story as a script; (6) *sponsored content*—providers partner with companies which sponsor a certain type of content or subject matter; and (7) *advertising*—using the model similar to that of conventional print publications.[29] Yet another on-line revenue variation was explored in the late 2000s and was still employed by *People* in 2014, the *freemium*—a combination of free and premium content, with the reader being charged for the latter.[30]

Regardless of the model used, there was evidence that venturing on-line could produce positive revenue results. From a large-scale study conducted in 2009 for a consortium of prominent magazine publishers, including Condé Nast, Hearst, Meredith, News Corporation and Time, Inc., researchers Martin Kon, Sujata Gosalia and Edouard Portelette estimated that, even with the above-mentioned cannibalization, digital magazines—particularly interactive ones—could have a bright future. The research projected a "potential for $3 billion in revenues from interactive periodicals by 2014. After accounting for potential cannibalization of some print products, the industry could realize $1.3 billion in incremental revenue." Further, the authors noted that "interactive periodicals can combine the best of the print and on-line worlds. More importantly for media companies, consumers are willing to pay for the experience."[31]

This may have been an overly rosy projection. Or perhaps not. Indeed, much of the conversation about economic activity on-line has been so imbued with wishful thinking that it was very hard to know. Magazine publishers with extensive experience had not in 2014 found a best-practices solution to the challenges of the Web. Perhaps Holmes was correct when he suggested in 2013 that there was "a truth that most publishers making the transition between print and digital try to hide: Nobody knows what works."[32] Robert Picard, one of the founders of the field of media economics, was clear about the needed executive emphasis. "In the end, however, the most important managerial activity," he wrote, "will be focusing on the questions of the extent and timing of [the digital] transformation that is appropriate for an existing company given its unique market conditions."[33]

If the magazine industry was somewhat at sea in the digital age, perhaps researchers in the academy were in some sense at least partially at fault. "A magazine's on-line presence is part of the publisher's strategy and needs to be carefully and systematically defined. It seems that academic research so far has failed to provide a coherent understanding of the situation," wrote Hanna-Kaisa Ellonen and Olli Kuivalainen. And the industry had certainly not done an exemplary job of helping itself. "The results of previous studies from the industry on the other hand," they noted, "suggest that magazine publishers have merely haphazardly listed multiple goals for their Web sites and have not carefully reflected on how to achieve them."[34]

Readers May Beg to Differ

Some have contended that emerging technologies have made it possible for magazines to create new and even more robust relationships with their readers. The argument centered on the claim that an enhanced interactivity via reader responses held out the promise of an enriched sense of community and a deepened bond between the publication and its readers. The expectation was that the Web would make possible, in the hopeful idiom of the late-1990s, the "development, growth and maintenance of distance-transcending relationships."[35]

In the years since the beginning of the new millennium, a number of major magazine publishers attempted to take advantage of the above presumed opportunities, but the results were quite modest and difficult to confidently quantify. Perhaps there was a fundamental misapprehension about the appetite for interactivity itself. In the rush to embrace the new, the new may have been over-valued. "One of the areas in which contentious predictions recur relates to the alleged antagonism between *passive* and *interactive* media. These distinctions generally take for granted that *passive* means outdated," wrote François Heinderyckx. "In other words, the assumption is that legacy media are passive not by choice but because they could not, at the time they were conceived, be anything else." Moreover, assumptions were relied on which did not prove helpful. "The presumption," Heinderyckx continued, "that the masses crave for interactivity and feel nothing but frustration while using passive media leads to a number of fundamental derived conjectures that aggravate our misrepresentation of the situation."[36]

Perhaps it was the *linearity* of print—and its somewhat ethereal but intuitively apparent benefits to the reader—which was missing from most considerations. Embedded in a magazine's editorial structure was a certain pace and flow that set the tone for the reader's experience, even when the publication was not read in lock-step from front to rear. As Heinderyckx wrote,

> The virtues of linearity are utterly and unfairly overlooked. Linear media, because they are offered at a particular moment and in a carefully prepared sequence, require some discipline and some concentration on the part of the audience. In turn, they limit distractions and encourage, or at least allow, attention, immersion even, and precious opportunities for contemplation. Linear media are also more likely to foster loyalty in an audience that enters into a pattern of regular scheduled exposure.[37]

Furthermore, a set of experiments in 2013 attempting to pursue the viability of group-sourcing an on-line magazine suggested the approach had little promise. The study by Tanja Aitamurto found that even though readers seemed to enjoy the process of *co-creation* with the magazine editors and felt a sense of ownership of the publication, the outcome proved to be a disappointment to both the journalists and the readers. It was felt that the structural components of the editorial content were poorly integrated, and the end result seriously challenged the argument that *open journalism* can be applied to the magazine form.[38]

In sum, if one thinks seriously about readers with an appetite for the kind of material that is to be found in the magazine form, it becomes almost self-evident that the connection between reader and the publication is a function of content rather than technology. Magazines claim a place in their readers' lives because they are, in Victor Navasky's words, an art form, not a delivery method. In the well-chosen words of Ben Smith, the unwavering editorial imperative is to present—report, edit, design and deliver—"stories that brilliantly answer a latent question and meet a curiosity readers didn't know they had."[39] Or to put a sharper point on the centrality of the editorial content, "Whether a long-form story is published in a magazine or on the web," wrote Jonathan Mahler, "its goal should be to understand and illuminate its subject, and maybe even use that subject to (subtly) explore some larger, more universal truths."[40]

Future Possibilities

It can easily be argued that, based on the unique relationship between the publications and their readers, the continuing survival of the magazine form in the brave new digital age is a given. In the fragmenting media world of ever more niches, the formula underlying most magazines' success—providing valuable content to a definable audience which advertisers regard as potential customers—appears to be viable in both the print and the digital realms. It seems unlikely that the magazine form in print will disappear. "Doomsday predictions proved unfounded," wrote Heinderyckx. "A new medium does impact the media ecosystem, sometimes significantly, but so far the successive 'new media' have combined and recombined more than they have substituted."[41]

Researching the questions related to the viability of those two platforms, as well as the ways in which magazine editors can take advantage of the new technological possibilities, will be a task for magazine professionals and researchers in the coming decades. One would be well-advised, however, to approach any consideration of transformative technology with some modesty. "A central point," wrote Abrahamson, "about the Internet's future is simply to underscore something we all know—and that is that we know nothing."[42]

In 2012 Tim Holmes and Liz Nice offered their insightful *General Theory of Magazines*, which states that magazines always target a precisely defined group of readers; base their content on the expressed and perceived needs, desires, hopes and fears of that defined group; develop a bond of trust with their readers; foster community-like interactions between themselves and their readers—and between their readers; and respond quickly and flexibly to changes in both their readership and society as a whole.[43]

To which should be appended the *Le Masurier Corollary*, which adds the attributes of seriality; finiteness; and the notion of consumption in "a mid-temporal media space, allowing time for contemplation and desire."[44]

In an effort to acknowledge and perhaps foreground the economic challenges which, intensified by technological change, now face the magazine profession, there might be some value in proposing a *Special Theory of Magazines*. Drawing on and further refining the general theory and its corollary, the special theory states the following: The dominant formula for magazine success in print or on-line, or both, is to provide specific information of clear perceived value to a definable readership (1) willing to pay for the information and (2) on whom advertisers want to focus their market efforts. Magazine practitioners and publishers who can meet the demands of the special theory are likely to not just survive but flourish.

It may serve only as oblique evidence, but even in the rarified precincts of the twenty-first-century New Age digiterati—imagine, for example, the technocentric world of the TED conferences—the magazine form will still find a way to earn its keep, resonating with readers in powerful ways. Even Emily McManus, who oversaw the TED.com Web site, seemed to agree when asked in 2012 for her underlying organizing principle. "We actually try," she said, "to be a magazine."[45]

Notes

1 Victor S. Navasky, "Editorial Note," *New York Review of Magazines* (New York: Columbia University Graduate School of Journalism, 2007), 1 <http://archives.jrn.columbia.edu/nyrm/2007/ednote.html>, accessed 10 November 2010.

2 Victor S. Navasky and Evan Cornog, eds., *The Art of Making Magazines: On Being an Editor and Other Views from the Industry* (New York: Columbia University Press, 2012), viii.

3 David Abrahamson, "Magazine Exceptionalism: The Concept, the Criteria, the Challenge," *Journalism Studies* 8.4 (July 2007): 669.

4 Lori Cole, "Magazine Modernism: Notes from the NEH Seminar," *Journal of Modern Periodical Studies* 2.1 (2011): 116 <http://muse.jhu.edu/journals/jmp/summary/v002/2.1.cole.html>, accessed 30 September 2012.

5 David Abrahamson, *Magazine-Made America: The Cultural Transformation of the Postwar Periodical* (Cresskill, NJ:: Hampton Press, 1996), 57–58.

6 Christopher Phin, "What Is a Magazine?" *Flipping Pages Blog*, 4 February 2013 <http://flippingpagesblog.com/what-is-a-magazine/>, accessed 14 February 2013.

7 Alan Rutter, "What Is a Magazine?" *Flipping Pages Blog*, 11 February 2013 <http://www.alanrutter.com/2013/what-is-a-magazine>, accessed 14 February 2013.

8 Tim Holmes, "Mapping the Magazine: An Introduction," in Tim Holmes, ed., *Mapping the Magazine: Comparative Studies in Magazine Journalism* (London and New York: Routledge, 2008), xiii. Emphasis this author's.

9 Abrahamson, "Magazine Exceptionalism," 669.

10 Jared Sparks, *The Writings of George Washington, Part V, July 1777 to July 1778* (Boston: Russell, Odiorne, and Metcalf, 1834), 296.

11 David Renard, ed., *The Last Magazine* (New York: Universe Publishing, 2006), 14.

12 Nick Hampshire, "The E-Paper Catalyst," in David Renard, ed., *The Last Magazine* (New York: Universe Publishing, 2006), 34.

13 David E. Nye, *American Technological Sublime* (Cambridge: MIT Press, 1994), ix. The author graciously credited Leo Marx, a professor at Amherst College during his undergraduate days in the 1960s, with first introducing him to the concept.

14 Stephen Driver and Andrew Gillespie, "The Diffusion of Digital Technologies in Magazine Print Publishing: Organizational Change and Strategic Choices," *Journal of Information Technology* 7.3 (1992): 158 <http://www.palgrave-journals.com/jit/journal/v7/n3/abs/jit199221a.html>, accessed 30 September 2012.

15 Tim Holmes, "Magazines in the Digital World," in Jenny McKay, ed., *The Magazines Handbook*, 3rd ed. (London: Routledge, 2013), 188.

16 Joy Enriquez, "Picking Up the Pages: Discussing the Materiality of Magazines," *Journal of Digital Research and Publishing* 2 (2009): 89.

17 Amanda MacArthur, "How American Adults Consume Magazines on Tablets," *Mequoda Tablet Study*, 20 May 2013 <http://www.mequoda.com/free-reports/mequoda-tablet-study/>, accessed 13 January 2014.

18 Deborah Corn, "A Troubling Sign for Tablet Magazines?" *Dead Tree Edition* (blog), 29 May 2013 <http://deadtreeedition.blogspot.com/2013/05/a-troubling-sign-for-tablet-magazines.html>, accessed 15 June 2013.

19 Hampshire, "The E-Paper Catalyst," 33.

20 "Bend Me, Shape Me, Anyway You Want Me," *Economist*, 22 January 2009 <http://www.economist.com/science/PrinterFriendly.cfm?story_id=12971020>, accessed 28 January 2009.

21 Quoted in Nick Bilton, "Waiting for Flexible Displays and Flexible Devices," *Bits* (blog), *New York Times*, 14 January 2010 <http://bits.blogs.nytimes.com/2010/01/14/flexible-displays-and-flexible-devices/>, accessed 30 September 2012.

22 Karen Rupp-Serrano, "From Gutenberg to Gigabytes: The Electronic Periodical Comes of Age," *American Periodicals* 4 (1994): 102.

23 William Zinsser, "Once Around the Sun," *American Scholar*, 29 April 2011 <http://theamericanscholar.org/once-around-the-sun/#.UynoVVyp07c>, accessed 19 February 2014.

24 Quoted in Jacob Bernstein, "A Crown Prince in a New Kingdom," *New York Times*, 18 August 2013, 11.

25 Jonathan Hochman, "The Cost of Pay-per-Click (PPC) Advertising—Trends and Analysis," Hochman Consultants (2014) <http://www.hochmanconsultants.com/articles/je-hochman-benchmark.shtml>, accessed 11 March 2014.

26 Daniel H. Simon and Vrinda Kadiyali, "The Effect of a Magazine's Free Digital Content on Its Print Circulation: Cannibalization or Complementarity?" *Information Economics and Policy* 19.3/4 (October 2007): 345.

27 Ulrich Kaiser and Hans Christian Kongsted, "Magazine 'Companion Websites' and the Demand for Newsstand Sales and Subscriptions," *Journal of Media Economics* 25.4 (2012): 184–197 <http://dx.doi.org/10.1080/08997764.2012.729545>, accessed 15 January 2014.

28 Erik Brynjolfsson and Andrew McAfee, *The Second Machine Age: Work, Progress, and Prosperity in a Time of Brilliant Technologies* (New York: W.W. Norton, 2014), 62.

29 Anna Hiatt, "The Future of Digital Longform," Tow Center of Digital Journalism, March 2014 <http://towcenter.org/future-digital-longform/>, accessed 5 March 2014.

30 "Reading Between the Lines," *Economist*, 26 March 2009 <http://www.economist.com/node/13362043/print?story_id=13362043>, accessed 31 March 2009.

31 Martin Kon, Sujata Gosalia and Edouard Portelette, *A New Digital Future for Publishers?* (New York: Oliver Wyman, 2009), 1 <http://www.oliverwyman.com/insights/publications/2009/dec/a-new-digital-future-for-publishers.html>, accessed 30 September 2012.

32 Holmes, "Magazines in the Digital World," 186–187.

33 Robert G. Picard, "Cash Cows or Entrecôte: Publishing Companies and Disruptive Technologies," *Trends in Communication* 11:2 (2003): 35.

34 Hanna-Kaisa Ellonen and Olli Kuivalainen, "Magazine Publishers and Their Online Strategies: Review and Implications for Research and Online-Strategy Formulation," *International Journal of Technology Marketing* 2.1 (2007): 97.

35 Matthew J. Smith, "Strands in the Web: Community-Building Strategies in Online Fanzines," *Journal of Popular Culture* 33.2 (Fall 1999): 87.

36 François Heinderyckx, "In Praise of the Passive Media," in Ilija Tomanić Trivundža, Nico Carpentier, Hannu Nieminen, Pille Pruulmann-Venerfeldt, Richard Kilborn, Ebba Sundin and Tobias Olsson, eds., *Past, Future and Change: Contemporary Analysis of Evolving Media Scapes* (Ljubljana, Slovenia: University of Ljubljana Press, 2013), 100.

37 Heinderyckx, "In Praise of the Passive Media," 106.

38 Tanja Aitamurto, "Balancing between Open and Closed: Co-creation in Magazine Journalism," *Digital Journalism* 1.2 (2013): 229–251 <http://www.tandfonline.com/doi/abs/10.1080/21670811.2012.750150#.Uys1g Vyp07c>, accessed 16 February 2014.

39 Ben Smith, "What the Longform Backlash Is All About," *Journalism, Deliberated* (blog), 26 January 2014 <https://medium.com/journalism-deliberated/958f4e7691f5>, accessed 20 March 2014.

40 Jonathan Mahler, "When 'Long-Form' Is Bad Form," *New York Times*, 24 January 2014 <http://www.nytimes.com/2014/01/25/opinion/when-long-form-is-bad-form.html>, accessed 25 January 2014.

41 Heinderyckx, "In Praise of the Passive Media," 100.

42 David Abrahamson, "The Visible Hand: Money, Markets, and Media Evolution," *Journalism & Mass Communication Quarterly* 75.1 (Spring 1998): 18.

43 Tim Holmes and Liz Nice, *Magazine Journalism*. Journalism Studies: Key Texts Series (Los Angeles and London: Sage, 2012), 110–111.

44 Megan Le Masurier, "What is a Magazine?" *TEXT* 25 (April 2014): 14.

45 Emily McManus quoted in Nathan Heller, "Listen and Learn," *New Yorker*, 9 and 16 July 2012, 73.

Bibliography

Abrahamson, David. "Magazine Exceptionalism: The Concept, the Criteria, the Challenge." *Journalism Studies* 8.4 (July 2007): 667–670.

Abrahamson, David. *Magazine-Made America: The Cultural Transformation of the Postwar Periodical*. Cresskill, NJ: Hampton Press, 1996.

Abrahamson, David. "The Visible Hand: Money, Markets, and Media Evolution." *Journalism & Mass Communication Quarterly* 75.1 (Spring 1998): 14–18.

Aitamurto, Tanja. "Balancing between Open and Closed: Co-creation in Magazine Journalism." *Digital Journalism* 1.2 (2013): 229–251 <http://www.tandfonline.com/doi/abs/10.1080/21670811.2012.75015 0#.Uys1gVyp07c>, accessed 16 February 2014.

"Bend Me, Shape Me, Anyway You Want Me." *Economist*, 22 January 2009 <http://www.economist.com/science/PrinterFriendly.cfm?story_id=12971020>, accessed 28 January 2009.

Bernstein, Jacob. "A Crown Prince in a New Kingdom." *New York Times*, 18 August 2013, 1(L), 11.

Bilton, Nick. "Waiting for Flexible Displays and Flexible Devices." *Bits* (blog). *New York Times*, 14 January 2010 <http://bits.blogs.nytimes.com/2010/01/14/flexible-displays-and-flexible-devices/>, accessed 30 September 2012.

Brynjolfsson, Erik and McAfee, Andrew. *The Second Machine Age: Work, Progress, and Prosperity in a Time of Brilliant Technologies*. New York: W.W. Norton, 2014.

Cole, Lori. "Magazine Modernism: Notes from the NEH Seminar." *Journal of Modern Periodical Studies* 2.1 (2011): 116–119 <http://muse.jhu.edu/journals/jmp/summary/v002/2.1.cole.html>, accessed 30 September 2012.

Corn, Deborah. "A Troubling Sign for Tablet Magazines?" *Dead Tree Edition* (blog), 29 May 2013 <http://deadtreeedition.blogspot.com/2013/05/a-troubling-sign-for-tablet-magazines.html>, accessed 15 June 2013.

Driver, Stephen and Gillespie, Andrew. "The Diffusion of Digital Technologies in Magazine Print Publishing: Organizational Change and Strategic Choices." *Journal of Information Technology* 7.3 (1992): 149–159 <http://www.palgrave-journals.com/jit/journal/v7/n3/abs/jit199221a.html>, accessed 30 September 2012.

Ellonen, Hanna-Kaisa and Kuivalainen, Olli. "Magazine Publishers and Their Online Strategies: Review and Implications for Research and Online-Strategy Formulation." *International Journal of Technology Marketing* 2.1 (2007): 81–100.

Enriquez, Joy. "Picking Up the Pages: Discussing the Materiality of Magazines." *Journal of Digital Research and Publishing* 2 (2009): 86–96.

Hampshire, Nick. "The E-Paper Catalyst." In Renard, David, ed. *The Last Magazine*. New York: Universe Publishing, 2006, 30–35.

Heinderyckx, François. "In Praise of the Passive Media." In Trivundža, Ilija Tomaniić; Carpentier, Nico; Nieminen, Hannu; Pruulmann-Venerfeldt, Pille; Kilborn, Richard; Sundin, Ebba; and Olsson, Tobias, eds. *Past, Future and Change: Contemporary Analysis of Evolving Media Scapes*. Ljubljana, Slovenia: University of Ljubljana Press, 2013, 99–108.

Heller, Nathan. "Listen and Learn." *New Yorker*, 9 and 16 July 2012, 69–77.

Hiatt, Anna. "The Future of Digital Longform." Tow Center of Digital Journalism, March 2014 <http://towcenter.org/future-digital-longform/>, accessed 5 March 2014.

Hochman, Jonathan. "The Cost of Pay-per-Click (PPC) Advertising—Trends and Analysis." Hochman Consultants, 2014 <http://www.hochmanconsultants.com/articles/je-hochman-benchmark.shtml>, accessed 11 March 2014.

Holmes, Tim. "Magazines in the Digital World." In Jenny McKay, ed. *The Magazines Handbook*. 3rd ed. London: Routledge, 2013, 186–203.

Holmes, Tim. "Mapping the Magazine: An Introduction." In Holmes, Tim, ed. *Mapping the Magazine: Comparative Studies in Magazine Journalism*. London and New York: Routledge, 2008, viii–xix.

Holmes, Tim and Nice, Liz. *Magazine Journalism*. Journalism Studies: Key Texts Series. Los Angeles and London: Sage, 2012.

Kaiser, Ulrich and Kongsted, Hans Christian. "Magazine 'Companion Websites' and the Demand for Newsstand Sales and Subscriptions." *Journal of Media Economics* 25.4 (2012): 184–197 <http://dx.doi.org/10.1080/08997764.2012.729545>, accessed 15 January 2014.

Kon, Martin; Gosalia, Sujata; and Portelette, Edouard. *A New Digital Future for Publishers?* New York: Oliver Wyman, 2009 <http://www.oliverwyman.com/insights/publications/2009/dec/a-new-digital-future-for-publishers.html>, accessed 30 September 2012.

Le Masurier, Megan. "What is a Magazine?" *TEXT* 25 (April 2014): 14.

MacArthur, Amanda. "How American Adults Consume Magazines on Tablets." *Mequoda Tablet Study*, 20 May 2013 <http://www.mequoda.com/free-reports/mequoda-tablet-study/>, accessed 13 January 2014.

Mahler, Jonathan. "When 'Long-Form' Is Bad Form." *New York Times*, 24 January 2014 <http://www.nytimes.com/2014/01/25/opinion/when-long-form-is-bad-form.html>, accessed 25 January 2014.

Navasky, Victor S. "Editorial Note." *New York Review of Magazines*. New York: Columbia University Graduate School of Journalism, 2007 <http://archives.jrn.columbia.edu/nyrm/2007/ednote.html>, accessed 10 November 2010.

Navasky, Victor S. and Cornog, Evan, eds. *The Art of Making Magazines: On Being an Editor and Other Views from the Industry*. New York: Columbia University Press, 2012.

Nye, David E. *American Technological Sublime*. Cambridge: MIT Press, 1994.

Phin, Christopher. "What Is a Magazine?" *Flipping Pages Blog*, 4 February 2013 <http://flippingpagesblog.com/what-is-a-magazine/>, accessed 14 February 2013.

Picard, Robert G. "Cash Cows or Entrecôte: Publishing Companies and Disruptive Technologies." *Trends in Communication* 11.2 (2003): 127–136.

"Reading Between the Lines." *Economist*, 26 March 2009 <http://www.economist.com/node/13362043/print?story_id=13362043>, accessed 31 March 2009.

Renard, David, ed. *The Last Magazine*. New York: Universe Publishing, 2006.

Rupp-Serrano, Karen. "From Gutenberg to Gigabytes: The Electronic Periodical Comes of Age." *American Periodicals* 4 (1994): 96–104.

Rutter, Alan. "What Is a Magazine?" *Flipping Pages Blog*. 11 February 2013 <http://www.alanrutter.com/2013/what-is-a-magazine>, accessed 14 February 2013.

Simon, Daniel H. and Kadiyali, Vrinda. "The Effect of a Magazine's Free Digital Content on Its Print Circulation: Cannibalization or Complementarity?" *Information Economics and Policy* 19.3/4 (October 2007): 344–361.

Smith, Ben. "What the Longform Backlash Is All About." *Journalism, Deliberated* (blog), 26 January 2014 <https://medium.com/journalism-deliberated/958f4e7691f5>, accessed 20 March 2014.

Smith, Matthew J. "Strands in the Web: Community-Building Strategies in Online Fanzines." *Journal of Popular Culture* 33.2 (Fall 1999): 87–99.

Sparks, Jared. *The Writings of George Washington, Part V, July 1777 to July 1778.* Boston: Russell, Odiorne and Metcalf, 1834.

Zinsser, William. "Once Around the Sun." *American Scholar,* 29 April 2011 <http://theamericanscholar.org/once-around-the-sun/#.UynoVVyp07c>, accessed 19 February 2014.

Supplemental Resources

Abrahamson, David, ed. *The American Magazine: Research Perspectives and Prospects.* Ames: Iowa State University Press, 1995.

Abrahamson, David. "Magazines: A Past in Paper and a Future on the Web." *Media Studies Journal* 13.2 (Spring/Summer 1999): 44–51.

Carr, David. "Print Starts to Settle into Its Niches." *New York Times,* 5 January 2014 <http://www.nytimes.com/2014/01/06/business/media/print-starts-to-settle-into-its-niches.html?ref=todayspaper>, accessed 6 January 2014.

Heikkilä, Heikki; Kunelius, Risto; and Ahva, Laura. "From Credibility to Relevance: Towards a Sociology of Journalism's 'Added Value.'" *Journalism Practice* 4.3 (2010): 274–284 <http://www.tandfonline.com/doi/abs/10.1080/17512781003640547#.UywpPFyp07c>, accessed 9 September 2012.

Hollander, Justin B. "Long Live Paper." *New York Times,* 9 October 2012 <http://www.nytimes.com/2012/10/10/opinion/long-live-paper.html>, accessed 15 October 2012.

Jue, Kaitlin. "Major Trends in Digital Magazines." B.S. in Graphic Communication thesis, California Polytechnic State University-San Luis Obispo, 2009 <http://digitalcommons.calpoly.edu/grcsp/2/>, accessed 30 September 2012.

Karp, John. "The Impact of Digital and Online Technology on Cross Media Periodicals." In Levenson, Harvey R., ed. *The Reality about the Promise of Printing in the Digital World.* California Polytechnic State University-San Luis Obispo, 2007, 18–39 <http://citeseerx.ist.psu.edu/viewdoc/download?doi=10.1.1.130.7331&rep=rep1&type=pdf>, accessed 20 September 2012.

Tarkiainen, Anssi; Ellonen, Hanna-Kaisa; and Kuivalainen, Olli. "Complementing Consumer Magazine Brands with Internet Extensions?" *Internet Research* 19.4 (2009): 408–424.

Zarem, Jane E. "All-Digital Magazines: New Opportunity or Last Hurrah?" *Folio:,* 3 April 2009 <http://www.foliomag.com/2009/all-digital-magazines#.UyxfhFyp07c>, accessed 30 September 2012.

Zimerman, Martin. "Periodicals: Print or Electronic?" *New Library World* 111.9/10 (2010): 426–433.

BIBLIOGRAPHY

Aaker, David A. *Managing Brand Equity: Capitalizing on the Value of a Brand Name*. New York: Free Press, 1991.

Aamidor, Abe; Kuypers, Jim A.; and Wiesinger, Susan. *Media Smackdown: Deconstructing the News and the Future of Journalism*. New York: Peter Lang, 2013.

AAS. "Historical Periodicals Collection." American Antiquarian Society <http://www.ebscohost.com/archives/featured-archives/american-antiquarian-society>, accessed 12 February 2014.

ABC-CLIO Greenwood. "Historical Guides to the World's Periodicals and Newspapers." ABC-CLIO <http://www.abc-clio.com/>, accessed 5 February 2015.

Abdollahyan, Hamid. "Gender and Generations Modes of Religiosity: Locality versus Globality of Iranian Media." *Journal of Media and Religion* 7.1/2 (2008): 4–33.

Abelman, Robert; Atkin, David; and Rand, Michael. "What Viewers Watch When They Watch TV: Affiliation Change as Case Study." *Journal of Broadcasting & Electronic Media* 41.3 (Summer 1997): 360–379.

Abernethy, Avery M. and Franke, George R. "The Information Content of Advertising: A Meta-Analysis." *Journal of Advertising* 25.2 (Summer 1996): 1–17.

"About ABM." ABM—The Association of Business Information & Media Companies <http://www.abmassociation.com/abm/About.asp>, accessed 14 January 2014.

"About BPA." BPA Worldwide <http://www.bpaww.com/Bpaww_com/Pages/AboutBPA.aspx>, accessed 18 April 2014.

"About Mission Training International." Mission Training International <http://mti.org>, accessed 30 November 2013.

"About RSAP." Research Society for American Periodicals <http://www.periodicalresearch.org>, accessed 22 May 2014.

Abrahamson, David, ed. *The American Magazine: Research Perspectives and Prospects*. Ames: Iowa State University Press, 1995.

Abrahamson, David. "Beyond the Mirror Metaphor: Magazine Exceptionalism and Sociocultural Change." *Journal of Magazine & New Media Research* 4.1 (Spring 2002): n.p.

Abrahamson, David. "Brilliant Fragments: The Scholarly Engagement with the American Magazine." In Abrahamson, David, ed. *The American Magazine: Research Perspectives and Prospects*. Ames: Iowa State University Press, 1995, xvii–xxi.

Abrahamson, David. "The Counter-Coriolis Effect: Contemporary Literary Journalism in a Shrinking World." In Bak, John S. and Reynolds, Bill, eds. *Literary Journalism across the Globe: Journalistic Traditions and Transnational Influences*. Amherst: University of Massachusetts Press, 2011, 79–84.

Abrahamson, David. "The Future of Magazines, 2010–2020." *Journal of Magazine & New Media Research* 10.2 (Spring 2009): 1–3.

Abrahamson, David. "Magazine Exceptionalism: The Concept, the Criteria, the Challenge." *Journalism Studies* 8.4 (July 2007): 667–670.

Abrahamson, David. *Magazine-Made America: The Cultural Transformation of the Postwar Periodical*. Cresskill, NJ: Hampton Press, 1996.

Abrahamson, David. "Magazines: A Past in Paper and a Future on the Web." *Media Studies Journal* 13.2 (Spring/Summer 1999): 44–51.

Abrahamson, David. "The Problem with Sources, a Source of the Problem." *Journal of Magazine & New Media Research* 9.1 (Fall 2006): 1–6.

Abrahamson, David. "Teaching Literary Journalism: A Diverted Pyramid?" *Journalism & Mass Communication Educator* 60.4 (Winter 2006): 430–434.

Abrahamson, David. "The Visible Hand: Money, Markets, and Media Evolution." *Journalism & Mass Communication Quarterly* 75.1 (Spring 1998): 14–18.

Abrahamson, David and Abusharif, Ibrahim N. "Literary Journalism in the Middle East: The Paradox of Arab Exceptionalism." In Keeble, Richard Lance and Tulloch, John, eds. *Global Literary Journalism: Exploring the Journalistic Imagination*. New York: Peter Lang, 2012, 23–38.

Abrahamson, David and Eddy, Nathan. Review of *Magazines That Make History: Their Origins, Development and Influence*. In *Journalism & Mass Communication Educator* 60.4 (Winter 2006): 441–443.

Abrams, Nathan. Commentary *Magazine 1945–59: "A Journal of Significant Thought and Opinion."* London: Vallentine Mitchell, 2007.

Abrams, Nathan. *Norman Podhoretz and* Commentary *Magazine: The Rise and Fall of the Neocons*. New York: Continuum, 2010.

ACEJMC. "2. Curriculum and Instruction." *ACEJMC Accrediting Standards*. Accrediting Council on Education in Journalism and Mass Communications <http://www2.ku.edu/~acejmc/PROGRAM/STANDARDS.SHTML#std2>, accessed 2 June 2014.

Adams, Mark. *Mr. America: How Muscular Millionaire Bernarr Macfadden Transformed the Nation through Sex, Salad, and the Ultimate Starvation Diet*. New York: HarperCollins Publishers, 2009.

"Adapting the Business Model." *Freemium Business Model* <http://freemiumbusinessmodel.com/adapting-the-business-model/>, accessed 7 December 2013.

Adler, Renata. *Gone: The Last Days of the* New Yorker. New York: Simon & Schuster, 1999.

Adrian, Lynne M. "'The World We Shall Win for Labor': Early Twentieth-Century Hobo Self-Publication." In Danky, James P. and Wiegand, Wayne A., eds. *Print Culture in a Diverse America*. Urbana: University of Illinois Press, 1998, 101–128.

Adsprouts. "*Elle* Magazine Media Kit." *Adsprouts: Just Media Kits* <http://justmediakits.com/mediakit/1224-elle.html>, accessed 19 February 2014.

AEJMC Magazine Division. "About the Journal." *Journal of Magazine & New Media Research* <http://aejmcmagazine.arizona.edu/journal.html>, accessed 2 June 2014.

AEJMC Magazine Division. "AEJMC Magazine Division Student Contest." 2012 <http://aejmcmagazine.arizona.edu/students.html>, accessed 2 June 2014.

Agee, Warren K.; Ault, Phillip. H.; and Emery, Edwin. "Magazines." *Introduction to Media Communications*. 12th ed. New York: Longman, 1997, 153–177.

Aitamurto, Tanja. "Balancing between Open and Closed: Co-creation in Magazine Journalism." *Digital Journalism* 1.2 (2013): 229–251 <http://www.tandfonline.com/doi/abs/10.1080/21670811.2012.750150#.Uys1gVyp07c>, accessed 16 February 2014.

Ala-Fossi, Marko; Bakker, Piet; Ellonen, Hanna-Kaisa; Küng, Lucy; Lax, Stephen; Sabada, Charo; and van der Wurff, Richard. "The Impact of the Internet on the Business Models in the Media Industries—A Sector-by-Sector Analysis." In Küng, Lucy; Picard, Robert G.; and Towse, Ruth, eds. *The Internet and the Mass Media*. Los Angeles, London: Sage Publications, 2008, 149–169.

Albarran, Alan B.; Anderson, Tonya; Garcia Bejar, Ligia; Bussart, Anna L.; Daggett, Elizabeth; Gibson, Sarah; Gorman, Matt; Greer, Danny; Guo, Miao; Horst, Jennifer L.; Khalaf, Tania; Lay, John Phillip; McCracken, Michael; Mott, Bill; and Way, Heather. "'What Happened to Our Audience?' Radio and New Technology Uses and Gratifications among Young Adult Users." *Journal of Radio Studies* 14.2 (November 2007): 92–101.

Albarran, Alan B.; Chan-Olmsted, Sylvia M.; and Wirth, Michael O., eds. *Handbook of Media Management and Economics*. Mahwah, NJ: Lawrence Erlbaum Associates, 2006.

Albaugh, Gaylord P. *History and Annotated Bibliography of American Religious Periodicals and Newspapers Established from 1730 through 1830*. Worcester, MA: American Antiquarian Society, 1994.

Aldoory, Linda and Toth, Elizabeth L. "An Exploratory Look at Graduate Public Relations Education." *Public Relations Review* 26.1 (Spring 2000): 115–125.

Aldrich, Robert. "Homosexuality and the City: An Historical Overview." *Urban Studies* 41.9 (August 2004): 1719–1737.

Alexander, Edward. Review of *Running Commentary: The Contentious Magazine that Transformed the Jewish Left into the Neoconservative Right*, by Benjamin Balint. In *Modern Judaism* 31.1 (February 2011): 103–108.

Alexander, Robert. "'My Story Is Always Escaping into Other People': Subjectivity, Objectivity, and the Double in American Literary Journalism." *Literary Journalism Studies* 1.1 (Spring 2009): 57–66.

Ali, Shahzad and Khalid. "US Mass Media and Muslim World: Portrayal of Muslim by '*News Week*' and '*Time*' (1991–2001)." *European Journal of Scientific Research* 21.4 (August 2008): 554–580.

Al-Kandari, Ali A.J. "Predicting the Clash of Civilizations: The Use and Impact of Religious Media in Kuwait." *Journal of Media and Religion* 10.4 (2011): 206–223.

Allan, Ken. "Conceptual Art Magazine Projects and Their Precedents." Ph.D. diss., University of Toronto, 2004.

Allan, Kenneth and Coltrane, Scott. "Gender Displaying Television Commercials: A Comparative Study of Television Commercials in the 1950s and 1980s." *Sex Roles* 35.3/4 (1996): 185–203.

Allen, Douglas E. and Anderson, Paul F. "Consumption and Social Stratification: Bourdieu's Distinction." *Advances in Consumer Research* 21.1 (1994): 70–74.

Allen, Gwen L. "Against Criticism: The Artist Interview in *Avalanche* Magazine, 1970–76." *Art Journal* 64.3 (Fall 2005): 50–61.

Allen, Gwen L. *Artists' Magazines: An Alternative Space for Art.* Cambridge: MIT Press, 2011.

Allen, Gwen L. "From Specific Medium to Mass Media: The Art Magazine in the 1960s and Early 1970s." Ph.D. diss., Stanford University, 2004.

Aloise-Young, Patricia A.; Slater, Michael D.; and Cruickshank, Courtney C. "Mediators and Moderators of Magazine Advertisement Effects on Adolescent Cigarette Smoking." *Journal of Health Communication* 11.3 (April/May 2006): 281–300.

Alsdurf, Phyllis Elaine. "*Christianity Today* Magazine and Late Twentieth-Century Evangelism." Ph.D. diss., University of Minnesota, 2004.

Alterio, Michael Moran. "Print Advertising Down in August, but Select Verticals Show Life." ABM—The Association of Business Information & Media Companies, 5 December 2012 <http://www.abmassociation.com/News/2936/Print-ad-sales-continue-downward-trend>, accessed 25 January 2013.

Altheide, David L. "The Mass Media and Terrorism." *Discourse & Communication* 1.3 (August 2007): 287–308.

Althusser, Louis. *Lenin and Philosophy, and Other Essays.* Translated by Ben Brewster. New York: Monthly Review Press, 2001. Originally published in 1968.

Altschull, J. Herbert. *Agents of Power: The Media and Public Policy.* White Plains, NY: Longman, 1995.

Alumkal, Antony W. "American Evangelicalism in the Post-Civil Rights Era: A Racial Formation Theory Analysis." *Sociology of Religion* 65.3 (Fall 2004): 195–213.

Alvesson, Mats. *Understanding Organizational Culture.* London: Sage, 2002.

American Civil Liberties Union (ACLU). "ACLU Women's Rights Victories." 31 December 1996 <https://www.aclu.org/womens-rights/aclu-womens-rights-victories>, accessed 06 September 2013.

Ammann, Rudolf. "Weblogs 1994–2000: A Genealogy." Ph.D. diss., University College London, 2013.

Anand, Anika. "Is Print Really Dying, or Just Getting Nichier?" *Upstart Business Journal*, 8 March 2013 <http://upstart.bizjournals.com/companies/media/2013/03/08/time-inc-no-sign-magazines-are-dead.html?page=all>, accessed 3 December 2013.

Anderson, Benedict. *Imagined Communities: Reflections on the Origin and Spread of Nationalism.* London and New York: Verso, 1983; Rev. ed. 2006.

Andsager, Julie L. and Powers, Angela. "Framing Women's Health with a Sense-Making Approach: Magazine Coverage of Breast Cancer and Implants." *Health Communication* 13.2 (2001): 163–185.

Andsager, Julie L. and Powers, Angela. "Social or Economic Concerns: How News and Women's Magazines Framed Breast Cancer in the 1990s." *Journalism & Mass Communication Quarterly* 76.3 (Autumn 1999): 531–550.

Angeletti, Norberto and Oliva, Alberto. *Magazines that Make History: Their Origins, Development, and Influence.* Barcelona: Editorial Sol 90 and Gainesville: University Press of Florida, 2004.

Anglo-American Cataloguing Rules. AACR2.org, 2006 <http://www.aacr2.org/>, accessed 16 April 2014.

Applegate, Edd, ed. *Literary Journalism: A Biographical Dictionary of Writers and Editors.* Westport, CT: Greenwood Press, 1996.

Applegate, James L. "Engaged Graduate Education: Skating to Where the Puck Will Be." *Spectra*, September 2001, 2–5.

Ardis, Ann. "Towards a Theory of Periodical Studies." Roundtable opening statement at the Annual Convention, Modern Language Association, January 2013.

Aris, Annet and Bughin, Jacques. *Managing Media Companies: Harnessing Creative Value.* Chichester, UK: John Wiley & Sons, 2005.

Arnheim, Rudolph. *Art and Visual Perception: A Psychology of the Creative Eye.* Berkeley: University of California Press, 1954, revised 1974.

Arnheim, Rudolph. *Visual Thinking.* Berkeley: University of California Press, 1969.

Aronson, Amy Beth. Review of *Shaping Our Mothers' World: American Women's Magazines*, by Nancy A. Walker. *American Periodicals* 12 (2002): 209–212.

Aronson, Amy Beth. "Still Reading Women's Magazines: Reconsidering the Tradition a Half Century after *The Feminine Mystique*." *American Journalism* 27.2 (Spring 2010): 31–61.

Aronson, Amy Beth. *Taking Liberties: Early American Women's Magazines and Their Readers*. Westport, CT: Praeger, 2002.

Arriaga, Ximena B. and Foshee, Vangie A. "Adolescent Dating Violence: Do Adolescents Follow in Their Friends,' Or Their Parents,' Footsteps?" *Journal of Interpersonal Violence* 19.2 (February 2004): 162–184.

ASBPE; Peck, Abe; LeBailly, Bob; Sherman, Robin; with Nesbitt, Mary. "Survey on Digital Skills and Strategies." Presentation by ASBPE—American Society of Business Publication Editors and Medill School and Media Management Center, Northwestern University, April 2010 <http://www.slideshare. net/asbpe/2010-0405asbpemedilldigitalskillsreport>, accessed 30 May 2014.

"ASBPE Ethics Advisories." ASBPE—American Society of Business Publication Editors <http://www. asbpe.org/ethics/asbpe-ethics-advisories-2>, accessed 14 January 2014.

"Asian Americans: A Mosaic of Faiths." Pew Research: Religion and Public Life Project. PewForum. org, 19 July 2012 <http://www.pewforum.org/Asian-Americans-A-Mosaic-of-Faiths.aspx>, accessed 15 June 2013.

"ASME's Top 40 Magazine Covers of the Last 40 Years." American Society of Magazine Editors <http:// www.magazine.org/asme/magazine-cover-contests/asmes-top-40-magazine-covers-last-40-years>, accessed 1 January 2013.

Atkin, Charles K.; Smith, Sandi W.; McFeters, Courtnay; and Ferguson, Vanessa. "A Comprehensive Analysis of Breast Cancer News Coverage in Leading Media Outlets Focusing on Environmental Risks and Prevention." *Journal of Health Communication* 13.1 (January/February 2008): 3–19.

Atton, Chris. "Alternative and Citizen Journalism." In Wahl-Jorgensen, Karin and Hanitzsch, Thomas, eds. *The Handbook of Journalism Studies*. International Communication Association Handbook Series. New York and Milton Park, UK: Routledge, 2009, 265–278.

Atton, Chris. "'Living in the Past'?: Value Discourses in Progressive Rock Fanzines." *Popular Music* 20.1 (January 2001): 29–46.

Aucoin, James L. "Journalistic Moral Engagement: Narrative Strategies in American Muckraking." *Journalism* 8.5 (October 2007): 559–572.

Audience Profile: Demographics. Economist Group, 2013 <http://www.economistgroupmedia.com/ research/audience-profile/demographics>, accessed 29 April 2013.

"Audience Profile: Overview." "Are You an Ideas Person?" Economist Group, 2013 <http://www.econo mistgroupmedia.com/research/audience-profile/>, accessed 29 April 2013.

"Audience Tipping Point, The." AffinityResearch.net, 19 December 2011 <http://www.affinityresearch. net/images/Tipping_Point.pdf>, accessed 14 March 2013.

Augspurger, Michael. *An Economy of Abundant Beauty*: Fortune *Magazine and Depression America*. Ithaca, NY: Cornell University Press, 2004.

Austin, Charles. "The History and Role of the Protestant Press." In Hubbard, Benjamin J., ed. *Reporting Religion: Facts and Faith*. Sonoma, CA: Polebridge Press, 1990, 108–117.

Axel Springer. "Our Media." <http://www.axelspringer.de/en/media/index.html>, accessed 20 February 2014.

Aynsley, Jeremy. "Fashioning Graphics in the 1920s: Typefaces, Magazines and Fashion." In Aynsley, Jeremy and Forde, Kate, eds. *Design and the Modern Magazine*. Manchester and New York: Manchester University Press, 2007, 37–55.

Aynsley, Jeremy and Forde, Kate. *Design and the Modern Magazine*. Manchester and New York: Manchester University Press, 2007.

"Azbee Awards." ASBPE—American Society of Business Publication Editors <http://www.asbpe.org/ azbee-awards>, accessed 14 January 2014.

Babbie, Earl. *The Practice of Social Research*. 11th ed. Belmont, CA: Thomson Wadsworth, 2007.

Bachechi, Kimberly. "Taking Care of Washington." *Journal of American Culture* 33.2 (June 2010): 126–138.

Bacon's Magazine Directory 2011. 59th ed. Chicago: Cision, 2010.

Baehr, Craig and Schaller, Bob. "Chunking and Hyperlinking." *Writing for the Internet: A Guide to Real Communication in Virtual Space*. Santa Barbara, CA: Greenwood Press, 2010, 111–124.

Baehr, Craig and Schaller, Bob. "Cognitive and Psychological Aspects of Online Writing." *Writing for the Internet: A Guide to Real Communication in Virtual Space*. Santa Barbara, CA: Greenwood Press, 2010, 187–198.

Baehr, Craig and Schaller, Bob. "New Media Theory." *Writing for the Internet: A Guide to Real Communication in Virtual Space.* Santa Barbara, CA: Greenwood Press, 2010, 15–32.

Bagdikian, Ben H. *The New Media Monopoly.* Boston: Beacon Press, 2004.

Bagehot, Walter. "The First Edinburgh Reviewers." *National Review* 1 (October 1855): 276.

Bailey, Kenneth D. *Typologies and Taxonomies: An Introduction to Classification Techniques.* Thousand Oaks: Sage Publications, 1994.

Bak, John S. "Introduction." In Bak, John S. and Reynolds, Bill, eds. *Literary Journalism across the Globe: Journalistic Traditions and Transnational Influences.* Amherst: University of Massachusetts Press, 2011, 1–20.

Bakhtin, M.M. *The Dialogic Imagination: Four Essays by M.M. Bakhtin.* Edited by Michael Holquist. Translated by Caryl Emerson and Michael Holquist. Austin: University of Texas Press, 1981.

Bakhtin, M.M. "The Epic and the Novel: Towards a Methodology for the Study in the Novel." In *The Dialogic Imagination: Four Essays by M.M. Bakhtin.* Edited by Michael Holquist. Translated by Caryl Emerson and Michael Holquist. Austin: University of Texas Press, 1981, 3–40.

Balint, Benjamin. *Running Commentary: The Contentious Magazine That Transformed the Jewish Left into the Neoconservative Right.* New York: PublicAffairs, 2010.

Ball, Benjamin. "Long-Form as Moral Category?" *Axon: Creative Explorations* 3.1 (March 2013) <http://www.axonjournal.com.au/issue-4/long-form-moral-category>, accessed 4 February 2014.

Ballaster, Ros; Beetham, Margaret; Frazer, Elizabeth; and Hebron, Sandra. *Women's Worlds: Ideology, Femininity and the Woman's Magazine.* Houndmills, Hampshire, UK: Palgrave Macmillan, 1991.

Bandura, Albert. "Social Learning Theory of Aggression." *Journal of Communication* 28.3 (September 1978): 12–29.

Baran, Stanley J. "Magazines." *Introduction to Mass Communication: Media Literacy and Culture.* 3rd ed. Boston: McGraw-Hill, 2004, 132–157.

Bardoel, Jo and Deuze, Mark. "'Network Journalism': Converging Competencies of Old and New Media Professionals." *Australian Journalism Review* 23.2 (December 2001): 91–103.

Barnett, Barbara. "Health as Women's Work: A Pilot Study on How Women's Magazines Frame Medical News and Femininity." *Women & Language* 29.2 (Fall 2006): 1–12.

Barney, Jay. "Firm Resources and Sustained Competitive Advantage." *Journal of Management* 17.1 (March 1991): 99–120.

Barney, Timothy. "Richard Edes Harrison and the Cartographic Perspective of Modern Internationalism." *Rhetoric & Public Affairs* 15.3 (Fall 2012): 397–433.

Barry, Thomas E.; Gilly, Mary C.; and Doran, Lindley E. "Advertising to Women with Different Career Orientations." *Journal of Advertising Research* 25.2 (April/May1985): 26–35.

Barsh, Joanna; Kramer, Emily E.; Maue, David; and Zuckerman, Neal. "Magazines' Home Companion." [Special Edition] *McKinsey Quarterly* 2 (Spring 2001): 82–91.

Barthel, Michael. "Magazines: Hey, Look at Us!" *Salon.com*, 23 August 2012 <http://www.salon.com/2012/08/23/magazines_hey_look_at_us/>, accessed 27 August 2012.

Barthes, Roland. *Image-Music-Text.* Essays Selected and Translated by Stephen Heath. New York: Hill and Wang, 1977.

Barton, Kristin M. "Reality Television Programming and Diverging Gratifications: The Influence of Content on Gratifications Obtained." *Journal of Broadcasting & Electronic Media* 53.3 (September 2009): 460–476.

Bashtavenko, Aleksey. *Principles of Typology.* Bloomington, IN: AuthorHouse, 2008.

Batchen, Geoffrey. "Observing by Watching: Joachim Schmid and the Art of Exchange." *Aperture*, Spring 2013, 46–49.

Bateman, David N. "The Employees' Right to Know the Issues and the Corporations' Responsibility to Communicate." *Journal of Business Communication* 14.2 (Winter 1977): 3–9.

Bateman, David N. and Miller, Jeffrey. "Employee Communication: Messages for the 1980s." *Journal of Business Communication* 18.3 (Summer 1981): 3–10.

Bateman, Scott; Mandryk, Regan L.; Gutwin, Carl; Genest, Aaron; McDine, David; and Brooks, Christopher. "Useful Junk? The Effects of Visual Embellishment on Comprehension and Memorability of Charts." In *Proceedings of the SIGCHI Conference on Human Factors in Computing Systems.* New York: Association for Computing Machinery, 2010, 2573–2582.

Baughman, James L. Review of *The Publisher: Henry Luce and His American Century*, by Alan Brinkley. *Journal of American History* 97.4 (2011): 1167.

Bazilian, Emma. "Home Improvement: With Luxury on the Upswing, Shelter Magazines are Raising the Roof." *Adweek*, 22 May 2012 <http://www.adweek.com/news/press/home-improvement-140629>, accessed 4 May 2014.

Bazilian, Emma. "Women's Service Mags Trade Housekeeping for Style." *Adweek*, 11 March 2013 <http://www.adweek.com/news/press/womens-service-mags-trade-housekeeping-style-147815>, accessed 11 March 2013.

Beaujon, Andrew. "The *New York Times* Bans Quote Approval." *MediaWire*. Poynter.org, 20 September 2012 <http://www.poynter.org/latest-news/mediawire/189170/the-new-york-times-bans-quote-approval.html>, accessed 1 October 2012.

Beck, Ulrich. *Risk Society: Towards a New Modernity*. Translated by Mark Ritter. London and Newbury Park, CA: Sage Publications, 1992.

Becker, Lee B. "Enrollments Increase in 1989, but Graduation Rates Drop." *Journalism Educator* 45.3 (Autumn 1990): 4–15.

Becker, Lee B.; Vlad, Tudor; and Desnoes, Paris. "Enrollments Decline Slightly and the Student Body Becomes More Diverse." *Journalism & Mass Communication Educator* 65.3/4 (Autumn/Winter 2010): 224–249.

Becker, Lee B.; Vlad, Tudor; and Olin, Devora. "2008 Enrollment Report: Slow Rate of Growth May Signal Weakening of Demand." *Journalism & Mass Communication Educator* 64.3 (Autumn 2009): 232–257.

Becker, Lee B.; Vlad, Tudor; Sholla, David; and Kalpen, Konrad. "Doctoral Programs in Communication: Updated Report for 2009–2010 Graduates, A Supplemental Report." 9 August 2012 <http://www.grady.uga.edu/annualsurveys/Doctoral_Survey/Doctoral_2010/DOCTO2010COMBINED.pdf>, accessed 21 January 2013.

Bedor, Emma and Tajima, Atsushi. "No Fat Moms! Celebrity Mothers' Weight-Loss Narratives in *People* Magazine." *Journal of Magazine & New Media Research* 13.2 (Summer 2012): 1–26 <http://aejmcmagazine.arizona.edu/Journal/Summer2012/BedorTajima.pdf>, accessed 10 August 2012.

Beetham, Margaret. *A Magazine of Her Own?: Domesticity and Desire in the Woman's Magazine, 1800–1914*. London, New York: Routledge, 1996.

Beetham, Margaret. "Towards a Theory of the Periodical as a Publishing Genre." In Brake, Laurel; Jones, Aled; and Madden, Lionel, eds. *Investigating Victorian Journalism*. Houndmills, UK: MacMillan Press, 1990, 19–32.

Beetham, Margaret and Boardman, Kay, eds. *Victorian Women's Magazines: An Anthology*. Manchester: Manchester University Press, 2001.

Behr, Peter. "Looking for Answers in the Enron Story: 'Start with a Pretty Straightforward Question.'" *Nieman Reports*, Summer 2002, 8–9.

Bekken, Jon. "The Invisible Enemy: Representing Labour in a Corporate Media Order." *Javnost-The Public* 12.1 (2005): 71–84.

Bell, J.H. and Pandey, U.S. "Gender-Role Stereotypes in Australian Farm Advertising." *Media Information Australia* 51 (February 1989): 45–49 <http://search.informit.com.au/documentSummary;dn=207931994074409;res=IELLCC>, accessed 21 May 2013.

Bell, Philip. "Content Analysis of Visual Images." In van Leeuwen, Theo and Carey, Jewitt eds. *Handbook of Visual Analysis*. Thousand Oaks, CA: Sage Publications, 2001, 10–34.

Bell, Philip and Milic, Marko. "Goffman's Gender Advertisements Revisited: Combining Content Analysis with Semiotic Analysis." *Visual Communication* 1.2 (June 2002): 203–222.

"Bend Me, Shape Me, Anyway You Want Me." *Economist*, 22 January 2009 <http://www.economist.com/science/PrinterFriendly.cfm?story_id=12971020>, accessed 28 January 2009.

Beniger, James R. "Communication–Embrace the Subject, Not the Field." *Journal of Communication* 43.3 (Summer 1993): 18–25.

Benjamin, Walter. *Illuminations*. Edited with Introduction by Hannah Arendt. Translated by Harry Zorn. London: Pimlico, 1999.

Benjamin, Walter. "The Work of Art in the Age of Mechanical Reproduction." *Illuminations: Essays and Reflections*. Edited by Hannah Arendt. Translated by Harry Zohn. New York: Schocken Books, 1968, 217–251.

Bennett, Paula Bernat. *Poets in the Public Sphere: The Emancipatory Project of American Women's Poetry, 1800–1900*. Princeton: Princeton University Press, 2003.

Bennion, Sherilyn Cox. *Equal to the Occasion: Women Editors of the Nineteenth-Century West*. Reno: University of Nevada Press, 1990.

Benson, Christopher D. and Whitaker, Charles F. "B2B: The Ultimate in Service Journalism." *Magazine Writing*. New York: Routledge, 2014, 275–284.

Benson, Christopher D. and Whitaker, Charles F. *Magazine Writing*. New York: Routledge, 2014.

Benyus, Janine M. *Biomimicry: Innovation Inspired by Nature*. New York: Morrow, 1997.

Bercovici, Jeff. "Did Sarah Palin Use *Newsweek* for Product Placement?" *Forbes*, 11 July 2011 <http://www.forbes.com/sites/jeffbercovici/2011/07/11/did-sarah-palin-use-newsweek-for-product-placement>, accessed 1 March 2013.

Bercovitch, Sacvan, ed. *Typology and Early American Literature*. Amherst: University of Massachusetts Press, 1972.

Berelson, Bernard. "What 'Missing the Newspaper' Means." In Lazarsfeld, Paul F. and Stanton, Frank N., eds. *Communications Research, 1948–1949*. New York: Harper & Brothers, 1949, 111–128.

Berelson, Bernard and Salter, Patricia J. "Majority and Minority Americans: An Analysis of Magazine Fiction." *Public Opinion Quarterly* 10.2 (Summer 1946): 168–190.

Berg, A. Scott. *Max Perkins, Editor of Genius*. New York: E.P. Dutton, 1978.

Berger, Eva and Naaman, Dorit. "Combat Cuties: Photographs of Israeli Women Soldiers in the Press since the 2006 Lebanon War." *Media, War & Conflict* 4.3 (December 2011): 269–286.

Berinato, Scott. "Red Gold Rush: The Copper Theft Epidemic." *CSO*, 1 February 2007 <http://www.csoonline.com/article/221225/red-gold-rush-the-copper-theft-epidemic>, accessed 21 May 2013.

Berkhout, Frans and Hertin, Julia. "De-Materialising and Re-Materialising: Digital Technologies and the Environment." *Futures* 36.8 (2004): 903–920.

Berman, Marshall. *All That Is Solid Melts into Air: The Experience of Modernity*. London: Verso, 1983.

Bernhard, Jim. *Porcupine, Picayune, and Post: How Newspapers Get Their Names*. Columbia: University of Missouri Press, 2007.

Berns, Nancy. "Women's Magazines: The Victim Empowerment Frame." *Framing the Victim: Domestic Violence, Media, and Social Problems*. Hawthorne, NY: Aldine de Gruyter, 2004, 55–81.

Berns, Sandra A. "To Speak as a Judge/Woman: A Different Voice." *To Speak as a Judge: Difference, Voice, and Power*. Aldershot, England and Brookfield, VT: Ashgate/Dartmouth, 1999, 193–213.

Bernstein, Jacob. "A Crown Prince in a New Kingdom." *New York Times*, 18 August 2013, 1(L), 11.

Berreby, David. "We Want Good Journalistic Practices. We Just Don't Want to Pay for Them." BigThink.com, 5 September 2012 <http://bigthink.com/Mind-Matters/we-want-good-journalistic-practices-we-just-dont-want-to-pay-for-them>, accessed 7 March 2013.

Berry, Leigh Talbert. "Comprehension and Recall of Internet News: A Quantitative Study of Web Page Design." *Journal of Magazine & New Media Research* 3.2 (Fall 2000): 1–26.

Betiku, Fehintola. "Hip-Hop Wild Child Azealia Banks Blows Up a Condom on Controversial Magazine Cover That's Been Banned in Seven Countries." *Mail Online*, 16 August 2012 <http://www.dailymail.co.uk/tvshowbiz/article-2189047/Azealia-Banks-controversial-magazine-cover-thats-banned-seven-countries.html>, accessed 1 March 2013.

Biagi, Shirley. "Magazines: Targeting the Audience." *Media/Impact: An Introduction to Mass Media*. 9th ed. Boston: Wadsworth Cengage Learning, 2010, 72–91.

Bidwell, John. "The *Engraver and Printer*, a Boston Trade Journal of the Eighteen Nineties." *Papers of the Bibliographical Society of America* 71 (January/March 1977): 29–48.

Bierstedt, Robert. "Nominal and Real Definitions in Sociological Theory." In Gross, Llewellyn, ed. *Symposium on Sociological Theory*. Evanston, IL: Row, Peterson, 1959, 121–144.

Bilton, Nick. "Waiting for Flexible Displays and Flexible Devices." *Bits* (blog). *New York Times*, 14 January 2010 <http://bits.blogs.nytimes.com/2010/01/14/flexible-displays-and-flexible-devices/>, accessed 30 September 2012.

Bird, S. Elizabeth. *For Enquiring Minds: A Cultural Study of Supermarket Tabloids*. Knoxville: University of Tennessee Press, 1992.

Bird, S. Elizabeth and Dardenne, Robert W. "Myth, Chronicle and Story: Exploring the Narrative Qualities of News." In Berkowitz, Dan, ed., *Social Meanings of News: A Text-Reader*. Thousand Oaks, CA: Sage, 1997, 333–350.

Bisaillon, Jocelyne. "Professional Editing Strategies Used by Six Editors." *Written Communication* 24.4 (October 2007): 295–322.

Biswas, Abhijit; Olsen, Janeen E.; and Carlet, Valerie. "A Comparison of Print Advertisements from the United States and France." *Journal of Advertising* 21.4 (December 1992): 73–81.

Bjork, Ulf Jonas. "'The Backbone of Our Business': American Films in Sweden, 1910–50." *Historical Journal of Film, Radio and Television* 15.2 (1995): 245–263 <http://www.tandfonline.com/doi/abs/10.1080/01439689500260151#.UZ0kj5VNzG4>, accessed 22 May 2013.

Bjork, Ulf Jonas. "'Have Gun, Will Travel': Swedish Television and American Westerns, 1959–1969." *Historical Journal of Film, Radio and Television* 21.2 (August 2001): 309–321.

Black, Jay and Bryant, Jennings. "Magazines." *Introduction to Media Communication*. 4th ed. Dubuque, IA: Brown & Benchmark, 1995, 121–150.

Blanchard, Deena; Erblich, Joel; Montgomery, Guy H.; and Bovbjerg, Dana H. "Read All About It: The Over-Representation of Breast Cancer in Popular Magazines." *Preventive Medicine* 35.4 (October 2002): 343–348.

Blom, Robin and Davenport, Lucinda D. "Searching for the Core of Journalism Education: Program Directors Disagree on Curriculum Priorities." *Journalism & Mass Communication Educator* 67.1 (Spring 2012): 70–86.

Blow, Richard. *American Son: A Portrait of John F. Kennedy, Jr.* New York: Henry Holt & Co., 2002.

Blumer, Herbert. *Symbolic Interactionism: Perspective and Method.* Berkeley: University of California Press, 1986.

Blundell, William E. *The Art and Craft of Feature Writing: Based on the* Wall Street Journal *Guide*. New York: Plume, 1988.

Blundell, William E. *Storytelling Step-by-Step: A Guide to Better Feature Writing.* New York: Dow Jones, 1986.

Boellstorff, Tom. "Zines and Zones of Desire: Mass-Mediated Love, National Romance, and Sexual Citizenship in Gay Indonesia." *Journal of Asian Studies* 63.2 (May 2004): 367–402.

Boers, Raoul; Ercan, Esra; Rinsdorf, Lars; and Vaaggan, Robert W. "From Convergence to Connectivism: Teaching Journalism 2.0." *On-line Journal of Communication and Media Technologies* 2.4 (October 2012): 52–64.

Bogart, Leo. "Magazines Since the Rise of Television." *Journalism Quarterly* 33.2 (Spring 1956): 153–166.

Bogus, Carl T. *Buckley: William F. Buckley Jr. and the Rise of American Conservatism.* New York: Bloomsbury Press, 2011.

Bohleke, Karin J. "Americanizing French Fashion Plates: *Godey's* and *Peterson's* Cultural and Socio-Economic Translation of *Les Modes Parisiennes*." *American Periodicals* 20.2 (2010): 120–155.

Bok, Edward W. *A Man from Maine.* New York: C. Scribner's Sons, 1923.

Bonham, Lorie. "Gender Images and Power in Magazine Advertisements: The Consciousness Scale Revisited." M.A. thesis, Georgia State University, 2005.

Bonsiepe, Gui. "Visual/Verbal Rhetoric." In Bierut, Michael; Helfand, Jessica; Heller, Steven; and Poynor, Rick. eds. *Looking Closer 3: Classic Writings on Graphic Design.* New York: Allworth, 1999, 167–173.

Boon, Susan D. and Lomore, Christine D. "Admirer-Celebrity Relationships among Young Adults: Explaining Perceptions of Celebrity Influence on Identity." *Human Communication Research* 27.3 (July 2001): 432–465.

Boorstin, Daniel J. "From Hero to Celebrity: The Human Pseudo-Event." *The Image: A Guide to Pseudo-Events in America.* New York: Vintage Books, 1992, 45–76.

Boorstin, Daniel J. "From News Gathering to News Making: A Flood of Pseudo-Events." *The Image: A Guide to Pseudo-Events in America.* New York: Vintage Books, 1992, 7–44.

Boorstin, Daniel J. *The Image: A Guide to Pseudo-Events in America.* New York: Vintage Books, 1992.

Boorstin, Daniel J. *The Image, or, What Happened to the American Dream.* New York: Atheneum, 1962.

Booth, Charles and Rowlinson, Michael. "*Management and Organizational History*: Prospects." *Management & Organizational History* 1.1 (2006): 5–30.

Booth, Douglas. "(Re)reading the *Surfers' Bible*: The Affects of *Tracks*." *Continuum: Journal of Media & Cultural Studies* 22.1 (February 2008): 17–35.

Bornstein, George and Williams, Ralph G., eds. *Palimpsest: Editorial Theory in the Humanities.* Ann Arbor: University of Michigan Press, 1993.

Bortree, Denise; Ahern, Lee; Dou, Xue; and Nutter Smith, Alexandra. "Framing Environmental Advocacy: A Study of 30 Years of Advertising in *National Geographic Magazine*." *International Journal of Nonprofit and Voluntary Sector Marketing* 17.2 (May 2012): 77–91.

Boston Public Health Commission. News Release 03–12–2009, "Public Health Commission Surveys Youths on Dating Violence." 12 March 2009 <http://www.bphc.org/Newsroom/Pages/TopStories View.aspx?ID=60>, accessed 2 October 2013.

Botta, Renée A. "The Mirror of Television: A Comparison of Black and White Adolescents' Body Image." *Journal of Communication* 50.3 (Summer 2000): 144–159.

Bourdieu, Pierre. *Distinction: A Social Critique of the Judgement of Taste.* Translated by Richard Nice. Cambridge, MA: Harvard University Press, 1984.

Bourdieu, Pierre. *The Field of Cultural Production: Essays on Art and Literature.* Edited by Randal Johnson. Cambridge: Polity Press, 1993.

Bourdieu, Pierre. "The Forms of Capital." In Richardson, John G., ed. *Handbook of Theory and Research for the Sociology of Education*. New York: Greenwood Press, 1986, 241–258.

Bourdieu, Pierre. *Outline of a Theory of Practice*. Translated by Richard Nice. Cambridge, UK and New York: Cambridge University Press, 1977.

Bourdieu, Pierre. "The Specificity of the Scientific Field and the Social Conditions of the Progress of Reason." *Social Science Information* 14.6 (1975): 19–47.

Bowallius, Marie-Louise. "Advertising and the Use of Colour in *Woman's Home Companion*, 1923–33." In Aynsley, Jeremy and Forde, Kate, eds. *Design and the Modern Magazine*. Manchester and New York: Manchester University Press, 2007, 18–36.

Bowden, Mark. "Nonfiction Storytelling." In Jackson, Dennis and Sweeney, John, eds. *The Journalist's Craft: A Guide to Writing Better Stories*. New York: Allworth, 2002, 59–78.

Bowen, Lawrence and Schmid, Jill. "Minority Presence and Portrayal in Mainstream Magazine Advertising: An Update." *Journalism & Mass Communication Quarterly* 74.1 (Spring 1997): 134–146.

Bowles, Dorothy A. and Bromley, Rebekah V. "Newsmagazine Coverage of the Supreme Court during the Reagan Administration." *Journalism Quarterly* 69.4 (Winter 1992): 948–959.

Boyd-Barrett, Oliver. "Media Imperialism Reformulated." In Thussu, Daya Kishan, ed. *Electronic Empires: Global Media and Local Resistance*. London: Arnold, 1998, 157–176.

Boynton, Robert S. "The New New Journalism, Circa 2011." Byliner, 15 September 2011 <https://www.byliner.com/robert-s-boynton/stories/the-new-new-journalism-circa-2011>, accessed 27 March 2013.

Boynton, Robert S., ed. *The New New Journalism: Conversations with America's Best Nonfiction Writers on Their Craft*. New York: Vintage Books, 2005.

Brake, Laurel. "Doing the Biz: Book-Trade and News-Trade Periodicals in the 1890s." *Media History* 4.1 (1998): 29–47 <http://www.tandfonline.com/doi/abs/10.1080/13688809809357934?journalCode=cmeh20#.UZqDe5VNzG4>, accessed 20 May 2013.

Brake, Laurel; Jones, Aled; and Madden, Lionel, eds. *Investigating Victorian Journalism*. New York: St. Martin's Press, 1990.

Brandth, Berit and Haugen, Marit S. "From Lumberjack to Business Manager: Masculinity in the Norwegian Forestry Press." *Journal of Rural Studies* 16.3 (2000): 343–355.

Bräuchler, Birgit and Postill, John. eds. *Theorising Media and Practice*. Anthropology of Media. Vol. 4. New York: Berghahn Books, 2010.

Breazeale, Kenon. "In Spite of Women: *Esquire* Magazine and the Construction of the Male Consumer." *Signs: Journal of Women in Culture and Society* 20.1 (Autumn 1994): 1–22.

Breen, Gerald-Mark and Matusitz, Jonathan. "Communicating the Negative Aspects of Pack Journalism to Media Reporters." *Global Media Journal* 7.12 (Spring 2008): 1–7.

Brennen, Bonnie S. "From Headline Shooter to Picture Snatcher: The Construction of Photojournalists in American Film, 1928–39." *Journalism* 5.4 (November 2004): 423–439.

Brennen, Bonnie S. and Hardt, Hanno, eds. *Picturing the Past: Media, History, and Photography*. Urbana: University of Illinois Press, 1999.

Bridges, Bill. "Teach Editing—If You Can." *Thinking Classroom*, July 2006, 45–46.

Briggs, Jean E. and Fleming, Charles A. "A Survey of Master's Programs Documents Diversity." *Journalism Educator* 49.2 (Summer 1994): 12–17.

Briggs, Mark. *Journalism Next: A Practical Guide to Digital Reporting and Publishing*. 2nd ed. Los Angeles: CQ Press, 2013.

Brinkley, Alan. *The Publisher: Henry Luce and His American Century*. New York: Alfred A. Knopf, 2010.

Briñol, Pablo and Petty, Richard E. "Source Factors in Persuasion: A Self-Validation Approach." *European Review of Social Psychology* 20 (2009): 49–96.

Britten, Bob. "Losing Control: Using Social Media to Engage and Connect." *Journal of Magazine & New Media Research* 14.2 (Fall 2013): 1–3.

Bromley, Michael and Purdey, Heather. "Journo-Morphosis: Today's New Media and the Education and Training of Tomorrow's 'Cool' Journalists." *Convergence, the International Journal of Research into New Media Technologies* 4.4 (December 1998): 77–93.

Brooks, Brian S. and Pinson, James L. *The Art of Editing in the Age of Convergence*. 9th ed. Boston: Pearson, 2009.

Brooks, Peter. "Outcomes, Testing, Learning: What's at Stake?" *Social Research* 79.3 (Fall 2012): 601–611.

Brooten, Lisa. "The Feminization of Democracy under Siege: The Media, 'The Lady' of Burma, and U.S. Foreign Policy." *NWSA Journal* [*National Women's Studies Association Journal*] 17.3 (Fall 2005): 134–156.

Brouwer, Daniel C. "Counterpublicity and Corporeality in HIV/AIDS Zines." *Critical Studies in Media Communication* 22.5 (December 2005): 351–371.

Brown, Helen Gurley. *I'm Wild Again: Snippets from My Life and a Few Brazen Thoughts.* New York: St. Martin's Press, 2000.

Brown, Micheal. "The Popular Art of American Magazine Illustration 1885–1917." *Journalism History* 24.3 (Autumn 1998): 94–103. Editor's Note: Article carries name spelled as Micheal; correct spelling is Michael.

Brown, Millward. "Do Men and Women Respond Differently to Ads?" *WPP* <http://www.wpp.com/wpp/marketing/advertising/do-men-and-women-respond-differently-to-ads/#>, accessed 6 September 2013.

Brown, Phil; Zavestoski, Stephen M.; McCormick, Sabrina; Mandelbaum, Joshua; and Luebke, Theo. "Print Media Coverage of Environmental Causation of Breast Cancer." *Sociology of Health & Illness* 23.6 (2001): 747–775.

Brown, Tina and Shetty, Baba. "A Turn of the Page for *Newsweek.*" *Daily Beast,* 18 October 2012 <http://www.thedailybeast.com/articles/2012/10/18/a-turn-of-the-page-for-newsweek.html>, accessed 5 September 2013.

Brown, William J. and Basil, Michael D. "Media Celebrities and Public Health: Responses to 'Magic' Johnson's HIV Disclosure and Its Impact on AIDS Risk and High-Risk Behaviors." *Health Communication* 7.4 (1995): 345–370.

Brown, William J.; Basil, Michael D.; and Bocarnea, Mihai C. "The Influence of Famous Athletes on Health Beliefs and Practices: Mark McGwire, Child Abuse Prevention, and Androstenedione." *Journal of Health Communication* 8.1 (2003): 41–57.

Brown, William J.; Basil, Michael D.; and Bocarnea, Mihai C. "Social Influence of an International Celebrity: Responses to the Death of Princess Diana." *Journal of Communication* 53.4 (December 2003): 587–605.

Brownson, Ross C.; Hartge, Patricia; Samet, Jonathan M.; and Ness, Roberta B. "From Epidemiology to Policy: Toward More Effective Practice." *Annals of Epidemiology* 20.6 (June 2010): 409–411.

Bruccoli, Matthew J. and Baughman, Judith S., eds. *The Sons of Maxwell Perkins: Letters of F. Scott Fitzgerald, Ernest Hemingway, Thomas Wolfe, and Their Editor.* Columbia: University of South Carolina Press, 2004.

Brunn, Stanley D. and Raitz, Karl B. "Regional Patterns of Farm Magazine Publication." *Economic Geography* 54.4 (October 1978): 277–290 <http://www.jstor.org/discover/10.2307/143279?uid=3739560&uid=2129&uid=2&uid=70&uid=4&uid=3739256&sid=21102309397127>, accessed 20 May 2013.

Brunner, Brigitta R. and Brunner Huber, Larissa R. "101 Ways to Improve Health Reporting: A Comparison of the Types and Quality of Health Information in Men's and Women's Magazines." *Public Relations Review* 36.1 (March 2010): 84–86.

Bruns, Axel. *Gatewatching: Collaborative Online News Production.* New York: Peter Lang, 2005.

Bryant, Jennings and Miron, Dorina. "Theory and Research in Mass Communication." *Journal of Communication* 54.4 (December 2004): 662–704.

Bryant, Mark, co-founder and editor-in-chief of Byliner. Interview by author. 26 February 2013.

Brynjolfsson, Erik and McAfee, Andrew. *The Second Machine Age: Work, Progress, and Prosperity in a Time of Brilliant Technologies.* New York: W.W. Norton, 2014.

Buckley, Craig. "From Absolute to Everything: Taking Possession in 'Alles Ist Architektur.'" *Grey Room* 28 (Summer 2007): 109–122.

Buckley, William F., Jr. *Miles Gone By: A Literary Autobiography.* Washington, DC: Regnery Publishing, Inc., 2004.

Buckley, William F., Jr. *Nearer, My God: An Autobiography of Faith.* New York: Doubleday, 1997.

Buckman, Robert T. "How Eight Weekly Newsmagazines Covered Elections in Six Countries." *Journalism Quarterly* 70.4 (Winter 1993): 780–792.

Bugeja, Michael. "Magazine." *World Book Encyclopedia.* Chicago: World Book, 2008, 42–45.

Bulla, David. "Media Convergence: Industry Practices and Implications for Education." Paper presented at the Annual Meeting, Association for Education in Journalism and Mass Communication, August 2002.

Burgin, Victor. "Paranoiac Space." In Taylor, Lucien, ed. *Visualizing Theory: Selected Essays from V.A.R., 1990–1994.* New York and London: Routledge, 1994, 230–241.

Burgin, Victor, ed. *Thinking Photography.* London: Macmillan, 1982.

Burnham, Linda Frye and Durland, Steven. *The Citizen Artist: 20 Years of Art in the Public Arena: An Anthology from High Performance Magazine 1978–1998*. Gardiner, NY: Critical Press, 1998.

Burr, Nelson R. *A Critical Bibliography of Religion in America*. Religion in American Life. Edited by James Ward Smith and A. Leland Jamison. Vol. 4. Princeton, NJ: Princeton University Press, 1961.

Burrelle's/Luce Media Directory. Livingston, NJ: Information Services, 2003.

Burriss, Larry L. and McComb, Don. "Use of Color in Three News Magazines to Identify Political Parties." *Journal of Visual Literacy* 21.2 (Autumn 2001): 167–176.

Burroughs, Henry D. *Close-Ups of History: Three Decades through the Lens of an AP Photographer*. Edited with Introduction by Margaret Wohlgemuth Burroughs. Columbia: University of Missouri Press, 2007.

Busby, Linda J. and Leichty, Greg. "Feminism and Advertising in Traditional and Nontraditional Women's Magazines 1950s–1980s." *Journalism Quarterly* 70.2 (Summer 1993): 247–264.

Buse, Peter. "Polaroid, *Aperture* and Ansel Adams: Rethinking the Industry-Aesthetics Divide." *History of Photography* 33.4 (November 2009): 354–369.

Buse, Peter. "The Polaroid Image as Photo-Object." *Journal of Visual Culture* 9.2 (August 2009): 189–207.

"Business Information Network." ABM—The Association of Business Information & Media Companies <http://www.abmassociation.com/abm/Business_Information_Network.asp>, accessed 14 January 2014.

Caddy, Adrian. "Be the Brand." *Fast Company*, 19 December 2007 <http://www.fastcompany.com/73124/be-brand>, accessed 12 December 2012.

Cafri, Guy and Thompson, J. Kevin. "Measuring Male Body Image: A Review of the Current Methodology." *Psychology of Men & Masculinity* 5.1 (2004): 18–29.

Cairo, Alberto. *The Functional Art: An Introduction to Information Graphics and Visualization*. Berkeley, CA: New Riders, 2013.

Calvi, Pablo. "Latin America's Own 'New Journalism.'" *Literary Journalism Studies* 2.2 (Fall 2010): 63–83.

Campbell, David. "The Iconography of Famine." In Batchen, Geoffrey; Gidley, Mick; Miller, Nancy K.; and Prosser, Jay, eds. *Picturing Atrocity: Photography in Crisis*. London: Reaktion Books, 2012, 79–91.

Campbell, Richard; Martin, Christopher R.; and Fabos, Bettina. "Magazines." *Media and Culture: Mass Communication in a Digital Age*. 9th ed. Boston: Bedford/St. Martin's, 2014, 312–343.

Cane, Aleta Feinsod and Alves, Susan, eds. *"The Only Efficient Instrument": American Women Writers and the Periodical, 1837–1916*. Iowa City: University of Iowa Press, 2001.

Canning, Peter. *American Dreamers: The Wallaces and Reader's Digest: An Insider's Story*. New York: Simon & Schuster, 1996.

Cantor, Geoffrey; Shuttleworth, Sally; and Topham, Jonathan R. "Representations of Science in the Nineteenth Century Periodical Press." *Interdisciplinary Science Reviews* 28.3 (September 2003): 161–168.

Card, Stuart K.; Mackinlay, Jock D.; and Shneiderman, Ben, eds. *Readings in Information Visualization: Using Vision to Think*. San Diego: Academic Press, 1999.

Cardoso, Carla Rodrigues. "The Future of Newsmagazines." *Journalism Studies* 11.4 (August 2010): 577–586.

Carli, Don. "Is Digital Media Worse for the Environment Than Print?" *MediaShift*, 31 March 2010 <http://www.pbs.org/mediashift/2010/03>, accessed 3 December 2012.

Carlson, Peter. "Magazine Tease a Rare Art Form." *Sun Sentinel*, 12 November 1997 <http://articles.sun-sentinel.com/1997–11–12/lifestyle/9711110381_1_orgasm-national-magazine-award-outdoor-life>, accessed 22 February 2013.

Carpenter, Joel A. "*Moody Monthly*, 1900-." In Lora, Ronald and Longton, William Henry, eds. *The Conservative Press in Twentieth-Century America*. Westport, CT: Greenwood Press, 1999, 103–111.

Carpenter, Serena. "An Application of the Theory of Expertise: Teaching Broad and Skill Knowledge Areas to Prepare Journalists for Change." *Journalism & Mass Communication Educator* 64.3 (Autumn 2009): 287–304.

Carr, David. "Business Is a Beat Deflated." *New York Times*, 2 November 2009, B1.

Carr, David. "How *Esquire* Survived Publishing's Dark Days." *New York Times*, 22 January 2012 <http://www.nytimes.com/2012/01/23/business/media/how-esquire-survived-publishings-dark-days.html?pagewanted=all&_r=0>, accessed 28 April 2013.

Carr, David. "Maturing as Publisher and Platform." *New York Times*, 21 May 2012, B1(L).

Carr, David. "Print Starts to Settle into Its Niches." *New York Times*, 5 January 2014 <http://www.nytimes.com/2014/01/06/business/media/print-starts-to-settle-into-its-niches.html?ref=todayspaper>, accessed 6 January 2014.

Carter, Graydon. "Print Is Dying . . . Really?" *Brandweek*, 29 March 2010, 37.

Castañeda, Laura; Murphy, Sheila; and Hether, Heather Jane. "Teaching Print, Broadcast, and Online Journalism Concurrently: A Case Study Assessing a Convergence Curriculum." *Journalism & Mass Communication Educator* 60.1 (Spring 2005): 57–70.

Catton, William R., Jr., and Dunlap, Riley E. "Environmental Sociology: A New Paradigm." *American Sociologist* 13.1 (1978): 41–49.

Caudill, Susan; Caudill, Ed; and Singletary, Michael W. "'Journalist Wanted': Trade-Journal Ads as Indicators of Professional Values." *Journalism Quarterly* 64.2/3 (Summer/Autumn 1987): 576–580, 633 <http://www.eric.ed.gov/ERICWebPortal/search/detailmini.jsp?_nfpb=true&_&ERICExtSearch_SearchValue_0=EJ370125&ERICExtSearch_SearchType_0=no&accno=EJ370125>, accessed 12 May 2013.

Ceasar, Stephen. "Hispanic Population Tops 50 Million in U.S." *Los Angeles Times*, 24 March 2011 <http://articles.latimes.com/2011/mar/24/nation/la-na-census-hispanic-20110325>, accessed 8 July 2013.

Celebitchy. "*Star* Magazine Seems to Suggest that Rihanna Had It Coming." *Cele|bitchy*, 25 February 2009 <http://www.celebitchy.com/38419/star_magazine_seems_to_suggest_rihanna_had_it_coming/>, accessed 2 October 2013.

Challinor, Mark. "Lessons for Newsmedia Companies from Around the Mobile Industry." INMA— International News Media Association, 19 February 2012 <http://www.inma.org/blogs/mobile-tablets/post.cfm/lessons-for-newsmedia-companies-from-around-the-mobile-industry>, accessed 7 December 2013.

Chamblee, Robert and Sandler, Dennis M. "Business-to-Business Advertising: Which Layout Style Works Best?" *Journal of Advertising Research* 32.6 (November/December 1992): 39–46 <http://www.researchgate.net/publication/232600298_Business-to-business_advertising_Which_layout_style_works_best>, accessed 29 May 2014.

Chandler, Alfred D., Jr. *The Visible Hand: The Managerial Revolution in American Business*. Cambridge, MA: Belknap Press, 1977.

Chandler, Daniel. "An Introduction to Genre Theory." Aberystwyth University, 1997 <http://www.aber.ac.uk/media/Documents/intgenre/chandler_genre_theory.pdf>, accessed 12 April 2014.

Chang, Jui-Shan. "Refashioning Womanhood in 1990s Taiwan: An Analysis of the Taiwanese Edition of *Cosmopolitan* Magazine." *Modern China* 30.3 (July 2004): 361–397.

Chang, Tsan-Kuo and Tai, Zixue. "Mass Communication Research and the Invisible College Revisited: The Changing Landscape and Emerging Fronts in Journalism-Related Studies." *Journalism & Mass Communication Quarterly* 82.3 (Autumn 2005): 672–694.

Chan-Olmsted, Sylvia M. *Competitive Strategy for Media Firms: Strategic and Brand Management in Changing Media Markets*. Mahwah, NJ: Lawrence Erlbaum Associates, 2006.

Chapman, Jane. "From India's Big Dams to Jungle Guerillas: Arundhati Roy and the Literary Polemics of Global versus Local." In Keeble, Richard Lance and Tulloch, John, eds. *Global Literary Journalism: Exploring the Journalistic Imagination*. New York: Peter Lang, 2012, 317–331.

Chapman, Michael, ed. *The Drum Decade: Stories from the 1950s*. 2nd ed. Pietermaritzburg, South Africa: University of KwaZulu-Natal Press, 2001.

Charbonnier, Éric and Heckmann, Corinne. "Women's Outcomes in Education and Employment: Strong Gains, but More to Do." *OECD EducationToday* (blog), 27 March 2012 <http://oecdeducationtoday.blogspot.com/2012/03/womens-outcomes-in-education-and.html>, accessed 6 September 2013.

"Charlie Sheen: 'It's Not an Act.'" *People*, 2 March 2011 <http://www.people.com/people/article/0,,20470054,00.html>, accessed 9 October 2013.

Charrier, Philip. "On Diane Arbus: Establishing a Revisionist Framework of Analysis." *History of Photography* 36.4 (November 2012): 422–438.

Chen, Peiqin. "Magazines: An Industry in Transition." In Scotton, James F. and Hachten, William A., eds. *New Media for a New China*. Oxford, UK: Wiley-Blackwell, 2010, 61–73.

Chen, Peiqin. "Social Movements and Chinese Literary Reportage." In Bak, John S. and Reynolds, Bill, eds. *Literary Journalism across the Globe: Journalistic Traditions and Transnational Influences*. Amherst: University of Massachusetts Press, 2011, 148–161.

Chen, Shawn. E-mails to author. Senior associate editor, Ulrich's Serials, New Providence, NJ: Serials Solutions, 6 March 2006, 14 July 2011.

Chen, Yongmin and He, Chuan. "Paid Placement: Advertising and Search on the Internet." NET Institute Working Paper No. 06–02 (September 2006): 1–29 <http://dx.doi.org/10.2139/ssrn.936472>, accessed 24 November 2012.

Cheney, Theodore A. Rees. *Writing Creative Nonfiction: Fiction Techniques for Crafting Great Nonfiction.* Berkeley, CA: Ten Speed Press, 2001.

Cheng, Hong. "'Holding Up Half the Sky'?: A Socio-Cultural Comparison of Gender-Role Portrayals in Chinese and U.S. Advertising." *International Journal of Advertising* 16.4 (1997): 295–319.

Cheng, Hong and Frith, Katherine Toland. "Going Global: An Analysis of Global Women's Magazine Ads in China" [on-line]. *Media International Australia, Incorporating Culture & Policy* Issue119 (May 2006): 138–151 <http://search.informit.com.au/documentSummary;dn=009938041484775;res=IELLCC>, accessed 8 February 2013.

Chi, Chia-Wen and Baldwin, Cecelia. "Gender and Class Stereotypes: A Comparison of U.S. and Taiwanese Magazine Advertisements." In Segal, Marcia Texler and Martinez, Theresa A., eds. *Intersections of Gender, Race, and Class: Readings for a Changing Landscape.* Los Angeles: Roxbury Publishing, 2007, 251–264.

Chia, Stella C. "Third-Person Perceptions about Idealized Body Image and Weight-Loss Behavior." *Journalism & Mass Communication Quarterly* 84.4 (Winter 2007): 677–694.

Chia, Stella C. and Wen, Nainan. "College Men's Third-Person Perceptions about Idealized Body Image and Consequent Behavior." *Sex Roles* 63.7/8 (October 2010): 542–555.

Chiang, Yung-chen. "Womanhood, Motherhood and Biology: The Early Phases of the *Ladies' Journal*, 1915–25." *Gender & History* 18.3 (November 2006): 519–545.

Chielens, Edward E., ed. *American Literary Magazines: The Eighteenth and Nineteenth Centuries.* New York: Greenwood Press, 1986.

Chielens, Edward E., ed. *American Literary Magazines: The Twentieth Century.* Westport, CT: Greenwood Press, 1992.

Chin, Carol C. "Translating the New Woman: Chinese Feminists View the West, 1905–15." *Gender & History* 18.3 (November 2006): 490–518.

"*China Computerworld* Online." IDG International Data Group <http://careers.idg.com/www/IDGProducts.nsf/ByKey/People's-Republic-of-China_WebSite_China-Computerworld-Online>, accessed 29 May 2014.

Chinn, Carl. *The Cadbury Story: A Short History.* Studley, UK: Brewin Books, 1998.

Chittal, Nisha. "Are Long and Short Form Writing Mutually Exclusive?" *MediaWire.* Poynter.org, 16 December 2011 <http://www.poynter.org/latest-news/making-sense-of-news/156361/are-long-and-short-form-writing-mutually-exclusive/>, accessed 1 December 2013.

Chittum, Ryan. "Bloomberg Investigates a 'Double Irish' Corporate Tax Scheme." *The Audit* (blog). *Columbia Journalism Review*, 24 May 2010 <http://www.cjr.org/the_audit/bloomberg_investigates_a_doubl.php>, accessed 29 November 2013.

Cho, Hyunyi; Lee, Seungyoon; and Wilson, Kari. "Magazine Exposure, Tanned Women Stereotypes, and Tanning Attitudes." *Body Image* 7.4 (September 2010): 364–367.

Chow, Jean. "Adolescents' Perceptions of Popular Teen Magazines." *Journal of Advanced Nursing* 48.2 (October 2004): 132–139.

Christ, William G. and Broyles, Sheri J. "Graduate Education at AEJMC Schools: A Benchmark Study." *Journalism & Mass Communication Educator* 62.4 (Winter 2008): 376–401.

Christensen, Nina. "Lust for Reading and Thirst for Knowledge: Fictive Letters in a Danish Children's Magazine of 1770." *The Lion and the Unicorn* 33.2 (April 2009): 189–201.

Christian, Georgia. "How Does Progressive Profiling Work and What Are the Benefits?" *Advertising Age*, 21 April 2011 <http://www.btobonline.com/apps/pbcs.dll/article?AID=/20110421/EMAIL06/304219997/0/SEARCH>, accessed 12 May 2013.

Christidou, Vasilia; Dimopoulos, Kostas; and Koulaidis, Vasilis. "Constructing Social Representations of Science and Technology: The Role of Metaphors in the Press and the Popular Scientific Magazines." *Public Understanding of Science* 13.4 (October 2004): 347–362.

Chuang, Angie and Roemer, Robin Chin. "The Immigrant Muslim American at the Boundary of Insider and Outsider: Representations of Faisal Shahzad as 'Homegrown' Terrorist." *Journalism & Mass Communication Quarterly* 90.1 (Spring 2013): 89–107.

Churchill, Suzanne W. and McKible, Adam. "Introduction." In Churchill, Suzanne W. and McKible, Adam. eds. *Little Magazines and Modernism: New Approaches.* Burlington, VT: Ashgate, 2007, 3–18.

Churchill, Suzanne W. and McKible, Adam. "Little Magazines and Modernism: An Introduction." *American Periodicals* 15.1 (2005): 1–5.

Churchill, Suzanne W. and McKible, Adam, eds. *Little Magazines and Modernism: New Approaches.* Burlington, VT: Ashgate, 2007.

Clair, Colin. *A History of European Printing*. London and New York: Academic Press, 1976.

Clampitt, Phillip G.; Crevcoure, Jean M.; and Hartel, Robin L. "Exploratory Research on Employee Publications." *Journal of Business Communication* 23.3 (Summer 1986): 5–17.

Clark, Daniel A. *Creating the College Man: American Mass Magazines and Middle-Class Manhood, 1890–1915*. Madison: University of Wisconsin Press, 2010.

Clark, Gary L.; Kaminski, Peter F.; and Brown, Gene. "The Readability of Advertisements and Articles in Trade Journals." *Industrial Marketing Management* 19.3 (August 1990): 251–260.

Clark, Jocalyn P. "Babes and Boobs? Analysis of JAMA Cover Art." *BMJ: British Medical Journal* 319.7225 (18–25 December 1999): 1603–1604.

Clark, Roy Peter. *How to Write Short: Word Craft for Fast Times*. New York: Little, Brown, 2013.

Clarke, Juanne N. "The Case of the Missing Person: Alzheimer's Disease in Mass Print Magazines 1991–2001." *Health Communication* 19.3 (2006): 269–276.

Clarke, Juanne N. "Childhood Depression and Mass Print Magazines in the USA and Canada: 1983–2008." *Child and Family Social Work* 16.1 (February 2011): 52–60.

Clarke, Juanne N. "The Paradoxical Portrayal of the Risk of Sexually Transmitted Infections and Sexuality in U.S. Magazines *Glamour* and *Cosmopolitan* 2000–2007." *Health, Risk & Society* 12.6 (December 2010): 560–574.

Clarke, Juanne N. "Portrayal of Childhood Cancer in English Language Magazines in North America: 1970–2001." *Journal of Health Communication* 10.7 (October/November 2005): 593–607.

Clarke, Juanne N. "The Portrayal of Depression in the Three Most Popular English-Language Black-American Magazines in the U.S.A.: *Ebony*, *Essence*, and *Jet*." *Ethnicity & Health* 15.5 (October 2010): 459–473.

Clarke, Juanne N. "Women's Work, Worry and Fear: The Portrayal of Sexuality and Sexual Health in U.S. Magazines for Teenage and Middle-Aged Women, 2000–2007." *Culture, Health & Sexuality* 11.4 (May 2009): 415–429.

Clarke, Juanne N. and Binns, Jeannine. "The Portrayal of Heart Disease in Mass Print Magazines, 1991–2001." *Health Communication* 19.1 (2006): 39–48.

Clarke, Juanne N. and Gawley, Adele. "The Triumph of Pharmaceuticals: The Portrayal of Depression from 1980 to 2005." *Administration & Policy in Mental Health & Mental Health Services Research* 36.2 (March 2009): 91–101.

Clarke, Juanne N.; McLellan, Lianne; and Hoffman-Goetz, Laurie. "The Portrayal of HIV/AIDS in Two Popular African American Magazines." *Journal of Health Communication* 11.5 (July/August 2006): 495–507.

Clarke, Juanne N.; Romagnoli, Amy; Sargent, Cristal; and van Amerom, Gudrun. "The Portrayal of Complementary and Alternative Medicine in Mass Print Magazines since 1980." *Journal of Alternative and Complementary Medicine* 16.1 (January 2010): 125–130.

Clarke, Juanne N.; van Amerom, Gudrun; and Binns, Jeannine. "Gender and Heart Disease in Mass Print Media: 1991, 1996, 2001." *Women & Health* 45.1 (2007): 17–35.

Claussen, Dane S. "*Broadcasting & Cable Magazine*: Serving Readers and/or Advertisers?" In Carter, Ginger R., ed. *Proceedings of the Southeast Colloquium*. Milledgeville, GA: George College and State University, 1998.

Claussen, Dane S. "Review of *The Layers of Magazine Editing* by Michael Robert Evans." *Journalism & Mass Communication Quarterly* 82.1 (Spring 2005): 221–222.

Claussen, Dane S. "'They're in for a Rude Awakening.'" *Journalism & Mass Communication Educator* 63.2 (Summer 2008): 103–106.

Clawson, Rosalee A. and Trice, Rakuya. "Poverty as We Know It: Media Portrayals of the Poor." *Public Opinion Quarterly* 64.1 (Spring 2000): 53–64.

Clay, Daniel; Vignoles, Vivian L.; and Dittmar, Helga. "Body Image and Self-Esteem among Adolescent Girls: Testing the Influence of Sociocultural Factors." *Journal of Research on Adolescence* 15.4 (2005): 451–477.

Clayman, Steven E. and Reisner, Ann. "Gatekeeping in Action: Editorial Conferences and Assessments of Newsworthiness." *American Sociological Review* 63.2 (April 1998): 178–199.

Cleveland, Paul. "The Effect of Technology on the Development of Magazine Visual Design Style." Ph.D. diss., Queensland College of Art, Griffith University, 2004.

Cleveland, Paul. "How Much Visual Power Can a Magazine Take?" *Design Studies* 26.3 (May 2005): 271–317.

Cleveland, Paul. "Style Based Automated Graphic Layouts." *Design Studies* 31.1 (January 2009): 3–25.

Click, J. William and Baird, Russell N. *Magazine Editing and Production*. 1st to 6th eds. Dubuque, IA, Madison, WI: Wm C. Brown / WCB Brown & Benchmark, 1974–1994.

Clifford, Stephanie. "Magazine Cover Ads, Subtle and Less So." *New York Times*, 12 June 2009, B3.

Clifford, Stephanie. "Making It Look Easy at the *New Yorker*." *New York Times*, 5 April 2010, B1.

Clinton, Patrick. *Guide to Writing for the Business Press*. Lincolnwood, IL: NTC Business Books, 1997.

CNN Library. "O.J. Simpson Fast Facts." CNN.com, 13 August 2013 <http://www.cnn.com/2013/04/12/us/o-j-simpson-fast-facts/index.html>, accessed 9 October 2013.

Cobb, Jasmine Nichole. "No We Can't!: Postracialism and the Popular Appearance of a Rhetorical Fiction." *Communication Studies* 62.4 (September/October 2011): 406–421.

Cobley, Paul and Haeffner, Nick. "Digital Cameras and Domestic Photography: Communication, Agency and Structure." *Visual Communication* 8.2 (May 2009): 123–146.

Cody, Michael. *Charles Brockden Brown and the Literary Magazine: Cultural Journalism in the Early American Republic*. Jefferson, NC: McFarland & Co., 2004.

Coffman, Elesha. "The Measure of a Magazine: Assessing the Influence of the *Christian Century*." *Religion and American Culture: A Journal of Interpretation* 22.1 (Winter 2012): 53–82.

Cohane, Geoffrey H. and Pope, Harrison G., Jr. "Body Image in Boys: A Review of the Literature." *International Journal of Eating Disorders* 29.4 (2001): 373–379.

Cohen, Judy. "White Consumer Response to Asian Models in Advertising." *Journal of Consumer Marketing* 9.2 (Spring 1992): 17–27.

Cohen, Patricia Cline; Gilfoyle, Timothy J.; and Horowitz, Helen Lefkowitz. *The Flash Press: Sporting Male Weeklies in 1840s*. New York and Chicago: University of Chicago Press, 2008.

Cohen, Philip, ed. *Devils and Angels: Textual Editing and Literary Theory*. Charlottesville: University Press of Virginia, 1991.

Cohn, Steve, ed. *The Most Intriguing and Top-Selling Magazine Covers*. Rockville, MD: Access Intelligence LLC, 2010.

Cohoon, Lorinda B. *Serialized Citizenships: Periodicals, Books, and American Boys, 1840–1911*. Lanham, MD: Scarecrow Press, 2006.

Cole, Lori. "Magazine Modernism: Notes from the NEH Seminar." *Journal of Modern Periodical Studies* 2.1 (2011): 116–119 <http://muse.jhu.edu/journals/jmp/summary/v002/2.1.cole.html>, accessed 30 September 2012.

Coleman, Renita and Colbert, Jan. "Grounding the Teaching of Design in Creativity." *Journalism & Mass Communication Educator* 56.2 (Summer 2001): 4–24.

Collins, Dana. "'No Experts—Guaranteed!': Do-It-Yourself Sex Radicalism and the Production of the Lesbian Sex Zine *Brat Attack*." *Signs: Journal of Women in Culture & Society* 25.1 (Autumn 1999): 65–89.

Collins, Jim. "Making It as a Freelancer." In Kramer, Mark and Call, Wendy, eds. *Telling True Stories: A Nonfiction Writers' Guide from the Nieman Foundation at Harvard University*. New York: Plume, 2007, 264–268.

Collins, Max Allan and Hagenauer, George. *Men's Adventure Magazines in Postwar America: The Rich Oberg Collection*. Koln and Los Angeles: Taschen, 2004.

Commission of the European Communities (CEC). Proposal for a Directive of the European Parliament and the Council on Waste Electrical and Electronic Equipment and on Restriction of the Use of Certain Hazardous Substances in Electrical and Electronic Equipment. Brussels, 13 June 2000.

Compaine, Benjamin M. *Consumer Magazines at the Crossroads: A Study of General and Special Interest Magazines*. White Plains, NY: Knowledge Industry Publications, 1974.

Compaine, Benjamin M. "How Special Interest and General Interest Magazines Differ." *The Business of Consumer Magazines*. White Plains, NY: Knowledge Industry Publications, 1982, 89–104.

Compaine, Benjamin M. "The Magazine Industry: Developing the Special Interest Audience." *Journal of Communication* 30.2 (June 1980): 98–103.

"Condé Nast Heritage." *Condé Nast* <http://www.condenast.com/about-us/heritage>, accessed 12 March 2014.

Condit, Celeste M.; Ofulue, Nneka; and Sheedy, Kristine M. "Determinism and Mass Media Portrayals of Genetics." *American Journal of Human Genetics* 62.4 (April 1998): 979–984.

"Conference Paper Abstracts." AEJMC—Association for Education in Journalism and Mass Communication <http://www.aejmc.org/home/scholarship/abstracts-archive/>, accessed 14 January 2014.

Congleton, W. Russell. "*Sword of the Lord*." In Fackler, P. Mark and Lippy, Charles H., eds. *Popular Religious Magazines of the United States*. Westport, CT: Greenwood Press, 1995, 457–462.

Connery, Thomas B. *Journalism and Realism: Rendering American Life*. Evanston, IL: Northwestern University Press, 2011.

Connery, Thomas B. "Research Review: Magazines and Literary Journalism, an Embarrassment of Riches." *Electronic Journal of Communication/La Revue Electronique de Communication* 4 (December 1994): 1–12.

Connery, Thomas B. "Research Review: Magazines and Literary Journalism, an Embarrassment of Riches." In Abrahamson, David, ed. *The American Magazine: Research Perspectives and Prospects*. Ames: Iowa State University Press, 1995, 207–216.

Connery, Thomas B., ed. *A Sourcebook of American Literary Journalism: Representative Writers in an Emerging Genre*. New York: Greenwood Press, 1992.

Connolly, John and Prothero, Andrea. "Green Consumption: Life-Politics, Risk and Contradictions." *Journal of Consumer Culture* 8.1 (March 2008): 117–145.

Cookman, Claude. "A Computer-Based Graphics Course and Students' Cognitive Skills." *Journalism & Mass Communication Educator* 53.3 (Autumn 1998): 37–49.

Cookman, Claude. "Gilles Caron and the May 1968 Rebellion in Paris." *History of Photography* 31.3 (Autumn 2007): 239–259.

Cookman, Claude. "Gilles Caron's Coverage of the Crisis in Biafra." *Visual Communication Quarterly* 15.4 (2008): 226–242.

Cookman, Claude. "Janine Niépce's Coverage of French Women's Lives and Struggle for Equal Rights." *Visual Communication Quarterly* 13.4 (2006): 202–223.

Cookman, Claude. "*Life* Visits 'Middletown': Trying to Repair America's Social Contract with Margaret Bourke-White's Photographs." *Visual Communication Quarterly* 18.4 (October/December 2011): 204–222.

Cooper, Roger; Potter, W. James; and Dupagne, Michel. "A Status Report on Methods Used in Mass Communication Research." *Journalism Educator* 48.4 (Winter 1994): 54–61.

Coover, Gail E. "Television and Social Identity: Race Representation as 'White' Accommodation." *Journal of Broadcasting & Electronic Media* 45.3 (Summer 2001): 413–431.

Corbett, Julia B. and Durfee, Jessica L. "Testing Public (Un)certainty of Science: Media Representations of Global Warming." *Science Communication* 26.2 (December 2004): 129–151.

Corn, Deborah. "A Troubling Sign for Tablet Magazines?" *Dead Tree Edition* (blog), 29 May 2013 <http://deadtreeedition.blogspot.com/2013/05/a-troubling-sign-for-tablet-magazines.html>, accessed 15 June 2013.

Corn, Wanda M. "Coming of Age: Historical Scholarship in American Art." *Art Bulletin*, June 1988, 188–207.

Cosgrove-Mather, Bootie and Watercutter, Angela. "Reduced Charges for Winona Ryder." *CBS News*, 18 June 2004 <http://www.cbsnews.com/news/reduced-charges-for-winona-ryder/>, accessed 7 April 2014.

Coté, Joseph A. "Clarence Hamilton Poe: The Farmer's Voice, 1899–1964." *Agricultural History* 53.1 (January 1979): 30–41 <http://www.jstor.org/discover/10.2307/3742857?uid=3739560&uid=2&uid=4&uid=3739256&sid=21102309582837>, accessed 20 May 2013.

Cottle, Simon. *Ethnic Minorities and the Media: Changing Cultural Boundaries*. Philadelphia: Open University Press, 2000.

Cottrell, Camille. "The Mainstreaming of Modern Art in America." Ph.D. diss., University of Georgia, 2002.

Coughlan, Sean. "Young People 'Prefer to Read on Screen.'" BBC, 16 May 2013 <http://www.bbc.co.uk/news/education-22540408>, accessed 7 December 2013.

Couldry, Nick and Markham, Tim. "Celebrity Culture and Public Connection: Bridge or Chasm?" *International Journal of Cultural Studies* 10.4 (December 2007): 403–421.

Couturier, Lynn E. "Considering the *Sportswoman*, 1924 to 1936: A Content Analysis." *Sport History Review* 41.2 (November 2010): 111–131.

Covert, Juanita J. and Dixon, Travis L. "A Changing View: Representation and Effects of the Portrayal of Women of Color in Mainstream Women's Magazines." *Communication Research* 35.2 (April 2008): 232–256.

Covert, Tawnya Adkins and Wasburn, Philo C. "Information Sources and the Coverage of Social Issues in Partisan Publications: A Content Analysis of 25 Years of the *Progressive* and the *National Review*." *Mass Communication and Society* 10.1 (December 2007): 67–94.

Coward, John M. "Making Images on the Indian Frontier." *Journalism History* 36.3 (Fall 2010): 150–159.

Coward, John M. "Making Sense of Savagery: Native American Cartoons in the *Daily Graphic*." *Visual Communication Quarterly* 19.4 (December 2012): 200–215.

Coward, John M. "Promoting the Progressive Indian: Lee Harkins and the *American Indian Magazine*." *American Journalism* 14.1 (1997): 3–18.

Cox, Howard. "Shaping a Corporate Identity from Below: The Role of the *BAT Bulletin*." *Management & Organizational History* 3.3/4 (August/November 2008): 197–215.

Coyle, Diane. *The Weightless World: Strategies for Managing the Digital Economy*. Cambridge, MA: MIT Press, 1998.

Craig, Robert. "Ideological Aspects of Publication Design." *Design Issues* 6.2 (Spring 1990): 18–27.

Craig, Steve, ed. *Men, Masculinity, and the Media*. Research on Men and Masculinities Series. Edited by Michael S. Kimmel. Vol. 1. Newbury, CA: Sage Publications, 1992.

Cramer, Clayton E. "Ethical Problems of Mass Murder Coverage in the Mass Media." *Journal of Mass Media Ethics* 9.1 (1994): 26–42.

Cramer, Janet M. "White Womanhood and Religion: Colonial Discourse in the U.S. Women's Missionary Press, 1869–1904." *Howard Journal of Communications* 14.4 (2003): 209–224.

Crane, Diana. "Gender and Hegemony in Fashion Magazines: Women's Interpretations of Fashion Photographs." *Sociological Quarterly* 40.4 (August 1999): 541–563.

Crawforth, Hannah. "Surrealism and the Fashion Magazine." *American Periodicals* 14.2 (2004): 212–246.

Crawshaw, Paul. "Governing the Healthy Male Citizen: Men, Masculinity and Popular Health in *Men's Health* Magazine." *Social Science & Medicine* 65.8 (October 2007): 1606–1618.

Crist, Eileen. "Limits-to-Growth and the Biodiversity Crisis." *Wild Earth*, Spring 2003, 62–65.

Cronin, Mary M. "Trade Press Roles in Promoting Journalistic Professionalism, 1884–1917." *Journal of Mass Media Ethics* 8.4 (Winter 1993): 227–238.

Cronin, Mary M. and Huntzicker, William E. "Popular Chinese Images and 'the Coming Man' of 1870: Racial Representations of Chinese." *Journalism History* 38.2 (Summer 2012): 86–99.

Crouse-Dick, Christine E. "Reframing the Domestic Angel: *Real Simple* Magazine's Repackaging of the Victorian-Era 'Angel in the House' Narrative." *Communication Studies* 63.4 (September/October 2012): 441–456.

Crouteau, David and Hoynes, William. *Media/Society: Industries, Images, and Audiences*. 2nd ed. Thousand Oaks, London and New Delhi: Pine Forge Press, 2000.

Crowley, David. *Magazine Covers*. London: Mitchell Beazley, 2003.

Crymble, Sarah B. "Contradiction Sells: Feminine Complexity and Gender Identity Dissonance in Magazine Advertising." *Journal of Communication Inquiry* 36.1 (January 2012): 62–84.

Cuillier, David and Schwalbe, Carol B. "GIFTed Teaching: A Content Analysis of 253 Great Ideas for Teaching Awards in Journalism and Mass Communication Education." *Journalism & Mass Communication Educator* 65.1 (Spring 2010): 22–39.

Cultural Dictionary. Dictionary.com, LLC. *American Heritage New Dictionary of Cultural Literacy*. 3rd ed. New York: Houghton Mifflin, 2005 <http://dictionary.reference.com/browse/The+business+of+America+is+business>, accessed 26 March 2014.

Currie, Dawn H. *Girl Talk: Adolescent Magazines and Their Readers*. Toronto: University of Toronto Press, 1999.

Cutler, Bob D.; Javalgi, Rajshekhar G.; and Erramilli, M. Krishna. "The Visual Components of Print Advertising: A Five-Country Cross-Cultural Analysis." *European Journal of Marketing* 26.4 (1992): 7–20.

Cutter, John A. "Specialty Magazines and the Older Reader." [Theme Issue: Images of Aging in Media and Marketing]. *Generations* 25.3 (Fall 2001): 13–15.

Czepiec, Helena and Kelly, J. Steven. "Analyzing Hispanic Roles in Advertising: A Portrait of an Emerging Subculture." *Current Issues & Research in Advertising* 6.1 (1983): 219–240.

Czitrom, Daniel J. *Media and the American Mind: From Morse to McLuhan*. Chapel Hill: University of North Carolina Press, 1982.

Daglas, Cristina. "Point of View: Examining the Magazine Industry Standard." Master's thesis, University of Missouri-Columbia, May 2009.

Dahlstrom, Michael F. and Ho, Shirley S. "Ethical Considerations of Using Narrative to Communicate Science." *Science Communication* 34.5 (October 2012): 592–617.

Dale, Carolyn and Pilgrim, Tim. *Fearless Editing: Crafting Words and Images for Print, Web, and Public Relations*. Boston: Pearson Education, 2005.

Dallmann, Katharina M. "Targeting Women in German and Japanese Magazine Advertising: A Difference-in-Differences Approach." *European Journal of Marketing* 35.11/12 (2001): 1320–1339.

Daly, Charles P.; Henry, Patrick; and Ryder, Ellen. *The Magazine Publishing Industry*. Boston, MA: Allyn and Bacon, 1997.

Daly, Charles P.; Henry, Patrick; and Ryder, Ellen. "Overview of Magazine Publishing." *The Magazine Publishing Industry*. Boston: Allyn and Bacon, 1997, 1–20.

D'Amico, Theodore F. "Magazines' Secret Weapon: Media Selection on the Basis of Behavior As Opposed to Demography." *Journal of Advertising Research* 39.6 (November/December 1999): 53–60.

Damon-Moore, Helen. *Magazines for the Millions: Gender and Commerce in the* Ladies' Home Journal *and the* Saturday Evening Post, *1880–1910*. Albany: State University of New York Press, 1994.

Daniel, Robert and Hagey, Keach. "Turning a Page: *Newsweek* Ends Print Run." *Wall Street Journal*, 26 December 2012, B.3.

Daniels, Elizabeth A. "The Indivisibility of Women Athletes in Magazines for Teen Girls." *Women in Sport & Physical Activity Journal* 18.2 (Fall 2009): 14–24.

Danky, James P. and Wiegand, Wayne A., eds. *Print Culture in a Diverse America*. Urbana: University of Illinois Press, 1998.

Dannefer, W. Dale and Poushinsky, Nicholas. "The C.B. Phenomenon, a Sociological Appraisal." *Journal of Popular Culture* 12.4 (Spring 1979): 611–619.

Danto, Arthur. "The Artworld." In Madoff, Steven Henry, ed. *Pop Art: A Critical History*. Berkeley: University of California Press, 1997, 269–278.

D'Aprix, Roger. "Communicators in Contemporary Organizations." In Reuss, Carol and Silvis, Donn, eds. *Inside Organizational Communication*. 2nd ed. London and New York: Longman, 1985, 15–29.

Darling-Wolf, Fabienne. *Imagining the Global: Transnational Media and Popular Culture Beyond East and West*. Ann Arbor: University of Michigan Press, forthcoming.

Darling-Wolf, Fabienne. "The Men and Women of *non-no*: Gender, Race, and Hybridity in Two Japanese Magazines." *Critical Studies in Media Communication* 23.3 (August 2006): 181–199.

Darling-Wolf, Fabienne and Mendelson, Andrew L. "Seeing Themselves through the Lens of the Other: An Analysis of the Cross-Cultural Production and Negotiation of *National Geographic*'s 'The Samurai Way' Story." *Journalism & Communication Monographs* 10.3 (Autumn 2008): 285–322.

Darnton, Robert. "What Is the History of Books?" In *The Kiss of Lamourette: Reflections in Cultural History*. New York: W. W. Norton & Co., 1990, 107–135.

Dates, Jannette L. and Barlow, William, eds. *Split Image: African Americans in the Mass Media*. 2nd ed. Washington, DC: Howard University Press, 1993.

David, Prabu. "Accuracy of Visual Perception of Quantitative Graphics: An Exploratory Study." *Journalism Quarterly* 69.2 (Summer 1992): 273–292.

Davidson, Laura; McNeill, Lisa; and Ferguson, Shelagh. "Magazine Communities: Brand Community Formation in Magazine Consumption." *International Journal of Sociology and Social Policy* 27.5/6 (2007): 208–220.

Davidson, Roei. "The Emergence of Popular Personal Finance Magazines and the Risk Shift in American Society." *Media, Culture & Society* 34.1 (January 2012): 3–20.

Davis, Anthony. "The Magazine World." *Magazine Journalism Today*. Oxford, UK: Heinemann Professional Publishing, 1988, 3–14.

Davis, Renette. "RDA Serials Cataloging: Changes from AACR2 to RDA." Library of Congress, PowerPoint. 22 September 2010 <http://www.loc/gov/catdir/cpso/RDAtest/RDAtest/rdatest.html>, accessed 16 April 2014.

Deal, Terrence E. and Kennedy, Allan A. *The New Corporate Cultures: Revitalizing the Workplace after Downsizing, Mergers, and Reengineering*. New York: Perseus Books, 1999.

de Almeida, Cristina. "The Rhetorical Genre in Graphic Design: Its Relationship to Design Authorship and Implications to Design Education." *Journal of Visual Literacy* 28.2 (Autumn 2009): 186–198.

de Burgh, Hugo. "Skills Are Not Enough: The Case for Journalism as an Academic Discipline." *Journalism* 4.1 (February 2003): 95–112.

De Decker, Kris. "The Monster Footprint of Digital Technology." Grosjean, Vincent, ed. *Low Tech Magazine*, 16 June 2009 <http://www.lowtechmagazine.com/2009/06/embodied-energy-of-digital-technology.html>, accessed 5 November 2012.Deeken, Aimee. "Service Upgrades." *Mediaweek*, 2 December 2002, 45–46f.

DeFleur, Melvin L. and Dennis, Everette E. "Magazines: Voices for Many Interests." *Understanding Mass Communication*. 6th ed. Boston: Houghton Mifflin, 1998, 97–126.

Delahaye, Agnès; Booth, Charles; Clark, Peter; Procter, Stephen; and Rowlinson, Michael. "The Genre of Corporate History." *Journal of Organizational Change Management* 22.1 (2009): 27–48.

de los Ríos, María Enriqueta Cortés. "Cognitive Devices to Communicate the Economic Crisis: An Analysis through Covers in the *Economist*." *Ibérica* 20 (Fall 2010): 81–106.

Dennis, Everette E.; Martin, Justin D.; and Wood, Robb. *Media Use in the Middle East: An Eight-Nation Survey*. Doha: Northwestern University in Qatar, 2013.

Dennis, Everette E.; Meyer, Philip; Sundar, S. Shyam; Pryor, Larry; Rogers, Everett M.; Chen, Helen L.; and Pavlik, John. "Learning Reconsidered: Education in the Digital Age—Communications, Convergence and the Curriculum." *Journalism & Mass Communication Educator* 57.4 (Winter 2003): 292–317.

Deslauriers, Marguerite. *Aristotle on Definition*. Leiden, The Netherlands: Brill, 2007.

Detweiler, Frederick G. *The Negro Press in the United States*. Chicago: University of Chicago Press, 1922.

Deveau, Vicki and Fouts, Gregory. "Revenge in U.S. and Canadian News Magazines Post 9/11." *Canadian Journal of Communication* 30.1 (2005): 99–109.

"Devil Wears Prada, The." Box Office Mojo <http://www.boxofficemojo.com/movies/?id=devilwearsprada.htm>, accessed 1 August 2013.

Devitt, Amy J. "A Theory of Genre." *Writing Genres*. Carbondale: Southern Illinois University Press, 2004, 1–32.

Dewan, Janet. "The Mourner: 'Red Man's Memories.'" *History of Photography* 15.2 (Summer 1991): 135–139.

Diamond, Daniel S. "A Quantitative Approach to Magazine Advertisement Format Selection." *Journal of Marketing Research* 5.4 (November 1968): 376–386.

Dianoux, Christian and Linhart, Zdenek. "The Effectiveness of Female Nudity in Advertising in Three European Countries." *International Marketing Review* 27.5 (2010): 562–578.

Dickerson, Dennis C. and Reid, Robert H., Jr. "*Christian Recorder*." In Fackler, P. Mark and Lippy, Charles H., eds. *Popular Religious Magazines of the United States*. Westport, CT: Greenwood Press, 1995, 162–167.

Dickson, David. "Weaving a Social Web—The Internet Promises to Revolutionize Public Engagement with Science and Technology." *Nature* 414.6864 (6 December 2001): 587.

Dickson, Thomas V. and Brandon, Wanda. "The Gap between Educators and Professional Journalists." *Journalism & Mass Communication Educator* 55.3 (Autumn 2000): 50–67.

Dickson, Thomas V. and Sellmeyer, Ralph L. "Green Eyeshades vs. Chi Squares Revisited: Editors' and JMC Administrators' Perceptions of Major Issues in Journalism Education." Paper presented at the Annual Meeting, Association for Education in Journalism and Mass Communication, August 1992 <http://eric.ed.gov/?id=ED349564>, accessed 2 June 2014.

Dictionary.com. s.v. "Public Affairs" <http://dictionary.reference.com/browse/public+affairs>, accessed 27 December 2012.

Dines, Gail and Humez, Jean M., eds. *Gender, Race, and Class in Media: A Critical Reader*. 3rd ed. Thousand Oaks, CA: Sage, 2011.

"Directory." Evangelical Press Association <http://www.evangelicalpress.com/member-list>, accessed 29 November 2013.

"*DisciplesWorld* Magazine, Website to Cease Publishing; Non-Profit to Dissolve." *DisciplesWorld*, 16 December 2009 <http://www.disciplesworldmagazine.com/node/7486>, accessed 28 November 2013.

Dixit, Nandan. "A Case Study of Uses and Gratification that People Seek from a Special Interest Computer Magazine." Master's thesis, San Jose State University, 1987.

Dobias, Karen S.; Moyer, Cheryl A.; McAchran, Sarah E.; Katz, Steven J.; and Sonnad, Seema S. "Mammography Messages in Popular Media: Implications for Patient Expectations and Shared Clinical Decision-Making." *Health Expectations* 4.2 (June 2001): 131–139.

Dobkin, Bethami A. *Tales of Terror: Television News and the Construction of the Terrorist Threat*. New York: Praeger, 1992.

Dominick, Joseph R. "Magazines." *The Dynamics of Mass Communication: Media in Transition*. 11th ed. New York: McGraw-Hill, 2011, 108–129.

Donaton, Scott; Crumley, Bruce; and Serafin, Raymond. "Hachette Signs Ford in Global Media Deal." *Advertising Age*, 10 February 1992, 3, 41.

Donohew, Lewis. "Newspaper Gatekeepers and Forces in the News Channel." *Public Opinion Quarterly* 31.1 (Spring 1967): 61–68.

Doss, Erika. "Introduction: Looking at *Life*: Rethinking America's Favorite Magazine, 1936–1972." In Doss, Erika, ed., *Looking at Life Magazine*. Washington, DC: Smithsonian Institution Press, 2001, 1–21.

Doty, D. Harold and Glick, William H. "Typologies as a Unique Form of Theory Building: Toward Improved Understanding and Modeling." *Academy of Management Review* 19.2 (1994): 230–251.

Douglas, George H. *The Smart Magazines: 50 Years of Literary Revelry and High Jinks at* Vanity Fair, *the* New Yorker, Life, Esquire, *and the* Smart Set. Hamden, CT: Archon Books, 1991.

Douglas, Mary and Wildavsky, Aaron. *Risk and Culture: An Essay on the Selection of Technical and Environmental Dangers.* Berkeley: University of California Press, 1982.

Dover, C.J. "The Three Eras of Management Communication." In Redding, W. Charles and Sanborn, George A., eds. *Business and Industrial Communication: A Source Book.* New York: Harper and Row, 1964, 61–65.

Downing, John D.H. "U.S. Media Discourse on South Africa: The Development of a Situation Model." *Discourse & Society* 1.1 (July 1990): 39–60.

Doyle, Gillian. "Managing Global Expansion of Media Products and Brands: A Case Study of FHM." *International Journal on Media Management* 8.3 (2006): 105–115.

Doyle, Gillian. *Understanding Media Economics.* London: Sage Publications, Ltd., 2002.

Draper, Jimmy. "'Gay or Not?!': Gay Men, Straight Masculinities, and the Construction of the *Details* Audience." *Critical Studies in Media Communication* 27.4 (October 2010): 357–375.

Dredge, Bart. "Company Magazines and the Creation of Industrial Cooperation: A Case Study from the Southern Textile Industry, 1880–1940." *Management & Organizational History* 3.3/4 (August/November 2008): 273–288.

Dreier, Peter. "How the Media Compound Urban Problems." *Journal of Urban Affairs* 27.2 (June 2005): 193–201.

Driver, Stephen and Gillespie, Andrew. "The Diffusion of Digital Technologies in Magazine Print Publishing: Organizational Change and Strategic Choices." *Journal of Information Technology* 7.3 (1992): 149–159 <http://www.palgrave-journals.com/jit/journal/v7/n3/abs/jit199221a.html>, accessed 30 September 2012.

Duffy, Brooke Erin. *Remake, Remodel: Women's Magazines in the Digital Age.* Urbana, Chicago and Springfield: University of Illinois Press, 2013.

Duhé, Sonya Forte and Zukowski, Lee Ann. "Radio-TV Journalism Curriculum: First Jobs and Career Preparation." *Journalism & Mass Communication Educator* 52.1 (Spring 1997): 4–15.

Duke, Lisa. "Black in a Blonde World: Race and Girls' Interpretations of the Feminine Ideal in Teen Magazines." *Journalism & Mass Communication Quarterly* 77.2 (Summer 2000): 367–392.

Dumeco, Simon. "Magazines Are Dead, or Why There's No Such Thing as a (Mere) Magazine Company Anymore." *Ad Age Media News,* 21 October 2012 <http://adage.com/article/the-media-guy/thing-a-mere-magazine-anymore/244851/>, accessed 9 July 2013.

Duncombe, Stephen. *Notes from Underground: Zines and the Politics of Alternative Culture.* London and New York: Verso, 1997.

Dunlap, Riley E. and Catton, William R. Jr. "What Environmental Sociologists Have in Common (Whether Concerned with 'Built' or 'Natural' Environments)." *Sociological Inquiry* 53.2/3 (April 1983): 113–135.

Dunleavy, Patrick. *Studying for a Degree in the Humanities and Social Sciences.* Basingstoke, UK: Macmillan Education Ltd., 1986.

Dunwoody, Sharon. "Scientists, Journalists, and the Meaning of Uncertainty." In Friedman; Sharon M.; Dunwoody, Sharon; and Rogers, Carol L., eds. *Communicating Uncertainty: Media Coverage of New and Controversial Science.* Mahwah, NJ: Lawrence Erlbaum Associates, 1999, 59–79.

Duperray, Stéphane and Vidaling, Raphaële, with Amara, Cécile; Ples, Agnieszka; and Wurst, Alain-Xavier. *Front Page: Covers of the Twentieth Century.* London: Weidenfeld & Nicolson, 2003.

"DuraBooks: A Revolutionary New Concept." Melcher Media <http://www.melcher.com/about-us/>, accessed 15 May 2014.

Durham, Meenakshi Gigi. "Girls, Media, and the Negotiation of Sexuality: A Study of Race, Class, and Gender in Adolescent Peer Groups." *Journalism & Mass Communication Quarterly* 76.2 (Summer 1999): 193–216.

Durham, Meenakshi Gigi. "Revolutionizing the Teaching of Magazine Design." *Journalism & Mass Communication Educator* 53.1 (Spring 1998): 23–32.

Dutta-Bergman, Mohan J. "The Readership of Health Magazines: The Role of Health Orientation." *Health Marketing Quarterly* 22.2 (2004): 27–49.

Dysart, Deborah. "Narrative and Values: The Rhetoric of the Physician Assisted Suicide Debate." *New Jersey Journal of Communication* 8.2 (Fall 2000): 155–172 <http://www.tandfonline.com/doi/abs/10.1080/15456870009367386#.UZxJX5VNzG4>, accessed 21 May 2013.

Earle, David M. *All Man!: Hemingway, 1950s Men's Magazines, and the Masculine Persona.* Kent, OH: Kent State University Press, 2009.

Earle, David M. *Re-Covering Modernism: Pulps, Paperbacks, and the Prejudice of Form*. Burlington, VT: Ashgate Publishing Company, 2009.

Edel, Leon. "Biography and the Science of Man." In Friedson, Anthony M. ed. *New Directions in Biography*. Honolulu: University Press of Hawaii, 1981, 1–11.

Edge, Marc. "Professionalism versus Pragmatism." *Media*, Fall/Winter 2003, 10–12.

Editorial. "The *Burlington Magazine*, March 1903–February 2004." *Burlington Magazine* 146.1211 (February 2004): 75.

"Editorial Guidelines: ASME Guidelines for Editors and Publishers." Updated May 2014. American Society of Magazine Editors <http://www.magazine.org/asme/editorial-guidelines>, accessed 26 May 2014.

Editors of *Sports Illustrated*. Sports Illustrated: *The Covers*. New York: *Sports Illustrated* Books, 2010.

Edwards, Janis L. "The Very Model of a Modern Major (Media) Candidate: Colin Powell and the Rhetoric of Public Opinion." *Communication Quarterly* 46.2 (Spring 1998): 163–176.

Edy, Carolyn M. "Women's Magazine Coverage of Heart Disease Risk Factors: *Good Housekeeping* Magazine, 1997 to 2007." *Women & Health* 50.2 (March 2010): 176–194.

Ehses, Hanno H.J. "Representing Macbeth: A Case Study in Visual Rhetoric." *Design Issues* 1.1 (Spring 1984): 53–63.

Einsiedel, Edna F. "Public Participation and Dialogue: A Research Review." In Bucchi, Massimiano and Trench, Brian, eds. *Handbook of Public Communication of Science and Technology*. New York: Routledge, 2008, 173–184.

Elam, Caroline. "'A More and More Important Work': Roger Fry and the *Burlington Magazine*." [Centenary Issue]. *Burlington Magazine* 145.1200 (March 2003): 142–152.

Elliott, Stuart. "Renaming the Circulation Overseer." *New York Times*, 14 November 2012 <http://www.nytimes.com/2012/11/15/business/media/renaming-the-audit-bureau-of-circulations.html?_r=0>, accessed 2 May 2014.

Ellis, Doug; Locke, John; and Gunnison, John, eds. *The Adventure House Guide to the Pulps*. Silver Spring, MD: Adventure House, 2000.

Ellis, Estelle. Interview with author, 19 March 1994, New York. Phone interview.

Ellonen, Hanna-Kaisa. "Exploring the Strategic Impact of Technological Change: Studies on the Role of Internet in Magazine Publishing." Ph.D. thesis, Lappeenranta University of Technology. *Acta Universitatis Lappeenrantaensis*. No. 261, 2007.

Ellonen, Hanna-Kaisa; Jantunen, Ari; and Kuivalainen, Olli. "The Strategic Impact of Internet on Magazine Publishing." *International Journal of Innovation and Technology* Management 5.3 (2008): 341–361.

Ellonen, Hanna-Kaisa; Kosonen, Miia; and Henttonen, Kaisa. "The Development of a Sense of Virtual Community." *International Journal of Web-Based Communities* 3.1 (2007): 114–130.

Ellonen, Hanna-Kaisa and Kuivalainen, Olli. "Exploring a Successful Magazine Web Site." *Management Research News* 31.5 (2008): 386–398.

Ellonen, Hanna-Kaisa and Kuivalainen, Olli. "Magazine Publishers and Their Online Strategies: Review and Implications for Research and Online-Strategy Formulation." *International Journal of Technology Marketing* 2.1 (2007): 81–100.

Ellonen, Hanna-Kaisa; Tarkiainen, Anssi; and Kuivalainen, Olli. "The Effect of Magazine Web Site Usage on Print Magazine Loyalty." *International Journal on Media Management* 12.1 (March 2010): 21–37.

Ellonen, Hanna-Kaisa; Tarkiainen, Anssi; and Kuivalainen, Olli. "The Effect of Website Usage and Virtual Community Participation on Brand Relationships." *International Journal of Internet Marketing and Advertising* 6.1 (2010): 85–105.

Ellonen, Hanna-Kaisa; Wikström, Patrik; and Jantunen, Ari. "Linking Dynamic Capability Portfolios and Innovation Outcomes." *Technovation* 29.11 (2009): 753–762.

Emanuel, Bárbara. "Rhetoric in Graphic Design." M.A. thesis, Hochschule Anhalt, Anhalt University of Applied Sciences, Dessau, Germany, 2010.

Enda, Jodi. "Campaign Coverage in the Time of Twitter." *American Journalism Review*, 25 August 2011 <http://www.ajr.org/article.asp?id=5134>, accessed 18 January 2013.

Endicott, R. Craig. "Top 300 Revenue a Record $32.5 Bil." *Advertising Age*, 20 September 2004 <http://adage.com/article/special-report-magazine-300/top-300-revenue-a-record-32-5-bil/100462/>, accessed 24 November 2012.

Endres, Kathleen L. "The Feminism of Bernarr Macfadden: *Physical Culture* Magazine and the Empowerment of Women." *Media History Monographs* 13.2 (2011): 2–14 <http://facstaff.elon.edu/dcopeland/mhm/mhmjour13-2.pdf>, accessed 27 November 2012.

Endres, Kathleen L. "'Help-Wanted Female': *Editor & Publisher* Frames a Civil Rights Issue." *Journalism & Mass Communication Quarterly* 81.1 (Spring 2004): 7–21.

Endres, Kathleen L. "Ownership and Employment in Specialized Business Press." *Journalism Quarterly* 65.4 (Winter 1988): 996–998 <http://connection.ebscohost.com/c/articles/14839741/ownership-employment-specialized-business-pressm>, accessed 28 May 2013.

Endres, Kathleen L. "Research Review: The Specialized Business Press." *Electronic Journal of Communication / La Revue Electronique de Communication* 4.2/4 (1994) <http://www.cios.org/EJCPUBLIC/004/2/004211.html>, accessed 12 May 2013.

Endres, Kathleen L. "Research Review: The Specialized Business Press." In Abrahamson, David, ed. *The American Magazine: Research Perspectives and Prospects.* Ames: Iowa State University Press, 1995, 72–83.

Endres, Kathleen L., ed. *Trade, Industrial, and Professional Periodicals of the United States.* Westport, CT and London: Greenwood Press, 1994.

Endres, Kathleen L. and Lueck, Therese L., eds. *Women's Periodicals in the United States: Consumer Magazines.* Westport, CT: Greenwood Press, 1995.

Endres, Kathleen L. and Lueck, Therese L., eds. *Women's Periodicals in the United States: Social and Political Issues.* Westport, CT: Greenwood Press, 1996.

Endres, Kathleen L. and Schierhorn, Ann B. "New Technology and the Writer/Editor Relationship: Shifting Electronic Realities." *Journalism & Mass Communication Quarterly* 72.2 (Summer 1995): 448–457.

Enriquez, Joy. "Picking Up the Pages: Discussing the Materiality of Magazines." *Journal of Digital Research and Publishing* 2 (2009): 86–96.

Entman, Robert M. "Framing: Toward Clarification of a Fractured Paradigm." *Journal of Communication* 43.4 (Autumn 1993): 51–58.

Entman, Robert M. "Framing U.S. Coverage of International News: Contrasts in Narratives of the KAL and Iran Air Incidents." *Journal of Communication* 41.4 (Autumn 1991): 6–27.

Entman, Robert M. *Projections of Power: Framing News, Public Opinion, and U.S. Foreign Policy.* Chicago: University of Chicago Press, 2004.

Esbester, Mike. "Organizing Work: Company Magazines and the Discipline of Safety." *Management & Organizational History* 3.3/4 (August/November 2008): 217–237.

Esteban-Bravo, Mercedes; Múgica, José M.; and Vidal-Sanz, Jose M. "Magazine Sales Promotion: A Dynamic Response Analysis." *Journal of Advertising* 38.1 (Spring 2009): 137–146.

European Media Management Education Association. "Seminal Reading on Media Management and Media Economics" <http://www.media-management.eu/member-directory/seminal-readings.html>, accessed 30 August 2013.

Evans, Curtis J. "White Evangelical Protestant Responses to the Civil Rights Movement." *Harvard Theological Review* 102.2 (April 2009): 245–273.

Evans, Harold. *Editing and Design: A Five-Volume Manual of English, Typography and Layout.* New York: Holt, Rinehart and Winston, 1972–1978.

Evans, Jessica. "Celebrity, Media and History." In Evans, Jessica and Hesmondhalgh, David, eds. *Understanding Media: Inside Celebrity.* Maidenhead, UK: Open University Press, 2005, 12–55.

Evans, Jessica and Hall, Stuart, eds. *Visual Culture: The Reader.* London, Thousand Oaks and New Delhi: Sage Publications, 1999.

Evans, Michael Robert. *The Layers of Magazine Editing.* New York: Columbia University Press, 2004.

Fackler, P. Mark and Lippy, Charles H., eds. *Popular Religious Magazines of the United States.* Westport, CT: Greenwood Press, 1995.

Fandrich, Ashley M. and Beck, Stephenson J. "Powerless Language in Health Media: The Influence of Biological Sex and Magazine Type on Health Language." *Communication Studies* 63.1 (January/March 2012): 36–53.

Farrar, Ronald T. "Magazines." *Mass Communication: An Introduction to the Field.* 2nd ed. Madison, WI: Brown & Benchmark, 1996, G.1–18.

Farrell, Amy Erdman. *Yours in Sisterhood: Ms. Magazine and the Promise of Popular Feminism.* Chapel Hill: University of North Carolina Press, 1998.

Farris, Paul W. and Parry, Mark E. "Clarifying Some Ambiguities Regarding GRP and Average Frequency: A Comment on 'GRP: A Case of Mistaken Identity.'" *Journal of Advertising Research* 31.6 (December 1991): 75–77.

Faust, Drew. "Educate Women; Change the World." *Harvard Gazette*, 22 March 2013 <http://www.harvard.edu/president/educate-women-change-world-ewha-womans-university>, accessed 27 February 2014.

Featherstone, Mike. "Global Culture: An Introduction." In Featherstone, Mike, ed. *Global Culture: Nationalism, Globalization and Modernity*. London: Sage, 1990, 1–14.

Felder, Lynda. *Writing for the Web: Creating Compelling Web Content Using Words, Pictures and Sound*. Berkeley, CA: New Riders Press, 2012.

Fell, Jason. "Michael Jackson's Death Spurs 'Biggest Newsstand Push' since Election." *Folio:*, 10 July 2009 <http://www.foliomag.com/2009/michael-jackson-death-spurs-biggest-newsstand-push-elections>, accessed 1 January 2013.

Feng, Yang and Frith, Katherine. "The Growth of International Women's Magazines in China and the Role of Transnational Advertising." *Journal of Magazine & New Media Research* 10.1 (Fall 2008): 1–14. <http://aejmcmagazine.arizona.edu/Journal/Fall2008/FengFrith.pdf>, accessed 21 September 2013.

Feng, Yang and Karan, Kavita. "The Global and Local Influences in the Portrayal of Women's Roles: Content Analysis of Women's Magazines in China." *Journal of Media and Communication Studies* 3.2 (February 2011): 33–44.

Fennis, Bob M. and Bakker, Arnold B. "'Stay Tuned—We Will Be Back Right after These Messages': Need to Evaluate Moderates the Transfer of Irritation in Advertising." *Journal of Advertising* 30.3 (Fall 2001): 15–25.

Ferguson, Denise P. "The Independent Catholic Press and Vatican II." In Winston, Diane H., ed. *The Oxford Handbook of Religion and the American News Media*. New York: Oxford University Press, 2012, 509–522.

Ferguson, Marjorie. *Forever Feminine: Women's Magazines and the Cult of Femininity*. London: Heinemann, 1982.

Ferris, Thomas. "*Christian Beacon*." In Lora, Ronald and Longton, William Henry, eds. *The Conservative Press in Twentieth-Century America*. Westport, CT: Greenwood, 1999, 141–153.

Festinger, Leon. *A Theory of Cognitive Dissonance*. Stanford, CA: Stanford University Press, 1957.

Few, Stephen. "The Chartjunk Debate: A Close Examination of Recent Findings." *Visual Business Intelligence Newsletter*, April/May/June 2011, 1–11 <http://www.perceptualedge.com/articles/visual_business_intelligence/the_chartjunk_debate.pdf>, accessed 28 May 2013.

Few, Stephen. "Data Visualization for Human Perception." In Soegaard, Mads and Dam, Rikke Friis, eds. *The Encyclopedia of Human-Computer Interaction*. 2nd ed. Aarhus, DK: The Interaction Design Foundation, 2013.

Few, Stephen. "Does GE Think We're Stupid?" *Visual Business Intelligence* (blog), 21 June 2011 <http://www.perceptualedge.com/blog/?p=995>, accessed 26 May 2013.

Few, Stephen. *Show Me the Numbers: Designing Tables and Graphs to Enlighten*. 2nd ed. Burlingame, CA: Analytics Press, 2012.

Filak, Vincent F. "Marriage, Magazines and Makeup Tips: A Comparative Content Analysis of *Brides* Magazine and *Glamour* Magazine." Paper presented at the Annual Meeting, Association of Education in Journalism and Mass Communication, August 2002.

Filak, Vincent F. "Words: The Foundation Stone of Journalism." In Quinn, Stephen and Filak, Vincent F., eds. *Convergent Journalism: An Introduction*. Burlington, MA and Oxford, UK: Focal Press, 2005, 39–52.

Finch, Christopher. *Norman Rockwell: 332 Magazine Covers*. New York: Abbeville Press/Random House Publishers, 1979.

Finders, Margaret J. "Queens and Teen Zines: Early Adolescent Females Reading Their Way toward Adulthood." *Anthropology & Education Quarterly* 27.1 (March 1996): 71–89.

Fink, Edward J. and Gantz, Walter. "A Content Analysis of Three Mass Communication Research Traditions: Social Science, Interpretive Studies, and Critical Analysis." *Journalism & Mass Communication Quarterly* 73.1 (Spring 1996): 114–134.

Finkelstein, David and McCleery, Alistair, eds. *The Book History Reader*. 2nd ed. London: Routledge, 2006.

Finkelstein, David and McCleery, Alistair. *An Introduction to Book History*. 2nd ed. London: Routledge, 2012.

FIPP. "Home." FIPP Research Forum <http://www.fippresearchforum.com/Home.asp>, accessed 29 May 2014.

FIPP—The Worldwide Magazine Media Association <http://www.fipp.com>, accessed 18 February 2013.

First Cover, and "Cover Look: First Blush," *Vogue*, March 2009, First Cover, 136.

Fish, Stanley E. "Interpreting the *Variorum*." *Critical Inquiry* 2.3 (Spring 1976): 465–485.

Fisher, William, ed. *Business Journals of the United States*. Westport, CT: Greenwood Press, 1991.

Fishkin, Shelley Fisher. "The Borderlands of Culture: Writing by W.E.B. Du Bois, James Agee, Tillie Olsen, and Gloria Anzaldúa." In Sims, Norman, ed. *Literary Journalism in the Twentieth Century*. New York: Oxford University Press, 1990, and Evanston, IL: Northwestern University Press, 2008, 133–182.

Flaherty, Francis. *The Elements of Story: Field Notes on Nonfiction Writing*. New York: Harper Perennial, 2009.

Flamiano, Dolores. "Too Human for Life: Hansel Mieth's Photographs of Heart Mountain Internment Camp." *Visual Communication Quarterly* 11.3/4 (Summer/Autumn 2004): 4–17.

Flamm, Matthew. "525 Magazines Died in 2008." *Crain's New York Business*, 6 February 2009 <http://www.crainsnewyork.com/article/20090206/FREE/902069972>, accessed 20 December 2012.

Fleming, Tyler and Falola, Toyin. "Africa's Media Empire: *Drum's* Expansion to Nigeria." *History in Africa* 32.1 (2005): 133–164.

Flournoy, Craig. "Covering a Mississippi Murder Trial: The Emmett Till Lynching." Paper presented at the Annual Meeting, Association for Education in Journalism and Mass Communication, August 2005.

Folio:. "Monetizing the Digital Revolution: Media Industry Benchmarks & Trends Study, Third Edition." Closed Survey <https://www.research.net/s.aspx?sm=HuPUyAZtUD4jVwk0hHQDjg_3d_3d,Red 7media.com>, accessed 29 May 2014.

Folkerts, Jean and Lacy, Stephen. "Magazines." *The Media in Your Life*. 2nd ed. Boston: Allyn & Bacon, 2001, 114–143.

Foote, Timothy. "There Goes (Varoom!) *Esquire* Magazine." *New York Times*, 13 August 1995, G9.

Ford, James L.C. *Magazines for Millions: The Story of Specialized Publications*. Carbondale: South Illinois University Press, 1969.

Ford, Jennifer. "Fashion Advertising, Men's Magazines, and Sex in Advertising: A Critical-Interpretive Study." Master's thesis, University of South Florida, 2008.

Ford, John B.; Voli, Patricia Kramer; Honeycutt, Earl D., Jr.; and Casey, Susan L. "Gender Role Portrayals in Japanese Advertising: A Magazine Content Analysis." *Journal of Advertising* 27.1 (Spring 1998): 113–124.

Forde, Kathy Roberts. *Literary Journalism on Trial: Masson v. New Yorker and the First Amendment*. Amherst: University of Massachusetts Press, 2008.

Forde, Kathy Roberts. "Profit and Public Interest: A Publication History of John Hersey's 'Hiroshima.'" *Journalism & Mass Communication Quarterly* 88.3 (Autumn 2011): 562–579.

Forde, Kathy Roberts and Ross, Matthew W. "Radio and Civic Courage in the Communications Circuit of John Hersey's 'Hiroshima.'" *Literary Journalism Studies* 3.2 (Fall 2011): 31–53.

Forsyth, David P. *The Business Press in America, 1750–1865*. Philadelphia: Chilton Books, 1964.

Fosdick, Scott. "The State of Magazine Research in 2008." *Journal of Magazine & New Media Research* 10.1 (Fall 2008): 1–4.

Fosdick, Scott and Cho, Sooyoung. "No Business Like Show Business: Tracking Commodification Over a Century of *Variety*." *Journal of Magazine & New Media Research* (Spring 2005): 1–14.

Foucault, Michel. *Power/Knowledge: Selected Interviews and Other Writings, 1972–1977*. Edited by Colin Gordon. Translated by Colin Gordon, Leo Marshall, John Mepham and Kate Soper. New York: Pantheon, 1980.

Foust, James C. and Bradshaw, Katherine A. "Something for the Boys: Framing Images of Women in *Broadcasting* Magazine in the 1950s." *Journalism History* 33.2 (Summer 2007): 93–100 <http://www.questia.com/library/1P3–1319083581/something-for-the-boys-framing-images-of-women-in>, accessed 21 May 2013.

Fox, Richard L.; Van Sickel, Robert W.; and Steiger, Thomas L. *Tabloid Justice: Criminal Justice in an Age of Media Frenzy*. Boulder, CO: Lynne Rienner Publishers, 2007.

Fraser, Kathryn. "The Makeover and Other Consumerist Narratives." Ph.D. diss., McGill University, 2002.

Frederiksen, Bodil Folke. "*Joe*, the Sweetest Reading in Africa: Documentation and Discussion of a Popular Magazine in Kenya." *African Languages and Cultures* 4.2 (1991): 135–155.

Freedman, Eric. "Union Magazines' Coverage of the NAFTA Controversy before Congressional Approval." *Journal of Labor Research* 25.2 (Spring 2004): 301–313.

Freedman, Robert, ed. *Best Practices of the Business Press*. Dubuque, IA: Kendall/Hunt Publishing Company, 2004.

Freemium. "Information for Business Owners." *Freemium Business Model* <http://freemiumbusinessmodel.com/>, accessed 7 December 2013.

Frey, Christopher. editor-in-chief of Hazlitt.com. Interview by author, 28 January 2013.

Freydkin, Donna. "Doctored Cover Photos Add Up to Controversy." *USA Today*, 17 June 2003, 3D.

Fried, Amy. "Terrorism as a Context of Coverage before the Iraq War." *International Journal of Press/Politics* 10.3 (Summer 2005): 125–132.

Friedland, Lewis A. and Webb, Sheila. "Incorporating Online Publishing into the Curriculum." *Journalism & Mass Communication Educator* 51.3 (Autumn 1996): 54–65.

Friedlander, Edward Jay and Lee, John. *Feature Writing: The Pursuit of Excellence.* 7th ed. Boston: Allyn & Bacon, 2011.

Friedlander, Edward Jay and Lee, John. *Feature Writing for Newspapers and Magazines: The Pursuit of Excellence.* 4th ed. New York: Longman, 2000.

Friedman, Barbara. "Unlikely Warriors: How Four U.S. News Sources Explained Female Suicide Bombers." *Journalism & Mass Communication Quarterly* 85.4 (Winter 2008): 841–859.

Friedman, Daniela B.; Laditka, James N.; Laditka, Sarah B.; and Mathews, Anna E. "Cognitive Health Messages in Popular Women's and Men's Magazines, 2006–2007." *Preventing Chronic Disease* 7.2 (March 2010): 1–10.

Friedman, Jon. "Magazines Have Questionable Covers." CBS.MarketWatch.com, 18 June 2004 <http://www.marketwatch.com/story/magazine-covers-should-answer-not-ask-questions>, accessed 18 June 2004.

Frisby, Cynthia. "Getting Real with Reality TV." *USA Today* (Magazine), September 2004, 50–54.

Frith, Katherine. "Globalising Women: How Global Women's Magazines in China and Singapore Transmit Consumer Culture" [on-line]. *Media International Australia, Incorporating Culture & Policy* Issue 133 (November 2009): 130–145.

Frith, Katherine. "Global Media Texts and Consumption: The Study of International Magazines." Paper presented at the Annual Meeting, International Communication Association, 2009.

Frith, Katherine. "Race and Ethnicity: A Comparison of Global and Local Women's Magazine Advertising in Singapore." Paper presented at the Annual Meeting, International Communication Association, June 2006.

Frith, Katherine and Feng, Yang. "Transnational Cultural Flows: An Analysis of Women's Magazines in China." *Chinese Journal of Communication* 2.2 (July 2009): 158–173.

Frith, Katherine; Feng, Yang; and Ye, Lan. "International Women's Magazines and Transnational Advertising in China." Paper presented at the Annual Meeting, Association for Education in Journalism and Mass Communication, August 2008.

Frith, Katherine; Shaw, Ping; and Cheng, Hong. "The Construction of Beauty: A Cross-Cultural Analysis of Women's Magazine Advertising." *Journal of Communication* 55.1 (March 2005): 56–70 <http://onlinelibrary.wiley.com/doi/10.1111/j.1460-2466.2005.tb02658.x/pdf>, accessed 2 June 2014.

Frith, Katherine and Wesson, David. "A Comparison of Cultural Values in British and American Print Advertising: A Study of Magazines." *Journalism Quarterly* 68.1/2 (Spring/Summer 1991): 216–223.

Frontani, Michael R. "'Beatlepeople': Gramsci, the Beatles, and *Rolling Stone* Magazine." *American Journalism* 19.3 (2002): 39–61.

Frus, Phyllis. *The Politics and Poetics of Journalistic Narrative: The Timely and the Timeless.* New York: Cambridge University Press, 1994.

Fry, Don and Clark, Roy Peter. "Return of the Narrative: the Rebirth of Writing in America's Newsrooms." *Quill,* May 1994, 27–28.

Fugate, Douglas L.; Decker, Philip J.; and Brewer, Joyce J. "Women in Professional Selling: A Human Resource Management Perspective." *Journal of Personal Selling & Sales Management* 8.3 (November 1988): 33–41.

Fujioka, Yuki. "Emotional TV Viewing and Minority Audience: How Mexican Americans Process and Evaluate TV News about In-Group Members." *Communication Research* 32.5 (October 2005): 566–593.

Gadney, Max; McCandless, David; Tufte, Edward; and Holmes, Nigel. "You Are Here." *Eye,* Winter 2012 <http://www.eyemagazine.com/feature/article/you-are-here>, accessed 15 March 2013.

Gale Directory of Publications and Broadcast Media. Detroit: Gale Cengage Learning, 2014.

Galin, Michal. "Magazine Ads that Drove Readers to the Web: MRI Starch Picks the 10 Most Effective Print to Online Ads." *Advertising Age,* 18 December 2008 <adage.com/article/media/magazine-ads-drove-readers-web/133258/>, accessed 12 November 2012.

Gallaugher, John; Auger, Pat; and BarNir, Anat. "Revenue Streams and Digital Content Providers: An Empirical Investigation." *Innovation & Management* 38.7 (August 2001): 473–485.

Gamson, Joshua. *Claims to Fame: Celebrity in Contemporary America.* Berkeley: University of California, 1994.

Gamson, Joshua. "Normal Sins: Sex Scandal Narratives as Institutional Morality Tales." *Social Problems* 48.2 (May 2001): 185–205.

Gannon, Susan R.; Rahn, Suzanne; and Thompson, Ruth Anne, eds. St. Nicholas *and Mary Mapes Dodge: The Legacy of a Children's Magazine Editor, 1873–1905*. Jefferson, NC: McFarland, 2004.

Gao, Yunxiang. "Nationalist and Feminist Discourses on *Jianmei* (Robust Beauty) during China's 'National Crisis' in the 1930s." *Gender & History* 18.3 (November 2006): 546–573.

Gardner, Eric. *Unexpected Places: Relocating Nineteenth-Century African American Literature*. Jackson: University Press of Mississippi, 2009.

Gardner, Jared. *The Rise and Fall of Early American Magazine Culture*. Urbana: University of Illinois Press, 2012.

Garnett, James L.; Marlowe, Justin; and Pandey, Sanjay K. "Penetrating the Performance Predicament: Communication as a Mediator or Moderator of Organizational Culture's Impact on Public Organizational Performance." *Public Administration Review* 68.2 (March/April 2008): 266–281.

Garvey, Ellen Gruber. *The Adman in the Parlor: Magazines and the Gendering of Consumer Culture, 1880s to 1910s*. New York: Oxford University Press, 1996.

Garvey, Ellen Gruber. "Foreword." In Harris, Sharon M., ed. *Blue Pencils and Hidden Hands: Women Editing Periodicals, 1830–1910*. Boston: Northeastern University Press, 2004, xi–xxiii.

Gattuso, Suzy; Fullagar, Simone; and Young, Ilena. "Speaking of Women's 'Nameless Misery': The Everyday Construction of Depression in Australian Women's Magazines." *Social Science & Medicine* 61.8 (October 2005): 1640–1648.

Gauntlett, David. *Media, Gender and Identity: An Introduction*. 2nd ed. London: Routledge, 2008.

Gauntlett, David. "Men's Magazines and Modern Masculinities." *Media, Gender and Identity: An Introduction*. 2nd ed. London and New York: Routledge, 2008, 164–189.

Gauntlett, David. "Women's Magazines and Female Identities." *Media, Gender and Identity: An Introduction*. 2nd ed. London and New York: Routledge, 2008, 190–222.

George-Palilonis, Jennifer and Spillman, Mary. "Interactive Graphics Development: A Framework for Studying Innovative Visual Story Forms." *Visual Communication Quarterly* 18.3 (2011): 167–177.

George-Palilonis, Jennifer and Spillman, Mary. "Storytelling with Interactive Graphics: An Analysis of Editors' Attitudes and Practices." *Visual Communication Quarterly* 20.1 (2013): 20–27.

Gerbner, George; Gross, Larry; Morgan, Michael; and Signorielli, Nancy. "The 'Mainstreaming' of America: Violence Profile No. 11." *Journal of Communication* 30.3 (Summer 1980): 10–29.

Gerlach, Peter. "Research about Magazines Appearing in *Journalism Quarterly*." *Journalism Quarterly* 64.1 (Spring 1987): 178–182.

Ghemawat, Pankaj. "The Cosmopolitan Corporation." *Harvard Business Review*, May 2011, 92–99.

Giddens, Anthony. *The Politics of Climate Change*. Cambridge, UK: Polity Press, 2009.

Gieryn, Thomas. "Boundaries of Science." In Jasanoff, Sheila; Markle, Gerald E.; Petersen, James C.; and Pinch, Trevor. *Handbook of Science and Technology Studies*. Rev. ed. London: Sage, 1995, 393–443.

Giggie, John M. "The African American Religious Press." In Winston, Diane H., ed. *The Oxford Handbook of Religion and the American News Media*. New York: Oxford University Press, 2012, 579–592.

Gilens, Martin. "Race and Poverty in America: Public Misperceptions and the American News Media." *Public Opinion Quarterly* 60.4 (Winter 1996): 515–541.

Gilgoff, Dan. "Evangelical Minister Jim Wallis Is in Demand in Obama's Washington." *U.S. News*, 31 March 2009 <http://www.usnews.com/news/religion/articles/2009/03/31/evangelical-minister-jim-wallis-is-in-demand-in-obamas-washington>, accessed 28 November 2013.

Gill, Brendan. *Here at the New Yorker*. New York: Random House, 1975.

Gill, Elizabeth A. and Babrow, Austin S. "To Hope or to Know: Coping with Uncertainty and Ambivalence in Women's Magazine Breast Cancer Articles." *Journal of Applied Communication Research* 35.2 (May 2007): 133–155.

Gill, Rosalind. *Gender and the Media*. Cambridge, UK: Polity Press, 2007.

Gill, Rosalind. "Gender in Magazines from *Cosmopolitan* to *Loaded*." *Gender and the Media*. Cambridge, UK: Polity Press, 2007, 180–217.

Gillett, Frank. "Why Tablets Will Become Our Primary Computing Device." *Frank Gillett's Blog*, 23 April 2012 <http://blogs.forrester.com/frank_gillett/12–04–23-why_tablets_will_become_our_primary_computing_device>, accessed 26 March 2013.

Gillmor, Dan. "Where Did 'Citizen Journalist' Come From?" *Center for Citizen Media* (blog), 14 July 2008 <http://citmedia.org/blog/2008/07/14/where-did-citizen-journalist-come-from/>, accessed 7 March 2013.

Gitlin, Todd. "Supersaturation, or, the Media Torrent and Disposable Feeling." *Media Unlimited: How the Torrent of Images and Sounds Overwhelms Our Lives*. New York: Metropolitan Books/Henry Holt, 2007, 12–70.

Glasser, Susan B. "Creating a Go-To Digital Destination for Foreign Affairs Reporting and Commentary." *Neiman Reports*, Fall 2010, 55–57.

Glasser, Theodore L. "Objectivity and News Bias." In Cohen, Elliot D., ed. *Philosophical Issues in Journalism*. New York: Oxford University Press, 1992, 176–183.

Gleditsch, Nils Petter. "The Most-Cited Articles in JPR." *Journal of Peace Research* 30.4 (November 1993): 445–449.

Gluch, Pernilla and Stenberg, Ann-Charlotte. "How Do Trade Media Influence Green Building Practice?" *Building Research & Information* 34.2 (2006): 104–117 <http://www.tandfonline.com/doi/abs/10.1080/09613210500491613>, accessed 24 January 2013.

Goffman, Erving. *Frame Analysis: An Essay on the Organization of Experience*. Cambridge, MA: Harvard University Press, 1974.

Goffman, Erving. *Gender Advertisements*. Cambridge, MA: Harvard University Press, 1979.

Goldman, Karen. "La Princesa Plastica: Hegemonic and Oppositional Representations of *Latinidad* in Hispanic Barbie." In Dines, Gail and Humez, Jean M., eds. *Gender, Race, and Class in Media: A Critical Reader*. 3rd ed. Thousand Oaks, CA: Sage, 2011, 375–382.

Gonser, Sarah. "Revising the Cover Story." *Folio:*, 1 March 2003, 20.

Goodman, J. Robyn. "Flabless Is Fabulous: How Latina and Anglo Women Read and Incorporate the Excessively Thin Body Ideal into Everyday Experience." *Journalism & Mass Communication Quarterly* 79.3 (Autumn 2002): 712–727.

Gordon, Jacob Barrie. "Can Sociologists Study Society in the Same Way that Scientists Study the Natural World?" Jake Gordon, 2002 <http://jakeg.co.uk/essays/science>, accessed 14 February 2014.

Gordon, Jane. "The Fears Aroused by a Fine Physique: Modern Men Face the Same Media Pressure to be Perfect that Women Have Long Endured." *The Daily Telegraph* (London, UK), 12 June 1996.

Gough-Yates, Anna. *Understanding Women's Magazines: Publishing, Markets and Readerships*. London and New York: Routledge, 2003.

Gourevitch, Philip, ed. *The Paris Review: Interviews*. Vol. 4. Edinburgh, UK: Canongate, 2009.

Grafton, Anthony. *The Culture of Correction in Renaissance Europe*. London: British Library, 2011.

Graham, Betsy P. *Magazine Article Writing*. 2nd ed. Fort Worth: Harcourt Brace Jovanovich, 1993.

Graham, Katharine. *Personal History*. New York: Alfred A. Knopf, 1997.

Graham, Lisa. "Gestalt Theory in Interactive Media Design." *Journal of Humanities & Social Sciences* 2.1 (2008): 1–12.

Gramsci, Antonio. *Selections from the Prison Notebooks of Antonio Gramsci*. Edited and Translated by Quintin Hoare and Geoffrey Nowell Smith. New York: International Publishers, 1971.

Grandy, Karen. "Busy Bee, Tough Mom, Farmer's Daughter: The Canadian Business Press Portrayal of Annette Verschuren." *Canadian Journal of Communication* 35.1 (2010): 49–62.

Grandy, Karen. "The Glossy Ceiling: Coverage of Women in Canadian and American Business Magazines." *Journal of Magazine & New Media Research* 14.1 (Spring 2013): 1–20 <http://aejmcmagazine.arizona.edu/Journal/Summer2013/Grandy.pdf>, accessed 21 September 2013.

Grandy, Karen. "Mother Load: Parental-Status References in Canadian Business Magazines." *Canadian Journal of Communication* 38.2 (2013): 245–254.

Grates, Gary. "Is the Employee Publication Extinct?" *Communication World*, December 1999–January 2000, 27–30.

Greco, Albert N. "The Economics of Books and Magazines." In Alexander, Alison; Owers, James; Carveth, Rod; Hollifield, C. Ann and Greco, Albert N., eds. *Media Economics: Theory and Practice*. 3rd ed. Mahway, NJ: Lawrence Erlbaum Associates, 2003, 127–147.

Greenberg, Bryan. "Different Voices, Same Script: How Newsmagazines Cover Media Consolidation Issues." Paper presented at the Annual Meeting, Association for Education in Journalism and Mass Communication, August 2001.

Greenberg, Susan. *Editors Talk about Editing*. New York: Peter Lang, forthcoming.

Greenberg, Susan. "The Hidden Art of Editing: Theory, History and Identity." Ph.D. Diss., University College London, 2013.

Greenberg, Susan. "Slow Journalism in the Digital Fast Lane." In Keeble, Richard Lance and Tulloch, John, eds. *Global Literary Journalism: Exploring the Journalistic Imagination*. New York: Peter Lang, 2012, 381–393.

Greenberg, Susan. "Theory and Practice in Journalism Education." *Journal of Media Practice* 8.3 (December 2007): 298–303.

Greenberg, Susan. "When the Editor Disappears, Does Editing Disappear?" *Convergence: The International Journal of Research into New Media Technologies* 16.1 (February 2010): 7–21.

Greenberg, Susan and Phelps, Christopher. "Poetics of Fact." *Times Higher Education*, 15 August 2010, 36.

Green Dude. "Paper or Digital: Which Format is Better for the Environment." Green Techno Log.com (blog), 25 February 2010 <http://www.greentechnolog.com/2010/02/paper_or_ digital_which_format_is_better_for_the_en.html>, accessed 30 October 2012.

Greenfeld, Karl Taro. "A Life after Wide Right." *Sports Illustrated*, 12 July 2004, 140.

Greening, Lorna A.; Greene, David L.; and Difiglio, Carmen. "Energy Efficiency and Consumption—The Rebound Effect—A Survey." *Energy Policy* 28.6/7 (2000): 389–401.

Greenpeace. *Dirty Data Timeline.* 29 May 2012 citing The Climate Group. "Smart 2020: Enabling the Low Carbon Economy in the Information Age." Greenpeace.org <http://www.greenpeace.org/international/en/campaigns/climate-change/cool-it/The-Dirty-Data-timeline/>, accessed 30 October 2012.

Greenwood, Keith. "Picturing Defiance: Visions of Democracy in Iran." *International Communication Gazette* 74.7 (November 2012): 619–635.

Greenwood, Keith and Smith, C. Zoe. "How the World Looks to Us." *Journalism Practice* 1.1 (January 2007): 82–101.

Gretton, Tom. "The Pragmatics of Page Design in Nineteenth-Century General-Interest Weekly Illustrated News Magazines in London and Paris." *Art History* 33.4 (September 2010): 680–709.

Griffin, Jeffrey L. and Stevenson, Robert L. "The Effectiveness of 'How Graphics' and Text in Presenting the News." *Visual Communication Quarterly* 1.2 (Spring 1994): 10–11, 16.

Griffin, Jeffrey L. and Stevenson, Robert L. "The Effectiveness of Locator Maps in Increasing Reader Understanding of the Geography of Foreign News." *Journalism Quarterly* 71.4 (Winter 1994): 937–946.

Griffin, Jeffrey L. and Stevenson, Robert L. "The Influence of Statistical Graphics on Newspaper Reader Knowledge Gain." Paper presented at the Annual Meeting, Association for Education in Journalism and Mass Communication, August 1992.

Griffin, Jeffrey L. and Stevenson, Robert L. "Influence of Text and Graphics in Increasing Understanding of Foreign News Context." *Newspaper Research Journal* 13.1/2 (Winter/Spring 1992): 84–99.

Griffin, Michael. "Picturing America's 'War on Terrorism' in Afghanistan and Iraq: Photographic Motifs as News Frames." *Journalism* 5.4 (November 2004): 381–402.

Griffin, Michael and Lee, Jongsoo. "Picturing the Gulf War: Constructing an Image of War in *Time*, *Newsweek*, and *U.S. News & World Report*." *Journalism & Mass Communication Quarterly* 72.4 (Winter 1995): 813–825.

Griffin, Robert J.; Dunwoody, Sharon; and Neuwirth, Kurt. "Proposed Model of the Relationship of Risk Information Seeking and Processing to the Development of Preventive Behaviors." *Environmental Research* 80.2 (February 1999): S230–S245.

Griffiths, John. "Exploring Corporate Culture: The Potential of Company Magazines for the Business Historians." *Business Archives: Sources and History* 78 (1999): 27–37.

Griffiths, John. "'Give My Regards to Uncle Billy . . .': The Rites and Rituals of Company Life at Lever Brothers, c.1900–c.1990." *Business History* 37.4 (October 1995): 25–45.

Grigoriadis, Vanessa. "What Does Tina Brown Have to Do to Get Some Attention?" *New York*, 10 June 2007 <http://nymag.com/news/features/33159/>, accessed 15 November 2012.

Grix, Jonathan. "Introducing Students to the Generic Terminology of Social Research." *Politics* 22.3 (2002): 175–186.

Grizzle, Raymond E.; Rothrock, Paul E.; and Barrett, Christopher B. "Evangelicals and Environmentalism: Past, Present, and Future." *Trinity Journal* 19.1 (Spring 1998): 3–27.

Gross, Gerald, ed. *Editors on Editing: What Writers Need to Know About What Editors Do.* New York: Grove Press, 1993.

Groth, Janet. *The Receptionist: An Education at the* New Yorker. Chapel Hill, NC: Algonquin Books of Chapel Hill, 2012.

Grove, Jaleen. "A Castle of One's Own: Interactivity in *Chatelaine Magazine*, 1928–35." *Journal of Canadian Studies/Revue d'études canadiennes* 45.3 (Fall 2011): 167–194.

Grow, Gerald. "Magazine Covers and Cover Lines: An Illustrated History." *Journal of Magazine & New Media Research* 5.1 (Fall 2002): 1–19.

"Growth of the Nonreligious." Pew Research: Religion and Public Life Project, PewForum.org, 2 July 2013 <http://www.pewforum.org/growth-of-the-nonreligious-many-say-trend-is-bad-for-american-society.aspx>, accessed 8 July 2013.

Grunwald, Edgar A. *The Business Press Editor*. New York: New York University Press, 1988.

Gryboski, Michael. "United Methodist Publication '*Reporter*' Founded in 1840s to Close." *Christian Post*, 17 May 2013 <http://www.christianpost.com/news/united-methodist-publication-reporter-founded-in-1840s-to-close-96140/>, accessed 29 November 2013.

Guidone, Lisa M. "The Magazine at the Millennium: Integrating the Internet." *Publishing Research Quarterly* 16.2 (Summer 2000): 14–33.

Gunn, Simon and Faire, Lucy. *Research Methods for History*. Edinburgh: Edinburgh University Press, 2012.

Gunn, Virginia. "McCall's Role in the Early Twentieth-Century Quilt Revival." *Uncoverings* 31 (December 2010): 11–64.

Gunther, Marc. "The Push to Create Original Magazines in Cyberspace: The Pioneers Have a Long Road Ahead—and Millions of Dollars Are at Stake." *Philly.com*, 9 August 1995 <http://articles.philly.com/1995–08–09/entertainment/25711011_1_internet-access-cyberspace-web-sites>, accessed 2 June 2014.

Gussow, Don. *The New Business Journalism: An Insider's Look at the Workings of America's Business Press*. San Diego: Harcourt Brace Jovanovich, 1984.

Gutierrez-Villalobos, Sonia; Hertog, James K.; and Rush, Ramona R. "Press Support for the U.S. Administration during the Panama Invasion: Analyses of Strategic and Tactical Critique in the Domestic Press." *Journalism Quarterly* 71.3 (Autumn 1994): 618–627.

Gutkind, Lee. *You Can't Make This Stuff Up: The Complete Guide to Writing Creative Nonfiction—from Memoir to Literary Journalism and Everything in Between*. Boston: Da Capo Press, 2012.

Gysels, Marjolein; Pool, Robert; and Nyanzi, Stella. "The Adventures of the Randy Professor and Angela the Sugar Mummy: Sex in Fictional Serials in Ugandan Popular Magazines." *AIDS Care* 17.8 (November 2005): 967–977.

Habermas, Jürgen. *The Structural Transformation of the Public Sphere*. Translated by Thomas Burger and Frederick Lawrence. Cambridge, MA: MIT Press, 1989.

Hafstrand, Helene. "Competitive Advantage in the Magazine Publishing Business—A Resource-Based Perspective." Paper presented at the 15th Nordic Conference on Media and Communication Research, Reykjavik, 10–13 August 2001.

Hage, Emily. "The Magazine as Strategy: Tristan Tzara's *Dada* and the Seminal Role of Dada Art Journals in the Dada Movement." *Journal of Modern Periodical Studies* 2.1 (2011): 33–53.

Haidarali, Laila. "Polishing Brown Diamonds: African American Women, Popular Magazines, and the Advent of Modeling in Early Postwar America." *Journal of Women's History* 17.1 (2005): 10–37.

Hall, Edward T. *The Hidden Dimension*. New York: Doubleday, 1969.

Hall, Ronald E. "The Ball Curve: Calculated Racism and the Stereotype of African American Men." *Journal of Black Studies* 32.1 (September 2001): 104–119.

Hall, Stuart. "Encoding/Decoding." In Hall, Stuart; Hobson, Dorothy; Lowe, Andrew; and Willis, Paul, eds. *Culture, Media, Language*. Birmingham, UK: Centre for Contemporary Cultural Studies, University of Birmingham, 1980, 128–138.

Hamilton, John Robert. "An Historical Study of Bob Pierce and World Vision's Development of the Evangelical Social Action Film." Ph.D. diss., University of Southern California, 1980.

Hamilton, Martha M. "What We Learned in the Meltdown: Financial Journalists Saw Some Trees but Not the Forest. Now What?" *Columbia Journalism Review*, January/February 2009, 36–39.

Hamilton, Nancy M. *Uncovering the Secrets of Magazine Writing: A Step-by-Step Guide to Writing Creative Nonfiction for Print and Internet Publication*. Boston: Pearson, 2005.

Hamlet, Janice D. "Assessing Womanist Thought: The Rhetoric of Susan L. Taylor." *Communication Quarterly* 48.4 (Fall 2000): 420–436.

Hampshire, Nick. "The E-Paper Catalyst." In Renard, David, ed. *The Last Magazine*. New York: Universe Publishing, 2006, 30–35.

Han, Chong-suk. "'Sexy Like a Girl and Horny Like a Boy': Contemporary Gay 'Western' Narratives about Gay Asian Men." In Dines, Gail and Humez, Jean M., eds. *Gender, Race, and Class in Media: A Critical Reader*. 3rd ed. Thousand Oaks, CA: Sage, 2011, 163–170.

Hannah, Leslie. *The Rise of the Corporate Economy*. London: Methuen, 1976.

Hansen, Evan. "Violations of Editorial Standards Found in *Wired* Writer's Blog." *Frontal Cortex* (blog). Wired.com, 31 August 2012 <http://www.wired.com/wiredscience/2012/08/violations-of-editorial-standards-found-in-wired-writers-blog/>, accessed 7 March 2013.

Hanson, Ralph E. Study Guide for "Chapter 5. Magazines: The Power of Words and Images," *Mass Communication: Living in a Media World.* 3rd ed. Washington, DC: CQ Press, 2011 <http://college.cqpress.com/sites/masscomm/Home/chapter5.aspx>, accessed 4 February 2013.

Harcup, Tony. "Alternative Journalism as Active Citizenship." *Journalism* 12.1 (January 2011): 15–31.

Harcup, Tony. "Hackademics at the Chalkface: To What Extent Have Journalism Teachers Become Journalism Researchers?" *Journalism Practice* 5.1 (August 2011): 34–50 <http://dx.doi.org/DOI: 10.1080/17512786.2010.493333>, accessed 20 October 2010.

Harless, James D. "The American Magazine: A Range of Reading." *Mass Communication: An Introductory Survey.* 2nd ed. Dubuque: Wm. C. Brown, 1990, 148–180.

Harp, Dustin; Loke, Jaime; and Bachmann, Ingrid. "Voices of Dissent in the Iraq War: Moving from Deviance to Legitimacy?" *Journalism & Mass Communication Quarterly* 87.3/4 (Autumn/Winter 2010): 467–483.

Harper, Charlotte. "What Is Longform Journalism?" *Editia,* 28 August 2012 <http://editia.com/what-is-longform-journalism/>, accessed 2 February 2014.

Harrigan, Jane T. and Dunlap, Karen Brown. *The Editorial Eye.* 2nd ed. Boston: Bedford / St. Martin's, 2003.

Harris, Christopher R. "Digitization and Manipulation of News Photographs." *Journal of Mass Media Ethics* 6.3 (1991): 164–174.

Harris, Mark. "A Shocking Truth." *IEEE Spectrum,* March 2012, 30–34, 57–58 <http://www.american-businessmedia.com/abm/C1A_Shocking_Truth.asp>, accessed 14 January 2014.

Harris, Sharon M., ed. With a Foreword by Gruber Garvey, Ellen. *Blue Pencils and Hidden Hands: Women Editing Periodicals, 1830–1910.* Boston: Northeastern University Press, 2004.

Harrison, Charles H. *How to Write for Magazines: Consumer, Trade, and Web.* Boston: Allyn & Bacon, 2002.

Harrison, Kristen. "The Body Electric: Thin-Ideal Media and Eating Disorders in Adolescents." *Journal of Communication* 50.3 (Summer 2000): 119–143.

Harrison, Kristen and Cantor, Joanne. "The Relationship between Media Consumption and Eating Disorders." *Journal of Communication* 47.1 (1997): 40–67.

Harrison, Kristen and Fredrickson, Barbara L. "Women's Sports Media, Self-Objectification, and Mental Health in Black and White Adolescent Females." *Journal of Communication* 53.2 (2003): 216–232.

Hart, Jack. "A Note from Jack Hart." *Storycraft: The Complete Guide to Writing Narrative Nonfiction.* Chicago: University of Chicago Press, 2011 <http://www.press.uchicago.edu/books/hart/index.html>, accessed 30 November 2013.

Hart, Jack. *Storycraft: The Complete Guide to Writing Narrative Nonfiction.* Chicago: University of Chicago Press, 2011.

Hart, Jack. *A Writer's Coach: An Editor's Guide to Words That Work.* New York: Pantheon Books, 2006.

Hartley, John. "Documenting Kate Moss." *Journalism Studies* 8.4 (2007): 555–565.

Hartley, John. *Uses of Television.* London and New York: Routledge, 1999.

Hartsock, John C. *A History of American Literary Journalism: The Emergence of a Modern Narrative Form.* Amherst: University of Massachusetts Press, 2000.

Hartsock, John C. "Note from the Editor." *Literary Journalism Studies* 1.1 (Spring 2009): 5.

Harwood, Jake. "Age Identification, Social Identity Gratifications, and Television Viewing." *Journal of Broadcasting & Electronic Media* 43.1 (Winter 1999): 123–136.

Harwood, Jake. "Age Identity and Television Viewing Preferences." *Communication Reports* 12.2 (Summer 1999): 85–90.

Harwood, Jake. "Viewing Age: Lifespan Identity and Television Viewing Choices." *Journal of Broadcasting & Electronic Media* 41.2 (Spring 1997): 203–213.

Harwood, Jake and Sparks, Lisa. "Social Identity and Health: An Intergroup Communication Approach to Cancer." *Health Communication* 15.2 (2003): 145–159.

Hatch, Nathan O. *The Democratization of American Christianity.* New Haven, CT: Yale University Press, 1989.

Hatton, Erin and Trautner, Mary Nell. "Equal Opportunity Objectification? The Sexualization of Men and Women on the Cover of *Rolling Stone.*" *Sexuality & Culture* 15.3 (September 2011): 256–278.

Haughney, Christine. "A Magazine Article on Race Sets Off an Outcry." *Media Decoder* (blog). *New York Times,* 24 March 2013 <http://mediadecoder.blogs.nytimes.com/2013/03/24/being-white-in-philly-article-brings-an-outcry/?_r=0>, accessed 2 January 2013.

Haughney, Christine. "*Newsweek* Plans Return to Print." *New York Times,* 3 December 2013 <http://www.nytimes.com/2013/12/04/business/media/newsweek-plans-return-to-print.html>, accessed 15 December 2013.

Haughney, Christine and Carr, David. "At *Newsweek*, Ending Print and a Blend of Two Styles." *Media Decoder* (blog). *New York Times*, 18 October 2012 <http://mediadecoder.blogs.nytimes.com/2012/10/18/newsweek-will-cease-print-publication-at-end-of-year/?ref=newsweekinc>, accessed 15 December 2013.

Hay, Vicky. *The Essential Feature: Writing for Magazines and Newspapers*. New York and Chichester, UK: Columbia University Press, 1990.

Haygood, Daniel Marshall. "Henry Luce's Anti-Communist Legacy: An Analysis of U.S. News Magazines' Coverage of China's Cultural Revolution." *Journalism History* 35.2 (Summer 2009): 98–105.

Hays, Robert G. and Reisner, Ann E. "Farm Journalists and Advertiser Influence: Pressures on Ethical Standards." *Journalism Quarterly* 68.1/2 (Spring/Summer 1991): 172–178.

He, Zhou. "Diffusion of Movable Type in China and Europe: Why Were There Two Fates?" *Gazette* 53.3 (1994): 153–173.

Heidenry, John. *Theirs Was the Kingdom: Lila and DeWitt Wallace and the Story of the* Reader's Digest. New York: W.W. Norton, 1993.

Heikkilä, Heikki; Kunelius, Risto; and Ahva, Laura. "From Credibility to Relevance: Towards a Sociology of Journalism's 'Added Value.'" *Journalism Practice* 4.3 (2010): 274–284 <http://www.tandfonline.com/doi/abs/10.1080/17512781003640547#.UywpPFyp07c>, accessed 9 September 2012.

Heinderyckx, François. "In Praise of the Passive Media." In Trivundža, Ilija Tomanić; Carpentier, Nico; Nieminen, Hannu; Pruulmann-Venerfeldt, Pille; Kilborn, Richard; Sundin, Ebba; and Olsson, Tobias, eds. *Past, Future and Change: Contemporary Analysis of Evolving Media Scapes*. Ljubljana, Slovenia: University of Ljubljana Press, 2013, 99–108.

Helal, Kathleen M. "Celebrity, Femininity, Lingerie: Dorothy Parker's Autobiographical Monologues." *Women's Studies* 33.1 (January/February 2004): 77–102.

Helfgott, Isadora Anderson. "Art and the Struggle for the American Soul: The Pursuit of a Popular Audience for Art in America from the Depression to World War II." Ph.D. diss., Harvard University, 2006.

Heller, Michael. "British Company Magazines, 1878–1939: The Origins and Functions of House Journals in Large-Scale Organisations." *Media History* 15.2 (2009): 143–166.

Heller, Michael. "Company Magazines 1880–1940: An Overview." *Management & Organizational History* 3.3/4 (August/November 2008): 179–196.

Heller, Michael. "Corporate Brand Building: Shell-Mex Ltd. in the Interwar Period." In Lopes, Teresa da Silva and Duguid, Paul, eds. *Trademarks, Brands, and Competitiveness*. London: Routledge, 2010, 194–214.

Heller, Nathan. "Listen and Learn." *New Yorker*, 9 and 16 July 2012, 69–77.

Heller, Steven. "Books: Authored/Edited/Coauthored." Hellerbooks.com <http://www.hellerbooks.com/docs/books.html>, accessed 21 June 2013.

Heller, Steven. *Merz to Émigré and Beyond: Avant-Garde Magazine Design of the Twentieth Century*. London: Phaidon Press, 2003.

Heller, Steven. *Nigel Holmes: On Information Design*. New York: Jorge Pinto Books, 2006.

Heller, Steven and Fernandes, Teresa. *Magazines Inside and Out*. Glen Cove, NY: PBC International, 1997.

Hendershot, Heather. *Shaking the World for Jesus: Media and Conservative Evangelical Culture*. Chicago: University of Chicago Press, 2004.

Henderson, Ann M. "Mixed Messages about the Meanings of Breast-Feeding Representations in the Australian Press and Popular Magazines." *Midwifery* 15.1 (March 1999): 24–31.

Hendrickson, Elizabeth Meyers. "Refresh: Examining the Production of Celebrity News in an Online Environment." Ph.D. diss., University of Missouri-Columbia, 2008.

Henriques, Diana. "Business Reporting: Behind the Curve," *Columbia Journalism Review*, November/December 2000, 18–26.

Herbst, Susan. "Disciplines, Intersections, and the Future of Communication Research." *Journal of Communication* 58.4 (December 2008): 603–614.

Herbst, Susan. "History, Philosophy, and Public Opinion Research." *Journal of Communication* 43.4 (Autumn 1993): 140–145.

Herbst, Susan. "Illustrator, American Icon, and Public Opinion Theorist: Norman Rockwell in Democracy." *Political Communication* 21.1 (2004): 1–25.

Hermes, Joke. *Reading Women's Magazines: An Analysis of Everyday Media Use*. Cambridge, UK: Polity Press, 1995.

Herran, Néstor. "'Science to the Glory of God': The Popular Science Magazine *Ibérica* and Its Coverage of Radioactivity, 1914–1936." *Science & Education* 21.3 (March 2012): 335–353.

Hertz, Todd and Guthrie, Stan. "Moody Closes Magazine, Restructures Aviation Program." *Christianity Today*, 1 February 2003 <http://www.christianitytoday.com/ct/2003/februaryweb-only/2–24–21.0.html>, accessed 29 November 2013.

Herzog, Herta. "What Do We Really Know About Daytime Serial Listeners?" In Lazarsfeld, Paul F. and Stanton, Frank N., eds. *Radio Research, 1942–1943*. New York: Duell, Sloan & Pearce, 1944, 3–33.

Herzog, Herta. "Why Do People Like a Program? Professor Quiz—A Gratification Study." In Lazarsfeld, Paul F. ed. *Radio and the Printed Page*. New York: Duell, Sloan & Pearce, 1940, 67–93.

Hesse, Douglas. "The Place of Creative Nonfiction." *College English* 65.3 (January 2003): 237–241.

Hessell, Nikki. "Riding the Rails with Robin Hyde: Literary Journalism in 1930s New Zealand." In Bak, John S. and Reynolds, Bill, eds. *Literary Journalism across the Globe: Journalistic Traditions and Transnational Influences*. Amherst: University of Massachusetts Press, 2011, 211–224.

Hester, Joe Bob and Gibson, Rhonda. "The Economy and Second-Level Agenda Setting: A Time-Series Analysis of Economic News and Public Opinion about the Economy." *Journalism & Mass Communication Quarterly* 80.1 (Spring 2003): 73–90.

Hewitt, Elizabeth. "Romances of Real Life; Or, the Nineteenth-Century American Business Magazine." *American Periodicals* 20.1 (2010): 1–22.

Hiatt, Anna. "The Future of Digital Longform." Tow Center of Digital Journalism, March 2014 <http://towcenter.org/future-digital-longform/>, accessed 5 March 2014.

Hiebert, Ray Eldon and Gibbons, Sheila Jean. "Books, Magazines and Newsletters." *Exploring Mass Media for a Changing World*. Mahwah, NJ: Lawrence Erlbaum, 2000, 166–186.

Hill, Anthony D. *Pages from the Harlem Renaissance: A Chronicle of Performance*. Studies in African and African-American Culture. Vol. 6. New York: Peter Lang, 1996 <http://www.peterlang.com/download/datasheet/46828/datasheet_69865.pdf>, accessed 28 May 2013.

Hill, Jan M. and Radimer, Kathy L. "Health and Nutrition Messages in Food Advertisements: A Comparative Content Analysis of Young and Mature Australian Women's Magazines." *Journal of Nutrition Education* 28.6 (November 1996): 313–320.

Hilty, Lorenz M. and Ruddy, Thomas F. "Towards a Sustainable Information Society." *Informatik/Informatique* 4 (August 2000): 2–9.

Hinnant, Amanda and Hudson, Berkley. "The Magazine Revolution, 1880–1920." In Christine Bold, ed. *The Oxford History of U.S. Popular Print Culture: 1860–1920*. Vol. 6. New York: Oxford University Press, 2012, 113–131.

Hirji, Faiza. "One Nation, Many Voices: The Muslim Press in the United States." In Winston, Diane H., ed. *The Oxford Handbook of Religion and the American News Media*. New York: Oxford University Press, 2012, 565–578.

Hirons, Jean. "Revising AACR2 to Accommodate Seriality: Report to the Joint Steering Committee on the Revision of AACR." *CONSER*, Library of Congress, April 1999 <http://www.rda-jsc.org/docs/ser-rep.pdf>, accessed 2 May 2014.

Hobsbawm, Eric and Ranger, Terence, eds. *The Invention of Tradition*. Canto ed. Cambridge, UK: Cambridge University Press, 1992.

Hobson, Kersty. "Competing Discourses of Sustainable Consumption: Does the 'Rationalisation of Lifestyles' Make Sense?" *Environmental Politics* 11.2 (Summer 2002): 95–120.

Hochman, Jonathan. "The Cost of Pay-per-Click (PPC) Advertising—Trends and Analysis." Hochman Consultants, 2014 <http://www.hochmanconsultants.com/articles/je-hochman-benchmark.shtml>, accessed 11 March 2014.

Hoffman, David. "D'Aprix Discusses Communication Awareness." *IABC Communication World*, November 1985, 14–16.

Hoffman-Goetz, Laurie. "Cancer Experiences of African-American Women as Portrayed in Popular Mass Magazines." *Psycho-Oncology* 8.1 (January/February 1999): 36–45.

Hoffman-Goetz, Laurie; Gerlach, Karen K.; Marino, Christina; and Mills, Sherry L. "Cancer Coverage and Tobacco Advertising in African-American Women's Popular Magazines." *Journal of Community Health* 22.4 (August 1997): 261–270.

Hoffman-Goetz, Laurie and MacDonald, Megan. "Cancer Coverage in Mass-Circulating Canadian Women's Magazines." *Canadian Journal of Public Health* 90.1 (January/February 1999): 55–59.

Hofstede, Geert. *Culture's Consequences: International Differences in Work-Related Values*. Abridged ed. Beverly Hills, CA: Sage Publications, 1984.

Holden, Vanessa. Interview with author, 13 June 2005, New York. Personal interview.

BIBLIOGRAPHY

Hollander, Justin B. "Long Live Paper." *New York Times*, 9 October 2012 <http://www.nytimes.com/2012/10/10/opinion/long-live-paper.html>, accessed 15 October 2012.

Hollifield, C. Ann. "The Specialized Business Press and Industry-Related Political Communication: A Comparative Study." *Journalism & Mass Communication Quarterly* 74.4 (Winter 1997): 757–772.

Hollinger, David A. "After Cloven Tongues of Fire: Ecumenical Protestantism and the Modern American Encounter with Diversity." *Journal of American History* 98.1 (June 2011): 21–48.

Holmes, Michael E.; Papper, Robert A.; Popovich, Mark N.; and Bloxham, Michael. *Middletown Media Studies: Observing Consumers and Their Interaction with Media, Concurrent Media Exposure*. Muncie, IN: Ball State University Center for Media Design, Fall 2006.

Holmes, Michael E.; Papper, Robert A.; Popovich, Mark N.; and Bloxham, Michael. *Middletown Media Studies II: Concurrent Media Exposure*. Muncie, IN: Ball State University Center for Media Design, 2006.

Holmes, Nigel. "Crashing through the Type." *Eye*, Winter 2012 <http://www.eyemagazine.com/feature/article/crashing-through-the-type>, accessed 12 March 2013.

Holmes, Nigel. *The Lonely Planet Book of Everything: A Visual Guide to Travel and the World*. Victoria, AUS: Lonely Planet, 2012.

Holmes, Tim. "Magazines in the Digital World." In Jenny McKay, ed. *The Magazines Handbook*. 3rd ed. London: Routledge, 2013, 186–203.

Holmes, Tim. "Mapping the Magazine: An Introduction." *Journalism Studies* 8.4 (August 2007): 510–521.

Holmes, Tim. "Mapping the Magazine: An Introduction." In Holmes, Tim, ed. *Mapping the Magazine: Comparative Studies in Magazine Journalism*. London and New York: Routledge, 2008, viii–xix.

Holmes, Tim and Nice, Liz. "The International Perspective." *Magazine Journalism*. Journalism Studies: Key Texts Series. Los Angeles and London: Sage, 2012, 109–119.

Holmes, Tim and Nice, Liz. *Magazine Journalism*. Journalism Studies: Key Texts Series. Los Angeles and London: Sage, 2012.

Holstead, Carol E. "What's Old Is New: The Need for Historical Inspiration in Contemporary Magazine Design." *American Periodicals* 7 (1997): 73–86.

Homans, Charles, executive editor of the *Atavist*. E-mail interview by author, 13 February 2013.

Hon, Linda Childers; Fitzpatrick, Kathy R.; and Hall, Margarete Rooney. "Searching for the 'Ideal' Graduate Public Relations Curriculum." *Journalism & Mass Communication Educator* 59.2 (Summer 2004): 126–142.

Hong, Jae W.; Muderrisoglu, Aydin; and Zinkhan, George M. "Cultural Differences and Advertising Expression: A Comparative Content Analysis of Japanese and U.S. Magazine Advertising." *Journal of Advertising* 16.1 (July 1987): 55–62, 68.

Hooper, Mark. "Who Says Print Is Dead?" *Guardian*, 3 June 2012 <http://www.theguardian.com/media/2012/jun/03/who-says-print-is-dead>, accessed 2 May 2014.

Hoover, Stewart M. "Mass Media and Religious Pluralism." In Lee, Philip, ed. *The Democratization of Communication*. Cardiff: University of Wales Press, 1995, 185–198.

Horppu, Marianne; Kuivalainen, Olli; Tarkiainen, Anssi; and Ellonen, Hanna-Kaisa. "Online Satisfaction, Trust and Loyalty, and the Impact of the Offline Parent Brand." *Journal of Product and Brand Management* 17.6 (2008): 403–413.

Horrigan, John B. *The Internet as a Resource for News and Information about Science*. Washington, DC: Pew Internet and American Life Project, 2006.

Houser, Craig. "The Politics of Scholarship: College Art Association and the Uneasy Relationship between Art and Art History 1911–1945." Ph.D. diss., City University of New York, 2011.

Hovland, Roxanne; McMahan, Carolynn; Lee, Guiohk; Hwang, Jang-Sun; and Kim, Juran. "Gender Role Portrayals in American and Korean Advertisements." *Sex Roles* 53.11/12 (December 2005): 887–899.

Hoy, Anne H. *The Book of Photography: The History, the Technique, the Art, the Future*. Washington, DC: National Geographic Society, 2005.

Hoyles, Anna. "Pickled Herrings and Politics: The Early Journalism of Moa Martinson." In Keeble, Richard Lance and Tulloch, John, eds. *Global Literary Journalism: Exploring the Journalistic Imagination*. New York: Peter Lang, 2012, 72–88.

Hu, Fan and Wang, Mena. "Beauty and Fashion Magazines and College-Age Women's Appearance-Related Concerns." Paper presented at the Annual Meeting, International Communication Association, May 2009.

579

Huang, Edgar Shaohua. "Readers' Perception of Digital Alteration in Photojournalism." *Journalism & Communication Monographs* 3.3 (Autumn 2001): 147–182.

Huang, Edgar Shaohua. "Where Do You Draw the Line?" *Visual Communication Quarterly* 7.4 (2000): 4–16.

Huang, Ying and Lowry, Dennis T. "An Analysis of Nudity in Chinese Magazine Advertising: Examining Gender, Racial and Brand Differences." *Sex Roles* 66.7/8 (April 2012): 440–452.

Hubbard, Benjamin J., ed. *Reporting Religion: Facts and Faith*. Sonoma, CA: Polebridge Press, 1990.

Hudson, Berkley. "Photojournalists." *Encyclopedia of Journalism*. Thousand Oaks, CA: Sage Publications, 2009.

Hudson, Berkley and Townsend, Rebecca. "Unraveling the Webs of Intimacy and Influence: Willie Morris and *Harper's* Magazine, 1967–1971." *Literary Journalism Studies* 1.2 (2009): 63–78.

Huff, Darrell. *How to Lie with Statistics*. New York: W.W. Norton, 1993.

Hughes, Marie Adele and Garrett, Dennis E. "Intercoder Reliability Estimation Approaches in Marketing: A Generalizability Theory Framework for Quantitative Data." *Journal of Marketing Research* 27.2 (May 1990): 185–195.

Hulsether, Mark. *Building a Protestant Left*: Christianity and Crisis *Magazine, 1941–1993*. Knoxville: University of Tennessee Press, 1999.

Humphrey, Sandi L. "Making Your Association Magazine Matter." Canadian Society of Association Executives CSAE/SCDA <http://www.csae.com/Resources/ArticlesTools/View/Articleid/19/Making-Your-Association-Magazine-Matter>, accessed 25 February 2014.

Hung, Kineta H.; Gu, Flora Fang; and Tse, David K. "Improving Media Decisions in China: A Targetability and Cost-Benefit Analysis." *Journal of Advertising* 34.1 (Spring 2005): 49–63.

Hung, Kineta H.; Li, Stella Yiyan; and Belk, Russell W. "Glocal Understandings: Female Readers' Perceptions of the New Woman in Chinese Advertising." *Journal of International Business Studies* 38.6 (November 2007): 1034–1051 <http://dx.doi.org/10.1057/palgrave.jibs.8400303>, accessed 3 February 2013.

Husni, Samir. *Launch Your Own Magazine. A Guide for Succeeding in Today's Marketplace*. Nashville: Hamblett House, 1998.

Husni, Samir. "'*Recoil*' and '*Highlights Hello*' Top My List of Most Notable Launches of 2012: New Magazines Wrap-Up; Mr. Magazine Style." *Mr. Magazine* (blog), 29 December 2012 <https://mrmagazine.wordpress.com/2012/12/29/recoil-and-highlights-hello-top-my-list-of-most-notable-launches-of-2012-new-magazines-wrap-up-mr-magazine-style/>, accessed 2 June 2014.

Husselbee, L. Paul and Stempel, Guido H., III. "Contrast in U.S. Media Coverage of Two Major Canadian Elections." *Journalism & Mass Communication Quarterly* 74.3 (Autumn 1997): 591–601.

Hutcheson, John; Domke, David; Billeaudeaux, Andre; and Garland, Philip. "U.S. National Identity, Political Elites, and a Patriotic Press Following September 11." *Political Communication* 21.1 (January/March 2004): 27–50.

Hutton, Deborah. "Raja Deen Dayal and Sons: Photographing Hyderabad's Famine Relief Efforts." *History of Photography* 31.3 (2007): 260–275.

"IALJS Homepage." International Association for Literary Journalism Studies <http://www.ialjs.org>, accessed 28 November 2013.

Ibanga, Imaeyen. "Obama's Choice to Bare Arms Causes Uproar." ABC News, 2 March 2009 <http://abcnews.go.com/GMA/story?id=6986019>, accessed 15 December 2013.

IDG. "IDG Total Portfolio." "Global Media Kit," IDG—International Data Group, 2014 <http://www.idg.com/www/home.nsf/BySection/Global_Media_Kit>, accessed 29 May 2014.

Ifezue, Alexander N. "What Makes an Effective Advertising for a Man or a Woman?" *Journal of Communication* [J *Communication*, India] 1.1 (July 2010): 13–18.

"Index Checklist: 100+ Under $100," *Vogue*. March 2009, 502.

Infotendencias Group. "Media Convergence." In Siapera, Eugenia and Veglis, Andreas, eds. *The Handbook of Global Online Journalism*. Chichester, UK: Wiley-Blackwell, 2012, 21–37.

Inness, Sherrie A. "Pretty Tough: The Cult of Femininity in Women's Magazines." In Carter, Cynthia and Steiner, Linda, eds. *Critical Readings: Media and Gender*. Issues in Cultural and Media Studies. Allan Stuart, ed. Maidenhead, UK: Open University Press, 2004, 123–142.

International Association for Literary Journalism Studies, "*Literary Journalism Studies* Selected Bibliography of Scholarship and Criticism." *Literary Journalism Studies* Updated 1 March 2012 <http://www.davidabrahamson.com/WWW/IALJS/LJS_Biblio_v120301.pdf>, accessed 17 January 2013.

Inzlicht, Michael; Tullett, Alexa M.; Legault, Lisa; and Kang, Sonia K. "Lingering Effects: Stereotype Threat Hurts More than You Think." *Social Issues and Policy Review* 5.1 (December 2011): 227–256.

"Iraq: Will There Be Light?" *IEEE Spectrum*, 1 February 2006 <http://spectrum.ieee.org/energy/the-smarter-grid/iraq-will-there-be-light>, accessed 31 May 2014.

Ireland, Sandra L. Jones. *Ethnic Periodicals in Contemporary America: Annotated Guide.* Westport, CT: Greenwood Press, 1990.

Ives, Nat. "Hearst Adds *Elle*, but New Global Footprint May Mean More in the Long Run." *Advertising Age*, 7 February 2011, 4.

Ives, Nat. "The Last Page: A Guide to Magazines that Have Ceased Publication." *Ad Age Media News*, 15 December 2009 <http:adage.com/article/media/a-guide-magazines-ceased-publication/132779/>, accessed 1 March 2014.

Ives, Nat. "Magazines: The A-list." *Advertising Age*, 6 October 2008, 1.

Ives, Nat. "Magazines Shape Up for Digital Future." *Advertising Age*, 17 April 2006 <http://adage.com/article/media/magazines-shape-digital-future/108620>, accessed 28 November 2013.

Ives, Nat. "Time Inc. CEO Laura Lang: Why We Changed Our Minds About the iPad." *Ad Age*, 14 June 2012 <http://adage.com/article/media/time-ceo-laura-lang-selling-ipad-subs/235381/>, accessed 19 May 2014.

Ives, Nat and Parekh, Rupal. "For Pubs, Going Global Comes with Challenges." *Advertising Age*, 14 June 2010, 17.

Izzo, Amanda. "Outrageous and Everyday: The Papers of Gloria Steinem." *Journal of Women's History* 14.2 (Summer 2002): 151–153.

Jabr, Ferris. "Why the Brain Prefers Paper." *Scientific American*, November 2013, 48–53.

Jackson, Dennis and Sweeney, John, eds. *The Journalist's Craft: A Guide to Writing Better Stories.* New York: Allworth Press, 2002.

Jackson, Sue. "'I'm 15 and Desperate for Sex': 'Doing' and 'Undoing' Desire in Letters to a Teenage Magazine." *Feminism & Psychology* 15.3 (August 2005): 295–313.

Jacobi, Peter. "The Art of Editing: It's the Editor's Job to Bring the Publication to Life, and by So Doing, Serve the Reader's Need—Issue, after Issue, after Issue." *Folio:*, July 1990, 102.

Jamison, Anne. "*Kmen*: A Faraway Magazine about Which We Know Nothing." *Comparative Literature Studies* 44.1/2 (January 2007): 51–66.

Janello, Amy and Jones, Brennon. *The American Magazine.* New York: Abrams and Magazine Publishers of America, 1991.

Jantunen, Ari; Ellonen, Hanna-Kaisa; and Johansson, Anette. "Beyond Appearances—Do Dynamic Capabilities of Innovative Firms Actually Differ?" *European Management Journal* 30.2 (Summer 2012): 141–155.

Järventie-Thesleff, Rita; Villi, Mikko; and Moisander, Johanna. "Traditional and Online Publishing in Juxtaposition—A Comparison of Change Management Practices." Paper presented at EMMA Annual Conference, Budapest, 10–12 February 2012.

Jayson, Sharon. "Family Life, Roles Changing as Couples Seek Balance." *USA Today*, 19 April 2009 <http://usatoday30.usatoday.com/news/health/2009-04-18-families-conf_N.htm>, accessed 06 September 2013.

Jeffers, Dennis W. "A Descriptive Study of Perceived Impact of Gender on Employment Status, Type of Work, Industry Relationships, Working Environment and Job Satisfaction in Livestock Industry Magazines." Paper presented at the Annual Meeting, Association for Education in Journalism and Mass Communication, August 1987 <http://catalogue.nla.gov.au/Record/5480309>, accessed 21 May 2013.

Jensen, Jakob D.; Bernat, Jennifer K.; Wilson, Kari M.; and Goonewardene, Julie. "The Delay Hypothesis: The Manifestation of Media Effects over Time." *Human Communication Research* 37.1 (October 2011): 509–528.

Jensen, Klaus Bruhn. "The Qualitative Research Process." In Jensen, Klaus Bruhn, ed. *A Handbook of Media and Communication Research: Qualitative and Quantitative Methodologies.* London and New York: Routledge, 2002, 235–253.

Jewitt, Carey, ed. *The Routledge Handbook of Multimodal Analysis.* 2nd ed. London: Routledge, 2013.

Jhally, Sut. *The Codes of Advertising: Fetishism and the Political Economy of Meaning in the Consumer Society.* New York: Routledge, Chapman and Hall, 1990.

Johansen, Peter. "'For Better, Higher and Nobler Things': Massey's Pioneering Employee Publication." *Journalism History* 27.3 (Fall 2001): 94–104.

Johansen, Peter. "Where's the Meaning and the Hope? Trends in Employee Publications." *Journal of Popular Culture* 29.3 (Winter 1995): 129–138.

Johanson, Katya. "Dead, Done For and Dangerous: Teaching Editing Students What Not to Do." *New Writing: The International Journal for the Practice and Theory of Creative Writing* 3.1 (April 2006): 47–55.

Johansson, Anette; Ellonen, Hanna-Kaisa; and Jantunen, Ari. "Magazine Publishers Embracing New Media: Exploring Their Capabilities and Decision Making Logic." *Journal of Media Business Studies* 9.2 (Summer 2012): 97–114.

Johansson, Anette and McKelvie, Alexander. "Unpacking the Antecedents of Effectuation and Causation in a Corporate Context." *Frontiers of Entrepreneurship Research* 32.17 (2012): Article 1.

Johansson, Tobias. "Lighting the Campfire: The Creation of a Community of Interest around a Media Company." *International Journal on Media Management* 4.1 (2002): 4–12.

Johnson, Abby Arthur and Johnson, Ronald Maberry. *Propaganda and Aesthetics: The Literary Politics of African-American Magazines in the Twentieth Century*. Amherst: University of Massachusetts Press, 1991.

Johnson, Branden B. "Further Notes on Public Response to Uncertainty in Risks and Science." *Risk Analysis* 23.4 (2003): 781–789.

Johnson, Carla. *21st Century Feature Writing*. Boston: Pearson, 2004.

Johnson, J. David and Meischke, Hendrika. "A Comprehensive Model of Cancer-Related Information Seeking Applied to Magazines." *Human Communication Research* 19.3 (March 1993): 343–367.

Johnson, John H., with Bennett, Lerone, Jr. *Succeeding Against the Odds: The Autobiography of a Great American Businessman*. New York: Amistad, 1992.

Johnson, Mark S. "Causes and Consequences of U.S. Chain Store Closings: Attributions in the Media." *Psychology & Marketing* 17.8 (August 2000): 721–743.

Johnson, Richard D. "Machlup and the Information Age." *Scholarly Publishing* 18.4 (July 1987): 271–276.

Johnson, Sammye. "The Art and Science of Magazine Cover Research." *Journal of Magazine & New Media Research* 5.1 (Fall 2002): 1–10.

Johnson, Sammye. "Overview of Research into the Magazine Form: The Relationship of Academic Scholarship to the Magazine Industry." Keynote Address, Mapping the Magazine 2 International Conference, Cardiff University, Cardiff, Wales, 15 September 2005.

Johnson, Sammye. "Why Should They Care? The Relationship of Academic Scholarship to the Magazine Industry." *Journalism Studies* 8.4 (August 2007): 522–528.

Johnson, Sammye and Prijatel, Patricia. "The Magazine as a Storehouse: The Scope of the Medium." The Magazine from Cover to Cover. 3rd ed. New York and Oxford: Oxford University Press, 2013, 2–21.

Johnson, Sammye and Prijatel, Patricia. *The Magazine from Cover to Cover*. 2nd ed. New York and Oxford: Oxford University Press, 2007.

Johnson, Sammye and Prijatel, Patricia. *The Magazine from Cover to Cover*. 3rd ed. New York and Oxford: Oxford University Press, 2013.

Johnston, Caitlin. "Second Chance." *American Journalism Review*, April/May 2012 <http://ajr.org/Article.asp?id=5278>, accessed 18 January 2013.

Johnston, Jane. "Changing Journalistic Environments." Review of *Feature Writing: Telling the Story*, 2nd ed., by Stephen Tanner, Molly Kasinger, and Nick Richardson. In *Text* 13.1 (April 2009) <http://www.textjournal.com.au/april09/johnston_rev.htm>, accessed 26 November 2013.

Jolliffe, Lee. "Research Review: Magazine Editors and Editing Practices." In Abrahamson, David, ed. *The American Magazine: Research Perspectives and Prospects*. Ames: Iowa State University Press, 1995, 51–71.

Jolliffe, Lee and Whitehouse, Virginia. "The Magazine as Mentor: A Turn-of-the-Century Handwritten Magazine by St. Louis Women Artists." *American Periodicals* 7 (1997): 48–72.

Jones, Bob and Brown, Stacy. *Michael Jackson: The Man behind the Mask*. New York: Select Books, 2005.

Jones, John. "Patterns of Revision in Online Writing: A Study of Wikipedia's Featured Articles." *Written Communication* 25.2 (April 2008): 262–289.

Joseph, Sue. "Supervising Life-Writing of Trauma in a Tertiary Setting." *Text* 15.2 (October 2011) <http://textjournal.com.au/oct11/joseph.htm>, accessed 13 January 2013.

Joshi, Suchi P.; Peter, Jochen; and Valkenburg, Patti M. "Ambivalent Messages in *Seventeen* Magazine: A Content Analytic Comparison of 1997 and 2007." *Journal of Magazine & New Media Research* 12.1 (Fall 2010): 1–20 <http://aejmcmagazine.arizona.edu/Journal/Fall2010/JoshiPeterValkenburg.pdf >, accessed 19 September 2012.

Joshi, Suchi P.; Peter, Jochen; and Valkenburg, Patti M. "Scripts of Sexual Desire and Danger in U.S. and Dutch Teen Girl Magazines: A Cross-National Content Analysis." *Sex Roles* 64.7/8 (April 2011): 463–474.

"*Journal of Public Affairs*: Description." Wiley <http://eu.wiley.com/WileyCDA/WileyTitle/productCd-PA.html>, accessed 27 December 2012.

Jue, Kaitlin. "Major Trends in Digital Magazines." B.S. in Graphic Communication thesis, California Polytechnic State University-San Luis Obispo, 2009 <http://digitalcommons.calpoly.edu/grcsp/2/>, accessed 30 September 2012.

Jung, Jaehee and Lee, Yoon-Jung. "Cross-Cultural Examination of Women's Fashion and Beauty Magazine Advertisements in the United States and South Korea." *Clothing & Textiles Research Journal* 27.4 (October 2009): 274–286.

Jung, Jaemin. "How Magazines Covered Media Companies' Mergers: The Case of the Evolution of Time Inc." *Journalism & Mass Communication Quarterly* 79.3 (Autumn 2002): 681–696.

Jussim, Lee. "Social Reality and Social Problems: The Role of Expectancies." *Journal of Social Issues* 46.2 (Summer 1990): 9–34.

Kachun, Mitch. "Interrogating the Silences: Julia C. Collins, 19th-Century Black Readers and Writers, and the *Christian Recorder*." *African American Review* 40.4 (Winter 2006): 649–659.

Kaiser, Ulrich. "Magazines and Their Companion Websites: Competing Outlet Channels?" *Review of Marketing Science* 4.3 (August 2006): 1–24.

Kaiser, Ulrich and Kongsted, Hans Christian. "Magazine 'Companion Websites' and the Demand for Newsstand Sales and Subscriptions." *Journal of Media Economics* 25.4 (2012): 184–197 <http://dx.doi.org/10.1080/08997764.2012.729545>, accessed 15 January 2014.

Kaiser, Ulrich and Wright, Julian. "Price Structure in Two-Sided Markets: Evidence from the Magazine Industry." *International Journal of Industrial Organization* 24.1 (January 2006): 1–28.

Kamhawi, Rasha and Weaver, David. "Mass Communication Research Trends from 1980 to 1999." *Journalism & Mass Communication Quarterly* 80.1 (Spring 2003): 7–27.

Kamiya, Gary. "Let Us Now Praise Editors: They May Be Invisible and Their Art Unsung. But in the Age of Blogging, Editors Are Needed More Than Ever." *Salon.com*, 24 July 2007 <http://www.salon.com/2007/07/24/editing/>, accessed 25 February 2013.

Kampe, Joan and Christenson, Lyn. "Publications: What's in the Package." In Reuss, Carol and Silvis, Donn, eds. *Inside Organizational Communication*. 2nd ed. London and New York: Longman, 1985, 129–144.

Kamrath, Mark L. and Harris, Sharon M., eds. *Periodical Literature in Eighteenth-Century America*. Knoxville: University of Tennessee Press, 2005.

Kanayama, Tomoko. "Magazine Coverage of Welfare Recipients 1969–1996: Media Rituals and American Society." *Journal of American and Canadian Studies* 21 (March 2004): 83–113.

Kanellos, Nicolás. "A Brief History of Hispanic Periodicals in the United States." In Kanellos, Nicolás, with Martell, Helvetia. *Hispanic Periodicals in the United States, Origins to 1960: A Brief History and Comprehensive Bibliography*. Houston: Arte Público Press, 2000, 3–8.

Kang, Mee-Eun. "The Portrayal of Women's Images in Magazine Advertisements: Goffman's Gender Analysis Revisited." *Sex Roles* 37.11/12 (December 1997): 979–996.

Kantar Media SRDS. "Homepage." SRDS.com <www.srds.com>, accessed 30 May 2014.

Kaplan, Elaine Bell and Cole, Leslie. "'I Want to Read Stuff on Boys': White, Latina, and Black Girls Reading *Seventeen* Magazine and Encountering Adolescence." *Adolescence* 38.149 (Spring 2003): 141–159.

Kaplan, John. "The *Life* Magazine Civil Rights Photography of Charles Moore 1958–1965." *Journalism History* 25.4 (Winter 1999/2000): 126–139.

Karan, Kavita and Feng, Yang. "International Women's Magazines in China: Global and Local Perspectives." *Chinese Journal of Communication* 2.3 (November 2009): 348–366.

Karp, John. "The Impact of Digital and Online Technology on Cross Media Periodicals." In Levenson, Harvey R., ed. *The Reality about the Promise of Printing in the Digital World*. California Polytechnic State University-San Luis Obispo, 2007, 18–39 <http://citeseerx.ist.psu.edu/viewdoc/download?doi=10.1.1.130.7331&rep=rep1&type=pdf>, accessed 20 September 2012.

Katz, Elihu; Blumler, Jay G.; and Gurevitch, Michael. "Uses and Gratifications Research." *Public Opinion Quarterly* 37.4 (Winter 1973): 509–523.

Katz, Elihu; Blumler, Jay G.; and Gurevitch, Michael. "Utilization of Mass Communication by the Individual." In Blumler, Jay G. and Katz, Elihu, eds. *The Uses of Mass Communications: Current Perspectives on Gratifications Research*. Beverly Hills, CA: Sage, 1974, 19–31.

Katz, Elihu; Gurevitch, Michael; and Haas, Hadassah. "On the Use of the Mass Media for Important Things." *American Sociological Review* 38.2 (April 1973): 164–181.

Katz, Jon. "Online or Not, Newspapers Suck." *Wired*, September 1994 <http://www.wired.com/wired/archive/2.09/news.suck.html>, accessed 2 January 2013.

Katz, Mira L.; Sheridan, Stacey; Pignone, Michael; Lewis, Carmen; Battle, Jamila; Gollop, Claudia; and O'Malley, Michael. "Prostate and Colon Cancer Screening Messages in Popular Magazines." *Journal of General Internal Medicine* 19.8 (August 2004): 843–848.

Kava, Ruth; Meister, Kathleen A.; Whelan, Elizabeth M.; Lukachko, Alicia M.; and Mirabile, Christina. "Dietary Supplement Safety Information in Magazines Popular among Older Readers." *Journal of Health Communication* 7.1 (January/February 2002): 13–23.

Kaye, Barbara K. and Johnson, Thomas J. "From Here to Obscurity? Media Substitution Theory and Traditional Media in an On-Line World." *Journal of the American Society for Information Science & Technology* 54.3 (February 2003): 260–273.

Kaye, Barbara K. and Johnson, Thomas J. "Online and in the Know: Uses and Gratifications of the Web for Political Information." *Journal of Broadcasting & Electronic Media* 46.1 (March 2002): 54–71.

Kazanjian, Dodie. *Alex: The Life of Alexander Liberman*. New York: Knopf, 1993.

Kazanjian, Dodie. Vogue: *The Covers*. New York: Abrams, 2011.

Keith, Susan and Schwalbe, Carol B. "Women and Visual Depictions of the U.S.-Iraq War in Print and Online Media." *Visual Communication Quarterly* 17.1 (January/March 2010): 4–17.

Keith, Susan; Schwalbe, Carol B.; and Silcock, B. William. "Visualizing Cross-Media Coverage: Picturing War across Platforms during the U.S.-Led Invasion of Iraq." *Atlantic Journal of Communication* 17.1 (January/March 2009): 1–18.

Kelly, James D. "The Effects of Display Format and Data Density on Time Spent Reading Statistics in Text, Tables and Graphs." *Journalism Quarterly* 70.1 (Spring 1993): 140–149.

Kelly, Kevin. "New Rules for the New Economy." *Wired*, 5.09 September 1997 <http://www.wired.com/wired/archive/5.09/newrules.html>, accessed 30 November 2012.

Kemp, Earl and Ortiz, Luis, eds. *Cult Magazines A to Z: A Compendium of Culturally Obsessive and Curiously Expressive Publications*. New York: Nonstop Press, 2009.

Kemsley, Viscount. *The Kemsley Manual of Journalism*. London: Cassell, 1950.

Kenney, Keith R. "Images of Africa in News Magazines: Is There a Black Perspective?" *Gazette* 54.1 (August 1995): 61–85.

Képes, György. *Language of Vision*. Chicago: Paul Theobald, 1944. Reissued: New York: Dover Publications, 1995.

Kerl, Alexander G. and Walter, Andreas. "Market Responses to Buy Recommendations Issued by Personal Finance Magazines: Effects of Information, Price-Pressure, and Company Characteristics." *Review of Finance* 11.1 (March 2007): 117–141.

Kessler, Eva-Marie and Schwender, Clemens. "Giving Dementia a Face? The Portrayal of Older People with Dementia in German Weekly News Magazines between the Years 2000 and 2009." *Journals of Gerontology, Series B: Psychological Sciences and Social Sciences* 67B.2 (March 2012): 261–270.

Kets de Vries, Manfred F.R. *The Leadership Mystique: A User's Manual for the Human Enterprise*. New York: Financial Times Prentice Hall, 2001.

Kilbourne, William E. "An Exploratory Study of the Effect of Sex Role Stereotyping on Attitudes toward Magazine Advertisements." *Journal of the Academy of Marketing Science* 14.4 (Winter 1986): 43–46.

Kim, Gyong Ho and Paddon, Anna R. "Digital Manipulation as New Form of Evidence of Actual Malice in Libel and False Light Cases." *Communications & the Law* 21.3 (September 1999): 57–73.

Kim, Hun Shik and Smith, C. Zoe. "Sixty Years of Showing the World to America: Pulitzer Prize Photographs, 1942–2002." *International Communication Gazette* 67.4 (August 2005): 307–323.

Kim, Mim-Sun. "A Comparative Analysis of Nonverbal Expressions as Portrayed by Korean and American Print-Media Advertising." *Howard Journal of Communications* 3.3/4 (Winter/Spring 1992): 317–339.

King, Elliot. *Free for All: The Internet's Transformation of Journalism*. Evanston, IL: Northwestern University Press, 2010.

King, Elliot. "Research Review: Issues in Magazine Journalism Education." In Abrahamson, David, ed. *The American Magazine: Research Perspectives and Prospects*. Ames: Iowa State University Press, 1995, 122–133.

King, Elliot. "The Role of Journalism History, and the Academy, in the Development of Core Knowledge in Journalism Education." *Journalism & Mass Communication Educator* 63.2 (Summer 2008): 166–178.

King, Emily. "*Time Out* Cover Design, 1970–1981." In Aynsley, Jeremy and Forde, Kate, eds. *Design and the Modern Magazine*. Manchester and New York: Manchester University Press, 2007, 56–74.

King, Erika G. and Wells, Robert A. "American Newsmagazine Coverage of the Persian Gulf War: The Parallels of World War II and Vietnam." *Southeastern Political Review* 22.2 (June 1994): 341–367.

King, John. *The Role of Mexico's Plural in Latin American Literary and Political Culture: From Tlatelolco to the "Philanthropic Ogre"* [in English]. Studies of the Americas. 1st ed. New York: Palgrave Macmillan, 2007.

Kinross, Robin. "The Rhetoric of Neutrality." *Design Issues* 2.2 (Autumn 1985): 18–30.

Kirk, Andy. *Data Visualization: A Successful Design Process*. Birmingham, UK: Packt Publishing, 2012.

Kirkpatrick, David. "B2B Marketing: 5 Privacy Factors to Consider When Using Marketing Automation." MarketingSherpa, 9 November 2011 <http://www.marketingsherpa.com/article/how-to/5-privacy-factors-to-consider>, accessed 31 May 2014.

Kitch, Carolyn. "'A Death in the American Family': Myth, Memory, and National Values in the Media Mourning of John F. Kennedy Jr." *Journalism & Mass Communication Quarterly* 79.2 (Summer 2002): 294–309.

Kitch, Carolyn. "Destructive Women and Little Men: Masculinity, the New Woman, and Power in 1910s Popular Media." *Journal of Magazine & New Media Research* 1.1 (Spring 1999): 1–15.

Kitch, Carolyn. *The Girl on the Magazine Cover: The Origins of Visual Stereotypes in American Mass Media*. Chapel Hill and London: University of North Carolina Press, 2001.

Kitch, Carolyn. "Making Scholarly Use of Magazines: What Counts Most? What Gets Left Out?" Invited panel presentation to the Magazine Division, Annual Meeting, Association for Education in Journalism and Mass Communication, August 2008.

Kitch, Carolyn. "'Mourning in America': Ritual, Redemption, and Recovery in News Narrative after September 11." *Journalism Studies* 4.2 (2003): 213–224.

Kitch, Carolyn. *Pages from the Past: History and Memory in American Magazines*. Chapel Hill: University of North Carolina Press, 2005.

Kitch, Carolyn and Hume, Janice. *Journalism in a Culture of Grief*. New York: Routledge, 2008.

Kitley, Philip. "*Playboy Indonesia* and the Media: Commerce and the Islamic Public Sphere on Trial in Indonesia." *South East Asia Research* 16.1 (March 2008): 85–116.

Klassen, Michael L.; Jasper, Cynthia R.; and Schwartz, Anne M. "Men and Women: Images of Their Relationships in Magazine Advertisements." *Journal of Advertising Research* 33.2 (March/April 1993): 30–39.

Klean Zwilling, Jillian. "A Feminist Icon in Uncharted Territory: The Public Memory of Gloria Steinem." Paper Presented at the Annual Meeting, International Communication Association, May 2009.

Knight, Jennifer L.; Giuliano, Traci A.; and Sanchez-Ross, Monica G. "Famous or Infamous? The Influence of Celebrity Status and Race on Perceptions of Responsibility for Rape." *Basic and Applied Social Psychology* 23.3 (September 2001): 183–190.

Knobloch-Westerwick, Silvia and Coates, Brendon. "Minority Models in Advertisements in Magazines Popular with Minorities." *Journalism & Mass Communication Quarterly* 83.3 (Autumn 2006): 596–614.

Knobloch-Westerwick, Silvia and Hastall, Matthias R. "Please Your Self: Social Identity Effects on Selective Exposure to News About In- and Out-Groups." *Journal of Communication* 60.3 (September 2010): 515–535.

Knobloch-Westerwick, Silvia and Hoplamazian, Gregory J. "Gendering the Self: Selective Magazine Reading and Reinforcement of Gender Conformity." *Communication Research* 39.3 (June 2012): 358–384.

Knopf, June S. "Images of Change: Magazine Cover Art of the Tumultuous Late Progressive Era." D.Litt., diss., Drew University, 2011.

Knox, Page Stevens. "*Scribner's Monthly*, 1870–1881: Illustrating a New American Art World." Ph.D. diss., Columbia University, 2012.

Kobak, James B. "Just What Is a Magazine?" *How to Start a Magazine and Publish It Profitably*. New York: M. Evans & Company, 2002, 17–18.

Kobré, Kenneth. *Videojournalism: Multimedia Storytelling*. Waltham, MA and Oxford, UK: Focal Press, 2012.

Kolbe, Richard H. and Albanese, Paul J. "Man to Man: A Content Analysis of Sole-Male Images in Male-Audience Magazines." *Journal of Advertising* 25.4 (Winter 1996): 1–20.

Koller, Veronika. "Designing Cognition: Visual Metaphor as a Design Feature in Business Magazines." *Information Design Journal + Document Design* 13.2 (2005): 136–150.

Kolodzy, Janet. "The Multimedia Story: How to Help Audiences Get What They Want and Need." *Practicing Convergence Journalism: An Introduction to Cross-Media Storytelling*. New York: Routledge, 2013, 133–147.

Kolodzy, Janet. *Practicing Convergence Journalism: An Introduction to Cross-Media Storytelling.* New York: Routledge, 2013.

Kon, Martin; Gosalia, Sujata; and Portelette, Edouard. *A New Digital Future for Publishers?* New York: Oliver Wyman, 2009 <http://www.oliverwyman.com/insights/publications/2009/dec/a-new-digital-future-for-publishers.html>, accessed 30 September 2012.

Kopnina, Helen. "Culture and Media: The Study of National Editions of a Fashion Magazine." *Studies in Communication Sciences* 7.1 (2007): 85–101.

Kopnina, Helen. "Education for Sustainable Development (ESD): The Turn Away from 'Environment' in Environmental Education." *Environmental Education Research* 18.5 (2012): 699–717.

Kopnina, Helen. "The Lorax Complex: Deep Ecology, Ecocentrism and Exclusion." *Journal of Integrative Environmental Sciences* 9.4 (December 2012): 235–254 <http://dx.doi.org/10.1080/1943815X.2012.742914>, accessed 31 January 2015.

Kopnina, Helen. "Toward Conservational Anthropology: Addressing Anthropocentric Bias in Anthropology." *Dialectical Anthropology* 36.1/2 (2012): 127–146.

Kopnina, Helen. "What Is (Responsible) Consumption? Discussing Environment and Consumption with Children from Different Socioeconomic Backgrounds in the Netherlands." *The Environmentalist* 31.3 (September 2011): 216–226.

Kopnina, Helen. "The World According to *Vogue*: The Role of Culture(s) in International Fashion Magazines." *Dialectical Anthropology* 31.4 (December 2007): 363–381.

Kopnina, Helen and Shoreman-Ouimet, Eleanor. *Environmental Anthropology: Future Trends.* Routledge Studies in Anthropology Series. New York and Oxford: Routledge, 2013.

Kopnina, Helen and Shoreman-Ouimet, Eleanor. *Environmental Anthropology Today.* New York and Oxford: Routledge, 2011.

Korinis, Mary; Korslund, Mary K.; Belli, Gabriella; Donohue, Joyce M.; and Johnson, Janet M. "Comparison of Calcium and Weight Loss Information in Teen-Focused Versus Women's Magazines over Two 4-Year Periods (1986–1989 and 1991–1994)," *Journal of Nutrition Education* 30.3 (May 1998): 149–154.

Korzeniowska, Victoria B. "Gender, Space and Identification in *Femmes du Maroc* and *Citadine.*" *International Journal of Francophone Studies* 8.1 (April 2005): 3–22.

Koschat, Martin A. and Putsis, William P., Jr. "Audience Characteristics and Bundling: A Hedonic Analysis of Magazine Advertising Rates." *Journal of Marketing Research* 39.2 (May 2002): 262–273.

Kosner, Edward. *It's News to Me: The Making and Unmaking of an Editor.* New York: Thunder's Mouth Press, 2006.

Kovach, Bill and Rosenstiel, Tom. *The Elements of Journalism: What Newspeople Should Know and the Public Should Expect.* New York: Three Rivers Press, 2007.

Kovach, Bill and Rosenstiel, Tom. *Warp Speed: America in the Age of Mixed Media Culture.* New York: Century Foundation Press, 1999.

Kozol, Wendy. "Domesticating NATO's War in Kosovo/a: (In)Visible Bodies and the Dilemma of Photojournalism." *Meridians: Feminism, Race, Transnationalism* 4.2 (2004): 1–38.

Kozol, Wendy. *Life's America: Family and Nation in Postwar Photojournalism.* Philadelphia: Temple University Press, 1994.

Kramarae, Cheris. "The Language and Nature of the Internet: The Meaning of Global." *New Media & Society* 1.1 (April 1999): 47–53.

Kramer, Mark. "Breakable Rules for Literary Journalists." In Sims, Norman and Kramer, Mark, eds. *Literary Journalism: A New Collection of the Best American Nonfiction.* New York: Ballantine Books, 1995, 21–34.

Kramer, Mark. "Narrative Journalism Comes of Age." *Nieman Reports,* Fall 2000, 5–8.

Kramer, Mark and Call, Wendy, eds. *Telling True Stories: A Nonfiction Writers' Guide from the Nieman Foundation at Harvard University.* New York: Plume, 2007.

Krause-Wahl, Antje. "Between Studio and Catwalk—Artists in Fashion Magazines." *Fashion Theory: The Journal of Dress, Body & Culture* 13.1 (March 2009): 7–27.

Kreiss, Daniel; Finn, Megan; and Turner, Fred. "The Limits of Peer Production: Some Reminders from Max Weber for the Network Society." *New Media & Society* 13.2 (March 2011): 243–259.

Kress, Gunther and van Leeuwen, Theo. *Reading Images: The Grammar of Visual Design.* 2nd ed. London and New York: Routledge, 2006.

Krishnan, Satya P.; Durrah, Tracy; and Winkler, Karen. "Coverage of AIDS in Popular African American Magazines." *Health Communication* 9.3 (1997): 273–288.

Kruip, Gudrun. "Restricted Support: The Role of the Axel Springer Verlag in the Process of Westernization." Paper presented at Conference, American Impact on Western Europe: Americanization and Westernization in Transatlantic Perspective, Washington, DC: German Historical Institute, 25–27 March 1999 <http://webdoc.sub.gwdg.de/ebook/p/2005/ghi_12/www.ghi-dc.org/conpotweb/western-papers/kruip.pdf>, accessed 22 July 2013.

Kuczynski, Alex. "How Magazines Stimulate Newsstand Sales." *New York Times*, 18 June 2001, C1–C2.

Kuhn, Martin. "Drawing Civil War Soldiers." *Journalism History* 32.2 (Summer 2006): 96–105.

Kuhn, Thomas S. *The Structure of Scientific Revolutions*. Chicago: University of Chicago Press, 1962.

Kuivalainen, Olli; Ellonen, Hanna-Kaisa; and Sainio, Liisa-Maija. "An Online Success Story: The Role of an Online Service in a Magazine Publisher's Business Model." *International Journal of E-Business Research* 3.3 (2007): 43–59.

Kumar, Deepa. *Outside the Box: Corporate Media, Globalization, and the UPS Strike*. Urbana: University of Illinois Press, 2007.

Küng, Lucy. *Strategic Management in the Media: Theory to Practice*. London: Sage Publications, 2008.

Kunkel, Thomas. "Eighty-Two and Counting: The Continuing Excellence of the *New Yorker*." *American Journalism Review*, 1 April 2007 <http://www.highbeam.com/Doc/1G1-162680245.html>, accessed 31 January 2013.

Kunkel, Thomas. *Genius in Disguise: Harold Ross of the* New Yorker. New York: Random House, 1995.

Kunkel, Thomas, ed. *Letters from the Editor: The* New Yorker's *Harold Ross*. New York: Modern Library, 2001.

Kurtz, Howard. *The Fortune Tellers: Inside Wall Street's Game of Money, Media, and Manipulation*. New York: Free Press, 2000.

Kurtz, Lester R. *Gods in the Global Village: The World's Religions in Sociological Perspective*. 2nd ed. Sociology for a New Century. Thousand Oaks, CA: Pine Forge Press, 2007.

Kwa, Chunglin. "The Taxonomic Style." *Styles of Knowing: A New History of Science from Ancient Times to the Present*. Translated by David McKay. Pittsburgh, PA: University of Pittsburgh Press, 2011, 165–195.

Kweon, Sanghee. "A Framing Analysis: How Did Three U.S. News Magazines Frame about Mergers or Acquisitions?" *International Journal on Media Management* 2.3/4 (Autumn/Winter 2000): 165–176.

La Pastina, Antonio and Quick, Brian. "An Exploration of Internet and Traditional Media Uses in the Rio Grande Valley." Paper presented at the Annual Meeting, International Communication Association, May 2004.

Labbe, Colleen P. and Fortner, Rosanne W. "Perceptions of the Concerned Reader: An Analysis of the Subscribers of E/The Environmental Magazine." *Journal of Environmental Education* 32.3 (March 2001): 41–46.

Labre, Magdala Peixoto and Walsh-Childers, Kim. "Friendly Advice? Beauty Messages in Web Sites of Teen Magazines." *Mass Communication and Society* 6.4 (Fall 2003): 379–396.

Lachover, Einat. "Influential Women: Feminist Discourse in Women's Business Magazines—The Case of Israel." *Communication, Culture & Critique* 6.1 (March 2013): 121–141.

Lacy, Sarah. "Byliner Launches with a Splash, Aims to Disrupt Long-Form Journalism." *TechCrunch.com*, 19 April 2011 <http://techcrunch.com/2011/04/19/byliner-launches-with-a-splash-aims-to-disrupt-long-form-journalism/>, accessed 25 February 2013.

Lamb, Chris. *Drawn to Extremes: The Use and Abuse of Editorial Cartoons*. New York: Columbia University Press, 2004.

Lamb, Yanick Rice. "All the News That Fits on Tablets: An Analysis of News Consumption and Best Practices." Paper presented at the Annual Meeting, Association of Education in Journalism and Mass Communication, August 2013.

Lamb, Yanick Rice and Desrosiers, Kendra. "The Seven Sisters and Their Siblings Go Digital: An Analysis of Women's Magazine Content on Websites, iPads and Cell Phones." In Langmia, Kehbuma; Tyree, Tia C.M.; O'Brien, Pamela; and Sturgis, Ingrid, eds. *Social Media: Pedagogy and Practice*. Lanham, MD: University of America Press Inc., 2014.

Lambiase, Jacqueline. "Promoting Sexy Images: Case Study Scrutinizes *Maxim*'s Cover Formula for Building Quick Circulation and Challenging Competitors." *Journal of Promotion Management* 13.1/2 (2007): 111–125.

Lambiase, Jacqueline and Reichert, Tom. "Sex and the Marketing of Contemporary Consumer Magazines: How Men's Magazines Sexualized Their Covers to Compete with *Maxim*." In Reichert, Tom and Lambiase, Jacqueline, eds. *Sex in Consumer Culture: The Erotic Content of Media and Marketing*. Mahwah, NJ: Lawrence Erlbaum Associates, 2006, 67–86.

Lamuedra Graván, María. "Comparative Study of Magazine Romantic Fiction, True Life Stories and Celebrity Stories: Utopia, Closure and Reader's Participation." Paper presented at Mapping the Magazine Conference, UK, 2008.

Landers, James. *The Improbable First Century of* Cosmopolitan *Magazine*. Columbia: University of Missouri Press, 2010.

Lane, W. Ronald; King, Karen Whitehill; and Reichert, Tom. "Using Magazines." *Kleppner's Advertising Procedure*. 18th ed. Upper Saddle River, NJ: Prentice Hall/Pearson, 2011, 319–355.

Lang, Annie. "Discipline in Crisis? The Shifting Paradigm of Mass Communication Research." *Communication Theory* 23.1 (February 2013): 10–24.

Lang, Annie and Yegiyan, Narine S. "Understanding the Interactive Effects of Emotional Appeal and Claim Strength in Health Messages." *Journal of Broadcasting and Electronic Media* 52.3 (September 2008): 432–447.

Langa, Helen. "'At Least Half the Pages Will Consist of Pictures': *New Masses* and Politicized Visual Art." *American Periodicals* 21.1 (2011): 24–49.

Langewiesche, William, author of Byliner e-book, *Finding the Devil*. Interview by author. 14 February 2013.

Langton, Loup. *Photojournalism and Today's News: Creating Visual Reality*. Chichester, UK: Wiley-Blackwell, 2009.

LaRocque, Paula. *The Book on Writing: The Ultimate Guide to Writing Well*. Arlington, TX: Grey and Guvnor Press, 2003.

LaRose, Robert. "The Problem of Media Habits." *Communication Theory* 20.2 (May 2010): 194–222.

Lasky, Julie. "A New Home Décor Magazine, but Why?" *New York Times*, 28 August 2013 <http://www.nytimes.com/2013/08/29/garden/a-new-home-decor-magazine-but-why.html?_r=0>, accessed 28 May 2014.

Lasorsa, Dominic L. "Sources, Credibility of." In *Encyclopedia of International Media and Communications*. Vol. 4. Johnston, Donald H., ed. San Diego, CA: Academic Press, 2003.

Lasorsa, Dominic L. and Dai, Jia. "Newsroom's Normal Accident? An Exploratory Study of 10 Cases of Journalistic Deception." *Journalism Practice* 1.2 (June 2007): 159–174.

Lasorsa, Dominic L. and Reese, Stephen D. "News Source Use in the Crash of 1987: A Study of Four National Media." *Journalism Quarterly* 67.1 (Spring 1990): 60–71.

Lassila-Merisalo, Maria. "Literary Journalism in Twentieth-Century Finland." In Bak, John S. and Reynolds, Bill, eds. *Literary Journalism across the Globe: Journalistic Traditions and Transnational Influences*. Amherst: University of Massachusetts Press, 2011, 184–207.

Lattin, Bohn David and Underhill, Steve. "The Soul of Politics: The Reverend Jim Wallis's Attempt to Transcend the Religious/Secular Left and the Religious Right." *Journal of Communication and Religion* 29.2 (November 2006): 205–223.

Law, Cheryl and Labre, Magdala Peixoto. "Cultural Standards of Attractiveness: A Thirty-Year Look at Changes in Male Images in Magazines." *Journalism & Mass Communication Quarterly* 79.3 (Autumn 2002): 697–711.

Lazarsfeld, Paul F. and Wyant, Rowena. "Magazines in 90 Cities—Who Reads What?" *Public Opinion Quarterly* 1.4 (October 1937): 29–41.

Le, Cuong Nguyen. *Asian American Assimilation: Ethnicity, Immigration, and Socioeconomic Attainment*. New York: LFB Scholarly Publishing, 2007.

Lebeck, Robert and von Dewitz, Bodo. *Kiosk: A History of Photojournalism*. Göttingen: Steidl, 2001.

Lee, Judith Yaross. "From the Field: The Future of *American Periodicals* and American Periodicals Research." *American Periodicals* 15.2 (2005): 196–201.

Lee, Ki-Young and Joo, Sung-Hee. "The Portrayal of Asian Americans in Mainstream Magazine Ads: An Update." *Journalism & Mass Communication Quarterly* 82.3 (Autumn 2005): 654–671.

Lee, Philip, ed. *The Democratization of Communication*. Cardiff: University of Wales Press, 1995.

Lee, Richard. "Botswana: Victory for Women's Rights in Botswana." *All Africa*, 3 September 2013 <http://allafrica.com/stories/201309040359.html>, accessed 1 March 2014.

Leggatt, Helen. "Digital Magazine Readers Want More Personalized Ads." *BizReport*, 7 February 2012 <http://www.bizreport.com/2012/02/digital-magazine-readers-want-more-personalized-ads.html>, accessed 7 December 2013.

Lehman, Daniel W. *Matters of Fact: Reading Nonfiction over the Edge*. Columbus: Ohio State University Press, 1997.

Lehrer, Jim. "The New Age of Journalism." NewsHour with Jim Lehrer, 19 January 2000 <http://www.pbs.org/newshour/bb/media/jan-june00/new_journalism_1–19.html>, accessed 20 February 2006.

Lehuu, Isabelle. *Carnival on the Page: Popular Print Media in Antebellum America*. Chapel Hill: University of North Carolina Press, 2000.

Le Masurier, Megan. "My Other, My Self: *Cleo* Magazine and Feminism in 1970s Australia." *Australian Feminist Studies* 22.53 (July 2007): 191–211.

Le Masurier, Megan. "What is a Magazine?" in "Australasian Magazines: New Perspectives on Writing and Publishing," ed. Rosemary Williamson and Rebecca Johinke, special issue, *TEXT* 25 (April 2014): 1–16, http://www.textjournal.com.au/speciss/issue25/LeMasurier.pdf.

Len-Ríos, María E.; Hinnant, Amanda; and Park, Sun-A. "Understanding How Health Journalists Judge Public Relations Sources: A Rules Theory Approach." *Public Relations Review* 35.1 (March 2009): 56–65.

Lepre, Carolyn and Bleske, Glen L. "Little Common Ground for Magazine Editors and Professors Surveyed on Journalism Curriculum." *Journalism & Mass Communication Educator* 60.2 (Summer 2005): 190–200.

Lester, Paul Martin. *Images that Injure: Pictorial Stereotypes in the Media*. Westport, CT: Praeger, 1996.

Leung, Louis. "College Student Motives for Chatting on ICQ." *New Media & Society* 3.4 (December 2001): 483–500.

Levin, Jack; Fox, James Alan; and Mazaik, Jason. "Blurring Fame and Infamy: A Content Analysis of Cover-Story Trends in *People* Magazine." *Internet Journal of Criminology* (2005): 1–17 <http://www.internetjournalofcriminology.com/index.html>, accessed 7 February 2015.

Levine, Lawrence W. *Highbrow/Lowbrow: The Emergence of Cultural Hierarchy in America*. Cambridge: Harvard University Press, 1988.

Levy, Mark R. "Watching TV News as Para-Social Interaction." *Journal of Broadcasting* 23.1 (1979): 69–80.

Lewin, Kurt. *Field Theory in Social Science: Selected Theoretical Papers*. Edited by Dorwin Cartwright. New York: Harper & Row, 1951.

Lewin, Kurt. "Frontiers in Group Dynamics: Concept, Method and Reality in Social Science; Social Equilibria and Social Change." *Human Relations* 1.5 (June 1947): 5–41.

Lewis, Michael M., ed. *Panic: The Story of Modern Financial Insanity*. New York: W.W. Norton, 2009.

Lewis, Peggy A. "Preaching, Praying and Strategic Media Planning: From Montgomery to Selma, How the Civil Rights Movement Forced Journalists to Do Their Job." Ph.D. diss., Howard University, 2013.

Lewis, Stanley T. "Periodicals in the Visual Arts." *Library Trends* 10.3 (1962): 330–352.

Li, Pin. "International Cooperation and Globalization of the Magazine Industry in China." *Publishing Research Quarterly* 24.1 (March 2008): 59–63.

Li, Shuang. "A New Generation of Lifestyle Magazine Journalism in China: The Professional Approach." *Journalism Practice* 6.1 (February 2012): 122–137.

Liddle, Dallas. *The Dynamics of Genre: Journalism and the Practice of Literature in Mid-Victorian Britain*. Charlottesville: University of Virginia Press, 2009.

Lieb, Thom. *All the News: Writing and Reporting for Convergent Media*. Boston: Pearson, 2009.

Leit, Richard A.; Gray, James J.; and Pope, Harrison G., Jr. "The Media's Representation of the Ideal Male Body: A Cause for Muscle Dysmorphia?" *International Journal of Eating Disorders* 31.3 (April 2002): 334–338.

Lind, Rebecca Ann, ed. *Race/Gender/Class/Media 3.0: Considering Diversity across Content, Audiences, and Production*. 3rd ed. New York: Pearson, 2013.

Lindner, Katharina. "Images of Women in General Interest and Fashion Magazine Advertisements from 1955 to 2002." *Sex Roles* 51.7/8 (October 2004): 409–421.

Linenthal, Edward Tabor. *The Unfinished Bombing: Oklahoma City in American Memory*. New York: Oxford University Press, 2001.

Lippy, Charles H., ed. *Religious Periodicals of the United States: Academic and Scholarly Journals*. Westport, CT: Greenwood Press, 1986.

Littell, Robert T. *The Men We Became: My Friendship with John F. Kennedy, Jr*. New York: St. Martin's Press, 2004.

Littlejohn, Stephen W. *Theories of Human Communication*. 4th ed. Belmont, CA: Wadsworth, 1992.

Litz, A. Walton. "Maxwell Perkins: The Editor as Critic." In Howard, Wm J. ed. *Editor, Author, and Publisher: Papers Given at the Editorial Conference, University of Toronto, November 1968*. Toronto: University of Toronto Press, 1969, 96–112.

Liu, Matthew Tingchi and Brock, James L. "Selecting a Female Athlete Endorser in China: The Effect of Attractiveness, Match-Up, and Consumer Gender Difference." *European Journal of Marketing* 45.7/8 (2011): 1214–1235.

Liu, Zhengjia and Rodriguez, Lulu. "Psychological and Social Motives for Fashion Magazine Use among Shanghai's Female College Students." *Journal of Magazine & New Media Research* 13.2 (Summer 2012): 1–17 <http://aejmcmagazine.arizona.edu/Journal/Summer2012/LiuRodriguez.pdf>, accessed 19 September 2012.

Lizzi, Giulio; Cantoni, Lorenzo; and Inversini, Alessandro. "When a Magazine Goes Online: A Case Study in the Tourism Field." In Law, Rob; Fuchs, Matthias; and Ricci, Francesco, eds. *Information and Communication Technologies in Tourism 2011: Proceedings of the International Conference.* 26–28 January 2011, Vienna, Austria: Springer-Verlag, 2011, 355–366.

Lois, George. *Covering the '60s: George Lois, the* Esquire *Era.* New York: The Monacelli Press, 1996.

Long, Michael. "Fonic Set for Exposure at Munich's Allianz Arena." *SportsPro,* 6 September 2013 <http://www.sportspromedia.com/news/fonic_set_for_exposure_at_munichs_allianz_arena>, accessed 05 September 2013.

Lora, Ronald and Longton, William Henry, eds. *The Conservative Press in Eighteenth- and Nineteenth-Century America.* Westport, CT: Greenwood Press, 1999.

Lora, Ronald and Longton, William Henry, eds. *The Conservative Press in Twentieth-Century America.* Westport, CT: Greenwood Press, 1999.

Losowsky, Andrew, ed. *We Love Magazines.* Luxembourg: Editions Mike Koedinger SA, 2007.

Lounsberry, Barbara. *The Art of Fact: Contemporary Artists of Nonfiction.* New York: Greenwood Press, 1990.

"Loving Touch: Magazines and CDs Get Luxurious." *Economist,* 8 April 2010 <http://www.economist.com/node/15871885>, accessed 26 May 2013.

Lowry, Dennis T. "Population Validity of Communication Research: Sampling the Samples." *Journalism Quarterly* 56.1 (Spring 1979): 62–68, 76.

Lu, Amy Shirong. "The Characteristics of Introductory Research Methods Courses in Mass Communication Doctoral Programs." *Journalism & Mass Communication Educator* 62.3 (Autumn 2007): 289–304.

Lucking-Reiley, David and Spulber, Daniel F. "Business-to-Business Electronic Commerce." *Journal of Economic Perspectives* 15.1 (Winter 2001): 55–68 <http://www.jstor.org/stable/2696539>, accessed 29 May 2014.

Lueck, Therese L. "Women's Moral Reform Periodicals of the 19th Century: A Cultural Feminist Analysis of the *Advocate.*" *American Journalism* 16.3 (Summer 1999): 37–52.

Lueders, Bill. *An Enemy of the State: The Life of Erwin Knoll.* Monroe, ME: Common Courage Press, 1996.

Lukovitz, Karlene. "Perception vs. Reality: Print's Power in a Digital Age." MPA—The Association of Magazine Media, 14 June 2013 <http://www.magazine.org/node/25206>, accessed 10 October 2013.

Lule, Jack. "Enduring Image of War: Myth and Ideology in a *Newsweek* Cover." *Journal of Popular Culture* 29.1 (Summer 1995): 199–211.

Lumme-Sandt, Kirsi. "Images of Ageing in a 50+ Magazine." *Journal of Aging Studies* 25.1 (January 2011): 45–51.

Lumpkins, Crystal Y.; Cameron, Glen T.; and Frisby, Cynthia M. "Spreading the Gospel of Good Health: Assessing Mass Women's Magazines as Communication Vehicles to Combat Health Disparities among African Americans." *Journal of Media and Religion* 11.2 (2012): 78–90.

Lundell, Åsa Kroon and Ekström, Mats. "The Complex Visual Gendering of Political Women in the Press." *Journalism Studies* 9.6 (2008): 891–910.

Lundmark, Carina. "The New Ecological Paradigm Revisited: Anchoring the NEP Scale in Environmental Ethics." *Environmental Education Research* 13.3 (July 2007): 329–347.

Lupton, Ellen. "Visual Dictionary." In Lupton, Ellen and Miller, J. Abbott, eds. *The ABC's of [Triangle, Square, Circle]: The Bauhaus and Design Theory.* London: Princeton Architectural Press, 1993.

Luther, Catherine A. and Rightler-McDaniels, Jodi L. "'More Trouble than the Good Lord Ever Intended': Representations of Interracial Marriage in U.S. News-Oriented Magazines." *Journal of Magazine & New Media Research* 14.1 (Spring 2013): 1–30 <http://aejmcmagazine.arizona.edu/Journal/Summer2013/Luther.pdf>, accessed 21 September 2013.

Lutz, Catherine A. and Collins, Jane L. *Reading* National Geographic. Chicago and London: University of Chicago Press, 1993.

Lynch, James and Schuler, Drue. "The Matchup Effect of Spokesperson and Product Congruency: A Schema Theory Interpretation." *Psychology & Marketing* 11.5 (September/October 1994): 417–445.

Lynch, Rene. "*Time* Magazine Breastfeeding Cover: A Shocking 'Stroke of Genius.'" *Los Angeles Times,* 11 May 2012 <http://articles.latimes.com/2012/may/11/nation/la-na-nn-time-magazine-breastfeeding-cover-20120511>, accessed 2 January 2014.

Maat, Henk Pander. "How Promotional Language in Press Releases Is Dealt With by Journalists: Genre Mixing or Genre Conflict?" *Journal of Business Communication* 44.1 (January 2007): 59–95.

MacArthur, Amanda. "How American Adults Consume Magazines on Tablets." *Mequoda Tablet Study,* 20 May 2013 <http://www.mequoda.com/free-reports/mequoda-tablet-study/>, accessed 13 January 2014.

MacDougall, A. Kent. "Clay Felker's *New York*." *Columbia Journalism Review*, March/April 1974, 36–47.

Macfarlane, John. "Editing a Magazine Is Like Conducting an Orchestra." *Toronto Life*, July 2006, 19.

Machin, David. "Building the World's Visual Language: The Increasing Global Importance of Image Banks in Corporate Media." *Visual Communication* 3.3 (October 2004): 316–336.

Machin, David and Niblock, Sarah. "The New Breed of Business Journalism for Niche Global News: The Case of Bloomberg News." *Journalism Studies* 11.6 (December 2010): 783–798.

Machin, David and Thornborrow. Joanna. "Branding and Discourse: The Case of *Cosmopolitan*." *Discourse & Society* 14.4 (2003): 453–471.

Machin, David and van Leeuwen, Theo. "Global Media: Generic Homogeneity and Discursive Diversity." *Continuum: Journal of Media & Cultural Studies* 18.1 (March 2004): 99–120.

Machin, David and van Leeuwen, Theo. "Global Schemas and Local Discourses in *Cosmopolitan*." *Journal of Sociolinguistics* 7.4 (November 2003): 493–512.

Machin, David and van Leeuwen, Theo. "Language Style and Lifestyle: The Case of a Global Magazine." *Media, Culture & Society* 27.4 (July 2005): 577–600.

Machlup, Fritz; Leeson, Kenneth; and Associates. "Scope, Structure, and Market of the Journal-Publishing Industry." *Information through the Printed Word: The Dissemination of Scholarly, Scientific, and Intellectual Knowledge*. Vol. 2, *Journals*. New York: Praeger, 1978, 3–37.

Machlup, Fritz; Leeson, Kenneth; and Associates. "Terminological Notes." *Information through the Printed Word: The Dissemination of Scholarly, Scientific, and Intellectual Knowledge*. Vol. 1, *Book Publishing*. New York: Praeger, 1978, 15–22.

MacKinnon, Kenneth. *Representing Men: Maleness and Masculinity in the Media*. New York: Oxford University Press, 2003.

Macleod, Colin. "Adspend in G7 Countries." *International Journal of Advertising* 23.4 (2004): 534–536.

Macmillan Publishers. Victor S. Navasky. *A Matter of Opinion*. Winner of the 2005 George Polk Book Award <http://us.macmillan.com/amatterofopinion/VictorNavasky>, accessed 19 February 2014.

Madden, Normandy. "Dentsu Builds Media Offices across Asia," *Ad Age Media News*, 28 April 2012 <http://adage.com/results?endeca=1&searchprop=AdAgeAll&return=endeca&search_offset=0&search_order_by=score&search_phrase=Dentsu+media/>, accessed 9 July 2013.

Madrigal, Alexis C. "The 12 Timeless Rules for Making a Good Publication." *Atlantic*, 11 November 2010 <http://www.theatlantic.com/technology/archive/2010/11/the-12-timeless-rules-for-making-a-good-publication/66444/>, accessed 25 February 2013.

Madsen, Ole Jacob and Ytre-Arne, Brita. "Me at My Best: Therapeutic Ideals in Norwegian Women's Magazines." *Communication, Culture & Critique* 5.1 (March 2012): 20–37.

"Magazine Industry Sectors." Magforum.com <www.magforum.com/sectors.htm>, accessed 8 February 2013.

"Magazine Media Brands See Advertising, Readership Growth during the First Half of 2013." MPA—The Association of Magazine Media, 9 July 2013 <http://www.magazine.org/mpa/magazine-media-brands-see-advertising-readership-growth-during-first-half-2013#sthash.CJJc7Gor.dpuf>, accessed 1 August 2013.

Magnussen, Anne. "Imagining the Dictatorship, Argentina 1981 to 1982." *Visual Communication* 5.3 (October 2006): 323–344.

Maguire, Miles. "Richard Critchfield: 'Genius' Journalism and the Fallacy of Verification." *Literary Journalism Studies* 1.2 (Fall 2009): 9–21.

Maguire, Miles and Maguire, Roberta S. "Building a Bibliography for the Study of Literary Journalism." *Literary Journalism Studies* 3.2 (Fall 2011): 123–124.

Maguire, Miles and Maguire, Roberta S. "Selected Bibliography of Scholarship and Criticism, Examining Literary Journalism: New Additions." *Literary Journalism Studies* 3.2 (Fall 2011): 126–127.

Maguire, Roberta S. "Riffing on Hemingway and Burke, Responding to Mailer and Wolfe: Albert Murray's 'Anti-Journalism.'" *Literary Journalism Studies* 2.2 (Fall 2010): 9–26.

Mahler, Jonathan. "When 'Long-Form' Is Bad Form." *New York Times*, 24 January 2014 <http://www.nytimes.com/2014/01/25/opinion/when-long-form-is-bad-form.html>, accessed 25 January 2014.

Mahrt, Merja. "The Attractiveness of Magazines as 'Open' and 'Closed' Texts: Values of Women's Magazines and Their Readers." *Mass Communication and Society* 15.6 (November/December 2012): 852–874.

Maier, Scott R. "Do Trade Publications Affect Ethical Sensitivity in Newsrooms?" *Newspaper Research Journal* 21.1 (Winter 2000): 41–50.

Major, Ann Marie. "'Problematic' Situations in Press Coverage of the 1988 U.S. and French Elections." *Journalism Quarterly* 69.3 (Fall 1992): 600–611.

Makemson, Harlen. "One Misdeed Evokes Another: How Political Cartoonists Used 'Scandal Intertextuality' against Presidential Candidate James G. Blaine." *Media History Monographs* 7.2 (2004/2005): 1–20.

Malkin, Amy R.; Wornian, Kimberlie; and Chrisler, Joan C. "Women and Weight: Gendered Messages on Magazine Covers." *Sex Roles* 40.7/8 (April 1999): 647–655.

Mallett, Daniel. "The Relationship of Screen-In Rates and Readership Levels in MRI and SMRB (Mediamark Research Inc., Simmons Market Research Bureau)." [Special Issue: The Growing Importance of Media Research]. *Journal of Advertising Research* 33.1 (1993): 18–22.

Maltby, John; Giles, David C.; Barber, Louise; and McCutcheon, Lynn E. "Intense-Personal Celebrity Worship and Body Image: Evidence of a Link among Female Adolescents." *British Journal of Health Psychology* 10.1 (2005): 17–32.

Mandese, Joe. "Simmons Adopts Rival's Audience Methodology: Magazine Research Change Will Cost Less." *Advertising Age*, 19 September 1994, 1.

Manganello, Jennifer A. "Teens, Dating Violence, and Media Use: A Review of the Literature and Conceptual Model for Future Research." *Trauma, Violence & Abuse* 9.1 (January 2008): 3–18.

Marable, Darwin. "Carl Mydans: An Interview." *History of Photography* 26.1 (2002): 47–52.

Marchand, Roland. *Creating the Corporate Soul: The Rise of Public Relations and Corporate Imagery in American Big Business.* Berkeley: University of California Press, 1998.

Marek, Jayne E. *Women Editing Modernism: "Little" Magazines and Literary History.* Lexington: University Press of Kentucky, 1995.

Marikar, Sheila. "Charlie Sheen's Long List of Legal Woes." *ABC NEWS*, 9 March 2011, 1–2 <http://abcnews.go.com/Entertainment/charlie-sheens-long-list-legal-woes/story?id=13075771>, accessed 8 October 2013.

Marino, Christina and Gerlach, Karen K. "An Analysis of Breast Cancer Coverage in Selected Women's Magazines, 1987–1995." *American Journal of Health Promotion* 13.3 (January/February 1999): 163–170.

Marino, Sal. *Business Magazine Publishing: Creative Ideas on Management, Editorial, Selling Space, Promotion . . . and Boosting Profits.* Lincolnwood, IL: NTC Business Books, 1992.

Marino, Sal. McAllister Top Management Fellowship winner speech given at the Medill School of Journalism, Northwestern University, Evanston, IL, 1985.

Markku, Ruotsila. "Carl McIntire and the Fundamentalist Origins of the Christian Right." *Church History* 81.2 (June 2012): 378–407.Marquis, Alice G. *Hopes and Ashes: The Birth of Modern Times, 1929–1939.* New York: The Free Press, 1986.

Marsden, George M. *Fundamentalism and American Culture: The Shaping of Twentieth-Century Evangelicalism: 1870–1925.* 2nd ed. New York: Oxford University Press, 2006.

Marshall, P. David. "New Media–New Self: The Changing Power of Celebrity." In Marshall, P. David, ed. *The Celebrity Culture Reader.* London: Routledge, 2006, 634–644.

Marten, James, ed. *Lessons of War: The Civil War in Children's Magazines.* Wilmington, DE: SR Books, 1999.

Martens, Peter. "Revisiting the Allegory/Typology Distinction: The Case of Origen." *Journal of Early Christian Studies* 16 (2008): 283–317.

Marti, Donald B. "Agricultural Journalism and the Diffusion of Knowledge: The First Half-Century in America." *Agricultural History* 54.1 (January 1980): 28–37 <http://www.jstor.org/discover/10.2307/3742591?uid=3739560&uid=2129&uid=2&uid=70&uid=4&uid=3739256&sid=21102317316437>, accessed 20 May 2013.

Martin, Christopher R. *Framed!: Labor and the Corporate Media.* Ithaca, NY: ILR Press/Cornell University Press, 2004.

Martin, Edwin. "On Photographic Manipulation." *Journal of Mass Media Ethics* 6.3 (1991): 156–163.

Martin, Kathleen. "How Far Really? Some Marketers Are Ditching the Old Sex Role Stereotypes, but Advertising Still Has a Long Way to Go." *Marketing Magazine*, 2 July 2001, 13–14.

Martin, Mary C. and Gentry, James W. "Stuck in the Model Trap: The Effects of Beautiful Models in Ads on Female Pre-Adolescents and Adolescents." *Journal of Advertising* 26.2 (Summer 1997): 19–33.

Martin, Shannon E. "Using Expert Sources in Breaking Science Stories: A Comparison of Magazine Types." *Journalism Quarterly* 68.1/2 (Spring/Summer 1991): 179–187.

Martínez, Katynka Zazueta. "*Latina* Magazine and the Invocation of a Panethnic Family: Latino Identity as It Is Informed by Celebrities and *Papis Chulos.*" *Communication Review* 7.2 (2004): 155–174.

Marty, Martin E. "The Protestant Press: Limitations and Possibilities." In Marty, Martin E.; Deedy, John G., Jr.; Silverman, David Wolf; and Lekachman, Robert, eds. *The Religious Press in America*. New York: Holt, Rinehart and Winston, 1963, 3–63.

Marty, Martin E.; Deedy, John G., Jr.; Silverman, David Wolf; and Lekachman, Robert. *The Religious Press in America*. New York: Holt, Rinehart and Winston, 1963.

Massé, Mark H. and Popovich, Mark N. "Accredited and Nonaccredited Media Writing Programs Are Stagnant, Resistant to Curricular Reform, and Similar." *Journalism & Mass Communication Educator* 62.2 (Summer 2007): 142–160.

Massé, Mark H. and Popovich, Mark N. "Assessing Faculty Attitudes toward the Teaching of Writing." *Journalism & Mass Communication Educator* 53.3 (August 1998): 50–64.

Massé, Mark H. and Popovich, Mark N. "The National Media Writing Faculty Study." *Journalism & Mass Communication Educator* 59.3 (Autumn 2004): 214–238.

Massie, Keith and Perry, Stephen D. "Hugo Gernsback and Radio Magazines: An Influential Intersection in Broadcast History." *Journal of Radio Studies* 9.2 (2002): 264–281.

Massoni, Kelley. *Fashioning Teenagers: A Cultural History of Seventeen Magazine*. Walnut Creek, CA: Left Coast Press, 2010.

Masteller, Richard N. "Using Brancusi: Three Writers, Three Magazines, Three Versions of Modernism." *American Art* 11.1 (Spring 1997): 46–67.

Mastro, Dana E. "A Social Identity Approach to Understanding the Impact of Television Messages." *Communication Monographs* 70.2 (June 2003): 98–113.

Matheu, Robert and Bowe, Brian J. Creem: *America's Only Rock 'N' Roll Magazine*. New York: Collins Living, 2007.

Mathur, Mahima and Chattopadhyay, Amitava. "The Impact of Moods Generated by Television Programs on Responses to Advertising." *Psychology & Marketing* 8.1 (Spring 1991): 59–77.

Matthews, H. Scott. "The Environmental Implications of the Growth of the Information and Communications Technology Sector." Paper presented to the Environment Directorate, OECD, Paris, 2001.

Mau, Heidi and Kitch, Carolyn. " 'No Longer Chasing Yesterday's Story': New Roles for Newsmagazines in the 21st Century." In Allen, Stuart, ed. *Routledge Companion to News and Journalism*. Rev. ed. London and New York: Routledge/Taylor & Francis, 2012, 649–660.

Maxwell, Kimberly A.; Huxford, John; Borum, Catherine; and Hornik, Robert. "Covering Domestic Violence: How the O.J. Simpson Case Shaped Reporting of Domestic Violence in the News Media." *Journalism & Mass Communication Quarterly* 77.2 (Summer 2000): 258–272.

Mayo, Charles and Pasadeos, Yorgo. "Changes in the International Focus of U.S. Business Magazines, 1964–1988." *Journalism Quarterly* 68.3 (Fall 1991): 509–514.

Maza, Erik. "Project Décor Reviving *Domino* Brand." *Women's Wear Daily*, 29 August 2013 <http://www.wwd.com/media-news/fashion-memopad/playing-dominoes-7103095>, 28 May 2014.

McAlexander, James; Schouten, John; and Koenig, Harold. "Building Brand Community." *Journal of Marketing* 66.1 (2002): 38–54.

McCabe, Katie. "Like Something the Lord Made." *Washingtonian*, August 1989, 108–111, 226–233.

McCandless, David. "The Beauty of Data Visualization." Talk presented at TEDGlobal 2010 Conference. Filmed July 2010. TED video, 17:56 <http://www.ted.com/talks/david_mccandless_the_beauty_of_data_visualization.html>, accessed 22 May 2013.

McCandless, David. Information Is Beautiful.net <http://www.informationisbeautiful.net/>, accessed 23 May 2013.

McCandless, David. *Information Is Beautiful*. 2nd ed. London: Collins, 2012.

McCandless, David. *The Visual Miscellaneum: A Colorful Guide to the World's Most Consequential Trivia*. New York: HarperCollins Publishers, 2009.

McChesney, Robert W. *Communication Revolution: Critical Junctures and the Future of the Media*. New York: The New Press, 2007.

McClister, Nell. "*Bomb* Magazine, Celebrating 25 Years." *New Art Publications* No. 96 (Summer 2006): 22–23.

McConnell, Jane S. "Choosing a Team for Democracy: Henry R. Luce and the Commission on Freedom of the Press." *American Journalism* 14.2 (Spring 1997): 148–163.

McCracken, Ellen. *Decoding Women's Magazines: From* Mademoiselle *to* Ms. Houndmills, Hampshire, UK: Palgrave Macmillan, 1992; Basingstoke, UK: Macmillan, 1993. New York: St. Martin's Press, 1993.

McCullough, Lynette S. and Taylor, Ronald K. "Humor in American, British, and German Ads." *Industrial Marketing Management* 22.1 (February 1993): 17–28 <http://www.sciencedirect.com/science/article/pii/001985019390016Z>, accessed 21 May 2013.

McCutcheon, Lynn E.; Lange, Rense; and Houran, James. "Conceptualization and Measurement of Celebrity Worship." *British Journal of Psychology* 93.1 (2002): 67–87.

McDaniel, Stephen R. "An Investigation of Match-Up Effects in Sport Sponsorship Advertising: The Implications of Consumer Advertising Schemas." *Psychology & Marketing* 16.2 (March 1999): 163–184.

McDonald, Willa. "Creditable or Reprehensible? The Literary Journalism of Helen Garner." In Bak, John S. and Reynolds, Bill, eds. *Literary Journalism across the Globe: Journalistic Traditions and Transnational Influences.* Amherst: University of Massachusetts Press, 2011, 260–275.

McDonough, William and Braungart, Michael, eds. *Cradle to Cradle: Remaking the Way We Make Things.* New York: North Point Press, 2002.

McDowell, Walter S. "Issues in Marketing and Branding." In Albarran, Alan B.; Chan-Olmsted, Sylvia M.; and Wirth, Michael O., eds. *Handbook of Media Management and Economics.* Mahwah, NJ: Lawrence Erlbaum Associates, 2006, 229–250.

McGann, Jerome. "Philology in a New Key." *Critical Inquiry* 39.2 (Winter 2013): 327–346.

McGaurr, Lyn. "Travel Journalism and Environmental Conflict: A Cosmopolitan Perspective." *Journalism Studies* 11.1 (February 2010): 50–67.

McIlroy, Thad. "The Future of Magazines." *The Future of Publishing,* 10 July 2013 <http://thefutureofpublishing.com/industries/the-future-of-magazines>, accessed 4 February 2013.

McIntyre, Douglas A. "Twelve Major Brands that Will Disappear." 24/7 Wall St., 15 April 2009 <http://247wallst.com/2009/04/15/twelve-major-brands-that-will-disappear/>, accessed 28 April 2013.

McIntyre, John E. *The Old Editor Says: Maxims for Writing and Editing.* Baltimore, MA: Apprentice House, 2013.

McKay, Jenny. "Åsne Seierstad and the Bookseller of Kabul." In Keeble, Richard Lance and Tulloch, John, eds. *Global Literary Journalism: Exploring the Journalistic Imagination.* New York: Peter Lang, 2012, 175–190.

McKay, Jenny. *The Magazines Handbook.* 2nd ed. London and New York: Routledge, 2006.

McKay, Jenny. *The Magazines Handbook.* 3rd ed. London and New York: Routledge, 2013.

McKay, Susan and Bonner, Frances. "Educating Readers: Breast Cancer in Australian Women's Magazines." *International Journal of Qualitative Studies in Education* 17.4 (July/August 2004): 517–535.

McKay, Susan and Bonner, Frances. "Telling Stories: Breast Cancer Pathographies in Australian Women's Magazines." *Women's Studies International Forum* 22.5 (September/October 1999): 563–571.

McKeen, William. "A Hunter S. Thompson Bibliography." [Special Issue: Hunter S. Thompson]. *Literary Journalism Studies* 4.1 (Spring 2012): 117–124.

McKeen, William. *Tom Wolfe.* New York: Twayne Publishers, 1995.

McKeen, William. "The Two Sides of Hunter Thompson." [Special Issue: Hunter S. Thompson] *Literary Journalism Studies* 4.1 (Spring 2012): 7–18.

McKeen, William. "The Wolfe Man." 2014 <http://www.williammckeen.com/Tom_Wolfe.html>, accessed 5 December 2012.

McKenzie, Donald F. *Bibliography and the Sociology of Texts: The Panizzi Lectures 1985.* Cambridge: Cambridge University Press, 1999.

McLeod, Jack M. and Becker, Lee B. "The Uses and Gratifications Approach." In Nimmo, Dan D. and Sanders, Keith R., eds. *Handbook of Political Communication.* Beverly Hills, CA: Sage, 1981, 67–99.

McMahon, Kathryn. "The *Cosmopolitan* Ideology and Management of Desire." *Journal of Sex Research* 27.3 (August 1990): 381–396.

McPhee, John. "Editors and Publisher." *New Yorker,* 2 July 2012, 32–38.

McPhee, John. "Progression." *New Yorker,* 14 November 2011, 36–41.

McPhee, John. "Structure: Beyond the Picnic-Table Crisis." *New Yorker,* 14 January 2013, 46–51.

McQuail, Denis. *Mass Communication Theory: An Introduction.* London and Beverly Hills, CA: Sage, 1st ed., 1983; 2nd ed., Newbury Park: 1987; 3rd ed. Thousand Oaks, 1994.

McQuail, Denis. *McQuail's Mass Communication Theory.* London and Thousand Oaks, CA: Sage, 4th ed., 2000; 5th ed., 2005; 6th ed., 2010.

McRobbie, Angela. *Feminism and Youth Culture: From 'Jackie' to 'Just Seventeen.'* Boston: Unwin Hyman, 1991.

McRobbie, Angela. Jackie: *An Ideology of Adolescent Femininity*. Birmingham, UK: The Centre for Contemporary Cultural Studies, University of Birmingham, 1978.

McRobbie, Angela. "Jackie: An Ideology of Adolescent Femininity." In Waites, Bernard; Bennett, Tony; and Martin, Graham, eds. *Popular Culture: Past and Present*. London: Open University Press, 1982, 263–283.

McRobbie, Angela. *Postmodernism and Popular Culture*. Florence, KY: Routledge, 1994.

McRobbie, Angela. "Young Women and Consumer Culture: An Intervention." *Cultural Studies* 22.5 (September 2008): 531–550.

McShane, Steven L. "Occupational, Gender, and Geographic Representation of Information Sources in U.S. and Canadian Business Magazines." *Journalism & Mass Communication Quarterly* 72.1 (Spring 1995): 190–204.

Meakin, Budgett. *Model Factories and Villages: Ideal Conditions of Labour and Housing*. London: T. Fisher Unwin, 1905.

Mehltretter, Sarah Ann. "Dorothy Day, the Catholic Workers, and Moderation in Religious Protest during the Vietnam War." *Journal of Communication and Religion* 32.1 (March 2009): 1–32.

Mehta, Ved. *Remembering Mr. Shawn's New Yorker: The Invisible Art of Editing*. Woodstock, NY: The Overlook Press, 1998.

Mellow, James R. *Walker Evans*. New York: Basic Books, 1999.

Meloy, Michelle L. and Miller, Susan L. "Words that Wound: Print Media's Presentation of Gendered Violence." In Humphries, Drew, ed. *Women, Violence and the Media*. Hanover, NH: University Press of New England, 2009, 29–56.

Melzer, Arthur M.; Weinberger, Jerry; and Zinman, M. Richard, eds. *Democracy and the Arts*. Ithaca, NY: Cornell University Press, 1999.

Mendelson, Andrew and Smith, C. Zoe. "Part of the Team: *Life* Photographers and Their Symbiotic Relationship with the Military during World War II." *American Journalism* 12.3 (1995): 276–289.

Mercado-Martinez, Francisco J.; Robles-Silva, Leticia; Moreno-Leal, Nora; and Franco-Almazan, Claudia. "Inconsistent Journalism: The Coverage of Chronic Diseases in the Mexican Press." *Journal of Health Communication* 6.3 (July/September 2001): 235–247.

Merriam-Webster's Collegiate Dictionary. 11th ed. Springfield, MA: Merriam-Webster, 2004.

Merrill, John C. "The Four Theories of the Press Four and a Half Decades Later: A Retrospective." *Journalism Studies* 3.1 (February 2002): 133–136.

Merrill, John C.; Lee, John D.; and Friedlander, Edward Jay. "Books and Magazines." *Modern Mass Media*. New York: Harper & Row, 1990, 140–168.

Mersey, Rachel Davis. *Can Journalism Be Saved? Rediscovering America's Appetite for News*. Santa Barbara, CA: Praeger, 2010.

Mersey, Rachel Davis. "The Identity Experience." In Peck, Abe and Malthouse, Edward C., eds. *Medill on Media Engagement*. New York: Hampton Press, 2010, 81–93.

Merton, Robert K. *On the Shoulders of Giants: A Shandean Postscript*. New York: Free Press, 1965.

Meyer, Michael. "Going to Great Lengths." *Columbia Journalism Review*, November/December 2012, 16–17.

Meyers, Erin. "'Can You Handle My Truth?': Authenticity and the Celebrity Star Image." *Journal of Popular Culture* 42.5 (2009): 890–907.

Mickey, Bill. "How Revenue Models Are Evolving for Online-Only Publishers." *Folio:*, 17 December 2012 <http://www.foliomag.com/2012/how-revenue-models-are-evolving-online-only-publishers#.Ut2yjtLnbDc>, accessed 2 June 2014.

Mickey, Bill. "Politico Plans Print Magazine Launch as It Passes 1,000 Pro Subscriber Mark." *Folio:*, 12 March 2013 <http://www.foliomag.com/2013/politico-plans-print-magazine-launch-it-passes-1–000-pro-subscriber-mark#.UVJJyI6wnTC>, accessed 27 March 2013.

Mierzjewska, Bozena I. and Hollifield, C. Ann. "Theoretical Approaches in Media Management Research." In Albarran, Alan B.; Chan-Olmsted, Sylvia M.; and Wirth, Michael O., eds. *Handbook of Media Management and Economics*. Mahwah, NJ: Lawrence Erlbaum Associates, 2006, 37–66.

Mikaelian, Allen. "Middlemen by Profession: Popular Fiction and the Rise of the In-House Book Editor." M.A. diss., Institute of English Studies, University of London, 1997.

Milavsky, J. Ronald. "Recent Journal and Trade Publication Treatments of Globalization in Mass Media Marketing and Social Change." *International Journal of Advertising* 12.1 (1993): 45–56 <http://www.internationaljournalofadvertising.com/ArticleViewer.aspx?ID=5418>, accessed 13 May 2013.

Millard, Jennifer E. and Grant, Peter R. "The Stereotypes of Black and White Women in Fashion Magazine Photographs: The Pose of the Model and the Impression She Creates." *Sex Roles* 54.9/10 (May 2006): 659–673.

Miller, James S. "White-Collar Excavations: *Fortune* Magazine and the Invention of the Industrial Folk." *American Periodicals* 13 (2003): 84–104.

Miller, Jon D. "Public Understanding of, and Attitudes toward, Scientific Research: What We Know and What We Need to Know." *Public Understanding of Science* 13.3 (July 2004): 273–294.

Miller, Laura. "There's More than *Manga*: Popular Nonfiction Books and Magazines." In Robertson, Jennifer, ed. *A Companion to the Anthropology of Japan*. Malden, MA: Blackwell Publishing, 2005, 314–326.

Miller, Monica K. and Summers, Alicia. "Gender Differences in Video Game Characters' Roles, Appearances and Attire as Portrayed in Video Game Magazines." *Sex Roles* 57.9/10 (November 2007): 733–742.

Millman, Gregory J. "No Longer Just Gray: Business Journalism Takes Off." *Financial Executive*, October 2006, 18–23.

Miner, Earl, ed. *Literary Uses of Typology from the Late Middle Ages to the Present*. Princeton, NJ: Princeton University Press, 1977.

Mirabella, Grace. *In and Out of Vogue: A Memoir*. New York: Doubleday, 1995.

Mitchell, Bill. "Recasting the Anonymous Source as 'Exceptional Event.'" *MediaWire*. Poynter. org, 18 June 2004 <http://www.poynter.org/content/content_view.asp?id=67304>, accessed 30 November 2012.

Mitchell, Pama A. "The Response of the Broadcasting and Advertising Trade Press to Television Blacklisting Practices, 1950–1956." *Mass Comm Review* 16.1/2 (1989): 63–69 <http://eric.ed.gov /?id=ED311487>, accessed 30 May 2014.

Mitchell, W.J.T. *Iconology: Image, Text, Ideology*. Chicago and London: University of Chicago Press, 1986.

Moeran, Brian. "More than Just a Fashion Magazine." *Current Sociology* 54.5 (September 2006): 725–744.

Moeran, Brian. "The Portrayal of Beauty in Women's Fashion Magazines." *Fashion Theory: The Journal of Dress, Body & Culture* 14.4 (December 2010): 491–510.

Mogel, Leonard. "Serial Rights, Foreign Licensing, and Publishing." *The Magazine*. 4th ed. Pittsburgh, PA: GATFPress, 1998, 147–151.

Mogel, Leonard. "What Is a Magazine?" *The Magazine*. 4th ed. Pittsburgh: GATFPress, 1998, 10–12.

Moldovan, Raluca. "A Tale of Two Clintons: Media Bias in the Coverage of Hillary Clinton's 2008 Presidential Campaign." *Studia Universitatis Babeş-Bolyai, Studia Europaea* 54.2 (2009): 41–60.

Mondini, Silvia; Favaro, Angela; and Santonastaso, Paolo. "Eating Disorders and the Ideal of Feminine Beauty in Italian Newspapers and Magazines." *European Eating Disorders Review* 4.2 (June 1996): 112–120.

Monk-Turner, Elizabeth; Wren, Kristy; McGill, Leanne; Matthiae, Chris; Brown, Stephan; and Brooks, Derrick. "Who Is Gazing at Whom?: A Look at How Sex Is Used in Magazine Advertisements." *Journal of Gender Studies* 17.3 (September 2008): 201–209.

Montgomery, M.R. "He Rules the *Atlantic* without Making Waves." *Boston Globe*, 7 March 1995, 55.

Moore, Carley. "Invasion of the Everygirl: *Seventeen* Magazine, 'Traumarama!' and the Girl Writer." *Journal of Popular Culture* 44.6 (December 2011): 1248–1267.

Moore, Roberta J. "The Beginning and Development of Protestant Journalism in the United States, 1743–1850." Ph.D. diss., Syracuse University, 1968.

Moorehead, Caroline. *Gellhorn: A Twentieth-Century Life*. New York: Henry Holt, 2003.

Morgan, Winona and Leahy, Alice M. "The Cultural Content of General Interest Magazines." *Journal of Educational Psychology* 25 (October 1934): 530–536.

Moriarty, Sandra E. and Popovich, Mark N. "Newsmagazine Visuals and the 1988 Presidential Election." *Journalism Quarterly* 68.3 (Fall 1991): 371–380.

Morimoto, Mariko and Chang, Susan. "Western and Asian Models in Japanese Fashion Magazine Ads: The Relationship with Brand Origins and International Versus Domestic Magazines." *Journal of International Consumer Marketing* 21.3 (July 2009): 173–187.

Morin, Monte. "Robert Downy Jr. Gets 3 Years in Prison." *Los Angeles Times*, 6 August 1999 <http:// articles.latimes.com/1999/aug/06/local/me-63303>, accessed 8 October 2013.

Morris, Pamela K. and Waldman, Jennifer A. "Culture and Metaphors in Advertising: France, Germany, Italy, the Netherlands, and the United States." *International Journal of Communication* 5 (2011): 942–968.

Morrish, John. *Magazine Editing: How to Develop and Manage a Successful Publication*. 2nd ed. London and New York: Routledge, 2003.

Morrisson, Mark S. *The Public Face of Modernism: Little Magazines, Audiences, and Reception, 1905–1920*. Madison: University of Wisconsin Press, 2001.

Morton, Leith. "The Concept of Romantic Love in the *Taiyō* Magazine 1895–1905." *Japan Review* 8 (1997): 79–103.

Morton, Thomas A. and Duck, Julie M. "Social Identity and Media Dependency in the Gay Community: The Prediction of Safe Sex Attitudes." *Communication Research* 27.4 (August 2000): 438–460.

Moses, Lucia. "'The *Economist*' Sets Digital Rate Base: Claims a First in the Magazine World." *Adweek*, 25 September 2012 <http://www.adweek.com/news/press/economist-sets-digital-rate-base-143969>, accessed 28 March 2013.

Moses, Lucia. "'*Lucky*' Mag's Technology Solution." *Adweek*, 16 July 2012 <http://www.adweek.com/news/press/lucky-mags-technology-solution-141910>, accessed 6 September 2013.

Moses, Lucia. "Tablets Helping Publishers Sell Back Issues." *Adweek*, 9 January 2012 <http://www.adweek.com/news/press/tablets-helping-publishers-sell-back-issues-137387>, accessed 26 April 2013.

Moss, Jean Russel. "Walking the Tightrope: The Story of Nursing as Told by Nineteenth-Century Nursing Journals." Ph.D. diss., The University of Iowa, 1987.

Mosse, David. *Cultivating Development: An Ethnography of Aid Policy and Practice.* London and Ann Arbor, MI: Pluto Press. 2005.

Moszkowicz, Julia. "Gestalt and Graphic Design: An Exploration of the Humanistic and Therapeutic Effects of Visual Organization." *Design Issues* 27.4 (Autumn 2011): 56–67.

Mott, Frank Luther. *A History of American Magazines.* Vol. 1, *A History of American Magazines, 1741–1850*; Vol. 2, *A History of American Magazines, 1850–1865*; Vol. 3, *A History of American Magazines, 1865–1885*; Vol. 4, *A History of American Magazines, 1885–1905*; Vol. 5, *A History of American Magazines, 1905–1930.* New York: D. Appleton, 1930; Cambridge, MA: The Belknap Press, 1938, 1938, 1957; Cambridge, MA: Harvard University Press, 1968.

Mott, Frank Luther. "Introduction." *A History of American Magazines 1741–1850.* Vol. 1. New York: D. Appleton, 1930, 1–9.

Mott, Frank Luther. "Unfinished Story; or, the Man in the Carrel." *Time Enough: Essays in Autobiography.* Chapel Hill: University of North Carolina Press, 1962, 169–180.

MPA—The Association of Magazine Media. "Magazine Media Readers Are Social." April 2012, 4, 9 <http://www.magazine.org/sites/default/files/SOCIAL-f5%20website.pdf>, accessed 8 January 2014.

MPA—The Association of Magazine Media. Twitter Infographic, 13 February 2014, 7:24 a.m. <https://twitter.com/mpamagmedia/status/433984949876584448/photo/1>, accessed 16 February 2014.

Mueller, Barbara. "Reaching African American Consumers: African American Shopping Behavior." In Dines, Gail and Humez, Jean M., eds. *Gender, Race, and Class in Media: A Critical Reader.* 3rd ed. Thousand Oaks, CA: Sage, 2011, 213–220.

Muniz, Albert and O'Guinn, Thomas. "Brand Community." *Journal of Consumer Research* 27.4 (2001): 412–432.

Murray, Ray. "Stalking the Paparazzi: A View from a Different Angle." *Visual Communication Quarterly* 18.1 (January 2011): 4–17.

Murray, Susan. "Digital Images, Photo-Sharing, and Our Shifting Notions of Everyday Aesthetics." *Journal of Visual Culture* 7.2 (2008): 147–163.

Mussell, James. "Nineteenth-Century Popular Science Magazines: Narrative and the Problem of Historical Materiality." *Journalism Studies* 8.4 (August 2007): 656–666.

Mussey, Dagmar and Hall, Emma. "Global Highlight: *Vanity Fair* in Germany." *Advertising Age*, 26 February 2007, 36.

Myers, David G. "The Decline and Fall of Literary Journalism." *Literary Commentary* (blog). *Commentary*, 8 June 2012 <http://www.commentarymagazine.com/2012/06/08/literary-journalism-then-now/>, accessed 6 January 2014.

Nacos, Brigitte L. "Terrorism as Breaking News: Attack on America." *Political Science Quarterly* 118.1 (Spring 2003): 23–52.

Nadesan, Majia Holmer. "*Fortune* on Globalization and the New Economy: Manifest Destiny in a Technological Age." *Management Communication Quarterly* 14.3 (February 2001): 498–506.

Najjar, Orayb Aref. "'The Editorial Family of al-Kateb Bows in Respect': The Construction of Martyrdom Text Genre in One Palestinian Political and Literary Magazine." *Discourse & Society* 7.4 (1996): 499–530.

Napoli, Philip M. "The Media Trade Press as Technology Forecaster: A Case Study of the VCR's Impact on Broadcasting." *Journalism & Mass Communication Quarterly* 74.2 (Summer 1997): 417–430 <http://jmq.sagepub.com/content/74/2/417.short>, accessed 25 January 2013.

Narunsky-Laden, Sonja. "Consumer Magazines in South Africa and Israel: Toward a Socio-Semiotic Approach to Magazine Research." *Journalism Studies* 8.4 (2007): 595–612.

Nasaw, David. *The Chief: The Life of William Randolph Hearst*. Boston: Houghton Mifflin, 2000.

National Directory of Magazines. "A Magazine for Everyone." 14 July 2011 <www.magazine.org/handbook_2010/2011>, accessed 12 November 2012.

National Directory of Magazines. New York: Oxbridge Communications, 2014.

Navasky, Victor S. "Editorial Note." *New York Review of Magazines*. New York: Columbia University Graduate School of Journalism, 2007 <http://archives.jrn.columbia.edu/nyrm/2007/ednote.html>, accessed 10 November 2010.

Navasky, Victor S. *A Matter of Opinion*. New York: Farrar, Straus and Giroux, 2005.

Navasky, Victor S. and Cornog, Evan, eds. *The Art of Making Magazines: On Being an Editor and Other Views from the Industry*. New York: Columbia University Press, 2012.

"Neal Awards." ABM—The Association of Business Information & Media Companies <http://www.abmassociation.com/abm/Neal_Awards2.asp>, accessed 30 May 2014.

Nelissen, Paul and van Selm, Martine. "Surviving Organizational Change: How Management Communication Helps Balance Mixed Feelings." *Corporate Communications: An International Journal* 13.3 (2008): 306–318.

Nelson, Daniel. *Managers and Workers: Origins of the Twentieth-Century Factory System in the United States, 1880–1920*. 2nd ed. Madison: University of Wisconsin Press, 1995.

Nelson, Michelle R. and Paek, Hye-Jin. "A Content Analysis of Advertising in a Global Magazine across Seven Countries: Implications for Global Advertising Strategies." *International Marketing Review* 24.1 (2007): 64–86.

Nelson, Michelle R. and Paek, Hye-Jin. "Cross-Cultural Differences in Sexual Advertising Content in a Transnational Women's Magazine." *Sex Roles* 53.5/6 (September 2005): 371–383.

Nettleton, Pamela Hill. "Domestic Violence in Men's and Women's Magazines: Women Are Guilty of Choosing the Wrong Men, Men Are Not Guilty of Hitting Women." *Women's Studies in Communication* 34.2 (Summer 2011): 139–160.

Nettleton, Sarah. "Governing the Risky Self: How to Become Healthy, Wealthy and Wise." In Petersen, Alan and Bunton, Robin, eds. *Foucault, Health and Medicine*. London: Routledge, 1997, 207–222.

Neuman, Fredric. "Changing Gender Roles in Marriage." *Fighting Fear* (blog). *Psychology Today*, 4 January 2013 <http://www.psychologytoday.com/blog/fighting-fear/201301/changing-gender-roles-in-marriage>, accessed 6 September 2013.

Neuman, W. Russell; Just, Marion R.; and Crigler, Ann N. *Common Knowledge: News and the Construction of Political Meaning*. Chicago: University of Chicago Press, 1992.

Neville, Helen A. and Pieterse, Alex L. "Racism, White Supremacy, and Resistance: Contextualizing Black American Experiences." In Neville, Helen A.; Tynes, Brendesha M.; and Utsey, Shawn O., eds. *Handbook of African American Psychology*. Los Angeles, CA: Sage, 2009, 159–272.

Nevins, Jess. *Pulp Magazine Holdings Directory: Library Collections in North America and Europe*. Jefferson, NC: McFarland, 2007.

Newbury, Darren. "Johannesburg Lunch-Hour 1951–1963." *Journalism Studies* 8.4 (August 2007): 584–594.

Newton, Isaac. Letter to Robert Hooke, 5 February 1676, as transcribed in *The Correspondence of Isaac Newton*, Vol. 1. H.W. Turnbull, ed. Cambridge, UK: Cambridge University Press, 1959, 416.

Newton, Julianne H. *The Burden of Visual Truth: The Role of Photojournalism in Mediating Reality*. Mahwah, NJ: Lawrence Erlbaum, 2001.

"The New York Times Launches E-Book Programs," Business Wire, 13 December 2012 <http://www.businesswire.com/news/home/20121213006180/en/York-Times-Launches-E-Book-Programs#.VMryz010wy4>, accessed 29 January 2015.

New York Magazine. Archives: Tom Wolfe <http://nymag.com/nymag/tom-wolfe/>, accessed 31 January 2014.

Nguyen, Thuc Doan. "*AudreyMagazine.com*: Portrayals of Asian American Women Online by Asian American Women." In Lind, Rebecca Ann, ed. *Race/Gender/Class/Media 3.0: Considering Diversity across Content, Audiences, and Production*. 3rd ed. New York: Pearson, 2013, 269–273.

Nichols, Heidi L. *The Fashioning of Middle-Class America*: Sartain's Union Magazine of Literature and Art and Antebellum Culture. New York: Peter Lang, 2004.

Nielsen. "Mobile Majority: U.S. Smartphone Ownership Tops 60%." Nielsen, 6 June 2013 <http://www.nielsen.com/us/en/newswire/2013/mobile-majority—u-s—smartphone-ownership-tops-60-.html>, accessed 7 December 2013.

Nikolaev, Alexander G. "Images of War: Content Analysis of the Photo Coverage of the War in Kosovo." *Critical Sociology* 35.1 (January 2009): 105–130.

Nisbet, Matthew C. and Scheufele, Dietram A. "What's Next for Science Communication? Promising Directions and Lingering Distractions." *American Journal of Botany* 96.10 (October 2009): 1767–1778.

"'Nones' on the Rise." Pew Research: Religion and Public Life Project, 9 October 2012 <http://www.pewforum.org/2012/10/09/nones-on-the-rise>, accessed 15 June 2013.

Noonan, Mark J. *Reading the* Century Illustrated Monthly Magazine: *American Literature and Culture, 1870–1893.* Kent, OH: Kent State University Press, 2010.

Nord, David Paul. "Intellectual History, Social History, Cultural History . . . and Our History." *Journalism Quarterly* 67.4 (Winter 1990): 645–648.

Nordland, Rod. "Portrait of Pain Ignites a Debate Over the Afghan War." *New York Times*, 5 August 2010, A6(L).

Norris, Vincent P. "Consumer Magazine Prices and the Mythical Advertising Subsidy." *Journalism Quarterly* 59.2 (Summer 1982): 205–211.

North, Robert C.; Holsti, Ole R.; Zaninovich, M. George; and Zinnes, Dina A. *Content Analysis: A Handbook with Applications for the Study of International Crisis.* Evanston, IL: Northwestern University Press, 1963.

Norton, Scott. *Developmental Editing: A Handbook for Freelancers, Authors, and Publishers.* Chicago: University of Chicago Press, 2009.

"Nothing to Shout About." *Economist*, 30 July 2009 <http://www.economist.com/node/14140373>, accessed 20 December 2012.

Nourie, Alan and Nourie, Barbara, eds. *American Mass-Market Magazines.* Westport, CT: Greenwood Press, 1990.

Nunberg, Geoffrey. "Farewell to the Information Age." In Nunberg, Geoffrey ed. *The Future of the Book.* Berkeley: University of California Press, 1996, 103–138.

Nuttall, Sarah. "Stylizing the Self: The Y Generation in Rosebank, Johannesburg." *Public Culture* 16.3 (Fall 2004): 430–452.

Nwafor, Okechukwu. "Of *Mutuality* and *Copying*: Fashioning *Aso Ebi* through Fashion Magazines in Lagos." *Fashion Theory: The Journal of Dress, Body & Culture* 16.4 (December 2012): 493–520.

Nye, David E. *American Technological Sublime.* Cambridge: MIT Press, 1994.

Nykanen, Kaisa; Suominen, Tarja; and Nikkonen, Merja. "Representations of Hysterectomy as a Transition Process in Finnish Women's and Health Magazines." *Scandinavian Journal of Caring Sciences* 25.3 (September 2011): 608–616.

"Obituaries: Gordon Parks (1912–2006)." *History of Photography* 30.3 (Autumn 2006): 283–284.

"Obituaries: Loomis Dean (1917–2005)." *History of Photography* 30.2 (Summer 2006): 185.

"Obituaries: Thomas J. Abercrombie (1931–2006)." *History of Photography* 30.3 (Autumn 2006): 283.

O'Callaghan, Jerome and Dukes, James O. "Media Coverage of the Supreme Court's Caseload." *Journalism Quarterly* 69.1 (Spring 1992): 195–203.

O'Dea, Dathalinn M. "Modernist Nationalism in *Dana: An Irish Magazine of Independent Thought* (1904)." *Éire-Ireland* 45.3/4 (Fall/Winter 2010): 95–123.

O'Donnell, Michael. "Teaching Publication Design with Desktop Technology." *Journalism Educator* 49.4 (Winter 1995): 47–56.

Oh, David Chison. "Complementary Objectivity and Ideology: Reifying White Capitalist Hierarchies in *Time* Magazine's Construction of Michelle Rhee." *Journal of Communication Inquiry* 34.2 (April 2010): 151–167.

Oh, Hyun Sook and Frith, Katherine. "Globalization and Localization in the Production Process of International Women's Magazines in Korea." Paper presented at the Annual Meeting, International Communication Association, May 2007.

Ohmann, Richard M. *Selling Culture: Magazines, Markets and Class at the Turn of the Century.* London and New York: Verso, 1996.

O'Keefe, Garrett J. and Sulanowski, Barbara K. "More Than Just Talk: Uses, Gratifications, and the Telephone." *Journalism & Mass Communication Quarterly* 72.4 (Winter 1995): 922–933.

Okker, Patricia. *Our Sister Editors: Sarah J. Hale and the Tradition of Nineteenth-Century American Women Editors.* Athens: University of Georgia Press, 1995.

Okker, Patricia, ed. *Transnationalism and American Serial Fiction.* New York: Routledge, 2012.

Olasky, Marvin. *Telling the Truth: How to Revitalize Christian Journalism*. Wheaton, IL: Crossway Books, 1996.

Ono, Kent A. and Phan, Vincent N. *Asian Americans and the Media*. Malden, MA: Polity Press, 2009.

On-line database: *American Periodical Series, 1740–1940*. Ann Arbor, MI: ProQuest, 2000.

Oppenheimer, Jerry. *Front Row: Anna Wintour, the Cool Life and Hot Times of Vogue's Editor-In-Chief*. New York: St. Martin's Press, 2005.

Oppenheimer, Jerry. *Martha Stewart—Just Desserts: The Unauthorized Biography*. New York: William Morrow and Company, 1997.

Oremus, Will. "Google Has Officially Eaten the Newspaper Industry." *Future Tense* (blog), *Slate.com*, 12 November 2012 <http://www.slate.com/blogs/future_tense/2012/11/12/google_ad_revenue_tops_entire_us_print_media_industry_chart.html>, accessed 2 June 2014.

Orth, Ulrich R., and Holancova, Denisa. "Men's and Women's Responses to Sex Role Portrayals in Advertisements." *International Journal of Research in Marketing* 21.1 (March 2004): 77–88.

Osterwalder, Alexander; Pigneur, Yves; and Tucci, Christopher. "Clarifying Business Models: Origins, Present and Future of the Concept." *Communications of the Association for Information Systems* 15 (May 2005): 1–25.

Ostler, Nicholas. *Empires of the Word: A Language History of the World*. New York and London: Harper Perennial, 2005.

Ouellette, Laurie. "Inventing the Cosmo Girl: Class Identity and Girl-Style American Dreams." *Media, Culture & Society* 21.3 (May 1999): 359–383.

Owen, Laura Hazard. "The Rise of E-Singles: It's a Long Story." *Business Week*, 31 December 2012, 1.

Owen, William. *Modern Magazine Design*. New York: Rizzoli, 1991.

Packer, Cathy and Gower, Karla K. "The Persistent Problem of Media Taxation: First Amendment Protection in the 1990s." *Journalism & Mass Communication Quarterly* 74.3 (Autumn 1997): 579–590.

Paden, William D. *An Introduction to Old Occitan*. New York: Modern Language Association of America, 1998, 3–9.

Paisley, William. "The Convergence of Communication and Information Science." In Edelman, Hendrik, ed. *Libraries and Information Science in the Electronic Age*. Philadelphia, PA: ISI Press, 1986, 122–153.

Palmer, Erik. "How to Read Richard Avedon." *Visual Communication Quarterly* 17.3 (July/September 2010): 147–161.

Palmgreen, Philip; Wenner, Lawrence A.; and Rosengren, Karl Erik. "Uses and Gratifications Research: The Past Ten Years." In Rosengren, Karl Erik; Wenner, Lawrence A.; and Palmgreen, Philip, eds. *Media Gratifications Research*. London: Sage, 1985, 11–37.

Panzer, Mary. *Things as They Are: Photojournalism in Context since 1955*. New York: Aperture, 2005.

Papper, Robert A.; Holmes, Michael E.; and Popovich, Mark N. "Middletown Media Studies: Media Multitasking . . . and How Much People Really Use the Media." *International Digital Media and Arts Association Journal* 1.1 (Spring 2004): 4–56.

Parameswaran, Radhika. "Local Culture in Global Media: Excavating Colonial and Material Discourses in *National Geographic*." *Communication Theory* 12.3 (August 2002): 287–315.

Parekh, Rupal. "Many Magazines Racing to Capitalize on Pinterest." *Ad Age*, 2 April 2012 <http://adage.com/article/media/magazines-racing-capitalize-pinterest/233865/>, accessed 28 April 2013.

Park, Jacob and Roome, Nigel. *The Ecology of the New Economy—Sustainable Transformation of Global Information, Communications and Electronics Industries*. Sheffield, UK: Greenleaf Publishing, 2002.

Parry, Sheila. "Finding a Global Voice for DP DHL's Internal Magazine." *Strategic Communication Management* 13.4 (June/July 2009): 24–27.

Pascale, Richard Tanner and Athos, Anthony G. *The Art of Japanese Management: Applications for American Executives*. New York: Simon and Schuster, 1981.

Pasqua, Thomas M., Jr.; Buckalew, James K.; Rayfield, Robert E.; and Tankard, James W., Jr. "Magazines." *Mass Media in the Information Age*. Englewood Cliffs, NJ: Prentice Hall, 1990, 66–83.

Pasternack, Steve and Utt, Sandra H. "Reader Use and Understanding of Newspaper Infographics." *Newspaper Research Journal* 11.2 (Spring 1990): 28–41.

Patel, Arti. "Time Inc.'s Cover Ads Cause Stir, But No Backlash." *Folio:*, 22 May 2014 <http://www.foliomag.com/2014/time-inc-s-cover-ads-cause-stir-no-backlash?hq_e=el&hq_m=2886693&hq_l=7&hq_v=289ee2c2f2#.U38ssyhuJU1>, accessed 22 May 2014.

Pathak, Shareen. "East Meets West in Nissan Social Media Bollywood Link." *Ad Age Media News*, 21, 9 April 2012 <http://adage.com/article/global-news/east-meets-west-nissan-social-media-bollywood-link/233980/>, accessed 9 July 2013.

Patmore, Greg and Rees, Jonathan. "Employee Publications and Employee Representation Plans: The Case of Colorado Fuel and Iron, 1915–1942." *Management & Organizational History* 3.3/4 (August/November 2008): 257–272.

Patten, Robert L. "When is a Book Not a Book?" *Biblion: The Bulletin of the New York Public Library* 4.2 (Spring 1996): 35–63.

Patterson, Benton Rain and Patterson, Coleman E.P. *The Editor-in-Chief: A Practical Management Guide for Magazine Editors.* Ames: Iowa State University Press, 1997.

Patterson, Cynthia. "'Illustration of a Picture': Nineteenth-Century Writers and the Philadelphia Pictorials." *American Periodicals* 19.2 (2009): 136–164.

Patterson, Cynthia Lee. *Art for the Middle Classes: America's Illustrated Magazines of the 1840s.* Jackson: University Press of Mississippi, 2010.

Pauly, John J. "Literary Journalism and the Drama of Civic Life: Keynote Address, IALJS, Brussels, Belgium, May 13, 2011." *Literary Journalism Studies* 3.2 (Fall 2011): 73–82.

Pauly, John J. "The Politics of the New Journalism." In Sims, Norman. *Literary Journalism in the Twentieth Century.* New York: Oxford University Press, 1990, and Evanston, IL: Northwestern University Press, 2008, 110–129.

Pavlik, John V.; Nwosu, Ikechukwu E.; and Ettel, Diana G. "Why Employees Read Company Newsletters." *Public Relations Review* 8.3 (1982): 23–33.

Payne, Gregg A.; Severn, Jessica J.H.; and Dozier, David M. "Uses and Gratifications Motives as Indicators of Magazine Readership." *Journalism Quarterly* 65.4 (Winter 1988): 909–913, 959.

Pearl, Monica B. "'What Strange Intimacy': Janet Flanner's Letters from Paris." *Journal of European Studies* 32.125/126 (September 2002): 303–318.

Peck, Abe. "The Utilitarian Experience." In Peck, Abe and Malthouse, Edward C., eds. *Medill on Media Engagement.* Cresskill: Hampton Press, 2010, 61–70.

Peck, Abe and Malthouse, Edward C., eds. *Medill on Media Engagement.* Cresskill: Hampton Press, 2010.

Peirce, Kate. "A Feminist Theoretical Perspective on the Socialization of Teenage Girls through *Seventeen* Magazine." *Sex Roles* 23.9/10 (November 1990): 491–500.

Peirce, Kate L. and Martinez, Gilbert D. "How We Learn to Teach: Trial by Fire, by the Seat of Our Pants and Other (More Scientific) Methods." *Journalism & Mass Communication Educator* 67.2 (Summer 2012): 134–144.

Pelizzari, Maria Antonella. "Photojournalism as Contemporary Artefact." Review of *Things as They Are: Photojournalism in Context since 1955*, by Mary Panzer. *History of Photography* 31.3 (Autumn 2007): 309–311.

"The People vs. Simpson." *People* Magazine, 10 October 1994 <http://www.people.com/people/archive/article/0,,20104089,00.html>, accessed 9 October 2013.

Perlmutter, David D. and Wagner, Gretchen L. "The Anatomy of a Photojournalistic Icon: Marginalization of Dissent in the Selection and Framing of 'a Death in Genoa.'" *Visual Communication* 3.1 (February 2004): 91–108.

Peteraf, Margaret. "The Cornerstones of Competitive Advantage: A Resource-Based Perspective." *Strategic Management Journal* 14.3 (1993): 179–191.

Peterfreund, Stanley. "Employee Publications: Deadly but Not Dead Yet." *Public Relations Journal* 30.1 (January 1974): 20–23.

Peters, Jeremy W. "Advertisement or *Vogue* Feature? You Decide." *Media Decoder* (blog). *New York Times*, 8 September 2010 <http://mediadecoder.blogs.nytimes.com/2010/09/08/advertisement-or-vogue-feature-you-decide/?_php=true&_type=blogs&_r=0>, accessed 15 December 2013.

Peters, Jeremy W. "*U.S. News & World Report* to Become Online Only." *New York Times*, 5 November 2010 <http:mediadecoder.blogs.nytimes.com/2010/11/05/u-s-news-to-cease-printing-become-online-only/?_r=0>, accessed 12 November 2012.

Peters, Jeremy W. "Web Focus Helps Revitalize the *Atlantic*." *New York Times*, 13 December 2010, B1.

Peters, Thomas J. and Waterman, Robert H., Jr. *In Search of Excellence: Lessons from America's Best Run Companies.* New York: Harper & Row, 1982.

Peterson, Carla L. *"Doers of the Word": African-American Women Speakers and Writers in the North (1830–1880).* New York: Oxford University Press, 1995.

Peterson, Christian A. "American Arts and Crafts: The Photograph Beautiful, 1895–1915." *History of Photography* 16.3 (Autumn 1992): 189–232.

Peterson, Robin T. "Consumer Magazine Advertisement Portrayal of Models by Race in the U.S.: An Assessment." *Journal of Marketing Communications* 13.3 (September 2007): 199–211.

Peterson, Robin T. "The Utilization of Ecological Themes in State and Local Government Tourism Magazine Commercials: An Assessment." *Journal of Hospitality & Leisure Marketing* 6.4 (2000): 5–16.

Peterson, Theodore. "Magazine." In Barnouw, Erik; Gerbner, George; Schramm, Wylbur; Worth, Tobia L.; and Gross, Larry, eds. *International Encyclopedia of Communications*. Vol. 2. New York: Oxford University Press, 1989, 463–468.

Peterson, Theodore. *Magazines in the Twentieth Century*. 1st, 2nd eds. Urbana: University of Illinois Press, 1956, 1964.

Pettersson, Rune. "Research in Information Design." *Journal of Visual Literacy* 26.1 (Spring 2006): 77–88.

Pew Research Center. "Overview." *The State of the News Media 2013: An Annual Report on American Journalism*. Washington, DC: Pew Research Center, 2013 <http://stateofthemedia.org/2013/overview-5/>, accessed 3 December 2013.

Pfau, Michael. "Epistemological and Disciplinary Intersections." *Journal of Communication* 58.4 (December 2008): 597–602.

Pfau, Michael; Haigh, Michel; Gettle, Mitchell; Donnelly, Michael; Scott, Gregory; Warr, Dana; and Wittenberg, Elaine. "Embedding Journalists in Military Combat Units: Impact on Newspaper Story Frames and Tone." *Journalism & Mass Communication Quarterly* 81.1 (Spring 2004): 74–88.

Phegley, Jennifer. *Educating the Proper Woman Reader: Victorian Family Literary Magazines and the Cultural Health of the Nation*. Columbus: Ohio State University Press, 2004.

Phillips, Angela. *Good Writing for Journalists*. London: Sage, 2007.

Phillips, Selene G.; Della, Lindsay J.; and Sohn, Steve H. "What Does Cancer Treatment Look Like in Consumer Cancer Magazines? An Exploratory Analysis of Photographic Content in Consumer Cancer Magazines." *Journal of Health Communication* 16.4 (April 2011): 416–430.

Phillips, Simon. "'Chemists to the Nation': House Magazines, Locality and Health at Boots The Chemists 1919–1939." *Management & Organizational History* 3.3/4 (August/November 2008): 239–255.

Phillpot, Clive. "Art Magazines and Magazine Art." *Artforum*, February 1980, 52–54.

Phin, Christopher. "What Is a Magazine?" *Flipping Pages Blog*, 4 February 2013 <http://flippingpagesblog.com/what-is-a-magazine/>, accessed 14 February 2013.

Picard, Robert G. "Cash Cows or Entrecôte: Publishing Companies and Disruptive Technologies." *Trends in Communication* 11.2 (2003): 127–136.

Picard, Robert G. *The Economics and Financing of Media Companies*. New York: Fordham University Press, 2002.

Picard, Robert G. "Unique Characteristics and Business Dynamics of Media Products." *Journal of Media Business Studies* 2.2 (2005): 61–69.

Piepmeier, Alison. *Girl Zines: Making Media, Doing Feminism*. New York: New York University Press, 2009.

Piepmeier, Alison. "Why Zines Matter: Materiality and the Creation of Embodied Community." *American Periodicals* 18.2 (2008): 213–238.

Pipps, Val; Walter, Heather; Endres, Kathleen; and Tabatcher, Patrick. "Information Recall of Internet News: Does Design Make a Difference? A Pilot Study." *Journal of Magazine & New Media Research* 11.1 (Fall 2009): 1–20.

Pitts, Melissa. "4 Reasons Pinterest Wins with Women (and Facebook Loses)." *Forbes*, 10 April 2012 <http://www.forbes.com/sites/gyro/2012/04/10/4-reasons-pinterest-wins-with-women-and-facebook-loses/>, accessed 7 December 2013.

Plakoyiannaki, Emmanuella and Zotos, Yorgos. "Female Role Stereotypes in Print Advertising: Identifying Associations with Magazine and Product Categories." *European Journal of Marketing* 43.11/12 (2009): 1411–1434.

Plotnik, Arthur. *The Elements of Editing: A Modern Guide for Editors and Journalists*. New York: Macmillan, 1982.

Podeschi, Christopher W. "The Culture of Nature and the Rise of Modern Environmentalism: The View through General Audience Magazines, 1945–1980." *Sociological Spectrum* 27.3 (March 2007): 299–331.

Poitras, Marc and Sutter, Daniel. "Advertiser Pressure and Control of the News: The Decline of Muckraking Revisited." *Journal of Economic Behavior & Organization* 72.3 (December 2009): 944–958.

Polsgrove, Carol. *It Wasn't Pretty, Folks, but Didn't We Have Fun? Esquire in the Sixties*. New York: W.W. Norton, 1995.

Pompilio, Natalie. "Graphics Evolution." *American Journalism Review*, April/May 2004, 9–10 <http://ajrarchive.org/article.asp?id=3642>, accessed 13 January 2014.

Pompper, Donnalyn. "Masculinities, the Metrosexual, and Media Images: Across Dimensions of Age and Ethnicity." [Special Issue, Fiction, Fashion, and Function: Gendered Experiences of Women's and Men's Body Image] *Sex Roles* 63.9 (2010): 682–696.

Pompper, Donnalyn and Koenig, Jesica. "Cross-Cultural-Generational Perceptions of Ideal Body Image: Hispanic Women and Magazine Standards." *Journalism & Mass Communication Quarterly* 81.1 (Spring 2004): 89–107.

Pompper, Donnalyn; Lee, Suekyung; and Lerner, Shana. "Gauging Outcomes of the 1960s Social Equality Movements: Nearly Four Decades of Gender and Ethnicity on the Cover of the *Rolling Stone* Magazine." *Journal of Popular Culture* 42.2 (2009): 273–290.

Pompper, Donnalyn; Soto, Jorge; and Piel, Lauren. "Male Body Image and Magazine Standards: Considering Dimensions of Age and Ethnicity." *Journalism & Mass Communication Quarterly* 84.3 (Autumn 2007): 525–545.

Pooley, Jefferson. "The New History of Mass Communication Research." In Park, David W. and Pooley, Jefferson, eds. *The History of Media and Communication Research: Contested Memories.* New York: Peter Lang, 2008, 43–69.

Pope, Harrison G., Jr.; Phillips, Katharine A.; and Olivardia, Roberto. *The Adonis Complex: The Secret Crisis of Male Body Obsession.* New York: Free Press, 2000.

Popovich, Mark N. "Research Review: Quantitative Magazine Studies, 1983–1993." In Abrahamson, David, ed. *The American Magazine: Research Perspectives and Prospects.* Ames: Iowa State University Press, 1995, 24–36.

Popp, Richard K. *The Holiday Makers: Magazines, Advertising, and Mass Tourism in Postwar America.* Baton Rouge: Louisiana State University Press, 2012.

Popp, Richard K. and Mendelson, Andrew L. "'X'-ing Out Enemies: *Time* Magazine, Visual Discourse, and the War in Iraq." *Journalism* 11.2 (April 2010): 203–221.

Porpora, Douglas V. and Nikolaev, Alexander. "Moral Muting in U.S. Newspaper Op-Eds Debating the Attack on Iraq." *Discourse & Communication* 2.2 (May 2008): 165–184.

Porter, Michael. *Competitive Advantage: Creating and Sustaining Superior Performance.* New York: Free Press, 1985.

Postman, Neil. *Amusing Ourselves to Death: Public Discourse in the Age of Show Business.* New York: Penguin Books, 1985, 2005.

Potter, Beth; Sheeshka, Judy; and Valaitis, Ruta. "Content Analysis of Infant Feeding Messages in a Canadian Women's Magazine, 1945 to 1995." *Journal of Nutrition Education* 32.4 (July/August 2000): 196–203.

Potter, W. James; Cooper, Roger; and Dupagne, Michel. "The Three Paradigms of Mass Media Research in Mainstream Communication Journals." *Communication Theory* 3.4 (November 1993): 317–335.

Power, J. Gerard; Murphy, Sheila T.; and Coover, Gail. "Priming Prejudice: How Stereotypes and Counter-Stereotypes Influence Attribution of Responsibility and Credibility among Ingroups and Outgroups." *Human Communication Research* 23.1 (September 1996): 36–58.

PPA Marketing. "The Case for Consumer Magazines," Powerpoint Presentation. PowerShow.com <http://www.powershow.com/view1/1e5ce9-MzY5M/Mixed_Media_Planning_powerpoint_ppt_presentation>, accessed 7 April 2014.

Pramling, Niklas and Säljö, Roger. "Scientific Knowledge, Popularisation, and the Use of Metaphors: Modern Genetics in Popular Science Magazines." *Scandinavian Journal of Educational Research* 51.3 (July 2007): 275–295.

Pratt, Cornelius B.; Ha, Louisa; and Pratt, Charlotte A. "Setting the Public Health Agenda on Major Diseases in Sub-Saharan Africa: African Popular Magazines and Medical Journals, 1981–1997." *Journal of Communication* 52.4 (December 2002): 889–904.

Prettyman, Gib. "*Harper's Weekly* and the Spectacle of Industrialization." *American Periodicals* 11 (2001): 24–48.

Price, Kenneth M. and Smith, Susan Belasco, eds. *Periodical Literature in Nineteenth-Century America.* Charlottesville: University Press of Virginia, 1995.

Price, Vincent. "Social Identification and Public Opinion: Effects of Communicating Group Conflict." *Public Opinion Quarterly* 53.2 (Summer 1989): 197–224.

Prijatel, Patricia. "Fleur's Folly?" *Print*, March/April 1995, 99–108, 110.

Prince, Gregory A. "'Let the Truth Heal': The Making of *Nobody Knows: The Untold Story of Black Mormons.*" *Dialogue: A Journal of Mormon Thought* 42.3 (Fall 2009): 74–100.

Prior-Miller, Marcia R. "Core Knowledge: Scholarly Research on Magazines." Invited panel presentation, Magazine Division, at the Annual Meeting, Association for Education in Journalism and Mass Communication, August 2008.

Prior-Miller, Marcia R. "An Organization Communication-Goals Theory of Magazine Types: Toward an Integrated Conceptual Framework of Magazine and Journal Periodicals as a Medium of Communication." Manuscript in preparation.

Prior-Miller, Marcia R. "Research Review: Issues in Magazine Typology." *Electronic Journal of Communication/La Revue Electronique de Communication* 4.2/4 (December 1994) <eric.ed.gov/?id=EJ494512>, accessed 30 May 2014.

Prior-Miller, Marcia R. "Research Review: Issues in Magazine Typology." In Abrahamson, David, ed. *The American Magazine: Research Perspectives and Prospects.* Ames: Iowa State University Press, 1995, 3–23.

Prior-Miller, Marcia R. and Associates. "Bibliography of Published Research on Magazine and Journal Periodicals." 8th ed. Research database. Ames: Iowa State University, last modified, 31 August 2012, MSWord file <mpm@iastate.edu>.

Prior-Miller, Marcia R. and Associates. "Bibliography of Published Research on Magazine and Journal Periodicals." 9th ed. Research database. Ames: Iowa State University, last modified, 31 August 2014, MSWord file <mpm@iastate.edu>.

Prior-Miller, Marcia R. and Esch, Kellie L. "A Census and Analysis of Journals Publishing Research about Magazines, 1977–1987." Paper presented at the Annual Meeting, Association for Education in Journalism and Mass Communication, August 1990.

Propp, V. *Morphology of the Folktale,* 2nd ed. Translated by Laurence Scott. Edited by Louis R. Wagner. Austin: University of Texas Press, 1968. Originally published in 1928.

Prusank, Diane T. "Masculinities in Teen Magazines: The Good, the Bad, and the Ugly." *Journal of Men's Studies* 15.2 (Spring 2007): 160–177.

Putnam, Robert D. "Technology and Mass Media." *Bowling Alone: The Collapse and Revival of American Community.* New York: Simon & Schuster, 2000, 216–246.

Pyka, Andrea; Fosdick, Scott; and Tillinghast, William. "Visual Framing of Patriotism and National Identity on the Covers of *Der Spiegel.*" Paper presented at the Annual Meeting, Association for Education in Journalism and Mass Communication, August 2010.

Quandt, Thorsten and Singer, Jane B. "Convergence and Cross-Platform Content Production." In Wahl-Jorgensen, Karin and Hanitzsch, Thomas, eds. *Handbook of Journalism Studies.* International Communication Association (ICA) Handbook Series, ed. Robert T. Craig. New York and London: Routledge, 2009, 130–144.

Quart, Alissa. "The Long Tale." *Columbia Journalism Review,* 20 September 2011 <http://www.cjr.org/reports/the_long_tale.php?page=all>, accessed 25 February 2013.

Quinn, Stephen. "What Is Convergence and How Will It Affect My Life?" In Quinn, Stephen and Filak, Vincent F., eds. *Convergent Journalism: An Introduction.* Burlington, MA and Oxford, UK: Focal Press, 2005, 3–19.

Quinn, Stephen and Filak, Vincent F., eds. *Convergent Journalism: An Introduction.* Burlington, MA and Oxford, UK: Focal Press, 2005.

Radway, Janice A. "Learned and Literary Print Cultures in an Age of Professionalization and Diversification." In Kaestle, Carl F. and Radway, Janice A. eds., *Print in Motion: The Expansion of Publishing and Reading in the United States, 1880–1940.* A History of the Book in America, David D. Hall, ed. Vol. 4. Chapel Hill: University of North Carolina Press, 2009.

Radway, Janice A. *Reading the Romance: Women, Patriarchy, and Popular Literature.* Chapel Hill: University of North Carolina Press, 1984.

Rahman, Bushra H. "Analysis of the Coverage of Muslim Political Women in *Time* and *Newsweek.*" *Journal of Media Studies* 25.1 (January 2010): 50–65.

Rahman, Mohmin. "Is Straight the New Queer? David Beckham and the Dialectics of Celebrity." *M/C Journal* 7.5 (November 2004): 1–5.

Rakow, Lana. "Feminists, Media, Freed Speech." *Feminist Media Studies* 1.1 (2001): 41–44.

Ramos, Howard; Ron, James; and Thoms, Oskar N.T. "Shaping the Northern Media's Human Rights Coverage, 1986–2000." *Journal of Peace Research* 44.4 (July 2007): 385–406.

Randle, Quint. "Gratification Niches of Monthly Print Magazines and the World Wide Web among a Group of Special-Interest Magazine Subscribers." *Journal of Computer-Mediated Communication* 8.4 (July 2003): Unpaginated [Open Access Journal, ICA].

Raphael, T.J. "Condé Nast: Print Isn't Dead for the Young, Yet." *Audience Development*, 30 May 2012 <http://www.audiencedevelopment.com/2012/cond+nast+print+isn+t+dead+young+yet#. UqO30WTF37A>, accessed 7 December 2013.

Raphael, Todd. "Web Publications." In Freedman, Robert, ed. *Best Practices of the Business Press*. Dubuque, IA: Kendall/Hunt Publishing, 2004, 121–130.

Reader, Bill and Moist, Kevin. "Letters as Indicators of Community Values: Two Case Studies of Alternative Magazines." *Journalism & Mass Communication Quarterly* 85.4 (Winter 2008): 823–840.

"Reading Between the Lines." *Economist*, 26 March 2009 <http://www.economist.com/node/13362043/ print?story_id=13362043>, accessed 31 March 2009.

Reaves, Shiela. "Digital Alteration of Photographs in Consumer Magazines." *Journal of Mass Media Ethics* 6.3 (September 1991): 175–181.

Reavy, Matthew. "Rules and the Real World: An Examination of Information Graphics in *Time* and *Newsweek*." *Visual Communication Quarterly* 10.4 (Autumn 2003): 4–10.

Reed, Barbara Straus. "The Antebellum Jewish Press: Origins, Problems, Functions." *Journalism Monographs* 139 (June 1993): 1–42.

Reichert, Tom and Carpenter, Courtney. "An Update on Sex in Magazine Advertising: 1983 to 2003." *Journalism & Mass Communication Quarterly* 81.4 (Winter 2004): 823–837.

Reichert, Tom and Zhou, Shuhua. "Consumer Responses to Sexual Magazine Covers on a Men's Magazine." *Journal of Promotion Management* 13.1/2 (January 2007): 127–144.

Reilly, Kevin S. "Dilettantes at the Gate: *Fortune* Magazine and the Cultural Politics of Business Journalism in the 1930s." *Business & Economic History* 28.2 (Winter 1999): 213–222.

Reimold, Daniel. *Journalism of Ideas: Brainstorming, Developing, and Selling Stories in the Digital Age*. New York and London: Routledge, 2013.

Reiss, Marguerite. "Nightmare Hunt." In Mueller, Larry and Reiss, Marguerite. *Bear Attacks of the Century: True Stories of Courage and Survival*. Guilford, CT: Lyons Press, 2005, 103–112.

Reissner, Stefanie C. "Patterns of Stories of Organisational Change." *Journal of Organizational Change Management* 24.5 (2011): 593–609.

Remnick, David. "Barbara Epstein: The Talk of the Town." *New Yorker*, 3 July 2006, 27.

Remnick, David. "Big Think Interview with David Remnick." BigThink.com, 22 April 2010 <http:// bigthink.com/videos/big-think-interview-with-david-remnick>, accessed 2 December 2013.

Renard, David, ed. *The Last Magazine*. New York: Universe Publishing, 2006.

Renard, David. "The Last Magazine (in Print)." In Renard, David, ed. *The Last Magazine*. New York: Universe Publishing, 2006, 14–15.

Reymond, Rhonda L. "Looking In: Albert A. Smith's Use of *Repoussoir* in Cover Illustrations for the *Crisis and Opportunity*." *American Periodicals* 20.2 (2010): 216–240.

Reynolds, Bill. "Adventures in Long-Form Magazine Editing." *J-Source*, 28 July 2009 <http://j-source.ca/ article/adventures-long-form-magazine-editing>, accessed 25 February 2013.

Reynolds, Bill. "The Missing Link in Literary Journalism." *Literary Journalism: The Newsletter of the International Association for Literary Journalism Studies*, Winter 2013, 1, 10.

Reynolds, Bill. "Recovering the Peculiar Life and Times of Tom Hedley and of Canadian New Journalism." *Literary Journalism Studies* 1.1 (Spring 2009): 79–104.

Reynolds, Paul Davidson. *A Primer in Theory Construction*. Indianapolis: Bobbs-Merrill, 1971.

Rhodes, Colin. "*Burlington* Primitive: Non-European Art in the *Burlington Magazine* before 1930." *Burlington Magazine* 146.1211 (February 2004): 98–104.

Rhodes, Leara D. "Inflight Magazines: Changing How Magazines Market to Travelers." *Journal of Magazine & New Media Research* 2.1 (Fall 1999): 1–22.

Rhodes, Leara D. "Magazines." In Thomas, Erwin K. and Carpenter, Brown H., eds. *Mass Media in 2025: Industries, Organizations, People and Nations*. Westport, CT: Greenwood Press, 2001, 39–49.

Rhodes, Leara D. "Magazines in Capitalist Russia: Impact of Political and Economic Transitions." Paper presented at the Annual Meeting, Association for Education in Journalism and Mass Communication, August 1997.

Rhodes, Leara D. "Research Review: An International Perspective on Magazines." In Abrahamson, David, ed. *The American Magazine: Research Perspectives and Prospects*. Ames: Iowa State University Press, 1995, 159–171.

Rhodes, Leara D. and Roessner, Amber. "Teaching Magazine Publishing through Experiential Learning." *Journalism & Mass Communication Educator* 63 (Winter 2009): 304–316.

Ricchiardi, Sherry. "Offscreen." *American Journalism Review*, October/November 2008 <http://www.ajr. org/article.asp?id=4602>, accessed 14 January 2013.

Ricci, Oscar. "Technology for Everyone: Representations of Technology in Popular Italian Scientific Magazines." *Public Understanding of Science* 19.5 (September 2010): 578–589.

Rich, Carole. *Writing and Reporting News: A Coaching Method.* 7th ed. Boston: Cengage Learning, 2013.

Richardson, Lyon N. *A History of Early American Magazines, 1741–1789.* New York: Thomas Nelson and Sons, 1931.

Richardson, Peter. *A Bomb in Every Issue: How the Short, Unruly Life of* Ramparts *Magazine Changed America.* New York: New Press, 2009.

Richter, David H. "Introduction." In Richter, David H., ed. *The Critical Tradition: Classic Texts and Contemporary Trends.* 3rd ed. Boston: Bedford/St. Martin's, 2007, 1–22.

Ricketson, Matthew. "The New Appreciation of Long-Form Journalism in a Short-Form World." In Ricketson, Matthew, ed. *Australian Journalism Today.* South Yarra, AUS: Palgrave Macmillan, 2012, 217–233.

Ricketson, Matthew. *Writing Feature Stories: How to Research and Write Newspaper and Magazine Articles.* Crows Nest, AUS: Allen & Unwin, 2004.

Riffe, Daniel; Lacy, Stephen; and Varouhakis, Miron. "Media System Dependency Theory and Using the Internet for In-Depth, Specialized Information." *Web Journal of Mass Communication Research* 11 (January 2008): 1–14.

Riley, Sam G., ed. *American Magazine Journalists, 1900–1960.* First Series. Detroit: Gale Research, 1990.

Riley, Sam G. *American Magazine Journalists, 1900–1960.* Second Series. *Dictionary of Literary Biography.* Vol. 91. Detroit: Gale Research, 1994.

Riley, Sam G., ed. *Corporate Magazines of the United States.* Westport, CT: Greenwood Press, 1992.

Riley, Sam G. and Selnow, Gary W., eds. *Regional Interest Magazines of the United States.* Westport, CT: Greenwood Press, 1991.

Ritter, Robert Mark. "The Transformation of Authority in Print and the Rise of House Style." D.Phil. diss., St. Anne's College, University of Oxford, 2010.

Rivers, Marcia Bolton. "Old, New, Borrowed, Read: The Powers and Problems of American Protestant Periodicals—Then and Now." Capstone research paper presented to Northeastern Seminary, 22 July 2004.

Roberts, Jeff John. "Hearst: Women Finally Embracing Online Magazines Thanks to 7-Inch Screens." *Gigaom* (blog), 12 February 2013 <gigaom.com/2013/02/12/women-finally-embracing-online-magazine-thanks-to-7-inch-screens-hearst-president/>, accessed 20 May 2014.

Roberts, Nancy L. "Firing the Canon: The Historical Search for Literary Journalism's Missing Links." *Literary Journalism Studies* 4.2 (Fall 2012): 81–93.

Roberts, Nancy L. "Journalism for Justice: Dorothy Day and the *Catholic Worker*." *Journalism History* 10.1/2 (Spring/Summer 1983): 2–9.

Robertson, Roland. "Glocalization: Time-Space and Homogeneity-Heterogeneity." In Featherstone, Mike; Lash, Scott; and Robertson, Roland, eds. *Global Modernities.* Theory, Culture & Society Series. Mike Featherstone, ed. London: Sage, 1995, 25–44.

Robinson, Andrew. Review of *Photographing America: Henri Cartier-Bresson and Walker Evans*, Agnès Sire, curator. *History Today* 59.11 (November 2009): 59.

Rodriguez, Lulu and Dimitrova, Daniela V. "The Levels of Visual Framing." *Journal of Visual Literacy* 30.1 (Spring 2011): 48–65.

Roessler, Patrick. "Global Players, Émigrés, and *Zeitgeist*: Magazine Design and the Interrelation between the United States and Germany." *Journalism Studies* 8.4 (August 2007): 566–583.

Rogers, Everett M. *A History of Communication Study: A Biographical Approach.* New York: The Free Press, 1994.

Rogers, T.B. *A Century of Progress, 1831–1931: Cadbury Bournville.* Chicago: Hudson & Kearns, 1931.

Rohlinger, Deana A. "Eroticizing Men: Cultural Influences on Advertising and Male Objectification." *Sex Roles* 46.3/4 (February 2002): 61–74.

Rojek, Chris. "Celebrity and Celetoids." *Celebrity.* London: Reaktion Books, 2001, 9–49.

Rojek, Chris. "Celebrity and Religion." *Celebrity.* London: Reaktion Books, 2001, 51–99.

Romanenko, Katerina. "Photomontage for the Masses: The Soviet Periodical Press of the 1930s." *Design Issues* 26.1 (Winter 2010): 29–39.

Rome, Dennis. *Black Demons: The Media's Depiction of the African American Male Criminal Stereotype.* Westport, CT: Praeger, 2004.

Rooks, Noliwe M. *Ladies' Pages: African American Women's Magazines and the Culture that Made Them.* New Brunswick, NJ: Rutgers University Press, 2004.

Rose, Rebecca. "You've Come a Long Way . . . Are Women Still Being Passed Over for the Top Magazine Editing Jobs? Or Are They Just Too Smart to Take It?" *Ryerson Review of Journalism*, Spring 2008 <http://www.rrj.ca/m4126/>, accessed 24 February 2013.

Rosenhouse, Jason and Branch, Glenn. "Media Coverage of 'Intelligent Design.'" *BioScience* 56.3 (March 2006): 247–252.

Ross, Lillian. *Here but Not Here: My Life with William Shawn and the* New Yorker. New York: Random House, 1998.

Rössler, Patrick; Bomhoff, Jana; Haschke, Josef Ferdinand; Kersten, Jan; and Müller, Rüdiger. "Selection and Impact of Press Photography: An Empirical Study on the Basis of Photo News Factors." *Communications: The European Journal of Communication Research* 36.4 (November 2011): 415–439.

Rothenberg, Tamar Y. *Presenting America's World: Strategies of Innocence in* National Geographic Magazine*, 1888–1945.* Aldershot, UK and Burlington, VT: Ashgate, 2007.

Rothman, Emily F.; Nagaswaran, Anita; Johnson, Renee M.; Adams, Kelley M.; Scrivens, Juliane; and Baughman, Allyson. "U.S. Tabloid Magazine Coverage of a Celebrity Dating Abuse Incident: Rihanna and Chris Brown." *Journal of Health Communication: International Perspectives* 17.6 (2012): 733–744.

Rothstein, Jandos. *Designing Magazines: Inside Periodical Design, Redesign, and Branding.* New York: Allworth Press, 2007.

Roush, Chris. "The Need for More Business Education in Mass Communication Schools." *Journalism & Mass Communication Educator* 61.2 (Summer 2006): 196–204.

Roush, Chris. *Profits and Losses: Business Journalism and Its Role in Society.* Oak Park, IL: Marion Street Press, 2006.

Roush, Chris. "Unheeded Warnings." *American Journalism Review*, December 2008/January 2009, 34–39.

Rover, Carla. "Inside the *Economist's* Digital Strategy." *Digiday*, 17 January 2012 <http://www.digiday.com/publishers/inside-the-economists-digital-strategy/>, accessed 27 March 2013.

Rowley, Karen M. and Kurpius, David D. "Separate and Still Unequal: A Comparative Study of Blacks in Business Magazines." *Howard Journal of Communications* 14.4 (October/December 2003): 245–255.

Rowlinson, Michael. "Public History Review Essay: Cadbury World." *Labour History Review* 67.1 (April 2002): 101–119.

Rowlinson, Michael; Booth, Charles; Clark, Peter; Delahaye, Agnès; and Procter, Stephen. "Social Remembering and Organizational Memory." *Organization Studies* 31.1 (January 2010): 69–87.

Rowlinson, Michael and Hassard, John. "The Invention of Corporate Culture: A History of the Histories of Cadbury." *Human Relations* 46.3 (March 1993): 299–326.

Roy, Stephannie C. "'Taking Charge of Your Health': Discourses of Responsibility in English-Canadian Women's Magazines." *Sociology of Health & Illness* 30.3 (April 2008): 463–477.

Royal, Cindy and Tankard, James W., Jr. "Literary Journalism Techniques Create Compelling *Blackhawk Down* Web Site." *Newspaper Research Journal* 25.4 (Fall 2004): 82–88.

Rožukalne, Anda. "Young People as a Media Audience: From Content to Usage Processes." *Central European Journal of Communication* 5.1 (2012): 105–120.

Rubin, Alan M. "Television Uses and Gratifications: The Interactions of Viewing Patterns and Motivations." *Journal of Broadcasting* 27.1 (Winter 1983): 37–51.

Ruggiero, Thomas E. "Uses and Gratifications Theory in the 21st Century." *Mass Communication and Society* 3.1 (Winter 2000): 3–37.

Ruggiero, Thomas E. and Yang, Kenneth C.C. "Latino Ethnic Identity, Linguistic Acculturation, and Spanish Language Media Preference." Paper presented at the Annual Meeting, International Communication Association, May 2009.

Rupp-Serrano, Karen. "From Gutenberg to Gigabytes: The Electronic Periodical Comes of Age." *American Periodicals* 4 (1994): 96–104.

Russell, Jennifer M. "'A Savage Place!': Hunter S. Thompson and His Pleasure Dome." *Literary Journalism Studies* 4.1 (Spring 2012): 37–50.

Russell, Karen Miller and Bishop, Carl O. "Understanding Ivy Lee's Declaration of Principles: U.S. Newspaper and Magazine Coverage of Publicity and Press Agentry, 1865–1904." *Public Relations Review* 35.2 (June 2009): 91–101.

Russell, Karen Miller and Lamme, Margot Opdycke. "Public Relations and Business Responses to the Civil Rights Movement." *Public Relations Review* 39.1 (March 2013): 63–73.

Rutenbeck, Jeff. "The Triumph of News over Ideas in American Journalism: The Trade Journal Debate, 1872–1915." *Journal of Communication Inquiry* 18.1 (Winter 1994): 63–79 <http://jci.sagepub.com/content/18/1/63.extract>, accessed 20 May 2013.

Rutter, Alan. "What Is a Magazine?" *Flipping Pages Blog*, 11 February 2013 <http://www.alanrutter.com/2013/what-is-a-magazine>, accessed 14 February 2013.

Ryan, Cynthia. "Struggling to Survive: A Study of Editorial Decision-Making Strategies at MAMM Magazine." *Journal of Business and Technical Communication* 19.3 (July 2005): 353–376.

Ryan, William and Conover, Theodore. *Graphic Communications Today*. 4th ed. Clifton Park, NY: Thomson/Delmar Learning, 2004.

Saab, A. Joan. *For the Millions: American Art and Culture between the Wars*. Philadelphia: University of Pennsylvania Press, 2004.

Sachs, Andrea. "Q & A: Isaiah Wilner." *Time*, 5 October 2006, 91.

Sacks, Robert M. "The Bleeding Edge." *Publishing Executive*, September 2012 <http://www.pubexec.com/article/bosacks-why-magazine-publishers-need-think-more-like-razor-companies#>, accessed 26 March 2013.

Sagendorf, Cathy and Moore, David. "Module 33: Newspapers." *CONSER Cataloging Manual*. Library of Congress, 2006 <http://www.loc.gov/acq/conser/pdf/CCM-Module-33.pdf>, accessed 18 April 2014.

Sagolla, Dom. *140 Characters: A Style Guide for the Short Form*. Hoboken, NJ: John Wiley & Sons, 2009.

Said, Edward. *Orientalism*. New York: Vintage Books, 1979.

Saliba, J. Keith and Geltner, Ted. "Literary War Journalism: Framing and the Creation of Meaning." *Journal of Magazine & New Media Research* 13.2 (Summer 2012): 1–19.

Saller, Carol Fisher. *The Subversive Copy Editor: Advice from Chicago*. Chicago: University of Chicago Press, 2009.

Sandler, Dennis M. and Secunda, Eugene. "Point of View: Blurred Boundaries—Where Does Editorial End and Advertising Begin?" *Journal of Advertising Research* 33.3 (May/June 1993): 73–80.

Santori, Flaminia Gennari. "Holmes, Fry, Jaccaci and the 'Art in America' Section of the *Burlington Magazine*, 1905–10." [Centenary Issue] *Burlington Magazine* 145.1200 (March 2003): 153–163.

Sar, Sela and Doyle, Kenneth O. "A Comparative Content Analysis of Cambodian and Thai Print Advertisements." In Keller, Punam A. and Rook, Dennis W., eds. *Advances in Consumer Research*. Vol. 30. Valdosta, GA: Association for Consumer Research, 2003, 223–229.

Sarachan, Jeremy. "The Path Already Taken: Technological and Pedagogical Practices in Convergence Education." *Journalism & Mass Communication Educator* 66.2 (Summer 2011): 160–174.

Sarasvathy, Saras. "Causation and Effectuation: Toward a Theoretical Shift from Economic Inevitability to Entrepreneurial Contingency." *Academy of Management Review* 26.2 (2001): 243–263.

Sarna, Jonathan D. "The American Jewish Press." In Winston, Diane H. ed. *The Oxford Handbook of Religion and the American News Media*. New York: Oxford University Press, 2012, 537–550.

Sass, Erik. "'Forbes' Reports 50% of Revs from Digital." *MediaDailyNews*. MediaPost, 17 October 2012 <http://www.mediapost.com/publications/article/185400/forbes-reports-50-of-revs-from-digital.html#axzz2NT0PUyM2>, accessed 14 March 2013.

Sasseen, Jane; Matsa, Katerina-Eva; and Mitchell, Amy. "News Magazines: Embracing Their Digital Future." *The State of the News Media 2013: An Annual Report on American Journalism*. Washington, DC: Pew Research Center, 2013 <http://stateofthemedia.org/2013/news-magazines-embracing-their-digital-future/>, accessed 3 December 2013.

Sasseen, Jane; Olmstead, Kenny; and Mitchell, Amy. "Digital: As Mobile Grows Rapidly, the Pressures on News Intensify." *The State of the News Media 2013: An Annual Report on American Journalism*. Washington, DC: Pew Research Center <http://stateofthemedia.org/2013/digital-as-mobile-grows-rapidly-the-pressures-on-news-intensify/>, accessed 1 August 2013.

Sassen, Saskia. "Digital Networks and the State: Some Governance Questions." *Theory, Culture & Society* 17.4 (August 2000): 19–33.

Saucier, Jason A. and Caron, Sandra L. "An Investigation of Content and Media Images in Gay Men's Magazines." *Journal of Homosexuality* 55.3 (July 2008): 504–523.

Sauer, Abe. "Straw Poll: Is GQ's Mila Kunis Cover a Stealth Starbucks Product Placement?" *Brand Channel*, 13 July 2011 <http://www.brandchannel.com/home/post/2011/07/13/GQ-Starbucks-Cover-Plays-With-Mag-Guidelines.aspx>, accessed 1 March 2013.

Saylor, Elizabeth A.; Vittes, Katherine A.; and Sorenson, Susan B. "Firearm Advertising: Production Depiction in Consumer Gun Magazines." *Evaluation Review* 28.5 (October 2004): 420–433.

Scanlon, Jennifer. *Bad Girls Go Everywhere: The Life of Helen Gurley Brown*. New York and Oxford: Oxford University Press, 2009.

Scanlon, Jennifer. *Inarticulate Longings: The* Ladies' Home Journal, *Gender, and the Promises of Consumer Culture*. London and New York: Routledge, 1995.

Schaab, Gertrud; Freckmann, Peter; Stegmaier, Ralph; and Ortwein, Sigrid. "Visualizing Germany via Maps in a Magazine: 'Fancy' Graphic Design as Compared to 'Proper' Cartography." Paper presented at the 24th International Cartographic Conference (ICC 2009). Santiago, Chile, November 2009.

Schein, Edgar H. *Organizational Culture and Leadership*. 3rd ed. London: Jossey-Bass, 2004.

Scherr, Arthur. Review of *The Chief: The Life of William Randolph Hearst*, by David Nasaw. *Midwest Quarterly* 45.3 (March 2004): 319–321.

Schickel, Richard. *Intimate Strangers: The Culture of Celebrity*. New York: Doubleday, 1985.

Schierhorn, Ann B. and Endres, Kathleen L. "Magazine Writing Instruction and the Composition Revolution." *Journalism Educator* 47.2 (Summer 1992): 57–64.

Schiffrin, Anya, ed. *Bad News: How America's Business Press Missed the Story of the Century*. New York: New Press, 2011.

Schiller, Dan. "Informational Bypass: Research Library Access to U.S. Telecommunications Periodicals." *Journal of Communication* 39.3 (September 1989): 104–109.

Schlenker, Jennifer A.; Caron, Sandra L.; and Halteman, William A. "A Feminist Analysis of *Seventeen* Magazine: Content Analysis from 1945 to 1995." *Sex Roles* 38.1/2 (January 1998): 135–149.

Schlesinger, Philip. *Media, State, and Nation: Political Violence and Collective Identities*. London, Thousand Oaks and New Delhi: Sage Publications, 1991.

Schmidt, Dorothy. "Magazines." In Inge, M. Thomas, ed. *Handbook of American Popular Culture*. Westport, CT: Greenwood Press, 1981, 137–162.

Schneirov, Matthew. *The Dream of a New Social Order: Popular Magazines in America, 1893–1914*. New York: Columbia University Press, 1994.

"Scholarly Journal." PennState Library <http://www.sgps.psu.edu/foweb/lib/scholarly-journal/index.html>, accessed 4 February 2013.

Scholes, Robert. "Modernist Art in a 'Quality' Magazine, 1908–1922." *Journal of Modern Periodical Studies* 2.2 (2011): 135–164.

Scholes, Robert and Wulfman, Clifford. *Modernism in the Magazines: An Introduction*. New Haven: Yale University Press, 2010.

Scholnick, Robert J. "*Scribner's Monthly* and the 'Pictorial Representation of Life and Truth' in Post-Civil War America." *American Periodicals* 1.1 (Fall 1991): 46–69.

Schooler, Deborah and Ward, L. Monique. "Average Joes: Men's Relationships with Media, Real Bodies, and Sexuality." *Psychology of Men & Masculinity* 7.1 (2006): 27–41.

Schramm, Wilbur. "Twenty Years of Journalism Research." [20th Anniversary Issue]. *Public Opinion Quarterly* 21.1 (Spring 1957): 91–107.

Schreiber, Rachel Lynn. "Constructive Images: Gender in the Political Cartoons of the *Masses* (1911–1917)." Ph.D. diss., Johns Hopkins University, 2008.

Schubert, William H. *Curriculum: Perspective, Paradigm, and Possibility*. New York: Macmillan Publishers, 1986.

Schudson, Michael. "News, Public, Nation." *American Historical Review* 107.2 (April 2002): 481–495.

Schudson, Michael. "Sex Scandals." In *Our National Passion: 200 Years of Sex in America*. Banes, Sally; Frank, Sheldon; and Horwitz, Tem, eds. Chicago: Follett Publishing, 1976, 41–57.

Schulman, Vanessa Meikle. "'Making the Magazine': Visuality, Managerial Capitalism, and the Mass Production of Periodicals, 1865–1890." *American Periodicals* 22.1 (2012): 1–28.

Schulten, Susan. "The Perils of *Reading National Geographic*." *Reviews in American History* 23.3 (1995): 521–527.

Schultze, Quentin J. *Christianity and the Mass Media in America: Toward a Democratic Accommodation*. East Lansing: Michigan State University Press, 2003.

Schultze, Quentin J. "Leading the Tribes out of Exile: The Religious Press Discerns Broadcasting." *Christianity and the Mass Media in America: Toward a Democratic Accommodation*. East Lansing: Michigan State University Press, 2003, 89–138.

Schultze, Quentin J. and Woods, Robert H., Jr., eds. *Understanding Evangelical Media: The Changing Face of Christian Communication*. Downers Grove, IL: IVP Academic, 2008.

Schwartz, Alexandra K. "Designing Ed Ruscha: The Invention of the Los Angeles Artist 1960–1980." Ph.D. diss., University of Michigan, 2004.

Schwartz, Joseph and Andsager, Julie L. "Four Decades of Images in Gay Male-Targeted Magazines." *Journalism & Mass Communication Quarterly* 88.1 (Spring 2011): 76–98.

Schwartz, Vanessa R. and Przyblyski, Jeannene M., eds. *The Nineteenth-Century Visual Culture Reader*. New York: Routledge, 2004.

Schwartz-DuPre, Rae Lynn. "Portraying the Political: *National Geographic*'s 1985 Afghan Girl and a U.S. Alibi for Aid." *Critical Studies in Media Communication* 27.4 (October 2010): 336–356.

Scott, David W. and Stout, Daniel A. "Religion on *Time*: Personal Spiritual Quests and Religious Institutions on the Cover of a Popular News Magazine." *Journal of Magazine & New Media Research* 8.1 (Spring 2006): 1–17.

Seale, Clive. "Cancer Heroics: A Study of News Reports with Particular Reference to Gender." *Sociology* 36.1 (2002): 107–126.

Sedgwick, Ellery. *The Atlantic Monthly, 1857–1909: Yankee Humanism at High Tide and Ebb*. Amherst: University of Massachusetts Press, 1994.

Seebohm, Caroline. *The Man Who Was* Vogue: *The Life and Times of Condé Nast*. New York: Viking Press, 1982.

Seelye, Katharine Q. "Lurid Numbers on Glossy Pages! (Magazines Exploit What Sells)." *New York Times*, 10 February 2006, A1(L).

Segel, Edward and Heer, Jeffrey. "Narrative Visualization: Telling Stories with Data." *IEEE Transactions on Visualization and Computer Graphics* 16.6 (November/December 2010): 1139–1148.

Seglin, Jeffrey L. "ASME is Really, Really Mad about Ads on Covers—and You Should Be, Too." *Folio:*, 17 April 2009 <http://www.foliomag.com/2009/asme-really-really-mad-about-ads-covers-and-you-should-be-too#.UT00lFfAHTo>, accessed 1 March 2013.

Seife, Charles. "Jonah Lehrer's Journalistic Misdeeds at Wired.com." *Slate.com*, 31 August 2012 <http://www.slate.com/articles/health_and_science/science/2012/08/jonah_lehrer_plagiarism_in_wired_com_an_investigation_into_plagiarism_quotes_and_factual_inaccuracies_.html>, accessed 11 November 2013.

Senat, Joey. "From Pretty Blondes and Perky Girls to Competent Journalists: *Editor & Publisher*'s Evolving Depiction of Women from 1967–74." Paper presented at the Annual Meeting, Association for Education in Journalism and Mass Communication, Chicago, 30 July–2 August 1997.

Senat, Joey and Grusin, Elinor Kelley. "Seeking a Theoretical Framework for Master's Programs in the 1990s." *Journalism Educator* 49.2 (Summer 1994): 18–28.

Sender, Katherine. "Gay Readers, Consumers, and a Dominant Gay Habitus: 25 Years of the *Advocate* Magazine." *Journal of Communication* 51.1 (March 2001): 73–99.

Sengupta, Rhea. "Reading Representations of Black, East Asian, and White Women in Magazines for Adolescent Girls." *Sex Roles* 54.11/12 (June 2006): 799–808.

Sennett, Richard. *The Corrosion of Character: The Personal Consequences of Work in the New Capitalism*. New York and London: W.W. Norton, 1999.

Server, Lee. *Danger Is My Business: An Illustrated History of the Fabulous Pulp Magazines, 1896–1953*. San Francisco: Chronicle Books, 1993.

Severin, Werner J. and Tankard, James W., Jr. *Communication Theories: Origins, Methods, and Uses in the Mass Media*. 5th ed. New York: Addison Wesley Longman, 2000.

Shabir, Ghulam; Ali, Shahzad; and Iqbal, Zafar. "U.S. Mass Media and Image of Afghanistan: Portrayal of Afghanistan by *Newsweek* and *Time*." *South Asian Studies* 26.1 (January/June 2011): 83–101.

Shapiro, Ivor. "Evaluating Journalism: Towards an Assessment Framework for the Practice of Journalism." *Journalism Practice* 4.2 (April 2010): 143–162.

Sharp, Naomi. "The Future of Longform." *Columbia Journalism Review*, 9 December 2013 <http://www.cjr.org/behind_the_news/longform_conference.php?page=all>, accessed 3 February 2014.

Shehata, Adam. "Facing the Muhammad Cartoons: Official Dominance and Event-Driven News in Swedish and American Elite Press." *International Journal of Press/Politics* 12.4 (October 2007): 131–153.

Shenhav, Yehouda and Weitz, Ely. "The Roots of Uncertainty in Organization Theory: A Historical Constructivist Analysis." *Organization* 7.3 (August 2000): 373–401.

Sheridan, Lorraine; North, Adrian; Maltby, John; and Gillett, Raphael. "Celebrity Worship, Addiction and Criminality." *Psychology, Crime & Law* 13.6 (December 2007): 559–571.

Sherman, Lee and Deighton, John. "Banner Advertising: Measuring Effectiveness and Optimizing Placement." *Journal of Interactive Marketing* 15.2 (Spring 2001): 60–64.

Sheth, Bhavin R.; Sharma, Jitendra; Rao, S. Chenchal; and Sur, Mriganka. "Orientation Maps of Subjective Contours in Visual Cortex." *Science* [New Series] 274.5295 (20 December 1996): 2110–2115.

Shiva, Vandana. *Monocultures of the Mind: Biodiversity and Biotechnology*. London, UK; Atlantic Highlands, NJ: Zed Books, 1993.

Shneiderman, Ben. "The Eyes Have It: A Task by Data Type Taxonomy for Information Visualizations." In *Proceedings of the IEEE Symposium on Visual Languages*. Los Alamitos, CA: IEEE Computer Society Press, 1996, 336–343.

Shoemaker, Pamela J. "Communication in Crisis: Theory, Curricula, and Power." *Journal of Communication* 43.4 (Autumn 1993): 146–153.

Shoemaker, Pamela J. and Reese, Stephen D. *Mediating the Message: Theories of Influence on Mass Media Content*. New York: Longman, 1996.

Shoop, Tiffany J.; Luther, Catherine A.; and McMahan, Carolynn. "Advertisement Images of Men and Women in Culturally Diverging Societies: An Examination of Images in U.S. and Japanese Fashion Magazines." *Journal of International Business and Economics* 8.3 (September 2008): 29–41 <http://www.freepatentsonline.com/article/Journal-International-Business-Economics/190616968.html>, accessed 6 September 2013.

Shore, Elliott; Fones-Wolf, Ken; and Danky, James P., eds. *The German-American Radical Press: The Shaping of a Left Political Culture, 1850–1940*. Urbana: University of Illinois Press, 1992.

Shuler, Sherianne. "Breaking Through the Glass Ceiling without Breaking a Nail: Women Executives in *Fortune* Magazine's 'Power 50' List." *American Communication Journal* 6.2 (Winter 2003): Unpaginated.

Shulman, Stuart W. "The Progressive Era Farm Press: A Primer on a Neglected Source of Journalism History." *Journalism History* 25.1 (Spring 1999): 26–35 <http://www.questia.com/library/1P3-42962816/the-progressive-era-farm-press-a-primer-on-a-neglected>, accessed 12 May 2013.

Siapera, Eugenia and Veglis, Andreas. "Introduction: The Evolution of Online Journalism." In Siapera, Eugenia and Veglis, Andreas, eds. *The Handbook of Global Online Journalism*, Chichester, UK: Wiley-Blackwell, 2012, 1.

Siddiqi, Mohammad A. "Muslim Media: Present Status and Future Directions." *Gazette* 47.1 (February 1991): 19–31.

Sigal, Leon V. *Reporters and Officials: The Organization and Politics of News Making*. Lexington, MA: D.C. Heath, 1973.

Signorielli, Nancy and Morgan, Michael. *Cultivation Analysis: New Directions in Media Effects Research*. Newbury Park, CA: Sage, 1990.

Silvennoinen, Hanna and Jantunen, Ari. "Dynamic Capabilities and Innovation in the Magazine Publishing Industry." Paper presented at the 23rd ISPIM Conference, Barcelona, Spain, 17–20 June 2012.

Silverstein, Brett; Perdue, Lauren; Peterson, Barbara; and Kelly, Eileen. "The Role of the Mass Media in Promoting a Thin Standard of Bodily Attractiveness for Women." *Sex Roles* 14.9/10 (May 1986): 519–532.

Simmons, Brian K. and Lowry, David N. "Terrorists in the News, as Reflected in Three News Magazines, 1980–1988." *Journalism Quarterly* 67.4 (Winter 1990): 692–696.

Simmons, Sherwin. "Photo-Caricature in the German Popular Press, 1920." *History of Photography* 20.3 (Autumn 1996): 258–264.

Simon, Daniel H. and Kadiyali, Vrinda. "The Effect of a Magazine's Free Digital Content on Its Print Circulation: Cannibalization or Complementarity?" *Information Economics and Policy* 19.3/4 (October 2007): 344–361.

Simon, Janice. "Introduction: American Periodicals and Visual Culture." *American Periodicals* 20.2 (2010): 117–119.

Simpson, George Gaylord. "Systematics, Taxonomy, Classification, Nomenclature." *Principles of Animal Taxonomy*. New York: Columbia University Press, 1961, 11.

Sims, Norman. "The Art of Literary Journalism." In Sims, Norman and Kramer, Mark, eds. *Literary Journalism: A New Collection of the Best American Nonfiction*. New York: Ballantine Books, 1995, 3–19.

Sims, Norman. "The Bomb." In *True Stories: A Century of Literary Journalism*. Evanston, IL: Northwestern University Press, 2007, 163–199.

Sims, Norman. "Joseph Mitchell and the *New Yorker* Nonfiction Writers." In Norman Sims, ed. *Literary Journalism in the Twentieth Century*. New York: Oxford University Press, 1990, and Evanston, IL: Northwestern University Press, 2008, 82–109.

Sims, Norman. *Literary Journalism in the Twentieth Century*. New York: Oxford University Press, 1990, and Evanston, IL: Northwestern University Press, 2008.

Sims, Norman. "New Generations." In *True Stories: A Century of Literary Journalism*. Evanston, IL: Northwestern University Press, 2007, 279–317.

Sims, Norman. "The Problem and the Promise of Literary Journalism Studies." *Literary Journalism Studies* 1.1 (Spring 2009): 7–16.

Sims, Norman. "Tourist in a Strange Land: Tom Wolfe and the New Journalists." *True Stories: A Century of Literary Journalism*. Evanston, IL: Northwestern University Press, 2007, 219–262.

Sims, Norman. *True Stories: A Century of Literary Journalism*. Evanston, IL: Northwestern University Press, 2007.

Sims, Norman. "A True Story." In *True Stories: A Century of Literary Journalism*. Evanston, IL: Northwestern University Press, 2007, 1–24.

Sims, Norman. "Writing Literary History . . . *The Promised Land*, and *The Big Test*, an Interview with Author . . . Nicholas Lemann." *Literary Journalism Studies* 3.1 (Spring 2011): 9–31.

Sine, Richard. "Who's Taking Care of Business? Editors Have a Hard Time Finding Qualified Applicants for Business Desk Jobs." *American Journalism Review*, August/September 2004, 20–21.

Singer, Jane B. "Online Journalists: Foundations for Research into Their Changing Roles." *Journal of Computer-Mediated Communication* 4.1 (September 1998): n.p. <http://onlinelibrary.wiley.com/doi/10.1111/j.1083–6101.1998.tb00088.x/full >, accessed 12 May 2004.

Singer, Jane B. and Ashman, Ian. "'Comment Is Free, but Facts Are Sacred': User-Generated Content and Ethical Constructs at the *Guardian*." *Journal of Mass Media Ethics* 24.1 (January/March 2009): 3–21.

Sire, Agnès, curator. *Henri Cartier-Bresson/Walker Evans: Photographing America 1929–1947*. London: Thames & Hudson, 2009.

Sivek, Susan Currie. "Editing Conservatism: How *National Review* Magazine Framed and Mobilized a Political Movement." *Mass Communication and Society* 11.3 (Autumn 2008): 248–274.

Skalli, Loubna H. *Through a Local Prism: Gender, Globalization, and Identity in Moroccan Women's Magazines*. Lanham, MD: Lexington Books, 2006.

Skok, David. "Aggregation Is Deep in Journalism's DNA." *Nieman Journalism Lab*, 27 January 2012 <http://www.niemanlab.org/2012/01/david-skok-aggregation-is-deep-in-journalisms-dna/>, accessed 11 August 2012.

Slater, David Jeremiah. "The American Girl, Her Life and Times: An Ideal and Its Creators, 1890–1930." Ph.D. diss., University of Minnesota, 2005.

Slawinski, Scott. *Validating Bachelorhood: Audience, Patriarchy, and Charles Brockden Brown's Editorship of the Monthly Magazine and American Review*. New York: Routledge, 2005.

Slovic, Paul; Finucane, Melissa L.; Peters, Ellen; and MacGregor, Donald G. "Risk as Analysis and Risk as Feelings: Some Thoughts about Affect, Reason, Risk, and Rationality." *Risk Analysis* 24.2 (April 2004): 311–322.

Smith, Ben. "What the Longform Backlash Is All About." *Journalism, Deliberated* (blog), 26 January 2014 <https://medium.com/journalism-deliberated/958f4e7691f5>, accessed 20 March 2014.

Smith, Elizabeth; Fleer, Josh; and Waters, Ken. "Deviating from the Pack: How Religious Publications Frame the AIDS in Africa Crisis." Unpublished paper, Pepperdine University, 2004.

Smith, Erin A. *Hard-Boiled: Working-Class Readers and Pulp Magazines*. Philadelphia: Temple University Press, 2000.

Smith, Glenn D., Jr. "'You Can Do Anything': The Agendas of Carolyn Bennett Patterson, *National Geographic*'s First Woman Senior Editor." *Journalism History* 37.4 (Winter 2012): 190–206.

Smith, Matthew J. "Strands in the Web: Community-Building Strategies in Online Fanzines." *Journal of Popular Culture* 33.2 (Fall 1999): 87–99.

Smith, Nicole E. "Stem Cell Research: Visual Framing of the Ethical Debate in *Time* and *Newsweek*." Paper presented to the Annual Meeting, Association for Education in Journalism and Mass Communication, August 2006.

Smith, Roland B. "The Genesis of the Business Press in the United States." *Journal of Marketing* 19.2 (October 1954): 146–151.

Smith, Shawn Michelle. "Obama's Whiteness." *Journal of Visual Culture* 8.2 (August 2009): 129–133.

Smith, Stacy L. and Granados, Amy D. "Content Patterns and Effects Surrounding Sex-Role Stereotyping on Television and Film." In Bryant, Jennings and Oliver, Mary Beth, eds. *Media Effects: Advances in Theory and Research*. 3rd ed. New York: Routledge, 2009, 342–361.

Smith, Susan Harris. *Plays in American Periodicals, 1890–1918*. New York: Palgrave Macmillan, 2007.

Smith, Terry. *Making the Modern: Industry, Art, and Design in America.* Chicago: University of Chicago Press, 1993.

Smith, Zoe. "Dickey Chapelle: Pioneer in Combat." *Visual Communication Quarterly* 1.2 (April 1994): 4–9.

So, C.Y.K. and Chan, J.M. "Evaluating and Conceptualizing the Field of Communication: A Survey of the Core Scholars." Paper presented at the Annual Meeting, Association for Education in Journalism and Mass Communication, August 1991.

So, Stella Lai Man. "A Comparative Content Analysis of Women's Magazine Advertisements from Hong Kong and Australia on Advertising Expressions." *Journal of Current Issues and Research in Advertising* 26.1 (Spring 2004): 47–58.

Soares, Isabel. "Literary Journalism's Magnetic Pull: Britain's 'New' Journalism and the Portuguese at the Fin-de-Siècle." In Bak, John S. and Reynolds, Bill, eds. *Literary Journalism across the Globe: Journalistic Traditions and Transnational Influences.* Amherst: University of Massachusetts Press, 2011, 118–133.

Söll, Änne. "Pollock in *Vogue*: American Fashion and Avant-Garde Art in Cecil Beaton's 1951 Photographs." *Fashion Theory* 13.1 (2009): 29–50.

Solomon, Martha M., ed. *A Voice of Their Own: The Woman Suffrage Press, 1840–1910.* Tuscaloosa: University of Alabama Press, 1991.

Solomon, William S. "News Frames and Media Packages: Covering El Salvador." *Critical Studies in Mass Communication* 9.1 (March 1992): 56–74.

Soloski, John. "On Defining the Nature of Graduate Education." *Journalism Educator* 49.2 (Summer 1994): 4–11.

Sontag, Susan. *Regarding the Pain of Others.* New York: Farrar, Straus and Giroux, 2003.

Sorensen, George. "Interdisciplinary Master's Program Serves Campus Well." *Journalism Educator* 28.3 (October 1973): 36–38.

Souder, William. *On a Farther Shore: The Life and Legacy of Rachel Carson.* New York: Crown, 2012.

Souza, Pete. "Kent Kobersteen: The New Director of Photography at *National Geographic.*" *Visual Communication Quarterly* 5.3 (Summer 1998): 3–8.

Spaeth, Jim; Holmes, Michael E.; Moult, Bill; and Bloxham, Michael. *Mind the Measurement Gap: Measured and Unmeasured Media Occasions.* Muncie, IN: Ball State University Center for Media Design, June 2006.

Sparks, Jared. *The Writings of George Washington, Part V, July 1777 to July 1778.* Boston: Russell, Odiorne and Metcalf, 1834.

[Special Issue, Children's Periodicals]. *American Periodicals* 22.2 (2012).

[Special Issue: Hunter S. Thompson] *Literary Journalism Studies* 4.1 (Spring 2012) <http://www.ialjs.org/?p=1495>, accessed 20 February 2014.

[Special Issue, Immigrant Periodicals]. *American Periodicals* 19.1 (2009).

Speck, Bruce W. *Editing: An Annotated Bibliography.* Westport, CT: Greenwood Press, 1991.

Speck, Bruce W.; Hinnen, Dean A.; and Hinnen, Kathleen. *Teaching Revising and Editing: An Annotated Bibliography.* Westport, CT: Greenwood Press, 2003.

Spees, Jennifer M. Greve and Zimmerman, Toni Schindler. "Gender Messages in Parenting Magazines: A Content Analysis." *Journal of Feminist Family Therapy* 14.3/4 (Fall/Winter 2002): 73–100.

Spence, Robert. *Information Visualization: Design for Interaction.* 2nd ed. Harlow, UK: Pearson Education Limited, 2007.

Spiegler, Marc. "Hot Media Buy: The Farm Report." *American Demographics,* October 1995, 18–19.

Spiker, Ted. "Cover Coverage: How U.S. Magazine Covers Captured the Emotions of the September 11 Attack—and How Editors and Art Directors Decided on Those Themes." *Journal of Magazine & New Media Research* 5.2 (Spring 2003): 1–18.

Spiker, Ted. "9/11 Magazine Covers." American Society of Magazine Editors <http://www.magazine.org/asme/magazine-cover-contests/9/11-magazine-covers>, accessed 11 September 2011.

Squires, Catherine R. and Jackson, Sarah J. "Reducing Race: News Themes in the 2008 Primaries." *International Journal of Press/Politics* 15.4 (October 2010): 375–400.

SRDS Business Media Advertising Source, Parts 1, 2. Vol. 95. Des Plaines, IL: Kantar/SRDS/Standard Rate & Data Service, 2013.

SRDS Consumer Media Advertising Source. Vol. 95. Des Plaines, IL: Kantar/SRDS/Standard Rate & Data Service, 2013.

Srisuwan, Paweena and Barnes, Stuart. "Predicting Online Channel Use for an Online and Print Magazine: A Case Study." *Internet Research* 18.3 (2008): 266–285.

Stabile, Carol A. "Getting What She Deserved: The News Media, Martha Stewart, and Masculine Domination." *Feminist Media Studies* 4.3 (November 2004): 315–332.

Stahl, Florian; Schäfer, Marc-Frederic; and Mass, Wolfgang. "Strategies for Selling Paid Content on Newspaper and Magazine Web Sites: An Empirical Analysis of Bundling and Splitting of News and Magazine Articles." *International Journal on Media Management* 6.1/2 (2004): 59–66.

Standard Periodical Directory. New York: Oxbridge Communications, 2014.

Stankiewicz, Julie M. and Rosselli, Francine. "Women as Sex Objects and Victims in Print Advertisements." *Sex Roles* 58.7/8 (April 2008): 579–589.

Stanko, Elizabeth. *Intimate Intrusions: Women's Experience of Male Violence*. London: Routledge & Kegan Paul, 1985.

Stanley, Alessandra. "Talk Ends and Spin Begins: Tina Brown Has No Regrets." *New York Times*, 20 January 2002 <http://www.nytimes.com/2002/01/20/us/talk-ends-and-spin-begins-tina-brown-has-no-regrets.html>, accessed 2 June 2014.

Starkman, Dean. *The Financial Crisis and the Disappearance of Investigative Journalism*. New York: Columbia University Press, 2014.

Starkman, Dean. "Ouryay Eatbay Just Ewblay Upyay: Ten Fundamentals for the Business Press Now." *The Audit* (blog). *Columbia Journalism Review*, 29 September 2008 <http://www.cjr.org/the_audit/ouryay_eatbay_just_ewblay_upya.php>, accessed 29 November 2013.

Starkman, Dean. "Power Problem: The Business Press Did Everything but Take On the Institutions that Brought Down the Financial System." *Columbia Journalism Review*, May/June 2009, 24–30.

Starkman, Dean. "Red Ink Rising: How the Press Missed a Sea Change in the Credit-Card Industry." *Columbia Journalism Review*, March/April 2008, 14–16.

"*Star* Magazine Seems to Suggest that Rihanna Had It Coming." *Star* Magazine [print edition], 2 March 2009, Front Cover.

"Star Power: Bonnie Fuller and the Feminist Case for Celebrity Journalism." *Economist*, 5 August 2004 <http://www.economist.com/node/3062089>, accessed 11 November 2012.

Startt, James D. and Sloan, Wm. David. *Historical Methods in Mass Communication*. Hillsdale, NJ: Lawrence Erlbaum Associates, Inc., 1989.

Steele, Janet. "Representations of 'the Nation' in *Tempo* Magazine." *Indonesia* 76 (October 2003): 127–145.

Steele, Jeanne R. and Brown, Jane D. "Adolescent Room Culture: Studying Media in the Context of Everyday Life." *Journal of Youth and Adolescence* 24.5 (1995): 551–576.

Steiger, Paul E. "Not Every Journalist 'Missed' the Enron Story." *Nieman Reports*, Summer 2002, 10–12.

Steinberg, Sigfrid H. *Five Hundred Years of Printing*. New ed. Revised by John Trevitt. London: British Library & Oak Knoll Press, 1955/1996.

Steiner, Linda. "Oppositional Decoding as an Act of Resistance." *Critical Studies in Mass Communication* 5.1 (March 1988): 1–15.

Steinfels, Peter. "Influential Christian Journal Prints Last Issue." *New York Times*, 4 April 1993 <http://www.nytimes.com/1993/04/04/us/influential-christian-journal-prints-last-issue.html>, accessed 29 November 2013.

Stephen, Leslie. "The Evolution of Editors." *Studies of a Biographer*. Vol. 1. New York: G. P. Putnam's Sons, 1907, 35–68.

Stepp, Carl Sessions. *Editing for Today's Newsroom: A Guide for Success in a Changing Profession*. 2nd ed. New York: Routledge, 2008.

Stepp, Carl Sessions. "Giving a Forgotten Visionary His Due." *American Journalism Review*, October/November 2006 <http://ajrarchive.org/article_printable.asp?id=4198>, accessed 27 January 2014.

Sterk, Helen M. "Faith, Feminism and Scholarship: The *Journal of Communication and Religion*, 1999–2009." [Special Issue]. *Journal of Communication and Religion* 33.2 (November 2010): 206–216.

Sterk, Helen M. "How Rhetoric Becomes Real: Religious Sources of Gender Identity." *Journal of Communication and Religion* 12.2 (September 1989): 24–33.

Stern, Bruce L.; Krugman, Dean M.; and Resnik, Alan. "Magazine Advertising: An Analysis of Its Information Content." *Journal of Advertising Research* 21.2 (April 1981): 39–44.

Stern, Paul C. "Toward a Coherent Theory of Environmentally Significant Behavior." *Journal of Social Issues* 56.3 (Fall/Sept. 2000): 407–424.

Stern Magazine. *Consumer Magazines in Europe*. Hamburg: Gruner + Jahr AG & Co., 1981.

Stevenson, Nick. *Understanding Media Cultures*. 2nd ed. London: Sage, 2002.

Stevenson, Thomas H. "Four Decades of African American Portrayals in Magazine Advertising." *Journal of Business & Economics Research* 7.3 (March 2009): 23–30.

Stibbe, Arran. "Health and the Social Construction of Masculinity in *Men's Health* Magazine." *Men and Masculinities* 7.1 (July 2004): 31–51.

Stoker, Kevin and Rawlins, Brad L. "The 'Light' of Publicity in the Progressive Era: From Searchlight to Flashlight." *Journalism History* 30.4 (Winter 2005): 177–188.

Stovall, James Glen. *Writing for the Mass Media*. 8th ed. Knoxville: University of Tennessee Press, 2012.

Strauss, David Levi. *Between the Eyes: Essays on Photography and Politics*. New York: Aperture, 2003.

Strauss, Neil. "The Ballad of Pamela Anderson and Tommy Lee." *Rolling Stone*, 10 May 2001, 1–5 <http://www.rollingstone.com/music/news/the-ballad-of-pamela-anderson-tommy-lee-20010510>, accessed 17 September 2013.

Streitmatter, Rodger. *Unspeakable: The Rise of the Gay and Lesbian Press in America*. Boston: Faber and Faber, 1995.

Stroyberg, Mik. "Social Sharing: The New Coffee Table Magazine Spread." *Adam Sherk* (blog), 4 December 2012 <http://www.adamsherk.com/publishing/mik-stroyberg-social-sharing-the-new-coffee-table-magazine-spread/>, accessed 15 December 2013.

Strube, Mania. "Entering Emerging Media Markets: Analyzing the Case of the Chinese Magazine Market." *International Journal on Media Management* 12.3/4 (December 2010): 183–204.

Stuhlfaut, Mark W. "Economic Concentration in Agricultural Magazine Publishing: 1993–2002." *Journal of Media Economics* 18.1 (2005): 21–33 <http://www.tandfonline.com/doi/abs/10.1207/s15327736me1801_2#preview>, accessed 21 May 2013.

Suggs, Henry Lewis, ed. *The Black Press in the Middle West, 1865–1985*. Westport, CT: Greenwood Press, 1996.

Sugiarto, Catur and De Barnier, Virginie. "Sexually Appealing Ads Effectiveness on Indonesian Customers." *European Journal of Business and Management* 5.9 (2013): 125–135 <http://www.iiste.org/Journals/index.php/EJBM/article/view/5133>, accessed 27 September 2013.

Sugiura, Ikuko. "Lesbian Discourses in Mainstream Magazines of Post-War Japan: Is *Onabe* Distinct from *Rezubian*?" *Journal of Lesbian Studies* 10.3/4 (2006): 127–144.

Sullivan, Paul W. "G.D. Crain Jr. and the Founding of '*Advertising Age*.'" *Journalism History* 1.3 (1974): 94–95.

Sultze, Kimberly. "Women, Power, and Photography in the *New York Times Magazine*." *Journal of Communication Inquiry* 27.3 (July 2003): 274.

Sumner, David E. "A Bibliography of American Magazine History." *The Magazine Century: American Magazines since 1900*. Mediating American History Series. New York: Peter Lang, 2010, 225–234.

Sumner, David E. "Letter from Our Division Head: Revisiting an Old Question." *Magazine Matter*, Spring 2000, 1.

Sumner, David E. *The Magazine Century: American Magazines since 1900*. Mediating American History Series. New York: Peter Lang, 2010.

Sumner, David E. "Magazine-Related Articles in *Journalism Mass Communications Quarterly* 1990 to 2010." <http://davidabrahamson.com/WWW/MAG2/Sumner_JMCQ_Magazine_Bibliography.pdf>, accessed 02 June 2014.

Sumner, David E. "Sixty-Four Years of *Life*: What Did Its 2,128 Covers Cover?" *Journal of Magazine & New Media Research* 5.1 (Fall 2002): 1–16.

Sumner, David E. "Theory? Bah Humbug!" *Journal of Magazine & New Media Research* 10.1 (Fall 2008): 1–2 <http://aejmcmagazine.arizona.edu/Journal/Fall2008/SumnerColumn.pdf>, accessed 9 September 2012.

Sumner, David. "Undergraduate Magazine Programs and Courses at U.S. Universities." <http://aejmcmagazine.arizona.edu/Students/magazine_programs.pdf>, accessed 2 June 2014.

Sumner, David E. "A Visit to the Condé Nast Library and Archives." *Journal of Magazine & New Media Research* 10.2 (2009) <http://aejmcmagazine.arizona.edu/journal/spring2009/Sumner.pdf>, accessed 20 February 2014.

Sumner, David E. and Miller, Holly G. *Feature and Magazine Writing: Action, Angle, and Anecdotes*. 3rd ed. Malden, MA and Chichester, UK: Wiley-Blackwell, 2013.

Sumner, David E. and Miller, Holly G. "Long-Form Digital Storytelling." *Feature and Magazine Writing: Action, Angle, and Anecdotes*. 3rd ed. Malden, MA and Chichester, UK: Wiley-Blackwell, 2013, 265–276.

Sumner, David E. and Rhoades, Shirrel. *Magazines: A Complete Guide to the Industry*. New York: Peter Lang, 2006.

Sunderland, Jane. "'Parenting' or 'Mothering'?: The Case of Modern Childcare Magazines." *Discourse & Society* 17.4 (July 2006): 503–527.

Sung, Yongjun and Hennink-Kaminski, Heidi J. "The Master Settlement Agreement and Visual Imagery of Cigarette Advertising in Two Popular Youth Magazines." *Journalism & Mass Communication Quarterly* 85.2 (Summer 2008): 331–352.

Suro, Roberto and Associates. "Changing Faiths: Latinos and the Transformation of American Religion." *Pew Forum on Religion & Public Life*. Washington, DC: Pew Research Center, March 2007 <http://www.pewforum.org/uploadedfiles/Topics/Demographics/hispanics-religion-07-final-mar08.pdf>, accessed 8 July 2013.

Swain, Bruce M. "Bernarr Macfadden." In Riley, Sam G., ed. *American Magazine Journalists, 1900–1960, First Series*. Dictionary of Literary Biography. Vol. 91. Detroit: Gale Research, 1990, 205–215.

Swain, Kristen Alley. "Proximity and Power Factors in Western Coverage of the Sub-Saharan AIDS Crisis." *Journalism & Mass Communication Quarterly* 80.1 (Spring 2003): 145–165.

Swanson, Carl with Larocca, Amy. "What Makes Bonnie Run?" *New York*, 14 July 2003 <http://nymag.com/nymetro/news/nedia/features/n_8946/>, accessed 29 January 2014.

Swartz, David R. "Identity Politics and the Fragmenting of the 1970s Evangelical Left." *Religion and American Culture: A Journal of Interpretation* 21.1 (Winter 2011): 81–120.

Sweeney, Michael S. "'Delays and Vexation': Jack London and the Russo-Japanese War." *Journalism & Mass Communication Quarterly* 75.3 (Autumn 1998): 548–559.

Sweeney, Sharienne. "The Inter-Media Agenda Setting Influence of Trade Publications." M.S. thesis, The Ohio State University, 1998.

Sweeney, Sharienne and Hollifield, C. Ann. "Influence of Agricultural Trade Publications on the News Agendas of National Newspapers and News Magazines." *Journal of Applied Communications* 84.1 (2000): 23–45.

Swithinbank, Tessa. *Coming Up from the Streets: The Story of the* Big Issue. London: Earthscan, 2001.

Sypeck, Mia Foley; Gray, James J.; and Ahrens, Anthony H. "No Longer Just a Pretty Face: Fashion Magazines' Depictions of Ideal Female Beauty from 1959 to 1999." *International Journal of Eating Disorders* 36.3 (2004): 342–347.

Tabeek, Melissa. "NYTimes: Consumer Now at Media's Center." *NetNewsCheck*, 27 March 2012 <http://www.netnewscheck.com/article/17769/ny-times-consumer-now-at-medias-center>, accessed 7 December 2013.

"Tabela Circulação Geral." *IVC*, May 2013 <http://www.publiabril.com.br/tabelas-gerais/revistas/circulacao-geral/imprimir>, accessed 19 April 2013.

Taft, William H. *American Magazines for the 1980s*. New York: Hastings House, 1982.

Tait, Lisa Olsen. "The *Young Woman's Journal*: Gender and Generations in a Mormon Women's Magazine." *American Periodicals* 22.1 (2012): 51–71.

Tajfel, Henri. "Social Identity and Intergroup Behaviour." *Social Science Information* 13.2 (April 1974): 65–93.

Tajfel, Henri and Turner, John C. "The Social Identity Theory of Intergroup Behavior." In Worchel, Stephen and Austin, William G., eds. *The Psychology of Intergroup Relations*, 2nd ed. Chicago: Nelson-Hall Publishers, 1986, 7–24.

Talese, Gay. "Frank Sinatra Has a Cold." *Esquire*, April 1966 <http://www.esquire.com/features/esq1003-oct_sinatra_rev_>, accessed 20 June 2013.

Tankard, James W., Jr. "Quantitative Graphics in Newspapers." *Journalism Quarterly* 64.2/3 (Summer/Fall 1987): 406–415.

Tanner, James T.F. "From the Editor." *American Periodicals: A Journal of History, Criticism, and Bibliography* 1.1 (Fall 1991): iii.

Tanner, Stephen; Kasinger, Molly; and Richardson, Nick. *Feature Writing: Telling the Story*. New York and Melbourne, AUS: Oxford University Press, 2009.

Tarkiainen, Anssi; Ellonen, Hanna-Kaisa; and Kuivalainen, Olli. "Complementing Consumer Magazine Brands with Internet Extensions?" *Internet Research* 19.4 (2009): 408–424.

Tassin, Algernon. *The Magazine in America*. New York: Dodd, Mead and Company, 1916.

Tay, Jinna. "'Pigeon-Eyed Readers': The Adaptation and Formation of a Global Asian Fashion Magazine." *Continuum: Journal of Media & Cultural Studies* 23.2 (April 2009): 245–256.

Taylor, Adam. "The Cover of this British Magazine about Olympic Censorship Could Be Banned Due to Olympic Censorship." *Business Insider*, 11 July 2012 <http://www.businessinsider.com/spectator-cover-olympic-censorship-2012-7>, accessed 4 March 2013.

Taylor, Charles R.; Landreth, Stacy; and Bang, Hae-Kyong. "Asian Americans in Magazine Advertising: Portrayals of the 'Model Minority.'" *Journal of Macromarketing* 25.2 (December 2005): 163–174.

Taylor, Jill Fenton and Carroll, John. "Corporate Cultural Narratives as the Performance of Organisational Meaning." *Qualitative Research Journal* 10.1 (2010): 28–39.

Taylor, Laramie D. "College Men, Their Magazines, and Sex." *Sex Roles* 55.9/10 (November 2006): 693–702.

Taylor, Orlando L. "What is the Discipline of Communication?" *Spectra*, April 1999, 2, 12.

Taylor, Steve. *100 Years of Magazine Covers*. London: Black Dog Publishing, 2006.

Tayman, John. "It's a Long Article. It's a Short Book. No, It's a Byliner E-Book." *Nieman Reports*, Winter 2011, 38.

Tebbel, John and Zuckerman, Mary Ellen. *The Magazine in America, 1741–1990*. New York and Oxford, UK: Oxford University Press, 1991.

Teece, David J. "Explicating Dynamic Capabilities: The Nature and Microfoundations of (Sustainable) Enterprise Performance." *Strategic Management Journal* 28.13 (December 2007): 1319–1350.

Tenore, Mallary Jean. "Byliner CEO Excited About 'Opportunity to Discover Some Great Writers.'" *MediaWire*. Poynter.org, 21 June 2011 <http://www.poynter.org/latest-news/top-stories/136421/byliner-ceo-were-really-excited-about-the-opportunity-to-discover-great-writers/>, 12 May 2014.

Tenore, Mallary Jean. "How Technology Is Renewing Attention to Long-Form Journalism." *MediaWire*. Poynter.org, 4 March 2011 <http://www.poynter.org/latest-news/top-stories/104962/how-technology-is-renewing-attention-to-long-form-journalism/>, accessed 25 February 2013.

Terry, Don. "An Icon Fades." *Columbia Journalism Review*, 16 March 2010 <http://www.cjr.org/feature/an_icon_fades_1.php?page=all>, accessed 15 December 2013.

Theodorson, George A. and Theodorson, Achilles G. *A Modern Dictionary of Sociology*. New York: Barnes & Noble Books, Division of Harper & Row, 1969.

Thomas, James J. and Cook, Kristin A., eds. *Illuminating the Path: The Research and Development Agenda for Visual Analytics*. Los Alamitos, CA: IEEE, 2005.

Thomas, Jeremy N. and Olson, Daniel, V.A. "Evangelical Elites' Changing Responses to Homosexuality 1960–2009." *Sociology of Religion* 73.3 (2012): 239–272.

Thomsen, Steven R. "Health and Beauty Magazine Reading and Body Shape Concerns among a Group of College Women." *Journalism & Mass Communication Quarterly* 79.4 (Winter 2002): 988–1007.

Thornton, Brian. "The Disappearing Media Ethics Debate in Letters to the Editor." *Journal of Mass Media Ethics* 13.1 (November 1998): 40–55.

Thornton, Brian. "The Murder of Emmett Till: Myth, Memory, and National Magazine Response." *Journalism History* 36.2 (Summer 2010): 96–104.

Thorson, Esther. "Reconceptualizing the Influence of the News Industry on Journalism Graduate Education." *Journalism & Mass Communication Educator* 60.1 (Spring 2005): 17–22.

"367 Magazines Closed in 2009 So Far." *Magazine Death Pool: "Who Will Be Next?"* (blog), 14 December 2009 <http://www.magazinedeathpool.com/magazine_death_pool/2009/12/367-magazines-closed-in-2009-so-far.html>, accessed 2 June 2014.

Thurlow, Crispin and Jaworski, Adam. "Communicating a Global Reach: Inflight Magazines as a Globalizing Genre in Tourism." *Journal of Sociolinguistics* 7.4 (November 2003): 579–606.

Tiggemann, Marika; Polivy, Janet; and Hargreaves, Duane. "The Processing of Thin Ideals in Fashion Magazines: A Source of Social Comparison or Fantasy?" *Journal of Social and Clinical Psychology* 28.1 (2009): 73–93.

Tiggemann, Marika; Slater, Amy; Bury, Belinda; Hawkins, Kimberley; and Firth, Bonny. "Disclaimer Labels on Fashion Magazine Advertisements: Effects on Social Comparison and Body Dissatisfaction." *Body Image* 10.1 (January 2013): 45–53 <http://www.sciencedirect.com/science/article/pii/S1740144512000952>, accessed 10 December 2012.

Tillinghast, William and McCann, Marie. "Climate Change in Four News Magazines: 1989–2009." *Online Journal of Communication and Media Technologies* 3.1 (January 2013): 22–48 <http://www.ojcmt.net/articles/31/312.pdf>, accessed 12 February 2013.

"TimeInc.: News/Business/Sports." TimeInc. <http://www.timeinc.com/brands/news-businessfinance.php>, accessed 13 January 2013.

Tiryakian, Edward A. "Typologies." In Sills, David L., ed. *International Encyclopedia of the Social Sciences*. Vol. 16. New York: MacMillan, 1968, 177–186.

Tobler, Kyle J.; Wilson, Philip K.; and Napolitano, Peter G. "Frequency of Breast Cancer, Lung Cancer, and Tobacco Use Articles in Women's Magazines from 1987 to 2003." *Journal of Cancer Education* 24.1 (March 2009): 36–39.

Tolstikova, Natasha. "*Rabotnitsa*: The Paradoxical Success of a Soviet Women's Magazine." *Journalism History* 30.3 (Fall 2004): 131–140.

Tonkonow, Leslie. *Multiple Exposure: The Group Portrait in Photography*. New York: Independent Curators, 1995.

"Top 500 Sites on the Web, The." Alexa <http://www.alexa.com/topsites>, accessed 2 June 2014.

Toulouse, Mark G. "*Christianity Today* and American Public Life: A Case Study." *Journal of Church and State* 35.2 (Spring 1993): 241–284.

Towers, Wayne M. "Uses and Gratifications of Magazine Readers: A Cross-Media Comparison." *Mass Comm Review* 13.1/2/3 (1986): 44–51.

Towers, Wayne M. and Hartung, Barbara. "Explaining Magazine Readership with Uses and Gratifications Research." Paper presented at the Annual Meeting, Association for Education in Journalism and Mass Communication, 1983.

Trachtenberg, Alan, ed. *Classic Essays on Photography*. New Haven: Leete's Island Books, 1980.

Trachtenberg, Alan. *Reading American Photographs: Images as History, Mathew Brady to Walker Evans*. New York: Hill and Wang, 1989.

Treme, Julianne. "Effects of Celebrity Media Exposure on Box-Office Performance." *Journal of Media Economics* 23.1 (2010): 5–16.

Triggs, Teal. "Scissors and Glue: Punk Fanzines and the Creation of a DIY Aesthetic." *Journal of Design History* 19.1 (2006): 69–83.

Trindade, Alice Donat. "What Will the Future Bring?" *Literary Journalism Studies* 4.2 (Fall 2012): 101–105.

Trouten, Douglas J. "The Development of Professionalization in the Evangelical Press Association." M.A. thesis, University of Minnesota, 1999.

Trumbo, Craig W. "Research Methods in Mass Communication Research: A Census of Eight Journals 1990–2000." *Journalism & Mass Communication Quarterly* 81.2 (Summer 2004): 417–436.

Tsai, Joyce. "*Der Kuckuck* and the Problem of Workers' Photography in Austria." *History of Photography* 29.3 (2005): 275–286.

Tuchman, Gaye. "Introduction: The Symbolic Annihilation of Women by the Mass Media." In Tuchman, Gaye; Daniels, Arlene Kaplan; and Benét, James, eds. *Hearth and Home: Images of Women in the Mass Media*. New York: Oxford University Press, 1978, 3–38.

Tucker, Amy. *The Illustration of the Master: Henry James and the Magazine Revolution*. Stanford, CA: Stanford University Press, 2010.

Tufte, Edward R. *Beautiful Evidence*. Cheshire, CT: Graphics Press, 2006.

Tufte, Edward R. *Envisioning Information*. Cheshire, CT: Graphics Press, 1990.

Tufte, Edward R. *The Visual Display of Quantitative Information*. Cheshire, CT: Graphics Press, 1983.

Tufte, Edward R. *The Visual Display of Quantitative Information*. 2nd ed. Cheshire, CT: Graphics Press, 2001.

Tufte, Edward R. *Visual Explanations: Images and Quantities, Evidence and Narrative*. Cheshire, CT: Graphics Press, 1997.

Turner, Graeme. "Understanding Celebrity." *Understanding Celebrity*. London: Sage, 2004, 3–27.

Turner, Melanie B.; Vader, Amanda M.; and Walters, Scott T. "An Analysis of Cardiovascular Health Information in Popular Young Women's Magazines: What Messages are Women Receiving?" *American Journal of Health Promotion* 22.3 (January/February 2008): 183–186.

Turow, Joseph. "The Magazine Industry." *Media Today: An Introduction to Mass Communication*. 3rd ed. New York: Routledge, Taylor & Francis, 2009, 342–374.

Tyler, Imogen and Bennett, Bruce. "'Celebrity Chav': Fame, Femininity and Social Class." *European Journal of Cultural Studies* 13.3 (2010): 375–393.

Tyler, Tom R. and Cook, Fay Lomax. "The Mass Media and Judgments of Risk: Distinguishing Impact on Personal and Societal Level Judgments." *Journal of Personality and Social Psychology* 47.4 (October 1984): 693–708.

Ubbens, Wilbert. Review of *The 'World-View' of the Axel Springer Publishing Company: Journalism between Western Values and German Traditions of Thought*, by Gudrun Kruip. *Communication Booknotes Quarterly* 31:1 (Winter 2000): 37–38.

Ukman, Lesa. *IEG's Complete Guide to Sponsorship: Everything You Need to Know about Sports, Arts, Event, Entertainment and Cause Marketing*. Chicago, IL: IEG, 1996.

Ulin, David L. "Literary Journalism Finds New Platforms: Byliner, the *Atavist* and *Virginia Quarterly Review* Take the Form into the Future." *Los Angeles Times*, 15 May 2011 <latimes.com/entertainment/news/books/la-ca-david-ulin-20110515,0,3634450.story>, accessed 25 February 2013.

Ulrich, Carolyn F. *Periodicals Directory: A Classified Guide to a Selected List of Current Periodicals Foreign and Domestic*. New York: R. R. Bowker, 1932.

Ulrich's Periodicals Directory 2014. Vol. 1. 52nd ed. New Providence, NJ: ProQuest, 2013. s.v. "*CIO Africa*."

Ulrich's Periodicals Directory 2014. Vols. 1–4. 52nd ed. New Providence, NJ: ProQuest, 2013.

Underwood, Doug. *Journalism and the Novel: Truth and Fiction, 1700–2000*. Cambridge: Cambridge University Press, 2008.

"United States—Consumer Magazines." *G2MI*, Global Media Market Intelligence <www.g2mi.com/country_sector_info.php?sectorName=%20Consumer%20magazines&countryName=United%20States&id=155>, accessed 8 February 2013.

University of North Carolina at Chapel Hill School of Journalism and Mass Communication. "1500s–1800s: History of Business Journalism." <http://www.bizjournalismhistory.org/main_frame.htm>, accessed 29 May 2014.

Unsworth, Michael E. *Military Periodicals: United States and Selected International Journals and Newspapers*. Westport, CT: Greenwood Press, 1990.

Updike, John. "Foreword." *Complete Book of Covers from the New Yorker, 1925–1989*. New York: Knopf, 1989.

U.S. Census Bureau. "Hispanic Americans by the Numbers." *InfoPlease* <http://www.infoplease.com/spot/hhmcensus1.html>, accessed 5 September 2013.

Usdansky, Margaret L. "The Emergence of a Social Problem: Single-Parent Families in U.S. Popular Magazines and Social Science Journals, 1900–1998." *Sociological Inquiry* 78.1 (February 2008): 74–96.

Utt, Sandra H. and Pasternack, Steve. "Infographics Today: Using Qualitative Devices to Display Quantitative Information." *Newspaper Research Journal* 14.3/4 (Summer/Fall 1993): 146–157.

Valanto, Vera; Kosonen, Miia; and Ellonen, Hanna-Kaisa. "Are Publishers Ready for Tomorrow? Publishers' Capabilities and Online Innovations." *International Journal of Innovation Management* 16.1 (February 2012): 1–18.

Vance, Laura. "Evolution of Ideals for Women in Mormon Periodicals, 1897–1999." *Sociology of Religion* 63.1 (Spring 2002): 91–112.

Van den Bulck, Hilde and Panis, Koen. "Michael as He Is Not Remembered: Jackson's 'Forgotten' Celebrity Activism." *Celebrity Studies* 1.2 (2010): 242–244.

van der Wurff, Richard. "Business Magazine Market Performance: Magazines for the Agricultural, Business Services, and Transportation Sectors in the Netherlands." *Journal of Media Economics* 18.2 (2005): 143–159 <http://www.tandfonline.com/doi/abs/10.1207/s15327736me1802_5?journalCode=hmec20#preview>, accessed 28 February 2014.

VanZile, Jon. "Direct Marketers Need to Understand Their Customer's Buying Journey." BtoB, *Ad Age*, 4 March 2013 <http://adage.com/article/btob/direct-marketers-understand-customer-s-buying-journey/289311/>, accessed 31 May 2014.

Varey, Richard J. and Lewis, Barbara R., eds. *Internal Marketing: Directions for Management*. London: Routledge, 2000.

Vayda, Andrew P. "Causal Explanation for Environmental Anthropologists." In Kopnina, Helen and Shoreman-Ouimet, Eleanor, eds. *Environmental Anthropology: Future Trends*. Routledge Studies in Anthropology Series. New York and Oxford: Routledge, 2013.

Verdon, Dan (editor of *DVM Newsmagazine*). Speech given at the Medill School of Journalism, Northwestern University, Evanston, IL, 5 February 2009.

Verrall, Krys. "*artscanada*'s 'Black' Issue: 1960s Contemporary Art and African Liberation Movements." *Canadian Journal of Communication* 36.4 (2011): 539–558.

Vigorito, Anthony J. and Curry, Timothy J. "Marketing Masculinity: Gender Identity and Popular Magazines." *Sex Roles* 39.1/2 (July 1988): 135–152.

Vincent, Cindy S. "*POOR Magazine* and Civic Engagement through Community Media." In Lind, Rebecca Ann, ed. *Race/Gender/Class/Media 3.0: Considering Diversity across Content, Audiences, and Production*. 3rd ed. New York: Pearson, 2013, 316–322.

Vitek, Jack. *The Godfather of Tabloid: Generoso Pope Jr. and the National Enquirer*. Lexington: University Press of Kentucky, 2008.

Vivian, John. "Magazines." *The Media of Mass Communication*. 8th ed. Boston: Pearson, 2007, 80–99.

Vlad, Tudor; Becker, Lee B.; Simpson, Holly; and Kalpen, Konrad. "Annual Survey of Journalism and Mass Communication Enrollments" <http://www.grady.uga.edu/annualsurveys/Enrollment_Survey/Enrollment_2012/Enroll12Merged.pdf>, accessed 8 March 2014.

Vogue. March 2009.

Vogue. "Photographers: Annie Leibovitz." Voguepedia <http://www.vogue.com/voguepedia/Annie_Leibovitz>, accessed 15 December 2013.

Vokey, Megan; Tefft, Bruce; and Tysiaczny, Chris. "An Analysis of Hyper-Masculinity in Magazine Advertisements." *Sex Roles* 68.9/10 (May 2013): 562–576.

Wakefield, Dan. "Harold Hayes and the New Journalism: *Esquire* Editor Encouraged a Generation of Writers to Experiment with Non-Fiction Techniques." *Nieman Reports* Summer 1992, 32–35.

Walker, John A. "Internal Memorandum." *Studio International* 192.983 (September/October 1976): 113–118.

Walker, John A. "Periodicals since 1945." In Fawcett, Trevor and Phillpot, Clive, eds. *The Art Press: Two Centuries of Art Magazines.* London: The Art Book Company, 1976, 45–52.

Walker, Nancy A. *Shaping Our Mothers' World: American Women's Magazines.* Jackson: University Press of Mississippi, 2000.

Wall, Melissa A. "The Rwanda Crisis: An Analysis of News Magazine Coverage." *International Communication Gazette* 59.2 (April 1997): 121–134.

Wallace-Sanders, Kimberly. *Mammy: A Century of Race, Gender, and Southern Memory.* Ann Arbor: University of Michigan Press, 2008.

Walsh-Childers, Kim; Edwards, Heather M.; and Grobmyer, Stephen. "Covering Women's Greatest Health Fear: Breast Cancer Information in Consumer Magazines." *Health Communication* 26.3 (April/May 2011): 209–220.

Walsh-Childers, Kim; Edwards, Heather M.; and Grobmyer, Stephen. "*Essence, Ebony* and O: Breast Cancer Coverage in Black Magazines." *Howard Journal of Communications* 23.2 (April/June 2012): 136–156.

Walter, Gerry. "The Ideology of Success in Major American Farm Magazines, 1934–1991." *Journalism & Mass Communication Quarterly* 73.3 (Autumn 1996): 594–608.

Walter, Tony. "Jade and the Journalists: Media Coverage of a Young British Celebrity Dying of Cancer." *Social Science and Medicine* 71.5 (2010): 853–860.

Wang, Jixiang. "Scientific, Technical, Medical and Professional Publishing." In Baensch, Robert E., ed. *The Publishing Industry in China.* New Brunswick: Transaction Publishers, 2003, 67–84.

Ward, Douglas B. "From Barbarian Farmers to Yeoman Consumers: Curtis Publishing Company and the Search for Rural America, 1910–1930." *American Journalism* 22.4 (Fall 2005): 47–67.

Ward, Douglas B. *A New Brand of Business: Charles Coolidge Parlin, Curtis Publishing Company, and the Origins of Market Research.* Philadelphia: Temple University Press, 2010.

Ware, Colin. *Information Visualization: Perception for Design.* 3rd ed. Waltham, MA: Morgan Kaufmann, 2012.

Ware, Colin. *Visual Thinking for Design.* Burlington, MA: Morgan Kaufmann, 2008.

Warwick, Claire; Terras, Melissa; and Nyhan, Julianne. *Digital Humanities in Practice.* London: Facet Books, 2012.

Waters, Ken. "Evangelical Magazines." In Woods, Robert H., Jr., ed. *Evangelical Christians and Popular Culture: Pop Goes the Gospel.* Vol. 3. Santa Barbara, CA: Praeger, 2013, 195–211.

Waters, Ken. "The Evangelical Press." In Winston, Diane H. ed. *The Oxford Handbook of Religion and the American News Media.* New York: Oxford University Press, 2012, 551–564.

Waters, Ken. "Pursuing New Periodicals in Print and Online." In Schultze, Quentin J. and Woods, Robert H., Jr., eds. *Understanding Evangelical Media: The Changing Face of Christian Communication.* Downers Grove, IL: IVP Academic, 2008, 71–84.

Waters, Ken. "Vibrant, but Invisible: A Study of Contemporary Religious Periodicals." *Journalism & Mass Communication Quarterly* 78.2 (Summer 2001): 307–320.

Waters, Ken. "*World Vision.*" In Fackler, P. Mark and Lippy, Charles H., eds. *Popular Religious Magazines of the United States.* Westport, CT: Greenwood Press, 1995, 537–542.

Weaver, David H. "Mass Communication Research at the End of the 20th Century: Looking Back and Ahead." In Leung, Kenneth W.Y.; Kenny, James; and Lee, Paul S.N., eds. *Global Trends in Communication Education and Research.* Cresskill, NJ: Hampton Press, 2006, 1–16.

Webb, Sheila M. "Art Commentary for the Middlebrow: Promoting Modernism and Modern Art through Popular Culture—How *Life* Magazine Brought 'The New' into Middle-Class Homes." *American Journalism* 27.3 (2010): 115–150.

Webb, Sheila M. "The Narrative of Core Traditional Values in Reiman Magazines." *Journalism & Mass Communication Quarterly* 83.4 (Winter 2006): 865–882.

Wei, Ran and Jiang, Jing. "New Media Advertising and Its Social Impact in China." In Cheng, Hong and Chan, Kara, eds. *Advertising and Chinese Society: Impacts and Issues* Copenhagen: Copenhagen Business School Press, 2009, 245–263.

Weick, Karl E. *Sensemaking in Organizations*. London: Sage, 1995.

Weinberger, Peter. "The *Philosophical Magazine* and the Periodic Table of Elements." *Philosophical Magazine* 92.13 (May 2012): 1727–1732.

Weiner, Camille Mary. "Artists as Authors: Three Los Angeles Art Periodicals of the 1970s." Master's thesis, University of Southern California, 2011.

Weisenfeld, Gennifer S. "'Touring Japan-as-Museum': *Nippon* and Other Japanese Imperialist Travelogues." *Positions: East Asia Cultures Critique* 8.3 (2000): 747–793.

Weitzer, Ronald and Kubrin, Charis E. "Breaking News: How Local TV News and Real-World Conditions Affect Fear of Crime." *Justice Quarterly* 21.3 (September 2004): 497–520.

Wekerle, Christine and Wolfe, David A. "Dating Violence in Mid-Adolescence: Theory, Significance, and Emerging Prevention Initiatives." *Clinical Psychology Review* 19.4 (June 1999): 435–456.

Welch, Mary and Jackson, Paul R. "Rethinking Internal Communication: A Stakeholder Approach." *Corporate Communications: An International Journal* 12.2 (2007): 177–198.

"Welcome to ARPA!" The Australasian Religious Press Association <http://www.arpanews.org>, accessed 29 November 2013.

Wells, Jonathan Daniel. "Introduction." In Minor, Benjamin Blake, ed. *The* Southern Literary Messenger, *1834–1864*. Columbia: University of South Carolina Press, 2007.

Welton, Caysey. "*Wired* Reveals Its Future Digital Content Strategy with 'Vision Quest.'" *Folio:*, 28 May 2013 <http://www.foliomag.com/2013/wired-reveals-its-future-digital-content-strategy-vision-quest#.Uh-SRaUyu5e>, accessed 28 May 2014.

Wesson, Matt. "Get More Data and Conversions with Progressive Profiling." Pardot, 21 March 2013 <http://www.pardot.com/forms/data-conversions-progressive-profiling/>, accessed 31 May 2014.

West, James L. W., III, *American Authors and the Literary Marketplace since 1900*. Philadelphia: University of Pennsylvania Press, 1988.

West, Richard Samuel. "The *Light* that Failed: The History of an Unknown Magazine that Published the Work of a Galaxy of Emerging Stars." *American Periodicals* 19.2 (September 2009): 189–212.

Westad, Anniken. "The Norwegian Magazine Industry: An Overview and Bibliographic Review." Paper presented to the Contemporary Magazine Publishing Research Roundtable, Iowa State University, December 2010.

Whannel, Garry. *Media Sport Stars: Masculinities and Moralities*. London: Routledge, 2002.

Wharton-Michael, Patty. "Print vs. Computer Screen: Effects of Medium on Proofreading Accuracy." *Journalism & Mass Communication Educator* 63.1 (Spring 2008): 28–41.

"What Is a Serial?" *CONSER Cataloging Manual*, Library of Congress <http://www.itsmarc.com/crs/mergedprojects/conser/conser/module_2_1__ccm.htm>, accessed 18 April 2014.

Wheeler, Britta B. "The Institutionalization of an American Avant-Garde: Performance Art as Democratic Culture, 1970–2000." *Sociological Perspectives* 46.4 (Winter 2003): 491–512.

Wheelock, John Hall, ed. *Editor to Author: The Letters of Maxwell E. Perkins*. Introduction by Marcia Davenport. 2nd ed. New York: Charles Scribner Sons, 1979.

White, David Manning. "The 'Gate Keeper': A Case Study in the Selection of News." *Journalism Quarterly* 27.4 (Fall 1950): 383–390.

Whitehead, Kally and Kurz, Tim. "Saints, Sinners and Standards of Femininity: Discursive Constructions of Anorexia Nervosa and Obesity in Women's Magazines." *Journal of Gender Studies* 17.4 (December 2008): 345–358.

Whitt, Jan. "A 'Labor from the Heart': Lesbian Magazines from 1947–1994." *Journal of Lesbian Studies* 5.1/2 (March 2001): 229–251.

Whitt, Jan. *Settling the Borderland: Other Voices in Literary Journalism*. Lanham, MD: University Press of America, 2008.

Whyte, Kenneth. *The Uncrowned King: The Sensational Rise of William Randolph Hearst*. Berkeley: Counterpoint, 2009.

Wikström, Patrik and Ellonen, Hanna-Kaisa. "The Impact of Social Media Features on Print Media Firms' Online Business Model." *Journal of Media Business Studies* 9.3 (2012): 63–80.

Wilk, Richard. "Consumption Embedded in Culture and Language: Implications for Finding Sustainability." *Sustainability: Science, Practice and Policy* 6.2 (2010): 38–48.

Wilkes, Lesley; Withnall, Janice; Harris, Rebecca; White, Kate; Beale, Barbara; Hobson, Jane; Durham, Marsha; and Kristjanson, Linda. "Stories about Breast Cancer in Australian Women's Magazines: Information Sources for Risk, Early Detection and Treatment." *European Journal of Oncology Nursing* 5.2 (June 2001): 80–88.

Wilkinson, Jeffrey S.; Grant, August E.; and Fisher, Douglas J. *Principles of Convergent Journalism.* New York: Oxford University Press, 2013.

Williams, Alex. "How a Science Journalist Created a Data Visualization to Show the Magnitude of the Haiti Earthquake." *Readwrite.com*, 12 January 2011 <http://readwrite.com/2011/01/12/how-a-science-journalist-creat>, accessed 24 May 2013.

Williams, Alex. "Secrets of the Stock Stars." *New York*, 18 January 1999 <http://nymag.com/nymetro/news/bizfinance/biz/features/1026/>, accessed 29 November 2013.

Williams, Angie; Ylänne, Virpi; Wadleigh, Paul Mark; and Chen, Chin-Hui. "Portrayals of Older Adults in UK Magazine Advertisements: Relevance of Target Audience." *Communications: The European Journal of Communication Research* 35.1 (March 2010): 1–27.

Williams, Gilbert Anthony. "The A.M.E. *Christian Recorder*: A Forum for the Social Ideas of Black Americans, 1854–1902." Ph.D. diss., University of Illinois, 1979.

Williams, Gilbert Anthony. "The Role of the *Christian Recorder* in the African Emigration Movement, 1854–1902." *Journalism Monographs* 111 (April 1989).

Williams, Iolo A. *The Firm of Cadbury, 1831–1931.* London: Constable and Co. Ltd., 1931.

Williams, Megan E. "The *Crisis* Cover Girl: Lena Horne, the NAACP, and Representations of African American Femininity, 1941–1945." *American Periodicals* 16.2 (2006): 200–218.

Williams, Peter; Tapsell, Linda; Jones, Sandra; and McConville, Kellie. "Health Claims for Food Made in Australian Magazine Advertisements." *Nutrition & Dietetics* 64.4 (December 2007): 234–240.

Williams, Raymond. "Film and the Dramatic Tradition." In Higgins, John, ed. *The Raymond Williams Reader*. Oxford, UK: Blackwell Publishers, Ltd., 2001, 25–41.

Williams, Raymond. "Drama in a Dramatised Society." In O'Connor, Alan, ed. *Raymond Williams on Television*. Toronto: Between the Lines, 1989, 3–5.

Williamson, Judith. *Decoding Advertisements: Ideology and Meaning in Advertising.* London: Calder and Boyars, 1978.

Willis, William James and Willis, Diane B. "Magazines and the Search for Specialization." *New Directions in Media Management*. Boston: Allyn & Bacon, 1993, 65–89.

Wilner, Isaiah. *The Man Time Forgot: A Tale of Genius, Betrayal, and the Creation of* Time *Magazine.* New York: HarperCollins, 2006.

Wilson, Christopher P. Review of *An Economy of Abundant Beauty*: Fortune *Magazine and Depression America*, by Michael Augspurger. *American Historical Review* 111.3 (June 2006): 856.

Wilson, Clint C., II; Gutiérrez, Félix; and Chao, Lena M. *Racism, Sexism, and the Media: The Rise of Class Communication in Multicultural America.* 3rd ed. Thousand Oaks, CA: Sage, 2003.

Wilson, Eric. "Fashion Changes, and So Do the Magazines." *New York Times*, 1 February 2012 <http://www.nytimes.com/2012/02/02/fashion/fashion-changes-and-so-do-the-magazines.html>, accessed 29 April 2013.

Wilson, John F. *British Business History, 1720–1994.* Manchester: Manchester University Press, 1995.

Wilson, Stan Le Roy. "Magazines: The Specialized Medium." *Mass Media/Mass Culture: An Introduction.* 2nd ed. New York: McGraw-Hill, 1992, 121–145.

Wimmer, Roger D. and Dominick, Joseph R. *Mass Media Research: An Introduction.* 9th ed. Boston, MA: Cengage Wadsworth Learning, 2011.

Winfield, Berry Houchin. "The Making of an Image: Hillary Rodham Clinton and American Journalists." *Political Communication* 14 (1997): 241–253.

Winston, Diane H., ed. *The Oxford Handbook of Religion and the American News Media.* New York: Oxford University Press, 2012.

Wintour, Anna. "Letter from the Editor: Vision Quests." *Vogue*, March 2009, 170, 178, 192.

Witte, Kim. "Putting the Fear Back into Fear Appeals—The Extended Parallel Process Model." *Communication Monographs* 59.4 (December 1992): 329–349.

Wojdynski, Bartosz W. "Graphical Depictions of Quantitative Data: Can Interactivity Affect Recall and Attitudes?" Paper presented at the Annual Meeting, Association for Education in Journalism and Mass Communication, August 2010.

Wolfe, Tom. Archive. *New York* Magazine <http://nymag.com/nymag/tom-wolfe/>, accessed 20 June 2013.

Wolfe, Tom. "The Birth of 'The New Journalism': Eyewitness Report by Tom Wolfe." *New York* Magazine, 14 February 1972 <http://nymag.com/news/media/47353/>, accessed 20 June 2013.

Wolfe, Tom. *The New Journalism*. With an Anthology edited by Wolfe, Tom and Johnson, E.W., eds. New York: Harper & Row, 1973.

Wolff, Alexander. "That Old Black Magic." *Sports Illustrated*, 21 January 2002, Unpaginated <http://sportsillustrated.cnn.com/vault/article/magazine/MAG1024790/index.htm>, accessed 18 September 2012.

Wolin, Lori D. "Gender Issues in Advertising—An Oversight Synthesis of Research: 1970–2002." *Journal of Advertising Research* 43.1 (March 2003): 111–129.

Wolman, David. "Journalism Done the *Atavist* Way." *Nieman Reports*, Winter 2011, 36–38.

Wolseley, Roland E. "Magazine Types." *Understanding Magazines*. Ames: Iowa State University Press, 1965, 255–355.

Wolseley, Roland E. "The Role of Magazines in the U.S.A." *Gazette* 23.1 (1977): 20–26.

Wolseley, Roland E. *Understanding Magazines*. Ames: Iowa State University Press, 1965.

Wood, Gaby. "The Quiet American." *Observer*, 9 September 2006.

Woods, Joshua. "What We Talk About When We Talk About Terrorism: Elite Press Coverage of Terrorism Risk from 1997 to 2005." *International Journal of Press/Politics* 12.3 (Summer 2007): 3–20.

Woods, Robert H., Jr., ed. *Evangelical Christians and Popular Culture: Pop Goes the Gospel*. Santa Barbara, CA: Praeger, 2013.

Woods, Stuart. "Random House of Canada Launches On-line Magazine as Part of Digital Overhaul." *Quill & Quire*, 23 August 2012 <http://www.quillandquire.com/digital-publishing-and-technology/2012/08/23/random-house-of-canada-launches-online-magazine-as-part-of-digital-overhaul/>, accessed 25 April 2014.

Woolley, John T. "Using Media-Based Data in Studies of Politics." *American Journal of Political Science* 44.1 (January 2000): 156–173.

Wörsching, Martha. "Gender and Images of Nature and Sport in British and German News Magazines: The Global and the National in Images of Advertising." *International Journal of Media and Cultural Politics* 5.3 (2009): 217–232.

Wright, Charles R. *Mass Communication: A Sociological Perspective*. 2nd, 3rd eds. New York: Random House, 1975, 1986.

Wright, Fred. "The History and Characteristics of Zines." *Zine & E-Zine Resource Guide* <http://www.zinebook.com/resource/wright1.html>, accessed 20 December 2012.

WWF. "Deforestation." The World Wide Fund for Nature. 2012 <http://wwf.panda.org/about_our_earth/about_forests/deforestation/>, accessed 30 November 2012.

Yaffa, Joshua. "The Information Sage." *Washington Monthly*, May/June 2011 <http://www.washingtonmonthly.com/magazine/mayjune_2011/features/the_information_sage029137.php?page=all>, accessed 13 January 2014.

Yagoda, Ben. *About Town: The* New Yorker *and the World It Made*. New York: Scribner, 2000.

Yagoda, Ben. "Preface." In Kerrane, Kevin and Yagoda, Ben, eds. *The Art of Fact: A Historical Anthology of Literary Journalism*. New York: Scribner, 1997, 13–16.

Yahr, Jayme Alyson. "The Art of the *Century*: Richard Watson Gilder, the Gilder Circle, and the Rise of American Modernism." Ph.D. diss., University of Washington, 2012.

Yang, Fang-Chih Irene. "International Women's Magazines and the Production of Sexuality in Taiwan." *Journal of Popular Culture* 37.3 (February 2004): 505–530.

Yarbus, Alfred L. *Eye Movements and Vision*. Translated by Basil Haigh. Translation Edited by Lorrin A. Riggs. New York: Plenum, 1967.

Yarrow, Andrew L. "The Big Postwar Story: Abundance and the Rise of Economic Journalism." *Journalism History* 32.2 (Summer 2006): 58–76.

Yates, JoAnne. *Control through Communication: The Rise of System in American Management*. Baltimore: Johns Hopkins University Press, 1989.

Yeager, Holly. "Crook on Broken 'Labour' Markets, Bartlett Notices That We're Getting Old, *WSJ* Notices Fannie and Freddie." *The Audit* (blog). *Columbia Journalism Review*, 24 May 2010 <http://www.cjr.org/the_audit/audit_dc_notes_crook_on_broken.php>, accessed 29 November 2013.

Yeager, Holly. "Jobs, Jobs, Jobs? As Press Coverage Falters, the Washington Conversation Keeps Shifting." *The Audit* (blog). *Columbia Journalism Review*, 18 May 2010 <http://www.cjr.org/the_audit/shifting_the_washington_conversation_to_jobs_again.php>, accessed 29 November 2013.

Yeomans, Liz. "Internal Communication." In Tench, Ralph and Yeomans, Liz, eds. *Exploring Public Relations*. 2nd ed. Harlow, UK: FT Prentice Hall, 2009, 316–337.

Yi, Youjae. "Contextual Priming Effects in Print Advertisements: The Moderating Role of Prior Knowledge." *Journal of Advertising* 22.1 (March 1993): 1–10.

Yin, Jaifei. "Beyond the Four Theories of the Press: A New Model for the Asian and the World Press." *Journalism & Communication Monographs* 10.1 (Spring 2008): 3–62.

Young, C. "Winona Ryder Busted for Shoplifting." *People*, 14 December 2001 <http://www.people.com/people/article/0,,623102,00.html>, accessed 10 October 2013.

Ytre-Arne, Brita. "'I Want to Hold It in My Hands': Readers' Experiences of the Phenomenological Differences between Women's Magazines Online and in Print." *Media, Culture & Society* 33.3 (April 2011): 467–477.

Ytre-Arne, Brita. "Positioning the Self: Identity and Women's Magazine Reading." *Feminist Media Studies* 14.2 (May 2014): 237–252.

Zarem, Jane E. "All-Digital Magazines: New Opportunity or Last Hurrah?" *Folio:*, 3 April 2009 <http://www.foliomag.com/2009/all-digital-magazines#.UyxfhFyp07c>, accessed 30 September 2012.

Zdovc, Sonja Merljak. "Željko Kozinc, the Subversive Reporter: Literary Journalism in Slovenia." In Bak, John S. and Reynolds, Bill, eds. *Literary Journalism across the Globe: Journalistic Traditions and Transnational Influences*. Amherst: University of Massachusetts Press, 2011, 238–259.

Zehle, Soenke. "Ryszard Kapuściński and the Borders of Documentarism: Toward Exposure without Assumption." In Bak, John S. and Reynolds, Bill, eds. *Literary Journalism across the Globe: Journalistic Traditions and Transnational Influences*. Amherst: University of Massachusetts Press, 2011, 276–294.

Zelizer, Barbie. *Taking Journalism Seriously: News and the Academy*. London: Sage, 2004.

Zeman, Scott C. "'Taking Hell's Measurements': *Popular Science* and *Popular Mechanics* Magazines and the Atomic Bomb from Hiroshima to Bikini." *Journal of Popular Culture* 41.4 (August 2008): 695–711.

Zhang, Bohai. "The Development of Business-to-Business Magazines in China." *Publishing Research Quarterly* 24.1 (March 2008): 54–58.

Zillmann, Dolf. "Excitation Transfer in Communication-Mediated Aggressive Behavior." *Journal of Experimental Social Psychology* 7.4 (July 1971): 419–434.

Zimerman, Martin. "Periodicals: Print or Electronic?" *New Library World* 111.9/10 (2010): 426–433.

Zimmerman, Amanda and Dahlberg, John. "The Sexual Objectification of Women in Advertising: A Contemporary Cultural Perspective." *Journal of Advertising Research* 48.1 (March 2008): 71–79.

Zinnbauer, Markus. "e-Newspaper: Consumer Demands on Attributes and Features." *JMM—The International Journal on Media Management* 5.2 (2003): 127–137 <http://www.tandfonline.com/doi/abs/10.1080/14241270309390026?journalCode=hijm20#preview>, accessed 12 May 2013.

Zinsser, William. "Once Around the Sun." *American Scholar*, 29 April 2011 <http://theamericanscholar.org/once-around-the-sun/#.UynoVVyp07c>, accessed 19 February 2014.

Zott, Christopher and Amit, Raphael. "Business Model Design: An Activity System Perspective." *Long Range Planning* 43.2 (2010): 216–226.

Zuckerman, Mary Ellen. *A History of Popular Women's Magazines in the United States, 1792–1995*. Westport, CT: Greenwood Press, 1998.

Zuckerman, Mary Ellen. *Sources on the History of Women's Magazines, 1792–1960: An Annotated Bibliography*. New York: Greenwood Press, 1991.

Zullow, Harold M. "Pessimistic Rumination in Popular Songs and Newsmagazines Predict Economic Recession via Decreased Consumer Optimism and Spending." *Journal of Economic Psychology* 12.3 (September 1991): 501–526.

LIST OF CONTRIBUTORS

David Abrahamson is a professor of Journalism and the Charles Deering Professor of Teaching Excellence at the Northwestern University's Medill School, where he teaches courses exploring the changing nature of long-form journalism. The co-editor of this volume, he is the author of *Magazine-Made America: The Cultural Transformation of the Postwar Periodical* (1996) and editor of *The American Magazine: Research Perspectives and Prospects* (1995). He is the general editor of the Northwestern University Press Visions of the American Press series, as well as past president of the International Association for Literary Journalism Studies and past head of both the Association for Education in Journalism and Mass Communication's Magazine and History divisions. He is also the past winner of the American Journalism History Association's *Sidney Kobre Award for Lifetime Achievement in Journalism History* and the AEJMC Magazine Division's *Educator of the Year* Award.

Dane S. Claussen is a visiting professor at the School of International Journalism and the Center for Global Opinion of China at Shanghai International Studies University, China. From 2001 to 2010, he was a professor of Communication in the School of Communication at Point Park University. He is the author of *Anti-Intellectualism in American Media: Magazines and Higher Education* (2004) and editor of three other books. From 2006 to 2012 he was the editor of *Journalism & Mass Communication Educator*, a refereed, quarterly journal published by the Association for Education in Journalism and Mass Communication. He has served as the head of the Magazine, Media Management and Economics, History, Mass Communication and Society and GLBT divisions of AEJMC. Before joining the academy, he was editor and publisher of daily, weekly, biweekly and monthly newspapers, magazines and newsletters.

Elizabeth Crisp Crawford is an assistant professor of Communication in the Department of Communication at North Dakota State University, where she teaches advertising courses. Her research focuses on message strategy and mass communication education, and she has published her research in academic journals including the *Journal of Health and Mass Communication*, *Electronic News*, *Journal of Radio and Audio Media* and *Asian Cinema*. She also advises the student Ad Club and National Student Advertising Competition team.

Michael F. Dahlstrom is an associate professor of Journalism and Mass Communication at the Greenlee School of Journalism and Communication at Iowa State University. He works with colleagues from social science and humanities fields to explore the complex communicative interactions between science and the public. His research has been published in leading journals in the communication field, and he currently sits on the executive board of the Communicating Science, Health, Environment and Risk Division of the Association for Education in Journalism and Mass Communication. His current research focuses on the effects of narrative structure on science perceptions and the biases inherent when attempting to perceive scientific topics beyond the realm of human scale.

Hanna-Kaisa Ellonen is a professor of Strategic Management of Innovations at the School of Business at the Lappeenranta University of Technology in Lappeenranta, Finland. Her research interests are in the areas of strategic management and technological change, particularly within the magazine publishing industry. Her work has been published in *Technovation*, the *International Journal on Media Management* and the *Journal of Media Business Studies*.

Bill Emmott was the editor-in-chief of the *Economist* from 1993 to 2006, having worked at that publication since 1980 in Brussels, Tokyo and London. He is the author of 13 books, including *Good Italy, Bad Italy: Why Italy Must Conquer Its Demons to Face the Future* (2012); *Rivals: How the Power Struggle between China, India and Japan Will Shape our Next Decade* (2008); and *Japan's Global Reach: The Influence, Strategies and Weaknesses of Japan's Multinational Corporations* (1993). He writes frequently for *La Stampa* in Italy and *Nikkei Business* in Japan. He serves as chairman of the London Library, as a trustee of the International Institute for Strategic Studies and most recently as chairman and co-founder of the Wake Up Foundation, a charity dedicated to education and communication about the decline of Western societies. With his co-founder, Annalisa Piras, he is now working on a film about the dangers of European disintegration and a book about the tasks facing the West as a whole.

Kathleen L. Endres is a distinguished professor of Communication in the School of Communication at the University of Akron. A trained historian, Endres does research on magazines, journalism history and women's studies. She is the author or editor of six books, has written many scholarly articles and book chapters and presented more than 100 convention papers. She is also an *Emmy* and *Telly* award-winning producer of documentaries. She teaches a variety of magazine, journalism history and writing courses.

Vincent F. Filak is an associate professor at the University of Wisconsin Oshkosh, where he is an award-winning teacher, researcher and media adviser. He teaches writing and editing courses and serves as the adviser to the school's award-winning newspaper, the *Advance-Titan*. He co-authored *Convergent Journalism: An Introduction* (2005) with Stephen Quinn and *The Journalist's Handbook for Online Editing* (2012) with Kenneth L. Rosenauer. He has extensively published research on issues of media convergence, e-learning, self-censorship and student journalism in numerous journals, including *Journalism & Mass Communication Quarterly*; *Journalism & Mass Communication Educator*; *Journalism: Theory, Practice and Criticism*; and the *British Journal of Social Psychology and Educational Psychology*.

Cheryl Renée Gooch is a professor of Mass Communication at Lincoln University of Pennsylvania. She teaches, conducts research and publishes in the areas of media and culture, ethnographic journalism, and communication and social change. Her recent scholarship explores how famed folklorist Joel Chandler Harris used his journalism to advocate for civil rights in the post-Reconstruction South. An avid genealogist, she is completing a work of narrative journalism that blends ethnography and oral history to chronicle six generations of Gooch family history. Before embarking on a career in higher education, she worked as a reporter for print and broadcast media.

Susan Greenberg is a senior lecturer/associate professor of English and Creative Writing at the University of Roehampton, London, where she teaches on publishing and innovative form in nonfiction. Before that she reported on central and eastern Europe and held a number of editing roles on newspapers, magazines and the Web. Her essay "Slow Journalism in the Digital Fast Lane" was published in *Global Literary Journalism: Exploring the Journalistic Imagination* (2012) and a book of interviews, *Editors Talk about Editing* is forthcoming. Other articles include "The Ethics of Narrative: A Return to the Source" in *Journalism: Theory Practice* *and Criticism*; "When the Editor Disappears, Does Editing Disappear?" in *Convergence*; and "Theory and Practice in Journalism Education" in the *Journal of Media Practice*. Greenberg is a founding member of the International Association of Literary Journalism Studies, a Senior Fellow of the Higher Education Academy and a member of the Higher Education committee of the United Kingdom's National Association of Writers in Education.

Michael Heller is a senior lecturer in Marketing at Brunel University in the United Kingdom. His research and teaching interests focus on branding, corporate identity and communications, integrated marketing communications and business history. He has taught at a number of major London universities including Queen Mary and Royal Holloway. He has published on a wide range of topics, including the history of clerical workers, company magazines, corporate branding, corporate social responsibility and the marketing of suburbia. He has researched major corporations in Britain, which include the Prudential Insurance Company, the Royal Bank of Scotland, Royal Dutch Shell, the British Broadcasting Corporation and Royal Mail, and he is currently writing a monograph on the history of public relations and corporate communications in Britain in the interwar period.

Elizabeth Meyers Hendrickson is an assistant professor in the E.W. Scripps School of Journalism at Ohio University, where she teaches courses related to the magazine industry. Her research focus is technological innovation within magazine content creation. Previous research includes "iPerceive: Platform Priorities and Workplace Innovation in America's Consumer Magazine Industry" in *Journal of the International Symposium on Online Journalism*, and "Economic Rationalism in Popular Culture: Celebrity Booking in America's Women's Magazines" in *Journal of Magazine & New Media Research*. During the 1990s, she worked as an entertainment editor in New York City for titles such as *Glamour* and *Ladies' Home Journal*.

Carol Holstead is an associate professor of Journalism at the University of Kansas, where she teaches courses in magazine writing, editing, publishing and design, as well as visual storytelling. She has written about design for *Folio*: magazine and has contributed chapters on magazine design to several encyclopedias, including Sage Publishing's *Encyclopedia of Journalism* (2009). She is a recipient of the *Budig Teaching Professorship in Writing* Award at the University of Kansas, as well as a recipient of a *Great Ideas for Teachers* Award from the Association for Journalism and Mass Communication, for an assignment she created for visual communication courses.

Berkley Hudson is an associate professor of Journalism in the magazine sequence of the Missouri School of Journalism at the University of Missouri, where he has taught since 2003. His scholarly research has been published in journals such as *Journalism History*, *Media History* and *Southern Cultures*, and he is currently the editor-in-chief of *Visual Communication Quarterly*. Prior to joining the academy, he worked for 25 years as a magazine and newspaper (*Los Angeles Times*) journalist.

Anette Johansson earned her doctorate in Business Administration at the Media Management and Transformation Center, Jönköping International Business School in Jönköping, Sweden. Currently she teaches marketing and entrepreneurship at the School of Engineering in Jönköping, Sweden, and her research interests include business development and innovation in the media industries and high-tech industries, with a particular focus on decision-making in situations of uncertainty. Her recent research examines different approaches to innovation in the Swedish magazine publishing industry and demonstrates how a combination of different decision-making approaches encourages innovation.

Elliot King is a professor of Communication and chair of the Department of Communication at Loyola University Maryland, where he founded the Digital Media Lab in 1995. He is also the executive chair of the Joint Journalism and Communication History Conference and the organizer of the Media History Exchange, an on-line social media network and archive for researchers exploring media issues. He is the author of *Key Readings in Journalism* (2012), *Free for All: The Internet's Transformation of Journalism* (2010) and *The Online Journalist* (1995). Among his current projects is a study of language use in newspapers using a framework that draws on concepts from content analysis, sociolinguistics and conceptual history.

Carolyn Kitch is a professor of Journalism at Temple University's School of Media and Communications. She also teaches in the school's Mass Media and Communication doctoral program and has been faculty director for the school's study-abroad programs in London and Dublin. In addition to numerous journal articles, she has published four books: *The Girl on the Magazine Cover: The Origins of Visual Stereotypes in American Mass Media* (2001); *Pages from the Past: History and Memory in American Magazines* (2005); *Journalism in a Culture of Grief*, co-authored with Janice Hume (2008); and *Pennsylvania in Public Memory: Reclaiming the Industrial Past* (2012). She is a former writer and editor for *Reader's Digest*, *McCall's* and *Good Housekeeping* magazines.

Helen Kopnina is a lecturer and the coordinator of the Sustainable Business Program at The Hague University of Applied Science in the Netherlands. She is the author of *East to West Migration* (2005), *Crossing European Boundaries: Beyond Conventional Geographical Categories* (2006), *Migration and Tourism: Formation of New Social Classes* (2007), *Health and Environment: Social Science Perspectives* (2010), *Environmental Anthropology Today* (2011), *Anthropology of Environmental Education* (2012), *Environmental Anthropology: Future Directions* (2013), *Sustainable Business: Key issues* (2014) and *Sustainability: Key Issues* (forthcoming, 2015).

Yanick Rice Lamb is an associate professor of Journalism in the Department of Media, Journalism and Film at Howard University, where she teaches courses in magazine writing and editing. Lamb is also adviser to the Howard University News Service and *101 Magazine*, a national publication for college students. She is on the editorial board of the *Journal of Magazine & New Media Research* and a Digitally Speaking columnist for *Howard Magazine*. Her research focuses on media management, particularly for magazines. She was an editor at the *New York Times* before joining the company's magazine division as a senior editor at *Child*. She went on to become founding editor of *BET Weekend* magazine, editor-at-large at *Essence* and editor-in-chief of *Heart & Soul*. She is co-founder of FierceforBlackWomen. com, an on-line health magazine. She is co-author of *Born to Win: The Authorized Biography of Althea Gibson* (2004) and *The Spirit of African Design* (1996).

Elizabeth A. Lance works as a research administrator at Northwestern University in Qatar. She holds a master's in journalism from the Missouri School of Journalism, where she served as the assistant editor of *Visual Communication Quarterly*. She was a Fulbright U.S. Student Fellow to Nepal in 2008–2009 and a recipient of a U.S. State Department Critical Language Scholarship to study in Bangladesh in 2012 and 2013. Her research interests include the American influence on journalistic practice in South Asia, representations of South Asia in the American press and the South Asian press in the Middle East.

Dominic L. Lasorsa is an associate professor of Journalism at the University of Texas at Austin. He co-authored *How to Build Social Science Theories* (2004) and the three-volume *National Television Violence Study* (1997–1998) and is co-editor of the forthcoming anthology from Taylor and Francis *Identity and Communication: New Agendas*. He has published original research in the *International Journal of Public Opinion Research*, *Journal of Media Economics*,

Journalism & Mass Communication Educator, Journalism & Mass Communication Quarterly, Journalism Practice, Journalism Studies, Newspaper Research Journal and other research journals. He has written entries for the *Encyclopedia of International Media and Communications, Encyclopedia of Political Communication, International Encyclopedia of Communication* and *Historical Dictionary of Political Communication*.

Carolyn Ringer Lepre is an associate professor and assistant dean of the Department of Communication at Marist College in New York, where she also directs the College's Honors Program. She is the co-author of *Diversity in U.S. Mass Media* (2012), a comprehensive look at issues regarding mass media portrayals of social groups within the mass media in the United States. Her research interests also include the representation of gender in magazines and the way health issues are framed in the press. She served as the 2010–2011 head of the AEJMC Magazine Division.

Kim Martin Long is the founding dean of Business and Humanities at Delaware Valley College in Bucks County, Pennsylvania, just north of Philadelphia. Having earned her Ph.D. in American literature at the University of North Texas, she taught and worked at Shippensburg University of Pennsylvania for 17 years, where she was a professor of English and then Associate Dean. Long was the founding manager editor of the journal *American Periodicals* and served as the Research Society for American Periodical's bibliographer for six years. She has also published on various American writers and is working on a manuscript of ecofeminism in American literature from 1850. She has chaired the MLA division on Ethnic Studies and is the treasurer for MELUS, Multi-Ethnic Literature of the United States.

Miles Maguire is a professor of Journalism at the University of Wisconsin Oshkosh, where he teaches writing, editing and reporting. He is the author of *Advanced Reporting: Essential Skills for 21st Century Journalism* (2014), and his research is focused in two interrelated areas: quality standards for news organizations and reporting methods. An associate editor of *Literary Journalism Studies*, he is currently working on a biography of Thomas Whiteside, the *New Yorker* writer whose articles were credited with bringing a halt to the use of Agent Orange. He was the founding editor of the Oshkosh Community News Network, a nonprofit on-line news organization. The *Knight-Batten* Awards has cited the OCNN's work as a notable innovation in journalism.

Rachel Davis Mersey is an associate professor at Northwestern University's Medill School of Journalism, Media, Integrated Marketing Communications. She is also the senior director of research at the university's Media Management Center and a fellow at the Institute for Policy Research. Her first book, *Can Journalism Be Saved? Rediscovering America's Appetite for News*, was published in 2010. In addition, her research has been published in journals across a variety of disciplines and presented at academic and industry conferences, including those for the Paley Center for Media in New York and the American Society of News Editors. She has also done work for the Newspaper Association of America on young adults and news and the Chicago Community Trust on local information needs. She is a past head of the AEJMC Magazine Division.

Cynthia Lee Patterson is an associate professor of English at the University of South Florida and the co-editor of *American Periodicals*, the scholarly journal of the Research Society for American Periodicals. Her book, *Art for the Middle Classes: America's Illustrated Magazines of the 1840s* (2010), won an honorable mention in the EBSCOhost/Research Society for American Periodicals book prize contest for 2010. A cultural historian by training, she teaches courses in professional and technical writing, visual culture studies and nineteenth-century American literature and culture.

Abe Peck is a professor *emeritus* of Journalism and the director of Business-to-Business Communication at the Medill School of Journalism at Northwestern University, as well as senior director for the university's Media Management Center specializing in B2B and Chinese media. He is the author of *Uncovering the Sixties: The Life and Times of the Underground Press* (1985, 1991) and co-editor of *Medill on Media Engagement* (2010). Professionally, he consults on strategic editorial performance across platforms, vision and mission statements, branding, magazine architecture, feature writing and ethics. He has led workshops in the United States, United Kingdom, China, Hong Kong, India, Malaysia, the Philippines and Qatar and has worked with more than 100 print magazines, Web sites and newspapers. He is the winner of a *Lifetime Achievement* Award of the American Society of Business Press Editors and the *Educator of the Year* Award from the Association for Education in Journalism and Mass Communication's Magazine Division. He is also in the Chicago Journalism Hall of Fame.

Marcia R. Prior-Miller is an associate professor emeritus of Journalism and Mass Communication at the Greenlee School of Journalism and Communication at Iowa State University, where she led the magazine program and developed and taught courses in contemporary magazine publishing, editorial strategies, and magazine and journal periodical research. Co-editor of this volume and author of "Issues in Magazine Typology," her published research and long-term research agenda focus on the sociology of the media, the question of magazine types and identifying and mapping the body of scholarly knowledge on magazine and journal periodicals. She is the compiler of the *Bibliography of Published Research on Magazine and Journal Periodicals*, now in its 9th edition, and serves on the editorial board of *Journalism & Mass Communication Quarterly*. Prior to joining the academy, her professional experience included advertising agency, public relations, magazine and book publishing, in profit and nonprofit, regional, national and international contexts.

Bill Reynolds is an associate professor of Journalism at the School of Journalism at Ryerson University, Toronto, Canada, where he teaches feature writing, magazine production and literary journalism. He is the co-editor of *Literary Journalism across the Globe: Journalistic Traditions and Transnational Influences* (2011). After receiving a Master of Arts in philosophy from University of Waterloo, he spent 15 years as a journalist, including a stint as editor of the Toronto alternative news and arts paper, *Eye Weekly*. In the past few years he has received the National Magazine Award and the Western Magazine Award for his feature writing, and for the past decade his research area has been literary journalism. He is currently the president of the International Association for Literary Journalism Studies.

Leara D. Rhodes is an associate professor of Journalism and Mass Communication in the Grady College of Journalism and Mass Communication at the University of Georgia. Her research focuses on media in transitional governments with emphasis on Haiti and the Caribbean. She is the author of *Democracy and the Role of the Haitian Media* (2001) and *The Ethnic Press: Shaping the American Dream* (2010). Her research is published in *Journalism & Mass Communication Quarterly*, *Journalism & Mass Communication Educator*, *Journal of Haitian Studies*, *Latin American Perspectives*, *Journal of Development Communication* and other journals as well as book chapters. She is a faculty member in the African Studies Institute and an affiliate faculty member of the Latin American and Caribbean Studies Institute, and she teaches magazine writing, publishing, international communications, race and gender in the media, and mass communication theory.

Lulu Rodriguez is a professor and director of Agricultural Communication, a program jointly administered by the College of Agriculture, Consumer and Environmental Sciences and the College of Media at the University of Illinois. She designs, implements and evaluates the impact of communication campaigns related to agriculture, renewable energy, the environment, food safety and food security. Her research focuses on the communication of risks related to scientific and technological breakthroughs, investigating people's basic mental models of hazard and their opinions about innovations that cause controversies or may be perceived as risky. Her research agenda includes examining and testing approaches that have the potential to improve society's ability to anticipate, diagnose, prioritize and respond to issues that confront, and often confound, risk managers. Rodriguez also conducts research on the visual representations of science and risk issues.

Michael Rowlinson is a professor of Organization Studies at the School of Business and Management, Queen Mary University of London. He has published widely on the relationship between history and organization theory in journals such as the *Academy of Management Review, Business History, Human Relations, Organization,* and *Organization Studies.* His research on organizational remembering concerns the representation of history by organizations, especially the dark side of their involvement in war, slavery and racism. This research has been published in journals such as *Critical Perspectives on Accounting, Journal of Organizational Change Management* and *Labour History Review.* His current interests include the methodology of interpretive historical research in organization studies. He is a co-editor for a Special Topic Forum of the *Academy of Management Review* on "History and Organization Theory."

Sela Sar is an associate professor of Advertising at the College of Media at the University of Illinois. He is a member of the editorial boards of the *Journal of Advertising* and the *International Journal of Advertising,* and he is a recipient of the *Journal of Advertising's Best Reviewer* Award for 2010. He is also an associate editor of the *Asian Journal of Communication.* He has published more than a dozen refereed journal articles in top journals, such as the *Journal of Advertising, Journal of Current Issues and Research in Advertising* and *Psychology and Marketing.* His research area involves examining the effects of mood and emotion on health and risk communication, and he teaches courses in advertising strategies, advertising research and psychology of advertising.

Carol B. Schwalbe is an associate professor of Journalism and the Soldwedel Family Professor of Journalism at the School of Journalism at the University of Arizona. She was the editor of the peer-reviewed *Journal of Magazine & New Media Research* and is a past head of the AEJMC Magazine Division. Her research focuses on the role of images in shaping ideas and public opinion during the early years of the Cold War, ethical concerns about publishing violent images and the visual framing of the Iraq War on the Internet. She teaches science journalism, feature writing, magazine photography and multimedia journalism. She has won numerous teaching awards, including the grand prize three times in the AEJMC *Great Ideas for Teachers* competition; first place in the AEJMC *Promising Professors* competition; first place in the AEJMC Teaching Committee's *Teaching Writing Across Media* competition; the *Excellence in Classroom Performance* at Arizona State University and the *Leicester and Kathryn Sherrill Creative Teaching* Award at the University of Arizona. Prior to joining the academy, she enjoyed a long professional career at *National Geographic.*

Isabel Soares is an assistant professor at the Institute for Social and Political Sciences at Universidade de Lisboa, University of Lisbon, where her teaching focuses on imperial studies emphasizing Great Britain and the Commonwealth and English as *lingua franca.* She has written extensively on British and Portuguese attitudes towards the Empire and on literary journalism in Portuguese and in the international scholarly journal *Literary Journalism Studies.* Her Ph.D. dissertation (2007) was the first research project concerning literary journalism in Portugal. She is a founding member and current officer of the International

Association for Literary Journalism Studies and a research fellow at the Center for Public Administration and Policies.

Ted Spiker is an associate professor of Journalism at the College of Journalism and Communications at the University of Florida, where he heads the Department of Journalism's magazine program. A former articles editor at *Men's Health* magazine, he has written for such publications as *Fortune, Reader's Digest, O The Oprah Magazine, Outside* and *Runner's World*. He is also co-author, with Dr. Mehmet Oz and Dr. Michael Roizen, of the *YOU: The Owner's Manual* series of health books. In addition, he is a past head of the AEJMC Magazine Division, and his article on how magazines portrayed September 11 on their covers was published in the *Journal of Magazine & New Media Research*.

Ken Waters is a professor of Journalism and chair of the Communication Division at Pepperdine University in Malibu, Calif. Waters has written extensively about the religious press in America, particularly those associated with the Protestant movement of Christianity. His most recent chapters on the future of evangelical periodicals appeared in a three-part series of books, *Evangelicals and Popular Culture* (2013), edited by Robert Woods and *The Oxford Handbook of Religion and the American News Media* (2012), edited by Diane Winston. Waters is also the author of "Vibrant, but Invisible: A Study of Contemporary Religious Periodicals," which appeared in *Journalism & Mass Communication Quarterly*. His other research interests are media ethics and magazine history.

Sheila M. Webb is an associate professor in the Department of Journalism at Western Washington University, where she teaches mass media research, mass media ethics and visual journalism—Web, multimedia, photo, magazine and print design. Her publications analyze the role of magazines in American life and culture from qualitative, historical and narrative perspectives and deal with how photographers, editors and publishers frame visuals and text. Her work also examines the themes of creation of community, identity formation and gender representation in the media. Her current line of research explores the reframing of community in legacy media's move to on-line formats. Her work has been honored with the 2010 *Mary Ann Yodelis Smith Award for Feminist Scholarship* and the 2011 *Covert Award* for the best article on mass communication history published in 2010. She has also worked in museums as an educator, curator and public information coordinator, specializing in the decorative arts, twentieth-century works on paper and photographs.

INDEX